The Descendants of Joshua and Diana (Adams) Hicks of Clermont County, Ohio

compiled by Betty Jo Stockton

based on a manuscript by
Orville W. Jones (1908-1996)

©Betty Jo Stockton, 2011

Table of Contents

Dedication I

Introduction iii

Background 1

Generation One - Joshua and Diana (Adams) Hicks 10

Generation Two - Children of Joshua and Diana Hicks 17

Generation Three - The grandchildren of Joshua and Diana Hicks 35

Generation Four: The great grandchildren of Joshua and Diana Hicks 87

Generation Five: The great great grandchildren of Joshua and Diana Hicks . . . 185

Generation Six: The 3rd great grandchildren of Joshua and Diana Hicks 304

Name Index 379

Place Index 427

Dedication

Orville William Hicks
(1908-1996)

To Orville William Hicks (1908-1996)
   ...whose manuscript on the Hicks family formed the nucleus of this book. Orville researched when it wasn't easy – before the internet, cheap phone calls and recent census records. Thanks also to his son Walter for sharing the manuscript.

To Elizabeth Sunshine (Stalder) Kieser
   ... my connection to the Hicks family. No better mother could exist. She remained active and interesting past her 95th year. Her stories made family history come alive for her descendants.

Betty Stalder Kieser (1913-2008)
Bob Kieser (1909-1995)

Introduction

This work is a collaboration of three researchers who never met each other. Only two of them had any contact, and that was minimal.

When I began my research, I knew only that my grandmother, Mollie Dell Levi's, mother was Mary Hite and that she had died young. As I researched, I found my grandmother's older sister, Irma Levi, in the 1880 Federal census with her parents, Frank and Lucy Levi, and with Frank's brother-in-law, Frank Hicks. Following up on this, I found that what I knew from my mother and her older brother was only half right. Yes, her mother had died young – but her name was Lucy Hicks. No one knows where Mollie's children got the name Mary Hits - but all of them believed it. Interestingly, the family Bible - which no one had checked - said that Frank Levi married Lucy Ann Hicks.

So I began to look for the Hicks family in Clermont County, Ohio, where my grandmother had grown up. I stumbled across IDI records in the LDS Family History Center, submitted by Norman Zezula. This was before the days of Internet and cheap phone calls, so I contacted the LDS church to see if they could put me in touch with Norman. I wrote to the address the church gave me in February 1992. Norman wrote back and then sent me a batch of information on the Hicks family that he'd been researching for years. He was especially thorough with land records in North Carolina and Ohio.

By 1999, I felt I had enough information to make a research trip to Ohio, so I let Norman know - still by letter. The night before I left, he phoned to say that he'd heard that Orville Jones in Neville, Ohio was writing a book about the Hicks family, could I check on that? Orville was a Hicks descendant through his father, whose great grandmother, Elizabeth Hicks, had married Henry Jones.

When I got to Clermont County, I found that Orville Jones had died in 1996, but the Hicks relatives I met thought that there **was** a book. "Would I like to meet Orville's son, Walter?" I never made contact with Walter in Ohio, but wrote to him when I got back to Florida. He generously sent me the manuscript that his father had almost completed on the Hicks family and gave me permission to publish it.

I can't determine how long Orville had been researching – but it was obviously a long time. Most of his work had been done through personal knowledge, letter writing, expensive phone calls and library research before computers and photocopy machines. He seemed to have updated it through about 1985. It was handwritten, with a unique numbering system, and not yet indexed.

I input all the information into the computer and began working towards publication. Each time I thought I was at a good stopping point, some new information became available, i.e. the 1920 & 1930 census were released, familysearch.org began offering wonderful records, etc. So I'd update and start my formatting again.

The folks I met in Ohio were extremely helpful. An Internet friend, Debbie Shaffer, helped me make contact with the Hicks cousins. Lvera Seipelt and her mother, Elizabeth (Hicks) Jennings, shared information, stories and photos. Donald Hicks drove me all over the county, showing me family cemeteries, farms and workplaces. Rosalene (Hicks) Burkirk gave me a photo of my great grandmother, Lucy Ann (Hicks) Levi – seemingly the only photo in existence of her. To all these folks — thanks!

Any genealogy is a "work in progress". Hopefully, others reading this work will offer corrections and updates so the second edition will be better. To protect the privacy of living individuals, anyone born after 1930 and for whom I have no death date, will be considered to be still living. Their personal information will not be included in this book. I may have more information on recent generations. Please contact me with questions, additions or corrections.

Betty Jo Stockton, 8501 Pajaro Ct, Orlando, FL 32836
bjstock@cfl.rr.com

Background Information

Very little is known about the life of Joshua Hicks, so any information here is based on a few known facts and records of others living during the same time frame. The parents and siblings of Joshua may never be known for certain. The Hicks appear in Surry County, North Carolina about 1791, but no one knows where they were before that. There had been a Samuel Hicks in Granville Co, NC in 1790 (about 100 miles east of Surry), but there is nothing to indicate this is the same one. Some family stories say the family came from Virginia; other say from Pennsylvania. There are no records that any of this Hicks family were involved in the Revolution, even though they were in the right age range.

We do know that a Joshua Hicks who fits the facts as we know them was living in Salisbury, Surry County, North Carolina in 1800, when he appears on the federal census. Another fact is that Joshua Hicks married Diana Adams in Rowan County, North Carolina on 19 Sep 1794. Rowan County is next to Surry. Later records show that the wife of Joshua is named Diana, which confirms this as our Joshua and Diana.

Norman Zezula and Orville Jones studied the records of Surry County in great depth. Because of the interconnections shown in land records as well as the sparse census records, they concluded that Samuel Hicks was the most likely father of Joshua. Benjamin, James, William, Polly and Eliza were possible siblings. See the following chapter for details on this research. Most of the family appears to have left this area by 1810. Since I cannot prove otherwise, I'm accepting this premise. If Samuel is Joshua's father, I find it strange that none of Joshua's descendants were named Samuel, even though the family re-used other family names frequently. Perhaps there was some falling out between father and son - or Joshua and Diana simply didn't like the name.

In 1850, Surry County was split, with the area south of the Yadkin River becoming Yadkin County. The part of Surry County where the Hicks family owned land is now in Yadkin County – in the area of the town of Yadkinville. Land records show the Hicks land as being in the areas of Deep Creek and Hunting Creek. This is an area of rolling hills and valleys. Deep Creek is considered to be a major creek - to the point that the town of Yadkinville draws its water supply from a dam on the Creek. Hunting Creek is further west and smaller. Both run to the Yadkin River.

This area of Surry County was prime farmland. Currently tobacco, grains and wine grapes are commercial crops there. Tobacco was probably a major crop in the 1800s as well.

Surry County farmland

Southwest corner of Yadkin County

Possible family of Joshua HICKS - Surry Co, NC

A. **Samuel[1] HICKS**, born[1, 2] abt 1745 of Surry Co, NC; died[3] aft 1806 of Surry Co, NC. He married **-?-**, born abt 1745.

> Very little is known of this Samuel Hicks. All information is based on land and tax records, which give no personal information. Because he was shown as over 45 in the 1800 census, he was obviously born before 1755. He was not in the 1790 census of Surry County, but might have been the Samuel Hicks who was in Granville County that year. Granville County is east of Surry County by about 100 miles. No record of his marriage has been found. Based on land records, he arrived in Surry County in 1790-1791, and was taxed on 600 acres of land in 1791. In 1800, he sold two parcels of land (100 acres each) to what was most likely his sons, William and Benjamin. In 1806, he sold 400 acres to what was probably another son, James. This probably was the final piece of his land. Joshua was witness to several of these land sales. The last record of Samuel in Surry County seems to be the 1806 acknowledgment of his land sale. He seemed to be settling his affairs, but whether that was because of ill health or an imminent move may never be known. Family relationships are based on proximity and involvement in each other's land sales. None of this is proven.@@

Possible children of Samuel HICKS:

1 **Joshua[2] HICKS**. [See following chapters]

b. **Benjamin[2] HICKS**, born[4] 1768 probably in. Surry Co, NC; died aft 1804. He married abt 1790.

> Benjamin Hicks, presumed brother of Joshua, was first noted in 1794 when he signed Joshua's marriage bond. Assuming that he was 21 at that time, he was born before 1773. His age in the 1800 census (between 26-45) could give him a birth date of 1755-1775. By 1800, he had 6 children under 10 years of age. He appears to have left Surry County before 1810. There is no Benjamin Hicks on the 1810 census that matches what we know of this Benjamin Hicks. @@

c. **James[2] HICKS**, born[5, 6, 7, 8] abt 1770 of Surry Co, NC; died aft 1830 of Surry Co, NC. He married[9] on 16 Oct 1799 in Surry Co, NC **Elizabeth DAVIS**, born bef 1780.

> James Hicks, presumed brother of Joshua, married later than Joshua, so is thought to have been younger. He married Elizabeth Davis in 1797. It appears from census records that they had one son by 1800, but had lost him by 1810. If it is the right family, there were children by 1830, but not necessarily his. He seems to be the only one of this group to have stayed in Surry County. No information is found after 1830. @@

d. **William[2] HICKS**, born[10] abt 1772 of Surry Co, NC; died aft 1810 in Iredell Co, NC. He married[11] on 31 Dec 1799 in Surry Co, NC **Ann DAVIS**, born bef 1780.

> William Hicks, presumed brother of Joshua, is believed to have been born about 1772. He appears to have moved to Iredell Co, NC before 1810. He was taxed on land in Surry from 1794-1799 and bought and sold land between 1800 and 1805. There were two marriages for William Hicks - (1) Ann Davis (31 Dec 1799) and (2) Polly Moss (28 May 1802). There are no records for William after 1810, but a Henry appears in 1820 - which might be another name for William. @@

e. **Eliza[2] HICKS**, born[12] abt 1774 of Surry Co, NC. She married[13] on 18 Jan 1797 in Surry Co, NC **Benjamin SPARKS**.

> Eliza Hicks, presumed sister of Joshua, was born about 1774. Elizabeth only appears in marriage records, with her marriage in 1797 to Benjamin Sparks. Following Nicholas through census shows the family remaining in Surry County through 1830. They had a number of children. @@

@@For more information, see research notes at the end of the chapter.

f. **Polly**[2] **HICKS**, born abt 1776 of Surry Co, NC. She married[14] on 15 Aug 1800 in Surry Co, NC **Elijah OLIVER**.

> Polly Hicks, presumed sister of Joshua, was born about 1776. Polly appears only in marriage records, with her marriage in 1800 to Elijah Oliver. The Oliver family was in Surry Co through 1810, but disappears after that. @@

Research notes for Background

<u>Notes for Samuel HICKS #A</u>

Relationship assumed based on available documents, but not proven.

Most information from Norman Zezula and Orville Jones' notes.

Birth: 1800 census ,Surry Co., NC (#662) indicates he is over 45

Marriage: no record found; prob. 1770 or before due to estimated ages of sons.

Death: alive in Surry Co., NC in May 1806 when he acknowledged a land sale.

On 14 Oct 1809, a Samuel Hicks married Lucy James (in Surry Co.) It is not known if this is the same Samuel.

Census:

1800: Surry Co., NC (#662) Samuel Hicks b. Bef. 1745; Son b. 1745-1764 [William?]

1810: Surry Co., NC (p 648) Samuel Hicks b. Bef. 1765; Wife b. 1765-1784 [Lucy James ?] No children [probably not the same Samuel - possibly a son?]

Chronology:

1790:		No Samuel Hicks in NC or VA census, or in any Surry record.
1791:		taxed in Surry on 600 acres (first Surry record found for him)
1792-1794:	" " " "	600 acres
1795:	" " " "	400 acres
1796:	" " " "	600 acres
1797-1798:	" " " "	400 acres
1799:	" " " "	300 acres
1800:	" " " "	300 acres; sold 2 parcels of land (one to William Hicks; the other to Benjamin Hicks probably his sons) (100 acres to each)

1804: Sold 42 acres in Surry; was a witness for a 8 May 1804 land transaction.

1805: Sold 400 acres in Surry to James Hicks (probably his son). this apparently was the remainder of his land holdings.

1806: In the May term, in open court, he acknowledged his mark on the sale document for the 400 acres sold in 1805.

Land: Samuel Hicks had a 242 acre land parcel on Hunting Creek in Surry Co, NC. After putting together a sketch based on the land description of several subsequent transactions, the following description of the original parcel has been concluded: From Jefferies' corner, N. 120 poles to a pine on Johnson's corner; then E. 56 poles to an oak ? on Laban Hicks line; then N. 40 poles; then E. 226 poles; then 17 degrees W. of due south to the "old line" (which line runs east and west thru Jefferies' corner); and then west along this "old line" back to the beginning (at Jefferies' corner).

In 1800, Samuel sold the western 100 acres to William Hicks; the central 100 acres to William Hicks, and retained the eastern 42 acres. The dividing lines were parallel to the 120 pole line that forms the western boundary of the original parcel. These dividing lines intersect the "old line" (the southern boundary of the original parcel) at 56 poles and at 156 poles east of the oak at Jefferies' corner. These dividing lines are perpendicular to the "old line." All 3 parcels are on Hunting Creek.

On 8 May 1804, Benjamin Hicks sold the eastern 22 acres of his land to William Hicks (thus moving

@@For more information, see research notes at the end of the chapter.

their common border to the west). In 1805 (3 Aug), William Hicks (by then "of Iredell Co.") sold his land to William Jeffery.

On 17 Oct of 1805, Benjamin Hicks sold his land to William Jefferies. In Dec 1804, Samuel Hicks sold his 42 acres (remaining to him of the original 242 acres) to Isaac Jones. On 17 Mar 1805, Samuel Hicks sold 400 acres to James Hicks. This land was on Deep Creek. However, it apparently wasn't far from the Hunting Creek parcel. Laban Hicks's land was also on Deep Creek; yet it appears that his land and Samuel's have a point of contact (an oak on Laban Hicks line). Samuel Hicks 400 acres may even have adjoined the 244 acre parcel on Hunting Creek. At any rate, the transaction for the 400 acres sold to James follows: 17 Mar 1805 for 100 pounds "On the waters of Deep Creek beginning at a black oak; runs south 17 degrees west 75 chains to a stake; west 45 chains to a ____ oak; north 71 chains to a pine; east to the beginning; containing in the whole 400 acres. Signed Samuel Hicks (by mark) (acknowledged in open court by Samuel Hicks in the May term of 1806, and ordered to be duely registered." [Norman Zezula notes]

Land: Summary:

28 Feb 1791 Laban Hicks enters 200 acres in Surry Co. on the waters of Hunting Creek and Deep Creek adjoining Edward Woolridge.(p 492, Land Entries)

Nov 1792 Laban Hicks enters 200 acres on the waters of Hunting Creek adjoining William Woodridge and himself (p 547, Land Entries)

24 Dec 1792 Laban Hicks rec'd 200 acres on Deep Creek

26 Jul 1800 Samuel Hicks to Benjamin Hicks: 100 acres on Hunting Creek (Samuel signs by mark; wit. James & Joshua Hicks)

26 Jul 1800 Samuel Hicks to William Hicks: 100 acres (Samuel signs by mark; wit. James & Joshua Hicks)

8 May 1804 Benjamin Hicks to William Hicks: 22 acres (Benjamin signs; wit. Samuel Hicks by mark, and Laban Hicks)

17 Oct 1804 Benjamin Hicks to William Jeffery, on the waters of North Hunting Creek: (Benjamin signs; wit Joshua Hicks)

10 Nov 1804 Samuel Hicks to Issac Jones: (Samuel signs by mark; wit. Laban Hicks)

10 Nov 1804 Laban Hicks sells 100 acres

12 Dec 1804 Samuel Hicks to Issac Jones: (Samuel signs by mark; wit. Laban Hicks

17 Mar 1805 Samuel Hicks to James Hicks: 400 acres (Samuel signs by mark; later acknowledged by him in open court)

3 Aug 1805 William Hicks of Iredell Co. to William Jeffery: (William by mark)

11 Nov 1807 Laban Hicks obtains 100 acres from the state on Cobbs Creek at 50 shillings per hundred acres
  Land: Deeds: 24 Dec 1792 Grant of 200 acres (10 pounds/ acre) to Laban Hicks [in Surry Co.] "on the waters of Deep Creek, beginning at a black oak, William Woolridges beginning corner, and runs North on Richard Bealock's? line 28 chains to a stake in William Terrel's [division?] line, known by the name of Aymes? Old Place; thence West on the same [heading?] by his corner 28 chains; and so on the same course 43 chains more to a pine; thence South 28 chains to a stake on the piney nobbs; thence East to the beginning." (has 12 months to register this deed)

26 Jul 1800 Samuel Hicks to Benjamin Hicks, both of Surry Co., 100 acres; cost 50 pounds: "On the waters of Hunting Creek, beginning at a ____ oak, William Hicks corner oak, West 100 poles to a ____ oak in that line; thence _____ [therewith?] said line South 160 poles to a ____ oak thru [old?] corner; then East 100 poles to a stake, William Hicks corner; then North with his line to the beginning." (wit. James & Joshua Hicks)

26 Jul 1800 Samuel Hicks to William Hicks, both of Surry Co. 100 acres; cost 50 pounds: " On the waters of Hunting Creek, beginning at a white oak, runs West 126 poles to a ____ oak; then South 160 poles to a stake in the old line; then along said line East 78 poles to a stake in the old corner; thence North 17 degrees East with the old line to the beginning." (wit. James & Joshua Hicks)

8 May 1804 Benjamin Hicks to William Hicks, 22 acres; cost 15 pounds: "On the waters of Hunting Creek,

beginning at a [post at?] William Hicks corner; runs West 10 poles to a post oak at Thomas Coffin's corner, then South 8 degrees West 164 poles to a stake in Woodridge's old line; thence East 33 poles to a stake: thence South 163 poles to the Beginning." (wit. Laban Hicks, Samuel Hicks)

17 Oct 1804 "Benjamin Hicks sells 80 acres on Hunting Creek to William Jeffery for 50 pounds current money of [NC?]: On the waters of North Hunting Creek adjoining Samuel Hicks and Issac Jones and John Brown, including the plantation whereon Thomas Coffin ?) now lives and bounded as follows: beginning at a ____ oak, running North 163 [poles?] to ____oak; then East 90 poles to a ____ oak; then South ___ degrees West 164 poles to a stake in the original line; then west to the beginning." (wit. Joshua Hicks)

10 Nov 1804 Laban Hicks sells 100 acres: "On the waters of Deep Creek containing 100 acres, beginning at a pine (?), Henry Jefferies (?) corner, runs West to said Hicks corner pine (?); then North (?) on his line 28 chains to his corner stake in William Woodridge's line; then West on the same 11.5 chains to a stake on Hill's line; then North on the same [heading?] ____ corner 58 chains to a pine; thence East 22.5 chains to a stake on Speer's line; thence on the same to the beginning.

12 Dec 1804 Samuel Hicks to Issac Jones, 42 acres: "On the waters of Hunting Creek, beginning at a ____ oak, [Jefferies corner ?], runs North 120 poles to a pine, Johnson's corner; then East 56 poles to a post (?) oak on Laban Hicks line; then South 120 poles to a Spanish oak in said _____ line; then west to the begining; containing in the whole 42 acres." (wit. Laban Hicks)

3 Aug 1805 William Hicks of Iredell Co. to William Jeffery, 100 acres: "On the waters of Hunting Creek joining Samuel Hicks', John Brown's, Richard Mesick's (?) line, beginning at a white oak, runs West 126 poles to a ___ oak; then South 160 poles to a stake in the old line; thence along the old line East 78 poles to a stake, the old corner; thence North 17 (?) degrees with the old line to the beginning."

17 Mar 1805 Samuel Hicks to William Hicks 400 acres; cost 100 pounds: "On the waters of Deep Creek, beginning at a black oak, runs South 17 degrees West 75 chains to a stake; West 45 chains to a ____ oak; North 71 chains to a pine; East to the beginning." "acknowledged in open court May term, 1806 by Samuel Hicks and ordered to be duely registered."

11 Nov 1807 Laban Hicks from the state for 50 shillings per 100 acres; 100 acres N 2528 (M:327): "On Cobb's Creek beginning at creek, stout oak in Spark's line; runs West one hundred and ___ poles to a black oak; thence South 114 (?) poles to a short oak; thence East 67 poles to a red oak; thence N 5 poles to a pine, John Rose's corner; then with his line 73 poles to a black oak; thence North to the beginning."

Samuel & William Hicks sign by mark. Apparently, Laban, Joshua, James, and Benjamin can write their own name.

Notes - LABAN HICKS: He is a neighbor of Samuel Hicks and his sons. His land and that of Samuel's original parcel touch at a corner (at least). Also, he is a witness for several land transactions involving Samuel and his sons. (two sales of Samuel to non family; Laban also is a co-witness with Samuel in the Benjamin to William sale. This all implies that they are related; Laban may be another son of Samuel. There are references to "Laban Sen." and "Laban Jun." in the records. Only a Laban Sr. is listed in the 1800 Census for Surry; However, only Laban Jr., (or just "Laban") is mentioned in the tax, deed and grant indexes. Clearly, Laban Jr. is the son of Laban Senior. The 1800 census lists only one Laban (in the 26-44 age group.) If this is Laban Jr., Laban Sr. is probably Samuel's brother, or possibly Samuel's father. If this is Laban Sr., he is probably an older son of Samuel. It should be noted that both Laban and Samuel appear first in Surry in 1791 (Laban entered land; both were taxed on their land). Additional members of this extended Hicks family do not appear in Surry Co. records until 1792 or later.

CHRONOLOGY for Laban:
  1791: enters 200 acres (from state); taxed on 400 acres
  1792: enters 100 acres; bought 200 acres
  1794: Laban Jr. taxed on 300 acres
  1795: Laban Jr. taxed on 300 acres
  1796: Laban Jr. taxed on 300 acres

1797-1800: Laban (no Jr. or Sr.) taxed on 300 acres

1800: Laban Sr., Surry census (26-44); no Laban Jr.

1804: Laban sells 100 acres; wit. to 3 land transactions involving Samuel, Benj. and Wm.

1807: Laban obtains 100 acres on Cobb's Creek from the state for 50 shillings.

Children: Benjamin, James, Joshua, and William are presumed to be Samuel's sons because of their close involvement in land transactions. The father sells 3 land parcels to 3 of his sons (James, Benjamin, and William). Benjamin sells part of his to William. They act as witnesses in the sales between father and son and between 2 brothers. Benjamin signs Joshua's marriage bond (in Rowan Co.). Only the "Laban Sr.-Laban Jr. problem" prevents listing Laban as another son at this time. The two possible daughters, Eliza and Polly, were obtained from Surry Co. marriage bonds. It is not certain that Samuel, and not Laban (or even Thomas, Nathanial, or John -- see "Other Hicks") is their father. This is a preliminary assumption because the marriage dates are consistent with this family.

Other Hicks: None of the Laban-Samuel Hicks family appears in Surry Co. prior to 1791. However, 5 other Hicks or HIX are listed in the county in previous records. None were in the Hunting Creek-Deep Creek area, except for James. The names of these five are: Thomas, Nathaniel, John, James, and Frederick Hicks.

1771-1772: Frederick Hicks in tax list: in 1771 with a "1" in a column (heading illegible); in 1772 with a "2" in a similar column (from the clerk of the House of Burgesses)

1782: James Hicks in tax list. No data is given for him; however, he is listed among people who are designated "Deep Creek." The names for "Capt. Wright's district" include: Philimon Halcourt (400 acres), Peter Myers (160 acres), Greenburg, Patterson (640), John Catten?, John Door?, James Hicks, George Hol____, _____, Thomas Gallium?, Lawrence Halcomb, Darrel? _____, .

1787: Thomas HIX listed in state census (no data)

1790: Census (Surry Co.):
  Nathaniel Hicks: 1 son under 16; 4 daughters; wife
  John Hicks: 1 Son over 16; 3 under; no daughters; wife
  Thomas Hicks: 7 sons over 16; 1 daughter; wife

1790-1793: John taxed; (1791 - on 23 acres;

1794 - on 150 acres)

1790-1791: Nathaniel taxed on 640 acres

1794: Nathaniel " " " " (did not check him for later years)

Other Hicks

1800: Census (Surry Co.): Nathaniel Hicks Jr: He & wife (both over 45); 3 young sons; 3 dau.

1800: Census (Iredell Co.) Henry Hicks: he over 45, wife 26-44; 1 son, 1 dau < 10; 1 son 10-16.

1801: Nathaniel HIX and wife buys 640 acres on Fall Creek from John August (Thomas HIX a witness) (I 202)

Thomas Hicks m. Elizabeth Deadman Bond Date: 29 Oct 1787; Rowan; Bondsman: Wm Hampton; Witness: Jno Macay

Note: Hicks, Elizabeth Jane: an account (under heading: "Accounts, Inventories, and Settlements") May 1894, agent - Sam'l Davis (gdsn?); file #691. (This probably is not a relative or a wife of Samuel Hicks)

Note:

1800 census: p. 662 - names in loose alphabetical order Hicks, Joshua 2 - - 1 - / 1 - 1 - - [under 10 / 10-16 / 16-26 / 26-45 / over 45] Samuel - - - 1 1 / - - - - - Benjamin 4 - - 1 - / 2 - 1 - - James - - - 1 - / - - - 1 - Laban Sr - - - 1 - / - - - - -

1810 census: (#686) Surry Co: John Hix: 1 son, 1 dau under 10; 4 sons 16-18; wife 26-44; his age apparently not given

1820 census: (#231) Iredell Co: Henry Hicks over 45, his wife 26-44, 2 sons 16-18, 1 dau 10-16; 2 slaves

1830 census: (#031) Iredell Co: Henry Hicks 50-60, son 20-30, female 50-60, 10-15, 20-30 (#032)

Iredell Co: Elijah Hicks--males: 2 (under 5); 2 (5-10), 1 (30-40); female: 2 (5-10), 1 (30-40) (#121)

Surry Co: Daniel Hicks--males: 1 (under 5), 1 (30-40), female: 2 (under 5), 2 (5-10), 1 (20-30)

Notes for Benjamin Hicks #b.

Most information from Norman Zezula

Birth: a preliminary estimate based on an attempt to assemble the family. He first appears in 1794 when he signs Joshua's marriage bond (Rowan Co., NC). Thus he was born before 1773. In the 1800 census, he is in the 26-45 age group--he is listed as married with 6 children under 10. Since he had 4 more children than did Joshua, while James had none and William was apparently living with his father, and unmarried, Benjamin is presumed to be the oldest of four sons. Since the 1800 census indicates that all four were born 1755-1774, Benjamin's birth year is estimated to be abt 1769. The other sons are put in order of their marriage dates. The two Hicks girls are assumed to have married a few years younger than did their brothers. With this adjustment, they were listed in probable birth order behind their four brothers.

Marriage: marriage date estimated based on his 6 children in the 1800 census He was probably married about or before 1790. His marriage does not appear in the Surry Co. marriage bonds. It is possible that he married before he came to Surry Co.

Death: aft 1804 (He sold his land in Surry Co. in Oct 1804)

Census:
- 1800: Surry Co., NC (#662) Benjamin Hicks b. 1755-1774 [probably before 1770] Wife b. 1774-1784; 4 sons born 1790-1800; 2 daughters born 1790-1800
- 1810: Benjamin apparently left Surry Co. about 1805, having sold his land in late 1804. He does not appear in the 1810 or later censuses for Surry. His father, his brothers (Joshua and William), and his "relative?" Laban Hicks all appear to have sold their land and left the county about this time. Only James appears to have stayed; he appears in the 1810-1830 Surry Co. census records. William apparently went to Iredell Co., NC; Joshua went to Clermont Co., OH; the others haven't been traced.
- 1820: Land: See notes for his father.

Chronology:
- 1794: First appears on the Surry Co. tax rolls
- 1799: Taxed on 100 acres
- 1800: bought 100 acres; taxed on 100 acres (prob. the 1799 land was this same parcel, i.e. he had 100 acres total); Census: with wife & 6 children under 10
- 1804: sold his land in an 80 acre and a 22 acre parcel

Note: Another Benjamin Hicks is in the 1850 census (Surry Co., NC (P207) Hicks, Benjamin 69 M (could be the son of the Benj. b. in 1768); Sarah 60 F; Solomon 25 M; Martha 23 F; Sally 18 F; Benjamin 17 M

Notes for James Hicks #c:

Birth: From provisional family group record (see Benjamin Hicks Notes for further information). First taxed in 1792 (thus at least 21 then)

Marriage: 16 Oct 1797 to Elizabeth Davis. Surry Co., NC marriage bond

Death: alive in the 1830 census (Surry Co.)

Census:
- 1800: Surry Co., NC (p 662) James Hicks b. 1756-1774; Wife Hicks b. 1756-1774; (no children indicated) (They are shown with 3 slaves.)
- 1810: Surry Co., NC (p 641) James Hicks b. 1765-1784; Wife b. bef. 1765; Son b. 1794-1800 (They are shown with 1 slave.)
- 1820: Surry Co. NC (p 680) James Hicks b. Bef. 1775; Wife b. bef. 1775 (They are shown with no children; 4 slaves.)
- 1830: Surry Co., NC (p 121) James Hicks b. 1770-1780; Wife?; b. 1750-1760 [sic]; Male b. 1815-1820; Male b. 1825-1830; Female b. 1780-1790 [relationship not known] (Presumably all are related; the "Female" may be the wife, sister, or sister-in-law; the two males may be her sons; the "wife" may be an aged mother-in law.)
- Surry Co., (p 153) Daniel Hicks b. 1790-1800; Wife b. 1800-1810; Daughter b. 1820-1825; Daughter b. 1820-1825; Son b. 1825-1830; Daughter b. 1825-1830; Daughter b. 1825-1830 (Relationship, if

any, to James Hicks is unknown.)

Chronology:
- 1792-1797: Taxed on 200 acres (Surry)
- 1797: Married in Surry Co.
- 1798: Taxed on 200 acres (Surry)
- 1800: Census (Surry); Witness land sales with Joshua Hicks (Samuel sold; Benjamin and William Hicks were the buyers)
- 1805: Samuel sold him 400 acres. (Surry)
- 1810: In census, one son (Surry Co.)
- 1820: In census (Surry)
- 1830: In census (Surry)

Notes for William Hicks #d.

Birth: Estimated from marriage order of brothers and sisters (See notes on "Children" for Samuel Hicks and notes on "Birth" for Benjamin Hicks)

Marriage: both from Surry Co, NC marriage bonds
  (1) Ann Davis (31 Dec 1799)
  (2) Polly Moss (28 May 1802)

It is possible that the first marriage may have been to another William Hicks (due to the time between the two marriages, and due to the belief that William was living with his father in the census (he first bought land later in 1800, although he was taxed --not on land-- since 1794). However no other William Hicks has been found.

Death: In 1810 census (Iredell, NC; p 190 (cannot locate in 1820 census)

Census
- 1800: Does not appear; believed to be with father
- 1810: Iredell Co., NC (p 190) William Hicks b. 1765-1784; Wife b. 1765-1784; Son b. 1794-1800; Son b. 1800-1810; Son b. 1800-1810; Son b. 1800-1810; Daughter b. 1800-1810; Daughter b. 1800-1810 (1 slave is indicated)
- 1810: Iredell Co., NC (p 031) Henry Hicks b. 1765-1784; Wife b. 1765-1784; Son b. 1794-1800; Son b. 1800-1810; Daughter b. 1800-1810 (Not sure if Henry is related)
- 1820: No William; Henry, Wife both over 45-- son, dau. (26-45), 2 slaves, (Iredell, p 231)};
  Elisha Hicks (26-44), Wife (16-26), 2 sons under 10) (Iredell, p 231)}
  (prob. another) William: (#708), Surry?: he, wife 16-26, 3 sons, 1 dau under 10; 1 slave
- 1830: No William; {Henry, Wife (50-60)-- son, dau. (20-30)-- dau. (10-15) (Iredell, p 031)}
  {Elijah Hicks, Wife (30-40), 2 sons, 2 dau.(5-10), 2 sons (0-5) (Iredell, p 031)}

Chronology:
- 1794-1799: Tax lists, Surry
- 1800: Not in census (probably enumerated with his father)
- 1800: Buys 100 acres from father (Surry)
- 1804: Buys 22 acres from Benjamin (Surry)
- 1805: Sells 100 acres in Surry (called William of Iredell in contract of sale) --3 Apr, to William Jefferies
- 1810: A William Hicks is in the Iredell census.

Notes for Eliza HICKS #e:

Birth: From marriage order of family (See notes on "Children" for Samuel Hicks & notes on "Birth" for Benjamin Hicks)

Marriage: Surry Co. Marriage bond 18 Jan 1797 to Benjamin Sparks

Census:
- 1800: Surry Co., NC (p 689) Benjamin SPARKS [No age given]; Wife b. 1755-1774 [Elizabeth]; Daughter b. 1790-1800 [abt 1798]; Son b. 1790-1800 [abt 1799]

1810: Surry Co., NC (p 680) Benjamin SPARKS [No age given]; Wife b. 1765-1784 [Elizabeth]; Daughter b. 1800-1810; Son b. 1800-1810 (Note that another source gives a different family pattern. 2 sons, 1 dau under 10; 1 son, 1 dau 10-16)

1820: Surry Co., NC (p 666) Benjamin SPARKS b. Bef. 1775; Wife b. Bef. 1775 [Elizabeth]; Daughter b. 1794-1804; Son b. 1794-1804; Son b. 1794-1804; Son b. 1804-1810; Son b. 1804-1810; Daughter b. 1804-1810

1830: Surry Co., NC (p 090) Benjamin SPARKS b. 1780-1790; Wife b. 1790-1800; Son b. 1800-1810; Daughter b. 1815-1830; Son b. 1810-1820; Son b. 1820-1825; Daughter b. 1820-1825; Daughter b. 1820-1825; Son b. 1825-1830; Daughter b. 1825-1830; Daughter b. 1825-1830

Notes for Polly HICKS #f

Birth: From marriage order of brothers and sisters (See notes on "Children" for Samuel Hicks and notes on "Birth" for Benjamin Hicks.)

Marriage: Surry Co., NC marriage bond 15 Aug 1800 to Elijah Oliver

Census

1800: Surry Co., NC (p 681) Elijah OLIVER b. 1755-1774 Wife b. 1755-1774 [Polly]

1810: Surry Co., NC (p 675) Elijah OLIVER b. 1784-1794 Wife OLIVER b. 1784-1794 (No children) (another extract shows he and wife over 45 with 2 sons 16-26)

1820: No Elijah or Polly OLIVER listed; there is a Betsy OLIVER for Surry (#692): she over 45, 2 sons (10-16), son, dau. (0-10) Clearly, this is not the OLIVER family of interest; Elijah or Polly do not appear in the 1830 or 1840 Surry Co. census)

End notes for Background

1. Surry Co, NC - Census - 1800 [M32, #32].
2. Surry Co, NC - Census - 1810 [M252, #43].
3. Surry Co, NC Land Records 1791-1807.
4. Surry Co, NC - Census - 1800 [M32, #32].
5. Ibid.
6. Surry Co, NC - Census - 1810 [M252, #43].
7. Surry Co, NC - Census - 1820 [M33, #82].
8. Surry Co, NC - Census - 1830 [M19, #125].
9. North Carolina Marriage Bonds, 1741-1868.
10. Iredell Co, NC - Census - 1810 [M252, #40].
11. North Carolina Marriage Bonds, 1741-1868.
12. Surry Co, NC - Census - 1800 [M32, #32].
13. North Carolina Marriage Bonds, 1741-1868.
14. Ibid

The First Generation - Joshua and Diana (Adams) Hicks

Joshua and Diana Hicks moved west to Ohio about 1806. Since there were very few records kept for pioneer families, much of the "story of Joshua" is based on a few facts and a great amount of conjecture.

Joshua and Diana almost definitely were in Surry County, North Carolina in 1800 for the census. They were married in neighboring Rowan County in 1794. That is all we know for certain. Some family stories say that this part of the Hicks family moved to Ohio because they were opposed to slavery in the South. There may be some truth to this, since the Underground Railroad for escaping slaves ran directly through the parts of Ohio where our folks lived.

Joshua and his family probably traveled to Ohio by horse and wagon and possibly by flatboat for the final part of the journey. If the 1806 migration date is correct, the family would have consisted of Diana, Joshua and six children under the age of 12. The migration route that seems most likely was via the Kanawa Trace through West Virginia, then by flatboat from Parkersburg down the Ohio River.

After the Revolution and lessening of tension with the Indian tribes, restless settlers were ready to move to Ohio and acquire cheap land. The route of Lewis' army during the Revolution proved that the route was feasible and was the most direct way there from SW Virginia and North Carolina. The New River rises in the mountains of western North Carolina, and travels northeast through southwestern Virginia, then turns northwest into what is now West Virginia. It cuts a deep gorge through the mountains before it is joined by the Gauley River, after which it becomes the Kanawha. From the point of this juncture, all the way to the its mouth opposite Gallipolis the Kanawha is a wide slow moving stream and is navigable throughout its entire course. The Kanawa River meets the Ohio River at Point Pleasant, Ohio.

The Kanawha Trace enters what is now West Virginia near the town of Peters town, about twenty-five miles west of Blacksburg, Virginia. It largely follows alongside the course of the New River, but at times it goes overland in places where the river makes a wide loop. From Peterstown to where the trail comes to the Falls of New River (where the Kanawha River Dam is now located) was eighty-one miles of rugged trail. At this point the river becomes navigable and some settlers would build flatboats to float down to Gallipolis. Others would continue on the trail alongside the river for the remaining eighty-two miles to the Ohio River.

Ohio River flatboat

The journey, as described by the Rummel Waybill, was divided into segments approximately equal to what could be traveled in a single day. The segments varied in length from three up to eighteen miles. The three-mile segment represents the Trace, just after it enters West Virginia at Peterstown. The last fifty-five miles before getting to the Ohio River opposite Gallipolis could be traversed in four days. The daily segments across what is now West Virginia add up to a total of 163 miles and would take 19 days.[1]

The writings of Katherine (Shinkle) Bolender describe the flatboat trip, "The trip down the Ohio river was a slow, meandering float, with the river surrounded by heavy forest. Danger lurked in the forest; danger from hostile Indians, bear and the wilderness itself". According to *The History of Clermont County, Ohio*, "the family lived on the flatboat ready to cut loose, at any Indian trouble.[2]"

When the family reached Franklin Township in Clermont County, they were on the frontier. Earliest settlers to the area had been there no more than 10 years, as the county was officially formed in 1800. There were no towns, simply individual farms hewn from the dense forest. Joshua and his sons probably cleared land, using the wood for building a log cabin and other household uses. It appears that Joshua simply settled on land for his first 8-10 years. There is no record of his buying land until 1815. The land he purchased may have been the land he had been living on, but there is no way to know. His land purchase was 126 acres along the Ohio River in the area of the current town of Rural. The land there now - as it probably was then - was a large area of flood plain along the river, then rising steeply above the river. This land was wonderful farmland, but flooded often.

Diana and Joshua produced a large family. There are no records that tell precisely who family members were, but there was apparently only one Hicks family in that area in that time period. Thus, any child of the right age is presumed to be theirs. There may have been a number of others who did not live long enough to leave any records, as conditions would have been very harsh and medical care practically non-existent.

Pioneer life must have been very difficult. Evert's *History of Clermont County, OH*, written in 1880, describes a day in the life of a pioneer women. "Rising in the morning at four, she built the fires, made up her own beds, awoke and dressed the children, made up the trundle-bed, shoved it under the big bed, put on the tea-kettle, and mixed the Indian meal for the johnny-cakes and corn-dodgers. This done, she prepared the frugal meal and set the table, after which she blew a merry peal on the tin horn to call the men to breakfast. Next she nursed the baby, but that could be done while she was knitting the socks and stockings. The men came in, and, springing up, she laid the sweet smiling little baby in the trough-cradle, and with one loving kiss she set the victuals on

Ohio log cabin built in early 1800s

the rude table, and jogged the cradle with her foot each time she passed to keep the baby calm. Breakfast over, the rustic dishes put away, the children sent to school or out to play, she sprinkled the linen on the grass, and now spinning is resumed. She takes the wheel out on the puncheon floor, takes her darling babe from the cradle, and, while her foot is busy with the treadle, it serves as a motion to quiet the little beauty, while singing and musing. But it is time to prepare dinner, and greens must be picked, potatoes washed, meat put on to boil, and venison or bear-meat to be broiled or baked; and if the husband is a good shot, a turkey is swung up before the large fireplace to broil. Then down to the wheel or into the loom, banging away as she sends the swiftly-flying shuttle through the double-threaded web. The horn is blown again, the victuals taken up, and the meal is eaten with the baby on the lap. The pewter dishes washed and put away, the floor must be scrubbed, for she has no carpet, and the bleaching cloth is to be watered again. Then back to the wheel till time for supper; which over, she goes to the pasture to milk the cows, puts the children to bed, and takes again to the ever-busy wheel until the husband retires to his couch. She must stop now, for he does not like the buzzing noise, but no bed comes to her relief yet, for the children's clothes are to be mended and stockings darned and thus she toils on until late in the night. Such was the life led by most of Clermont's pioneer mothers.[3]"

At the same time, the men and boys were clearing fields, building shelter, hunting for game for the table as well as planting crops to get them through the winter and possibly have something to sell. The pioneer life was from "can see" in the morning until "can't see" at night.

Obviously, Joshua and Diana were up to the challenge. They went on to have a total of 12 known children, many of whom remained to farm in Clermont – following in their parents' footsteps. They married children of other pioneer families – and built a community. Both Joshua and Diana lived into their 80s.

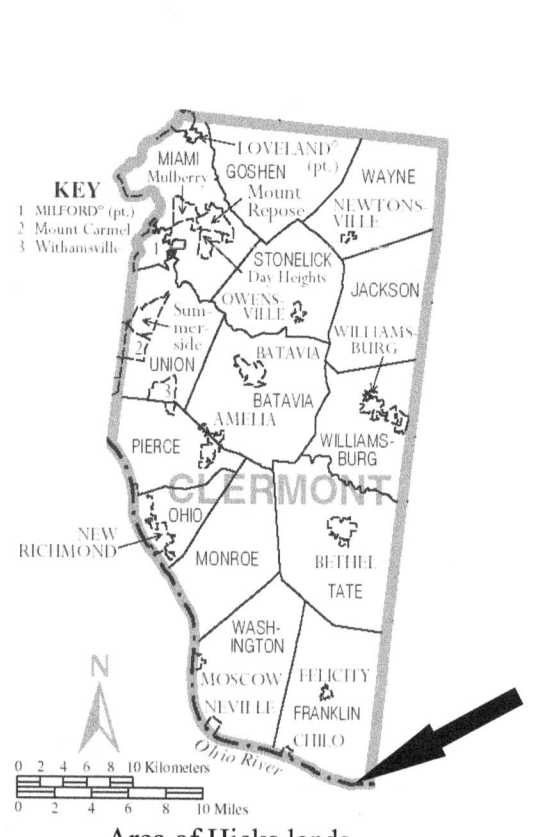

Area of Hicks lands
Clermont Co, OH

Land record - Joshua Hicks' 1st land purchase in Clermont Co, OH - 1815, p. 1

Land record - Joshua Hicks' 1st land purchase in Clermont Co - 1815, p. 2

The First Generation
Joshua and Diana (Adams) Hicks

1. **Joshua**[1] **HICKS**, born[4] about 1765 probably in Surry Co, NC; died about 1848 in Clermont Co, OH, possibly son of Samuel HICKS. He married[5] on 19 Sep 1794 in Rowan Co, NC **Diana ADAMS**, born[6] 1768 in VA; died aft 1850 probably in Clermont Co, OH.

Joshua was born in North Carolina about 1765, possibly the son of Samuel Hicks [see background chapter]. He was taxed on land in Surry Co, NC in 1797 and was on the 1800 census there. He married Diana Adams in 1794 in neighboring Rowan Co, NC. The family apparently migrated to Clermont County, OH about 1804-5. Joshua purchased 126 acres in 1815 in Franklin Township, Clermont Co, OH. He probably farmed the land but few details are known about him. He sold part of his land to his son Henry in 1820 and the remainder to son Joshua, Jr in 1840. They probably continued to live with Joshua Jr. and his wife until Joshua Sr. died about 1845. Then, Joshua Jr. sold the land and moved to Edgar Co, Illinois about 1849. At that time, Diana probably moved in with her daughter, Nancy and her husband, Nelson Newkirk. Nancy died in 1846 and Nelson remarried in 1847, but Diana continued living there with her grandchildren and former son-in-law. @@

Children of Joshua HICKS and Diana ADAMS were as follows:

+ 2   i   **Henry**[2] **HICKS**.
+ 3   ii   **Ruth**[2] **HICKS**.
+ 4   iii   **Elijah**[2] **HICKS**.
+ 5   iv   **Lydia**[2] **HICKS**.
+ 6   v   **Mary**[2] **HICKS**.
+ 7   vi   **Elizabeth 'Betsy'**[2] **HICKS**.
+ 8   vii   **Margaret**[2] **HICKS**.
+ 9   viii **James**[2] **HICKS**.
+ 10   ix   **William**[2] **HICKS**.
+ 11   x   **Nancy**[2] **HICKS**.
+ 12   xi   **Joshua**[2] **HICKS**.
  13   xii   **daughter**[2] **HICKS**, born about 1819 in OH.
              No record found for this child except for the 1820-1840 census record of her father, in which she is referred to only as a female in a certain age group. Comparison of marriage and other records of Clermont Co, OH, has led to the probable identification of all other children of Joshua Hicks and Diana Adams except for this 12th child. She does not appear in the 1850 census; thus, it is concluded that she died before 1850.

Research Notes for Generation 1

<u>Notes for Joshua HICKS #1</u>

Most information from Norman Zezula and from Orville Jones notes.
Birth: Paid taxes on land in 1792 (Surry Co, NC). Thus he was at least 21 then. Census records of 1830 & 1840 for Clermont Co, OH indicate he was born between 1760-1770
Marriage: Rowan Co, NC marriage bond (Benjamin Hicks also signs). 19 Sep 1794. State of North Carolina, Rowan county. "Know all men by these presents, that we Joshua Hicks & Benjamin Hicks of said county are held and firmly bound unto his Excellency Richd. D. Spaight Esquire, Governor Captain-General and Commander in Chief of the state aforesaid, in the full and just sum of 500 pounds current money of the state aforesaid to be paid to his Excellency the governor, his successors or assigns: To the which payment well and truly to be made and done, we bind ourselves, our heirs, Ex C___, Administrators and assigns, jointly and

severally, firmly by ____ Sealed with our ___ and dated this nineteenth day of Sept in the nineteenth year of Independence of this state. Anno Domini one thousand seven hundred and ninety four. The condition of the above Obligation is such, That whereas the above bound Joshua Hicks has made application for a licence of marriage to be celebrated between him and Diana Adams of the county aforesaid: now in case it shall not appear hereafter, that there is any lawful cause to obstruct the said marriage intended to be _ad and solemn ___ then the above Obligation to be void otherwise to remain in full force and _____. Joshua Hicks [seal] Signed sealed and delivered in the presence of J. Troy, D. C.; Benj Hicks [seal]

Death: His son, Joshua, his son's wife, Sarah, and his wife (or widow) sold 73.5 acres in 1845. This was apparently the family homestead that he and Diana sold to Joshua Jr. in 1840. It is concluded that Diana held a mortgage on it as Joshua's widow. The death of Joshua Sr. is concluded from the fact that he didn't sign. Administration papers for Joshua are indicated for the year 1848 in Clermont Co, OH. The actual papers are missing except for a few receipts. (Orville Jones' Notes)

Children: Surmised from study of the Hicks family in Clermont Co, OH. Records correlated include marriage, land, census, and death records of the children.

Chronology:
- 1792-1797: taxes paid in Surry Co, NC
- 1793: First taxed specifically on land in Surry Co, NC
- 1794: Marriage in Rowan Co, NC -- Benjamin Hicks witnessed
- 1798: taxed on 250 acres of land in Surry Co, NC.
- 1799-1800: taxed on 300 acres of land in Surry Co, NC.
- 1800: Census, Surry Co, NC (same page as Samuel, James, Benjamin, and Laban Hicks)
- 1800: Witnessed land transaction in Surry Co, NC.
- 1804: Witnessed land transaction in Surry Co, NC.
- 1805: Probable date of move to OH
- 1806: Daughter (Mary Hicks Robinson) born in OH according to her death record. (14 Feb)
- 1810: Not in the NC census. The 1810 census for OH was destroyed.
- 1815: bought 126 acres from Jas. Kerr in Clermont Co, OH One of 4 families mentioned by Everts as having settled in Franklin township "early after the War of 1812" *History of Clermont Co, Ohio*, Everts.
- 1816,1817,1819: taxed on 100 acres (John Neville, orig. proprietor)
- 1820: Census, Clermont Co, OH
- 1826: landowner in Franklin township, Clermont Co, OH; Everts, ibid.
- 1827: land sale to Henry Hicks of 59 acres (from Joshua and Diana Hicks) (In 1843, Henry sold this same land to William Hicks.)
- 1830: Census, Clermont Co, OH
- 1840: Census, Clermont Co, OH.
- 1840: land sale of 73.5 acres to Joshua Hicks Jr. (Joshua and Diana Hicks both sign) (Platting done by Orville Jones shows that this is the remaining portion of the 1815 purchase of 126 acres)
- 1845: land sale of this 73.5 acres ("Joshua and Sarah Ann and Diana Hicks sign; Sarah Ann apparently is the wife of Joshua Jr. and his mother, Diana, is apparently a widow who held a mortgage as the survivor of Joshua Sr. Sold to Chris Houser. Deed signed by Joshua, Sarah [his wife] and Diana [his mother]
- 1845: Probable date of death of Joshua Hicks.
- 1848: administration papers of Joshua's estate are indicated for this date. However, the papers are missing.
- 1854: land sale (sheriff's sale) of 8 acres belonging to Joshua Hicks and others not named. This was sold by the sheriff as a result of a suit (no details given) Only a few receipts survive, one of which is a receipt for court costs in a suit brought by Elijah Hicks against Alex Johnston, Joshua's administrator (and son-in-law). The sheriff described the land as 10 acres less 2 acres previously sold to Elijah.

Census:

1800: Surry Co, NC Joshua Hicks b. 1755-1774 [Joshua b. about 1765]; Wife b. 1774-1784 [Diana b. 1768]; Son b. 1790-1800 [Henry b. about 1795]; Daughter b. 1790-1800 [Ruth b. 28 Aug 1797]; Son b. 1790-1800 [Elijah b. 2 Apr 1799]

1810: (This census no longer exists for OH)

1820: Franklin Township, Clermont, OH (p. 19) Joshua Hicks b. Bef. 1785; Wife b. 1785-1794 [Diana b. 1768]; Son b. 1794-1804 [Henry b. About 1795]; Daughter b. 1794-1804 [Ruth b. 28 Aug 1797]; Son b. 1794-1804 [Elijah b. 2 Apr 1799]; Daughter b. 1794-1804 [Lydia b. 1 Sep 1802]; Daughter b. 1804-1810 [Betsy b.1804]; Daughter b. 1804-1810 [Mary b. 14 Feb 1806]; Son b. 1804-1810 [William b. About 1810]; Son b. 1810-1820 [James b. 30 Oct 1811]; Daughter b. 1810-1820 [Margaret b. 1812]; Son b. 1810-1820 [Joshua b. 1815]; Daughter b. 1810-1820 [Nancy b. 1817]; Daughter b. 1810-1820 [? b. About 1819] (Note: 3 persons of this household engaged in agriculture)

1830: Franklin Twp, Clermont, OH (#258). Joshua Hicks b. 1760-1770; Wife b. 1770-1780 [Diana b.1768]; Daughter b. 1810-1815 [Mary b. 14 Feb 1806]; Son b. 1800-1810 [William b. About 1810]; Son b. 1810-1815 [James b. 30 Oct 1811]; Son b .1815-1820 [Joshua b. 1815]; Daughter b. 1815-1820 [Nancy b. 1817]; Daughter b. 1815-1820 [b. About 1819] (Note: 5 older children and Margaret married prior to 1830 according to their marriage records. Apparently, a daughter was born after 1815. She is assigned the birth year of 1819 until further information is obtained.

1840: Franklin Township, Clermont, OH (#176). Joshua Hicks b. 1760-1770; Wife b. 1770-1780 [Diana b. 1768]; Son b. 1800-1810 [William b. About 1810]; Son b. 1810-1820 [Joshua b. 1815]; Daughter b. 1810-1820 [Nancy b. 1817]; Daughter b. 1820-1825 (Note: Henry Hicks, Joshua Hicks, and Alexander Johnson are listed consecutively in the census roll-- this implies they are neighbors. James Hicks is listed 2 pages previously in the census. Henry, Mrs. Margaret Johnson, and James are Joshua's children.) (It is possible that the last-unnamed-daughter is in fact Joshua Jr.'s wife Sarah. Their marriage date has not been found. Joshua Jr. did buy his parents 73.5 acre homestead in 1840; presumably, his parents continued to reside there. Joshua Jr. and his wife, Sarah sold this land in 1845.

1850: Joshua Hicks Sr. died about 1848, but his wife, Diana Hicks is listed at age 82 with the Nelson Newkirk family (see notes on Diana Adams and Nancy Hicks).

Note: Could find no record of Joshua buying or selling land in Surry Co, NC.

Notes for Diana ADAMS #1s

Birth: 1850 census, Tate township, Clermont, OH #1167. Diana Hicks listed with Nelson Newkirk family. Diana is identified as Nelson's mother-in-law, age 82; b. VA

Death: Probably shortly after the 1850 census (age 82); she doesn't appear in the 1860 census.

Note: Diana and Joshua sold the family homestead to Joshua Jr. in 1840. They probably continued to live with Joshua Jr. and his wife until Joshua Sr. died. Then, Joshua Jr. sold the land and moved to Edgar Co, Illinois about 1849. At that time, Diana probably moved in with her youngest daughter (?), Nancy and her husband, Nelson Newkirk. Nancy died in 1846. Nelson remarried in 1847, but Diana continued living there with her grandchildren and former son-in-law. (See Notes for Nancy Hicks)

---

1. Elvick, Neil. *The Kanawha Trace.*
<www.galliagenealogy.org/History/kanawha.htm>

2. Everts, ***History of Clermont County, OH***, 1880.

3. Everts, ***History of Clermont County, OH***, 1880. p. 51.

4. Surry Co, NC Land Records 1791-1807.

5. North Carolina Marriage Bonds, 1741-1868.

6. Clermont Co, OH - Census - 1850 [M432; #667].

The Second Generation
Children of Joshua and Diana Hicks

Most of this second generation remained in Clermont County and were farmers as their father had been. Joshua sold his land to his sons – beginning with 59 acres to Henry in 1827. Henry later sold this to his brother William. In 1840, Joshua, Sr. sold the remainder of the land to his son Joshua, Jr. This land remained in the family until at least 1895, when it is shown on a Clermont County land map.

Daughter, Betsy, and her husband, Levi Hopkins, continued in the Hicks' pioneering spirit and moved further west – first to Iowa before 1860 and then on to Kansas by 1880. Son Joshua farmed in Clermont County for a while, then migrated west to Edgar County, Illinois about 1850. Daughter Nancy died young and, after her death, her husband, Nelson Newkirk, their children and his second wife moved to Iowa.

Clermont County had become increasingly settled, so there were more people around during this generation. The township of Franklin, where the Hicks first settled, had grown. An 1826 listing of property owners totaled over 500, including Joshua and Elijah Hicks, Levi Hopkins (husband of Betsy Hicks) and John Tatman (husband of Ruth Hicks). There were two villages in the township, Felicity and Chilo.

Some of the family began to spread out through Clermont County. Lydia Hicks and her husband Reuben Tatman were in Tate Township (just north of Franklin Township) by 1850. Betsy Hicks and her husband, Levi Hopkins, were also in Tate Township, before they moved to Iowa. James Hicks moved across the river to Kentucky by 1850.

Most of the Hicks children had large families, so the family was expanding rapidly. The twelve children of Joshua and Diana Hicks had produced almost 60 grandchildren.

Evidently the children were fairly successful farmers. When Elijah died in 1853, his property appraisal included: 1 spinning wheel; 1 stove; 1 Bible; 1 cow; 2 beds; bedstead and bedding; the clothing and wearing apparel of the family; 1 table; 6 chairs; 6 knives and forks; 6 plates; 1 sugar dish; 1 milk pot; 15 spoons; the clothes, wearing apparel of the widow; 12 hogs worth $20.00; 2.5 acres corn 15.00; potato patch 3.00; 1 stand bees 4.00. August 19, 1853

Ohio River farmland

Area of Hicks Land in Franklin Township

Generation 2

2. Henry² HICKS (Joshua¹), born[1] about 1795 in Surry Co, NC; died[2] aft 1843. He married[3] on 25 Apr 1822 in Clermont Co, OH **Betsy UTTER**, born 1804 in Clermont Co, OH; died bef 1840, daughter of Joseph UTTER and Elizabeth BURKE.

Henry Hicks was born about 1795 probably in Surry Co, NC. He moved with his family to Ohio about 1803-5; then purchased 59 acres of land in Franklin Township, Clermont Co, OH from his father in 1820. He probably farmed the land, but no specific information has been found. He married Betsy Utter in Clermont Co in 1822. Betsy's brother Col. Dowty Utter, was an important local political figure, who later ran for governor and lost by one vote. Betsy was not on the 1840 census, so she probably died between 1830 and 1840. Henry did not appear on the 1850 census, so may have died between 1843 and 1850. @@

Children of Henry HICKS and Betsy UTTER were:
- 14 i **Daughter³ HICKS**, born est 1823.
  Census: 1830, Clermont Co, Franklin Township, p. 263 shows Henry Hicks; a wife and female child 5-10 years old

3. Ruth² HICKS (Joshua¹), born 28 Aug 1797 in Surry Co, NC; died 3 Nov 1874 in Tate Twp, Clermont Co, OH; buried in Bethel, Cemetery, Tate Twp, Clermont Co, OH. She married[4] on 19 Dec 1822 in Clermont Co, OH **John TATMAN**, born 5 Nov 1797 in KY; died 26 May 1875 probably in Clermont Co, OH; buried in Bethel Cemetery, Tate Twp, Clermont Co, OH.

Ruth Hicks was born about 1797 in North Carolina, probably Surry Co, and migrated to Ohio with her family 1803-1806. She married John Tatman late in 1822. John Tatman was a farmer, born in Kentucky in 1797. Ruth's sister Lydia married Reuben Tatman, who may be a sibling of John. @@

Children of Ruth HICKS and John TATMAN were:
- + 15 i **Lucinda³ TATMAN**.
- + 16 ii **Dianna³ TATMAN**.
- + 17 iii **George Washington³ TATMAN**.
- + 18 iv **Sarah A.³ TATMAN**.
- + 19 v **John³ TATMAN**.
- + 20 vi **William Oliver³ TATMAN**.
- + 21 vii **Mary³ TATMAN**.
- + 22 viii **Elijah³ TATMAN**.
- 23 ix **Benjamin F.³ TATMAN**, born 1837 in Clermont Co, OH; died 7 Oct 1864 in Andersonville Prison, GA.
  Jones notes: "Served Co C., 153 OVI; Captured at Hammachs Mill, WV; d. in Andersonville prison 10/7/1864; no children". *Prisoners who died at Andersonville Prison, Atwater List* (13000 names) gives: Tattman, B. 153, Co C, died Oct 7, diarrhea[5].
- 24 x **Amanda C.³ TATMAN** [1124], born 1853 in Clermont Co, OH.
  Notes: She was in the 1860 census as 7 year old, but not found after that.

4. Elijah² HICKS[6] (Joshua¹), born[7] 2 Apr 1799 probably in. Surry Co, NC; died[8] 3 Jul 1853 in Clermont Co, OH; buried in Mt. Pleasant Cemetery, Clermont Co, OH. He married[9] on 28 Feb 1823 in Bracken Co, KY **Nancy MELVIN**, born[10] 24 Jun 1806 in MD; died about 1903 probably in Mason Co, KY; buried in a small cemetery in Aberdeen, Brown Co, OH.

Elijah Hicks was born in North Carolina, probably in Surry County, in 1799. He migrated with his family to Clermont Co, OH about 1803-1805. In 1823 he married Nancy Melvin of Bracken County, KY – which lies directly across the Ohio River from Clermont Co, OH. Nancy may have been a twin of John Melvin – who

@@ More information can be found in research notes at the end of this chapter.

signed her marriage bond. Elijah was listed as a bricklayer in the 1850 census. He died in 1853; leaving Nancy a widow for almost 50 years. She lived with her daughter Callie, wife of Frank Jones in 1870; then with her daughter, Mary and her husband, William Jones, in 1880. By 1900, she was living with her grandson, George Jones, in Mason Co, KY. According to Jones' notes, "Nancy died 1903 at Maysville, KY. Buried in little riverbank cemetery at Aberdeen, OH – very small, near the river and the old road." She was present at the 50th anniversary party of her son Henry Melvin. Photo on page 37. @@

Children of Elijah HICKS and Nancy MELVIN were:
- 25 i   **John³ HICKS**[11], born 13 Oct 1824 in Clermont Co, OH; died 28 Dec 1863 in Rebel Prison, Richmond, VA.@@
- + 26 ii   **Henry Melvin³ HICKS**.
- + 27 iii   **Mary³ HICKS**.
- + 28 iv   **Elizabeth³ HICKS**.
- + 29 v   **Nancy³ HICKS**.
- + 30 vi   **Joshua³ HICKS**].
- + 31 vii   **James³ HICKS**.
- + 32 viii   **Elijah³ HICKS**.
- + 33 ix   **Martha Ann³ HICKS**.
- + 34 x   **William Stephen³ HICKS**.
- + 35 xi   **Orestes Marion Polk³ HICKS**.
- 36 xii   **George W. HICKS**[12], born 30 Mar 1847 in Clermont Co, OH; died aft 1882. No children. @@
- + 37 xiii   **Caroline Rebecca J.³ HICKS**.

5. Lydia² HICKS (Joshua¹), born 1 Sep 1802 in Surry Co, NC; died[13] 29 Nov 1861 in Clermont Co, OH; buried in Tate Cemetery Clermont Co, OH. She married[14] on 12 Apr 1828 in Clermont Co, OH **Reuben TATMAN**, born 1800/10 in NC or KY; died bef 1840 probably in Clermont Co, OH.

Lydia Hicks was probably the last of the Hicks children to be born in North Carolina. If so, she would have been a toddler at the time of the family's migration to Ohio. She married, in 1828, Reuben Tatman. Jones notes give his birthplace as North Carolina, but census records on his children give a birthplace as Kentucky. Reuben died young, so little is known of him. Lydia evidently maintained her own home until the children were grown. In 1860, she was living with her son James and his family and was listed as a 58-year old cigar maker. James was a cigar manufacturer; his mother and his wife were both working for him. @@

Children of Lydia HICKS and Reuben TATMAN were:
- + 38 i   **James³ TATMAN**.
- + 39 ii   **Lucinda³ TATMAN**.
- 40 iii   **Eliza³ TATMAN**, born Jul 1836 in Clermont Co, OH; died 20 Aug 1914 in City Infirmary, Cincinnati, Hamilton, OH; buried 22 Aug 1914 in Bethel Tate Cemetery. Not married. @@.

6. Mary² HICKS (Joshua¹), born 12 Feb 1803 in Clermont Co, OH; died[15] 3 May 1878 in Clermont Co, OH; buried in Bethel Tate Cemetery, Bethel OH. She married[16] on 15 Nov 1838 in Clermont Co, OH **John W. ROBINSON**, born 17 Dec 1817 in OH; died 11 Mar 1882 in Tate Twp, Clermont Co, OH; buried in Bethel Cemetery, Tate Twp, Clermont Co, OH.

Death records of Mary Hicks show that she was born in Ohio. There is some question about this, as her father Joshua signed documents in North Carolina in 1804. Mary's tombstone and death certificate give her birth as 1803. The birthplace on her death certificate was probably incorrect. She married John Robinson in Clermont Co in 1838. John Robinson was a farmer and fairly prosperous, as he had land worth $2000 and a personal wealth of $600 in 1860. @@

@@ More information can be found in research notes at the end of this chapter.

Children of Mary HICKS and John W. ROBINSON were:
+ 41 i   **Alonzo³ ROBINSON**.
+ 42 ii   **Melissa Jane³ ROBINSON**.
+ 43 iii **Nancy Emily³ ROBINSON**.
  44 iv **Mary Eliza³ ROBINSON**, born 4 Feb 1848 in Clermont Co, OH; died 6 Aug 1867; buried in Bethel Tate Cemetery. Not married
  45 v   **Alfonso³ ROBINSON**, born 1852 in Clermont Co, OH. Not married.
       Census: 1880 Tate, Clermont, OH, p. 271. James Holliday 41; Adaline M. Holliday 37; Alfonso Robinson 28, single, boarder, OH/OH/OH, farmer; Mary Utter 16.
       1900 not found
+ 46 vi **Margaret Missouri³ ROBINSON**.

7. Elizabeth 'Betsy'² HICKS[17, 18] (Joshua¹), born[19] 4 Dec 1804 in Surry Co, NC; died[20] 23 Apr 1880 in Haven, Reno Co, KS; buried in an unmarked grave 4½ m. south of Haven KS. She married[21] on 14 Nov 1822 in Clermont Co, OH **Levi HOPKINS**[22, 23], born 3 Jan 1803 in Bourbon Co, KY; died[24] 24 Apr 1883 in Haven, Reno Co, KS; buried in unmarked grave 4½ m. south of Haven KS.

Betsy Hicks was probably the last child of the Hicks family to be born in North Carolina. She married Levi Hopkins in 1822. Levi was a shoemaker by trade. The family was among the early members of the first Methodist Church organized in Clermont Co, The Sugar Tree Wesleyan Methodist Church, sw of Bethel. The family moved to Wapello Co, IA by 1860; then to Haven, Reno Co, KS in 1875. Kendell Griggs, a descendant, wrote a book in about 1984 ***Levi W. & Sarah E. (Carter) Hopkins, their ancestors & descendants*** about this family. @@

Children of Elizabeth 'Betsy' HICKS and Levi HOPKINS were:
+ 47 i   **Joshua H.³ HOPKINS**.
+ 48 ii **Mary³ HOPKINS**.
+ 49 iii **Diana³ HOPKINS**.
  50 iv **Elizabeth Ann³ HOPKINS**, born 31 Jul 1837 in Clermont Co, OH; died 15 Mar 1844 in Clermont Co, OH. Jones notes: "died at age 6"; Griggs book gives dates and "Died at age 7"
+ 51 v   **Levi Whitcomb³ HOPKINS**.

8. Margaret² HICKS (Joshua¹), born[25] 29 Oct 1810 in Clermont Co, OH; died[26] 29 Mar 1890 in Felicity, Clermont Co, OH. She married[27] on 27 Mar 1828 in Clermont Co, OH **Alexander JOHNSTON**, born about 1809 in Scotland; died[28] 17 Jul 1879 in Tate Twp, Clermont, OH.

Margaret Hicks married Alexander Johnston in 1828 in Clermont Co, OH. Alexander was born in Scotland and was a blacksmith by trade (as was his son, William). He was administrator of the will of his father-in-law, Joshua Hicks. His death certificate gave his occupation as a farmer. @@

Children of Margaret HICKS and Alexander JOHNSTON were:
+ 52 i   **William J.³ JOHNSTON**.

9. James² HICKS (Joshua¹), born 30 Oct 1811 in Clermont Co, OH; died 26 Jul 1850 in Clermont Co, OH; buried in Amelia Cemetery. He married[29] on 31 May 1838 in Hamilton Co, OH **Caroline WHETSTONE**, born 7 Oct 1822 in Cincinnati, Hamilton Co, OH; died 6 Aug 1894 probably in Amelia, Clermont Co, OH; buried Aug 1894 in Amelia Cemetery, Amelia, Clermont Co, OH.

James Hicks married Caroline Whetstone in 1838. He was listed as a lumber merchant in the only census he was on that gives an occupation. He moved to Newport, Campbell Co, KY before 1850 with his wife and children. After his death, Caroline and her children moved back to Clermont Co, OH. @@

@@ More information can be found in research notes at the end of this chapter.

Children of James HICKS and Caroline WHETSTONE were:
+ 53 i **Ann Maria³ HICKS**.
+ 54 ii **Sarah³ HICKS**.
+ 55 iii **William J.³ HICKS**.
   56 iv **Mary J.³ HICKS**, born about 1845 possibly in Clermont Co, OH; died 2 Feb 1932 in Amelia, Clermont Co, OH. She married **Benneville KLINE**[30], born about 1821 in PA; died 3 Jan 1898 in Amelia, Clermont Co, OH. No children. @@
+ 57 v **Georgia Anna³ HICKS**.
+ 58 vi **James Reuben³ HICKS**.

10. **William² HICKS** (Joshua¹), born about 1816 in OH?; died[31, 32]bef Sep 1850 in Campbell Co, KY. He married about 1846 **Harriet Mary BAXTER**, born about 1825 in VA.

There is some question about the life of this William Hicks. If he is the William Hicks who went to Campbell Co, KY and married Harriet Baxter, he was a lawyer (as were two of his sons). Later research by Orville Jones made him question this – and he believes that "our" William Hicks married Johanna West and later settled in Dublin, IN. This is still in question as your compiler has found nothing yet to substantiate his theory. Research will continue. Until further information is found, we will include this family as the correct one. @@

Children of William HICKS and Harriet Mary BAXTER were:
   59 i **James Walter³ HICKS**, born about 1843 in OH.
Jones notes: "not with Harriet, William & Louis in 1870; a James W. Hicks, Pvt, age 18, enlisted in Co F, 89th OVI on 8/12/1862. Missing 9/20/1863 at Chicamauga - no further record. This is the same company in which Elijah Hicks was a Lt before promotion to Capt & was mostly Clermont County names. 89th served in 31 battles in the West including Sherman's march to the sea."
+ 60 ii **William Alexander³ HICKS**.
+ 61 iii **Louis³ HICKS**.

11. **Nancy² HICKS** (Joshua¹), born 1817 in Clermont Co, OH; died 1 Dec 1846, probably in Clermont Co, OH; buried in Mt. Pleasant Cem, Clermont Co, OH. She married[33] on 20 Sep 1840 in Clermont Co, OH **Nelson NEWKIRK**, born 21 Sep 1819 in IN; died 6 Apr 1905 in Drakesville, Davis Co, IA; buried in Drakesville, Davis Co, IA.

Nancy Hicks and Nelson Newkirk were married in 1840 in Clermont Co, OH. After Nancy's death in 1846, Nelson Newkirk married Eliza Giles. Nancy's widowed mother, Diana (Adams) Hicks, lived with her son-in-law and second wife in 1850. After Diana's death, Nelson and his family moved to Whitley, Moultrie Co, IL in 1866 and then to Center, Appanoose Co, IA. Jones notes say that he lived in Drakesville, Davis Co, IA, but the census of 1880 and 1900 show his family in Center, IA. Nelson was a farmer and carpenter. @@

Children of Nancy HICKS and Nelson NEWKIRK were:
   62 i **Harriet Eliza³ NEWKIRK**, born 1841 in Clermont Co, OH.
Jones notes: "shown in 1850 & 1860 census. Mrs Howard Johnston, a granddaughter, says she never heard of her of her father speak of her and no reference to her in the papers that were in his Bible""
   63 ii **John C.³ NEWKIRK**, born 1843 in Clermont Co, OH; died 6 Apr 1863, at Stone River, TN during the Civil War.
Jones notes: "Enlisted 8/20/1862, Co H, 59th OVI; served at Lavergne & Stone River TN; d. at Stone River of Typhoid Fever"
+ 64 iii **William David³ NEWKIRK**.

@@ More information can be found in research notes at the end of this chapter.

12. **Joshua² HICKS** (Joshua¹), born about 1815 in OH; died before 1900 in Elbridge Twp, Edgar Co, IL. He married on 28 Mar 1844 in Clermont Co, OH **Sarah Ann MORGAN**, born Dec 1824 in PA; died 18 Nov 1909 in Elbridge Twp, Edgar Co, IL; buried Nov 1909 in New Providence Cemetery, Elbridge, IL. @@

Joshua Hicks, the youngest son of Joshua and Diana Hicks, bought 73 acres from his father in 1840. He sold that land and moved first to Campbell Co, KY before 1850 and then to Elbridge, Edgar Co, IL before 1860. He was a large property owner there and he operated a store, a sawmill, and a large orchard.

Children of Joshua HICKS and Sarah Ann MORGAN were:

- 65 i **William³ HICKS**, born Jan 1845 in Clermont Co, OH; died 1906 in Elbridge Twp, Edgar Co, IL.
  Jones notes: "A Civil War veteran; resided at the homestead with his mother; never married"
- 66 ii **James Alphonse³ HICKS**, born 1847 in Clermont Co, OH; died 1899.
  Jones notes: "resided in Elbridge Twp; never married"
- + 67 iii **Charles James³ HICKS**.
- + 68 iv **Albert Alden³ HICKS**.
- + 69 v **Mary Elizabeth³ HICKS**.
- 70 vi **Martha E.³ HICKS**, born Apr 1862 in Elbridge Twp, Edgar Co, IL; died 4 Feb 1924; buried in Highland Lawn Cem, Terre Haute, IN. She married in 1901 **Anderson Alford WOLFE**, born 6 Dec 1873 in IL. Jones notes: "no children"
  Census: 1910 Terre Haute Ward 7, Vigo, IN, p. Anderson A Wolfe 37, IL/IL/IL, foreman - stamping mill; Martha E 43. IL/OH/PA; married 10 years, no children.
    1920 May be the Martha E. Wolfe, 52, living in Oakwood, Vermilion, IL. She a farmer - general farm, widowed, IL/OH/IL
- + 71 vii **Sherman³ HICKS**.

Research Notes for Generation 2

<u>Notes for Henry HICKS #2</u>

Much of this information is from Norman Zezula and from Orville Jones notes.

Birth: Estimate based on the 1800 census of Surry Co, NC (showing that Joshua had 3 children under 10 years); the marriage date of Henry's parents (1794), and the identification of two other children born to Henry's parents: Ruth Hicks b. 28 Aug 1797 & Elijah Hicks b. 2 Apr 1799. The conclusion that Henry was a son of Joshua Hicks is based on the study of Clermont Co, OH marriage, land, and census records. For example, in 1827, Joshua & Diana Hicks sold 59 acres to Henry, and in 1840 sold the remaining 73.5 acres of their land to Joshua Hicks Jr. Henry sold his land (in 1843) to William Hicks. All evidence indicates Henry, Joshua Jr., and William are brothers. Joshua Hicks Sr., Henry, and Alexander Johnston (husband of Margaret Hicks) are listed consecutively in the 1840 census, suggesting they are neighbors. In the 1820 census, there is only one Hicks family in Clermont Co. (i.e. Joshua Hicks). In 1830, there are only 3 Hicks families: those of Joshua and 2 of his sons: Henry and Elijah.

Marriage: Married 25 Apr 1822 to Betsy Utter. Clermont Co, OH marriage records (v 2 p 31)

Death: Alive in 1843 when he sold his land. Does not appear on 1850 census in Clermont Co, OH

Chronology:
- 1822: Married in Clermont County.
- 1825-1830: Clerk of Franklin Township, Clermont, OH.
- 1827: Bought 59 acres from Joshua & Diana Hicks
- 1830: Census, Franklin Township (p. 263) next to Elijah Hicks; a wife and child (5-10 years old) were indicated.
- 1834: Indentured this 59 acres of land to R. Chalfant for $200.
- 1836: (or before) apparently redeemed his indentured land
- 1840: Census, Franklin, Clermont Co.; alone, aged 40-50
- 1843: sold the 59 acres to William Hicks (no wife signed) Apparently Henry left the area (not in the 1850 census.)
- 1850: Not found

Land:
- 1827: bought 59 acres from Joshua and Diana Hicks (vol. Y23, p 105)
- 1834: Indentured (mortgaged?) this 59 acres for $200. (I2 33 p. 115) 26 Dec 1834 to Robert Chalfant: [Henry Hicks sells] all that tract or parcel of land lying in the said county of Clermont and state of OH-- On the waters of the Ohio River. Beginning at two ashes and an elm, thence South 46 E. 53 poles to a stone in the branch-- thence N. 46 E 50 poles to a stone on the East side of the state road, thence N 46 W 9 poles to a stone on the West side of the road. Then N 46 E. 39 poles to a stone. Then South 46 E. 9 poles to a stone. Then N 46 E 96 poles to two beeches and a sugar tree and a stone in the patent line. Then South 45 W. 180 poles to the beginning-- containing fifty-nine acres and twelve poles be. the same more or less, it being the same tract of land where the said Henry Hicks now resides... ... the said Henry Hicks together with his wife who hereby relinquishes her right of dower... ... The conditions of the foregoing indenture is such that in case the said Henry Hicks, his heirs, admrs., exrs., or assigns shall well and truly pay to the said R. Chalfant, his heirs or assigns the sum of two hundred dollars on or before the first day of January one thousand eight hundred and thirty six, according to a written bond given by the said Henry Hicks to the said Robert Chalfant bearing [?] even date herewith. Then and in that case, this indenture shall be void and of no effect. Otherwise to remain in full force and virtue in law and equity. In testimony whereof. the said Henry Hicks has hereunto set his hand and seal the date first written. Henry Hicks [no wife signs]

Notes for Betsy UTTER #1s

Betsy's brother Col. Dowty Utter, was an important local political figure, who later ran for governor. (He failed, by one vote, to get the Democratic nomination) *History of Clermont Co, OH* - Everts

Not in 1840 census with Henry.

Information on Betsy's birth date & place and mother are from the WorldConnect Site "JMG" posted 11/2004 - accessed 11/09. Not documented!

Notes for Ruth HICKS #2

Birth: Calculated from age given in Clermont Co. death record (consistent with the census records for Tate Township, Clermont, OH)

Marriage: Clermont Co, OH marriage record (v 2, p 46) "Ruth Hicks to John Tatman, 19 Dec 1822 by Isaac Mitchell, JP"

Death: Clermont Co. death record (indicates birth in S. Carolina.) "77y, 2m, 8d; res. Tate Township; married; d. Tate township, Clermont Co, OH"

Burial: Jones Notes

Spouse: John Tatman b. 5 Nov 1797 in Kentucky; d. 26 May 1875; buried in Bethel Tate Cemetery

Land:
- 1832: John Tatman and Elijah Hicks bought 190 acres jointly (from Robert Chalfant)
- 1836: 105 acres was deeded from Elijah Hicks to John Tatman and back again (possibly a maneuver to clear title) Elijah is John's brother-in-law.

Census:
- 1830: Tate Township, Clermont, OH. John Tatman b. 1790-1800 [b.1798]; Wife b. 1800-1810 [Ruth b. 28 Aug 1797]; Son b. 1825-1830; Son b. 1825-1830; Daughter b. 1825-1830; Daughter b. 1825-1830
- 1840: Tate Township, Clermont, OH, p 151. John Tatman b. 1790-1800; Wife b. 1790-1800 [Ruth b. 28 Aug 1798]; Daughter b. 1820-1825; Daughter b. 1820-1825; Son b. 1825-1830; Son b. 1825-1830; Daughter b. 1825-1830; Son b. 1830-1835; Daughter b. 1830-1835; Son b. 1835-1840; Daughter b. 1835-1840; Son b. 1835-1840
- 1850: Tate Township, Clermont, OH. John Tatman 52, farmer, $ 2100, illiter. [b. 1798]; Ruth 52, illiter. NC [b. 1798]; George W. 23, OH [b. 1827]; John 20, OH [b. 1830]; Oliver 18, OH [b. 1832]; Mary 17, OH [b. 1833]; Elijah 15, OH [b. 1835]; Benjamin, 13 OH [b. 1837]
- 1860: Tate Twp, Clermont, OH. John Tatman 62, farmer, KY; Ruth 63 NC; George W. 32, farmer, OH; Mary 26, OH; Elijah 25, OH; Amana 7, OH. Value of land & personal property - $3600 / $600
- 1870: Tate Township, Clermont, OH. John Tatman, 72, M, Retired farmer, KY; Ruth, 72, F, NC; Elijah 35, M, OH; Sarah A,. 29 F, OH; Fanny, 6, OH; Dau ?? 1 F, OH; Effie, 1; Missouri Fitzpatrick 22; John Fitzpatrick 16. Note: Elijah Tatman and his family were living with his parents, brother Oliver next door; John Fitzpatrick was their grandson, son of daughter, Diana; Missouri is a granddaughter, daughter of their daughter Sarah.
- 1880 - not found.

Question? Are John Tatman who married Ruth Hicks and Reuben Tatman who married Lydia Hicks siblings?

Notes for Elijah HICKS #4

Bible Records: Hicks Bible. Loose paper in Hicks Bible states "Elijah Hicks was born April 2, 1799; Died July 3 1853. Also: Elijah Hicks Senior died July 3, 1853"

Birth: Tombstone (Hicks Bible gives 1797; 1850 census gives 1799)

Marriage: Bracken Co, KY Marriage record: Elijah Hicks to Nancy "Melville". Bracken Co. marriage bond is dated 28 Feb 1823 (no date given by Hicks Bible)

Death: Tombstone, Mt. Pleasant Cemetery; administration papers dated 19 Aug 1853; they are in Clermont Co, OH.

Census:
- 1830: Clermont Co, OH. This census lists Elijah, a wife, 2 sons, and 2 daughters. All are in age groups consistent with birth dates given by the Hicks Bible.
- 1840: Clermont Co, OH. Elijah Hicks: age: 40-50; wife, age: 30-40 (Nancy, b. 1806); 3-Sons age: 0-5 (James; Elijah; 1 other male); 4-Sons age: 5-10 (Joshua; 3 other males); 1-Son age: 15-20 (John, b. 1824); 3-Daughters age: 0-5 (Martha; 2 other females); 4-Daughters age: 5-10 (Nancy; 3 other females); 1-Daughter age: 15-20 (1 other female) Note: Henry b. June 1826; Mary b. 1827; Elizabeth b. 1829 are not listed in their correct age groups. Allowing for this, there are still 3 extra males and 4 extra females. They may be the children of Elijah's brother, Henry (shown with no wife or children in the 1840 census)
- 1850: Franklin Township, Clermont, OH. Elijah Hicks 51, Bricklayer, $500, NC; Nancy 44, MD; John 25, farmer, OH; Henry M. 24, Bricklayer, OH; Joshua 17, Laborer, OH; James 14, OH; Elijah 12, OH; Martha 11, OH; William 8, OH; Erastus 5, OH; George W. 3, OH; James White 19, laborer;
- 1860: Franklin township, Clermont, OH. Nancy Hicks 54, MD; Wm. Hicks 19, OH, Farm labor; O. M. P. Hicks 14, OH; George W. Hicks 12, OH; Caroline Hicks 7, OH
- 1870: Maysville, Mason Co, KY p. 5. Frank Jones 30, OH, blacksmith; Callie, 18, OH; Nancy Hicks 63, MD. (Indexed as Frank James on Ancestry.com) This would be Nancy's daughter, Caroline Rebecca.
- 1880: Rural, Clermont, OH, p 650. William Jones, 58, OH/OH/OH; Mary, 52, wife, OH/-/MD; Nancy Hicks, 73, mother-in-law, MD/MD/MD
- 1900: Maysville, Mason, KY, p 31. on E. 3rd St., George Jones, ___ 1871 OH; Susan?; wife, Feb 1873, KY; -?-, son. May 1891, KY; Nancy Hicks, grandmother, Jun 1806, MD. [Writing on census is barely legible]

Land:
1832: Elijah Hicks & John Tatman (apparently his brother-in-law) bought 190 acres from R. Chalfant in Nathaniel Gest's survey.
1836: Elijah Hicks & John Tatman deeded 105 acres back & forth (apparently to clear title)
1836: Elijah Hicks sold 2.5 acres to Alex Johnston (apparently another brother-in-law)
1841: (17 Sep) Elijah & Nancy Hicks sell 81.5 acres to David Fee in Survey 964 for $800.00
1842: (26 Apr) Elijah Hicks to Charles Rice, 5.5 acres

Will: Clermont Co, OH Book A1:44. 8 Aug 1853. Administration Papers of Elijah Hicks (no will found) We the undersigned appraisers of the estate of Elijah Hicks, deceased, after being duly sworn, have made an inventory and appraisement thereof as follows:

1 R____ Share Plow worth 15.00;   1 Shovel Plow 7.50;
1 lot double & single _____ 12.55; 1 Ax 6.00
1 Lot of tools 10.00

The following are the debts to said estate

Debtor	How Secure	Date Orig Sum	Sum	Probably Payable
____ Craig	Book acct.?;	1 Oct 1848	$400.00	...;
Bill "	"	15 Sep 1848	3.00 ... & 64 bushels;	
John Thomas	" "	1847	11.50	doubtful;
_____	" "		11.17;	$11.12
_____	" "		2.00	doubtful;
_____	" "	1841	40.26	
S. Mattels?;	" "	---	12.00.	

The deceased having left a widow and minor children, we set off to? the following property without appraising these papers as directed by statute: 1 spinning wheel; 1 stove; 1 Bible; 1 cow; 2 beds; bedstead and bedding; 1 _____; the clothing and wearing apparel of the family; 1 table; 6 chairs; 6 knives and forks; 6 plates; 6 _____; 1 sugar dish; 1 milk pot; 15 spoons; the clothes, wearing apparel of the widow. The following is a schedule of property and C? [Chattel?] belonging to the estate of Elijah Hicks, deceased, set off by the undersigned for support of Nancy Hicks, widow, and Martha Ann Hicks, Joshua Hicks, William Hicks, E.M.P. Hicks and George W. Hicks and C.R.J. Hicks, his minor children: 12 hogs worth $20.00; 2.5 acres corn 15.00; potato patch 3.00; 1 stand bees 4.00. We certify that there is no other personal property of a suitable kind to set of to the widow and children, and that the further sum of $408.00 is necessary for their support, and we allow the same out of any moneys or property belonging to said estate. August 19, 1853 William Waterfield; P. Shinkle; Harrison Yates

***Note**: Callie Hicks Lingenfelser (age 96 in 1972) is a daughter of James Hicks and a grand daughter of Elijah Hicks. She reported that her sister, Minnie, claimed (as a result of unspecified research) that Elijah's father was Joshua.

Notes for Nancy MELVIN #4s

Birth: Hicks Bible; consistent with 1850, 1860, 1880 Clermont Co, OH; 1900 census– Maysville, Mason, KY (ED 91, sh 31, line 18), with grandson, George Jones); b. Jun 1806, MD. All cited census records give a Maryland birthplace.

Bible Records: Hicks Bible in possession of Elizabeth (Hicks) Jennings [copy sent to me by Lvera Jennings Seipelt, Georgetown OH]. Loose paper in Hicks Bible states "Nancy Melvin was born June 24, 1801.

Death: "Nancy died 1903 at Maysville, KY. Buried in little riverbank cemetery at Aberdeen OH. Jones notes:"very small, near the river and the old road".

Family: Apparently her brother is John Melvin. A John Melvin signed her marriage bond. In the 1850 census, Clermont Co, OH John Melvin (with wife Susan, 41, and daughter Margaret, 19) is listed age 44, b. MD. Also, a James Melvin, age 21, b., KY (with wife Susan age 17) is listed. James corresponds in age to a son in the 1840 Clermont Co, OH census. Also, Rebecca died 5 Jul 1855, age 22y 3m 9d. George B. Melvin died 12 Jul 1855 (her child). (tombstone, Old Bethel Cemetery, Clermont, OH.)

Census

- 1860: Franklin twp, Clermont, OH, p. 512. Nancy Hicks 54, MD; Wm. Hicks 19, OH, Farm labor; O. M. P. Hicks 14, OH; George W. Hicks 12, OH; Caroline Hicks 7, OH.
- 1870: Maysville, Mason Co, KY, p. 5. Frank Jones 30, OH, blacksmith; Callie, 18, OH; Nancy Hicks 63, MD. Indexed as Frank James on Ancestry.com. Callie is Nancy's daughter Caroline Rebecca.
- 1880: Rural, Clermont, OH, p 650. William Jones, 58, OH/OH/OH; Mary, 52, wife, OH/-/MD; Nancy Hicks, 73, mother-in-law, MD/MD/MD
- 1900: Maysville, Mason, KY, p.31. E. 3rd St. George Jones B., 28, Aug 1871, OH; Lutie; wife, 27, Feb 1873, KY; Harold, 9, May 1891, son, KY; Nancy Hicks, 93, grandmother, Jun 1806, MD/MD/MD, widow

Notes for John HICKS #25

Information from Norman Zezula says he died of starvation in Prison Camp in Richmond, VA during the Civil War; buried Oakwood Cemetery, Richmond, VA. "The day after the battle of Chickamauga [GA], his regiment (59th OVI) was assigned to prevent the Rebs from crossing the bridge of the Chickamauga River. During this assignment, the regiment lost 2 officers, 15 men captured -- one may have been John."

Bible Records: Hicks Bible in possession of Elizabeth (Hicks) Jennings [copy sent to me by Lvera Jennings Seipelt, Georgetown OH]. Loose paper in Hicks Bible states, "John Hicks was born October 13, 1824 -- note beside name in different handwriting says barely legible -- see note on death below"

Marriage: Probably not married. No indication in Hicks Bible or Clermont Co. / Brown Co. marriage records. Census records show that in 1850 he lived with his parents.

Death: Roster of OH Soldiers, 1861-1865. Hicks Bible states he died in Andersonville Prison, GA. of starvation "in 1865?" He actually died in rebel prison in Richmond on 28 Dec 1863. Orville Jones notes say "buried Oakwood Cemetery".

Census:
- 1850 Clermont Co, OH. Elijah Hicks 51, NC; wife Nancy 44, MD; John 25; Henry M. 24, NC; Joshua 17, NC; James 14; Elijah 12; Martha 11; William 8; Erastes M. P. 5; George W. 3; James White 19 (laborer). Children b. OH.
- 1860 not found on census in Clermont or surrounding counties.

Military: He enlisted 12 Sep 1861 in Co. A, OH Vol. Inf. On 31 Oct 1861, he transferred to Co. C. Subsequently, he was captured and died in rebel prison (reportedly of starvation) on 28 Dec 1863. Apparently, the family harbored long term bitterness over the manner of his death. Laura Behan Zink related (in 1988) the following incident: Shortly before he died (in 1950), Harvey Henry Hicks (Laura's grandfather) asked her what she intended to name her soon-to-be-born son. She responded that they were considering "Jeffery". "Jeffery?", he said. "Jeffery" "That's Jeff! My uncle starved to death in rebel prison under Jeff Davis and ..." He became increasingly agitated. Laura named her son "Donald."

Notes for George W. HICKS #36

Jones notes say "named in his father's estate papers as under 21"

Census:
- 1850 Franklin Twp, Clermont, OH (#1774). Elijah Hicks 51, bricklayer, $500; NC; Nancy 44, MD; John 25, farmer, OH; Henry M. 24, bricklayer, OH; Joshua 17, laborer, OH; James 14, OH; Elijah 12, OH; Martha 11, OH; William 8, OH; Erastus 5, OH; George W. 3, OH; James White 19, laborer;
- 1860 Franklin Twp, Clermont, OH, p. 512. Nancy Hicks 54, MD; Wm. Hicks 19, OH, Farm labor; O. M. P. Hicks 14, OH; George W. Hicks 12, OH; Caroline Hicks 7, OH;
- 1870 Maysville Ward 4, Mason, KY, p. 434. Emile Martin 56, saddler, France; Eliza Martin 30; Duke Martin 7; George Martin 3; Cyntha Warbleton 58, KY; Margaret Rasp 20, KY; George Hicks 23, single, saddler, OH/OH/OH. [Eliza Martin is the sister-in-law and Cyntha Warbleton the mother-in-law of George's brother Elijah; his wife Victoria's family.]
- 1880 not found in KY or OH.
- *1880 Rockford, Caldwell, MO, p. 416. George W. Hicks 35, farmhand; Margaret Hicks 32; William H. Hicks 12; Moses E. Hicks 8; Bertha Hicks 4. All OH/OH/OH

[*possible - age & birthplace fit, but if child William is 12 - he should have been on the 1870 census]

Hicks Bible - Loose paper in Hicks Bible states "George W. Hicks was born March 30, 1847"

Marriage: There is no indication that he ever married. His 1880 census cannot be located. He does appear on the 1871-1875, & 1880-1881 yearly tax lists of Mason Co, KY. No wife is indicated in these lists.

Death: The 1881 tax list of Mason Co, KY is the latest record found of him, unless he is the George in MO in 1880.

Tax Lists:
Mason Co, KY tax lists 1871-1875; 1880-1881. Appears in the lists: 1871-1875; 1880-1881 (gap in collection) He does not appear in 1882 or later lists. In militia until 1875. First shown with property in 1875 (1 horse, $75.; $50. gold, etc.; In 1880, he had 4 acres worth $60.; no animals shown. In 1881, he had 4 acres and a horse worth $40. He does not appear in 1882 or later. His brothers, Orestes Polk, William, and James are found in these tax lists for the same period.

Letter: George W. Hicks, Maysville, Mason, Ky. to Henry Melvin Hicks in Rural, Clermont, OH. The text follows: *7 Oct 1874 Dear Brother, Hope this may find all well as it leaves all at present. My health is about as usual. Henry, I have not rec'd that money yet, and as I made arrangements to use it the 1st of this month, it will put me to considerable trouble if I don't get it. As you know, I discounted it heavy in order to make sure of getting it at that time. I got the balance I lacked [?] for 30 days, which is now overdue. If you have not sent it yet, please do so as soon as possible. Enclosed find one of Mr. Pelham's [?] cards. The price of his moveable _____ hives is 3.00. Write soon. Your bro. George W. Hicks* (Letter in possession of Blaine Hicks in 1976; photocopy in possession of Norman Zezula)

Notes for Lydia HICKS #5

Information from Norman Zezula and from Jones notes.

Birth: Tombstone (calculated). Father did not move to OH (from NC) until 1804-1806. The 1850 census gives NC as her birthplace.

Marriage: Clermont Co, OH marriage records (v 2, p 257); by deacon of Methodist Episcopal Church. "Lydia Hicks to Reuben Tatman, 12 Apr 1828, by Peter Hastings, L.D.M.E.C.". Information from Jones notes.

Death: Tombstone, Tate Cemetery, Tate Township, Clermont, OH. (d. 29 Nov 1861; age 59y, 2m, 28d; ie a calculated birth of 1 Sep 1802)

Census

1830: Franklin Township, Clermont, OH, p. 261. Reuben Tatman, b. 1800-1810; Wife b. 1800-1810; Son b. 1826-1830 [James b. 1830]

1840: Franklin Township, Clermont, OH, p 150. Lydia Tatman, b. 1800-1810; Son b. 1830-1835; Daughter b. 1830-1835; Daughter b. 1835-1840

1850: Tate Twp, Clermont Co, OH, p. 360. Lydia Tatman, 47, $500, NC, illiterate; James 20, OH; Lucinda 17, OH; Eliza B. 15, OH. [next to Elijah Tatman 36, Dortha 73 VA; Margaret 30, Joseph 10, Frank M. 8. all but Dortha b. OH]

1860: Clermont Co, Tate Twp, OH. James Tatman, 30, cigar manufacturer, $250/300, OH; Mary Ann, 29, cigar maker, IN; James S. 5; Lydia Ann 2; Lydia, 58, cigar maker, NC; Eliza E. 25, cigar maker. All b. OH except Mary Ann & Lydia.

Notes for Reuben TATMAN #5s

Information from Norman Zezula and from Orville Jones notes.

Marriage: Clermont Co, OH marriage records (v 2, p 257)--by deacon of Methodist Episcopal Church. "Lydia Hicks to Reuben Tatman 12 Apr 1828 by Peter Hastings, L.D.M.E.C." Information from Jones notes

Question: Are John Tatman who married Ruth Hicks and Reuben Tatman who married Lydia Hicks siblings?

Notes for Eliza TATMAN #40

Census

1900 Tate Twp, Clermont Co, OH, p. 242a. Luc___ Brittingham, Head, F, Oct 1832, wd, OH/KY/NC, 4 (?) ch / 4 living, washerwoman, owns home; Eliza Tatman, sister, Jul 1836, 63, single, OH/KY/NC, can read & speak English but not write.

1910 Tate Twp, Clermont Co, OH, p. 4B. Lucindy Brittingham 77; Eliza S Tatman 75. No occ for either.

Death*: Eliza Tatman, d. 20 Aug 1914, City Infirmary, Cincinnati, Hamilton, OH, Birth Jul 1834, Ohio; Age at death 79 years; Single; Street address: 814 West Liberty St.; Occ: Housewife; Burial 22 Aug 1914, Bethel, OH. Ohio Deaths, 1908-1953 <fsbeta.familysearch.org>

*Note: this may not be right person, but most facts fit. Birth is wrong year, but right month.

Notes for Mary HICKS #6

Information from Norman Zezula and from Jones notes.

Birth: Tombstone calculations show 12 Feb 1803 as birth date. Jones notes gave birth as 14 Feb 1806.

Marriage: Clermont Co, OH marriage record (v 3, p 167) "15 Nov 1838 Mary Hicks to John Robinson by Washington B. Utter, JP"

Death: Jones notes - tombstone states: "3 May 1875 72y 2m 19d" (Bethel Tate Cemetery, Tate Township, Clermont Co, OH) Note: She is buried with her husband (same stone) and next to Ruth Tatman and her husband. Ruth is almost certainly her sister.

Census

1840: Ohio Township, Clermont, OH. John W. Robinson b. 1800-1810 [b. 1810]; Wife b. 1810-1820 [Mary b. 14 Feb 1806]; Son b. 1830-1835; Daughter b. 1830-1835; Daughter b. 1835-1840; Son b. 1835-1840; Son b. 1835-1840; Son b. 1835-1840

1850: Franklin twp, Clermont, OH. John W. Robinson 33, farmer $1400; Mary 42; Alonzo 12; Melissa J. 8; Missorn?; 6; Nancy E. 3; Mary E. 1; all b. in OH

1860: Clermont Co, OH. J. W. Robinson 50, farmer $2000/600 PA; Mary 50; Alvin?; 20; Malissa 17; Emily 16; Alfred? 12 Female [sic]; ? 10 M; (other notes from this census indicate: "Missouria 16; Emily 12, Alf____ 10)

1870: Not found

Notes for John W. ROBINSON #6s

Information from Norman Zezula and from Jones notes

Note: **History of Clermont Co, OH** by _Everts, p. 255. "In April 1816, J. W. Robinson settled in the village of Batavia. At first he was a carpenter; then a businessman. He had a son, W. W. Robinson and a daughter, Mrs. Geo. W. Dennison. J. W. moved to Missouri in the 1840s." John W. Robinson may be another son of this J. W. Robinson.

Notes for Elizabeth 'Betsy' HICKS #7

Information from Norman Zezula and from Jones notes. Also from book: **Levi W. & Sarah E. (Carter) Hopkins, their ancestors & descendants** by Kendall Griggs, 1613 E. 35th, Hutchison, KS 67502

Marriage 14 Nov 1822; "Betsy Hicks to Levi Hopkins by Joseph Utter, JP". Clermont Co, OH marriage record (v 2, p 37 or 47). [Jones notes say 1841 but that cannot be correct]

Birth: 1850 census, with husband, Levi Hopkins, Tate Township, Clermont, OH. They lived next to Nelson Newkirk's family that included Nelson's mother-in-law (and Betsy's mother), Diana Hicks; the census states Betsy's birthplace is NC.

Death: Alive at the time of the 1850 census; she may be the Elizabeth Hopkins listed in the 1900 census (Zanesville, Muskingum, OH); the birth date of June 1804 is consistent with the 1850 census; however, the 1900 census lists her birthplace as MD, not NC. This could be due to her being a boarder living with an apparently unrelated family.

Census: 1830: not found

1840: Tate Township, Clermont, OH. Levi Hopkins b. 1801-1810; Wife b. 1801-1810; Daughter b. 1821-1825 [About 1823]; Daughter b. 1826-1830; Son b. 1836-1840; Daughter b. 1836-1840

1850: Tate Township, Clermont, OH (#720) Levi Hopkins, 47, farmer KY; Elizabeth 46 NC; Levi W. 10 OH (Living next to the Nelson Newkirk family which includes Diana Hicks, the mother of Betsy and mother-in-law of Nelson). Census indicates Betsy is insane.

1860: Adams Twp, Wapello Co, IA, p. 695. Levi Hopkins 57, farmer, KY $1000, 200; Elizabeth Hopkins 50, NC.

1870: Drakesville, Davis, IA. Levi Hopkins 68, teamster, KY; Elizabeth 68, NC; Levi W 30, OH, shoemaker; Sarah 31, England; Sarah L 9; Clara E 7; George W 3; William L 1. Children are Levi W's, b. IA.

1880: Sumner, Reno, KS. p. 1. Levi W. Hopkins 40, KY/KY/PA, occ: farmer/prof: physician; Sarah 40, Eng/Eng/Eng; Lavina 18, IA/OH/Eng, school teacher; George W. 13, IA/OH/Eng, farm labor; Wm. L. 10, IA/OH/Eng, farm labor; Gertie M. 1, KS/OH/Eng; Levi 77, KY/KY/PA, shoe maker, widowed. [Betsy evidently died before the census in 1880]

Land: There was a Levi Hopkins, listed as a property owner in Franklin township, Clermont Co, OH in 1876. **History of Clermont Co, OH**, Everts.

Notes for Levi HOPKINS #7s

"Levi was a shoemaker by trade. Among the early members of the 1st Methodist church organized in Clermont Co, The Sugar Tree Wesleyan Methodist Church, sw of Bethel. Family moved to Wapello Co, IA by 1860; then to Haven, Reno Co, KS in 1875." from Kendall Griggs book, **Levi W. & Sarah E. (Carter) Hopkins, their ancestors & descendants** about this family, about 1984.

Notes for Margaret HICKS #8

Information from Norman Zezula and Orville Jones notes.

Birth: Clermont Co, death record (calculated as 29 Oct 1810). The year is given as 1812 in the 1880 Census (Felicity, Clermont, OH; #37) An 1811 birth year would imply that James Hicks, whose birth (inscribed on his tombstone-- 30 Oct 1811) is her twin. An 1810 birth date would imply that William is her twin.

Marriage: Clermont Co, OH marriage record (v 5, p 127) - 27 Mar 1828 "Margaret Hicks to Alexander Johnston [sic]"

Death: Clermont Co, OH death record (p 39): Margaret H. Johnson, 1890 Mar 29; wid. 79y, 5m, 0d; d. Felicity, b. Clermont Co."

Census

1840: Franklin Twp, Clermont, OH, p 176. Alexander Johnson b. 1800-1810; Wife b. 1810-1820 [Margaret b. 1812]; Male b. 1820-1825 [too old to be son?]; Son b. 1825-1830 (next to Joshua Hicks and Henry Hicks)

1850: Franklin Twp, Clermont, OH, #765. Alexander Johnson 44, Blacksmith, $1350 OH; Margaret 39, OH; Illiterate; William J. 21, Blacksmith OH; Mary Manning 17, OH; Samuel Bolan 14, OH; Tabitha Leypole 10, OH

1860: Alexander not found. Clermont Co, OH, #1165. Margaret Johnson, 59, weaver; alone b. Pa.; 500/100; no obvious relatives near her (on previous page is Franklin Johnson, a blacksmith. This is probably the wrong Margaret)

1870: Felicity, Clermont, OH, p 2. Wm. J. Johnson M 42, OH, blacksmith 700 250; Mary A. 37, OH; Lucy F. 16, OH; Alexander M. 13, OH, attends school; Jennie F. 10, OH, attends school; Frank M. 8, OH, attends school; Anna F. 4, OH; Elizabeth F. 1, OH; Margaret F. 58, OH, lives with son.

1880: Felicity, Clermont, OH (#37) William J. Johnson 50, Blacksmith, OH; Mary 45 wife; Alexander 23 son; Nancy J. 21, daughter; Anna B. 14, daughter; Mary E. 11, daughter; Bart. 8, son; Margaret H. (or A.) 68, mother

Spouse: Alex Johnston b. 1806 OH; d. 1853. Orville Jones notes.

Notes for Alexander JOHNSTON #8s

Jones notes: "Margaret was with Wm J. Johnston, Franklin Twp 1880; gave OH as birthplace in both 1870 & 1880. He died 1853; gave mother & father as b. SC"

Will: He was administrator of the estate of Joshua Hicks Sr. In this capacity, he was apparently sued by Elijah Hicks (in what may have been merely a legal ploy to clear title.)

Land: Elijah Hicks sold 2.5 acres to him in 1836. (Jones notes)

Death: Alex Johnston, Male, Death: 17 Jul 1879 Tate Tp, Clermont, OH, Age: 70; Birth: 1809 Scotland; Occ: farmer; Widowed. Ohio Deaths and Burials, 1854-1997 <pilot.familysearch.org>

Notes for James HICKS #9

Information from Norman Zezula and Orville Jones notes.

Marriage: 31 May 1838 James Hicks to Caroline Whetstone in Hamilton Co, OH.

Birth: Tombstone; place given in 1850 census in Newport, Campbell, KY

Death: Tombstone (Amelia Cemetery, Amelia, Clermont, OH). The tombstone has birth dates & death dates of both husband and wife as well their daughter, Anna Maria White.

Census

1840: Clermont Co, OH James Hicks, b. 1810-1820; Wife, b. 1810-1820, Daughter b. 1835-1840 [Manda]

1850: Newport, Campbell, KY. James Hicks 38 M Lumber Merchant OH.; Caroline 28 F OH; Manda? 11, F, OH [Anna Marie?]; Sarah 9, F, OH; Wm. 7, M, OH; Mary 5, F, OH; Georgia Anna 3, F, OH. He apparently moved to KY between the last time he was mentioned in a Clermont Co record - 1847 and 1850.

1860: not found

1870: Batavia Twp, Clermont Co, OH. p. 22; Caroline Hicks 46, keep house, OH; Mary Hicks, 22, seamstress, OH

1880 Batavia, Twp, Clermont Co, OH, p. 13A. Caroline Hicks, 58, widow, keeping house, OH/OH/OH; Mary J. dau, 32, at home, OH/OH/NY; James R., son, 29, Grocer & P.M. [postmaster?], OH/OH/OH

Note: "Anna Marie White (26 Mar 1839- 21 Nov 1882)" is on same tombstone as James and Caroline Hicks. She is the "Manda" mentioned in the 1850 census. The tombstone dates are consistent with the census age.

Marriage: Clermont Co, OH marriage record show: "Ann Maria Hicks, 19, to William H, White, 20; 7 Oct 1857 (v 7, p 234)
Land: Jones notes "Owned property at Moscow, Washington Township, Clermont, OH at the time he died. James was living in Newport KY when he sold Moscow lot 21, in 1849."

Notes for Mary J. HICKS #56

Probate: 1932 Will [Clermont Co, OH] of Mary H. Kline names: Nieces - Carrie Smith of Richmond, IN; Georgie Hicks Belden of Dublin, IN; Mina White of New Rochelle, NY; Ella Gleason of New Rochelle, NY; Mina White of Williamsburg; Nephews: John R. Miller of Chicago; Dr. Wm M. Hicks of Cincinnati; Gordon R. Hicks - Friend: Nettie Chatterton; Amelia M. E. Church; Amelia IOOF cemetery; Nephew: Albert Cochler of Madisonville; Brother: Wm J. Hicks of Dublin IN; James R. Hicks of Amelia.

1941 Administration Docket: Niece: Mina White Adams of Williamsburg; Gr-niece - Mina White of Williamsburg; gr-niece Marie Gregg of Batavia; gr-nephew Lawrence White of Williamsburg; gr-nephew Nich. White of Williamsburg; nephew: John R. Miller, 343 S. Dearborn, Chicago; nephew: Wakefield King of Leonidas MI; niece: Bessie King Robertson of Leonidas MI; nephew: Robert A. Hicks of Cambridge City IN; niece: George Belden of Dublin; niece: Marie (& James) Gregg of Batavia.

Jones notes: "Kline owned acreage in present Amelia. Kline Av goes through his land; Mary Hicks was his second wife"

Census
  1880: Amelia, Clermont, OH, p. 230B. Benneville Kline, Other, 59, PA/PA/PA, Occ: Real Estate Agt; Mary Kline, Other, 54, OH/OH/OH; with Henry Hancock, Head, 51, MD/MD/MD, Occ: farmer; wife Martha. Also Nancy Swem, Other, Widow, 75, OH/NJ/NJ.
  1900: Pierce, Clermont, OH, p. 7B. Mary Kline 55, Dec 1844, OH, widow; farmer.
  1910: not found
  1920: Amelia, Clermont, OH, p. 1A. Mary H Kline 74, OH, No occ.
  1930: Amelia, Clermont, OH, p. 1B. Mary Kline 83; James Fisher 75, cousin, companion - in home. Both OH/OH/OH.

Notes for William HICKS #10

Information from Norman Zezula and Orville Jones notes.
Probably married Harriet Baxter. [see note below]
Birth: Surmised from 1820-1840 census records and comparison with the other children in the family.
Census
  1850: Newport, Campbell, KY, p. 14. William Hicks 42, lawyer; Margaret 30; Walter 7; Alexander 5; Louisa 6/12, KY. All but baby b. OH.
  1860: Batavia, Clermont, OH (657); Harriet Hicks, 38, $1500/$2160, b. OH; James Walter, 15, OH; William A. 14, OH; Lewis 11, OH.
  1870: Batavia, Clermont, OH, p. 14. Harriet Hicks 47, VA, housekeeping,; William A 24, at school, OH; Lewis 20, OH, works on farm
  1880: Amelia, Clermont, OH, p. 3. Harriett Hicks 55, widow, VA/VT/MD, keeping house; William 34, single, attorney, OH/NC/VA; Louis 30, single, OH/NC/VA, attorney;
  1900: Batavia, Clermont, OH, p. 16. Louis Hicks 49, Sep 1850, attorney at law; Josephine 48, Jun 1851; Sarah L 14, Feb 1886; Anna B Hopkins 50, Jul 1849, OH/OH/OH, sis-in-law, single.
Death: Will probate date (Campbell Co, Ky.)
Will: Will probated first in Sept Court of Campbell Co, KY 1850, and then a certified copy probated 3 Apr 1852. in Clermont Co, OH. (Book G, P 31; 1852, Clermont Co). The will states: I, William Hicks, do hereby convey the right, title, and free use of all my property to my wife Harriet Hicks to have and to hold and to make use of the same so long as she remains my widow. In case she marries, it is my will that she shall retain one-third part after my just debts are paid; the two-thirds shall be devoted to the use of my children. It is my will that the business existing under the firm of Hicks & McRay and Co. shall continue so long as the said

company shall deem it safe and profitable. Made this 3 Sep 1850.

Note: This may be the wrong William Hicks. Orville Jones (1984) now thinks that the correct William went to Dublin, IN, (near Richmond). Orville thinks that the above ("wrong"?) William is one of the Brown Co. Hicks'. In that case, the "correct William may have been the one who married Joanna West. (md. 3 Mar 1846--Clermont Co, Marriage. record.) also a possible marriage to Elizabeth Judd, 1 Sep 1854; he a widower, 39, she 18) Clermont Co marriage record (v 6, p 175)

Marriage: From Jones notes.

Notes for Harriet Mary BAXTER #10s

"Harriet gave birthplace as West Virginia on census. Granddaughter Helen gave it as NC on William Alex's death record" - Orville Jones notes.

Orville Jones gives the children as: William, Louis, Ruth, and Alfred. The firm mentioned in the will may be a law firm.

Notes for Nancy HICKS #11

Information from Norman Zezula and Orville Jones notes.

Marriage: 20 Sep 1840 to Nelson Newkirk, Clermont Co. by W. P. Utter, J.P. Clermont Co, OH marriage record (v 3, p 233)

Birth: Census records of Clermont Co, OH (1820-1840; with her parents) and comparison with the known data for the rest of Joshua Hicks children led to this birth year estimate. Her name was determined from the Clermont Co marriage record (v 3, p 233). The fact that she was a daughter of Joshua Hicks and Diana Adams was established by the listing of Diana Hicks (Joshua's widow) with the Nelson Newkirk family in the 1850 census "Diana Hicks, age 82, b. VA; identified as Nelson's mother-in-law". Nelson is listed in 1859 with his second wife; Nancy (Hicks) Newkirk died in 1847.

Census:

- 1850: Tate Township, Clermont, OH Nelson Newkirk 30, IN, farmer; Eliza 30, OH; Eliza 9, OH; John L. 7, OH; William D. 5, OH; James 1, OH; Diana Hicks 82, VA. Eliza, John L, and William D. are apparently children of Nelson and Nancy. They were born before Nancy's death in 1846; Nelson and Eliza Giles were married in 1847.
- 1860: Tate, Clermont, OH, p. 25 Nelson Newkirk 41, farmer; Eliza 39; Hariet E 19; John C 17, farmer; William D 15, farmer; James N 12; Francis M 10; Albert L 8; Charles 4; Daniel E 1. All b. OH.
- 1870: Whitley, Moultrie, IL, p. 22. Nelson Newkirk 50, farmer; Eliza 48; William D 25, works on farm; James N 22, works on farm; Frank 19, works on farm; Albert L 18, works on farm; Charles 13, works on farm; Daniel L 12, works on farm. All b. OH.
- 1880: Center, Appanoose, IA, p. 15. Nelson Newkirk 58, farmer; Eliza 56; Francis M. 28, at home - asthma; Charley 23, school teacher; Daniel L. 21, school teacher All b. OH. Eliza's parents born Eng/NC.
- 1900: Center, Appanoose, IA, p. 5. A[lbert] L. Newkirk, 43, Oct 1854, OH/OH/OH, carpenter; Margaret, 44, Nov 1855, 1 ch / 0 living; A. N. Newkirk, 80, Nov 1819, Widowed, no occ; Smith Smith, boarder 9/12, Mar 1900, IA/IA/IA.

Death: Jones notes give the death date and states she is buried in Mt. Pleasant Cemetery, Clermont Co, a few feet from her brother, Elijah Hicks. Tombstone gives death as 1 Dec 1846, age 29.

Spouse: Nelson Newkirk married his second wife, Eliza Giles, on 30 Sep 1847 in Clermont Co.

Moved: In 1866, the Newkirk family moved to Illinois and then to Drakesville, Iowa.

Children: John C. served in Co. H, 59th OVI; died at Stone River, TN 1862. William D. was also in Co. H, 59 OVI; He received a disability discharge (pension papers). He married in Illinois and had 4 daughters. One of these, Cora Johnston was still living in Ottumwa, Iowa on 23 Oct 1974 (age 90 years). Orville Jones corresponded with her on that date, and obtained the above information from her. She has never heard of "Harriet" [sic] (prob. means "Hannah"), the 3rd child of Nelson Newkirk and Nancy Hicks. The William D. Newkirk Bible does not mention her. She may have married or died in Clermont Co. prior to 1866. (Jones notes)

Notes for Nelson NEWKIRK #11s
Jones notes includes his birth, death, remarriage to Eliza Giles 9/30/1847. Diana (Adams) Hicks [his former mother-in-law] continued to live with him. Diana was listed as age 82 in 1850.

Notes for Joshua HICKS #12
Information from Norman Zezula and from Orville Jones notes. "Removed to Elbridge Twp, Edgar Co, IL in late 1849-early 1850. Large property owner there, he operated a store, a sawmill, and a large orchard. She died 11/18/1909, buried New Providence Cemetery, Elbridge Twp, Edgar Co, IL."
Birth: estimated based on 1850-1880 census records (1850 Newport, Campbell, Ky.; p 2, #27; 1860: Elbridge Township, Edgar, Illinois; p 134, #964; 1870: ibid.--p 17, #129; 1880: ibid. p 22, #199). Analysis of parent's 1820-1830 census records of Clermont Co, OH and Clermont Co land transactions (in which Joshua and Diana Hicks sell Joshua Jr. 73.5 acres in 1840, and Joshua Jr., his wife, and Diana Hicks - probably as Joshua's survivor - sell the same parcel). Clermont Co Deeds; from Jones notes.
Marriage: to Sarah Ann (see land transaction); probably married in 1844, since birth of first known child was 1845.
Death: He is in the 1880 census; but does not appear with his wife and family in the 1900 census (Sarah marked "widow") Edgar Co, IL (ED 64, sh 10A; #210)
Census
  1840: Cannot locate - probably living with his parents; his father indicates a son in 30-39 age group -- which fits Joshua.
  1850: Campbell Co, KY p 2. Joshua Hicks 34, miller, NJ; Sarah 28, OH; Wm 5, OH; A. 3, KY; "Layfiett" ? 1, KY
  1860: Elbridge Township, Edgar, IL, p 134-135. Joshua Hicks 45?, OH, farmer, $300/480 [5 may be 8]; Sarah A. 35?, NJ [5 may be 8]; William R. 15?, OH [5 may be 3]; James A. 13?, OH; Charley 7?, IL; Albert 3?, IL; Mary 9/12, IL (The ages were hard to read; the interpretations were influenced by the ages given in other census years.) Apparently, "Layfiet" b. 1849 and died before 1860
  1870: Elbridge Township, Edgar, IL, p. 17. Joshua Hicks 54 OH, farmer; Sarah 45 OH [prob. b. in NJ]; James A. 22 OH; Charles 15 OH; Albert 13 OH; Mary 11 OH; Martha 9 IL; Sherman? 5 IL
  1880: Elbridge Township, Edgar, IL p 22. Joshua Hicks 65, farmer, OH/MD/ NC; Sarah 55, wife, NJ/NJ/NJ; William R. 35, Single, son, farm labor, OH/OH/NJ; Alonzo 32, single, son, OH/OH/NJ; Charles J. 25 M single, son, School teacher, OH/OH/NJ; Martha 18, F, Single, daughter, At home IL/-/-; Sherman 15, M, single, son, Farm labor, IL/-/-. (Note: Alonzo in 1880 may be the same as James A. in 1870. Both have the same birth year. The middle initial of James is "A" which may stand for "Alonzo." Another son, Albert, is listed next to Joshua.)
  1900: Elbridge Township, Edgar, IL, p. 10A. Sarah Hicks, 75, Dec 1824, wid., farmer, PA /NJ/NJ; William 55, Jan 1845, son, farmer, OH/OH/PA; Martha 38, Apr 1862, dau, IL/OH/PA; Sherman, 35, Mar 1865, son, IL/OH/PA (The census indicates Sarah had 9 children; 6 are still alive. She is listed next to the household of Albert Hicks, her son.)
Land: 1840 - Joshua Hicks Jr. buys 73.5 acres from Joshua and Diana Hicks in Clermont Co, OH. 1845--Joshua and Sarah Ann Hicks and Diana Hicks sell this same 73.5 acres. Diana prob. held a mortgage as the survivor of Joshua Sr.
Info: John Hicks farm journal of Jan 11, 1898 says " Uncle Josh Hicks came by".

Notes for Sarah MORGAN #12s

Obituary: Sarah Hicks [***Terre Haute [IN] Tribune***, Friday, November 19, 1909]

Mrs. Sarah Hicks Dies Paris, Ill., Nov. 19 -- The death of Mrs. Sarah Hicks occurred Thursday night at the home of her daughter, Mrs. H. C. Clark, on aVnce (sic) avenue. Some few days ago she suffered a stroke of paralysis and never rallied from the shock. The deceased was born in Ohio 86 years ago and came to this county when a child. For several years she lived on a farm south of Vermillion, and after the death of her husband, a few years ago, took up her residence in this city with her daughter, Mrs. Clark. The deceased leaves 3 children, Mrs. Angel Wolfe, of Terre Haute; Sherman Hicks, of Terre Haute, and Mrs. Clark, of Paris. The funeral will be held from the home of Mrs. Clark Sunday afternoon. <genealogytrails.com/ill/edgar/obituaries>

End notes: Generation Two

1. Surry Co, NC - Census - 1800 [M32, #32].
2. Clermont Co, OH Land Records.
3. Clermont Co, OH Marriage Books.
4. Ibid.
5. ***Prisoners who died at Andersonville Prison, Atwater List***
6. Hicks Family Bible (loose paper).
7. Hicks Family Bible.
8. Ibid.
9. Bracken Co, KY Marriage Records.
10. Hicks Family Bible.
11. Hicks Family Group Sheet - Elijah Hicks.
15 Hicks Family Bible (loose paper).
13. Hicks, Lydia - tombstone.
14. Clermont Co, OH Marriage Books.
15. Tombstone - Bethel Tate Cemetery, Tate Twp., Clermont Co, OH.
16. Clermont Co, OH Marriage Books.
17. Information on the Hopkins family is from Kendall Griggs's book: ***Levi W. & Sarah E. (Carter) Hopkins, their ancestors & descendants***
18. Wapello Co, IA - Census - 1860.
19. Hopkins Family Bible as reproduced in ***Levi W. & Sarah E. (Carter) Hopkins***.
20. Ibid.
21. Clermont Co, OH Marriage Books.
22. Wapello Co, IA - Census - 1860 [M653, #343].
23. Hopkins Family Bible as reproduced in ***Levi W. & Sarah E. (Carter) Hopkins***.
24. Ibid.
25. Hicks, Margaret - Tombstone.
26. Clermont Co. OH Death Record.
27. Clermont Co, OH Marriage Books.
28. Ohio Deaths & Burials, 1854-1997.
29. Marriage Index: Selected Counties of Ohio, 1789-1850 [Genealogy.com database].
30. Ibid.
31. Campbell Co, KY Court Records.
32. Clermont Co, OH Will Book.
33. Clermont Co, OH Marriage Books.

The Third Generation
The grandchildren of Joshua and Diana Hicks

The grandchildren of Joshua and Diana Hicks were no longer pioneers. Clermont County, though it was (and still is) rural and mostly farmland, now had towns and roads. Steamboats landed several times a day at Chilo and Smith's Landing, bringing supplies, visitors, and news.

Tobacco had become the major farm crop, with large warehouses available for storage and sales. Several mills were built in the area, making life easier on the residents.

The hamlet of Rural (the town closest to the Hicks land), at the mouth of Bullskin Creek, on the Ohio River, was laid out on the 24th and 25th of November, 1845. The lots were numbered from 1 to 60, and were of variable size. The streets running parallel with the river were named Front, Broadway, and Third; and the intersecting streets received the names of Water, Pine, and Western Row. For a short time the place had a promising growth and was the center of a great deal of business. By 1880 other points had taken the lead, and the hamlet in 1880 contained about twenty houses, a store, tobacco warehouse, and a few mechanic shops.

There were schools and churches now, so social life improved. Some of the earlier settlers had built large homes. Franklin Township had a population of 2,219 in 1840 and 3,402 by 1880. The Ohio River was important to most activities in the county. It was the major transportation route, but it also flooded regularly, sometimes inundating homes and farms. Many years the crops had to be replanted due to flooding.

While most of the family remained in or near Clermont County, others spread out across the country. A number of family left the farms and moved to the "big city" - Cincinnati, about 20 miles west. Nancy (Hicks) Owens moved to Illinois; Martha (Hicks) Vermillion moved across the river to Mason Co, KY. After the death of Elijah Hicks, his widow, Victoria, moved to St Louis with her married daughter, then westward to Seattle, Washington.

This generation of Hicks descendants were of military age for the Civil War, and many served. The 153rd Ohio Volunteer Infantry Regiment formed in Clermont County and many of the Hicks sons, sons-in law and grandsons enlisted. Some served only three months, but others served much longer. John Hicks, son of Elijah, died in a Confederate Prison in Richmond; while his cousin Benjamin Tatman, son of Ruth (Hicks) Tatman, died at Andersonville. John Newkirk, son of Nancy (Hicks) Newkirk died at the Battle of Stone River, TN. Elijah Hicks, son of Elijah, served as an officer in the OVI, but received a serious head wound. This wound caused mental problems and he eventually was committed to the State Hospital. Many families had several sons serving.

This Civil War letter was from Polk Hicks to his brother, Henry (in possession of Blaine Hick's widow, Elsie in 1988.) It has a Nashville, Tenn. postmark, and was addressed to Henry in Rural, OH. The text follows:

23 April 1860 - Camped on Stone River

Dear brother,

I take this opportunity of addressing a few lines. I am well and hope these few lines will find you enjoying the Lord's blessing. I received your letter and was glad to hear from you. I lost your letter I got so that I could not answer it right. Henry, I hear that they are about to start Josh off to the Confederacy and that they have taken his name down. I think Josh has turned to be a union [?] man lately from the last letter I got from _____. There is no news to communicate. Henry, I would like to come home for a while, but there is no chance to do so.

We are attending the general, yet I don't know when we will leave. We may stay here all summer. One of

the boys in our company died today with pneumonia. We have lost six or seven with it since we came to this camp. Henry, I want you to write often for it is a satisfaction [?] to have a letter from my family to read. Write soon and let me know all of the news about home. Henry, I will send you a genuine Confederate bill of five dollars that I got here at Stone River [?]. It is genuine -- made in the CSA.
Well, I must close for it is getting dark. No more at present, but I remain your affectionate brother,
Polk Hicks

P.S. Direct to Co. A, 27th [?] regt. -- OH Vol. -- 2 brigade, B division, left wing, Army of the Cumberland [?] [it could be 59th regt.]

Battle at Lookout Mountain

The Rural, OH area was active in the Underground Railroad movement – helping fleeing slaves reach freedom. We don't know if the Hicks were involved, but they may have been.

Ulysses S. Grant was born in Point Pleasant in Clermont County. His home may have been typical of the area.

Boyhood home of Ulysses S. Grant

Nancy (Melvin) Hicks
(1806-1903)

Henry Melvin Hicks (1826-1905)

Hannah F. (Owens) Hicks
(1821-1907)

Elizabeth (Hicks) Jones (1829-1872)

4 generation photo. Henry Jones Age 78, William A Jones 52, Albert E. Jones 28, & Ralph C. Jones 7 - abt 1902

Generation 3

15. Lucinda[3] **TATMAN** (Ruth[2] HICKS, Joshua[1]), born 1824 in OH; died 1867/70. She married on 13 Feb 1845 in Clermont Co, OH **William MANNING**, born 1 Mar 1815 in OH; died aft 1870, son of John MANNING III and Jane BERRY.

Lucinda Tatman, granddaughter of Joshua Hicks, married William Manning. Both were from Clermont County, so it is possible that they knew each other as children. They married in 1845 and had 7 children. We have been unable to find any further information on daughters, Sarah Elizabeth, born 1854, and Lulu, born 1867. In 1850, John Manning, possibly William's father, lived with them. William Manning was a farmer. Son George W. "removed to Missouri; two sons", accord to Orville Jones, but we have been unable to locate him. @@

Children of Lucinda TATMAN and William MANNING were:
+ 72 i   **Francis M.**[4] **MANNING**.
+ 73 ii   **Mary A. 'Mollie'**[4] **MANNING**.
+ 74 iii   **John Wesley**[4] **MANNING**.
   75 iv   **George W.**[4] **MANNING**, born 1851 in OH. Jones notes: "removed to Missouri; two sons"
   76 v   **Sarah Elizabeth**[4] **MANNING**, born 1853 in OH. Not found on census after 1870 - either married young or died young.
+ 77 vi   **Charles William**[4] **MANNING**.
   78 vii **Lulu May**[4] **MANNING**, born 1867 in OH. Not found on census after 1870 - either married young or died young.

16. Diana[3] **TATMAN** (Ruth[2] HICKS, Joshua[1]), born 14 Mar 1825 in Clermont Co, OH; died 16 May 1867 probably in Brown Co, OH; buried in Old Nicholsville Cemetery, Clermont Co, OH. She married on 2 Dec 1848 in Clermont Co, OH **Zachariah FITZPATRICK**, born 20 May 1826 in Nicholsville, Clermont Co, OH; died 24 Jul 1867; buried in Old Nicholsville, Clermont Co, OH, son of Solomon FITZPATRICK and Sarah DONHAM.

Diana Tatman, probably named for her grandmother Diana (Adams) Hicks, married Zachariah Fitzpatrick. They stayed in Clermont Co, where Zachariah Fitzpatrick was a blacksmith. Diana's sister, Sarah, married Zachariah's brother, John. After both Diana and Zachariah died about 1867, the ten children lived with relatives and neighbors. The 1870 census showed them spread out over Clermont County. We have found no records of sons, Samuel and Zachariah, who must have left the area after their parents' death. @@

Children of Dianna TATMAN and Zachariah FITZPATRICK were:
+ 79 i   **Homer Jerome**[4] **FITZPATRICK**.
+ 80 ii   **Sarah Ellen**[4] **FITZPATRICK**.
   81 iii   **Samuel**[4] **FITZPATRICK**, born 1851 in OH. No known children.
           Census: 1870 not found in OH or KY
           1880 - may be the Samuel Fitzpatrick in Saint Louis, Saint Louis, MO, p. 490 age 28, b. OH living with brother, Edward, 30 (possibly George E.?). Both are painters, OH/IA/IA. birthplace is right, but parents' birthplaces are not. No other information found.
+ 82 iv   **George E.**[4] **FITZPATRICK**.
   83 v   **Zachariah**[4] **FITZPATRICK**, born 30 Apr 1856; died 1 Jul 1867; buried in Old Nicholsville. No known children.
   84 vi   **Mary Olive**[4] **FITZPATRICK**, born 18 Sep 1858 in Clermont Co, OH; died 3 Feb 1908; buried in Old Nicholsville. No children. @@
+ 85 vii **Walter**[4] **FITZPATRICK**.
   86 viii **John S.**[4] **FITZPATRICK**, born 1863 in OH. No children.@@
   87 ix   **Ida Blanche**[4] **FITZPATRICK**, born 6 Jun 1863 in Brown Co, OH; died 17 Jun 1937 in Batavia

@@For more information on this family, see research notes at the end of this chapter.

Clermont Co, OH. No children.

Ida Fitzpatrick was only 4 when her parents died. She and her sister, Sarah, went to live with her aunt and uncle, John & Jane Tatman. John Tatman was the brother of Ida's mother, Diana Tatman Fitzpatrick. In 1880, she was living with the family of her uncle John McNair. Her brother Walter was there with her. In 1910, she was living with Dr. Mary Crane, a physician. She remained in that household as housekeeper until at least 1930. @@

88 x **Ruth L.**[4] **FITZPATRICK**, born 3 Aug 1865 in Clermont Co, OH; died 17 Jan 1920 in Batavia Clermont Co, OH. No children. @@

Ruth L. Fitzpatrick went to live with her uncle [her mother's brother] Washington Tatman's family after the death of her parents. She was a school teacher, never married.

89 xi **Gertrude**[4] **FITZPATRICK**, born 1866 in Clermont Co, OH; died 1937; buried in Old Nicholsville.

Gertrude Fitzpatrick may be the same person as Ruth #88. The death certificate for Ruth gives her middle name as Gertrude. Ruth is not found on census after 1870 – Gertrude was found on both 1880 and 1900. Jones notes lists them as two separate daughters and gives a death date of 1937 for Gertrude. I cannot confirm this, so until proven otherwise, we'll leave them that way. @@

17. **George Washington**[3] **TATMAN** (Ruth[2] HICKS, Joshua[1]), born 15 Jul 1827 in Clermont Co, OH; died 16 Feb 1899; buried in Bethel Tate Cemetery. He married on 30 Sep 1866 in Clermont Co, OH **Edith HARRIS**, born 10 Sep 1838 in OH; died 20 Apr 1873; buried in Bethel Tate Cemetery.

George Washington Tatman was the oldest son of Ruth (Hicks) Tatman. He served in Co. C, of the 153rd Regiment, Ohio Volunteer Infantry. This was one of the 100 day regiments called up in 1864 in hopes of ending the War. His brother Elijah was in the same unit. Evidently he came back without injury, since he didn't receive a pension. After the death of his wife Edith in 1873, Washington lived with his brother Elijah.@@

Children of George Washington TATMAN and Edith HARRIS were:
90 i **Grace**[4] **TATMAN**, born 9 Oct 1872; died 6 May 1873; buried in Bethel Tate Cemetery.
91 ii **Infant**[4] **TATMAN**, died 13 Feb 1869, buried in Bethel Tate Cemetery.

18. **Sarah A.**[3] **TATMAN** (Ruth[2] HICKS, Joshua[1]), born 1828 in OH; died 1890; buried in Old Nicholsville, Clermont Co, OH. She married on 18 Apr 1847 in OH **John FITZPATRICK**, born 6 Apr 1820 in Clermont Co, OH; died 9 Mar 1911 in Tate Twp, Clermont Co, OH; buried in Old Nicholsville Cemetery, Clermont Co, OH, son of Solomon FITZPATRICK and Sarah DONHAM.

Sarah married John Fitzpatrick, who was the brother of Zachariah Fitzpatrick, who had married Sarah's sister Diana. [brothers married sisters]. John was a farmer in Clermont County all his life. Many of their children remained single and were still living with their father when he died in 1911. @@

Children of Sarah A. TATMAN and John FITZPATRICK were:
92 i **Randolph**[4] **FITZPATRICK**, born 1849; died bef 1870. Never married
93 ii **Missouri "Sue"**[4] **FITZPATRICK**, born 1850; died 4 Jun 1928 in Clermont Co, OH.
Missouri never married and lived with her brothers after her father's death. In 1900, Ruth and her sister Missouri were living in Cincinnati, where both were dressmakers.@@
94 iii **Sarah R.**[4] **FITZPATRICK**, born 1852.
Jones notes: "in 1860 census but not in 1870". This is incorrect, as she was living with her uncle, John Tatman in 1870. Not found after that. @@
95 iv **Ruth E.**[4] **FITZPATRICK**, born Oct 1854 in OH; died 1905; buried in Old Nicholsville. No children.
Jones notes: "resided (1892) at 1525 Central Ave, Cincinnati, OH; not married". In 1900

@@For more information on this family, see research notes at the end of this chapter.

Ruth and her sister Missouri were living in Cincinnati, where both were dressmakers. Both were single. @@

96 v **William B.**[4] **FITZPATRICK**, born 16 Aug 1855; died 23 Dec 1900 in Dayton OH; buried in Old Nicholsville. No children.
William Fitzpatrick remained on the family farm for many years, where he was listed as "farm labor". The Ancestry family tree of Krysten Stabler gives his death as 25 Dec 1900, Dayton, Greene Co, OH. No documentation. He was not found in the 1900 census. Never married.

+ 97 vi **John Lee**[4] **FITZPATRICK**.

98 vii **Mary Emma**[4] **FITZPATRICK**, born Mar 1858 in OH; died 1905; buried in Old Nicholsville. No children.
Discrepancy: The 1850-1880 census shows Emma as born 1858; 1900 show her as born Mar 1848. Ancestry family tree of Krysten Stabler give her death as 24 Dec 1904. No documentation. Emma was still single and living on the family farm in 1900. Not found in 1910.

99 viii **Benjamin F.**[4] **FITZPATRICK**, born Jan 1860; died 9 May 1936 in Tate Twp, Clermont Co, OH. No children.
Ben Fitzpatrick was still on the family farm in 1930, living with his unmarried siblings. He was a farmer. Never married. @@

100 ix **Reece**[4] **FITZPATRICK**, born 1862; died 1890; buried in Old Nicholsville. He married on 27 Apr 1890 in Clermont Co, OH **Callie MANNING**, born 7 Jan 1870 in Pt. Isabel OH; died 23 Oct 1966; buried in Greenwood Cemetery, Montgomery, AL, daughter of George W. and Mary MANNING. No children.

101 x **Minnie L.**[4] **FITZPATRICK**, born 15 Mar 1865 in OH; died[34] 19 Feb 1937 in New Richmond, Clermont Co, OH; buried 22 Feb 1937 in Nicholsville, OH.
Jones notes: "not married"; Single, living with father & siblings in 1900 census and with brothers after that – probably still on the family farm.
Death: Ohio Deaths 1908-1953 <pilot.familysearch.org>: Lists parents; "single". Death certificate signed by brother Oliver.

102 xi **Oliver L**[4] **FITZPATRICK**, born 7 Jul 1867 in Clermont Co, OH; died 23 Nov 1945 Cincinnati, OH. No children.
Notes: Single, living with father & siblings in 1900 census; Jones notes: "living with Alonzo Robinson [a first cousin 1x removed] in 1880"; later he was living on the family farm with his father and still later with his siblings. Never married.
Death: Oliver Fitzpatrick d. 23 Nov 1945, Cincinnati, Hamilton, OH; b. 07 Jul 1867, Clermont Co, OH; Age 78 years; Parents: John Fitzpatrick; Sarah Tatman. Ohio Deaths, 1908-1953 <beta.familysearch.org>

103 xii **Charles C.**[4] **FITZPATRICK**, born 1868. No known children.
Jones notes: "Resided in St. Louis; believe this to be Clifford who resided 1525 Central, Cincinnati, OH in 1892".
Census: 1870 not on census with family, should have been a 2 year old there.
1880 living on family farm with father & siblings.
1900 may be the Charles Fitzpatrick who was in Great Falls, Cascade Co, MT, as a boarder, b. Sep 1865, single, OH/OH/OH. Occ: smelter? (lab). A Harry Fitzpatrick, 27, b. Ireland, immigrated 1873, is in same household & same occupation.

+ 104 xiii **John Sherman**[4] **FITZPATRICK**.

@@For more information on this family, see research notes at the end of this chapter.

19. John[3] TATMAN, (Ruth[2] HICKS, Joshua[1]), born 16 Mar 1830 in Clermont Co, OH; died[35] 28 Mar 1913 in Tate, Clermont, OH; buried 2 Apr 1913 in Bethel Tate Cemetery, Clermont Co, OH. He married (1) on 25 Nov 1852 in Clermont Co, OH **Jane MCNAIR**, born 4 May 1834 in Clermont Co, OH; died 25 Apr 1897; buried in Bethel Tate Cemetery, daughter of Archibald and Mary MCNAIR; (2) abt 1898 in Clermont Co, OH **Melita or Melissa ANDERSON**, born 30 Jul 1850 in Clermont Co, OH; died[36] 7 Aug 1918 in Monroe Twp., Clermont, OH; buried 9 Aug 1918 in Bethel Tate Cemetery, daughter of William ANDERSON and Mary KING. @@

Children of John TATMAN and Jane MCNAIR were:

+ 105 i **William W.[4] TATMAN**.
+ 106 ii **Mary A.[4] TATMAN**.
   107 iii **Archibald[4] TATMAN**, born 1862 in Clermont Co, OH; died 1896; buried in Batavia. He married on 8 Nov 1894 in Clermont Co, OH **Mary W. PETERSON**, born 17 Nov 1870 in Williamsburg, Clermont Co, OH; died 1936; buried in Batavia, daughter of William PETERSON and Maggie PETERSON. No children.
       Archibald Tatman married in 1894 and died two years later. Evidently they had a child, but the child was not living in 1900. His wife, Mary, remarried after 1900.
   108 iv **Harriet[4] TATMAN**, born 1865 in Clermont Co, OH; died 1868. No children.
+ 109 v **Maud Blanche[4] TATMAN**.
+ 110 vi **Lewis G.[4] TATMAN**.
+ 111 vii **John Charles[4] TATMAN**.
+ 112 viii **Florence J.[4] TATMAN**.
   113 ix **Oliver[4] TATMAN**, born 18 Jan 1874 in Clermont Co, OH; died[37] 12 Dec 1952 in Chillicothe, Ross, OH; buried 15 Dec 1952 in Grandview Cemetery, Chillicothe, OH. He married on 19 Oct 1909 in Ross County, OH **Florence E. WILSON**, born 1877 in Chillicothe, OH. No children.
       Oliver was a physician, who was living with his aunt and uncle in Brown Co, OH in 1900 and a farm laborer- possibly while a student. By 1910, he was listed as a physician and was living with another aunt in Ross Co, OH. By 1920, he was living with his wife Florence, but next door to the aunt. He remained in Chilicothe, Ross Co, OH until his death in 1952. @@

20. William Oliver[3] TATMAN (Ruth[2] HICKS, Joshua[1]), born 1831 in Clermont Co, OH; died 9 Mar 1876; buried in Bethel Tate Cemetery. He married (1) on 10 Nov 1853 in Clermont Co, OH **Barbara ALTMAN**, born 1832 in Clermont Co, OH; died 1854; buried in Bethel Tate Cemetery; (2) bef 1860 **Elizabeth HANCOCK**, born abt 1848; died 29 May 1868; buried in Bethel Tate Cemetery; (3) bef 1870 **Melita or Melissa ANDERSON**, born 30 Jul 1850 in Clermont Co, OH; died[38] 7 Aug 1918 in Monroe Twp., Clermont, OH; buried 9 Aug 1918 in Bethel Tate Cemetery, daughter of William ANDERSON and Mary KING.

William Oliver Tatman was a farmer for most of his life, although in 1860 he was listed as a cigar maker. He had three wives, outliving two of them. After he died, his widow, Melita, married his brother, John. He had probably 6 children, but it is unsure which children went with which mother. I've make a "best guess".

Children of William Oliver TATMAN and Elizabeth HANCOCK were:

   114 i **Annie L.[4] TATMAN**, born 1860 in Clermont Co, OH; died abt 1880.
       Jones notes: "died at about 20 years"
+ 115 ii **Ledora Estelle[4] TATMAN**.
+ 116 iii **Arizona T. "Arra"[4] TATMAN**.

@@For more information on this family, see research notes at the end of this chapter.

Children of William Oliver TATMAN and Melita or Melissa ANDERSON were:
+ 117 i **Caroline 'Callie'**[4] **TATMAN**.
  118 ii **Ruie**[4] **TATMAN**, born abt Sep 1871 in Clermont Co, OH; died[39] 20 Feb 1941 in Bethel, Clermont, OH; buried 21 Feb 1941 in Monroe Cem. She married (1) on 14 Feb 1892 in Clermont Co, OH **Harry N. TAYLOR**, born Nov 1861 in OH, son of Frank TAYLOR and Martha BROWNEN; (2) on 24 Jul 1915 in Clermont Co, OH **Harvey J. BRETZ**, born 13 Feb 1869 in Laurel OH; died[40] 17 Sep 1958 in Cincinnati, Hamilton, OH. No children. @@
  119 iii **Lurena Dee**[4] **TATMAN**, born 10 Jun 1874 in Bethel, OH; died 7 Mar 1960 in Clermont Co, OH. She married on 5 Nov 1914 in Clermont Co, OH **John Eselman EMMONS**, born 25 Nov 1867 in Bethel, OH; died[41] 12 Oct 1938 in Bethel, Clermont, OH; buried 15 Oct 1938 in Bethel Cemetery, Clermont, OH, son of David EMMONS and Martha MCNUTT. No children. @@

21. **Mary**[3] **TATMAN** (Ruth[2] HICKS, Joshua[1]), born 19 May 1833 in Clermont Co, OH; died 8 Jan 1895; buried in Bethel Tate Cemetery. She married on 14 Mar 1864 in Clermont Co, OH **John MCNAIR**, born 21 Apr 1832 in Scotland; died 27 Mar 1910 in Tate, Clermont Co, OH; buried 29 Mar 1910 in Bethel Cemetery, Clermont, OH, son of Archibald and Mary MCNAIR.

After the death of her sister, Diana, Mary and her husband, John McNair, took in some of Diana's children. John was a farmer. @@

Children of Mary TATMAN and John MCNAIR were:
  120 i **Infant**[4] **MCNAIR**, born est 1865; died 1 Jan 1865.
+ 121 ii **Ulysses Grant**[4] **MCNAIR**.
  122 iii **Infant**[4] **MCNAIR**, born est 1869; died 1 Sep 1870.
+ 123 iv **Benjamin Edwin**[4] **MCNAIR**.

22. **Elijah**[3] **TATMAN** (Ruth[2] HICKS, Joshua[1]), born 8 Jun 1835 in Clermont Co, OH; died 5 Feb 1902; buried in Bethel Tate Cemetery. He married on 24 Jun 1863 in Clermont Co, OH **Sarah Ann RUSH**, born 26 Jan 1844 in Clermont Co, OH; died 26 Jul 1914 in Bethel, Clermont, OH; buried 28 Jul 1914 in Bethel Tate Cemetery, daughter of Thornton RUSH and Mary "Polly" FEE.

Elijah, like most of his family, was a farmer in Clermont County. During the Civil War, he enlisted in Company C, 153rd Infantry Regiment Ohio on 10 May 1864 and served as a private until September of 1864. His brother George was in the same unit. He lived next door to John Fitzpatrick, his brother-in-law. George evidently worked with him on the farm for a while. @@

Children of Elijah TATMAN and Sarah Ann RUSH were:
  124 i **Hattie**[4] **TATMAN**, born 7 Aug 1863 in Clermont Co, OH; died 11 Jul 1868; buried in Bethel Tate Cemetery. No children.
+ 125 ii **Fanny**[4] **TATMAN**.
+ 126 iii **Effie**[4] **TATMAN**.
+ 127 iv **Carrie**[4] **TATMAN**.
+ 128 v **John Warren**[4] **TATMAN**.
  129 vi **Solon Elijah**[4] **TATMAN**, born 2 Aug 1882 in Clermont Co, OH; died 1942; buried in Bethel Tate Cemetery. No children.
  Jones notes: "not married". Solon was a shoemaker by trade. When he registered for the draft in 1918, he listed his closest relative as his sister, Carrie Holland. @@

26. **Henry Melvin**[3] **HICKS** (Elijah[2], Joshua[1]), born[42, 43] 29 Jun 1826 in Bethel, Clermont Co, OH; died 15 Nov 1905 in Franklin, OH. He married[44] on 22 Dec 1850 in Bracken Co, KY **Hannah Francis OWENS**[45], born 5 Dec 1821 in Augusta, Bracken Co, KY; died 3 Nov 1907 in Franklin, Clermont, OH. @@

@@For more information on this family, see research notes at the end of this chapter.

Henry Melvin Hicks was a farmer like most of his family. He was also postmaster of Rural, Clermont Co, OH (at that time called Smith's Landing) from 1869-1871. His wife, Hannah Francis Owens, was from Bracken Co, KY, directly across the Ohio River from Clermont County. Her brother, William, signed their marriage bond. William had married Henry's sister, Nancy, a few years earlier. The couple celebrated their 50th wedding anniversary in 1900. Photos and clipping on page 88-89 tell of that event. Henry is the ancestor of the compiler of this book.

Children of Henry Melvin HICKS and Hannah Francis OWENS were:
+ 130 i **Orestes Daily "O.D."[4] HICKS**.
   131 ii **Sarah Francis[4] HICKS**[46], born[47] 5 Dec 1853 in Clermont Co, OH; died Feb 1859 in Clermont Co, OH.
      Bible Records: Hicks Bible in possession of Elizabeth (Hicks) Jennings, Georgetown, OH August, 1998. [copy sent to me by Lvera Jennings Seipelt, Georgetown OH]. "Sarah Frances Hicks was Born Dec 5 at 12 Oclock PM 1853. Sarah Frances Hicks died February 1854 (Burned) Age 4 years.
+ 132 iii **Elijah Franklin[4] HICKS**.
+ 133 iv **Lucy Ann[4] HICKS**.
+ 134 v **Mary Elizabeth[4] HICKS**.
+ 135 vi **Harvey Henry[4] HICKS**.
+ 136 vii **John James[4] HICKS**.

27. **Mary[3] HICKS**[48, 49] (Elijah[2], Joshua[1]), born 29 Nov 1827 in Clermont Co, OH; died aft 1900; buried in Mt Pleasant Cemetery, Clermont Co, OH. She married on 1 Feb 1843 in Clermont Co, OH **William JONES**, born 18 Jan 1821 in Clermont Co, OH; died 21 Oct 1891 in Clermont Co, OH; buried in Mt Pleasant Cemetery, Clermont Co, OH.

Mary Hicks married William Jones in 1843. There were several Hicks/Jones marriages. Orville Jones notes that William was a brother of Henry Jones, who married Mary's sister, Elizabeth. William was a farmer. In 1880, Mary's widowed mother, Nancy, was living with the Jones family. The 1900 census states that Mary had 4 children and 2 were living. There is no information about the "missing" child. @@

Children of Mary HICKS and William JONES were:
+ 137 i **Minerva Elizabeth[4] JONES**.
+ 138 ii **Samantha Jane[4] JONES**.
   139 iii **James[4] JONES**, born 1854 in Clermont Co, OH; died 1860/70 in Clermont Co, OH.

28. **Elizabeth[3] HICKS**[50, 51] (Elijah[2], Joshua[1]), born[52] 26 Oct 1829 in Clermont Co, OH; died[53] 23 Feb 1872 in Franklin Twp, Clermont Co, OH; buried in Mt Pleasant Cemetery, Clermont Co, OH. She married[54] on 20 Sep 1846 in Clermont OH **Henry JONES**[55], born 22 Feb 1825 in OH; died 10 Nov 1904 of Rural, Clermont Co, OH; buried in Mt. Pleasant Cemetery, Clermont Co, OH, son of John JONES and Mary CHAPMAN.

Elizabeth Hicks married Henry Jones, who according to Orville Jones, was a brother to William Jones, who married Elizabeth's sister, Mary. Henry was a farmer. After Elizabeth's death and the youngest children were out of the house, he lived with his son James. @@

Children of Elizabeth HICKS and Henry JONES were:
+ 140 i **James Marcellus[4] JONES**.
   141 ii **John Knox[4] JONES**, born 12 Dec 1848 in OH; died 17 Feb 1866; buried in Mt Pleasant Cemetery, Clermont Co, OH. No children.
      In 1850 census--Tate twp, Clermont, OH (# 715); age 1. Information from Jones book & Jones notes
+ 142 iii **William A.[4] JONES**.

@@For more information on this family, see research notes at the end of this chapter.

+ 143 iv **Elijah Hicks**[4] **JONES**.
144 v **Clinton**[4] **JONES**, born 13 May 1854 in Clermont Co, OH; died 1 Oct 1855 in Clermont Co, OH. This child was in Orville Jones notes; not in Jones Book. Does not appear in any census records
+ 145 vi **George Washington**[4] **JONES**.
+ 146 vii **Doctor Albert**[4] **JONES**.
+ 147 viii **Minerva Isadora 'Dora'**[4] **JONES**.
148 ix **Francis McClellen 'Mack'**[4] **JONES**, born 18 Feb 1863 in Clermont Co, OH.
Notes: 1870 census lists a "Francis", age 7, male. This birth date given in Orville Jones notes; not mentioned in Jones Family book - no record of death.
149 x **Lewis Edward**[4] **JONES**, born 11 Nov 1865 in Clermont Co, OH; died 19 Jun 1867; buried in Mt Pleasant Cemetery, Clermont Co, OH.
Jones book gives birth/death dates; Jones notes do not mention him
150 xi **Finley James**[4] **JONES**, born 1867 in OH.
Census: 1870 Franklin twp., Clermont Co, OH; age 3. Name in 1870 census could not be read. Jones book lists a "Finley James, no dates, died young"
151 xii **Orpha Grace**[4] **JONES**, born 28 Oct 1870 in Clermont Co, OH; died abt 1960 in near Portland OR. She married **Frank TRACY**. No children. @@
Orpha Jones married Frank Tracy and moved west. In 1910, they were in Nebraska; by 1920, they were in Careyhurst, Converse, WY. Orpha died in Portland, OR. Orpha's sister, Dora, lived with them in Nebraska and evidently remained there when Orpha McCabe moved west. Dora's son James Robert lived with Orpha and Frank in Wyoming. Frank was a storekeeper.

29. **Nancy**[3] **HICKS**[56] (Elijah[2], Joshua[1]), born 27 Oct 1831 in Clermont Co, OH; died 25 Jan 1865 in Mattoon, Coles Co, IL. She married[57] on 21 Jul 1847 in Clermont Co, OH **William F. OWENS**, born 1824 in KY; died 6 Oct 1873 in Mattoon, Coles Co, IL. @@

Nancy Hicks married William F. Owens, who was probably the brother of Nancy's brother Henry's wife, Hannah. William Owens was a farmer. The family moved to Illinois before 1860. Nancy died in Mattoon, IL in 1865. After her death, William married Mrs Lucinda Clark and had two more children. No record has been found of Lucinda after William's death.

Children of Nancy HICKS and William F. OWENS were:
152 i **James H.**[4] **OWENS**, born 1848 in OH.
Possible marriages: Illinois Statewide Marriage Index, 1763-1900. J H Owens to Catharine Coon 1874-12-24 Coles Co, IL; James Owens to Elizabeth Tierney 1861-02-07 Coles Co, IL. Not located after 1860 on census records.
153 ii **John W.**[4] **OWENS**, born abt Mar 1850 in OH. No other information found.
+ 154 iii **Mary**[4] **OWENS**.
155 iv **Isabel**[4] **OWENS**, born abt 1854 in OH. No further information in Jones notes.
It appears that Isabel Owens married Solomon Ray in Coles Co, IL. If this is the correct family, they had a family as shown in the census records shown in research notes below. @@
156 v **Joshua**[4] **OWENS**, born abt 1856 in OH.
157 vi **Nancy J.**[4] **OWENS**, born abt 1858 in IL.
+ 158 vii **Josephine**[4] **OWENS**, born about 1859 in IL.
Living with sister Mary and her husband Peter Mason in 1880.
159 viii **Emma**[4] **OWENS**, born abt 1861 in Illinois.
Living with sister Mary and her husband Peter Mason in 1880.
Census: 1880 Mattoon, Coles, IL, p. 198. Peter Mason 41, Can/Can/Can; Mary Mason 29, OH/KY/OH; Peter Mason 19; Rosa Mason 18; Julia Mason 16; Carrie Mason 14; Nannie

@@For more information on this family, see research notes at the end of this chapter.

Mason 11; Freddie Mason 8; Ida Mason 6; Josie Mason 3; Josie Owens 21, sis in law, IL/KY/OH; Emma Owens 19, sis in law, IL/KY/OH

30. **Joshua[3] HICKS** (Elijah[2], Joshua[1]), born[58] 16 Dec 1833 in Clermont Co, OH; died[59] 6 Dec 1906 in Cincinnati, Hamilton Co, OH; buried in Watkins Hill Cemetery. He married (1)[60] on 20 Jun 1858 in Clermont Co, OH **Minerva MARSHALL**, born 1830 probably in OH; died 1870/80; (2) in abt 1890 **Esther M. BARNES**, born 10 Oct 1853 in Charleston, OH. @@

Joshua Hicks was listed as a plasterer in census records. Jones notes say that he was a Civil War veteran, but I can find no record of service. He married Minerva Marshall in 1858 and had four children. Minerva died between 1870 and 1880. Joshua married Esther Barnes in 1890. The 1900 census shows that Esther had one child, but none living. Since she was single in 1880 and listed as Ester Barnes, she probably had not been married before – the child likely was Joshua's.

Children of Joshua HICKS and Minerva MARSHALL were:
+ 160 i **Mary Emma[4] HICKS**.
  161 ii **Anna L.[4] HICKS**, born 1859 in OH.
      Notes: Birth 1860: Franklin twp., Clermont Co, OH; # 1283; age 1. No further information.
+ 162 iii **Nancy B.[4] HICKS**.
  163 iv **Ida[4] HICKS**, born 1866 in Clermont Co, OH; died bef 1870.
      Birth: 1870 census- OH twp., Clermont Co, OH; age 4. Jones notes: "not shown in 1880 census so believe died young"

31. **James[3] HICKS**[61] (Elijah[2], Joshua[1]), born[62] 29 Feb 1836 in Clermont Co, OH; died 3 Jun 1924 in Clermont Co, OH; buried in Maysville, Mason Co, KY. He married [63] on 19 Nov 1857 in Clermont Co, OH **Emily Ann BURNS**, born 29 Nov 1839 in Bracken Co, KY; died[64] 11 Apr 1917 in Mason Co, KY; buried in Maysville, Mason Co, KY, daughter of John Campbell BURNS and Jane MELVIN.

James was listed with various occupations: journeyman wagon maker in 1870; plough shop in 1880; moulder in a foundry in 1910; pattern maker on his death records. It is likely that Emily's mother, Jane Melvin, is related to the other Melvins connected to the Hicks family. Nancy Melvin's marriage to Elijah Hicks was in Bracken Co, so she was probably from there.

Children of James HICKS and Emily Ann BURNS were:
  164 i. **Cora Jane[4] HICKS**, born 10 Feb 1860 in Aberdeen, Brown Co, OH; died 1890 probably in Cincinnati, Hamilton Co, OH. She married on 14 Aug 1883 in Maysville, Mason Co, KY **William H. DAVIS**, born Est 1860. No children.
      Birth:1880 census, Mason Co., KY; age 20 Jones notes: gives middle name; "resided Cincinnati, OH, d. 1890. No children."
  165 ii **Charley Frank[4] HICKS**, born 2 Sep 1862 in Aberdeen, Brown Co, OH; died 1864 probably in Aberdeen, Brown Co, OH.
+ 166 iii **Nora Sureanth[4] HICKS**.
  167 iv **Minnie Martin[4] HICKS**, born 26 Mar 1867 in Aberdeen, Brown Co, OH; died 20 Jun 1944 in Maysville, Mason Co, KY; buried 29 Jun 1944 in Maysville, Mason Co, KY.
      Minnie Hicks never married and lived with her father until his death; then with her sister Nora. She was a practical nurse. @@
+ 168 v **William Pearce[4] HICKS**.
+ 169 vi **Callie James[4] HICKS**.

32. **Elijah[3] HICKS**[65] (Elijah[2], Joshua[1]), born[66] 22 Oct 1837 in Clermont Co, OH; died[67] 14 Dec 1888 in Athens, Clermont Co, OH. He married[68] on 5 Jun 1866 in Mason Co, KY **Victoria E. WARBINGTON**, born 2 Mar 1844 in OH; died 1 Sep 1916 in Seattle, King Co, WA, daughter of Joseph WARBINGTON and

@@For more information on this family, see research notes at the end of this chapter.

Cynthia FIRESTONE.

Elijah Hicks was a wagon maker by occupation. He served in the Civil War, in Co. I, 22nd Regt, OH Infantry as a corporal and later was promoted to lieutenant, then captain in Co C of the same regiment. He received a severe head wound from shell splinters at Missionary Ridge and was mustered out in 1864. His head wounds led to dizzy spells; he later became violent, and was eventually committed (after 1870) to the state mental hospital in Athens, OH where he died. After Elijah entered the mental hospital, Victoria lived first with her mother in Kentucky, then with her married daughter, Lida, in Saint Louis, MO and later in Seattle, WA. Victoria died in Seattle. @@

Children of Elijah HICKS and Victoria E. WARBINGTON were:
+ 170 i **Lida H.**[4] **HICKS**.

33. Martha Ann[3] **HICKS** (Elijah[2], Joshua[1]), born[69] 12 Feb 1840 in Clermont Co, OH; died aft 1900. She married[70, 71] on 31 May 1855 in Mason Co, KY **John B. VERMILLION**, born[72] 1831 in Mason Co, KY; died aft 1910, son of Mary VERMILLION.

Martha Hicks married John Vermillion in 1855 and then moved to Platte Co, MO before 1870. By 1880, Martha was back in Clermont Co, OH, living next to her brother, Henry, and was listed on the census as divorced. By 1900, Martha is listed as married (in Ohio), while John, in Missouri, is listed as widowed. It is the belief of Orville Jones that the couple were separated rather than divorced, with the older children staying with their father in Missouri and the younger ones returning to Ohio with their mother. John was a farmer. @@

Children of Martha Ann HICKS and John B. VERMILLION were:
171 i **Child**[4] **VERMILLION**, born abt 1855. Listed in Jones notes. No other information.
172 ii **Lilly Or Julie**[4] **VERMILLION**, born abt 1857 in KY. No other information found
173 iii **William**[4] **VERMILLION**, born abt 1859 in KY. William appears in the 1860 census as a 1 year old, but never after that.
174 iv **Nancy Or Mary**[4] **VERMILLION**, born 1861 in KY. No other information found - married or died?
175 v **U. S. Grant**[4] **VERMILLION**, born 1866 in OH. No further information found.
Living next to his father in Platte Co, MO in 1900, carpenter, single.
Kansas State Census, 1915. Wendell, Thomas Co. Grant Vermillion 49, farmer.
+ 176 vi **Edgar Newton**[4] **VERMILLION**.
177 vii **John C.**[4] **VERMILLION**, born Aug 1870 in MO.
With his mother in Ohio in 1880 and 1900. No definitive information after that.
178 viii **Charles H.**[4] **VERMILLION**, born Oct 1877 in Platt City, Platte Co, MO. He married[73] on 1 Jan 1906 in Kansas City, Wyandotte, KS **Olive A. DROWN**, born 1883 in Kansas?. No known children.
In 1920 Charles was in the National Military Home, Leavenworth, KS. His wife was given as Olive, of Kansas City, MO. @@

34. William Stephen[3] **HICKS**[74] (Elijah[2], Joshua[1]), born[75] 10 Jan 1842 in Clermont Co, OH; died 6 Apr 1920 in Maysville, Mason Co, KY; buried 7 Apr 1920 in Maysville, Mason Co, KY. He married[76] on 5 Jun 1870 in Mason Co, KY **Elizabeth Ann MEENACH**, born 20 Jan 1840 in KY; died 17 Mar 1921 in Detrich, Mason Co, KY; buried 19 Mar 1921 in Maysville Cemetery, daughter of J. H. MEENACH and Eliza COLBURN.

William Stephen Hicks was a farmer in Mason Co, Kentucky - across the Ohio River from Clermont Co, OH. He married Elizabeth Meenach (sometimes spelled Meerach) in 1870. Later, Elizabeth's brother William married Nancy Hicks, daughter of Joshua Hicks, and therefore William's niece. William served in the Civil War enlisting in 5th OH Vol., Co. A on 10 Sep 1861 at age 18 and mustered out 29 Nov 1864,

@@For more information on this family, see research notes at the end of this chapter.

at the end of his service. He also enlisted in Co. I, 22nd OVI for 3 months, 27 days with his brothers Polk and James. He received a disability for chronic sore eyes.

    Children of William Stephen HICKS and Elizabeth Ann MEENACH were:

+ 179 i **Caroline Wise**[4] **HICKS**.
+ 180 ii **William H.**[4] **HICKS**.
    181 iii **Alif Maude**[4] **HICKS**, born 1877 in KY.
        Birth: 1880 census, Mason Co., KY, p 50 No other information found. A correction on Ancestry.com gives first name as Olive.
+ 182 iv **Arthur S.**[4] **HICKS**.

35. Orestes Marion Polk[3] **HICKS**[77] (Elijah[2], Joshua[1]), born 2 Jan 1845 in Rural, Clermont Co, OH; died 17 Nov 1902 in OH; buried in Greenlawn Cemetery, Columbus, OH. He married[78] on 13 Mar 1866 in Clermont Co, OH **Levina Caroline UTTER**, born 11 Dec 1845 in Chilo, Clermont Co, OH; died 22 May 1928 in Columbus, Franklin, OH; buried in Greenlawn Cemetery, Columbus, OH, daughter of John UTTER and Levina COCKRELL.

Polk Hicks was a farmer first in Mason Co, KY in 1870 and 1880. By 1900, he was in Columbus, OH, where he was working as a gardener. He lived next door to his married daughter, Lavinia. After his death, his widow Caroline ran a boarding house in Columbus. Polk Hicks enlisted in Co. I, 22nd OVI for 3 months with his brothers James and Elijah. He was wounded - "lance in shoulder" - and received a pension for his disability.

    Children of Orestes Marion Polk HICKS and Levina Caroline UTTER were:

+ 183 i **Lavina Britana**[4] **HICKS**.
+ 184 ii **Nancy Olivia**[4] **HICKS**.
    185 iii **Frank St. Clair**[4] **HICKS**, born 23 May 1872 in Maysville, Mason Co, KY. He married abt 1905 **Beryl L. _?_**, born abt 1883 in Ohio. No children.
        Jones notes say "not married" for Frank, but census records show him in Columbus, OH with wife Beryl. Death records confirm this marriage. After his wife's death, he lived with his widowed sister, Olivia. Frank was a tailor by profession. @@
+ 186 iv **Elsie**[4] **HICKS**.
    187 v **Walter Polk**[4] **HICKS**[79], born 3 Mar 1878 in Maysville, Mason Co, KY; died[80] 19 Jul 1942 in Columbus, Franklin Co, OH; buried 21 Jul 1942 in Glen Rest Cemetery. He married bef 1920, divorced **Mayme GOEDJKA**, born abt 1877 in Ohio.
        Walter Hicks had a variety of jobs over the years. In 1900, he was a 22-year-old machinist. By 1920, he was a cigar dealer and in 1930 was a salesman of wearing apparel. His draft registration gave his occupation as simply "salesman". His wife was evidently Marjorie, but called Mayme. He was divorced by 1930. @@
+ 188 vi **Clarence Malcolm**[4] **HICKS**.

37. Caroline Rebecca J.[3] **HICKS**[81] (Elijah[2], Joshua[1]), born 1 Nov 1851 in Clermont Co, OH; died abt 1928 probably in Columbus, Franklin Co, OH. She married[82] on 20 May 1869 in Clermont Co, OH **Thomas Franklin JONES**, born 10 Feb 1840 in Clermont Co, OH; died 10 Feb 1916 in Union Twp, Clermont Co, OH; buried in Mr Moriah Cemetery, Clermont Co, OH, son of Isaac JONES and Nellie BARTLOW.

Caroline Rebecca Hicks was the youngest child of Elijah Hicks. She married Thomas Franklin Jones, a younger cousin to John, the father of Henry & William Jones. Thomas served in Co A, 59th Ohio Volunteer Infantry. He was captured in September 1863 at Chicamauga Bridge, GA and mustered out May 9, 1865 at Clermont. He was a blacksmith at Maysville KY and later at Mt Carmel, OH. @@

@@For more information on this family, see research notes at the end of this chapter.

Children of Caroline Rebecca J. HICKS and Thomas Franklin JONES were:

+ 189 i **William P.**[4] **JONES**, born 20 Jun 1870; died 28 Aug 1871.
+ 190 ii **George B.**[4] **JONES**.
+ 191 iii **Irma Clare**[4] **JONES**.
   192 iv **Minnie Ward "Wardy"**[4] **JONES**, born 28 Mar 1888.
         Jones notes: "not married - 1919"

38. **James**[3] **TATMAN** (Lydia[2] HICKS, Joshua[1]), born 1830 in Clermont Co, OH; died abt 1869/70. He married on 21 Nov 1852 in Clermont Co, OH **Mary Ann ROSS**, born 1830 in Indiana.

Little is known about James Tatman, who married Mary Ann Ross in 1851. James was listed as a cigar manufacturer in 1860. His mother, Lydia, was living with him – both his wife and mother were listed as cigar makers. This was possibly a home business. Mary Tatman was living in Davies Co, IN in 1870. She probably went home to live after she was widowed in 1870. @@

   Children of James TATMAN and Mary Ann ROSS were:
+ 193 i **James Sylvester**[4] **TATMAN**
+ 194 ii **Lydia Ann**[4] **TATMAN**.
+ 195 iii **Franklin Ulyses**[4] **TATMAN**.

39. **Lucinda**[3] **TATMAN** (Lydia[2] HICKS, Joshua[1]), born 18 Oct 1833 in Clermont Co, OH; died[83] 10 Oct 1912 in Felicity, Clermont Co, OH; buried in Bethel Tate Cemetery She married on 8 Nov 1852 in Clermont Co, OH **William Brown BRITTINGHAM**, born abt 1922 in Washington, DC; died bef 1900 in OH. @@

Lucinda Tatman married William Brittingham, who was born in Washington, DC. In 1860, they lived next to her brother James, and probably had a cigar manufacturing business together. William was still working with cigars in 1870, but by 1880 was listed as a shoe maker. After William's death, Lucinda supported herself and her sister Eliza as a "washerwoman" @@

   Children of Lucinda TATMAN and William Brown BRITTINGHAM were:
+ 196 i **Cornelia Blanche**[4] **BRITTINGHAM**.
+ 197 ii **James Winfield**[4] **BRITTINGHAM**.
+ 198 iii **Lydia May**[4] **BRITTINGHAM**.

41. **Alonzo**[3] **ROBINSON** (Mary[2] HICKS, Joshua[1]), born 27 Oct 1848 in Clermont Co, OH; died[84] 26 Jun 1913 in Cincinnati, Hamilton, OH; buried 28 Jun 1913 in New Richmond, OH. He married (1) on 8 May 1862 in Clermont Co, OH **Laura A. MCGRAW**, born 1 Jan 1846 in OH; died 6 Feb 1868; (2) aft 1868 **Dian** _?_, born Jul 1852 in OH. @@

Alonzo Robinson, son of Mary Hicks Robinson, remained in Clermont Co and was a leaf tobacco dealer. There is no proof, but it seems likely that he may have worked with others in the family who were cigar manufacturers. His wife Laura died in 1868 and he had remarried by 1900. @@

   Children of Alonzo ROBINSON and Laura A. MCGRAW were:
   199 i **Clairmore**[4] **ROBINSON**, born 22 Feb 1863; died 1 Jul 1863; buried in Mt. Pleasant.
   200 ii **Lillie L.**[4] **ROBINSON**, born abt 1866 in Clermont Co, OH. No other information found

42. **Melissa Jane**[3] **ROBINSON** (Mary[2] HICKS, Joshua[1]), born 6 Dec 1842 in Clermont Co, OH; died 6 Aug 1870; buried in Bethel Tate Cemetery She married on 16 Oct 1862[85] in Clermont Co, OH **James T. UTTER**, born 1834. @@

There is little information available about this family. They were married in 1862; Melissa died in 1870. They could not be found on census records.

@@For more information on this family, see research notes at the end of this chapter.

Children of Melissa Jane ROBINSON and James T. UTTER were:
+ 201 i **Missouri Mary**[4] **UTTER**.

43. Nancy Emily[3] **ROBINSON** (Mary[2] HICKS, Joshua[1]), born 15 Jun 1846 in Clermont Co, OH; died 1 Feb 1877[86]; buried in Bethel Tate Cemetery She married on 9 Dec 1867[87] in Clermont Co, OH **Robert MCNAIR**, born 1841 in Scotland, son of Archibald and Mary MCNAIR. @@
Nancy Robinson died young so little is known about her family.

Children of Nancy Emily ROBINSON and Robert MCNAIR were:
202 i **Charles**[4] **MCNAIR**, born 1869.
Census: 1880 Tate, Clermont, OH, p. 272. Thomas J. Nichols 48; Jennie A. Nichols 48; William W. Nichols 22; Lora Mattox 17; Charles Mcnair 11, farm labor, OH/OH/OH. [may not be right person, but name & age match]
1900 not found
203 ii **Alexander H.**[4] **MCNAIR**, born 5 Jun 1873 in Clermont Co, OH.
Notes: Not found on any census records

46. Margaret Missouri[3] **ROBINSON** (Mary[2] HICKS, Joshua[1]), born 1 Sep 1844 in Clermont Co, OH; died 2 Mar 1883 probably in Clermont Co, OH; buried in Bethel Tate Cemetery She married[88] on 14 Feb 1866 in Clermont, OH **John CANN**, born Oct 1838 in OH; died 1903; buried in Bethel Tate Cemetery. @@

Margaret Missouri Robinson married John Cann in 1866. John was a farmer and also a native of Clermont County. After Margaret's death in 1883, John remarried to Ella Tompkins and had several more children.

Children of Margaret Missouri ROBINSON and John CANN were:
204 i **Robert Clayton or Clinton**[4] **CANN**, born 7 Jan 1867 in Clermont Co, OH; died 1 Mar 1892 in Laurel, Clermont, OH; buried in Bethel Tate Cemetery No children.
Death: Clayton Cann; d. 14 Mar 1892 Laurel, Clermont, OH; Age: 25; Birth: 1867. Ohio Deaths and Burials, 1854-1997 <pilot.familysearch.org>
205 ii **Melissa Blanche**[4] **CANN**, born 1869 in Clermont Co, OH; died in Sioux City, IA. She married abt 1905 in Thermopolis, WY **Christopher CHAPMAN**, born Est 1869; died bef 1910. No children.
After she was widowed, Blanche lived with her sister Belle in Sioux City, IA @@
206 iii **Otto Willard**[4] **CANN**, born Feb 1870 in Clermont Co, OH; died in WY. He married in Thermopolis, WY **(---) KEESTER**, born Est 1870. No children.
Jones notes: "no children"
Census: 1900 Thermopolis, Fremont, WY, p. 5B. Willard O Cann 30, Feb 1870, single, OH/OH/OH, bookkeeper. Not found after 1900.
207 iv **Annie L.**[4] **CANN**, born 6 Nov 1871 in Clermont Co, OH; died 29 Apr 1875; buried in Bethel Tate Cemetery
Birth: Female Cann; b. 06 Nov 1871 Monroe, Clermont, OH; Father: John T. Cann; Mother: Margret Missouri Robinson. Ohio Births and Christenings, 1821-1962 <familysearch.org>.
No other information found
208 v **Missouri Belle**[4] **CANN**, born 25 Jan 1878 in Washington Tp, Clermont, OH. She married in Thermopolis, WY **Myron WHEELER**, born abt 1874 in Pennsylvania, son of George WHEELER. No children.
Myron was a storekeeper in Sioux City, IA. Belle's sister, Blanche lived with the family for a number of years.@@

@@For more information on this family, see research notes at the end of this chapter.

47. Joshua H.[3] HOPKINS (Elizabeth 'Betsy'[2] HICKS, Joshua[1]), born 22 Sep 1823 in Brown Co, OH; died 3 Feb 1890; buried in Union Cemetery, Batavia OH. He married 29 Feb 1846 in Clermont Co, OH **Electra Collins FOSTER**, born est. 1823; died abt 1893; buried in Union Cemetery, Batavia, OH. @@

Jones notes:"Joshua Hopkins was a tailor and also owned a hotel in Amelia in 1882. He lived between Amelia & Batavia"[89]

Children of Joshua H. HOPKINS and Electra Collins FOSTER were:

209 i **Annabell[4] HOPKINS**, born Jul 1849 in OH; died 28 Aug 1931 in Clermont Co, OH. No children.
Annabelle never married. She lived with her sister, Sarah Hicks, for most of her life. She worked as a dressmaker. @@

210 ii **Sarah F.[4] HOPKINS**, born 8 Sep 1849 in Amelia, Clermont Co, OH; died 1888; buried in Batavia, Clermont Co, OH. She married on 27 May 1885 in Newport KY **Louis HICKS** (see #61), born 8 Sep 1849 in Amelia, Clermont Co, OH; died[90] 24 Feb 1920 in Batavia, Clermont, O; buried 26 Feb 1920 in Batavia, Clermont Co, OH, son of William HICKS and Harriet Mary BAXTER.
Jones notes: "1st wife Sarah & 2nd wife Josephine were sisters"

211 iii **Josephine[4] HOPKINS**, born 25 Aug 1851 in Amelia, Clermont Co, OH; died 28 Jan 1941 in Batavia, Clermont, OH; buried in Batavia, Clermont Co, OH. She married bef 1894 in Brown Co?, OH **Louis HICKS**, born 8 Sep 1849 in Amelia, Clermont Co, OH; died 24 Feb 1920 in Batavia, Clermont, O; buried 26 Feb 1920 in Batavia, Clermont Co, OH, son of William HICKS and Harriet Mary BAXTER
After the death of his wife, Sarah, Louis Hicks married Sarah's sister Josephine. His sister-in-law, Annabelle, lived with this family most of her life. @@

212 iv **Carrie[4] HOPKINS**, born 1857; died 14 Oct 1886 in Amelia, Clermont, OH.
Death: Carrie E. Hopkins, d. 14 Oct 1886, Amelia, Clermont, OH, Age 28; Birth date 1858 Amelia; single. Ohio Deaths and Burials, 1854-1997 <pilot.familysearch.org>

48. Mary[3] HOPKINS (Elizabeth 'Betsy'[2] HICKS, Joshua[1]), born 27 Jan 1825 in Clermont Co, OH; died 11 Nov 1894; buried in Drakesville, Davis Co, IA. She married on 3 Sep 1840 in Clermont Co, OH **William H. KLINGLER**, born abt 1815 in Ohio; died 22 Aug 1885; buried in Drakesville, Davis Co, IA.

Mary Hopkins married William Klinger and moved to Davis Co, IA before 1860. Mary's parents moved to Iowa about the same time, and later moved on to Kansas, while Mary, her sister Diane, and some extended family remained in Iowa. William Klinger was a farmer.[91] @@

Children of Mary HOPKINS and William H. KLINGLER were:
213 i **Minerva E[4] KLINGLER**, born abt 1842 in Ohio. No further information found.
+ 214 ii **Mary E.[4] KLINGLER**.

49. Diana[3] HOPKINS (Elizabeth 'Betsy'[2] HICKS, Joshua[1]), born 26 Dec 1826 in Clermont Co, OH; died 1 Sep 1897 probably in Drakesville, Davis Co, IA; buried in Drakesville, Davis Co, IA. She married on 26 Mar 1853 **Arthur W. STEWART**, born 1828 in Ohio; died 10 Dec 1887 probably in Drakesville, Davis Co, IA; buried in Drakesville, Davis Co, IA.

Diana Hopkins married Arthur Stewart, who was listed as a "master blacksmith" in the 1860 census. Diana probably moved with her family to Iowa and married Arthur there. After her mother's death and her father's move to Kansas, the Stewarts remained in Iowa. @@

@@For more information on this family, see research notes at the end of this chapter.

Children of Diana HOPKINS and Arthur W. STEWART were:

215 i **Mary E.**[4] **STEWART**, born abt 1854; died 31 Mar 1863.
Notes: Griggs book: "d. 31 Mar 1863 at age 9"

216 ii **James W.**[4] **STEWART**, born abt 1857 in Iowa; died 28 Feb 1863.

+ 217 iii **John M.**[4] **STEWART**.

51. Levi Whitcomb[3] **HOPKINS** (Elizabeth 'Betsy'[2] HICKS, Joshua[1]), born 5 Jan 1840 in Clermont Co, OH; died 3 Dec 1883 in Reno Co, KS. He married on 29 Sep 1859 in Wapello Co, IA **Sarah Elizabeth CARTER**, born 15 Jun 1839 in Upwell, England; died 19 Sep 1919 in Haven, Reno Co, KS.

Levi W. Hopkins evidently moved to Reno Co, Kansas when his father did before 1880. Levi had married Sarah Carter, a native of England, in 1859 and he, with his wife and 4 children, lived with his parents in Iowa in 1870. Levi was listed as a farmer in 1860, a teamster in 1870 and a farmer & "prof physician" in 1880. After Levi's death, Sarah lived with her daughter, Clara, in 1900 and then with her grandson, George, in Oklahoma in 1910. @@

Children of Levi Whitcomb HOPKINS and Sarah Elizabeth CARTER were:

+ 218 i **Sarah Lavina**[4] **HOPKINS**.
+ 219 ii **Clara Elizabeth**[4] **HOPKINS**.

220 iii **George Wesley**[4] **HOPKINS**, born 3 Jul 1866 in Wapello, Louisa Co, IA; died 1884 in California. No children.
Notes: Information from Kendall Griggs' book. Jones notes: "not married"

221 iv **William Lincoln**[4] **HOPKINS**, born 3 Jul 1879 in Davis Co, IA; died[92] 24 Mar 1952 in Orlando, Orange Co, FL. He married on 17 Mar 1903 **De Leo RHODES**, born 12 Aug 1877; died[93] 1964 in Orlando, Orange Co, FL No children. @@.

+ 222 v **Gertrude May**[4] **HOPKINS**.
+ 223 vi **Walter Ralph**[4] **HOPKINS**.

52. William J.[3] **JOHNSTON** (Margaret[2] HICKS, Joshua[1]), born 1828/30 in Clermont Co, OH; died 1883. He married[94] on 6 Jan 1853 in Clermont Co, OH **Mary MANNING**, born 1833 in Clermont Co, OH; died 29 Jan 1923.

William Johnston was a blacksmith like his father. The family lived in Felicity, OH. After William's father's death in 1879, his mother, Margaret, lived with them, probably until her death in 1890. After Williams's death, several of Mary's children and grandchildren lived with her. @@

Children of William J. JOHNSTON and Mary MANNING were:

+ 224 i **Lucinda Margaret**[4] **JOHNSTON**.
+ 225 ii **William Alexander**[4] **JOHNSTON**.

226 iii **Nancy Jane 'Jennie'**[4] **JOHNSTON**, born 18 Apr 1859 in Clermont Co, OH; died[95] 4 Jul 1926 in Washington Twp, Clermont Co, OH; buried 6 Jul 1926 in Mt. Pleasant Cemetery, Clermont Co, OH. Not married.
Jones notes: "not married; reside Light St, 1900; seamstress". Lived with her mother.
Death: Nancy Jane Johnston, d. 04 Jul 1926, Washington, Clermont, OH; b. 18 Apr 1859 Ohio; age 67 years 2 months 16 days; Single; Occ: Domestic; Burial: 6 Jul 1926, Mt. Pleasant Cemetery; Father: Wm. Johnston, b. OH; mother: Mary Manning, b. OH. Signed by sister Annie Utter. Ohio Deaths, 1908-1953 <beta.familysearch.org>.

227 iv **Frank**[4] **JOHNSTON**, born 1862 in Clermont Co, OH; died 1889; buried in Mt. Pleasant.
Jones notes: "not married"

+ 228 v **Annie Belle**[4] **JOHNSTON**.
+ 229 vi **Mary Elizabeth**[4] **JOHNSTON**.

@@For more information on this family, see research notes at the end of this chapter.

230 vii **Aterburt Elliot "Burt"⁴ JOHNSTON**, born 1872 in Clermont Co, OH; died 1903; buried in Mt. Pleasant.

Jones notes: "not married". Burt was living at home in 1900 and listed as a clerk.

231 viii **William⁴ JOHNSTON**, born 4 Mar 1872 in Clermont Co, OH.

In Jones notes. Does not appear on any census. May be another name for listed child. Birth year is same as Burt's; name corresponds to William Alexander.

53. Ann Maria³ HICKS (James², Joshua¹), born 26 Mar 1839 probably in Clermont, OH; died 21 Nov 1882; buried in Amelia, Clermont Co, OH. She married⁹⁶ on 7 Oct 1857 in Clermont Co, OH **William H. WHITE**, born 3 Mar 1837 probably in Clermont, OH; died⁹⁷ 6 Aug 1912 in Williamsburg, Clermont; buried 9 Aug 1912 in Williamsburg, Clermont Co, OH, son of Joseph WHITE and Elmirah FISHER.

Anna Marie White is buried with her parents, James and Caroline Hicks, in Amelia and has a large monument. She was listed on the census as Manda. William White was a grocer in 1870, a farmer in 1880, and was listed as a merchant on his death certificate. @@

Children of Ann Maria HICKS and William H. WHITE were:

+ 232 i **Ella F.⁴ WHITE**.
+ 233 ii **James Hicks⁴ WHITE**.
   234 iii **Mina Bell⁴ WHITE**, born 14 Nov 1871 in Williamsburg, Clermont Co, OH. No children. Mina lived with her sister Ella Gleason in 1900; with her father in 1910 and with her widowed sister-in-law, Maggie White in 1930. Her occupation was given as saleslady and as a stenographer. @@

54. Sarah³ HICKS (James², Joshua¹), born Apr 1843 probably in Clermont Co, OH. She married abt 1869 **Edward N. KING**⁹⁸, born Apr 1844 in England; died 1 Sep 1937.

Sarah Hicks was evidently called Sallie. The presence of a "stepson", John Miller, raises a question. Was Sarah married before and had a child, John Miller, born abt 1864 OH? We cannot locate them on the 1870 census, which might answer the question. Based on the 1910 census, when she said she had been married 41 years, the marriage date to Edward King was about 1869. Where were they in 1870? In 1910, Sarah was enumerated in both North Dakota (in April) and Michigan (in May). She was evidently visiting her daughter Bessie in April. Edward King had immigrated from England in 1859 and was a flour miller. @@

Children of Sarah HICKS and Edward N. KING were:

+ 235 i **Bessie⁴ KING**.
+ 236 ii **Wakefield Edward⁴ KING**.

55. William J.³ HICKS (James², Joshua¹), born Jul 1843 probably in Clermont Co, OH. He married on 18 May 1871 in Clermont Co, OH **Clara HOPKINS**, born Nov 1847 in Ohio; died bef 1920, daughter of Robert A and Mariah HOPKINS.

William Hicks was a flour & grain dealer in 1880 & 1900; a retailer - flour & feed in 1910. His wife Clara died before 1920, but no records have been found. The family evidently moved to Indiana between 1871, when they were married, and the 1880 census. @@

Children of William J. HICKS and Clara HOPKINS were:

   237 i **Carrie⁴ HICKS**, born Mar 1872 in Ohio. She married on 14 Jun 1894 in Wayne Co, IN **Elmer J. SMITH**, born Mar 1872 in Indiana, son of George C. and Martha E. SMITH. Mentioned in 1932 Will of Mary H. Kline. @@
+ 238 ii **Robert A.⁴ HICKS**.

@@For more information on this family, see research notes at the end of this chapter.

239 iii **Georgia**[4] **HICKS**, born May 1879 in Indiana; died[99] 1954 in Orange Co, FL. She married abt 1924 **Guy Joseph BELDEN**, born 11 May 1878 in Vevay, Wayne Co, IN; died[100] 1952 in Orange Co, FL, son of Moore H and Rosa BELDEN
Jones notes: "Resided (1932) Dublin, IN; m. ___ Belden"
Mentioned in 1932 Will of Mary H. Kline and 1941 Admin Docket "Georgia Hicks Belden of Dublin"
Census: 1930 Dublin, Wayne Co, IN, p. 4A gives spouse as Guy J. Belden, 51, born in Indiana, married age 45, retail merchant (grocery store); wife Georgie, 50, married age 44, born Indiana, parents born in Ohio.
Death: Georgia H. Belden; Death Date: 1954; Orange Co, FL. FL Death Index [Ancestry.com]

57. **Georgia Anna**[3] **HICKS** (James[2], Joshua[1]), born abt 1847 probably in Clermont Co, OH. She married **Albert Butler SMITH**.

Jones notes give their only child as Carrie, living in Richmond, IN in 1932 when she was mentioned in her aunt, Mary Kline's, will. All the records found show Albert and Georgiana with a daughter, Luella, b. 1869 and living in Cincinnati. Albert B. Smith is listed as a teamster. He died before 1900, as Georgiana is listed as a widow in the 1900 census. @@

Children of Georgia Anna HICKS and Albert B. SMITH were:
+ 240 i **Luella**[4] **SMITH**.
Jones notes: "resided (1932) in Richmond, IN". Mentioned in 1932 Will of Mary H. Kline
Error: Jones notes seem to have Luella Smith confused with Carrie (Hicks) Smith, dau. of William J. Hicks of Wayne Co, IN. Luella's children numbered 240a and 240b.

58. **James Reuben**[3] **HICKS** (James[2], Joshua[1]), born 23 Dec 1850 in Newport, Campbell Co, KY; died[101] 7 Apr 1938 in Amelia, Clermont Co, OH; buried 11 Apr 1938 in IOOF Cemetery, Amelia, Clermont Co, OH. He married on 27 Jan 1885 in Clermont Co, OH **Anna Bertrand MORSE**, born abt 1861 in OH; died aft 1938, daughter of Increase MORSE and Caroline BERTRAND.

James R. Hicks was a merchant and had his own dry goods store in Amelia, OH. Later he had a tomato canning business. He married Anna Morse @@

Children of James Reuben HICKS and Anna Bertrand MORSE were:
+ 241 i **William Morse**[4] **HICKS**.
  242 ii **James R.**[4] **HICKS**, born 25 Jul 1886 in Amelia, Clermont Co, OH; died 27 Jul 1886.
  Included in Jones notes. Does not appear on any records.
  243 iii **Gordon Benevil**[4] **HICKS**, born[102] Oct 1890 in Amelia, Clermont Co, OH.

60. **William Alexander**[3] **HICKS** (William[2], Joshua[1]), born 28 Nov 1845 in Newport, Campbell Co, KY; died 10 Dec 1929; buried in Laurel Cemetery, Madisonville, OH. He married on 12 Dec 1883 in Clermont Co, OH **Nettie W. WHITAKER**, born 9 Nov 1846 in Batavia, OH; died 5 Jan 1927 in Cincinnati, Hamilton Co, OH; buried in Laurel Cemetery, Madisonville, OH, daughter of Joseph T. WHITAKER and Rosana WAGLEMAN

William Hicks was a lawyer and had his own law office in the Cincinnati area. His brother Louis and his son Lewis were also lawyers. @@

Children of William Alexander HICKS and Nettie W. WHITAKER were:
  244 i. **Louis Raymond**[4] **HICKS**, born Mar 1886 in OH; died 1959; buried in Laurel Cemetery, Madisonville OH. He married bef 1920 **Ruth wife of Lewis HICKS**, born abt 1891 in Chicago, IL; died 10 Feb 1970 in Madiera, Hamilton Co, OH; buried in Laurel Cemetery, Madisonville OH.

@@For more information on this family, see research notes at the end of this chapter.

Jones notes: "no children"

Census: 1920, Cincinnati, Hamilton, OH, p. 11. Ray Hicks 44, lawyer, OH/KY/OH; Ruth J. 39, IL/OH/OH. married aged 33/29.

1930 Cincinnati, Hamilton, OH, p. 6A. Ray Hicks 44, lawyer; Ruth J 39, IL.

Not found on WW I Draft Registration

245 ii **Helen R.**[4] **HICKS**, born Sep 1891 in OH. No other information found.

Jones notes: "she married -?- Brunk at Cincinnati; he was killed in auto accident. She went to Texas and married -?- Dodson". She was still living at home in 1920 and could not be found in 1930. No other information found.

61. **Louis**[3] **HICKS**[103] (William[2], Joshua[1]), born 8 Sep 1849 in Amelia, Clermont Co, OH; died[104] 24 Feb 1920 in Batavia, Clermont, O; buried 26 Feb 1920 in Batavia, Clermont Co, OH. He married (1) on 27 May 1885 in Newport KY **Sarah F. HOPKINS**[105] (see #210), born 8 Sep 1849 in Amelia, Clermont Co, OH; died 1888; buried in Batavia, Clermont Co, OH, daughter of Joshua H. HOPKINS and Electra Collins FOSTER; (2)[106] bef 1894 in Brown Co?, OH **Josephine HOPKINS**, born 25 Aug 1851 in Amelia, Clermont Co, OH; died 28 Jan 1941 in Batavia, Clermont, OH; buried in Batavia, Clermont Co, OH, daughter of Joshua H. HOPKINS and Electra Collins FOSTER.

Louis Hicks, like his brother William, was a lawyer. He married first Sarah Hopkins and, after her death, married Sarah's sister Josephine. Annabelle, sister to Sarah and Josephine, lived with the family for many years. @@

Children of Louis HICKS and Sarah F. HOPKINS were:

246 i **Sarah Louise**[4] **HICKS**[107], born 12 Feb 1886 in Batavia, Clermont Co, OH; died Jan 1972; buried in Batavia, Clermont Co, OH.

Jones notes: "resided on Spring St, Batavia; not married"

Census: 1930 Batavia, Clermont, OH, p. 10A. Josephine Hicks 78; Louise Hicks 42, dau, stenographer - shoe manuf. co; Annabelle Hopkins 82, sister. All OH/OH/OH

64. **William David**[3] **NEWKIRK** (Nancy[2] HICKS, Joshua[1]), born 31 Dec 1844 in Bethel, Clermont Co, OH; died 26 Nov 1932 in Ottumwa, Wapello Co, IA; buried in Drakesville, Davis Co, IA. He married on 13 May 1873 in Sullivan, IL **Sarah Emaline WATKINS**, born 28 Mar 1853 near Sullivan, Moultrie Co, IL; died 4 Jul 1921; buried in Drakesville, Davis Co, IA.

William Newkirk enlisted in Co H, 59th Ohio Volunteer Infantry in September, 1861. After the War, he moved to Moultrie, IL - probably with his parents - and married Sarah there. Sometime between 1897 and 1900, the family moved to Drakesville, IA. William was a farmer. In 1925, William's parents were living with him in Ottumwa, IA.@@

Children of William David NEWKIRK and Sarah Emaline WATKINS were:

+ 247 i. **Edward**[4] **NEWKIRK**.
+ 248 ii **Mary Ellen**[4] **NEWKIRK**.
+ 249 iii **Cora**[4] **NEWKIRK**.
  250 iv **Nancy**[4] **NEWKIRK**, born 25 Feb 1887 in Moultrie Co, IL; died 7 Mar 1972; buried in Agency, IA. She married on 16 Jun 1916 in Ottumwa, IA **William PARKER**[108], born 3 Nov 1881 in Iowa; died 10 Jan 1942; buried in Agency, IA.

Jones notes: "no children"; No other information found.

67. **Charles James**[3] **HICKS** (Joshua[2], Joshua[1]), born 9 Jun 1852 in Elbridge Twp, Edgar Co, IL; died 23 Sep 1893; buried in New Providence Cemetery. He married after 1880 **Sarah Ellen REED**, born Oct 1861 in Illinois.

Jones notes: "resided near Vermillion, IL; Helped operate his father's saw mill in the winter months and

@@For more information on this family, see research notes at the end of this chapter.

threshed in the summer with the steam tractor from the saw mill. Worked in the Dakota grain fields". After his death, his wife Ella worked as a seamstress to support their children. @@

    Children of Charles James HICKS and Sarah Ellen REED were:

+ 251 i **Verna**[4] **HICKS**.
  252 ii **daughter**[4] **HICKS**, born est. 1882.
  253 iii **Harry**[4] **HICKS**, born Jun 1887 in IL.
      May be the Harry Hicks, of Attica, Fountain Co, IN who registered for WW I draft in 1942. Born June 1888, Paris, IL, farmer, self employed, contact: Bertha Hicks. Red hair, blue eyes, light complexion, 5' 10", 145 lbs.
+ 254 iv **Mary Cecil**[4] **HICKS**.
  255 v **Paul**[4] **HICKS**, born 16 Aug 1892 in Paris, Edgar Co, IL. Not married.
      Jones notes: "not married"
      Census: 1920 May be the Paul Hicks in Libertyville, Lake Co, IL, age 27, welder - electric road, wife Eleanor. Both IL/IL/IL.
      Military: WWI Draft Registration [Ancestry.com] gives Paul Hicks, age 24, b. Paris, IL, 16 Aug 1892, living at 1469 Chase, Terre Haute, IN. Machinist, married, military service: private, Marine Corp, US Navy. length of service illegible. Contact: wife, name not given. Tall, slender, brown eyes, auburn hair. Registered: June 1917.

68. Albert Alden[3] **HICKS** (Joshua[2], Joshua[1]), born 25 Jun 1857 in Elbridge Twp, Edgar Co, IL; died 19 Jan 1907; buried in New Providence Cemetery He married on 27 Oct 1878 in Elbridge Twp, Edgar Co, IL **Sadie Bell ROBERTS**, born 10 Jun 1858; died[109] 22 Jun 1937 in Edgar Co, IL.

Jones notes: "died in a train explosion near Sanford, IL when returning on a train from Terre Haute IN. Partner to his brother, Charles J., in the threshing business". After Albert's death, Sadie remained on the farm until her death. @@

    Children of Albert Alden HICKS and Sadie Bell ROBERTS were:

  256 i **Roscoe**[4] **HICKS**, born 23 Jan 1880 in Elbridge Twp, Edgar Co, IL; died 11 Jul 1953. He married on 20 Nov 1917 **Grace TUCKER**, born abt 1893 in Nevada.
      Jones notes: "no children"
      Census: 1920 Elbridge, Edgar, IL. p. 8a. Roscoe Hicks, 39, head, farmer, general farm, IL/IL/OH; Gracie, 27, wife, NV/IL/IL
      1930 District 6, Elbridge, Edgar, IL. Roscoe Hicks, 50, married age 37, IL/OH/IL, farmer; wife Grace, 37, married at age 25, NV/IL/IL.
      Military: WW II Draft Registration, 1942 [Ancestry.com] shows name, no middle initial, b. 23 Jan 1880, Edgar Co, IL. Self employed, contact: G. A. Hicks, Paris, IL. 5' 10", 225 lbs, blue eyes, brown hair, ruddy complexion.
+ 257 ii **Glenn Alvin**[4] **HICKS**.
  258 iii **Blanche E.**[4] **HICKS**, born 10 Oct 1883; died 12 Mar 1888.
      Notes: "Willard Burnett Hicks, was the son of Charles Jefferson Hicks, who was the son of Albert Alden Hicks who was the son of Joshua Hicks". Information from Marsha Gillespie <tomargill@centurytel.net>, 9/25/2005
  259 iv **Curtis Ivan**[4] **HICKS**, born 3 May 1889 in Edgar Co, IL; died 27 Sep 1967 in Contra Costa Co, CA; buried in San Francisco, CA.
      Lived on the family farm until at least 1930.
      Military: WW II Draft Registration - 1942 [Ancestry.com] gives birth date & place, residence: Elbridge, Edgar Co, IL. Name as Ivan Curtis Hicks, contact Roscoe Hicks, Paris, IL. 6'; 208 lbs, ruddy complexion, blue eyes, brown & gray hair.

          @@For more information on this family, see research notes at the end of this chapter.

Death: Ivan C Hicks; SS#: 305240837; Male; Birth: 3 May 1889, Illinois; Death: 27 Sep 1967, Contra Costa, CA. California Death Index, 1940-1997 [ancestry.com]
Discrepancy: Jones notes gave death as 24 Sep 1967, San Francisco, CA; CA Death index gives 27 Sep 1967 Contra Costa, CA.

+ 260 v **Charles Jefferson**[4] **HICKS**.
  261 vi **Julian Stephen**[4] **HICKS**, born 24 Jan 1899 in Illinois; died[110] Sep 1981 in Terre Haute, Vigo Co, IN. He married[111] on 5 Feb 1925 in Vigo, IN **Margaret Faye HALL**, born 21 Aug 1905 in Terre Haute, IN; died[112] 9 Apr 1999 in Terre Haute, Vigo, IN, daughter of George O'Neal HALL and Monone May WATTS. No children.
Julian was a mail carrier in 1930.
Census: 1930 Terre Haute, Vigo, IN. p. 17A. Julian S Hicks 31, mail carrier - govt, IL/OH/OH; Margart F 24. IN/IL/IL, laborer - food products; married 5 years.
Marriage: Julian S. Hicks, b. 24 Jan 1899, IL; Bride: Faye Hall, b. 21 Aug 1905, Terre Haute, IN; Marriage: 5 Feb 1925, Vigo, Indiana; Groom's parents: Albert A. Hicks; Sadie Bell Roberts; Bride's parents: George O'Neal Hall; Monone May Hall; both single. Indiana Marriages, 1780-1992 <fsbeta.familysearch.org>
Marriage (1903) of Margaret's sister May gives mother's maiden name as Watts.
Not found on WW I Draft records

69. Mary Elizabeth[3] **HICKS** (Joshua[2], Joshua[1]), born abt 1860 in Elbridge Twp, Edgar Co, IL; died 1931; buried in Little Grove Cemetery, Edgar Co, IL. She married (1)[113] on 28 Nov 1878 in Edgar Co, IL **Herbert FARNHAM**, born est. 1859; died bef 1908; (2) on 12 Apr 1908 in Paris, IL **Harvey CLARK**, born Est. 1859; died aft 1930.

Mary E. Hicks married Herbert Farnham, a farmer in Edgar Co, IL in 1878. After his death (before 1900), she married Harvey Clark. It was a second marriage for each of them. In 1930, Mary was listed as divorced; Harvey, living in the same town, was listed as widowed. Mary had 3 children but none of them were living in 1910. @@

Children of Mary Elizabeth HICKS and Herbert FARNHAM were:
  262 i **Erma**[4] **FARNHAM**, born Oct 1879 in Illinois.
Census 1880 - Stratton, Edgar, IL p. 239C. Herbert Farnham, Head, 24, IL/IL/MO, Occ: farmer; Mary, Wife, 20, IL/OH/VT, Occ: Keeping House, Erma, Dau, 7/12, b. Oct, IL/IL/IL 1900: not found. No marriage or death information found.

71. Sherman[3] **HICKS** (Joshua[2], Joshua[1]), born Mar 1865 in Elbridge Twp, Edgar Co, IL; died 1932; buried in New Providence Cemetery. No known children, but Jones notes indicate a daughter.
Jones notes: "little known of him as he was a wanderer. Was married at one time, but nothing known."
Census: 1920 Terre Haute, Vigo Co, IN, p. 8B. May be the Sherman Hicks, 54, living alone, farmer, born in IL, parents both born in Ohio,. Birth date is about right. Single.

Children of Sherman HICKS were:
  263 i **Daughter**[4] **HICKS**, born abt 1890.

@@For more information on this family, see research notes at the end of this chapter.

Research notes for Generation Three

<u>Notes for Lucinda TATMAN #15</u>
Jones notes: "Resided (1870) at Tate Twp; John Manning, b. 1770 in NJ, lived with William & Lucinda in 1850"

<u>Notes for William MANNING #15s</u>
Census
- 1850 Franklin Twp, p. 408. William Manning 36, farmer; Lucinda 26; Francis M 3; Mary A 2; John W 10/12; John Manning 80 b. NJ, no occ. All others b. OH.
- 1860 Tate Twp, Clermont Co, OH; p. 307. William Manning 44, farmer; Lucinda 35; Francis M 14; Mary A 12; John W 10; George W 7; Sarah E 6; Charles W. 4. All born OH.
- 1870 Tate Twp, Clermont Co, OH. Wm Manning, 55, farmer, 8000, 600; Mollie, 22, keep house; Elizabeth, 17, asst. keeping house; Frank, 23, works on farm; John, 20, works on farm; George, 19, works on farm; Charles, 14, works on farm; Lulu, 3; All born OH
- 1880 could be the William Manning, age 61, with wife Mary D. living in Washington Twp, Clermont Co, OH; farmer, father b. NJ., mother b. VA. If so, this is a second marriage.

<u>Notes for Dianna TATMAN #16</u>
Jones notes: "Resided in Brown Co at the time of death - 1867"

<u>Notes for Zachariah FITZPATRICK #16s</u>
Name and dates from tombstone in Nicholsville, OH Cemetery.

FITZPATRICK

Sarah Donham 1800-1851   Solomon 1793-1868

Their Children

William 1818-1906	Hannah 1832-1898
John 1820-1912	Margaret 1834-1892
Elizabeth 1821-1843	Solomon 1837-1881
Emerine 1823-1840	Hugh 1839-1856
Able 1824-1831	Jonathan 1842-1864
Zachariah 1826-1867	Sarah Jane 1845-1932

Census
- 1850 Tate, Clermont, OH, p. 360. Zachariah Fitzpatrick 24, OH, blacksmith; Dianna Fitzpatrick 25; Sarah E Fitzpatrick 3/12. Next to John Fitzpatrick, 26, also a blacksmith.
- 1860 Monroe, Clermont, Oh, p. 427. Zack Fitzpatrick 34, blacksmith; Diana Fitzpatrick 34; Sarah E Fitzpatrick 10; Jerome H Fitzpatrick 8; George E Fitzpatrick 6; John L Fitzpatrick 3; Mary O Fitzpatrick 1. All b. OH.

<u>Notes for Mary Olive JONES #84</u>
Children were living with relatives and neighbors in 1870 after death of both parents in 1867.
Jones notes "died at George's home; not married; with Thos. Hodges in 1870;

Census
- 1870 Monroe, Clermont, OH, p. 181. Thomas Hodges 47, farmer; Mary J Hodges 47; John Hodges 19; Franklin T Hodges 16; Jacob Hodges 6; Olive Fitzpatrick 12 Ollie may be a distant cousin to the Hodges.
- 1880 Monroe, Clermont, OH, p. 174. Alonzo F. Robinson 38; Dean M. Robinson 28; Lillie L. Robinson 14; Ollie Fitzpatrick 22, servant. 2 doors from her brother Homer Jerome & family. "Ollie is a 1st cousin once removed of Alonzo".
- 1900 not found; not with Robinson family.

Notes for Ida Blanche FITZPATRICK #8

Children were living with relatives and neighbors in 1870 after death of both parents in 1867.
Jones notes: "teacher in Columbus, OH; lived with Dr. Mary Crane; not married"

Census:

1870 Tate, Clermont, OH, p. 309A Living with John & Jane Tatman - Jane is his sister. John Tatman 40, farmer, Jane Tatman 36; William Tatman 17; John C Tatman 13; Mary R Tatman 11; Archibald Tatman 8; Maud Tatman 5; Louis Tatman 3; Sarah Fitzpatrick 20, servant; Ida B Fitzpatrick 7; Archibald McNair 40, farm labor, SCO. [Sarah & Ida Fitzpatrick are nieces of John Tatman, their mother's brother]

1880, Tate, Clermont, OH, p.264. John McNair 47, farmer, Scotland; Mary McNair 47; Grant McNair 14; Eddie McNair 9; Walter Fitzpatrick 19, nephew; Ida Fitzpatrick 17, niece. [Mary Tatman McNair is a sister of Diana Fitzpatrick, deceased mother of Walter & Ida Fitzpatrick.]

1900 Tate, Clermont, OH, p. 6A. John McNair 68, Apr 1832, Sco, widowed, farmer; Ida Fitzpatrick, niece, 36, Jul 1863, single.

1910 Columbus Ward 11, Franklin, OH, p. 2B. James M Crane 63, shoemaker - own shop; Mary D Crane 56, doctor - home office, OH/Ire/Ire; Matson H Crane 32, baggage master - railroad; Hazel F Crane 20, music teacher - private family; Ida Fitzpatrick 46, servant - private family. All OH/OH/OH except Mary.

1920 Columbus Ward 14, Franklin, OH, p. 3B. Dr. Mary Crane 55, physician - at home; Matson Crane 40, baggage master - railroad; Roxy Brandman 20, boarder, cashier - express co; Ida Fitzpatrick 56, housekeeper - priv family

1930 Columbus, Franklin, OH, p. 7A. Mary D Crane 70, widow, physician - medical; Charles Mcintyer 50, son in law, road inspector - state employed; Hazel Mcintyer 30, welfare worker - state welfare; Ida Fitchpatrick 50, housekeeper - private family.

Death: Ida B. Fitzpatrick b. 17 Jul 1862 Ohio; d. 17 Jun 1937, Batavia, Clermont, OH; Age: 74 years 11 months; Female; single; Burial: 19 Jun 1937, Nicholsville, OH; Father: Zachariah Fitzpatrick b. Ohio; Mother: Diana Tatman b. Ohio. Ohio Deaths, 1908-1953 <pilot.familysearch.org>

Notes for John S. Fitzpatrick #86:

Children were living with relatives and neighbors in 1870 after death of both parents in 1867.

Census

1870 Tate Twp., Clermont, OH (#221) John Tatman 72, Retired Farmer, KY; Ruth 72, NC; Elijah 35, OH; Sarah A. 29, OH; Fanny 6, OH; Dau ?? 1, OH; Effie 1; Missouri Fitzpatrick 22; John Fitzpatrick 16. (Note: Elijah Tatman and his family living with his parents, brother Oliver next door) [John Fitzpatrick is John Tatman's grandson, son of his deceased daughter, Diana; Missouri is granddaughter, daughter of his daughter Sarah.]

1880 not found. There are a number of John Fitzpatricks, but none in Clermont - and nothing that would identify one of the others as the right John Fitzpatrick.

Notes for Ruth L Fitzpatrick #88:

Possibly same person as Ruth Gertrude Fitzpatrick. Jones notes: "teacher, not married"

Census:

1870 Tate, Clermont, OH, p. 307. Washington Tatman 44, farmer; Edith Tatman 30; Ruth L. Fitzpatrick 5

1880 not found

Discrepancy: Jones notes give Ruth Gertrude Fitzpatrick. Gertrude is sister to Ruth. 1870 census gives Ruth's middle initial as L. I'm not sure which of the two was the teacher and unmarried or if both were the same person.

Death: Ruth Gertrude Fitzpatrick, b. 02 Jul 1866 OH; d. 17 Jan 1920, Batavia, Clermont, OH; Age: 54 years 5 months 14 days; Single; Teacher; Burial: 19 Jan 1920, Nicholsville Cemetery; Father: Zachariah Fitzpatrick b. OH; Mother: Diana Tatman b. OH. Ohio Deaths, 1908-1953 <pilot.familysearch.org>

Notes for Gertrude FITZPATRICK #89:
Jones notes: "with Walter Burke in 1880, Tate Twp" listed as housekeeper.
Census
- 1880 Tate, Clermont, OH, p. 264. Walter W. Burke 51, farmer; Rebecca Burke 46; James Burke 16; Gertie Fitzpatrick 14, servant.
- 1900 Tate Twp, Clermont Co, OH, p. 229a. Walter W. Burke, head, Sep 1828, 71, wid., OH/OH/NJ, farmer; Gertrude Fitzpatrick,, Jul 1866, 33, single, housekeeper.

Notes for George Washington TATMAN #17
Jones notes: "Civil War - Was a private in Co. C, 153 OVI; The 153rd Regiment, Ohio Infantry (National Guard), Co. C, 153 Ohio Voluntary Infantry was one of the 100-day regiments called up in the spring of 1864 to support the Union's final push to achieve victory over the Confederate armies and bring an end to the War. They were involved in a number of engagements in northern Virginia and southern Maryland. His brother Elijah was in the same unit."
Resided with brother Elijah in 1880
Census
- 1870 Tate, Clermont, Oh, p. 307. Washington Tatman 44, farmer; Edith Tatman 30; Ruth Fitzpatrick 5. [George W. Tatman was uncle of Ruth - her mother's brother]
- 1880 Tate, Clermont, OH p. 270. Elija Tatman 44, OH/KY/NC, farmer; Sarah A. Tatman 39; Fanny Tatman 16; Effie Tatman 10; Carrie Tatman 7; John W. Tatman 4; George W. Tatman 53, brother, farmer, widowed.

Notes for Sarah A. TATMAN #18
Sarah married John Fitzpatrick, who was the brother of Zachariah Fitzpatrick, who married Sarah's sister Diana. [brothers married sisters}
Information: Ancestry family tree of Krysten Stabler give Sarah's death as 1 Apr 1890, Nicholsville, Clermont OH. No proof included

Notes for John FITZPATRICK #18s
Census
- 1850 Tate, Clermont Co, OH, p. 360A. John Fitzpatrick 27, farmer; Sarah Fitzpatrick 22; Missouri Fitzpatrick 2; Randolph Fitzpatrick 1
- 1860 Monroe, Clermont, OH, p. 436. John Fitzpatrick 40, farmer; Sarah Fitzpatrick 32; Missouri Fitzpatrick 12; Randolph Fitzpatrick 11; Sarah R Fitzpatrick 8; Ruth E Fitzpatrick 6; Wm B Fitzpatrick 5; Mary E Fitzpatrick 2; Benj F Fitzpatrick 4/12
- 1870 Monroe, Clermont Co, OH, p. 197A. John Fitzpatrick 49, carpenter; Sarah Fitzpatrick 42; Missouri A Fitzpatrick 22; Ruth E Fitzpatrick 16; William B Fitzpatrick 14, farm labor; Mary E Fitzpatrick 12; Benjamin F Fitzpatrick 10; Recce Fitzpatrick 8;; John S Fitzpatrick 6; Minnie L Fitzpatrick 5; Oliver L Fitzpatrick 3. All b. OH.
- 1880 Williamsburg, Clermont, OH, p. 372A. John Fitzpatrick 58, farmer; Sarah Fitzpatrick 51, OH/KY/NC; Missouri S. Fitzpatrick 30, dressmaker; Ruth Fitzpatrick 25; William B. Fitzpatrick 24, laborer; Emma Fitzpatrick 22, laborer; Benj. F. Fitzpatrick 20, laborer; Reese Fitzpatrick 19, laborer; Sherman Fitzpatrick 19, laborer; Minnie L. Fitzpatrick 14; Oliver L. Fitzpatrick 13, farm help; Charles C. Fitzpatrick 12
- 1900 - Clermont Co, Tate Twp. p. 241a. HH#41- John Fitzpatrick, head, 80, Apr 1820, widowed, OH/KY/OH, owns farm w/ mortgage; Emma, dau, Mar 1848, 52, single; Ben F., son, Jan 1860, 40, farmer; Minnie L., dau, Mar 1865, 35, single; Oliver L., son, Jul 1867, 32, single, farmer; William H., brother, Jun 1818, 82, OH/KY/OH. Children all OH/OH/OH. (next to bro-in-law, Elijah Tatman)
- 1910 Tate, Clermont Co, OH, p. 1A. John Fitzpatrick 90, OH/VA/OH, widowed, no occ; Missouri Fitzpatrick 62; Benjamin Fitzpatrick 50, farmer; Minnie L Fitzpatrick 44; Oliver D Fitzpatrick 42, farmer. Children all single.

Death: John Fitzpatrick b. 07 Apr 1820 Ohio; 09 Mar 1911 Tate, Clermont, OH; Death Age: 90 years 11 months 3 days; Widowed; Carpenter; burial 12 Mar 1911 Nicklesville Cemetery; Father: Saulman Fitzpatrick b. KY; Mother: Sarah Donham. Ohio Deaths, 1908-1953 <pilot.familysearch.org>

Notes for Missouri FITZPATRICK #93
Jones notes: "resided (1901) at 1525 Central Ave, Cincinnati, OH". Never married.
Census:
- 1900 Cincinnati Ward 15, Hamilton, OH, p. 7A. Ruth Fitzpatrick 45, Oct 1854, OH, dressmaker; Missouri Fitzpatrick 52, sister, Feb 1848, dressmaker; Clifford Fitzpatrick, brother, 28, Jul 1871, dry goods clerk.
- 1910 Tate, Clermont Co, OH, p. 1A. John Fitzpatrick 90, OH/VA/OH, widowed, no occ; Missouri Fitzpatrick 62; Benjamin Fitzpatrick 50, farmer; Minnie L Fitzpatrick 44; Oliver D Fitzpatrick 42, farmer. Children all single.
- 1920 Tate, Clermont Co, OH, p. 5B. Ben F Fitzpatrick 60, farmer; Missouri A Fitzpatrick 71; Oliver S Fitzpatrick 51, farmer; Minnie S Fitzpatrick 54. All OH/OH/OH
- 1930 Tate, Clermont Co, OH, p. 6A. Ben Fitzpatrick 70, OH/KY/OH, farmer; Minnie Fitzpatrick 65, OH/KY/OH; Oliver Fitzpatrick 62, farmer, OH/KY/OH; John Fitzpatrick 14, nephew

Death: OH Deaths <Ancestry.com> gives date and place, no other information.

Notes for Sarah R. FITZPATRICK #94
Census
- 1860 Monroe, Clermont, OH, p. 436. John Fitzpatrick 40, farmer; Sarah Fitzpatrick 32; Missouri Fitzpatrick 12; Randolph Fitzpatrick 11; Sarah R Fitzpatrick 8; Ruth E Fitzpatrick 6; Wm B Fitzpatrick 5; Mary E Fitzpatrick 2; Benj F Fitzpatrick 4/12
- 1870 Tate, Clermont, OH, p. 309A Living with John & Jane Tatman (John is her uncle, her mother's brother) John Tatman 40, Farmer, Jane Tatman 36; William Tatman 17; John C Tatman 13; Mary R Tatman 11; Archibald Tatman 8; Maud Tatman 5; Louis Tatman 3; Sarah Fitzpatrick 20, servant; Ida B Fitzpatrick 7; Archibald McNair 40, farm labor, SCO.
- 1880 not found

Notes for Ruth E. FITZPATRICK #95
Census: 1900 Cincinnati Ward 15, Hamilton, OH, p. 7A. Ruth Fitzpatrick 45, Oct 1854, OH, dressmaker; Missouri Fitzpatrick 52, sister, Feb 1848, dressmaker; Clifford Fitzpatrick, brother, 28, Jul 1871, dry goods clerk.

Notes for Benjamin FITZPATRICK #99
Census
- 1920 Tate, Clermont Co, OH, p. 5B. Ben F Fitzpatrick 60, farmer; Missouri A Fitzpatrick 71; Oliver S Fitzpatrick 51, farmer; Minnie S Fitzpatrick 54. All OH/OH/OH
- 1930 Tate, Clermont Co, OH, p. 6A. Ben Fitzpatrick 70, OH/KY/OH, farmer; Minnie Fitzpatrick 65, OH/KY/OH; Oliver Fitzpatrick 62, farmer, OH/KY/OH; John Fitzpatrick 14, nephew

Notes for John TATMAN #19
Jones notes: "Owned 335 acres, ½ mi N of SaltAir - 1900; m2 to his brother Oliver's widow, Malita."
Census
- 1870 Tate, Clermont, OH, p. 309A John Tatman 40, Farmer, Jane Tatman 36; William Tatman 17; John C Tatman 13; Mary R Tatman 11; Archibald Tatman 8; Maud Tatman 5; Louis Tatman 3; Sarah Fitzpatrick 20, servant; Ida B Fitzpatrick 7; Archibald McNair 40, farm labor, SCO. [Sarah & Ida Fitzpatirck are nieces, children of John's sister Diana]
- 1880 Tate, Clermont Co, OH., p. 271. John Tatman 50, farmer; Jane Tatman 46; Charles Tatman 22, farmer; Mollie Tatman 20; Archy Tatman 17; Maud Tatman 14; Lewis Tatman 12; Florence Tatman 9; Oliver Tatman 6; Archy McNair 52, brother in law, widowed, farm labor. Jane & Archy b. Scotland,

others b. OH.

1900 Tate, Clermont Co, OH, p. 2B. John Tatman 70, OH/KY/NC, farmer; Milila Tatman 49; Lewis Tatman 32, son, farmer; Louise Tatman 30, dau-in-law; John Colyer 21, farm labor; Dwight Tatman 11/12, grandson.

1910 Not found.

Death: John Tatman d. 28 Mar 1913, Tate, Clermont OH; b. 16 Mar 1830, OH. 83 yr, 13 day, married, farmer, bur 2 Apr 1913, Bethel. Father: John Tatman; Mother: Ruth Hicks. Ohio Deaths 1908-1953<pilot.familysearch.org>

Notes for Melita or Melissa ANDERSON #19s

Jones notes: "M2 - John Tatman, brother of her deceased husband, Oliver"

Marriage: date based on 1870 census

Death: Melita Tatman, widow, parents: William Anderson, b. VA; Mary King b. VA; Burial: Bethel, OH. Informant: Elmer Taylor, New Richmond, OH. Ohio Deaths 1908-1953 <pilot.familysearch.org>.

Notes for Oliver TATMAN #113

Census

*1900 Lewis, Brown, OH, p. 8A. Louis Carter 33; Sada Carter 30; Olive Tatman 25, Feb 1875, OH/OH/OH, farm labor. *may not be correct person - about the right age and Brown County borders Clermont.

1910 Chillicothe Ward 3, Ross, OH, p. 7B. Emma J Kopp 63, widow, no children; Florence W Tatman 34, niece, m 0 years, no children; Oliver P Tatman 36, nephew, physician; Susan Briggs 67, sister, single. All OH/OH/OH

1920 Chillicothe Ward 3, Ross, OH, p. 1A. Oliver Tatman 45, physician - gen practice; Florence Tatman 43. Next to Emma J. Kopp & Susan Briggs.

1930 Chillicothe, Ross, OH, p. 7B. Oliver P Tatman 55, OH/OH/Sco, physician; Florence Tatman 53, OH/OH/OH.

Marriage: Oliver P. Tatman, b. 1874 Batavia, Ohio, Age 35; Bride: Florence E. Wilson, b. 1877, Chillicothe, O., Age 32; Marriage: 19 Oct 1909, Ross County, OH; Groom's Father: John Tatman; Mother: Jane McNair; Bride's parents not given; both single. Ohio Marriages, 1800-1958 <fsbeta.familysearch.org>

Military: Not on WW I draft registration

Death: Oliver P. Tatman, d. 12 Dec 1952, Chillicothe, Ross, OH; b. 18 Jan 1874, OH; Age 78 years 10 months 24 days; burial: 15 Dec 1952, Grandview, Chilicothe, OH; occ: physician, M.D., father: John Tatman; mother: Jane McNair. Ohio Deaths, 1908-1953 <fsbeta.familysearch.org>

Notes for Ruie TATMAN #118

Census: 1880 Tate, Clermont, OH, p. 270. Melita Tatman 29, widow; Orie Tatman 15, dau; Callie Tatman 10; Ruie Tatman 8; Lurena Tatman 5; George Tatman 26, farmer.

1900 Monroe Twp, Clermont Co, OH, p. 154. Harry Taylor, Nov 1861; 38, mar. 3 yr, OH/OH/OH, farmer; Ruie, Sep? 1871, 28, no ch, OH/OH/OH; Dede Tatman, sis-in-law, Jun 1874, 26, single, OH/OH/OH. (next to family of Elmer Taylor, b. 1865)

1910 Tate, Clermont, OH, p. 1A. Harry N Taylor 48, general farmer; Rouie Taylor 38, no children.

1920 Franklin, Clermont, OH, p. 5B. Harvey J Bretz 50, farmer, OH/Ger/OH; Ruie Bretz 48; Harvy W Bretz 26, single, farmer - home farm.

1930 Bethel, Clermont, OH, p. 2B. Harvey Bretz 60, carpenter - home, OH/Ger/Ger; Ruie Bretz 59

Death: Ruie Bretz, d. 20 Feb 1941 Bethel, Clermont, OH; b. abt 1872; Age: 69 years; married; Spouse: H. J. Bretz; parents: Oliver Tatman; Meledia Pemduson; housewife. Ohio Deaths 1908-1953 <familysearch.org>

Note: Mothers of children presumed based on best knowledge of marriage dates. Since several are adopted, these may be wrong.

Notes for Lurena Dee TATMAN #119

Jones notes: "no children"; with brother-in-law Harry Taylor in 1900 census.

Census: 1900 Monroe Twp, Clermont Co, OH, p. 154. Harry Taylor, Nov 1861; 38, mar. 3 yr, OH/OH/OH, farmer; Ruie, Sep? 1871, 28, no ch, OH/OH/OH; Dede Tatman, sis-in-law, Jun 1874, 26, single, OH/OH/OH. (next to family of Elmer Taylor, b. 1865.)

1910 not found

1920 Tate, Clermont, OH, p. 6A. John E Emm* 52, real estate - own office; Lorena D Emm* 45. Both OH/OH/OH

1930 Bethel, Clermont, OH, p. 8B. John E Emmens 62, insurance agent; Lorena Emmens 55. M. 15 years.

Death: Lorena D Emmons b. 1875, res: Clermont Co, OH; D. 7 Mar 1960, Clermont Co, OH, age 85, widowed. Ohio Deaths, 1908-1932, 1938-1944, and 1958-2007 [ancestry.com]

Notes for Mary TATMAN #21

Census: 1870 Tate Twp., Clermont Co, OH, p. 309a. John McNair, 38, farmer, $6000, $600, born Scotland; Polly, 36, keep house; Grant, 4; Walter Fitzpatrick, 9. All born OH except John.

1880, Tate, Clermont, OH, p.264. John McNair 47, farmer, Scotland; Mary McNair 47; Grant Mc Nair 14; Eddie McNair 9; Walter Fitzpatrick 19, nephew; Ida Fitzpatrick 17, niece

1900 Tate, Clermont, OH, p. 6A. John McNair 68, Apr 1832, Sco, widowed, farmer; Ida Fitzpatrick niece, 36, Jul 1863, single. Next to Grant McNair; Edwin McNair.

Notes for John MCNAIR #21s

Death Certificate gives name, birth & death date, age 77 yr, 11mo, 6 da. Widowed, farmer, parents: Archibald and Mitchel. All b. Scotland. Ohio Deaths 1908-1953 <pilot.familysearch.org>

Notes for Elijah TATMAN #22

Jones notes: "served in Co. C, 153 OVI; resided in Salt Air, later #198 at Bethel"

Military: American Civil War Soldiers [ancestry.com] gives: Elijah Tatman, Enlistment Date: 2 May 1864; Union; Ohio; Enlisted as a Private on 2 May 1864 at the age of 29. Enlisted in Company C, 153rd Infantry Regiment, Ohio on 10 May 1864. Mustered Out Company C, 153rd Infantry Regiment Ohio on 9 Sep 1864 at Camp Dennison, OH.

Census: 1880 Tate, Clermont, OH, p. 270. Elija Tatman 44, OH/KY/NC, farmer; Sarah A. Tatman 39; Fanny Tatman 16; Effie Tatman 10; Carrie Tatman 7; John W. Tatman 4; George W. Tatman 53, brother, farmer, widowed.

1900 Tate Twp, Clermont Co, OH p. 241a. Elijah Tatman,. head, Jun 1835, 64, mar 36 yr, OH/KY/NC, Farmer, owns farm; Sara Ann, wife, Jan 1841, 59; 6 ch - 5 living, OH/ Misio?;/IN; Warren J., son, Oct 1875, 24, S, OH/OH/OH; shoemaker/cutter; Solon J. son, Aug 1882, 17, at school. Next to his sister Sarah Fitzpatrick's, widower & family.

1910 Tate Twp, Clermont Co, OH. Sarah A Tatman 69, widow, OH/MO/OH, 6 ch / 5 living, own income; Solon E Tatman 27, shoemaker - factory.

Notes for Sarah Ann RUSH #22s

Death: Sallie Tatman, d. 27 Jul 1914, Bethel, Clermont, OH; b. 27 Jan 1841 Ohio; Age at death: 73 years 6 months, Widowed; Occ: Housekeeping; Residence: Bethel, Ohio; Bur: 28 Jul 1914, Bethel, Ohio; Bethel Cemetery; Father: Thomas Rush, b. Ohio; Mother: Mary Fee, b. Ohio. Ohio Deaths 1908-1953 <pilot.familysearch.org>

Notes for Solon Elijah TATMAN #129

Census: 1930 Chicago, Cook, IL, p. 11B. Solon Tatman 42, single, OH/OH/OH, cutter- shoe factory.

Military: WWI Draft Registration [Ancestry.com] Solon Elijah Tatman, age 36, b. Aug 2, 1882, Shoe Worker - Elbinger Shoe Manufacturing Co, Lebanon, OH. Closest relative: Carrie Holland, Bethel, OH. Tall, slender, brown eyes, brown hair. Registered Sep 1918.

Notes for Henry Melvin HICKS #26

Bible Records: Hicks Bible in possession of Elizabeth (Hicks) Jennings, Georgetown, OH August, 1998. [copy sent to me by Lvera Jennings Seipelt, Georgetown OH]. "Henry M. Hicks was Born June 29 1826. Henry Melvin Hicks died 6A. M. November 15th 1905; age 79 yrs." Also on loose paper found in Bible.

Photo: Photocopy of photo of him (with wife) as elderly man in my files. I also have an original photo of him slightly younger, from collection of Molly Levi labeled "Grandpa Hicks". Also in photo of their 50th anniversary, 1900, page 89. Article on page 88.

Information from Norman Zezula says he was a farmer. He was postmaster of Rural, Clermont Co, OH from 1869-1871.

Marriage: Bracken Co, KY Marriage bond. (19 Dec 1850); actual marriage was 22 Dec (Hicks Family Bible). Bond signed by Henry M. Hicks and William F. Owens.

Health: 1880 census shows him as disabled by consumption.

Death: Clermont Co, OH death record. "Age 79y 4m 16d, farmer, res. Rural, OH; d. in Franklin twp., Clermont Co, OH"

Census:
 1860 Franklin Twp, Clermont, OH, p. 525. Henry M. Hicks 33, farmer, $150, OH; Hannah, 38, KY; Orestes D. 8, OH; Frank 4, OH; Lucy A. 3, OH; Mary E. 11/12, OH
 1870 Franklin Twp, Clermont, OH, p. 73B. Henry M. Hicks 44; Hannah F. 48; Orestes D. 18; Elijah 14; Lucy 12; Mary E. 10; Harvey H. 8; John James 6
 1880 Rural, Franklin Twp., Clermont, OH, p 67D. Henry Hicks, 53, farmer, OH/NC/MD; Hannah 58, KY/PA/MD; Mary E. 20; Franklin 24 butcher; Harvey H. 18; John J. 15.
 1900 Rural, Franklin Twp., Clermont, OH, p. 5. Henry Hicks, 73, June 1826; md. 50 yr. OH/NC/MD; Hannah, 77, Dec 1822, KY/MD/MD (7 children [sic], 5 living; he an apiarist?[beekeeper?])

Occupation: Henry was postmaster for Rural from 1869-1871. The post office was officially named "Smith's Landing". *History of Clermont Co, OH* - Everts.

Newspaper article: *Golden Anniversary. "Uncle Hy" M. Hicks and his aged and estimable companion, who was Miss Hannah F. Owens, have lived happily and peacefully together for fifty long eventful years. And on last Saturday, Dec 22 [1901], the golden anniversary of the marriage event in their lives was celebrated most delightfully by an ingathering of the children and grandchildren at their pleasant home on Locust Hill, just below Rural. There were present upon the joyous occasion: O. D. Hicks and wife and daughter, Miss Edna, of this place; H. H. Hicks and family of Utopia and their daughter, Mrs. Mary Joslin and four daughters of New Richmond; Mrs. Mary Jones and grandson, Clifford Houser; E. F. Hicks and wife and little son; J. J. Hicks and wife; H. C. Duvall and wife; and Chas. Fry and wife, all of Rural; and Mr James Melvin of Brooksville, KY. The latter named was also present at the wedding fifty years ago, which was performed at the old Owens homestead opposite Utopia in Kentucky. The light hearted company included one sister, four sons, one daughter and eleven grandchildren, and all enjoyed the day and event quite royally. A bounteous dinner was spread to the enjoyment of the guests, and of this we speak as one having authority, touching its merits. Our thanks for a box of the delicious cake is hereby extended. Mr. O. D. Hicks, the photographer, secured a number of excellent group pictures as mementoes of this occasion of much joy and thanksgiving.*

Notes for Hannah Francis OWENS #26s

Photo: Photocopy of photo of her (with husband) as elderly woman in my files. I also have an original photo of her in middle age, from Molly Levi, labeled "Grandma Hicks".

Bible Records: Hicks Bible in possession of Elizabeth (Hicks) Joslin, Georgetown, OH August, 1998. [copy sent to me by Lvera Jennings Seipelt, Georgetown OH]. "Hannah F. Hicks was born December 5, 1821. Hannah Francis Hicks died November 1907 Age 86 years."

Death: Clermont Co, OH death rec. "Hannah Francis Hicks, female, d. Franklin twp., OH on 3 Nov 1907, age 85y 10m 28d; b. Bracken Co, KY; old age; res. Franklin twp." Calculated birth of 6 Dec 1821.

Parents: 1880 census shows father b. PA, mother b. MD.

***Note**: "Fanny Owens died 20 Jul 1869, age 84" (handwritten note by Lucy M. F. Hicks; transmitted from Minnie Hicks Behan to her daughter, Marjorie Rogers) Calculated date of birth: 20 Jul 1785. Francis apparently is the grandmother of Hannah. The census suggests that both Hannah's parents died between 1839 and 1850. Francis "Fanny" Owens was raising her grandchildren in Bracken Co, KY in 1850 and 1860.
Letter: (From Hannah to a son) (blanks indicate holes in letter) Locus Hill Oct 6 1885 My Dear Son As I have not got an answer for my last letter, under the circumstances I will write to you again. I was out to Mary's three weeks and your Pa was taken sick and _____ and I had to_____ _____ _____ was sick____ _____ not heard from her since I left her. I am uneasy about her. Your Pa is better now. He was very sick for three or four weeks. Frankly Johny wants to go to Lebanon one term this winter and he can't raise the money. He wants to know if you can get him some. If you don't owe him enough, let it go on my account as I promised him I would help him if he would stay at home this summer. I would have had enough but I had to help pay the interest on the place and pay for Tom. Johny wants to start for Lebanon the first of next month. If you can get him 25 dollars, he can get the rest. Harvey says for you to get the Curier (sic) out of the office and read it. He wants to know if you found out any more about Edgar's Tobacco, and frankly I want to know when you are coming home to stay or not as your Pa _____ will be able to work _____ do_____ There is (sic) apples _____ enough to keep three or four men busy _____ to pick apples as soon as he gets well. He has been sick since he came home. I am going to weaving _____ morning again. Good night son Hope to see you soon from your loving mother, H. F. Hicks

Notes for Mary HICKS #27
Hicks Bible "Mary Hicks was born November 29, 1827 -- note beside name in different handwriting says W. Jones"
Marriage: Married William Jones 1 Feb 1843 Clermont Co, OH (marriage record (v 3, p 319)
Census: 1850 Franklin Twp, Clermont, OH, #801 William Jones 29; Mary 22; Minerva 6; Samantha 2/12 [prob. b. Aug 1850]
  1860 Franklin Twp, Clermont, OH, #1272; William Jones 39 M Farmer $1,100; $555; Mary 32 F; Minerva 16 F School; Samantha 10 F School; Frank? 6 M School
  1870 Franklin Twp., Clermont, OH, #631. William Jones 49 OH; Mary 42 OH; Samantha 20 OH
  1880 Rural, Clermont, OH, p. 650. William Jones 58, OH/OH/MD; Mary 52, wife, OH/OH/MD; Nancy Hicks, 73, mother-in-law, MD/MD/MD.
  1900 Franklin, Clermont, OH p. 6. Mary Jones, 72, Nov 1827, widow, OH/SC/MD. Farm owned free and clear; unrelated boarder lives with her. Married 40 year, 4 children; 2 living

Notes for William JONES #27s
Information from Norman Zezula and from Jones notes: "Wm Jones b. 1/18/1821 at Clermont; d. 10/21/1891. Both buried Mt. Pleasant. No stone for Mary. Resided at Rural & Neville"
Death: 1900 census shows Mary as a widow.

Notes for Elizabeth HICKS #28
Jones notes "Both buried at Mt Pleasant Cemetery. No stone for Henry."
Hicks Bible: Loose paper in Hicks Bible states "Elizabeth Hicks was born October 26, 1829. -- note beside name in different handwriting says H. Jones"
Marriage: Elizabeth Hicks to Henry Jones, 20 Sep 1846. Clermont Co, OH marriage record (v 4, p 64) [Henry is a brother to William, who married her sister, Mary]
Jones Book, p. 69, mentions child Ulysses Chilton; "Died young"; not in Jones notes.
Death: Clermont Co, OH death record (buried Mt. Pleasant Cemetery, Clermont Co, OH) "wife of Henry Jones, d. 23 Feb 1872; age 42y 6m 10d; white, married; born & died in Franklin twp, Clermont, OH; parents: E. Hicks, Nancy Melvin" (p 60, #1437) The calculated birth date is 13 Aug 1829 vs the Hicks Bible of 26 Oct 1829.

Census
- 1850 Tate Twp, Clermont, OH (#715). Henry Jones, 24, Laborer, OH; Elizabeth Jones 19. OH; James M Jones 2, OH; John Jones 1 OH
- 1860 Rural, Clermont, OH, p. 509. Henry Jones 35, Farmer; Elizabeth Jones 30; John Jones 11; William S. Jones 8; Elijah Jones 7; George W. Jones 3; D. Jones 2 (m); Minerva Jones 4/12
- 1870 Franklin Twp., Clermont, OH, p. 82B. Henry Jones 45, farmer; Elizabeth Jones 40; William A Jones 19, works on farm; Elizah H Jones 17, works on farm; George W Jones 14, works on farm; Albert Jones 12; Manervia Jones 10; Francis Jones (m) 7; Finley E Jones 3
- 1880 Franklin, Clermont Co, OH, p. 43B. Henry Jones 53, farmer; M. Isadore Jones 20; Orpha Jones 9.
- 1900 Neville, Clermont, OH, p. 4A. James M Jones 52, Dec 1847, farmer; Mary E Jones 46, Feb 1854, 7 ch/7 living; Gary G Jones 18, Jan 1882, farm labor; Carl R Jones 15, Nov 1884, farm labor; Ethel G Jones 13, Feb 1887; Larence M Jones 9, Jun 1890; Mary C Jones 7, Sep 1992; Audrey L Jones 6, Feb 1994; Jenevieve S Jones 4, Jan 1996; Henry Jones 75, Feb 1825, father, widowed.

Notes for Henry JONES #28s
Birth/Death: *Clermont Co, OH in 1980*, compiled by the Clermont Co Genealogical Society. "Henry Jones married 12 Oct 1846 Elizabeth Hicks. She: 23 Oct 1829-23 Feb 1872; He: 22 Feb 1825-10 Nov 1904. Both buried Mt Pleasant Cemetery; lived near Rural." (This book incorrectly gives their marriage date as 12 Oct 1846 (actual 20 Sep 1846), and his wife's birth as 23 Oct 1826 (actual 26 Oct 1826).

Notes for Orpha Grace JONES #151
Jones book lists as "b. Nov 1870; married Frank Tracy. They reside (1930) near Wayne, NE". Jones notes give "in 1930 they resided near Wayne, NE. At the time of her death about 1960 (could be 50), she resided at Portland OR.

Census
- 1910 Winside, Wayne, NE, p. 3A. Frank S Tracy 43, post master - Uncle Sam; Grace O Tracy 39, m. 7 yrs, no children; Dora Mccabe 49, sister in law, widowed, 1 child living
- 1920 Careyhurst, Converse, WY, p. 3A. Frank S Tracey 53, IA/Ire/NY, store keeper - gen merchandise; Orplia G Tracey 49; James R McCabe 5, nephew, WY/Wis/Wis; Amber C Fezer 31
- 1930 Orpha, Converse, WY, p. 1B. Frank S Tracy 64, IA/Ire/NY, merchandise - grocery; Orpha G Tracy 59, OH/OH/OH, m. age 31; Robert J McCabe 15, nephew, WY/IA/NE

Notes for Nancy HICKS #29
Jones notes. "Not mentioned in father's estate papers [1853], which names his children under 21."
Loose paper in Hicks Bible states "Nancy Hicks was born October 27, 1831.
Marriage: 21 Jul 1847, Clermont Co, OH. Marriage record (v 4, p 87) as listed in *Clermont Co OH Marriage Records 1800-1850*, by the Clermont Co, OH Gen. Soc) ("Owens" spelled "Ownes")
Family: Not with parents in 1850 census; It was once thought that she had died before 1850, since no marriage was located, none was indicated in the Hicks Bible, and she did not appear with her parents in the 1850 census. However, her 1847 marriage was found in *Clermont Co., Ohio Marriage Records, 1800-1850*. A Nancy Owens (age 19) was found with her husband in the 1850 census. A William F. Owens signed the marriage bond of Henry Melvin Hicks and Hannah Francis Owens. Apparently, two Hicks children married two Owens children. (The F. may stand for Francis). William F. Owens was born in KY, and also fits an age gap in the Owens family group that includes Hannah and those listed with Francis Owens in KY in the 1850 census.

Census
- 1850 Franklin twp, Clermont, OH, p 393. William F. Owens, 26, KY farmer, $200; Nancy 19, OH; James H. 2, OH; John W. 6/12, OH [b. abt Mar 1850]
- 1860 Township 7 Range 6 E, Effingham, IL, p. 1125 Wm Owen 34, KY, farmer; Nancy Owen 26, OH, domestic; James H Owen 12; John W Owen 10; Merry E Owen 8; Isabell Owen 6; Joshua Owen 4; Nancy? J Owen 2 IL. Ch b. OH, except youngest b. IL.

1870 Mattoon, Coles, IL, p. 199. William Owens 50, KY, day laborer; Lucinda Owens 29, KY; Joshua Owens 13, OH; Josephine Owens 10, OH; Emma Owens 7 IL; Gertrude Owens 3 IL; Sidney Owens 8/12 IL; Susan Wethers 22 IN; Mary Clark 10 IN; Lola Clark 7 IN; Thedora Payne 3/12 IL.

Information on death date & place from Alan Case via Ancestry.com message board.

Migration to IL about 1858 based on birth places of children. Nancy age 2 in 1860 is only child born in Illinois.

Notes for William OWENS #29s

Marriage2: William F Owens to Mrs Lucinda Clark 1865-10-04; Coles Co. Illinois Statewide Marriage Index, 1763-1900

Information on death date & place from Alan Case via Ancestry.com message board. Ancestry.com. Family Tree of Alan Case give father of William as James D Owens d. 1823; mother Frances.. no documentation.

Notes for Isabel OWENS #155.

It appears that Isabel Owens married Solomon Ray in Coles Co, IL. If this is the correct family, they had a family as shown in the census records below. Since I'm not sure of this, I have not recorded this family in the database. Jones notes did not have information on marriage or family.

Marriage: Illinois Statewide Marriage Index, 17631900. Soloman Ray to Belle Owens, 1879-07-04, Coles Co, IL. This marriage does not appear on the Illinois Marriage 1851-1900 list at Ancestry.com

Census

1870 Clay, Morgan, IN, p. 375. Elisha Ray 40; Martha J Ray 29; Solomon Ray 15; Erasmus Ray 10; Margaret Ray 9; Emma Ray 3; Ida Ray 3; Benjamin Cumins 20

* 1880 Arcola, Douglas, IL, p. 19A. Solomon Ray 24, hired man, IN/KY/IN; Belle Ray 23, laborer's wife, IL/KY/KY *

*1900 Chicago Ward 25, Cook, IL, p. 15A. Solomon Ray 46, Feb 1854, IN/IN/IN, engineer __y; Belle M Ray 45, Sep 1855, m. 11 yrs; Roy W Ray 19, Oct 1880; Ralph Ray 17, Jun 1882. Boys b. IL.

*may not be correct people

Notes for Joshua HICKS #30

Married Minerva Marshall, 20 Jun 1858, Clermont Co, OH

Death: 6 Dec 1906 in Cincinnati, Hamilton Co, OH; buried Watkins Hill Cemetery. Source ***T. B. White Funeral Home Records***.

Hicks Bible in possession of Elizabeth (Hicks) Jennings, Georgetown, OH. [copy sent to me by Lvera Jennings Seipelt, Georgetown OH]. Loose paper in Hicks Bible states "Joshua Hicks was born December 16, 1833"

Marriage1: Clermont Co, OH marriage record (v 7, p 304)--"Joshua Hicks (23) to Minerva A. Marshall (27), 20 Jun 1858

Census:

1860 Franklin Twp, Clermont, OH, p. 519. Joshua Hicks, 27, Plasterer, $100; Minerva 30; Mary E. 3; Anna L. 1. All b. OH

1870 Ohio Twp, Clermont, OH, p. 219B. Joshua Hicks 37, Jour. Plasterer; Minerva 39; Mary E. 12; Anna L. 11; Nancy 8; Ida 4.

1880 Ohio, Clermont, OH, p. 219C. Joshua Hicks 46, brick mason, OH/ME, widowed; Nancy Hicks 18, daughter. Image very light, illegible.

1900 Sophia St., New Richmond, Ohio Twp, Clermont, OH, p. 16. Joshua Hicks, Dec 1833, plasterer, married. 10 yrs. OH/MD/MD; Ester, Oct 1853 OH, 1 ch / 0 living.

Jones notes "He resided in New Richmond on Pleasant St, 1900.

Military: Civil war veteran. He is mentioned as being "about to start off to the Confederacy and that they have taken his name down" in a letter (28 Apr 1860) from George W. Hicks to his brother Henry. See "Letter" under George W. Hicks notes. [Compiler's note - no record of Civil War service found.]

Land: A property owner in Franklin Twp., Clermont, OH in 1876 (survey # 4847). ***History of Clermont Co., OH***, Everts

Notes for Minerva MARSHALL #30s
Jones notes "Minerva died between 1870-1880 - Joshua a widower in 1880 (Jun 24)
Death: 1900 census - New Richmond, Clermont Co, OH shows Joshua with second wife of 10 years, Ester.

Notes for Esther M. BARNES #30s2
Jones notes: "indicates she had 1 child who died before the 1900 census. It is not known if Joshua Hicks was the father, or if Esther was previously married." Possibly divorced - cannot decipher Jones notes.
Census
  1880 Charlestown, Portage, OH, p. 233. Newton Barnes 73, farmer, MA; Lorinda Barnes 66; Ester Barnes 26, OH; Emery Barnes 32; Charlie Barnes 2, OH, grandson; Almira Hall 75, sister in law.

Notes for James HICKS #31
Hicks Bible in possession of Elizabeth (Hicks) Jennings [copy sent to me by Lvera Jennings Seipelt, Georgetown OH]. Loose paper in Hicks Bible states "James Hicks was born February 29, 1836"
Marriage: James Hicks (age 21) to Emma Ann Burns (age 17) 19 Nov 1857, Clermont Co marriage record (v 7, p 246)
Death: Kentucky death record, "born Clermont Co, OH; parents: Elijah Hicks b. SC; Nancy Melvin, b. MD; widower; pattern maker; Minnie Hicks, informant" (birth date agrees with Hicks Bible)
Occupation: journeyman wagon maker (1870); plough shop, 1880; moulder in a foundry (1910 census record); pattern maker (death record)
Census:
  1860 Nicholsville, Monroe Twp., Clermont, OH; No. 2, p. 426. James Hicks 24 OH (James had $800. in real estate; $200 personal); Emily A. 20 b. KY; Corrie 4/12 OH; Elijah Hicks 22 b. OH, brother, OH
  1870 Monroe Twp., Clermont, OH, p. 34. James Hicks 35, Journeyman wagon maker, OH; Emma 30, KY; Cora 10, OH; Nora 5, OH; Minnie 3, OH.
  1880 Chester, Mason, KY, p. 379A. James Hicks 44, Plough shop, OH/OH/OH; Emma 40, Keeps house, KY/KY/KY; Cora 20, dau, at home, OH/KY/KY; Nora 15, dau, school; Minnie 13, dau,, school; William 8, son; Carrie 4 dau; Campbell Burns, 70, Fa-In-Law, gardener, KY/KY/KY (Central Ave.)
  1900 Dist 8, Mason Co., KY, p. 2A. James Hicks, 64, Feb 1836, OH/MD/MD, pattern maker; Emma A,, 60,. Nov 1839, wife, KY/KY/KY; Minnie M,. 33, Mar 1867, dau, OH/OH/KY, dressmaker (md. 42 yrs.; 6 children, 4 living.) Living next to daughter, Nora Hutchison and family.
  1910 Dieterich, Mason Co., KY, p. 2A. James Hicks 74, md 52 yrs, moulder in a foundry, b. OH; Emma 70. (6 children; 4 living), b. OH; Minnie M. 41, dau., dressmaker, b. KY.
  1920 Dieterich, Mason Co, KY, p. 5A. James Hicks 83, OH/MD/MD, widowed, no occ; Minnie W., 48, dau; single, KY/OH/ KY, clerk - druggist.
Tax Lists: 1882 (Mason Co, KY) He lived near Polk Hicks. James had 3 children in the 6-20 yr age group
1883: Voter (no other information)
1884: Voter (no other information)
1890: (Mason Co., Ky; Item 3 on microfilm) He lived in Maysville (precinct 4) near Polk Hicks. He had land worth $500.
  *Note: A child of James Hicks & Emma Burns died in Brown Co, OH (1870) #34
Military: Civil War (Union); no data, of Chester, Mason, KY (source unknown.-- prob. a census of civil war veterans in Mason Co.--also lists bros. Polk and William)
Children: "Lingenfelser?" written in the spouse section for Caroline in the Hicks Bible extracts and notes of Lucy Hicks Meeker. This is the surname of a daughter of James Hicks (Callie Lingenfelser) with whom Orville Jones reported a correspondence in 1972 (she age 96 then). (This corresponds to a "Carrie Hicks" age 4 in the 1880 census. She was thus born in 1876, which would make her 96 in 1972, as Orville Jones reported.)

Jones notes: "in 1881, James lived at Chester, Mason Co, KY. Brown Co records show a child born 1/6/1870 to James & Emma"

Norman Zezula notes: "reported that he was a Civil War veteran in 1890 Census of Veterans. Did not indicate his unit, but reported a service related disability (apparently an eye problem)."

Notes for Emily Ann BURNS #31

Info on birth, death from Jones notes. Emma on some records. Her father was Campbell Burns, b. 1810 in KY. (with James Hicks in 1880 census.)

Census: 1850 Bracken Co, KY. John C. Burnes 35, farmer; Jane Barnes 27; Emily Barnes 11; Mary Barnes 9; Serepttia Barnes 6; John Barnes 2. All b. KY.

Death: in 1910 census; husband died a widower on 3 Jun 1924. Probably the HICKS, Emily who died in Mason Co, KY 11 Apr 1917.

Death: Mrs Emily Hicks, d. 11 Apr 1917, Mason Co, KY. b. 29 Nov 1839; Bracken Co, KY; married. Father Campbell Burns; mother Jane Melvin, both b. KY. Informant: Miss Minnie Hicks. Kentucky Death Records, 1852-1953 [Ancestry.com]

Notes for Minnie Martin HICKS #167

Census:1930, KY, Mason, Dist 21, p. 28. Minnie Hicks. 61, single, Living with Edward & Nora Hutchison (Nora is Minnie's sister). Occ: practical nurse.

Death: Minnie M. Hicks, age 77, d. 24 Jun 1944, Maysville, Mason Co, KY; b. 26 Mar 1864, OH. Father: James Hicks; Mother: Emily Burns. Informant: Mrs William Lingensfelser; buried Maysville. Kentucky Death Records, 1852-1953 [Ancestry.com]

Notes for Elijah HICKS #32

Hicks Bible- Loose paper in Hicks Bible states "Elijah Hicks was Born October 22, 1837"

Marriage: Hicks Bible; Mason Co., KY marriage bond dated 4 Jun 1866 - Elijah Hicks, C. B. Worthington sign; from *History of Maysville & Mason Co, KY.* pt. 9, p 391.

Marriage: Mason Co Marriage Bond, V. 7, p. 393. Elijah, age 28, a carriage maker, resident of Nicholsville, Clermont, OH; Victoria, age 22, b. Clermont Co. First marriage for both. Groom's parent's both born MD; bride's parents b. OH. Married at Mrs. Warbinton's in Maysville, KY, 5 Jun 1866, witness: E. Hicks; attest: C. B. Warbinton.

Death: Athens Co, OH death rec. "Elijah Hicks Jr., married, age 53y; res. Clermont Co, OH (from "Probate, Athens, OH", p 234)

Military: Jones notes give: Elijah was a bodyguard to General Fremont when with Benton's Cadets. He was listed on the original roster of Co. I, 22nd reg., OH Inf.(a 3 month Co.) His brother William was in the same unit. He was a corporal in Co. I, and later a captain in Co. C, 89th Ohio Volunteer Infantry. He became a captain, received head wounds from shell splinters at Missionary Ridge (Civil War), and resigned due to this disability. His head wounds led to dizzy spells; he later became violent, and was eventually committed (after 1870) to the state mental hospital in Athens, OH where he died.

25 Jan 1863--1st Lt. 89 OVI

19 Mar 1864--Captain 89 OVI

19 Apr 1864--resigned (presume due to wounds)

The 89th OVI was mostly recruited from rural areas of Clermont Co, Highland Co., and Ross Co., OH. It was organized Aug 1862. By Sep 1862, it was sent to W. Virginia to reinforce Gen. Roscrans. In Sep 1863 it was involved in the battle of Chicamauga, and later at Chattanooga, or "Mission Ridge."

Census:
- 1850 Clermont Co, OH. Elijah Hicks 51; wife Nancy 44; John 25; Henry M. 24; Joshua 17; James 14; Elijah 12; Martha 11; William 8; Erastes M. P. 5; George W. 3; James White 19 (laborer).
- 1860 Nicholsville, Monroe Twp, Clermont, OH; No. 2; James Hicks 24 OH (James had $800 in real estate; $200 personal); Emily A. 20 b. KY; Corrie 4/12 OH; Elijah Hicks 22 b. OH (brother) OH
- 1870 Monroe Twp, Clermont, OH, p. 34. Elijah Hicks 32, works at wagon making, $750/$200 b. OH; Victoria E., 25, b. OH; Lida H. 3 b. OH

Land: A property owner in Franklin twp, Clermont Co, OH in 1876 *History of Clermont Co, OH*, Everts

Marriage: Marriage may have been in Mason Co, KY Norman Zezula reports a marriage bond there.

Notes for Victoria E. WARBINGTON #32s

Jones notes gives birthdate; "she died 9/1/1916 at Seattle, WA at the home of her daughter. James H. Wilson was attorney for Victoria in 1890 when she applied for Widows Pension from Seattle"

Census:
- 1850 Franklin, Clermont, OH, p.384a. Joseph Warbinton 39, farmer; Cynthia 38; John J 12; Eliza 10; Charles B 8; Julia Norris 20; Victoria E Warbinton 6; Emma B Warbinton 4.
- 1870 Maysville, Mason, KY, p. 173. Cyntha Warbington 47, PA; Eliza J 20; Charles B 17, day labor; Victoria 16; Emma B 14, Eliza Campbell 22, seamstress, KY. Ch. b. OH.
- 1880 Maysville, Mason, KY, p. 349C. Victora Hicks 35, sis in law, widow; Lida Hicks 13, niece; w/ Emile Martin 67; Eliza J. 40; Samuel D. 17; George H. 13; Joseph E. 7; Cinta Warbinton 68, mother in law.
- 1900 St Louis City, St Louis, MO, p. 1A, Robert J Wilson 38, OH/Ire/Ire, real estate agt; Lida H 32; Marie H 8; Victoria E Hicks 56, mother in law; George H Martin 32, Jan 1868, cousin, KY/Fra/OH, inspector - railroad

Death: Victoria E. Hicks, d. 1 Sep 1916, Seattle, King, WA; b. abt 1844, age 72 years 5 months 10 days. Mother: Cynthia Firestone. [index only, no certificate]. Washington Death Certificates 1907-1960. <pilot.familysearch.org>

Notes for Martha Ann HICKS #33

Married John B. Vermillion, 31 May 1855.

Hicks Bible - Loose paper in Hicks Bible states "Martha Hicks was born February 12, 1840 -- note beside name in different handwriting says John Vermillion"

Marriage: John B Vermillion, age 24; est. birth year: 1829, Bracken Co, Residence: Mason Co; Spouse: Martha Hicks, age 15, est. birth year: 1838; marriage: 31 May 1853, Mason Co, KY. Kentucky Marriage Records, 1852-1914 <ancestry.com>

Jones notes say "divorced"

Death: Martha was in the 1900 census in Miami Co, OH. John was listed as widowed in 1910.

Census:
- 1860 Lower District, Mason, KY, p. 189. Jno Vermillion 29, KY, farmer; Martha 20, OH; Lilly 3, OH; Wm 1, KY.
- 1870 Weston, Platte, MO, p. 477B. John Vermillion 38; Martha Vermillion 30; Julie B Vermillion 13; Mary A Vermillion 9; Edgar Vermillion 7; Ignatius Vermillion 5. Mary Vermillion, 76, living next door with family of Timothy & Nancy Haunch? (may not be right family; some names match; birthplaces match)
- 1880 Franklin, Clermont Co., OH, p. 67D. Martha Vermillion, 39, OH/NC/MD; Nancy, 19, KY/KY/OH; U. S. Grant, 14 S, OH/KY/OH; Edgar N. 10, OH/KY/OH; John C. 9, OH/KY/OH; Charles 3, MO/KY/OH. (census indicates divorce; they appear to live next door to her brother, Henry M. Hicks)

1900 Piqua City, Miami, OH, p. 4A. Martha Vermillion, 60, Feb 1840, OH; John C., 29, Aug 1870, son, MO [sic]; Charles H., 22, Oct 1877, son, MO. [The census lists her as married 45 years, not as widowed or divorced. This supports the belief that they were separated. It also states that Martha had 8 children; 6 are still alive]

1910 not found

Death: Not on Ohio Death Index 1908-1953.

*Note: Hicks Bible extract has "Maysville, KY." written below Martha Hicks; "Vermillion" indicated as her husband.

Notes for John B. VERMILLION #33s

Census:

1900 Carroll, Platte, MO, p. 3A. Grant Vermillion 34, Aug 1865, MO/MO/MO, single, carpenter. Next to John Vermillion, 66, Dec 1833, widowed, farm labor, KY/KY/KY.

1910 Kansas Ward 3, Wyandotte, KS, p. 9B. Edgar Vermillion 48, farmer, OH/KY/OH; Nora 33, KS/KS/KS, m. 16 yr; 10 ch / 6 living; Clarence 14; Clara 9; Ruth 7; Joseph 3; Edna 2; Willie 1; John Vermillion 77, widowed, KY/OH/KS. Kids: KS/OH/KS

1920 not found

Possible Child: Martha J. Vermillion; Marriage: 18 Jan 1892, Mt Vernon, Lawrence, MO, Spouse: Van Tindell; Father: John Vermillion. Missouri Marriage Records, 1805-2002 [Ancestry.com]

Death: Vermillion Family Tree [ancestry.com] gives his death as Nov 1913, Kansas City Ward, Wyandotte, KS. Gives father as John; mother Mary Newman. No documentation.

Notes for Charles Vermillion #178

Census: 1920 National Military Home, Leavenworth, KS, p. 22A. Chas H Vermillion 43, MO/OH/OH; married, helper - hospital.

1930 National Military Home, Leavenworth, KS, p. 28B. Charles Vermillion, 54, m. age 26; occ: elevator oper., MO/OH/OH

Marriage: Charles H. Vermillion, b. 1877, age 29; to Olive A. Drown, b. 1883, age 23; 1 Jan 1906, Kansas City, Wyandotte, KS. Kansas Marriages, 1840-1935 <fsbeta.familysearch.org>

Military: U.S. Army, Register of Enlistments, 1798-1914 [ancestry.com] Charles Vermillion, b. abt 1876 MO; res: Parkville MO; enlisted Cincinnati, OH 1899. laborer. Also enlisted 1903, age 26 5/12, in Cincinnati. Discharged Oct 19 1904, K. C.

Information: Admitted to the U.S. National Homes for Disabled Volunteer Soldiers in Leavenworth, KS in 1921, his wife Olive was living in Kansas City. He was in and out of the home until at least 1931. No record of his death there. Description: 5' 8", dark complexion, iron grey hair, cannot read & write, occ: carpenter, married, nearest relative: wife Olive, living at 1218 Oak St (basement), KC, MO. Disabilities when admitted - chronic rheumatism.

Notes for William Stephen HICKS #34

Married "Elizabeth Meeriach 5 Jun 1870" - Hicks Bible

Bible Records: Loose paper in Hicks Bible states "William Hicks was born January 10, 1842."

Jones notes say: "both buried Maysville Cemetery; Elizabeth was a sister to Wm Meeriach"

Death: Kentucky death record, "William Stephen Hicks, b. 10 Jan 1842; parents: Elijah Hicks, NC and Nancy Melvin, MD"

Census:

1880 Orangeburg, Mason, KY, p. 40. William S Hicks 38, Labors on farm, OH/OH/OH; Elizabeth 38, Wife KY/KY/KY; Caroline W. 8, Dau, KY/KY/OH [sic]; William H. 4, Son, KY/KY/KY; Alif? Maude 3, Son [sic] KY/KY/KY; Arthur S. 2, Son, KY/KY/ KY,

1900 District 8, Mason Co., KY, p.6.. William Hicks, 58, Jan 1842, OH; Elizabeth A. 60, Jan 1840, KY (md. 30 yrs.; 4 children, 3 living); Arthur S. 22, Mar 1878, KY, brick burner

1910 Mason Co., KY. William S. Hicks 68, OH/OH/OH, farmer; Elizabeth H. 70, KY/KY/KY; Arthur

32, KY/OH/KY burner? in brickyard. (md. 40 yrs.; 3 children living)

1920 Dietrich, Mason Co, KY William S. Hicks, 78, OH/NC/MD, no occ; Elizabeth A. 80, KY/KY/KY. Living next to daughter, Caroline Brubaker & her family.

Military: Civil War: Enlisted 24 Apr 1861 Co. I (served 3 months); Enlisted 10 Sep 1861 (5th OH Vol., Co., A; age 18; mustered out 29 Nov 1864 (end of service). Also Co. I, 22nd OVI for 3m 27d; res. Orangeburg pct. disability: chronic sore eyes, schictis U ? (1890 civil war veterans census; also listed are his bros, Polk and James)

Occupation: Farmer (death record states "retired farmer")

Tax-list: Mason Co., KY. In militia, 1872-1875

1872: (With his brother, Polk) 13 acres on the OH River ($50.) 2 horses ($100.); 2 cows ($10.); $10. gold & silver, watches, clocks; 500 bushels corn?; total assets (at 45%) $300.

1873: (With Polk) same as 1872 except land is $150. and gold (watches?) are $40.

1874; 1 horse worth $35. (With brothers Polk, George W.) 13 acres worth $150.

1875: 1 horse ($50.); voter; appears to be still associated with his brothers in the 13 acres

1879: 4 acres ($500); 1 horse ($40); voter; 1 child:(6-20 years)

1880: 4 acres ($60); 1 horse ($40); 1 WM, 1 WF, 2 children (6-20)

1881: same, except no wife or children indicated.

1882: 5 acres ($75); 1 horse ($50); 1 hog ($15); 1 cow; (40%? value total $130.); voter; 2 children (6-20 years)

1884: 13 acres in precinct 9 ($260); 1 horse ($40); $305. total assessed; 4 children (6-20 years)

Note: Another William Hicks is listed with l horse ($75); 2 cattle ($10); buggies, carriages, etc. ($30); $115. total; 10 hogs, 4000 lbs tobacco, 200 bushels corn; is in militia (did not copy year--prob. not ours)

Possible marriage: William Hicks to Telitha Burns, 26 Feb 1865. *Bracken Co, KY. Marriages 1796-1851*.

Marriage Bond, Mason Co, KY Marriage Book, v. 9, p. 94. "5 Jun 1870. William S. Hicks, of Mason Co, KY, age 28, farmer, b. Clermont Co, OH. Father b. N. C.; mother b. MD. Bride: Elizabeth Ann Meenach of Mason Co, KY, age 30, b. Mason Co, KY; father b. Lewis Co, KY; mother b. US. Married at James H. Meenach's, Mason Co, KY. Wm. S. Hicks; attest : A. C. Respose. J. H. Meenach signed bond.

Death: William Stephens Hicks, Death: 6 Apr 1920, Mason Co, KY; Age: 78; Birth: 10 Jan 1842, Clermont, Ohio; Father: Elijah Hicks b. NC; Mother Nancy Melvin, b. MD. Kentucky Death Records, 1852-1953 [ancestry.com]

Notes for Elizabeth Ann MEENACH #34s

Jones notes, "Elizabeth was a sister to William Meeriach who married Nancy Hicks."

Death: Mrs Elizabeth Ann Hicks [Mrs Elizabeth Ann Meenach], d. 17 Mar 1921, Mason; res: Mason; Age: 81, widow; b. 20 Jan 1840, KY; Father: J H Meenach, b. KY; mother: Eliza Colburn, b. KY. Informant: Arthur Hicks, Planton?, PA. Kentucky Death Records, 1852-1953 [ancestry.com]

Information: via email: "Before I send you the line I want to explore something and give you a little background. I believe you have another connection to this family. The Meenach line came out of Pennsylvania and settled Kentucky about 1795. James, seven sons and one daughter (no wife mentioned). I descend from his son James Harvey Meenach (1788) and James Harvey Meenach Jr. (abt 1810). Jr. married the daughter (Elizabeth b. 1810-1815) of Oliver C. Colburn (b abt 1791) who came to Kentucky about 1810-1814 from Maine. They had four daughters and one son (from whom I descend). She died and he married Elizabeth Ballou and they had two children, a girl and a boy (William Harvey Meenach), the one who married Nancy Hicks, dau of Joshua, son of Elijah. Williams half sister, I recently figured out, married a William S. Hicks (born Jan. 1842 - from 1900 census) in Jan. 1870. Looking at the children of Elijah Hicks and Nancy Melvin, I notice a William Stephen, born Jan. 10, 1842. Believing there is no such thing as coincidence, I have to believe he is the uncle of the Nancy Hicks (daughter of his brother Joshua) who married William Harvey Meenach and his marriage to William's older half sister is how he met his wife Nancy. William and Elizabeth had two boys and two girls. I have only been able to track one line, from their son Arthur (before I found your posting). He married, in 1918, Ada Porter and had a little girl, Betty

Ann in Feb. 1919. I found a World Tree source (turns out it was you) that claims she died Feb. 20. 1920. In the 1920 census, which was taken effective Jan. 1 that year, you will find all three plus her mother and married sister, obviously there to help care for her. Thanks to that, you can find little Betty Ann with assurance in 1930 as she is the care of her aunt, Etta Benfield in Beaver Co. PA. As you did not list Betty Ann, I thought maybe you did not have her in your files. In any event, she connects to my line as well as yours. Did you know about Betty Ann? Now, as I was writing this, I found your extensive OneWorldTree listing on this line. You call Elizabeth Mericach but she is also Meenach and William's half sister. I notice you claim five children for Wm and Eliz. I am puzzled about Elsie Hicks who was born about 1875. She is not with the family in 1880 (Mason County, Orangeburg Pct., KY). Are you sure she is connected to the family? Best regards, Bob Houston, Scottsdale, Arizona

<u>Notes for Orestes Marion Polk HICKS #35</u>
Jones notes: "Went to Columbus, OH in 1898; resided at 34 N. Front St"
Photocopy of photo of him in my files.
Hicks Bible: Loose paper in Hicks Bible states "Orestes M. P. Hicks born January 2, 1845."
Marriage: Clermont Co, OH marriage record (v 9, p 199) "Marion Orestes Polk Hicks, 21 to Caroline Utter, 20"
Census
  1870 Orangeburg, Mason, KY, p. 487. Marian Hicks 25, farm labor; Caroline Hicks 24; Brittania Hicks 3; Wm Hicks 28, farm labor. All OH/OH/OH
  1880 Orangeburg pct. 9, Mason, KY, p. 478B. Polk Hicks 35, farmer, OH/OH/MD; Caroline Hicks 34, OH/OH/MD; Brittana Hicks 12, OH/OH/OH; Olevia Hicks 10, KY/OH/OH; Frank Hicks 8, KY/OH/OH; Elsie Hicks 6, KY/OH/OH; Polk Hicks 2, KY/OH/OH; George Burr 22, son [sic], farm laborer, KY/KY/KY.
  1900 Columbus, Franklin Co, OH. Poke Hicks, b. Jun 1845, age 55, m. 36 yr, OH/NC/MD, gardener; Lavinia, b. Dec 1846, 54, 9 ch/ 6 liv; OH/OH/OH; Frank, May 1873, 27, KY/OH/OH, tailor; Walter P., Mar 1878, 22, machinist; Clerance M., Oct 1883, 16, tailor. Next to Edward _ Tudor, Nov 1867, 33, m. 10 yr, tailor; Lavina, b. Aug 1862, 31, 1 ch/ 1 liv, OH/OH/OH; C. Nora, dau, Jul 1891, 8. [Lavinia is dau of Poke Hicks]. Also Morton Mergard 30, Jan 1870, KY/Ger/Ger, tailor; Olivia Mergard 28, Jun 1871, KY/OH/OH; John Partello 50, roomer; Gomer Delay 39, roomer. M 2 years, no children [Olivia is also dau of Poke & Lavina]
  1910 Columbus Ward 8, Franklin, OH, p. 1A. Caroline Hicks 62, OH/OH/OH, widow, keeper - boarding house. Next to dau. Lavina Tudor.
Tax List: 1872-1875; 1879-1883 in Mason Co, Ky. tax lists.
  In militia until at least 1875; not in militia in 1879
  1872: Polk and William Hicks had 13 acres on the OH river (worth $50); 2 horses (worth $100); 2 cows (worth $10); $10. gold & silver; watches; clocks; 500 bushels of corn; total assessed $300.
  1873: same except land assessed at $150; and $40 gold (or gold watches)
  1874: Orestes with 1 horse worth $50; 100 bushels of corn and nothing else. appears to have one child: (6-20) He and his brothers, William and George have 13 acres worth $150.
  1875: He and his brothers, William and George have 13 acres worth $100., and total assets of $600.
  1879: 13 acres ($130); 1 horse $40; 50 bushels wheat
  1880 4 acres worth $60; 1 horse worth $40; a wife and 4 children (6-20 years)
  1881: same except land worth $100; the horse worth $50.
  1882: 1 horse worth $25; legal voter
  1883: 1 horse worth $60. (a legal voter) 4 children (6-20)
  1890: In Mason Co, KY; in militia; no taxables listed; no children in age group 6-20.
Military: Civil War (Union); Pvt. Co. A., OVI, 59th regt. (12 Mar. ? 1861-1864; 3y 1m 19d), of Chester, Mason, KY. Disability, Lance? in shoulder. His brothers. James and William are also listed. 1890 Veteran's census.

Letter: Civil War letter from Polk Hicks to his brother, Henry (in possession of Blaine Hick's widow, Elsie [1988]. It has a Nashville, Tenn. postmark, and was addressed to Henry in Rural, OH. The text follows: *23 April 1860 - Camped on Stone River. Dear brother, I take this opportunity of addressing a few lines. I am well and hope these few lines will find you enjoying the Lord's blessing. I received your letter and was glad to hear from you. I lost your letter I got so that I could not answer it right. Henry, I hear that they are about to start Josh off to the Confederacy and that they have taken his name down. I think Josh has turned to be a union [?] man lately from the last letter I got from _____. There is no news to communicate. Henry, I would like to come home for a while, but there is no chance to do so. We are attending the general, yet I don't know when we will leave. We may stay here all summer. One of the boys in our company died today with pneumonia. We have lost six or seven with it since we came to this camp. Henry, I want you to write often for it is a satisfaction [?] to have a letter from my family to read. Write soon and let me know all of the news about home. Henry, I will send you a genuine Confederate bill of five dollars that I got here at Stone River [?]. It is genuine -- made in the CSA. Well, I must close for it is getting dark. No more at present, but I remain your affectionate brother, Polk Hicks P.S. Direct to Co. A, 27th [?] regt. -- OH Vol. -- 2 brigade, B division, left wing, Army of the Cumberland [?] [it could be 59th regt.]*

Notes for Levina Caroline UTTER

Jones notes gives birth & death date, first name Levinia; "buried Green Lawn Cemetery, Columbus"

Census: 1920 Columbus Ward 12, Franklin, OH. Oliva Margard 48, widow, KY/KY/OH; Carolina Hicks 74, mother, widow, OH/OH/OH; Frank Hicks 46, brother, widow, KY/KY/OH; Gladys Margard 18, dau, OH/KY/KY; Ware H Margard 13, son, OH/KY/KY

Death: Levina Caroline Hicks, d. 22 May 1928. Columbus, Franklin, OH, age 82; b. 1846, Ohio; Burial 25 May 1928; Occ: Housekeeper; Widowed; Spouse: Polk Hicks; Father: John Utter; b. Ohio; Mother: Levina Cockrell b. Ohio. Ohio Deaths and Burials, 1854-1997 <fsbeta.familysearch.org>

Notes for Frank S. HICKS #185

Jones notes: "Not married"

Census

1910 Columbus, Franklin Co, OH, p. 2A. Frank S Hicks 36, KY/KY/VA, tailor - men's clothes; Beryl L Hicks 27, OH/OH/OH. m. 5 years, no children.

1920 Columbus Ward 12, Franklin, OH, p. 2B. Oliva Margard 48, widow, KY/KY/KY/OH; Carolina Hicks 74, mother, widow, OH/OH/OH; Frank Hicks 46, brother, widow, KY/KY/OH; Gladys Margard 18, dau, OH/KY/KY; Ware H Margard 13, son, OH/KY/KY

1930 Columbus, Franklin, OH, p. 16A. Olivia N Magard 59, landlady - rooming house; Wayne H Magard 23, presser - dry cleaning; Frank S Hicks 57, brother, salesman - clothing, divorced; Earl Brill 23, roomer; Everett Wilson 22, roomer; Charles Snedik 18, roomer; Thomas Bunton 37, roomer; William Bunton 36, roomer

Death: Frank S. Hicks, b. 23 May 1873, Maysville, KY; d. 22 Feb 1945, Marion Twp, Franklin, OH; Age: 71 years 8 months 29 days; Married; Spouse: Beryl Hicks; Father: O. M. P. Hicks; Mother: Lavina Utter. Ohio Deaths, 1908-1953 <fsbeta.familysearch.org>

Death: OH Deaths & Burials 1854-1997 <beta.familysearch.org> gives marital status as divorced, retired tailor.

Notes for Walter Polk HICKS #187

Census

1920 Columbus, Franklin Co, OH, p. 6B. Walter P Hicks 41, KY/OH/OH, dealer - cigars; Marjorie Hicks 42, OH/Hanover, Ger/Ger, salesman [sic] - dry goods.

1930 Columbus, Franklin Co, OH, p. 21A. Hotel Fort Hayes. Walter P. Hicks, 51, guest, divorced, KY/OH/OH, salesman - wearing apparel

Military: World War I Draft Registration Cards, 1917-1918 [ancestry.com] Walter Polk Hicks, age 40, b. 3 Mar 1878; res: N. 20th St, Columbus, Franklin Co, OH; no occ.; nearest relative: Mayne Goedjka Hicks,

same address; med height & build; blue eyes, dk brown hair. Regis: 12 Sep 1918, Columbus, OH.
Death: Walter P. Hicks, d. 19 Jul 1942, Columbus, Franklin Co., OH; b. 3 Mar 1878, Maysville, KY; 64 year, 4 mo, 16 days; divorced; Address: 318 E. Broad St; Occ: Salesman; burial: 21 Jul 1942, Glen Rest Cemetery; Spouse: Mayme Hicks; parents: Orestus Hicks, b. Rural, OH; Caroline Utter, b. Rural, OH. Ohio Deaths, 1908-1953 <fsbeta.familysearch.org>

Notes for Caroline Rebecca J. HICKS #37
Marriage: Norman Zezula gives: "Married 20 May 1889"; another source gives 25 May 1869
Norman Zezula notes: "resident of OH in 1916 when she applied for a widow's pension (6 Mar 1916) - husband served in Co. A, 59th OVI. "
Loose paper in Hicks Bible states "Caroline R. J. Hicks was born November 1, 1851 -- note beside name in different handwriting says Thomas Jones"
Death: Maysville KY or Columbus, OH on 22 May 1928 (Jones notes) Cannot locate record
*Note: "Lingenfelser?" written in the spouse section for Caroline in the Hicks Bible extracts and notes of Lucy Hicks Meeker. This is the surname of a daughter of James Hicks (Callie Lingenfelser) with whom Orville Jones reported a correspondence in 1972 (she age 96 then).

Notes for Thomas Franklin JONES #37s
Jones notes say "Thomas Franklin Jones was the son of Isaac, a younger cousin to John, who was the father of Henry & William. Mary Jones married John Hicks. She was the daughter of Asbury Jones of Bridgville, KY, a Confederate soldier and son of Isaac. They went to Stateline, MO. Thomas served in Co A, 59th OVI. He was a blacksmith at Maysville KY and later at Mt Carmel, OH. Captured 9/22/1863 at Chicamauga Bridge, GA; mustered out 5/9/1865 at Clermont. Susannah West, another cousin m 8/15/1850 to Thomas Hicks of Lewis Twp, Brown Co, OH. They went to Douglas Co, IL in 1860 or later"
Norman Zezula notes: "applied for invalid's pension 17 Nov 1882 while a KY resident."
Marriage: Clermont Co, OH. marriage record (p 608)
Land: A Thomas Jones is indicated as a property owner in Franklin. twp, Clermont Co, OH in 1876.
History of Clermont Co., Ohio, Everts
Census
   1870 Maysville, Mason Co, KY p. 5. Frank Jones 30, OH, blacksmith; Callie, 18, OH; Nancy Hicks 63, MD. (Indexed as Frank James on Ancestry.com) Callie is Nancy's daughter, Caroline Rebecca.
   1880 not found in KY or OH.
   1900 not found in KY or OH
   1910 Cincinnati Ward 24, Hamilton, OH, p. 16. Thomas F Jones 70, OH/OH/OH, blacksmith; Caroline 58, OH/NC/MD; Wardie 22, dau, tailoress.
Death: Thomas F. Jones, d. 10 Feb 1916, Union, Clermont, OH; b. 10 Feb 1840, OH; Age 76; Occupation: Blacksmith; Burial: 13 Feb 1916, Mt Moriah Cemetery; Father: Isaac Jones b. OH; mother: Nellie Bartlow, b. OH. Informant: Caroline Jones [wife]. OH Deaths 1908-1953 <familysearch.org>

Notes for James TATMAN #38
Census
   1860 Tate Twp, Clermont Co, p. 582. James Tatman, 30, cigar manufacturer, $250/300, OH; Mary Ann, 29, cigar maker, IN; James S. 5; Lydia Ann 2; Lydia, 58, cigar maker, NC; Eliza E. 25, cigar maker. All b. OH except Mary Ann & Lydia.
   1870 Mary Tatman living in Washington, Davies Co., IN, with children James, 15; Lydia, 12; Franklin, 4?
Note: The Ancestry.com website of Kevin Meade <KevinCMeade@aol.com> 3/2004 gives information on this family."

Notes for Mary Ann ROSS #38s
   Not found in Indiana in 1880. Possibly died or remarried

Notes for Lucinda TATMAN #39
Census:
- 1860 Tate Twp, Clermont Co, OH. William B. Brittingham, 38, cigar manufacturer, Wash DC; Lucinda 27, OH; Cornelia 6, OH. (next to bro-in-law, James Tatman, 30, cigar manufacturer)
- 1870 Tate, Clermont, OH, p. 327. Wm Brittingham 58, cigar? maker, D.C.; Lucinda 37; Jane C 16; Winfield 8; May 6; May 3; all b. OH except father.
- 1880 Clermont Co Tate Twp, p. 273. William Brittineham 60, shoe maker; Lucinda 47; James W. 18; Mollie 13; Nelly Altman 6, granddaughter
- 1900 Clermont Co Tate Twp, p. 242a. Luc___ Brittingham, Head, F, Oct 1832, 6, wd, OH/KY/NC, 4 (?) ch/ 4 living, washerwoman, owns home; Eliza Tatman, sister, Jul 1836, 63, single, OH/KY/NC, can read & speak English but not write.
- 1910 Clermont Co Tate Twp, p. 4B. Lucindy Brittingham 77; Eliza S Tatman 75. no occ for either.

Death: Ohio Death Index, 1908-1932 [Ancestry.com]. Gives only date and place.

Notes for Alonzo ROBINSON #41
Residence: Jones notes: "resided at Salt Air; m2 to Dian b. 1852"
Census:
- 1880 Clermont, Monroe Twp, p. 174A. Alonzo F. Robinson, head, 38, OH/OH/OH, dealer in Leaf tobacco; Dean M., wife, 28, OH/MD/OH, keeping house; Lillie L., dau, 14, OH/OH/OH, at school; Ollie Fitzpatrick, other, 22, OH/OH/OH, servant.
- 1900 New Richmond, Clermont, OH, p. 37. Alvin Robinson 56, Oct 1843, OH/PA/MD, leaf tobacco dealer; Dean, 47, Jul 1852, OH/MD/MD; she has no children.
- 1910 Cincinnati, Hamilton, OH, p. 13. Alonzo Robinson 61, inspector - lumber yard; Dean Robinson 57. His 2nd marriage, her 1st. Married 30 years, she has no children.

Death: Alonzo Robinson, d. 26 Jun 1913, Cincinnati, Hamilton, OH; b. 27 Oct 1848, OH; Age: 64 years 7 months 19 da; Married; Laborer; Res: 13 Armorey Ave, Cincinnati, OH; Burial 28 Jun 1913, New Richmond, OH; Father: John Robinson; mother: Mary Hicks. Ohio Deaths, 1908-1953 <familysearch.org>

Notes for Melissa Jane ROBINSON #42
Census: not found
Marriage: James I Utter, b. 1834, age 28 to Malissa I Robinson, b. 1842, age 20; Marriage:16 Oct 1862 Clermont, OH. Ohio Marriages, 1800-1958 <beta.familysearch.org>
Death: Melissa Utter, d. 8 Jul 1870, Tate Twp, Clermont, OH; Age: 27; Birth: 1843, Tate; Widowed. Ohio Deaths and Burials, 1854-1997 <fsbeta.familysearch.org>

Notes for Nancy Emily ROBINSON #43
Marriage: Robert McNair, b. 1841, age 26 to Nancy E. Robinson, b. 1846, age 21; Marriage 9 Dec 1867, Clermont County, OH. Ohio Marriages, 1800-1958 <beta.familysearch.org>
Death: Nancy E McNair, d. 01 Feb 1877, Clermont Co., OH; Age 30; b. 1847, OH; married. Ohio Deaths and Burials, 1854-1997 <beta.familysearch.org>
Census
- 1850 Tate Twp, Clermont Co, OH, p. 21B. Archibald McNair, 52, Mary 50; Archibald, 22; Hugh, 19; John 17; Jane, 15; Robert, 11; James, 9; Mary, 4; Jane Mitchell, 44. All b. Scotland except Mary, 4, b. OH. Father and older boys are farmers; Hugh is a blacksmith.
- 1860 Tate, Clermont, OH, p. 277. Archibald McNair 62, farmer; Mary McNair 55; John McNair 26, farmer; Robert McNair 21, farmer; James McNair 17, farmer; Mary McNair 14, OH; Jane Mitchell 50. All but Mary McNair b. Scotland.
- 1870 Monroe, Clermont, OH, p. 193. Robert McNair 40, farmer, Scotland; Emily McNair 30; Charles McNair 1

1880 Monroe, Clermont, OH, p. 174. William W. Tatman 26, farmer; Alice Tatman 25; Helena Tatman 8M; Robert McNair 40, uncle, OH/OH/OH [may be wrong Robert - or birthplace may just be wrong.]
1900 not found

Notes for Margaret Missouri ROBINSON #46
Census:
1870 Monroe, Clermont, OH, p. 194. John Cann 31, farmer; Margaret M Cann 25; Robert C Cann 3; Melissa B Cann 2; Clinton Cann 3/12, b. Feb; Mary C Mcgonagle 12, servant; Lewis Halfhill 30, farm labor.
1880 Washington, Clermont, OH, p. 314. John Cann 40, farmer; Margaret M. Cann 35; Robert C. Cann 13; Mellissa B. Cann 11; Ott Cann 10; Missouri B. Cann 2; Elisa A. Capwell 15, farmer.
Marriage: John Cann to Margaret Missouri Robinson; Marriage: 14 Feb 1866, Clermont, OH. Ohio Marriages, 1800-1958 <pilot.familysearch.org>

Notes for John CANN #46s
Jones notes: "he remarried"
Census:
1860 Franklin, Clermont, OH, p. 523. Robert Cann 44, farmer, KY; Cina Cann 45; John Cann 21; Wm Cann 21; Christian Cann 15; Irwin Cann 13; George Cann 9; Emma Cann 7; Anna Cann 3; Simon Cann 17. Other b. OH. Older boys "farm hands"
1900 Monroe Twp, Clermont Co OH, p. 154 John Cann, Oct 1838, 61, mar. 16 yr, OH/OH/OH, farmer; Ella, wife, Feb 1846, 34, 3 ch/3 liv; Grover Mar 1885, 15, son; Clyde, Nov 1886, 13, son, 13; Faye, Mar 1889, 11, dau. All b. OH. (near McNairs & Taylors)

Notes for Melissa Blanche CANN #295
Jones notes: "no children"
Census:
1910 Murray Ward 1, Salt Lake, UT, p. 1B. Myron Wheeler 36, engineer - stationary, PA; Belle M Wheeler 32, m. 5 yrs; Blanche Chapman 42, sis-in-law. None have children.
1920 Sioux City Precinct 7, Woodbury, IA, p. 13A. Myron Wheeler 45, proprietor - confectionery store, PA; Belle Wheeler 41, proprietor - confectionery store, OH; Blanche Chapman 51, sis-in-law, OH.
1930 Sioux City Dist 53, Woodbury, IA, p. 13A. Myron Wheeler 56, news dealer - news store & cigars, PA; Belle Wheeler 52, salesman - news store & cigars, OH; Blanche Chapman 60, sis-in-law, OH, child's nurse - private family, widow; Harvey Weisinger, 61, half brother, single, manager - fire b__?__; Helen Williams, 30, single, roomer, teacher - public school.

Notes for Missouri Belle CANN #208:
Jones notes: "no children; after her husband's death she lived with her sister, Blanche, at Sioux City, IA"
Birth: Missouri Belle Cann; Birth: 25 Jan 1878, Washington Twp, Clermont, OH; father: John Cann; mother: Mary M. Robinson. Ohio Births and Christenings, 1821-1962 <pilot.familysearch.org>
Census:
1910 Murray Ward 1, Salt Lake, UT, p. 1B. Myron Wheeler 36, engineer - stationary, PA; Belle M Wheeler 32, m. 5 yrs; Blanche Chapman 42, sis-in-law. None have children.
1915 IA State census, Sioux City. Belle Wheeler, 37, b. OH, Methodist, 4 yr in IA, 4 yr college, married.
1920 Sioux City Precinct 7, Woodbury, IA, p. 13A. Myron Wheeler 45, proprietor - confectionery store, PA; Belle Wheeler 41, proprietor - confectionery store, OH; Blanche Chapman 51, sis-in-law, OH.
1930 Sioux City Dist 53, Woodbury, IA, p. 13A. Myron Wheeler 56, news dealer - news store & cigars, PA; Belle Wheeler 52, salesman - news store & cigars, OH; Blanche Chapman 60, sis-in-law, OH, child's nurse - private family, widow; Harvey Weisinger, 61, half brother, single, manager - fire b__?__; Helen Williams, 30, single, roomer, teacher - public school.

Notes for Joshua H. HOPKINS #47
Census
- 1850 Batavia, Clermont, OH, p. 301B. Joshua H Hopkins 26, tailor; Electra C Foster 23; Anabell Hopkins 3. All b. OH.
- 1860 Batavia, Clermont, OH, p. 321. Joshua H Hopkins 36, taylor; Electra Hopkins 32; Anabelle Hopkins 13; Josephine Hopkins 8; Sallie Hopkins 5; Carrie Hopkins 3
- 1870 Batavia, Clermont, OH, p. 9A. Joshua H Hopkins 46, farmer (possibly tanner); Electra Hopkins 42; Anna B Hopkins 20; Josephine Hopkins 18; Sallie Hopkins 15; Caroline Hopkins 13. All b. OH.
- 1880 Amelia, Clermont, OH, p. 230B. Joshua Hopkins 56; Electra Hopkins 52; Anabelle Hopkins 32; Sallie Hopkins 26; Carrie Hopkins 22; Josephine Smith 28; Bessie Smith 1
- 1900 not found

Jones notes, "Lived in Clermont Co, OH between Amelia & Batavia. A tailor & hotel owner in Amelia in 1882."

Notes for Annabell HOPKINS #209:
Griggs book: "Annabell Hopkins never married"
Census: 1920 Batavia, Clermont, OH, p. 7B. Anabelle Hopkins 72, single, dressmaker - private family; Louis Hicks 70, bro-in-law, no occ; Josephine Hicks 68, sister; Louise Hicks 32, niece, stenographer - shoe factory
- 1930 Batavia, Clermont, OH, p. 10A. Josephine Hicks 78; Louise Hicks 42, dau, stenographer - shoe manuf. co; Annabelle Hopkins 82, sister. All OH/OH/OH

Death: 28 Aug 1931, Clermont Co, OH. Ohio Deaths, 1908-1932, 1938-1944, and 1958-2002 <ancestry.com>

Notes for Josephine HOPKINS #211:
Jones notes: "1st wife Sarah & 2nd wife Josephine were sisters"
Kendall Griggs book gives, "Josephine m. 1 a Mr Smith, who died before 1894. They had one child, Bessie, who died in 1897. 1900 census gives Josephine's birth as June 1851, OH; her sister Anna B. Hopkins as July 1849.

Census
- 1900 Batavia, Clermont, OH, p. 16. Louis Hicks 49, Sep 1850, attorney at law; Josephine 48, Jun 1851; Sarah L 14, Feb 1886; Anna B Hopkins 50, Jul 1849, OH/OH/OH, sis-in-law, single,
- 1910 Batavia, Clermont, OH, p. 8A. Louis Hicks 60, lawyer; Josephine M Hicks 58, 2 ch / 1 living; Sarah L Hicks 24, stenographer - wheel factory; Annabel Hopkins 62, sis-in-law
- 1920 Batavia, Clermont, OH, p. 7B. Anabelle Hopkins 72, single, dressmaker - private family; Louis Hicks 70, bro-in-law, no occ.; Josephine Hicks 68, sister; Louise Hicks 32, niece, stenographer - shoe factory
- 1930 Batavia, Clermont, OH, p. 10A. Josephine Hicks 78; Louise Hicks 42, dau, stenographer - shoe manuf. co; Annabelle Hopkins 82, sister. All OH/OH/OH

Death: Josephine Hicks, d. 26 Jun 1851, Batavia, OH, spouse: Louie Hicks. Widow, parents: Joshua Hopkins & Electra Foster. signed by Louis Hicks. Ohio Deaths 1908-1953 <pilot.familysearch.org>

Notes for Mary HOPKINS #48
Census
- 1850 Franklin, Clermont, OH, p. 387. William H Clingler 34, farmer; Mary Clingler 25; Minerva E Clingler 8; Mary E Clingler 6. All b. OH.
- 1860 Soap Creek, Davis, IA. p 17. W H Klingler 44, farmer; Mary E 34; Mary 16. All b. OH
- 1870 Drakesville, Davis, IA, p. 36A. William H Kleingler 49, farmer; Mary Kleingler 40; Sarah E Carpenter 12, servant
- 1880 Drakeville, Davis, IA Wm. H. Klinger 64; Mary Klinger 54; Mary Floyd 13, adopted child. writing very faded, illegible.

Notes for Diana HOPKINS #49
Census
 1860 Drakesville, Davis, IA, p. 875. Arthur W Stewart 32, OH, master blacksmith; Diana Stewart 32, OH; Mary E Stewart 6, IA; James W Stewart 3, IA.
 1870 Drakesville, Davis, IA, p. 40A. Arthur M Stewart 41, blacksmith; Diana Stewart 41; John Stewart 6
 1880 Drakesville, Davis, IA, p. 107A. Arthur Stewart 52, blacksmith, OH/VA/VA; Dianna Stewart 53, OH/KY/NC; John M. Stewart 15, IA
 Iowa State Census, 1895. Diana Stewart, Age: 68; Race: White; Birthplace: Ohio; Residence: Ottawa, Wapello, IA. [This is the town where her son John was enumerated in 1900]

Notes for Arthur W. STEWART #49s
Death: Arthur W. Stewart, d. 10 Dec 1887; Birth Date: 1828; Cemetery: Drakesville, wife: Diana. Grave Stone Records of Davis County, Iowa. Iowa Cemetery Records [Ancestry.com]

Notes for Levi Whitcomb HOPKINS #51
Information from book *Levi W. & Sarah E. (Carter) Hopkins, their ancestors & descendants* by Kendall Griggs, Hutchison, KS. Levi is his great great grandfather.
Census: 1860 Adams Twp, Wapello Co, IA, p. 704. Levi Hopkins 20, farmer, OH, $100; Sarah Hopkins 21, England. Married within year.
 1870 Drakesville, Davis Co, IA. p.13. Levi Hopkins 68, KY, teamster; Elizabeth 68, NC; Levi W 30, shoemaker, OH; Sarah 31, Eng; Sarah L 9, IA; Clara E 7, IA; George W 3, IA; William L 1, IA.
 1880 Sumner, Reno, KS. p. 1. Levi W. Hopkins 40, KY/KY/PA, occ: farmer/ prof. physician; Sarah 40, Eng/Eng/Eng; Lavina 18, IA/OH/Eng, school teacher; George W. 13, IA/OH/Eng, farm labor; Wm. L. 10, IA/OH/Eng, farm labor; Gertie M. 1, KS/OH/Eng; Levi 77, KY/KY/PA, shoe maker, widowed.
Land: There was a Levi Hopkins listed as a property owner in Franklin twp, *History of Clermont Co., OH*, Everts.

Notes for Sarah Elizabeth CARTER #51s
Information from Kendall Griggs book
Census:
 1900 Haven, Reno, KS. Clara Mithel 37, Jan 1863, widow, IA/OH/Eng; Ray 17, Sep 1882, KS/IA/IA, farm labor; Elmer 15, Jun 1884; Jessie 13, Sep 1886; George 12, Mar 1888; Sarah Hopkins, 60, Jun 1839, mother, widow, Eng/Eng/Eng; William Hoppins, brother, 30, Jul 1869, farmer, IA; Gertrud Hoppins, sister, 21, Apr 1879, sch teacher, IA; Walter Hopkins, brother, 17, Jul 1882, KS.
 1910 Darling, Muskogee, OK, p. 14. George H Mitchell 22, farmer; Mary Neoma 15, wife, KS/PA/IN; Clara 46, mother, widow; Elmer 25, brother, farmer; Sarah Hapkins 70, grandmother, widow.

Notes for William L. HOPKINS #221
Jones notes: "no children"; some information from Kendall Griggs' book
Census
 1900 Haven, Reno, KS p. Clara Mithel 37, Jan 1863, widow, IA/OH/Eng; Ray 17, Sep 1882, KS/IA/IA, farm labor; Elmer 15, Jun 1884; Jessie 13, Sep 1886; George 12, Mar 1888; Sarah Hopkins, 60, Jun 1839, widow, Eng/Eng/Eng; William Hopkins, brother, 30, Jul 1869, farmer, IA; Gertrud Hoppins, sister, 21, Apr 1879, sch teacher, IA; Walter Hopkins, brother, 17, Jul 1882, KS.
 1910 not found
 1920 Liberty, Pawnee, OK, William L Hopkins 50, farmer, IA/OH/Eng; Deleo 42, KS/IA/NY; Leslie F 5, nephew, OK/KS/NY.
 1930 Orlando, Orange, FL, Ellen Rhoades 75, NY/NY/VT; Vernon Rhodes 5, grandson, FL/KS/KS; William L Hopkins 61, son in law, laborer - odd jobs; De Leo Hopkins 52, dau; Leslie Hopkins 15, grandson, OK/KS/NY. FL

FL State Census
- 1935 Orange Co, precinct 27, p. 5. W. L. Hopkins, 65, b. IA, 8th grade education, laborer ; Beleo, 57, b. Kansas, high school education, housewife.
- 1945 Orange Co, precinct 17, p. 74. W. L. Hopkins, 75, b. IA, grade school education, retired; De Leo, 67, b. Kansas, high school education, housewife

Military: Not found on WW I Draft Registration

Death: William Lincoln Hopkins, d. 1952; Orange Co, FL. Florida Death Index, 1877-1998 [ancestry.com]

Notes for William J. JOHNSTON #52

Jones notes: "a blacksmith; resided in Franklin Twp 1870; his mother Margaret with him; also in 1880."

Census
- 1850 Franklin Twp, Clermont, OH, p. 383A. Alexander Johnson 44, blacksmith, $1350, OH; Margaret, 39, OH, illiterate; William J. 21, blacksmith, OH; Mary Manning 17, OH; Samuel Bolan 14, OH; Tabitha Leypole 10, OH
- 1870 Felicity, Clermont, OH, p 2. Wm. J. Johnson 42, OH, blacksmith 700 250; Mary A., 37, OH; Lucy 16, OH; Alexander 13 OH, attends school; Jennie 10, OH, attends school; Frank 8, OH, attends school; Anna 4, OH; Elizabeth 1, OH; Margaret 58, OH, lives with son.
- 1880 Felicity, Clermont, OH, p. 42D. William J. Johnston 50, blacksmith, OH; Mary 45, wife; Alexander 23, son; Nancy J. 21, daughter; Anna B. 14, daughter; Mary E. 11, daughter; Bart. 8, son; Margaret H. (or A.) 68, mother
- 1900 Franklin, Clermont, OH, p. 12. Mary Johnson 65, Dec 1834, 7 ch/5 liv; Jennie 40, Apr 1859, single, teacher; Anni B 30, Sep 1865; Birt 28, Mar 1872, single, clerk; Delia Lanham 19, Mar 1881, gr-dau. [dau of deceased daughter Lucy Lanham]
- 1910 Franklin, Clermont, OH, p. 4B. Mary M Johnson 76, widow; Alex W Johnson 53, son, widowed, blacksmith; Jennie Johnson 52, dau, single; Lena M Johnson 27, grand dau, single.
- 1920 Felicity, Franklin Twp, Clermont Co, OH, p. 8a. Mary Johnston, Head, 87, widowed, OH/OH/OH, housekeeper, own house. Jennie, daughter, 66, single, OH/OH/OH, no occ

Notes for Mary MANNING #52

Residence: Jones notes: "resided (1900) Light St, Felicity, OH"

Death: Ohio Deaths, 1908-1932, 1938-1944, and 1958-2002 [Ancestry.com] gives date & place of death, no details.

Notes for Ann Maria HICKS #53

Death: before 1900 - William listed as widowed in 1900 census.
Buried with parents in Amelia IOOF cemetery. Large monument.

Notes for William H. WHITE #53s

Census
- 1870 Williamsburg, Clermont, OH, p. 438. William White 31, grocer; Anna M White 30; Ella White 11; James H White 9; Mina B White 1/12. All b. OH.
- 1880 Batavia, Clermont Co, OH, p.10D. William H. White, head, 43, OH, farmer; Maria White, wife, 41, OH; James White, son, 20, OH; Mina White, son, 10, OH; Elnira White, mother, Widow, 77, MA; Jacob Potter, other, M, Single, 33, OH.
- 1900 Williamsburg, Clermont, OH, p. 12A. William White 63. Mar 1837, widowed, no occ. OH/MA/MA
- 1910 Williamsburg, Clermont, OH, p. 5A. William H White 73, laborer; Mina B White 38, dau, single.

Death: Ohio Death Certificate at <pilot.familysearch.org>. Gives parents as Joseph White & Elmira Fisher, occ: merchant, "widower", signed by son James White.

Notes for Mina Bell WHITE #234

Jones notes: "resided 1910 in Hamilton Co, OH with the Gleasons"
Mentioned in 1932 Will of Mary H. Kline - as niece Mina White & in 1941 Administration Docket as Mina

White Adams of Williamsburg

Birth: Mina Belle White, b. 14 Nov 1869, Williamsburg, Clermont, OH, Father: William White; Mother: Anna M. Hicks. Ohio Births & Christening 1821-1962 <pilot.familysearch.org>

Census

1930 Williamsburg, Clermont, OH, p. 3B. Maggie P White 62, widow, OH/MO/OH; Mina P White 35, single; Mina B White 59, sister in law, single, stenographer - chair factory. next to Nicholas White, 31, proprietor - chair factory.

Marriage - Mina evidently married to a ___ Adams, between 1932 and 1941, based on Administrative Docket of aunt, Mary Kline.

No marriage record or death information found.

Notes for Sarah HICKS #54

Jones notes: "Lists as Sallie M.; Resides (1910) at Leonidas, St Josephs Co, MI"

Census

1880 Dublin, Wayne, IN, p. 132. E. N. King 38, Eng, miller; Sarah King 39; Bessie King 3; Wakefield King 1; John Miller 14, stepson, OH, farmhand. Wakefield is shown as having consumption.

1900 Leonidas, Saint Joseph, MI, p. 2A. Edward N King 56, Apr 1844, Eng/Eng/Eng, imm 1859, flour mill & f__; Sarah N King 57, Apr 1843, OH/OH/KY, m. 30 yrs; Bessie V King 21, Oct 1878, IN; Wakefield King 20, Nov 1879, IN, flour mill laborer

1910 Leonidas, St Joseph, MI, p. 8A. (3 May 1910) Edward N King 68, Eng/Eng/Eng, miller - __ mill; Sarah King 69, OH/OH/OH, m. 41 yrs, 5 ch / 3 living. Son Wakefield is next door. Wakefield E King 31, IN/Eng/OH, miller; Grace King 32, MI/NY/MI, m. 4 yr, 1 child; Harlan King 3

1910 Gilbert, Rolette Co, ND, p. 3A. (17 Apr 1910) William Robertson 32, physician, WI/WI/WI; Bessie Robertson 32, IN/Eng/OH, m. 4 yrs, no children; Sara King 69, mother, OH/Eng/NY, 4 ch/3 liv; Pearson Briggs 52, boarder. [Evidently Sarah was in ND in April and was enumerated there; then included in the Michigan census in May as well]

Question? Was Sarah married before? That seems to be the only explanation for a stepson - unless the census taker wrote it wrong. If so, the first marriage was to a Miller. John Miller, stepson, b. abt 1866; Sarah m. Edward abt 1896.

Notes for Edward N. KING #34s

Edward King had immigrated from England in 1859, was naturalized and was a flour miller.

Death: Edward N. King; d. 28 Nov 1918, Leonidas, St. Joseph, MI; Age 76; Birth: 1842, England; Occ: Miller; Widowed; Father: Edward King; Mother: Sarah Hicks. [note - this has to be in error - his spouse was Sarah Hicks - not his mother - unless there was a real coincidence] Michigan Deaths and Burials, 1800-1995 <beta.familysearch.org>

Notes for William J. HICKS #55

Jones notes give birth as 1846; "Resided (1910) in Wayne Co, IN (Richmond area); was in Dublin in 1894." Mentioned in 1932 Will of Mary H. Kline: "Brother William J. Hicks of Dublin IN"; not in 1941 Admin. Docket.

Marriage: Groom: William Hicks b. 1846 Age: 25; Bride: Clara Hopkins b. 1850; Age: 21; Marriage: 18 May 1871 Clermont County, Ohio Collection: Ohio Marriages, 1800-1958 <pilot.familysearch.org>

Census

1880 Dublin, Wayne, IN, p. 129. William Hicks 36, flour & feed dealer; Clara 32; Carrie 8, OH; Robert 6, OH; Georgiana 1, IN.

1900 Jackson, Wayne, IN, p. 12B. William J Hicks 56, Jul 1843, grain dealer, OH; Clara 52, Nov 1847, 3 ch / 3 living; Georgia 21. May 1879, IN.

1910 Dalton Ward 4, Wayne, IN, p. 6B. William J Hicks 66, retailer - flour & feed; Clara 62, 3 ch / 3 living, m. 38 years; Georgia 30, dau, single, no occ.

1920 Jackson, Wayne, IN, p. 11A. Wm J Hicks 76, widower, no occ., OH/OH/OH; Georgeta 40, dau, single, no occ., IN/OH/OH.
 1930 Not found.
No death information found.

Notes for Clara HOPKINS #55s
William was listed as a widower on the 1920 census of Jackson, Wayne Co, IN.
Census:
 1860 Batavia, Clermont, OH, p. 311. Robert A Hopkins 39, hotel keeper; Mariah M Hopkins 37; Charles B Hopkins 14, painter; Clara P Hopkins 12; Mary P Hopkins 10; Margaret E Hopkins 8; William Hopkins 4; Julia T Hopkins 2; Benjamin Hopkins 23. All b. OH.
No positive death information found. May be the Clara P. Hicks who died in Wayne Co, IN - undated - aged 69. This would give a death date of 1916. Wayne Co, IN Death Records Index, 1882-1920. [Ancestry.com]

Notes for Carrie HICKS #237
Compiler's notes: the Jones notes had this one confused.. listing Carrie Smith as the daughter of Georgian Hicks & Albert B. Smith. Census research shows that the daughter of Georgiana & Albert B. Smith was Luella. Carrie Hicks, daughter of William J. Hicks, married Elmer J. Smith and lived in Richmond, IN.
Jones notes: "resided (1932) in Richmond, IN"
Mentioned in 1932 Will of Mary H. Kline "niece, Carrie Smith of Richmond, IN"
Marriage: Carrie M. Hicks to Elmer J. Smith; 14 Jun 1894, Wayne County, Indiana: W. P. A. County Clerk's Office, Book: C- R p. 67. [ancestry.com]
Census
 1880 Centerville, Wayne, IN, p. 215. George C. Smith 34, blacksmith; Martha E. Smith 29; Effa E. Smith 9; Elmer B. Smith 8; Lew S. Smith 6
 1900 Richmond, Wayne, IN, p. 5B. Elmer J Smith 28, Mar 1872, IN, salesman - dry goods; Carrie M Smith, 28, Mar 1872, OH. M. 6 years, no children.
 1910 Richmond Ward 7, Wayne, IN, p. 1A. Elmer J Smith 38, salesman - dry goods; Carrie M Smith 37, m. 15 years, no children.
 1920 Richmond Ward 7, Wayne, IN, p. 128. Elmer J Smith 46. salesman - dry goods store; Carrie M Smith 47, OH/OH/OH.
 1930 Richmond, Wayne, IN, p. 16B. Elmer J Smith 58, IN/IN/OH, salesman - furniture store; Carrie M Smith 57, OH/OH/OH; Martha E Smith 79. mother, widow, OH/OH/OH; Effie E Smith 59, sister, cashier - dry goods store, single.

Notes for Georgia Anna HICKS #57
Jones notes: "Resided (1910) in Hamilton Co, OH"
Census
 1870 Cincinnati Ward 8, Hamilton, OH, p. 153. Albert Smith 26, teamster; Georgeana Smith 23; Luella Smith 3; Hicks William Smith 26, laborer. [probably Georgia's brother, William Hicks] All b. OH.
 1880 Cincinnati, Hamilton, OH, p. 534. Albert Smith 37, teamster; Georgina Smith 32; Luiela Smith 12. All b. OH.
 1900 Cincinnati Ward 30, Hamilton, OH, p. 5a. Georgiana Smith 52, widow, Nov 1847, 1 ch / 1 living; Luella Smith 30, Jun 1869, dau, m. 9 years, 2 ch / 2 living; Georgiana Booso 12, Sep 1887, gr dau; Albert Koehler 6, July 1893, gr son, at school. No occ. for any of them.
 1910 Cincinnati Ward 24, Hamilton, OH, p. 6A. Georgiania Smith 63, widow - own income, 1 child / 1 living; Fannie C Burns 42, m3, 7 yrs, 3 ch / 2 living; Georgiania Borso 22, granddau; Albert S Koehler 16, grandson. All b. OH; no occ for any of them.
 1920 Cincinnati Ward 24, Hamilton, OH, p. 7A. Georgiana Smith 71, widow,

Notes for Albert Butler SMITH #57s
Census: 1870 Batavia, Clermont, OH, p. 10A. Amos Smith 51; Caroline A Smith 47; Albert B Smith 26, teamster; Catharine A Smith 16; Saml A Vanzant 26; Emma Vanzant 21

Notes on Luella SMITH. #240
Jones notes: "resided (1932) in Richmond, IN". Mentioned in 1932 Will of Mary H. Kline"
Note: I believe he is incorrect with this child. The Carrie Smith (#237) in Richmond, IN is the wife of Elmer J. Smith, daughter of William J. Hicks & Clara Hopkins. She is the one in Mary Kline's will.
Notes: The census records consistently mentions only a daughter named Luella, b 1873. Georgiana has only one child. See census records of mother for more information. Luella Smith apparently married three times (-?- Borso, George Koehler and Henry T. Bruns) and had children by two of the husbands. The children were Georgiana Borso? born Sept 1887 and Albert Koehler, born July 1893. "Albert Cockler of Madisonville" in mentioned in the 1941 Administration papers of Mary Kline.
Marriage3: Henry T. Bruns, b. 1873 Cinti, O., age 31, single; to Luella Koehler, b. 1871 OH, age 33; m. Sep 1904, Hamilton Co, OH. Groom's parents: Jno. B. Bruns; Katherine G. Broxtermann; bride's parents: Albert Smith; Georgie Hicks, Divorced; Bride's Previous Husband: Koehler. Ohio Marriages, 1800-1958 <beta.familysearch.org>
Death: Lulu Koehler, d. 31 Jan 1930, Cincinnati, Hamilton, OH; b. 12 Jun 1873, Cincinnati, O.; age 56 years 7 mo 19 days, Widowed; Address: 1635 Republic; Occ: Housework; Burial 03 Feb 1930, Spring Grove Cemetery; Spouse: George Koehler; parents: Albert Butler Smith; Georgana Hicks. Ohio Deaths 1908-1953 <familysearch.org>

Notes for James Reuben HICKS #58
Jones notes: "Operated a store in Amelia - Main St near Kline Ave"
Census
1900 Pierce, Clermont, OH, p. 9A. James R Hicks 49, Nov 1850, KY, dry goods merchant; Anna M Hicks 39, Jan 1861, OH/NH/KY; Maris M Hicks 12, Sep 1887, OH; Gordon B Hicks 9, Oct 1890, OH; Nellie M Jenkins 15, servant, Sep 1884, OH/OH/OH.
1910 Pierce, Clermont, OH, p. 1B. James R Hicks 59, OH/MA/OH, retail merchant - general store; Anna M Hicks 48; William M Hicks 22, no occ; Gordon B Hicks 19, no occ.; Nellie Jenkins 25, servant. M 24 rs; 3 ch / 2 living.
1920 Amelia, Clermont, OH, p. 1A. James R Hicks 67, tomato canner; Annie Hicks 57; Gordon Hicks 27, clerk - wholesale grocery; Nellie Chatterton 35, domestic. Next to Mary Kline, his sister.
1930 Amelia, Clermont, OH, p. 1B. James Hicks 79, no occ; Anna Hicks 69; Nellie Chatterton 42, servant. Near Mary Kline, 83.
Mentioned in 1932 Will of Mary H. Kline - "Brother James R. Hicks of Amelia"; not in 1941 Admin. Docket.
Death: James Ruben Hicks, d. 07 Apr 1938, Amelia, Clermont, OH; b. 24 Nov 1850, Newport, Campbell, Ky.; Age: 87 years 3 months 14 days; Married; Address: Main St. and Kline Ave.; Occ: merchant and canner; Burial: 11 Apr 1938, I.O.O.F. Cemetery, Amelia, OH; Spouse: Anna Bertran Morse Hicks; Father: James Hicks, b. West Virginia; Mother: Caroline Whetstone, b. Newport, KY; Informant: W. Morse Hicks [son]. Ohio Deaths, 1908-1953 <pilot.familysearch.org>.

Notes for Anna Bertrand MORSE #58s
Census:
1870 Pierce, Clermont, OH, p. 248. Increase Morse 63, ret grocer, NH,; Caroline Morse 40; Caroline Morse 18; John H Morse 13; Annie Morse 10; Cynthia Morse 6; John Craig 49. Other b. OH.
1880 Amelia, Clermont, OH, p. 230. Caroline Morse 49, widow, OH/MD/MD; Annie Morse 18, dau, OH/NH/OH; Jessie Morse 15, dau; Carrie Caley 27, dau; Carrie Caley 7, gr dau; Mary Caley 4, gr dau
No death information found

Notes for Gordon Benavil HICKS #243

Census

1900 Pierce, Clermont, OH, p. 9A. James R Hicks 49, Nov 1850, KY, dry goods merchant; Anna M Hicks 39, Jan 1861, OH/NH/KY; Maris M Hicks 12, Sep 1887, OH; Gordon B Hicks 9, Oct 1890, OH; Nellie M Jenkins 15, servant, Sep 1884, OH/OH/OH.

1910 Pierce, Clermont, OH, p. 1B. James R Hicks 59, OH/MA/OH, retail merchant - general store; Anna M Hicks 48; William M Hicks 22, no occ; Gordon B Hicks 19, no occ.; Nellie Jankins 25, servant. M 24 rs; 3 ch / 2 living.

1920 Amelia, Clermont, OH, p. 1A. James R Hicks 67, tomato canner; Annie Hicks 57; Gordon Hicks 27, clerk - wholesale grocery; Nellie Chatterton 35, domestic. Next to Mary Kline, his sister

1930 not found in OH/KY

This son not on Jones notes. Appears on 1910-1930 census.

Mentioned in 1932 Will of Mary H. Kline - nephew Gordon R. Hicks

Military: World War I Draft Registration Cards, 1917-1918 [ancestry.com] Gordon Benavil Hicks, age 26, b. 16 Dec 1890, Amelia, OH; occ: clerk - J. M. Short Co; single, no dependents; med height & build; blue eyes, blond hair, no disabilities. Reg: Amelia, OH; 5 Jun 1917

Military: Ohio Military Men 1917-18. Gordon B. Hicks; Serial Number: 2427626; W; Residence: Amelia, OH; Enlistment Division: National Army; Enlistment: Batavia, O. 25 Apr 1918; Birth Place: Amelia, O. Birth Date / Age: 27 5/12 Years; Assignments: 158 Depot Brigade to 19 Aug 1918; Co F 309 Supply Train to Discharge; Private, first class 19 May 1919. American Expeditionary Forces 16 Sept 1918 to 27 June 1919. Honorable discharge 5 July 1919. Volume #: 8

Notes for William Alexander HICKS #60

Jones notes: "resided (1929) at 4716 Ward St, Madisonville, OH; in Batavia 1900"

Discrepancy: 1900 census give birth date as Nov 1846. Jones notes give this date

Census:

1860 Batavia, Clermont, OH (0 657); Harriet Hicks, 38, $1500/$2160 b. OH; James Walter, 15, OH; William A. 14, OH; Lewis 11, OH.

1870 Batavia, Clermont, OH, p. 14. Harriet Hicks 47, VA, housekeeping; William A 24, at school, OH; Lewis 20, OH, works on farm

1880 Amelia, Clermont, OH, p. 3. Harriett Hicks 55, widow, VA/VT/MD, keeping house; William 34, single, attorney, OH/NC/VA; Louis 30, single, OH/NC/VA, attorney

1900 Columbia, Hamilton, OH, p. 27. William A Hicks 53, Nov 1846, attorney, OH/OH/VA; Nettie 52, Nov 1847, OH/OH/OH; Louis R 14, Mar 1886; Helen R 8., Sep 1891. M 17 yrs, 2 ch/2 liv.

1910 Columbia, Hamilton, OH. p. 8. W A Hicks 64, OH/OH/VA, lawyer; Nettie 63; L R 24, lawyer; Helen R 15.

1920 Cincinnati Ward 2, Hamilton, OH, p. 21. William A Hicks 73, lawyer; Nettie 72; Lewis R 33, lawyer; Ruth 30, dau-in-law; Hellen R 28, no occ.

Marriage: William A. Hicks b. 1862; Res. of Clermont Co, Ohio; Age: 21; Bride: Nettie Whittaker, b. 1864; Res. of Clermont Co, Ohio, Age: 19; Marriage: 12 Dec 1883, Clermont Co., OH. Ohio Marriages, 1800-1958 <pilot.familysearch.org>

Notes for Nettie W. WHITAKER 60s

Death: Nettie Hicks, d. 05 Jan 1927, Cincinnati, Hamilton, OH; Birth: 9 Nov 1846, Batavia, OH; Age: 80 years 1 month 26 days, Married; Street address: 4716 Ward; Occ: Housewife; Burial: 8 Jan 1927, Spring Grove Cemetery; Spouse :W. A. Hicks; parents: Joseph T. Whitaker, b. Batavia, OH; Rosana Wagleman, b. Clermont Co. Ohio Deaths, 1908-1953 <fsbeta.familysearch.org>

Notes for Louis HICKS #61

Jones notes: "attorney at Batavia; 1st wife Sarah & 2nd wife Josephine were sisters"

Census

 1900 Batavia, Clermont, OH, p. 16. Louis Hicks 49, Sep 1850, attorney at law; Josephine 48, Jun 1851; Sarah L 14, Feb 1886; Anna B Hopkins 50, Jul 1849, OH/OH/OH, sis-in-law, single,

 1910 Batavia, Clermont, OH, p. 8A. Louis Hicks 60, lawyer; Josephine M Hicks 58, 2 ch / 1 living; Sarah L Hicks 24, stenographer - wheel factory; Annabel Hopkins 62, sis-in-law

 1920 Batavia, Clermont, OH, p. 7B. Anabelle Hopkins 72, single, dressmaker - private family; Louis Hicks 70, bro-in-law, no occ.; Josephine Hicks 68, sister; Louise Hicks 32, niece, stenographer - shoe factory

Death: Ohio Death Certificate at <pilot.familysearch.org> gives wife as Jossie, occ. lawyer; mother as Harriet Mary Baxter.

Notes for Sarah F. HOPKINS #61s

Jones notes: "1st wife Sarah & 2nd wife Josephine were sisters"

Notes for Josephine HOPKINS #61s2

Jones notes: "1st wife Sarah & 2nd wife Josephine were sisters"

Kendall Griggs book "Josephine m. 1 a Mr Smith, who died before 1894. They had one child, Bessie, who died in 1897.

1900 census gives Josephine's birth as June 1851, OH. Her sister Anna B. Hopkin's as born July 1849.

Death. Josephine Hicks, d. 26 Jun 1851, Batavia, OH; spouse: Louie Hicks. Widow, parents: Joshua Hopkins & Electra Foster. Signed by Louis Hicks. OH Deaths 1908-1953 <pilot.familysearch.org>

Notes for William David NEWKIRK #64

Jones notes: "Enlisted 9/21/1861, Co H. 59th OVI, pensioned. Served at Piketon, KY. Removed abt 1865 to Moultrie Co, IL, near Windsor. Abt 1889, removed to Drakesville, IA"

Census:

 1880 Whitley, Moultrie, IL, p. 485. William D. Newkirk, 35, farmer, OH/OH/OH; Sarah E. Newkirk 25, IL/KY/KY; Edward Newkirk 5, IL/OH/KY; Mary E. Newkirk, 9m, IL/OH/KY, b. Aug.

 1900 Drakesville, Davis, IA, p. 1. Wm O Newkirk 55, Dec 1845, farmer, OH/OH/OH; Sarah ? 47, Mar 1853, IL/KY/KY, 4 ch / 4 living; Mollie E 20, IL, Aug 1879; Cora 15, Aug 1884; Nancy 13, Feb 1887. Children b. IL.

 1910 Drakesville, Davis, IA, p. 1. William D Newkirk, 65, own income; Sarah E 56, 4 ch/4 liv; m. 36 yrs

 1920 Drakesville, Davis, IA, p. 2B. William D Newkirk, 75, no occ, Sarah E 66; Mildred Cox 12, gr-dau.

 1930 Ottumwa, Wapello, IA, p. 8A. William Parker 48, IA/IA/IA, handironer - laundry; Nannie 43, IL/OH/IL; W D Newkirk, 85, father in law, OH/OH/OH, no occ.

Iowa State Census

 1915, Drakesville, Davis Co, IA. Wm D. Newkirk, age 70, meatman, unemployed 10 months, b. OH. Married, 25 yrs in IA. Military - Civil War, 59th OH, Co H.

 1925 Drakesville, Davis Co, IA. Wm D Newkirk, 80; father: Nelson Newkirk, mother: Nancy Hicks; Mildred Cox 17, granddau., b. IA, father: James Cox b MO, mother: Mollie Newkirk, b. IL.

Death: Wm. D. Newkirk b. 1845; d. 26 Nov 1932; Cem: Drakesville; wife: Emma. Iowa Cemetery Records [WPA]

Notes for Charles J. HICKS #67

Jones notes: "resided near Vermillion, IL; Helped operate his father's saw mill in the winter months and threshed in the summer with the steam tractor from the saw mill. Worked in the Dakota grain fields"

Census

 1900 Elbridge, Edgar, IL, p. 25. Ella Hicks 38, Oct 1861, widow, 4 ch / 4 living, dressmaking; Verna A 13, Nov 1886; Harry 12, Jun 1887; Mary Cecil 10, Feb 1890; Paul 7, Aug 1892. All b. IL/IL/IL.

1910 Paris Ward 4, Edgar, IL, p. 4a. Ella Hicks 47, seamstress, 5 ch / 4 living; Harry 21, driver; Cecil 20, stenographer - publishing co; Paul 17, driver?

1920 not found

No death information found.

Notes for Albert Alden HICKS #68

Jones notes: "died in a train explosion near Sanford, IL when returning on a train from Terre Haute IN. Partner to Charles J. in the threshing business"

Census

1880 Elbridge, Edgar Co IL, p. 55B Albert Hicks, 22, IL; Sadie Hicks, Wife, 21, OH; Roscoe B. Hicks, Son, 4 mo, IL

1900 Edgar County, IL, p. 50a Albert A Hicks, head, Jun 1851, 42, mar. 22 yr, IL/OH/OH, farmer, owns farm; Sadie, wife, Jun 1858, 41, mar 22 yr, 6 ch/5 living, OH/OH/OH; Roscoe, son, Jun 1880, 20, single, farm laborer; Glen, son, Nov 1881, 18 single, farm laborer; Curtis, son, May 1889, 11, single, attended school 8 months; Charles, son, Sept 1894, 5; Julian, son, Jan 1898, 2. Children all b. IL.

Notes for Sadie Bell ROBERTS 68s

Census

1910 Elbridge, Edgar, IL, p. 26. Sadie B Hicks 52, widow, 6 ch / 5 living, OH/OH/OH, farmer - general farm; Roscoe 30, IL/IL/OH, farmer - general farm; Curtis J 20, laborer - odd jobs; Charley 15; Julian S 11

1920 Elbridge, Edgar, IL, p. 25. Sadie B Hicks 61, no occ; Curtis 30, laborer - odd jobs; Julian 21, laborer - farm.

1930 - Elbridge, Edgar, IL, p. 9B. Sadie B Hicks 71, farmer, general farm, widow; Curtiss Hicks 40, farm labor, single.

Death: Sadie B Hicks 1937-06-22, Edgar Co, IL. Illinois Statewide Death Index 1916-1950.

Notes for Mary Elizabeth HICKS #69

Census

1880 - Stratton, Edgar, IL p. 239C. Herbert Farnham, Head, 24, IL/IL/MO, Occ: Farmer; Mary, Wife, 20, IL/OH/VT, Occ: Keeping House, Erma, Dau, 7/12, b. Oct, IL/IL/IL

1900 Paris, Edgar, IL, p. 14. Mary Farnham 46, b. Nov 1859, IL/ OH/NJ, widow, 2 ch / 0 living, no occ. [may not be right person]

1910 Paris Ward 4, Edgar, IL, p. 6A. H C Clark 56, farmer; Mary E Clark 50; Nellie Clark 26, single, music teacher. m2 for each of them; m. 2 yrs, Mary has 3 ch/0 living;

1920 Paris Ward 4, Edgar, IL, p. 17. Harvey Clark 66, IN/IN/VA, farmer; Mary 62, IL/KY/KY; Millie 39, IL/IN/IL, school teacher.

1930 Paris Ward 4, Edgar, IL p. 2. Mary E Clark 70, IL/OH/NJ, divorced, no occ. (Harvey Clark is in same town, listed as widowed, with daughter, Millie.)

Notes for Herbert FARNHAM 59s

Census: 1880 Stratton, Edgar Co, IL; p. 239C. Herbert Farnham, Head, 24, IL/IL/MO, Occ: Farmer; Mary, wife, 20, IL/OH/VT, Occ: Keeping House, Erma, Dau, 7/12, b. Oct, IL/IL/IL

Notes for Harvey CLARK 59s2

Census:

1880 Edgar, Edgar, IL, p. 33C. Harvy C. Clark 26, farmer; S. Belle Clark 26; Millie McAdams 19, boarder; Orman Morrison 18, boarder. All b. IN.

1900 Edgar, Edgar, IL, p. 6A. Harvey C Clark 46, Sep 1854, farmer, IN/IN/VA; Nellie B Clark 20, Aug 1880; Lettie M Clark 12, Oct 1888; Frank Griffith 12, servant.

End notes: Generation 3

34. Ohio Deaths 1908-1953.
35. Ohio Deaths 1908-1953.
36. Ibid.
37. Ohio Deaths 1908-1953. .
38. Ibid.
39. Ibid.
40. Ohio Deaths, 1908-1932, 1938-1944, and 1958-2002.
41. Ohio Deaths 1908-1953.
42. Hicks Family Bible.
43. Hicks Family Bible (loose paper).
44. Bracken Co, KY Marriage Bonds.
45. Hicks Family Bible.
46. Ibid.
47. Ibid
48. Hicks Family Bible (loose paper).
49. Hicks Family Group Sheet - Elijah Hicks.
50. Hicks Family Group Sheet - Elijah Hicks.
51. Clermont County, Ohio 1980 Vol 1.
52. Hicks Family Bible (loose paper).
53. Clermont Co. OH Death Record.
54. Clermont Co, OH Marriage Books.
55. Clermont County, Ohio 1980 Vol 1.
56. Hicks Family Bible (loose paper).
57. Clermont Co, OH Marriage Books.
58. Hicks Family Bible (loose paper).
59. White, T. B. Funeral Home Records.
60. Clermont Co, OH Marriages 1850-1874.
61. Zezula - Notes - abt 1990.
62. Hicks Family Bible (loose paper).
63. Clermont Co, OH Marriages 1850-1874.
64. Kentucky Death index, 1911-2000.
65. Zezula - Notes - abt 1990.
66. Hicks Family Bible (loose paper).
67. Probate, Athens, OH.
68. History of Maysville & Mason Co, KY
69. Hicks Family Bible (loose paper).
70. Clermont Co, OH Marriages 1850-1874.
71. Mason Co, KY Marriage Index.
72. Ibid.
73. Kansas Marriages, 1840-1935.
74. Mason Co, KY - Census - 1880.
75. Hicks Family Bible (loose paper).
76. Mason Co, KY Marriage Bonds.
77. Hicks Family Bible (loose paper).
78. Clermont Co, OH Marriages 1850-1874.
79. World War I Draft Registration Cards, 1917-1918.
80. Ohio Deaths 1908-1953.
81. Hicks Family Bible (loose paper).
82. Clermont Co, OH Marriages 1850-1874.
83. Ohio Deaths, 1908-1932, 1938-1944, and 1958-2002.
84. Ohio Deaths 1908-1953.
85. Ohio Marriages, 1800-1958
86. Ohio Deaths and Burials, 1854-1997
87. Ohio Marriages, 1800-1958
88. Ibid
89. Griggs, *Levi W. & Sarah E. (Carter) Hopkins, their ancestors & descendants.*
90. Ohio Deaths 1908-1953.
91. *Levi W. & Sarah E. (Carter) Hopkins, their ancestors & descendants.*
92. Florida Death Index.
93. Ibid.
94. Clermont Co, OH Marriage Books.
95. Ohio Deaths 1908-1953.
96. Clermont Co, OH Marriages 1850-1874.
97. Ohio Deaths 1908-1953.
98. Bracken Co, KY Marriage Bonds.
99. Florida Death Index.
100. Ibid.
101. Ohio Deaths 1908-1953.
102. Ohio Military Men, 1917-18.
103. *Levi W. & Sarah E. (Carter) Hopkins, their ancestors & descendants.*
104. Ohio Deaths 1908-1953.
105. *Levi W. & Sarah E. (Carter) Hopkins, their ancestors & descendants.*
106. Ibid.
107. Ibid.
108. World War I Draft Registration Cards, 1917-1918.
109. Illinois Statewide Death Index, 19161950.
110. Social Security Death Index.
111. Indiana Marriages, 1780-1992.
112. Social Security Death Index.
113. Illinois Marriage Records 1851-1900.

Generation Four
The great grandchildren of Joshua and Diana Hicks

This generation was born before, during or soon after the Civil War. Some served in the military, while the some of the younger of the generation grew up without fathers - or without healthy fathers as a result of the War.

Hicks home place - about 1900

The United States was growing and new areas opened for settlement. While many of this generation stayed in Clermont County, others moved to cities or settled in more western areas. No one seems to have moved east; only a few moved south - i.e. John Lee Fitzpatrick and his cousin, Sarah (Fitzpatrick) Higgins, moved to the Birmingham area of Alabama. By now Hicks descendants were in Ohio, Iowa, Illinois, Indiana, Kentucky, Kansas, Missouri and Washington state.

The population of Clermont County continued to grow, but it remained mostly farmland. A map of Clermont shows the Hicks family still along the Ohio River in 1891 – probably on part of the original land. John James and Elijah Franklin Hicks (John & Frank), sons of Henry Melvin Hicks, had married sisters (Georgia & Melissa Beeker) and lived side by side. The house was well up the hill, with the rich bottom land along the river used for growing crops. Many other familiar names – families connected to the Hicks by marriage – were nearby.

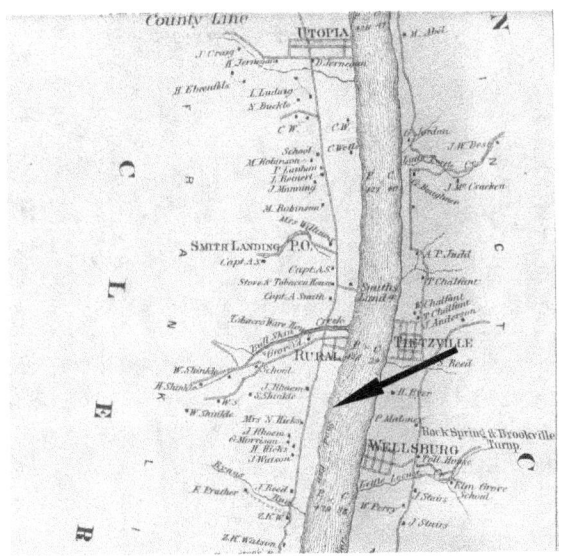

Ohio River map, 1891 -
Hicks land just below Rural

Hicks homes on the hill - bottom land below

Golden Anniversary.

1900

"Uncle Hy" M. Hicks and his aged and estimable companion, who was a Miss Hannah F. Owens, have lived happily and peaceful together for fifty long eventful years. And on last Saturday, December 22, the golden anniversary of the marriage event in their lives was celebrated most delightfully by an ingathering of the children and grandchildren at their pleasant home on Locust Hill, just below Rural. There were present upon the joyous occasion, O. D. Hicks and wife and daughter, Miss Edna, of this place; H. H. Hicks and family, of Utopia; and their daughter, Mrs. Mary Joslin and four daughters of New Richmond; Mrs. Mary Jones and grandson, Clifford Houser, E. F. Hicks and wife and little son, J. J. Hicks and wife, H. C. Duvall and wife and Chas. Fry and wife, all of Rural; and Mr. James Melvin of Brooksville, Ky. The latter named was also present at the wedding fifty years ago, which was performed at the old Owens homestead opposite Utopia in Kentucky. This light hearted company included one sister, four sons, one daughter and eleven grandchildren, and all enjoyed the day and event quite royally. A bounteous dinner was spread to the enjoyment of the guests, and of this we speak as one having authority, touching its merits. Our thanks for a box of the delicious cake is hereby extended. Mr. O. D. Hicks, the photographer, secured a number of excellent group pictures as mementoes of this occasion of much joy and thanksgiving.

Lucy Ann (Hicks) Levi 1857-1888

Frank & Melissa Hicks; John & Georgia Hicks w/ daughter, Marcella; Elizabeth Beeker. About 1910

50th Anniversary Party - Henry Melvin & Hannah Frances (Owens) Hicks - Dec 1900

Children in front row (l to r): Rella Joslin, Eva Joslin, —, —, Adlora Joslin, — , ----, Archie Joslin, —, Edna Joslin?, Hurdes Hicks. Adults (l. to r.) John Hicks, Georgia Hicks, — , ---- , ---- , Frank Hicks, Mary Joslin, Frances Owens (mother of Hannah Hicks), ---- , ----, ---- , ---- , ----, James Owens, ---- , ----, Henry Melvin Hicks, Hannah Frances (Owens) Hicks

Harvey Hicks 1862-1950

James Marcellus Jones
1847-1925

Generation 4

72. Francis M.[4] **MANNING** (Lucinda[3] TATMAN, Ruth[2] HICKS, Joshua[1]), born Nov 1844 in OH; died bef 1920 probably in Hamilton Co, OH. He married on 9 Sep 1877 in Clermont Co, OH **Caroline HANLEY**, born 14 Apr 1853 in Bethel, Clermont Co, OH; died[114] 3 Apr 1944 in St. Bernard, Hamilton Co, OH; buried 6 Apr 1944 in Bethel Cemetery, Clermont Co, OH, daughter of Redmond HANLEY and Margaret LIMING.

Francis Manning was a farmer in the Spann area of Clermont Co, OH until about 1910, when the family moved to the Cincinnati area and he worked in a factory. After his death (before 1920), his widow Caroline lived with her married daughter, Ethel Tekulve, until her death in 1944. @@

Children of Francis M. MANNING and Caroline HANLEY were:
- \+ 264 i **Cora**[5] **MANNING**.
- 265 ii **Lucinda**[5] **MANNING**, born Sep 1880 in OH. On 1900 census; no further information found.
- \+ 266 iii **Walter**[5] **MANNING**.
- 267 iv **Grace**[5] **MANNING**, born Apr 1890 in OH. No children
- 268 v **William**[5] **MANNING**[115], born 11 May 1891 in Bethel, Clermont Co, OH; died 3 May 1931 in Cincinnati, Hamilton, OH; buried in Bethel, Clermont Co, OH. @@
- \+ 269 vi **Ethel M.**[5] **MANNING**.

73. Mary A. 'Mollie'[4] **MANNING** (Lucinda[3] TATMAN, Ruth[2] HICKS, Joshua[1]), born 20 Jun 1848 in OH; died[116] 2 Sep 1913 in Miami Twp, Clermont Co, OH; buried 4 Sep 1913 in Pt. Isabel OH. She married on 27 Jan 1874 in Clermont Co, OH **John S. PATTISON**, born Mar 1846 in OH; died 1906; buried in Pt. Isabel, OH.

Mollie Manning married John Pattison, a farmer in Clermont County. No earlier records have been found for John Pattison, although census records indicate that he was born in Ohio. They were the parents of seven children. @@

Children of Mary A. 'Mollie' MANNING and John S. PATTISON were:
- 270 i **Clarence E.**[5] **PATTISON**, born 17 Nov 1874 in Bethel, Clermont Co, OH; died[117] 25 Oct 1951 in Cincinnati, Hamilton Co, OH; buried 29 Oct 1951 in Bethel Tate Cemetery Clarence never married. He taught school at Van Wert, OH. He was living in Cincinnati at the time of his death; a retired teacher. @@
- \+ 271 ii **Edward H.**[5] **PATTISON**.
- 272 iii **Myrtle Elizabeth**[5] **PATTISON**, born 11 Jun 1879 in Clermont Co, OH; died 11 Jun 1956; buried in Bethel Tate Cemetery She married abt 1910 **Clarence Homer REINHARDT**[118, 119], born 15 Jan 1889 in Bethel, Clermont Co, Ohio; died 24 Apr 1963 in Cincinnati, Hamilton, OH, son of Frank REINHARDT and Rachel PRICE.
  Jones notes: "no children; resided at Branch Hill; in Cincinnati OH in 1942". In 1920, Myrtle, 40 & single [but with her married name], was living with her married brother, Ross, in Covington, KY. By 1930 she had married Clarence Reinhardt and was back in Clermont Co, OH. @@
- \+ 273 iv **Ross John**[5] **PATTISON**.
- \+ 274 v **Walter Cleavland**[5] **PATTISON**.

@@For more information, see research notes at end of chapter.

     275   vi   **Dale Lester**[5] **PATTISON**[120, 121], born 1 Oct 1887 in Bethel, Clermont Co, OH; died 3 Dec 1959 in Cincinnati, Hamilton, OH; buried in Bethel Tate Cemetery. **Jones notes:** "no children". Dale Pattison was a shoe salesman in Cincinnati in 1917 and a shoe merchant in Huntington, WV in 1930. By 1942, he was working at a men's shop in Cincinnati. @@

+   276   vii   **Frank Lee**[5] **PATTISON**.

74. John Wesley[4] **MANNING** (Lucinda[3] TATMAN, Ruth[2] HICKS, Joshua[1]), born Aug 1849 in OH; died bet 1900-1908. He married on 12 Mar 1874 in Clermont Co, OH **Laura Francis VICKROY**, born 19 Jan 1851; died[122] 13 Jun 1923 in Bethel, Clermont Co, OH; buried 15 Jun 1923, daughter of William VICKROY and Nellie PATTISON.

John Manning and his wife Laura lived in Williamsburg, Clermont Co, OH, where John was a farmer. His farm was near that of his brother, Charles. After John's death, Laura lived with her brother and sister. @@

    Children of John Wesley MANNING and Laura Francis VICKROY were:

+   277   i   **Orville Lorain**[5] **MANNING**.

77. Charles William[4] **MANNING** (Lucinda[3] TATMAN, Ruth[2] HICKS, Joshua[1]), born 15 Oct 1855 in OH; died[123] 28 Feb 1947 in Williamsburg Twp, Clermont, OH. He married on 20 Sep 1878 in Clermont Co, OH **Edith L. RILEY**, born May 1858 in OH; probably died bef 1908.

Charles Manning was a farmer in the Williamsburg area. He and his wife Edith had 7 children, 6 of whom were living in 1910. Charles lived to be over 91 years old. @@

    Children of Charles William MANNING and Edith L. RILEY were:

+   278   i   **Ora Chasse**[5] **MANNING**.

+   279   ii   **Iva Lou**[5] **MANNING**.

+   280   iii **Chilton H.**[5] **MANNING**.

     281   iv **Tell**[5] **MANNING**, born 10 Jan 1887; died 10 Nov 1889; buried in Concord Cemetery.

     282   v   **Howard Metzzar**[5] **MANNING**, born 14 Feb 1888 in Clermont Co, OH.
Military: World War I Draft Registration Cards, 1917-1918 [ancestry.com] Howard Metzzar Manning, b. 14 Feb 1888; res: Clermont, Co, OH

     283   vi **Walter L**[5] **MANNING**[124], born 15 Jul 1892 in Clermont Co, OH; died 28 Apr 1966 in Hamilton Co, OH; buried in Bethel Tate Cemetery
Jones notes: "not married" @@

+   284   vii **Raleigh Clark**[5] **MANNING**.

+   285   viii **Lowell Burns**[5] **MANNING**.

79. Homer Jerome[4] **FITZPATRICK** (Dianna[3] TATMAN, Ruth[2] HICKS, Joshua[1]), born 23 Oct 1849/51 in Clermont Co, OH; died 18 Jun 1935 in Amelia, Clermont Co, OH; buried in Old Nicholsville Cemetery He married abt 1876 in IN **Susan A. TEVEBAUGH**, born 17 Oct 1854 in IN; died[125] 17 Jul 1931 in Batavia, Clermont Co, OH; buried 19 Jul 1931 in Nicholsville, OH, daughter of John TEVEBAUGH and Miriam SAGASER.

Homer Fitzpatrick worked as a farm laborer in 1870, then had his own farm by 1880, with both his brother John and father-in-law, John Tevebaugh, living with the family. In 1900, he was farming in Newport, KY. By 1910, he was back in Clermont Co, OH where he lived till his death. @@

@@For more information, see research notes at end of chapter.

Children of Homer Jerome FITZPATRICK and Susan A. TEVEBAUGH were:
>   286   i   **Ora D.**[5] **FITZPATRICK**, born 17 Apr 1881; died 28 Sep 1882; buried in Old Nicholsville.
> + 287   ii   **Pearl Diana**[5] **FITZPATRICK**.
> + 288   iii **John Charles**[5] **FITZPATRICK**.

80. Sarah Ellen[4] **FITZPATRICK** (Dianna[3] TATMAN, Ruth[2] HICKS, Joshua[1]), born Jan 1850 in OH; died[126] 11 May 1921 in Blount Co, AL. She married on 17 Feb 1874 in Clermont Co, OH **Samuel Oliver HIGGINS**, born 26 Oct 1849 in New Richmond, OH; died[127] 5 Feb 1929 in Garden City, Cullman, AL, son of William HIGGINS and Nancy Ann COFFMAN.

Sarah's mother Diana (Tatman) Fitzpatrick died young and the children were split among family and neighbors. Sarah and her sister Ida lived with their uncle, John Tatman. Sarah married Samuel Oliver Higgins and moved to Alabama soon thereafter. Samuel farmed in Morgan, Blount and Cullman Counties of Alabama. @@

Children of Sarah Ellen FITZPATRICK and Samuel Oliver HIGGINS were:
> + 289   i   **Guy**[5] **HIGGINS**.
>   290   ii   **Claude C.**[5] **HIGGINS**, born 1876 in AL; died 1893.
>   Appears only on 1880 census - Morgan, AL, p. 79. Samuel O. Higgins 30, farmer, OH/OH/MD; Sarah E. Higgins 30; Guy Higgins 5; Claud C. Higgins 4; Burton Higgins 2; Fredrick A. Higgins 8M, AL/OH/OH. Other OH/OH/OH
>   Not with family 1900 - census indicated that 3 children have died. He may have been one of them. Information from great granddaughter gives: Claude E. Higgins b 1876, d 1893
> + 291   iii **Frank**[5] **HIGGINS**.
> + 292   iv   **Burton**[5] **HIGGINS**.
>   293   v   **Frederick**[5] **HIGGINS**, born abt 1879 in AL; died 1882.
>   Appears only on 1880 census,
>   Not with family 1900 - census indicated that 3 children have died. He may have been one of them. Great granddaughter gives "Frederick Allen Higgins b 1879, d 1882"
> + 294   vi   **William Zachary**[5] **HIGGINS**.
> + 295   vii **Leroy**[5] **HIGGINS**.
> + 296   viii **James Monroe**[5] **HIGGINS**.

82. George E.[4] **FITZPATRICK** (Dianna[3] TATMAN, Ruth[2] HICKS, Joshua[1]), born 8 Jan 1854 in Clermont Co, OH; died 28 Oct 1940. He married **Sadie HANLEY**, born 8 Jul 1855 in Clermont Co, OH; died 17 Jul 1931.

After the death of his mother when George was about 13, he lived with what was probably neighbors, William and Mary Anderson. The Andersons were the parents of Melita, wife of George's uncle, William O. Tatman. George could not be found on the 1880 and 1900 census, so he may have left the area. He returned by 1910 and married Sarah Hanley. They had one son, Hanley. George was a farmer. @@

Children of George E. FITZPATRICK and Sadie HANLEY were:
> + 297   i   **Hanley**[5] **FITZPATRICK**.

85. Walter[4] **FITZPATRICK** (Dianna[3] TATMAN, Ruth[2] HICKS, Joshua[1]), born 1861 in Clermont Co, OH; died bef 1910 in GA or CO. He married **Addie -?-**, born Oct 1866 in Georgia.

@@For more information, see research notes at end of chapter.

After the death of his parents in about 1867, Walter lived with his uncle, John McNair, and worked on his farm for at least 10 years. By 1900, he was in Georgia, where he probably married Addie -?-. Addie was listed as a widow in the 1910 census of Denver, Colorado. No marriage or death information has been found. @@

    Children of Walter and Addie FITZPATRICK were:
- 298 i **Ethel**[5] **FITZPATRICK**, born Jan 1891 in AL.
- 299 ii **Mabel**[5] **FITZPATRICK**, born May 1896 in AL.

97. John Lee[4] **FITZPATRICK** (Sarah A.[3] TATMAN, Ruth[2] HICKS, Joshua[1]), born 13 Oct 1856 in Ohio; died 24 Jun 1929 in Montgomery, Montgomery Co, AL; buried in Oakwood Cemetery, Montgomery AL. He married on 30 Sep 1891 in Clermont Co, OH **Margaret M. MANNING**, born 5 Jul 1870 in Pt. Isabel OH; died 20 Jun 1949; buried in Oakwood Cemetery, Montgomery AL, daughter of George W. and Mary MANNING.

John L. Fitzpatrick moved to Alabama, probably soon after his marriage in 1891. He was a real estate agent in Montgomery, AL. His wife Margaret, called Maggie, was a sister to Callie Manning who married John's brother, Reece. Margaret's sisters, Eliza and Georgia, were living with the family in 1900. @@

    Children of John Lee FITZPATRICK and Margaret M. MANNING were:
- 300 i **Hal**[5] **FITZPATRICK**, born Jun 1895 in AL.
  Appears on 1900 census with parents. Does not appear on any other census or on Jones notes - died young? The 1910 census shows that 2 of Margaret's 4 children have died.
- + 301 ii **John Lee**[5] **FITZPATRICK Jr**.
- + 302 iii **Homer Tatman**[5] **FITZPATRICK**.

104. John Sherman[4] **FITZPATRICK** (Sarah A.[3] TATMAN, Ruth[2] HICKS, Joshua[1]), born 10 Aug 1863 in Nicholsville OH; died 17 Oct 1937 in Cincinnati, Hamilton, OH; buried 20 Oct 1937 in Bethel, Clermont, OH. He married on 26 Mar 1899 in Clermont Co, OH **Nora B. VAIL**, born 25 Jun 1873 in Harlington, OH

Sherman Fitzpatrick was a farmer and lived in Clermont Co, OH most of his life. By 1930, he was working as a landscape gardener on a private estate. @@

    Children of John Sherman FITZPATRICK and Nora B. VAIL were:
- + 303 i **Daisy B.**[5] **FITZPATRICK**.
- 304 ii **Gail A.**[5] **FITZPATRICK**, born abt 1903 in OH. Appeared on 1910 & 1920 census. No other information found
- 305 iii **Zelphia E.**[5] **FITZPATRICK**, born 29 Apr 1907 in OH. Appeared on 1910 & 1920 census No record of marriage or death.
  Birth: Zelphia Fitzpatrick, Female, 29 Apr 1907; parents: Sherman Fitzpatrick & Nora Vail. Ohio Births and Christenings, 1821-1962 <pilot.familysearch.org>
- 306 iv **John Willard**[5] **FITZPATRICK**, born 22 Jun 1915 in Clermont Co, OH; died[128] Jan 1979 in Cincinnati, Hamilton Co, OH.
  Census 1930 Tate, Clermont Co, OH, p. 6A. Ben Fitzpatrick 70, OH/KY/OH, farmer; Minnie Fitzpatrick 65, OH/KY/OH; Oliver Fitzpatrick 62, farmer, OH/KY/OH; John Fitzpatrick 14, nephew. No other information found

@@For more information, see research notes at end of chapter.

105. William W.[4] TATMAN (John[3], Ruth[2] HICKS, Joshua[1]), born Sep 1853 in Clermont Co, OH; died 23 Mar 1923. He married on 19 Dec 1878 in Clermont Co, OH **Alice M. TAYLOR**, born 11 Nov 1853 in Clermont Co, OH; died 31 Jan 1908, daughter of Arnold and Martha TAYLOR.

William Tatman was a farmer and probably farmed in Clermont County his whole life. None of his daughters ever married. They remained at home and probably kept the farm after the deaths of their parents. @@

    Children of William W. TATMAN and Alice M. TAYLOR were:
- 307 i **Helena "Lena"[5] TATMAN**, born 23 Sep 1879 in Clermont Co, OH; died 16 Aug 1922 in Monroe Twp, Clermont Co, OH; buried 18 Aug 1922 in Nicholsville, OH.
  Birth: Lena Tatman, b. 23 Sep 1879, Laurel, Clermont, OH, Father William Tatman; Mother Alice Taylor. Ohio Births and Christenings, 1821-1962 <familysearch.org>
  Death: Lena Tatman, d. 16 Aug 1922, Monroe, Clermont, OH. b. 23 Sep 1879, OH. 42 yr, 8 mo, 23 da. single, occ: housework; bur 18 Aug 1922, Nicholsville, OH. Father William Tatman; mother: Alice Taylor, both b. OH. OH Deaths 1908-1953. <familysearch.org>
- 308 ii **Bessie[5] TATMAN**, born Apr 1881 in OH; died 4 Apr 1960 in Bethel, Clermont Co, OH. **Jones notes**: "not married".
  Census: 1930 Monroe, Clermont, OH, p. 4A. Bessie Tatman 48; Jennie M Tatman 46. Both single, Occ on both - "incidental - cows & poultry". Next to Frank Tatman and family.
  Death: Bessie Tatman, b. 1882; Res: Clermont Co, OH; d. 4 Apr 1960, Long term care facilities, Clermont Co, OH, age 78, never married. Ohio Deaths, 1908-1932, 1938-1944, and 1958-2007 [Ancestry.com]
- 309 iii **Jennie[5] TATMAN**, born 28 Aug 1883 in Monroe Twp, Clermont, OH; died 15 May 1957 in Brown Co OH. Jones notes: "not married". See older sister for census information.
- + 310 iv **John Franklin[5] TATMAN**.

106. Mary A.[4] TATMAN (John[3], Ruth[2] HICKS, Joshua[1]), born 3 Dec 1858 in Clermont Co, OH; died 8 May 1929 in Tate, Clermont, OH; buried 12 May 1929 in Bethel Tate Cemetery She married on 4 Sep 1887 in Clermont Co, OH **Clifford John SWING**, born 7 Feb 1857 in OH; died 28 Jun 1951 in Bethel, Clermont, OH; buried 30 Jun 1951 in Bethel Tate Cemetery. He was the son of Charles W. SWING and Anna O. HANNAH

Mary Tatman, called Mollie, married Clifford Swing in 1887. Cliff Swing was a teacher for a while, as were some of his sons. By 1910, Clifford was listed as a farmer. @@

    Children of Mary A. TATMAN and Clifford John SWING were:
- + 311 i **Glen O'Hara[5] SWING**.
- 312 ii **Edna B[5] SWING**, born 8 Dec 1891 in Clermont Co, OH; died 1968; buried in Bethel Tate Cemetery. Jones notes: "not married". Lived with her parents until at least 1930.
- 313 iii **Archie T.[5] SWING**, born 1893 in Clermont Co, OH; died 1894; buried in Bethel Tate Cemetery. Jones notes: "died at age 9 months"
- + 314 iv **Phillip B.[5] SWING**.
- + 315 v **John Charles[5] SWING**.

109. Maud Blanche[4] TATMAN (John[3], Ruth[2] HICKS, Joshua[1]), born 5 Aug 1865 in Clermont Co, OH; died 21 Jan 1915 in Tate, Clermont, OH; buried 23 Jan 1915. She married on 3 Mar 1886 in Clermont Co, OH **John H. TAYLOR**, born 4 Mar 1856 in Clermont Co, OH; died 7 Dec 1926 in Tate, Clermont Co, OH; buried 9 Dec 1926 in Bethel, Clermont, OH, son of Arnold TRESTTIN and Martha TAYLOR.

@@For more information, see research notes at end of chapter.

Maude Tatman lived in Clermont County all of her life. She married John Taylor, a farmer. They had seven children, all of whom lived to adulthood. @@

    Children of Maud Blanche TATMAN and John H. TAYLOR were:

316 i **Goldie Louise**[5] **TAYLOR**, born 2 Nov 1886 in Clermont Co, OH; died 29 Jun 1963 in Clermont Co, OH; buried in Bethel Tate Cemetery
Jones notes: "Not married"
Death: Goldie L Taylor, b. 1887; res: Clermont Co, OH; Death 29 Jun 1963, home, Clermont Co, OH, age 76; never married. Ohio Deaths, 1908-1932, 1938-1944, and 1958-2007 [Ancestry.com]

+ 317 ii **Charles Harrison**[5] **TAYLOR**.

318 iii **Howard Tatman**[5] **TAYLOR**[129], born 22 May 1890 in Bethel, Clermont Co, OH; died 4 Jan 1922 in Dayton State Hospital, Van Buren, OH.
Jones notes: "Not married"
Military: World War I Draft Registration Cards, 1917-1918 [Ancestry.com] Howard Tatmon Taylor, age 27, b. 22 May 1890, Bethel, OH; Res: Bethel, Clermont, OH; farmer - near Bethel; single; military service: private, Co K, 3 years, State of Ohio; med height & build; light blue eyes, dk brown hair. no disabilities; regis: 5 Jun 1917, West Tate, Clermont Co, OH.
Death: Howard Taylor, d. 04 Jan 1922, Dayton State Hospital, Van Buren Twp, Montgomery, OH; Birth 22 May 1891, OH; single, farmer, res: Dayton, OH; former residence: Bethel, OH; age: 31 years 7 months 12 days; Burial 05 Jan 1922, Bethel, Ohio; Father John Taylor, b. OH; mother unknown, b. OH. Ohio Deaths 1908-1953 Death Certificate <pilot.familysearch.org>

+ 319 iv **Alice B.**[5] **TAYLOR**.

320 v **Archie McNair**[5] **TAYLOR**, born 6 Nov 1895 in Bethel, Clermont, OH; died 5 Oct 1932 in Bethel, Clermont, OH; buried 7 Oct 1932 in Bethel, Clermont, OH.
Jones notes: "Not married"
Census: 1930 Tate, Clermont, OH, p. 7B. Archie Taylor 34, farmer; Charles Taylor 42, brother, salesman - automobile. Both single.
Military: WWI Draft Registration [Ancestry.com] Archie McNair Taylor, age 23, b. Nov 6, 1899, Bethel OH. Occ: Fireman, Penn RR. Co, Cincinnati, single. Med height, med build lt blue eyes, lt brown hair. registered 5 Jun 1917.
Death: Archie M Taylor, d. 05 Oct 1932, Cincinnati, Hamilton, OH; Birth: 06 Nov 1885, Est. 1896, Ohio; Age: 36 years, Single, Farmer; Res: Bethel, OH; Bur: 7 Oct 1932, Bethel Cem; Father: John H Taylor, OH; Mother: Maud Tatman, OH. Cause of death: homicide - hit on head with automobile crank. Ohio Deaths 1908-1953 <pilot.familysearch.org>

+ 321 vi **George Richard**[5] **TAYLOR**.
+ 322 vii **John Kenneth**[5] **TAYLOR**.

110. **Lewis G.**[4] **TATMAN** (John[3], Ruth[2] HICKS, Joshua[1]), born 28 Nov 1867 in Clermont Co, OH; died[130] 3 Feb 1949 in Cincinnati, Hamilton, OH; buried 5 Feb 1949 in Bethel Tate Cemetery He married on 5 May 1898 in Clermont Co, OH **Jane Louise BOGGESS**, born 24 Jan 1870 in Clermont Co, OH; died 17 Mar 1949 in Bethel, Clermont Co, OH; buried 19 Mar 1949 in Bethel Tate Cemetery, Clermont Co, OH, daughter of Arch BOGGESS and Caroline ANDERSON.

Lewis Tatman was a farmer and probably inherited his parent's farm. In 1900, he and his wife lived with his parents on the farm. @@

@@For more information, see research notes at end of chapter.

Children of Lewis G. TATMAN and Jane Louise BOGGESS were:

323 i **Dwight Harrison**[5] **TATMAN**, born 30 Jun 1899 in OH; died 27 Feb 1975 in New Richmond, Clermont, OH. He married[131] on 10 Oct 1918 in Newport, Campbell, KY **Mabel MEEKER**, born May 1899 in OH, daughter of William D. MEEKER and Mary GARRISON. No children. @@

111. **John Charles**[4] **TATMAN** (John[3], Ruth[2] HICKS, Joshua[1]), born 1857 in Clermont Co, OH; died 1906; buried in Batavia. He married on 10 Aug 1880 in Clermont Co, OH **Ann M. NICHOLS**, born 11 Jun 1863 in Clermont Co, OH; died 29 Dec 1937; buried in Batavia OH, daughter of Perry and Nettie NICHOLS

Jones notes: "Charles Tatman was the sheriff of Clermont County". He was a farmer and tobacco merchant. @@

Children of John Charles TATMAN and Ann M. NICHOLS were:

324 i **Mary Louise**[5] **TATMAN**, born 31 Jul 1883 in Clermont Co, OH. She married on 14 Jun 1902 in Clermont Co, OH **George Bennett HATFIELD**, born 2 Dec 1875 in Withamsville OH, son of J. C. Hatfield and Mary Bennett.

No known children. No death information found. George did graduate work at Harvard, was a college professor and Congregational clergyman. He was president of Kingfisher College in Oklahoma in 1908. They were living in Pittsburgh, PA in 1930.

112. **Florence J.**[4] **TATMAN** (John[3], Ruth[2] HICKS, Joshua[1]), born 29 Mar 1871 in Clermont Co, OH; died 22 Mar 1919; buried in Bethel Tate Cemetery She married on 4 Oct 1891 in Clermont Co, OH **Walter C. FRAZIER**, born 29 Oct 1866 in Clermont Co, OH; died 5 Jun 1961; buried in Bethel Tate Cemetery

Florence Tatman married Walter Frazier, a Clermont County farmer. After Florence's death, Walter married Minnie -?- in about 1929. @@

Children of Florence J. TATMAN and Walter C. FRAZIER were:

325 i **Raymond T.**[5] **FRAZIER**, born 2 Jun 1892 in Clermont Co, OH; died 14 Sep 1915; buried in Bethel Tate Cemetery. He married **Lulu REMLEY**, born 20 Jun 1889 in Ohio; died[132] 12 Jun 1982 in Brown Co, OH, daughter of John REMLEY and Leanna DUGAN.
Jones notes: "No children". No death information found. This death date from Jones notes.

326 ii **Mildred**[5] **FRAZIER**, born 10 Jul 1902 in Clermont Co, OH; died 15 Nov 1949. She married on 19 Nov 1922 in Cincinnati, Hamilton Co, OH **Louis F. GOTOS**[133], born 2 Sep 1897 in Puerto Rico, USA; died[134] 3 Apr 1984 in Milford, Clermont Co, OH, son of Josephine -?- GOTOS. No known children.
Census: 1930 Norwood, Hamilton, OH, p. 12B. Louis Gotos 31, Puerto Rico /Spain/Puerto Rico, machinist - machine shop; Mildred L Gotos 27; Annabel Frazier 17, sister in law, assorter - ___ car co.

327 iii **Anna Belle**[5] **FRAZIER**, born 28 Oct 1912 in Clermont Co, OH.
Jones notes: "Resides (1973) at 6549 Nuncey, Mariemont, OH". Living with married sister, Mildred Gotos, in 1930. No other information.

@@For more information, see research notes at end of chapter.

115. Ledora Estelle[4] TATMAN (William Oliver[3], Ruth[2] HICKS, Joshua[1]), born 17 Jul 1862 in Clermont Co, OH; died[135] 20 Aug 1935 in Amelia, Clermont, OH; buried 22 Aug 1935 in Amelia Meth Cemetery, Amelia, Clermont Co, OH. She married on 22 Oct 1886 in Clermont Co, OH **Charles Wilmer HUTSON**, born 30 Sep 1859 in Clermont Co, OH; died 9 Dec 1947 in Amelia, Clermont Co, OH; buried in Amelia Meth. Cemetery, Amelia, Clermont Co, OH, son of William HUTSON and Susan KINDRICK.

Ledora "Dora" Tatman married Charles Hutson, a farmer in Clermont County. In 1920, Charles and Dora were living with their son, Carlos, in Van Buren, OH and Charles was a coal dealer. By 1930, they were back in Clermont County, where Carlos has a confectionary restaurant and Charles was a laborer. @@

Children of Ledora Estelle TATMAN and Charles Wilmer HUTSON were:
+ 328   i   **Carlos Stanley[5] HUTSON**.

116. Arizona T. "Arra"[4] TATMAN (William Oliver[3], Ruth[2] HICKS, Joshua[1]), born 2 Mar 1865 in Clermont Co, OH; died 16 Feb 1933; buried in Amelia Meth. Cemetery, Amelia, Clermont Co, OH. She married on 31 Dec 1882 in Clermont Co, OH **John F. HUTSON**, born May 1862 in Clermont Co, OH; died 1954; buried in Amelia Meth. Cemetery, Amelia, Clermont Co, OH.

Arizona "Arra" Tatman married John F. Hutson, whose brother Charles had married her sister Ladora. John was a farmer in Clermont County. The two families lived next to each other. @@

Children of Arizona T. "Arra" TATMAN and John F. HUTSON were:
+ 329   i   **Estella H.[5] HUTSON**.
  330   ii **Lena Bell[5] HUTSON**, born 14 Sep 1886 in Amelia, Clermont Co, OH.
           Jones notes: "Resides at Williamsburg, OH; no children"
           Birth: Lena Bell Hutson, b. 14 Sep 1885, Batavia Twp, Clermont, Ohio; parents: John Hutson; Anna Tatman: Ohio Births and Christenings, 1821-1962 <familysearch.org>. No death information found.
+ 331   iii **William Oliver[5] HUTSON**.
+ 332   iv **Gladys E.[5] HUTSON**.

117. Caroline 'Callie'[4] TATMAN (William Oliver[3], Ruth[2] HICKS, Joshua[1]), born 8 Oct 1869 in OH; died 27 Nov 1942 in Christ Hospital, Cincinnati, Hamilton, OH; buried 30 Nov 1942 in Bethel, Clermont Co, OH. She married on 8 Jul 1894 in Clermont Co, OH **Elmer TAYLOR**, born 15 Oct 1865 in Clermont Co, OH; died[136] 16 Apr 1929 in Monroe Twp, Clermont, OH; buried 18 Apr 1929 in Bethel, Clermont Co, OH, son of Frank TAYLOR and Martha BROWNEN.

Callie Tatman married Elmer Taylor, a farmer in Monroe, Clermont County. They lived near Salt Air. In 1920, their married daughter, Ethel, her husband Fred Witschzger and granddaughter Lela lived with Callie and Elmer. Callie's unmarried daughter, Lelah, was living with her widowed mother in 1930, after Fred's death a year earlier. @@

Children of Caroline 'Callie' TATMAN and Elmer TAYLOR were:
  333   i   **Lelah T.[5] TAYLOR**, born 1897 in Clermont Co, OH; died 13 Sep 1978 in Cincinnati, Hamilton, OH. She married in 1934 in Newport KY **Edward RIESINGER**[137, 138], born 2 Feb 1884 in Brown Co, OH; died 21 Jan 1960 in Clermont Co, OH, son of Chris RIESINGER and Lydia MOHR. No known children.
           Jones notes: "she resides (1973) at Brown Co, OH"

@@For more information, see research notes at end of chapter.

       Death: Lelah T Reisinger, b. 1897; res: Clermont Co, OH; d. 13 Sep 1978, Univ Hospital, Cincinnati, OH; age 81, widowed. Ohio Deaths, 1908-1932, 1938-1944, and 1958-2007 [Ancestry.com]

+   334   ii   **Ethel G.**[5] **TAYLOR**.

121. Ulysses Grant[4] **MCNAIR** (Mary[3] TATMAN, Ruth[2] HICKS, Joshua[1]), born 2 May 1866 in Clermont Co, OH; died 17 Sep 1942 in Tate, Clermont Co, OH; buried 19 Sep 1942 in Bethel Tate Cemetery He married on 25 Dec 1895 in Clermont Co, OH **Alma R. WOOD**, born 5 Aug 1873 in Clermont Co, OH; died 16 Sep 1940 in Tate, Clermont Co, OH; buried 18 Sep 1940 in Bethel Tate Cemetery, daughter of John WOOD and Rachiel MCCARTER.

Grant McNair was apparently a farmer in Clermont County his whole life. He married Alma Wood and had one son, John Lawrence. They lived next to his father, John McNair. @@

    Children of Ulysses Grant MCNAIR and Alma R. WOOD were:

  335   i   **John Lawrence**[5] **MCNAIR**, born 23 Apr 1898 in Bethel, Clermont Co, OH; died[139, 140] 10 Aug 1992 in Bethel, Clermont Co, OH. He married on 21 Apr 1928 in Brown Co, OH **Flora GRAY**, born 18 Dec 1899 in Hamersville, OH; died[141, 142] 5 May 1974 in Cincinnati, Hamilton, OH.
        Jones notes: "resides (1974) at Kennedy Ford Rd, Bethel, OH; no children" @@

123. Benjamin Edwin[4] **MCNAIR** (Mary[3] TATMAN, Ruth[2] HICKS, Joshua[1]), born 1 Sep 1870 in Clermont Co, OH; died 25 Mar 1942 in Bethel, Clermont, OH; buried 27 Mar 1942 in Bethel Tate Cemetery. He married on 18 May 1898 in Clermont Co, OH **Stella LLOYD**, born Aug 1872 in OH; died 24 Jan 1958 in Cincinnati, Hamilton, OH.

Benjamin Edwin (or Edward) McNair appears to have gone by his middle name. Most census years and his death records give his name as Edwin. He was a farmer in Clermont County. In 1930, he was working as a janitor - public building and his wife, Stella, as a nurse with a private family. @@

    Children of Benjamin Edwin MCNAIR and Stella LLOYD were:
+   336   i   **Lloyd Edwin**[5] **MCNAIR**.

125. Fanny[4] **TATMAN**[143] (Elijah[3], Ruth[2] HICKS, Joshua[1]), born 20 May 1863 in Clermont Co, OH; died 21 Feb 1944 in Ravenna, Portage, OH; buried 23 Feb 1944 in Talmadge, OH. She married on 6 Sep 1893 in Clermont Co, OH **William E. NORRIS**, born 20 May 1862 in Glasgow, Scotland; died 19 Feb 1943 in Westfield, Medina, OH.; buried 22 Feb 1943 in Talmadge, OH, son of Hugh NORRIS.

Fanny Tatman married William Norris, who had immigrated from Scotland in 1888 on the ship Anchoria and was a naturalized US citizen. He was a blacksmith working for the railroad in Cincinnati and later in a machine shop in St Clair. By 1930, Hugh and Fanny were living with their son, Hugh, and his family in Akron, OH. @@

    Children of Fanny TATMAN and William E. NORRIS were:
+   337   i   **Hugh Elijah**[5] **NORRIS**.

126. Effie[4] **TATMAN** (Elijah[3], Ruth[2] HICKS, Joshua[1]), born 20 Aug 1870 in Clermont Co, OH; died 8 Oct 1931 in Bethel, Clermont Co, OH; buried 10 Oct 1931 in Bethel Tate Cemetery She married on 23 Mar 1896 in Clermont Co, OH **Charlie E. DURHAM**, born 16 Nov 1860 in Cherry Grove OH; died 6 Feb 1941 in Cincinnati, Hamilton, OH; buried 8 Feb 1941 in Bethel Cemetery, Clermont Co, OH, son of John DURHAM and Mary JONES.

@@For more information, see research notes at end of chapter.

Effie Tatman, daughter of Elijah, married Charles Durham in 1896. Charles was a farmer - having a general farm / dairy farm. Charles Durham's mother was Mary Jones, but it is not known if she was related to the other Jones families who married Hicks. @@

 Children of Effie TATMAN and Charlie E. DURHAM were:
338 i **Warren Tatman[5] DURHAM**, born 22 Jan 1898 in Clermont Co, OH; died[144, 145] Sep 1978 in Bethel, Clermont Co, OH. He married aft 1930 **Eleanor SWING**, born 1 Sep 1905 in Clermont Co, OH. No children.
  Jones notes: "resides (1974) at 467 Diana Av, Batavia, OH; no children"
  Military: WWI Draft Registration [Ancestry.com] Warren Tatman Durham, Akron, Summit, OH; age 20, B. 22 Jan 1898, occ. Rubber worker - Goodrich, Akron, OH. Father: Charles E. Durham, Tall, slender, brown eyes, black hair. Registered Sep 1918.
  Census: 1930 Columbia, Hamilton, OH, p. 8B. Warren T. Durham 32, single, gardener - private estate
  Death: Warren T Durham b. 1898; Res: Clermont Co, OH; Death: 5 Sep 1978, Home, Clermont County, OH; married. Ohio Deaths, 1908-1932, 1938-1944, and 1958-2002 [Ancestry.com]
+ 339 ii **Phillip T.[5] DURHAM**.

127. Carrie[4] TATMAN (Elijah[3], Ruth[2] HICKS, Joshua[1]), born 2 Aug 1872 in Clermont Co, OH; died 1956. She married on 11 Mar 1900 in Clermont Co, OH **Archie G. HOLLAND**, born 19 Jan 1873 in Clermont Co, OH; died 9 Nov 1974 in Clermont Co, OH; buried in Concord Cemetery, Williamsburg Twp, OH, son of Thomas HOLLAND and Anna Rebecca BRAGDON.

Carrie Tatman grew up in Clermont County and married Archie Holland, who was a farmer. @@

 Children of Carrie TATMAN and Archie G. HOLLAND were:
340 i **Keith Thomas[5] HOLLAND**, born 19 Jun 1907 in Clermont Co, OH; died[146] 25 Aug 1993 in Clermont Co, OH. He is listed as widowed on death records, but no marriage records have been found.
  Death: Ohio Deaths 1908-1932, 1938-1944, and 1958-2007 gives full name; parents as Holland / Tatman; "widowed"; Occ: govt, supervisor, place of death: Mercy Hospital, Clermont Co. [Ancestry.com]
  SS Death index gives Bethel as place of death

128. John Warren[4] TATMAN (Elijah[3], Ruth[2] HICKS, Joshua[1]), born 20 Oct 1875 in Clermont Co, OH; died[147] 12 Nov 1961 in Kettering, Montgomery Co, OH; buried in Bethel Tate Cemetery He married on 9 Jun 1903 in Clermont Co, OH **Edith PHILLIPS**, born 20 Sep 1882 in Clermont Co, OH; died 1972; buried in Bethel Tate Cemetery, dau of Thomas PHILLIPS and Georgia FEE.

Warren Tatman was a street car conductor in Van Buren township, Montgomery Co, OH – about 50 miles north of Clermont County, in the Dayton area. Edith Taylor's family lived next door to Warren's cousin, William Tatman. @@

 Children of John Warren TATMAN and Edith PHILLIPS were:
341 i **Russell Paul[5] TATMAN**, born 7 May 1905 in Cincinnati, Hamilton Co, OH; died 28 Dec 1908 in Monroe Twp, Clermont Co, OH.

@@For more information, see research notes at end of chapter.

342 ii **Margaret⁵ TATMAN**, born est. 1907. She married aft 1930 **Robert GOINGS**, born est.1907. Jones notes: "resides (1973) at 1489 Melrose Av, Dayton OH 45409". No further information.

130. Orestes Daily "O.D."⁴ HICKS (Henry Melvin³, Elijah², Joshua¹), born[148] 23 Dec 1851 in Clermont Co, OH; died 14 Nov 1934 in Felicity, Clermont Co, OH; buried 15 Nov 1934 in Felicity, Clermont Co, OH. He married on 9 Jun 1875 in Clermont Co, OH **Hattie Sarah STEWART**, born 16 Jul 1855 in Chilo, Clermont Co, OH; died 20 Sep 1905 in Felicity, Clermont Co, OH; buried[149] 23 Sep 1905 in Sewanie Cemetery, Felicity OH.

O. D. Hicks was a farmer as well as a professional photographer and took a number of pictures of the family. He married Hattie Stewart and had one child, Edna, who was a professional gospel singer before her marriage. At the time of his death, he had a "notions shop" in Felicity. @@

Children of Orestes Daily "O.D." HICKS and Hattie Sarah STEWART were:
+ 343 i **Hattie Edna⁵ HICKS**.

132. Elijah Franklin⁴ HICKS (Henry Melvin³, Elijah², Joshua¹), born[150] 18 Dec 1855 in near Rural, Clermont Co, OH; died[151] 6 Feb 1935 in Felicity, Clermont Co, OH; buried 9 Feb 1935 in Felicity Inc Cemetery, Clermont Co, OH. He married (1) on 13 Jan 1889 in Clermont Co, OH **Addie FENTON**, born Est. 1855; died bef 1897; (2) on 26 May 1897 in Hamilton Co, OH **Melissa BEEKER**, born 8 Sep 1865 in Rural, Clermont Co, OH; died[152] 2 May 1949 in Felicity, Clermont Co, OH; buried 1949 in Felicity Inc Cemetery, Clermont Co, OH, daughter of William BEEKER and Elizabeth BRADSHAW.

Frank Hicks was a farmer in Clermont County for all of his life, with a farm next to his brother John. Frank and John had married sisters – Frank married Melissa Beeker and John married Georgia Beeker. Frank had a earlier marriage to Addie Fenton, but Addie must have died before 1897. The only child of that marriage, an unnamed daughter, died at the age of eight days. A photo of the two couples is at the beginning of this chapter, on page 85. @@

Children of Elijah Franklin HICKS and Addie FENTON were:
344 i **Daughter⁵ HICKS**, born 23 Sep 1889; died 1 Oct 1889 in Franklin Twp, Clermont, OH. **Death:** Clermont Co, OH death rec.--" Hicks, _____; female; d. 1 Oct 1889 in Franklin twp.; 0y 0m 8d; parents: Frank Hicks, Ida Fenton [sic]"

Children of Elijah Franklin HICKS and Melissa BEEKER were:
+ 345 i **Hurdes Beeker⁵ HICKS**.
+ 346 ii **Irlene Evelyn⁵ HICKS**.
+ 347 iii **Georgia Elizabeth⁵ HICKS**.

133. Lucy Ann⁴ HICKS[153] (Henry Melvin³, Elijah², Joshua¹), born 29 Sep 1857 probably in Felicity, Clermont Co, OH; died[154] 3 Jul 1888 in Felicity, Clermont Co, OH; buried 7 Jul 1888 in Felicity Inc Cemetery She married on 1 Apr 1877 in Felicity, Clermont Co, OH **Francis Marion 'Frank' LEVI**, born[155] 26 Mar 1854 in Clermont Co, OH; died[156, 157] 2 Oct 1933 in Orlando, Orange Co, FL; buried 3 Oct 1933 in Greenwood Cemetery, Orlando, FL, son of Willis LEVI and Hulda FANCHER.

Lucy Hicks married Frank Levi and had three children. They lived in Mt Orab, Brown Co, OH. Lucy died of consumption at the age of 31, leaving three young children. Shortly after that, Frank married Mary Emma Townsley, who had been the Sunday School teacher of Lucy Hicks. Emma raised the children as her own. In about 1918, Frank and Emma moved to Orlando, FL, where Frank was a very successful real estate agent and land speculator. He lost everything in the Florida "land bust" of 1928

@@For more information, see research notes at end of chapter.

and later lived with his daughter Mollie Stalder and her family. After his death, Emma remained with the Stalder family until her death in 1940. Photo of Lucy on page 88; Emma, Frank and his grandson, Curtis Stalder, are in the group photo on page 187 @@

    Children of Lucy Ann HICKS and Francis Marion 'Frank' LEVI were:

+   348   i   **Irma Clair**[5] **LEVI**.
+   349   ii   **Clyde Harvey**[5] **LEVI**.
+   350   iii   **Mollie Dell**[5] **LEVI**. [grandmother of the compiler of this book]

134. Mary Elizabeth[4] **HICKS** (Henry Melvin[3], Elijah[2], Joshua[1]), born[158] 25 Apr 1860 in Clermont Co, OH; died 29 Jun 1955 in New Richmond, Clermont Co, OH; buried 2 Aug 1955 in Green Mound Cemetery, New Richmond, Clermont Co, OH. She married[159] on 5 Dec 1880 in Clermont Co, OH **John D. JOSLIN**[160], born 25 Feb 1855 in Felicity, Clermont Co, OH; died 25 Aug 1891 in Clermont Co, OH, son of Jeremiah and Emirilla JOSLIN.

Mary Elizabeth Hicks married John Joslin in 1880 at the age of 20. When John died in 1891, Elizabeth was pregnant with her 8th child (with 1 set of twins). In 1900, the three older children were apparently supporting the family by working in a wool factory. In later years, she lived with her married children. She died at the age of 95. @@

    Children of Mary Elizabeth HICKS and John D. JOSLIN were:

     351   i   **Eva May**[5] **JOSLIN**, born 18 Jun 1882 in OH; died 18 May 1912.
                     Notes from Lvera (Jennings) Seipelt 1998 list "Children of Mary Elizabeth Hicks Joslin: Eva M. Joslin (deceased - no heirs). Never married. Jones notes: gives name, birth, "not married." Not on Ohio Death Index - did she die elsewhere?

+   352   ii   **Archibald D. "Archie"**[5] **JOSLIN**.

     353   iii   **Emarilla 'Rella'**[5] **JOSLIN**, born 10 Oct 1885 in Washington Twp, Clermont Co, OH; died[161] 21 Mar 1919 in Norwood, Hamilton, OH; buried 24 Mar 1919 in New Richmond, Clermont Co, OH. She married on 29 Jun 1908 in Clermont Co, OH **Carl DAWSON**, born 9 Jun 1882 in New Richmond, Clermont Co, OH; died[162] 13 Feb 1929 in Hamilton Co, OH; buried in New Richmond, Clermont Co, OH, son of Charles W. DAWSON and Emma PIGMAN. No children.
                     Rella married Carl Dawson, who the proprietor of a grocery store. She died at the age of 35, probably of tuberculosis . @@

     354   iv   **Frances Emma**[5] **JOSLIN**, born 10 Oct 1885. Jones notes give name, birth, no other info; twin to Rella.

     355   v   **Ella**[5] **JOSLIN**, born 31 Mar 1887 in Washington Twp, Clermont Co, OH; died abt 1887. Jones notes give birth date, "died young" (may be same person as "Lucy")

     356   vi   **Lucy**[5] **JOSLIN**, born 8 Jun 1887 in Pt Isabel, Clermont Co, OH; died 10 May 1888 in Washington Twp. Clermont Co, OH.
                     Notes: This child inferred from the fact that 5 children are listed in the 1900 census, while the 1910 census lists 3 children and states that Mary Joslin had 6 children, 3 of whom are still living.
                     Birth: Lucy Joslin, d. 10 May 1888, age 0 yr, 11 mo, 10 da. Died of lung disease; b. Pt Isabel, Clermont Co; d. Washington Twp, Clermont Co. Calculated birth date: 8 Jun 1887. Parents not listed on death record, but they were living in this town and there is a gap in children that this birth would fit. Later census infers this birth. Possibly same person as "Ella" listed by Orville Jones with same birth year, "died young"

+   357   vii   **Edna Clare**[5] **JOSLIN**.

@@For more information, see research notes at end of chapter.

+ 358 viii **Adlara Leona 'Addie'**[5] **JOSLIN**.

135. **Harvey Henry**[4] **HICKS** (Henry Melvin[3], Elijah[2], Joshua[1]), born[163] 21 Jan 1862 in Clermont Co, OH; died[164] 26 Jun 1950 in Norwood, Hamilton Co, OH; buried 28 Jun 1950 in Utopia, Clermont Co, OH. He married on 3 Feb 1885 in Clermont Co, OH **Margaret Sarah WELLS**, born 12 Jun 1864 in Utopia, Clermont Co, OH; died[165] 30 Jul 1931 in Norwood, Hamilton Co, OH; buried 1 Aug 1931 in Higginsport, Brown Co, OH, daughter of John Levi WELLS and Mary JERNEGAN.

Harvey Henry Hicks was a farmer, school teacher and fruit tree salesman. He sold fruit trees for Stark Nurseries and was one of their best salesmen. He is the great grandfather of Norman Zezula, a contributor to this book. Photo on page 89. @@

Children of Harvey Henry HICKS and Margaret Sarah WELLS were:

+ 359 i **Lucy Mary Francis**[5] **HICKS**.
+ 360 ii **Harvey John**[5] **HICKS**.
+ 361 iii **Minnie Clara**[5] **HICKS**.
  362 iv **Blaine Melvin**[5] **HICKS**, born 15 Sep 1895 in Rural, Clermont Co, OH; died 18 Aug 1985 in Cincinnati, Hamilton Co, OH. He married (1) on 14 Aug 1919 in Hamilton Co, OH **Laura Francis RUMMEL**, born 9 Nov 1896 in Bond Hill OH; died 27 Feb 1952 in Norwood, Hamilton Co, OH, daughter of Arthur RUMMEL and Frances RETTICH; (2) on 31 Jul 1956 **Elsie Glendora PRICE**, born 14 Nov 1904 in Terre Hautte, IN; died[166] Apr 1993 in Cincinnati, Hamilton Co, OH, daughter of Robert and Estelle M. PRICE. No children.
  Blaine Hicks was married twice. He worked as a mill worker, a glazier and real estate broker. At the time of his death in 1985, his occupation was given as "forestry". He served in Co. C, 154th Infantry, U. S. Army in France during World War I. In 1942, he was described as 5' 8 ½", 183 lbs, gray eyes, brown hair, dark complexion. @@
+ 363 v **Dion Williams**[5] **HICKS**.
  364 vi **Bryon**[5] **HICKS**, born 7 Nov 1898 in Franklin Twp, Clermont Co, OH; died 7 Jun 1899 in Clermont Co, OH.
  Birth: Clermont Co, OH birth cert. (v 1896, p 80). "Byron Hicks, b. Franklin twp, Clermont Co, OH; male; parents: H.H. Hicks, Maggie Wells."
  Death: Hicks Family Bible (no civil death record can be located). His birth is indicated, but no date is given.
  Jones notes: "died young"

136. **John James**[4] **HICKS** (Henry Melvin[3], Elijah[2], Joshua[1]), born[167] 18 Oct 1864 in near Rural, Clermont Co, OH; died[168] 30 Jan 1935 in Chilo, Clermont Co, OH; buried[169] 2 Feb 1935 in Felicity, Clermont Co, OH. He married on 27 Mar 1893 **Emma Georgia Anna BEEKER**, born 11 May 1867 in OH; died 2 Aug 1928 in Felicity, Clermont Co, OH; buried[170] 4 Aug 1928 in Felicity Cemetery, Clermont Co, OH, daughter of William BEEKER and Elizabeth BRADSHAW.

John Hicks was a farmer who lived in Clermont County all his life. He and his brother Frank married sisters - John married Georgia Beeker; Frank married Melissa Beeker - and lived side by side. The land they farmed may have been part of the original land purchased by their great grandfather, Joshua, in 1815. John kept a detailed farm journal for 40 years. Photos of the Hicks home and of the Hicks families can be found at the beginning of this chapter. John and Georgia had two adopted children, Marcella and Raymond. @@

@@For more information, see research notes at end of chapter.

Children of John James HICKS and Emma Georgia Anna BEEKER were:

365 i **Marcella Delores**[5] **HICKS**, born 31 Oct 1908 in Clermont Co, OH; died 25 Oct 2000 in Ripley, Brown Co, OH. Adopted daughter. Never married.
Notes: Photocopy of photo of Elizabeth, Erlene & Marcella Hicks as young girls in my files. Living in Clermont Co, OH August 1998.
Jones notes: "resides (1984) Georgetown OH"
Death: Social Security Death Index: Marcella Hicks, #272-12-2259; Ripley, Brown, OH; Born: 31 Oct 1908; Died: 25 Oct 2000.

366 ii **Raymond**[5] **HICKS**, born 16 Oct 1913 in Cincinnati, Hamilton Co, OH; died 15 Jan 1922 in Franklin, Clermont Co, OH; buried 17 Jan 1922 in Felicity, OH. Never married.
Notes: Adopted; died young
Death: Raymond Hicks; Death: 15 Jan 1922 Franklin, Clermont, OH; Birth: 16 Oct 1913. Cincinnati; child adopted; Age: 8 years 2 months 29 days; Burial: 17 Jan 1922, Felicity, OH. Cause of death: pneumonia. Ohio Deaths, 1908-1953 <familysearch.org>

137. **Minerva Elizabeth**[4] **JONES** (Mary[3] HICKS, Elijah[2], Joshua[1]), born 10 Apr 1844 in Clermont Co, OH; died[171] 6 Jul 1935 in Clovis, Fresno Co, A. She married (1) in 1861 in ?Clermont Co, OH **Francis M. HOUSER**, born abt 1841 in OH; died bef 1866, son of Nancy HOUSER; (2) on 2 Sep 1866 in ?Clermont Co, OH **Andrew Jackson BROADWELL**, born 1836 in Rural, Clermont Co, OH; died bef 1930 in Modesto, Stanislaus Co, CA, son of Lindley and Susan BROADWELL.

Minerva Jones was married twice, her first husband, Francis Houser, dying soon after their marriage. Her second husband was Andrew J. Broadwell. The family moved to Missouri, then Arizona and to California by 1910. Andrew was a dry goods merchant. @@

Children of Minerva Elizabeth JONES and Francis M. HOUSER were:

367 i **William Clifford**[5] **HOUSER**, born 9 Mar 1862 in ?Clermont Co, OH.
Jones notes: "not married."
Census: 1900 not found

+ 368 ii **Mary Frances**[5] **HOUSER**.

Children of Minerva Elizabeth JONES and Andrew Jackson BROADWELL were:

+ 369 i **Lindley Edward**[5] **BROADWELL**.
+ 370 ii **Herbert Fay**[5] **BROADWELL**.
371 iii **Raymond D.**[5] **BROADWELL**, born 26 Jul 1872 in Rural, Clermont Co, OH. Jones notes: "not married". Does not appear on any census with this name. Age corresponds to Arsemia in 1880 census; Rawley in 1900
372 iv **Lawrence**[5] **BROADWELL**[172], born 25 Dec 1874 in Rural, Clermont Co, OH; died[173] 12 Jun 1948 in Los Angeles, CA. Not married.
Lawrence Broadwell was a bee keeper. He lived with his brother Nathan in 1920, but could not be found in the 1930 census. @@
+ 373 v **Percival**[5] **BROADWELL**.
+ 374 vi **Nathaniel Dale**[5] **BROADWELL**.

138. **Samantha Jane**[4] **JONES** (Mary[3] HICKS, Elijah[2], Joshua[1]), born 4 Apr 1850 in Rural, Clermont Co, OH. She married on 25 Aug 1870 in Clermont Co, OH **William Joseph HELVERING**, born 8 Jun 1846 in Circleville, Pickaway Co, OH.

@@For more information, see research notes at end of chapter.

Samantha Jones was a teacher and William was town marshals in Felicity abt 1880. The family moved to Marshall Co, KS abt 1885; to Beattie, Marshall Co, KS in 1930.

Children of Samantha Jane JONES and William Joseph HELVERING were:

+ 375 i **Edwin G.[5] HELVERING**.
 376 ii **Lillian Gertrude[5] HELVERING**, born 7 Sep 1873; died 15 Jun 1878.
  All info from Orville Jones notes
 377 iii **Guy Tresillian[5] HELVERING**, born 10 Jan 1878 in Felicity, Clermont Co, OH; died 4 Jul 1946 in Washington, D.C; buried in Marysville, Marshall Co, KS. He married abt 1910 **Tinnie KOESTER**, born abt 1878 in Kansas, daughter of Charles and Sylvia KOESTER.
  Guy Helvering attended the University of Kansas at Lawrence; was graduated from the law department of the University of Michigan at Ann Arbor in 1906. He was elected US Representative from Kansas from 1913 to 1919. He was mayor of Salina, KS 1826-1830; Democratic State Chairman in 1930-1934 and a Federal Judge from 1843 until his death in 1946.
  Jones notes: "Studied law. County Attorney of Marshall Co KS for 4 years. Corp. Co. M, 22nd Kansas Infantry in Spanish War. Attorney & banker at Saline, KS. No children." @@
 378 iv **Robert Louis[5] HELVERING**, born 27 Jan 1883 in Neville, Clermont Co, OH; died 1961 in ?Marysville, KS. He married on 18 Oct 1911 **Elsie KAHLKE**, born 14 Feb 1887 in Kansas; died[174] 1 Apr 1980 in Marysville, Marshall Co, KS, daughter of Fred and Metha KAHLKE.
  Jones notes: "m. 18 Oct 1911 to Elsie Kahlke. Attorney at Marysville, KS. She resided (1972) at 1007 Elm St, Marysville KS 66508. He died 1961. No children. " @@
 379 v **Mary Alma[5] HELVERING**, born 19 Nov 1888 in Beattie, Marshall Co, KS. She married on 28 Jun 1917 **Roy Williard MOTES**[175], born 12 Feb 1886 in Kansas, son of Arthur O. and Leatha MOTES.
  Jones notes: "m. 6/28/1917 to Roy W. Motes. Postmistress at Beattie, KS 1914-18. No children. She resided (1972) at 1430 Chicago Cir, Homecrest, Evanston, IL 60201" @@

140. **James Marcellus[4] JONES**[176, 177](Elizabeth[3] HICKS, Elijah[2], Joshua[1]), born 6 Dec 1847 in Rural, Clermont Co, OH; died[178] 26 Nov 1925 in Rural, Clermont Co, OH; buried in Mt Pleasant Cemetery, Clermont Co, OH. He married on 27 Feb 1872 in Clermont Co, OH **Mary Elizabeth SHINKLE**[179], born 27 Feb 1854 in OH; died abt 1905 in Rural, Clermont Co, OH; buried in Mt Pleasant Cemetery, Clermont Co, OH, daughter of Solomon and Mary R. SHINKLE.

James Marcellus Jones was a farmer in Clermont County. He was recorded as James some census years and Marcellus in others, so he may have been called either one. He married Mary Elizabeth Shinkle, daughter of a pioneer Clermont family. Photo of him on page 89; of his daughters on page 186.. @@

Children of James Marcellus JONES and Mary Elizabeth SHINKLE were:

+ 380 i **Beatrice Gertrude[5] JONES**.
+ 381 ii **Effie Maud[5] JONES**.
+ 382 iii **Lola Agnes[5] JONES**.
+ 383 iv **Orville Guy[5] JONES**.
+ 384 v **Carl Raymond[5] JONES**.
+ 385 vi **Ethel Grace[5] JONES**.

@@For more information, see research notes at end of chapter.

+ 386 vii **Lawrence Marcellus**[5] **JONES**.
387 viii **Mary Elizabeth**[5] **JONES**, born[180] 19 Sep 1892 in Clermont Co, OH; died[181] 20 Jul 1980 in Cincinnati, Hamilton, OH; buried in Bethel Tate Cemetery She married on 16 Oct 1920 in Clermont Co, OH **Olin Kennedy NEAL**[182, 183], born 20 May 1895 in Brown Co, OH; died[184] 30 Jul 1965 in Clermont Co, OH; buried in Bethel Tate Cemetery, son of William B. and Eliza Jane NEAL.
Jones notes: "He died abt 1965; buried Bethel Tate; she resides (1972) at Bethel OH [crossed out] d. 1980; no children"
Census 1930 Symmes, Hamilton, OH, p. 3B. K Olin Neal 34, woodworker - wood manuf.; Mary Neal 37. Both OH/OH/OH. He m. age 24; she 27.
Death: Mary J Neal, b. 1893, OH; res: Cincinnati, Hamilton Co, OH; d. 20 Jul 1980 at home; age at death 87; widowed. Ohio Deaths, 1908-1932, 1938-1944, and 1958-2007 [ancestry.com]
388 ix **Audrey Lucille**[5] **JONES**, born[185] 19 Feb 1894 in Clermont Co, OH; died 1963; buried in Mt Pleasant Cemetery, Clermont Co, OH
Jones notes: "Not married"
Census: 1920 Norwood Ward 1, Hamilton, OH, p. 2A. Charles Knodel 58; Anna Knodel 56; Marie Knodel 22, clerk - lithograph co; Audrey Jones 25, boarder, single, employee - lithograph co
1930 not found
+ 389 x **Genevieve Shinkle**[5] **JONES**.

142. **William A.**[4] **JONES** (Elizabeth[3] HICKS, Elijah[2], Joshua[1]), born[186] 8 Jan 1851 in Clermont Co, OH; died 14 Feb 1938 in Cincinnati, Hamilton, OH; buried in Mt Moriah Cemetery, Clermont Co, OH. He married on 4 Mar 1874 **Frances ESSEX**, born 12 Feb 1852; died 20 Nov 1930 in Cincinnati, Hamilton, OH; buried 24 Nov 1930 in Mt. Moriah, OH, daughter of Albert ESSEX and Joanna BROADWELL.

William Jones was a school teacher in Clermont County in 1880. He and his family moved to Cincinnati before 1900 and he became a "motorman" for the Cincinnati street railroad. Joanna, the mother of Frances Essex, was a sister to Andrew Jackson Broadwell [#37s]. William Jones and Minerva Jones, who married secondly, Andrew J. Broadwell, were cousins, both grandchildren of Elijah Hicks. [Brother & sister married cousins].

Children of William A. JONES and Frances ESSEX were:
+ 390 i **Albert Essex**[5] **JONES**.
+ 391 ii **Hertha Katherine**[5] **JONES**.
+ 392 iii **Jessie Agnes**[5] **JONES**.
+ 393 iv **Anna Grace**[5] **JONES**.
394 v **Archie C.**[5] **JONES**, born 26 Mar 1883 in Clermont Co, OH; died 16 Feb 1905 probably in Cincinnati, Hamilton Co, OH.
Jones notes give birth date; Jones book gives death date. No other information. Appears with parents only in 1900 census.
+ 395 vi **Stella Blanche**[5] **JONES**.
396 vii **Lucy Florence**[5] **JONES**, born 30 Oct 1891. She married **J. E. STREITMEIR**. Jones notes: "resided at Cincinnati, married J. E. Streitmeir, no children." Not found on census records with this or any other closely related spelling

@@For more information, see research notes at end of chapter.

143. **Elijah Hicks⁴ JONES**¹⁸⁷ (Elizabeth³ HICKS, Elijah², Joshua¹), born 15 Sep 1852 in Clermont Co, OH; died Jan 1913 in near New Richmond, Clermont Co, OH. He married on 17 Mar 1875 in Clermont Co, OH, divorced **Julia WILLIAMS**, born 14 May 1854 in Ohio; died 5 Aug 1936 in New Richmond, Clermont Co, OH; buried in Greenmound Cemetery, daughter of Oliver P. and Deborah WILLIAMS.

Elijah Hicks Jones married Julia Williams in 1875. They were divorced by 1910 and the children lived with their mother. In 1910, Julia was listed as divorced - while Elijah was single. Elijah was a laborer, probably on a farm. Jones notes say that Elijah Hicks Jones drowned in the Ohio River in 1913 "near New Richmond". His death record is in Campbell Co, KY, which is directly across the Ohio River from New Richmond.

Children of Elijah Hicks JONES and Julia WILLIAMS were:

- 397 i **Dollie M.⁵ JONES**, born 18 Jan 1876 in Ohio; died 21 Feb 1946 in New Richmond, Clermont Co, OH. Not married.
  Jones notes: "resided at New Richmond, OH; not married"; Jones book gives "lived (1930) 420 Front St, New Richmond"
  Death: Dollie Jones, d. 21 Feb 1946, New Richmond, Clermont, OH; Birth: 18 Jan 1876, Ohio; Age: 70 years 1 month 3 days; Father: Elijah A Jones; Mother: Julia Williams. Ohio Deaths, 1908-1953 <pilot.familysearch.org>
- + 398 ii **Alfred William⁵ JONES**.
- 399 iii **Jessie⁵ JONES**, born 7 Jan 1881 in New Richmond, Clermont Co, OH; died 29 Jul 1966 in Clermont Co, OH. Jones notes: "not married"
  Death: Jessie Jones, b. 1881 Clermont, Ohio; d. 29 Jul 1966 Clermont County, OH. Ohio Deaths, 1908-1932, 1938-1944, and 1958-2007 [Ancestry.com]
- 400 iv **Stanley Lee⁵ JONES**, born 10 Jan 1883 in New Richmond, Clermont Co, OH; died 25 Dec 1940 in Kenton Co, KY. He married abt 1915 **Sarah RAHILLY**, born abt 1888 in Canada. No children. @@
- + 401 v **Howard Hicks⁵ JONES**.
- + 402 vi **Clifford O.⁵ JONES**.
- 403 vii **Chesley L.⁵ JONES**¹⁸⁸, ¹⁸⁹, born 7 Apr 1896 in New Richmond, Clermont Co, OH; died¹⁹⁰ Jan 1978 in New Richmond, Clermont Co, OH. He married on 6 Jun 1934 in Clermont Co, OH **Mrs. Anna E. RARDIN**, born 8 Oct 1893 in Silverton, Hamilton Co, OH; died¹⁹¹ Feb 1981 in New Richmond, OH. No known children. @@

145. **George Washington⁴ JONES** (Elizabeth³ HICKS, Elijah², Joshua¹), born 20 Jan 1856 in Clermont Co, OH; died 14 Aug 1942 in Balinas?, CO. He married on 14 Dec 1876 in Clermont Co, OH **Laura A. SHINKLE**, born 21 May 1855 in Clermont Co, OH; died 31 Jan 1926 in Keith, Ramsey Co, ND.

George Washington Jones was a blacksmith by trade, but also worked at farming, painting and as a retail merchant. He and his family moved from Ohio to Nebraska and then to North Dakota. He died in either Colorado or California. Jones notes are not clear and no death record has been found in either place. @@

Children of George Washington JONES and Laura A. SHINKLE were:

- + 404 i **Leontine Orrene⁵ JONES**.
- + 405 ii **Roxy Dale⁵ JONES**.
- + 406 iii **Edith Mary⁵ JONES**.

@@For more information, see research notes at end of chapter.

146. Doctor Albert[4] JONES (Elizabeth[3] HICKS, Elijah[2], Joshua[1]), born 25 Jan 1858 in Clermont Co, OH; died 9 Aug 1942. He married on 16 Jun 1880 **Lucy E. STRAHAN**, born 16 Jan 1859 in Illinois; died 20 Apr 1925, daughter of James and Francis STRAHAN.

"Doc" Jones (according to the Jones notes) was "a street car conductor and for several years was the Secretary of the Street Railway Union in Cincinnati, OH". The *Compendium of History of Nebraska*[192] says that he "is the seventh son in a family of eight sons and two daughters born to his parents; in view of the supposed healing qualities of the seventh son he was baptized Doctor Albert Jones". He worked for two years on a ranch in Texas, then farmed in Iowa for a few years. The family had moved on to Strahan, Wayne County, NE by about 1892. He was a prosperous farmer there and represented his county in the legislature during the years 1896-1898. @@

Children of Doctor Albert JONES and Lucy E. STRAHAN were:
+ 407 i **Marcellus Findly**[5] **JONES**.
+ 408 ii **Gayle E.**[5] **JONES**.
+ 409 iii **Jay Miller**[5] **JONES**.
+ 410 iv **Roscoe Otis**[5] **JONES**.
   411 v **Beulah Madge**[5] **JONES**, born 26 Jan 1890; died 5 Jun 1891.
       Info from Orville Jones notes.
+ 412 vi **Albert Doctor**[5] **JONES**.
+ 413 vii **Dorothy F.**[5] **JONES**.

147. Minerva Isadora 'Dora'[4] JONES (Elizabeth[3] HICKS, Elijah[2], Joshua[1]), born 21 Mar 1859 in Clermont Co, OH; died 19 Sep 1944. She married **James Baxter MCCABE**, born Feb 1856 in Illinois; died bef 1910, son of Wilber and Harriet E. **MCCABE**. @@

Dora Jones and her husband, Baxter McCabe, lived in Texas in 1900. Baxter was a "hardware merchant". After Baxter's death (before 1910), Dora moved to Nebraska and was living with her sister Grace. In 1930, Dora was in Iola, Kansas, probably with her brother, Frank.

Children of Minerva Isadora 'Dora' JONES and James Baxter MCCABE were:
+ 414 i **Raymond**[5] **MCCABE**.

154. Mary[4] OWENS (Nancy[3] HICKS, Elijah[2], Joshua[1]), born Dec 1852 in OH. She married on 30 May 1868 in Coles Co, IL **Peter MASON**, born abt 1836 in Canada; died bef 1900 probably in Illinois.

Mary Owens married Peter Mason, a Canadian, in 1868. Peter had been married first to Rosa Guyette and probably widowed, as he had four children when he married Mary. They then had eight more children before Peter died in 1899/1900. Mary supported her family as a "washerwoman" and seamstress. @@

Children of Mary OWENS and Peter MASON were:
   415 i **Nancy**[5] **MASON**, born abt 1869 in Coles Co, IL.
   416 ii **Freddie**[5] **MASON**, born Jun 1873 in Coles Co, IL.
   417 iii **Ida M.**[5] **MASON**, born Feb 1876 in Coles Co, IL.
       Notes: Possible marriage: Ida M. Mason to Frank J. Price; Jun 25, 1896 Sangamon Co,
       IL. Illinois Marriages, 1851-1900 [Ancestry.com]
   418 iv **Ada F.**[5] **MASON**, born Aug 1884 in Coles Co, IL.
   419 v **Mary C.**[5] **MASON**, born Jun 1886 in Coles Co, IL.
   420 vi **Vera F.**[5] **MASON**, born Feb 1894 in Coles Co, IL.

@@For more information, see research notes at end of chapter.

421　vii　**Claude F.**[5] **MASON**, born Jul 1899 in Coles Co, IL.
422　viii　**Josie**[5] **MASON**, born abt 1877 in Coles Co, IL.

158. Josephine[4] **OWENS** (Nancy[3] HICKS, Elijah[2], Joshua[1]), born Jul 1863 in Effingham, IL; died 11 Feb 1926; buried in Mount Hope Cemetery She married (1) on 24 Jan 1888 in Coles Co, IL **William GUYETTE**, born 1836 in St Johns, Canada; died 26 Feb 1896 in Mattoon, Coles, IL, son of Augustus GUYETTE and Adaline HOUKE; (2) on 22 Nov 1899 in Coles Co, IL **Benedict DURHAM**, born May 1854 in IL; died bef 1920.

Josephine "Josie" W Owens was living with her sister Mary (Owens) Mason in 1880. She married 1st William Guyette (who may have been related to her brother-in-law, Peter Mason's, deceased 1st wife Rosa Guyette). William died young, leaving Josie with 3 small children. Then Josie married Benedict Durham. @@

　　Children of Josephine OWENS and William GUYETTE were:
+　423　i　**Selma**[5] **GUYETTE**.
+　424　ii　**Raymond Joseph**[5] **GUYETTE**.
　　425　iii　**Ethel D.**[5] **GUYETTE**, born Feb 1896 in IL No children.

160. Mary Emma[4] **HICKS** (Joshua[3], Elijah[2], Joshua[1]), born 10 Sep 1858 in Rural, Clermont Co, OH; died[193] 23 Feb 1934 in New Richmond, Clermont, OH; buried 25 Feb 1934 in Watkins Hill Cemetery She married (1) on 28 Aug 1879 in Clermont Co, OH **Taylor B. HOLDERFIELD**, born est. 1858; died bef 1900 in Salem IL, son of William and America HOLDERFIELD; (2) on 14 Sep 1902 in Clermont Co, OH **Andrew A. LIGHT**, born 26 Mar 1856 in New Richmond, Clermont Co, OH; died 5 May 1942 in Cincinnati, Hamilton, OH; buried in Watkins Hill Cemetery, son of Benjamin LIGHT.

Mary Emma Hicks was a school teacher after the death of her husband, Taylor Holderfield. Taylor was a dentist. The family lived in Salem, IL in 1880. Taylor was "a graduate of the Cincinnati College of Dentistry and was convicted of larceny and sentenced to one year in State's Prison" in 1886. Emma returned to Clermont County, OH and remarried to Andrew Light, a farmer in Clermont County. @@

　　Children of Mary Emma HICKS and Taylor B. HOLDERFIELD were:
+　426　i　**Gussie E.**[5] **HOLDERFIELD**.
+　427　ii　**Ethel**[5] **HOLDERFIELD**.

162. Nancy B.[4] **HICKS** (Joshua[3], Elijah[2], Joshua[1]), born 23 Mar 1862 in New Richmond, Clermont Co, OH; died 6 Mar 1939 in Maysville, Mason Co, OH; buried 9 Mar 1939 in Maysville Cemetery Mason Co, KY. She married on 15 Jul 1884 in Clermont Co, OH **William Harvey MEENACH**, born 17 Dec 1850 in Mason Co, KY; died 4 Feb 1932 in Mason Co, KY; buried 4 Feb 1932 in Maysville Cemetery, Mason Co, KY, son of J. H. MEENACH and Elizabeth BALLON.

Nancy Hicks married William Harvey Meenach, who was the half brother of Elizabeth Meenach, wife of Nancy's uncle, William Stephen Hicks. Elizabeth and William H. were both children of J. H. Meenach. @@

　　Children of Nancy B. HICKS and William Harvey MEENACH were:
+　428　i　**Mary Edna H.**[5] **MEENACH**.
　　429　ii　**Harry Gordon**[5] **MEENACH**[194], born 27 Jul 1887 in Maysville, Mason Co, KY; died 1 Jan 1966 in Dayton, Montgomery, OH. He married abt 1913 **Rose BORNHORST**, born 23 Apr 1889 in St. Marys, Auglaize Co, OH; died 11 Mar 1946 in Dayton, Montgomery, OH, daughter of Henry BORNHORST and Catherine SEVERING. No children. @@

@@For more information, see research notes at end of chapter.

166. **Nora Sureanth**[4] **HICKS** (James[3], Elijah[2], Joshua[1]), born 17 Jan 1865 in Aberdeen, Brown Co, OH; died 28 May 1930 in Mason Co, KY; buried 30 May 1930 in Maysville, Mason Co, KY. She married on 21 Oct 1886 in Maysville, Mason Co, KY **Edward White HUTCHISON**, born 15 Aug 1860 in Mayslick, Mason Co, KY; died 23 Apr 1949 in Mason Co, KY; buried in Maysville, Mason Co, KY, son of William HUTCHISON and Mary E. WORTHINGTON. @@

Children of Nora Sureanth HICKS and Edward White HUTCHISON were:

+ 430   i   **Celia Mae**[5] **HUTCHISON**.
+ 431   ii   **Edward Roy**[5] **HUTCHISON**.

168. **William Pearce**[4] **HICKS** (James[3], Elijah[2], Joshua[1]), born 17 Aug 1872 in Aberdeen, Brown Co, OH; died 26 Dec 1962 in Cincinnati, Hamilton Co, OH. He married (1), divorced **Lillian [Emma?] DUNBAR**, born est. 1872; (2) on 18 Feb 1919 in Houston, TX **Frances [King] MILLER**, born 31 May 1875 in Cincinnati, Hamilton Co, OH.

William P. Hicks was a moulder by profession, working in an iron factory. He married twice - first to Lillian Dunbar by whom he had four children, three surviving to adulthood. After they divorced, he married a widow, Mrs. Frances (Miller) King, who had two children. @@

Children of William Pearce HICKS and Lillian [Emma?] DUNBAR were:

   432   i   **Floriene**[5] **HICKS**, born Est. 1903; died bef 1910; buried in Maysville Cemetery Mason Co, KY. Jones notes: "Died at 11 years, buried Maysville [KY] Cemetery"
+ 433   ii   **Leslie Brand**[5] **HICKS**.
+ 434   iii   **Hazel**[5] **HICKS**.
+ 435   iv   **William M.**[5] **HICKS**.

169. **Callie James**[4] **HICKS** (James[3], Elijah[2], Joshua[1]), born 26 Jun 1876 in Aberdeen, Brown Co, OH; died[195] 5 May 1979 in Sun City, Maricopa Co, Arizona. She married[196] on 2 Feb 1898 in Maysville, Mason Co, KY **William LINGENFELSER**, born 2 Aug 1873 in Aberdeen, Brown Co, OH; died 4 Sep 1964 in Maysville, Mason Co, KY, son of George LINGENFELSER and Margaret MILLER.

Callie Hicks died in Sun City, Arizona at the age of 102. She and her husband William Lingenfelser lived in Mason County, KY where William died in 1964. William was a farmer and later a butcher. Callie apparently moved to Arizona after William's death. Both of her children lived to be over 100. @@

Children of Callie James HICKS and William LINGENFELSER were:

   436   i   **Emma Margaret**[5] **LINGENFELSER**, born 5 Jul 1899 in Maysville, Mason Co, KY; died 9 Apr 2001 in in Sun City, Maricopa Co, AZ. Jones notes: "Resides (1972) 10513 Clair Dr, Sun City, AZ; not married".
Emma was a school teacher and lived with her parents in 1930. She evidently moved with her mother to Arizona after her father's death.

   437   ii   **Eugene William**[5] **LINGENFELSER**, born 3 Feb 1903 in Maysville, Mason Co, KY; died 7 Mar 2004 in Wickenburg, Maricopa, AZ. He married (1) in 1925 **Neva MERS**, born 1898 in KY; died 1931 in Elizaville, Fleming Co, KY; (2) in 1933, divorced **Eva M. BECKNER**, born 25 May 1903; died 6 Mar 1993; buried in Connersville, Fayette Co, IN; (3) on 21 Dec 1955 **Odessa BACON**, born[197] 27 May 1906; died[198] Feb 1983 in Rushville, Rush Co, IN; (4) abt 1984 **Kathryn R. RICHTER**. No children.

@@For more information, see research notes at end of chapter.

Eugene Lingenfelser was a grocer in Indiana and moved to Arizona in 1998, probably with his mother and sister. He owned a coin shop in Sun City, Arizona. He died just short of his 101st birthday. @@

170. **Lida H.**[4] **HICKS** (Elijah[3], Elijah[2], Joshua[1]), born 21 Mar 1867 in Nicholsville, Clermont Co, OH; died after 1930. She married[199, 200] on 18 Jul 1889 in Maysville, Mason Co, KY **Robert J. WILSON**, born Jul 1861 in Adams Co, OH; died 25 Dec 1931 in Seattle, King, WA, son of John WILSON and Jane MCKOULE.

Lida Hicks and her mother, Victoria, lived with Victoria's sister, Eliza Martin, and her family after her father's death. She married Robert Wilson, a real estate and insurance agent. By 1900, they had moved to St Louis, MO, and then to Seattle, WA by 1910. Victoria lived with the Wilson family until her death. Lida was living in 1930, but no record has been found of her death. @@

   Children of Lida H. HICKS and Robert J. WILSON were:
+ 438   i   **Maria H.**[5] **WILSON**.

176. **Edgar Newton**[4] **VERMILLION** (Martha Ann[3] HICKS, Elijah[2], Joshua[1]), born Apr 1863 in OH; died[201] 12 Dec 1954 in Houston, Harris Co, TX; buried 15 Dec 1954 in Forest Park Cemetery, Houston, TX. He married on 7 May 1893 in Jackson, Kansas City, MO **Nora Ellen SMITH**, born 9 Nov 1876 in MO; died 2 Dec 1930 in Kansas City, Jackson, MO; buried 5 Dec 1930 in Mt Hope Cemetery, Kansas City, MO, daughter of James and Ruth Anna SMITH.

Edgar Vermillion held a number of jobs - cabinet maker, farmer, laborer in can company and owner of a confectionery shop. He married Nora Ellen Smith. They lived in the Kansas City area. @@

   Children of Edgar Newton VERMILLION and Nora Ellen SMITH were:
+ 439   i   **Clarence Vern**[5] **VERMILLION**.
+ 440   ii   **Clara Belle**[5] **VERMILLION**.
   441   iii **Ruth M.**[5] **VERMILLION**, born 17 Dec 1902 in MO; died 15 Aug 1998 in KS.
              Notes: "Ruth b. 17 Dec 1902, MO; d. 15 Aug 1998, Kansas, married Alvin".
   442   iv   **Joseph E.**[5] **VERMILLION**, born 16 Dec 1913 in KS; died Jan 1982 in TX. Notes: "Joe or Joseph b.16 Dec 1913 Kansas, d. Jan 1982, TX. married to Gloria." Info from Verna Ruth (Vermillion) Coleman (granddaughter of Edgar Vermillion).
   443   v   **Edna P.**[5] **VERMILLION**, born 24 Feb 1906 in Kansas; died 1 Nov 1985 in Drakesville, Davis Co, IA. She married **Roscoe RUDD**, born 25 Aug 1901 in Iowa; died 1 Sep 1984 in Drakesville, Davis Co, IA, son of Henry RUDD and Ina CLARKSON.
              Notes: "Edna C. b. 1908, Kansas; d. unknown; married Roscoe Rudd", from Verna Ruth (Vermillion) Coleman, granddaughter of Edgar Vermillion.
              Census: 1930 Soap Creek, Davis, IA, p. 3B. Roscoe Rudd 27, IA/IA/WI, farmer; Edna C. Rudd 23, IA/IA/IA. Next to Henry & Ina Rudd, probably his parents.
              Death: Social Security Death Index: Edna Rudd; Birth Date: 12-24-1906; Death Date: 11-1-1985; Age: 79; Issued: Iowa; Died: Drakesville, IA
   444   vi   **Willie**[5] **VERMILLION**, born abt 1909 in KS. Notes: Not found after 1910 on US census; not on 1915 Kansas State Census - presume he died between 1910 and 1915.
+ 445   vii **Frank Marvin**[5] **VERMILLION**.
   446   viii **John A.**[5] **VERMILLION**, born abt 1915 in KS; died in OR. Notes: "John or Johnny, b. 1914 Kansas; d. unknown, Oregon, married to Juanita (2nd spouse). Info from Verna

@@For more information, see research notes at end of chapter.

Ruth (Vermillion) Coleman - granddaughter of Edgar Vermillion. May be the John Vermillion, b. 09 Mar 1914; d. Oct 1986, Gresham, Multnomah, OR; card issued Texas.

179. **Caroline Wise**[4] **HICKS** (William Stephen[3], Elijah[2], Joshua[1]), born 7 Jul 1871 in Maysville, Mason Co, KY; died[202] 29 Oct 1952 in Cleveland Heights, Cuyahoga Co, OH; buried 1 Nov 1952 in Maysville Cemetery Mason Co, KY. She married on 11 Sep 1898 in Maysville, Mason Co, KY **James Kyle BRUBAKER**, born 30 Dec 1867 in Sheridan Coal Works, Lawrence Co, OH; died 12 Jun 1922 in Detrich, Mason Co, KY; buried 14 Jun 1922 in Maysville Cemetery, Maysville, KY, son of David T BRUBAKER and Salome Arzela CLARKE.

Caroline "Carrie" Hicks married James Brubaker, a farmer in Mason County, KY. After the death of her husband, Carrie lived with her daughter, Bessie Owens, in Butler County, OH. @@

Children of Caroline Wise HICKS and James Kyle BRUBAKER were:
+ 447 i   **Maud Ella**[5] **BRUBAKER**.
+ 448 ii   **Bessie Salome**[5] **BRUBAKER**.
+ 449 iii **Arthur B.**[5] **BRUBAKER**.
+ 450 iv   **Cecil N.**[5] **BRUBAKER**.
+ 451 v   **Kyle Evans**[5] **BRUBAKER**.

180. **William H.**[4] **HICKS** (William Stephen[3], Elijah[2], Joshua[1]), born Aug 1876 in Mason Co, KY; died[203] 11 Feb 1925 in Mason Co, KY; buried in Maysville Cemetery, Mason Co, KY. He married on 26 Jan 1898 in Maysville, Mason Co, KY, divorced **Ella YANCEY**, born 31 Mar 1878 in Lewis Co, KY; died Mar 1967 in Maysville, Mason Co, KY; buried in Maysville Cemetery, Mason Co, KY, daughter of Andrew Jackson YANCEY and Catherine ALLEN

Both William H. Hicks and his wife Ella were osteopaths, practicing in Maysville, KY. They were divorced before 1920. They both attended the School of Osteopathy in Macon, Missouri. @@

Children of William H. HICKS and Ella YANCEY were:
452 i   **Georgia Kathryn**[5] **HICKS**, born 30 Apr 1900 in Washington KY; died[204] 21 Aug 1924 in Boyd Co, KY. She married on 3 Jun 1915 in Maysville, Mason Co, KY **Paul Hargis EASTHAM**[205], born 25 Aug 1884 in Cattletsburg KY; died[206] 14 Oct 1930 in Boyd Co, KY, son of D. D. EASTHAM and Emma V KINCAID. No children @@
Jones notes: "No children"
Question as to date of marriage given in Jones notes - she was living with her mother in 1920, age 19, and as Georgie Hicks; he was living with widowed mother & aunt.
Death: Georgia Kathryn Eastham, b. 30 Apr 1900 KY; d. 21 Aug 1924 Boyd Co, KY; Age: 24; Father: W H Hicks b. KY; Mother: Ella Yancy b. KY. Kentucky Death Records, 1852-1953 <ancestry.com>
453 ii   **Stanley Markham**[5] **HICKS**, born 10 May 1902; died 13 Sep 1954.
Jones notes: "Not married"
Census: 1930 Mason Co, KY, Dist 4, p. 4. Stanley Hicks, 22, lodger, farm operator, farm of Thomas Finn.

182. **Arthur S.**[4] **HICKS** (William Stephen[3], Elijah[2], Joshua[1]), born Mar 1878 in Maysville, Mason Co, KY; died Dec 1946 in Haywood, NC. He married on 2 Apr 1918 in Maysville, Mason Co, KY. No death information has been located. **Adah H. PORTER**, born Feb 1888 in Maysville, Mason Co, KY; died

@@For more information, see research notes at end of chapter.

10 Feb 1920; buried in Maysville Cemetery Mason Co, KY, daughter of Samuel and Mary M. PORTER; married (2) on 21 Mar 1926 in Haywood, Chatham, NC, Mary Kate THOMAS,

Arthur Hicks worked as a policeman at a steel company in 1920. After his wife, Adah, died, their daughter Betty was living with her aunt, Etta Benfield, in Beaver Co, PA. The obituary of his sister Caroline (Hicks) Brubaker gives his death as December 1946 in Haywood, NC. @@

Children of Arthur S. HICKS and Adda H. PORTER were:
454 i **Betty Ann**[5] **HICKS**, born Feb 1919 in Pennsylvania.
Census: 1930 Aliquippa, Beaver, PA, p. 1A. Esky F Benfield 41, NC/NC/NC; Etta Benfield 48, KY/KY/KY; Betty A Hicks 11, niece, PA/KY/KY

183. **Lavina Britana**[4] **HICKS** (Orestes Marion Polk[3], Elijah[2], Joshua[1]), born 9 Aug 1867 in Clermont Co, OH; died 22 Sep 1949 in Columbus, Franklin, OH. She married abt 1890 **Edward N. TUDOR**, born 7 Nov 1867 in KY; died 29 Nov 1917; buried in Greenlawn Cemetery, Columbus, OH, son of Thomas TUDOR and Caroline WHITE.

Lavinia Hicks seems to have gone by a number of versions of her name - Lavinia, Brittania and "Bittie" were all listed on the census. She married Edward Tudor, whose father was from South Africa. Lavinia lived with her daughter and son-in-law through most census years. She ran a boarding house in Columbus, OH. @@

Children of Lavina Britana HICKS and Edward N. TUDOR were:
455 i **C. Nora**[5] **TUDOR**, born 8 Jul 1891; died[207] Oct 1978 in Westerville, Franklin Co, OH. She married **William SOUDERS**. No known children.

184. **Nancy Olivia**[4] **HICKS** (Orestes Marion Polk[3], Elijah[2], Joshua[1]), born 19 Jun 1870 in Maysville, Mason Co, KY; died 14 Nov 1937 in Marble Cliff, Franklin, OH; buried 16 Nov 1937 in Greenlawn Cemetery, Columbus, OH. She married on 27 Oct 1898 in Columbus, Franklin Co, OH **Martin H. MERGARD**, born 25 Jan 1871 in Maysville, Mason Co, KY; died 7 Jun 1908 in Columbus, Franklin Co, OH; buried 10 Jun 1908, son of Henry MERGARD and Elizabeth SMITT.

Nancy Olivia Hicks married Martin Mergard, a tailor, and was widowed young, with two children under 10. She ran a rooming house in Columbus, OH. Her son, Wayne, and brother, Frank, lived with her for many years. @@

Children of Nancy Olivia HICKS and Martin H. MERGARD were:
+ 456 i **Gladys Lee**[5] **MERGARD**.
457 ii **Wayne H.**[5] **MERGARD**, born 09 Aug 1906 in Ohio; died 16 Mar 1966 in Columbus, Franklin Co, OH.
Notes: Death records say he was married, but no information has been located.
Death: Wayne H Mergard, b. 1907; Res: Columbus, Franklin, OH; Death: 16 Mar 1966, OSU Medical Ctr, Columbus (Pt), OH; Age at Death: 59; Married. Ohio Deaths, 1908-1932, 1938-1944, and 1958-2007 [ancestry.com]
SS Death Index: Wayne Mergard; b. 09 Aug 1906; d. Mar 1966; age 59; Columbus, Franklin, OH; card issued: Ohio; #275-01-1337

@@For more information, see research notes at end of chapter.

186. **Elsie**[4] **HICKS** (Orestes Marion Polk[3], Elijah[2], Joshua[1]), born 24 Mar 1874 in Maysville, Mason Co, KY; died 6 Apr 1903 in Columbus, Franklin Co, OH; buried in Greenlawn Cemetery. She married[208] on 24 Aug 1898 in Maysville, Mason Co, KY **Joseph J. LINGENFELSER**, born abt 1874 in Mason Co, KY; died 1938, son of George LINGENFELSER and Margaret MILLER.

Elsie Hicks married Joseph Lingenfelser, an engineer, but only lived a few years after her marriage. Joseph remarried after her death and had two more sons. @@

    Children of Elsie HICKS and Joseph J. LINGENFELSER were:
- 458   i   **Stanley Joesph**[5] **LINGENFELSER**, born 20 Jul 1899; died abt 1934. He married abt 1921 **Margaret _?_**, born abt 1896 in New Jersey

   Jones notes: "Resided New Jersey, married but no children"

   Census: 1920 not found in KY or NJ; not with father's family in Mason Co, KY

      1930 Dist 118, Jersey City, Hudson Co, NY, p. 41. Stanley Lingenfelser, 30, KY/KY/KY, carpenter - construction; Margaret 34, NJ/-/NJ

   Military: World War I Draft Registration Cards, 1917-1918 [ancestry.com] Stanley Joseph Lingenfelser, age 19, b. 20 Jul 1899; res: Jersey City, Hudson Co, NJ; occ: carpenter - H. Kopphers Co; relative: Mr. Joseph Lingenfelser, Maysville, KY; med height & build; brown eyes & black hair. Regis: 12 Dec 1918, location not given.

188. **Clarence Malcolm**[4] **HICKS** (Orestes Marion Polk[3], Elijah[2], Joshua[1]), born 9 Oct 1882 in OH; died 7 Feb 1925 in Columbus, Franklin, OH; buried in East Lawn Cemetery, Columbus OH. He married (1) abt 1905 **Mary L. -?-**, born abt 1886 in Ohio. **(2) Ruth MORRISON**, born 19 Jan 1898 in OH; died 30 Mar 1957; buried in East Lawn Cemetery, Columbus OH

Clarence Hicks, a tailor by trade, married first Mary L. -?- and had one daughter, Dona. Mary evidently died between 1910 and 1920, since Clarence was married to Ruth "Babe" Morrison by 1920 and had 3 more children. After Clarence's death, Ruth remarried Paul R. Hott. @@

    Children of Clarence Malcolm HICKS and Mary L. wife of Clarence HICKS were:
- 462   i   **Dona L.**[5] **HICKS**, born abt 1906 in Ohio. No further information.

    Children of Clarence Malcolm HICKS and Ruth MORRISON were:
- +   459   i   **Clarence M.**[5] **HICKS II**.
- +   460   ii   **Norma**[5] **HICKS**.
- +   461   iii   **Marilyn**[5] **HICKS**.

190. **George B.**[4] **JONES** (Caroline Rebecca J.[3] HICKS, Elijah[2], Joshua[1]), born 22 Aug 1871 in Kentucky. He married bef 1891, divorced **Susan/Lutie -?-**, born Feb 1873 in Kentucky.

George was listed as a blacksmith in the 1900 census, with a wife, son and his grandmother, Nancy Hicks, living with them. By 1910, Lutie and Harold are in OH and she is listed as divorced. No other information has been located @@

    Children of George B. and Lutie JONES were:
- 463   i   **Harold**[5] **JONES**, born Feb 1891 in Kentucky.

@@For more information, see research notes at end of chapter.

191. **Irma Clare**[4] **JONES** (Caroline Rebecca J.[3] HICKS, Elijah[2], Joshua[1]), born 22 Dec 1879 in Ohio. She married[209] (1) on 16 Jan 1902 in Brown County, OH **Everett COCHRAN**, son of John M. COCHRAN and Queen STEELE, divorced; (2)[210] on 25 Dec 1907 in Hamilton County, OH **Frederick Cole HELMICK**, born 13 Aug 1879 in West Virginia, son of Dexter HELMICK and Katherine COLE.

Irma Clare Jones married first, Everett Cochran, but was divorced by 1907 when she married Fred Helmick. Fred was manager of a planing mill. Irma's mother, Caroline Hicks, and her unmarried sister, Minnie, lived with the Helmick family. @@

Children of Irma Clare JONES and Fred Cole HELMICK were:
- 464   i   **Escalene R**[5] **HELMICK**, born 1911 in Ohio.
- 465   ii   **Thomas**[5] **HELMICK [twin]**, born 29 Aug 1913 in Clarksburg, Harrison, WV.
- 466   iii   **Wardie**[5] **HELMICK [twin]**, born 29 Aug 1913 in Clarksburg, Harrison, WV.

193. **James Sylvester**[4] **TATMAN** (James[3], Lydia[2] HICKS, Joshua[1]),, born 17 Aug 1855 in Clermont Co, OH; died 3 Jan 1918 in Kingfisher, Kingfisher Co, OK. He married **Elizabeth JOHNSON**, born 5 Feb 1869 in Tennessee, and died 27 Jun 1954, Kingfisher, Kingfisher Co, OK.

Jones notes had nothing about this family. Information is from Kevin Meade <kevinmeade@aol.com>.

Children of James Sylvester TATMAN and Elizabeth JOHNSON were:
- 193a   I   Mariam TATMAN was born 18 Feb 1897, and died 23 Jan 1898.
- 193b   ii   Clarice TATMAN was born 5 Mar 1899 in Kingfisher, Kingfisher Co, OK, and died 2 Jun 1980

194. **Lydia Ann**[4] **TATMAN** (James[3], Lydia[2] HICKS, Joshua[1]), born 1858 in Clermont Co, OH; died 19 Jun 1938 in Harris Co, TX. She married (1) on 1 Sep 1883 in Owen County IN **William GIBSON**, born Oct 1834 in Indiana; (2) on 22 Sep 1878 in Davies Co, IN **Joseph ROGERS**, born abt 1879 in South Carolina.

Lydia Tatman married first, Joseph Rogers, and had two sons, Thomas Rotheus and Frank Tatman, who died young. Joseph probably died (possibly divorced) before 1883 when she married William Gibson. She was living in Indiana for both marriages, but was in the Indian Territories with William Gibson by 1900; in Galveston, TX by 1910; in El Paso, TX in 1920 and Houston, TX by 1930. Joseph Rogers was a county surveyor; William Gibson, a carpenter. After the death of William, Lydia lived with her sons and grandsons. @@

Children of Lydia Ann TATMAN and Joseph ROGERS were:
- + 469   i   **Rotheus Thomas**[5] **ROGERS**.
- 469a   ii   **Frank Tatman ROGERS** born 17 Nov 1880 in Spencer, Owen Co, IN, and died 24 Nov 1882 in Spencer, Owen Co, IN. Not in Jones notes - info from Kevin Meade.

Children of Lydia Ann TATMAN and William GIBSON were:
- 467   i   **Kenneth**[5] **GIBSON**[211], born 18 Jul 1886 in Springfield, MO; died[212] 18 Apr 1968 in Los Angeles CA. He married bef 1930 **Gertrude -?-**, born 28 Oct 1886 in Arkansas; died[213] Feb 1968 in El Paso, El Paso, TX. No known children. @@
- 468   ii   **Mary May**[5] **GIBSON**, born 13 Sep 1889 in Logan, Lawrence Co, MO, and died 9 Aug 1977 in Galveston, Galveston Co, TX. She married abt 1911 **Rudolph BOOK** b: 5 May 1890 in Richland, PA and died Aug 1973 in Galveston, TX. One child **Theodore R. BOOK** b: 12 Jul 1918 in El Paso Co, TX, Not in Jones notes - info from Kevin Meade.

@@For more information, see research notes at end of chapter.

195. Franklin Ulyses⁴ TATMAN²¹⁴ (James³, Lydia² HICKS, Joshua¹), born 2 Dec 1862 in Bethel, Clermont Co, OH; died²¹⁵ 30 Sep 1934 in Chicago, Cook Co, IL; buried in Fairview Cemetery, Coffeyville, Montgomery Co, KS. He married on 8 Mar 1886 in Lincoln, Logan Co, IL **Flora Catherine LEWIS**, born Sep 1866/67 in Lincoln, Logan Co, IL; died Jan 1951 in Coffeyville, Montgomery Co, KS; buried in Fairview Cem, Coffeyville, KS, daughter of Decatur and Mary A. LEWIS.

Frank Tatman was a tailor who lived in the Indian Territory in 1900, then moved to Montgomery County, KS. He was in El Paso TX in 1930, where he was a freight broker. His obituary states that "He was a member of Roosevelt's Rough Riders in the Spanish-American War". @@

Children of Franklin Ulyses TATMAN and Flora Catherine LEWIS were:
- \+ 470 i **Frank L.⁵ TATMAN**.
- 471 ii **James⁵ TATMAN**²¹⁶, born²¹⁷ abt 1890. Meade notes: "died young, but not sure of birth or death dates". Does not appear on any census lists.
- 472 iii **Florence⁵ TATMAN**²¹⁸, born 13 Jun 1896 in OK; died 15 Oct 1904; buried in Fairview Cemetery, Coffeyville, Montgomery Co, KS. No further information.
- \+ 473 iv **Richard Bryon⁵ TATMAN**.
- \+ 474 v **William Jennings⁵ TATMAN**.

196. Cornelia Blanche⁴ BRITTINGHAM (Lucinda³ TATMAN, Lydia² HICKS, Joshua¹), born 8 Sep 1854 in Clermont Co, OH; died²¹⁹ 4 Jun 1926 in Madison, Boone, WV; buried in Bethel Tate Cemetery. She married on 25 Aug 1872 in Clermont Co, OH **John Wesley ALTMAN**, born abt 1853 in OH; died bef 1900; buried in Bethel Tate Cemetery

Cornelia Brittingham married John Altman, who, according to Orville Jones, was "shot by customer in his barber shop". Cornelia was listed as a "cigar roller" in the 1900 census. @@

Children of Cornelia Blanche BRITTINGHAM and John Wesley ALTMAN were:
- \+ 475 i **Nelly⁵ ALTMAN**.
- 476 ii **Bailey W.⁵ ALTMAN**, born Mar 1878 in OH.
  Not in Orville Jones notes and not on WW I Draft Registration
- 477 iii **Anna May⁵ ALTMAN**, born²²⁰ 8 Nov 1881 in Felicity, Clermont Co, OH; died 1958 in Detroit, MI; buried in Bethel Tate Cemetery She married **Henry KELLEY**, born est 1881. Jones notes: "resided in Detroit; no children"
  Census: 1930 Madison, Boone, WV, p. 8B. Samuel J Altman 46, divorced, OH/OH/OH, carpenter - building construction; Anna M Kelley 48, sister, OH, divorced, saleswoman - retail dry goods.
- 478 iv **Samuel J.⁵ ALTMAN**, born 1 Jan 1884 in Brown Co, OH; died²²¹ 12 Jan 1947 in Tate Twp, Clermont, Ohio; buried in Bethel Tate Cemetery Jones notes: "resided at Rt 2, Bethel, OH; no children"
  Census 1930 Madison, Boone, WV, p. 8B. Samuel J Altman 46, divorced, OH/OH/OH, carpenter - building construction; Anna M Kelley 48, sister, OH, divorced, saleswoman - retail dry goods
  Death: Samuel J. Altman, single, occ: farmer; parents: John W. Altman, b. IN; Cornelia Brittingham, b. OH. Burial: Bethel, OH. Informant: Mrs. Lou Hall, Bethel, OH. Ohio Death Certificate <www.familysearch.org>.
  Evidently was married at some point before 1930; shown as divorced in 1930 census. No marriage record found;
  Not found on WW I Draft Registration 1917-18; 1942 WW II registration.

@@For more information, see research notes at end of chapter.

+ 479 v **Millie Lou⁵ ALTMAN**.

197. James Winfield⁴ BRITTINGHAM (Lucinda³ TATMAN, Lydia² HICKS, Joshua¹), born 3 Aug 1861 in Bethel, Clermont Co, OH; died²²² 4 Feb 1943 in Norwood, Hamilton, OH; buried 7 Feb 1943 in Nicholsville, OH. He married (1) on 30 Nov 1891 in Clermont Co, OH **Mary "Mollie" CARR**, born Dec 1867 in Kentucky; died prob. bef 1920; (2) bef 1920 **Elizabeth Margaret WARE**, born 18 Sep 1863 in Pendleton Co KY; died 16 Feb 1941 in Hanover, Butler, OH; buried 18 Feb 1941 in Millville, OH, daughter of John WARE and Mabala DANS [DAVIS?]

James Brittingham was listed as a barber in 1900, who was a machinist in 1910 and a shoe maker with his own shop in 1920 and 1930. He was born in Clermont County, lived in Hamilton, Butler Co, OH most of his adult life, but died in Cincinnati. @@

Children of James Winfield BRITTINGHAM and Mary "Mollie" CARR were:

+ 480 i **William Karl⁵ BRITTINGHAM**.
  481 ii **Dorothy Louise⁵ BRITTINGHAM**, born 21 Dec 1893 in Clermont Co, OH; died bef 1974. She married (1) abt 1913 in Butler Co, OH, divorced **Ernest Gustav NAGEL**, born 6 Dec 1894 in Hamilton, OH; (2) on 30 Mar 1921 in Hamilton Co, OH **Edward A. BLANEY**, born 1869 in OH; possibly (3)²²³ on 30 Mar 1921 in Hamilton County, OH **Jasper HAMILTON M.D.**, born abt 1893. No known children. Living in Los Angeles, CA in 1974. @@
  482 iii **Marie⁵ BRITTINGHAM**, born 3 Aug 1895 in Hurlington, Clermont Co, OH; died²²⁴ Aug 1975 in Torrance, Los Angeles, CA. She married **Otis BENNETT**²²⁵, born abt 1895; died in IN.
  Jones notes: "she resides (1974) at California; he died in IN; son - unnamed"
  Census 1920 not found
  *1930 Charleston, Coles, IL, p. 17A. Otis Bennett 30, IL, shoemaker - shoe factory; Marie Bennett 25, IL, shoemaker - shoe factory; Billie Bennett 8. [*May not be right family - names match, but dates & birthplace don't]
+ 483 iv **Bryan James⁵ BRITTINGHAM**.

198. Lydia May⁴ BRITTINGHAM (Lucinda³ TATMAN, Lydia² HICKS, Joshua¹), born 1857 in Clermont Co, OH; died 1938; buried in Felicity Cemetery, Felicity OH. She married on 4 Sep 1898 in Clermont Co, OH **George M. WALKER**, born 23 Sep 1861 in Felicity, Clermont, OH; died 26 Jan 1928 in Felicity, Clermont, OH; buried 29 Jan 1928 in Felicity Cemetery, Felicity OH, son of John and Melissa G. WALKER.

May Brittingham married George Walker, a farmer and carpenter. They had one child, Melissa, who was a school teacher. @@

Children of Lydia May BRITTINGHAM and George M. WALKER were:

+ 484 i **Melissa L.⁵ WALKER**.

201. Missouri Mary⁴ UTTER (Melissa Jane³ ROBINSON, Mary² HICKS, Joshua¹), born 1864 in IN; died bef Jun 1900; buried in Bethel Tate Cemetery She married **John S. ALTMAN**, born Aug 1841 in OH; died 1919.

Practically no conclusive information has been located for Missouri and John Altman. John was listed as a widower in 1900, so Missouri evidently died before then. This may be the same John Altman who was married to Priscilla Salt and had children Guy and Maud. If so, he was a Civil War veteran and was admitted to the Dayton Home for Disabled Veterans in 1903. He died there in 1919. Benefits were paid

@@For more information, see research notes at end of chapter.

to daughter, Maud (a daughter from his first marriage), who was living in Cincinnati, OH. He was a widower. @@

    Children of Missouri Mary UTTER and John S. ALTMAN were:
- 485   i   **Pearl More**[5] **ALTMAN**, born 8 Sep 1884 in Clermont Co, OH.
  Notes: no other information found
- 486   ii   **Lloyd Robison**[5] **ALTMAN**, born 10 May 1890 in Bethel, Clermont Co, OH; died[226] 24 Apr 1915 in Cincinnati, Hamilton Co, OH; buried 27 Apr 1915 in Bethel Tate Cemetery
  Death: Lloyd R. Altman, d. 24 Apr 1915, Tuberculous Sanitarium, Cincinnati, OH. Occ - Clerk, RR Office, parents: John Altman, b. IN; Mary Utter, b. OH. Burial: Bethel, OH. Ohio Deaths 1908-1953 <pilot.familysearch.org>
  Not found on WW I Draft Registration; 1942 WW II registration.

214. Mary E.[4] **KLINGLER**[227] (Mary[3] HOPKINS, Elizabeth 'Betsy'[2] HICKS, Joshua[1]), born 30 Sep 1844 probably in Clermont Co, OH; died 1914, in Ottumwa, IA; buried in Drakesville, Davis Co, IA. She married 13 Oct 1868 in Davis Co, IA **Joseph WEINY**, born 1832; died 9 Dec 1910, probably in Ottumwa, IA; buried in Drakesville, Davis Co, IA.

Mary Klingler apparently lived in Davis Co, IA most of her life. She moved to Iowa with her parents before 1860, married there and then moved to Ottumwa in Wapello Co by 1910. She married Joseph Weiney, a carpenter, and had one daughter, Ella. @@

    Children of Mary E. KLINGLER and Joseph WEINY were:
- 487   i   **Ella**[5] **WEINY**, born abt 1875. No known children. Her husband had children from an earlier marriage.
  Marriage: L. E. Breeding, b. 1874, Fremont, IA, age 42; to Ella Weiny, b. 1874, Bloomfield, IA, Age: 42; Marriage: 08 Jun 1916, Ottumwa, Wapello, Iowa; Groom's Father: A. Breeding; Mother: P. Putman; Bride's Father: Jno. Weiny; Mother: Mary Klinger; both single. Iowa Marriages, 1809-1992 <familysearch.org>
  Census:
  - 1910 Wyacondah, Davis, IA, p. 6B. Samuel E Breeding 36, farmer; Zella A Breeding 35; James H Breeding 11; Hallie Breeding 10; Herman Breeding 8; Daisy Breeding 6; Ida Breeding 3
  - 1920 Wyacondah, Davis, IA, p. 5A. Lem Breeding 45, farmer; Ella Breeding 45; James Breeding 21, teacher - public schools; Herman Breeding 18; Iola Breeding 12; Daisey Breeding 16.
  - 1930 Wyacondah, Davis, IA, p 2B. Samuel E Breeding 55, IA/IN/IN, farmer - general farm; Ella Breeding 56. Samuel 1st m. age 21; Ella 1st married at 42. Obviously he was married before - children are from first marriage.

217. John M.[4] **STEWART** (Diana[3] HOPKINS, Elizabeth 'Betsy'[2] HICKS, Joshua[1]), born Jan 1865 in IA; buried in Ottumwa, IA. He married 27 Jun 1894, in Ottumwa, Wapello Co, IA **Carrie VINSON**, born Apr 1867 in Indiana, daughter of John VINSON and Mary F. BRUCE.

John Stewart was a carpenter. He married Carrie Vinson and had a daughter, Melva. @@

    Children of John M. STEWART and Carrie VINSON were:
- \+   488   i   **Melva E.**[5] **STEWART**.

@@For more information, see research notes at end of chapter.

218. **Sarah Lavina**[4] **HOPKINS** (Levi Whitcomb[3], Elizabeth 'Betsy'[2] HICKS, Joshua[1]), born Aug 1861 in Drakesville, Davis Co, IA; died 5 May 1953 in Hunter, Garfield Co, OK; buried in White Cemetery, Hunter OK. She married on 22 Mar 1885 in Reno Co, KS **Thomas Hale BENSON**, born 12 Nov 1869 in McLean Co, IL; died 15 Feb 1912 in Hunter, Garfield Co, OK; buried in White Cemetery, Hunter OK, son of George Hale BENSON and Neety Ann ROBINSON.

Sarah Hopkins married Thomas Hale Benson in 1885 in Reno Co, Kansas and soon thereafter moved to Garfield Co, OK. Thomas was a farmer and manager of a general store. After his death, Sarah ran an apartment building. Most information is from the Grigg's book[228]. @@

Children of Sarah Lavina HOPKINS[229] and Thomas Hale BENSON were:

+ 489 i **Ida May**[5] **BENSON**.
+ 490 ii **Lettie Pearl**[5] **BENSON**.
+ 491 iii **Roy Douglas**[5] **BENSON**.
   492 iv **Lois Maurietta**[5] **BENSON**, born 8 Nov 1905 in Hunter, Garfield Co, OK; died 14 Apr 1978. She married on 2 Aug 1924 in Los Angeles, Los Angeles Co, CA **Raymond BROWN**, born abt 1890. No other information found.
Notes: Not found in 1930 census. Could be the Lois Brown, 22, in Enid, Garfield Co, OK; boarder ; with Carl G. Brown, 24, and George D. 7/12. Carl is a telephone lineman. m. 3 years.

219. **Clara Elizabeth**[4] **HOPKINS** (Levi Whitcomb[3], Elizabeth 'Betsy'[2] HICKS, Joshua[1]), born 19 Jan 1863 in Wapello, Louisa Co, IA; died 14 Jan 1956 in Liberal, Seward Co, KS; buried in Haven/Priest Cemetery, Haven, Reno Co, KS. She married on 3 Jun 1879 in Reno Co, KS **William Joseph MITCHELL**, born 20 Nov 1854 in Fayette Co, IA; died 6 Nov 1887 in Haven, Reno Co, KS, son of Roland and Polly MITCHELL.

Clara Hopkins married at age 16 to William Mitchell, a farmer who was about 10 years older than she was. William died in 1887, leaving Clara a 24-year old widow, with 4 very young children. Her brothers William & Walter, as well as her sister Gertrude, lived with her in 1900, probably helping out on the farm. She lived with her son, George, in 1910 & 1930. She probably remarried a -?- Wall, as she was listed as Clara Wall in 1930, but no other record has been found. @@

Children of Clara Elizabeth HOPKINS and William Joseph MITCHELL were:

+ 493 i **Oran Ray**[5] **MITCHELL**.
   494 ii **Elmer C.**[5] **MITCHELL**, born Jun 1884 in KS. Jones notes: "not married"
      Census: 1910 Darling, Muskogee, OK, p. 14. George H Mitchell 22, farmer; Mary Neoma 15, wife, KS/PA/IN; Clara 46, mother, widow; Elmer 25, brother, farmer; Sarah Hapkins 70, grandmother, widow.
      1920 May be the Elmer C. Mitchell in Dist 212, El Cajon, San Diego, CA in 1920, age 35, KS/IA/IA, farmer - hay farm, single
      1930 - May be the Elmer C. Mitchell in Dist 3, El Cajon, San Diego, CA in 1930, age 44, KS/IA/IA, salesman - groceries, single.
      Not found on draft registration cards
+ 495 iii **William Jesse**[5] **MITCHELL**.
+ 496 iv **George Henry**[5] **MITCHELL**.

@@For more information, see research notes at end of chapter.

222. Gertrude May⁴ HOPKINS (Levi Whitcomb³, Elizabeth 'Betsy'² HICKS, Joshua¹), born 1 Apr 1879 in Reno Co, KS; died 14 Jul 1969 in Liberal, Seward Co, KS; buried in Tyrone, OK. She married on 29 Apr 1903 in Haven, Reno Co, KS **Frederick Julian SHUMWAY**[230], born 11 Apr 1878 in Pratt Co, KS; died 24 Oct 1936 in Tyrone, Texas Co, OK; buried in Tyrone, Texas Co, OK.

Gertrude Hopkins and her brothers William & Walter lived with her widowed sister, Clara Mitchell, in Haven KS in 1900. She was a school teacher at that time. After her marriage to Fred Shumway, a carpenter, the family lived in Pratt, Kiowa, Sedgwick & Stevens Counties in Kansas. @@

Children of Gertrude May HOPKINS and Frederick Julian SHUMWAY were:

497 i **Ivan Vernon⁵ SHUMWAY**[231], born 19 Feb 1904 in Turon, Pratt Co, KS; died 29 Nov 1978 in Wichita, Sedgwick Co, KS; buried in Kechi, KS Cemetery He married on 27 May 1933 in Kechi, KS **Harriet Mildred HAASE**, born 25 Dec 1908 in El Dorado, KS; died[232] 5 Oct 1999 in Wichita, Sedgwick Co, KS. No further information.

498 ii **Lora Irene⁵ SHUMWAY**[233], born 4 Feb 1907 in Turon, Pratt Co, KS; died[234] 7 Jun 1997 in Mcpherson, Mcpherson, KS. She married on 28 Oct 1934 in Wichita, KS **Joseph Benjamin MAPP**, born 9 Nov 1900 in Weatherford, Parker Co, TX; died 29 Jul 1949 in Tyrone, Texas Co, OK; buried in Tyrone, Texas Co, OK, son of Charlie E. and Cora M. MAPP.
Death: Social Security Death Index: Irene MAPP b. 04 Feb 1907; d. 07 Jun 1997, Mcpherson, Mcpherson, KS; #447-38-6789; issued: Oklahoma

223. Walter Ralph⁴ HOPKINS[235] (Levi Whitcomb³, Elizabeth 'Betsy'² HICKS, Joshua¹), born 29 Jul 1882 in Reno Co, KS; died 1 May 1958 in Orla Vista, Orange Co, FL. He married (1) on 29 Jan 1911, divorced **Elizabeth HOLME**, born 15 Jun 1892 in New York; died 1971 in Utica, Oneida Co, NY; (2) on 26 Jun 1922 in Winfield, KS **Julia Rebica BRAGG**, born 9 Apr 1906 in Thomas, Custer Co, OK; died 16 Jun 1971 in Antioch, Contra Costa Co, CA; buried in Fresno, Fresno Co, CA.

Walter Hopkins lived with his widowed sister, Clara Mitchell in 1900. He married twice and was probably divorced from each. It is not clear as to which wife was the mother of Walter's son Leslie, but Elizabeth seems more likely. Leslie was living with his uncle, William Hopkins, at the time of the 1920 & 1930 census, so may have been raised by his uncle. @@

Children of Walter Ralph HOPKINS and Elizabeth HOLME were:

499 i **Leslie Frederick⁵ HOPKINS**, born 26 May 1914 in Pawnee, Pawnee Co, OK; died 6 Aug 2003, Gainesville, Alachua Co, FL. He married on 3 Sep 1940 **Katheryn WILLIAMS**. No further information.
Notes: Jones notes are not clear on this family. I believe that this is the correct placement, but cannot be positive. Leslie was apparently raised by his uncle, William Lincoln Hopkins.
Census: 1920 Liberty, Pawnee, OK, p. William L Hopkins 50, farmer, IA/OH/Eng; Deleo 42, KS/IA/NY; Leslie F 5, nephew, OK/KS/NY.
1930 Orlando, Orange, FL, p. Ellen Rhoades 75, NY/NY/VT; Vernon Rhodes 5, grandson, FL/KS/KS; William L Hopkins 61, son in law, laborer - odd jobs; De Leo Hopkins 52, dau; Leslie Hopkins 15, grandson, OK/KS/NY.
Death: Leslie F Hopkins, b. 26 May 1914; d. 06 Aug 2003; age 89, Gainesville, Alachua, FL; card issued: Florida; SS #266-14-8792 [SS Death Index]

@@For more information, see research notes at end of chapter.

Children of Walter Ralph HOPKINS and Julia Rebica BRAGG were:
- 500 i **Gladys Mary Rosezella**[5] **HOPKINS**, born 2 Nov 1924 in Pawnee, Pawnee Co, OK; died 17 Oct 1927. No other information.
- 501 ii **Preston Dale**[5] **HOPKINS**[236], born 26 Aug 1927 in Pawnee, Pawnee Co, OK; died 05 Sep 2005, Oakley, Contra Costa, CA. No other information.
  Death: SS Death Index: Preston D Hopkins, b. 26 Aug 1927; d. 05 Sep 2005; age 78; Oakley, Contra Costa, CA; issued California; #573-24-7914

224. Lucinda Margaret[4] **JOHNSTON** (William J.[3], Margaret[2] HICKS, Joshua[1]), born 29 Nov 1853 in Clermont Co, OH; died 2 Mar 1883; buried in Mt. Pleasant. She married on 26 Oct 1878 in Clermont Co, OH **John LANHAM**, born 24 Jul 1855.

Lucinda Johnston married John F. Lanham and remained in Clermont Co, OH - probably her whole life. John was a laborer in a livery stable in 1880. Lucinda died young, leaving two young daughters. In 1900 Adelia was living with her grandmother, Mary Johnston; Mollie was already married.

Children of Lucinda Margaret JOHNSTON and John LANHAM were:
- \+ 502 i **Mollie E.**[5] **LANHAM**.
- 503 ii **Adelia F.**[5] **LANHAM**, born 1881 in Felicity, Clermont Co, OH; died 17 Nov 1970 in Cincinnati, Hamilton Co, OH; buried in Felicity Cemetery, Felicity, Clermont Co, OH. She married on 19 Aug 1908 in Clermont Co, OH **Bruce T. DAUGHTERS**[237], born 26 Feb 1877 in Clermont Co, OH; died[238] 21 Jul 1950 in Felicity, Clermont, OH; buried 24 Jul 1950 in Felicity Cemetery, Felicity, Clermont Co, OH, son of Turpin DAUGHTERS and Elizabeth WEDDING. No children.
  Jones notes: "resided at Cincinnati, OH; no children"
  Census: 1910 Franklin, Clermont, OH, p. 2B. Bruce L Daughters 33, tonsorial care - barber; Delia F Daughters 29. All OH/OH/OH. married 1 year, no children. Next to Elizabeth Daughters, 62. probably his mother.
  1920 Franklin, Clermont, OH, p. 12A. Bruce Daughters 42, barber - own shop; Delia Daughters 38.
  1930 Felicity, Clermont, OH, p. 12B. Bruce T Daughters 53, barber - barber shop; Delia F Daughters 49. Married ages 31 & 27.
  Marriage: Bruce Daughters, 31, b. 1877, Clermont, OH to Delia Lanham 27; b. 1881, Felicity, OH. Marriage Date: 19 Aug 1908, Clermont, OH; groom's father: Turpin Daughters; mother: Elizabeth. Bride's father: John Lanham; mother: Lucy Johnson. Ohio Marriages, 1800-1958 <pilot.familysearch.org>
  Death: Delia F. Daughters, b. 1881, d. 17 Nov 1970, Christ Hospital, Cincinnati, OH. Age 89, widow. Ohio Deaths, 1908-1932, 1938-1944, & 1958-2002 [ancestry.com].

225. William Alexander[4] **JOHNSTON** (William J.[3], Margaret[2] HICKS, Joshua[1]), born 19 Dec 1856 in Clermont Co, OH; died 16 Mar 1918 in Franklin Twp, Clermont, OH; buried in Mt. Pleasant. He married on 31 Oct 1880 in Clermont Co, OH **Anne ADRIAN**, born Mar 1858; died bef 1910, daughter of William and Sophia ADRIAN.

Alexander Johnston was a blacksmith by trade. After his wife Anne died (before 1910), Alexander and his daughter, Lena, lived with his mother, Mary Johnston. @@

Children of William Alexander JOHNSTON and Anne ADRIAN were:
- 504 i **Mary M.**[5] **JOHNSTON**, born est 1882. Jones notes: "died infancy"

@@For more information, see research notes at end of chapter.

505 ii **Lena**[5] **JOHNSTON**, born 17 Nov 1882 in Clermont Co, OH; died 22 Feb 1920 in Franklin, Clermont, OH; buried 24 Feb 1920 in Felicity, Clermont, OH. She married[239] on 19 Feb 1914 in Hamilton County, OH **Sidney MARKSBERRY**, born 8 Aug 1874 in Clermont Co, OH; died 9 Aug 1951; buried in Felicity Cemetery, Felicity, Clermont Co, OH, son of William MARKSBERRY and Cynthia BRUEN. No known children. Sidney had been married before; all the children seem to be from his first marriage to Emma MAYNES. He was widowed by 1910. @@

228. Annie Belle[4] **JOHNSTON** (William J.[3], Margaret[2] HICKS, Joshua[1]), born 2 Sep 1865 in Clermont Co, OH; died 18 Jun 1931 in Franklin, Clermont, Ohio; buried in Chilo Cemetery She married on 8 Jun 1902 in Clermont Co, OH **Morgan UTTER**, born 5 Nov 1853 in Clermont Co, OH; died 24 Jan 1937; buried in Chilo Cemetery; son of Washington UTTER and Mary MORGAN.

Anna Johnston married Morgan Utter, as his second wife. No records have been found for his first marriage. He was single and living at home in 1880, not found on the 1900 census and married to Anna by 1910. He was a farmer. Jones notes state that Anna Utter was a teacher. @@

Children of Annie Belle JOHNSTON and Morgan UTTER were:
+ 506 i **Lucy**[5] **UTTER**.
+ 507 ii **Mary Morgan**[5] **UTTER**.
+ 508 iii **Robert Alexander**[5] **UTTER**.

229. Mary Elizabeth[4] **JOHNSTON** (William J.[3], Margaret[2] HICKS, Joshua[1]), born 27 Jun 1869 in Felicity, Clermont Co, OH; died 27 Jan 1960 in Brown County, OH. She married on 13 Feb 1889 in Clermont Co, OH **Henry Harrison STEVENS**, born 20 Oct 1852 in Kentucky; died 16 Dec 1916 in Felicity, Clermont, OH; buried in Felicity, Clermont Co, OH, son of Samuel STEVENS and Jane LANE.

Mary Elizabeth "Lizzie" Johnston lived to be 90 years of age. She had married Harry Stevens at age 18 and had two sons. After Harry's death, she was manager of a telephone company. Harry was a photographer and later a telephone operator. @@

Children of Mary Elizabeth JOHNSTON and Henry Harrison STEVENS were:
509 i **Charles Richard**[5] **STEVENS**[240], born 15 Nov 1889 in Felicity, Clermont Co, OH; died[241] 1 Jul 1973 in Clermont Co, OH; buried in Felicity Cemetery, Felicity, Clermont Co, OH. Never married.
Jones notes: "US Army, WW I"
Military: World War I Draft Registration Cards, 1917-1918 [ancestry.com]. Charles Richard Stevens, age 27, b. 15 Nov 1889, Felicity, OH; res: Cincinnati, Hamilton, OH; occ: piano worker, Baldwin Piano Co; single, med height & build; grey eyes, lt brown hair. Regis: Cincinnati, Hamilton, OH 5 Jun 1917.
Ohio Soldiers in WWI, 1917-1918 [ancestry.com] Charles R. Stevens, Age: 28 8/12 Years; b. abt 1889, Felicity, OH; Enlistment: 22 Jul 1918, Cincinnati, OH; National Army LB 4; Comments: 45 Co 12 Training Battalion 156 Depot Brigade to 24 July 1918; Battery C, 10 Battalion, Field Artillery Replacement Draft Cp Jackson; Summary Court to 7 Sept 1918; 2 Battery Cp Jackson Summary Court Sept Automatic Replacement Draft to 29 Sept 1918; Honorable discharge 28 May 1919,
Death: Charles R Stevens, b. 1890; Res: Clermont Co, OH; Death Date: 1 Jul 1973, Long-Term Care Facilities, Clermont Co, OH. Ohio Deaths, 1908-1932, 1938-1944, and 1958-2007 [Ancestry.com]
+ 510 ii **Henry Johnston**[5] **STEVENS**.

@@For more information, see research notes at end of chapter.

232. Ella F.[4] WHITE (Ann Maria[3] HICKS, James[2], Joshua[1]), born Sep 1858 in OH; died 1938; buried in New Rochelle, NY. She married on 10 Sep 1878 in Clermont Co, OH **John C. GLEASON**, born Nov 1859 in Clermont Co, OH; died 1920 in New Rochelle, Westchester Co, NY; buried in New Rochelle, Westchester Co, NY.

Ella White married John Gleason and moved with him to New Rochelle, NY before 1910. John had worked for the railroad in Ohio, but was a real estate agent in New Rochelle. @@

    Children of Ella F. WHITE and Jno. C. GLEASON were:
+   511 i **Caroline Marie[5] GLEASON**.
    512 ii **Guy[5] GLEASON**, born abt 1882 in OH; died in New Rochelle, Westchester Co, NY. Jones notes: " married; no children"
          Birth: Guy L. Gleason, b. 4 Feb 1884, Williamsburg, Clermont, Ohio; father: John C. Gleason; mother: ___ White, Ohio Births and Christenings, 1821-1962 <fsbeta.familysearch.org>
          Living in New Rochelle, Westchester Co, NY in 1930, with mother Ella, truck driver. not found on WW I Draft Registration or Ohio Death Records

233. James Hicks[4] WHITE (Ann Maria[3] HICKS, James[2], Joshua[1]), born Sep 1861 in OH; died 1928; buried in Williamsburg. He married on 5 Nov 1884 in Clermont Co, OH **Margaret Pearl ATCHLEY**, born Oct 1866 in OH; died 1958; buried in Williamsburg, Clermont Co, OH, daughter of Daniel and Mary ATCHLEY.

James White was a manufacturer of chairs. Several of his children also worked in the chair factory and his sister in law, Mina White, was a stenographer there. After his death, his son, Nicholas, ran the factory. @@

    Children of James Hicks WHITE and Margaret Pearl ATCHLEY were:
+   513 i **Marie W.[5] WHITE**.
    514 ii **Charles A.[5] WHITE**, born 1888 in Williamsburg, Clermont Co, OH; died 1888 in Williamsburg, Clermont Co, OH; buried in Williamsburg Cemetery.
    515 iii **Lawrence Webster[5] WHITE**[242], born 5 Mar 1889 in Williamsburg, Clermont Co, OH; died 27 Jun 1949; buried in Williamsburg Cemetery. He married on 22 Jun 1910 in Clermont Co, OH **Mabel LEEDS**, born 2 Jun 1892 in New Harmony, IN; died 4 Oct 1979 in Clermont Co, OH. No children.
          Jones notes: "she resides (1974) at 194 N. Front St, Williamsburg, OH; no children"
          Mentioned in 1941 Admin Docket "gr nephew Laurence White of Williamsburg" but not in 1932 Will of Mary H. Kline
          Census 1920 Williamsburg, Clermont, OH, p. 11B. Lawrence White 32, OH, manager - chair factory; Mabel L White 28, OH.
          1930 Williamsburg, Clermont, OH, p. 1B. Lawrence W White 43, manager - chairs; Mable L White 38, OH.
          Discrepancy: 1900 census and draft registration gives birth as Mar 1887; Jones notes give 1889.
          Military: World War I Draft Registration Cards, 1917-1918 [ancestry.com] Lawrence Webster White, age 30, b. 5 Mar 1887, Williamsburg, OH; res: Williamsburg, Clermont, OH; occ: manufacturer & miller - J. A. White & self; married; med height, stout, blue eyes, black hair; Regis: Williamsburg, OH, 2 Sep - no year given.
          No death information found.

                        @@For more information, see research notes at end of chapter.

516 iv **Mina P.**[5] **WHITE**, born 28 Jun 1891 in Williamsburg, Clermont Co, OH; died 18 Aug 1965 in Clermont Co, OH; buried in Williamsburg Cemetery. Never married.
    Mentioned in 1932 Will of Mary H. Kline as gr niece Mina White of New Rochelle, NY; 1941 Admin Docket as Gr-niece Mina White of Williamsburg
    Living in Williamsburg, OH in 1930 Maggie, 62, daughter Mina, 35, & sister in law Mina, 59, who is a stenographer, chair factory. Living next door to son, Nicholas, proprietor, chair factory.
    Death: Mina P White b. 1891; res: Clermont Co, OH; d. 22 Aug 1965, home, Clermont Co, OH, age 74. Ohio Deaths, 1908-1932, 1938-1944, and 1958-2002 [Ancestry.com]

517 v **Russell L.**[5] **WHITE**, born 17 Oct 1892 in Williamsburg, Clermont Co, OH; died 1902 in Williamsburg Twp, Clermont, OH; buried in Williamsburg Cemetery
    Notes: 1900 census gives birth as Mar 1892.
    Death: Russell White d. 2 Feb 1902 Williamsburg Twp, Clermont, OH, age 9. B. 1893. Ohio Deaths and Burials, 1854-1997 <pilot.familysearch.org>

+ 518 vi **Nicholas James**[5] **WHITE**.

235. Bessie[4] **KING** (Sarah[3] HICKS, James[2], Joshua[1]), born Oct 1878 in Indiana. She married on 26 May 1901 in Saint Joseph, Berrien, MI **William Fernando ROBERTSON**, born 1 Dec 1877 in Wisconsin; died 1925/30 in North Dakota.

Bessie King married William F. Robertson in St Joseph, Michigan. Both William and Bessie were "of Chicago, IL" at the time of their marriage. William's occupation was physician and Bessie was listed as a music teacher. After their marriage, they moved to Rollette Co, ND, where William was both a physician and president of a bank.@@

    Children of Bessie KING and William Fernando ROBERTSON were:
    519 i **Robert K.**[5] **ROBERTSON**, born abt 1913 in North Dakota.

236. Wakefield Edward[4] **KING** (Sarah[3] HICKS, James[2], Joshua[1]), born 23 Nov 1878 in Indiana. He married on 27 Jun 1905 in Mendon, St Joseph, MI **Grace M MAUFORT**, born abt 1878.

Wakefield King was a miller like his father. He appeared to have spent most of his life in Leonidas, Michigan. He married Grace Manfort/Maufort and had two children.@@

    Children of Wakefield Edward KING and Grace M MAUFORT were:
    520 i **Harlan E.**[5] **KING**, born abt 1907 in Michigan. He married abt 1920 **Gladys -?-**, born abt 1903 in Wisconsin.
        Census: 1930 Chicago, Cook, IL, p. 10B. Harlan E King 23, MI/IN/MI, bookkeeper - auto part sup co.; Gladys R King 28, WI/Nor/WI, file clerk - school supply, married age 22/27
    521 ii **Glada**[5] **KING**, born abt 1911 in Michigan. She married abt 1920 in Michigan **Gay WARREN**, born abt 1905 in Michigan.
        Census 1930 Leonidas, St Joseph, MI, p. 5A. Wakefield King 51, IN/Eng/OH, miller - flour mill; Grace M King 52, MI/NY/MI, m. age 26/27; Gay L Warren 25, son-in-law, MI/MI/MI, laborer - odd jobs; Glada L Warren 19, dau. Parents married age 24/19

@@For more information, see research notes at end of chapter.

238. Robert A.[4] HICKS (William J.[3], James[2], Joshua[1]), born Jul 1874 in OH. He married[243] on 25 Dec 1897 in Wayne Co, IN **Nora HUDDLESTON**, born Jan 1877 in Indiana, daughter of Rollin HUDDLESTON and Mary FURY.

Robert Hicks was a banker by profession and apparently lived in Wayne Co, IN all his working life. He and wife, Nora, had two daughters, Helen and Eva Lou.@@

    Children of Robert A. HICKS and Nora HUDDLESTON were:

522 i **Helen[5] HICKS**, born Jun 1899 in IN. Notes: "My Royal Family" - on Ancestry.com lists Robert's daughter Helen b. 1899; d. 1952, unmarried. No documentation.
    *Death: Helen Hicks b. 06 Feb 1897; d. Mar 1979; age 82; Bremen, Marshall, IN; card issued: Illinois; #351-18-1229 [*may not be right person..]

523 ii **Eva Lou[5] HICKS**, born abt 1906 in IN. No other information.

240. Luella[4] SMITH (Georgia Anna[3] HICKS, James[2], Joshua[1]), born 12 Jun 1873 in Cincinnati, OH; died 31 Jan 1930 in Cincinnati, Hamilton, OH; buried 3 Feb 1930 in Spring Grove Cemetery. She married (1) bef 1887 **-?- BORSO**; (2) bef 1893, divorced **George KOEHLER**; (3) in Sep 1904 in Hamilton Co, OH **Henry T. BRUNS**.

Luella Smith married three times and had children from two of the marriages. She apparently lived with her widowed mother, Georgianna, for much of her life. Because the children were discovered late in the compiling process, they are numbered with their mother's number, plus a and b, rather than renumbering the whole book. @@

    Children of Luella SMITH and -?- BORSO were:
    240a i **Georgiana[5] BORSO**, born Sep 1887 in Ohio.

    Children of Luella SMITH and George KOEHLER were:
    240b i **Albert[5] KOEHLER**, born Jul 1893 in Ohio.

241. William Morse[4] HICKS[244] (James Reuben[3], James[2], Joshua[1]), born 8 Sep 1887 in Amelia, Clermont Co, OH; buried in Spring Grove Cemetery, Cincinnati OH. He married on 27 Dec 1917 in Clermont Co, OH **Elizabeth B. MCDONALD**, born 16 Nov 1895 in Newark, Essex Co, NJ; died 1931; buried in Spring Grove Cemetery, Cincinnati OH.

William Morse Hicks was a physician and served as a Captain during World War I. His service included time in France where he was awarded the French Croix de Guerre with bronze star. He and his wife Elizabeth had 3 children, two daughters and a son. @@

    Children of William Morse HICKS and Elizabeth B. MCDONALD were:

524 i **William Morse[5] HICKS Jr**, born 17 Mar 1924.
    Jones notes: "resides (1993) in Victoria, TX; wife Dorothy; in a deed to O. Hutson in 1949, Wm & Dorothy witnessed in Bernalillo Co, NM (Albuquerque area)"

525 ii **Frances[5] HICKS**, born 2 Oct 1925.
    Jones notes: "resides (1993) in Avon Park, FL; married ___ Frazier"

@@For more information, see research notes at end of chapter.

> 526 iii **Eleanor**[5] **HICKS**, born 15 Mar 1929 in Cincinnati, Hamilton Co, OH.
> Jones notes: "resides (1993) at 6427 Ridge Cir, San Antonio, TX 98233; (Putt) after Eleanor in his notes - nickname or marriage?

247. Edward[4] **NEWKIRK** (William David[3], Nancy[2] HICKS, Joshua[1]), born 19 Jun 1874 in Moultrie Co, IL; died 11 May 1959. He married on 20 Oct 1897 in Bloomfield, IL **Elizabeth HARRIS**, born est.1874; died 16 Jan 1939.

Edward Newkirk, though born in Illinois, lived his adult life in Davis Co, Iowa. He was a farmer all his life. @@

> Children of Edward NEWKIRK and Elizabeth HARRIS were:
> 527 i **Raymond E.**[5] **NEWKIRK**, born 27 May 1901 in Iowa; died 11 Mar 1964.
> **Death**: SS Death Index gives: Raymond Newkirk b. 27 May 1901; d. Mar 1964; age 62; place not specified; card issued Iowa; #483-18-8874

248. Mary Ellen[4] **NEWKIRK** (William David[3], Nancy[2] HICKS, Joshua[1]), born 14 Aug 1879 in Moultrie Co, IL; died 8 Dec 1912. She married on 22 Mar 1903 in Drakesville, Davis Co, IA **James Hansford COX**[245], born 16 Dec 1882 in MO.

Mollie Newkirk married James H. Cox, who worked for the railroad in 1910. By 1920, the family had moved to Sheridan Co, Kansas, where James was listed as a farmer. @@

> Children of Mary Ellen NEWKIRK and James Hansford COX were:
> 528 i **Roy W.**[5] **COX**, born est 1904.
> Jones notes: "resides (1974) at 917 Locust St, apt 128, Des Moines, IA - answered phone, ill health & no interest"
> **Census**
> 1920 Capital, Hutchinson, SD, p. 6. Howard W Johnston 38, farmer - general farm; Cora 35, IL/OH/IL; Doyle H 10, IA; Verle E 8, SD; Loren K 5, SD; Roy W Cox 16, IA, nephew, farm labor [son of Cora's sister Mary Ellen].
> *1930 Des Moines, Polk, IA, p. 20A. Roy W Cox 24, IA/IA/NY, laborer - warehouse; Mary A Cox 23, IA/IA/IA; James R Cox 9/12; Joseph W Couch 21, brother in law. *may not be right family; birthplace of mother is wrong.
> *Death: May be: SS Death Index: Roy Cox b. 02 Mar 1906; d. Mar 1982, Des Moines, Polk, IA; #481-26-5801; issued: Iowa
> 529 ii **Inez**[5] **COX**, born abt 1906 in IA.
> 530 iii **Mildred**[5] **COX**, born abt 1908 in IA.
> IA State Census: 1925 Drakesville, Davis Co, IA. Wm D Newkirk 80, father: Nelson Newkirk, mother: Nancy Hicks; Mildred Cox 17, granddau., b. IA, father: James Cox b MO, mother: Mollie Newkirk, b. IL
> 530a iv **Edwin COX**, born abt 1919, prob Sheridan Co, KS. No other information.

249. Cora[4] **NEWKIRK** (William David[3], Nancy[2] HICKS, Joshua[1]), born 11 Aug 1884 in Moultrie Co, IL; died Apr 1982 in Bloomfield, Davis, IA. She married on 11 Mar 1907 in Drakesville, Davis Co, IA **Howard Washington JOHNSTON**[246], born 20 Jun 1881 in Mt Carroll, Carroll Co, IL; died Jan 1985 in Bloomfield, Davis, IA, son of George and Kate JOHNSTON.

@@For more information, see research notes at end of chapter.

Cora Newkirk and her husband Howard Johnston were married in Iowa, but moved to South Dakota soon afterward. Howard Johnston was listed as a farmer in both 1920 and 1930. They returned to Iowa before 1974, and both died in Bloomfield – Cora at age 97 and Howard at age 103. @@

    Children of Cora NEWKIRK and Howard Washington JOHNSTON were:
+   531 i   **Doyle Howard[5] JOHNSTON**.
+   532 ii   **Verle[5] JOHNSTON**.
+   533 iii **Loren K.[5] JOHNSTON**.

251. Verna[4] HICKS (Charles James[3], Joshua[2], Joshua[1]), born Nov 1886 in IL; died[247] Oct 1970 in Paris, Edgar Co, IL. She married on 12 Sep 1909 in Paris, IL **William Lafayette WHEELER**, born[248] 18 Jun 1884 in IL.

Verna Hicks married William Wheeler in Edgar Co, IL, where William was a mail clerk for at least 30 years. They had one daughter, Elizabeth. @@

    Children of Verna HICKS and William Lafayette WHEELER were:
    534 i   **Elizabeth P.[5] WHEELER**, born abt 1919 in IL.

254. Mary Cecil[4] HICKS (Charles James[3], Joshua[2], Joshua[1]), born Feb 1890 in Illinois; died aft 1930. She married on 12 Aug 1912 **Chester SMITTKAMP**, born[249] 28 Sep 1887 in Redmon, IL; died[250] 16 Mar 1931 in Paris, Edgar Co, IL, son of Joseph and Sabin SMITTKAMP.

Mary Cecil Hicks, called Cecil, married Chester Smittkamp, a farmer, and evidently lived in Edgar Co, IL all their lives. They had 3 children. @@

    Children of Mary Cecil HICKS and Chester SMITTKAMP were:
    535 i   **Charles[5] SMITTKAMP**, born abt 1915 in IL.
    536 ii   **Chester Allen[5] SMITTKAMP**, born 1 Jan 1918 in IL; died 27 Mar 2010 in Terre Haute, Vigo, IN.
           Death: SS Death Index: Chester Allen Smittkamp; #323-20-6480; Last Residence: 47805 Terre Haute, Vigo, Indiana; Born: 1 Jan 1918; Died: 27 Mar 2010; SSN issued: Illinois
    537 iii **James[5] SMITTKAMP**, born 24 May 1924 in IL; died 11 May 1995 in Paris, Edgar Co, IL.
           Death: Probably the James E. Smittkamp on SS Death Index: James E Smittkamp b. 24 May 1924; d. 11 May 1995; Paris, Edgar, IL

257. Glenn Alvin[4] HICKS (Albert Alden[3], Joshua[2], Joshua[1]), born 25 Nov 1882, probably in Edgar Co, IL; died 5 Mar 1954. He married **Mayme Ethel HALL**, born 5 Mar 1884 in Terre Haute, Vigo Co, IN; died 21 Jan 1959.

Glenn A. Hicks was a farmer in Edgar Co, IL, apparently for his whole life. He was of medium height and build, with brown eyes and slightly balding hair at age 36. No further information is known about this family. @@

    Children of Glenn Alvin HICKS and Mayme Ethel HALL were:
    538 i   **Ruth[5] HICKS**, born abt 1907 in Illinois.
    539 ii   **Merle[5] HICKS**, born abt 1908 in Illinois.

@@For more information, see research notes at end of chapter.

540 iii   **Mabel**[5] **HICKS**, born abt 1910 in Illinois.

541 iv   **Wendell**[5] **HICKS**, born abt 1914 in Illinois; died 30 Aug 1996 in Beecher, Illinois Co, IN. Jones notes: "resides (1984) at Rt 1, Box 40, Beecher, Illinois 60401". May be the Wendell Hicks who died 30 Aug 1996 in Beecher, Illinois Co, IN. SS Death Index gives birth date as 1914.

542 v   **Miriam**[5] **HICKS**, born abt 1916 in Illinois.

543 vi   **EmIllinois**[5] **HICKS**, born abt 1919 in Illinois.

544 vii   **Mary E.**[5] **HICKS**, born abt 1922 in Illinois.

545 viii   **Richard A.**[5] **HICKS**, born abt 1925 in Illinois.

260. **Charles Jefferson**[4] **HICKS** (Albert Alden[3], Joshua[2], Joshua[1]), born 12 Sep 1894 in Elbridge Co, IL; died[251] 4 Jul 1976 in Dennison, Clark Co, IL. He married on 11 Sep 1915 **Edna CLEM**, born 21 Jul 1894 in IL; died 4 Sep 1938 in Edgar Co, IL, daughter of Willes A and Nancy E. CLEM.

Charles Hicks was a farmer in Clark Co, IL. Jones notes state "4 sons; names not listed". Census records indicate sons Albert, Bernard and Bennett. No further information on this family. @@

    Children of Charles Jefferson HICKS and Edna CLEM were:

       546 i   **Willis Albert**[5] **HICKS**, born 19 Mar 1916 in IL; died 28 Jan 2008 in Denver, Denver Co, CO.

           Death: SS Death Index gives: Willis A Hicks, b. 19 Mar 1916; d. 28 Jan 2008 Denver, Denver, CO #339-03-4702; issued: Illinois

       547 ii   **Bernard Russell**[5] **HICKS**, born 19 Sep 1919 in IL; died 24 Jun 1994 in Dennison, Clark, IL.

           Military: World War II Army Enlistment Records, 1938-1946 [Ancestry.com] Bernard R Hicks b. 1919 Illinois; res: Edgar Co, Illinois; Enlistment: 5 Mar 1941, Paris, IL; Branch: Infantry; Grade: Corporal; National Guard (Officers, Warrant Officers, and Enlisted Men); Education: 3 years of high school; Civil Occupation: Attendants, filling stations and parking lots; Single, without dependents; Height: 70; Weight: 155

           Death: SS death index gives: Bernard Hicks, b. 21 Sep 1919; d. 24 Jun 1994 Dennison, Clark, IL #326-14-9775; issued: Illinois

+   548 iii   **Willard Burnett**[5] **HICKS**.

@@For more information, see research notes at end of chapter.

Research Notes for Generation 4

Notes for Francis M. MANNING #74

Jones notes: "Resided at Spann"

Census:

1880 OH, Clermont Co, Tate Twp. p. 264. Francis M. Manning 32, farmer; Caroline 26; Cora 2, dau; May 13, sister

1900 Pierce Twp. Clermont Co, OH, p. 198. Francis Manning 55, Nov 1844, OH/OH/OH, farmer, m. 28 yr ; Caroline E 47, Apr 1853, OH/PA/OH, 6 ch, 5 liv.; Lucinda 19, Sep 1880; Walter 15, Nov 1884; Grace 10, Apr 1890; William 8, May 1892; Ethel 5, Jun 1894.

1910 Millcreek, Hamilton Co, OH p. 4A. Francis Manning 62, laborer - factory, m. 32 yr; Carolina 56, wife, 6 ch/4 liv, Grace 22, William 19; Ethel 17; Alpha Fagin 12, granddaughter. Son Walter, 26, is two houses away.

Not in Ohio Death Index 1908-1953.

Notes for Caroline HANLEY #71s

Death: Caroline H. Manning, 700 E. Ross Ave, St Bernard, Hamilton Co, OH. B. 4/14/1853 Bethel, Clermont Co, OH; d. 4/3/1944, age 90 yr, 11 mo, 20 days. Father: Redmond Hanley; mother: Margaret Liming, b. Hamersville, OH. Widowed; Spouse: Francis M. Manning. Burial: Bethel Cemetery; Informant: Mrs Ethel Tekulve, same address. <familysearch.org>

Census:

1920 Cincinnati Ward 26, Hamilton Co, OH, p. 1A. William B. Tekulve 29, OH/Ger/Ger, boiler maker - iron works; Ethel 25, William A. 2 6/12, Mildred E. 8/12?; Caroline Manning, 66, widow, mother in law.

1930 St Bernard, Hamilton Co, OH, p. 19B. William B Tekulve 39, boiler maker - sheet metal; Ethel E 35; William N 13; Mildred E 10; Mary F. 7 4/12; Carolina Manning 75. mother in law.

Notes for William MANNING #268

Military: World War I Draft Registration Cards, 1917-1918 [Ancestry.com] William Manning, age 26, b. 11 May 1891, South Bamton, OH; res: Cincinnati, Hamilton Co, OH; occ: messenger - postal delivery; single; relatives: parents; disability - right arm missing; med height, slender, blue eyes, light hair; regis: 5 Jun 1917, Cincinnati, OH.

Death: William Manning, d. 03 May 1931 Cincinnati, Hamilton, OH; b. 11 May 1891, Bethel, OH; Age: 39 years 11 months 22 days; Single; Address: 5525 Vine St. St. Bernard, OH; Occ: Laborer; Burial: 6 May 1931, Bethel, OH; Father: Francis Manning, b. Bethel, Ohio; Mother: Caroline Hanley, b. Bethel, Ohio. Ohio Deaths, 1908-1953 <fsbeta.familysearch.org>

Discrepancy: 1900 census gives birth as May 1892; death record gives 11 May 1891

Notes for Mary A. 'Mollie' MANNING #73

Census:

1880 Tate, Clermont, OH, p. 272. John Pattison 34 , farmer; Mary A. Pattison 30; Clarence Pattison 5; Edward Pattison 3; Lizzie M. Pattison 1; James L. Beall 32, farm labor. All b. OH.

1900 Monroe Twp, Clermont Co, OH, Page 143. HH#130. John S. Pattison 54, Mar 1846, farmer, with wife Mary 51, Jun 1848; Clarence 25, Nov 1874, school teacher, Myrtle 20, Jun 1879; Walter 15, Mar 1883; Dale 12, Oct 1887; Frank 8, Oct 1891. Last 3: "at school". Married 26 years; 7 children, all living.

1910 Ohio, Clermont, OH, p. 5B. Marry A Patson 60, widow, 7 ch/7 living; Dale L Patson 22, salesman - retail hardware; Frank L Patson 18. All OH/OH/OH

Death: Mary A. Pattison, b. 20 Jun 1849, OH; d. 2 Sep 1913, Miami, Clermont Co, OH, age 65/2/12. Widow, Father: William Maning, b. OH; mother: __ Tatman, b. OH. Buried: Pt Isabel, OH, 4 Sep 1913.

-128-

Informant: E. H. Pattison, Owensville, OH. [probably son Edward H. Pattison]. Ohio Deaths 1908-1953 <pilot.familysearch.org>

Notes for Clarence E. PATTISON #270:
Jones notes: "not married; taught school at Van Wert, OH"; on 1900 census with parents.

Census:
- 1920 E. Cleveland Ward 3, Cuyahoga, OH p. 14B. Clarence E. Pattison, 45, teacher, boarding with John A. McKenney, 34, mech. engineer.
- 1930 E. Cleveland Ward 3, Cuyahoga, OH, Dist 603, p. 1B. Clarence E. Pattison, 55, single, teacher - public schools. Boarding with Ira J. Emery.
- 1910 A Clarence Pattison, 45, is boarding with Walter Bullard in Middletown, Burler Co, OH. [p. 4A, HH#75] Occ: toolman. Has wife Lorette, children Daisy 4, James 4/12. Probably not same person, but possible.

Death: Clarence E. Pattison, b. 17 Nov 1874 Bethel, OH; d. 25 Oct 1951, Cincinnati, OH. Res: 3626 Zumstein Ave, Cincinnati. Single, Teacher - retired. Father: John S. Pattison; Mother: Mary E. Manning. Informant Mrs Myrtle E. Rumhardt. OH Deaths 1908-1953 <pilot.familysearch.org>

Notes for Myrtle E. PATTISON #272
Jones notes: "no children; resided at Branch Hill; in Cincinnati OH in 1942"

Census:
- 1920 Covington, Kenton Co, KY, p. 1. Ross Pattison, 37, fireman, city; Ann, wife, 32; Robert, son, 7 7/12; Myrtle Reinhardt, sister, 40 [43?], single.
- 1930 Moscow, Clermont Co, OH p. 2B. Clarence H Reinhardt 42, OH/Ger/OH, machinist - state highway; Myrtle 48, OH/OH/KY, m. age 28. Elizabeth St.

Notes for Dale L. PATTISON #275
Jones notes: "no children"

Census:
- 1920 not found.
- 1930 Huntington, Cabell Co, WV, p. 4B. Dale L. Pattison, 42, shoe merchant.; roomer in home of Samuel Sayres.

Military: World War I Draft Registration Cards, 1917-1918 [Ancestry.com] Dale Lester Pattison; age 29, b. 1 Oct 1887, Bethel, OH; res: Cincinnati, Hamilton Co, OH; occ: salesman - Petter Shoe Co; single, med height, slender, blue eyes, brown hair. Regis: Cincinnati, Hamilton Co, OH, 5 Jun 1917.

Military: World War II Draft Registration Cards, 1942 [Ancestry.com]. Dale Lester Pattison, age 54, b. 1 Oct 1887, Bethel, Clermont Co, OH; Res: Wm H. Taft Rd, Cincinnati, OH; relative: sister Mrs. Myrtle Reinhart, same address; occ: McDivitts Men's Shop, Cincinnati

Death: Dale L Pattison, b. 1887, Male; res: Cincinnati, Hamilton Co, OH; d.. 3 Dec 1959, Cincinnati, OH. age 72; Never Married. Ohio Deaths, 1908-1932, 1938-1944, and 1958-2007 [Ancestry.com]

Notes for John Wesley MANNING #74
Jones notes: "resided Williamsburg"

Census:
- 1880 Williamsburg, Clermont, OH, p. 374. John Manning 29, farmer; Laura 28; Orville 4. Next door to Charles Manning.
- 1900 Williamsburg East, Clermont, OH, p.312. John W. Manning, head, Aug 1849, 50, married 26 yr, OH/OH/OH, farmer; Laura F?, wife, Jan 1851, 49, Mar 26 yr, 1 ch/ 1 liv, OH/OH/OH; Orville, son, Feb 1876, 24, single, OH/OH/OH, school teacher. Two houses from Charles Manning.
- 1910 Not found; son Orville is living with in-laws, Wright Sprague, in Williamsburg, Clermont OH. Wife Laura is with her brother, Thomas, and sister, Malvina, and is listed as a widow.

Death: Not found in Ohio Deaths 1908-1953, so probably died between 1900-1908. His wife, Laura, was listed as a widow on the 1910 census.

Notes for Laura Francis VICKROY #74s

Census:

1870 Tate, Clermont, OH, p. 318. Ellen Vickrey 52, farm manager; Malvina Vickrey 23; Thomas Vickrey 21; Laura Vickrey 19. All b. OH.

1910 Tate, Clermont, OH, p. 2A. Thomas H Vickrey 51, single; Melvinie Vickrey 63, sister; Laura Manning 49. sister, widow

1920 Tate, Clermont, OH, p. 4B. Laura F Manning 67, widow, OH/OH/OH; Vina E Vickroy 75, sister.

Death: Laura Francis Manning, widow, b. Jan 19, 1851, OH; d. June 13, 1923, aged 72, 4, 28. Informant: O. L. Manning, Williamsburg, OH. Buried Bethel Cemetery. OH Death 1908-1953 <pilot.familysearch.org>;

Notes for Charles William MANNING #77

Census:

1900 Williamsburg East, Clermont, OH, p. 312. Charles W. Manning, head, Oct 1855, 45, married 22 yr, OH/OH/OH, farmer; Edith L., wife, May 1858, 42, m. 22 yr, 7 ch/ 6 liv, OH/OH/-; Ora C., son, Oct 1879, 20, single, OH/OH/OH, farm laborer; Chilton, son, Sep 1882, 17, single, day labor: Walter L. son, Mar 1892, 8, single, at school; Lowell B., son, Dec 1896, 3; Raleigh H., son, Dec 1896. Two houses from John Manning.

1910 Williamsburg, Clermont County, OH, p 7B. Charles W Manning 54, farmer - gen. farm; Edith L 53, m. 31 yr, 7 ch/6 liv; Chilton H 27, farm labor; Walter 18, farm labor; Lowell 13; Raleigh 13.

1920 Tate, Clermont, OH, p. 9A. Charles Manning 64, no occ; Edith 61; Chilton H 36, motorman - street railway; Walter 27, motorman - street railway;; Lewell 23, worker - rubber factory.

1930 - not found.

Death: Charles William Manning, b. 25 Oct 1855, OH; d. Feb 28, 1947, Williamsburg, Clermont Co, OH. age 91 yrs, 4 mo, 13 days; widowed, wife: Edith. Parents: William Manning; Melinda Tatman. Informant: Chilton Manning, Bethel, OH. Buried: Bethel Cemetery, 4 Mar 1947. Ohio Deaths 1908-1953 <pilot.familysearch.org>

Burial: Bethel Cemetery, Tate Twp, Clermont, Ohio; Sec. 9, Lot 78, Grave 1-5

Notes for Edith L. RILEY #77s

Probably died before 1908 as she wasn't on Ohio Death Index 1908-1953.

Notes for Walter L. MANNING #283

Census:

1930 Highland Park, Wayne, MI, p. 13A. Wm Burkhardt 61; Alena Burkhardt 54; Robert Vandergriff 34; Betty Vandergriff 9; Wilma Burkhardt 20; Walter Manning 37, single, OH/OH/OH, lodger, motorman - street railroad.

Military: Walter L. Manning, Serial Number: 2930739; Residence: 2112 Freeman Ave., Cincinnati, O.; Enlistment Division: National Army; Enlistment Location: Cincinnati, O.; Enlistment Date: 27 Jun 1918; Birth Place: Bethel, O.; Assigns Comment: 158 Depot Brigade to Discharge Private Honorable discharge 14 Dec 1918. Ohio Military Men, 1917-18 [Ancestry.com]

Death: Walter L Manning b. 1892, Clermont Co, OH; d. 28 Apr 1966, Hamilton Co, OH; Age 74; never married. Burial: Bethel Cemetery, Tate Twp, Clermont, OH, Sec. 9, Lot 78, Grave 1-5. Ohio Deaths, 1908-1932, 1938-1944, and 1958-2007 [Ancestry.com]

Notes for Homer Jerome FITZPATRICK #79

Jones notes: "with Rebecca Frazier in 1870"

Census:

1870 Tate, Clermont Co, OH. Working as an 18-year old farm laborer on farm of Rebecca Frazier, 70.

1880 Monroe, Clermont Co, OH, p. 174A. Jerome H. Fitzpatrick 28 farmer, OH/KY/OH; Susan Fitzpatrick 24, VA/KY/OH; John Fitzpatrick 23, brother, farm labor, OH/OH/VA; John Cecebaugh 80, f-in-law, VA/VA/VA

1900 Hayfield, Campbell, KY, p. 17B. Jerome H Fitzpatrick 48, Oct 1851, farmer; Susan A Fitzpatrick 45, Oct 1854; Pearl D Fitzpatrick 17, Dec 1882; John C Fitzpatrick 11, Oct 1888; Walter Willis 21, hired man

1910 Batavia, Clermont, OH, p. 7A. Homer Fitzpatrick 58, OH/OH/OH, farmer, m. 34 yrs; Susana Fitzpatrick 56, 3 ch / 2 living, IN/PA/KY; Pearl Fitzpatrick 26, accountant - art manuf.; Charles Fitzpatrick 21, laborer

1920 Batavia (Clermont) OH, p. 3A. Jerome H Fitzpatrick 68, farmer; Susie A Fitzpatrick 65; Ruth Fitzpatrick 57, sister.

1930 Batavia (Clermont) OH, District 3, p. 173. Homer Fitzpatrick, 78, farmer; Susan, 75, b. IN; Charles J, 44, son, widowed, veterinary surgeon; Wayne N, 8, grandson.

Notes for Susan A. TEVEBAUGH #79s

Jones notes give birth as 8 Jul 1855 in VA; death certificate gives 17 Oct 1854 in IN.

Death: Ohio Death Certificate <pilot.familysearch.org>. Gives parents as John Tevebaugh & Miriam Sagaser, both b. PA.

Census:

1860 Ninevah, Johnson, IN show parents as John Tevebough, b. abt 1800 VA; mother Marion, b. abt 1818 KY

1870 Deer Creek, Cass.,IN. Working as a 16 year old domestic servant in home of William Britton. John Tevebaugh, 21, is working as a hired hand a few houses away. Her father, John 70, is living with the Sagaser family in the same area, probably with his wife's family.

Notes for Sarah Ellen FITZPATRICK #80

Jones notes: "removed to Birmingham, AL 1876"

Census:

1870 Tate, Clermont, OH, p. 309A. Living with John & Jane Tatman. John Tatman 40, Farmer, Jane Tatman 36; William Tatman 17; John C Tatman 13; Mary R Tatman 11; Archibald Tatman 8; Maud Tatman 5; Louis Tatman 3; Sarah Fitzpatrick 20, servant; Ida B Fitzpatrick 7; Archibald McNair 40, farm labor, SCO. [Sarah & Ida Fitzpatrick are nieces of John Tatman, their mother's brother]

1880 Beat 2, Morgan, AL, p. 79. Samuel O. Higgins 30, farmer, OH/OH/MD; Sarah E. Higgins 30; Guy Higgins 5; Claud C. Higgins 4; Burton Higgins 2; Fredrick A. Higgins 8M, AL/OH/OH. Other OH/OH/OH

1900 Blountsville, Blount, AL, p. 1B. Samuel O Higgins 50, Oct 1849, mail contractor, OH/NC/Ger; Sarah E Higgins 50, Jan 1850, OH/OH/OH; Wm Z Higgins 16, May 1884, AL/OH/OH; Leroy Higgins 14, Feb 1886, AL/OH/OH; James M Higgins 10, Feb 1890, AL/OH/OH. 8 ch / 5 living; m. 26 years

1910 Garden City, Cullman, AL, p. 3A. Samuel O Higgins 60, OH/NJ/Ger, farmer; Sarah E Higgins 60; James M Higgins 20, son, AL, telegrapher - r.r.; m. 36 yrs, 8 children, 5 living.

1920 Garden City, Cullman, AL, p. 2A. Samuel Higgins 70, OH/Eng/Eng, farmer; Sarah Higgins 70, OH/Eng/Eng.

1930 not found

Death: Sarah Ellen Higgins, d. 11 May 1921, Blount, AL; Age: 71y 3m 19d; Est. Birth Date 1850; Spouse: Samuel O. Higgins; Father: Zacharia Fitzpatrick; Mother: Diana Tattman. Alabama Deaths, 1908-1974 <fsbeta.familysearch.org>

Notes for Samuel Oliver HIGGINS #80s
Census: 1850 Washington, Clermont, OH, p. 46A. William J Higgins 30; Nancy A Higgins 27; Adeline E Higgins 5; Mary E Higgins 3; Samuel C Higgins 0; Abraham Cosman 64; Hannah Higgins 17
Death: Samuel Oliver Higgins, d. 5 Feb 1929, Garden City, Cullman, AL. Age at Death 79y 3m 10d; b. 26 Oct 1849, New Richmond, OH, Widowed; spouse: Sarah Ellen Higgins; Father: William Higgins, b. NC; Mother: Nancy Ann Coffman, b. Germany; Occ: Farmer; Burial: Garden City Cremation, 6 Feb 1929. Alabama Deaths, 1908-1974 <fsbeta.familysearch.org>

Notes for George E. FITZPATRICK #82
Children of Zach & Dianna Fitzpatrick were divided among different relatives and neighbors in 1870 after death of both parents in 1867.
Living with family of William Anderson, Tate Twp, Clermont Co 1870, p. 319 ; parents of Milita (Anderson) Tatman?
Census:
- 1870 Tate, Clermont, OH, p. 319. William Anderson 69; Mary Anderson 58; Margaret Anderson 19; George Fitzpatrick 16
- 1880 & 1900 not found
- 1910 Tate, Clermont, OH, p. 10B. George E Fitzpatrick 53, farmer; Sarah F Fitzpatrick 53, OH/PA/OH; Hanley G Fitzpatrick 7. All b. OH. M. 9 yrs, 1 child.
- 1920 Tate, Clermont, OH, p. 4B. George E Fitzpatrick 65, farmer; Sarah F Fitzpatrick 63; Hanley G Fitzpatrick 17, farmer.
- 1930 Tate, Clermont, OH, p. 2B. George G Fitzpatrick 76, farmer; Hanley L Fitzpatrick 74, wife; Hanley G Fitzpatrick 28, farmer.

Death: George E. Fitzpatrick, b. Jun 1854 OH; d. 30 Oct 1940, Tate Twp, Clermont, OH; Age: 86 years; Widowed; Occ: Farmer; Res: Bethel, Ohio; Burial: 1 Nov 1940, Bethel Cemetery; Spouse: Sadie Fitzpatrick; parents: Zacheriah Fitzpatrick, b. Ohio; Dianne Tatman, b. OH. Ohio Deaths, 1908-1953 <familysearch.org>

Notes for Sadie HANLEY #82s
Death: Sarah F. Fitzpatrick, b. 5 Jan 1856 OH; d. 25 Sep 1931 Tate, Clermont, OH; Age: 75 years; Married; Burial: 27 Sep 1931, Bethel Cemetery; Father: Redman Hanley, b. PA; Mother: M. Linning, b. Ohio. Ohio Deaths, 1908-1953 <pilot.familysearch.org>

Notes for Walter FITZPATRICK #85
Children were living with different relatives and neighbors in 1870 after death of both parents in 1867. Jones notes: "resided (1892) in Montgomery AL; with John McNair in 1870 & 1880; 2 dau."
Census:
- 1870 Tate, Clermont, OH, p. 309. John Mcnair 38, farmer, Scotland; Polly Mcnair 36; Grant Mcnair 4; Walter Fitchpatrick 9.
- 1880 Tate, Clermont, OH, p. 264. John Mc Nair 47, farmer, Scotland; Mary Mc Nair 47; Grant Mc Nair 14; Eddie Mc Nair 9; Walter Fitzpatrick 19, nephew; Ida Fitzpatrick 17, niece
- 1900 Augusta Ward 1, Richmond, GA, p. 24A. Walter S Fitzpatrick 39, Apr 1861, OH/OH/OH, mirror restoration?; Addie Fitzpatrick 33, Oct 1866, GA/GA/GA; Ethel G Fitzpatrick 9, Jan 1891, AL; Mabel L Fitzpatrick 4, May 1896, AL.

1910 Denver, Denver, CO, p. 5G. Addie Fitzpatrick 40; widow, GA, keeper - rooming house; Ethel Fitzpatrick 19, AL/OH/GA, dressmaker; Mable Fitzpatrick 13, AL/OH/GA; John D Stipp 16, boarder, laborer - freight office; Daniel W Stipp 21, boarder, laborer - freight office.

1920 not found - remarried or died?

Notes for John Lee FITZPATRICK #97

Census

1880 not found; not living with parents.

1900 Montgomery Ward 2, Montgomery, AL, p. 6A. John L Fitzpatrick 38, Oct 1861, OH, real estate; Maggie Fitzpatrick 28, Jul 1871; Hal Fitzpatrick 4, Jun 1895, AL; Lizzie M Manning 24, Dec 1875, boarder; Georgia Manning 22, Mar 1878, boarder. Other OH/OH/OH

1910 Montgomery Ward 2, Montgomery, AL, p. 35A. J L Fitzpatrick 54, OH, real estate agent; Mrs M M Fitzpatrick 38; J L Fitzpatrick Jr 9, AL; H T Fitzpatrick 2, AL. 4 ch / 2 living.

1920 not found

1930 Montgomery, Montgomery, AL, p. 2A. Maggie Fitzpatrick 56, OH, widow; Homer Fitzpatrick 27, AL/OH/OH, office clerk - railroad.

Death: John L. Fitzpatrick; Death: Jun 1929, Montgomery, AL. Alabama Deaths, 1908-59 <familysearch.org>

Notes for Margaret M. MANNING #97s

Census: 1880 Franklin, Clermont, OH, p. 53D. Geo. W. Manning 39; Mary E. Manning 33; Cally Manning 10; Maggie M. Manning 8; Angie D. Manning 7; Eliza Manning 4; Georgia Manning 2

Notes for John Sherman FITZPATRICK #104

Census

1900 Monroe, Clermont, OH, p. 4A. Sherman Fitzpatrick 36, farmer; Nora Fitzpatrick 22. M. 1 year, no children.

1910 Monroe, Clermont, OH, p. 6A. Sherman Fitzpatrick 45; Nora Fitzpatrick 34; Daisie B Fitzpatrick 4; Gail A Fitzpatrick 7; Zelphia E Fitzpatrick 3. M. 11 yrs, 4 ch / 3 living. Sherman's occ not legible - Grand - routable?. All OH/OH/OH.

1920 Batavia, Clermont, OH, p. 7A. John S Fitzpatrick 56, carpenter - house, OH/OH/AL; Lenora L Fitzpatrick 43; Galen A Fitzpatrick 18, sewing - coat factory; Zelphia Fitzpatrick 12; John Fitzpatrick 4 4/12; Daisy B Singler 19, dau, married; George Singler 1 2/12, nephew. Others OH/OH/OH. Husband of Daisy might be Edwin Singler, 22, who was living with his parents, Edward & Catherine in Monroe; listed as married.

1930 Cincinnati, Hamilton, OH, p. 4B. John Fitzpatrick 68, landscape gardener - private estate; Norah Fitzpatrick 53; John Fitzpatrick 14

Discrepancy - Jones notes give birth as 1864; death certificate gives 1863.

Death: John Sherman Fitzpatrick, d. 17 Oct 1937, Cincinnati, Hamilton, OH; Birth 10 Aug 1863, OH. Age 74 years 2 months 7 days; Widowed; Landscape Gardener; Burial: 20 Oct 1937 Bethel, O.; Spouse: Lenora Fitzpatrick; Father: John S. Fitzpatrick, b. OH; mother: Sarah Tatman, b. OH. Informant: Mrs. Edwin Singler. [dau]   Ohio Deaths, 1908-1953 <pilot.familysearch.org>.

Notes for Nora B. VAIL #104s

May be the Norah Vale in Monroe, Clermont Co, OH 1880. B. abt 1872, parents John & Sarah Vale. May be the Nora Fitzpatrick who died in Cincinnati, OH on 9 Aug 1942; but the death certificate of Sherman in 1937 listed him as widowed.

Notes for William W. TATMAN #105
Jones notes: "resided 1880 in Monroe Twp."
Census:
- 1900 Tate Twp, Clermont, OH, p. 144 William Tatman, Head, Sep 1853, 46, married 26 yr, OH/OH/Scot, farmer, owns farm; Alice, wife, Nov 1853, 46, married 26 yr, 4 ch/ 4 living, OH/OH/OH; Lena, dau, Sep 1879, 20; Bessie, dau, Apr 1881, 19; Jennie, dau, Apr 1883, 17; Frank son, Mar 1885, 15. 3 younger ch. "at school"; children all OH/OH/OH.
- 1910 Monroe, Clermont, OH. p. 4A. William W Tatman 56, widowed, farmer; Lena Tatman 30; Bessie Tatman 29; Jennie M Tatman 27; John F Tatman 26, no occ.
- 1920 Monroe, Clermont, OH, p. 4A. William W Tatman 56, OH/OH/Sco, widowed, farmer; Lena Tatman 30; Bessie Tatman 29; Jennie M Tatman 27; John F Tatman 25. Children all single, OH/OH/OH, no occ.

Notes for Alice M. TAYLOR #105s
Census: 1870 Monroe, Clermont, OH, p. 181B. Arnold F Taylor 51, farmer; Martha Taylor 45; George Taylor 18; Alice Taylor 16; John Taylor 14; Frank Taylor 11; Harvey Taylor 8; Elmer Taylor 4. All b. OH.

Notes for Mary A. TATMAN #106
Death: Mary R. Swing, d. 08 May 1929; Tate, Clermont, OH; b. 03 Dec 1859, OH. Age at death: 69 years 5 months 5 days; Burial: 12 May 1929; Bethel, O. Spouse: Clifford J. Swing; Father: John Tatman, b. Ohio; Mother Jane McNair, b. Scotland. Ohio Deaths 1908-1953 <pilot.familysearch.org>
Name given as Mollie R. on 1910 census.

Notes for Clifford John SWING #106s
Census:
- 1900 Tate, Clermont Co, OH, p. 11B. Cliff J Swing 43, Feb 1857, OH/OH/OH, school teacher; Mollie R Swing 40; Glenn O Swing 10; Edna B Swing 8; Phil M Swing 5; John C Swing 1
- 1910 Tate, Clermont Co, OH, p. 11B. Clifford J Swing 53, farmer - general farm; Mary R Swing 50; Glenn O Swing 20, school teacher - public school.; Edna B Swing 18; Phil B Swing 15; John C Swing 11
- 1920 Tate, Clermont Co, OH, p. 5A. Clifford J Swing 62, farmer - general farm; Mary R Swing 61; Edna B. Swing 28; Phil B Swing 24, school teacher - public school; John C Swing 20, rubber worker - factory.
- 1930 Tate, Clermont Co, OH, p. 6A. Clifford Swing 72, farmer; Edna Swing 38, dau, single

Death: Clifford John Swing d. 28 Jun 1951, Bethel, Clermont, OH; b. 07 Feb 1857, Ohio; Age at death: 94 years; Father: Charles W. Swing; Mother: Anna O. Hannah. Ohio Deaths 1908-1953 <pilot.familysearch.org>

Notes for Maud Blanche TATMAN #109
Census:
- 1900 Tate Twp, Clermont Co, OH, John H. Taylor, Head, 44, Mar 1856, married 14 yr, OH/OH/OH, owns farm; Maud B. wife, 39, Aug 1860, 6 children/6 living, OH/OH/Scot; Goldia L, dau, 13, Nov 1886, at school; Charly H. son, 11, Aug 1888, school; Howard T. son, 10, May 1890, school; Alice B. dau. 7, Mar 1893, school; Archie M. son, 4, Nov 1895; George R. son, 2, May 1898. Children all b. OH.
- 1910 Tate, Clermont, OH, p. 11B; John H Taylor 54, farmer; Maud B 44, 7 ch / 7 living; Goldie L 23, school teacher; Charles H 21, farmer; Howard T 19; Alice B 17; Archie M 14; George R 11; John K 8. All OH/OH/OH except Maud's mother b. Scotland.

Death: Maud B. Taylor, d. 21 Jan 1915, Tate, Clermont, Ohio; b. 5 Aug 1865 Ohio; Age at death: 49 years 5 months 15 days, Married; Housekeeper; Residence: Tate, Clermont, OH; Burial: 23 Jan 1915; Father: John Tatman, b, OH; Mother: Jane ___, b, Ohio. Ohio Deaths 1908-1953 Death Certificate <pilot.familysearch.org>

Notes for John H. TAYLOR #109s
Census: 1920 Tate, Clermont, OH, p. 6B. John H Taylor 63, widowed, no occ; Goldie L 33, no occ; Charles H 31, farmer; Howard T 29, farmer; Alice B Crane 26, dau, divorced; Agnes C Crane 7, grdau; Archie M. 24, fireman - railroad; George R 21, rubber worker - factory; John K 17.

Notes for Lewis G. TATMAN #110
Jones notes: "received the home farm of 92½ acres."
Census:
- 1900 Tate Twp, Clermont Co, OH. p. 2B. John Tatman 70, Mar 1830, OH/KY/NC, farmer; Milila 49, Jul 1851; Lewis 32 (son), Nov 1867; Louise 30 (d-in-law), Jan 1879; John Colyer 21, boarder, May 1879, farm labor; Dwight 11/12, (grandson) Jun 1899.
- 1910 Monroe, Clermont, OH. Louis G Tatman 41, farmer; Jane L 40; Dwight 10.
- 1920 Tate, Clermont, OH. Lewis G Tatman 52, farmer; J Louise 49; Dwight H 20, rubber worker - factory.
- 1930 Tate, Clermont, Ohio Lewis G Tatman 62, farmer; J Louise 60.

Death: Ohio Death Certificate <pilot.familysearch.org>. Gives father as John Tatman; mother: Jane McNair.

Notes for Jane Louise BOGGESS #110s
Death: Ohio Death Certificate <pilot.familysearch.org>. Gives parents as Arch Bogess & Caroline Anderson; "widow"

Notes for Dwight H. TATMAN #323
Jones notes: "Resided (1973) at Rt 232 SW of Bethel, corner of Rt 232 & 222; She resides (1975) at Green Bay WI; No children"
Military: WWI Draft Registration 1918. (Ancestry.com) Dwight Harrison Tatman, birth: Jun 30, 1898; farmer. Med. height, med build, blue eyes, light hair. Poor copy.
Census:
- 1920 Tate, Clermont, OH, p. 5B. Louis G Tatman 52, farmer; J Louise Tatman 49; Dwight H Tatman 20, married, rubber worker - factory.
- 1930 Cincinnati, Hamilton, OH, p. 5A. D. H. Tatman, 30, single, member of firm - auto industry, guest at Queen City Hotel run by John J. & Agnes Fitzgerald.

Marriage: Dwight Tatman b. 1899; age 19; to Mabel Meeker b. 1899, age 19; married 10 Oct 1918, Newport, Campbell, KY. Groom's parents: L. G. & Louise Tatman; Bride's parents: Wm. D. & Mary Meeker. Kentucky Marriages, 1785-1979 <pilot.familysearch.org>
Death: Dwight H Tatman, b. 1900; Death Date: 27 Feb 1975, Clermont County Mercy Hospital; Age 75; Married. Ohio Deaths (Ancestry.com)
SS Death index gives: Dwight Tatman; Birth: 30 Jun 1899; Death: Feb 1975, New Richmond, Clermont, OH

Notes for John Charles TATMAN #111
Jones notes: "sheriff of Clermont Co."
Census: 1900 Batavia, Clermont, OH, p. 11A. J C Tatman 42, Aug 1857. tob[acco]. merchant; Anna Tatman 36, Jun 1863; Mary L Tatman 16, Jul 1883. All OH/OH/OH. Married age 18, 1 child/1 living.

Notes for Ann M. NICHOLS #111s

Census: 1870 Ohio, Clermont, OH, p. 227A. Perry J Nichols 30, atty at law; Nettie Nichols 26; Annie Nichols 7; Lewis H Nichols 5; Carrie Nichols 4; Nellie Nichols 1; Alice Gilmore 19, apt. in ___; Eva Hannah 17, domestic serv.

Notes for Florence J. TATMAN #112

Marriage: Walter C. Frazier to Florence J. Tatman, b. 1872; Age 19; Marriage: 4 Oct 1891, Clermont Co., OH. Ohio Marriages, 1800-1958 <beta.familysearch.org>

Census:

1900 Tate, Clermont, OH, p. 2B. Walter P Frazier 33, Oct 1866, farmer, OH/OH/OH; Florence Frazier, Mar - no age or date, OH/OH/Sco; Ray T Frazier 8, Jan 1892; Henry Hackman 38, boarder, MO. M. 9 yrs, 1 child.

1910 Tate, Clermont, OH, p. 1A. Walter C Frazier 43, farmer; Florence J. Frazier 39; Ray R Frazier 17; Mildred L Frazier 7. 3 ch / 2 living [indexed by Ancestry.com as Reagan]

Death: Florence J. Frazier, d. 22 Mar 1919, Bethel Vil, Clermont Co., OH; b. 28 Mar 1872 OH; Age: 46 years 11 months 25 days; Married; Burial: 24 Mar 1919, Bethel, Oh; Spouse: Walter Frazier; Father: John Tatman; b. OH; Mother: Jane Mcnair, b. OH. Ohio Deaths, 1908-1953 <pilot.familysearch.org>

Notes for Walter C. FRAZIER #112s

Census: 1920 Tate, Clermont, OH, p. 14A. Walter C Frazier 53, widowed, farmer; Mildred L Frazier 17, dau; Anabel Frazier 7, dau.

1930 Bethel, Clermont, OH, p. 4B. Walter Frazier 63, no occ; Minne Frazier 47, wife. She m. age 46.

Notes for Ledora Estelle TATMAN #115

Death: Ladora E. Hutson, d. 20 Aug 1935, Amelia, Clermont, OH; b. 17 Jul 1862 Ohio; Death Age 73 years 1 month 3 days; Married; occ: House Work; Burial: 22 Aug 1935, Amelia, OH; Spouse: Charles W. Hutson; Father: Oliver Tatman, b. OH; mother: Eliza Hancock, b. OH. Ohio Deaths, 1908-1953 <fsbeta.familysearch.og>

Notes for Charles Wilmer HUTSON #115s

Census:

1870 Franklin, Clermont, OH, p. 60A. William Hutson 37; Susan Hutson 31; Sarah L Hutson 15; Clara B Hutson 13; Charles Hutson 11; John Hutson 8; Ida M Hutson 5; Flora Hutson 3; Walter Hutson 3/12

1900 Pierce, Clermont, OH, p. 5A. Charles Hutson 39, Sep 1860, farmer; Ledora Hutson 39, Jul 1862, m. 11 yrs, 1 child; Carlos Hutson 3, Jul 1896; Sarah Canter 48, sister, May 1852, widowed, 2 ch / 1 liv.

1910 Pierce, Clermont, OH, p.1B. Charles W Hutson 48; Ladora E Hutson 47, 2 ch / 1 living; Karlos S Hutson, 14

1920 Van Buren, Montgomery, OH, p. 21A. Carlos S Hutson 25, stockman - cash register co; Blanche Hutson 21, wife; Dora Hutson 52, mother; Charles W Hutson 58, father, coal dealer; Alberta Hutson 28, wife [question: does Carlos really have two wives?]

1930 Amelia, Clermont, OH, p. 2B. Carlos Hutson 34, restaurant - confectionery; Blanche Hutson 32; Ruth Hutson 5, dau; Alice Hutson 3, dau; Charles Hutson 70, father, laborer; Ladora Hutson 68, mother. All b. OH

Death: Chas. W. Hutson, d. 9 Dec 1947 Amelia, Clermont, OH; Birth: 30 Sep 1859 Clermont Co. OH; Age: 88 years 2 months 9 days, widowed; Spouse: Ladora Tattman; Father: Wm Oliver Hutson; Mother: Susan Kindrick; occ: coal business. Ohio Deaths, 1908-1953 <pilot.familysearch.org>

Notes for Arizona T. "Arra" TATMAN #116
Census:
- 1900 Pierce, Clermont, OH, p. 5A. John F Hutton 38, May 1862, farmer; Arizona Hutton 35, Mar 1865; Stella Hutton 16, Sep 1883; Lena B Hutton 14, Sep 1885; William Hutton 13, Mar 1887; Gladys Hutton 11, Nov 1888.
- 1910 Pierce, Clermont, OH, p. 1B. John F Hutson 44, farmer; Arza Hutson 45; Ladora E Hutson 19; Lena B Hutson 24, teacher - public school; Gladys E Hutson 21, stenographer - art manufacturer. 4 ch/ 4 living. Others OH/OH/OH. next to Charles Hutson, 48, OH/OH/KY [brother?; Ladora is listed as a daughter, but doesn't fit exactly - possibly Stella]
- 1920 Amelia, Clermont, OH, p. 1B. John F Hutson 56, laborer - coal yard, OH/OH/KY; Arra Hutson 53; Lena B Hutson 33, teacher - public school.
- 1930 Amelia, Clermont, OH, p. 1B. John Hutson 66, coal supply; Ara Hutson 65; Ida Hutson 65, sister. All OH/OH/OH.

Notes for Caroline 'Callie' TATMAN #117
Jones notes: "resided near Salt Air"
Census:
- 1900 Monroe, Clermont, OH, p. 11A. Elmer Taylor 34, Oct 1866, farmer; Callie Taylor 30, Oct 1869; Ethel Taylor 4, Mar 1897; Lelah Taylor 3, Mar 1897; Geo Fitzpatrick 49, Jun 1830, cousin, farm hand; Grace Carnes 17, Oct 1882, servant, housekeeper.
- 1910 Monroe, Clermont, OH, p. 4A. Elmer Taylor 44, farmer; Callie Taylor 40, 2 ch / 2 living; Ethel Taylor 14; Lelah Taylor 13
- 1920 Monroe, Clermont, OH, p. 2B. Elmer Taylor 54, farmer; Calla Taylor 50; Lella M Taylor 22, dau; Fred T Witschzger 24, son in law, farmer; Ethel G Witschzger 24, dau; Lela Eleanor Witschzger 1, gr dau. All b. OH.
- 1930 Bethel, Clermont, OH. Callie H Taylor 60, widow; Lela Taylor 33, single, bookkeeper - garage.

Death: Callie Taylor, d. 27 Nov 1942, Cincinnati, Hamilton, OH; b. 8 Oct 1869, OH; Age: 73 years; Widowed; Res: Main St., Bethel, OH; Bur: 30 Nov 1942, Bethel; Spouse: Elmer Taylor; Father: Oliver Tatman, b. OH; Mother: Elita Anderson, b. OH. Ohio Deaths 1908-1953 <familysearch.org>

Notes for Elmer TAYLOR #117s
Callie was listed as a widow on the 1930 census.
Death: Elmer Taylor, d. 16 Apr 1929, Monroe Twp, Clermont, OH; Birth: 15 Oct 1865, Ohio; Age at death: 63 yrs, 6 mo, 1 da; married; Occ: Farmer; Burial: 18 Apr 1929, Bethel, Ohio; Spouse: Callie Taylor; parents: Frank Taylor, b. OH; Martha Brownen, b. OH. Ohio Deaths 1908-1953 [pilot.familysearch.org]

Notes for Ulysses Grant MCNAIR #121
Census:
- 1900 Tate, Clermont, OH, p. 6A. Grant Mcnair 34, May 1866, m. 4 years, farmer; Alma R. Mcnair 27, Aug 1872, 1 ch/1living; John L. Mcnair 2, Apr 1898. Next to John McNair & Ida Fitzpatrick; Edwin McNair.
- 1910 Tate, Clermont, OH, p. 10A. V Grant Mcnair 44, farmer, m. 14 yr; Dollie Mcnair 37, 1 ch/1 living; J Lawrence Mcnair 12.
- 1920 Tate, Clermont, OH, p. 4A. Ulysses G Mcnair 53, farmer - general farm; Alma R Mcnair 47
- 1930 Tate, Clermont, OH, p. 3A. Grant N Mcnair 63, farmer - general farm, OH/Sco/OH; Alma R Mcnair 57.

Death: Ulysses Grant Mcnair, d. 17 Sep 1942, Tate, Clermont Co, OH; b. 2 May 1866, OH; Age: 76 years, Widowed, Bur. 19 Sep 1942, Bethel Cemetery; Spouse: Alma Mcnair; parents: John Mcnair, b. OH; Mary Tatman, b. OH. Informant: Lloyd McNair [nephew]. Ohio Deaths 1908-1953 <familysearch.org>

Notes for Alma R. WOOD #121s

Death: Alma R. Mcnair, d. 16 Sep 1940 Tate, Clermont, OH; b. 05 Aug 1872 OH; Age: 68 years, Married, Housewife; Res: Bethel, Ohio; Burial: 18 Sep 1940, Bethel; Spouse: Grant Mcnair; Father John Wood, b. OH; Mother: Rachiel Mccarter b. OH. Ohio Deaths 1908-1953 <pilot.familysearch.org>

Notes for John L. MCNAIR #335

Jones notes: "resides (1974) at Kennedy Ford Rd, Bethel, OH; no children"

Census:

- 1920 Akron Ward 7, Summit, OH, p. 5A. Edward Stevens 46; J Lawrence Mcnair 21, boarder, laborer, rubber fact, single, OH/OH/OH.
- 1930 Norwood, Hamilton, OH, p. 31B. John L Mcnair 32, commercial traveler - Weatherstrip Co; Flora T Mcnair 30, bookkeeper - jewelry co. Both OH/OH/OH.

Military: WWI Draft Registration [Ancestry.com] John Lawrence Mcnair, Clermont, OH, b. 23 Apr 1898. Barely legible. Occ: Rubber Worker, Firestone Rubber, Akron, OH. Nearest relative: Alma McNair, Bethel, OH. tall, slender, blue eyes, lt brown hair.

Death: John Lawrence McNair, b. 23 Apr 1898, Clermont Co, OH; Res: Clermont; Death: 10 Aug 1992, Long-Term Care Facilities, Brown Co, OH. Age: 94; Injury in Ohio; #377-09-0671. Ohio Deaths, 1908-1932, 1938-1944, and 1958-2002 [Ancestry.com]

Notes for Benjamin Edwin MCNAIR #123

Jones notes give middle name as Edward; census & death certificate list name as Edwin.

Census:

- 1900 Tate, Clermont, OH, p. 6A. Edwin Mcnair 29, Sep 1780, m. 2 years, farmer; Stella Mcnair 27, Aug 1872, 1 ch/1living; Lloyd H Mcnair 0/12, May 1900. Next to John McNair & Ida Fitzpatrick.
- 1910 Batavia, Clermont, OH, p. 3A. Edward Mcnair 39, farmer, m. 12 yrs; Stella Mcnair 35; Lloyd Mcnair 9; Manda Lloyd 52, sis-in-law, widowed; Robert Lloyd 44, bro-in-law, single, laborer - home farm
- 1920 B Edwin Mcnair 48, farmer - general farm; S Stella Mcnair 46; Lloyd E Mcnair 19, worker - rubber factory
- 1930 Tate, Clermont, OH, p. 7A. Edward McNair 59, janitor - public building; Stella McNair 55, nurse - private family.

Death: Benjamin Edwin Mcnair d. 25 Mar 1942, Bethel, Clermont Co, OH; b. Sep 1870, OH; Age: 71 years, Married, Burial. 27 Mar 1942, Bethel Cemetery; Spouse: Stella Mcnair; parents: John Mcnair, b. OH; Jane Tatman b. OH. Informant: Lloyd McNair [son]. Ohio Deaths 1908-1953 <familysearch.org>

Notes for Stella LLOYD #123s

Death information from Ancestry's Ohio Deaths - gives name, death date, birth year, residence: Clermont, d. Christ Hospital, Cincinnati, widowed.

Notes for Fanny TATMAN #125

Census:

- 1910 Cincinnati Ward 4, Hamilton, OH, p. 6B. William Norris 48, Sco/Eng/Sco, blacksmith - railroad, imm. 1888 / naturalized; Fannie Norris 44; Hugh Norris 11
- 1920 St Clair, Butler Co, OH, p 9B. William Norris, 55, with wife Fannie, 53. Born Scotland, immigrated 1889, naturalized 1891. Blacksmith, machine shop. Son Hugh was in Akron as a 21 yr old boarder.
- 1930 Akron, Summit, OH, p. 48A. Hugh L Norris 31, OH/Sco/OH, printer - print shop; Carrie L Norris 33, PA/PA/PA; Robert H Norris 3; Fannie Norris 66, OH/OH/OH, mother; William Norris 68, father, Sco/Sco/Sco, imm. 1897, naturalized, no occ.

Death: Fannie Norris, d. 21 Feb 1944, Ravenna, Portage, OH; b. 20 May 1863, Clairmont [sic] Co, OH. Age: 80 years 9 months 1 day, Widowed, Housewife, Residence: Ravenna, Portage, OH; Burial: 23 Feb 1944, Talmadge, OH. Father: Elijah Tatman b. Ohio; Mother: Sarah Ruole [sic], b. Oh. Ohio Deaths 1908-1953 <pilot.familysearch.org> [mother should be Sarah Rush]

Notes for William E. NORRIS #125s
Immigration: Wm E Norris; Arrival: 27 Mar 1888; Birth: abt 1865; Age: 23; Place of Origin: Scotland; Port of Departure: Glasgow, Scotland; Arrival: New York; Ship Name: Anchoria. New York Passenger Lists, 1820-1957 [Ancestry.com]
Death: William E. Norris, d. 19 Feb 1943, Westfield, Medina, OH; b. 20 May 1862, Glasgow, Scotland; Age at death: 80 years 8 months 11 days, Married, Blacksmith. Residence: Westfield, Medina, Ohio Burial: 22 Feb 1943, Talmadge, OH. Spouse: Fanny; Father: Hugh, b. Glasgow, Scotland. Ohio Deaths 1908-1953 <pilot.familysearch.org>

Notes for Effie TATMAN #126
Census:
  1900 Tate, Clermont, OH, p. 8A. Charles E Durham 39, Nov 1861?, farmer; Effie Durham 31, Aug 1869; Warren T Durham 2, Jun 1898. All OH/OH/OH
  1910 Tate, Clermont, OH, p. 1B. Charles C Durham 49, farmer - dairy farm; Effie Durham 40, 1 ch / 1 living; Warren F Durham 12
  1920 Tate, Clermont, OH, p. 2A. Charles E Durham 59, farmer - general farm; Effie Durham 50; Philip Durham 8.
  1930 Tate Clermont, OH, p. 2B. Charles E Durham 69, farmer - general farm; Effie T Durham 60; Phillip T Durham 18. (Indexed as Denham by Ancestry.com)
Death: Effie Tatman Durham; d. 08 Oct 1931, Tate Twp, Clermont Co, OH; b. 14 Aug 1869, Ohio; Age: 62 years; Married; Bur: 10 Oct 1931 Bethel; Spouse: Chas. Durham; Father: L. Tatman b. OH; Mother: not known. Informant: Phillip Durham, Bethel OH. Ohio Deaths 1908-1953 <familysearch.org>

Notes for Charlie E. DURHAM #126s
Census: 1880 Tate, Clermont, OH, p. 265. John Durham 54, farmer; Elizabeth Durham 53; Alice Durham 22; Charley Durham 19; Ellsworth Durham 17.
Death: Charles E. Durham, d. 6 Feb 1941 Cincinnati, Hamilton, OH; b. 07 Nov 1860, OH; Age: 80 years; Widowed; Occ: Retired Farmer; Res: Bethel, Ohio; Burial: 8 Feb 1941, Bethel Cemetery; Spouse: Effie Durham; Father: John Durham, b. OH; Mother: Mary Jones, b. OH. Ohio Deaths 1908-1953 <pilot.familysearch.org>
Discrepancy: Jones notes gave birth as 16 Nov 1860; death certificate gives 7 Nov.

Notes for Carrie TATMAN #127
Marriage: Archie G. Holland, b. 1873, Bethel, Ohio; Age: 27; Bride: Carrie Tatman, b. 1873, Salt Air, Ohio, Age: 27; Marriage: 11 Mar 1900, Clermont, OH; Groom's Father: Thomas Holland; Mother: Rebecca Bragdon; Bride's Father: Elijah Tatman; Mother: Sarah Kuch. Both single. Ohio Marriages, 1800-1958 <pilot.familysearch.org>

Notes for Archie G. HOLLAND
Census
  1900 Willamsburg, Clermont, OH. p. 2. Archie Holland 29, Jan 1873, farmer; Carrie 27, wife, Aug 1873, Ethel 20, Nov 1879, sister. All b. OH. parents b. OH. At same address with Tomas Holland 66, Jul 1833, OH/OH/PA, farmer; Anna R., wife 52, Oct 1847. OH/OH/OH. Nearby: Allen V Holland 39, Dec 1860, farmer, OH/OH/OH; Lilly 33, Dec 1866, wife, KY/KY/OH; Eva 30, Sep 1869, boarder; Carrie Deel 22, Aug 1877, servant.

1910 Williamsburg, Clermont, OH, p. 11. Archie G Holland 37, farmer; Carrie 37; Keith T. 2. Next to Thomas 77, OH/MD/VA, own income; Rebecca A., 62, OH/OH/OH. m. 43 yrs, 3 ch/3 living.

1920 Williamsburg, Clermont, OH, p. 3. Archie Holland 46, farmer; Carrie 47; Keith 12; Anna 72, mother, widow. All OH/OH/OH. Allen, 59, is widowed and boarding on the farm of Lachlan? Kennedy, p. 8.

1930 Williamsburg, Clermont, Oh, p. 7B. Archer Halland 57, farmer; Carrie Halland 57; Keith T Halland 22, no occ. All b. OH

Military: WWI Draft Registration [Ancestry.com] Archie G Holland, Clermont, OH, age 45, b. 18 Jan 1873, farmer, Bethel, OH. Wife: Carrie Holland. Med height, slender, blue eyes, brown hair. Reg: Sept 1918.

Death: Archie G Holland, b. 1874; Res: Clermont, OH; d. 9 Nov 1974, Home, Clermont Co, OH; widowed, age at death: 100. Ohio Deaths, 1908-1932, 1938-1944, 1958-2007 <pilot.familysearch.org>

Notes for John Warren TATMAN #128

Jones notes: "resided (1973) on A__ Bantan-Glover Rd, Clermont Co, OH" [this is obviously wrong, since Warren died in 1961 – perhaps his family lived here. @@

Marriage: Warren Tatman, b. 1876, Clermont Co., OH, age: 27 to Edith Phillips, b. 1883, Clermont Co., OH, age 20; Marriage: 9 Jun 1903, Clermont Co, OH; Groom's parents: Elijah Tatman, Sarah Rush; Bride's parents: Thomas Phillips, Georgia Fee. both single. Ohio Marriages, 1800-1958 <familysearch.org>

Military: WWI Draft Registration [Ancestry.com] John Warren Tatman, age 42, b. 20 Oct 1875, Montgomery, OH. Conductor - Cincinnati Dayton Tractor Co, res R 16, Dayton, OH. Closest relative: Edith B. Tatman. Med height, slender, brown eyes, brown hair. Registered Sept 1918.

Census:

1910 Monroe, Clermont, OH, p. 1A. Thomas Philips 46, farmer; Georgia Philips 43; Edith Philips 17; Jessie Philips 14; Warren Philips 10. Living next door to William & Alice Tatman - William is a cousin to Warren.

1920 Van Buren, Montgomery, OH, p. 8B. Warren Tatman 44, conductor - street car; Edith Tatman 37; Margurite Tatman 9; Robert Tatman 3

1930 Van Buren, Montgomery, OH, p. 8B. G Warren Tatman 54, conductor - electric railroad; Edith Tatman 47; Margaret L Tatman 19; Robert P Tatman 14

Death: John W Tatman, b. 1875; Res: Kettering, Montgomery Co, OH; d. 12 Nov 1961 - home; married. Ohio Deaths, 1908-1932, 1938-1944, and 1958-2002 [Ancestry.com]

Notes for Edith PHILLIPS #128s

Death: may be the Bessie E Tatman b. 1882; res: Dayton, Montgomery Co, OH; d. 22 Nov 1972 Middletown, Butler Co, OH. Ohio Deaths, 1908-1932, 1938-1944, and 1958-2002 [Ancestry.com]

Notes for Orestes Daily "O.D." HICKS #130

Jones notes say "b. 12-23-1854, Clermont Co, M. 7/8/1875 to Harriet Sarah Stewart"

Bible Records: Hicks Bible in possession of Elizabeth (Hicks) Joslin, Georgetown, OH August, 1998. [copy sent to me by Lvera Jennings Seipelt, Georgetown OH]. "Orestes Daily Hicks was Born December 23 at 9 oclock pm 1851"

Church: Trustee's Report of Christian Church, Rural, OH -- O. D. Hicks, secretary. 6 Sep 1880.

Census:

1880 Rural, Clermont, OH, p. 67D. Erastus D. HICKS 28, farmer; Hattie S. 25; Hattie E. 3

1900 Felicity, Franklin twp, Clermont, OH, p. 60. Erastus D. HICKS 48, Dec 1851 OH, photographer; Hattie S. 44, Jul 1855 OH; Edna S. 22, Sep 1877 OH (md. 25 yrs.; 1 child, still living; own home debt free)

1910 Felicity, Clermont, OH, p. 42. Orestes D. HICKS 58, no occ, OH/OH/KY; Edna 32 Evangelist, singer, OH/OH/KY (Orestes a widower, Edna is single)

The Hicks Bible indicates Orestes was a photographer in Felicity.

Note: Molly Dell Levi Stalder (in 1909) mentions visiting Uncle O.D. and Edna.

Occupation: A farmer in 1880, a photographer by or before 1900. His death record indicates he was a merchant and had a "notions shop."

Death: Orestes D. Hicks, d. 14 Nov 1934 Felicity Village, Clermont, OH; wife: Hattie Hicks; parents: Henry M. Hicks, Hannah Owens; he b. OH in 23 Dec 1851. Age: 72 years 8 months 18 days. Occ: merchant - notions & shoes. Burial: Felicity, OH 16 Nov 1934. Edna H. Hite of Felicity signed the death certificate. Ohio Deaths 1908-1953 <pilot.familysearch.org>

Notes for Hattie Sarah STEWART #130s

Marriage: IGI Batch 7534302 -25 (#884698) Submission of Norman Zezula

Death: Absent from 1910 census, Felicity; husband listed as widower in 1934 on his OH death rec.

Children: Only one child listed in the 1880 census (Rural, Clermont, OH; # 325),

Burial: Hattie S. Hicks, b. Chilo, OH; last residence Felicity. B. 16 Jul 1855; d. 20 Sep 1905 of paralysis. Parents Wm R. & Eliza Stuart. Interred on lot of H. F. Hicks. Undertaker, W. P. Mefford. Permit obtained by O. L. Hicks. Sewanie Cemetery Record, Sewanie Lodge, No 95, I. O. O. F. <Cincinnati Library>

Notes for Elijah Franklin HICKS #132

Photos: I have a photocopy of photo of him in my files. Also photocopy of photo of family farm in Rural. I believe that Lvera Hicks has the original. Also group photo of extended family taken on occasion of his brother, John J. Hicks birthday abt 1913. Also of two couples, John James & wife, Georgia Beeker; Elijah Franklin and wife Melissa Beeker with their mother in law Elizabeth (Bradshaw) Beeker (reproduced on page 88) . Also photo of him in play of some sort.

Census

1880 Green Twp, Brown Co, OH. Francis M Levi 26, w. Lucy A. 26, dau. Erma 1; brother in law Frank Hicks, 24.

1900 Clermont, Franklin Twp, p. 58a. Frank Hicks, head, 44, Dec 1855, mar. 3 yr, OH/OH/KY; Farmer, owns farm; Melissa wife, 34, Sep 1865, mar 3 yr, 1 ch, 1 living; OH/Ger/OH; Herdes, son, 1, Jul 1898, OH/OH/OH. Next to father Henry.

1910 Franklin, Clermont, OH, p. 12-5A. Frank E Hicks 54, OH/OH/KY, farmer, m2, 13 years; Malissa Hicks 44, OH/Ger/OH, m1, 3 ch/3 living; Hurdes B Hicks 11; Irlene E Hicks 6; Elizabeth G Hicks 2; Elizabeth Beeker 72, widow, m-in-law, OH/OH/OH.

1920, Franklin South, Clermont Co, OH., p. 4. Frank Hicks, 64, M . OH, OH, KY. no occ. Melissa (wife), 53, OH, GER/GER. Irlene, dau, 15; Elizabeth, 22. Next to Hurdus Hicks; Johnnie Hicks.

1930 Franklin, Clermont, OH, p. 193, Dist 5. Eligha Hicks, 75, farmer; Melissa Hicks 65. Eligha's parents b. Germany; Melissa's father b. Germany. [birthplace of Elijah's parents is incorrect]

Bible Records: Hicks Bible in possession of Elizabeth (Hicks) Joslin, Georgetown, OH, August, 1998. "Elijah Franklin Hicks was Born Dec 18 at 10 Oclock A M 1855 Tuesday"

Burial: Felicity Incorporated Cemetery, Clermont Co, OH On one stone: Elizabeth Bradshaw, wife of Wm Beeker 1837-1912; Dora H. their Dau 1863-1882; John J. Hicks 1864-1935, Georgia B. his wife 1867 - 1928; E. Franklin Hicks 1855-1935, Melissa B. his wife 1865-1949.

Obituary: unnamed local paper, Feb 1935. *"Elijah Franklin, second son of Henry M. and Hannah Owens Hicks, was born on a farm overlooking the Ohio River, near Rural, OH, Dec 18, 1855. He spent his early years in school and after reaching manhood selected agriculture as his life work. He was a great reader and always kept himself in touch with all the current events. He had a remarkable knowledge of the Bible, of which he made a careful study. In early life he united with the Christian Church at Mt Pleasant transferring this membership to the Rural Church of Christ as soon as it was established. This Church he*

served as Sunday School Supt, teacher, deacon and elder. In later years, when the Rural Church was not having services, he placed his membership in the Church at Felicity.
He lived an honest, upright life and was respected by all.
On the morning of Feb y, 1935, he quietly closed his eyes her to open them in the glad homeland. This was just one week after the passing of his youngest brother, John, and 2½ months after that of his oldest brother, Orestes, their separation here being very brief.
Those who are left to miss him are his wife, Melissa Beeker Hicks to whom he was married May 26 1897..Three children: Hurdes Hicks of Rural, Mrs Erlene Devore of _____ and Mrs Elizabeth Jennings of Utopia, one brother, H. H. Hicks of Norwood, one sister, Mrs. Mary Joslin of New Richmond, nine nieces and nephews, and a host of other relatives, friends and neighbors.

Note: Mollie Dell Levi Stalder (in 1909) mentions visiting "Aunt Melissa" Hicks, RR1, Chilco, OH
Marriage: (1) Adie Fenton - Clermont Co marriage record (not listed in Bible) (2) Melissa Beeker - Hicks Bible and Hamilton Co. marriage record (LDS FHL microfilm 44262; item 2; pt. 56; #319)
Death: 6 Feb 1935. Edward Franklin Hicks [sic], Chilo, OH, RFD #1. Male, white, married, wife Melissa Hicks. Birth date not given, age at death, 70, 1, 18. Retired Farmer. Birthplace: OH; parents: Henry Hicks, b. Bethel, OH; Hannah Owens, b. KY; informant: Melissa Hicks; Chilo, OH RR #1. Burial: Felicity OH 2/9/1935. Undertaker: L. M. Broadwell & Son, Felicity OH. Cause of Death: Influenza complicated by Broncho pneumonia. Ohio death certificate
Occupation: retired farmer at death; a butcher in 1880
Residence: At death he lived in Chilo, Franklin Twp, Clermont, OH. Previously resided in Rural, Clermont Co. and in Brown Co, OH

Notes for Addie FENTON #132s
Marriage: Clermont Co marriage records: "E. F. Hicks and Adie Fenton, 13 Jan 1889". No indication of this marriage in the Hicks Bible.
Census: 1910 census indicates Melissa is E. F. Hicks' second wife.
Death: Assume Addie died before her husband's second marriage in 1897 to Melissa.

Notes for Melissa BEEKER #132s2
Census: 1870 Franklin, Clermont, OH, p. 72. William Becker 39, Bavaria, works in vineyard; Elizabeth Becker 46; Dora B Becker 7; Melissa Becker 4; Georgia E Becker 3
Death: Melissa Hicks, b. 8 Sep 1865; d. 2 May 1949, Felicity, Clermont, OH, age 83 years 7 months 24 days. Gives birthplace as Ohio; father as William Beeker; mother Elizabeth Bradshaw. [birth places not given]. <pilot.familysearch.org>
Burial: Felicity Incorporated Cemetery, Clermont Co, OH On one stone: Elizabeth Bradshaw, wife of Wm Beeker (possibly Becker) 1837-1912; Dora H. their Dau 1863-1882; John J. Hicks 1864-1935, Georgia B. his wife 1867 - 1928; E. Franklin Hicks 1855-1935, Melissa B. his wife 1865 - 1949. FHL film #0862016 p.60
Obituary: unnamed local paper, May, 1949. *Melissa Beeker was born to William and Elizabeth Bradshaw Beeker at Rural, O.; on Sept 8, 1865, and departed this life May 2, 1949 at the age of 83 years, 7 months and 24 days. Her twin brother passed away at the age of six months. Her sister, Georgia, was the last living member of her immediate family and they were a great comfort to one another until her passing in 1928. She was united in holy matrimony to E. Franklin Hicks on May 26, 1897 and to this union were born three children; one son and two daughters. She was a devoted wife and mother. She endured long illness with cheerfulness and was often in a mirthful mood. Her husband preceded her in death, passing away February 6, 1935. Surviving her are three children, Hurdes Hicks of Chilo; Irlene DeVore, Felicity; and Elizabeth Jennings, Higginsport; 11 grandchildren; five great grandchildren and a host of other relatives and friends.*

Note: Her mother is Elizabeth Beeker, b. 1838 in OH. (1910 census--Franklin twp, Clermont Co, OH; p 48, line 131. She apparently is the daughter of Clement Bradshaw Jr. Clement Bradshaw Jr. married Judith Broshears in 1822 (Bracken Co. Ky. marriage bond dated 16 Apr 1822) They were the grandparents of the sisters Melissa and Georgia Beeker, who married the brothers Elijah & John James Hicks.

Notes for Lucy Ann HICKS #133

Bible Records: Hicks Bible "Lucy Ann Hicks was Born Sept 29 at 2 Oclock PM 1857"
Marriage: IGI, Frank M. Levi married Lucy A. Hicks, 1 April 1877, Clermont Co, OH. #7534302 -25.
Photograph: of Lucy as young adult, sent by Rosalene (Hicks) Buskirk, 12/98.
Confusion here: Death certificate of Mollie Dell Levi Stalder lists her mother as Mary Hite (info given by oldest son Curtis; other Stalder children say their grandmother was Mary Hite, but she had died before they were born.) Frank's 2nd wife was Mary Emma Townsley, who had been Lucy's Sunday School teacher. She raised the children. Family Bible of Mollie Dell Levi states that her children are grandchildren of Frank M. Levi and Lucy Hicks. A cousin, Emma Hicks, married Charles Hite; perhaps that is where the name came from. There is no question that Lucy Hicks is the mother of Mollie Levi.
Census: 1880 Green Twp, Brown Co, OH, p.3. Francis M Levi 26, w. Lucy A. 26; dau. Erma 1; brother
    in law Frank Hicks, 24.
Death: Tombstone: Felicity Inc. Cemetery (no death record has been located)
Burial: Sewanie Cemetery Record, Sewanie Lodge #95, I. O. O. F. Clermont Co, OH, Application for burial. Lucy A. Levi, b. Clermont Co, O. Last residence: Ivanhoe, Hamilton Co, OH; b. 29 Sep 1857; d. 4 Jul 1888. Disease: Consumption. Parents: H. M. & H. F. Hicks. Interred on lot of Frank Levi; undertaker J. L. Brannock. 7 July 1888.

Notes for Francis Marion 'Frank' LEVI #133s

Occupation: Grocer in OH before moving to FL; realtor who lost everything in "land bust' in FL. Blonde, blue eyes. Have his business card in file. M. 2 Mary Emma Townsley. Curtis Directory 1870 lists Frank Levi as Cabinet maker, works NWC. May not be same person.
Photograph of Frank Levi in files; also group photo of Hicks family which includes Frank & Emma Levi (abt 1910) and Frank's grandson, Curtis Stalder, as a toddler.
Marriage: IGI, Frank M. Levi married Lucy A. Hicks 1 April 1877, Clermont Co, OH. #7534302 -25.
Bible Records: Family Bible [in possession of Betty Jo Stockton] lists children, grandchildren, marriages.
Census:
  1870 Franklin Township, Clermont Co, OH. p. 45. Willis Levi 48, farm labor, b. KY; Huldy 48, keep
    house, b. OH; Amanda 22, helps mother, b. OH; John 19, common labor; Francis 16, common labor;
    Sarah Day 52, lives with son, b. IN - cannot read or write; Mary Levi 2, b. OH.
  1900 Norwood, Hamilton Co, OH, p. 6B. Frank M. Levi, Mar 1854, OH/KY/OH; Mary E. Aug 1850,
    wife, OH/PA/PA; Irma C. Aug 1878 dau; Harvey C. Apr 1881 son; Mollie D. Sep 1884 dau. Living
    on Sherman Ave. Children b. OH.
  1910 Millcreek, Norwood, Hamilton Co, OH. Francis M. Levi, 57; wife Mary E., 59, m. 22 yr, no
    children; dau - Mollie D 25.
  1920 Orlando, Orange, FL. p. 16B. Frank M Levi 65, OH/KY/OH, real estate; Mary E Levi 69,
    OH/PA/PA. 204 Schultz? St - between Jackson & Church.
  1930 Orlando, Orange, FL., p. 9A. Frank M Levi 80, no occ; Mary E Levi 79. 429 Ruth St
Land Records: 1889 (687/45? Hamilton Co, OH) Frank M. Levi & Mary E, his wife, sell land in Section 3, Millcreek Twp, Hamilton Co. 1/24/1904 [152/525]
  Willis Levi, resident of Felicity, deeds real estate in Felicity to John J. Levi, reserves use for life. 1/24/1904 [152/52?]
  Willis Levi deeds real estate near Felicity to John J. Levi of Clermont & Frank M. Levi of Hamilton Co, reserves use for life. 5/26/1915 [177/45 or 115]

John J. Levi sells ½ interest in property in Felicity, which came from Willis Levi, to Frank M. Levi of Hamilton Co, OH

Death: Frank M. Levi; res. Peel Ave; male, white, married (wife Emma Levi); born 26 Mar 1854; death: 28 Sep 1933; age 79 years, 6 mo, 6 days. Occupation: real estate. Born: Clermont Co, OH. Father -?- Levi, b. KY; mother "don't know"; cause of death: obstructions of bowels. Dr: S. Miles Robinson, Orlando. Informant: Mrs. B. Stalder, Rt 1, Box 8, Orlando. Certificate #15910, Orange County, FL.

Tombstone: Felicity Inc. Cemetery states: 1854-19__) . Frank is not buried there - had moved to FL. First wife, Lucy Ann (Hicks) Levi, is buried there.

Burial: Greenwood Cemetery, Orlando, 3 Oct 1933. Undertaker: Carey Hand, Orlando." Listed in Greenwood Cemetery Office Records as buried next to Odd Fellows monument in Greenwood. No stone visible, 1997, but listed in card file in cemetery office. Records show he bought six lots in Old Fellows section.

Death: Letter from Molly Levi to family in Ohio telling of death of "Dad Levi" 2 Oct 1932.

Notes for Mary Elizabeth HICKS #134

Molly Dell Levi Stalder (in 1909) mentions Aunt Mary Joslin, New Richmond OH, b. 25 Apr 1860.

Bible Records: Hicks Bible: "Mary Elizabeth Hicks was Born April 25 at 9 Oclock pm 1860 Wednesday.

Marriage: Clermont Co marriage record - "John D. Jaslin [sic] to Mary E. Hicks, 5 Dec 1880"

Census:

- 1900 New Richmond, Clermont Co, OH, p. 5. Mary Joslin, Apr 1860, OH, widow, no occ; Eva M. 18, May 1882, dau, OH, wool twister; Archie D. 16, Feb 1884 son, OH, wool carder; Rella, 14, Oct 1885, dau, OH, wool twister; Edna C. Apr 1889 dau, OH; Addie L. Sep 1892 dau. OH (living on Willow St.; 6 children, 5 living)
- 1910 Ohio twp, Clermont, OH, p 61. Mary E. Joslin, 49, widow, OH/OH/KY, no occ; Eva C. 27, twister - woolen mill; Lina C. 20, teacher - public school; Leona 18 (6 children, 3 living; "Lina"="Edna"; "Leona" = "Addie")
- 1920 Sycamore, Hamilton, OH, p. 3A. Howard West 27, laborer - farm manager; Lora West 28; Marian West 6/12; Mary Joslin 59, m-in-law, widowed
- 1930 Phoenix, Maricopa, AZ, p. 1A. W B Edwards 66, inspector - cement co, KY/KY/KY; Edna C Edwards 40; Mary Joslin 69, m-in-law.

Death: OH death record - "Mary E. Joslin, d. 29 Jul 1955 in New Richmond, Clermont Co, OH; widow; b. 25 Apr 1860 in OH; parents: Henry Hicks, Hannah Owens"

Obituary: 30 Jul 1955 Cincinnati paper (unnamed). *Mary E. Joslin, (nee Hicks) of New Richmond, OH, mother of Adlora West & mother-in-law of Mrs. Josephine Joslin, grandmother of Mrs. Howard (Elizabeth) Hayden & Mrs. Robert (Marion) Sterrett July 29, 1955. Funeral services at the Lew F. White Memorial Funeral Home, New Richmond Tuesday Aug 2 at 10:30 am.*

Notes for John D. JOSLIN #134s

Jones notes give birth date, death date; 'buried Zion Cemetery'

Health: Norman Zezula notes: tuberculosis afflicted many of the Joslin family. John D. Joslin died in his mid-30s of it; at least one child (Lucy) died of "lung disease". According to family tradition, his son Archie died of it and one daughter, Edna, had it so bad that, a few years after her marriage, her family moved to Phoenix, AZ due to her health requiring a drier climate".

Notes for Emarilla JOSLIN #353:

Married Carl Dawson

Jones notes: gives birth, marriage, spouse "no ch."

Census:
- 1900 New Richmond, Clermont Co, OH, p. 5. Mary Joslin, 40, Apr 1860, OH; Eva M., 18, May 1882 dau, OH; Archie D., 16, Feb 1884, son, OH; Rella, 14, Oct 1885, dau, OH; Edna C., 10, Apr 1889, dau, OH; Addie L., 7, Sep 1892, dau, OH. (live on Willow St.; 6 children, 5 living)
- 1910 New Richmond, Clermont, OH;, p. 61. Carl, 28, proprietor, retail grocery. Married 1 year. Rella J., wife, 24, no occ. Living next to Charles Dawson, 61, postmaster, Emma 51, Allen H. 22; Margaret 20; Russell 19.

Photograph: In photograph of Hicks family on the birthday of John James Hicks - 1914/1915.

Notes from Lvera (Jennings) Seipelt 1998 list "Children of Mary Elizabeth Hicks Joslin: Rella Dawson (Deceased - no heirs)"

Death: Rella Dawson, d. 21 Mar 1919, Norwood, Hamilton, OH; b. 10 Oct 1885, OH; Age: 33 years 5 months 11 days; Married; Occ: Housework; Bur: 24 Mar 1919, New Richmond, OH; parents: John Joslin; b. OH; Mary Hicks b. OH. Cause of death: pulmonary tuberculosis. Ohio Deaths 1908-1953 <familysearch.org>

Notes for Harvey Henry HICKS #135

Married Margaret Sarah Wells "Maggie", 3 Feb 1885

Photocopy of photo of him in my files.

Great grandfather of Norman Zezula, who said "he was a farmer, schoolteacher, nurseryman and fruit tree salesman."

Note: Molly Dell Levi Stalder (in 1909) mentions "Uncle Harvey Hicks, Norwood, OH, b. 1/21/1862".

Birth: Hicks Family Bible. Harvey Henry Hicks was Born January 21, 1862. At 11 oclock a. m. Tuesday

Marriage: Clermont Co, OH marriage record (# 321). "at Utopia, Clermont, OH at her mother's home" - according to family tradition as related by her daughter, Minnie (Hicks) Behan, to Norman Zezula in 1979.

Death: Ohio death certificate: "Harvey Henry Hicks, d. 25 Jun 1950 in Norwood, Hamilton, OH; b. 21 Jan 1862 in OH; widower, retired; parents: Henry Hicks (b. OH), Hannah Owens (b. KY); burial: Utopia, Brown Co, OH. Informant: Dion H. Hicks (son).

Census:
- 1900 Franklin twp, Clermont, OH, p. 8. Henry Hicks 38, Jan 1862, OH/OH/KY, day laborer; Margaret 36, Jun 1864, OH/PA/OH; Lucy M. 14, Nov 1885, OH; Harvey J. 10, Aug 1889 OH; Minnie C. 6, Oct 1893, OH; Blaine 4, Sep 1895, OH; Dion 1, Nov 1898, OH (7 children, 5 living [sic]; rents home)
- 1910 Cincinnati, Hamilton Co, OH p.156, Section Ave. Harvey H. Hicks, 48, packer (teacher?) lithographer; Margaret S. 46; Harvey J. 20; Minnie C. 15; Blaine M. 14; Dion W. 11. (7 children, 5 [sic] living; married 25 yrs.)
- 1920 Norwood Ward 4, Hamilton, OH, p. 6. Harvey Hicks 68, shipping clerk - bank; Margaret 64; Dione 21, occ: illegible.
- 1930 Norwood, Hamilton, OH, p. 125. Harvey Hicks, 68, nursery man; wife Margaret, 65; son Dion 30, salesman, advertising; Madeline, d-in law, 22; grson Dion, 7/12 b IN

Bible Records: Hicks Bible in possession of Elizabeth (Hicks) Joslin, Georgetown, OH August, 1998. "Harvey Henry Hicks was Born January 21 at 11 oclock A.M. 1842. Tuesday."

Occupation: schoolteacher; salesman for Stark Nursery. He received a write up (that included his picture) in the company publication for being one of the top salesman of Stark fruit trees in OH. (A photocopy of this is in the possession of Norman Zezula.)

Notes for Margaret Sarah WELLS #135s
Birth: Wells Family Bible; Hicks Family Bible
Photo: In 5 generation photo on page 186.
Death: Margaret Sarah Hicks, lived at 5341 Ralston Ave, Norwood, OH, b. 12 Jun 1863 in Utopia, Clermont Co, OH; d. 30 Jul 1931, Norwood, Hamilton, OH. parents: John L. Wells, b. PA; Mary Jernegan, b. Amelia, Clermont, OH; housewife; burial: Higginsport, Brown, OH. Informant: H. H. Hicks. Ohio Deaths 1908-1953 [pilot.familysearch.org]
Note: The Hicks Bible indicates she d. 31 Jul 1931; the OH death record states 30 Jul 1931.

Notes for Blaine Melvin HICKS #362:
Jones notes: "resides at 2232 Hannaford, Norwood, OH. Laura d. 2/27/1952; b. 11/9/1896 at Cincinnati, no ch. US Army - WWI"
Birth: Hicks Family Bible; no civil birth record exists. Blaine stated that he was born in Rural, Clermont, OH (Rural is in Franklin Twp. and is the likely birth town of his brothers and sisters)
Marriage: (1) Laura Rummel - Hamilton Co, OH marriage record (v 300, p 231) - "Blaine Melvin Hicks (age 23 on 15 Sep 1918; b. Rural, OH; parents: Harvey H. Hicks, Margaret Wells; res. Norwood, Hamilton, OH; a glazier) to Laura Francis Rummel (age 22 on 9 Nov 1918; Bond Hill, OH; parents: Arthur Rummel, Frances Rettesh; stenographer; res. Norwood, OH." (She d. 27 Feb 1952 - OH death certificate)
   (2) Elsie Glendora Price - from personal knowledge of Blaine Hicks (oral to Norman Zezula in 1979)
Census:
   1920 Norwood Ward 4, Hamilton, OH, p. 5B. Blaine M Hicks 24, mill worker - sash & door co; Laura Hicks 23. Both OH/OH/OH
   1930 Norwood, Hamilton, OH, p. 19A. Blaine M Hicks 34, broker - real estate; Laura Hicks 33. Both OH/OH/OH
Military: WW I Draft Registration [Ancestry.com] Blaine Melvin Hicks, Rolston Ave, Norwood, OH. B. 15 Sep 1895, Rural, OH. Occ: glaser, Norwood Sash & Window, single. Medium height, stout build, black hair, black eyes. Age 21, 5 Jun 1917.
Military: U.S. World War II Draft Registration Cards, 1942. Blaine Melvin Hicks, Hannaford Ave, Norwood, OH. b. Rural, OH, 15 Sep 1895. Contact: Laura Frances Hicks, same address. Employer: Besuden Nurseries, Cincinnati, OH. 5' 8½ ", 183 lbs, gray eyes, brown hair, dark complexion. Reg: 27 Apr 1942.
Military: He served in World War I in France (Co. C, 154th Inf). Norman Zezula has a photocopy of a brief letter (including the envelope) from Pvt. D. H. Rummel to Pvt. Blaine Hicks that was dated 20 Sep 1918. The letter was written merely to give Blaine his address - "I will not write very much as you may not get this letter" - and asks "How do you like army life?"
Military: WW I - Blaine M. Hicks, W, 5113 Rolston Ave., Norwood, O; Enlisted Norwood, O. 28 May 1918; b. Rural, O. 15 Sept 1895. Serial Number: 3095885. "Assignments: 159 Depot Brigade to 17 June 1918; Co C 154 Infantry to 8 Nov 1918; Co C 162 Infantry to Discharge Private, first class 1 Sept 1918; Corporal 15 Oct 1918. American Expeditionary Forces, 6 Aug 1918 to 19 Feb 1919. Honorable discharge 1 March 1919. Volume #: 8. Ancestry.com "Ohio Military Men, 1917-18".
Death: Personal knowledge of Norman Zezula (the death was on a Sunday in August 1985; probably on 18 or 25 Aug); Social security death index agrees with birth date; gives Aug 1985 for death date. His second wife (Elsie) is still living (March 1989)
Death: Blaine M Hicks, b. 1896 Ohio; Residence: Norwood, Hamilton Co, Ohio; Death: 18 Aug 1985, Jewish Hospital, Cincinnati, Hamilton, OH. Married. Industry of Decedent: Forestry. Ohio Deaths, 1908-1932, 1938-1944, and 1958-2007 [Ancestry.com]

Notes for John James HICKS #136
Photocopies of photos of him in my files. Also group photo of extended family taken on occasion of his birthday abt 1913. Photocopy of photo of his farm. Also of two couples, John James & wife, Georgia

Beeker; Elijah Franklin and wife Melissa Beeker with their mother in law Elizabeth (Bradshaw) Beeker. Also photo of him in play of some sort.

Bible Records: Hicks Bible in possession of Elizabeth (Hicks) Jennings, Georgetown, OH August, 1998. [copy sent to me by Lvera Jennings Seipelt, Georgetown OH]. "John James Hicks was born October the 18, 1864 Teusday [sic] evening at 4 oclock.

Marriage: to Emma Georgia Anna Beeker, 27 Mar 1893 - Clermont Co marriage record (v 22, p 24)

Census:
 1900 Clermont Co, OH, John Hicks, Oct 1864, married 7 yrs; Georgia, May 1867; Elizabeth Beeker, Oct 1837, married 39 yrs; 5 children, 3 living. All born in OH; Elizabeth's parents born in KY
 1920, Franklin South, Clermont Co, OH, p. 4. Johnnie Hicks, 55, M, OH/OH/KY, farmer. Georgia (wife), 52, OH/GER/GER. Marcella, dau, 11; Raymond, 6. next to Hurdus Hicks; Frank Hicks.
 1930 Franklin, Clermont, OH, p. 193 [3A] John Hicks, 65, farmer; Marcella Hicks 22, daughter. Next to brother, Eligha Franklin (Frank) Hicks.

Occupation: farmer

Death: OH death certificate: John J. Hicks, d. 30 Jun 1955 in Clermont Co, Franklin Twp, town of Chilo; b. 16 Oct 1864 in Clermont Co, OH; parents: Henry M. Hicks, b. Bethel, OH; Hannah F Owens, b. Augusta, KY. His widow was Georgia Hicks. He was a farmer. Informant: Marcella D. Hicks, Chilo, OH. Burial: Felicity, OH, 2 Feb 1935. Undertaker: L. M. Broadwell & Son, Felicity, OH. Cause of death: Influenza complicated by Broncho pneumonia.

Burial: Felicity Incorporated Cemetery, Clermont Co, OH   On one stone: Elizabeth Bradshaw, wife of Wm Beeker 1837-1912; Dora H., their Daughter 1863-1882; John J. Hicks 1864-1935, Georgia B. his wife 1867-1928; E. Franklin Hicks 1855-1935, Melissa B., his wife 1865-1949

Obituary: unnamed local paper, Feb 1935. *"John James Hicks, youngest child of Henry M. and Hannah Owens Hicks, was born on the banks of the Ohio River, near Rural, Ohio, Oct 18, 1864.*

He was a quiet studious lad spending his early years in school and helping on the farm. After completing his common school course, he attended Valparaiso, Ind. Normal School and Together with his brother, O. D. Hicks and his wife and a number of neighbors, took the Chautauqua course, then quite popular.

At the age of 16 he gave his heart to his Master and united with the Rural Church of Christ, and remaining true to that faith through all the years, serving the Church as Sunday School Superintendent, teacher and elder.

Being deeply interested in agriculture, he became a member of Felicity Grange No. 1950.

On March 27, 1893, he was united in marriage with Miss Georgia Beeker. Their love and loyalty were ideal and was severed here by the death of the wife, August 2, 1928, but his love for her extended across the vale.

Unto their home and love came Marcella and Raymond and upon these two he lavished his love, tenderness and kindliness. Raymond went to the Heavenly home Jan. 15, 1922.

On the morning of Jan 30, 1935, his quiet spirit took its flight to be with his Lord and her "he had loved and lost awhile."

Those who remain to miss him are Marcella, two brothers, E. F. Hicks of Rural and H. H. Hicks of Norwood, one sister, Mrs. Mary Joslin of New Richmond, one sister-in-law, Mrs. E. F. Hicks and twelve nieces and nephews, and a host of other relatives, friends and neighbors, whose lives have been enriched by his"

<u>Notes for Emma Georgia Anna BEEKER #136s</u>

Death: Ohio Death Certificate <pilot.familysearch.org>. Gives father as Wm Beeker, b. Germany; mother Lida Bradshaw, b. OH. Occ: housewife;

Obituary: mentioned in obit of her sister, Melissa, in unnamed local paper, Feb 1935. Her death date is given in obit of husband, John James Hicks.

Obituary: Georgia B. Hicks was born near Rural, on the 11th of May 1867, and spent her life at or near the same with the exception of a few months. At 4 minutes before 1:00 on the morning of August 2nd [1924], she passed away, in her home she loved so well. .. On the 27th day of March 1893, she was united in marriage to John J. Hicks. Marcella, at the age of four years, came to their home and heart and remained a constant companion and source of pleasure to the end. One wish was fulfilled, to see Marcella graduated from Felicity High School. Another wish, to see Marcella graduated from her chosen profession was unfilled.. The love of children and their presence brought Raymond to our home on the 17th of March 1919, being 5 years old. He brought sunshine and gladness by his bright and smiling face and childish talk. On Jan 15, 1922, the Lord called him and we had to submit to his will. [undated, unknown paper]

Note: Molly Dell Levi Stalder (in 1909) mentions visiting Uncle John and Aunt Georgie.

Notes for Minerva Elizabeth JONES #137

Jones notes: "b. 4/10/1844 at Clermont Co; m1 1861 to F. M. Houser who died; m2: 9/2/1866 to Andrew Jackson Broadwell [b. 1836 at Rural OH]; Removed to Downing MO in 1882 and lived there till 1897. In 1897 moved to Arizona. In 1907, moved to Modesto CA, where he died abt 1930. She was living in Ceres?; CA in 1930.

Obituary: *"Mrs. Minerva Broadwell of Clovis, is summoned in Clovis July 6, Mrs Minerva Elizabeth Broadwell, 91, Died today in the home of a son Perce Broadwell, here, Mrs. Broadwell had lived in California.. 28 years. She was a native of Ohio. Surviving her are five sons, Lindsley Broadwell of Iowa, H.S. Broadwell of Missouri, Lawrence and N. D. of Ceres, and Perce Broadwell of Clovis, California; and one daughter, Mrs. Frankie Ross of Iowa.* Note from Laurie Ichters, granddaughter of Perce Broadwell. "The year might have been 1935. I don't have the Bible, but this clipping was in it; no dates. They also lived in Arizona some of the time."

Census:

- 1870 Franklin, Clermont, OH, p. 59A. Andrew Broadwell 33, retail dry goods merchant; Manerva Broadwell 26; Lindley Broadwell 3; Herbert Broadwell 8/12 [b. Sept]; Frances Houser 7, attending school.
- 1880 Franklin, Clermont, OH, p. 65D. Jackson J. Broadwell 44, dry goods merchant, OH/NJ/NJ; Menerva E. Broadwell 36; Leander E. Broadwell 12; Hilbert F. Broadwell 10; Arsnenia Broadwell 7 (m); Lawrence Broadwell 5; Purcell Broadwell 3; Cliffered Houser 18, step son; Mary F. Houser 16, step daughter. All b. OH. [all Broadwell children are boys; b. OH.]
- 1900 Totten, Lonoke, AR, p. 5B. M J Broadwell 70, Feb 1830, farmer; Minnie Broadwell 69, Apr 1831 MO, 7 ch/6 living; Rawley Broadwell 19; Lawrence Broadwell 15; Preston Broadwell 13; Nathan N Broadwell 9; Robert Broadwell 6.
- 1910 Turlock, Stanislaus, CA, p. 9A. Dell Broadwell 29, farmer; Elva Broadwell 28, AR/MO/MO, m. 10 yrs, 4 ch / 4 living; Imogen Broadwell 9, AR; Eunice Broadwell 4, AR; Romba Broadwell 3, AR; Lionel Broadwell 1 8/12, CA; Andrew J Broadwell 74, own income, OH/NJ/NJ; Minerva Broadwell 66, own income, OH/OH/OH
- 1920 Precinct 10, Maricopa, AZ, p. 17A. Perce Broadwell 43, farmer, OH/OH/OH; Nettie Broadwell 39, IL/OH/US; Harold Broadwell 18, AR; Catherine Broadwell 14, AR; Eugenia Broadwell 12, AR; Chester Broadwell 8 5/12, CA; Glenn Broadwell 1 4/12, AZ; Minerva Broadwell 75, widow. Next to Nathan Broadwell, 38 (another son)
- 1920 Precinct 10, Maricopa, AZ, p. 17A. Nathan Broadwell 38, farmer; Elva H Broadwell 37; Imogene Broadwell 18; Eunice Broadwell 14; Romba Broadwell 12; Lionel Broadwell 10; Karylton Broadwell 1/12]; Lawrence Broadwell 45. brother.

1930 Clovis, Fresno, CA, p. 11B. Perce Broadwell 53, farmer; Nellie E Broadwell 49; Kathleen A Broadwell 24, bookkeeper - electric office; Chester Broadwell 18; Glenn W Broadwell 11; Minerva Broadwell 85, mother.

Notes for Francis M. HOUSER #137s

Census: 1860 Franklin, Clermont, OH. Nancy A Howser 40; Francis M Howser 19; Isaac R Howser 18; George W Howser 17; Mary E Howser 15; Sarah E Howser 13; Wm Howser 12; Sylvester J Howser 10

Notes for Andrew Jackson BROADWELL #137s2

Jones notes: "b. 4/10/1844 at Clermont Co. m1 1861 to F. M. Houser who died; m2 9/2/1866 to Andrew Jackson Broadwell [b. 1836 at Rural OH]; Removed to Downing MO in 1882 and lived there till 1897. In 1897 moved to Arkansas. In 1907, moved to Modesto, CA, where he d. abt 1930. She was living in Ceres? CA in 1930

Census: 1860 Franklin, Clermont, OH, p. 510. Lindley Broadwell 74, retired from business; Susan Broadwell 64; Nathaniel Broadwell 35, farmer; Louisa Broadwell 22; Andrew J Broadwell 24, merchant; Ferdinand Broadwell 21, no business; Joanna Essecks 37, domestic duties; Frances Essecks 8; Albert L Essecks 6

Notes for Lawrence BROADWELL #372:

Jones notes: "not married; resided (1929) at Montesano (Chehalis) WA"

Census: 1920 Precinct 10, Maricopa, AZ, p. 17A. Nathan Broadwell 38, farmer; Elva H Broadwell 37; Imogene Broadwell 18; Eunice Broadwell 14; Romba Broadwell 12; Lionel Broadwell 10; Karylton Broadwell 1/12; Lawrence Broadwell 45. brother, bee man.

1930 not found

Military: World War I Draft Registration Cards, 1917-1918 [ancestry.com]. Lawrence Broadwell, age 44, b. 25 Dec 1874, res: Crown Landing, Stanislaus, CA; occ: bee keeper; contact: A. J. Broadwell, Clovis Farms, CA; 5' 9", 150 pounds, brown eyes, black hair; reg: 12 Sep 1918, Stanislaus Co, CA.

Death: Lawrence Broadwell, b. 25 Dec 1874; d. 12 Jun 1948, Los Angeles, CA. California Death Index [Archives.com]

Notes for Samantha Jane JONES #138

Jones notes "Samantha Jane, b. 4/4/1850 at Rural, OH; m. 8/25/1870, Clermont to Wm Joseph Helvering, b. 6/8/1846 at Circleville, OH. Removed to Marshall Co, KS abt 1885; Beattie (Marshall) KS in 1930. She was a teacher at Felicity; Wm was town marshall at Felicity abt 1880."

Census

1880 Felicity, Clermont, OH, p. 43. Wm. J. Helvering 33, OH/OH/PA, marshall of Felicity; Nancy J. Helvering 30; Edwin G. Helvering 9; Guy P. Helvering 2.

1900 Guittard, Marshall, KS, p. 6A. William J Helvering 53, Jun 1846, OH/MD/PA; Samantha J Helvering 50, Apr 1850; Alma M Helvering 11, Nov 1888. 5 ch/ 4 living; m. age 29.

1910 Guittard, Marshall, KS, p. 5A. William J Helvering 64, OH/MD/MD, truck gardener; Samantha J Helvering 60, OH; Robert Helvering 27, OH, lawyer - general practice; Alma Helvering 21, KS. 5 ch / 4 living.

1920 Guittard, Marshall, KS, p. 4A. William Helvering 73, OH/MD/MD, postmaster; Samantha Helvering 69

1930 Beattie, Marshall, KS, p. 3A. William Helvering 83, OH/PA/PA, no occ.; Samatha Helvering 79, OH

Kansas State Census

1 Mar 1895, Beattie, KS. W J Helvering 49, OH, old soldier, honorably discharged - 20 Sep 1864; S J Helvering 45; Guy Helvering 16; Robert Helvering 2; Alma Helvering 6, KS. All but Alma b. OH.

1 Mar 1905. W J Helvering 58, OH, truckster; S J Helvering 54; Guy Helvering 26; Robert Helvering 21; Alma Helvering 16, KS. All but Alma b. OH.

1915 Beattie, KS. W J Helvering 68, OH; S J Helvering 64, OH; Alma Helvering 26, KS; Murtle Marlow 23, KS, school teacher.

1925 Beatie, KS. W J Helvering 78, labor; Samantha J Helvering 75

No death information found

Notes for William Joseph HELVERING #138s
Marshall at Felicity in 1880. Postmaster in Guittard, KS in 1920.
No death information found

Notes for Guy HELVERING #377:
Jones notes: "Studied law. County Attorney of Marshall Co KS for 4 years. Corp. Co. M, 22nd Kansas Infantry in Spanish War. Attorney & banker at Saline, KS. No children."

Census

1900 Guittard, Marshall, KS, p. 5B. Guy Helvering, 22, Jan 1878, OH/OH/OH, weigh master - elevator; Amasa S Trosher, 25, partner, saloon keeper; Ephraim L Conger, 27, partner, barber; Howard Kingman, 26, partner, editor. All single.

1910 Marysville Ward 4, Marshall, KS, p. 24B. Guy F Helvering 32, OH/OH/OH, county attorney; Tinnie L Helvering 32, KS/Ger/IL, m. 0 years; Jennie L Konter [Koester] 30, sister in law, KS/Ger/IL; Emma Crome 16, servant, KS/Ger/Ger.

1920 Marysville, Marshall, KS, p. 25B. Guy T Helvering 42, banker; Tinnie L Helvering 43, occ music?; Arthur J Scott 38, bro-in-law, internal rev. collector; Jennie L Scott 39, sis-in-law

1930 Salina, Saline, KS, p. 8B. Guy L Helvering 50, president - bank; Tinnie Helvering 50

Military: World War I Draft Registration Cards, 1917-1918 [ancestry.com] Guy Tressillian Helvering, age 40, b. 10 Jan 1878; res: Marysville, Marshall, Kansas. Occ: member of Congress, US Capitol, Washington, DC; Contact: Trinnie Helvering; Med height, stout build, brown eyes & hair. Regis: Sep 3, 1918, Wash D.C.

Marriage: Guy T. Helvering, b. 1878, age 32; to Tinnie Ludawine Koester, b. 1878; age 32; Marriage: 16 Mar 1910, Marshall, Kansas. Kansas Marriages, 1840-1935 <fsbeta.familysearch.org>

Biography: Biographical Directory of the United States Congress, 1774-2005 [ancestry.com] *Guy Tresillian Helvering; Birth: 10 Jan 1878; Death: 4 Jul 1946; Elected Office(s): Representative, President; Elected Date(s): 4 Mar 1913; State: Kansas, Ohio, Michigan, Washington Biography: a Representative from Kansas; born in Felicity, Clermont County, Ohio, January 10, 1878; moved to Kansas in 1887 with his parents, who settled in Beattie, Marshall County; attended the public schools; during the Spanish-American War enlisted as a corporal in Company M, Twenty-second Regiment, Kansas Infantry, and served from May 12 to November 3, 1898; attended the University of Kansas at Lawrence; was graduated from the law department of the University of Michigan at Ann Arbor in 1906; was admitted to the bar in the same year and commenced practice in Marysville, Kans.; prosecuting attorney of Marshall County 1907-1911; unsuccessful Democratic candidate for election in 1910 to the Sixty-second Congress; elected as a Democrat to the Sixty-third, Sixty-fourth, and Sixty-fifth Congresses (March 4, 1913-March 3, 1919); unsuccessful candidate for reelection in 1918 to the Sixty-sixth Congress; moved to Salina, Saline County, Kans., and became engaged in banking; Democratic State chairman 1930-1934; mayor of Salina, Kans., from February 15, 1926, until his resignation on December 8, 1930; State highway director in 1931 and 1932; appointed Commissioner of Internal Revenue by President Franklin D. Roosevelt in 1933 and served until his appointment as a Federal district judge for Kansas in 1943, in which capacity he was serving at the time of his death in Washington, D.C., on July 4, 1946; interment in Marysville Cemetery, Marysville, Kans.*

Notes for Robert Louis Helvering #378

Jones notes: "m. 10/18/1911 to Elsie Kahlke. Attorney at Marysville, KS. No ch. She resided (1972) at 1007 Elm St, Marysville KS 66508. He d. 1961."

Census
- 1900 St Joseph Ward 5, Buchanan, MO, p. 19B. John Balsiger 38; Robt Helvering 17, Jan 1883, roomer, at school, OH/OH/OH
- 1910 Guittard, Marshall, KS, p. 5A. William J Helvering 64, OH/MD/MD, truck gardener; Samantha J Helvering 60, OH; Robert Helvering 27, OH/OH/OH, lawyer - general practice; Alma Helvering 21, KS. 5 ch / 4 living.
- 1920 Marysville, Marshall, KS, p. 3B. Fred Kahlke 56, elevator operator; Metha Kahlke 52; Robert L Helvering 36, son-in-law, lawyer - own office; Elsa Helvering 32, dau, KS/Ger/Ger
- Kansas State Census 1 Mar 1895, Beattie, KS. W J Helvering 49, OH, old soldier, honorably discharged 20 Sep 1864; S J Helvering 45; Guy Helvering 16; Robert Helvering 2; Alma Helvering 6, KS. All but Alma b. OH. 1 Mar 1905 . W J Helvering 58, OH, truckster; S J Helvering 54; Guy Helvering 26; Robert Helvering 21; Alma Helvering 16, KS. All but Alma b. OH.

Military: World War I Draft Registration Cards, 1917-1918 [ancestry.com] Robert Lewis Helvering, age 25, 27 Jan 1883; lawyer - self employed; contact: Mrs. R. L Helvering, Marysville, KS; med height, stout, grey eyes, brown hair.

Notes for Mary Alma HELVERING #379

Jones notes: "m. 6/28/1917 to Roy W. Motes. Postmistress at Beattie, KS 1914-18. No children. She resided (1972) at 1430 Chicago Cir, Homecrest, Evanston, IL 60201"

Census
- 1900 Lulu, Mitchell, KS, p. 2A. Arther O Motes 46; Letha E Motes 39; Huldiah J Motes 17; Effie M Motes 16; Ray W Motes 14, Feb 1886; James E Motes 10; Nora E Motes 9
- 1910 Murry, Marshall, KS. Roy W Motes 24, ?undertaker -furniture store; Effie Motes 26, sister, saleswoman, furniture store.
- 1920 Murray, Marshall, KS, p. 1A. Roy Motes 32, KS/IA/MO, cashier - 1st Natl bank; Alma Motes 31, KS/OH//OH
- 1930 Axtell, Marshall, KS, p. 2A. Roy Motes 44, cashier - bank, KS/IA/IA; Alma Motes 38, KS/OH/OH. Married ages 32/28. Index as Moter.

Kansas State Census
- 1905 Lulu, Mitchell, KS. A O Motes 52, farmer; Letha Motes 47; Roy Motes 19, farmer; Earl Motes 15; Nora Motes 13
- 1915 Axtell, Marshall, KS. Roy W Motes 29, clerk; Effie M Motes 31, dealr?
- 1925 Axtell, Marshall, KS, p. 16. Roy Motes 39, banking cashier; Alma Motes 35, bank accountant

Notes for James Marcellus JONES #140

Jones Family book[252]: "James Marcellus, b. 6 Dec 1847 at Rural, OH; m. 27 Feb 1872 to Mary Elizabeth Shinkle, b. 27 Feb 1854, d. abt 1905. He d. 26 Nov 1925. Farmer at Clermont Co, OH. buried at Mt Pleasant Cemetery, near Felicity, OH. In 1903, they were living on Maple Creek near Neville, OH."
Same information in Orville Jones notes.

Census:
- 1870 Franklin, Clermont, OH, p. 65B. Solomon Shinkle 57, farmer; Mary R Shinkle 50; Leroy R Shinkle 18; Mary E Shinkle 16; Matilda Chapman 21, domestic servant; Morsellas Jones 22, farm labor.
- 1880 Washington, Clermont, OH,, p. 327. James M. Jones 31, farmer; Mary E. 26, Beratrice G. 4; Effie M. 2; Lola A. Jones 7m. All b. OH

1900 Neville, Clermont, OH, p. 4A. James M Jones 52, Dec 1847, farmer; Mary E 46, Feb 1854, m. 27 yrs, 7 ch/7 living; Gary G. 18, Jan 1882, farm labor; Carl R. 15, Nov 1884, farm labor; Ethel G. 13, Feb 1887; Larence M. 9, Jun 1890; Mary C. 7, Sep 1892; Audrey L. 6, Feb 1894; Jenevieve S. 4, Jan 1896; Henry Jones 75, Feb 1825, OH/OH/PA, widowed. Other OH/OH/OH.

1910 Tate, Clermont, OH, p. 2A. Marcellus Jones 62, OH, widowed, farmer; Ethel S 23; Mary E. 17; Audrey L. 16; Jennie V. 14. Children all single, no occ.

1920 - not found

Death: James Marcellus Jones; d. 26 Nov 1925, Cincinnati, Hamilton, OH; b. 6 Dec 1847, OH; Age: 77 years 11 months 20 days; Widowed; Address: 3600 Newton Ave; Farmer; Burial: 29 Nov 1925, Mount Pleasant Cemetery: Spouse: Mary Elizabeth Jones; Father: Henry Jones b. OH; Mother: Mary Hicks, b. OH. Ohio Deaths 1908-1953 <pilot.familysearch.org>

Notes for Mary Elizabeth SHINKLE #140s
Census: 1870 Franklin, Clermont, OH, p. 65B. Solomon Shinkle 57, farmer; Mary R Shinkle 50; Leroy R Shinkle 18; Mary E Shinkle 16; Matilda Chapman 21, domestic servant; Morsellas Jones 22, farm labor.

Notes for William A. JONES #142
Information from Jones book,[253] "born 8 Jan 1851; married 4 Mar 1874 to Frances Essex, b. 12 Feb 1852. Resides [1927] at 4512 Plainville Rd, Cincinnati, OH"

Info from Jones notes: "d. 1/7/1945 (possibly 43). Both buried Mt Moriah Cemetery; Resided on Plainville Rd, Cincinnati, OH."

Census

1880 Neville, Clermont, OH, p. 339D. William A. Jones, 29, school teacher, OH/OHOH; Frances Jones, wife, 28, Keeping House, OH/NY/OH; Albert E. Jones, son, 5, OH/OH/OH; Uertha K. Jones, dau, 3, OH/OH/OH; Jessie A. Jones, dau, 1, OH/OH/OH

1900 Cincinnati Ward 26, Hamilton, OH, p. 2A. William A Jones 49, Jan 1851, OH/OH/OH, motorman - street r.r.; Francis Jones 48, Feb 1852, OH/NY/OH; Jessie Jones 21, Dec 1878, OH; A Grace Jones 18, Jun 1881, OH, bookkeeper; Archie C Jones 17, Mar 1883; Stella B Jones 16, Nov 1884; Lucy F Jones 8, Oct 1881; Jos E Snyder 35, roomer, May 1865, motorman

1910 Cincinnati Ward 26, Hamilton, OH, p. 9B. William A Jones 59, motorman - street rwy; Frances Jones 58, 7 ch / 6 living, m. 36 yrs; Walker Bertlesman 21, son-in-law, OH/Ger/OH, machinist - furniture Co; Lucy F Bertlesman 18, dau.

1920 Cincinnati Ward 26, Hamilton, OH, p. 2B. William A Jones 68, motorman - street car; Frances Jones 68

1930 Cincinnati, Hamilton, OH, p. 41A. William H Jones 79, no occ; Francis Jones 78

Marriage: William A. Jones to Frank Essex 4 Mar 1874 Clermont County, OH. Ohio Marriages, 1800-1958 <pilot.familysearch.org>

Death: Wm. A. Jones, b. 8 Jan 1851, Clermont Co, OH; d. 14 Feb 1938, Cincinnati, Hamilton, OH; Age: 87 yrs 1 mo 6 da; Widowed; Street Address: 3770 Drakewood Dr; Retired; Burial: 17 Feb 1938, Mt. Moriah; Spouse: Frances; parents: Henry Jones b, OH; Elizabeth Hicks, b. OH. Ohio Deaths, 1908-1953 <pilot.familysearch.org>

Discrepancy: Jones notes give death as 7 Jan 1945 (43?) - death certificate give 14 Feb 1938 Cincinnati, Hamilton, OH.

Notes for Frances ESSEX #142s

Census

1850 Anderson, Hamilton, OH, p. 174A. Albert Essex 32, doctor, NY; Joanna Essex 27, OH.

1860 Franklin, Clermont, OH, p. 510. Lindley Broadwell 74, retired from business; Susan Broadwell 64; Nathaniel Broadwell, 35, farmer; Louisa Broadwell 22; Andrew J Broadwell, 24, merchant; Ferdinand Broadwell, 21, no business; Joanna Essecks, 37, domestic duties; Frances Essecks, 8; Albert L Essecks 6

1870 Franklin, Clermont, OH, p. 59A. Lindley Broadwell 84, NJ; Susan Broadwell 74, NJ; Joana Essecks 47, OH; Frances Essecks 18; Albert L Essecks 16. Next to Andrew J. Broadwell.

Death: Francis Jones, b. 12 Feb 1852, Clermont Co, OH; d. 20 Nov 1930, Cincinnati, Hamilton, OH; Age: 78 years 9 months 8 days; married; address: 4512 Plainville Road; Burial: 24 Nov 1930, Mt. Moriah, OH; Spouse: Wm. A. Jones; parents: Albert Essex b. NY; Joan Broadwell, b. OH. Ohio Deaths, 1908-1953 <pilot.familysearch.org>

Notes for Elijah Hicks JONES #143

Information from Jones book[254] "b. 15 Sep 1852; m. to Julia Williams, b. 14 May 1854. He was drowned in the OH River near New Richmond OH in Jan 1913."

Census:

1880 Franklin, Clermont, OH, p. 62B. Hicks Jones, 27, OH/OH/OH, farmer, Julia Jones, wife, 26, OH/OH/OH, Keeps House; Dolly Jones, dau, 4; Alford Jones, son, 1.

1900 New Richmond, Clermont, OH, p. 5B. Elijah Jones 47, Sep 1852, day laborer; Julia Jones 46, May 1854, 7 ch/7 living; Dollie 24, Jan 1876; Alfred W 21, Feb 1879, laborer - saw mill; Jesse 19, Jan 1881, dau; Stanley L 17, Jan 1883, tinner; Howard 13, Jan 1887; Clifford 7, Aug 1892; Chesley 4, Apr 1896. All OH/OH/OH.

1910 Monroe Twp, Clermont Co, OH, p. 4A. Elijah Hicks Jones, 57, OH/OH/OH, single, laborer - working out. [Julia, "divorced", and the children were also in Clermont Co - in Ohio township, which is next to Monroe.]

Death: Elijah Hicks Jones, d. 1913, Campbell, Kentucky; Father: Henry Jones; Mother: Elizabeth Hicks. Kentucky Deaths and Burials, 1843-1970 <beta.familysearch.org>

Discrepancy: Jones notes give death as near New Richmond; Kentucky Death Records give place as Campbell Co, KY. Campbell County is directly across the Ohio River from New Richmond, OH; Jones notes gives date of marriage as 17 March 1875

Notes for Julia WILLIAMS #143s

Census:

1860 Higginsport, Brown, OH, p. 386. Oliver P Williams 36, tradesman; Deborah Williams 32; Emerson Williams 15; Hester Williams 7; Julia Williams 6; Hanson Williams 4; Joseph Williams 2. All b. OH.

1870 Franklin, Clermont, OH, p. 84. Debra Williams 43; Hester Williams 17, helps mother; Julia Williams 16; Hanson Williams 14, works on farm; Joseph Williams 12; Jesse Williams 8; Oliver Williams 5; Charles Williams 3. All b. OH.

1880 & 1900 - see spouse.

1910 Ohio twp, Clermont Co, OH. p. 2B. Julia Jones 56, divorced, no occ, 7 ch/7 living; Dollie Jones 34, spinner - woolen mill; Jessie Jones 28, spinner - cotton mill; Howard Jones 22, laborer - transfer company; Clifford Jones 17, laborer - soap company; Chesley Jones 14. [Elijah Hicks Jones, "single", also lives in Clermont Co, laborer - working out]

1920 Ohio, Clermont, OH, p. 11B. Julia Jones 64, widow, no occ; Dollie 45, spinner - woolen factory; Jessie Alfred 37, dau, finisher - hosiery mill; Howard 32, no occ; Chesley 33, machinist - car shop. All children single.

1930 New Richmond, Clermont, OH, p. 3A. Julia Jones 75, widow; Dollie Jones 50; Jessie Jones 42, finisher - hosiery mill; Howard Jones 38, laborer - lumber yard; Chester Jones 32, painter.

Death: Julia W Jones, d. 05 Aug 1936, New Richmond, Clermont, OH; b. 14 May 1854 Ohio; Age: 82 years 2 months 21 days; Widowed; Occ: Housework; Burial: 7 Aug 1936, G.. Mound Cem; Spouse: E Hicks Jones; Father: Olioce P Williams, b. Ohio; Mother: Cornelia Klugan, b. Ohio. Ohio Deaths, 1908-1953 <pilot.familysearch.org>

Notes for Stanley Lee JONES #400

Jones notes: "m. Sarah Raleigh; both deceased; no children; resided at Covington, KY"

Census

1920 Covington Ward 5, Kenton, KY, p. 7B. John Rahilly 51, Can/Ire/Ire, Machinist - railroad, imm. 1889; Sarah Rahilly 57; William Rahilly 21, KY, Machinist - railroad; Stanley Jones 37, son in law, auto - metal worker, OH/OH/OH; Sadie C Jones 33, dau, Can.

1930 Covington, Kenton, KY, p. 10B. Stanley L Jones 47, OH, sheet metal worker; Sarah K Jones 37, Canada, clerk - shoe store. Married age 31/21.

Military: WW I Draft Registration: Stanley Lee Jones, age 36, b. Jan 10, 1882, New Richmond, Clermont Co, OH. Sheet metal worker, Troy Manuf. Co, Miami, OH. Contact: Mrs Julia Jones, New Richmond, OH. Registered Batavia, OH, Sept 1918.

Death: Stanley L Jones d. 25 Dec 1940; Kenton Co, KY; Age: 57; Residence: Kenton. Kentucky Death Index, 1911-2000.

Notes for Chesley JONES #403:

Jones notes: "m. 6/6/1934 to Mrs. Anna E. Rardin at Clermont Co. No children. Reside (1972) at 707 Pike St, Milford, OH"

Military: World War I Draft Registration Cards, 1917-1918 [ancestry.com] Chesley Jones, age 21, b. 7 Apr 1896, Richmond, OH; res: St Bernard?, Hamilton Co, OH; occ: oil si__ filer - Proctor & Gamble; single, med height & build; brown eyes & hair; regis: St Bernard, OH, Jun 1917.

Military: WW I - Chesley Jones; Serial Number: 244788; Residence: New Richmond, O. Enlistment: Regular Army Enlistment; Location: Fort Thomas, Ky. Date: 05 Nov 1917 Birth Place: New Richmond, O.; Birth Date/Age: 21 6/12 Years; Assignment: Co C 30 Engineers to 17 May 1918; Motor Transport Corps Army Post Office 907 to 15 Dec 1918; Postal Express Service American Expeditionary Forces to 1 May 1919; Army Service Corps American Expeditionary Forces to Discharge Private St Mihiel; Meuse-Argonne. American Expeditionary Forces 26 Feb 1918 to 13 July 1919. Honorable discharge 21 July 1919. Vol#: 9

Death: Chesley L Jones b. 1897; Residence: Clermont Co, OH; d. 23 Jan 1978, Long-Term Care Facilities, Hamilton County, OH; Age: 81; Married. Ohio Deaths, 1908-1932, 1938-1944, and 1958-2007 [Ancestry.com]

Notes for George Washington JONES #145

Information from Jones book[255] "b. 20 Jan 1856; m. Dec 14 1876 to Laura A. Shinkle [b. 21 May 1855]. Farmer at Rural, OH. Removed to Wayne, NE and from there to Keith, Ramsey Co, ND, where she d. 31 Jan 1926.

Info from Jones notes: gives date of G. W.'s death as 8/14/1942 at Balinas, Col (could be Cal)

Census:

1880 Franklin, Clermont, OH Page 66A. Geo. W. Jones, 24, Blacksmith, OH/OH/OH; Laura A. Jones, Wife, 25, OH/OH/OH, Keeps House; Leonteen Jones, Dau, 3, OH/OH/OH; Roxey Jones, Dau, 4, OH/OH/OH

1900 Wilbur, Wayne, NE, p. 2A. George W Jones 49, Jan 1856, farmer, Laura A 45, May 1855; Edith M 12, Sep 1887, CO; O M Jones 37, Feb 1863, brother, farm laborer. 2 houses from dau Roxy Jones.

1910 Wayne Ward 2, Wayne, NE, p. 13A. George W Jones 54, m. 34 yrs, painter; Laura 54, 3 ch/3 living; Edith 22

1920 Leith, Grant, ND, p. 8B. George W Jones 64, merchant - retail; Laura A 64.

1930 Leith, Grant, ND, p. 2a. W George Jones 74, widowed, retired merchant.

Notes for Laura A. SHINKLE #145s

Death: Laura A Jones, d. 1/31/1926, Grant Co; Female; 70 Years; b. 5/21/1855 ND, Grant Co. North Dakota Dept of Health. <https://secure.apps.state.nd.us/doh/certificates/deathCertSearch.htm>

Notes for Doctor Albert JONES #146

Information from Jones book[256] gives first initial as "D"; "b. 25 Jan 1858; m. 16 Jun 1880 to Lucy E. Strahan [b. 16 Jan 1859; d. 20 Apr 1925]. He was a street car conductor and for several years was the Secretary of the Street Railway Union in Cincinnati, OH"

Jones notes give first name as Doctor; death date

Census:

1880 Silver Creek, Mills, IA. Doc Jones, 22, OH, working as farm laborer on farm of Henry Donner. [census taken 6 June 1880 - he was married 16 June 1880]

1900 Strahan, Wayne, NE, p. 8B. D A Jones 42, Jan 1858, OH/MD/MD; Lucy E Jones 41, Jan 1859; M J Jones 17, July 1882, IA, farm labor; Gale E Jones 16, Mar 1884, IA; J C M Jones 14, Sep 1885, IA; R O Jones 11, Dec 1888, IA; D A Jones 8, Jun 1892, NE. 6 ch/ 5 living, m. 19 yrs.

1910 Wayne Ward 3, Wayne, NE, p. 17B. Doctor A Jones 52, own income, OH/OH/OH; Lucy Jones 51, IL/IN/IN; Albert Jones 18, NE; Dorotha Jones 8, NE.

1920 Wayne, Wayne, NE, p.7B. Doc A Jones 61, no occ; Lucy E Jones 60, IL; Dorothy Jones 18, NE; George Sherbahn 38, son-in-law, inspector - house, PA/PA/PA; Gail Sherbahn 36, dau, IA/OH/IL; Bernadine Sherbahn 9, dau, NE; Donald Sherbahn 7, son, NE.

1930 Wayne, Wayne, NE, p. 1B. D A Jones 72, farmer, widowed; Albert Jones 37, son, laborer ___ job; Edna Jones 37, dau-in law, saleslady - dry goods; Marion Jones 14, grandson; June Jones 12, granddau; Neva Jones 11, granddau; Bonnell Jones 8, granddau; George Sherbahn 43, son-in-law, __?__ - carnival; Gail Sherbahn 46; Bernadine Sherbahn 19, dau in law; Donald Sherbahn 17, grandson; Betty Meister 4 2/12, granddau; Cora Pratt 60, lodger.

Biography: *Doctor A. Jones. Mr. Doctor A. Jones, a prosperous retired farmer now residing in Wayne, is the seventh son in a family of eight sons and two daughters born to his parents; and in view of the supposed healing qualities of the seventh son he was baptized Doctor Albert Jones. His parents, Henry and Elizabeth (Hicks) Jones, were natives of Maryland and Ohio respectively; the former died in 1906, the latter about 1868.*

Mr. Jones was born in Clermont county, Ohio, January 25, 1858, and there reared. At the age of twenty, he went to Texas and for two years was employed on the ranch of Atterburg Brothers, riding the range as a cowboy in Texas and Oklahoma for two years. Coming to Mills county, Iowa, for a time he was employed at farm labor and then rented land and farmed for a year or two prior to his moving to Nebraska in 1889. He purchased a half-section three miles west of Wayne, and lived here nearly twenty years, making farming a very successful vocation. In 1908, he purchased a fine dwelling adjoining Court Square in the city of Wayne, and gives his personal attention to his farming interests near the city.

Mr. Jones was married in Mills county, Iowa, June 16, 1880, to Miss Lucy E. Strahan, who was born in Henderson county, Illinois. Her parents, J. M. and Frances (Davis) Strahan moved to eastern Iowa in 1865, and later on out to Mills county, where she and Mr. Jones met. Of six children born to Mr. and Mrs. Jones, all are living; they are: Marcellus F., who is running the home farm; Gale, who is the wife of George Sherbohrn, resides in Wayne; Jay, is farming four miles west of Wayne; Roscoe returned to the former residence of the family in Mills county, Iowa, and engages in farming there; Albert, who is an expert motorist, acts as his father's chauffeur in his business trips through the country; and Dorothy, the youngest, is still in school.

Deer and antelope were extinct in the region when Mr. Jones came to Wayne county, but they were plentiful in Texas when he was employed there on the ranch. Much of the country throughout northeastern Nebraska was open prairie at the time Mr. Jones settled, here. In the period he has been a resident of the cornhusker's state, he has seen all this change-where was once open country covered with waving prairie grasses, are now to be seen highly tilled farms, miles of trees, substantial and elegant farm dwellings; big red barns, sheds, stacks of grain, and herds of cattle and horses; a country teeming with wealth and enjoying a prosperity that few sections can equal anywhere within the national domain.

Mr. Jones is a democrat, and represented his county in the legislature during the years 1896, 1897 and 1898. He is a member of the Modern Woodmen of America and the Eagle lodges. **Compendium of History, Reminiscence and Biography of Nebraska***, 1912.*

Notes for Lucy E. STRAHAN #146s
Info from Jones book & Jones notes
Census: 1870 Silver Creek, Mills, IA, p. 101. James Strahan 40, farmer, IN; Francis Strahan 36, NY; Lucy Strahan 11, IL; Lorella Strahan 7; Frances Strahan 4; Rosetta Strahan 1; John Strahan 20.

Notes for Minerva Isadora 'Dora' JONES #147
Jones book says b. 21 Mar 1859; m. James McCabe. They reside (1930) at Iola (Allen) KS.
Jones notes give nickname as "Dora"; death date
Census
  1900 Alvin, Brazoria, TX, p. 4B. Baxter Mccabe 44, Feb 1856, IL, IL/KY, salesman - hardware; Dora Mccabe 40, Mar 1860, OH/OH/OH, I child; Raymond Mccabe 12, Aug 1877, IA.
  1910 Winside, Wayne, NE, p. 3A. Frank S Tracy 43, post master - Uncle Sam; Grace O Tracy 39, m. 7 yrs, no children; Dora Mccabe 49, sister in law, widowed, 1 child living
  1920 Norfolk Ward 2, Madison, NE, p. 3A. Dora Meccabe 59, widow, OH/OH/OH, saleslady - corset co; lodger with August Arnecke 37
  1930 Iola, Allen, KS, p. 5A. Dora Mc Cabe 70, widow; Francis M McCabe 67, brother, single. Neither has occupation; Both OH/OH/OH. [this may be Dora's brother, Frank Jones]

Notes for James Baxter MCCABE #147s
Census
  1870 Rushville, Schuyler, IL, p. 173B. Wilber Mccabe 41, KY, farmer; Harriet E Mccabe 37, IL; George W Mccabe 17, IL; James B Mccabe 14, IL.
  1880 Malvern, Mills, IA, p. 359. J. B. Mccabe 24, IL/OH/KY, single, hardware merchant; George Mccabe 28, brother, hardware merchant, IL/OH/KY

Notes for Mary OWENS #154
Marriage: Peter Mason to Mary E Owens, 1868-05-30; Coles Co, IL [Illinois Statewide Marriage Index, 1763-1900]
Census
  1870 Mattoon, Coles, IL, p. 224B. Peter Mason 34, rr laborer, Can; Mary Mason 19, OH; Peter Mason 11; Rosa Mason 8; Julia Mason 6; Carrie Mason 4; Nancy Mason 1. Children b. IL. Children must be his from previous marriage; Nancy is probably hers.
  1880 Mattoon, Coles, IL, p. 198. Peter Mason 41, Can/Can/Can; Mary Mason 29, OH/KY/OH; Peter Mason 19; Rosa Mason 18; Julia Mason 16; Carrie Mason 14; Nannie Mason 11; Freddie Mason 8; Ida Mason 6; Josie Mason 3; Josie Owens 21, sis in law, IL/KY/OH; Emma Owens 19, sis in law, IL/KY/OH

1900 Mattoon, Coles, IL, p. 26B. Mary E Mason 47, Dec 1852, widow, washwoman, 7 ch/5 living; Fred A Mason 26, Jun 1873, painter; Edmund J Mason 11, Oct 1882, painter; Ida M Mason 24, Feb 1876, seamstress; Ada F Mason 15, Aug 1884, saleslady - dry goods; Mary C Mason 13, Jun 1886; Vera F Mason 6, Feb 1894; Claude F Mason 1, Jul 1899

1910 Chicago Ward 7, Cook, IL, p. 15A. Mary Mason 58, seamstress - retail dry goods, 7 ch / 5 living; Ida Mason 34, seamstress - retail dry goods; Dewey M Platt 24, son-in-law, salesman - retail dry goods, IL/OH/OH; Mary Platt 23, dau, m. 4 years, 2 ch / 1 living; Vera Mason 15, operator - phone co; Joseph Platt 1 1/12, grandson; Claude Mason 12

1920 May be the Mary D. Mason, 67, widow, OH/OH/VA listed as a patient at Oak Forest Institution, Bremen, Cook Co, IL, p. 29B.

*1930 possibly the Mary Mason in Kansas, Edgar Co, IL; age 77, widow, OH/NJ/OH, housekeeper. [*probably a different Mary.]

Notes for Peter MASON #154s
Death: Mary is listed as a widow in the 1900 census.
Info from Dean Demos, "married Peter Mason".
Census: 1860 Mattoon, Coles, IL, p. 52. Peter Mason 24, day laborer, East Canada; Rosa Mason 16, West Canada; Peter Mason 1, IL.

Notes for Josephine OWENS #158
Marriage1: William Guyette, to Josie Owens, 1888-01-24; Coles
Marriage2: Benedict Durham to (Mrs) Josie Owens Guyett, 1899-11-22; Coles. Illinois Statewide Marriage Index, 17631900
Biography: Information from great grandson-in-law, Alan Case of Columbus, OH, via Ancestry Message Board. "Josephine Owens was the daughter of William Owens and Nancy Hicks. She married William Guyette who was the Great Grandfather to my Wife, Linda Guyette Case. Her grandfather was Raymond Guyette (1892 to 1952). Her Grandfather had two children: Edward W. Guyette, her father, and Raymond Guyette, her uncle."
Census:
1880 Mattoon, Coles, IL, p. 198. Peter Mason 41, Can/Can/Can; Mary Mason 29, OH/KY/OH; Peter Mason 19; Rosa Mason 18; Julia Mason 16; Carrie Mason 14; Nannie Mason 11; Freddie Mason 8; Ida Mason 6; Josie Mason 3; Josie Owens 21, sis in law, IL/KY/OH; Emma Owens 19, sis in law, IL/KY/OH

1900 Mattoon, Coles, IL. p. 26B. Benedict Durham, 46, May 1854, carpenter; Josie M Durham 36, Jul 1863, IL; Selena H., dau 10, Dec 1889, Raymond, son, 8, May 1892; Ethel D. 4, Feb 1886, dau. m. 12 yrs, 3 ch / 3 living. [The children's surname should be Guyette as they are from her 1st marriage.]

1910 East St Louis Ward 6, St Clair, IL, p. 3B. Benedict Durham 55, carpenter - house; Josephine Durham 44; Selina Guyette 20, stenographer - steam railway, step dau; Raymond Guyette 17, clerk - steam railway, stepson. Married 10 yrs; 2nd marriage for each of them.

1920 East St Louis Ward 6, St Clair, IL, p. 4B. Josephine Durham, 52, widow, IL/OH/IN, packer - candy factory.

Notes for William GUYETTE #158s1
William may have been a sibling of Rosa Guyette, 1st wife of his brother-in-law, Peter Mason.
Information from Alan Case, Columbus, OH via Ancestry.com. His wife, Linda, is ggranddaughter of William Guyette & Josie Owens.

Notes for Benedict DURHAM #158s2
Information from great grandson via Ancestry Message Board.
Census: 1920 - Josephine listed as widow.

Notes for Mary Emma HICKS #160

Jones notes: "she was a school teacher. M1 to Taylor B. Holderfield, a dentist. He d. at Salem IL. M2 to Andrew A. Light"

Census

1880 Salem, Marion, IL, p. 193. Taylor B. Holderfield 31, dentist, OH/OH/OH; Emma 22, OH/OH/OH; Gussie E. 1/12, b. May, IL/OH/OH

1900 New Richmond, Clermont, OH, p. 5A. Mary E Holderfield 41, Sep 1858, OH/OH/KY, widow, 2 ch / 2 living, school teacher; Gussie E 20, May 1880; Ethel 18, Feb 1882, IL/OH/OH. Next to Elizabeth Joslin.

1910 Ohio, Clermont, OH, p. 1A. Andrew A Light 54, farmer; Emma 51. m2 for each of them; m. 5 years; living next to daughter: Gussie & John Gilfillen, their dau. Ethelene, 4.

1920 Ohio, Clermont, OH, p. 2B. Andy Light 62, salesman - creamery, OH/US/Wales; Emma 61; John Gilfilen 40, son-in-law, widowed, foreman - novelty co, OH/MD/OH; Etheleen Gilfillen 13, grandchild.

1930 New Richmond, Clermont, OH, p. 18A. Andrew Light 73, woodworker - coat hanger mill, OH/OH/Wales; Mary E Light 71, OH/OH/KY.

Death: Death Certificate gives name as Mary E. Light, spouse: Andrew A. Light, parents Joshua Hicks & Minerva Marshall, "married", date of death, burial. Informant: A. A. Light. Ohio Deaths 1908-1953 <pilot.familysearch.org>.

Notes for Taylor B. HOLDERFIELD #160s1

Jones notes: "Mary Emma Hicks M1 to Taylor B. Holderfield; He d. at Salem IL; a dentist."

Article in **Chicago Tribune**, 26 Feb 1886, "Centralia, ILL, Feb 25 - [special] *At Salem today, Taylor Holderfield, a well known dentist, graduate of the Cincinnati College of Dentistry, was convicted of larceny and sentenced to one year in State's Prison.*"

Emma Holderfield is listed as a widow in the 1900 census.

Notes for Andrew A. LIGHT #160s2

Jones notes: "Mary Emma Hicks. M2 to Andrew A. Light"

Census:

1860 Ohio twp, Clermont, OH, p. 230. Benjamine Light 54, farmer, NY; Mary 45, NY; John 23; Andy 4; Benjamine 1; Richard Lewis 24, farm labor; William Launsbery 22, farm labor; Mary Carter 18. Children b. OH.

1870 Ohio twp, Clermont, OH, p. 229. Benjamin Light 65, farmer, OH; Esther 50, OH; Andrew E 14, works on farm, OH. Next to John Light, 33, farm labor & his family.

Death: Ohio Death Certificate gives parents as Benjamin Light and "don't know"; spouse Mary Emma Light, "widowed", retired farmer. b. OH. Informant: Mrs A. J. Beckman [step-daughter], same address: 650 W. McMicken, Cincinnati, OH. <pilot.familysearch.org>.

Notes for Nancy B. HICKS #162

Info from Jones notes: birth date, spouse

Death: Mrs Nancy B Meenach, [Mrs Nancy B Hicks]; d. 6 Mar 1939, Mason Co, Residence: Mason; Age: 76, b. 23 Mar 1862, New Richmond, OH; Spouse: William H Meenach; Father: George Hicks. b. OH; Mother: Minerva Marshall; b. OH. Kentucky Death Records, 1852-1953. [Ancestry.com]

Notes for William Harvey MEENACH #162S

Jones notes: "John Hicks diary mentions Wm Meeriack dropping by 11/30/1900"

Census:

1900 Maysville, Mason, KY, p. 33B. W H Meinach 49, Dec 1850 KY, laborer; Nackie Meinach 38, Mar 1862, OH; Mary E Meinach 14, Apr 1886 KY; Harry G Meinach 12 Jul 1887, KY. m. 16 yr, 2 ch/2 living

1910 Dieterich, Mason, KY, p. 2B. William Menack 55, traveling salesman; Maxey Menack 45; Harry Menack 25; Edna Cablish 23, dau, m. 4 yrs, 1 child; Fred Cablish 27, son in law, plumber; Evelyn Cablish 3, gr dau. All b. KY.

1920-1930 not found

Jones notes say "Elizabeth was a sister to Wm Meeriach

Name on marriage bond is Meenach.

Death: William Harvey Meenach, Death: 2 Feb 1932, Mason, 81; Birth: 17 Dec 1850, Mason, KY; Spouse: Nancy Hicks; Father: James Harvey Meenach; b. Mason, KY; Mother: Elizabeth Ballon, b. US. Informant: Mrs R. F. Kablish [dau. Edna]. Kentucky Death Records, 1852-1953 [Ancestry.com].

Information via email: *"Before I send you the line I want to explore something and give you a little background. I believe you have another connection to this family. The Meenach line came out of Pennsylvania and settled Kentucky about 1795. James, seven sons and one daughter (no wife mentioned). I descend from his son James Harvey Meenach (1788) and James Harvey Meenach Jr. (abt 1810). Jr. married the daughter (Elizabeth b. 1810-1815) of Oliver C. Colburn (b abt 1791) who came to Kentucky about 1810-1814 from Maine. They had four daughters and one son (from whom I descend). She died and he married Elizabeth Ballou and they had two children, a girl and a boy (William Harvey Meenach), the one who married Nancy Hicks, dau of Joshua, son of Elijah. Williams half sister, I recently figured out, married a William S. Hicks (born Jan. 1842 (from 1900 census) in Jan. 1870. Looking at the children of Elijah Hicks and Nancy Melvin, I notice a William Stephen, born Jan. 10, 1842. Believing there is no such thing as coincidence, I have to believe he is the uncle of the Nancy Hicks (dau of his brother Joshua) who married William Harvey Meenach and his marriage to Williams older half sister is how he met his wife Nancy. William and Elizabeth had two boys and two girls. I have only been able to track one line, from their son Arthur (before I found your posting). He married in 1918, Ada Porter and had a little girl, Betty Ann in Feb. 1919. I found a World Tree source (turns out it was you) that claims she died Feb. 20. 1920. In the 1920 Census , which was taken effective Jan. 1 that year, you will find all three plus her mother and married sister, obviously there to help care for her. Thanks to that, you can find little Betty Ann with assurance in 1930 as she is the care of her aunt, Etta Benfield in Beaver Co. PA. As you did not list Betty Ann, I thought maybe you did not have her in your files. In any event, she connects to my line as well as yours. Did you know about Betty Ann? Now, as I was writing this, I found your extensive OneWorldTree listing on this line. You call Elizabeth Mericach but she is also Meenach and William's half sister. I notice you claim five children for Wm and Eliz. I am puzzled about Elsie Hicks who was born about 1875. She is not with the family in 1880 (Mason County, Orangeburg Pct., KY) number 469. Are you sure she is connected to the family. Best regards, Bob*

Notes for Harry G. MEENACH #429

Jones notes: "Married Rose -?-; resided Dayton, OH"

Census

1920 Dayton Ward 4, Montgomery, OH, p. 6A. H G Marnach 32, KY/KY/OH, plumber - factory; Rose Marnach 31; Tully Marnach 14, nephew, OH/OH/OH; Barbara Miller 60, lodger

1930 Dayton, Montgomery, OH, p. 7A. Harry G Meenach 42, KY/KY/OH, manager - autos; Rose Meenach 41, OH/OH/OH.

Military: World War I Draft Registration Cards, 1917-1918 [ancestry.com] Harry Meenach, age 30, b. 27 May 1887, Maysville, KY; res: Dayton, Montgomery, OH; occ: plumber; dependents: wife & wife's nephew. Short, stout, brown hair & eyes. Regis: 5 Jun 1917, Dayton, OH.

Military: World War II Draft Registration Cards, 1942 [ancestry.com] Harry Gordon Meenach, age 54, b. 27 Jul 1887, Maysville, Mason Co, KY; res: Union, Miami co, Ohio; Relative: Rose Meenach; occ: farming - southern Miami Co, OH.

Death: Harry G Meenach, b. 1888; Res: St Marys, Auglaize, OH; d. 1 Jan 1966, Good Samaritan Hospital, Dayton, Montgomery, OH; Age: 78; Widowed. Ohio Deaths, 1908-1932, 1938-1944, and 1958-2007 [ancestry.com]

Notes for Nora Sureanth HICKS #166
Death: KY Death Index gives: Hutchison Nora H, Age 70, Mason; 05-28-1930
Death: Nora Hicks Hutchison, b. 17 Jan 1860, OH; d. 28 May 1930, Mason Co, KY. Parents: James Hicks; Emma Barnes. Buried Maysville, KY 30 May 1930. Kentucky Death Records, 1852-1953 [Ancestry.com]
Census:
  1900 Magisterial District 8, Mason, KY, p. 2A. Edward Hutchison 39, OH, cigar maker; Nora 35; Celia M 12; Roy E 7. Living next to James Hicks, Nora's father.
  1910 Dieterich, Mason, KY. Edward W Hutchison 49, cigar maker; Nora L 44; Roy 17. 4 ch/2 living.
  1920 Dietrich, Mason, KY, p. 5A. Edward W Hutchison 59, cigar maker; Nora L 54. Next to James Hicks, Nora's father.
  1930 Dist 21, Mason, KY, p. 28. Edward Hutchison, 68, KY/OH/KY, janitor - public school; Nora, wife, 63, OH/OH/OH, no occ; Minnie Hicks. 61, single, sis-in-law; Occ: practical nurse.

Notes for Edward White HUTCHISON #166s
Jones notes: "cigar maker, resided at Mays Lick; bur Maysville"
Death: KY Death Index gives: Hutchison Edward W; age 88; Mason; 4-23-1949
Death: Edward White Hutchison; d. 23 Apr 1949, Mason; Residence: Mason (lifetime); Age: 88; widower, retired cigar maker; b. 15 Aug 1860, Mason, KY. Parents: William Hutchison; Mary E Worthington. Informant: Roy Hutchison; Burial: Maysville, KY. Kentucky Death Records, 1852-1953 [Ancestry.com]

Notes for William Pearce HICKS #168
Jones notes: M1 Lillian Dunbar; M2 2/18/1919 to Frances (Miller) King at Houston TX [she b. 5/31/1875 Cincinnati]; dau of 2nd wife - Mrs Helen Shoher, 750 NE 40th St, Apt 450, Boca Raton FL 33422. Geneva Wehmeyer, 5225 Carthage Av, Norwood was executor. Maier & Mathews attys [case 233205]. William resided with Robert & Genevieve Wehmeyer at time of his death. Clifford and Helen King were children of Frances from her 1st marriage, their father being deceased""
Census
  1900 not found in KY or OH.
  1910 Newport, Campbell Co, KY, p. William P Hicks 38, OH/KY/KY10B, machine moulder - foundry; Lilly 36, KY/KY/KY; Leslie B 4, male; Hazel L 11/12. m. 14 yr; 3 ch/2 living.
  1920 Houston Ward 3, Harris, TX, p. 2a. William P Hicks 47, KY/OH/KY, moulder - iron; Fannie M Hicks 44; Helen King 11, OH, step dau.
  1930 Norwood, Hamilton, OH, p. 34B. William Hicks 57, moulder - foundry, KY/OH/US; Fanny Hicks 54, OH/ LS?/Ger. Age at 1st marriage William 46 / Fannie 19.

Notes for Lillian [Emma?] DUNBAR #168s
Census: 1930 Cleveland, Cuyahoga, OH. Emma Hicks 56, widowed, gen housework - private house; William Hicks 16; Hazel Faloon 21, dau, married (at age 16), saleslady - dry goods.

Notes for Callie James HICKS #169
Jones notes: give birth date, spouse; "resided for a time at Connorsville, IN. In 1972, resided at 10513 Clari, Sun City Ariz 85351"
Alive in 1972; Orville Jones corresponded with her then (age 96)
Death: Lingenfelser, Callie; b. 25 Jul 1876; May 1979; 102; Sun City, Maricopa, AZ; issued: Arizona. #527-88-6025. Social Security Death Index <rootsweb.com>

Census
- 1900 Mason Co, KY, p.13. Will Lingenfelser, Jul 1873, KY/Ger/MD; Callie W, Jul 1876, OH/KY/ KY; Margarete D, Jul 1899, KY. Married 3 yrs., 1 ch / 1 living next to: John Lingenfelser, Apr 1837 Germany; Margarete, Apr 1838, MD/Ger/Ger; Frank, Mar 1866, KY; George, Aug 1872, KY; Minnie, Jun 1880, KY; (mar. 33 yrs. 7 children, all living). John and Margarete are presumably the parents of Will
- 1910 Magisterial District 5, Mason, KY, p. 8A. William Lingenfelser 36, farmer, KY/Ger/Ger; Callie 34, KY/OH/OH; Margaret 13, KY; Eugene 6, KY. 2 ch / 2 living. M. 12 years.
- 1920 Washington, Mason, KY, p. 12B. Wm Lingenfelser 46, farmer; Callie 43; Margaret 20; Eugene 15. Next to George Lingenfelser 48; on other side: Frank Lingenfelser 56. [his brothers]
- 1930 Maysville, Mason, KY, p. 2A. Wm H Lingenfelser 54, meat cutter - meat market; Callie J 51; Emma M 39, dau, single, teacher - college.

Marriage: to William Lingenfelser on 2 Feb 1898 in Maysville, KY. He 24, butcher; she 21. Mason Co Marriage Rec. Vol. 21, p. 602.

Marriage Bond. Wm. Lingenfelser & Callie Hicks. Mason Co, KY, 2 Feb 1898. Res. near Maysville, KY; age 24, butcher; b. near Maysville. Father, b. Germany; mother, b. Boston, MA. Callie, b. near Maysville, age 21. 1st marriage for both. Bond by William & Joseph Lingenfelser.

*Note: "Lingenfelser ?" written in the spouse section for Caroline in the Hicks Bible extracts and notes of Lucy Hicks Meeker. This is the surname of a daughter of James Hicks (Callie Lingenfelser) with whom Orville Jones reported a correspondence in 1972 (she then age 96).

Notes for William LINGENFELSER #169s
Jones notes: 'he died 9/3/1864 ; buried Maysville". [Note: this is before he was born - maybe 1964?]

Notes for Eugene William LINGENFELSER #437
Jones notes: "Resides (1972) at Rt 1, Box 21 Rushville, IN 46173; no children"
Ancestry OneWorld Tree gives wives as: 1925 - Neva Mers 1898-1931 (Neva died 5 months pregnant of pneumonia, Elizaville, Fleming, KY); 1933 - Eva M. Beckner 1903-1993, d. 6 Mar 1993 in Connersville, Fayette, IN; 21 Dec 1955 - Odessa Bacon 1906-1983 (Odessa was buried in Maysville, Mason Co, KY; d. 22 Feb 1983 in Rushville, Rush, IN); Kathryn Richter. No documentation. Info from Catherine Theresa Lingenfelser, 2007.
- **Census**: 1930 Milton, Wayne, IN, p. 5B. Eugene Lingenfelser 26, retail merchant - own grocery, m. age 21; Neva Lingenfelser 32. Both KY/KY/KY.

U.S. Public Records Index [Ancestry.com] E W Lingenfelser; Birth: Feb 1903; Address: PO Box 511, Milton, IN. 47357-0401 (1992);   Rr 1 PO Box 235, Rushville, Indiana 46173-1201 (1985)

Death: Social Security Death Index: Eugene W. Lingenfelser; #311-34-6624; Last Residence: Wickenburg, Maricopa, AZ; Born: 3 Feb 1903; Died: 7 Mar 2004; SSN issued: Indiana (1951)

Obituary: *The Wickenburg Sun* [week of March 10, 2004]. *Eugene "Gene" Lingenfelser, co-owner of Katy and Gene's Coins and Collectibles on Wickenburg Way, died Sunday, March 7, 2004, in a Sun City Hospice just 33 days after his 101st birthday. The popular centenarian, known for his sense of humor and positive outlook on life, was a fixture at the shop run by he and his wife of 20 years, Katy. He was at the shop six days a week, often in his chair in front of the store greeting passersby. His wife recalled the time a few months ago when two out-of-towners, apparently used to the store front stuffed images so often seen around the Southwest, stopped in front of her husband and one of them said, "Oh look, this one looks real." "Gene just broke out laughing and almost gave them a heart attack," she said. Born in Maysville, Ky. on Feb. 3. 1903, he was in the grocery business, owning and operating supermarkets in Indiana for some 50 years before his retirement in 1952. He was a member of the Clarksburg, Indiana Christian Church for 42 years and was a Lifetime Charter Member of the Fraternal Order of Eagles, Lodge 1065 in Connersville, Ind. He and his wife Katy moved to Wickenburg in 1998. He is survived by several step-children and grandchildren and his wife, the former Kathryn R. Richter, who said, "Gene's last* *words were for his close friends. They were, 'Tell my friends to avoid the Wahoo.'" Funeral services by Frey Funeral Home this week were private.*

Notes for Lida H. HICKS #170
Norman Zezula notes: "Lida married Robert J. Wilson in Maysville, Mason Co, KY on 18 Jul 1889. Robert was born in Adams Co, OH but was a resident of Seattle, WA and a lawyer. After Elijah was institutionalized, Lida & her mother Victoria went to Maysville where they appear with her Victoria's sister's family (Emile & Ellen Martin) in the 1880 census."

Census

1880 Maysville, Mason, OH. Victora Hicks 35, sis in law, widow; Lida Hicks 13, niece; with Emile Martin 67; Eliza J. 40; Samuel D. 17; George H. 13; Joseph E. 7; Cinta Warbinton 68, mother in law.

1900 St Louis City, St Louis, MO. Robert J Wilson 38, Jul 1861, OH/Ire/Ire, real estate agt; Lida H 32, Mar 1868, OH; Marie H 8, Feb 1892; Victoria E Hicks 56, Mar 1844, mother in law; George H Martin 32, Jan 1868, cousin, KY/Fra/OH, inspector - railroad

1910 Seattle Ward 14, King, WA, p 4A. Robert J Wilson 49, booker - real estate, OH/Eng/Eng; Lida H 43, OH/OH/OH, 1 ch / 1 living; Marie H 18, dau, WA/OH/OH ; Victory E Hicks 66, mother, widow, OH/OH/OH, 1 ch / 1 living.

1920 Seattle, King, WA, p. 3B. Robert J Wilson 59, OH/Ire/Ire, insurance agent; Lida 52, OH/OH/OH; Harold E Kerry 29, son in law, MI/Eng/Scot, salesman - paper; Marie Kerry 27, daughter, WA/OH/OH

1930 Seattle, King, WA, p. 36A. Robert J Wilson 69, salesman - insurance, OH/Ire/Ire; Lida H Wilson 63; Frank Aubell 52, roomer, postman - US mail, MI/Ger/MI.

Notes for Robert J. WILSON #170s
Jones notes: "m. 7/18/1889 to Robert J. Wilson [b. 1861 Adams Co OH] at Maysville KY. Resided (1916) at 6555 19th Ave NE, Seattle, WA; boy & girl dead"

Marriage Bond, Mason Co, KY. Robt J. Wilson with Geo H. Martin as surety. Marriage of Robt J. Wilson & Lida H. Hicks. 18 July 1889. Robert, age 28, b. Adams Co, OH; residence: Seattle, WA. Lawyer. Father & mother, b. Ireland. Lida H. Hicks, b. Nicholasville, OH, age 22, res: Maysville, KY. 1st marriage for both. Married at residence of Mr. Martin on S---stone St, Maysville, KY, 18 Jul 1889.

Census: 1900 Seattle, King, WA shows another Robert Wilson, b. Aug 1860, head, married 15 yrs, Fireman - Steamboat; wife Lida, b. Feb 1867, 33, mar. 15 yr, 2 ch/2 living; Lena, dau, July 1891, 8; Ora B., dau, Jun 1894, 5. All PA/PA/PA. Apparently not related.

Death: Robert J. Wilson, d. 25 Dec 1931, Seattle, King, WA; b. abt 1860, age 71 yr, 5 mo, 3 da. Parents: John Wilson & Jane Mckoule; spouse Lida H. Wilson. Washington Death Certificates 1907-1960 [pilot.familysearch.org> [index only, no certificate]

Notes for Edgar Newton VERMILLION #176
Census

1900 Kansas City, Jackson County, MO, Ward 10, p. 280. Edgar Vermillion, April 1863, 37, married 7 years, b. OH, MO/OH. Cabinet maker, rents home. Wife Nora , Nov 1876, 23, b. KS/KS/KS, 4 ch/2 living; Clarence, May 1894, 5, son, MO; Nora, dau, Apr 1899, 1, KS. Agnes Ave.

1910 Kansas City Ward 3, Wyandotte, KS, p. 9B. Edgar Vermillion 48, farmer, OH/KY/OH; Nora 33, KS/KS/KS; Clarence 14; Clara 9; Ruth 7, MO; Joseph 3; Edna 2; Willie 1; John Vermillion 77, KY/OH/KS. M 16 yr; 10 ch/6 living. Kids other than Ruth, b. KS

1920 Kansas City, Wynadotte Co, KS, 41 Precinct, p. 289. Edgar Vermillion, age 54, b. OH, parents b. KY, OH, laborer in Can Co; wife Nora, children: Ruth 17 b. MO, Joseph 12 b. KS, Edna 11, Frank 8, John 5. Rest of children b. KS.

1930 Kansas City, Wyandotte, KS, p. 43A. Edgar Vermillion 68, owner - confectionery; Nora 53; Joseph 23, clerk - Westinghouse office; Frank 18; John 16; Martha Vermillion 90, mother, widow.

Kansas State census
- 1915 Kansas City, Ward 3, KS. E N Vermillion 52, laborer; N E Vermillion 38; Clara B Vermillion 14; R M Vermillion 12; J E Vermillion 8; Edna P Vermillion 7; F M Vermillion 3; John A Vermillion 1
- 1925. Bonner Springs, Wyandotte Co, KS. Edgar N Vermillion 59, carpenter - Chase Bag Co; Nora E 48, cook - Myron Greens; Joseph E 18, candy maker; Frank M 13; John A 10

Death: no information located. This date from granddaughter.

Info: Vermillion Family Tree [ancestry.com] gives marriage to Nora Ellen Smith, 1893; death as 12 Dec 1954, Houston, Harris Co, TX. No documentation.

Information on birth & death date is from Verna Ruth (Vermillion) Coleman - granddaughter of Edgar Vermillion. "They were married May 7, 1893 in Jackson, Kansas City, Missouri". This according to MO Marriage records, 1805-2002 John B. parents: John Vermillion b. 1790, Mary Newman b. 1796 and grandparents Edward Vermillion b. 1744; d. 1810; married to Mildred Vermillion. Mildred and Edward were 1st cousins."

Notes for Nora Ellen SMITH #176

Information on birth & death date is from Verna Ruth (Vermillion) Coleman, granddaughter of Edgar Vermillion.

Death: Nora Ellen Vermillion, 2235 Richwood, Kansas City, MO; b. 9 Nov 1876; d. 2 Dec 1930; spouse: Edgar Vermillion; parents: James Smith & Ruth Anna ?. Buried Mt Hope Cem, 5 Dec 1930. Death Certificate <www.sos.mo.gov>.

Notes for Caroline Wise HICKS #179

Jones notes: "Resided in Maysville; both buried in Maysville Cemetery"

Death: Carrie Wise Brubaker, d. 29 Oct 1952, Cleveland Heights, Cuyahoga, OH; b. 7 Jul 1871, Maysville Ky; Age: 81 years; widowed; Father: Wm. S. Hicks; Mother: Bettie Meinach. Ohio Deaths, 1908-1953 <familysearch.org>

Census:
- 1900 Magisterial District 8, Mason, KY, p. 6B. James Brubaker 32, Dec 1867, OH, farmer; Carrie W Brubaker 28, Jul 1871, KY; Lillia M Brubaker 10/12, Jul 1899, KY; m. 2 yrs, 1 child.
- 1910 Maysville Ward 5, Mason, KY, p. 3A. James K Brubaker 41, carpenter; Carrie Brubaker 38; Maud E Brubaker 10; Arthur Brubaker 8; Bessie Brubaker 8; Cecil Brubaker 5; Evans Brubaker 2. married 11 yrs, 5 children.
- 1920 Dietrich, Mason Co, KY. James K. Brubaker, 51, OH/OH/OH, carpenter; Carrie W., wife, 48, KY/OH/KY; Maudella E., dau, 20, S, KY/OH/KY; Arthur, son, 18, S, ships clerk - warehouse?; Bessie S, 18, Cecil N., 15; Kyle E., 11. Living next to Carrie's parents William S. & Elizabeth Hicks.
- 1930 Seven Mile, Butler, OH, p. 1A. Robert B Owens 34, TN/TN/TN, welder - automobile factory; Bessie 28; Alice 7, PA; Carrie Brubaker 58, mother in law.

Obituary: *Mrs. Carrie Brubaker Dies; Burial Here [10-30-1952]. Mother of W. A. and C. N. Brubaker Expires Early Wednesday in Cleveland. Mrs. Carrie Hicks Brubaker, 80, widow of J. K. Brubaker and a native Maysvillian, expired early Wednesday in Cleveland, O, where she alternated residence with her two daughters. She was the mother of W. Arthur Brubaker, Kentucky Utilities office manager here, and Cecil N. Brubaker, a vice president of the Browning Manufacturing company. Mrs. Brubaker had not been really well during the past few years but when she retired Tuesday night, she seemed to be feeling quite well. Death was attributed to coronary thrombosis. Although she had been away from Maysville most of the time since her husband passed away on June 12, 1922, Mrs. Brubaker often returned here and is well and lovingly remembered. She was a member of Trinity Methodist church. One whose gentle manner and sweet simplicity endeared her to all, Mrs. Brubaker was a woman of superior character. She had many friends and she richly deserved the for she had a heart fully of sympathy for others and a kindness about her that set her apart as a truly good woman. At the news of her passing, poignant regret will be* *experienced by those who had the deepest admiration for her. Born July 7, 1873, the deceased was the daughter of the late William H. and Elizabeth Meenach Hicks. Her parents also had two sons, Dr. W. H. Hicks, Maysville osteopath who died in February of 1925, and Arthur S. Hicks, of Haywood, NC, who passed away in December, 1948. In addition to her two sons in Maysville, the deceased leaves another son, Evans Brubaker, of Hamilton, O., and two daughters, Mrs. Robert Brown Owen, twin sister of the KY Utilities office manager, and Mrs. James E. Roden, also of Cleveland. It was at the Owen home that Mrs. Brubaker passed away. Also surviving are seven grandchildren.*

Notes for James Kyle BRUBAKER #179s
Death: James Kyle Brubaker, d. 12 Jun 1922, Mason Co, KY; Age: 54; b. 30 Dec 1867, Ohio; Father: David T Brubaker b. OH; Mother: Arzela Clarke, b. OH. occ: carpenter. Kentucky Death Records, 1852-1953 [Ancestry.com]

Notes for William H. HICKS #180
Jones notes: "Resided at Maysville, KY; son & dau deceased; both Wm & Ella were osteopaths"
Census
  1900 Washington, Mason, KY. William Hicks 24, Aug 1876, school teacher, KY/KY/KY; Ella 22, Mar 1878, KY/VA/VA; Georgia 1/12, Apr 1900, KY/KY/KY
  1910 Washington, DC, Precinct 1. p. 9. Wm J Nicks 34, KY, physician - ostopathy; Ella T 32; Geo K 10; Stanley M. 8. All b. KY.
  1920 Maysville, Mason Co, KY, p. 4. William A Hicks 44, div, doctor - ostopathy; Edward Linville 33, roomer, ?-music; Richard Shaniara 32, roomer, ? - music.
Not found on WW I Draft Registration.
Marriage: W. H. Hicks, b. 1876; age 22 to Ella Yancey, b. 1879, age 19. Marriage Date: 25 Jan 1898. Kentucky Marriages, 1785-1979. <familysearch.org>
Death: W H Hicks, Death: 11 Feb 1925 Mason Co, KY; Age: 50. Kentucky Death Index, 1911-2000 [ancestry.com]
Death: Dr W H Hicks; d. 11 Feb 1925, Mason Co, age 49; b. 5 Aug 1875, Mason Co, KY; father: Wm S. Hicks, b. OH; mother: Elizabeth A Munhill, b. Mason, Kentucky. Occ: osteopath. Divorced. Informant: A. G? Hicks, Moncure, NC. Kentucky Death Records, 1852-1953 [ancestry.com]

Notes for Ella YANCEY #181s
Census
  1920 Maysville, Mason, KY, p. 8. Ella Y Hicks 41, div, KY/VA/WV, doctor - osteopath, Georgie 19; Markham 17, salesman - shoe store; Francis Wright 16; Ella M Allen 58, roomer.
  1930 Maysville, Mason, KY, p. 8. Ella Y. Hicks, un, wid, physician - osteopath
Death: SSDI gives Ella Hicks, born 31 Mar 1878, died Mar 1967; Maysville, Mason, KY; #402-54-3354; card issued in Kentucky
Obituary: *Dr. Ella Y. Hicks, who practiced osteopathy in Maysville for almost 50 years, died at noon Monday at the Mary L. Eddy Nursing Home in Lexington. She was nearing her 89th birthday. Dr. Hicks, whose offices were at 216 Court Street, entered the nursing home in late September 1957. She had retired from her profession earlier in the year after 49 years of practice. She had opened offices here in June 1908, after completing training at the School of Oasteopathy, Macon, Missouri, and from then until failing health forced her retirement had a large clientele.*
Dr. Hicks had known the heartbreak of losing an only daughter and an only son, Mrs. Georgia (Paul) Eastham, of Ashland, died August 21, 1924, and Stanley Markham Hicks, September 13, 1954. Their father, the late Dr. William H. Hicks, was also a long-time Maysville osteopath who also received his training at the Missouri school. The widely known woman osteopath was a Lewis Countian by birth. Born March 31, 1878, she was the next to the last of the ten children of Andrew Jackson and Catherine Allen Yancey who migrated to Kentucky from Virginia soon after their marriage. Survivors are one sister, Mrs.

Charles B. Day of Maysville, three nieces and five nephews; Mrs. Madison D Lindsay, of Lewisburg, Mrs. W.G. Bradford, Maysville; Mrs. James N Kirk, of Mason county; Fred R. Day, Richmond; George Yancey, Lexington; Louis Yancey, Miami, FL; and Clarence and Russell Ensor, both of Mason County. Burial will be in Maysville Cemetery.

Notes for Arthur S. HICKS #182
Jones notes: "Resided in Maysville; no children"
Military: World War I Draft Registration Cards, 1917-1918. [ancestry.com] Arthur Stanley Hicks, age 40, b. 2 Mar 1878; res: Maysville, Mason, KY; occ: engine coler [sic], - C & O R.R.; nearest relative: Adah G. Hicks, Maysville. (Back of card missing)
Census
  1920 Clairton, Allegheny, PA, p. 17B. Arthur S Hicks 40, KY/KY/KY, policeman - steel co.; Ada S Hicks 30, KY/KY/KY; Betty Ann Hicks 11/12, PA; Etta M Benfield 37, sister-in-law, married, no occ.; Mary M Porter 66, mother in law, widow, no occ.
  1930 Aliquippa, Beaver, PA, p. 1A. Esky F Benfield 41, NC/NC/NC, contractor- construction co; Etta Benfield 48, KY/KY/KY; Betty A Hicks 11, niece, PA/KY/KY
  1930 Haywood, Chatham, NC, p. 2A. Arther Hicks 52, farmer, KY; Kate Hicks 44, NC; saleslady - gen store
Marriage2: Arthur S Hicks, b. 1881. age 45 to Mary Kate Thomas, b. 1886, Age: 40; Marriage Date: 21 Mar 1926, Haywood, Chatham, NC; Groom's parents: W. S. Hicks / Bettie A. Hicks; Bride's parents: J J Thomas / Nola Thomas. North Carolina Marriages, 1759-1979 <familysearch.org>
Death: Obituary of his sister, Caroline Brubaker, gives his death as Dec 1946 in Haywood, NC.

Notes for Adah H. PORTER #182s
Census: 1910 Maysville Ward 2, Mason, KY, p. 4A. Samuel Porter 56, blacksmith - carriage factory; Mary Porter 56; Etta Porter 26; William Porter 24; Ada Porter 22, saleslady - confectionery store; Katie Porter 19. All KY/KY/KY

Notes for Lavina Britana HICKS #183
Census: 1900 Columbus, Franklin Co, OH, p. 4A. Edward _ Tudor, Nov 1867, 33, m. 10 yr, tailor; Lavina, b. Aug 1862, 31, 1 ch/ 1 liv, OH/OH/OH; C. Nora, dau, Jul 1891, 8. Next to Lavina's parents Poke & Lavinia Hicks.
  1910 Columbus Ward 8, Franklin, OH, p. 1A. Edward M Tudor 43, KY/Eng/Eng, bookkeeper - real estate; Linina B Tudor 40, KY/KY/OH, keeper - boarding house; William Sonders 20, son in law, clerk - cigar store, TN/OH/OH; Lenora Sonders 18, dau, KY/KY/KY; Phillip R Bunn 50, boarder, laborer - odd jobs; William Kankin 45, boarder, laborer - odd jobs. Next to Lavina's mother, Caroline Hicks, 62, widow, keeper of boarding house.
  1920 Columbus Ward 12, Franklin, OH, p. 7A. William A Souder 29, TN, merchant - dyeing co; Senora Souder 28; Bittie Tudor 51, widow, — in- law; Charles F Weaver 54, roomer, clerk - postal; Elsworth Stewart 56, roomer, painter - house.
  1930 Columbus, Franklin, OH, p. 10A. Wm A Souders 40, TN/OH/TN, salesman - advertising; Lenora Souders 39; Brittania Tudor 60, m-in-law, widow
Death: Lavina Tudor, d. 22 Sep 1949, Columbus, Franklin, OH; age 82; b. 09 Aug 1867, Shilo, OH; Father: O. M. P. Hix; mother: Lavina C. Hutter. Ohio Deaths, 1908-1953 <pilot.familysearch.org>

Notes for Edward N. TUDOR #183s
Death: Edward N. Tudor, d. 29 Nov 1917, Columbus, Franklin, OH; b. 07 Nov 1866 KY; Age: 51 years 22 days; Burial: 1 Dec 1917; Father: Thomas Tudor, b. South Africa; Mother: Caroline White, b. KY. Ohio Deaths, 1908-1953 <fsbeta.familysearch.org>

Notes for Nancy Olivia HICKS #184

Census

1900 Columbus Ward 12, Franklin, OH, p. 4A. N. Fremont St. Morton Mergard 30, Jan 1870, KY/Ger/Ger, tailor; Olivia Mergard 28, Jun 1871, KY/OH/OH; John Partello 50, roomer; Gomer Delay 39, roomer. M 2 year, no children; in same household with sister Lavinia Tudor & parents Polk & Carolina Hicks.

1910 not found

1920 Columbus Ward 12, Franklin, OH, p. 2B. N. 5th St. Oliva Margard 48, widow, KY/KY/OH, housekeeper - private family; Carolina Hicks 74, mother, widow, OH/OH/OH; Frank Hicks 46, brother, widow, KY/KY/OH; Gladys Margard 18, dau, OH/KY/KY; Wayne H Margard 13, son, OH/KY/KY

1930 Columbus, Franklin, OH, p. 16A. Gay Street. Olivia N Magard 59, landlady - rooming house, KY/OH/OH, married; Wayne H Magard 23, presser - dry cleaning, OH/KY/KY; Frank S Hicks 57, brother, salesman - clothing, divorced; Earl Brill 23, roomer; Everett Wilson 22, roomer; Charles Snedik 18, roomer; Thomas Bunton 37, roomer; William Bunton 36, roomer

Death: Nancy Olevia Mergard, d. 14 Nov 1937, Marble Cliff, Franklin, OH; b. 19 Jun 1870, Maysville, KY; Age: 67 years 4 months 28 days; Widowed; Street address: 1970 Cardigian Ave; Burial: 16 Nov 1937 Greenlawn; Spouse: Morton H. Mergard; Father: E. P. Hicks b. Ohio; Mother: Levina Carolina Ulter; informant Mrs. W. L. Omert, same address. Ohio Deaths, 1908-1953 <fspilot.familysearch.org>

Notes for Martin H. MERGARD #184s

Census 1880 Maysville, Mason, OH, p. 389. Henry Merguard 43, Prussia, tailor; Maggie Merguard 22, Bavaria; Henry Merguard 10; Mattie Merguard 8; Hermann Merguard 5; Emma Merguard 1

Death: Martin H. Mergard d. 07 Jun 1908 Columbus, Franklin Co, OH, Burial date 10 Jun 1908; Age 37; b 25 Jan 1871 Maysville, Ky; occ: Tailor; Married; Father Henry Mergard; b. Germany; Mother Elizabeth Schmitt b. Germany. Ohio Deaths and Burials, 1854-1997 <fspilot.familysearch.org>

Notes for Elsie HICKS #186

Birth: 1880 census - Orangeburg pct 9, Mason, KY - indicates "Elsie" is a "son"

Marriage: Elise Hicks, 23, dau of William Hicks & Elizabeth Meeriach, m. 24 Aug 1898 to Joseph J. Lingenfelser, 24, by Roman Catholic priest at his home in Maysville, KY. Joseph, b. Mason Co, KY; Engineer. his father b. Germany; mother, b. Baltimore, MD; Elise b. Maysville, Mason Co, KY, parents b. same. Mason Co, Marriages, v. 22, p. 122.

Census: 1900, Columbus, Franklin Co, OH. Elsie Lingenfelser, head, 25, b. Mar 1875, m. 2 yr, housework; son Stanley 11/12, b. Jul 1899, KY. near her father Poke Hicks and family and Lavinia Tudor (her sister). All under same dwelling number (may have been a boarding house). Joseph not found in US.

Death: Elsie Lingenfelser, d. 06 Apr 1903 Columbus, Franklin, OH; Burial: 7 Apr 1903; Age 29; Birth: 1874 Kentucky; Married; Father: Polk Hicks; Mother: Lovina C. Hicks. Ohio Deaths and Burials, 1854-1997 <fsbeta.familysearch.org>

Notes for Joseph J. LINGENFELSER #186s

Jones notes: "Joseph remarried 9/1/1904 to Lulu Trisler, d. 1938"

Census:

1910 Maysville, Mason Co, KY. Joseph Lingenfelser, 34, m2, stationary engineer; wife Lulu, 33, her 1st marriage, m. 5 yr, 2 ch / 2 living. Sons Gordon 4, Edward 2; Stanley 10 (son of Elsie)

1920 Maysville, Mason Co, KY, p. 1B. Joseph Lingenfelser 43, KY/Ger/Ger, laborer - county roads; Lula Lingenfelser 42; Gordon Lingenfelser 13; Edward Lingenfelser 11; William Lingenfelser 8; Nellie Trisler 22, sister-in-law. All except Joseph - KY/KY/KY.

1930 Maysville, Mason Co, KY, p. 1A. Joseph J Lingenfelser 52, engineer - road machine; Lula Lingenfelser 49; Wm Lingenfelser 19; Nellie B Trisler 32

Notes for Clarence Malcolm HICKS #188

Census
1910 Columbus Ward 8, Franklin, OH, p. 2B. Clarence M Hicks 27, KY/KY/KY, tailor - tailor shop; Mary L Hicks 24, OH/OH/OH; Dona L Hicks 4, OH. m. 5 years, 1 child
1920 Columbus Ward 5, Franklin, OH, p. 7B. C Clarence M Hicks 35, dry cleaners - laundry co, KY/KY/KY; Ruth B Hicks 21, OH/OH/OH; Clarence Hicks 5/12, OH

Military: World War I Draft Registration Cards, 1917-1918 [ancestry.com] Clarence Malcolm Hicks, age 35, b. 9 Oct 1883; res: Columbus, Franklin Co, OH; occ: dry cleaners - Capitol City Laundry; contact: Ruth Babe Hicks; short, med. build, gray eyes, black hair. Regis: 12 Sep 1918, Columbus, OH.

Death: Clarence M. Hicks, d. 8 Feb 1925, Columbus, Franklin, OH; Birth: 9 Oct 1885 Maysville, KY; Age: 39 years 3 months 29 days; address: Cassady Ave & 9th Ave; Occ: Manager Dry Cleaning; Burial 12 Feb 1925, East Lawn Burial Park; Spouse: Ruth Babe Hicks; Father: Polk Hicks b. Clermont Co. OH; mother: Caroline Utter. OH Deaths 1908-1953 <familysearch.org>

Discrepancy: Jones notes gave death as 7 Feb 1925.

Notes for Ruth MORRISON #188s

Census: 1930 Mifflin, Franklin, OH, p. 14A. Paul R Hott 30, musician - orchestra; Ruth B Hott 31; Clarence M Hicks 10, stepson; Norma C Hicks 8, step-dau; Marilyn J Hicks 6, step dau; Mary Kitzmiller 70, aunt. All OH/OH/OH.

Notes for George B. JONES #190

Jones notes: "m. to W. Chinger at Maysville, KY"; gave birth year as 1872.

Census
1900 Maysville, Mason, KY, p. 31. E. 3rd St. George Jones, 28, Aug 1871 KY/OH/OH, blacksmith; Susan?; wife, Feb 1873, KY/KY/KY; Harold, son, May 1891, KY; Nancy Hicks, g mother Jun 1806 MD/MD/MD, widow.
1910 not found. His wife is listed as divorced; she & son are in Portsmouth Ward 1, Scioto, OH, p. 7A. Lutie Jones 36; KY/KY/KY, divorced, 2 ch /1 living, dressmaker; Harold Jones 17, machinist - plow factory, KY/OH/KY.

Notes for Irma Clare JONES #191

Jones notes: "b. 12/22/1879; m. to Fred C. Helmick

Marriage1: Everett Cochran b. 08 Jun 1879, Ripley, Brown Co., OH, age 22; Bride: Irma Clare Jones, b. 22 Dec 1879, Aberdeen, Brown Co, Ohio, age 22, Marriage: 16 Jan 1902, Brown County, OH. Groom's Father: John M. Cochran; Groom's Mother: Queen Steele; Bride's Father: Thomas F. Jones, Bride's Mother: Caroline B. Hicks; both single. Ohio Marriages, 1800-1958 <familysearch.org>

Marriage2: Frederick Cole Helmick, b. W. Va; Bride: Irma C. Jones, b. 1879, OH, age 28; Marriage: 25 Dec 1907, Hamilton County, OH; Groom's parents: Dexter; Katherine Cole; Bride's parents: T. F.; Bride's C. R. J. Hicks; Groom - Single; Bride - Divorced; Bride's Previous Husband's Name: Cochoran. Ohio Marriages, 1800-1958 <beta.familysearch.org>

Census:
1910 Clay, Ritchie, WV, p. 7A. Virginia S Wilson 69; Agnes E Wilson 45; Mandal Wilson 29; Eugene L Olephant 58; Flora Olephant 34; Winfred F Knight 27; Clara Knight 26; Frederick C Helmick 34, WV/WV/WV, manager - planing mill; Erma C Helmick 30, roomer, KY/NC/OH, m. 2 years, no children.
1920 Flint Ward 5, Genesee, MI, p. 18B. Fred C Helmick 43, WV/WV/WV, woodworking - planing mill; Irma C Helmick 40, OH/OH/OH; Escalene R Helmick 9, OH/WV/OH; Frank T Helmick 3 5/12,

WV/WV/OH; Wardie Helmick 3 5/12, dau, WV/WV/OH; Caroline R Jones 69, OH/SC/MD, Mother in law, widowed; Minnie W Jones 31, sister in law, KY/OH/OH, single, practical nurse.

  1930 Flint, Genesee, MI, p. 3A. Fred C Helmick 54, woodworker - lumber co, WV/WV/WV; Enna Helmick 50, OH/OH/OH; Essulene Helmick 19; Frank Helmick 13; Ward Helmick 13, dau; Caroline Jones 79, laborer - domestic, OH/NC/OH, widowed; Minnie Jones 43, no occ., KY/OH/OH, single

Notes for Fred Cole HELMICK #191s

Military: WW I Draft registration: barely legible. William Frederick Helmick, b. 13 Aug 1879, rest illegible.

Birth: Probably the Fred W. Helmick in Mill Creek, Hamilton, OH in 1880, age 11 months, son of Fred W. & Dora Helmick. no other information found

Child: Birth of child: Thomas Helmick, b. 29 Aug 1913 Clarksburg, Harrison, WV; father: Fred C Helmick; mother Irma Helmick. West Virginia Births, 1853-1930 <beta.familysearch.org>

Notes for Lydia Ann TATMAN #194

Marriage1: Lydia A Tateman to Joseph Rogers, 22 Sep 1878, Daviess County, IN. Index to Marriage Record 1850 - 1920 Inclusive Vol 3: W. P. A. Original Record Located: County Clerk's Office

Marriage2: Lydia A Rogers to William Gibson, 1 Sep 1883, Owen County, Indiana. Source: Index to Marriage Record 1850 - 1920 Inclusive Vol 31 W. P. A.

Census

  1880 Spencer, Owen, IN, p. 306. Joseph L. Rogers 27 SC/SC/SC, co. surveyor; Lydda Rogers 21, OH/OH/IN; Rotheus Rogers 8M, dau [sic], b. Sep, IN/SC/OH

  1900 South McAlester, Choctaw Nation, Indian Territory, p. 17. William Gibson 65, Oct 1834, IN/IN/IN, carpenter, m. 17 yrs; Lydia E Gibson 43, Sep 1858, OH/OH/OH; Rotheus Rogers 20, Oct 1879, IN/IN/OH, boarder crossed out - maybe son written over; Keneth E Gibson 14, Jul 1885, son, MO/IN/OH, newsboy; Mary May Gibson 10, Sep 1889, dau, MO/IN/OH

  1910 Galveston Ward 10, Galveston, TX, p. 8A. Thomas R Rogers 30, IN/SC/OH, forwarding - freight agent, m. 5 yrs; Syrene Rogers 29, wife, TX/MO/TN, 3 ch/3 living; Evalyan Rogers 4. OK; Loclins L Rogers 3, dau, TX; Paul G Rogers 1 6/12, TX; Lydia B Gibson 59, mother, OH/OH/IN, widow, 4 ch/3 living; Kenneth C Gibson 23, son, MO/IN/OH, check clerk - railroad; Mary M Gibson 20, dau, MO/IN/OH, stenographer - office.

  1920 El Paso Precinct 7, El Paso, TX, p. 7B. Lydia A Gibson 60, OH/OH/OH, widow; Thomas R Rogers 40, son, widowed, IN/SC/OH, contractor - own office; Evelyn R Rogers 14, granddau, OK/IN/TX; Locleus L Rogers 13, granddau, TX/IN/TX; Paul G Rogers 11, grandson, TX/IN/TX; Mary M Rogers 9, granddau, TX/IN/TX; Claris L Rogers 7, granddau, TX/IN/TX. Rogers is crossed out - so surname of all may be Gibson

  1930 Houston, Harris, TX, p. 23A. Lydia Gibson 71, OH, widow; John B Winn 27, TX/TN/TX, grandson in law; Evalyn Winn 24, OK/IN/TX, granddau; Kenneth R Winn 5, TX, gr grandson; John H Winn 2/12, TX, gr grandson; Joseph B Ahlschies 23, grandson in law, TX/TX/TX; Claris Ahlschies 18, granddau, TX/IN/TX; Joseph B Ahlschies 1 4/12, gr grandson; Mary M Rogers 19, granddau, TX/IN/TX. Children b. TX

Death: Mrs. Lydia Ann Gibson, d. 19 Jun 1938, Harris Co, TX.

Death of spouse: May be the John William Gibson who died in Galveston, TX on 31 Oct 1919. Texas Death Index, 1903-2000. [Ancestry.com]

Notes for Kenneth GIBSON #467s

Census

  1920 El Paso Precinct 13, El Paso, TX, p. 18A. William Young 50, painter - house; Rose Young 40; Iva A Young 19, single, operator - telephone; Kenneth E Gibson 34, son in law, MO, married, mechanic - garage. All except Kenneth Eng/Eng/Eng, imm. 1912, citizenship pending.

1930 El Paso, El Paso, TX, p. 15B. Kenneth Gibson 40, MO/MO/MO, manager - express co; Gertrude Gibson 38, AR/AR/AL, stenographer - express co, m. age 28; Lyman Lenfesty 12, son, CA/CA/MO; Virginia B Hawkins 2 10/12, TX/VA/TX; Fredrick R Burow 28, son, MN/MN/MN

Military: World War I Draft Registration Cards, 1917-1918 [ancestry.com] Kenneth E Gibson, age 30, b. 18 Jul 1886, Springfield, MO; res: Lake Valley, NM; truck driver, Southwestern Wrecking Co; single; tall, med. build, gray eyes, light hair, slightly bald. Reg: Sierra, NM 6 May 1917.

Residence: Living in El Paso, 1960 when brother Thomas Rogers died.

Death: Kenneth E Gibson, #526031451; b. 18 Jul 1886, Missouri; d. 18 Apr 1968, Los Angeles CA; Mother's Maiden Name: Tatman. California Death Index, 1940-1997 [ancestry.com]

Notes for Franklin Ulyses TATMAN #195

Census: 1880 Anderson, Madison, IN, p. 233A. Frank Tatman 20, boarder, single, OH/OH/OH, tailor.

1900 South McAlester, Choctaw Nation, Indian Territory, p. 75A. Frank Tatman 36, Dec 1863, OH/OH/OH, tailor, m. 15 yrs; Flora Tatman 33, Sep 1866, 3 ch / 3 living, IL/OH/OH; Frank Tatman 14, Aug 1885, IL/OH/IL; Florence Tatman 3, Jun 1896, Indian Ty; Richard B Tatman 11/12, Jun 1899, Indian Ty.

1910 Coffeyville Ward 4, Montgomery, KS, p. 4A. F U Tatman 46, bookkeeper - Ice co, OH; Flora Tatman 42, IL/VA/IL, proprietor - restaurant, 5 ch / 3 living; Dick Tatman 11, KS; William Tatman 7, KS

1920 Coffeyville Ward 2, Montgomery, KS, p. 4A. Frank U Tatman 56, manager - bakery; Florence E Tatman 50; Richard B Tatman 20, OK, manager - Benery? Electric; William J Tatman 16, KS, apprentice - elec? bakery

1930 El Paso, El Paso, TX, p. 13A. R Richard Tatman 32, OK/OH/IL, broker - freight car? lots; B Nell Tatman 32, Tx/US/US; U Franklin Tatman 66, father, married, OH/OH/IN, broker - freight car? lots.

Info: Kevin Meade 3/2004, adds "3rd child of James Tatman and Mary Ann Ross is Franklin Ulyses Tatman, born Dec 2, 1862 in Bethel, Clermont Co, OH. Franklin married Flora Catherine Lewis in Lincoln, Logan Co, IL; he died in 1934 in Chicago, Cook Co, Illinois (lived in Coffeyville, KS)."

Obituary: *Coffeyville man succumbs to Stroke in Chicago where he was attending Code meeting. Frank Ulysis Tatman, 71, whose home here in Coffeyville was 207 West 7th Street died in Chicago, Ill. where he suffered a paralytic stroke. He was engaged in the real estate and freight forwarding business in El Paso, Texas, and was attending a freight forwarding Code meeting in Chicago. Mr. Tatman was born 12-2-1862 at Bethel, Ohio, and was left an orphan at the age of 8. He came to Coffeyville from McAlester, Okla. He was a member of Roosevelt's Rough Riders in the Spanish-American War, and was the only volunteer to be admitted to the army in McAlester. He was a member of the Elks Lodge in Coffeyville. Mr. Tatman was married in 1886 at Lincoln, Illinois to Flora Catherine Lewis, who survives. He leaves 2 sons- Richard Bryon Tatman of El Paso, Texas, and William Jennings Tatman of Coffeyville, a sister Mrs. Lydia Gibson of Houston, Texas, 4 grandchildren, 2 great-grandchildren. Mr. Tatman's 2 sons went to Chicago on learning of his illness and were with him when he died. They will accompany the body to Coffeyville and it is scheduled to arrive tomorrow morning by way of Katy Railroad. Mrs. R. B. Tatman arrived from El Paso this morning, while Mrs. Gibson, sister of Mr. Tatman, accompanied by her son, T. R. Rodgers, both of Houston, Texas will arrive in Coffeyville tomorrow. Burial will be in Fairview Cemetery in Coffeyville. Funeral arrangements all incomplete.*

Obituary: *El Paso Herald-Post (El Paso, Texas) 1 Oct 1934 F. U. Tatman Dies: El Paso Business Man Victim of Stroke While on Visit. Frank U. Tatman, El Paso business man, died yesterday afternoon in Chicago where he was visiting at the Century of Progress before leaving for Coffeyville, Kan., to see relatives. Mr. Tatman died of pneumonia resulting from a paralytic stroke. Mr Tatman was joint owner, with his son, R. B. Tatman, of the R T. R. Rogers Package Car Co. in El Paso. He made his home at 2818 ½ N. Piedras St. He was born in Bethel, O., and has been a resident of El Paso since 1922. Mr Tatman is survived by his widow, Mrs. Florence Tatman, of Coffeyville; his son in El Paso and another son*

William of Coffeyville; 2 nephews, K. E. Gibson of El Paso and T. R. Rogers; and 2 nieces, Mrs. R. Book and Lydia Gibson of Houston.

Info: Meade notes: "Franklin Ulyses Tatman b. Dec 2, 1862 in Bethel, Clermont Co, Ohio. Died 1934 in Chicago, Cook Co, IL and buried in Fairview Cemetery, Coffeyville, Montgomery Co, KS. Frank married Flora Catherine Lewis, daughter of Decatur and Mary A. Lewis. Flora was born either Sept 1866 or Sept 1867? in Lincoln, Logan Co, IL. She died January 1951 in Coffeyville, Montgomery Co, KS and buried in Fairview Cemetery, Coffeyville, Montgomery Co, KS. They were married on March 8, 1886 in Lincoln, Logan Co, IL. One more thing about Frank U. Tatman was that he was part of Theodore Roosevelt's Rough Riders of 1899. He served in Troop M under Cpt Robert H. Bruce as Corporal and joined on May 14th at Muskogee, Indian Territory (Oklahoma now). He lived in South McAlester at the time he joined. I don't know when his parents died exactly, but his mother had died by the time he was 8. I also think I found him in the 1880 census in Anderson, Madison Co, IN as a boarder. The 1880 census has that Frank Tatman as a tailor and so does the 1900 census, so I think it's a match."

Death: Franklin U. Tatman M/W 1934-09-30 Cook Co, Chicago, IL. Illinois Statewide Death Index

Notes for Flora Catherine LEWIS #195s

Census: 1880 Lincoln, Logan, IL, p. 213. Decatur Lewis 46, VA/Wales/MD, carpenter; Mary A. Lewis 36, OH/PA/PA; Clara Lewis 18 Marshal M. Lewis 16, works in soda water; Flora C. Lewis 13; Mabel Lewis 11. Children all b. IL.

Notes for Cornelia Blanche BRITTINGHAM #196

Census

1880 Felicity, Clermont, OH, p. 49B John Wesley Altman, 27, OH / PA/ MD, barber; Corna J., wife, 26, OH/ VA/ OH, Keeps House; Nellie J, dau, 6, OH/ OH /OH; Bailey W., son, 2, OH/ OH/ OH; May Brittenhaus, sister-in-law, 16, OH/ VA/ OH

1900 Cincinnati Ward 15, Hamilton, OH, p. 7A. Corna J Altman 47, Sep 1852, widow, 5 ch / 5 living; Bailey Altman 22, Mar 1878, insurance solicitor; Aurelia M Altman 18, Nov 1881, cigar roller; Samuel Altman 16. Jan 1884, bartender; Louisa Altman 11, Sep 1888; Grace Carr 15, Dec 1884, boarder, cigar roller.

1910 not found

1920 Scott, Boone, WV, p. 22A. Sam Altman 36, single, clerk - pool room; C A Altman 65, mother, widow. Both OH/OH/OH.

Death: Cornelia Blanche Altman, d. 4 Jun 1926, Boone, WV; age: 72 years 8 months 27 days; Father: William Brittingham;; mother: Lieu Tatman. West Virginia Deaths, 1853-1970 <fsbeta.familysearch.org>

Discrepancy: Jones notes give fist name Jane Cornelie; WV Death records give Cornelia Blanche.

Notes for John Wesley ALTMAN #196s

Jones notes: "shot by customer in his barber shop"

Notes for James Winfield BRITTINGHAM #197

Mollie's surname from Jones notes - may be wrong.

Marriage2: James Winfield Brittingham b. 1862 Clermont Co, Ohio, Age: 52; Bride: Elizabeth Margaret Ware, b. 1864 Pendleton Co, Ky., age 50; Marriage: 14 May 1914, Butler, Ohio; Groom's Father: Wm. Brittingham, Mother: Lucinda Tatman; Bride's Father: John Ware. Mother: Mabala Dans. Ohio Marriages, 1800-1958 <pilot.familysearch.org>

Census

1900 Tate, Clermont, OH, p. 2B. James W Brittingham 38, Aug 1861, OH/VA/OH, barber; Mollie 32, Dec 1867, KY/OH/KY, m. 10 years, 4 ch / 4 living; Willie 7, Jul 1892; Louise 6, Jun 1893; Marrie 4, Aug 1895; Bryan 3, Apr 1897

1910 Hamilton Ward 4, Butler, OH, p. 4B. James Brittingham 49, machinist - shop, OH/OH/OH; Mollie 38, KY/KY/KY, 4 ch / 4 living; William 20, cabinet maker; Louise 18; Marie 16; Bryan 15; Mamie 16, dau in law. (wife of William), OH/OH/OH.

1920 Hamilton Ward 1, Butler, OH, p. 2A. James Brittingham 58, OH/MD/OH, shoemaker - own shop; Elizabeth 56, KY/KY/KY

1930 Hamilton, Butler, OH, p. 17B. James Brittingham 68, OH/OH/OH, shoe maker - shoe repair shop; Elizabeth 66, KY/KY/KY; Theodore Taylor 43, stepson, KY/KY/KY, shoe maker - shoe repair shop; Andrew Wicklery 62, lodger, OH/Ger/Ger, laborer - odd jobs.

Death: James W. Brittingham, b. 3 Aug 1861 Bethel, OH; d. 4 Feb 1943, Norwood, Hamilton Co, OH. spouse: Elizabeth Ware; father: William Brittingham; Mother: Lucinda Tattman. Widowed, no occ. Living in Millville, OH. Burial: Nicholsville, OH, 7 Feb 1943. Informant: Bryan Brittingham. Ohio Death Certificate <pilot.familysearch.org>.

Notes for Mary "Mollie" CARR #197s

James W. Brittingham was married to Elizabeth by 1920, so assume that Mollie had died. Not proven. No other information found

Notes for Elizabeth Margaret WARE #197s2

Jones notes: "Elizabeth Margaret (Ware) Taylor"

May be the Elizabeth Ware, 6, in Precinct 8, Pendleton, KY, 1910 with parents John & Mahala

Must have had a prior marriage to ___ Taylor, as death certificate lists father as John Ware.

Death: Elizabeth Brittingham, d. 16 Feb 1941 Hanover, Butler, OH; Birth: Sep 18 1863, Campbell Co, KY; father: John Ware b. OH; mother: .. Davis, b. KY; spouse: James Brittingham. Burial: Millville, OH 18 Feb 1941; 77 yrs 4 mo 28 da; Informant: Theodore Taylor. Ohio Deaths, 1908-1953 <familysearch.org>

Notes for Dorothy Louise BRITTINGHAM #481

Jones notes: "resides (1974) at 500 N. Normandie Av, Los Angeles, CA 90004"

Census: 1920-1930 not found

Marriage 1: 26 Nov 1913; Ernest Gustav Nagel b. Hanover Tp, Ohio; to Dorothy Louise Brittingham b. Bethel, Ohio; Age: 20; Marriage: Butler Co, OH; Groom's parents: Wm. Nagel; Lucy Schultheiss; Bride's parents: James W. Brittingham; Mary Carr. Ohio Marriages, 1800-1958 <pilot.familysearch.org>

Marriage2: Groom: Edward A. Blaney, b. 1869 OH, age 52; Bride: Dorothy Louise Brittingham, b. 1894 Harington, OH, age: 27; Marriage: 30 Mar 1921 Hamilton Co, OH. Groom's parents: Geo S. Blaney; Margaret Schatzman; Bride's parents: James W. Brittingham; Mary .. Carr; Groom: Divorced; Bride: Divorced; Bride's Previous Husband's Name: Nagel. Ohio Marriages, 1800-1958 <familysearch.org>

Discrepancy - Jones notes give spouse as Jasper Hamilton - marriage date is date of marriage to Edward Blaney (above). No Jasper Hamilton located.

Notes for Lydia May BRITTINGHAM #198

Census

1900 Franklin, Clermont, OH, p. 13B. George Walker 38, Sep 1861, OH/KY/KY, farmer; May Walker 35, Feb 1865, OH/OH/OH. M. 1 yr, no children.

1910 Franklin, Clermont, OH, p. 2A. George M Walker 38, carpenter - house; Lydia M Walker 46; Melissa R Walker 9

1920 Franklin, Clermont, OH, p. 12A. George Walker 61, carpenter - house; May Walker 55, teacher - public school; Malissa Walker 19, teacher - public school

Not on Ohio Death Index 1908-1953

Notes for George M. WALKER #198s
Death: George M. Walker b. 23 Sep 1861 Felicity, Ohio; d. 26 Jan 1928 Felicity, Clermont, Ohio; Age: 66 years 4 months 3 days; Occ: Carpenter; Burial: 29 Jan 1928 Felicity, O.; spouse: May Walker; Father: John Walker b. KY; mother: Melissa G, b. OH. Ohio Deaths, 1908-1953 <pilot.familysearch.org>

Notes for Missouri Mary UTTER #201
Jones notes: "his second wife; resided near Wiggonsville"

Notes for John S. ALTMAN #201s
Census: [*may not be right person]
 *1880 Tate, Clermont, OH, p. 271B. John Altman 37; Percilla Altman 33; Maud Altman 10; Guy Altman 8; Ray Altman 2; Sallie Salt 34, sister.
 1900 Ohio, Clermont Co, Tate Twp, Page 233a, John Altman, Aug 1841, 58, wd, OH/PA/OH, music teacher; Pearl M. dau, Sep 1884, 15, OH/OH/IN; Lloyd R., May 1890, 10, at school; OH/OH/IN.
 *1910 Jefferson, Montgomery, OH. Natl. Military Home. John Altman, 68, OH/PA/OH, Inmate, Widowed

Notes for Mary E. KLINGLER #214
Census
 1870 Bloomfield, Davis, IA, p. 19A. Joseph Weiney 37, carpenter, OH; Mary E Weiney 26, OH.
 1880 Bloomfield, Davis, IA, p. 74c. Joseph Werny 47. Carpenter, PA; Mary Werny 36, OH.[where is Ella? She should have been there as a 5 year old.]
 1900 Bloomfield, Davis, IA, p. 10B. Joseph Weiny 67, Nov 1832, PA/PA/PA, carpenter; Mary Weiny 57, Sep 1842, OH/OH/OH; Ellen Weiny 26, Feb 1874, IA/IA/IA, single.
 1910 Ottumwa, Wapello, IA, p. 9A. Joseph Weiny, 77, 2nd marriage, married 41 yrs, born PA, no occ.; Mary E, 66, 2nd marriage, born OH, 1 child/1 living; Ella, dau, 36, single, b. IA, foreman, laundry.
Iowa State Census
 1885 Bloomfield, David, IA, p. 71. Joseph Weiny 52, PA, carpenter; Mary Weiny 41, IA; Ellen Weiny 10.
 1905 Ottumwa, Wapello, IA. Joseph Weiny; Mary E. Weiny; Ella Weiny
Marriage: Joseph Weiney to Mary E. Klingler; Marriage: 13 Oct 1868, Davis, Iowa. Iowa Marriages, 1809-1992 <familysearch.org>
IA Marriage Index shows a marriage of Mary Klinger to Daniel Leighty on 31 Aug 1871 in Polk Co, IA. Probably not related.
Death: Mary E. Weiny, d. 27 Apr 1914 Ottumwa, Center; buried: 27 Apr 1914, Drakeville, IA; Age: 70; b. 30 Sep 1843, Ohio; Retired; Widowed; father: Wm. Kluiger, b. Ohio; Mother: Mary Hopkins. Iowa Deaths and Burials, 1850-1990 <familysearch.org>
Death Index: Mary E. Weiny; Death Date: 1914; Page #: 139; Birth Date: 1843; Cemetery: Drakesville Grave Stone Records of Davis County, Iowa [Ancestry.com]
Discrepancy: birth & death dates do not agree with census or Jones notes.

Notes for Joseph WEINY #214s
Marriage 1: Joseph Weiney to Amanda Lane; Marriage: 20 Mar 1855, Davis, IA. Iowa Marriages, 1809-1992 <familysearch.org>
Death: Joseph Weiny; Death: 9 Dec 1910; Birth Date: 1838; Cemetery: Drakesville. Grave Stone Records of Davis County, Iowa; copied by Graves Registration W. P. A. Project [Ancestry.com]
IA State Census
 1856 Bloomfield, Davis, IA, p. 578. Joseph Winey 23, PA, carpenter; Amanda Winey 20, ME.

Notes for John M. STEWART #217
Griggs book, "John M. Stewart married and had at least 2 children - Carrie & Melva"
Census
- 1900 Ottumwa, Wapello, IA. p. 4B. John F Stewart 35, Jan 1865, IA/OH/OH, carpenter; Carrie B Stewart 30, Apr 1867, IN/IN/IN; Melva E Stewart 5, May 1895, IA
- 1910 Center, Wapello, IA, p. 2B. John M Stewart 40, carpenter - railroad; Carrie V Stewart 40, married 15 yrs, 1 child; Melvae Stewart 14.
- 1920 Ottumwa, Wapello, IA, p. 3. John M. Stewart, 54, IA/OH/OH, carpenter, foreman R.Y, Carrie V., wife, 50, IN/IN/IN.
- 1930 Burlington, Des Moines, IA, p. 15A. John M Stewart 64, carpenter - house builder, IA/IN/IN; Carrie V Stewart 59, IN/IN/IN; Marilynne S Smith 10, gr dau, IA/TX/IA; Robert B Smith 7, gr son, NY/TX/IA

Iowa State Census, 1895: John Stewart; Age: 30; Race: White; Birthplace: Davis Co IA; Residence: Ottawa, Wapello

Marriage: J. M. Stewart, b. 1855. Iowa. Age: 39; Bride: Carrie Vinson, b. 1869, Ind, Age: 25; Marriage: 27 Jun 1894, Ottumwa, Wapello, IA; Groom's Father: A.W. Stewart; Mother: Dina Hopkins; Bride's Father: John Vinson; Mother: Mary F. Bruce. Iowa Marriages, 1809-1992 <familysearch.org>

Ed. note: I suspect that the Griggs book is incorrect on this one; Carrie is his wife & Melva their only child.

Notes for Carrie V. wife of John STEWART #217s
Iowa State Census, 1895. Carrie Stewart, 24; Birthplace: Ind; Residence: Ottawa, Wapello

Notes for Sarah Lavina HOPKINS #218
Griggs book[257]: "Came to Sumner Twp, Reno Co, KS in Aug 1876"
Discrepancy: 1900 census Noble, Garfield, OK, gives birth date as Aug 1861. Griggs book gives 15 Aug 1856.
Census
- 1900 Noble, Garfield, OK, p. 4. Thomas Benson 39, Nov 1860, IL/IL/IL, farmer; Sarah L 38, Aug 1861, IA/OH/Eng; Ida M 13, Jul 1886, KS/IL/IA; Lettie P 11, Feb 1889, KS/IL/IA; Roy D 4, Oct 1895, KS/IL/IA.
- 1910 Hunter, Garfield, OK, p. 8A. Hale T Benson 49, IL/IL/IL, manager - gen store; Sarah L Benson 48; Lettie P Benson 21, KS, saleswoman - dept store; Roy D Benson 14, OK; Lois M Benson 4, OK
- 1920 Enid Ward 5, Garfield, OK, p. 9B. Sarah L Benson 58, IA/OH/Eng, widow, proprietor - apt house; Lois M Benson 14, OK
- 1930 not found

Notes for Clara Elizabeth HOPKINS #219
Census
- 1880 Haven, Reno, KS. William Mitchell 26, farming, IA/PA/NY; Clara E. 17, IA/Eng/PA. Next to R. N. Mitchel [father?] 54, PA/France/ NH, farmer; Polly 54, NY/NH/NH; Oliver 20, IA/PA/NH, farm labor.
- 1900 Haven, Reno, KS. Clara Mithel 37, Jan 1863, widow, IA/OH/Eng; Ray 17, Sep 1882, KS/IA/IA, farm labor; Elmer 15, Jun 1884; Jessie 13, Sep 1886; Gorge 12, Mar 1888; Sarah Hopkinks, 60, Jun 1839, widow, Eng/Eng/Eng; William Hoppinks, brother, 30, Jul 1869, farmer, IA; Gertrud Hoppinks, sister, 21, Apr 1879, sch teacher, IA; Walter Hoppinks, brother, 17, Jul 1882, KS.
- 1910 Darling, Muskogee, OK, p. 14. George H Mitchell 22, farmer; Mary Neoma 15, wife, KS/PA/IN; Clara 46, mother, widow; Elmer 25, brother, farmer; Sarah Hapkins 70, grandmother, widow.
- 1920 - not found in KS or OK. May have remarried -?- Wall.

1930 Spring, Butler, KS, p. 1. George H Mitchell 42, farm operator; M Neoma 35, KA/PA/IN; Pearl H 19, OK/KS/KS; George L 7, KS/KS/KS; Clara E Wall 67, mother, IA/OH/Eng; Leon G M Chumina 17, hired man, CO/US/US.

Notes for William Joseph MITCHELL #219s
Census: 1860 Illyria, Fayette, IA, p. 226. Roland Mitchell 36, PA; Polly Mitchell 35, NY; Susan Mitchell 15; John Mitchell 12; Jane Mitchell 10; Wm Mitchell 7, IA; Rowland Mitchell 5; Benjiman Mitchell 3; Oliver Mitchell 2/12 [may not be right family but places of birth match]

Notes for Gertrude May HOPKINS #222
Census
1900 Haven, Reno, KS p. 10B. Clara Mithel 37, Jan 1863, widow, IA/OH/Eng; Ray 17, Sep 1882, KS/IA/IA, farm labor; Elmer 15, Jun 1884; Jessie 13, Sep 1886; Gorge 12, Mar 1888; Sarah Hopkinks, 60, Jun 1839, widow, Eng/Eng/Eng; William Hoppinks, brother, 30, Jul 1869, farmer, IA; Gertrud Hoppinks, sister, 21, Apr 1879, sch teacher, IA; Walter Hoppinks, brother, 17, Jul 1882, KS.
1910 Haynesville, Pratt, KS, p. 8. Fred Shumway 32, KS/IL/IL, carpenter; Gertrude 31, KS/OH/Eng; Ivan 6, KS; Irene 3, KS
1920 Wellsford, Kiowa, KS. p. 22. Fred Shumway 41, farmer; Gertrude 40; Ivan 15; Irene 12
1930 Wichita, Sedgwick, KS p. 32B. Fred Shumway 52, no occ.; Gertrude 51; Ivan 26, mail carrier; Irene 23. [Indexed on Ancestry.com as Sumway].
Kansas State Census: 1915 Vorhees, Stevens Co, KS. Fred Shumway 36; Gertrude 35; Ivan 11; Irene 8

Notes for Frederick Julian SHUMWAY #222s
Military: World War I Draft Registration Cards, 1917-1918 [ancestry.com] Fred Julian Shumway; age 40; res: Tyrone, Texas Co, OK; farmer, contact: Gertrude Shumway, Tyrone, OK; med height & build, brown eyes, black hair; regis: 12 Sep 1918, Stevens Co, KS

Notes for Walter Ralph HOPKINS #223
Jones notes are not clear on this family. I believe that this is the correct placement, but cannot be positive. Son Leslie was evidently raised by his uncle, William L. Hopkins. He was with them for the 1920 census in Pawnee, Oklahoma & 1930 census in Orange Co, FL.
Discrepancy: Jones notes give middle name as Ray; Draft Registration gives Ralph.
Census
1900 Haven, Reno, KS p. Clara Mithel 37, Jan 1863, widow, IA/OH/Eng; Ray 17, Sep 1882, KS/IA/IA, farm labor; Elmer 15, Jun 1884; Jessie 13, Sep 1886; George 12, Mar 1888; Sarah Hopkinks, 60, Jun 1839, widow, Eng/Eng/Eng; William Hoppinks, brother, 30, Jul 1869, farmer, IA; Gertrud Hoppinks, sister, 21, Apr 1879, sch teacher, IA; Walter Hoppinks, brother, 17, Jul 1882, KS
1910 Darling, Muskogee, OK, p. 18B. Walter R Hopkins 27, KS/-/IA, farmer.
1920 Pawnee, Pawnee, OK, p. 25B. Chas L Haun 32, laborer - cigar plant; Lena Haun 27; [22] Walter Hopkins 43, roomer, divorced, MO/MO/KS, no occ.
1930 Shawnee, Pottawatomie, OK, p. 11B. W R Hopkins 47, KS, Machinist - Railroad shop; Julia Hopkins 24; Preston Hopkins 2 9/12; Cecil Pefah [illegible] 20, niece, married age 17; May Lena Pefah 11/12, dau. All but Walter b. OK.
Military: World War I Draft Registration Cards, 1917-1918 [ancestry.com] Walter Ralph Hopkins, age 36, b. 29 Jul 1882; res: Pawnee, Pawnee Co, OK; occ: Engineer - Pawnee City; relative: Elizabeth Hopkins - wife; med height, slender, blue eyes, black hair; regis: 12 Sep 1918 Pawnee.

Notes for Lucinda Margaret JOHNSTON #224
Death: date from Jones notes.

Notes for John LANHAM #224s
Census
1870 Franklin, Clermont, OH p. 23 - may be the John F. Lanham, 14, works in __ mill. With parents William & Virginia. Birthplaces of parents match known information.
1880 Felicity, Clermont, OH, p. 1. John D. Lanham 23, laborer in livery stable, OH/OH/VA; Lucinda M. 26, OH/OH/OH; Mollie E. 8
1900 not found
Not found on Ohio Death Index 1908-1953. May be the John Lanham in the index who died 11 Feb 1914 in Clermont, b 4 May 1840; Laborer. Informant: Mary Melvin.

Notes for William Alexander JOHNSTON #225
Census:
1900 Monroe Twp, Clermont Co, OH, p. 144; HH#11. Alexander Johnston, Dec 1856, 43, mar 19 yr, OH/OH/OH, blacksmith, owns home; Anna, Mar 1858; 41, mar 19 yr, 3 ch, 1 living; Lena Johnston, Nov 1882, 17, dau. single, OH/OH/OH.
1910 Franklin, Clermont, OH, p. 4B. Mary M Johnson 76, widow; Alex W Johnson 53, son, widowed, blacksmith; Jennie Johnson 52, dau, single; Lena M Johnson 27, grand dau, single.
Marriage: Alex Johnson to Annie Adrien; 31 Oct 1880, Clermont County, OH; Ohio Marriages, 1800-1958 <familysearch.org>
Death: William Alexander Johnson, d. 16 Mar 1918, Franklin Twp, Clermont, OH; b. 18 Dec 1856, OH; Age: 61 years 2 months 27 days; Widowed; occ: Blacksmith; Burial: 18 Mar 1918, Mt. Pleasant; Father: William Johnson, b. OH; mother: Mary Manning, b. OH. Informant: Elizabeth Stevens [sister]. Ohio Deaths, 1908-1953 <familysearch.org>

Notes for Anne ADRIAN #225
Not found in Ohio Death Index

Notes for Lena JOHNSTON #505
Census:
1910 Franklin, Clermont, OH, p. 4B. Mary M Johnson 76, widow; Alex W Johnson 53, son, widowed, blacksmith; Jennie Johnson 52, dau, single; Lena M Johnson 27, grand dau, single.
1920 Franklin, Clermont Co, OH. Sidney Marksberry 44, farmer; Lena Marksberry 37; Ray Marksberry 22, farmer; Viola Marksberry 19; Anna Marksberry 14; Russel B Marksberry 2 8/12, grandson, KY
Marriage: Sidney Marksberry, b. 1876 KY, Age: 38; to Lena Johnston, b. 1883 Felicity, Ohio; Age: 31; Marriage: 19 Feb 1914, Hamilton Co, OH; Groom's parents: William Marksberry; Cynthia Bruen; Bride's parents: Alex Johnston; Anna Adrian; Groom: widowed; Bride: single. Ohio Marriages, 1800-1958 <familysearch.org>
Death: Lena M. Marksberry; death: 22 Feb 1920, Franklin, Clermont, OH; Birth: 17 Nov 1882, OH; age: 37 years 3 months 5 days; Married; Burial: 24 Feb 1920, Felicity, Oh; Father: Alex Johnston, b. OH; Mother: Anna Adrian, b. OH. Informant: Mary Johnston, Felicity, OH. Ohio Deaths, 1908-1953 <pilot.familysearch.org>

Notes for Sidney MARKSBERRY #505s
Census:
1880 Milford, Bracken, KY, p. 527. William Marksbery 35; Cynthia Marksbery 33; Amos Marksbery 13; Albert Marksbery 10; James Marksbery 9; Sidney Marksbery 6; Martha Marksbery 3; Willis Marksbery 3M

1900 Brooksville, Bracken, KY, p. 5B. Sidney Marksbary 24, Aug 1875, farmer, mar. 6 yrs.; Emmie Marksbary 21, July 1874, 4 ch / 2 living; Essee Marksbary 5, Apr 1895; RayMarksbary 2, Feb 1898; Maria Manes 78, 1822, widow, grandmother. All KY/KY/KY.

1910 Franklin, Clermont, OH, p. 3A. Sidney Marksbury 34, KY, widowed, farmer; Essie Marksbury 14, dau; Roy Marksbury 12; Viola Marksbury 8; Annie Marksbury 6; James Foley 43, step father, farmer, 1st marriage; Cynthia Foley 66, mother, m. 23 yrs, 2nd marriage, 3 ch / 3 living. All b. KY, parents b. KY

1920 Franklin, Clermont Co, OH. Sidney Marksberry 44, farmer; Lena Marksberry 37; Ray Marksberry 22, farmer; Viola Marksberry 19; Anna Marksberry 14; Russel B Marksberry 2 8/12, grandson, KY

1930 Washington, Clermont, OH, p. 7A. Sidney Marksbury 45; Martha Marksbury 72. [May be wrong person - wrong age & Mother's name, but in right place]

Military: World War I Draft Registration Cards, 1917-1918. Sidney Marksberry, age 43, b. 8 Aug 1875, res: Bethel, Clermont Co, OH; farmer - self employed, signed by mark. Nearest relative: Lena J. Marksberry, Bethel. Med Height & build, grey eyes, black hair. Reg: Batavia, OH 12 Sep 1918.

Death: Sidney Marksberry, d. 9 Aug 1951, Cincinnati, Hamilton, OH; b. 8 Aug 1875, KY; Age: 76 years 1 day; Father: Wm Marksberry; Mother: Cynthiana Bruice

Notes for Annie Belle JOHNSTON #228

Jones notes: "resided Light St, Felicity, OH 1900; teacher"

Census

1910 Washington, Clermont, OH, p. 3A. Morgan Utter 55, farmer; Anna Utter 44; Lucy Utter 6; Mary Utter 5; Robert Utter 3; Oliver Boughner 20, hired man. Married 8 years, his 2nd, her 1st.

1920 Washington, Clermont, OH, p. 6B. Morgan P Utter 64; Anna B Utter 54; Lucy F Utter 16; Mary M Utter 13; Robert A Utter 12

1930 Washington, Clermont, OH, p. 3B. Morgan P Utter 76, farmer; Anna B Utter 64; Robert A Utter 23, machinist - automobile. All OH/OH/OH

Marriage: Morgan P. Utter, b. 1853, Clermont Co., OH, Age: 49; Bride: Anna B. Johnston, b. 1865, Felicity, OH, Age: 37; Marriage: 8 Jun 1902, Clermont, OH; Groom's parents: Washington Utter, Mary A. Mergan; Bride's parents: W. J. Johnston, Mary Manning; Groom: Widowed; Bride: Single. Ohio Marriages, 1800-1958 <familysearch.org>

Death: Anna Utter, d. 18 Jun 1931, Franklin, Clermont, OH; b. 6 Sep 1865, Felicity, OH; Age: 65 yrs 9 mo 12 da; Married; Housewife; Burial: 21 Jun 1931, Chilo, OH; Spouse: Morgan Utter; Parents: Wm. Johnson; b. OH; Mary Manning, b. OH. Informant: Robert Utter [son] Ohio Deaths 1908-1953 <familysearch.org>

Notes for Morgan UTTER #228s

Death: Morgan P. Utter, d. 24 Jan 1937, New Market Tp., Highland, OH; b. 05 Nov 1853; Age: 83 years 2 months 19 days; Widowed; Farmer; Burial: 26 Jan 1937, IOOF, Chilo, OH; Father: Washington Utter, b. OH; Mother: Mary Morgan, b. OH. Ohio Deaths, 1908-1953 <familysearch.org>

Notes for Mary Elizabeth JOHNSTON #229

Jones notes: "4 more children; names not given"

Discrepancy on birth date between census [1881] & Jones notes [1869]. 1900 census gives year as 1881 but age 29, which would be birth year of 1871 - more likely.

Birth: Mary E. Johnston; Female; Birth: 27 Jun 1869, Felicity, Clermont, OH; Father: William Johnston; Mother: Mary Manning. Ohio Births and Christenings, 1821-1962. <familysearch.org>

Census

1900 Felicity, Franklin Twp, Clermont Co, OH, p. 14. Walnut St. Harry H. Stevens, Head, 47, Oct 1852, mar. 11 yr, KY/KY/KY, photographer, rents home; Lizzie, wife, 29, Jun 1881, mar. 11 yr, 2 ch, 2 liv;

Charles R. son, 9, Nov 1891, OH/KY/OH, st school; Henry J., son, 5, Jan 1895, OH/KY/OH; Frances, m, Oct 1841, 58, bro, single, KY/KY/KY, photography

1910 Franklin, Clermont, OH, p. 5B. Harry H Stevens 57, telephone operator; Elizabeth M Stevens 40; Charles R Stevens 20, OH, laborer - factory; Henry J Stevens 12, KY; Francis M Stevens 68, brother, KY, widowed, laborer - odd jobs.

1920 Batavia, Batavia Twp, Clermont Co, OH. p. 4b. Elizabeth Stevens, Head, 49, widowed, OH/OH/OH, manager, telephone. Marion, m, 78, bro-in-law, KY/KY/KY, no occ.

1930 not found

Death: Mary E Stevens, b. 1870, Residence: Clermont Co, OH; d. 27 Jan 1960, Brown County General Hospital, Brown County, OH; age 90, widow. Ohio Deaths, 1908-1932, 1938-1944, and 1958-2007 [Ancestry.com]

Notes for Henry Harrison STEVENS #229s

Death: - Henry Harrison Stevens, d. 11 Dec 1916 Felicity, Clermont, OH; b. 15 Oct 1852 KY; Age: 64 yrs 1 mo 26 da; Married; Occ: Telephone Manager; Burial: 13 Dec 1916, V.C.O? Cemetery, Felicity, O.; parents: Samuel Stevens b. Ky; Jane Lane b. Ky. Informant: Elizabeth Stevens. Ohio Deaths, 1908-1953 <pilot.familysearch.org>

Notes for Ella F. WHITE #232

Jones notes: "resided 1880 in Bing Twp; 1910 in Hamilton Co, OH; removed to New Rochelle, NY"
Mentioned in 1932 Will of Mary H. Kline - "niece Ella Gleason", but not in 1941 Administration Docket

Census

1880 Williamsburg, Clermont, OH, p. 388. John C. Gleason 23, OH/Ire/Ire, telegraph operator; Ella F. Gleason 20; Carrie M. Gleason 4M.

1900 Cincinnati Ward 2, Hamilton, OH, p. 7B. John C Gleason 40, Nov 1859, OH/Ire/Ire, supt _?_ R.R.; Ella F Gleason 41, Sep 1858; Caroline M Gleason 18, Feb 1881; Guy O Gleason 16, Feb 1883; Mina B White 29, Nov 1870, sis-in law, single, saleslady; Bertha Stillwell 21, Jul 1878, servant.

1910 New Rochelle Ward 2, Westchester, NY, p. 11A. John C Gleason 51, real estate - buyer; Ella F Gleason 51; Guy S Gleason 26, real estate office

1920 New Rochelle Ward 1, Westchester, NY, p. 7A. John C Gleason 63, real estate agent; Ella F Gleason 59; Mina B White 48, sis in law, single; Kenneth L Bigger 22, lodger; chauffeur - rubber co

1930 not found

Marriage: John C. Gleason to Ella F. White, b. 1859, age 19. Marriage: 10 Sep 1878, Clermont Co., OH. Ohio Marriages, 1800-1958 <familysearch.org>

Notes for James Hicks WHITE #233

Census

1900 Williamsburg, Clermont, OH, p. 11A. James H White 38, Sep 1861, manufacturer; Maggie White 33, Oct 1866; Marie White 15, May 1885; Laurence White 13, Mar 1887; Niny [Mina] White 9, May 1885; Russel White 8, Mar 1892.

1910 Williamsburg, Clermont, OH, p. 1B. James H White 48, manufacturer - chairs; Maggie P White 44; Lawrence W White 23, bookkeeper, chair factory; Mina P White 18; Nicholas J White 12; Carl Gorebrund 60, servant, MD/Ger/Ger

1920 Williamsburg, Clermont, OH, p. 8A. James H White 56, OH, manufacturer - chairs; Margaret P White 42; Mina P White 25; Carl Grobrund 64, hired man, laborer - garden. Son Nicholas and family lived next door. Nicholas was a bookkeeper, chair factory.

1930 Williamsburg, Clermont, OH, p. 3B. Maggie P White 62, widow, OH/MO/OH; Mina P White 35, single; Mina B White 59, sister in law, single, stenographer - chair factory. next to Nicholas White, 31, proprietor - chair factory [son].

Death: May be the James H. White who died in Hamilton Co, OH 31 Jul 1928. Ohio Deaths [Ancestry.com]

Notes for Margaret Pearl ATCHLEY #233s
Census: 1870 Williamsburg, Clermont, OH, p. 431. Daniel Atchley 31; Mary Atchley 23; Minnie Atchley 5; Maggie Atchley 3; Nancy Erwin 31
No death records found

Notes for Bessie KING #235
Jones notes: "resided (1932) in Leonidas, MI"
Mentioned in 1941 Admin Docket "niece Bessie King Robertson of Leonidas, MI" but not in 1932 Will of Mary H. Kline
Marriage: W.F. Robertson, res: Chicago, IL, age 24 years; b. 1877, Wisconsin, occ: medicine; Bride: Bessie King of Chicago, IL, age 24 years; b. 1877, IN, music teacher; Marriage 26 May 1901 Saint Joseph, Berrien, MI. groom's parents: Fred, Ella; bride's parents: E. N., ___ Hicks. Michigan Marriages, 1868-1925 <fspilot.familysearch.org>
Census
  1910 Gilbert, Rolette, ND, p. 3A. William Robertson 32, physician, WI/WI/WI; Bessie Robertson 32, IN/Eng/OH, m. 4 yrs, no children; Sara King 69, mother, OH/Eng/NY, 4 ch/3 liv; Pearson Briggs 52, boarder.
  1920 Rolette, Rolette, ND, p. 8A. William F Robertson 43, WI/WI/WI, president - bank; Bess V Robertson 43, IN/Eng/OH; Robert K Robertson 7, ND.
  1930 Rolette, Rolette, ND, p.2B. Bessie Robertson 52, widow, IN/Eng/OH; Robert K Robertson 17, ND. no occ. for either.
North Dakota State Census
  1915 Rolette, Rollette, unpaged. Wm. F. Robertson; Bessie L. Robertson; Robert K. Robertson. 1 male child under 5, 1 male 30-60, 1 female 30-60.
  1925 Rolette, Rollette, p. 6. Wm. F. Robertson, 47: Bessie L. Robertson, 47, Robert K. Robertson, 12.

Notes for William Fernando ROBERTSON #235s
Military: WW I Draft Registration: William Fernando Robertson; Rolette, ND; Birth: 1 Dec 1877, age 40, occ. banking & medicine - Selff? Natl Bank; medium height & build, black hair, blue eyes. Contact: Mrs Bessie L. Robertson.

Notes for Wakefield Edward KING #236
Jones notes: "resided (1932) in Leonidas, MI"
Mentioned in 1941 Admin Docket "nephew Wakefield King of Leonidas, MI", but not in 1932 Will of Mary H. Kline
Marriage: Wakefield E King, age 26 years, b. 1879, Indiana, miller; Bride: Grace M Maufort, age 27, b. 1878, Michigan; Marriage 27 Jun 1905, Mendon, St Joseph, Michigan; Groom's parents: E. M. King; ___ Hicks; bride's parents: J.. Maufort, ___ Uptegrove. Both reside Leonidas, MI. Michigan Marriages, 1868-1925 <fsbeta.familysearch.org>
Census
  1910 Leonidas, St Joseph, MI, p. 8A. Wakefield E King 31, IN/Eng/OH, miller; Grace King 32, MI/NY/MI, m. 4 yr, 1 child; Harlan King 3. Next to father Edward.
  1920 Leonidas, St Joseph, MI, p. 2A. Wakefield King 41, miller - flour mill; Grace King 42, MI/NY/MI; Harlan King 12, MI; Glada King 9, MI
  1930 Leonidas, St Joseph, MI, p. 5A. Wakefield King 51, IN/Eng/OH, miller - flour mill; Grace M King 52, MI/NY/MI, m. age 26/27; Gay L Warren 25, son-in-law, MI/MI/MI, laborer - odd jobs; Glada L Warren 19, dau. Married at age 24/19

Military: WW I Draft Registration: Wakefield Edward King, Leonidas, St Joseph, MI, b. 23 Nov 1879, age 39, flour miller - self employed, med height & build, green eyes. Contact: Mrs. Grace King.
No death information found.

Notes for Robert A. HICKS #238
Jones notes: "1932, Cambridge City IN"
Mentioned in 1941 Admin Docket "nephew Robert A. Hicks of Cambridge City, IN" but not in 1932 Will of Mary H. Kline

Census
  1900 Jackson, Wayne, IN, p. 5B. Robert A Hicks 25, Jul 1874, bank clerk, m. 2 years; Nora L 23, 2 ch / 2 living, Jan 1877; Helen C 11/12, Jun 1899.
  1910 Mt Auburn Ward 2, Wayne, IN, p. 10B. Robb A Hicks 35, cashier - bank; Nora 33; Helen 10; Eve Lou 4
  1920 Jackson, Wayne, IN, p. 6B. Robert Hicks 45, OH/OH/OH, banker - Natl Bank; Nora 42, IN/IN/IN; Helen 20, IN; Eva Lou 14, IN.
  1930 Mt Auburn, Wayne, IN, p. 2A. Robert A Hicks 55, banker; Nora H 53; Helen C 30; Eva Lou 24, personal shopper - dept store.

Marriage: Robert A. Hicks to Nora L. Huddleston; 25 Dec 1897 Wayne County, Indiana. Index to Marriage Record 1860 - 1920 Inclusive Vol W. P. A. Original Record Located: County Clerk's O Book: C- S p. 82 Indiana Marriage Collection, 1800-1941 [ancestry.com]

Information: "My Royal Family" - tree of blaatann on Ancestry.com gives death as 1953 in Cambridge City, Wayne Co, IN. Gives Nora's parents as Rollin M Huddleston & Mary J. Fury. No documentation.

Notes for Luella SMITH #240
Jones notes had this daughter confused with Carrie Hicks, daughter of William J. Hicks - who married Elmer J. Smith and lived in Richmond, IN.

Marriage: Henry T. Bruns, b. 1873 Cinti, OH, age 31, single; Bride: Luella Koehler, b. 1871 OH, age 33; m. Sep 1904, Hamilton Co, OH. Groom's parents: Jno. B. Bruns; Katherine G. Broxtermann; Bride's parents: Albert Smith; Georgie Hicks - Divorced; Bride's Previous Husband's Name Koehler. Ohio Marriages, 1800-1958 <beta.familysearch.org>

Ohio Death record for Lulu Koehler give her parents as Albert Smith & Georgiana Hicks.

Death: Lulu Koehler, d. 31 Jan 1930, Cincinnati, Hamilton, OH; b. 12 Jun 1873, Cincinnati, O; age 56 yrs 7 mo 19 da, widowed; Address 1635 Republic; Occ: Housework; Burial 03 Feb 1930, Spring Grove Cemetery; Spouse: George Koehler; parents: Albert Butler Smith; Georgana Hicks. OH Deaths 1908-1953 <familysearch.org>

Evidently Luella was married three times and had children by two husbands.

Census:
  1900 Cincinnati Ward 30, Hamilton, OH, p. 5a. Georgiana Smith 52, widow, Nov 1847, 1 ch / 1 living; Luella Smith 30, Jun 1869, m. 9 years, 2 ch / 2 living; Georgiana Booso 12, Sep 1887; Albert Koehler 6, July 1893. No occ.
  1910 Cincinnati Ward 24, Hamilton, OH, p. 6A. Georgiania Smith 63, widow - own income, 1 child / 1 living; Fannie C Burns 42, dau, m3, 7 yrs, 3 ch / 2 living; Georgiania Borso 22, granddau; Albert S Koehler 16, grandson. All b. OH; no occ for any of them.
  1920 Not found

Notes for William Morse HICKS #241
Mentioned in 1932 Will of Mary H. Kline as "Dr. Wm. M Hicks of Cincinnati
Birth: William Morse Hicks, b. 08 Sep 1887, Pierce Twp, Clermont, OH; Father: Jas. R. Hicks; Mother: Annie Morse. Ohio Births and Christenings, 1821-1962 <pilot.familysearch.org>

Military: Ohio Military Men, 1917-18. William M. Hicks, Captain; Residence: Amelia, OH; Birth Place: Amelia, OH; Birth Date: 8 Sept 1888. Assigns Comment: 1 Lieutenant MC 13 June 1917 from Officers' Reserve Corps Fort Benj Harrison Ind June --/17 to Sept --/17. Captain 23 June 1918. 145 Field Hospital 112 Sanitary Train to --; Medical Department 146 Infantry to Discharge Columbus O; Cp Sheridan Ala; Cp Lee Va; American Expeditionary Forces Meuse-Argonne; Ypres-Lys; Defensive Sector. American Expeditionary Forces 15 June 1918 to 31 March 1919. Honorable discharge 29 Apr 1919. Awarded or Award French Croix de Guerre with bronze star.

not on WW I Draft registration - already serving?

Census

1920 Cincinnati Ward 2, Hamilton, OH, p. 3A. William Hicks 32, physician - private practice, OH/KY/OH; Elizabeth Hicks 24, NJ/Can/Can

1930 Cincinnati, Hamilton, OH, p. 2B. William M Hicks 42, physician - medical; Elizabeth Hicks 34; William Hicks 6; Frances A Hicks 4; Eleanor Hicks 1; June A Ramsey 27, servant. All but Elizabeth b. OH.

No death information found

Notes for Elizabeth B. MCDONALD #241s

Death: Elizabeth Macdonald Hicks, d. 21 Jan 1931, Cincinnati, Hamilton, OH; Est. Birth Year: 1896, Newark, NJ; death age: 35 years 2 months 5 days; burial: 23 Jan 1931, Oak Grove Cem; Married; Spouse: Dr. W. Morse Hicks; parents: John Macdonald, b. Canada; Francis Newcomb, b. Canada. Ohio Deaths, 1908-1953 <fsbeta.familysearch.org>

Notes for Edward NEWKIRK #247

Census

1900 Cleveland, Davis, IA, p. 3 Edward Newkirk 26, Jun 1873, farmer; Elizabeth 30, Mar 1870, IN/IN/IN, Married 2 years, no children.

1910 Perry, Davis, IA, p. 6. Edward Newkirk 35, farmer, IL/unk/unk; Elizabeth H 38, IN/KY/IN; Ray E 8; Nancy E Harris 71, Mo-in-law, widow, own income, IN/IN/KY.

1920 Marion, Davis, IA, p. 7. Edward Newkirk 45, IL/OH/IL, farmer; Elisbeth 46, IN/KY/IN; Raymond E 18, IA,/IL/IN, laborer.

1930 Marion, Davis, IA, p. 5. Edward Newkirk 55, IL/OH/IL, farmer - general farm; Elisbeth 57, IN/KY/IN; Raymond E 28, IA,/IL/IN, laborer - general farm

Notes for Mary Ellen NEWKIRK #248

Census:

1910 Drakesville, Davis, IA, p. 2. James H Cox 28, section foreman - railroad, MO/MO/MO; Mollie 29, IL/OH/OH, 3 ch / 3 living; Roy W 6; Ineze L 4; Mildred 2. Children b. IA.

1920 Kenneth, Sheridan, KS, p. 9B. James H. Cox 38, MO/US/US, farmer; Nellie Cox 28 MO/IL/MO; Inez Cox 14, IA/MO/IA; Edwin Cox 1 6/12, KS/MO/MO

Notes for James Hansford COX #248s

IA State Census: 1905 Fox River, Davis Co, IA. James Cox; Mollie Cox, R. W. Cox. PO - Burch or Bunch.

Military: WW I Draft Registration Cards, 1917-1918 [ancestry.com] James Hansford Cox; age 36, b. 16 Dec 1882; farmer, res: Grainfield Gove, Sheridan, Kansas; contact: Mrs. Nellie Cox; dark blue eyes, dk brown hair. Registered: 12 Sep 1918, Sheridan Co, KS.

Notes for Cora NEWKIRK #249
Jones notes: "resides (1974) at 407 Walnut, Bloomfield, IA 52537"
Census
   1910 Drakesville, Davis, IA, p. 9. Howard W Johnston 28, farmer - general farm, IL/IL/IL; Cora 25, IL/OH/IL; Doyle H 10/12 (in May 1910). Married 3 years.
   1920 Capital, Hutchinson, SD, p. 6. Howard W Johnston 38, farmer - general farm; Cora 35; Doyle H 10, IA; Verle E 8, SD; Loren K 5, SD; Roy W Cox 16, IA, nephew, farm labor.
   1930 Washington, Bon Homme, SD, p. 3. Howard W Johnston 48, farmer - general farm; Cora 45; Doyle 20; Verle 18; Loren 15.
Death: SS Death Index gives: Cora Johnston, b. 11 Aug 1884; d. Apr 1982; age 97; Bloomfield, Davis, IA; issued Iowa; #480-80-8440

Notes for Howard Washington JOHNSTON #249s
Census: 1900 Marshall, Pocahontas, IA, p. 14B. George Johnston 42, Jun 1857, IL/Sco/Sco, farmer; Kate Johnston 43, Mar 1847, IL/PA/Ger; Howard Johnston 18, Jun 1881, IL/IL/IL, farm labor; Ora Johnston 16; George Johnston 15; Pearl Johnston 3
Military: World War I Draft Registration Cards, 1917-1918 [ancestry.com] Howard Washington Johnston, age 37, b. 20 Jun 1881; res: Olivet, Hutchinson, SD, occ: farming; relative: Cora Johnston; med height & build, grey eyes, black hair; regis: Hutchinson, SD, 12 Sep 19__
Death: SS Death Index gives: Howard Johnston, b. 20 Jun 1881; d. Jan 1985; age 103; Bloomfield, Davis, IA; issued Iowa; #485-42-7696

Notes for Verna HICKS #251
Census
   1910 Paris Ward 4, Edgar, IL, p. 8. Wm Wheeler 24, ___ - mail clerk; Verna [indexed as Rema] 23.
   1920 Paris Ward 2, Edgar, IL, p. 11. William L Wheeler 35, mail clerk - railroad; Verna 33; Elizabeth P 3/12. All IL/IL/IL.
   1930 Paris, Edgar, IL, p. 25. William L Wheeler 45, railroad mail clerk; Verna A 43; Elizabeth P 10
Death: Social Security Death Index gives death date and place; #335-38-2219. No other detail.

Notes for William Lafayette WHEELER #251s
Military: WW I Draft Registration [Ancestry.com] gives middle name Lafayette, middle name of wife may be Anna, birth date, Occupation: postal clerk, railroad. Medium build, medium height, black hair & eyes.

Notes for Mary Cecil HICKS #254
Census
   1920 Symmes, Edgar, IL, Chester Smittkamp, 32, head, farmer, stock farm, IL/OH/IL; Cecil, wife, 30, IL/IL/IL; Charles, son, 5 3/12; Allen, son, 2.
   1930 Symmes, Edgar, IL, p. 9. Chester Smittkamp 42, farmer - general farm; Cecil 40; Charles 15; Allen 11; James 5

Notes for Chester SMITTKAMP #254s
Military: World War I Draft Registration [Ancestry.com] gives date & place of birth; occupation: farmer; Medium height & build; blue eyes, lt brown hair. Living in Paris, IL; wife & child.
Census
   1900 Symmes, Edgar, IL Joseph Smittkemp 37, OH; Sabin 35, May 1865, IL; Chester A 14, Sep 1888; John O. 8, Jun 1891; Fredrick F 9, May 1891
   1910 Symmes, Edgar, IL, p. 26. Joseph Smitthamp 48, farmer; Sophia 44; Chester A 22, works on farm; John O 17, works on farm;; Fred F 10, works on farm.
Death: Chester Smittkamp, 1931-03-16, Paris, Edgar [Co], IL

Notes for Glenn Alvin HICKS #257

Census

- 1900 Elbridge, Edgar, IL, p 50a. Albert A. Hicks, head, Jun 1851, 42, mar. 22 yr, IL/OH/OH, farmer, owns farm; Sadie, wife, Jun 1858, 41, mar 22 yr, 6 ch/5 living, OH/OH/OH; Roscoe, son, Jun 1880, 20, single, farm laborer; Glen, son, Nov 1881, 18, single, farm laborer; Curtis, son, May 1889, 11, single, attended school 8 months; Charles, son, Sept 1894, 5; Julian, son, Jan 1898, 2. Children all b. IL.
- 1910 Elbridge, Edgar, IL, p. 28. Glen A Hicks 28, farmer-gen. farm; Mary E 24; Ruth E 3; Merle F 2; Mayble E 6. Married 4 years, 3 ch / 3 living.
- 1920 Elbridge, Edgar, IL,, p. 43. Glen A. Hicks, 38, farmer-gen. farm; Mayme 34, Ruth 13, Merle (f) 12, Mabel 10, Ethel 8, Wendell 5, Miriam 3 7/12, Emil 11/12. All b. IL, parents b. IL, except for Glen whose mother was b. OH.
- 1930 Elbridge, Edgar, IL, p. 1. G A Hicks 48, farmer - general farm; Mame 44; Ruth 23, waitress - hotel dining; Merle 22, mounter - Westinghouse Electric; Mable 20, ?supply girl - Westinghouse Electric; Ethel 18; Wendall 15, farm labor; Miriam 13; Emil 11; Mary E 8; Richard A 5. All b. IL, children all single.

Military: World War I Draft Registration Cards, 1917-1918 [Ancestry.com] Glen Alvin Hicks; age 36; b. 25 Nov 1881; res: Edgar Co, IL; farmer; closest relative: Mayme Hicks. Dk Brown eyes, slightly bald, med heights & build. Registered: Edgar Co, IL, 12 Sep 1918.

WW II Draft Registration - 1942 [Ancestry.com] gives Glenn Alvin Hicks, age 60, b. 25 Nov 1881, res: Paris, Edgar Co, IL, self employed, contact: Rosco Hicks, Paris, IL. 5' 7", brown eyes, bald, dark complexion.

Notes for Charles Jefferson HICKS #260

Jones notes: "4 sons"; names not listed

Census

- 1920 Wabash Twp, Clark Co, IL. ED 20, Sheet 2a. County Line Rd, HH 26. Charles Hicks, 25, head, IL/IL/IL, farmer, general farm; Edna, wife, 25, IL/IL/IL; Albert, son, 3; Bernard, son, 3/12; Bennett, son, 3/12. Children: IL/IL/IL
- 1930 Wabash Twp, Clark Co, IL. District 16, p. 11A. Charles Hicks, 35, head, farmer, general farm; Edna, 35, wife; Willis A., son, 14; Bernard R., son, 10; Burnett W., son, 10. all IL/IL/IL. Both age 20 at marriage.

Military: World War I Draft Registration Cards, 1917-1918 [Ancestry.com] Charles Hicks, age 22; b. 12 Sep 1894; res: Dennison, IL; born in Elbridge, IL; farmer; wife and 1 child; tall, med. build, brown eyes, black hair. Regis: Clark Co, IL Jun 5 1917.

WW II Draft Registration 1942 [Ancestry.com] Charles Jefferson Hicks, Dennison, Clark Co, IL; b. 12 Sep 1894, Edgar, IL. Contact: Burnett Hicks, Dennison, IL; self employed, 5' 11", 155 lbs, hazel eyes, gray hair, light complexion

Notes for Edna CLEM #260s

Census:

- 1900 Symmes, Edgar, IL, p. 9A. Willes A Clem 31, farmer, IL/OH/NC; Nancy E Clem 25, IL/IN/OH; Ethel Clem 4; Edna Clem 4, Jul 1895

Death: IL Death Index gives Edna C. Hicks; 1938-09-04; Edgar County, IL

End notes: Generation 4

114. Ohio Deaths 1908-1953.
115. World War I Draft Registration Cards, 1917-1918.
116. Ohio Deaths 1908-1953.
117. Ibid
118. World War I Draft Registration Cards, 1917-1918.
119. World War II Draft Registration Cards, 1942.
120. World War I Draft Registration Cards, 1917-1918.
121. U.S. World War II Draft Registration Cards, 1942.
122. Ohio Deaths 1908-1953.
123. Ibid
124. Ohio Military Men, 1917-18.
125. Ohio Deaths 1908-1953.
126. Alabama Deaths, 1908-1974.
127. Ibid.
128. Social Security Death Index.
129. World War I Draft Registration Cards, 1917-1918.
130. Ohio Deaths 1908-1953.
131. Kentucky Marriages, 1785-1979.
132. Ohio Deaths, 1908-1932, 1938-1944, and 1958-2002.
133. World War I Draft Registration Cards, 1917-1918.
134. Ohio Deaths, 1908-1932, 1938-1944, and 1958-2002.
135. Ohio Deaths 1908-1953.
136. Ibid.
137. World War I Draft Registration Cards, 1917-1918.
138. U.S. World War II Draft Registration Cards, 1942.
139. Social Security Death Index.
140. Ohio Deaths, 1908-1932, 1938-1944, and 1958-2002 [database on-line].
141. Social Security Death Index.
142. Ohio Deaths, 1908-1932, 1938-1944, and 1958-2002.
143. Ohio Deaths 1908-1953.
144. Social Security Death Index.
145. Ohio Deaths, 1908-1932, 1938-1944, and 1958-2002 [database on-line].
146. Ibid.
147. Ibid.
148. Hicks Family Bible.
149. Sewanie Cemetery Record, Sewanie Lodge #95 IOOF.
150. Hicks Family Bible.
151. Clermont Co. OH Death Record.
152. Ohio Deaths 1908-1953.
153. Hicks Family Bible.
154. Sewanie Cemetery Record, Sewanie Lodge #95 IOOF.
155. Levi Family Bible.
156. Levi, Francis M. - Death Certificate.
157. Levi Family Bible.
158. Hicks Family Bible.
159. Clermont County, OH Marriage Books.
160. Zezula - Notes - abt 1990.
161. Ohio Deaths 1908-1953.
162. Ibid.
163. Hamilton Co. OH Death Record.
164. Ibid.
165. Ibid.
166. Social Security Death Index.
167. Hicks Family Bible.
168. Clermont Co. OH Death Record.
169. Felicity, OH Inc. Cemetery - Tombstone.
170. Clermont Co, OH Cemeteries.
171. Broadwell, Minerva (Jones) - Obituary.
172. World War I Draft Registration Cards, 1917-1918.
173. California Death Index.
174. Social Security Death Index.
175. World War I Draft Registration Cards, 1917-1918.
176. Clermont County, Ohio 1980 Vol 1.
177. Jones Family.
178. Ohio Deaths 1908-1953.
179. Clermont County, Ohio 1980 Vol 1.
180. Ibid.
181. Ohio Deaths, 1908-1932, 1938-1944, and 1958-2002.
182. World War I Draft Registration Cards, 1917-1918.
183. U.S. World War II Draft Registration Cards, 1942.
184. Ohio Deaths, 1908-1932, 1938-1944, and 1958-2002.
185. Clermont County, Ohio 1980 Vol 1.
186. *Jones Family* book by Orville Jones.
187. Clermont Co, OH - Census - 1880 [T9; #1000].
188. Ohio Military Men, 1917-18.
189. World War I Draft Registration Cards, 1917-1918.
190. Social Security Death Index.
191. Ibid.
192. *Compendium of History, Reminiscence and Biography of Nebraska*, 1912.
193. Ohio Deaths 1908-1953.
194. World War I Draft Registration Cards, 1917-1918.
195. Social Security Death Index.
196. Mason Co, KY Marriage Bonds.
197. Social Security Death Index.
198. Ibid.
199. Zezula - Notes - abt 1990.
200. Mason Co, KY Marriage Bonds.

201. Texas Death Certificate.
202. Ohio Deaths 1908-1953.
203. Kentucky Death index, 1911-2000.
204. Kentucky Death Records, 1852-1953.
205. World War I Draft Registration Cards, 1917-1918.
206. Kentucky Death Records, 1852-1953.
207. Social Security Death Index.
208. Mason Co, KY Marriage Bonds.
209. Ohio Marriages, 1800-1958.
210. Ibid
211. World War I Draft Registration Cards, 1917-1918.
212. California Death Index.
213. Social Security Death Index.
214. Meade, Kevin.
215. Illinois Statewide Death Index, 19161950.
216. Meade, Kevin.
217. Ibid.
218. Ibid.
219. West Virginia Deaths 1853-1970.
220. Ohio Births and Christenings 1821-1962.
221. Ohio Deaths 1908-1953.
222. Ibid.
223. Ohio Marriages, 1800-1958.
224. Social Security Death Index.
225. World War I Draft Registration Cards, 1917-1918.
226. Ohio Deaths 1908-1953.
227. Information on the Hopkins family is from Griggs, Wendell. *Levi W. & Sarah E. (Carter) Hopkins, their ancestors & descendants.*
228. Ibid
229. Information on the Hopkins family is from Griggs, Wendell. *Levi W. & Sarah E. (Carter) Hopkins, their ancestors & descendants.*
230. World War I Draft Registration Cards, 1917-1918.
231. Levi W. & Sarah E. (Carter) Hopkins, their ancestors & descendants.
232. Social Security Death Index.
233. Levi W. & Sarah E. (Carter) Hopkins, their ancestors & descendants.
234. Social Security Death Index.
235. Levi W. & Sarah E. (Carter) Hopkins, their ancestors & descendants.
236. Levi W. & Sarah E. (Carter) Hopkins, their ancestors & descendants..
237. World War I Draft Registration Cards, 1917-1918.
238. Ohio Deaths 1908-1953.
239. Ohio Marriages, 1800-1958.
240. World War I Draft Registration Cards, 1917-1918.
241. Ohio Deaths, 1908-1932, 1938-1944, and 1958-2002.
242. World War I Draft Registration Cards, 1917-1918.
243. Indiana Marriage Collection, 1800-1941.
244. Ohio Military Men, 1917-18.
245. World War I Draft Registration Cards, 1917-1918.
246. Ibid.
247. Social Security Death Index.
248. World War I Draft Registration Cards, 1917-1918.
249. Ibid.
250. Illinois Statewide Death Index, 19161950.
251. Social Security Death Index.
252. Jones, Orville. *Jacob Jones Family*, 1992. Unpublished manuscript.
253. Jones, Orville. *Jacob Jones Family*, 1992. Unpublished manuscript.
254. Jones, Orville. *Jacob Jones Family*, 1992. Unpublished manuscript.
255. Jones, Orville. *Jacob Jones Family*, 1992. Unpublished manuscript
256. Ibid
257. Griggs, Kendall. *Levi W. & Sarah E. (Carter) Hopkins, their ancestors & descendants*

Generation Five

The great great grandchildren of Joshua and Diana Hicks

The great great grandchildren of Joshua and Diana Hicks were scattered all over the United States, although the trend in movement was almost always westward.

Some of the men of this generation were involved with World War I, either in the military or with military-related occupations. Many were included in the World War I Draft registration in 1917-1918, which gave physical descriptions and occupations.

A number of the families remained on farms – in Ohio, Missouri, Nebraska and other western states. Other occupations included everything from dentists and bank presidents to farmers and mechanics.

Several families migrated to retirement areas of Arizona, Florida and southern California. There were very few states, other than those on the east coast, that did not have descendants of the Hicks family.

Many descendants remained in or near Clermont County, Ohio. Some descendants worked what may have been the same land their pioneer ancestors had farmed.

Eugene and Elizabeth (Hicks) Jennings
before 1984

William Benjamin & Mollie Dell
(Levi) Stalder, Jacksonville, FL
abt 1940

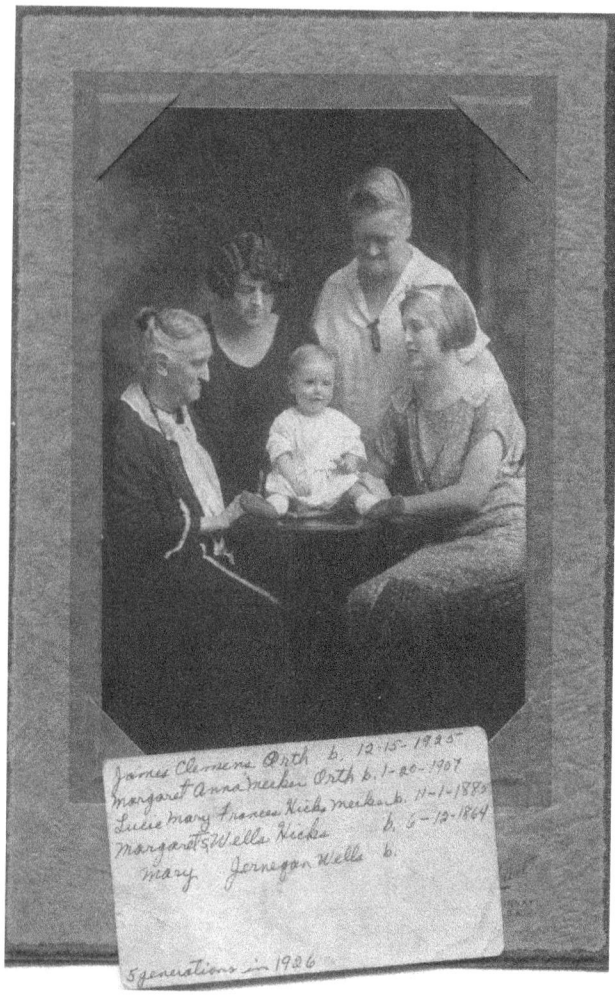

5 Generations - James Clarence Orth; Margaret Anna Meeker Orth; Lucie Mary Frances Hicks Meeker; Margaret Wells Hicks; Mary Jernegan Wells

Clark family photo. Emmet, Roscoe, Georgia, Leta & Cecil in center. Abt 1905, Nebraska

Guy Higgins (1874-1951)

Daughters of James Marcellus Jones - Audrey, Mary, and Genevieve - abt 1900, Clermont Co, OH.

Frank M & Ruth Vermillion

Back row: Hurdes Beeker Hicks, Elijah Franklin Hicks; Frank Levi; O. D. Hicks; Bodman Hite; Howard West; John James Hicks; Emma Levi; Carl Dawson. Middle row: Rella (Joslin) Dawson; Mary Elizabeth (Hicks) Joslin; Melissa (Beeker) Hicks; Edna (Joslin) Edwards; Adlora (Joslin) West; Emma Georgiana (Beeker) Hicks. Front row: Curtis Stalder; Georgia Elizabeth Hicks; Irlene Hicks; Marcella Hicks. Clermont Co, OH, abt 1913.

Point Pleasant flood, Clermont Co, OH - 1937

Hicks family home, Rural, Ohio abt 1900.

Generation 5

264. Cora⁵ MANNING (Francis M.⁴, Lucinda³ TATMAN, Ruth² HICKS, Joshua¹), born 10 Jan 1878 in Clermont Co, OH; died before 1900 in Ohio. She married on 19 Jan 1899 in Clermont Co, OH **Charles R. FAGIN**, born 13 Mar 1875; died²⁵⁸ 1 Nov 1916 in Cincinnati, Hamilton, OH.

Cora Manning married Charles Fagin and evidently died very young, leaving a daughter Alpha. Charles remarried and had several more children by 1910. @@

Children of Cora MANNING and Charles R. FAGIN were:

549 i **Alpha⁶ FAGIN**, born abt 1898 in OH. She married James Finley of Savannah, GA on 11 Dec 1917. Not further information has been found on this family.
  Birth: Alpha Fagin, female, b. 18 Oct 1897; father Charles R. Fagin; mother Cora Manning. Ohio Births and Christenings, 1821-1962 <pilot.familysearch.org>
  Census: 1900 not found. Her father, Charles, is living with his mother, Elizabeth, and is widowed.
    1910 census shows Alpha Fagin, age 12, living with her grandparents, Francis & Caroline Manning.
    1920 not found in Ohio, KY or Georgia
  Marriage: James Finley, b. 05 Mar 1888, Savannah, GA to Alpha M. Fagin, b. 18 Oct 1897, Ten Mile, Ohio, age 20; Marriage: 11 Dec 1917, Hamilton, OH; Groom's Father: Joseph I. Finley; Mother: Josephine Oswalt; Bride's Father: Charles Fagin; Mother: Cora Manning; both single. Ohio Marriages, 1800-1958. <familysearch.org>

266. Walter⁵ MANNING (Francis M.⁴, Lucinda³ TATMAN, Ruth² HICKS, Joshua¹), born 25 Nov 1883 in Cincinnati, Hamilton Co, OH; died²⁵⁹ 18 Jan 1913 in Cincinnati, Hamilton Co, OH; buried 22 Jan 1913 in Bethel, Cemetery, Tate Twp, Clermont Co, OH. He married on 24 Dec 1906 in Clermont Co, OH **Laura A. WILLS**, born 13 Jul 1889 in Brown Co, OH.

Walter Manning worked as a laborer in the Proctor & Gamble factory. He died at the age of 30 of tuberculosis. His widow Laura remarried Albert Klapper before 1930.@@

Children of Walter MANNING and Laura A. WILLS were:

550 i **William Francis⁶ MANNING**, born 21 Feb 1907 in Clermont Co, OH; died 4 Nov 1989 in Montgomery, Hamilton Co, OH. No known children.
  Census:
    1910 Millcreek, Hamilton Co, OH, p. 4A; HH#70. Walter Manning, 26, labor-factory, Laura 21, OH/KY/OH; Francis 3, son; Mildred 2; Elvina Welch 17 sister in law. Ohio
    1920 may be the Francis Manning, 12, who was an inmate at the Natl Council of the Jr. O. of the U.S. of N. A Home, U. A. M., in Tiffin, Seneca, OH, p. 14B. [Junior Order United American Mechanics Children's Home]
    1930 Cincinnati, Hamilton, OH, p. 7A. Albert Klapper 37, janitor - club house; Laura Klapper 37; Francis Manning 21, stepson, chauffeur - gas? company.
  Death: Francis William Manning, b. 21 Feb 1907, Ohio; res: Cincinnati, Hamilton, OH; death: 4 Nov 1989, Bethesda North Hospital, Montgomery, Hamilton Co, OH, age 82; Widowed; Occ: Telephone installers and repairers. Ohio Deaths, 1908-1932, 1938-1944, and 1958-2007 [Ancestry.com]

551 ii **Mildred⁶ MANNING**, born abt 1908 probably in Cincinnati, Hamilton Co, OH. Notes: Not found on 1920 census or Ohio Death Index. May have married.

@@See research notes at end of chapter.   ##Born after 1930 & possibly living.

269. **Ethel M.**[5] **MANNING** (Francis M.[4], Lucinda[3] TATMAN, Ruth[2] HICKS, Joshua[1]), born 15 Jun 1894 probably in Cincinnati, Hamilton Co, OH; died 26 Dec 1993 in Blue Ash, Hamilton Co, OH. She married bef 1918 **William Bernard TEKULVE**[260], born 9 Aug 1891 in Reading, OH; died 25 Jan 1974 in Silverton, Hamilton Co, OH, son of Herman and Mary TEKULVE.

Ethel Manning was a homemaker, living in the Cincinnati area most of her life. She married William Tekulve, who worked as a boiler maker. He was the son of German immigrant. @@

Children of Ethel M. MANNING and William B TEKULVE were:

552 i **William A.**[6] **TEKULVE**, born abt 1917 in OH; died 8 Sep 1967 in Cincinnati, Hamilton, OH. **Death:** William Tekulve, b. 1917; Res: St Bernard, Hamilton Co, OH; Death: 8 Sep 1967, Veterans Adm. Med. Ctr, Cincinnati, OH; Age: 50; Never married Ohio Deaths, 1908-1932, 1938-1944, and 1958-2007 [Ancestry.com]

553 ii **Mildred E.**[6] **TEKULVE**, born abt 1919 in OH. No other information found

554 iii **Mary F.**[6] **TEKULVE**, born abt 1923 in OH. No other information found

271. **Edward H.**[5] **PATTISON** (Mary A. 'Mollie'[4] MANNING, Lucinda[3] TATMAN, Ruth[2] HICKS, Joshua[1]), born 20 Apr 1877 in Clermont Co, OH; died 8 Sep 1961 in Cincinnati, Hamilton Co, OH; buried in Bethel Tate Cemetery He married on 1 Sep 1901 in Clermont Co, OH **Jennie Irene MCKIBBEN**, born 18 Apr 1883 in Flag Springs KY; died[261] 9 Jun 1950 in Cincinnati, Hamilton Co, OH; buried 10 Jun 1950 in Bethel Tate Cemetery, daughter of Albert MCKIBBEN and Thresia ROSS.

Edward Pattison was an educator all his life, beginning as a teacher and ending as Superintendent of Clermont County schools. He served in the Kentucky Infantry, Spanish American War. @@

Children of Edward H. PATTISON and Jennie Irene MCKIBBEN were:
+ 555 i **Stanley Edward**[6] **PATTISON**.
+ 556 ii **Thelma Myrtle**[6] **PATTISON**.
+ 557 iii **Eunice Irene**[6] **PATTISON**.
+ 558 iv **John W.**[6] **PATTISON**.

273. **Ross John**[5] **PATTISON** (Mary A. 'Mollie'[4] MANNING, Lucinda[3] TATMAN, Ruth[2] HICKS, Joshua[1]), born 20 Apr 1882 in Clermont Co, OH; died 3 May 1948. He married on 9 Aug 1911 in New Richmond, Clermont Co, OH **Ann C. NEISER**, born[262] 18 Apr 1887 in Camp Springs KY; died[263] May 1982 in Covington, Kenton Co, KY.

Ross Pattison was a fireman in Covington, KY for a number of years. He and his wife, Ann, had one son, Robert. @@

Children of Ross John PATTISON and Ann C. NEISER were:
+ 559 i **Robert John**[6] **PATTISON**.

274. **Walter Cleavland**[5] **PATTISON**[264] (Mary A. 'Mollie'[4] MANNING, Lucinda[3] TATMAN, Ruth[2] HICKS, Joshua[1]), born 15 Apr 1885 in Clermont Co, OH; died[265] Jan 1973 in Sylvania, Lucas Co, OH. He married (1)[266] on 19 Aug 1905 in Hamilton, OH **Minnie M. BOWER**, born May 1882 in OH; died before 1915, daughter of Jerry BOWER and Samatha SHAW; (2)[267] on 2 Dec 1915 in Hamilton Co, OH **Mada Mary KUHN**, born 1891 in Cincinnati, Hamilton Co, OH; died[268] Nov 1963 in Toledo, Lucas Co, OH, daughter of George KUHN and Mary RAMMINGER.

Walter Pattison worked as a drop forger in the automotive industry. He married first, Minnie M. (Bowers) Brummel, a widow. She had one daughter; she and Walter had two more daughters. After

@@See research notes at end of chapter.   ##Born after 1930 & possibly living.

Minnie's death, Walter married Mada Kuhn and had at least five sons. Walter's widowed daughter, Edith, and her four children lived with his family in 1930.

Children of Walter Cleavland PATTISON and Minnie M. BOWER were:
+   560   i   **Grace**[6] **PATTISON**.
+   561   ii   **Edith May**[6] **PATTISON**.

Children of Walter Cleavland PATTISON and Mada Mary KUHN were:

562 i   **Elmore Walter**[6] **PATTISON**, born 1916 in OH; died[269] 1955 in Dade Co, FL. Jones notes: "WW II; Captured at Bataan, released at war's end in poor health, d. FL"
Military: Elmore W Pattison b. 1916 Ohio; Res: Cuyahoga, OH; Enlistment Date: 28 Mar 1941 Cleveland OH; Branch Immaterial - Warrant Officers, USA; Grade: Private; Component: Selectees (Enlisted Men); Source: Civil Life; Education: 2 years of high school; Civil Occupation: Cooks, except private family; Marital Status: Single, without dependents; Height: 65; Weight: 134. U.S. World War II Army Enlistment Records, 1938-1946 [Ancestry.com]
Death: Elmore Walter Pattison, Death Date: 1955; Miami, Dade Co, FL. Florida Death Index, 1877-1998 [Ancestry.com]

563 ii   **Herbert Leroy**[6] **PATTISON**, born 1918 in Cincinnati, Hamilton Co, OH; died 1941/45 in USS Tumey, WW II.
Jones notes: "Navy Water Tender 2C; lost when the USS Tumey went down in WW II"

564 iii   **George E.**[6] **PATTISON**, born 1920 in OH.
Jones notes: "US Navy Air Force". No military records found. No death information found.

565 iv   **Albert P.**[6] **PATTISON**, born 24 Mar 1922; died[270] 23 Feb 1993 in Ottawa Lake, Monroe Co, MI. He married on 23 Mar 1957 in Ottawa Lake, MI **Hilda Mae OLICH**, born 22 Feb 1927.
Jones notes: "resides (1973) at 8421 Head o'Lake Rd, Ottawa Lake, MI 49257; Air Force Sergeant, WW II; no children"
Military: U.S. World War II Army Enlistment Records, 1938-1946 [Ancestry.com] Albert F Pattison, b. 1922, Ohio; Res: Lucas Co, OH; Enlistment: 31 Oct 1942 Camp Perry, Lacarne, Ohio; Branch: Air Corps, Enlistment for the duration of the War or other emergency, plus six months, subject to the discretion of the President or otherwise according to law; Component: Army of the United States - includes the following: Voluntary enlistments effective December 8, 1941 and thereafter; One year enlistments of National Guardsman whose State enlistment expires while in the Federal Service; Officers appointed in the Army of; Source: Civil Life; Education: 4 years of high school; Civil Occupation: Semiskilled mechanics and repairmen, n.e.c.; Marital Status: Single, without dependents; Height: 67; Weight: 131

566 v   **Edwin L.**[6] **PATTISON**, born 1923 in OH.

567 vi   **Walter**[6] **PATTISON**, born 28 Apr 1927 in Washington Twp, Lucas, OH; died 28 Apr 1927 in Washington Twp, Lucas, OH; buried 29 Apr 1927 in Memorial Park.
Death: Male Pattison, b. 28 Apr 1927 Wash Twp; d. 28 Apr 1927 Washington Twp, Lucas, OH; bur 29 Apr 1927, Memorial park; Father: Walter Pattison b. Ohio; Mother: Nada Kuhn b. OH. Collection: Ohio Deaths and Burials, 1854-1997 <pilot.familysearch.org>

@@See research notes at end of chapter.   ##Born after 1930 & possibly living.

276. **Frank Lee⁵ PATTISON**²⁷¹ (Mary A. 'Mollie'⁴ MANNING, Lucinda³ TATMAN, Ruth² HICKS, Joshua¹), born 17 Oct 1891 in Salt Air, Clermont Co, OH; died 18 May 1954. He married on 18 Aug 1925 in Cleveland, Cuyahoga Co, OH **Delores Naomi BUCEY**, born 13 Jun 1903 in Wellsville, Columbiana Co, OH; died²⁷² 1 Mar 1988 in East Cleveland, Cuyahoga Co, OH, daughter of Fredrick and Lois BUCEY.

Frank Pattison was a pharmacist, living in several counties in Ohio. He served in World War I, working at the Base Hospital in Sherman, OH. He married Delores Bucey and had one daughter, Patricia. @@

  Children of Frank Lee PATTISON and Delores Naomi BUCEY were:
+   568 i   **Patricia⁶ PATTISON**.

277. **Orville Lorain⁵ MANNING**²⁷³ (John Wesley⁴, Lucinda³ TATMAN, Ruth² HICKS, Joshua¹), born 20 Feb 1876 in Clermont Co, OH; died 27 Nov 1959 in Cincinnati, Hamilton, OH; buried in Concord Cemetery. He married on 4 Jun 1905 in Clermont Co, OH **Margaret R. SPRAGUE**, born 19 Aug 1876 in Baywood, Clermont Co, OH; died 14 Aug 1963 in Clermont Co, OH; buried in Concord Cemetery, daughter of Wright SPRAGUE and Rebecca HOMAN.

Orville Manning was listed as a teacher in 1910 and 1930; as a farmer in 1920 and on his draft registration in 1918. His daughter Onmeta (with a variety of spellings) was also a teacher. @@

  Children of Orville Lorain MANNING and Margaret R. SPRAGUE were:
    569 i   **Onneita⁶ MANNING**, born 12 Mar 1907 in Clermont Co, OH; died 1970; buried in Concord Cemetery. Jones notes: "m. -?- Summers"
        Death: Onneita M Summers, b. 1908; Res: Clermont; d. 3 Oct 1970, Mercy Hosp Anderson; Hamilton Co; Age: 62; Married. Ohio Deaths, 1908-1932, 1938-1944, and 1958-2007. [Ancestry.com]
    570 ii **Dane C.⁶ MANNING**, born 6 Nov 1909; died²⁷⁴ 26 Sep 1988 in Warren, Macomb Co, MI. Jones notes: "resides (1973) at 30592 St. Onge St, Warren, MI 48093"

278. **Ora Chasse⁵ MANNING** (Charles William⁴, Lucinda³ TATMAN, Ruth² HICKS, Joshua¹), born 7 Oct 1879 in Clermont Co, OH; died²⁷⁵ 22 Jun 1939 in Tate, Clermont, Ohio; buried 24 Jun 1939 in Bethel Tate Cemetery He married (1) abt 1908 in Ohio **Velma PATTERSON**, born 3 Aug 1889; died²⁷⁶ 13 Feb 1920 in Tate Twp, Clermont Co, OH; buried 16 Feb 1920 in Bethel Tate Cemetery, daughter of John PATTERSON and Nancy MCCLELLAN; (2) on 12 Nov 1921 in Clermont Co, OH **Lilla B. WALKER**, born May 1879, daughter of Lewis WALKER and Mahala PATTEN.

Ora Manning was a farmer, apparently living in Clermont Co his whole life. His first wife, Velma, died in 1920, leaving 3 young children. Ora remarried in 1921 to Lida Walker, who was the widow of Alfonso Jacobs. @@

  Children of Ora Chasse MANNING and Velma PATTERSON were:
+   571 i   **John C.⁶ MANNING**.
    572 ii **Glenn⁶ MANNING**, born 23 Jun 1910 in Tate Twp, Clermont Co, OH; died 21 Jun 1967 in Fairfax OH.
        Jones notes: "divorced (no wife's name given)" May be the Glenn H. Manning in Cleveland, Russell Co, VA in 1930 - a boarder with Dotson family, age 19, occ: railroading, steam engine.
+   573 iii **Ruth N.⁶ MANNING**.

@@See research notes at end of chapter.   ##Born after 1930 & possibly living.

279. **Iva Lou**[5] **MANNING** (Charles William[4], Lucinda[3] TATMAN, Ruth[2] HICKS, Joshua[1]), born 29 Oct 1881 in Clermont Co, OH; died 18 Sep 1969 in Chevioti, Hamilton Co, OH; buried in Concord Cemetery. She married on 1 Apr 1900 in Clermont Co, OH **Miles Robert DEEL**, born 26 Jul 1878 in Baywood, Clermont Co, OH; died 29 Jun 1951 in Williamsburg, Clermont, OH; buried 2 Jul 1951 in Concord Cemetery, Clermont Co, OH, son of Collins DEEL and Ella BRICKER.

Iva Manning married Miles Deel (spelled several different ways) at the age of 19. Miles worked as a farmer and later as county surveyor. A note from a great granddaughter says that he was a politician and changed his name from Deel to Deal. @@

Children of Iva Lou MANNING and Miles Robert DEEL were:

574 i   **Docia**[6] **DEEL**, born abt 1907 in OH. Jones notes: "resides (1951) at Burbank, CA; m. ___ Hanch"; no other information found

575 ii   **Mildred**[6] **DEEL**, born Est. 1908 in OH; died 1908. Notes: does not appear on census records.

576 iii   **Marjorie**[6] **DEEL**, born abt 1912 in OH. Jones notes: "resides (1951) at 2632 Hemlock, Cincinnati, OH; m. ___ Bruche?"; no other information found

577 iv   **Estell**[6] **DEEL**, born 7 Sep 1908 in Williamsburg, Clermont, OH; died 1 Jun 1909 in Williamsburg, Clermont, OH. Notes: Ohio Death Certificate Digital image at <pilot.familysearch.org>

578 v   **Edna Edith**[6] **DEEL**, born 15 Feb 1914 in Williamsburg, Clermont Co, OH. Jones notes: "resides (1951) at 621 Trenton, Cincinnati, OH; m. ___ Peters". No other information found

579 vi   **Charles Collins**[6] **DEEL**, born 18 May 1916 in Williamsburg, Clermont Co, OH; died[277] 5 Jul 1953 in Cincinnati, Hamilton Co, OH; buried in Bethel Cemetery, Clermont, OH. He married **Jewel Virginia SMITH**, born 10 Aug 1917 in Kentucky; died 5 Dec 1996 in Hamilton Co, OH; buried in Bethel Cemetery, Clermont, OH.
Jones notes: "resides (1951) at Amelia, OH"
Death: Charles Collins Deal; d. 5 Jul 1953, Good Samaritan Hospital, Cincinnati, Hamilton Co, OH; Birth: 18 May 1916, OH; age: 37 years; Father: Miles Deal; Mother: Iva Manning. Res: Amelia, OH. Occ: truck driver - Richter Concrete; informant: Mrs. Jewel Deal. Ohio Deaths, 1908-1953 <familysearch.org>

280. **Chilton Henry**[5] **MANNING** (Charles William[4], Lucinda[3] TATMAN, Ruth[2] HICKS, Joshua[1]), born 13 Feb 1885 in Bethel, OH; died[278] 3 Aug 1962 in Cincinnati, Hamilton, OH; buried in Bethel Tate Cemetery He married on 2 Nov 1925 in Clermont Co, OH **Mary Ann WISBY**, born 16 Feb 1905 in Bethel, OH; died aft 1962, daughter of Charles L. and Ida A. WISBY.

Chilton Manning did not married until he was 42; his bride was 21. Chilton evidently worked on the family farm as a young adult, but was working as a motorman - street railway by 1920. He was working as a carpenter in 1930. @@

Children of Chilton H. MANNING and Mary Ann WISBY were:

580 i   **Elizabeth**[6] **MANNING**, born abt Jun 1928 in OH.

581 ii   **Chilton**[6] **MANNING Jr**, born 30 Dec 1929 in Bethel, Clermont Co, OH; died[279] 30 Dec 1929 in Bethel, Clermont Co, OH; buried 31 Dec 1929 in Bethel, OH.
Death: Chilton Manning Jr, b. 30 Dec 1929, Bethel, OH; d. 10 hr; Parents: Chilt H. Manning; Mary Wisby. Informant: Chilt H. Manning, Bethel, OH; Buried: Bethel Cemetery 12/31/1929. <pilot.familysearch.org>

582 iii   **James Chilton**[6] **MANNING**, born 30 Nov 1930 in Clermont Co, OH.

@@See research notes at end of chapter.   ##Born after 1930 & possibly living.

583 iv **Forest**[6] **MANNING**, born 22 Feb 1932 in Clermont Co, OH; died 22 Feb 1932 in Bethel, Clermont Co, OH; buried 22 Feb 1932 in Bethel Cem., Bethel, OH.
Death: Forest Manning; d. 22 Feb 1932, Bethel, Clermont, Ohio; b. 22 Feb 1932, OH; Age: 1 day; Male; Burial: 22 Feb 1932, Bethel Cem; Father: C.H. Maning; b. Ohio; Mother: Mary Wisby, b. OH; cause of death: prematurity. Ohio Deaths, 1908-1953 <pilot.familysearch.org>

584 v **Ida Laron**[6] **MANNING**, born 24 Jan 1933 in Cincinnati, Hamilton, OH; died 25 Jan 1933 in Cincinnati, Hamilton, OH.
Death: Female Manning, d. 25 Jan 1933, Cincinnati, Hamilton, OH; b. 24 Jan 1933, Cincinnati, Hamilton, OH; Age: 14 hours; Female; Residence: Batavia, Ohio; Burial: 27 Jan 1933 Cemetery: Bethel; Father: Chilton Henry Manning, b. Bethel, Ohio; Mother: Mary Wisby, b. Bethel, Ohio. Cause of death: prematurity. Ohio Deaths, 1908-1953 <pilot.familysearch.org>

284. Raleigh Clark[5] **MANNING**[280, 281] (Charles William[4], Lucinda[3] TATMAN, Ruth[2] HICKS, Joshua[1]), born 14 Dec 1896 in Bethel, OH; died 18 Jan 1957. He married on 28 Jan 1919 in Clermont Co, OH **Hazel Marie BOICE**, born 2 Jun 1900 in Bethel, OH; died[282] 27 Jul 1976 in Bethel, Clermont Co, OH, daughter of Charles M. BOICE and Mary E. CORNELL.

Raleigh Manning was a farmer in Clermont Co, OH. He and Hazel had 4 children. @@

Children of Raleigh Clark MANNING and Hazel Marie BOICE were:

585 i **Mary**[6] **MANNING**, born 15 Nov 1919 in Clermont Co, OH; died[283] May 1979 in Tucson, Pima Co, AZ. She married **unknown KLINK**, born Est. 1919. Jones notes: " resided (1957) at 437 E. Navajo Tr, Tuscon, AZ"

586 ii **Robert Chilton**[6] **MANNING**, born 22 Feb 1922 in Bethel, OH; died 18 Nov 1967 in Clermont Co, OH. He married on 22 May 1942 in Clermont Co, OH **Dorthea Bernadina MASON**, born 4 Jun 1924 in Cincinnati, Hamilton Co, OH, daughter of Fred MASON and Edith CASE. Jones notes: "she resides (1973) at 304 N. Charity, Bethel, OH"
Death: SS Death Index: Robert Manning b. 25 Feb 1922; d. Nov 1967; no location given; card issued in OH.
Death: Robert C Manning, b. 1922; Res: Clermont Co, OH; d. 18 Nov 1967, Clermont Co, OH; Age: 45; Married. Ohio Deaths, 1908-1932, 1938-1944, and 1958-2007 [Ancestry.com]

587 iii **Norma Jean**[6] **MANNING**, born 14 Aug 1927 in Clermont Co, OH. She married on 17 Jul 1948 in Clermont Co, OH **Stanley H. BERRY**, born 19 May 1922 in Pt. Isabel OH; died[284, 285] 10 Nov 1973 in Brown Co, OH, son of Hargus and Milie BERRY. Jones notes: "resides (1973) at Bethel Williamsburg Pike". No death information found

588 iv **Wanda Lee**[6] **MANNING**, born 29 Mar 1931 in Clermont Co, OH. She married **unknown WAYBRIGHT**. Jones notes: "resided (1957) at 2434 Robertson, Norwood, OH"

285. Lowell Burns[5] **MANNING** (Charles William[4], Lucinda[3] TATMAN, Ruth[2] HICKS, Joshua[1]), born 14 Dec 1896 in Bethel, Clermont Co, OH; died 12 Jan 1925 in Akron, Summit, OH; buried in Concord Cemetery. He married Harriet M **COWLING**, born 1902.

Children of Lowell Burns MANNING were:

589 i **Geneva Grace**[6] **MANNING**, born 1921; died 2001 Jones notes: "resides (1973) at Akron, OH"

287. Pearl Diana[5] **FITZPATRICK** (Homer Jerome[4], Dianna[3] TATMAN, Ruth[2] HICKS, Joshua[1]), born 12 Dec 1882 in Mt. Orab, Clermont Co, OH; died[286] 7 Jan 1972 in Hamilton Co, OH. She married on

@@See research notes at end of chapter.   ##Born after 1930 & possibly living.

8 Jun 1918 in Clermont Co, OH **Edward WOLF**, born 15 Sep 1882 in Amelia, Clermont Co, OH; died[287] May 1976 in Loveland, Clermont Co, OH, son of John Adam WOLF and Katharine MILLER.

Children of Pearl Diana FITZPATRICK and Edward WOLF were:
+   590   i   **Charles Edward[6] WOLF**.

288. **John Charles[5] FITZPATRICK** (Homer Jerome[4], Dianna[3] TATMAN, Ruth[2] HICKS, Joshua[1]), born 8 Oct 1888 in Batavia OH; died[288, 289] 23 Aug 1973 in Amelia, Clermont Co, OH; buried in Batavia Cemetery. He married (1) on 23 Sep 1916 in Clermont Co, OH **Ella Marie NICHOLS**, born 12 Sep 1895 in Batavia, Clermont Co, OH; died 30 May 1928 in Cincinnati, Hamilton Co, OH; buried 2 Jun 1928 in Batavia, Clermont Co, OH, daughter of Clayton B. NICHOLS and Maude HITCH; (2) on 30 Jan 1932 in Clermont Co, OH **Fannie L. BECKETT**, born 16 Jun 1888 in Hamersville OH; died[290] 30 Jun 1952 in Amelia, Clermont Co, OH; buried 3 Jul 1952 in Batavia Union Cemetery, Clermont Co, OH; (3) on 15 Jul 1953 in Clermont Co, OH **Mrs. Mabel WEST**, born 23 Jun 1897 in New Richmond, Clermont, OH.

John Charles Fitzpatrick was a veterinarian, living in Clermont Co, OH all of his life. He was married to Ella Nicols, who died young, leaving him with a son, Wayne, who was only 7 when his mother died. John married two more times, possibly outliving both those wives. @@

Children of John Charles FITZPATRICK and Ella Marie NICHOLS were:
+   591   i   **Wayne Nichols[6] FITZPATRICK**.

289. **Guy[5] HIGGINS** (Sarah Ellen[4] FITZPATRICK, Dianna[3] TATMAN, Ruth[2] HICKS, Joshua[1]), born 21 Dec 1874 in AL; died 5 Jun 1951 in Clanton, Chilton, AL. He married **Elizabeth L. FULLER**, born Nov 1876 in GA, daughter of John P. FULLER.

Guy Higgins moved with his parents to Alabama about 1876. Guy worked for the railroad as a station agent in 1900, but was manager of a lumber company by 1918. Photo, page 186. @@

Children of Guy HIGGINS and Elizabeth L. FULLER were:
   592   i   **John Burton[6] HIGGINS**, born Aug 1898 in AL.
        Notes: If the family found in the 1930 census is the correct one, there were children of this family. With no confirmation, that family is included only in these notes here.
        Jones notes: "resides (1973) at 103 8th St N., Clanton, AL 35045; attorney"
        1900 census gives name as John Burton Higgins; Jones notes give John M. Higgins
        Census:
        1920 Clanton, Chilton, Al, p. 3A. Burt Higgins, 21, single, boarder, purchasing agent - lumber. Not found in 1930 census. His uncle is John Burton Higgins, b. 1878.
        1930 Clanton, Chilton, Al, p. 11B. J B Higgins 31, occ: lumber, married age 25; Gussie Higgins 30; Martha Higgins 4; John Burton Higgins 1 1/12; Gussie Rainer Higgins 1/12; Charlie Williams 38, black, helper; Della Williams 37, black. **not certain that this is right person, but age & occupation fits; name of son is family name.
   593   ii   **Sarah E.[6] HIGGINS**, born abt 1909 in AL; died[291] 20 Feb 1911 in Chilton, AL.
        Notes: Family tree online gives death as 1913 - checking further.
        Death: Sarah Elizabeth Higgins, d. 20 Feb 1911, Chilton, AL, age 2; b. 1909 AL; parents: Guy Higgins, b. AL / Elizabeth Higgins. Alabama Deaths and Burials, 1881-1952 <familysearch.org>
   594   iii   **Guy[6] HIGGINS Jr**, born 1910 in Alabama; died[292] 22 Aug 1913 in Clanton, Chilton, AL.

@@See research notes at end of chapter.   ##Born after 1930 & possibly living.

Death: Guy Higgins Jr., d. 22 Aug 1913, Clanton, Chilton, AL; Age 3; Birthdate 1910 Ala.; Father: Guy Higgins, b. AL; mother: Elizabeth Higgins, b. AL. Alabama Deaths and Burials, 1881-1952 <fsbeta.familysearch.org>

291. **Frank**[5] **HIGGINS** (Sarah Ellen[4] FITZPATRICK, Dianna[3] TATMAN, Ruth[2] HICKS, Joshua[1]), born Est. 1876; died bef 1973; buried in Old German Cemetery, Garden City AL. He married unknown.

Jones notes: "resided at Deatsville, AL; RR telegrapher; lumber business late; buried in Old German Cemetery, Garden City, AL". None of the information found on Frank Higgins is definitive. If the information found is correct, then he had additional children [see reference notes], but they have not been added to the database until proof is found. It is possible that this is a duplicate of one of the previously listed sons. @@

 Children of Frank HIGGINS were:
  595* i **Mary Ellen**[6] **HIGGINS**, born Est. 1900. Jones notes: "resides (1973) at Thorsby, AL; two marriages - names not given"; no other information found
  596* ii **Elizabeth**[6] **HIGGINS**, born Est. 1900. Jones notes: "resides (1973) at Birmingham, AL"; no other information found. *This may be with the wrong family

292. **Burton**[5] **HIGGINS** (Sarah Ellen[4] FITZPATRICK, Dianna[3] TATMAN, Ruth[2] HICKS, Joshua[1]), born 28 Aug 1877 in Bethel, Clermont Co, OH; died[293] 21 Feb 1947 in Thorsby, Chilton, AL; buried in Deatsville Cemetery, Deatsville, AL. He married on 24 May 1899 in Elmore Co, AL **Eula Pugh RAWLINSON**, born 17 Nov 1879 in Deatsville, AL; died 11 Dec 1952 in Thorsby, Chilton Co, AL, daughter of Frank B. RAWLINSON and Ellen Christina JACKSON; adopted by W. W. Myrick.

Burt Higgins worked for the railroad as well as farming. He did not appear with his family on the 1900 census - was he with a relative somewhere? He and his wife Eula had 4 children. @@

 Children of Burton HIGGINS and Eula Pugh RAWLINSON were:
+ 597 i **Frank Oliver**[6] **HIGGINS**.
 598 ii **William**[6] **HIGGINS**, born abt 1904 in Alabama.
 599 iii **Mary**[6] **HIGGINS**, born abt 1905 in Alabama.
 600 iv **Elizabeth**[6] **HIGGINS**, born abt 1908 in Alabama.

294. **William Zachary**[5] **HIGGINS**[294] (Sarah Ellen[4] FITZPATRICK, Dianna[3] TATMAN, Ruth[2] HICKS, Joshua[1]), born 27 May 1884 in Decatur, AL; died[295] 27 Feb 1973 in Birmingham, Jefferson, AL. He married abt 1907 **Edith Elizabeth QUINN**, born abt 1890 in Alabama; died[296] 17 Jul 1958 in Birmingham, Jefferson, AL, daughter of John V. QUINN and Martha COFFEE.

William Z. Higgins was involved with the railroad most of his working life, working as a telegraph operator. Nothing more is known of this family. @@

 Children of William Zachary HIGGINS and Edith Elizabeth QUINN were:
 601 i **Lida Frances**[6] **HIGGINS**, born abt 1909 in Alabama.
 602 ii **William S**[6] **HIGGINS**, born abt 1912 in Alabama.
 603 iii **Virginia**[6] **HIGGINS**, born abt 1914 in Alabama.
 604 iv **Edith L.**[6] **HIGGINS**, born abt 1916 in Alabama.
 605 v **Edward N**[6] **HIGGINS**, born abt 1919 in Alabama.
 606 vi **?Leroy?**[6] **HIGGINS**, born abt 1926 in Alabama.
 607 vii **__ne**[6] **HIGGINS**, born abt 1929 in Alabama.

@@See research notes at end of chapter. ##Born after 1930 & possibly living.

295. Leroy⁵ HIGGINS (Sarah Ellen⁴ FITZPATRICK, Dianna³ TATMAN, Ruth² HICKS, Joshua¹), born Feb 1886 in Alabama; died[297] 20 Nov 1951 in Birmingham, Jefferson, AL. He married[298] on 8 Nov 1913 in Cullman Co, AL **Lelah COBB**, born abt 1893 in Alabama.

Leroy Higgins, like many of his family, worked for the railroad. He was a telegraph operator for the Louisville & Nashville Railroad. Nothing more is known about this family. @@

Children of Leroy HIGGINS and Lelah COBB were:
- 608 i **Pearce C.⁶ HIGGINS**, born abt 1915 in Alabama.
- 609 ii **Martha F.⁶ HIGGINS**, born abt 1918 in Alabama.
- 610 iii **William K.⁶ HIGGINS**, born abt 1922 in Alabama.

296. James Monroe⁵ HIGGINS (Sarah Ellen⁴ FITZPATRICK, Dianna³ TATMAN, Ruth² HICKS, Joshua¹), born 24 Feb 1890 in Garden City, Culman Co, AL; died Aug 1971. He married **Jane -?-**, born abt 1889 in Alabama.

James Higgins, like most of his family, worked for the railroad most of his life. He was a telegraph operator, then a ticket agent and later station agent. Nothing more is known of this family. @@

Children of James Monroe HIGGINS and Jane wife of James M. HIGGINS were:
- 611 i **Roy F.⁶ HIGGINS**, born abt 1913 in Alabama.
- 612 ii **James M.⁶ HIGGINS**, born abt 1915 in Alabama.
- 613 iii **Milton S.⁶ HIGGINS**, born abt 1917 in Alabama.
- 614 iv **Ruth E.⁶ HIGGINS**, born abt 1918 in Alabama.
- 615 v **Eugene H⁶ HIGGINS**, born abt 1920 in Alabama.
- 616 vi **Morris W⁶ HIGGINS**, born abt 1922 in Alabama.
- 617 vii **Herman A⁶ HIGGINS**, born abt 1928 in Alabama.

297. Hanley⁵ FITZPATRICK[299] (George E.⁴, Dianna³ TATMAN, Ruth² HICKS, Joshua¹), born 25 May 1902 in Tate Twp, Clermont Co, OH; died[300] 30 Jul 1992 in Williamsburg, Clermont Co, OH. He married (1) in 1940 in Maysville, Mason Co, KY, divorced **Bernice DAUGHERTY**, born Est. 1902; (2) 1 Aug 19__ in Brown Co, OH **Airee? SEWARD**.

Hanley Fitzpatrick was still living with his parents in 1930 and listed as a farmer. Jones notes: "Resided (1973) at Bethel, OH"; gave death as 1 Oct 1959. The Social Security Death Index gives his death as 30 Jul 1992 in Williamsburg, Clermont Co, OH.

Children of Hanley FITZPATRICK and Bernice DAUGHERTY were:
- 618 i **George⁶ FITZPATRICK**, born Est. 1941. Jones notes: "Resided (1973) at Short's Dr, Mt. Washington, Cincinnati, OH 45230"
- 619 ii **Sadie Christine⁶ FITZPATRICK**, born Est. 1941. She married **Jean BOWMAN**, born Est. 1941. Jones notes: "Resided (1973) at 5635 Alvina St, Cincinnati, OH 45230; (1984) 3840 Laurenceburg Rd, E'town"

301. John Lee⁵ FITZPATRICK Jr (John Lee⁴, Sarah A.³ TATMAN, Ruth² HICKS, Joshua¹), born 28 Jul 1900 in Montgomery, AL; died 19 Jan 1957 in Montgomery, Montgomery, AL; buried in Greenwood Cemetery, Montgomery, AL. He married on 22 Jun 1922 **Mary Laverne TANKERSLEY**, born 24 Mar 1905 in Alexander City, AL; died 16 Jun 1964.

@@See research notes at end of chapter.   ##Born after 1930 & possibly living.

John L. Fitzpatrick, Jr. worked for the Western of Alabama Railroad for a number of years. He married Laverne Tankersley about 1924 and had two daughters. @@

Children of John Lee FITZPATRICK Jr and Mary Laverne TANKERSLEY were:
+   620   i   **Mary Laverne**[6] **FITZPATRICK**.
+   621   ii   **Sandra Louise**[6] **FITZPATRICK**.

302. Homer Tatman[5] **FITZPATRICK** (John Lee[4], Sarah A.[3] TATMAN, Ruth[2] HICKS, Joshua[1]), born 3 Apr 1908 in Montgomery, AL; died 14 Apr 1971 in Montgomery, Montgomery Co, AL; buried in Oakwood Cemetery, Montgomery, AL. He married on 18 Jun 1940 in Montgomery, Montgomery Co, AL **Jessie Lee DORRIS**, born 30 May 1921 in New Orleans, LA.

Homer Fitzpatrick worked as a clerk for the railroad in 1930. @@

Children of Homer Tatman FITZPATRICK and Jessie Lee DORRIS were:
622   i   **Linda Margaret**[6] **FITZPATRICK**, ##. She married **Herbert Donald RICKLES**, born 3 Jun 1931 in Griffin, GA; died 26 Sep 1973. Jones notes: " reside (1973) at 411 W. Hillsboro St, El Dorado, AR; no children"
623   ii   **Terry Baxter**[6] **FITZPATRICK**, ##. He married **Linda MILLER**.
Jones notes: "resides (1973) at 7247 Opaekaa St, Honolulu, HI 96825"

303. Daisy B.[5] **FITZPATRICK** (John Sherman[4], Sarah A.[3] TATMAN, Ruth[2] HICKS, Joshua[1]), born abt 1901 in OH; died 25 May 1964 in Clermont Co, OH. She married on 7 Jun 1918 in Newport, Campbell, KY **Edwin Joseph SINGLER**[301], born 20 Dec 1897 in Ohio; died 12 Aug 1966 in Clermont Co, OH, son of Edward and Katherine SINGLER.

Daisy Fitzpatrick married Edwin Singler in Newport, KY (across the Ohio River from Clermont Co, OH). In 1918, Edwin as listed as a farmer in Clermont Co, OH; in the 1930 census, he was a tinner - building. @@

Children of Daisy B. FITZPATRICK and Edwin Joseph SINGLER were:
624   i   **George**[6] **SINGLER**, born abt 1920 in OH; died 25 Apr 1976 in Clermont Co, OH.
Notes: Ohio Deaths <ancestry.com> gives death date 25 Apr 1976, married, died in Clermont Co, OH.
625   ii   **Anthony**[6] **SINGLER**, born abt 1921 in OH; died 23 Aug 1986 in Cincinnati, Hamilton, OH.
Notes: Ohio Deaths <ancestry.com> gives death date 23 Aug 1986, married, died in Cincinnati, Hamilton Co, OH.
626   iii   **Gladys**[6] **SINGLER**, born abt 1923 in OH.
627   iv   **Donald**[6] **SINGLER**, born 6 Aug 1925 in Cincinnati, Hamilton, OH; died 1 May 2002 in Cincinnati, Hamilton, OH.
Notes: Ohio Deaths <ancestry.com> gives death date 1 May 2002, married, died in Cincinnati, Hamilton Co, OH. Father's name Singler; mother's name Fitzpatrick.
628   v   **Charles**[6] **R. SINGLER**, born 23 Apr 1927 in Cincinnati, Hamilton, OH; died 20 Aug 1947 in Cincinnati, Hamilton, OH.
Death: Charles R. Singler, d. 20 Aug 1947, Cincinnati, Hamilton, OH; b. 23 Apr 1927, Cincinnati, OH; Age: 20 years 3 months 27 days; single; parents: Edwin Singler / Daisy Fitzpatrick; veteran of War II; accidental drowning, no occupation. Ohio Deaths, 1908-1953 <familysearch.org>

@@ See research notes at end of chapter.   ## Born after 1930 & possibly living.

310. **John Franklin⁵ TATMAN** (William W.⁴, John³, Ruth² HICKS, Joshua¹), born 1 Mar 1885 in Salt Air Clermont Co, OH; died 1959. He married on 25 May 1916 in Clermont Co, OH **Anna Rebecca SIMMONS**, born 23 Nov 1884 in Laurel OH; died³⁰² Dec 1972 in Cincinnati, Hamilton Co, OH, daughter of William D SIMMONS and Mary E. ALLEN.

Frank Tatman was a farmer in Clermont Co. His wife, Anna, was a teacher before they were married. @@

Children of John Franklin TATMAN and Anna Rebecca SIMMONS were:
- 629 i **William Durwood⁶ TATMAN**, born 5 Nov 1919 in Clermont Co, OH; died³⁰³ Jul 1977 in Cincinnati, Hamilton Co, OH. He married abt 1950, divorced **Eloise -?-**, born 31 Dec 1916; died 20 May 2010 in Harrison, Hamilton, OH.
  Jones notes: "resides (1973) at 5589 Glenway, Cincinnati, OH; m. to Eloise -?-"
  Divorce: William B Tatman, b. 1918; Times Married: 1; Res: Cincinnati, Hamilton; Spouse: Eloise H Tatman, b. 1916; Spouse - Times Married: 2; Spouse's Residence: Cincinnati, Hamilton; Marriage Duration (Years): 24; Number of Minor Children: 2; Grounds for Divorce: Willful Absence; To Whom Decree Granted: Wife; County of Decree: Hamilton; Decree Date: 28 Feb 1974 Ohio Divorce Index, 1962-1963, 1967-1971, 1973-2007 [ancestry.com]
  Death: William Tatman, b. 1920, res: Cincinnati, OH; d. 19 Jul 1977, Univ Hosp, Cinci General, age at death: 57. Ohio Deaths, 1908-1932, 1938-1944, and 1958-2007 [ancestry.com]

311. **Glen O'Hara⁵ SWING** (Mary A.⁴ TATMAN, John³, Ruth² HICKS, Joshua¹), born 9 Dec 1889; died³⁰⁴ 14 Nov 1962 in Kenton Co, KY. He married abt 1918 **Linda COUREY**, born abt 1892 in KY; died 2 Dec 1964 in Campbell Co, KY.

Glen Swing was an educator, starting as a teacher in Clermont Co, OH, then in Covington, KY - later becoming superintendent of schools in Covington. At the time he registered for the draft in 1918, he was a student instructor in Math, having graduated from OH State in 1917. @@

Children of Glen O'Hara SWING and Linda COUREY were:
- 630 i **Kenneth⁶ SWING**, born 29 Oct 1919 in OH; died³⁰⁵ Mar 1975.
  Jones notes: "resides (1973) at 25 Fairway Ct, Hamilton, OH 45013"
  Does not appear on any census records with family;
- 631 ii **Marguerite R⁶ SWING**, born 24 Dec 1924 in Kenton Co, KY.
  Jones notes: "resides (1973) at Covington, KY"
  Birth: Marguerite R Swing, Birth: 24 Dec 1924, Kenton Co, KY; Mother: Linda Courey; Kentucky Birth Index, 1911-1999 [ancestry.com]

314. **Phillip B.⁵ SWING** (Mary A.⁴ TATMAN, John³, Ruth² HICKS, Joshua¹), born 20 Mar 1895; died³⁰⁶ 11 Apr 1985 in Beachwood, Cuyahoga Co, OH. He married **Julia PAGE**, born³⁰⁷ 2 May 1902 in OH; died³⁰⁸ Mar 1982 in Beachwood, Cuyahoga Co, OH.

Phillip Swing was a school teacher in 1920 and treasurer for a coal company in 1930. He was living in Shaker Heights, OH in 1973. @@

Children of Phillip B. SWING and Julia PAGE were:
- 632 i **Mary Louise⁶ SWING**, born abt Oct 1924 in OH. Jones notes: "married to __ Robinson; reside 1985 at CA"

@@ See research notes at end of chapter.   ## Born after 1930 & possibly living.

633 ii   **Katherine Jane**[6] **SWING**, born abt Jul 1926 in OH.

634 iii   **Page**[6] **SWING**.

315. John Charles[5] **SWING** (Mary A.[4] TATMAN, John[3], Ruth[2] HICKS, Joshua[1]), born 10 Apr 1899 in OH; died 7 May 1990[309], no place given. He married abt 1925 in OH **Gladys -?-**, born abt 1901 in OH.

On his World War I draft registration in 1918, John was listed as a farmer, in partnership with his father. In 1930, he was a messenger with an express company. @@

Children of John Charles SWING and Gladys wife of John C. SWING were:

635 i   **Barbara**[6] **SWING**. Jones notes: "Attending college 1973"

317. Charles Harrison[5] **TAYLOR** (Maud Blanche[4] TATMAN, John[3], Ruth[2] HICKS, Joshua[1]), born 1 Aug 1888 in Clermont Co, OH; died 12 Feb 1970 in Brown Co, OH. He married on 15 Aug 1932 in Brooksville KY **Gladys Armelda PAELTZ**, born 6 Aug 1893 in Pekin OH; died 16 Jan 1992 in Brown Co, OH, daughter of Charles PAELTZ and Emma GATES.

Charles Taylor served in the American Expeditionary Forces in World War I. After the war, he was listed on the 1930 as an automobile salesman. @@

Children of Charles Harrison TAYLOR and Gladys A. PAELTZ were:

636 i   **Sally L.**[6] **TAYLOR**, born 26 Jun 1934; died 26 Jun 1934 in Bethel, Clermont , OH.

319. Alice B.[5] **TAYLOR** (Maud Blanche[4] TATMAN, John[3], Ruth[2] HICKS, Joshua[1]), born 25 Mar 1893 in Bethel, Clermont Co, OH; died 15 Sep 1944 in Bethel, Clermont Co, OH; buried in Bethel Tate Cemetery She married (1) on 19 Jul 1911 in Hamilton Co, OH, divorced **Forest T. CRANE**[310], born 21 Jan 1893 in Bethel, Clermont Co, OH, son of Wiley E. CRANE and Lena THIES; (2) bef 1931 **Estel Rosco BECK**, born 16 Mar 1882 in Bethel, Clermont Co, OH; died[311] 25 Jun 1940 in Bethel, Clermont Co, OH; buried 28 Jun 1940 in Bethel Cemetery, Clermont Co, OH, son of Horace J. BECK and Phoebe WINTERROD; (3) on 24 Nov 1943 in Clermont Co, OH **Malcolm NEWKIRK**, born 3 Mar 1892 in Butler, Pendleton, KY; died 1972, son of James NEWKIRK and Nanney BONER.

Alice Taylor was married three times. The first to Forest Crane ended in divorce, producing 1 daughter, Alice. The second, to Estel Beck, ended when Estel committed suicide. Alice had one son, Richard, from this marriage. The third, to Malcomb Newkirk lasted until Alice's death. Malcolm remarried after her death.

Children of Alice B. TAYLOR and Forest T. CRANE were:

+   637 i   **Agnes Cleo**[6] **CRANE**.

Children of Alice B. TAYLOR and Estel Rosco BECK were:

+   638 i   **Richard Taylor**[6] **BECK**.

321. George Richard[5] **TAYLOR** (Maud Blanche[4] TATMAN, John[3], Ruth[2] HICKS, Joshua[1]), born 28 May 1898 in Ohio; died 11 Feb 1967 in Akron, Summit Co, OH. He married **Esther E. STEPHENS**, born 6 May 1902 in Ohio; died 22 Feb 1965 in Akron, Summit Co, OH.

George Taylor worked in the auto industry as a young adult - as a rubber worker in a factory in 1920 and as president of an automobile company in 1930. He married Esther Stephens and was the father of 3 children. @@

@@ See research notes at end of chapter.   ## Born after 1930 & possibly living.

Children of George Richard TAYLOR and Esther E. STEPHENS were:
- 639 i **Patricia Ann⁶ TAYLOR**, born abt Feb 1929 in OH. Jones notes: "Not married, 1979; resides (1979) 535 Hatch Rd, Wadsworth, OH"; 1930 census, Akron, shows her as 1 3/12.
- 640 ii **Gene Richard⁶ TAYLOR**, ##. Jones notes: "Not married, 1979; resides (1979) 19 Goodhue Dr, Akron OH 44313"
- + 641 iii **Gwen⁶ TAYLOR**.

322. John Kenneth⁵ TAYLOR (Maud Blanche⁴ TATMAN, John³, Ruth² HICKS, Joshua¹), born 2 May 1902 in Bethel, OH. He married aft 1930 in Putnam, CT **Grace ORR**, born 9 Jan 1909 in S. Attleboro, MA, daughter of Charles ORR and Laura BRIEN.

John Taylor worked as an automobile salesman in 1930. He was living with his brother, George, at the time. @@

Children of John Kenneth TAYLOR and Grace ORR were:
- 642 i **J. Dwight⁶ TAYLOR**, ##. Jones notes: "resides (1973) at 2128 GreenWay Dr, Uniontown, OH 44685"
- 643 ii **Charles T.⁶ TAYLOR**, ##. Jones notes: "resides (1973) at 55 E. York St, Apt 22, Akron OH 44310"

328. Carlos Stanley⁵ HUTSON³¹² (Ledora Estelle⁴ TATMAN, William Oliver³, Ruth² HICKS, Joshua¹), born 4 Jul 1895 in Batavia, Clermont Co, OH; died³¹³, ³¹⁴ Jan 1973 in Amelia, Clermont Co, OH. He married on 19 Apr 1919 in Clermont Co, OH **Blanche HENDRIXSON**, born 1898 in Hamilton Co, OH; died³¹⁵ 28 May 1973 in Hamilton Co, OH, daughter of Chas. F. HENDRIXSON and Minnie SOLWALL.

Carlos Hutson held a variety of jobs – self employed real estate agent in 1917; stock man in a cash register company in 1920; working in a confectionery restaurant in 1930. He was described in 1917 as small and slender. @@

Children of Carlos Stanley HUTSON and Blanche HENDRIXSON were:
- + 644 i **Ruth⁶ HUTSON**.
- + 645 ii **Alice Mae⁶ HUTSON**.
- + 646 iii **Harriet⁶ HUTSON**.

329. Estella H.⁵ HUTSON (Arizona T. "Arra"⁴ TATMAN, William Oliver³, Ruth² HICKS, Joshua¹), born 27 Sep 1883 in Clermont Co, OH; died 1957; buried in Amelia Meth. Cemetery, Amelia, Clermont Co, OH. She married³¹⁶ on 18 Jan 1903 in Clermont, OH **Samuel GLOVER**³¹⁷, born 18 Feb 1879 in Clermont Co, OH; died 22 Dec 1930 in Amelia, Clermont, OH; buried in Amelia Meth. Cemetery, Amelia, Clermont Co, OH, son of Samuel H. GLOVER and Sarah Elizabeth ROUSCH.

Estella Hutson married Samuel Glover, who had served as a bugler in the Spanish American War. Samuel was listed as a house painter in 1910, a house carpenter in 1920 and a meat cutter in 1930. @@

Children of Estella H. HUTSON and Samuel GLOVER were:
- + 647 i **Samuel Hodgson⁶ GLOVER**.
- 648 ii **Mary Elizabeth⁶ GLOVER**, born³¹⁸ 16 Jun 1904 in Clermont Co, OH; died³¹⁹ 21 Mar 1913 in Amelia, Clermont, OH; buried in Amelia Meth. Cem., Amelia, OH.
  Birth: Mary E. Glover, b. 16 Jun 1904; father: Samuel Glover; mother: Estella Hudson Ohio Births and Christenings, 1821-1962 <pilot.familysearch.org>

@@ See research notes at end of chapter.   ## Born after 1930 & possibly living.

Death: Mary Elizabeth Glover, died 21 Mar 1913, Amelia, Clermont, Ohio; Born: 16 Jun 1904, Ohio; Age: 8 years 9 months 5 days; Burial: 22 Mar 1913, Amelia, OH; Father: Samuel H. Glover b. Ohio; Mother: Estella Glover, b. Ohio. Cause of death: diphtheria. Ohio Deaths, 1908-1953 <pilot.familysearch.org>

+   649   iii   **Julia Elsie**[6] **GLOVER**.
+   650   iv   **Dorothy H.**[6] **GLOVER**.
+   651   v   **Charles Lee**[6] **GLOVER**.

331. William Oliver[5] **HUTSON** (Arizona T. "Arra"[4] TATMAN, William Oliver[3], Ruth[2] HICKS, Joshua[1]), born 13 Mar 1887 in Batavia, Clermont Co, OH. He married on 14 Sep 1909 in Clermont Co, OH **Imo FERRIE**, born 1891 in Williamsburg, Clermont Co, OH.

William Hutson was a real estate agent in 1918-1930. In 1910, he was listed as a retail merchant - groceries. He was described in 1918 as "short, slender, brown eyes, dark brown hair". @@

Children of William Oliver HUTSON and Imo FERRIE were:

    652   i   **Jennie Mae**[6] **HUTSON**, born 2 Oct 1912 in Amelia, Clermont Co, OH; died[320] 16 Dec 2000 in Hamilton Co, OH. She married **William LIPPS**, born 1911 in Ohio; died 17 Jul 1986 in Cincinnati, Hamilton Co, OH.
Jones notes: "resides (1973) at 20 E. Main, Amelia"
Death: Jennie Mae Lipps [Jennie Mae Hutson], b. 2 Oct 1912, Clermont, OH; Res: Clermont Co, OH; d. 16 Dec 2000; Mercy Hospital, Hamilton Co, OH. Age: 88, Father's surname: Hutson; Mother's Maiden Name: Ferrie. Ohio Deaths, 1908-1932, 1938-1944, and 1958-2007 [Ancestry.com]

332. Gladys E.[5] **HUTSON** (Arizona T. "Arra"[4] TATMAN, William Oliver[3], Ruth[2] HICKS, Joshua[1]), born 17 Nov 1889 in Amelia, Clermont Co, OH; died[321] 19 Aug 1945 in Amelia, Clermont, OH. She married on 10 May 1913 in Clermont Co, OH **Clifford Behymer MYRICK**[322], born 11 Mar 1889 in Mt Holly, Clermont Co, OH; died[323] 23 Apr 1930 in Cincinnati, Hamilton, OH, son of Enock MYRICK and Hariet BEHYMER.

Gladys Hutson was a school teacher. She married Clifford Myrick, who was also a teacher in 1920. Later Clifford was a butcher in a meat market. @@

Children of Gladys E. HUTSON and Clifford Behymer MYRICK were:
+   653   i   **Kenneth H.**[6] **MYRICK**.

334. Ethel G.[5] **TAYLOR** (Caroline 'Callie'[4] TATMAN, William Oliver[3], Ruth[2] HICKS, Joshua[1]), born 16 Sep 1895 in Salt Air OH; died 30 Nov 1969 in Cincinnati, Hamilton, OH. She married on 12 May 1917 in Clermont Co, OH **Frederick Thurman WITSCHGER**[324], born 13 Nov 1895 in Cincinnati, Hamilton Co, OH; died[325] 29 Nov 1996 in Clark Co, OH.

Ethel Taylor married Fred Witschger, who worked on her father's farm in 1920 and was manager of a grocery store in 1930. At the time of his death is 1996 (age 101), he was listed as a machinist in the printing industry@@

Children of Ethel G. TAYLOR and Frederick Thurman WITSCHGER were:

    654   i   **Lila Eleanor**[6] **WITSCHGER**, born abt 1919 in OH. She married **Jack REINSTATLER**. Jones notes: "Reside (1973) at 2045 Sunset Dr, Hamilton, OH"
    655   ii   **Alice L.**[6] **WITSCHGER**, born abt 1923 in OH. Jones notes: "Resides FL"

@@ See research notes at end of chapter.   ## Born after 1930 & possibly living.

336. Lloyd Edwin[5] MCNAIR (Benjamin Edwin[4], Mary[3] TATMAN, Ruth[2] HICKS, Joshua[1]), born 24 May 1900 in Clermont Co, OH; died 19 Oct 1951[326] in Cincinnati, Hamilton, OH. He married on 23 Jul 1925 in Clermont Co, OH **Irene Caroline BECKTOLD**, born 22 Aug 1899 in Cincinnati, Hamilton Co, OH; died[327] 16 Jun 1988 in Williamsburg, Clermont Co, OH.

Lloyd McNair was killed in a tractor accident in October 1951. In 1930, he was listed as proprietor - insurance agency @@

Children of Lloyd Edwin MCNAIR and Irene Caroline BECKTOLD were:
+ 656 i **Jessie Elizabeth (Betty)[6] MCNAIR**.
  657 ii **Lois Evelyn[6] MCNAIR**, born 4 Apr 1929 in Williamsburg, Clermont Co, OH. She married on 21 Jul 1951 in Clermont Co, OH **Walter James SCHAUSEN**, born 20 Apr 1927 in Chicago, Cook Co, IL. Jones notes: "resides (1973) at 3996 Washington Av, Elmhurst (Chicago) IL"
  658 iii **Margaret Ann[6] MCNAIR**, ##. She married **Walter Raymond CHIARA**, born 4 Jan 1929 in Cleveland, Cuyahoga Co, OH. Jones notes: "resides (1973) at 3416 Cornwall Dr, Lexington, KY"

337. Hugh Elijah[5] NORRIS[328] (Fanny[4] TATMAN, Elijah[3], Ruth[2] HICKS, Joshua[1]), born 4 Jan 1899 in Clermont Co, OH; died[329, 330] 6 Aug 1994 in Akron, Summit Co, OH. He married **Carrie L. -?-**, born abt 1896 in PA; died[331] 23 Aug 1977 in Cuyahoga Falls, Summit Co, OH.

Hugh Norris was a printer, working for a printing company and later as a printing press operator for a newspaper. His World War I Draft registration described him as medium height, slender build with black hair and brown eyes. @@

Children of Hugh Elijah NORRIS and Carrie L. wife of Hugh E NORRIS were:
  659 i **Robert H.[6] NORRIS**, born abt 1927 in OH. Jones notes: "resides (1974) at Cuyahoga Falls, OH"

339. Phillip T.[5] DURHAM (Effie[4] TATMAN, Elijah[3], Ruth[2] HICKS, Joshua[1]), born 16 Sep 2008 in Bethel, OH; died 16 Sep 2008; age 96 in Portland, Jay, IN. He married on 26 Jun 1935 in Bethel, OH **Gretchen L. BURNGROVER**, born 7 Dec 1919 in Brown Co, OH, died 16 Sep 2006 in Portland, Jay Co, IN.

Phillip Durham was a retired Lieutenant Colonel - Chaplain, as well as a preacher in the Christian Church. He was living in Panama City, FL in 1974. He and his wife Gretchen were in Portland, Jay Co, IN by 1992 and both died there. @@

Children of Phillip T. DURHAM and Gretchen L. BURNGROVER were:
  660 i **Rogers Lynde[6] DURHAM**, ##. Jones notes: "resides (1974) at Centerville, IN; m. Janice -?-"
  661 ii **David Joe[6] DURHAM**, ##. Jones notes: "resides (1974) at Huntington Beach, CA; m. Fenka ?"
  662 iii **Charles Elliott[6] DURHAM**, ##. Jones notes: "resides (1974) at Huntington Beach, CA; m. Edith ?;-"

@@ See research notes at end of chapter.   ## Born after 1930 & possibly living.

343. **Hattie Edna**[5] **HICKS** (Orestes Daily "O.D."[4], Henry Melvin[3], Elijah[2], Joshua[1]), born 13 Sep 1877 in Clermont Co, OH; died 23 Sep 1938 in Felicity, Clermont Co, OH; buried 27 Sep 1938 in Felicity, Clermont Co, OH. She married on 1 Jun 1913 in Felicity, Clermont Co, OH **Charles Bodman HITE**, born 11 May 1867 in Brown Co, OH; died 21 Dec 1925 in Felicity, Clermont Co, OH; buried in Felicity, Clermont Co, OH, son of James HITE and Elizabeth DUGAN.

Hattie Hicks was listed as an evangelical singer in the 1910 census. After her husband's death in 1925, she and daughter, Elizabeth, lived with her father. In 1930, Hattie was listed as a music teacher. @@

Children of Hattie Edna HICKS and Charles Bodman HITE were:
+   663   i   **Elizabeth Stewart**[6] **HITE**.

345. **Hurdes Beeker**[5] **HICKS** (Elijah Franklin[4], Henry Melvin[3], Elijah[2], Joshua[1]), born[332, 333] 20 Jul 1898 in Clermont Co, OH; died[334] 6 Jul 1984 in Clermont Co, OH; buried in Shinkles Ridge Cemetery He married (1) on 1 Mar 1919, divorced **Bessie Marie RODGERS**, born 3 Oct 1899 in Salt Air OH; died 1966; buried in Chilo Cemetery; (2) on 30 Dec 1939 **Susan Ann DUGAN**, born est. 1898.

Hurdes Hicks apparently was a farmer all his life, as well as Sexton for the Chilo Cemetery and a boatsman on the Ohio River. He married and divorced Bessie Rogers, by whom he had 4 children. He later married Susan Dugan. He was described in 1918 as med. height & build; brown eyes & hair. @@

Children of Hurdes Beeker HICKS and Bessie Marie RODGERS were:
+   664   i   **Melissa Rosaline**[6] **HICKS**.
        665   ii   **Opal Louise**[6] **HICKS**[335], born 5 Oct 1922 in OH; died Fall, 1923 in OH.
                     Hicks Bible: "Born to Mr. Hurdes Beeker Hicks and Mrs Bessie Hicks (nee Rogers) Opal Louise Hicks October 5, 1922 (died Fall, 1923)"
+   666   iii   **Morris Hurdes**[6] **HICKS**.
+   667   iv   **Donald Rogers**[6] **HICKS**.

Children of Hurdes Beeker HICKS and Susan Ann DUGAN were:
+   668   i   **Barbara Ann**[6] **HICKS**.

346. **Irlene Evelyn**[5] **HICKS**[336] (Elijah Franklin[4], Henry Melvin[3], Elijah[2], Joshua[1]), born 11 Feb 1904 in Rural, Clermont Co, OH; died[337] 8 Jan 2002 in Bradenton, Manatee Co, FL. She married[338] on 4 Jun 1924 in Felicity, Clermont Co, OH **Herbert Leroy DEVORE**, born 17 Mar 1906 in Georgetown, Brown Co, OH; died[339] 22 Nov 1970 in Felicity, Clermont Co, OH; buried in Felicity, Clermont Co, OH, son of Lewis Abner DEVORE and Stella Rosetta SHAW.

Irlene Hicks married Herbert Devore, who was a farmer and dairy farmer in Clermont County. After her husband's death, she moved to Bradenton, FL, where she died at age 97. @@

Children of Irlene Evelyn HICKS and Herbert Leroy DEVORE were:
+   669   i   **Eva Irlene**[6] **DEVORE**.
+   670   ii   **John Wilson "J. W."**[6] **DEVORE**.
        671   iii   **Melissa Rosetta**[6] **DEVORE**, born 7 Apr 1933 in OH; died[340] 11 Apr 1933 in Felicity, Clermont Co, OH; buried in Felicity, Clermont Co, OH.
                     Jones notes: "died in infancy"
                     Death: Melissa Rosetta Devore, d. 11 Apr 1934 Franklin, Clermont, Ohio; b. 7 Apr 1934; Age at death: 5 days; Burial: 12 Apr 1934, Felicity, Ohio; Parents: Herbert Devore / Irlene Hicks. Ohio Deaths 1908-1953 <familysearch.org>

@@ See research notes at end of chapter.   ## Born after 1930 & possibly living.

672 iv **Gerald Lee⁶ DEVORE**, born 17 May 1943 in Felicity, Clermont Co, OH; died³⁴¹ 23 Sep 2007 in Bradenton, Manatee, FL. Jones notes: "not married - 1972"
Death: Social Security Death Index. Gerald Devore b. 17 May 1943; d. 23 Sep 2007, Bradenton, Manatee, FL 34208; SS#287-38-0842, issued Ohio

347. **Georgia Elizabeth⁵ HICKS**³⁴² (Elijah Franklin⁴, Henry Melvin³, Elijah², Joshua¹), born 25 Jun 1908 in Rural, Clermont Co, OH; died³⁴³ 22 May 2000 in Georgetown Brown Co, OH. She married on 10 Mar 1928 in Batavia, Clermont Co, OH **Eugene Martin JENNINGS**, born 18 May 1904 in Brown Co, OH; died 31 Jan 1984 in Georgetown, Brown Co, OH; buried 4 Feb 1984 in Shinkles Ridge Cemetery, Brown Co OH, son of Emerson Everett JENNINGS and Lillie Mae SCOTT.

Elizabeth Hicks married Eugene Jennings and lived in Georgetown, Brown Co, OH. Eugene Jennings was a farmer. Elizabeth lived to be 91 years old. Interview in 1999 added information for this book. Photo on page 185. @@

Children of Georgia Elizabeth HICKS and Eugene Martin JENNINGS were:
+ 673 i **Lvera Adrienne⁶ JENNINGS**.
+ 674 ii **Irma Claire⁶ JENNINGS**.
+ 675 iii **Ivetta Faye⁶ JENNINGS**.
+ 676 iv **Eugene Martin⁶ JENNINGS 2nd**.

348. **Irma Clair⁵ LEVI** (Lucy Ann⁴ HICKS, Henry Melvin³, Elijah², Joshua¹), born 22 Aug 1878 in Clermont Co, OH; died³⁴⁴ 13 Sep 1928 in York, Ontario, Canada. She married (1)³⁴⁵ in 1909 in OH? **George Walter WALSH Jr**, born Jan 1886 in Minnesota; died³⁴⁶ 2 Sep 1913 in Seattle, King Co, WA, son of George Walter WALSH and Stella CABANNE; (2) bef 1921 **David Watson SYMONS**³⁴⁷, born 12 Aug 1875 in Canada; died aft 1948.

Irma Levi married first George Walsh and had two sons. After George's death in 1913, she married Watson Symons, a Canadian. She died in Ontario, Canada. The family spent winters in Florida when the boys were young. Betty (Stalder) Kieser remembered them well and fondly. @@

Children of Irma Clair LEVI and George Walter WALSH Jr were:
677 i **Walter Cabanni⁶ WALSH**, born 2 Aug 1910 in Washington.
Notes: Betty (Stalder) Kieser spent time with him as children during the time his family lived in St Petersburg, FL area. She kept in touch for years, but has lost contact now (1998). See video interview with Betty (Stalder) Kieser Spring 1998. Not found on 1930 census - possibly in Canada?
678 ii **Francis Marion 'Frank'⁶ WALSH**, born 17 Mar 1912 in Seattle, King Co, WA. Notes: Betty Kieser kept in touch for years, but has lost contact now (1998). See video interview with Betty (Stalder) Kieser Spring 1998. Not found on 1930 census - in Canada?

Children of Irma Clair LEVI and David Watson SYMONS were:
679 i **Robert Kenneth⁶ SYMONS**, born³⁴⁸ 11 May 1921; died³⁴⁹ Apr 1993 in Stockton, San Joaquin Co, CA.
Death: SS Death Index gives: Robert K Symons; b. 11 May 1921; d. Apr 1993; age 71; Stockton, San Joaquin, CA; card issued: Montana; SS# 517-05-2926

@@ See research notes at end of chapter.   ## Born after 1930 & possibly living.

349. **Clyde Harvey**[5] **LEVI**[350, 351] (Lucy Ann[4] HICKS, Henry Melvin[3], Elijah[2], Joshua[1]), born 16 Apr 1881 in Cincinnati, Hamilton Co, OH; died 8 Jan 1948 in Omaha, Douglas Co, NE. He married 22 Dec 1902 in Newport, Campbell Co, KY **Pearl Roser AUSTIN**[352], born 5 Mar 1877 in KY; died 22 Jan 1953 in Omaha, Douglas Co, NE, daughter of William and Mitilda AUSTIN.

Clyde Harvey Levi left home as a young man and traveled extensively. He was a printer and a showman with a traveling carnival. In 1918, he was described as "med height & build, blue eyes, lt brown hair". @@

Children of Clyde Harvey LEVI and Pearl R. AUSTIN were:
+ 680 i **Harvey Clyde**[6] **LEVI II**.
   681 ii **Irma Crystal**[6] **LEVI**, born abt 1905 in OH; died abt Nov 1957 in IN. She married **George DAVIS**, born 1905.
Notes: Names, no other information in Bible of Mollie Dell Levi.
"Died Nov/Dec 1957 in IN, buried IN". Marriage, death info from nephew, Lane Levi.

350. **Mollie Dell**[5] **LEVI**[353, 354] (Lucy Ann[4] HICKS, Henry Melvin[3], Elijah[2], Joshua[1]), born[355, 356] 7 Sep 1884 in Felicity, Clermont Co, OH; died[357] 7 Oct 1947 in Jacksonville, Duval, Co, FL. She married[358] on 25 Jun 1910 in Hamilton Co, OH **William Benjamin STALDER**[359, 360], born[361] 19 Aug 1878 in Dillsboro, Dearborn Co, IN; died[362] 27 Aug 1948 in Jacksonville, Duval Co, FL, son of William Henry Harriston STALDER and Medora BOARDMAN.

Mollie Levi married Ben Stalder in 1910 at age 26; Ben was 32. When the family moved to Orlando, FL in 1921, they had 7 children under 10, with the baby, Madge, being only 6 weeks old. Ben Stalder was a carpenter and house builder, whose business was destroyed by the Florida Land Bust which preceded the Great Depression. The family lost everything - including their home. When oldest son, Curtis, landed a well paying job in Jacksonville, the whole family moved north - except for daughter Elizabeth who stayed behind to marry. This is the family of the compiler. Photo on page 185; of their adult children on page 304. @@

Children of Mollie Dell LEVI and William Benjamin STALDER were:
   682 i **Curtis Clyde**[6] **STALDER**, born 26 Aug 1911 in Norwood, Hamilton Co, OH; died 13 Jan 1996 in Orlando, Orange Co, FL; cremated. He married on 19 Sep 1968 in Lexington KY **Florence Madlyn FRENCH**, born 3 Jan 1917; died 28 Jan 2000 in Canton, NC.
Notes: Living in Orlando, 1995. Worked for Greyhound Bus Line for all of his career. Lived in GA, IL, TN; retired to Orlando, FL / summered in NC. Married 1968 to Madlyn French, widow of his friend Charlie Forester.
+ 683 ii **Elizabeth**[6] **STALDER**.
+ 684 iii **Jeanette**[6] **STALDER**.
   685 iv **William Francis**[6] **STALDER**, born 23 Jul 1916 in Madeira, Hamilton Co, OH; died 5 Mar 2005 in New Smyrna, Volusia Co, FL. He married on 13 Oct 1949 in New Smyrna, FL **Frances HADLEY**, born 30 Aug 1919; died 10 Jun 2008 in New Smyrna, Volusia Co, FL; adopted daughter of Ashton West HADLEY and Bertha May GODING. @@
+ 686 v **Grace Olive**[6] **STALDER**.
+ 687 vi **Ruth Marilyn**[6] **STALDER**.
+ 688 vii **Mary Madge**[6] **STALDER**.
   689 viii **Richard Benjamin**[6] **STALDER**, born 8 Jun 1927 in Orlando, Orange Co, FL; died 12 Mar 2010 in Jacksonville, Duval Co, FL. He married (1) on 19 Apr 1952 in Jacksonville, Duval Co, FL **Caroline DAY**, born 2 Aug 1927; died 6 Nov 1997 in Jacksonville, Duval Co, FL; (2) aft 1997 **Taeko SHEE**, born 16 Oct 1924 in Japan. @@

@@ See research notes at end of chapter. ## Born after 1930 & possibly living.

352. Archibald D. "Archie"⁵ JOSLIN (Mary Elizabeth⁴ HICKS, Henry Melvin³, Elijah², Joshua¹), born³⁶³ 21 Feb 1884 in Washington Twp, Clermont Co, OH; died 18 Aug 1918 in Tate Twp, Clermont, OH; buried 19 Aug 1918 in New Richmond, Oh. He married on 16 Jun 1914 in Cincinnati, Hamilton Co, OH **Josephine RATCLIFF**, born 21 Apr 1884 in Flag Springs, KY; died 17 Jan 1986 in Clermont Co, OH, daughter of Charles and Cynthia J. RATCLIFF.

Archie Joslin joined the Army in 1908 and was stationed in North Carolina. He was described as "blue eyes, light brown hair, fair skin, 5' 9" tall". He died at age 34 of tuberculosis. His death certificate says his mother was Emerilla Phillips - perhaps adopted - or a mistake@@

   Children of Archibald D. "Archie" JOSLIN and Josephine RATCLIFF were:
+ 690 i   **Elizabeth⁶ JOSLIN**.

357. Edna Clare⁵ JOSLIN³⁶⁴ (Mary Elizabeth⁴ HICKS, Henry Melvin³, Elijah², Joshua¹), born³⁶⁵ 17 May 1889 in Washington Twp, Clermont Co, OH; died³⁶⁶ Nov 1931 in Phoenix, Maricopa Co, AZ; buried in Phoenix, AZ. She married on 19 Jun 1924 in Phoenix, AZ **William EDWARDS**, born 1864 in KY.

Edna Joslin married William Edwards, who was a cement inspector. Edna taught school before her marriage. She moved to Phoenix, AZ before 1920. @@

   Children of Edna Clare JOSLIN and William EDWARDS were:
  691 i   **Mary⁶ EDWARDS**, ##.

358. Adlara Leona 'Addie'⁵ JOSLIN (Mary Elizabeth⁴ HICKS, Henry Melvin³, Elijah², Joshua¹), born³⁶⁷ 18 Sep 1891 in Rural, Clermont Co, OH; died³⁶⁸ Mar 1971 in Cincinnati, Hamilton Co, OH. She married on 2 Apr 1914 in Clermont Co, OH **Howard Arlie WEST**³⁶⁹, born 27 Feb 1893 in Mt Zion, OH; died³⁷⁰ 17 Jun 1976 in Cincinnati, Hamilton Co, OH; buried in Mt Zion Cemetery

Addie Joslin married Howard West, a farmer in New Richmond, OH. They had a daughter, Marian. @@

   Children of Adlara Leona 'Addie' JOSLIN and Howard Arlie WEST were:
+ 692 i   **Marian⁶ WEST**.

359. Lucy Mary Francis⁵ HICKS (Harvey Henry⁴, Henry Melvin³, Elijah², Joshua¹), born 1 Nov 1885 in Franklin Twp, Clermont Co, OH; died 29 Aug 1964 in Cincinnati, Hamilton Co, OH; buried 1 Sep 1964 in Rest Haven Cemetery, Hamilton Co, OH. She married on 24 Dec 1905 in Hamilton Co, OH **James Clarence MEEKER**, born 5 Apr 1886 in Clermont Co, OH; died³⁷¹ 10 Apr 1961 in Norwood, Hamilton Co, OH, son of Napoleon MEEKER and Cynthia MURRAY.

Lucy Hicks was an early family historian and put together a family history - whereabouts currently unknown. Her husband, Clarence Meeker, worked in the lumber industry. Photo on page 186. @@

   Children of Lucy Mary Francis HICKS and James Clarence MEEKER were:
+ 693 i   **Margaret Anna⁶ MEEKER**.
  694 ii   **Roy Murray⁶ MEEKER**, born 15 May 1908 in Cincinnati, Hamilton Co, OH; died 20 Sep 1988 in Cincinnati, Hamilton Co, OH.
           Birth: Lucy Hicks Meeker (his mother) supplied this birth date as part of the genealogy data she presented to members of the extended family.
           Notes from Lvera (Jennings) Seipelt 1998 list "Lucy Meeker (Deceased 1964); Children: Roy Meeker (deceased - no children)"
           Jones notes: "US Army 101st; Capt at Bastagne; not married; resides with sister, Margaret"

@@ See research notes at end of chapter.   ## Born after 1930 & possibly living.

695 iii **Ruth Melvin⁶ MEEKER**, born 15 May 1908 in Cincinnati, Hamilton Co, OH; died 3 Sep 1977 in Los Angeles, Los Angeles Co, CA; buried in St Louis, MO. She married on 26 Jun 1929 in Cincinnati, Hamilton Co, OH **Laverne Joseph HOCK**, born 1 Jan 1902 in IL; died 1964; buried in St Louis, MO, son of Frank and Lena HOCK. No children
Birth: Lucy Hicks Meeker (her mother) supplied this birth date as part of the genealogy data she presented to members of the extended family. The memorial card distributed at her funeral, and the social security death index agree with this birth date.
Notes from Lvera (Jennings) Seipelt 1998 list "Lucy Meeker (Deceased 1964); Children: Ruth Hock (deceased - no children)"
Census: 1930 Norwood, Hamilton, OH, p. 4B. Lavern J Hock 29, IL/IL/IL, blacksmith - factory; Ruth M Hock 21, OH/OH/OH
Death: Memorial card distributed at her funeral
Jones notes: "resided (1972) Los Angeles, CA; no children"

+ 696 iv **Rachel Matilda⁶ MEEKER**.
+ 697 v **Robert⁶ MEEKER**.

360. Harvey John⁵ HICKS (Harvey Henry⁴, Henry Melvin³, Elijah², Joshua¹), born 12 Aug 1889 in Utopia, Clermont Co, OH; died 1979 in Cincinnati, Hamilton Co, OH; buried 24 Feb 1979 in Mt. Moriah, Withamsville, Clermont Co, OH. He married on 9 May 1917 in Clermont Co, OH **Ida Beulah GREEN**, born 20 Mar 1891 in Somerset, KY; died bef 1979, dau of **George Green** and **Laura Vaudal.**

Harvey Hicks enlisted in the Army in 1917. He later attended Officer's Candidate School and was commissioned as a 2ⁿᵈ Lieutenant in the Army. He was assigned to Texas where he trained soldiers during World War I. @@

Children of Harvey John HICKS and Ida Beulah GREEN were:
+ 698 i **Helen⁶ HICKS**.
+ 699 ii **Henrietta⁶ HICKS**.
+ 700 iii **Harriet JoAnn⁶ HICKS**.

361. Minnie Clara⁵ HICKS (Harvey Henry⁴, Henry Melvin³, Elijah², Joshua¹), born 15 Oct 1893 in Franklin Twp, Clermont Co, OH; died 26 Feb 1983 in Cincinnati, Hamilton Co, OH; buried 1 Mar 1983 in Rest Haven, Evendale, Hamilton Co, OH. She married on 3 Feb 1917 in Cincinnati, Hamilton Co, OH **John Joseph BEHAN**, born 23 Dec 1891 in Strokestown, Roscommon, Ireland; died 21 Feb 1955 in Norwood, Hamilton Co, OH; buried 23 Feb 1955 in Rest Haven Cemetery, Hamilton, OH, son of **Patrick Behan** and **Anna Gannon**

Minnie Hicks married John Behan, who had immigrated from Ireland in 1913. He was a machinist at the time of their marriage and later worked as a glazier in a planing mill. @@

Children of Minnie Clara HICKS and John Joseph BEHAN were:
+ 701 i **John Phillip⁶ BEHAN**.
+ 702 ii **Dorothy Ann⁶ BEHAN**.
+ 703 iii **Laura Margaret⁶ BEHAN**.
+ 704 iv **Donald James 'Bud'⁶ BEHAN**.
  705 v **Richard Melvin⁶ BEHAN**, born 21 Oct 1925 in Norwood, Hamilton Co, OH; died³⁷² 24 Dec 2002 in Jacksonville, Duval Co, FL.

@@ See research notes at end of chapter.   ## Born after 1930 & possibly living.

Jones notes: "career navy man - retired; not married; resides (1972) 2413 Norwood Av, Norwood, OH"

Birth: OH birth certificate:"Richard Melvin Behan, male, b. 25 Feb 1925 at 5312 Section Ave., Norwood, Hamilton, OH (at parents res.); parents: "John Behan (white, 34, b. Ireland, glazier at Norwood Sash and Door); Minnie Hicks (white, 33, b. KY [sic])"

+ 706 vi **Marjorie Claire "Margie"⁶ BEHAN**.
   707 vii **Lawrence Harvey⁶ BEHAN**, born 27 May 1932 in Cincinnati, Hamilton Co, OH; died 22 May 1933 in Cincinnati, Hamilton Co, OH.

Birth: OH birth certificate: "Lawrence Harvey Behan b. 27 May 1932, Cincinnati, Hamilton, OH; male; legitimate; parents: John Joseph Behan (white, 38; b. Strokestown, Ireland; carpenter at Norwood Sash and Door); Minnie Hicks, white, 37, b. Clermont Co, OH); res. 5312 Section Ave., Norwood, OH; his mother's 7th child--all living (b. at Bethesda Mat. Hosp.)"

Death: OH death certificate: "Lawrence Behan, d. 22 May 1933 at Children's Hospital in Cincinnati, Hamilton Co, OH, male, white; b. 27 May 1932 in Norwood, Hamilton Co, OH; parents: John Behan (b. Ireland), Minnie Hicks (b. Clermont Co, OH); res, 5312 Section Ave, Norwood, OH; bur. Calvary Cemetery"

363. **Dion Williams⁵ HICKS** (Harvey Henry⁴, Henry Melvin³, Elijah², Joshua¹), born 7 Nov 1898 in Franklin Twp, Clermont Co, OH; died 11 Jan 1960 in Cincinnati, Hamilton Co, OH; buried 14 Jan 1960 in St Peter & Paul, Reading OH. He married on 18 Sep 1928 **Madelyn VASKE**, born 3 Dec 1905 in Millhouser, IN; died 18 Jul 1988 in OH.

Dion Hicks was listed as an advertising salesman in 1930. At the time of his death in 1960, he was a presser in a tailor shop. He and his wife Madelyn had two sons. @@

Children of Dion Williams HICKS and Madelyn VASKE were:
+ 708 i   **Dion⁶ HICKS Jr.**
+ 709 ii **Daniel⁶ HICKS**.

368. **Mary Frances⁵ HOUSER** (Minerva Elizabeth⁴ JONES, Mary³ HICKS, Elijah², Joshua¹), born 4 Jul 1863 in Clermont Co, OH; died aft 1930. She married on 25 Jan 1883 in Downing, MO **George Allen ROSS**, born Apr 1861 in Ohio; died abt 1926 in Keokuk, Lee Co, IA.

Mary Frances Houser moved with her family to Missouri after her mother remarried. She married George Ross, who was a furniture maker. The Ross family moved to Keokuk, IA before 1910. @@

Children of Mary Frances HOUSER and George Allen ROSS were:
   710 i   **Edna Pauline⁶ ROSS**, born Oct 1883 in Missouri. She married bef 1925 **Glen W. CLARK**, born 27 Jan 1893 in Bonaparte, IA, son of John and Christie CLARK. No children.

Census: 1910 Keokuk Ward 4, Lee, IA, p. 9B. John H Clark 46; Christy L Clark 38; Glynn W Clark 17, alkali room - cereal plant; Mark H Clark 12; Benjaman M Clark 5
1920 Keokuk Ward 4, Lee, IA, p. 7A. Glen Clark 26, IA/IA/IA, steam fitter; Edna Clark 36, MO/OH/OH. Next to John (56) & Christie (48) Clark, Glen's parents.
1930 Great Falls, Cascade, MT, p. 12A. Glenn W Clark 37, IA, steam fitter - plumbing; Edna R Clark 46, MO.
+ 711 ii **Archie Milton⁶ ROSS**.

@@ See research notes at end of chapter.   ## Born after 1930 & possibly living.

712 iii **Welthie**[6] **ROSS**, born Sep 1888 in Missouri. Notes: not with family in 1921 - probably married.
+ 713 iv **Alma J.**[6] **ROSS**.
+ 714 v **William Clifford**[6] **ROSS**.
   715 vi **Walter H.**[6] **ROSS**, born abt 1901 in Missouri.
Iowa State Census 1915 Keokuk, Lee, IA, unp. Walter H. Ross, 18, at school, single. Not found on 1930 census.

369. Lindley Edward[5] **BROADWELL** (Minerva Elizabeth[4] JONES, Mary[3] HICKS, Elijah[2], Joshua[1]), born 28 Jun 1867 in Clermont Co, OH; died 14 Apr 1959 in Ames, Story Co, IA; buried in Ames Memorial Cemetery, Story Co, IA. He married on 12 Oct 1902 **Mae ZIMMERMAN**, born 9 May 1878 in Adair Co, MO; died 27 Jun 1945 in Ames, Story Co, IA; buried in Ames Memorial Cemetery, Story Co, IA.

Lindley Broadwell was working as a draftsman for the highway commission in 1930. He and his family lived in Ames, Iowa. @@

   Children of Lindley Edward BROADWELL and Mae ZIMMERMAN were:
   716 i **Lindley E.**[6] **BROADWELL**, born 8 Jan 1904 in Kirskville, MO; died[373] 4 Dec 1982 in Ames, Story Co, IA; buried in Ames Memorial Cemetery, Story Co, IA. He married **Elsie CARLSON**, born 1913; died 1993; buried in Ames Memorial Cemetery, Story Co, IA.
Death: Social Security Death Index gives: Lindley Broadwell, b. 08 Jan 1904; d. Dec 1982 Ames, IA; #483-20-6286; Issued: Iowa;
Occupation: Manager ISU (Iowa State University?) Bookstore.
Birth place, death date, spouse's surname, occupation from tombstone in Ames Memorial Cemetery, Ames, IA and burial records from cemetery. Survivors Elsie Carlson, spouse; Judy Kochel & Terry Benson (daughters?)
+ 717 ii **Ruby**[6] **BROADWELL**.
   718 iii **Leon**[6] **BROADWELL**, born abt 1911 in Iowa.
   719 iv **Andrew**[6] **BROADWELL**, died 1919 in Higley, Maricopa, AZ.
Death: Andrew Broadwell d. 1919 Higley, Maricopa, AZ; Father: Lindsley Broadwell; Mother: Not Known. Arizona Deaths, 1870-1951

370. Herbert Fay[5] **BROADWELL** (Minerva Elizabeth[4] JONES, Mary[3] HICKS, Elijah[2], Joshua[1]), born 26 Sep 1869 in Clermont Co, OH; died 10 Jan 1964 in Haven Rest Home, Greentop, MO; buried Coffey Cem, Schuyler Co, MO. He married[374] on 19 Apr 1891 in Schuyler Co, MO **Sarah Millie PINDELL**, born 12 Nov 1867 in OH; died[375] 21 Apr 1936 in Independence, Schuyler Co, MO; buried 24 Apr 1936 in Coffey Cemetery, daughter of Miqual M. PINDELL and Jennie BRADEY.

H. Fay Broadwell served as Secretary of State Senate of Missouri 1920-1924. He was listed as a farmer on every census. @@

   Children of Herbert Fay BROADWELL and Sarah Millie PINDELL were:
+ 720 i **Chester Allen**[6] **BROADWELL**.
   721 ii **Mabel**[6] **BROADWELL**, born 7 Mar 1894 in Missouri; died[376] 2 Oct 1987 in Missouri. She married on 22 Feb 1919 in Schuyler Co, MO **Clinton O. KETCHUM**[377], born 15 Feb 1896 in Downing, MO.

@@ See research notes at end of chapter.   ## Born after 1930 & possibly living.

Notes: SS Death Index gives Mabel Ketchum, b. 3-7-1894; d. 10-2-1987; Age: 93; Res: Columbia, MO

+ 722 iii **Harry**[6] **BROADWELL**.
+ 723 iv **Orma**[6] **BROADWELL**.
   724 v **Clyde Lawrence**[6] **BROADWELL**, born 12 Apr 1900 in MO; died 1923 probably in Downing, Schuyler Co, MO.
Military: WW I Draft Registration gives name as Clyde Lawrence Broadwell, age 18, date & place of birth, medium height, slender build, hazel eyes, lt brown hair. Registered 7 Sep 1918.
Death / Burial: Coffey Cemetery, Downing Mo - Broadwell, Clyde L. 1900 - 1923
   725 vi **Perley L**[6] **BROADWELL**, born abt 1903 in MO. He married abt 1927 **Grace -?-**, born abt 1905 in IA.
Census: 1930 Mason City, Cerro Gordo, IA, p. 24A. Perley Broadwell, 27, MO/OH/KY, no occ.; Grace Broadwell 23, IA/IA/IA.

373. Percival[5] **BROADWELL**[378] (Minerva Elizabeth[4] JONES, Mary[3] HICKS, Elijah[2], Joshua[1]), born 8 Jan 1877 in Rural, Clermont Co, OH; died[379] 20 Apr 1944 in Fresno, CA. He married on 30 Dec 1900 in Carlisle KS **Nettie E. WILSON**, born 30 Jul 1880 in Illinois; died[380] 18 Dec 1963 in Fresno, CA.

Percy Broadwell was listed as a farmer on all census records, though Jones notes state that he was a miller. He married in Kansas, but lived in California and Arizona. He was described in 1917 as "tall, slender, light brown eyes, black hair". @@

Children of Percival BROADWELL and Nettie E. WILSON were:
+ 726 i **William Harold**[6] **BROADWELL**.
   727 ii **Kathleen**[6] **BROADWELL**, born abt 1906 in AR. She married on 15 May 1965 in Fresno, CA **Carl FOSTER**, born 7 Nov 1896 in Missouri; died[381] 11 Sep 1969 in Fresno, CA.
Marriage: Kathleen A Broadwell; b. 1906, Age: 59; Spouse: Carl Foster, b. 1896, Age: 69; Marriage Date: 15 May 1965, Fresno, CA California Marriage Records [archives.com]
*****Death**: Kathleen A Foster, b. 9-29-1905; d. 1-27-2001, Age: 96; Clovis, CA. Social Security Death Index *may not be right person, but likely.
   728 iii **Eugenia**[6] **BROADWELL**, born abt 1908 in AR. Notes: no other information found
   729 iv **Chester A.**[6] **BROADWELL**, born 20 Aug 1911 in CA; died 3 Oct 1983 in Fresno, CA.
Death: Chester A Broadwell, b. 20 Aug 1911, CA; d. 3 Oct 1983, Fresno, CA, age 72; Mother's Maiden Name: Wilson. California Death Index [archives.com]
   730 v **Glenn**[6] **BROADWELL**, born abt 1918 in AZ. No other information found

374. Nathaniel Dale[5] **BROADWELL**[382, 383] (Minerva Elizabeth[4] JONES, Mary[3] HICKS, Elijah[2], Joshua[1]), born 4 Apr 1881 in Rural, Clermont Co, OH; died[384] 1 Mar 1966 in Ceres, Stanislaus, CA. He married on 4 Dec 1900 in Grannis, AK **Elva Helen CLARK**[385], born 4 Sep 1882 in Arkansas; died 20 May 1953 in Stanislaus, CA.

Nathaniel Dale Broadwell seems to have been called both Nathan and Dale. He was a farmer, both in Central California and in the Phoenix area of Arizona. In 1918, he was described as "med height; med. build; brown hair & eyes"@@

@@ See research notes at end of chapter. ## Born after 1930 & possibly living.

Children of Nathaniel Dale BROADWELL and Elva Helen CLARK were:
+ 731 i **Beulah Imogene⁶ BROADWELL**
+ 732 ii **Eunice⁶ BROADWELL**. Note: this family was not in Jones notes.
+ 733 iii **Romba⁶ BROADWELL**.
   734 iv **Cecil Lionel⁶ BROADWELL**, born 11 Mar 1909 in California; died³⁸⁶ 6 Oct 1990 in Stanislaus, CA.
Census: 1930 Sacramento, Sacramento, CA, p. 9A. Harry A Jones 21, KS/OH/CA, inspector - state agriculture?; Romba L Jones 32, AR/-/AR; Harriet L Jones 2 4/12, CA; Kent H Jones 4/12, CA; Cecil L Broadwell 21, brother-in law, CA, clerk - grocery
Death: Cecil Lionel Broadwell, b. 11 Mar 1909, CA; d. 6 Oct 1990, Stanislaus, CA; Age: 81; Mother's Maiden Name: Clark. California Death Index [archives.com]
+ 735 v **Karylton Victor⁶ BROADWELL**.

375. Edwin G.⁵ HELVERING (Samantha Jane⁴ JONES, Mary³ HICKS, Elijah², Joshua¹), born 24 Jun 1871 in Rural, Clermont Co, OH; died living in 1930 in Newport News, VA. He married on 17 Nov 1897 in Newport News, VA **Ida WILLIAMS**, born Feb 1871 in VA.

Edwin Helvering was a machinist and later an inspector at the ship yard in Newport News, VA. He married Ida (Williams) McGregor, probably a widow. Kenneth may have been his son - or may be hers from her earlier marriage - but carried the name Helvering. @@

Children of Edwin G. HELVERING and Ida WILLIAMS were:
   736 i **Kenneth M.⁶ HELVERING**, born Jan 1894 in VA.
Notes: May be from her previous marriage - date in 1900 census shows he was born before marriage to Helvering, presume he was adopted since he carried the name Helvering; WW I Draft records gives his birth as 1898 - which would be after the marriage to Helvering.
Military: World War I Draft Registration Cards, 1917-1918 [ancestry.com] Kenneth Helvering, age 20, b. 17 Jan 1898, res: Newport News, VA; "not working at present on account of health"; contact: Mrs. E. G. Helvering, Newport News, VA; Med height & build, gray eyes, dk. brown hair. Disability: Cast in left eye from air gun. Reg: 12 Sep 1918, Newport News, Warwick Co, VA.
No other information found

380. Beatrice Gertrude⁵ JONES (James Marcellus⁴, Elizabeth³ HICKS, Elijah², Joshua¹), born³⁸⁷ 9 Aug 1875 in Clermont Co, OH; prob died bef 1908. She married on 27 Oct 1895 in Clermont Co, OH **Wilbur Glenn WOOD**, born Jan 1872 in OH; died Jan 1960 in Osceola Co, FL.

Gertrude Jones died young, leaving two or three young daughters. Her husband, Wilbur Wood, married again and moved first to Tennessee and later to Florida. @@

Children of Beatrice Gertrude JONES and Wilbur G. WOOD were:
+ 737 i **Effie Blanche⁶ WOOD**.
   738 ii **Ruth Merrel⁶ WOOD**, born 15 Jul 1901 in Pt Isabel OH.
Jones notes: "Resides (1972) at Box 535, Middleboro, KY"
Birth: Ruth Merrel Wood; b. 15 Aug 1901; Father: Wilber Glenn Wood; Mother: Gertrude Beatrice Jones. Ohio Births and Christenings, 1821-1962 <fsbeta.familysearch.org>

@@ See research notes at end of chapter. ## Born after 1930 & possibly living.

Census: 1930 Jellico, Campbell, TN, p. 15A. Lloyd Baird 33, comptroller - wholesale hardware, TN/TN/TN; Effie Baird 33; Glenna Baird 4 5/12; Merrie Wood 22, sister in law, stenographer - dry goods store. No death information found

    739 iii **Alpha M**[6] **WOOD**, born abt 1908 in OH. Notes: May be the child of 2nd wife Katherine.

381. Effie Maud[5] **JONES** (James Marcellus[4], Elizabeth[3] HICKS, Elijah[2], Joshua[1]), born[388] 7 Aug 1877 in Clermont Co, OH; died[389, 390] 20 Dec 1909 in Monterey, Clermont Co, OH. She married on 27 Oct 1895 in Clermont Co, OH **Lewis O. MCMAHON**, born Sep 1867 in OH; died aft 1930.

Effie Maud Jones died in childbirth at the age of 32. Her husband, Lewis McMahan, was a merchant, with a general store. Lewis married Nona Spriggs on 18 Jun 1921 in Butler County, OH. @@

    Children of Effie Maud JONES and Lewis O. MCMAHON were:

+ 740 i **Wilbur Lewis**[6] **MCMAHON**.
   741 ii **Byron Jones Ozar**[6] **MCMAHAN**, born 18 Apr 1898 in Lausche, OH; died[391] 16 Jul 1963 in Hamilton, Butler Co, OH. He married on 8 Feb 1937 in Franklin Co, IN **Gladys R. BOWLING**, born 21 Mar 1906 in Fleming, KY; died[392, 393] 23 May 1973 in Hamilton, Butler Co, OH, daughter of Elijah BOWLING and Louisa MILLER. Jones notes: "Married Gladys -?-. They had no children; she had two children"
          Military: WW I Draft Registration: Byron Jones Mcmahan, Lawshee, Adams Co, OH; Age: 20, Birth: 18 Mar 1898; Occ: Rodman - Air Nitrate Corporation, Ancor, Hamilton, OH. Relative: Lewis McMahan, Lawshee, Adams, OH; tall, slender, brown eyes, black hair. Reg 10 Sep 1918, Ancor, OH. [Ancestry.com]
          Marriage: Byron J Mcmahan, b. 18 Mar 1898, Cincinnati, OH; Residence: Hamilton OH; Father: Lewis Mcmahan; Mother: Maude Jones; Bride: Gladys R Bowling (or Boling), b. 21 Mar 1906, Fleming, KY; Bride's Residence: Laurel, IN; Bride's Number of Marriage: 1; Bride's Father: Elijah Bowling; Mother: Louisa Miller; Marriage: 8 Feb 1937 Franklin,, IN. Indiana Marriages, 1811-1959
          Census: 1920 Norwood Ward 4, Hamilton, OH, p. 12B. Byron Mcmahan 21, boarder, clerk - office fixtures
          1930 St. Clair, Butler, OH, p. 5A. Louis Mcmahan 62, proprietor - general store; Nona Mcmahan 44; Byron Mcmahan 31, salesman - radio.<pilot.familysearch.org>
+ 742 iii **Lola Gayle**[6] **MCMAHAN**.
+ 743 iv **Sarah Elizabeth**[6] **MCMAHAN**.

382. Lola Agnes[5] **JONES** (James Marcellus[4], Elizabeth[3] HICKS, Elijah[2], Joshua[1]), born[394] 20 Oct 1880 in Clermont Co, OH; died 1946. She married (1) in Jun 1900, divorced **Joseph Patrick MYLER**[395], born 29 Dec 1875 in Ohio; died 14 Oct 1959 in Cincinnati, Hamilton, OH, son of Patrick and Hannah MYLER; (2) **Nathaniel T. DAILY**, born 27 Jul 1856 of Williamsburg; died 23 May 1929 in Williamsburg, Clermont, OH.

Lola Jones married Joseph Myler, a policeman, by whom she had two children. She was divorced by 1920 and working as a servant in the home of Nathaniel Daily, an undertaker, who she later married. @@

    Children of Lola Agnes JONES and Joseph Patrick MYLER were:
+ 744 i **Hannah Elizabeth**[6] **MYLER**.

@@ See research notes at end of chapter.   ## Born after 1930 & possibly living.

  745 ii **Joseph**[6] **MYLER Jr**, born 7 Apr 1911 in Cincinnati, Hamilton, OH; died 7 Apr 1911 in Cincinnati, Hamilton, OH; buried in Calvary Cemetery, Cincinnati, OH.
     Death: OH Death Certificate <www.pilot.familysearch.org> "stillbirth, 12 pound baby". Gives parents as Joseph Myler, b. Cincinnati, OH; Lola Jones, b. Neville, OH.

383. Orville Guy[5] **JONES**[396, 397] (James Marcellus[4], Elizabeth[3] HICKS, Elijah[2], Joshua[1]), born 10 Jan 1882 in Clermont Co, OH; died Jan 1940 in Clermont Co, OH. He married on 7 Oct 1906 in Clermont Co, OH **Lora ROGERS**, born 30 Jul 1889 in Downing, Schuyler Co, MO; died[398, 399] 27 Dec 1979 in Cincinnati, Hamilton Co, OH; buried in Laurel Cemetery.

Orville Guy Jones was the father of Orville Jones, who collected the data that served as the nucleus for this book. He was a street car conductor in Cincinnati, OH. He was described in 1918 as "med height & build, grey eyes, brown hair". @@

 Children of Orville Guy JONES and Lora ROGERS were:
+ 746 i **James Paul**[6] **JONES**.
+ 747 ii **Orville William**[6] **JONES**.
+ 748 iii **Hilda Louise**[6] **JONES**.

384. Carl Raymond[5] **JONES**[400] (James Marcellus[4], Elizabeth[3] HICKS, Elijah[2], Joshua[1]), born[401] 25 Nov 1884 in Clermont Co, OH; died abt 1955. He married in Apr 1908 **Lavinia ROBINSON**, born 23 Aug 1887 in OH; died 5 Jan 1976 in Los Angeles, CA, daughter of Winfield and Martha J. ROBINSON.

Carl Jones worked on a ranch in Sonoma, CA before returning to Cincinnati, where he was a varnish maker. @@

 Children of Carl Raymond JONES and Lavinia ROBINSON were:
+ 749 i **Alice Agnes**[6] **JONES**.

385. Ethel Grace[5] **JONES** (James Marcellus[4], Elizabeth[3] HICKS, Elijah[2], Joshua[1]), born[402] 12 Feb 1887 in Clermont Co, OH; died 25 Dec 1963 in Dayton, Montgomery Co, OH; buried in Mt Orab OH. She married on 11 Jun 1910 in Clermont Co, OH **Calvin BECKELHIMER**, born 1 Oct 1885 in Felicity, Clermont Co, OH; died[403] 17 Jul 1946 in Scott Twp, Brown, OH; buried 20 Jul 1946 in Mt Orab, OH, son of George W BECKELHEIMER and Elisabeth Ann SUTTON.

Ethel Jones married Calvin Beckelhimer, whose parents were early settlers of Clermont Co. Calvin was a farmer. @@

 Children of Ethel Grace JONES and Calvin BECKELHIMER were:
+ 750 i **Calvin Marcellus**[6] **BECKELHIMER**.
+ 751 ii **Harry Raymond**[6] **BECKELHIMER**.
+ 752 iii **Mary Elizabeth**[6] **BECKELHIMER**.
  753 iv **Harriet**[6] **BECKELHIMER**, born abt 1914 in OH.
     Notes: John Tippet says "Harriet Beckelhimer is or may be still living." Tippet Home Page <www.johntippet.com>
+ 754 v **Jack Jones**[6] **BECKELHIMER**.

386. Lawrence Marcellus[5] **JONES**[404] (James Marcellus[4], Elizabeth[3] HICKS, Elijah[2], Joshua[1]), born[405] 5 Jun 1890 in Clermont Co, OH; died[406] 1 Jul 1964. He married (1) **Margaret SHARP**; (2) aft 1930 **Mary -?-**.

@@ See research notes at end of chapter. ## Born after 1930 & possibly living.

Lawrence Jones, a carpenter by trade, married first Margaret Sharp, by whom he had one son. After her death (before 1918), Lawrence and his son James lived with his sister, Ethel Beckelheimer in 1920 and boarded in Kenton Co, KY in 1930. He married Mary -?- after 1930 and had 3 more children. @@

    Children of Lawrence Marcellus JONES and Margaret SHARP were:
+   755   i   **James Marcellus^6 JONES**.

    Children of Lawrence Marcellus JONES and Mary UNKNOWN were:
+   756   i   **Beryl Josephine^6 JONES**.
+   757   ii   **John Lee^6 JONES**.
   758   iii **Audrey Lynn^6 JONES**. Jones notes: "Resides (1972) with her mother; not married"

389. Genevieve Shinkle^5 JONES (James Marcellus^4, Elizabeth^3 HICKS, Elijah^2, Joshua^1), born^{407} 24 Jan 1896 in Clermont Co, OH; died^{408} Jan 1996 in Cincinnati, Hamilton Co, OH. She married on 27 Oct 1917 in Clermont Co, OH **George Thomas HODGES**, born 1 Sep 1896 in Camp Dennison OH; died Aug 1968 in Cincinnati, Hamilton, OH, son of Frank T. and Alice HODGES.

Genevieve Jones married George Hodges, who was a machinist in 1920 and a postal carrier in 1930. Genevieve died days before her 100th birthday. Photo with sisters on page 186. @@

    Children of Genevieve Shinkle JONES and George Thomas HODGES were:
+   759   i   **Virginia Marylin^6 HODGES**.

390. Albert Essex^5 JONES (William A.^{4}, Elizabeth^3 HICKS, Elijah^2, Joshua^1), born 7 Dec 1874 in Clermont Co, OH; died^{409} 1 Jun 1962 in Deer Park, Hamilton Co, OH; buried in Mt Moriah Cemetery, Clermont Co, OH. He married (1) abt 1894 **Irene KEITHLER**, born 20 May 1874 in Brown Co, OH; died^{410} 9 Jan 1912 in Cincinnati, Hamilton, Co OH, daughter of Riley KEITHLER and Sarah Rebecca BLACK,; (2) on 9 Sep 1915 **Mabel I. THORNTON**, born 10 Dec 1890 in Clermont Co, OH; died 8 Apr 1995 in Montgomery, Hamilton Co, OH.

Albert Jones was a street car conductor in Cincinnati and for several years was President of the Street Railway Workers Union. @@

    Children of Albert Essex JONES and Irene KEITHLER were:
+   760   i   **Ralph Charles^6 JONES**.
   761   ii   **Forrest Allen^6 JONES**, born 16 Oct 1904 in Cincinnati, Hamilton Co, OH; died Mar 1956 in Chicago, Cook Co, IL. Jones notes: "Resided Chicago; no children; wife's name unknown but deceased before 1972". May be the Forrest A. Jones living in Hamilton, Mercer Co, NY, p. 8A in 1930, boarder, inspector - adding machines, OH/OH/OH

    Children of Albert Essex JONES and Mabel I. THORNTON were:
   762   i   **Lois Marie^6 JONES**, born 6 Jul 1916 in Brown Co, OH; died 4 Jun 1972 in Norfolk, VA. She married on 19 Jul 1941 in Cincinnati, Hamilton Co, OH **Wayne W. WOLFORD**, born in AL.
Jones notes: "Resided 238 N. Blake Rd, Norfolk, VA 23505; no children"
   763   ii   **Helen Alberta "Peach"^{6} JONES**, born 10 Nov 1927 in Cincinnati, OH. Jones notes: "Resides (1972) at 7534 Hopkins Rd, Maineville, OH. No children"

391. Hertha Katherine^5 JONES (William A.^{4}, Elizabeth^3 HICKS, Elijah^2, Joshua^1), born 10 Jan 1877 in Clermont Co, OH. She married in Nov 1897 **Charles E. WILLIAMS**, born 2 Dec 1874 in Virginia.

@@ See research notes at end of chapter.   ## Born after 1930 & possibly living.

Hertha Katherine Jones seems to have been called Hertha, Katherine and Katie. She married Charles Williams, who worked in the baggage area of the railroad. @@

    Children of Hertha Katherine JONES and Charles E. WILLIAMS were:
+   764   i   **Leta Grace[6] WILLIAMS**.
+   765   ii   **Ezra Glenn Dale "Jack"[6] WILLIAMS**.

392. Jessie Agnes[5] JONES (William A.[4], Elizabeth[3] HICKS, Elijah[2], Joshua[1]), born 11 Dec 1878 in Clermont Co, OH; died 27 Jan 1922 in Sycamore Twp, Hamilton, OH; buried in Pleasant Ridge Presb. Cemetery, Cincinnati OH. She married on 25 Dec 1909 **Charles Edwin BROWN**, born 28 Jan 1874 in Cuyahoga Co, OH; died 9 Mar 1935 in Cincinnati, Hamilton, OH; buried in Spring Grove Cemetery; son of Andrew BROWN and Rachael WORKMAN.

Jessie Jones married Charles Brown, a carpenter / cabinet maker. They had 2 daughters and 1 son. @@

    Children of Jessie Agnes JONES and Charles E. BROWN were:
-    766   i   **Dorothy Jean[6] BROWN**, born 22 Feb 1918 in Norwood, Hamilton Co, OH; died[411] 17 Sep 2003 in Clermont Co, OH. She married on 11 May 1940 in Kenton Co, KY **Dow Enzor "Jack" SATTERFIELD**, born 28 Mar 1912 in Smith Co, TN; died[412] Jul 1973 in Loveland, Clermont Co, OH.
  Jones notes: "Resides (1972) at 354 Field Crest Ln, Miamiville, OH; no children"
  Death: Dorothea Satterfield [Dorothea Brown], b. 22 Feb 1918, OH; res: Clermont Co, OH; d. 17 Sep 2003, nursing home, Clermont Co, OH; age 85; Farther's surname: Brown; Mother: Jones; widowed, 1 year college. Ohio Deaths, 1908-1932, 1938-1944, and 1958-2007 [ancestry.com]
-    767   ii   **Marjorie Lenore[6] BROWN**, born 21 Mar 1919 in Norwood, Hamilton Co, OH; died[413] 15 Mar 2004 in Clermont Co, OH.
  Jones notes: "Resides (1972) at 4129 O'Leary Av, Deer Park, OH; not married"
  Death: Marjorie Lenora Brown, b. 26 Mar 1920, OH; d. 15 Mar 2004, Clermont Co, OH; father's name: Brown; mother: Jones; never married. Ohio Deaths, 1908-1932, 1938-1944, and 1958-2007 [ancestry.com]
+   768   iii   **William Charles[6] BROWN**.

393. Anna Grace[5] JONES (William A.[4], Elizabeth[3] HICKS, Elijah[2], Joshua[1]), born 29 Jun 1881 in Clermont Co, OH; died 11 Nov 1971; buried in Laurel Cemetery, Madisonville OH. She married (1) on 26 Jun 1902 **Samuel Elmore MELVIN**, born 19 Mar 1874 in Clermont Co, OH; died 11 Apr 1937 in Cincinnati, Hamilton, OH; buried 14 Apr 1937 in Laurel Cemetery, Madisonville OH, son of James S. MELVIN and Sarah Ella LAUGH; (2) aft 1937 **Oscar W. MCCALLA**, born abt 1881.

Anna Jones married first, Samuel Melvin, who worked as a door watchman and timekeeper. In 1920, she was working at a drug store. After Samuel's death, she married Oscar McCalla, with whom her first husband had boarded before their marriage. @@

    Children of Anna Grace JONES and Samuel Elmore MELVIN were:
+   769   i   **Rosslyn Earl[6] MELVIN**.

@@ See research notes at end of chapter.   ## Born after 1930 & possibly living.

395. **Stella Blanche**^{5} **JONES** (William A.^{4}, Elizabeth^3 HICKS, Elijah^2, Joshua^1), born 10 Nov 1884 in Clermont Co, OH; died 5 Jan 1967 in Cincinnati, Hamilton, OH. She married on 3 Jun 1907 **Joseph Warren PUGH**, born 30 Sep 1879 in Belfontaine, OH; died 28 Mar 1952 in Jefferson Twp, Montgomery, OH, son of James B. PUGH and Mary B. SUTTLES.

Stella Jones married Joseph Pugh, who was both a painter and brakeman on the steam railroad. Joseph died of a broken neck in a fall from wheelchair at age 72 at the VA Hospital.@@

Children of Stella Blanche JONES and Joseph Warren PUGH were:
+ 770 i **Carl Starner**^{6} **PUGH**.

398. **Alfred William**^{5} **JONES**^{414} (Elijah Hicks^4, Elizabeth^3 HICKS, Elijah^2, Joshua^1), born 27 Feb 1879 in New Richmond, Clermont Co, OH; died 27 Dec 1968 in Cincinnati, Hamilton Co, OH; buried in Watkins Hill Cemetery He married abt 1905 **Grace Bell WARD**, born 21 Dec 1881 in Ohio; died 21 Aug 1913 in Pierce, Clermont Co, OH; buried 24 Aug 1913 in Watkins Hill Cemetery

Alfred Jones married Grace Ward, who died young, leaving 4 young children. After her death, Alfred disappeared from records. The children were scattered among relatives and others. @@

Children of Alfred William JONES and Grace Bell WARD were:
+ 771 i **Julia M.**^{6} **JONES**.
  772 ii **Alfred W.**^{6} **JONES Jr.**, born abt 1907 in OH. He married in Cincinnati, Hamilton Co, OH **Hazel KIRTLEY**, born 1908.
  Jones notes: "Resides (1972) at 2543 Melrose Cir, Norwood, OH"
  Jones books give birth year as 1908; he was 3 in the 1910 census, so estimate a 1907 birth year - brother Roy was 2 in 1910.
  Census:
  1920 Pierce, Clermont, OH. Alfred Jones 12 & Julia Jones 13 were with William H. 74 & Sallie Simmons 67, listed as niece and nephew.
  1930 not found.
  May be the Alfred W. Jones who died 13 Jun 1974 in Cincinnati, OH. Birth year is given as 1908.
  773 iii **Roy E.**^{6} **JONES**, born abt 1908. He married in Cincinnati, Hamilton Co, OH **Hazel PLANCK**.
  Jones notes give birth year as 1911; 1910 census lists him as 2 years old.
  Census:
  1920 Pierce, Clermont, OH. Roy Jones, 11, was a boarder with George W. & Zouella Snider.
  *1930 New Richmond, Clermont, OH, p. 5A. Joseph Boots 29; Verlie Boots 26; Monard Boots 8; Dolvia Boots 6; Roy Jones 23, boarder, OH/KY/KY
  *may not be correct person. age and place is right; birthplace of parents is not.
+ 774 iv **Leona I.**^{6} **JONES**.
  775 v **Stanley Hicks**^{6} **JONES**, born 29 Jan 1912; died 9 Mar 1913 in New Richmond, Clermont Co, OH; buried^{415} 11 Mar 1913 in Watkins Hill Cemetery.

@@ See research notes at end of chapter.   ## Born after 1930 & possibly living.

401. Howard Hicks⁵ JONES (Elijah Hicks⁴, Elizabeth³ HICKS, Elijah², Joshua¹), born 29 Jun 1887 in New Richmond, Clermont Co, OH; died⁴¹⁶ 13 Feb 1967 probably in New Richmond, Clermont Co, OH; buried in Watkins Hill Cemetery He married aft 1930 **Beulah Gladys ABERCROMBIE**, born est 1890; died aft 1973.

Howard Jones lived with his mother after his parents divorced. He married Beulah Abercrombie after 1930 and had five children. He was listed as a laborer on all the census records. @@

Children of Howard Hicks JONES and Beulah Gladys ABERCROMBIE were:
- + 776 i **Julia Marie⁶ JONES**.
-    777 ii **Paul Ralph⁶ JONES**, ##. Jones notes: "reside (1973) at Sutton Ave - Bethel OH [crossed out]"
-    778 iii **Frank⁶ JONES**, ##. Jones notes: "resides (1973) at New Richmond, OH [crossed out]"
-    779 iv **Howard Stanley⁶ JONES**, ##. Jones notes: "reside (1973) at Williamsburg, OH"
-    780 v **Pauline Joyce⁶ JONES**, ##. She married **Milton SCHAEFER**. Jones notes: "reside (1973) at Goshen, OH"

402. Clifford O.⁵ JONES⁴¹⁷ (Elijah Hicks⁴, Elizabeth³ HICKS, Elijah², Joshua¹), born 3 Aug 1892 in New Richmond, Clermont Co, OH. He married in 1910/12 **Althea WALKER**, born 16 Feb 1896 in Sterling, Brown Co, OH, daughter of Ora W. WALKER and Pervilla K LEONARD.

Clifford Jones married Aletha Walker and fathered two children. They were divorced before 1930 and Aletha married Frank Dunn. Clifford disappeared from records. In 1917, Clifford was described as "med height & build, brown eyes & hair." @@

Children of Clifford O. JONES and Althea WALKER were:
- + 781 i **Jessie Marie⁶ JONES**.
-    782 ii **Earl⁶ JONES**, born 1915; died abt 1915. Jones notes: "Died young"

404. Leontine Orrene⁵ JONES (George Washington⁴, Elizabeth³ HICKS, Elijah², Joshua¹), born 29 Aug 1877 in Clermont Co, OH; died 11 Apr 1964 in Marin Co, CA; buried in Colmer? CA. She married on 5 Feb 1896 in Wayne NE **James Emmet CLARK**, born 13 Dec 1874 in Oakland, IA; died 30 Jan 1953 in Marin Co, CA; buried in Colmer? CA.

Leta Jones and her family were pioneers in North Dakota, moving there with her husband before 1910. Emmet Clark was a farmer. Sometime before 1953, Emmet and Leta moved to Marin Co, CA where they both died. Photo of family on page 186. @@

Children of Leontine Orrene JONES and James Emmet CLARK were:
-    783 i **Orville Dale⁶ CLARK**, born 23 Jan 1897; died 3 Mar 1897. Notes: "Died young"
- + 784 ii **Georgia Gladys⁶ CLARK**.
- + 785 iii **Cecil Emmett⁶ CLARK**.
- + 786 iv **Roscoe Glenn⁶ CLARK**.
- + 787 v **Edith Zeta Mabel⁶ CLARK**.

405. Roxy Dale⁵ JONES (George Washington⁴, Elizabeth³ HICKS, Elijah², Joshua¹), born 16 Feb 1880 in Clermont Co, OH. She married on 6 Dec 1898 in Wayne NE **William Jacob EVANS**, born 6 Mar 1877 in PA.

Roxy Jones married William Jacob Evans, a farmer. They lived in Wayne County, Nebraska. @@

@@ See research notes at end of chapter.   ## Born after 1930 & possibly living.

Children of Roxy Dale JONES and William Jacob EVANS were:
- 788 i **Gayle Orene**[6] **EVANS**, born 16 Jul 1899 in Wayne, Wayne Co, NE.
  Jones notes: "not married; resides (1974) at 2444 Central Ave, Almeda, CA"
  Census: 1930 Minneapolis, Hennepin, MN, p. 39A. James A Bauer 38, MN/Ger/Ger, salesman - insurance; Ellen I Bauer 29, WI/Ire/Can; Orene Evens 30, lodger, single, NE/OH/OH, saleslady - retail grocer. [may not be right person, but most facts fit]
- 789 ii **Faye Opal**[6] **EVANS**, born 13 Aug 1901 in Wayne, Wayne Co, NE; died bef 1974. She married on 19 Dec 1940 in Wayne NE **Glenn V. CHICHESTER**, born 28 May 1901 in Wayne, Wayne Co, NE; died May 1968 in Hood River, Hood River, OR, son of Eliphalet L and Bethriah S CHICHESTER.
  Jones notes: "no children"
- \+ 790 iii **Laura Mona**[6] **EVANS**.
- \+ 791 iv **Dale Elizabeth**[6] **EVANS**.
- 792 v **Wilma Jesse**[6] **EVANS**, born 6 Mar 1908; died[418] Jan 1987 in Portland, Multnomah Co, OR. She married aft 1930 **Donald HODGES**, born[419] 26 Jul 1922; died[420] Oct 1969 in Portland, Multnomah Co, OR.
  Jones notes: "resides (1974) at 10 NW 20th St, Portland, OR 97209. No children"
- \+ 793 vi **Grace**[6] **EVANS**.
- \+ 794 vii **Dorthea Gladys**[6] **EVANS**.
- \+ 795 viii **Rex Willard**[6] **EVANS**.

406. Edith Mary[5] **JONES** (George Washington[4], Elizabeth[3] HICKS, Elijah[2], Joshua[1]), born 16 Sep 1887 in Wray, Yuma Co, CO; died 5 Sep 1961 in Custer Co, MT; buried Sep 1961 in Lewiston, MT. She married on 20 Aug 1916 in Leith ND **John WILL**, born 21 Jan 1894 in Menno, Hutchison Co, SD; died 23 Jul 1982 in Great Falls, Cascade, MT; buried in Lewiston MT, son of Gottlieb and Fredericka WILL.

Edith Jones was born in Colorado, married in North Dakota and died in Montana. Her husband, John Will, was a retail merchant, postmaster and bank examiner through the years. @@

Children of Edith Mary JONES and John WILL were:
- \+ 796 i **Izeta Mae**[6] **WILL**.
- \+ 797 ii **Wanda Fae**[6] **WILL**.
- 798 iii **Warren Howard**[6] **WILL**, born 11 Jan 1921.
  Jones notes: "resides (1974) at 106 Hillcrest Dr, Lewiston, MT 59457; m. Vera -?-"

407. Marcellus Findly[5] **JONES** (Doctor Albert[4], Elizabeth[3] HICKS, Elijah[2], Joshua[1]), born 7 Jul 1881 probably in Silver Creek, Mills Co, IA; died 28 Jan 1964 in Los Angeles, CA. He married on 15 Sep 1909 **Bertha Mabel CHERRY**, born 5 Mar 1885 in NE; died aft 1930 probably in California.

Marcellus Jones was a farmer, first in Nebraska and later in South Dakota. In 1918, he was described as "medium build; medium height; blue eyes; brown hair" @@

Children of Marcellus Findly JONES and Bertha Mabel CHERRY were:
- 799 i **Clinton**[6] **JONES**, born 20 Jun 1908 probably in Wayne Co, NE; died 22 Feb 1990.
  Death: Social Security Death Index - Probably the Clinton A Jones who was b. 20 Jun 1908; d. 22 Feb 1990 w/ no location given; card issued in South Dakota. Birth date matches.
- 800 ii **Marcellus**[6] **JONES**, born 25 Mar 1910 probably in Wayne Co, NE.

@@ See research notes at end of chapter.   ## Born after 1930 & possibly living.

801 iii **Dale**[6] **JONES**, born 11 Feb 1915 probably in Wayne Co, NE.
No other information found

802 iv **Floyd Claire**[6] **JONES**, born 20 Jan 1917 probably in Wayne Co, NE; died[421] 28 Mar 1988 in Arcata, Humboldt Co, CA.
Death: Floyd Claire Jones, #504032356; Birth: 20 Jan 1917, Nebraska; Death: 28 Mar 1988, Humboldt Co, CA. Mother's Maiden Name: Cherry. California Death Index, 1940-1997 [Ancestry.com]

803 v **Lloyd**[6] **JONES**, born 20 Jan 1917 probably in Wayne Co, NE; died[422] Sep 1983 in Paradise, Butte Co, CA.

804 vi **Helen Frances**[6] **JONES**, born 7 Dec 1921 probably in Wayne Co, NE.

408. Gayle E.[5] **JONES** (Doctor Albert[4], Elizabeth[3] HICKS, Elijah[2], Joshua[1]), born 12 Mar 1883 probably in Silver Creek, Mills Co, IA. She married on 2 Sep 1908 **George Garfield SHERBAHN**[423], born 22 Sep 1881 in Pennsylvania.

Gayle Jones married George Sherbahn, who was a house inspector in 1920 and worked with a carnival in 1930. They apparently lived in Wayne Co, NE all their lives. @@

Children of Gayle E. JONES and George Garfield SHERBAHN were:

805 i **Bernadine L.**[6] **SHERBAHN**, born 5 May 1910 in Wayne, Wayne Co, NE; died 5 Sep 2005 in Wayne, Wayne Co, NE. She married on 2 Sep 1936 in Creighton, NE **Harold E. WEST**, born 2 Aug 1907; died[424] Sep 1972 in Wayne, Wayne Co, NE.
Jones notes. "he d. 1972; she resides (1975) at 308 E. 8th, Wayne, NE 68787"
Death: SS Death Index gives Bernadine West, b. 5 May 1910; d. 5 Sep 2005, age 95; Wayne, Wayne, NE; issued Nebraska; #507-01-9685

+ 806 ii **Donald G.**[6] **SHERBAHN**.

807 iii **Geraldine**[6] **SHERBAHN**, born 27 Dec 1914; died 1 Jan 1915.

409. Jay Miller[5] **JONES** (Doctor Albert[4], Elizabeth[3] HICKS, Elijah[2], Joshua[1]), born 19 Sep 1885 in IA; died 19 Oct 1928. He married on 2 Sep 1908 **Fern BARLEY**, born 22 Oct 1889 in Missouri, daughter of S. M. and Emma BARLEY.

Jay Miller Jones was a farmer in Nebraska and later worked as a real estate broker in Iowa. In 1918, he was working in auto sales and repair and was described as "tall, med build, blue eyes, light hair". @@

Children of Jay Miller JONES and Fern BARLEY were:

808 i **Dorothy F.**[6] **JONES**, born 2 Sep 1909.

809 ii **James M.**[6] **JONES**, born 13 Jul 1912.
Info from Jones notes. "James Marcellus?"; may be the Jay Jones who died Sep 1981 in Pomona (Los Angeles) CA - SS Death Index.

410. Roscoe Otis[5] **JONES**[425] (Doctor Albert[4], Elizabeth[3] HICKS, Elijah[2], Joshua[1]), born 23 Dec 1888 in Wayne, Wayne Co, NE; died[426] 4 Aug 1968 in Wayne, Wayne Co, NE. He married on 4 Mar 1909 **Ellen Mae MORGAN**, born 1 May 1891 in Harlan, Shelby Co, IA; died 9 Apr 1968.

Orville Jones states that Roscoe was born in Nebraska, but the census and draft records give his birth place as Malvern, IA. He married Ellen Morgan and had 4 children before 1917. His draft registration in 1917 describe him as "tall, med build, blue eyes, brown hair". @@

@@ See research notes at end of chapter.   ## Born after 1930 & possibly living.

Children of Roscoe Otis JONES and Ellen Mae MORGAN were:
- + 810 i **Mildred Gayle⁶ JONES**.
- 811 ii **Jean Eleanor⁶ JONES**, born 26 Jan 1912 in Wayne, Wayne Co, NE; died[427] Oct 1977 in San Diego, San Diego Co, CA.
    Jones notes. "resides (1976) at Chula Vista, CA; not married"
- + 812 iii **Elizabeth Jane⁶ JONES**.
- + 813 iv **Robert Otis⁶ JONES**.
- + 814 v **Elva Mae⁶ JONES**.
- + 815 vi **Billy Morgan⁶ JONES**.
- + 816 vii **Joan Faye⁶ JONES**.
- + 817 viii **Shirley Lou⁶ JONES**.

412. **Albert Doctor⁵ JONES**[428] (Doctor Albert⁴, Elizabeth³ HICKS, Elijah², Joshua¹), born 8 Jun 1893 in Wayne, Wayne Co, NE; died 24 Jan 1955 in Downey, Los Angeles Co, CA. He married on 17 Oct 1912 in Hartington, NE **Edna Fae PRATT**, born 8 Jul 1892 in Illinois; died[429] 3 Apr 1981 in Los Angeles, CA, daughter of Ed PRATT and Cora BLOODHART.

Albert Jones, like most of his family, was a farmer in Nebraska. He and his wife Edna both died in Los Angeles, CA @@

Children of Albert Doctor JONES and Edna Fae PRATT were:
- 818 I **Marion Francis⁶ JONES**, born 4 Jan 1916 in Wayne, Wayne Co, NE; died 3 Sep 1970 in Downey, Los Angeles Co, CA. He married on 6 Feb 1943 in Los Angeles, Los Angeles Co, CA **Julia Olive HALL**, born 17 Sep 1915.
    Death: Marion F Jones,# 508056758; Birth: 4 Jan 1916, Nebraska; Death 3 Sep 1970, Los Angeles, CA. California Death Index, 1940-1997 [Ancestry.com]
- + 819 ii **June Gayle⁶ JONES**.
- + 820 iii **Neva Mae⁶ JONES**.
- + 821 iv **Bonnell Elizabeth⁶ JONES**.

413. **Dorothy F.⁵ JONES** (Doctor Albert⁴, Elizabeth³ HICKS, Elijah², Joshua¹), born 25 Mar 1902 in Nebraska; died 15 Dec 1927 probably in Wayne Co, NE. She married on 27 Sep 1923 **John August MEISTER**[430], born 15 Oct 1893 in West Point, Cuming Co, NE; died[431] 29 Dec 1971 in Ottertail, Otter Tail, MN.

Little is known of Dorothy Jones. Her daughter, Betty, was living with her grandparents in 1930; John was not found in that census. John Meister died in Minnesota. @@

Children of Dorothy F. JONES and John August MEISTER were:
- 822 i **Betty Frances⁶ MEISTER**, born 9 Jan 1926.
    Notes: Living with grandfather, aunts & uncles in Wayne, NE in 1930 census, 4 2/12.
- 823 ii **Patricia Yvonne⁶ MEISTER**, born 12 Dec 1927. Jones notes: "died young"

414. **Raymond⁵ MCCABE** (Minerva Isadora 'Dora'⁴ JONES, Elizabeth³ HICKS, Elijah², Joshua¹), born Aug 1887 in Iowa. Living with parents in Brazoria Co, TX in 1900. No other information found.

Children of Raymond MCCABE were:
- 824 i **Robert⁶ MCCABE**, born abt 1915 in Wyoming.
    Jones notes: "mother died when he was very young. Lived with the Traceys"

@@ See research notes at end of chapter.   ## Born after 1930 & possibly living.

Orpha (Jones) Tracy was the sister of Dora (Jones) McCabe; thus Robert's aunt.

Census: 1920 Careyhurst, Converse, WY, p. 3A. Frank S Tracey 53, IA, store keeper; Orplia G 49, OH; James R Mc Cabe 5, nephew, WY/WI/WI; Amber C Fezer 31, boarder.

1930 Orpha, Converse, WY, p. 1B. Frank S Tracy 64, merchandise - groceries; Orpha G Tracy 59; Robert J McCabe 15, nephew, WY/IA/NE.

Death: may be James Robert McCabe, d. 4 Feb 1990, Lane Co, OR; b. 11 Dec 1914; age 75, spouse Evelly. Oregon Death Index, 1903-98

423. Selma[5] GUYETTE (Josephine[4] OWENS, Nancy[3] HICKS, Elijah[2], Joshua[1]), born Dec 1889 in Illinois; died[432] 3 Oct 1944 in E. St Louis, St Clair, IL. She married **Hershel William REEVES**[433], born 17 Jun 1884 in Georgia.

Selma Guyette married Herschel Reeves, who worked with livestock - as a "mule saleman" in 1918. The family lived in East St Louis, Illinois. @@

Children of Selma GUYETTE and Hershel William REEVES were:
- 825 i   **Leatha[6] REEVES**, born abt 1915 in IL.
- 826 ii **Hershell[6] REEVES**, born 28 Jun 1917 in IL; died Feb 1987 in Belleville, St Clair, IL.
  Death: SS Death Index gives Herschel Reeves, b. 28 Jun 1917; d. Feb 1987, Belleville, Saint Clair, IL; #327-03-1702; issued: Illinois
- 827 iii **Floyd L[6] REEVES**, born abt 1924 in IL.
- 828 iv **Norman H.[6] REEVES**, born abt 1926 in IL.

424. Raymond Joseph[5] GUYETTE (Josephine[4] OWENS, Nancy[3] HICKS, Elijah[2], Joshua[1]), born 27 May 1892 in Mattoon, Coles, IL; died 19 Apr 1952 in St Louis, MO; buried 23 Apr 1952 in Belleville, IL. He married on 9 Mar 1911 in Belleville, IL **Sydonia R LEPAGE**, born 29 Aug 1893 in IL; died Feb 1989 in E. St Louis, St Clair, IL.

Raymond Guyette worked in the stock yards in St Louis. He was described in 1917 as "medium height, slender, dk brown eyes & hair" @@

Children of Raymond Joseph GUYETTE and Sydonia R LEPAGE were:
- 829 i   **Raymond J.[6] GUYETTE**, born 29 May 1911 in IL; died Apr 1967 in IL.
  Notes: Information from great grandson via Ancestry Message Board and Case Family Tree [Ancestry.com]
- + 830 ii **Edward W.[6] GUYETTE**.

426. Gussie E.[5] HOLDERFIELD (Mary Emma[4] HICKS, Joshua[3], Elijah[2], Joshua[1]), born 11 May 1880 in Salem, Marion Co, IL; died 17 Dec 1918 in New Richmond, Clermont, OH; buried in Greenmound.Cemetery, New Richmond, OH. She married on 14 Aug 1904 in Clermont Co, OH **John Graham GILFILLEN**[434], born 11 Jun 1879 in Moscow, Clermont Co, OH, son of August and Marie GILFILLEN.

Gussie Holderfield died of pneumonia after giving birth to her third child. Her husband, John Gilfillen, and daughter, Ethelene, were living with Gussie's parents in 1920; the baby Mary was not found unless she was living with Gussie's sister Ethel Beckman and enumerated as Gussie P. age 1. Ethelene and Mary Jane Beckman were enumerated in Ethel's home in 1930; Ethel and her husband August Beckman may have adopted their nieces. John Gilfillen remarried Carrie Judd and had two more children. @@

@@ See research notes at end of chapter.   ## Born after 1930 & possibly living.

Children of Gussie E. HOLDERFIELD and John Graham GILFILLEN were:

831 i **Ethelene**[6] **GILFILLEN**, born 8 Sep 1906 in New Richmond, Clermont Co, OH; died 3 Jan 1990 Daytona Beach, Volusia Co, FL.[435].
Jones notes: "Resides (1972) at 3738 Darwin, Cheriot, OH; no children"
May be same person as Ethelene Beckman #834.
Census: 1930 not found... possibly the Ethelene Beckman enumerated with August & Ethel Beckman. Dates match. (Ethel was her mother's sister).
Death: SS Death Index: Ethelene Beckman, b. 08 Sep 1905; d. 03 Jan 1990, age 84; Daytona Beach, Volusia, FL; issue Ohio; #269-03-9615

832 ii **Emma Lucille**[6] **GILFILLEN**, born 28 Aug 1911 in New Richmond, Clermont Co, OH; died 19 Jul 1912 in New Richmond Clermont Co, OH.
Death: Emma Lucille Gilfillen, b. 28 Aug 1911, OH; d. 19 Jul 1913, Clermont, Greene, OH; age 1 year 10 months 21 days; Residence: Clermont, OH; Burial: 22 Jul 1913; Father John G. Gilfillen, b. OH; Mother: Jussie Holderfield, b. IL Ohio Deaths, 1908-1953 <pilot.family search.org>.

833 iii **Mary Jane**[6] **GILFILLEN**, born 15 Dec 1918 in New Richmond, Clermont Co, OH; died[436] May 1994 in Daytona Beach, Volusia, FL. She married on 23 Nov 1946 in Cincinnati, Hamilton Co, OH **George W. DEWALD**, born 27 Feb 1917 in Cincinnati, Hamilton Co, OH; died 16 May 1986 in Volusia Co, FL.
May be the same person as Mary Jane Gifillen/Beckman #835
Jones notes: "Resides (1972) at Miami Beach, FL; no children"
Death: Mary Jane Dewald; d. 30 May 1994; Volusia Co, FL; age 76; b. 15 Dec 1917. FL Death Index
Question: where was she on the 1920 census? Probably the Mary Jane Beckman enumerated with August & Ethel Beckman in 1930; possibly the Gussie P. Beckman, age 1, with the Beckmans in 1920. (Ethel was her mother's sister).

427. Ethel[5] **HOLDERFIELD** (Mary Emma[4] HICKS, Joshua[3], Elijah[2], Joshua[1]), born 8 Feb 1882 in Cincinnati, Hamilton Co, OH; died 27 Jan 1937 in Cincinnati, Hamilton, OH; buried 30 Jan 1937 in Spring Grove Cemetery, Cincinnati OH. She married **August John BECKMAN**, born 2 Oct 1883 in Cincinnati, Hamilton Co, OH; died 20 Mar 1971.

Ethel Holderfield married August Beckman, a roofer in Cincinnati, OH. They probably adopted - or at least raised - Ethelene and Mary Jane, the daughters of her deceased sister, Gussie. Ages, dates and names match; Jones notes say she had no children. @@

Children of Ethel HOLDERFIELD and August John BECKMAN were:

834 i **Etheline**[6] **BECKMAN**, born abt 1907 in OH.
Notes: This is probably her sister Gussie's child (see #831)- either adopted after Gussie's death or simply raised by the Beckmans. She shows up on the 1930 census as Etheline Beckman. The 1920 census shows Ethelene Gilfillan, living with her father and grand parents, same age. Jones' records say that Ethel & August Beckman had no children.
Death: Ethelene Beckman, b. 8 Sep 1905, d. 3 Jan 1990; Daytona Beach, Volusia, FL; #269-03-9615; issued Ohio. Social Security Death Index <rootsweb.com>
Death: Ethelene Beckman, Death Date: 3 Jan 1990, Volusia Co, FL; Age: 83; Birth Date: 8 Aug 1906. FL Death Index
Jones notes: "Resided at New Richmond, OH; no children"

@@ See research notes at end of chapter.   ## Born after 1930 & possibly living.

Census: 1930 Cincinnati, Hamilton, OH, p. 5A. August J Beckman 47, tinner - roofing company; Ethel 48; Etheline 23, clerical work - roofing co; Mary Jane 11. Next to William (81) & Lena (78) Beckman. Both b. OH, parents b. Germany.

- 835 ii **Mary Jane[6] BECKMAN**, born abt 1918 in OH.
  Notes: This is probably her sister Gussie's child (see #833), either adopted after Gussie's death or simply raised by the Beckmans. She shows up on the 1930 census as Mary Jane Beckman. Jones notes say that Ethel & August Beckman had no children.

- 836 iii **Gussie P.[6] BECKMAN**, born 1919 in OH.
  * **Death:** Gussie M Beckman, b. 1921; Res: Cincinnati, Hamilton, OH; d. 10 Oct 1978, Jewish Hospital, Cincinnati, OH; age 57, divorced. Ohio Deaths, 1908-1932, 1938-1944, and 1958-2007 [ancestry.com] (*Possible)

428. Mary Edna H.[5] MEENACH (Nancy B.[4] HICKS, Joshua[3], Elijah[2], Joshua[1]), born Apr 1886 in KY; died 3 Feb 1970 in Jefferson Co, KY; buried in Maysville Cemetery, Maysville, KY. She married abt 1906 in Maysville, Mason Co, KY **Robert Fredrick CABLISH**[437], born 22 Feb 1883 in Maysville, Mason Co, KY; died 5 Aug 1946 in Maysville, Mason Co, KY; buried 8 Aug 1946 in Maysville Cemetery, Maysville KY, son of Jacob CABLISH and Margaret BODEY.

Edna Meenach married Robert Cablish, who was a grocer in Maysville, KY. They had one daughter, Evelyn. @@

Children of Mary Edna H. MEENACH and Robert Fredrick CABLISH were:
+ 837 i **Evelyn C.[6] CABLISH**.

430. Celia Mae[5] HUTCHISON (Nora Sureanth[4] HICKS, James[3], Elijah[2], Joshua[1]), born 12 Dec 1887 in Maysville, Mason Co, KY; died[438] 9 Oct 1972 in Mason Co, KY; buried in Maysville Cemetery Mason Co, KY. She married **Charles Marshall COOPER**[439], born 18 Jan 1882 in Maysville, Mason Co, KY; died[440] 31 Aug 1940 in Maysville, Mason Co, KY; buried 2 Sep 1940 in Maysville, Mason Co, KY, son of Charles H. COOPER and Emma V. HARRIS.

Celia May Hutchison married Marshall Cooper, who worked for the railroad. Both of their children died young, Milton at age 18 and Frances at age 20. They remained in Mason Co, KY all their lives. @@

Children of Celia Mae HUTCHISON and Charles Marshall COOPER were:
- 838 i **Milton Hutchison[6] COOPER**, born Sep 1901; died[441] 15 Apr 1919 in Maysville, Mason Co, KY; buried 17 Apr 1919 in Maysville, Mason Co, KY.
  Jones notes: "Died at age 8" [should be age 18]
  Death: Milton Hutchison Cooper, d. 15 Apr 1919, Mason Co, KY; Age: 18; b. Sep 1901, Maysville, KY; single, no occ., cause of death: pneumonia; parents: Marshall Cooper, b. KY; Celia Mae Hutchison. Burial: Maysville, KY. KY Deaths, 1852-1953 [Ancestry.com]

- 839 ii **Frances Marshall[6] COOPER**, born 25 Jul 1909 in Maysville, Mason Co, KY; died[442] 18 Jul 1930 in Maysville, Mason Co, KY; buried 21 Jul 1930 in Maysville, Mason Co, KY. She married abt 1928 **Lovell EASYBUCK**, born[443] 22 Nov 1907 in Kentucky; died[444] 9 Aug 1995 in Maysville, Mason Co, KY, son of Joe EASYBUCK and Elizabeth POHLMAN.
  Jones notes: "Died at age 21, no children"
  Death: Frances Marshall Easybuck, d. 18 Aug 1920, Mason Co, KY; Age: 20. b. 25 Jul 1909, Maysville, KY. spouse: Lovel Easybuck. Father: Marshall Cooper, b. KY; mother:

@@ See research notes at end of chapter.   ## Born after 1930 & possibly living.

May Hutchison. Informant: Lovel Easybuck. Burial: Maysville, KY. Kentucky Death Records, 1852-1953 [Ancestry.com]. SS Death Index adds middle initial M.
Census: 1930 Mason Co, KY. Lovel Easybuck, 22, farmer, KY/KY/Ger; Frances M. 21.

431. **Edward Roy^5 HUTCHISON**[445] (Nora Sureanth^4 HICKS, James^3, Elijah^2, Joshua^1), born 13 Aug 1892 in Mayslick, Mason Co, KY; died 25 Jan 1981 in Maysville, Mason Co, KY. He married on 8 Aug 1914 in Maysville, Mason Co, KY **Lena BREEZE**, born 24 Feb 1896 in Kentucky; died[446] 25 Jun 1996 in Maysville, Mason Co, KY.

Roy Hutchison worked with cars - as a mechanic and a chauffeur. He married Lena Breeze and they had 7 children. In 1917, he was described as "tall, med build, grey eyes, dk brown hair". @@

Children of Edward Roy HUTCHISON and Lena BREEZE were:
- + 840 i **Mildred B.^{6} HUTCHISON**.
- + 841 ii **John or Jack^6 HUTCHISON**.
- + 842 iii **Ruth Lenora^6 HUTCHISON**.
- + 843 iv **Effie Nolean^6 HUTCHISON**.
- 844 v **William E.^{6} HUTCHISON**, born abt Feb 1927 in Mason Co, KY.
  Jones notes: "Not married (1972)"
- + 845 vi **Robert L.^{6} HUTCHISON**.
- 846 vii **Glenn^6 HUTCHISON**. He married on **Betty J. WATSON**.
  Jones notes: "Resides (1972) 1157 Lewisburg Rd, Washington Court House, OH. 43160; served 4 years in USAF. Both are teachers, he is superintendent of 2 Washington Court House schools. No children"

433. **Leslie Brand^5 HICKS** (William Pearce^4, James^3, Elijah^2, Joshua^1), born 5 Jun 1905 in Maysville, Mason Co, KY; died[447] 11 Nov 1961 in Cleveland, Cuyahoga, OH. He married (1) on 6 Jun 1925 in Cleveland, Cuyahoga Co, OH **Margaret GLENN**, born 3 Feb 1904 in Jeanette, PA, daughter of James P. GLENN and Margaret RUDGERS; (2) on 29 Jul 1949 in Cleveland, Cuyahoga Co, OH **Betty AUSTIN**, born 28 Mar 1921 in Cleveland, Cuyahoga Co, OH; died in aft 1973; (3) **Mildred E. MITCHELL**, died aft Nov 1961.

Leslie Hicks married Margaret Glenn and had a number of children. There was probably a divorce, as Margaret was listed as the widow of Robert Kelso in 1971. Leslie married Betty Austin in 1949. His 1961 obituary gave his wife as Mildred E, so he obviously married again. @@

Children of Leslie Brand HICKS and Margaret GLENN were:
- 851a vi **Glenn KELLY**, born abt 1923. Not in Jones notes, but listed on 1930 census and in father's obituary. Glenn Kelly (along with 3 Hicks boys) is listed in 1971 obit of Robert Kelso as a stepson.
- + 847 i **Leslie William^6 HICKS**.
- + 848 ii **David Lee^6 HICKS**.
- + 849 iii **Robert James^6 HICKS**.
- + 850 iv **Becky Sue^6 HICKS**.
- 851 v **Lynda Lee^6 HICKS**, ##.
  Jones notes: "resides (1973) at 5461 Alexander, Parma, OH. Not married 1973"

@@See research notes at end of chapter.   ##Born after 1930 & possibly living.

434. Hazel⁵ Lee HICKS (William Pearce⁴, James³, Elijah², Joshua¹), born 9 Jan 1909 in Maysville, Mason Co, KY; died⁴⁴⁸ 7 Mar 1993 in Oberlin, Lorraine Co, OH. She married on 27 Mar 1929 in Cleveland, Cuyahoga Co, OH **John R. FALOON**, born 28 Dec 1905 in Cleveland, Cuyahoga Co, OH; died 3 Jul 1965 in Cleveland, Cuyahoga, OH, son of John R. and Francis FALOON.

Hazel Hicks married John Faloon but was still living with her widowed mother in the 1930 census. She was listed as Hazel Faloon and married, but John, living with his parents, was listed as single. Hazel was working as a dry good saleslady; John was a truck driver. @@

Children of Hazel HICKS and John R. FALOON were:
+ 852 i   **Janet Lea⁶ FALOON**.
+ 853 ii **Richard Lee⁶ FALOON**.

435. William M.⁵ HICKS (William Pearce⁴, James³, Elijah², Joshua¹), born 16 Feb 1914 in Hamilton, Butler Co, OH; died⁴⁴⁹ 18 Feb 1998 in N. Olmsted, Cuyahoga Co, OH. He married on 12 Dec 1937 in Cleveland, Cuyahoga Co, OH **Margaret Ethel HICKS**, born 9 Jan 1909 in Maysville, Mason Co, KY; died 1 Jun 1999 in San Pedro, Los Angeles Co, CA..

William Hicks married Margaret Ethel Hicks, who appears to be unrelated. He was a machine operator, in the automobile industry. Ethel moved to California before her death in 1999. @@

Children of William M. HICKS and Margaret Ethel HICKS were:
+ 854 i   **Janie Marie⁶ HICKS**.
+ 855 ii   **Jeanette Merle⁶ HICKS**.
  856 iii **William Merle⁶ HICKS Jr**, ##.

438. Maria H.⁵ WILSON (Lida H.⁴ HICKS, Elijah³, Elijah², Joshua¹), born abt 1892 in WA; died 18 Jan 1947 in Seattle, King Co, WA. She married abt 1918 in WA? **Harold Edwin KERRY**, born 8 Jan 1890 in MI; died Apr 1984 in Sun City, Maricopa, AR, son of Aaron KERRY and Jane MCCRACKEN.

Maria Wilson married Harold E Kerry, who was a paper salesman in 1920 and lumber exporter in 1930. Harold evidently did a good bit of traveling, as he was found on several passenger lists. He moved to Arizona sometime after his wife's death. @@

Children of Maria H. WILSON and Harold Edwin KERRY were:
  857 i **Harold E.⁶ KERRY Jr**, born abt Jan 1928 in WA.
           Note: may be the Harold E Kerry, b. 10 December 1928; d. 15 April 2005 Riverside, CA; Card issued: Washington. SS# 538-22-1059. Issued: Washington

439. Clarence Vern⁵ VERMILLION⁴⁵⁰ (Edgar Newton⁴, Martha Ann³ HICKS, Elijah², Joshua¹), born 17 May 1895 in Smithville, KS; died⁴⁵¹ 10 Apr 1986 in Los Angeles, Los Angeles, CA. He married abt 1926 **Leila HERRIOT**, born 1887 in Kansas, daughter of Oscar E. and Alice L. HERRIOT.

Clarence Vermillion was listed as an electrician in 1920 and salesman "radio course" in 1930. He was "night wire chief for the Home Telephone Co in 1917" and claimed exemption on the draft registration "to help keep up telephone service for the nation". He had previously served in the military for 2 years as a seaman, electrician. @@

@@See research notes at end of chapter.   ##Born after 1930 & possibly living.

Children of Clarence Vern VERMILLION and Leila HERRIOT were:
- 858 i **John E.^{6} VERMILLION**, born abt 1935 in Kansas.
- 859 ii **Shirley L.^{6} VERMILLION**, born abt 1929 in Kansas.

440. Clara Belle^5 VERMILLION (Edgar Newton^4, Martha Ann^3 HICKS, Elijah^2, Joshua^1), born 9 Mar 1901 in Kansas; died 21 Feb 1994 in Texas. She married abt 1920 **John Ire Chester DAVIS**^{452}, born 26 Mar 1899 in Missouri.

Clara Vermillion married Chester Davis, who was a farm laborer in 1920. Before her marriage, Clara worked as a mail opener in a mail order business. A grand niece says she was married twice, but her death information is as Clara Davis. @@

Children of Clara Belle VERMILLION and John Ire Chester DAVIS were:
- 860 i **Harold A.^{6} DAVIS**, born abt 1921 in Missouri.
- 861 ii **Allie M.^{6} DAVIS**, born abt 1924 in Missouri.

445. Frank Marvin^5 VERMILLION (Edgar Newton^4, Martha Ann^3 HICKS, Elijah^2, Joshua^1), born 23 May 1911 in Kansas City, KS; died 5 Jan 1993 in Houston, TX. He married aft 1930 **Ruth Mildred WILLIAMS**, born 18 Jul 1915 in Kansas; died 18 Apr 2002 in Hempstead, Waller, TX.

Frank Vermillion was still living with his parents in 1930, aged 18, and was not yet employed. He worked for Westinghouse Electric in Houston, TX many years. Photo on page 186. @@

Children of Frank Marvin VERMILLION and Ruth Mildred WILLIAMS were:
- 445a a **Linda Lou Vermillion**, ##; married, divorced.
- 445b b **Clyde Edgar VERMILLION**, ##; married **Susan Dianne LASSITER**. Served in Army Reserve.
- 445c c **Barbara Ellen VERMILLION** ##; married Ben -?-.
- 862 i **Verna Ruth^6 VERMILLION**, ##; married **Larry COLEMAN**. Verna Coleman provided information for this book.

447. Maud Ella^5 BRUBAKER (Caroline Wise^4 HICKS, William Stephen^3, Elijah^2, Joshua^1), born 31 Jul 1899 in Maysville, Mason Co, KY; died^{453} 22 May 1988 in Cleveland, Cuyahoga Co, OH. She married on 13 Mar 1920 in Flemingsburg KY **James E. RODEN**^{454}, born 28 Apr 1890 in Maysville, Mason Co, KY; died^{455} 3 May 1966 in Cleveland, Cuyahoga Co, OH; buried in Cleveland, Cuyahoga Co, OH, son of James and Susan RODEN.

Maude Brubaker married James Roden, who was widowed with a young daughter. They lived in Mayfield Heights, OH, where James was supervisor of a hospital laundry in 1930.

Children of Maud Ella BRUBAKER and James E. RODEN were:
- \+ 863 i **Kenneth Windsor^6 RODEN**.
- \+ 864 ii **Eleanor Bernice^6 RODEN**.

@@See research notes at end of chapter.   ##Born after 1930 & possibly living.

448. **Bessie Salome**[5] **BRUBAKER** (Caroline Wise[4] HICKS, William Stephen[3], Elijah[2], Joshua[1]), born 26 Jul 1901 in Maysville, Mason Co, KY; died[456] 26 Sep 1990 in -. She married on 29 Jul 1921 in Cleveland, Cuyahoga Co, OH **Robert Brown OWENS**, born 1 May 1895 in Mt Pleasant, TN; died[457] 18 Feb 1955 in VA.

Bessie Brubaker was a twin to Arthur. She married Robert Owen, who in 1930 worked as a welder in an automobile factory. Robert was born in Tennessee, lived in Alabama in 1918, and died in Virginia. @@

Children of Bessie Salome BRUBAKER and Robert Brown OWENS were:
- 865　i　**Alice Lorraine**[6] **OWEN**, born 28 Dec 1922 in Clairton, Allegheny Co, PA.
  Jones notes: "Resides (1972) at 1017 Pembrook, Cleveland Hgts, OH"

449. **Arthur B.**[5] or **William Arthur BRUBAKER** (Caroline Wise[4] HICKS, William Stephen[3], Elijah[2], Joshua[1]), born 26 Jul 1901 in Maysville, Mason Co, KY; died 4 Nov 1968 in Mason Co, KY. He married abt 1925 in Maysville, Mason Co, KY **Evelyn DONALD**, born[458] 7 Mar 1904; died[459] Nov 1993 in Maysville, Mason Co, KY.

Orville Jones listed him as Arthur B, but the Social Security & KY Death Indexes give his name as William Arthur. He is Bessie's twin, which is confirmed in his mother's obituary. In 1930, Arthur was working for a milk company. His mother's obituary in 1952 states that he is office manager for Kentucky Utilities in Maysville, KY. @@

Children of Arthur B. BRUBAKER and Evelyn DONALD were:
- +　866　i　**Evelyn Ann**[6] **BRUBAKER**.

450. **Cecil N.**[5] **BRUBAKER** (Caroline Wise[4] HICKS, William Stephen[3], Elijah[2], Joshua[1]), born 16 Jul 1904 in Maysville, Mason Co, KY; died[460] 11 Dec 1966; buried in Maysville, Mason Co, KY. He married in 1922 in West Union OH **Grace WALLINGFORD**, born 27 Aug 1900/03 in Maysville, Mason Co, KY; daughter of George WALLINGFORD and Anna DAWSON.

Cecil Brubaker was an office manager for a pulley manufacturer in 1930. He and his wife, Grace, had two daughters and lived in Maysville, KY. His mother's obituary in 1952 states that he is a vice president of the Browning Manufacturing company in Maysville. @@

Children of Cecil N. BRUBAKER and Grace WALLINGFORD were:
- 867　i　**Nancy B.**[6] **BRUBAKER**, born est. 1923.
  Jones notes: "Resides (1972) in Maryland."
- 868　ii　**Harriet J.**[6] **BRUBAKER**, born abt 1924 in KY.

451. **Kyle Evans**[5] **BRUBAKER** (Caroline Wise[4] HICKS, William Stephen[3], Elijah[2], Joshua[1]), born 7 Mar 1908 in Maysville, Mason Co, KY; died 19 Jun 1957. He married (1) in 1925, divorced **Esther CONOLD**, born abt 1908, daughter of Arthur and Marie L CONOLD (2) in Aug 1952 **Mrs Hazel IHLE**, born abt 1908.

Evans Brubaker had an auto repair garage, "Brubaker's Garage", in Hamilton, OH. He married and divorced Esther Conold and later married Mrs. Hazel Ihle. At the time of his mother's death in 1952, he was living in Hamilton, OH.@@

@@See research notes at end of chapter.　##Born after 1930 & possibly living.

Children of Kyle Evans BRUBAKER and Esther CONOLD were:
- 869 i **Eileen**[6] **BRUBAKER**, born Jan 1926. She married **Raymond SCHROER**. Jones notes: "Resides (1972) at 5529 Liberty-Fairfield Rd, Hamilton, OH 45011"
- + 870 ii **Shirley**[6] **BRUBAKER**.

456. Gladys Lee[5] **MERGARD** (Nancy Olivia[4] HICKS, Orestes Marion Polk[3], Elijah[2], Joshua[1]), born 14 Aug 1900 in Columbus, OH; died[461] Mar 1965 in Broward Co, FL. She married on 6 May 1921 in Columbus, Franklin Co, OH **Winfield Leroy OHMERT**[462], born 22 Feb 1882 in Dubuque, IA; died[463, 464] Nov 1975 in Dade Co, FL, son of George and Elizabeth OHMERT.

Gladys Mergard married Winfield Ohmert, as his 2nd wife. He was a teacher at the time and later was president of a training school. The 1930 census shows both daughters the same age, so they may have been twins. The daughters may have been from the first marriage, as they were born before the date of his marriage to Gladys. After Gladys died, he married again in Florida. @@

Children of Gladys Lee MERGARD and Winfield Leroy OHMERT were:
- 871 i **Alice**[6] **OHMERT**, born abt 1920 in OH.
- 872 ii **Olive**[6] or **Ailine OHMERT**, born abt 1920 in OH.

459. Clarence M.[5] **HICKS II** (Clarence Malcolm[4], Orestes Marion Polk[3], Elijah[2], Joshua[1]), born est. 1920. He married unknown. Jones notes: "married 2 times, both in Columbus - names not given"; no marriages found in Ohio

Children of Clarence M. HICKS II were:
- 873 i **Daughter**[6] **HICKS**, born est. 1940.
- + 874 ii **Clarence M.**[6] **HICKS III**.

460. Norma[5] **HICKS** (Clarence Malcolm[4], Orestes Marion Polk[3], Elijah[2], Joshua[1]), born est. 1922. She married **Thomas Kelly HILL**, born est. 1922.

Norma Hicks was living with her mother and step-father, a musician, in 1930. She may be the Norma Hill who died in Virginia Beach in Oct 1994. @@

Children of Norma HICKS and Thomas Kelly HILL were:
- + 875 i **Thomas Kelly**[6] **HILL II**.

461. Marilyn[5] **HICKS** (Clarence Malcolm[4], Orestes Marion Polk[3], Elijah[2], Joshua[1]), born 27 Jan 1924 in Columbus, Franklin Co, OH; died 8 Sep 2010 in Columbus, OH. She married (1) in 1940 in Flemingsburg KY **Walter WILKES**; (2) abt 1962 (divorced 1970), Richard **DISBRO**, born abt 1924.

Marilyn Hicks was married twice and had two sons.@@

Children of Marilyn HICKS and Walter WILKES were:
- + 876 i **Walter H.**[6] **WILKES Jr.**.
- 877 ii **William Paul**[6] **WILKES**.
    Jones notes: "resides (1976) at 812 S. Waverly Rd, Columbus, OH 43027"

@@See research notes at end of chapter.   ##Born after 1930 & possibly living.

469. **Rotheus Thomas**[5] **ROGERS** (Lydia Ann[4] TATMAN, James[3], Lydia[2] HICKS, Joshua[1]), born 29 Oct 1879 in Indiana; died[465] 30 Oct 1960 in Houston, Harris Co, TX. He married abt 1905 **Syrene McADOO**, born 8 Mar 1881 in Mt Pleasant, Titus Co, TX; died 5 Mar 1914 in Galveston, Galveston Co, TX, daughter of **Robert** and **Laura McADOO**.

Thomas Rogers married Syrene McAdoo, who died at age 33, leaving him with five young children. The family lived with Thomas' mother, Lydia Gibson, in 1910 and 1920. Thomas worked with freight distribution. @@

Children of Rotheus Thomas ROGERS and Syrene wife of Thomas ROGERS were:

+ 878 i **Evalyn R.**[6] **ROGERS**.
+ 879 ii **Locleus L**[6] **ROGERS**.
   880 iii **Paul G.**[6] **ROGERS**, born abt 1909 in Texas.
       Census: 1930 Houston, Harris, TX, p. 37A. Carl C Russell 30, painter & paper hanger; Gladys Russell 30; Margaret Russell 10; Paul Rogers 18, TX/TX/TX, lodger, paper hanger
   881 iv **Mary M**[6] **ROGERS**, born abt 1911 in Texas.
+ 882 v **Claris**[6] **ROGERS**.

470. **Frank L.**[5] **TATMAN** (Franklin Ulyses[4], James[3], Lydia[2] HICKS, Joshua[1]), born 26 Aug 1862 in Bethel, Clermont Co, OH; died[466] 18 Sep 1924 in Tacoma, Pierce Co, WA. He married bef 1909 **Ethel May SCHAUFLER**.

Frank Tatman was both a tailor and a longshoreman on the docks of Washington State. He was killed in a fall from a shipping wharf. @@

Children of Frank L. TATMAN and Ethel May SCHAUFLER were:

   883 i **Leone Helen**[6] **TATMAN**[467], born 30 Sep 1909 in Pratt, Pratt Co, KS; died 9 Jan 1994 in Chicago, Cook Co, IL; buried 16 Jan 1994 in Homewood, Cook Co, IL.
       Meade notes: "Frank and Ethel had 2 girls: 1. Leone Helen Tatman, b. Sept 30, 1909 in Pratt, Pratt Co, KS and d. Jan 9, 1994 in Chicago, Cook Co, IL. She was buried on Jan 16, 1994 in Homewood, Cook Co, IL. She was also married to Nicholas Roberts, but I don't believe they had any children."
+ 884 ii **Florence Marie**[6] **TATMAN**.

473. **Richard Bryon**[5] **TATMAN**[468, 469] (Franklin Ulyses[4], James[3], Lydia[2] HICKS, Joshua[1]), born 27 Jun 1899 in OK; died 6 Aug 1964 in El Paso, TX. He married (1) abt 1921 **Nell Beatrice MIXON**, born 15 Oct 1896 in Quanah, TX; died 10 Dec 1956 in El Paso, El Paso, TX; buried 12 Dec 1956 in Restlawn Mem Park, daughter of William Henry MIXON and Mary Alice MCELREATH; (2) bef 1957 prob in El Paso, TX **Ruby Edith CAMPBELL**.

Richard Tatman worked in the freight forwarding business and was active in the Masonic Lodge. He lived in El Paso, TX for 41 years. @@

Children of Richard Bryon TATMAN and Nell Beatrice MIXON were:

   885 i **Richard Frank**[6] **TATMAN**, ##.
       Birth: Richard Frank Tatman, b. ##; parents: Richard B Tatman; Nell Beatrice Mixon. Texas Birth Index [Ancestry.com]

@@See research notes at end of chapter.   ##Born after 1930 & possibly living.

Newspaper: *El Paso Herald-Post* (El Paso, TX) 18 Nov 1954. *Attends Kemper. Frank Tatman, son of Mr & Mrs R. B. Tatman of 3900 N. Stanton street, is one of several first year cadets at The Kemper School, Boonville, MO, advanced to Phase II New Cadet on the basis of efficiency, attitude and conduct. Tatman is a high school junior. He is active in swimming and track.*

El Paso Herald-Post (El Paso, TX) 10 Jun 1961. *Cadet Richard Frank Tatman, son of Mr & Mrs R. B. Tatman of 6204 Pinehurst road, has been graduated from the Kemper Military School.*

474. **William Jennings[5] TATMAN**[470] (Franklin Ulyses[4], James[3], Lydia[2] HICKS, Joshua[1]), born 22 Jul 1903 in Coffeyville, Montgomery Co, KS; died May 1966. He married abt 1923 **Marjorie Francis WISE**, born abt 1903 in Kansas; married (2) **Ola ARCHER**, born abt 1911.

William Tatman worked at an oil refinery in 1930. The Kansas State census in 1925 gave his occupation as a fireman. He was a private in the Army Air Corp during World War II. @@

Children of William Jennings TATMAN and Marjorie Francis WISE were:
- 886 i **Gayl[6] TATMAN**, born abt 1925 in Kansas.
- 887 ii **Richard[6] TATMAN**, born abt 1928 in Kansas.

475. **Nelly[5] ALTMAN** (Cornelia Blanche[4] BRITTINGHAM, Lucinda[3] TATMAN, Lydia[2] HICKS, Joshua[1]), born 21 Jul 1873 in Clermont Co, OH; died[471] 11 Feb 1946 in Loveland, Clermont, OH; buried in Pekin Cemetery, Pt Isabell, OH. She married **Richard T. DAY**[472], born 29 Aug 1873 in Pt. Isabell, Ohio; died[473] 23 Apr 1952 in Loveland, Clermont, OH; buried in Pekin Cemetery, Pt Isabell, OH, son of Harrison and Jenny DAY.

Nelly Altman married Richard Day; the family remained in Clermont Co, OH and nearby Cincinnati. Richard worked with horses most of his life. @@

Children of Nelly ALTMAN and Richard T. DAY were:
- 888 i **Roy E.[6] DAY**, born 1892 in Ohio; died 1897 in Ohio; buried in Pt. Isabel.
- 889 ii **Ruth[6] DAY**, born Apr 1894 in OH.
  Notes: May be same person as Ruth below, but census dates do not agree with Orville's dates. not found on 1920 or 1930 census
- 890 iii **Mary[6] DAY**, born 11 Oct 1895 in Clermont Co, OH. She married aft 1930 -?- **KIDDER**, born est. 1895.
  Census 1930 Cincinnati, Hamilton, OH, p. 12A. Richard Day 57, church janitor; Nellie 57; Mary 34, single, chemist - lab. All b. OH.
  Jones notes: "resided in Cincinnati"; no other information found
- 891 iv **Cleon Joseph[6] DAY**, born 29 Oct 1897 in Clermont Co, OH; died[474] 3 Jun 1920 in Cincinnati, Hamilton Co, OH; buried 7 Jun 1920 in Point Isabel, Clermont Co, OH.
  Notes: Listed as daughter on 1900 & 1910 census. Not found on WW I Draft Registration.
  Death: Cleone Joseph Day, d. 3 Jan 1920, Cincinnati, Hamilton, OH. b. 29 Nov 1897, Clermont Co, OH. Parents: Richard Day & Nellie Altman both b. Clermont, OH. burial Point Isabel Clermont Co, 7 Jun 1920. Laborer; single, age 22, cause of death: accidental wound to head. <pilot.familysearch.org>
- + 892 v **Dorothy[6] DAY**.

@@See research notes at end of chapter.   ##Born after 1930 & possibly living.

893	vi	**Harry A.⁶ DAY**, born 1902; died 1906; buried in Pt. Isabel.
894	vii	**Samuel G.⁶ DAY**, born 1909; died 1912; buried in Pt. Isabel. **Death**: Samuel G. Day; b. 21 Sep 1909, Cincinnati, Hamilton, OH; d. 17 Jul 1912, Cincinnati, Hamilton Co, OH; burial:18 Jul 1912, Bethel, OH; parents: Richard Day, Nellie Altman. Ohio Deaths, 1908-1953 <familysearch.org>
+ 895	viii	**Ruth⁶ DAY**.

479. Millie Lou⁵ ALTMAN (Cornelia Blanche⁴ BRITTINGHAM, Lucinda³ TATMAN, Lydia² HICKS, Joshua¹), born 3 Sep 1888 in Brown Co, OH; died⁴⁷⁵ 27 Jun 1977 in Sardinia, Brown Co, OH. She married in 1907 in Cincinnati, Hamilton Co, OH **Cicero Malcomb HALL**⁴⁷⁶, born 22 Jun 1885 in Pike Co, KY; died⁴⁷⁷ 30 Dec 1936 in Perry Township, Gallia, OH; buried 2 Jan 1937 in Bethel Tate Cemetery, son of Manuel HALL and Lou Elizabeth or Selena OSBORNE.

Millie Altman married Cicero Hall, a dentist from West Virginia. He practiced in Boone Co, WV for over 50 years. The couple had two adopted children. @@

Children of Millie Lou ALTMAN and Cicero Malcomb HALL were:
+ 896 i **Cicero⁶ HALL**.
+ 897 ii **Mildred Ruth⁶ HALL**.

480. William Karl⁵ BRITTINGHAM⁴⁷⁸ (James Winfield⁴, Lucinda³ TATMAN, Lydia² HICKS, Joshua¹), born 3 Jul 1892 in Pt Isabel, Clermont Co, OH; died⁴⁷⁹ 6 Apr 1940 in Los Angeles, CA. He married **Emma -?-**, born abt 1894 in Ohio.

William Brittingham served in the Marine Corp in World War I. He was described in 1917 as " tall, slender, black hair & eyes". @@

Children of William Karl and Emma BRITTINGHAM were:
898 i **Naomi⁶ BRITTINGHAM**, born abt 1916 in Ohio.
899 ii **Helen⁶ BRITTINGHAM**, born abt 1919 in Ohio.
900 iii **Robert⁶ BRITTINGHAM**, born abt 1922 in Ohio.

483. Bryan James⁵ BRITTINGHAM⁴⁸⁰, ⁴⁸¹(James Winfield⁴, Lucinda³ TATMAN, Lydia² HICKS, Joshua¹), born 15 Apr 1896 in Hurlington, Clermont Co, OH; died⁴⁸² Oct 1970 in Lomita, Los Angeles Co, CA. He married (1)⁴⁸³ on 25 Dec 1917 in Hamilton Co, OH **Gladys PARKER**, born Feb 1895 in Cincinnati, Hamilton Co, OH; died 22 Jul 1918 in Cincinnati, Hamilton Co, OH; buried 24 Jul 1918 in Mt Orab, Clermont Co, OH, daughter of John W. PARKER and Jennie HIGGINS; (2) abt 1924 **Eva -?-**, born abt 1902 in KY.

Bryan Brittingham served in the infantry during World War I. He was a corporal and served in France. He was described in 1917 as "tall, slender, brown eyes, lt brown hair". @@

Children of Bryan James and Eva BRITTINGHAM were:
901 i **Mary L.⁶ BRITTINGHAM**, born abt 1929 in OH.

484. Melissa L.⁵ WALKER (Lydia May⁴ BRITTINGHAM, Lucinda³ TATMAN, Lydia² HICKS, Joshua¹), born 30 Dec 1900 in Felicity, Clermont Co, OH; died⁴⁸⁴ Feb 1980 in Evansville, Vanderburgh Co, IN. She married on 4 May 1923 in Clermont Co, OH **Frank CLEMENT**, born 27 Oct 1899 in North Loop, NE.

@@See research notes at end of chapter.   ##Born after 1930 & possibly living.

Melissa Walker married Frank Clement, who was a superintendent in bridge construction. In 1930, the family was in Wrightville, PA. @@

  Children of Melissa L. WALKER and Frank CLEMENT were:
+   902   i   **Shirley⁶ CLEMENT**.

488. Melva E.⁵ STEWART (John M.⁴, Diana³ HOPKINS, Elizabeth 'Betsy'² HICKS, Joshua¹), born May 1895 in IA. She married bef 1920 **Clarence SMITH**, born abt 1896 in IA or TX.

Melva Stewart married Clarence Smith from Texas. In 1920, the family was living in Manhattan, NY, where Clarence was a teacher. In 1930, the children were with their grandparents; we can find no further information on Melva and Clarence. @@

  Children of Melva E. STEWART and Clarence SMITH were:
  903   i   **Marilyn⁶ SMITH**, born abt 1920 in Iowa.
  904   ii   **Robert B.⁶ SMITH**, born abt 1923 in New York.

489. Ida May⁵ BENSON⁴⁸⁵ (Sarah Lavina⁴ HOPKINS, Levi Whitcomb³, Elizabeth 'Betsy'² HICKS, Joshua¹), born 29 Jul 1886 in Reno Co, KS; died 10 May 1947 in Hunter, Garfield Co, OK; buried in White Cemetery, Hunter, Garfield Co, OK. She married on 24 Feb 1899 in Hunter, Garfield Co, OK **Orie William GRIGGS**⁴⁸⁶, ⁴⁸⁷, born 7 Apr 1879 in Monroe, Marion Co, IA; died 22 Aug 1928 in Covina, Los Angeles Co, CA; buried in White Cemetery, Hunter, Garfield Co, OK, son of William and Phoebe GRIGGS.

Ida Benson married Orie Griggs, a farmer from Iowa. The family lived in Garfield, OK. Orie died in 1928 in California; Ida either remained in or returned to Oklahoma. @@

  Children of Ida May BENSON and Orie William GRIGGS were:
+   905   i   **William Lloyd⁶ GRIGGS**.
+   906   ii   **Lois Marie⁶ GRIGGS**.
  907   iii   **Leta P.⁶ GRIGGS**, born abt Feb 1920 in OK.
      Notes: On 1930 census with widowed mother, Ida May Griggs and sister Lois, in Noble, Garfield Co, KS. No other information.

490. Lettie Pearl⁵ BENSON⁴⁸⁸ (Sarah Lavina⁴ HOPKINS, Levi Whitcomb³, Elizabeth 'Betsy'² HICKS, Joshua¹), born 10 Feb 1889 in Reno Co, KS; died 17 Jun 1973; buried in Evergreen Cemetery, Colorado Springs, CO. She married on 27 Oct 1912 in Enid, Garfield Co, OK **Paul Prosper PENNINGTON**⁴⁸⁹, ⁴⁹⁰, born 26 Aug 1887 in Marion Co, KS; died 16 Nov 1972 in Colorado Springs, El Paso Co, CO; buried in Evergreen Cemetery, Colorado Springs, CO, son of J. A. and Octavia H PENNINGTON.

Lettie Benson married Paul Pennington, a farmer from Garfield, OK. By 1930, the family had moved to Colorado Springs, CO, where Paul was a carpenter. @@

  Children of Lettie Pearl BENSON and Paul Prosper PENNINGTON were:
  908   i   **Wayne Benson⁶ PENNINGTON**, born 17 Aug 1915 in Hunter, Garfield Co, OK; died 16 May 1982 in Pueblo, CO. He married⁴⁹¹ on 19 May 1940 in Colorado Sp, CO **Dorothy Louise WOODEN**, born 29 Apr 1920 in Colorado Sp, CO; died 29 Dec 1992 in Pueblo, Pueblo Co, CO.
      Notes: "3 children."

@@See research notes at end of chapter.   ##Born after 1930 & possibly living.

909   ii   **Wilma June**[6] **PENNINGTON**[492], born 22 Feb 1925 in Enid, Garfield Co, OK; died 22 Jan 1979 in Falls Church, VA; buried in Rockland, La Cross Co, WI. She married on 29 Jun 1944 in Colorado Springs, CO **Stanton Ray GAYLORD**, born 30 Sep 1923 in Rockland, La Cross Co, WI, son of Cecil R and Lilian GAYLORD
Jones notes: "Stan living in Ft White FL 1994. 5 children."

491. Roy Douglas[5] **BENSON**[493] (Sarah Lavina[4] HOPKINS, Levi Whitcomb[3], Elizabeth 'Betsy'[2] HICKS, Joshua[1]), born 26 Sep 1895 in Hunter, Garfield Co, OK; died 7 Dec 1960 in Enid, Garfield Co, OK; buried in White Cemetery, Hunter, Garfield Co, OK. He married on 19 Feb 1921 in Hunter, Garfield Co, OK **Alta COGSWELL**, born 14 Nov 1898 in Hunter, Garfield Co, OK; died 6 Jul 1984 in Enid, Garfield Co, OK; buried in White Cemetery, Hunter, Garfield Co, OK, daughter of William and Jennie COGSWELL.

Roy Benson was a manager of a retail store in 1920; a grocery salesman in 1930. He was described as "medium height, slender build, blue eyes, brown hair".

Children of Roy Douglas BENSON and Alta COGSWELL were:
910   i   **Douglas Dean**[6] **BENSON**[494], born 26 Sep 1918 in Enid, Garfield Co, OK; died 1 Sep 1979 in Enid, Garfield Co, OK; buried in White Cemetery, Hunter, Garfield Co, OK. He married on 12 Jul 1939 in Hunter, Garfield Co, OK **Betty Ruth MOORE**, born 19 Feb 1921 in Hunter, Garfield Co, OK; died 6 Feb 1990 in Enid, Garfield Co, OK; buried in White Cemetery, Hunter, Garfield Co, OK.
Notes: Children & grandchildren named in Griggs book

493. Oran Ray[5] **MITCHELL**[495, 496] (Clara Elizabeth[4] HOPKINS, Levi Whitcomb[3], Elizabeth 'Betsy'[2] HICKS, Joshua[1]), born 6 Sep 1882 in Reno Co, KS; died 29 Mar 1978 in Pharr, Hidalgo Co, TX; buried in McAllen, Hidalgo Co, TX. He married on 19 Jan 1910 **Gracia GORDON**, born 3 Feb 1887 in Nickerson, KS; died 18 Sep 1988 in Littleton, CO; buried in McAllen, TX.

Oran Mitchell was a letter carrier in 1918 and an auto mechanic in 1930. He was described in 1918 as "tall, slender, blue eyes, dark brown hair; disability: heart & lungs weak". @@

Children of Oran Ray MITCHELL and Gracia GORDON were:
911   i   **Roy J.**[6] **MITCHELL**, born abt 1914 in CA.
912   ii   **Helen L.**[6] **MITCHELL**, born abt Mar 1919 in CA.

495. William Jesse[5] **MITCHELL**[497] (Clara Elizabeth[4] HOPKINS, Levi Whitcomb[3], Elizabeth 'Betsy'[2] HICKS, Joshua[1]), born 11 Sep 1886 in Haven, Reno Co, KS. He married on 7 Jul 1908 **Ida May PRENE**, born Jun 1892 in Kansas, daughter of Frank and Emma J PRENE.

Jesse Mitchell was a farmer in Reno, KS. He was described as "tall, med build, blue eyes, light hair, bald." @@

Children of William Jesse MITCHELL and Ida May PRENE were:
913   i   **Viola M**[6] **MITCHELL**, born abt 1913 in KS.
914   ii   **Junior**[6] **MITCHELL**, born abt 1922 in KS.
915   iii   **Wilma**[6] **MITCHELL**, born abt 1924 in KS.

@@See research notes at end of chapter.   ##Born after 1930 & possibly living.

496. George Henry⁵ MITCHELL⁴⁹⁸ (Clara Elizabeth⁴ HOPKINS, Levi Whitcomb³, Elizabeth 'Betsy'², HICKS, Joshua¹), born 30 Mar 1888 in Haven, Reno Co, KS. He married on 6 Sep 1908 **Mary Neoma PRENE**, born Oct 1894 in KS, daughter of Frank and Emma J PRENE.

George Mitchell was a farmer in 1910 & 1930, and a carter for a salt plant in 1920. In 1910, his mother, grandmother and brother were all living with him and Neoma. He was described as "med height & build; blue eyes, lt brown hair". @@

Children of George Henry MITCHELL and Mary Neoma PRENE were:
- 916   i   **Hazel Pearl⁶ MITCHELL**, born abt 1911 in OK.
- 917   ii   **Glenn⁶ MITCHELL**, born abt 1914 in Kansas.
- 918   iii   **George L.⁶ MITCHELL**, born abt 1923 in Kansas.

502. Mollie E.⁵ LANHAM (Lucinda Margaret⁴ JOHNSTON, William J.³, Margaret² HICKS, Joshua¹), born 3 Mar 1872 in Felicity, Clermont Co, OH; died 9 May 1945 in Springfield, Hamilton Co, OH. She married on 18 Mar 1891 in Clermont Co, OH **William KURTZ**, born 10 Sep 1866 in Chilo, Clermont Co, OH; died 23 Jan 1928 in Cincinnati, Hamilton, OH; buried 25 Jan 1928 in Vine St Hill, Cincinnati, OH.

Mollie Lanham married William Kurtz, who worked at a variety of jobs - stableman, night watchman, garage manager. In 1930, widowed Mollie had her 11 year old twin granddaughters living with her. @@

Children of Mollie E. LANHAM and William KURTZ were:
- \+   919   i   **Marie L.⁶ KURTZ**.
- \+   920   ii   **Harry W.⁶ KURTZ**.

506. Lucy Florence⁵ UTTER (Annie Belle⁴ JOHNSTON, William J.³, Margaret² HICKS, Joshua¹), born 27 Jun 1903 in Clermont Co, OH. She married on 4 Sep 1920 in Clermont Co, OH **Harold M. EDWARDS**, born 15 May 1902 in Brown Co, OH; died⁴⁹⁹ May 1975 in Felicity, OH, son of Arch and Mary A. EDWARDS; (2) on 2 Oct 1979 in Clermont Co, OH **Louis A. AYERS**, born abt 1901 in Ohio; died 11 Jul 1988 in Cincinnati, Hamilton Co, OH.

Lucy Utter married Harold Edwards, a Clermont County farmer. After his death, she married again - at age 76 - to Louie Ayers. She lived to be 95. @@

Children of Lucy UTTER and Harold M. EDWARDS were:
- 921   i   **Galen Harold⁶ EDWARDS**, born 12 Aug 1921 in Clermont Co, OH. He married (1) **Wanita HUFF**, born est. 1921; (2) **Anna STATZMAN**.
  Jones notes: "resides (1974) at 13655 Fellrath Rd, Taylor, MI 48180; served in Air Force, WW II"
- 922   ii   **Robert Merrill⁶ EDWARDS**, born 20 Jan 1924 in Clermont Co, OH. He married on 5 Feb 1941 in Clermont Co, OH **Martha M. STAATS**, born 5 Feb 1926 in Point Pleasant, Clermont Co, OH, daughter of William C. and Louella M. STAATS.
  Jones notes: "resides (1974) at 5814 Portsmouth Dr, Tampa, FL 33615; served in US Navy, WW II". May be the Robert G Edwards b. 20 Jan 1924; 25 May 2002 on SS death index. Birth date agrees. No death location given; card issued in OH.

@@See research notes at end of chapter.   ##Born after 1930 & possibly living.

923   iii   **Harry Morgan**[6] **EDWARDS**, born 29 Nov 1926 in Covington, Kenton Co, KY; died[500] 25 Sep 1999 in Felicity, Clermont Co, OH. He married on 3 Jun 1950 in Clermont Co, OH **Lilian RUDD**, born 22 Aug 1932 in Citusso?, KY.
         Jones notes: "resides (1974) at US Rt 133 near Felicity, OH; served in US Navy, WW II"

924   iv   **Lois Lucille**[6] **EDWARDS**, born 22 Jun 1930 in Clermont Co, OH; died 12 Nov 2003 in Bethel, Clermont Co, OH. She married on 4 Dec 1948 in Clermont Co, OH **John Holton POSTON Jr**, born 10 Sep 1926 in Falmouth, Pendleton Co, KY, son of John and Stella POSTON.
         Jones notes: "resides (1974) at Schaller Rd, Rt 1, Bethel, OH; he served in US Navy, WW II"
         SS Death Index gives: Lois E. Poston, b. 22 Jun 1930; d. 12 Nov 2003, age 73, Bethel, Clermont, OH; card issued in Kentucky; #401-32-3439

507. Mary Morgan[5] **UTTER** (Annie Belle[4] JOHNSTON, William J.[3], Margaret[2] HICKS, Joshua[1]), born 7 Feb 1905 in Clermont Co, OH; died[501] 3 Jul 1998 in Dayton, Campbell Co, KY. She married **Jeremiah L. WING**, born 1903 in Cincinnati, Hamilton Co, OH; died 11 Nov 1960, Norwood, Hamilton Co, OH.

Mary Utter married Jerry Wing, who was a truck driver in Dayton, KY in 1930. They evidently lived in Norwood, OH for a while, as Jerry died there in 1960. Mary was back in Dayton, KY, when she died in 1998. @@

   Children of Mary Morgan UTTER and Jeremiah L. WING were:
     925   i   **Catharine Anna**[6] **WING**, born abt 1928. Jones notes: "m -?- Wiseman"
     926   ii   **Jerry Laurence**[6] **WING**, born abt 1930.
     927   iii   **John Raymond**[6] **WING**. Jones notes: "graduate of West Point Academy"
     928   iv   **Robert Ralph**[6] **WING**. Jones notes: "served in US Army; died"

508. Robert Alexander[5] **UTTER** (Annie Belle[4] JOHNSTON, William J.[3], Margaret[2] HICKS, Joshua[1]), born 29 Mar 1907 in Clermont Co, OH; died[502] Apr 1973 in Felicity, Clermont Co, OH. He married on 8 Sep 1934 in Maysville, Mason Co, KY **Margarite TURNER**, born 3 Apr 1912 in Germantown, Bracken Co, KY.

Robert Utter was an automobile mechanic in 1930, living at home at age 23. He and his wife Margarite had two sons. @@

   Children of Robert Alexander UTTER and Margarite TURNER were:
     929   i   **Robert Eugene**[6] **UTTER**, ##. He married **Linda Carol DAVIS**. Jones notes: "career Air Force, Major; no children"
+   930   ii   **Edward M.**[6] **UTTER**.

510. Henry Johnston[5] **STEVENS** (Mary Elizabeth[4] JOHNSTON, William J.[3], Margaret[2] HICKS, Joshua[1]), born 8 Jan 1895 in Falmouth, KY; died 31 May 1964 in Cincinnati, Hamilton, OH; buried in Felicity Cemetery, Felicity, Clermont Co, OH. He married on 28 Feb 1916 **Lulu O. REED**, born 3 May 1895 in Clermont Co, OH; died 1 May 1971 in Clermont Co, OH; buried in Felicity Cemetery, Felicity, Clermont Co, OH.

Johnson Stevens worked for the Felicity & Bethel Railroad in 1918 and was a dry cleaning agent in 1930. He was described in 1918 as "short, slender, blue eyes, light hair" @@

@@See research notes at end of chapter.   ##Born after 1930 & possibly living.

Children of Henry Johnston STEVENS and Lulu O. REED were:
- 931 i **Elizabeth E.**[6] **STEVENS**, born 17 Oct 1916 in Felicity, Clermont Co, OH; died 8 Feb 2010 in Cincinnati, Hamilton, OH. She married on 16 Aug 1941 in Cincinnati, Hamilton Co, OH **Jack Willis HILGE**, born 26 Jun 1918 in Cincinnati, Hamilton Co, OH; died[503] 23 Oct 1999 in Cincinnati, Hamilton Co, OH, son of Herman H. and Mary HILGE.
  Jones notes: "resides (1974) at1095 Rosetree Ln, Cincinnati, OH 45230; no children"
  Death: SS Death Index gives, Elizabeth E. Hilge, b. 17 Oct 1916; d. 28 Feb 2010, age 93, Cincinnati, Hamilton, OH; issued: Ohio #272-24-2672
- + 932 ii **Charles E.**[6] **STEVENS**.
- 933 iii **Margie Garnet**[6] **STEVENS**, born 13 Jun 1921 in Felicity, Clermont Co, OH; died 24 Jul 1929 in Felicity, Clermont Co, OH; buried 27 Jul 1929 in Felicity Cemetery, Felicity, Clermont Co, OH.
  Death: Margie Garnet Stevens, d. 24 Jul 1929, Felicity, Clermont, OH; b. 13 Jun 1921, Felicity, OH; Age: 8 years 1 month 11 days; Res: Felicity, Clermont, OH; Burial: 27 Jul 1929, Felicity, OH; Father: H. J. Stevens, b. Falmouth Ky; Mother: Lulu Reed b. OH. Cause of death: Tetanus. Ohio Deaths, 1908-1953 <familysearch.org>
- + 934 iv **Wilma J.**[6] **STEVENS**.
- + 935 v **Lloyd J.**[6] **STEVENS**.
- + 936 vi **Delia**[6] **STEVENS**.

511. Caroline Marie[5] **GLEASON** (Ella F.[4] WHITE, Ann Maria[3] HICKS, James[2], Joshua[1]), born 17 Feb 1880 in Williamsburg, Clermont Co, OH; died 1960 in New Rochelle, Westchester Co, NY. She married abt 1900 **William S. CHARLES**, born abt 1872 in Richmond, Wayne Co, IN; died 1961 in New Rochelle, Westchester Co, NY; buried in New Rochelle, NY.

Caroline Gleason married William Charles who was a building contractor. The family moved to New Rochelle, NY before 1930. @@

Children of Caroline Marie GLEASON and William S. CHARLES were:
- 937 i **Mary Louise**[6] **CHARLES**, born abt 1910 in Norwood, Hamilton Co, OH.
  Jones notes: "resides (1974) at Oxford, OH (resident at Minmick Hall, Miami University); not married"

513. Marie W.[5] **WHITE** (James Hicks[4], Ann Maria[3] HICKS, James[2], Joshua[1]), born May 1885 in Williamsburg, Clermont Co, OH; died 26 Jun 1965 in Cincinnati, Hamilton Co, OH; buried in Batavia, OH. She married[504] on 19 Mar 1907 in Clermont Co, OH **George Woodlief GREGG**[505], born[506] 16 Jan 1882 in Batavia, Clermont Co, OH; died[507] Nov 1970 in Batavia, Clermont Co, OH; buried in Batavia, son of R. W. C. GREGG and Clara WOODLIEF.

Marie White married George Gregg, a farmer in Clermont Co, OH. By 1930, George was proprietor of an oil station. @@

Children of Marie W. WHITE and George Woodlief GREGG were:
- + 938 i **Clarke W.**[6] **GREGG**.
- + 939 ii **James Woodlief**[6] **GREGG**.
- 940 iii **George Whitlock**[6] **GREGG**[508], born 28 May 1916 in Clermont Co, OH; died 11 Aug 1916 in Batavia, Clermont, OH; buried in Williamsburg Cemetery

@@See research notes at end of chapter.   ##Born after 1930 & possibly living.

Birth / Death: George Whitlock Gregg, d. 11 Aug 1916 Batavia, Clermont, OH; b. 28 May 1916 Clermont Co.; Death Age: 2 months 13 days; Burial: 12 Aug 1916 Winsburg; Father: Geo. W. Gregg, b. Clermont Co.; Mother: Marie White, b. Clermont Co. Ohio Deaths, 1908-1953 <pilot.familysearch.org>

518. **Nicholas James^5 WHITE**[509] (James Hicks^4, Ann Maria^3 HICKS, James^2, Joshua^1), born 10 Sep 1897 in Williamsburg, Clermont Co, OH; died 12 Feb 1960 in Hamilton Co, OH; buried in Williamsburg Cemetery He married in Sep 1919 in Delaware OH **Lucille C. CHATTERTON**, born abt 1895, daughter of **Harry CHATTERTON and Sadie MOYER**.

Nicholas White took over management of Williamsburg Chair Co, the family chair factory, after his father's death; he had been bookkeeper before that. He was described in 1918 as "med height & weight; brown eyes & hair". @@

   Children of Nicholas James WHITE and Lucille C. CHATTERTON were:
+   941 i **James Chatterton^6 WHITE**.
+   942 ii **Nicholas Lawrence^6 WHITE**.

531. **Doyle Howard^5 JOHNSTON** (Cora^4 NEWKIRK, William David^3, Nancy^2 HICKS, Joshua^1), born 22 Jun 1909 in Bloomfield, Davis Co, IA; died[510] Nov 1984 in Cornelius, Washington Co, OR. He married on 15 May 1937 in Cornelius, OR **Helen L. SIMANTEL**, born 20 Nov 1912 in Illinois, died 18 Jan 2007 in Gaston, Washington Co, OR; daughter of George J. and Bertha SIMANTEL.

Doyle Johnston moved with his family to South Dakota as a young child. He died in Cornelius, Oregon. He was working on the family farm in Bon Homme Co, SD in 1930. @@

   Children of Doyle Howard JOHNSTON and Helen L. SIMANTEL were:
+   943 i **Gary Doyle^6 JOHNSTON**.
    944 ii **Gloria Jane^6 JOHNSTON**, born 3 Dec 1945 in Hillsboro, Washington Co, OR. Jones notes: "resides (1974) at 4435 NE 73rd Ave, Portland, OR 97218; married -?- Birchard"

532. **Verle^5 JOHNSTON** (Cora^4 NEWKIRK, William David^3, Nancy^2 HICKS, Joshua^1), born 28 May 1911 in Olivet, Hutchison Co, SD; died[511] Mar 1985 in Bloomfield, Davis Co, IA. He married on 24 Jan 1940 in Lancaster, MO **Gertrude WIEDENBACK**, born 6 Aug 1915 in Olivet, Hutchison Co, SD; died 10 Dec 2009 in Bloomfield, Davis, IA, daughter of Emil and Emma WIEDENBACK.

Verle Johnston moved with his parents to South Dakota, as a young child. He married in Missouri in 1941 and died in Iowa. @@

   Children of Verle JOHNSTON and Gertrude WIEDENBACK were:
+   945 i **Barbara^6 JOHNSTON**.
+   946 ii **Judith Kae^6 JOHNSTON**.

@@See research notes at end of chapter.   ##Born after 1930 & possibly living.

533. Loren K.[5] JOHNSTON (Cora[4] NEWKIRK, William David[3], Nancy[2] HICKS, Joshua[1]), born 11 Aug 1914 in Olivet, Hutchison Co, SD; died[512] 27 Jan 1992 in Scotland, Bon Homme Co SD. He married on 18 Jun 1937 in Scotland, SD **Ina Blanche BEHL**, born 13 Jul 1915 in Scotland, Bon Homme Co SD, died 16 Sep 2006 in Scotland, Bon Homme Co SD; daughter of George and Meredith BEHL.

Loren Johnston married Ina Behl, who had also grown up in Scotland, SD. They apparently remained in Scotland all their lives. @@

Children of Loren K. JOHNSTON and Ina B. BEHL were:
- 947 i **Bonitta K.[6] JOHNSTON**, Jones notes: "resides (1974) at Orient (Polo) SD 57467; not married"
- 948 ii **Gordon K.[6] JOHNSTON**, Jones notes: "resides (1974) at 2718 Stone Cir, Minnetonka, MN 55343; served in Viet Nam; m.Genevieve -?-"

548. Willard Burnett[5] HICKS (Charles Jefferson[4], Albert Alden[3], Joshua[2], Joshua[1]), born 19 Sep 1919 in Illinois; died 1 Jun 1974 in New Goshen, IN. He married **Lena Gwendolyn COX**, born abt 1920; buried 18 May 2010.

Willard Hicks married Lena Cox and had two children. @@

Children of Willard Burnett HICKS and Lena Gwendolyn COX were:
- 949 i **Marsha Rose[6] HICKS**.
- 950 ii **Gary Lynn[6] HICKS**.

@@See research notes at end of chapter.   ##Born after 1930 & possibly living.

Research notes for Generation 5

Notes for Cora MANNING #264
Information from Jones notes.
Death: bef 1900, as Charles is listed as widowed in 1900 census .

Notes for Charles R. FAGIN #264s
Census
  1900 Pierce, Clermont, OH, p. 1A. Elizabeth Fagin 61; Burl P Fagin 34, widowed, laborer in brick yard; James Fagin 26, single, machinist; Charles Fagin 25, Mar 1875, widowed, machinist, OH/VA/OH.
  1910 Pierce, Clermont, OH, p. 6B. Charles R Fagin 35, OH/WV/OH, 2nd marriage, engineer in brick yard; Berdie Fagin 27, OH/OH/OH, 1st marriage, 5 ch/ 2 living; Stanley W Fagin 8; Hazel L Fagin 1 5/12; Huldah Pullin 60, aunt, single.
Death: Charles R. Fagin, d. 1 Nov 1916, Cincinnati, Hamilton, OH; b. 17 Mar 1875, Clermont County; Age: 41 years 7 months 15 days; Married; Occ: Brick Burner; Res: New Palestine, OH; Burial: 3 Nov 1916; Free Mile Cemetery, Clermont Co.; Father: David M. Fagin, b. Clermont County; Mother: Elizabeth Jackson, b. Clermont County. Informant: James F. Fagin, New Palestine, OH. Ohio Deaths 1908-1953 <familysearch.org>

Notes for Walter MANNING #266
Census: 1910 Millcreek, Hamilton Co, OH, p. 4A. Walter Manning, 26 , labor-factory, Laura 21, OH/KY/OH; Francis 3, son; Mildred 2; Elvina Welch 17 sister in law. Ohio
Death: Walter Manning, b. 25 Nov 1883; d. 18 Jan 1913 Cincinnati, OH. 1269 State Ave. Married. Father Francis M. Manning b. Clermont, OH; Caroline Hanley b. Clermont, OH. Occupation: Laborer - Proctor & Gamble. Cause of death: Pulmonary Tuberculosis. Informant W. J. Wirwel, 652 State Ave. Ohio Deaths 1908-1953 <pilot.familysearch.org>

Notes for Laura A. WILLS #266s
Census
  *1920 Cincinnati Ward 1, Hamilton, OH, p. 4B. Albert C Klapper 25, millwright - candy co; Laura Klapper 25. Both b. OH.
  1930 Cincinnati, Hamilton, OH, p. 7A. Albert Klapper 37, janitor - club house; Laura Klapper 37; Francis Manning 21, stepson, chauffeur - gas? company.
*__Death:__ Laura Klapper, b. 1889, Hamilton, Ohio; d. 24 Jul 1969, Hamilton County, OH, widow, age at death 80.   * may not be right person.

Notes for Ethel M. MANNING #269
Census
  1920 Cincinnati Ward 26, p. 1A. William B. Tekulve 29, OH/Ger/Ger, boiler maker - iron works; Ethel 25, William A. 2 6/12, Mildred E. 8/12?; Caroline Manning, 66, widow, mother in law.
  1930 St Bernard, Hamilton Co, OH, p. 19B, HH #245.William B Tekulve 39; Ethel E 35; William N 13; Mildred E 10; Mary F. 7 4/12; Carolina Mannruz [Manning] 75. mother in law.
Signed death certificate of Caroline Hanley Manning 1944.
Death: Ethel M Tekulve [Ethel M Manning], b. 15 Jun 1894, OH; d. 26 Dec 1993, Long-Term Care Facilities, Blue Ash, Hamilton Co, OH. Age: 99; Father's Surname: Manning; Mother's Maiden Name: Hauly; Widowed; Housewife/ Homemaker. Ohio Deaths, 1908-1932, 1938-1944, and 1958-2007 [Ancestry.com]

@@See research notes at end of chapter.   ##Born after 1930 & possibly living.

Notes for William Bernard TEKULVE #269s

Census: 1900 Mill Creek, Hamilton, OH, p. 17A. Henry Tekulva 52, Ger/Ger/Ger, imm. 1825, day labor; Mary Tekulva 41, OH/Ger/Ger; Anthony Tekulva 20, OH; Benjiman Tekulva 14, AL; Elizibeth Tekulva 10, AL; William Tekulva 8, OH; Henry Tekulva 6, OH; Mary Tekulva 5/12, OH.

Military: World War I Draft Registration Cards, 1917-1918 [ancestry.com] William Bernard Tekulve, age 26, b. 9 Aug 1890. Reading, OH; res: St Bernard, Hamilton Co, OH; occ: boiler maker - Proctor & Gamble Co; married - wife and child; med height & build, blue eyes, brown hair; regis: 5 Jun 1917, St Bernard, OH.

Death: William B Tekulve, b. 1891; Residence: St Bernard, Hamilton Co, OH; d. 25 Jan 1974, Long-Term Care Facilities, Silverton, Hamilton Co, OH; Age: 83; married. Ohio Deaths, 1908-1932, 1938-1944, and 1958-2007 [Ancestry.com]

Notes for Edward H. PATTISON #271

Jones notes: "Supt of Clermont schools; Co K, 2nd Regt KY Infantry - Spanish War"; not in Clermont Co for 1900 census .

Census

1910 Union Twp, Clermont, OH. p. 7B, Edward H Pattison 32, teacher - public school; Jennie I 26; Stanley E 9; Thelma M 7.

1920 Tate Twp, Clermont, OH. p. 1A. Edward Pattison, 42, Supt public schools; Gennie I, 36; Stanley E 17; Thelma M 16; Eunice T 3 8/12; John W 1 9/12.

1930 Bethel, Clermont, OH, p. 11A. 423 Main St. Edward Pattison, 52; Irene 46; Eunice 18; John 11. Occ: Supt. public schools.

Military: World War I Draft Registration Cards, 1917-1918 [ancestry.com] Edward Pattison, age 41, b. 20 Apr 1877; res: Moscow, Clermont, OH; occ: supt - various boards of education; relative: Jennie Irene Pattison, same residence; med height & build; blue eyes, brown hair; regis: Batavia, Clermont Co, OH, 12 Sep 1918.

Death: 8 Sep 1961, Veteran's Admin Center, Cincinnati, OH, widowed. Ohio Deaths, 1908-1932, 1938-1944, and 1958-2002 <ancestry.com>

Notes for Jennie Irene MCKIBBEN #271s

Death: Jennie Irene Pattison, 423 S. Main, Bethel. b. 18 Apr 1883, KY; D. 9 Jun 1950, Christ Hospital, Cincinnati, OH. Married. Father Albert McKibben; Mother Thresia Ross. Informant E. H. Pattison. Buried Bethel Cemetery 6/10/1950. <pilot.familysearch.org>

Notes for Ross John PATTISON #273

Census

1900 Connersville, Fayette, IN, p. 9A. Hiram L Snake 40; Alice M Snake 39; Claud A Snake 18; Floyd H Snake 16; Pearl B Snake 14; Frank Silcott 20, furniture maker; Ross Pattison 18, Apr 1882, boarder, single, furniture maker, OH/OH/OH

1910 not found

1920 Covington, Kenton Co, KY, p. 1. Ross Pattison 37, fireman - city; wife Ann 32; son Robert 7 7/12; Myrtle Reinhardt, sister, 40 [43?], single

1930 Covington, Kenton Co, KY, p. 7A. Ross Pattison 47, fireman for the city; Ann 42, KY; Robert 17.

Military: Not found on WW I or WW II draft registration

Death: Ross J Pattison, d. 3 May 1948, Kenton Co, KY; age: 66; residence: Kenton Co, KY. Kentucky Death Index, 1911-2000

Notes for Ann C. NEISER #273s
Jones notes: "she resides (1973) at 1308 Greenup St, Covington, KY"

Notes for Walter Cleavland PATTISON #274
Jones notes: "Resides: (1973) at Montrie Co. Care Center, Sylvania OH. M1?, bur at Mt Washington Cem; M2 to Mada Kuhn; 3 daughters - names not given."
Birth: Walter C. Pattison, male, born 15 Apr 1885 Tate, Clermont, OH; Father: J. S. Pattison; Mother: Mary A. Manning. Ohio Births and Christenings, 1821-1962 <pilot.familysearch.org>
Census:
- 1910 Cincinnati, Hamilton Co, OH, p. 7A. Walter Pattison 25, Drop hammer man, forging; Minnie M, 27, 3 ch, 3 living, m. 5 years (his 1st, her 2nd); stepdau, Alma J. Brumell?, 7; dau Grace Pattison, 4; Edith M. Pattison 2. All b. OH.
- 1920, Toledo, Lucas Co, OH, p. 10B. Walter C Pattison 34, dropforger - automotive; Mada 28; Edith May 12; Elmore Walter 3 8/12; Herbert Le Roy 1. Hattie Smith, 71, at same address, also listed as head.
- 1930 Bedford, District 5, Monroe Co, MI. p. 14b. Walter C. Pattison 45, wife Mada 37, sons Elmore W. 13, Herbert L. 12, George E. 10, Albert F. 8, Edwin L. 6. Also Walter's daughter Edith M. Harris, widow, w/ dau Rose M. 6, sons Carl W. 5, Charles E. 2, James F. 4/12. All OH/OH/OH, except -?- Harris (deceased spouse of Edith) who was b. MI. Walter's occupation - Drop Forger, Automobile Factory.

Marriage1: Groom: Walter Cleavland Pattison, b. 1884, OH; Age: 21; to Minnie Brunell, b.1884, Cincinnati, OH; Age: 21; Marriage: 19 Aug 1905, Hamilton, OH; Groom's parents: Jno; Mary Manning; Bride's parents: Jerry Bowers; C Shaw; Groom: Single; Bride: Widowed. Ohio Marriages, 1800-1958 <familysearch.org>
Marriage2: Walter C. Pattison, b. 1885, Clermont County, OH, age 30; to Mady Kuhn, b. 1891, Cincinnati, OH, age 24; Marriage: 2 Dec 1915, Hamilton Co, OH; Groom's parents: John Pattison; Mary Manning; Bride's parents: George Kuhn, Mary Ramminger; Groom's Marital Status: Widowed. Ohio Marriages, 1800-1958 <pilot.familysearch.org>
Military: World War I Draft Registration Cards, 1917-1918 [ancestry.com] Walter Cleveland Pattison, age 33, b. 15 Apr 1885, OH; res: Toledo, Lucas Co, OH; occ: drop forging - Overland; relative: Mada Mary Pattison, wife; height 5' 7", med build, grey eyes, brown hair; regis: 12 Sep 1918, Toledo, OH.
Death of child: Male Pattison, b. 28 Apr 1927, Wash Twp; d. 28 Apr 1927, Washington Twp, Lucas, OH; bur 29 Apr 1927, Memorial park; Father: Walter Pattison b. Ohio; Mother: Nada Kuhn b. OH: Ohio Deaths and Burials, 1854-1997 <pilot.familysearch.org>
Death: Walter C. Pattison, b. 1886; res: Lucas Co, OH; d. 7 Apr 1973, St Lukes Hospital, Maumee, Lucas Co, OH. Age: 87; Widowed. Ohio Deaths, 1908-1932, 1938-1944, and 1958-2007 [Ancestry.com]

Notes for Minnie M. BOWER #274s1
Census: 1900 Cincinnati Ward 1, Hamilton, OH, p. 3B. John Schott 30, blacksmith; Samatha Schott 40, m. 3 yrs, 5 ch / 4 living; Oliver Schott 9, step son; Harry Bower 22, step son, day labor; Minnie Bower 18, May 1882, step dau, cigar roller; Jennie Bower 16, step dau, cigar roller; Cora Schott 19, sister, cigar roller
Death: no death records found.

Notes for Mada Mary KUHN #274s2
Marriage: Mady Kuhn, b. 1891, Cincinnati, OH; marriage: 2 Dec 1915, Hamilton County, OH; parents: George Kuhn, Mary Ramminger; spouse: Walter C. Pattison; parents: John Pattison, Mary Manning; groom - widowed. Ohio Marriages, 1800-1958 <familysearch.org>
Death: Mada M Pattison, b. 1892; Residence: Lucas Co, OH; Death: Nov 1963, Toledo, Lucas Co, OH; age 71; Married. Ohio Deaths, 1908-1932, 1938-1944, and 1958-2002 <ancestry.com>

Notes for Frank Lee PATTISON #276
Jones notes: "she resided (1973) at 1138 Sylvania Rd, Cleveland Hghts, OH 44672"
Census
- 1920 Bellaire Ward 4, Belmont, OH, p. 6B. Cora B Barrett 42; Hary E Shepherd 51; Frank L Pattison 28, single, pharmacist - drug store, OH/OH/OH; Louise Shear 27
- 1930 Cleveland, Cuyahoga, OH, p. 1B. Frank L Patteson 37, m. age 32, pharmacist - drug store; Dolores Patteson 27. Both OH/OH/OH.

Military: World War I Draft Registration Cards, 1917-1918 [ancestry.com] Frank Lee Pattison, age 25, b. 17 Oct 1892, Bethel, OH; res: Cincinnati, Hamilton Co, OH; occ: student - first year pharmacy, Ohio State; single; Military: student ___ infantry. Short, med build, brown hair, blue eyes. Regis: Cincinnati, OH, undated.

Military service: WW I - Frank L. Pattison; Serial Number: 3527022; Enlistment: National Army Location: Cincinnati, O. Date: 26 Jun 1918; Residence: 1517 Ruth Ave., Cincinnati, O.; Birth Place: Saltair, OH; Birth Date : 17 Oct 1892; Assignment: 9 Co 3 158 Depot Brigade to 14 July 1918; Medical Department Base Hospital Cp Sherman O to Discharge Private, first class 1 Nov 1918. Honorable discharge 23 July 1919. Volume # 13

Notes for Delores Naomi BUCEY #276s
Jones notes gives first name as Doris.
Census: 1910 Wellsville Ward 2, Columbiana, OH, p. 5A. Fredrick Bucey 30, OK/OH/IN, motorman - railroad; Lois? S Bucey 25; Naoma D Bucey 6; Ruth M Bucey 1. Other b. OH.
Death: Dolores B Pattison, b. 1904, OH; res: Cleveland Heights, Cuyahoga Co, OH; d. 1 Mar 1988, East Cleveland, OH, widowed. Ohio Deaths, 1908-1932, 1938-1944, and 1958-2007 [ancestry.com]

Notes for Orville Lorain MANNING #277
Census
- 1910 Williamsburg, Clermont, OH, p. 5B, HH # 123. Wright Sprague 71, farmer; Rebecca 68; Orville L Maning 35, teacher, son-in law; Margaret R Maning 35, dau; Waunita Maning 3, gr-dau; Dana C Manning 6/12, gr-son; William G Homan 73 bro-in-law.
- 1920 Williamsburg, Clermont, OH, p. 2B. Orville Manning 43, farmer; Margaret Manning 43; Oneita Manning 12; Dane Manning 10. All OH/OH/OH
- 1930 - Williamsburg, Clermont, OH,- District 27, p. 9b. Orville Manning 54, Margaret 54, Onmeta 23, Dana (son) 20. Orville & Onmeta are teachers, public school.

Military: World War I Draft Registration Cards, 1917-1918 [ancestry.com] Orville Lorain Manning, age 42, b. 20 Feb 1876; res: Williamsburg, Clermont, OH; occ: farmer; relative: Margaret Manning; tall, slender, grey eyes & hair. Regis: 12 Sep 1918, Batavia, Clermont Co, OH.

Death: Orville L Manning, b. 1876; Residence: Clermont, OH; d. 27 Nov 1959, Christ Hospital, Cincinnati, Hamilton Co, OH. Age: 83; Married. Ohio Deaths, 1908-1932, 1938-1944, and 1958-2007 [Ancestry.com].

Notes for Margaret R. SPRAGUE #277
Death: Margaret R Manning, b. 1876; res: Clermont Co, OH; d. 14 Aug 1963, Clermont Co, OH, age: 87; widowed. Ohio Deaths, 1908-1932, 1938-1944, and 1958-2007 [Ancestry.com]

Notes for Ora Chasse MANNING #278
Census
- 1910 Williamsburg, Clermont, OH, p. 7B. Ora C Manning 30, farmer; Velma Manning 21; John Manning 1 6/12. All OH/OH/OH. m. 2 years.

1920 Williamsburg, Clermont, OH, p. 4a; Orie Manning 40, Velma 31, John 11, Glenn 9, Ruth 4 11/12. Orie a farmer, general farm. All OH/OH/OH

1930 not found

Military: World War I Draft Registration Cards, 1917-1918 [Ancestry.com] Ora Chase Manning, age 30, b. 7 Oct 1879; res: Bethel, Clermont, OH; farmer - Bethel, OH; relative: Velma Manning; height: 5' 10"; slender, blue eyes, brown hair; regis: 12 Sep 1918, Batavia, Clermont, OH.

Death: Ora C. Manning, b. 7 Oct 1879, OH; d. 22 Jun 1929, Bethel, Clermont Co, OH; age 59. widowed, wife: Lida. Parents: Charles Manning; Edith Riley. Buried: Bethel Cemetery 6/24/1939. Informant: Mrs Lida Manning, Bethel, OH. Ohio Deaths 1908-1953 <familysearch.org>

Notes for Velma PATTERSON #278s

Death: Velma Manning, b. 3 Aug 1889, OH; d. 13 Feb 1920, Bethel, Clermont Co, OH. age 31. Married, spouse: Ora. Parents: John Patterson; Nancy McClellan; Informant: Ora Manning, Bethel, OH. Buried: Bethel Cemetery 2/16/1920.OH <pilot.familysearch.org>

Notes for Lilla B. (Walker) JACOBS #278s2

Jones notes list name as Lilla (Lida?) B. (Walker) Jacobs

Marriage1: Lida B. Walker, b. 1879, Clermont to Alfonso C. Jacobs. Married: 7 Sep 1904, Clermont Co, OH. Bride's parents: Lewis Walker, Mahala Patten. Ohio Marriages, 1800-1958 <familysearch.org>

Notes for Iva Lou MANNING #279

Census

1900 Cincinnati Ward 22, Hamilton, OH, p. 2B. Miles Dell 22, Jun 1877, day labor; Iva R Dell 18, Sep 1881. Married 0 years; no children. Both OH/OH/OH.

1910 Williamsburg, Clermont, OH, p. 6B. Miles R Deel 32, farmer; Iva L Deel 28, 4 ch / 1 living; Dorcia Deel 3. Next to Orlando Manning, 39 - possible relation?

1920 Williamsburg, Clermont, OH, p. 4A. Miles R Deal 43, farmer; Iva Deal 38; Dorcia Deal 13; Marjorie Deal 8; Edna Deal 5; Charles Deal 3 8/12. Next to Orie & Velma Manning; Rolland Manning a few houses away.

1930 Williamsburg, Clermont, OH, p. 7A. Miles R Deal 52, surveyor - county; Iva L Deal 48; Dorcia A Deal 22, teacher - public school; Marjorie L Deal 18, packer - Medovine Co; Edna E Deal 16; Charles C Deal 13

Marriage: Miles R. Deel, b. 1875, Baywood, OH, Age: 25; to Iva L. Manning b. 1881, Baywood, OH, Age: 19; Marriage: 1 Apr 1900 Clermont, OH; Groom's parents: Collins S. Deel,: Ella Brocker; Bride's parents: Charles Manning; Elizabeth V. Riley. Ohio Marriages, 1800-1958 <pilot.familysearch.org>

Death: Iva L. Deal; b. 1882, res: Hamilton Co, OH; widow; d. 18 Sep 1969 in long term care, Cheviot, Hamilton Co, OH. age 87. Ohio Deaths, 1908-1932, 1938-1944, and 1958-2002 <ancestry.com>

Notes for Miles Robert DEEL #279s

In Jones notes: "I wrote you last summer and let you know about Miles R. Deel. I am the great-granddaughter of Miles. My grandmother is his daughter and she is still living.

I believe I told you the story of how Miles Deel changed his last name to Deal. Because he was a politician. So his children and wife were Deal. Miles and Iva had 6 children. Dorcia Deal born 1907 and died 1959; Marjorie Deal born 1912 and died 1997 Estell (a boy) born 1908 and died 1909; Charles Collins Deal born 1916 and died 1953 - he married Jewell Virginia (Smith) born 1917 and died 1996. Buried Bethel Cemetery, Clermont, Ohio. Sec, 10A, Lot 36, Grave 4 & 5. Mildred Deal born 1902 and died 1908 and then my grandmother. Miles Robert Deal's wife was IVA Lou Manning (not, Ina), Iva's parents, Charles W. Manning and Edith (Riley) Manning, are buried at Bethel Cemetery, Tate Twp, Clermont, OH, Sec. 9, Lot 78, Grave 1-5. Also, Walter Manning is buried there - Iva's brother. Melissa Great-granddaughter of Miles Robert Deal and Iva Lou (Manning) Deal, 5/1/2003.

Military: World War I Draft Registration, 1917-1918 Miles Robert Deel, Clermont Co, OH, b. 26 Jul 1877; age 41; farmer; tall, med build, blue eyes, brown hair. Nearest relative: Iva Deal. Sept 12, 1918, Batavia, OH.

Death: Miles Robert Deal, d. 29 Jun 1951, Williamsburg, Clermont, OH; b. 26 Jul 1878, OH. Father: Collins Deal; mother: Ella Bricker. Ohio Deaths 1908-1953 <pilot.familysearch.org>.

Notes for Chilton H. MANNING #280

Jones notes: "resided (1900) at Baywood"

Census

1910 Williamsburg, Clermont Co, OH, p 7B. Charles W Manning 54, farmer - gen. farm; Edith L 53, m. 31 yr, 7 ch/6 liv; Chilton H 27, farm labor; Walter 18, farm labor; Lowell 13; Raleigh 13.

1920 Tate, Clermont County, OH, p. 9A. Charles Manning 64, no occ; Edith 61; Chilton H 36, motorman - street railway; Walter 27 motorman - street railway;; Lewell 23, worker - rubber factory.

1930 Bethel, Clermont Co, OH, p. 1A. East St. Chilton Manning 47, carpenter - house, age 42 at marriage; Mary 26, age 21 at marriage; Elizabeth 1 10/12

Military: World War I Draft Registration Cards, 1917-1918 [Ancestry.com] Chilton Henry Manning, b.13 Feb 1883; res: Bethel, Clermont Co, OH; farmer; mother - Edith Manning; med height & build; grey eyes, brown hair. Regis: 7 Sep 1918, Batavia, Clermont Co, OH.

Death: Chilton H. Manning, b. 1883; male; residence: Clermont Co, OH; d. 3 Aug 1962, Bethesda Oak Hospital, Cincinnati, Hamilton Co, OH. Age: 79, married. Ohio Deaths, 1908-1932, 1938-1944, and 1958-2007 [Ancestry.com].

Notes for Mary Ann WISBY #280s

Census: 1910 Tate, Clermont, OH, p. 4B. Charles L Wisby 31, second laster - shoe factory; Ida A Wisby, 33, m. 7 years, 3 ch / 2 living; Mary A Wisby, 6; Willard R Wisby 1 11/12; Eliza A Wisby 72, mother, 6 ch/ 3 living. All OH/OH/OH.

No death information found

Notes for Raleigh Clark MANNING #284

Jones notes: "she resides (1972) at Bethel, OH"

Census

1920 Williamsburg, Clermont, OH, p. 4a. Rolland Manning 23, farmer, Hazel 19, May L. 1/12.

1930 Williamsburg, Clermont, OH, p. 7A. Raleigh C Manning 33; Hazel M Manning 29; Mary L Manning 10; Robert C Manning 8; Norma J Manning 2. Indexed Mannino on Ancestry.

Military: World War I Draft Registration Cards, 1917-1918 [Ancestry.com] Raleigh Manning, age 21, b. 14 Dec 1896, Bethel, OH; res: Bethel, Clermont, OH; farmer; relative: Charles Manning, Bethel; grey eyes, lt brown hair; other lines illegible.

Military: U.S. World War II Draft Registration Cards, 1942 [Ancestry.com] Raleigh Clark Manning, age 45, b. 14 Dec 1896, Clermont Co, OH; res: McMurchy St, Bethel, Clermont, OH; contact: Mrs. Hazel Manning, Bethel, OH. Self employed.

Notes for Hazel Marie BOICE #284s

Jones notes: "she resides (1972) at Bethel, OH"

Census: 1900 Tate, Clermont, OH, p. 4A. Charles C Boice 38, Sep 1861; Mary E Boice 36, Jun 1864; Myrtie M Boice 16, Apr 1884; Archie L Boice 8, Feb 1882; Flossie L Boice, age & date illegible; Hazle M Boice 0, Jun 1900.

1910 Tate, Clermont, OH, p. 1B. Charles C Boice 49, OH/OH/OH, janitor - sematory [sic]; Marry E Boice 46, OH/OH/Eng, 5 ch / 4 living, m. 27 years; Myrtie M Boice 26, watter - hottel [sic]; Archie S Boice 18, shoemaker - factory; Flossie Boice Sr. 18; Hazel M Boice 10. Children all b. OH.

Notes for Lowell Burns MANNING #285

Census
- 1920 Tate, Clermont County, OH, p. 9A. Charles Manning 64, no occ; Edith 61; Chilton H 36, motorman - street railway; Walter 27 motorman - street railway; Lewell 23, worker - rubber factory. [note - Lowell is enumerated in both Clermont & Summit Co, OH]
- 1920 Akron, Summit Co, OH, p. 20b. Lowell Manning 23, a single boarder, working in rubber factory.

Military: WW I Draft Registration: Lowell Burns Manning, RR2, Bethel, OH. B. 14 Dec 1896. Bethel OH. Contact: C. M. Manning, Bethel. Occ: farmer, self employed, age 21, blue eyes, Lt brown hair, no disability, 5 Jun 1918.

Military: Ohio Soldiers in WWI, 1917-1918 [Ancestry.com] Lowell B. Manning; Age: 22; Birth: 14 Dec 1896 Bethel, Ohio, USA; Enlistment: 27 Aug 1918, Batavia, OH; National Army. 159 Depot Brigade to Discharge Private Honorable discharge 21 Dec 1918.

Death: Lowell Burns Manning, d. 12 Jan 1925, Akron, Summit, OH; b. 14 Dec 1897, OH; Age: 27 years 28 days; Divorced; address: 643 Johnston; Occ: Rubber Worker - Goodyear; Burial: 13 Jan 1925, Bethel, OH; parents: Charles Manning, b. Ohio; Edith Riley, b. Ohio. Ohio Deaths, 1908-1953 <familysearch.org>

Discrepancy - Death record give birth as 1897; military records give 1896 as does the 1900 census

Notes for Pearl Diana FITZPATRICK #287

Death: gives "widowed", d. Jewish Hospital, Hamilton Co, OH, 7 Jan 1972. OH Deaths 1908-1932, 1938-1944, and 1958-2007 [Ancestry.com]

Death: SS Death Index: Pearl Wolf; b. 12 Dec 1882; d. Jan 1972; 45102 Amelia, Clermont, OH

Notes for Edward WOLF #287s

Census
- 1900 Batavia, Clermont, OH, p. 10A. Adam Wolf 65, Sep 1834, Germany, imm. 1868, na, farmer, m. 24 yrs.; Katherine Wolf 43, Jun 1850, Germany, imm 1870, 7 ch / 2 living; Edward Wolf 16, Sept 1883; *Illie Wolf 13, Jan 1887, children b. OH.
- 1920 Batavia, Clermont, OH, p. 9A. Adam Wolf 75, no occ.; Katharine Wolf 59; Edward Wolf 26, farm labor - home farm
- 1920 Batavia, Clermont, OH, p. 1A. Edward Wolf 37, farmer, OH/Ger/Ger; Pearl Wolf 37, OH/OH/IN; Charles E Wolf 9/12
- 1930 Batavia, Clermont, OH, p. 9B. Edward Wolf 46; Pearl Wolf 47; Charles Edward Wolf 11

Birth: (probably) Edward Wolf, b. 15 Sep 1883, Batavia Twp, Clermont, OH; Father: Adam Wolf; Mother: Katharine Miller. Ohio Births and Christenings, 1821-1962. <pilot.familysearch.org>

Military: World War I Draft Registration Cards, 1917-1918 [Ancestry.com] Edward Wolf, age 22 [38?], b. 15 Sep 1884; res: Amelia, Clermont, OH; farmer - self employed; contact: Pearl Diana Wolf, Amrlia; tall, med build, blue eyes, lt brown hair. Regis: 12 Sep 1918, Batavia, OH.

Death: SS Death index: Edward Wolf b. 07 Sep 1882; d. May 1976; Loveland, Clermont, OH.

Notes for John Charles FITZPATRICK #288

Jones notes: "resides (1973) at Amelia, OH; veterinarian"

Birth: John Charles Fitzpatrick; Male; b. 08 Oct 1888, Batavia Twp, Clermont, OH; parents: Jerome Homer Fitzpatrick; Susan Terebaugh. Ohio Births and Christenings, 1821-1962 <familysearch.org>

Discrepancy - Jones notes gave birth year as 1889.

Census
- 1920 Batavia, Clermont, OH, p. 5B. John C Fitzpatrick 31, doctor - veterian [sic]; Ella M Fitzpatrick 24. Both OH/OH/OH
- 1930 Batavia, Clermont, OH, District 3, p. 173. Homer Fitzpatrick, 78, farmer; Susan, 75, b. IN; Charles J, 44, son, widowed, veterinary surgeon; Wayne N, 8, grandson.

Military: World War I Draft Registration Cards, 1917-1918 [Ancestry.com] John Charles Fitzpatrick, b. 8 Oct 1889, Batavia, OH; veterinarian; married, res: Batavia, Clermont OH; medium height, slender, blue eyes, brown hair. Registered: Amelia, OH, 5 Jun 1917.

Death: SS Death Index gives: John Fitzpatrick, b. 8 Oct 1888; d. Aug 1973; age 84; Amelia, Clermont, OH; issued Ohio; #295-34-1570

Death: John C Fitzpatrick, b. 1889; res: Clermont Co, OH; d. 23 Aug 1973, Bethesda Oak Hospital, Cincinnati, OH; age 84; widowed. Ohio Deaths, 1908-1932, 1938-1944, and 1958-2007 [Ancestry.com]

Notes for Ella Marie NICHOLS #288s
Death: Ella Fitzpatrick, d. 29 May 1928, Cincinnati, Hamilton, OH; b. 12 Sep 1895, Batavia, OH; Age: 32 yrs 8 mo 17 da; married; Res: Amelia, OH; Burial: 2 Jun 1928 Batavia, OH; Spouse: J. C. Fitzpatrick; parents: Clayton B. Nichols, b. OH; Maude Hitch ,b. OH. Ohio Deaths, 1908-1953 <familysearch.org>
Discrepancy: Jones notes gave death as 30 May 1922; OH Death records give 29 May 1928.

Notes for Fannie L. BECKETT #288s2
Jones notes gave birth year as 1889. This date from death certificate.
Death: Fannie B. Fitzpatrick, b. 16 Jun 1888, OH; d. 30 Jun 1952, Amelia, Clermont, OH, age 64; former school teacher; parents: Harry Beckett / Lida Duckett. Ohio Deaths, 1908-1953 <familysearch.org>

Notes for Guy HIGGINS #289
Census
- 1900 Clanton, Chilton, AL, p. 4B. Guy Higgins 25, Dec 1874, OH/OH/OH, station agent - r.r.; Lizzie Higgins 23, Nov 1876, GA/GA/AL; John Burton Higgins 1, Aug 1898, AL/OH/GA; John P Fuller 61, f-in-law, widowed, GA/GA/GA.
- 1910 Precinct 4, Chilton, AL, p. 5B. Guy Higgins 36, manager - lumber company; Elizabeth L Higgins 34; John B Higgins 11; Sarah E Higgins 1; John P Fuller 72. m. 16 yrs, 2 children / 2 living
- 1920 not found

Military: WW I Draft Registration: Guy Higgins, age 43; Chilton, AL; b. 21 Dec 1874; occ: lumber manuf & farming; closest relative: wife, Elizabeth Higgins. Med. height; med build; grey eyes; brown hair. 9/12/1918.

Information: Tatman Family Tree on Ancestry.com has more information on this family - undocumented. Site owner, Alexander Tatman, gives Elizabeth's middle name as Linda; other children: infant b/d 1896; Guy Higgins, Jr. 1911-1913, Frances Cullen Higgins 1913-1979 (m. Clayton Bland 1901-1945); Paul Edward Koeppel 1908-1971 - living child w. Koeppel). Guy's death as 6 May 1951 in Clanton, Chilton Co, AL; Elizabeth's death as 1966 in Redding, Shasta Co, CA. Two other wives: Louise Donnaly - 1 child; Mary Davis - 3 children/ 2 living, son Guy Moore 1925 - 2005. Has photos.

Death: Guy Higgens, d. 05 Jun 1951, Clanton, Chilton, AL; Age: 76y 5m 14d; est. Birth date 1875; Father: Samuel O. Higgens; Mother: Sarah Ellen Fitzpatrick; Burial: Clanton, AL, 7 Jun 1951. Alabama Deaths, 1908-1974 <fsbeta.familysearch.org>

Notes for Frank HIGGINS #291
Jones notes: "resided at Deatsville, AL; RR telegrapher; lumber business late; buried in Old German Cemetery, Garden City, AL"
Census: Does not appear with family on census - probably one of the listed sons under a different name. The following records are possibilities, none are confirmed to be this Frank, but are likely based on age and locale.
Census:
   1900 Cooper, Chilton, AL, p. 8A. Frank Higgins 27, Oct 1872, no occ, AL/GA/-; Annie Higgins 18, Feb 1882, AL/AL/AL
   1920 Clanton, Chilton, AL, p. 4B. Frank F Higgins 47; Anie M Higgins 38; Inez Higgins 18; Glenn Higgins 17; Joe Higgins 15; Maury Higgins 12, son.
   1930 Clanton, Chilton, AL, p. 14A. Frank B Higgins 56, farmer, AL/AL/AL; Annie Higgins 46; Maury Higgins 21, son.
Marriage: B. F. Higgins, b. 1873, age 26; Bride: Annie White, b. 1881; Age: 18; Marriage: 6 Aug 1899, Chilton Co., Alabama
Military: [Possible]: World War I Draft Registration Cards, 1917-1918 [Ancestry.com] Robert Franklin Higgins, age 41, b. 6 Nov 1876; res: Birmingham, Jefferson Co, AL; occ: salesman & collector - Matthews & Lively; contact: Annie Higgins, wife; med height, slender, lt blue eyes; dk brown hair; regis: 12 Sep 1918, Birmingham.

Notes for Burton HIGGINS #292
Census
   1910 Birmingham Ward 15, Jefferson, AL, p. 19B. Burt Higgins 32, OH/OH/OH, dispatcher - railroad; Eula Higgins 30, AL/AL/AL, m. 11 year, 4 ch / 4 living; Frank Higgins 10; William Higgins 6; Mary Higgins 5; Elizabeth Higgins 2; William W Myrick 73, uncle, widowed, 2 child/ 2 living, no occ, AL/AL/AL. children b. AL
   1920 not found
   1930 Thorsby, Chilton, AL, p. 4A. Burton Higgins 52, farmer - general farm; Eula P Higgins 50; Guy L Higgins 17, salesman - newspapers; A Jack Higgins 12; Ellen C Rollinson 78, widow, mother in law, AL/SC/SC
Marriage: Burt Higgins to Eula P Myrick; Marriage Date: 24 May 1899; Elmore Co, AL. Alabama Marriage Collection, 1800-1969 [Ancestry.com]
Military: World War I Draft Registration Cards, 1917-1918 [Ancestry.com] Burt Higgins, age 41, b. 28 Aug 1877, res: Deatsville, Elmore Co, AL; farmer - self employed & railroad operator - Land? N. RR; relative: Eula Higgins. Med height; stout, blue eyes, brown hair; Regis: 12 Sep 1918, Elmore Co, AL.
Death: Burt Higgins, d. 21 Feb 1947, Thorsby, Chilton, AL; Age at death: 69y 5m 24d; est. birth: 1878; Spouse: Eula Higgins; Father: Samual O. Higgins; Mother: Sarah Ellen Fitzpatric. Alabama Deaths, 1908-1974 <fsbeta.familysearch.org>

Notes for Eula Pugh RAWLINSON #292
"Ella Pugh Rollison was the daughter of Frank B. Rollinson, who was killed by lightning. She was adopted by W. W. Myrick when she was 9. She had a twin sister." - from a granddaughter.
Death certificate of son Frank gives mother's name as maiden name as Rawlinson.
Death: Eula P Higgins, d. 11 Dec 1952; Chilton Co, AL. Alabama Deaths, 1908-59 [Ancestry.com]
Death: Eula Pugh Higgins, d. 11 Dec 1952 Thorsby, Chilton, AL; Age: 73y 24d; Est. Birth Date 1879; Father: Frank Rawlinson; Mother: Ellen C. Jackson. Alabama Deaths, 1908-1974 <familysearch.org>

Notes for William Zachary HIGGINS #294

Census: 1910 Birmingham Ward 12, Jefferson, AL, p. 19A. William Z Higgins 25, telegraph operator; Edith O Higgins 20; Lida France Higgins 11/12; m. 3 years.

1920 Birmingham, Jefferson, AL, p. 10B. William Z Higgins 34, AL/OH/OH, telegraph operator - railroad; Edith E Higgins 39; Leda B Higgins 10; William S Higgins 8; Virginia Higgins 6; Edith L Higgins 4 1/12 ; Edward N Higgins 10/12. Others AL/AL/AL

1930 Birmingham, Jefferson, AL, p. 45A. William Z Higgins 46, telegraph operator; Edith Higgins 50; Lyda F Higgins 20, technician - doctor's office; William Higgins 18; Virginia Higgins 16; Lucille Higgins 14; ____ ?Leroy? Higgins 4, son; __ne Higgins 9, dau

Military: World War I Draft Registration Cards, 1917-1918 [Ancestry.com] William Zachariah Higgins, age 34, b. 27 May 1884; res: Birmingham, Jefferson, AL; occ: railroad telegraph operator - Birmingham Terminal Co. Contact: Edith Elizabeth Higgins, wife; tall, med. build, brown eyes, dk brown hair; regis: 12 Sep 1918, Birmingham, AL.

Death: William Z. Higgins, d. 27 Feb 1973, Birmingham, Jefferson, AL; Age at Death: 88y; b. 27 May 1884, Decatur, Alabama; Widowed; father: Samuel O. Higgins; mother: Sarah Fitzpatrick. Alabama Deaths, 1908-1974 <fsbeta.familysearch.org>

Notes for Edith Elizabeth QUINN #294s

Death: Edith Elizabeth Higgins, d. 17 Jul 1958, Birmingham, Jefferson, AL; Age at Death: 77y; est. birth date 1881; parents: John V. Quinn; Martha Coffe. Alabama Deaths, 1908-1974 <familysearch.org>

Notes for Leroy HIGGINS #295

Census

1910 not found in Alabama

1920 Culman, Culman Co, AL, p. 7A. Leroy Higgens 33; Lillah Higgens 26; Pearry Higgens 5; Martha Higgens 2 1/12

1930 Birmingham, Jefferson, AL, p. 23A. Le Roy Higgins 44, AL/OH/OH, operator - telegraph office; Lelah Higgins 36, AL/AL/AL, m. age 20; C Pearce C Higgins 15; Martha F Higgins 12; William K Higgins 9. Children b. AL.

Marriage: Leroy Higgins, b. 1886, Age: 27; Bride: Lela Cobb, b. 1893; Age: 20; Marriage: 8 Nov 1913, Cullman Co, AL. Alabama Marriages, 1816-1957 <familysearch.org>

Military: World War I Draft Registration Cards, 1917-1918 [Ancestry.com] Lee Roy Higgins, age 32, b. 17 Feb 1886; res: Birmingham, Jefferson, AL; occ: telegrapher - Louisville & Nashville R. R.; contact: Lela Estelle Higgins, wife; Med height, slender, blue eyes, light hair; regis: Birmingham, 5 Sep 1918.

Death: Leroy Higgins, d. 20 Nov 1951, Birmingham, Jefferson, AL; Age: 65y; Est. Birth Date: 1886; parents: Samuel O. Higgins; Sara Ellen Fitzpatrick. Alabama Deaths, 1908-1974 <familysearch.org>

Notes for James Monroe HIGGINS #296

Census

1920 Blount Springs, Blount, AL, p. 15B. James M Higgins 29, AL/OH/OH, ticket agent - railroad; Jane Higgins 31, AL/OH/OH; Roy Higgins 7; James Higgins 5; Milton Higgins 3 2/12; Ruth Higgins 2 4/12. Children b. Alabama

1930 Blount Springs, Blount, AL, p. 1A. James M Higgins 40, station agent - railroad. age 22; Irene L Higgins 41, AL/AL/AL, m. age 23; Roy F Higgins 17; James M Higgins 16; Milton S Higgins 13; Ruth E Higgins 12; Eugene H Higgins 10; Morris W Higgins 8; Herman A Higgins 2 6/12; Lillian Dunman 17, niece. next to John R. Dunman, 47.

Military: World War I Draft Registration Cards, 1917-1918 [Ancestry.com] James Monroe Higgins, b. 24 Feb 1890 Garden City, Cullman, AL; age 27, telegraph operator - L.W. R. R. co. Married, wife & 3 children; tall, med build, gray eyes, dark hair. 6/5/1917 Cullman, AL.

Information from Linda Collins (Aug 2010) gives: Samuel Oliver Higgins and Sarah Ellen Fitzpatrick had the following children: #1. Guy Higgins b 1874; d 1951; #2. Claude E. Higgins b 1876; d 1893; #3. Burton (no middle name) Higgins b 1877 d 1947 (my great grandfather); #4. Frederick Allen Higgins b 1879; d 1882; #5. Rosalia Higgins b 1881; d 1882; #6. William Z. Higgins b 1884; #7. Lee Roy Higgins b 1886; #8. James Monroe Higgins b 1890; d 1971
Death: SS Death Index: James Higgins; b. 24 Feb 1890; d. Aug 1971; age 81; Thorsby, Chilton, AL; Long-time or retired railroad workers; #704-05-3540

Notes for Hanley FITZPATRICK #297
Death: Hanley Fitzpatrick, b. 25 May 1902; d. 30 July 1992, Clermont, Ohio; #402-26-3306; Issued: Kentucky. Social Security Death Index <rootsweb.com>

Notes for John Lee FITZPATRICK Jr #301
Census
  1910 Montgomery Ward 2, Montgomery, AL, p. 35A. J L Fitzpatrick 54, OH, real estate agent; Mrs M M Fitzpatrick 38; J L Fitzpatrick Jr 9, AL; H T Fitzpatrick 2, AL. 4 ch / 2 living.
  1920 not found
  1930 Montgomery, Montgomery, AL, p. 11B. John L Fitzpatrick 29, clerk - steam railroad, AL/OH/OH; Laverne Fitzpatrick 25, TX/AL/AL; Mary Fitzpatrick 5, AL/AL/TX
Military: John Lee Fitzpatrick, Jr, age 18; b. 28 Jul 1900, railroad clerk - Western of AL Railroad; nearest relative: John Lee Fitzpatrick, Mobile St, Montgomery, AL; medium height and build; brown hair and eyes. Regis: 12 Sep 1918, Montgomery, AL. WW I Draft Registration [Ancestry.com]
Death: John L. Fitzpatrick, d. 19 Jan 1957 Montgomery, Montgomery, AL; Age: 56y; Est. Birth Date: 1901; parents: John L. Fitzpatrick; Maggie Manning. Alabama Deaths, 1908-1974 <familysearch.org>

Notes for Mary Laverne TANKERSLEY #301s
Jones notes: "she resided (1973) at 3455 S. Perry St, Montgomery AL 36105; she d. 6/16/1964" Question - dates?

Notes for Homer Tatman FITZPATRICK #302
Census
  1910 Montgomery Ward 2, Montgomery, AL, p. 35A. J L Fitzpatrick 54, OH, real estate agent; Mrs M M Fitzpatrick 38; J L Fitzpatrick Jr 9, AL; H T Fitzpatrick 2, AL. 4 ch / 2 living.
  1920 not found
  1930 Montgomery, Montgomery, AL, p. 2A. Maggie Fitzpatrick 56, OH, widow; Hamer Fitzpatrick 27, single, AL/OH/OH, office clerk - railroad.
Death: Homer T. Fitzpatrick, d. 14 Mar 1971 Montgomery, Montgomery, AL; Age: 62y Est. Birth Date: 1909; Spouse: Mary L. Fitzpatrick; parents: John L. Fitzpatrick / Maggie Manning. Alabama Deaths, 1908-1974 <pilot.familysearch.org>

Notes for Jessie Lee DORRIS #302s
  Jones notes: "she resides (1973) at 3 Montview Ct, Montgomery AL 36105"

Notes for Daisy B. FITZPATRICK #303
Census
  1920 Batavia, Clermont, OH, p. 7A. John S Fitzpatrick 56, carpenter - house, OH/OH/AL; Leorna L Fitzpatrick 43; Galen A Fitzpatrick 18, sewing - coat factory; Zelphia Fitzpatrick 12; John Fitzpatrick 4 4/12 ; Daisy B Singler 19, dau, married; George Singler 1 2/12, nephew. Others OH/OH/OH. Daisy's husband Edwin Singler, 22, living with his parents Edward & Catherine in Monroe - married.
  1930 Cincinnati, Hamilton, OH, p. 2B. Edwin Singler 32, tinner - building; Daisy Singler 30; George Singler 10; Anthony Singler 9; Gladys Singler 7; Donald Singler 4 7/12; Charles Singler 2 11/12

Marriage: Edwin Singler, b. 1897, age 21; Bride: Daisy Fitzpatrick, b. 1897, age 21. Marriage: 7 Jun 1918, Newport, Campbell, KY; Parents of groom: Edward Singler; Katherine Singler; parents of bride Sherman Fitzpatrick; Len... Fitzpatrick; both single. Kentucky Marriages, 1785-1979 <familysearch.org>
Death: Ohio Deaths <ancestry.com> gives death date 25 May 1964, married, died in Clermont Co, OH.

Notes for Edwin Joseph SINGLER
Military: World War I Draft Registration Cards, 1917-1918 [Ancestry.com] Edwin Joseph Singler, b. 20 Dec 1897; res: New Richmond, Clermont, OH; occ: farmer; contact: Edward Singler, New Richmond; tall, stout, blue eyes, brown hair; resis: 12 Sep 1918, Batavia, Clermont, OH.
Death: Ohio Deaths <ancestry.com> gives death date 12 Aug 1966, widowed, d. in Clermont Co, OH.

Notes for John Franklin TATMAN #310
Military: WWI Draft Registration [Ancestry.com] John Franklin Tatman, age 33, b. 1 Mar 1885, farmer - William Tatman, tall, slender, blue eyes, brown hair, registered Sept 1918.
Census
  1920 Monroe, Clermont, OH, p. 3A. Frank Tatman 34, farmer; Anna Tatman 35; Durwood Tatman 2/12
  1930 Monroe, Clermont, OH, p. 4A. Frank J Tatman 45, farmer; Anna R Tatman 45; W Durwood Tatman 10; Mary Simmons 81, widowed, mother in law. All OH/OH/OH
Marriage: John Franklin Tatman, b. 1885 Salt Air, Clermont, OH, age 25; bride: Anna Rebecca Simmons, b. 1885, Laurel, OH, age 24. m. 25 May 1910, Clermont, OH. Groom's parents: William W. Tatman; Alice Taylor; Bride's parents: William D. Simmons & Mary Elizabeth Allen. Both single. <familysearch.org>

Notes for Anna Rebecca SIMMONS #310s
  Census 1910 Monroe, Clermont, OH, p. 5B. William D Simmons 70; Mary E Simmons 62; Anna R Simmons 25, single, teacher - rural school.

Notes for Glen O'Hara SWING
Jones notes: "Superintendent of Schools, Covington, KY"
Census
  1920 Covington Ward 6, Kenton, KY, p. 7B. Glenn Swing 30, OH/OH/OH, engineer - elec?___; Linda Swing 28, KY/OH/IA; Kenneth Swing 11/12, OH.
  1930 Covington Ward 6, Kenton, KY, p. 17B. Glenn O Swing 40, teacher - school; Linda Swing 39; Kenneth E Swing 10, OH; Margurite R Swing 5, KY
Military: WWI Draft Registration [Ancestry.com] Glenn Ohara Swing, age 27, b. 9 Dec 1889, Bethel, OH; Occ: Student Instructor in Math (M. A. 17), Ohio State Univ, Columbus, OH. Single. Military: Student Cadet, Infantry, OSU. Med height, stout, grey eyes, black hair. Reg: Jun 1917.
Military: World War 1 - 5 Obsn Battery Field Artillery Central Officer' Training School 1918; discharge 4 Dec 1918 to accept Commission. Enlisted 12 Aug 1918, Batavia, OH.
Death: Glenn O Swing; **Death**: 14 Nov 1962, Kenton Co, Age: 72; Residence: Kenton. Kentucky Death Index, 1911-2000 [Ancestry.com]

Notes for Linda COUREY
Death: *Linda C Swing, 2 Dec 1964; Campbell Co, KY; Age: 73; Residence: Campbell Co. KY Death Index, 1911-2000 [Ancestry.com]   *may not be right person, but name is right and age is close

Notes for Phillip B. SWING #314
Jones notes: "Resided (1973) at19101 Van Aken Blvd, Shaker Hgts, OH; US Army WW I"
Jones notes: "not married". I believe this is wrong...based on 1930 census and family trees online.

Military: WWI Draft Registration [Ancestry.com] Phillip C. Swing, b. 16 Aug 1897, Bethel, OH; Employer: William J. Swing, RR 3, Bethel. Single. Med height, medium build, grey eyes, light hair. Registered Jun 1918

Military: World War 1 - 3 Ambulance Co, Ypres-Lys; Meuse-Argonne, American Expeditionary Forces 1918-1919. Enlisted 12 May 1917, Cincinnati, OH.

Census
  1920 Tate, Clermont Co, OH, p. 5A. Clifford J Swing 62, farmer - general farm; Mary R Swing 61; Edna B Swing 28; Phil B Swing 24, school teacher - public school; John C Swing 20, rubber worker - factory.
  1930 Lakewood, Cuyahoga, OH, p. 9B. Phillip B Swing 35, treasurer - coal company; Julia E Swing 27; Mary Louise Swing 5 6/12; Katherine Swing 3 9/12.

Notes for Julia PAGE #314s
SS Death Index gives Julia Swing, b. 02 May 1902 d. Mar 1982 44122, Beachwood, Cuyahoga, OH.

Notes for John Charles SWING #315
Jones notes: "Resides (1973) at 6375 Evergreen Dr, Independence OH 44131"
Birth: John Charles Swing, b. 10 Apr 1899; parents: Clifford John Swing; Mary R. Talanan. Ohio Births and Christenings, 1821-1962 <familysearch.org.>
Military: WWI Draft Registration [Ancestry.com] John Charles Swing, New Richmond, OH. age 19, b. Apr 10, 1899, farming - partnership with father, New Richmond OH. Nearest relative: Clifford Swing. Tall, slender, blue eyes, brown hair. Registered Sept 1918.
Census: 1930 Lakewood, Cuyahoga, OH, p. 4B. John C Swing 30, messenger - express company, OH/OH/OH, m. age 25; Gladys Swing 29.
Marriage: Marriage date based on age at marriage listed in 1930 census .

Notes for Gladys wife of John C. SWING #315s
No other information found.

Notes for Charles Harrison TAYLOR #317
Jones notes: "US Army WW I, 330 Infantry; she resides (1973) at 250 E. Plane St, Bethel, OH"
Military: WWI Draft Registration [Ancestry.com] Charles Harrison Taylor, age 28, b. Aug 1, 1888, Bethel, OH; farmer, self employed; single, military service: private, Co K, 1 Reg, state of Ohio, 3 years. med height; slender build, lt blue eyes, lt brown hair. Registered 5 Jun 1917.
Military Service: World War I - Co D 330 Infantry to Discharge; Private, first class - 5 Dec 1917; Corporal - 2 Feb 1918; Sergeant - 16 Nov 1918. American Expeditionary Forces - 12 June 1918 to 30 Jan 1919. Honorable discharge - 13 Feb 1919.
Census: 1930 Tate, Clermont, OH, p. 7B. Archie Taylor 34, farmer; Charles Taylor 42, brother, salesman - automobile. Both single.
Death: Charles H Taylor, b. 1889; res: Clermont Co, OH; d. 12 Feb 1970, Brown Co, OH; age 81; married. Ohio Deaths, 1908-1932, 1938-1944, and 1958-2007 [Ancestry.com]

Notes for Gladys A. PAELTZ #317
Jones notes: " she resides (1973) at 250 E. Plane St, Bethel, OH"
Census: 1900 North Washington, Clermont, OH, p. 5A. Charlie J Paeltz 38, OH/Ger/Ger, farmer; Emma L Paeltz 37; Minnie Paeltz 11; Louise Paeltz 8; Gladdis Paeltz 6, Aug 1893; Neomi Paeltz 4. Others OH/OH/OH.
Death: Gladys Armilda Taylor, b. 6 Aug 1893, OH; res: Clermont Co, OH; d. 16 Jan 1992, Brown Co, OH; Father's Surname: Paeltz; Mother's Maiden Name: Gates; Widowed; Education: 12; Industry of Decedent: Elementary and secondary schools - Bookkeepers, accounting, and auditing clerks. Ohio Deaths, 1908-1932, 1938-1944, and 1958-2007 [Ancestry.com]

Notes for Alice B. TAYLOR #319

Estel's death certificate gives wife as Alice Crane Beck... 2nd marriage?

Census:
- 1920 Tate, Clermont, OH, p. 6B. John H Taylor 63, widowed, no occ; Goldie L 33, no occ; Charles H 31, farmer; Howard T 29, farmer; Alice B Crane 26, dau, divorced; Agnes C Crane 7, grdau; Archie Mc 24, fireman - railroad; George R 21, rubber worker - factory; John K 17
- 1930 Bethel, Clermont, OH, p. 2A. Estel J Beck 48, inspector - pub. highway, m age 24; Alice Beck 37, m. age 37; Charles H Beck 17, son; Julia Beck 16, dau; Agnes Crane 18, step daughter. All OH/OH/OH.

Death: Alice Newkirk, b. 25 Mar 1892, OH; d. 15 Sep 1944, Bethel, Clermont Co, OH; married, housewife. Spouse Mack E. Newkirk; father John H. Taylor; mother Maude Tatman; both parents b. OH; burial 17 Sep 1944, Bethel, OH. OH Death Index 1908-1953 <pilot.familysearch.org>

Notes for Forest Theis CRANE #319s1

Census:
- 1900 Tate, Clermont, OH, p. 1B. George Crane 61; Maranda Crane 57; Wiley E Crane 31, son, widow; Cortland C Crane 24, son; Forest T Crane 6, grandson; Birtha R Crane 4, granddau.
- 1910 Tate, Clermont, OH, p. 2B. Wiley E Crane 41, widowed, farmer, Forest T Crane 16, son; Jonnie Marshall 31, boarder; Mannie Marshall 28; Gailon Marshall 4

Military: World War I Draft Registration Cards, 1917-1918 [Ancestry.com] Forrest Theis Crane, age 23, b. 21 Jan 1894, Bethel, OH; clerk - Fay Egan Co, Scioto, OH; married, tall, medium, blue eyes, d. brown hair. Regis 5 Jun 1917, Cincinnati, Hamilton, OH

Marriage: Marriage record in 1911 give his age as 18. Parents W. E. Crane & Lena Theis. Marriage date 19 Jul 1911, Hamilton, OH

Birth: Ohio Births & Christenings 1821-1962 gives Forest Theis Crane; birth date 21 Jan 1893, parents: Wilen Ellsworth Crane; Lena Thies.

Notes for Estel Rosco BECK #319s2

Military: WW I Draft Registration (Ancestry.com) shows middle name Rosco, b. 16 Mar 1882, Bethel, OH; Age 36; Occupation: ___ Feed Dealer [self employed]; nearest relation: Hannah Louise Beck, Bethel, OH; medium height, small build, brown hair & eyes. Registered Sept 12, 1918 in Batavia, OH.

Census
- 1900 Tate, Clermont, Ohio, p. 13A. Horace Beck 62,7/1837, m. 19 yrs, insurance agent;, OH/OH/NJ; Phebe J Beck 47, 8/1852, 4 ch/3 living, IN/OH/IN; Estel P Beck 18, 3/1882, at school; Angie C Beck 16, 6/1883; Clara E Beck 15 3/1885; Walter Rader 20, boarder, 4/1880, VA/VA/VA, works in shoe factory
- 1910, Tate, Clermont, OH, p. 11A. Estel Beck 28, insurance agent, m. 4 years; Louise 23, no children.
- 1920, Tate, Clermont, OH, p. 13B. Shows Estel R. Beck, 37, OH/OH/IN; merchant - coal & feed; Louise R. 32; Charles H. 7; Julia R. 6.
- 1930 Bethel, Clermont, OH, p. 2A. Estel J Beck 48, inspector - pub. highway; Alice 37, Charles H 17; Julia 16; Agnes Crane 18, step dau.

Death: Death certificate gives name of wife as Alice Crane Beck; parents as Horace Beck and __Winterrode. Occupation: State Highway. Cause of death: gunshot wound in head - suicide

Notes for Malcolm NEWKIRK #319s3

Census
- 1900 Butler, Pendleton, KY, p. 8B. James Newkirk 37, Jan 1863, KY, farmer; Nannie Newkirk 34, May 1866, KY; Edith Newkirk 14; Maysel Newkirk 10; Malcum Newkirk 8, Mar 1892, KY; Elizabeth Newkirk 6. All KY/KY/KY

1930 Rushville, Rush, IN, p. 20B. Malcom Newkirk 38, KY/KY/KY, cabinet maker - furniture factory, m. age 21; Nora Newkirk 37, KY/KY/KY; James Newkirk 15, IN; Charles Newkirk 10, IN

Marriage: Malcolm Newkirk, b. 3 Mar 1892, KY; res: Rush Co, IN, parents: James Newkirk; Nanney Boner; bride: Nora Bates, b. 7 Jul 1892, KY, res: Rush, IN; parents: Chas. L. Bates; Barbara Kemper; marriage: 12 Jun 1913, Rush Co, IN. Indiana Marriages, 1811-1959. <www.familysearch.org>

Military: World War I Draft Registration Cards, 1917-1918 [Ancestry.com] Malcon Newkirk, age 25, b. 3 Mar 1892, Butler, KY; res: Rushville, Rush Co, IN; laborer - Innes Pearce & Co, married; dependents: wife & child; med height & build, blue eyes, lt brown hair. Regis: Rushville, Rush Co, IN, 5 Jun 1917.

Death: no death information found; this date from Jones notes.

Birthplace: Jones notes gave birthplace as Falmouth, KY.

Notes for George Richard TAYLOR #321

Jones notes: "Resided at Akron, OH"

Military: WWI Draft Registration [Ancestry.com]: George Richard Taylor, age 20, b. 28 May 1898, farmer - John Taylor, Bethel, OH. Med height, med. build, grey eyes, brown hair. Registered 1918. Registrar: Phillip C. Swing.

Census:

1920 Tate, Clermont, OH, p. 6B. John H Taylor 63, widowed, no occ; Goldie L 33, no occ; Charles H 31, farmer; Howard T 29, farmer; Alice B Crane 26, dau, divorced; Agnes C Crane 7, grdau; Archie Mc 24, fireman - railroad; George R 21, rubber worker - factory; John K 1

1930 Akron, Summit, OH, p. 11B. George R Taylor 31, president - automobile, m. age 28; Esther E Taylor 27; Patricia A Taylor 1 3/12; John K Taylor 27, brother, salesman - automobile, single. Esther's mother b. PA; others all OH.

Death: George R Taylor, b. 1899; res: Akron, Summit Co, OH; d. 11 Feb 1967 Akron, OH; age 68; married. Ohio Deaths, 1908-1932, 1938-1944, and 1958-2007 [Ancestry.com]

Notes for Esther E. STEPHENS #321s

Death: Esther E Taylor, b. 1903; res: Akron, Summit, OH; d. 22 Feb 1965, Akron, OH, age 62; married. Ohio Deaths, 1908-1932, 1938-1944, and 1958-2007 [Ancestry.com]

Notes for John Kenneth TAYLOR #322

Jones notes: "Resides (1973) at 14404 Sarabande Way, Sun City AZ 85351"

Census: 1930 Akron, Summit, OH, p. 11B. George R Taylor 31, president - automobile, m. age 28; Esther E Taylor 27; Patricia A Taylor 1 3/12; John K Taylor 27, brother, salesman - automobile. single; Esther's mother b. PA; others all OH.

Death: no death information found.

Notes for Grace ORR #322s

Census: 1910 Attleborough, Bristol, MA, p. 14A. Charles F Orr 38, proprietor - dye house; Laura Orr 35; Blache Orr 10; Charlie F Orr 5; Grace Orr 1 2/12, MA/MA/Can

Death: Grace Orr Taylor, d. 18 Nov 2003, age 94, Fairlawn, Summit Co, OH; b. 18 Jan 1909. Father's Surname: Orr; Mother's Maiden Name: Brien; Widowed; Education: 4 years college. Ohio Deaths, 1908-1932, 1938-1944, and 1958-2007 [Ancestry.com]

Notes for Carlos Stanley HUTSON #328

Census:
- 1920 Van Buren, Montgomery, OH, p. 21A. Carlos S Hutson 25, stockman - cash register co; Blanche Hutson 21, wife; Dora Hutson 52, mother; Charles W Hutson 58, father, coal dealer; Alberta Hutson 28, wife [does he really have two wives?]
- 1930 Amelia, Clermont, OH, p. 2B. Carlos Hutson 34, restaurant - confectionery; Blanche Hutson 32; Ruth Hutson 5, dau; Alice Hutson 3, dau; Charles Hutson 70, father, laborer; Ladora Hutson 68, mother. All b. OH

Birth: Carlos Stanley Hutson b. 04 Jul 1895; Father: Charles Wilber Hutson. Ohio Births and Christenings, 1821-1962 <pilot.familysearch.org>

Military: World War I Draft Registration Cards, 1917-1918 [Ancestry.com] Carlos Stanley Hutson, age 22, b. 4 Jul 1895, Amelia, OH; res: Amelia, Clermont, OH; occ: Real estate agent - self employed, Cincinnati, OH; single; small, slender, brown eyes, black hair; regis: 5 Jun 1917, Amelia, OH.

Death: Carlos S Hutson, b. 1896; Res: Clermont Co, OH; d. 30 Jan 1973, Mercy Hosp Anderson, Hamilton County, OH. age 77, married. Ohio Deaths, 1908-1932, 1938-1944, and 1958-2007 [Ancestry.com]

Notes for Blanche HENDRIXSON #328s

Census: 1900 Cincinnati Ward 22, Hamilton, OH, p. 7B. Charles Hendrixson 24, Apr 1876, TX/TX/TX, machinist; Minnie Hendrixson 23, Jan 1877, OH/Ger/MO; Allice Hendrixson 4, Feb 1896; Blanch Hendrixson 2. Mar 1898; Clark Hendrixson 0/12, Mar 1900.

Marriage: Ohio Marriage records <pilot.familysearch.org> for Blanche & Carlos Hutson gives her parents as Chas. F. Hendrixson and Minnie Solwall

Residence: Jones notes: "she resides (1973) at 10 Hopkins, Amelia, OH"

Death: Blanche Hutson, b. 1898; res: Clermont Co, OH; d. 28 May 1973, Mercy Hosp Anderson, Hamilton Co, OH; age 75; widowed. Ohio Deaths, 1908-1932, 1938-1944, and 1958-2007 [Ancestry.com]

Notes for Estrella HUTSON #329

Marriage: Samuel H. Glover, b. 1875, Cincinnati, age 28; Bride: Estella L. Hutson b. 1884, Clermont Co, age 19; married: 18 Jan 1903, Clermont, Ohio. Groom's parents: Samuel Glover; Elizabeth Roush; Bride's parents: John Hutson; Ora Tatman; both single. Ohio Marriages, 1800-1958 <pilot.familysearch.org>

Census
- 1910 Pierce, Clermont, OH, p. 1A. Samuel H Glover 30, OH/IL/OH, painter - house; Estella L Glover 26; Samuel H Glover 7; Mary E Glover 6; Julia E Glover 4; Dartha H Glover 2
- 1920 Amelia, Clermont, OH, p. 1B. Samuel H Glover 40, carpenter - house; Estella L Glover 36; Hodgson J Glover 16; Elsie Julia Glover 13; Dorothy H Glover 12; Charles Lee Glover 9
- 1930 Amelia, Clermont, OH, p. 2A. Samuel Glover 51, meat cutter - butcher shop; Estella Glover 46; Dorothy Glover 21, teacher - public school; Charles Glover 19, foreman - pottery; Mary Coate 21, boarder, teacher - public school.

Notes for Samuel GLOVER #329s

Jones notes: "42nd OH Vol. Infantry, Spanish War - Bugler"

Military: not found on WW I Draft registration - possibly exempt because of Spanish War Service?

Death: Samuel H. Glover, d. 22 Dec 1930, Amelia, Clermont, OH; b. 18 Feb 1879 OH; age: 51 yrs 10 mo 4 da; married; occ: Meat Cutter; burial: 24 Dec 1930, Amelia, OH. Spouse: Stella Glover; parents: Samuel H. Glover, b. IL; Sarah E. Rousch, b. OH. Ohio Deaths, 1908-1953 <pilot.familysearch.org>

Notes for William Oliver HUTSON #331

Marriage: William O. Hutson, b. 1886 Amelia, Ohio, Age: 23; bride: Imo Ferree, b. 1891, Williamsburg; age 18; Marriage Date: 14 Sep 1909 Clermont, OH; Groom's Father: John F. Hutson; Mother: Arra Tatman. Ohio Marriages, 1800-1958 <pilot.familysearch.org>

Census
- 1910 Batavia, Clermont, OH, p. 2A. William Hutto 23, retail merchant - groceries; Imo Hutto 18. Both OH/OH/OH
- 1920 Amelia, Clermont, OH, p. 1A. William O Hutson 32, agent - real estate; Imo Hutson 28; Jennie May Hutson 7. Next to David Hutson, 68, merchant grocery store, Effie, 42, dau, single.
- 1930 Amelia, Clermont, OH, p. 3A. William Hutson 43, broker - real estate; Imo Hutson 38; Jennymae Hutson 17

Military: World War I Draft Registration Cards, 1917-1918 [Ancestry.com] William Oliver Hutson, age 30, b. 14 Mar 1887, Amelia, OH; res: Amelia, Clermont, OH; occ: real estate agent - self employed, Cincinnati, OH; dependents - wife and child; short, slender, brown eyes, dk brown hair; regis: 5 Jun 1917, Amelia, OH

Death: no death information found

Notes for Imo FERRIE #331s

Death: no death information found

Notes for Gladys E. HUTSON #332

Birth: Gladys Hutson b. 17 Dec 1888, Batavia Twp, Clermont, Ohio; Father: John Hutson; mother: Annie Tatman. Ohio Births and Christenings, 1821-1962 <familysearch.org>

Census
- 1920 Tate, Clermont, OH, p. 10B. Clifford Myrick 30, teacher - public school; Gladys Myrick 31; Kenneth Myrick 4 11/12. All OH/OH/OH.
- 1930 Amelia, Clermont, OH, p. 1A. Clifford Myrick 41, butcher - meat market; Gladys Myrick 41; Kenneth Myrick 15

Death: Gladys E. Myrick, d. 19 Aug 1945, Amelia, Clermont, OH; b. 17 Nov 1888, Amelia, OH; Age: 56 years 9 months 2 days; widowed; occ: school teacher; spouse: Clifford Myrick; father: John F. Hutson; Mother: Arra Tatman; burial: Mt Mariah. Ohio Deaths, 1908-1953 <fsbeta.familysearch.org>

Notes for Clifford Behymer MYRICK #332s

Census: 1900 Monroe, Clermont, OH, p. 2A. Enoch Myrick 51, Dec 1848, farmer; Hariet Myrick 51, July 1848, 4 ch/ 2 living, m. 23 yrs; Merta Myrick 21, Mar 1879, school teacher; Clifford Myrick 11, Mar 1889, OH/OH/OH

Military: World War I Draft Registration Cards, 1917-1918 [Ancestry.com] Clifford Behymer Myrick, age 28, b. 11 Mar 1889, Mt Holly, OH; res: Mt Holly, Clermont Co, OH; occ: farmer; dependents: wife & child; med height & build, blue eyes, brown hair; reg: 5 Jun 1917, Clermont Co, OH.

Death: Clifford Myrick, d. 23 Apr 1930, Cincinnati, Hamilton, OH; Est. Birth Year 1889; Age 41 years 1 month 12 days; Married; occ: butcher; Spouse: Gladys Myrick; parents: Enoch Myrick; Harriet Behymer. Ohio Deaths, 1908-1953 <fsbeta.familysearch.org>

Notes for Ethel G. TAYLOR #334

Census:
- 1920 Monroe, Clermont, OH, p. 2B. Elmer Taylor 54, farmer; Calla Taylor 50; Lella M Taylor 22, dau; Fred T Witschzger 24, son in law, farmer; Ethel G Witschzger 24, dau; Lela Eleanor Witschzger 1, gr dau. All b. OH.

1930 Cincinnati, Hamilton, OH, p. 21B. Frederick T Witschger 34, manager - grocery store; Ethel Witschger 34; Lela E Witschger 11; Alice L Witschger 7.

Death: Ethel Witschger, b. 1895; res: Hamilton Co, OH; d. 30 Nov 1969, Bethesda Oak Hospital, Cincinnati, OH; age 74; married. Ohio Deaths, 1908-1932, 1938-1944, and 1958-2007 [Ancestry.com]

Notes for Frederick Thurman WITSCHGER #334s

Military: World War I Draft Registration Cards, 1917-1918 [Ancestry.com] Fred Thurman Witschger, age 21, b. 13 Nov 1895; Cincinnati, OH; res: Moscow, Clermont, OH; occ: farmer; exemptions: wife & food producer; Med height & build, blue eyes, brown hair. Regis: Moscow, Clermont Co, OH, 5 Jun ___

Death: Fred P Witschger, b. 13 Nov 1895, Cincinnati, OH; d. 29 Nov 1996, Clark Co, OH; age 101; father: Witschger; mother: Frazier; widowed, machinist - printing industry. Ohio Deaths, 1908-1932, 1938-1944, and 1958-2007 [Ancestry.com]

Notes for Lloyd Edwin MCNAIR #336

Jones notes: "killed in a tractor accident 10/23/1951, bur. Burg. [Williamsburg?]; she resides (1973) at 180 3rd, Williamsburg"

Discrepancy: Jones notes give death as 10/23/1951 - OH Death Records give 19 Oct 1951.

Birth: Lloyd E. Mcnair; Male; 24 May 1900; Father: Edwin Mcnair; Mother: Stella Lloyd. Ohio Births and Christenings, 1821-1962 <pilot.familysearch.org>

Census: 1930 Williamsburg, Clermont, OH, p. 11A. Lloyd E Mcnair 29, proprietor - Insurance agency; Irene C Mcnair 29; Betty J Mcnair 3 6/12; Lois E Mcnair 11/12

Death: Lloyd E. Mcnair b. 24 May 1900 Ohio; d. 19 Oct 1951 Cincinnati, Hamilton, OH; Death Age: 51 years; Father: Edw. Mcnair; Mother: Stella Lloyd. Ohio Deaths, 1908-1953 <familysearch.org>

Notes for Irene Caroline BECKTOLD #336s

Jones notes: "she resides (1973) at 180 3rd, Williamsburg"

Notes for Hugh Elijah NORRIS #337

Jones notes: "resides (1973) at 1108 Burkhardt Av, Akron, OH 44301; printer"; Jones notes did not have birth or death info on Hugh.

Birth & death date and place are from Social Security Death index and Ohio Death Index.

Census: 1920, Akron, Summit, OH,. Hugh Norris, 21, lodger, co__sitor, Printing Co.

1930 Akron, Summit, OH, p. 48A. Hugh L Norris 31, OH/Sco/OH, printer - Print shop; Carrie L Norris 33, PA/PA/PA; Robert H Norris 3; Fannie Norris 66,OH/OH/OH, mother; William Norris 68, father, Sco/Sco/Sco, imm. 1897, naturalized, no occ.

Military: WW I Draft registration gives name as Hugh Elijah Norris, age 19. Confirms birth date; living on W. 7th St, Cincinnati (Hamilton) OH. Occupation: printer, Woodrow Printing Co; Nearest relative: Nell E. Norris, same address. Medium height, slender build, black hair, brown eyes. Registered Sept 1918.

Death: Hugh Elijah Norris; b. 4 Jan 1899, Clermont, OH. d. 6 Aug 1994, Long-Term Care Facilities, Akron, Summit Co, OH. Age: 95; Widowed; Education: 10; Occ: Printing press operators - Newspaper publishing and printing. Ohio Deaths, 1908-1932, 1938-1944, and 1958-2002 [Ancestry.com]

Notes for Carrie L. wife of Hugh E NORRIS #337s

Not found on Ohio Death Index 1908-1953 <pilot.familysearch.org>

Death: Carrie L Norris, b. 1896; Res: Cuyahoga Falls, Summit Co, OH. d. 23 Aug 1977, Cuyahoga Falls, Summit Co, OH. Age: 81; Married. Ohio Deaths, 1908-1932, 1938-1944, and 1958-2002 [Ancestry.com]

Notes for Phillip T. DURHAM #339
Jones notes: "resides (1974) at 1814 St Andrews Blvd, Panama City, FL 32401; retired Lt Col - Chaplain; Christian Church Preacher"
Death: SS Death Index gives: Philip T Durham; b. 31 Dec 1911; 16 Sep 2008; age 96; Portland, Jay, IN; card issued: Washington; #531-16-2261

Notes for Gretchen BURNGROVER #339s
Death: Gretchen B. Durham; b. 03 Nov 1916; d. 16 Sep 2006; age 89; Portland, Jay Co, IN; card issued: Colorado. Social Security Death Index
Obituary: Gretchen L. Durham, 89. Portland - *Gretchen Lucille Durham, 89, passed away Saturday, September 16, 2006.* Star Press, Muncie, IN [Ancestry.com]

Notes for Hattie Edna HICKS #343
Jones notes: gives first name as Myrtle; "resided at Felicity"
Photocopy of photo of her in my files (poor copy, in group of four girls - others unidentified)
Marriage: Not married in 1910 census; signs her father's death certificate in 1934 as "Edna Hite."
Census
   1910 Felicity, Clermont, OH (pg. 42) Orestes D. Hicks 58, no occ, OH/OH/KY; Edna 32, Evangelist - singer, OH/OH/KY (Orestes a widower, Edna is single)
   1920 Franklin, Clermont, OH, p. 9B. Charles Hite 51, salesman - grocery store; Edna Hite 42; Orestus Hicks 68, father, widowed, merchant - grocery store, OH/OH/KY; Elizabeth Hite 6, dau.
   1930 Felicity, Clermont, OH, p. 1A. Orestes D Hicks 78, widowed, merchant - notions; Edna S Hite 52, widow, teacher - music; Elizabeth S Hite 15
Discrepancy: Death certificate gives name as Edna S; Jones notes gives name as Hattie Edna. He may have had her mixed up with her mother Hattie.
Occupation: Evangelist, singer (1910 census)
Notes from Lvera (Jennings) Seipelt 1998 list "Edna Hite deceased 1938. Child: Elizabeth Fugatt Poston (Deceased 1980's); Children: Nancy Wilson, Patricia Schwartz, Kenneth Poston"
Death: Edna S. Hite; d. 24 Sep 1938 Felicity, Clermont, OH; Birth: 13 Sep 1877 Ohio; Age: 61 years 11 days; widowed; Occ: At Home; Res: Felicity, O.; Burial: 27 Sep 1938, Felicity, OH; Spouse: Chas. B. Hite; parents: O. D. Hicks b. OH; Hattie Stuart b. OH. Ohio Deaths 1908-1953 <pilot.familysearch.org>

Notes for Charles Bodman HITE #343s
Jones notes: "9th child of James and Elizabeth (Dugan) Hite"
Death: Chas. Bodman Hite; d. 21 Dec 1925, Felicity, Clermont, OH; b. 11 May 1867, Higginsport, OH; age: 58 yrs 7 mo 10 da; Occ: Merchant; Bur: 23 Dec 1925, Felicity, O. Spouse: Edna S. Hite; parents: James M. Hite, b. VA; Elizabeth Dugan, b. OH. Ohio Deaths 1908-1953 <familysearch.org>

Notes for Hurdes Beeker HICKS #345
Jones notes. "m1 to Bessie Marie Rogers at Augusta KY; div 1938; m2 to Susan Ann Dugan. Bessie d. 1977, bur at Chilo Cemetery Resided (1971) at Rural, OH."
Birth, marriage, death information from Lvera Seipelt, dau of his sister Elizabeth.
Photocopy of photo of him in my files.
Census
   1920, Franklin South, Clermont Co, OH., p. 4. Hurdus Hicks, 21, M . OH/OH/OH, laborer. Bessie , wife, 20, OH/OH/OH. next to Frank Hicks; Johnnie Hicks.
   1930 Franklin South, Clermont Co, OH., p. 2B. Hurdis Hicks 31, truck farmer; Bessie M Hicks 30; Rosalane M Hicks 9; Maurite H Hicks 5.

Bible Records: Hicks Bible last known in possession of Addie Joslin West [copy sent to me by Lvera Jennings Seipelt, Georgetown OH]. "Born to Mr. Elijah Franklin Hicks and Mrs. Melissa Hicks: Hurdis Beeker Hicks was born July 20, 1898. Mr. Hurdes Beeker Hicks was united in marriage to Miss Bessie Marie Rogers March 1, 1919. Born to Mr. Hurdes Beeker Hicks and Mrs Bessie Hicks (nee Rogers) Melissa Rosaline Hicks, May 3, 1920; Opal Louise Hicks, October 5, 1922 (died fall 1923); Maurice Hurdes Hicks, Sept 11, 1924; Donald Rogers Hicks, Mon. Sept 15, 1930"
Listed as Orestes B. in 1910 census.
Military: World War I Draft Registration Cards, 1917-1918 [Ancestry.com] Hurdes Beeker Hicks, age 20, b. 20 Jul 1898; farmer - Frank Hicks; contact: Frank Hicks, Chilo, Clermont, OH; med. height & build; brown eyes & hair. Regis: 12 Sep 1918, Batavia, OH.
Notes from Lvera (Jennings) Seipelt 1998 list "Children of Hurdes Beeker Hicks: Rosalene Buskirk, Morris Hicks, Donald Hicks, Barbara Hall"
Death: 7 Jul 1984, Clermont County Mercy Hospital, married, age 85. Ohio Deaths, 1908-1932, 1938-1944, and 1958-2002 [Ancestry.com]
Obituary: *Hurdes Beeker Hicks, age 85 years, 11 months, 18 days of Chilo, OH, departed this life on July 7, 1984 at Clermont Co Hospital, Batavia, OH. He was born July 20, 1898 near Rural, Franklin Township, Clermont Co, OH, the son of Elijah Franklin and Melissa Beeker Hicks. On March 1, 1919, he was united in marriage to Bessie Marie Rodgers and to this union were born two daughters and two sons: Melissa Rosalene Buskirk of New Richmond: Opal Louise, deceased in 1923; Morris Hurdes Hicks of Ocala, FL and Donald Rodgers Hicks of Felicity, OH. On Dec 30, 1939, he was married to Susan Ann Dugan and to this union was born one daughter, Barbara Ann Hall of Felicity, OH. Also surviving are two sisters: Mrs Irlene DeVore of Bradenton, FL and Mrs. Elizabeth Jennings of Georgetown, OH; 10 grandchildren and 11 great grandchildren, plus a host of nieces, nephews and cousins. He was baptized in the Ohio River and a member of Shinkle's Ridge Christian Church. During World War II, he worked at Allis-Chalmers in Cincinnati. He then began farming again and also delivered the Sunday Enquirer for 12 year. He was Chilo Cemetery Sexton. His love of the Ohio River and boats was a great part of his life. He worked on the towboat, Wm Penn, and the dredge Tabor at Portsmouth, which traveled both the Ohio River and the Mississippi as far as New Orleans. During the numerous floods, he used his boat to move many neighbors and their belongs to higher ground. He was highly respected in the community and portrayed a life of strength and courage. Services were held July 10, 1984 at Kennedy-Steven Funeral Home in Bethel, OH and interment in Shinkle's Ridge Cemetery near Higginsport, OH.*

Notes for Bessie Marie RODGERS #345s1
  "divorced 1938"

Notes for Susan Ann DUGAN #345s2
  Jones notes give surname as Dugan

Notes for Irlene Evelyn HICKS #346
Info from Orville Jones notes. "resides (1972) Poplar St, Felicity, OH
Lvera (Jennings) Seipelt's notes (1999): "restaurant; living in Bradenton, FL 1999"
Census: 1930 Franklin, Clermont, OH, p. 2B. Herbert L Devore 24, farmer; Irlene E Devore 26; Eva D Devore 5 [Ancestry.com has it indexed as Devose]
Photocopy of photo of Elizabeth, Irlene & Marcella Hicks as young girls in my files.
Birth, marriage, death information from Lvera Seipelt, dau of Elizabeth (Hicks) Jennings.
Bible Records: Hicks Bible: "Born to Mr. Elijah Franklin Hicks and Mrs. Melissa Hicks: Irlene Evelyn Hicks was born Feb 11, 1904. Irlene Evelyn Hicks was united in marriage to Herbert L. DeVore June 4, 1924. Born to Mr & Mrs Herbert DeVore: Eva Irlene DeVore March 16, 1925; J. W. (John Wilson) DeVore June 7, 1931; Melissa Rosetta DeVore April 7, 19__ (died Apr 11, 1938)."

Death: SS Death Index gives: Irlene Devore, b. 11 Feb 1904; d. 8 Jan 2002; age 97; Bradenton, Manatee, FL; card issued: Ohio; #272-32-8208.

Notes for Herbert Leroy DEVORE #346s
  Lvera (Jennings) Seipelt's notes (1999): "farmer, hauled milk in bulk; restaurant"

Notes for Georgia Elizabeth HICKS #347
Jones notes: "resides (1972) at Shinkles Ridge Rd, Brown Co, OH.
Census: 1930 Lewis, Brown, OH, p. 1A. Eugene Jennings 24, farmer; Elizabeth Jennings 21; Elvira
  Jennings 11/12
Photocopy of photo of Elizabeth, Erlene & Marcella Hicks as young girls in my files.
Bible Records: "Born to Mr. Elijah Franklin Hicks and Mrs. Melissa Hicks: Georgia Elizabeth Hicks was born June 25th 1908"
Living in Georgetown, OH in August, 1998. Visited her there. She has family Bible.
Lvera Seipelt's notes: "farmer's wife"; gives baptism dates.
Obituary: *Georgia Jennings, 91. Georgia Elizabeth Jennings, 91, of Georgetown, died Monday, May 22, 2000, at the Brown Co General Hospital in Georgetown. She was born on June 25, 1908, the daughter of the late Elijah Franklin and Melissa (Beeker) Hicks. She was also preceded in death by her brother Curtis B. Hicks. Mrs. Jennings was a homemaker and member of the Shinkles Ridge Church. She is survived by 3 daughters and one son-in-law, Irma Purdy of Georgetown, Ivetta Fridge of Ripley, and Lvera and Victor Seipelt of Georgetown; one son, Eugene M. Jennings, Jr. of Georgetown; 12 grandchildren; 20 great great grandchildren; 7 great great grandchildren; one sister, Irlene Devore of Bradenton, FL; one cousin, Marcella Hicks of Georgetown; and a special care giver, Mary Louise Mitchell. Interment will be in the Shinkles Ridge Cemetery in Georgetown.*

Notes for Eugene Martin JENNINGS #347s
  Lvera Seipelt's notes: "farmer"; gives baptism dates.

Notes for Irma Clair LEVI #348
M1: George Walsh, 1909 - sons Walter Cabanni [2 Aug 1910] and Francis Marion (Frank) [b. 17 Mar 1912]. M2: David Watson Symon - son Robert Kenneth [b. 5/11/?] George Walsh d. 1913 in Seattle.
Birth, Marriage: from Bible of Mollie Dell Levi, in possession of Betty Kieser (1998)
Discrepancy: family records give birth as 22 Aug 1878; Ontario Death index gives birth as 27 Aug 1881
Census:
  1900 Columbia, Norwood, Hamilton Co, OH. Francis Marion Levi 46, W. Mary E., 49; children: Irma
    C 21, Harvey C. 19, Mollie D 15.
  1910 Seattle Ward 10, King, WA, p. 5A. George W Walsh Jr 24, MN/ME/MO, salesman - auto supplies;
    Irma Walsh 27; married 0 years.
  1920 Seattle, King Co, WA, p. 4. George Walsh 67, b Maine; Stella 6,3 b. MO; Irma, dau, 37, OH;
    Francis, gr-son, 7, b. WA; Walter, gr-son, 9, b. WA. Also David Symons, 42, widowed, a tailor, b.
    Canada and John Symons, 20, single, b. OH, a bank clerk.
  1930 not found - in Canada?
Letter 8 Sep 1948 from Watson Symonds, 10 S. Main St, Butte, MT - says he celebrated his 73rd birthday on Aug 12. Mentions seeing Frank in his last days of his life; No mention of Walter. "Bob is still in California and is driving a Greyhound bus.. address 2051 Telegraph Ave, Oakland, CA."; "Sally [second wife?] is well..has her only son living here in Butte."]
Letter signed Henriette & Judy, who seem to be widow & daughter of Walter Walsh - written from Toronto, Canada, Jan. 1945 to Aunt Mollie [Stalder]. Asks "did Walt look like his mother?" Would guess Judy to be toddler, based on context of letter. Mentions "Frank & Betty"

Death: Irma Clair Symons, d. 13 Sep 1928 York, Ontario, Canada; Age at death: 47 years 23 days; Birth: 27 Aug 1881 Cincinnati USA; Father: Frank M Levi. Ontario Death Records 1869-1947 <pilot.familysearch.org>

Notes for George Walter WALSH Jr #348s1
An auto salesman in 1910.

Notes for David Watson SYMONS #348s2
Birth, Marriage: from Bible of Mollie Dell Levi, in possession of Betty Kieser
Military: World War I Draft Registration Cards, 1917-1918 [Ancestry.com] David Watson Symons; age 43, b. 12 Aug 1875; res: Lelah, Yakima, WA; rancher - self employed; contact: Emma Symons; med height & build; blue eyes, bald. Regis: 12 Sep 1918, no place given.
Census:
   1900 Butte Ward 3, Silver Bow, MT, p. 4B. Walter D. Symmes, b. Aug 1875, Canada, married, tailor, roomer
   1910 N Yakima Ward 5, Yakima, WA, p. 8A. David Symons, 34, roomer in hotel, married, 11 yrs, 2 ch / 2 living, cutter - tailor shop
   1920 Seattle, King Co, Washington. ED 208. sh 4. George Walsh 67 b Maine; Stella 63 b. MO; Irma dau 37 OH; Francis GS 7 b. WA; Walter GS 9, b. WA. Also David Symons, 42, widowed, a tailor b. Canada, naturalized, imm. 1906 and John Symons, 20, single, b. OH, a bank clerk.
Letter 8 Sep 1948 from Watson Symons, 10 S. Main St, Butte, MT - says he celebrated his 73rd birthday on Aug 12.. Mentions seeing Frank in his last days of his life; No mention of Walter. "Bob is still in California and is driving a Greyhound bus.. address 2051 Telegraph Ave, Oakland, CA."; "Sally [second wife?] is well..has her only son living here in Butte."]
Description: Betty (Stalder) Kieser remembered that "Uncle Watson was bald and very fair - so he always wore a hat - even while swimming."

Notes for Clyde Harvey LEVI #349
Itinerant actor ... Disappeared as young man.. In 1998, via the internet, I made contact with Lane Levi, grandson of Clyde Harvey Levi. He has given me photos and information on his family. They now pronounce the name Lee' vee. (His father and sister Mollie used Lee' I.)
Married Pearl who was living in Indianapolis, IN in about 1940. (RR 17) Certificates from Common School 1 Jun 1895 - Hamilton Co, Cincinnati; Norwood Public School 3 Jun 1892 from grade D to C (with honors)
Census:
   1910 Cincinnati Ward 16, Hamilton, OH, p. 4B. Harvey C Levy 28, foreman - printing? office; Pearl R Levy 28 KY; Harvey C Levy Jr 6; Irma C Levy 5. Indexed in Ancestry as Harvy C Very. Married 7 years, 2 ch / 2 living.
   1920 Cincinnati, Hamilton Co, OH. #1392. ED 276, 5, 14.Clad Levi, 38m, B. OH. Printer, renting on 8th St.; wife Pearl 42f, b. KY parents b. KY; Clad H, Jr 16m b. OH in school; Irma 15f b. OH in school; Lillie Austin 63 b. KY, parents b. KY. [mother in law].
   1930 Harlingen, Cameron, TX, p. 9B. Harvey C Levi 49, OH/OH/OH, roomer in hotel, married, showman - own show
Birth-Marriage: from Bible of Mollie Dell Levi, in possession of Betty Kieser
Marriage: H. Clyde Levi, b. 1880, age 22; spouse: Pearl Roser Austin; marriage: 22 Dec 1902; Newport, Campbell, KY. Kentucky Marriages, 1785-1979 <familysearch.org>
Children: Harvey Clyde; Irma Crystal. Names, no other information in Bible of Mollie Dell Levi.
Death: Died 1948 in Omaha. Buried there with wife Pearl. Marriage, death info from grandson, Lane Levi, "Grandfather Clyde was involved with the carnivals & traveled around the country running a swing ride"

Military: World War I Draft Registration Cards, 1917-1918 [Ancestry.com] Harvey Clyde Levi, age 37, b. 16 Apr 1881; res: Cincinnati, Hamilton, OH; occ: monotype operator - Bararach? Printing Co; wife: Pearl Levi; med height & build, blue eyes, lt brown hair. Regis: 12 Sep 1918, Cincinnati, OH.

Notes for Pearl Roser AUSTIN #349s
Census:
  1880 Mason Co, KY William Austin 31M b. in Ky; Mitilda Austin 24F B. Ky; Pearl 4F b. KY; Charles R. Austin 8 Mo 1880 b. Ky
  1930 may be the Pearl Levi, 48, married, living with Emil & Leanna Liska in Chicago, IL. Listed as sister in law. Next to Guy Austin, 42, b. IL.
Other information from Lane Levi, grandson of Clyde & Pearl.

Notes for Mollie Dell LEVI #350
Birth: from Bible of Mollie Dell Levi Stalder, in possession of Betty Stalder Kieser.
Note: Spent time before marriage in 1910 in Felicity Oh visiting with Aunt Laura. Mentions visiting Grandpa Levi, Uncle John, Uncle Frank, Uncle O.D., Aunt Georgie, Uncle Curt.
Census:
  1920 Madeira, Hamilton, OH, p. 6B. Wm B Stalder 41, woodworker - H.P. Lumber Co; Mollie D Stalder 36; Curtis C Stalder 8; Elizabeth Stalder 6; Jeanette Stalder 5; Wm F Stalder 3; Grace O Stalder 1; Ruth Stalder 0. Next to his sister Medora Thompson and her family; his mother, Medora Cooper, was living with the Thompsons.
  1930 Orlando, Orange Co, FL, p. 4B. William B Stalder 51, age at marriage 35, IN/PA/IN, carpenter - house; Nellie D Stalder 46, age at marriage 24, OH/OH/OH; Curtis C Stalder 18, bookkeeper - motor transport; Elizabeth Stalder 17; Jennette Stalder 15; William Stalder 13; Grace Stalder 11; Ruth Stalder 10; Madge Stalder 5; Richard Stalder 2 10/12; Medora Cooper 81, mother, IN/IN/NY. Children b. OH, except for Richard, b. FL.
  1935 FL State Census, Orange Co, FL. W. B. Stalder, 56, husband, high school education, carpenter; Mrs. W. B. Stalder 50, wife, OH, high school education; D.J. Cooper 86, mother, high school education, retired; Mrs. Frank M. Levy 85, step mother in law; Bettie Stalder 22, dau, bookkeeper; Jeanette Stalder 21, salesclerk; Billie Stalder 19, paperman; Grace Stalder 17, nursemaid; Ruth Stalder 16, student; Madge Stalder 14, student; Dickie Stalder 8, b. FL, student.
  1945 FL State Census, Duval Co, FL. William B. Stalder 66, 9th grade, clerk; Mollie D. 60, 12th grade, wife, Curtis C 34, 12th grade, Army Air corps; William F. 29, Army Air Corps; Frances H. 23, 12th grade, steno, NH; Mary M. 22, 12th grade, steno; Richard B. 18, FL, 12th grade, student; also married dau Grace - Euthan A. Windham 29, GA, 10th grade, army; Grace O. 26, 12th grade, clerk; Marilyn G. 3, child. Living as 1200 LeMer, Jacksonville, FL.
Note: Interview with Elizabeth (Stalder) Kieser, oldest daughter of family, 1998. "Family moved to FL in 1921 after a miserable winter, with continually sick children. They came by train with 7 children ranging from Curtis at 10 to Madge, an infant of six weeks. [complete interview on video tape in possession of Betty Jo Stockton]
Death: Death Certificate of Mollie D. Stalder, Duval Co, FL #19525. 7 Oct 1947. Mollie D. Stalder, white female. Married, husband William B. Stalder (aged 69). Born 7 Sep 1884, Mt Orab, Ohio. Aged 63. Housewife, dau of Frank M. Levi b. OH & Mary Hite [sic]; b. OH. Informant Curtis C. Stalder, 1200 La Mee Ave. Burial: 9 Oct 1947, Oaklawn.
Obituary from *Florida Times Union* 8 Oct 1947. **Funeral Services Scheduled Today for Mrs. Stalder**. *Funeral services will be held at 3 p.m. today of Mrs Mollie D. Stalder, 63, of 1200 LaMee Ave, who died in a local hospital Tuesday... Mrs Stalder was a native of Ohio and had lived in Florida for the past 26 years, moving to Jacksonville from Orlando in 1935. She was a Methodist and was active in Garden Club work. Surviving are her husband, William B. Stalder; three sons, Curtis and Richard Stalder of this city,*

and William Stalder of Orlando; five daughters: Mrs. Emmett Rhodes of Tallahassee, Mrs E. A. Windham of Jacksonville; Mrs E. E. Watkins of Donaldson, GA; Mrs Robert S. Keiser [sic] of Orlando and Mrs John Washell of Dowlestown, PA, and several grandchildren.

Notes for William Benjamin STALDER #350s

Was carpenter, cabinet maker and gardener. Built Sears "pre-fab" houses in OH. Moved from Cincinnati, OH in Spring, 1921

Marriage: Hamilton Co, OH. Marriage license in possession of Betty Kieser. states, Wm. D. Hurdis, Probate Judge, No witnesses. Family says marriage was in Covington, KY. Aunt Frances (Hadley) Stalder gives wedding date as 22 Jun 1909.

Military: World War I Draft Registration Cards, 1917-1918 [Ancestry.com] William Benjamin Stalder, age 40, b. 19 Aug 1878; res: Madisonville, Hamilton Co, OH; occ: foreman - Norwood Sash & Door; contact: Mollie Stalder, Madisonville, OH; short, med build; brown eyes, dark hair; regis: Norwood, OH, 12 Sep 1918.

Death: Death Certificate: Duval Co, FL. File #15929. 27 Aug 1948 8:45 pm. St Vincent's Hospital. White Male, widowed, b. August 19, 1878, aged 70 years 8 days. Born Wilmington, IN. Occupation Carpenter. Wife: Mollie D. Stalder, deceased. Informant Curtis Stalder, 1200 LaMee, Jax. Burial 30 Aug 1948, Oaklawn Cemetery.

Obituary: **William B. Stalder to be buried today**. Jacksonville Times Union, Aug 28, 1948. *Funeral services for William B. Stalder, 70, of 1200 LaMee Ave, who died Friday, will be conducted at 4 p.m. today in the Robert M. Naugle Mortuary, with burial following in Oaklawn Cemetery. ...Mr Stalder, a native of Indiana, had lived in Jacksonville since 1935. He is survived by three sons, Richard Stalder, an employee of The FL Times-Union, Curtis Stalder of Jacksonville, and William Stalder of Orlando; five daughters: Mrs. Emmett Rhodes of Tallahassee, Mrs E. A. Windham of Jacksonville; Mrs E. E. Watkins of Donaldson, GA; Mrs Robert S. Keiser of Orlando and Mrs John Washell of Dowlestown, PA, and several grandchildren.*

Notes for William Francis STALDER #685

Married Frances Hadley, New Smyrna, FL, 13 Oct 1949. No children. Bill served in the Army Air Corp, WW II. He was a natural mechanic and could fix anything. When he was very young - 6^{ish} - his grandpa Levi had a Model A that had to be cranked to start. He always had trouble starting it - so would yell for "Billie" to come start his car for him. Worked for Chrysler (Automobile) as parts manager; after retirement, had bike shop; then lawn mower repair business. Excelled at stained glass and made most of the windows for his church. Family has a number of his stained glass pieces. He and Frances were avid golfers most of their lives.

Anniversaries *Daytona Beach News-Journal* (FL) - October 15, 2000

Stalder-60th Frances and William F. Stalder of New Smyrna Beach celebrated their 60th wedding anniversary Oct. 13 with a luncheon at a local restaurant with family members from Jacksonville, Orlando and Lakeland. The former Frances Hadley was born in Boston and met her husband, a native of Cincinnati, Ohio, at Florida Motor Lines Bus Station in Daytona Beach, where he was working. They were married Oct. 13, 1940, at St. Paul's Episcopal Church in New Smyrna. Mrs. Stalder lived in New Smyrna Beach for a number of years and attended Live Oak Street school, graduating in 1937. She worked for SunTrust Bank of Orlando for 29 years, retiring in 1980. Her husband was a parts manager at Orlando Motors for 22 years, and later was self-employed as owner of Bill's Bike and Mower Shop in Orlando for 10 years. The couple moved to New Smyrna Beach from Orlando in 1989. Her hobbies include working crossword puzzles and reading, and her husband enjoys stained glass and woodworking. Both like to travel.

Notes for Richard Benjamin STALDER #689
Married 19 Apr 1952 to Caroline Day (b. 2 Aug 1927). No children. Married 2 - Taeko _?_ Shee, widow of Warde Shee, abt 1998. He quit high school before graduating to join the Army "because he was afraid that the war was going to be over before he got there". He was a reporter for the Stars and Stripes Army newspaper during the war. He went back to graduate after the war. Dick worked as a reporter, later city editor for the FL Times Union newspaper for all his life, starting as a copy boy.
Obituary: Richard B. Stalder: 1927-2010 ***Florida Times Union***, March 16, 2010
Richard B. Stalder, a longtime reporter and city editor at The Florida Times-Union, died of cardiopulmonary arrest at Baptist Medical Center on Friday. He was 82. Memorialization was by cremation, and there will be no funeral at his request. A native of Orlando, Mr. Stalder lived in Jacksonville since 1934. Before World War II, he delivered papers on the Southside. He served with the 4th Armored Division in Germany in 1945 and 1946 and attended Jacksonville Junior College, now Jacksonville University. From 1952 to 1957 he served in the Marine Corps Reserve. Mr. Stalder joined the news staff at The Times-Union in 1947 as a copy boy and worked his way up, serving as a police, general assignments and Beaches reporter before being named night city editor in 1966. He became city editor Jan. 1, 1972, and served until 1977 when he left the company. Mr. Stalder then worked as an appliance salesman for the former Pic 'N Save discount chain. His first wife, Caroline Stalder, died in 1997. Mr. Stalder is survived by his second wife of 10 years, Taeko Stalder.

Notes for Archibald D. "Archie" JOSLIN #352
Census: 1910 Fort Caswell, Brunswick, NC, p. 16B. Arch D. Joslin, 26, OH/OH/OH, single, corporal, soldier, US Army.
Married Josephine Ratcliff, who d. 17 Jan 1986, New Richmond, OH. Interment Greenmound Cemetery. Josephine was mother of late Elizabeth Hayden, grandmother of Bob, John, Jim Hayden & Jane Wilson; 9 great grandchildren.
Notes from Lvera (Jennings) Seipelt 1998 list "Children of Mary Elizabeth Hicks Joslin: Archie Joslin (Deceased) - child Elizabeth Hayden (d. 1975)"
Jones notes: gives birth date, marriage, spouse, death date "she resides (1972) at 350 Hamilton Av, New Richmond, OH"
Birth: Joslin, ___. b. Feb 21, 1884, Washington Twp, Clermont, OH; Male, white. Parents: John D. Joslin & Mary Hix [sic]. Clermont Co, OH Birth records, Vol 3, p. 136
Military: Arch D. Joslin, enlisted Sept 4, 1908, born Rural, OH, age 24 6/12, occ: soldier; blue eyes, lt brown hair, fair, 5' 9"; discharged Ft Caswell, NC, Last assignment - 63rd Cal 6/5/08. U.S. Army, Register of Enlistments, 1798-1914 [Ancestry.com].
Death: Arch D. Joslin, d. 18 Aug 1918, Tate Twp, Clermont, OH; b. 21 Feb 1884, OH; Age: 34 yrs 5 mo 25 da; Occ: St. Car Motorman; Burial date: 19 Aug 1918, New Richmond, OH. Parents: John Joslin, b. Ohio; Emmerilla Phillips, b. Ohio. OH Deaths 1908-1953 <familysearch.org>

Notes for Josephine RATCLIFF 352s
Jones notes give birth date, marriage, spouse, death date "she resides (1972) at 350 Hamilton Av, New Richmond, OH"
Death: Josephi Joslin, b.1886, KY; Res: Clermont, OH. Death 17 Jan 1986, Clermont Co, OH. Age: over 100 years, Widowed. Ohio Deaths, 1908-1932, 1938-1944, and 1958-2002 [Ancestry.com]

Notes for Edna Clare JOSLIN #357
M. Wm. B. Edwards, Phoenix, AZ 19 Jun 1924 [info from Lvera Seipelt notes]
Birth: Adlara Leona Joslin, b. Sep 18, 1891, Franklin Twp, Clermont, OH; Female, white. Parents: John Joslin & Mary Hicks. Clermont Co, OH Birth records, Vol 5, p. 153
Census
  1920 Phoenix, Maricopa, AZ, p. 9A. Edna C Joslin 31, teacher - city schools; Frances E Miller 24, lodger, OH/Eng/OH.
  1930 Phoenix, Maricopa, AZ, p. 1A. W B Edwards 66, inspector - cement co, KY/KY/KY, age at 1st marriage 22; Edna C Edwards 40, age at marriage 35; Mary Joslin 69, m-in-law, widow.
Notes from Lvera (Jennings) Seipelt 1998: "Children of Mary Elizabeth Hicks Joslin: Edna Edwards (Deceased 1931 - no heirs)
Photograph: In photo of Hicks family in 1914/1915
From Jones notes: "lived in Phoenix, AZ & buried there. School teacher. no ch."
Norman Zezula's notes: in Phoenix AZ City Directory 1930-32. William a cement inspector; Edna not listed 1932.
Death: Edna C. Edwards, d. 1921, Phoenix, Maricopa, AZ; parents: John Joslin; Mary Hicks. Arizona Deaths, 1870-1951 <beta.familysearch.org>

Notes for Adlara Leona 'Addie' JOSLIN #358
Adlora on Lvera's list. M. Howard West 2 Apr 1914; Dau. Marian m. Starrett. d. 14 Aug 1989.
Census:
  1920 Sycamore, Hamilton, OH, p. 3A. Howard West 27, laborer - farm manager; Lora West 28; Marian West 6/12; Mary Joslin 59, m-in-law, widowed.
  1930 Cincinnati, Hamilton, OH, p. 26A. Howard West 36, OH/Ire/OH, inspector - automobile; Lora West 38; Marian West 10.
Notes from Lvera (Jennings) Seipelt 1998 lists "Children of Mary Elizabeth Hicks Joslin: Adlora West (deceased); child: Marian Starret (deceased); 4 children.
Jones notes: gives name, birth, marriage, his death; "resides (1972) at 6950 Roe St, Cincinnati, OH"
Marriage: Minnie Clara (Hicks) Behan told Norman Zezula (before 1979) that the Hicks Bible was in the pos. of Addie West. Presumably, this is the married name of Addie Joslin.
Photograph: As young mother in photo of Hicks family abt 1914.
Death Notice: *Lora J. West, (Nee Joslin), wife of the late Howard West, devoted mother of Mrs. Robert (Marian) Starret, grandmother of Virginia Schmidt, Donna Reed, Robert, Thomas and Charles Starrett and survived by ___ great grandchildren. Apr 7 1962, Residence: Madison? Place.* [undated, unnamed paper].

Notes for Howard Arlie WEST #358s
Jones notes gives name, birth, marriage, his death;
Photograph: in photo of Hicks family, abt 1914.
Military: World War I Draft Registration Cards, 1917-1918 [Ancestry.com] Howard Arlie West, b. 22 Feb 1893, Clermontville, OH; res: New Richmond, OH. Farmer - self employed; dependents: wife and mother; short, stout, brown eyes, black hair; Regis: 5 Jun 1917, Laurel, Clermont, OH.

Notes for Lucy Mary Francis HICKS #359
Jones notes: "resided Norwood"
Birth: Clermont Co, OH birth cert. (v 1886, p 118) "Franklin twp, Clermont Co, OH, female; parents: H. H. Hicks, Maggie Wells." The date agrees with that given in the Hicks Family Bible.

Census:
- 1910 Cincinnati, Hamilton, OH. Clarence M. Meeker 24; Lucie M. 24; Margaret A 3; Ruth M. 1 11/12; Roy M.1 11/12 (all b. OH; md. 4 yrs., 3 children, all living)
- 1920 Cincinnati Ward 13, Hamilton, OH, p. 10A. Clarence Meeker 34m, millwright - lumber co; Lucie Meeker 34; Margaret Meeker 12; Roy M Meeker 11; Ruth M Meeker 11; Robert W Meeker 8; Rachael M Meeker 8. [indexed on Ancestry.com as Muker]
- 1930 Norwood (Hamilton) OH, p. 29B. Clarence Meeker 44, contractor, house; Lucie, 44; Roy 21, no occ.; Robert 18, laborer, golf links.

Marriage: Hamilton Co, OH marriage record (#108)--"Clarence Meeker (19, b. Clermont Co, OH; parents, Napoleon Meeker, Cynthia Murray; a porter) to Lucy Hicks (20, b. Clermont Co, OH; parents: Harvey Hicks, Mary Wells; a saleslady). Both are residents of Norwood, OH; neither married previously. Married by Rev. John Berry of the M E Church."

Death: OH death certificate: "Lucie Mary Meeker, d. Aug 29, 1964 in Cincinnati, Hamilton, OH; b. 1 Nov 1885 in Clermont Co, OH; parents: Harvey Hicks, Margaret Wells; widow; res. 5438 Norwood Ave, Norwood, Ham., OH; informant was Roy Meeker, 5439 Hunter Ave., Norwood, OH."

Note: She compiled a collection of family history which is referred to in this present family history as "Lucy's Data" or as "Lucie (Hicks) data." She also had possession of the Jernegan Family Bible, from which she extracted data and distributed it to interested relatives.

Notes from Lvera (Jennings) Seipelt 1998 list "Lucy Meeker (Deceased 1964); Children: Margaret Orth; Roy Meeker (deceased - no children); Ruth Hock (deceased - no children); Rachel Norman; Robert Meeker (Deceased 1984); children: Shirley; William R; Harvey John Hicks (deceased); children: Helen Luckey, Henrietta Wenger, Jo Ann McCracken. Child: Elizabeth Fugatt Poston (Deceased 1980's); Children: Nancy Wilson, Patricia Schwartz, Kenneth Poston"

Notes for James Clarence MEEKER #359s

Military: WW II Draft Registration 1942 [Ancestry.com] Clarence J. Meeker, 5438 Hunter Ave, Norwood, OH; b. 5 Apr 1886, Brown Co, OH. Age 56. Contact: Mrs Lucy Meeker; own business; 6' 1"; 200 lbs, blue eyes, brown hair, ruddy complexion, April 1942.

Obituary: *Meeker, Clarence, beloved husband of Lucie Hicks Meeker; devoted father of Mrs. Margaret Orth, Mrs. Ruth Hock, of Los Angeles, CA; Mrs. Rachel Norman of St Louis, MO; Roy Meeker of Chicago, IL and Robert Meeker; also survived by 7 grandchildren and 11 great grandchildren; Monday April 10, 1961; residence: 5348 Hunter Av, Norwood. [unnamed paper, undated]*

Notes for Harvey John HICKS #360

Birth: Clermont Co birth certificate (v 1886, p 126) "Harvey Hicks, Utopia [sic] Clermont Co, OH; male; parents: H. H. Hicks, Maggie Wells." The date agrees with that given by the Hicks family Bible.

Marriage: Hamilton Co. marriage license application and certificate (v 281, p 285) "Harvey J. Hicks (27 on 15 Aug 1916, res. Norwood, Hamilton Co, OH; parents: Harvey H. Hicks, Margaret Wells; to Ida Beulah Greene (26 on 20 Mar 1917, res. Cincinnati, Hamilton Co, OH; parents: Geo. Greene, Laura Vaudal?)"

Notes from Lvera (Jennings) Seipelt 1998 list "Harvey John Hicks (deceased); children: Helen Luckey, Henrietta Wenger, Jo Ann McCracken."

Jones notes: "resided (1972) Methodist Home, 5343 Hamilton Cin? 45224"; WWI, Lt, US Army."

Census:
- 1920 Cincinnati Ward 13, Hamilton, OH, p. 10B. Harvey J Hicks 29, OH/OH/OH, salesman - brokerage; Beulah 28, KY/VA/VA; Helen 1 3/12 OH.
- 1930 Cincinnati, Hamilton, OH, p. 21A. Harvey J Hicks 40, manager - bond; Beulah 39; Helen 11; Henrietta 10; Joan 4 6/12.

Not on WW I Draft Registration 1917 or WW II in 1942.

Military: 18 May 1917 to 10 Jan 1919 (army; honorable discharge) He spent WW I training soldiers in Texas. He never got overseas.
Military: Ohio Military Men, 1917-18. Harvey John Hicks; 2nd Lieutenant; Race: W; Residence: Cincinnati, O.; Enlistment Division: National Guard Enlistment, Cincinnati, O. 18 May 1917; Birth Place: Utopia, O / Age: 27 11/12 Years; Assignments: Co F 1 Infantry ONG (Co H 147 Infantry) to 19 June 1918; Machine Gun 4 Officers' Training School Cp Hancock Ga to Discharge Corporal 6 Jan 1915; Sergeant 14 July 1917. Honorable discharge 15 Sept 1918 to accept Commission 2 Lieutenant Infantry 16 Sept 1918 from National Guard 4 Officers' Training School Cp Hancock Ga 15 May 1918 to 16 Sept 1918. Co B 45 Machine Gun Battalion to --; 80 Infantry to Discharge Cp Hancock Ga; Cp Logan Tex; Cp Grant Ill. Honorable discharge 6 Jan 1919. Vol: 8
Death: OH death record: "Harvey John Hicks, male, white; d. 22 Apr 1979 in Cincinnati, Hamilton, OH; b. 12 Aug 1889 in OH; widowed; parents: Harvey H. Hicks, Margaret Wells; self employed gardener; res. 5343 Hamilton Ave, Cincinnati, Hamilton Co, OH;# 301-03-3853; informant: Henrietta Wegner, 1962 Wanninger Lane, Cincinnati, OH."
Burial: Mt. Moriah Cemetery, Withamsville, Clermont Co, OH (sect. 2, row 29, grave # 15)

Notes for Minnie Clara HICKS #361
Birth: Clermont Co birth certificate: (v 1886, p 131) "Minna Hicks, b. Franklin twp, Clermont Co, OH; female; parents: H. H. Hicks, Maggie Wells."
Marriage: "John Behan, 22 on 23 Dec 1916, b. Ireland, to Minnie Hicks, 23 on 15 Oct 1916, b. Clermont Co, OH; married by Benard J. Beckemeyer, a Roman Catholic priest. .... Hamilton Co, OH marriage license for "John Behan and Minnie Hicks." It has a handwritten notation added to it stating: "marriage solemnized 3 Feb 1917, Rev. B. J. Breckemyer." .... Hamilton Co, OH. Hamilton Co, OH marriage certificate: (v 279, #101)
Marriage application: "John Behan, res. Norwood, OH, a machinist; parents: Patrick Behan, Anna Gannon; to Minnie Hicks, res. Norwood, OH; parents: Harvey Hicks, Margaret Wells." Photocopies of all three documents are in the possession of Norman Zezula.
Jones notes: "resides (1972) at 2413 Norwood Av, Norwood, OH."
Census
  1920 Norwood Ward 4, Hamilton, OH, p. 7B. John J Behan 25, Ire/Ire/Ire, immigrated 1913?, naturalization "pa"; Minnie 26, OH/OH/OH; John P 2 2/12; Dorothy 1
  1930, Norwood, Hamilton, OH. p. 33A. John Behan, 36, born Ireland, immigrated in 1913; wife Minnie, 36; John P. 12; Dorothy A, 11; Laura M., 9; Donald J, 6; Richard 4; Marjorie, 2. John was a glazier in a planing mill.
Death: OH death certificate: "Minnie Clara Behan, female, d. 26 Feb 1983 in Cincinnati, Hamilton Co, OH, white; b. 15 Oct 1893, OH; parents: Harvey Hicks, Margaret Wells; widow; res. 2005 Seymour, Cincinnati, OH.; informant was Donald J. Behan."

Notes for John Joseph BEHAN #361s
Birth: Four Mile House parish church certificate of birth & baptism. Kilbride (RC) parish (certificate extract dated 1948). A copy is in the possession of Norman Zezula (grandson). This church is near Strokestown.
Death: OH death certificate: "John Joseph Behan, d. 23 Feb 1955 at 2413 Norwood Ave., Norwood, Hamilton Co, OH; b. 23 Dec 1892 [sic]; parents: Patrick Behan, Ann Gannon; Glazier for Cincinnati Sash and Door; # 228-03-9507; res. of Norwood Ave. address for 15 yrs.; informant was Minnie Behan."
Military: WW I Draft Registration [Ancestry.com] John Joseph Behan, b. 23 Dec 1894, Ireland, Medhedant?, living in Norwood, Hamilton Co, OH, age 23. Occ: box nailer - Globe Werner?, married, medium height, slender build, brown hair, black eyes.

Notes for Dion Williams HICKS #363
Info from Norman Zezula
Birth: "Dion Hicks b. Franklin twp, Clermont Co, OH; male; parents: H. H. Hicks, Maggie Wells." Clermont Co, OH birth certificate (v 1896, p 80). The date agrees with that given by the Hicks Family Bible.
Marriage: Lucy (Hicks) Meeker, his sister, gave the date and wife's name in the genealogy summary she compiled for and distributed to the extended Hicks family (copy in possession of Norman Zezula). The Hicks Bible extracts that she made names his wife (Madelyn Vaske), but gives no marriage date or place. (family tradition states that the marriage took place in Hamilton or Clermont Co, OH; however, no record has been found).
Jones notes: "resided (1972) 203 W. 69th, Cincinnati, OH"
Census: 1930 Norwood Hamilton OH, p. 31A. Harvey Hicks 68, nursery man; wife Margaret 65; son Dion 30, salesman, advertising; Madeline, d-in law, 22; Dion, grson, 7/12, b IN
Military: World War I Draft Registration Cards, 1917-1918 [Ancestry.com] Gives name as Dion Williams Hicks, living in Norwood, OH, age 19, foreman, shipping dept - coal? co; Contact: Margaret Hicks, Norwood. Tall, medium build, blue eyes, brown hair. 12 Sep 1918.
Death: "Dion Williams Hicks, d. 11 Jan 1960 in Cincinnati, Hamilton Co, OH; b. 7 Nov 1898; parents: Harvey Henry Hicks, Marguerite Wells [sic]; married, male, white; res. 203 W. 69th St., Cincinnati. 16, OH; a presser for a tailor shop; #290-24-0940; informant was Madelyn Hicks. [i.e., his wife]." OH death certificate

Notes for Madelyn VASKE #363s
Death: Social Security Death Index; birth agrees exactly
May be the Lena Vaske, age 4, in Marion, Decatur Co, IN in 1910, with parents Frank & Lena Vaske.

Notes for Mary Frances HOUSER #368
Jones notes: "m. 1/25/1883 to Geo. A. Ross at Downing, MO. Removed to Keokuk, IA where he d. abt 1926"
Census: 1900 Fabius, Schuyler, MO, p. 2A. G A Ross 39, Apr 1861, OH/OH/OH, furniture merchant; Francis Ross 36, Jul 1863; Edna Ross 16, Oct 1883, MO; Archie Ross 14, Sep 1885, MO; Welthie Ross 11, Sep 1888, MO; Alma Ross 6, Nov 1893, MO; Willis Ross 4, Oct 1895, MO; Lillie Brawdwell 13, niece, Mar 1887, MO. Married 17 years, 5 children / all living.
 1910 Keokuk Ward 5, Lee, IA, p. 1A. Geo Allen Ross 49, OH/OH/OH, laborer - rug factory; Mary F Ross 46, OH/OH/OH, 6 children/6 living; Pauline Ross 26, clerk - wall paper; Archie M Ross 24, laborer - rug factory; Alma Ross 16; William C Ross 14; Walter H Ross 9; Eugene Broadwell 21, boarder, MO, married, ball player - city team. Children all b. MO.
 1920 Keokuk Ward 2, Lee, IA, p. 8A. Geo A Ross 58, miller - cereal plant; Mary F Ross 56; Clarence H Mars 31, son in law, ND, plate maker - dental lab; Alma J Mars 26; Clayton R Mars 2 9/12, IA; Wm C Ross 24, machinist - rug factory; Walter H Ross 18, laborer - govt ?lock?
 1930 Keokuk, Lee, IA, p. 22A. Archie Ross 45, MO/OH/OH, no occ, m. age 34; Mame Ross 47, IA/OH/MO; Milton Ross 9, IA/MO/IA; Francis Ross 67, mother, OH/OH/OH, widowed.
 Iowa State Census 1925 Keokuk, Lee, IA, unp. George A Ross 63; Frankie M Ross 61; William Ross 29; Glen W Clark 36, son in law; Edna R Clark 41, dau.

Notes for Lindley Edward BROADWELL #369
Census: 1930 Ames, Story, IA, p. 11B. Lindley E Broadwell 61, salesman - dept store; Mae Broadwell 51; Lindley E Broadwell 25, draftsman - highway commission; Leon R Broadwell 19
Death date from tombstone in Ames Memorial Cemetery, Ames, IA.
Marriage date from burial information - City of Ames Cemetery. Ames, IA. Survivors: Mae Broadwell - spouse; Lindley Jr, Leon, Ruby Clark, Ruth Schard, Harriett Felenz, Lillian McCaffrey.

Notes for Mae ZIMMERMAN #369s
Census*: 1880 Pettis, Adair, MO, p. 58C. Grafton Zimmerman 40, miller, MD/PA/MD; Martha E. Zimmerman 44, OH/OH/OH; James B. Zimmerman 20; Catharine E. Zimmerman 14; Alfred C. Zimmerman 12; Emma Zimmerman 9; John Zimmerman 4; Nettie M. Zimmerman 2. Children b. MO. [*may not be correct family]
Death date from tombstone in Ames Memorial Cemetery, Ames, IA.

Notes for Herbert Fay BROADWELL #370
Jones notes: "m. 4/19/1891 to Sarah Millie Pindell. A school teacher at Queen City, MO. Was Sec of State Senate of Missouri, 1920-1924"
Census:
- 1900 Independence, Schuyler, MO, p. 6B. Fay H Broadwell 30, Sep 1869, OH, farmer; Millie S Broadwell 32, Nov 1867, OH; Chester A Broadwell 7, Oct 1892, MO; Mabel Broadwell 6, Mar 1894, MO; Harry Broadwell 4, Nov 1895, MO; Orma Broadwell 2 (f) Aug 1897, MO; Baby Broadwell 1/12 (m), Apr 1900, MO. 7 ch / 5 living. Married 9 yr, 7 ch / 5 living.
- 1910 Independence, Schuyler, MO p. 2A. Herbert F Broadwell 40, farmer; Sarah M Broadwell 41, 8 ch/6 living; Chester A Broadwell 17, farm labor; Mable Broadwell 16; Harry Broadwell 14, farm labor; Orma Broadwell 12; Clyde L Broadwell 10; Perley L Broadwell 7
- 1920 Independence, Schuyler, MO, p. 5B, Herbert F Broadwell 50, farmer; Sarah M Broadwell 51; Harry Broadwell 24, farmer; Clyde L Broadwell 19, farmer; Perley L Broadwell 16, farmer.
- 1930 Independence, Schuyler, MO, p. 8B. H Fay Broadwell 60, farmer; S Millie Broadwell 61

Marriage: H F Broadwell, Age: 21; Birth Date: abt 1870; Marriage: 14 Apr 1891 Schuyler County, MO; Spouse: Sarah M Pendell, Age: 22. Marriage book says "of Downing, MO" for both. Missouri Marriage Records, 1805-2002 [ancestry.com]
Politics: H. Fay Broadwell; Position: Official Reporter; Residence: Queen City; Officer of the Senate. Missouri State Offices Political and Military Records, 1919 - 1920 [ancestry.com]

Notes for Sarah Millie PINDELL #370s
Coffey Cemetery - Downing MO (Located South of Downing, MO
  Sarah M Broadwell   1867 - 1936   Mother

Notes for Percival BROADWELL #373
Jones notes: "m. 12/30/1900 to Nettie E. Wilson at Carlisle, KS. Removed to Clovis CA in 1907. A miller"
Census: 1900 Not found; not with family in Arkansas.
- 1910 Township 2, Fresno, CA, p. 13B. Percy Broadwell 33; Nettie Broadwell 29; Harold Broadwell 8; Kathleen Broadwell 4; Eugenia Broadwell 2
- 1920 Precinct 10, Maricopa, AZ, p. 17A. Perce Broadwell 43, farmer, OH/OH/OH; Nettie Broadwell 39, IL/OH/US; Harold Broadwell 18, AR; Catherine Broadwell 14, AR; Eugenia Broadwell 12, AR; Chester Broadwell 8 5/12, CA; Glenn Broadwell 1 4/12, AZ; Minerva Broadwell 75, widow. Next to Nathan Broadwell, 38 (his brother)
- 1930 Clovis, Fresno, CA, p. 11B. Perce Broadwell 53, farmer; Nellie E Broadwell 49; Kathleen A Broadwell 24, bookkeeper - electric office; Chester Broadwell 18; Glenn W Broadwell 11; Minerva Broadwell 85, mother.

Military: World War I Draft Registration Cards, 1917-1918 [Ancestry.com] Perce Broadwell, b. 8 Jan 1877; res: Higley, Maricopa, Arizona. Relative: Mrs. Nettie E. Broadwell, wife, same res. Farmer, self employed; tall, slender, light brown eyes, black hair. Reg: 12 Sep 1918.
Death: Perce Broadwell, b. 8 Jan 1877, OH; d. 20 Apr 1944 Fresno, CA; Age: 67; Mother's Maiden Name: Jones; Father's Last Name: Broadwell. California Death Index [archives.com]

Notes for Nettie E. WILSON #373s
Death: Nettie E Broadwell, b. 30 Jul 1880, Illinois; d. 18 Dec 1963, Fresno, CA; Age: 83; Mother's Maiden Name: Deatley. California Death Index [archives.com]

Notes for Nathaniel Dale BROADWELL #374
Jones notes: "m. 12/4/1900 to Elva Helen Clark at Grannis, AK. Resided (1929) at Modesto, CA. Salesman"
Census:
- 1910 Turlock, Stanislaus, CA, p. 9A. Dell Broadwell 29, farmer; Elva Broadwell 28, AR/MO/MO, m. 10 yrs, 4 ch / 4 living; Imogen Broadwell 9, AR; Eunice Broadwell 4, AR; Romba Broadwell 3, AR; Lionel Broadwell 1 8/12, CA; Andrew J Broadwell 74, own income, OH/NJ/NJ; Minerva Broadwell 66, own income, OH/OH/OH
- 1920 Precinct 10, Maricopa, AZ, p. 17A. Nathan Broadwell 38, farmer, OH/OH/OH; Elva H Broadwell 37, AR/MO/MO; Imogene Broadwell 18, AR; Eunice Broadwell 14, AR; Romba Broadwell 12, AR; Lionel Broadwell 10, CA; Karylton Broadwell 1/12, son, AZ; Lawrence Broadwell 45. brother, OH, burman?. Living next to brother Perce - their mother living with Perce.
- 1930 Turlock, Stanislaus, CA, p. 1A. Dale Broadwell 49, farmer; Elva H Broadwell 48; Kariylton V Broadwell 10, son.

Military: World War I Draft Registration Cards, 1917-1918 [Ancestry.com] Nathaniel Dale Broadwell, b. 4 Apr 1881, age 37; res: Clovis, Fresno, CA, farmer, relative: Elva Helen Broadwell, Clovis, CA; med height; med. build; brown hair & eyes. Registered: 12 Sep 1918.
Military: U.S. World War II Draft Registration Cards, 1942 [Ancestry.com] Nathaniel Dale Broadwell, b. 4 Apr 1881, age 61; b. Rural, Claremont Co, OH; Residence: Ceres, Stanislaus, CA; Person who will always know your address: Lawrence Broadwell, Ceres, CA. Self employed
Death: Nathaniel Broadwell, b. 4 Apr 1881; d. 1 Mar 1966; Age: 85; Last Known Residence: Ceres, CA Social Security Death Index [Archives.com]

Notes for Elva Helen CLARK #374s
Death: Elva Helen Broadwell, b. 4 Sep 1882, Arkansas; d. 20 May 1953 Stanislaus, CA; Age: 71; Mother's Maiden Name: Gibbons; Father's Last Name: Clark. California Death Index [Archives.com]

Notes for Edwin G. HELVERING #375
Jones notes: "m. 11/17/1897 to Mrs. Ida McGregor at Newport News VA. No Ch. Resided (1930) at Newport News"
Census
- 1900 Newport News Ward 5, Newport News City, VA, p. 11A. Edw* Helvering 24, Jun 1870, OH/OH/OH, machinist; Ida Helvering 29, Feb 1871, VA/VA/VA, m. 3 years, 2 ch/1 living; Kenneth M Helvering 6, Jan 1894, VA/OH/VA; Maral Williams 57, mother in law, widow, VA/VA/VA.
- 1910 not found
- 1920 Elizabeth City, Wythe Co, VA, p. 6A. Edward G Helvering 48, govt inspector - ship yard; Ida Helvering 45; [48]; Kenneth Helvering 20.
- 1930 Newport News, Newport News, VA, p. 9B. Ervin G Helvering 58, mech inspector - shipping yard; Ida Helvering 59; Kenneth M Helvering 33, married, no occ. Indexed as Helferiey

Notes for Beatrice Gertrude JONES #380
Jones notes give first name, birth date, spouse, marriage date
Marriage: W. G. Wood to Gertrude Jones; 27 Oct 1895, Clermont, OH. Ohio Marriages, 1800-1958 <familysearch.org>
Census: 1900 N. Washington, Clermont, OH. Wilber G Wood 28, Jan 1872, OH/OH/OH, Gertrude
   B. 24, Aug 1875; Effie 3, Mar 1897. M. 5 yrs, 2 ch / 1 living.
Death: Not found in OH Death Records

Notes for Wilbur Glenn WOOD #380s
Jones notes give name, marriage date
Not found in WW I Draft Registration 1917-18
Census:
  1910 Tate, Clermont, OH. p. 9B. Wilber G Wood 38, laborer - saw mill; Katherine Wood 34; Effie B
    Wood 13; Murel Wood 8; Alpha M Wood 1 10/12. Married 2 years, his 2nd, her 1st. Children 8/8
    living (doesn't compute - perhaps is an S or 0 with line through it)
  1920 Dayton, Rhea, TN, p. 2A. Wilber G Wood 45, retail merchant - grocery & novelty; Katie Wood
    44; Merrell Wood 18; Alpha Wood 11
  1930 St Cloud, Osceola, FL, p. 1B. W G Wood 58, m. age 24, carpenter - house; Kathryn M Wood 54,
    m. age 32; Alphe M Wood 21, single
Death: Wilber Glenn Wood; Death: Jan 1960; Osceola Co, FL Florida Death Index <ancestry.com>

Notes for Effie Maud JONES #381
Jones notes give first name, birth date, spouse, marriage date
Census: 1900 Jackson, Clermont, OH, p. 6A. Lewis Mcmahan 32, Sep 1867, merchant; Maud E
   Mcmahan 22, Aug 1877; Wilber L Mcmahan 3, Jul 1897; Byron J Mcmahan 2, Mar 1898.
Death: Maud Effie Mcmahan, d. 29 Aug 1909, Monterey, Clermont, OH; b. 7 Aug 1877, Clermont Co,
OH; Age: 32 years 22 days; Married; Housewife; Bur: 1 Sep 1909, Clarke Cem; Parents: Marcellus Jones,
b. OH / Elizabeth Shinkle, b. OH. Ohio Deaths 1908-1953 <familysearch.org>

Notes for Lewis O. MCMAHON #381s
Jones notes give name, marriage date
Census:
  1910 Meigs, Adams, OH, p. 11A. Louis O Mcmahan 42, retail merchant - general store; Wilbur
    Mcmahan 14; Byron Mcmahan 12; Gayle Mcmahan 9; Sarah Mcmahan 1; Sarah E Brewer 32,
    domestic. [52?]
  1920 Jacksonville, Adams, OH, p. 6B. L O Mcmahan 52, widow, merchant - general store; Gayle
    Mcmahan 19; Sarah Mcmahan 11
  1930 St. Clair, Butler, OH, p. 5A. Louis Mcmahan 62, proprietor - general store; Nona Mcmahan 44;
    Byron Mcmahan 31, salesman - radio.
Death: no death information found

Notes for Lola Agnes JONES #382
Jones notes give first name, birth date, spouse, marriage date, death year.
Census
  1900 Cincinnati, Hamilton, OH. p. 3A. Lola Jones 20, Oct 1880, working as servant for William &
    Fannie Biddle.
  1910, Cincinnati Ward 1, Hamilton, OH p. 8A. Joseph P Myler 34, OH/Ire/NY, policeman - city; Lola
    30; Elizabeth 2.
  1920 Williamsburg, Clermont, OH, p. 10A. Nathaniel Daily 63, widowed, undertaker; Lola A Myler 40,
    divorced, servant - private home; Elizabeth H Myler 12

1930 Sabina, Clinton, OH, p. 9B. Lola Dailey, 50, widowed
Not found on SSDI or Ohio Death Index. Possibly remarried.

Notes for Joseph Patrick MYLER #382s1

Jones notes: gives name, "div"

Census: 1900 Cincinnati Ward 26, Hamilton, OH, p. 10A. Patrick Mylor 59, policeman, Ire/Ire/Ire; Hannah Mylor 56, NY/Ire/Ire; Joseph Mylor 24, motorman - street rry, Dec 1925, OH; Emma Mylor 20; Katie A Mylor 18; Frank Mylor 14

Military: World War I Draft Registration Cards, 1917-1918 [Ancestry.com] Joseph Patrick Myler, age 42, b. 29 Dec 1875; res: Cincinnati, Hamilton Co, OH; occ: policeman - Cincinnati Police Dept; relative: Patrick Myler, Cincinnati, OH; tall, med build, grey eyes, brown hair, 1 finger crippled. Regis: 12 Sep 1918, Cincinnati, OH.

Death: Joseph Myler b. 1875; Res: Cincinnati, Hamilton, OH; d. 14 Oct 1959, Daniel Drake Memorial Hospital, Cincinnati; Age: 84; Widowed. Ohio Deaths, 1908-1932, 1938-1944, and 1958-2007 [Ancestry.com]

Notes for Nathaniel T. DAILY #382s2

Jones notes: gives name as W. T. Daily, death date, "undertaker"

Death: This is probably Nathaniel T. Dailey, for whom Lola was working in 1920. Death date & occupation match. b. 27 Jul 1856; d. 23 May 1929, Williamsburg, Clermont, OH. Spouse's name is Lola. Parents: Nathaniel Dailey, NY; Emma Dailey, OH. He was listed as widowed in the 1920 census. OH Death Certificate

Lola is widowed in the 1930 census.

Notes for Orville Guy JONES #383

Marriage: Guy Jones, age 24, b. 1882 Neville, OH; parents: Marcellus Jones, Elizabeth Shinkle; spouse: Lora Rogers, age 19, b. MO; parents: John Rogers, Sarah Davis; Marriage: 7 Oct 1906, Clermont County, OH; Ohio Marriages, 1800-1958 <familysearch.org>

Census
  1910 Cincinnati Ward 2, Hamilton Co, OH, p. 4A. Guy A Jones 28, OH/OH/OH, conductor - street railroad; Lora Jones 20, MO/OH/OH; Paul Jones 3; Orville Jones 2; Lawrence Jones 19, brother, car? repairman - own? shop; Frank Redgen 18, brother in law, MO/OH/OH, ___ factory
  1920 Cincinnati Ward 2, Hamilton, OH, p. 9B. Guy O Jones 37, conductor - street car; Lora Jones 30; Paul Jones 12; Orville Jones 11; Hilda Jones 6. next to Sarah Rogers, 73, widow, OH/OH/OH [possibly Lora's mother]
  1930 Cincinnati Ward 2, Hamilton, OH, p.232A. Gay O Jones 48, conductor - street railroad; Lora Jones 40; Paul Jones 23, salesman - lumber co; Orville Jones 21, city s___; Hilda Jones 16

Military: World War I Draft Registration Cards, 1917-1918 [Ancestry.com] Guy Orville Jones, age 36, b.10 Jan 1882; Res: Cincinnati, Hamilton Co, OH; occ: street car conductor - Auto Trac Co; relative: Lora Rogers Jones, wife; med height & build, grey eyes, brown hair. Reg: 10 Sep 1918, Cincinnati, OH.

Death: no death information found

Jones book gives "He was a street car conductor for the Cincinnati Transit System."

Notes for Lora ROGERS #383s

Jones book "After her husband's death, Lora ran her own seamstress business and was an employee at a florist in Madisonville"

Death: SS Death Index gives: Lora Jones b. 30 Jul 1889; d. Dec 1979; age 90; Cincinnati, Hamilton, OH; issued: Ohio; #273-24-9198

Death: Lora R Jones, b. 1889 Missouri; res: Cincinnati, Hamilton Co, OH; d. 27 Dec 1979, Mercy Hosp Anderson, Hamilton Co, OH; age 90, widow. Ohio Deaths, 1908-1932, 1938-1944, and 1958-2007 [Ancestry.com]

Discrepancy - Jones notes give death year as 1980; SS & Ohio Death index give 1979.

Notes for Carl Raymond JONES #384

Discrepancy - Jones notes give birth as 10 Jan 1882; 1900 census gives Nov 1884. 1884 would agree with 1920 census .WW II Draft Registration gives 25 Nov 1884.

Census:
- 1910 Glen Ellen, Sonoma, CA, p. 15A. Carl Jones 25, laborer on ranch; Lavina Jones 22.Both OH/OH/OH
- 1920 Cincinnati Ward 3, Hamilton, OH, p. 7A. Carl Jones 35, varnish maker - varnish co.; Lavina Jones 32; Alice Jones 3. All OH/OH/OH
- 1930 Cincinnati Ward 3, Hamilton, OH, p. 6A. Carl Jones 45, varnish maker - varnish co.; Lavina Jones 42; Alice Jones 13

Military: Carl Raymond Jones, age 57, b. 25 Nov 1884, Clermont Co, OH; res: Cincinnati, OH; occ: Foy Paint Co. Contact: Lavinia Jones. U.S. World War II Draft Registration Cards, 1942 [Ancestry.com]

Death: No death information found

Notes for Lavinia ROBINSON #384s

Jones notes: "living in Los Angeles, CA 1972

Census: 1900 Jefferson, Adams, OH, p. 2A. Winfield S Robinson 38; Martha J Robinson 34; George A Robinson 15; Arthur C Robinson 14; Lavina B Robinson 12, Aug 1887, OH; Martha E Robinson 11; Willis J Robinson 6; Homer E Robinson 5; William J Robinson 3; Ida A Robinson 4/12

Death: Lavina B Jones, SS#: 268052219; b. Ohio; d. 5 Jan 1976 Los Angeles, CA. California Death Index <Ancestry.com>

Notes for Ethel Grace JONES #385

All info from Orville Jones notes

Notes for Calvin BECKELHIMER #385s

From Jones book: "Calvin Beckelhimer; b. circa 1885; m. Ethel Jones; d. 20 Jul 1946; bur. circa 20 Jul 1946 in Mt Orab Cemetery, Green Township, Brown County, OH. Son of George Washington Beckelhimer & Elizabeth Ann Sutton"

Military: WW I Draft Registration [Ancestry.com] Calvin Beckelhimer, 32, b. 1 Oct 1885. Living in Burlington, Boone Co, OH. Farmer, closest relation: Ethel Beckelhimer. Medium height, medium build, brown eyes, dark hair. Registered at Burlington, KY 9/12/1918.

Census
- 1900, Neville, Clermont Co, OH. p. 4A. George W Beckelhimer 62, 1/1838, OH/VA/OH, farmer, m. 31 yrs; Elisabeth Beckelhimer 53 2/1847, OH/OH/OH, 11 ch, 7 living; Birtha Beckelhimer 23; George Beckelhimer 21; Wilson Beckelhimer 16; Calvin Beckelhimer 14, 10/1885, farm labor; Mary E Beckelhimer 12; Eva Beckelhimer 9.
- 1920 Burlington, Boone, KY; Page: 10A. Middle Creek Rd. Calvin Beckelheimer 33, OH/KY/OH, farmer; Ethel Beckelheimer 32; Calvin Jr. Beckelheimer 7; Harriet Beckelheimer 6; Laurence M Jones 29, b-in-l, farmer; James Jones 5, nephew; James M Jones 73, f-in-law, widowed; Mary Jones 27, s-in-law.
- 1930 Union, Warren, OH, p. 2B. Calvin Beckelhimer 44, farmer; Ethel G Beckelhimer 43; Calvin M Beckelhimer 17; Harry R Beckelhimer 16; Mary E Beckelhimer 8; Jack J Beckelhimer 4

Death: Calvin Beckelhimer, b. 1 Oct 1885, Adams Co, OH; d. 17 Jul 1946, Scott Twp, Brown, OH. Parents: George Beckelhimer & Elizabeth Sutton; Wife: Ethel Beckelhimer; Occ: farmer. Ohio Death Index <familysearch.org>.

Notes for Lawrence Marcellus JONES #386

Jones notes: m1 Margaret Sharp, who died; m2 Mary -?-. She resides (1972) at Milford, OH

Census
  1920 Burlington, Boone, KY, p. 10A. Calvin Beckelheimer 33; Ethel Beckelheimer 32; Calvin Beckelheimer 7; Harriet Beckelheimer 6; Lawrence M Jones 29, bro-in-law, widowed; James Jones 5, nephew; James M Jones 73, father in law; Mary Jones 27, sis-in-law
  1930 Covington, Kenton, KY, p. 4A. Minnie D Tingle 50; James C Tingle 19; Adna Davidson 40; Richard Davidson 74; Lawrence Jones 39, widowed, lodger, carpenter - contractor; James Jones 15, boarder, KY/OH/TN.

Military: World War I Draft Registration Cards, 1917-1918 [Ancestry.com] Lawrence Marcellus Jones, age 27, b. 5 Jun 1890, near Neville OH; res: Maysville, Mason Co, KY; occ: carpenter - Bates & Rogers Co; dependents: 1 child & father; married; med height & build; brown eyes & hair; regis: undated.

Notes for Genevieve Shinkle JONES #389

Jones notes: "She resides (1972) at Cincinnati O with her daughter"

Census: 1920 Symmes, Hamilton, OH, p. 5A. Geo F Hodges 23, machinist - tool shop; Jenevieve Hodges 23.
  1930 Cincinnati, Hamilton, OH, p. 15A. Thomas Hodges 36, letter carrier - post office; Genevieve Hodges 35; Virginia Hodges 6. All OH/OH/OH

Death: SS Death Index: Genevieve J. Hodges b. 24 Jan 1896; Jan 1996; Cincinnati, Hamilton, OH.

Death: Genevieve J Hodges [Genevieve J Jones], b. 24 Jan 1896, Clermont, OH; d. 13 Jan 1996, Butler Co, OH. Age: 99; #286-20-5798; Father: Jones; Mother: Beckelheimer; Widowed; Education: 8. Ohio Deaths, 1908-1932, 1938-1944, and 1958-2007 [Ancestry.com]

Notes for George Thomas HODGES #389s

Census: 1900 Williamsburg, Clermont, OH, p. 6B. Frank Hodges 45, farmer; Alice Hodges 27; George Hodges 3. All b. OH; m. 5 years, 1 child.

Military: World War I Draft Registration Cards, 1917-1918 [Ancestry.com] Geo Thomas Hodges, b. 1 Sep 1896, Camp Dennison, OH; father b. Nicholsville, OH; employer - F. T. Hodges, father; contact: Genevieve Hodges, wife; res: Camp Dennison, OH; grey brown eyes; lt. brown hair; regis: Norwood, Hamilton Co, OH, 5 Jun 1918.

Death: Social Security Death Index - George Hodges; #294-24-6286; Last Residence: Cincinnati, Clermont, OH; b. 1 Sep 1896; d. Aug 1968; issued: Ohio

Notes for Albert Essex JONES #390

Information from Jones book "M1 to Irene Keethler [b. 4/19/1874]; m2 Mabel Irene Thornton. He was a street car conductor in Cincinnati and for several years was President of the Street Railway Workers Union. Lived (1929) at 1639 Daumer in Cincinnati"

Jones notes: "d. 6/1/1962; buried Mt Moriah Cem; Mabel resides (1972) at 4168 O'Leary, Deer Park, OH"

Census
  1900 Cincinnati Ward 26, Hamilton, OH, p. 1A. Albert E Jones 28, Dec 1874, OH, conductor - street r.r.; Irene Jones 26, May 1874, OH; Ralph Jones 4, Jan 1896 OH; Marian Gillena 30, boarder, Aug 1873, Eng, saleslady dry goods.
  1910 Cincinnati Ward 2, Hamilton, OH, p. 1A. Albert E Jones 35, conductor - street railway; Irene Jones 35, m. 15 yrs, 2 ch / 2 living; Ralph C Jones 14; Forest A Jones 5. All OH/OH/OH.

1920 Cincinnati Ward 3, Hamilton, OH, p. 3A. Albert E Jones 45, conductor - street railway; Mabel Jones 29; Forest Jones 15; Lois Jones 3 5/12. All OH/OH/OH.

1930 Cincinnati, Hamilton, OH, p. 22A. Albert E Jones 55, conductor - street railway; Mabel I Jones 30; Louise Jones 14; Helen L Jones 2; Anna Thornton 42, sister; Bertha M Ellsberry 22, cousin, mailer - advertising. All OH/OH/OH.

Notes for Irene KEITHLER #390s

Census: 1880 Green, Brown, OH, p. 67A. Riley W. Keethler 35, farmer; Sarah R. Keethler 33; Ida J. Keethler 11; Emery E. Keethler 10; William W. Keethler 7; Irena Keethler 6; Mcdonold Keethler 4; Daniel S. Keethler 2. All b. OH.

Death: Irene Jones, d. 9 Jan 1912, Cincinnati, Hamilton, OH; b. 20 May 1874, Brown Co, OH; Age: 37 years 7 months 20 days; Married; Housewife; Burial: 11 Jan 1912, Mt. Orab, OH; Father: Riley Keethler, b. Brown Co, OH; Mother: Sarah Rebecca Black, b. Ohio. Ohio Deaths 1908-1953 <familysearch.org>

Notes for Mabel I. THORNTON

Death . Mabel Irene Jones, b. 20 Dec 1890, Clermont Co, OH; d. 8 Apr 1995, Montgomery, Hamilton Co, OH. Age 104. Father's name: Thornton; mother: Carter; widow. Ohio Deaths, 1908-1932, 1938-1944, and 1958-2002 <ancestry.com>

Notes for Hertha Katherine JONES #391

Jones notes - first name seems to be Hertha; Uertha K. on 1880 census .

Census

1900 Civil District 4, Claiborne, TN, p. 7A. Chas E Williams 25, Dec 1874, VA; Hertha K Williams 23, Jan 1877, OH; Leta Grace Williams 1, Dec 1898, TN. M. 2 years, 1 child, no occ.

1910 Green, Hamilton, OH, p. 11A. Charles E Williams 35, VA/VA/VA, baggage handler - depot; Katherine Williams 33; Leta Williams 11; Glendale Williams 6. OH/OH/OH for others.

1920 Cincinnati Ward 12, Hamilton, OH, p. 1A. Charles E Williams 44, checkman - r.r. depot; Katie H Williams 41; Glen D Williams 16

1930 Cincinnati, Hamilton, OH, 3B. Charles E. Williams 55, checkman - depot; Katherine H. Williams 53; Jack G. Williams, 26, lawyer - law practice. next to son in law - Tate Steele 38, machinist - lumber co; Lela G Steele 31; Shirley J Steele 8; Charles W Steele 5.

Notes for Jessie Agnes JONES #392

Census

1920 Norwood Ward 4, Hamilton, OH, p. 9A. Charles E Brown 43, OH, machine operator - machine co; Jessie A Brown 41, OH; Dorothy Brown 1 10/12

1930 Deer Park, Hamilton, OH, p. 24B. Charles E Brown 50, OH, cabinet maker - furniture plant; Josie Brown 32, wife, KY; Dorothy Brown 12; Margie Brown 10; Billy Brown 8; Wilburn Specht 18, nephew

Death: Jesse A. Brown, b. 11 Dec 1878, Liberty, OH; d. 27 Jan 1922, Sycamore Twp, Hamilton, OH; Age: 43 years 1 month 16 days; Married; Address: Monroe St; Occ: House Work; Burial: 30 Jan 1922 Pleasant Ridge Cem; Spouse: Charles E. Brown; Father: William ... Jones b. Pleasant ..., PA; Mother: Francis Essex, b. Pleasant ..., PA. Ohio Deaths, 1908-1953 <familysearch.org>

Notes for Charles Edwin BROWN #392s

Death: Charles Edwin Brown, b. 31 Jan 1874, Cleveland, OH; d. 9 Mar 1935, Cincinnati, Hamilton, OH; Age: 56 years 1 month 10 days; Married; Address: 4129 E OLeary Ave; Occ: Carpenter; Res: Deer Park; Burial: 13 Mar 1935, St. Joseph; Spouse: Josie Brown; Father: Andrew Brown, b. Pike, OH; Mother: Rachael Workman, b. Highland City, OH. Ohio Deaths, 1908-1953 <familysearch.org>

Notes for Anna Grace JONES #393
Jones notes: "resided at Madisonville OH (1972); d. 11/22/1971, bur. Laurel Cem, Madisonville, OH.

Census
- 1910 Cincinnati Ward 2, Hamilton, OH, p. 9B. Samuel Melvin 35, OH/OH/OH, timekeeper - whole dry goods; Anna G Melvin 28; Roslyn Melvin 7; John Dooley 35, lodger, teamster - horse mover; married 7 years, 1 child. All OH/OH/OH.
- 1920 Cincinnati Ward 13, Hamilton, OH, p. 6A. Samuel E Melvin 44, door watchman - paper towel fac; A Grace Melvin 38, toilet goods agency - drug store; Rosslyn E Melvin 16, son, machine band woodworking.
- 1930 Cincinnati, Hamilton, OH, p. 13A. Samuel Melvin 55, doorkeeper - dept store; Grace Melvin 47; William Harves 51, boarder.

Notes for Samuel Elmore MELVIN #393s
Jones notes. "bur. Laurel Cemetery, Madisonville, OH."
Census: 1880 Neville, Clermont, OH, p. 341. James S. Melvin 29, farmer, OH/MD/OH; Sallie A. Melvin 30; John H. Melvin 9; Winnie Melvin 7; Samuel E. Melvin 5; Ada E. Melvin 1
- 1900 Cincinnati Ward 8, Hamilton, OH, p. 5B. Oscar Mccalla 30; Samuel Melvin 25, lodger, OH/OH/OH, porter.

Death: Samuel Elmore Melvin, d. 11 Apr 1937, Cincinnati, Hamilton, OH; b. 19 Mar 1875, Clermont Co, OH; Age: 62 years 23 days; Married; address: 6710 Roe St.; Occ: Doorman; Burial: 14 Apr 1937; Cemetery: Laurel; Spouse: Anne Grace Melvin; Parents: James S. Melvin, b. Brown Co, OH / Sally Laugh, b. Clermont Co, OH. OH Deaths, 1908-1953 <familysearch.org>

Notes for Stella Blanche JONES #395
Jones notes. "resided at Madisonville, OH"

Census
- 1910 Cincinnati Ward 19, Hamilton, OH, p. 6A. Joseph W Pugh 30, OH/OH/OH, painter - house; Stella B Pugh 25; Starner D Pugh 2
- 1920 Marion Ward 3, Marion, OH, p. 3B. Joseph W Pugh 40, brakeman - steam railroad; Stella B Pugh 35; Starner D Pugh 11
- 1930 Cincinnati, Hamilton, OH, p. 41A. Joseph W Pugh 50, painter - house; Stella B Pugh 45; Carl S Pugh 22, accountant - radio parts.

Death: Stella Pugh, b. 1885; Res: Cincinnati, Hamilton Co, OH; Death: 5 Jan 1967, Long-Term Care Facilities, Cincinnati, Hamilton Co, OH. Age: 82, Widowed. Ohio Deaths, 1908-1932, 1938-1944, and 1958-2007 [Ancestry.com]

Notes for Joseph Warren PUGH #395s
Jones notes. "resided at Madisonville, OH"
Discrepancy: Jones notes give birth as 19 Mar 1875; WW I Draft registration gives 30 Sep 1879.
Military: WW I Draft Registration [Ancestry.com] Joseph Warren Puch, Hamilton Co, OH. age 38, b. 30 Sep 1879, brakeman - Erie Railroad, Marion, OH. Nearest relative: Mrs Estella Pugh. Med height, stout, blue eyes, brown hair. Regis: Sept 1918, Norwood, OH.
Death: Joseph W. Pugh, d. 28 Mar 1952, Jefferson Twp, Montgomery, OH, Birth: 30 Sep 1879, Bellefontaine, OH. Age: 72 years 5 months 28 days, married; Father: James B. Pugh; Mother: Mary B. Suttles. Died at VA Hospital, broken neck in fall from wheelchair. Usual residence: Madisonville, Hamilton Co, OH. Ohio Deaths, 1908-1953 <pilot.familysearch.org>

Notes for Alfred William JONES #398

Jones notes: "resided at Cincinnati; married Grace Ward; both bur Watkins Hill; he d. 12/27/68?"
Jones book gives "lived (1933) Cincinnati, OH". Another child, Loretta, d. in infancy - no dates.

Census:

1910 Millcreek, Hamilton, OH, p. 11B. Arthur W Jones 31, laborer - soap factory, m. 5 years; Grace B 29, 6 ch /4 living; Julia M 4; Alfred W 3; Roy E 2; Leona I. 5/12.

1920 Alfred not found; children scattered among relatives and others.

1920 Pierce, Clermont, OH. Alfred not found. Children: Alfred Jones 12 & Julia Jones 13 were with William H. 74 & Sallie Simmons 67, listed as niece and nephew. Roy Jones, 11, was 5 houses away as a boarder with George W. & Zouella Snider. Leona Jones, 10, was with Elijah & Hattie Reeves, listed as grandniece.

1930 not found

Military: World War I Draft Registration Cards, 1917-1918 [Ancestry.com] Alfred William Jones, age 40, b. 27 Feb 1878; res: Cincinnati, Hamilton, OH; occ: hyd___ worker - Proctor & Gamble; nearest relative: Julia Jones, New Richmond, OH; short, slender, brown eyes & hair; regis: Cincinnati, OH 12 Sep 1918.

Death: Alfred W. Jones, b. 1879; Res: Cincinnati, Hamilton, OH; d. 27 Dec 1968, Cincinnati. Age 89, widowed. Ohio Deaths, 1908-1932, 1938-1944, and 1958-2002 [Ancestry.com]

Notes for Grace Bell WARD #398

Death: Grace Bell Jones; d. 21 Aug 1913, Pierce, Clermont, OH; b. 21 Dec 1881, OH; Age: 31 yrs 7 mo 26 days; Married; Occ: Housekeeper; Burial 24 Aug 1913, Watkins Hill Cemetery. Father: John Ward, OH; Mother: Ella Welch, OH. Ohio Deaths 1908-1953 <familysearch.org>

Notes for Howard Hicks JONES #401

Jones notes: "m. Beulah Gladys Abercrombie; 3 sons, 2 girls. She resides (1973) at New Richmond"

Military: WW I Draft Registration: Howard Jones, age 20, b. 29 Jun 1887, New Richmond, OH. unemployed, single. Medium build, medium height, brown hair, brown eyes. Registered Jun 1917.

Census:

1910 Clermont Co, OH. p. 2B. Julia Jones 56, divorced, no occ, 7 ch/7 living; Dollie Jones 34, spinner - woolen mill; Jessie Jones 28, spinner - cotton mill; Howard Jones 22, laborer - transfer company; Clifford Jones 17, laborer - soap company; Chesley Jones 14. [father, Elijah Hicks Jones, p. 4A - also lives in Clermont Co, laborer - working out]

1920 Ohio, Clermont, OH, p. 11B. Julia Jones 64, widow, no occ; Dollie 45, spinner - woolen factory; Jessie Alfred 37, finisher - hosier mill; Howard 32, no occ; Chesley 33, machinist - car shop. All ch single.

1930 New Richmond, Clermont, OH, p. 3A. Julia Jones 75, widow; Dollie Jones 50; Jessie Jones 42, finisher - hosiery mill; Howard Jones 38, laborer - lumber yard; Chester Jones 32, painter. All ch single.

Death: Howard H Jones, b. 1888; Res: Clermont; d. 13 Feb 1967, home - Clermont Co, OH; Age: 79; Married. Ohio Deaths, 1908-1932, 1938-1944, and 1958-2002 [Ancestry.com]

Notes for Clifford O. JONES #402

Jones notes: "m. Aletha Walker; divorced, Clifford's whereabouts unknown.

Census

1920 St Bernard Ward 2, Hamilton, OH, p. 6A. Clifford Jones 28, pipe fitter - glue works; Aletha Jones 23; Jessie Jones 6; Earl Jones 2 11/12. All OH/OH/OH

1930 not found

Military: World War I Draft Registration Cards, 1917-1918 [Ancestry.com] Clifford O Jones, age 25, b. 3 Aug 1892, New Richmond, Ohio; res: St Bernard, Hamilton Co, OH; occ: laborer - Proctor & Gamble; dependents: wife & 2 children; med height & build, brown eyes & hair; regis: 5 Jun 1917, St Bernard, OH.

Notes for Althea WALKER #402s

Jones notes: "m. Aletha Walker; divorced, Clifford's whereabouts unknown. She remarried to Frank Dunn. (1972) 4227 29th St, Cincinnati"; Jones book says "lived (1930) New Richmond, OH"

Birth: Aletha Walker, b. 16 Feb 1896, Sterling, Brown, Ohio; Father: Ora W Walker; mother: Pervilla K Leonard. Ohio Births and Christenings, 1821-1962 <pilot.familysearch.org>

Census

 1900 Williamsburg, Clermont, OH, p. 10B. Orie N Walker 27, Jul 1872, engineer; Rewilla Walker 26, Apr 1872; Iola Walker 5, Feb 1895; Aletha Walker 4, Feb 1896; May Walker 1/12, May 1899. All OH/OH/OH

 1920 St Bernard Ward 2, Hamilton, OH, p. 6A. Clifford Jones 28, pipe fitter - glue works; Aletha Jones 23; Jessie Jones 6; Earl Jones 2 11/12

 1930 Cincinnati, Hamilton, OH, p. 1B. Frank L Dunn 37, shirt cutter - shirt factory; Aletha E Dunn 34; Jessie M Jones 16, step dau, clerk - dry cleaner

Notes for Leontine Orrene JONES #404

Jones notes: "m. 2/5/1896 to James Emmet Clark at Wayne NE [b. 12/13/1874 at Oakland IA]. Resided (1930) at Leith ND. She d. 4/11/1964; h. d. 1/30/1953. Both bur Colmer? CA"

Death: Leta O Clark; d. 11 Apr 1964 Marin Co; b. 29 Aug 1877, Ohio. California Death Index, 1940-1997 [Ancestry.com]

Notes for James Emmet CLARK #404s

Census

 1900 Wilbur, Wayne, NE, p. 3B. James E Clark 25, farmer, IA/PA/OH; Led O Clark 22, OH/OH/OH; Georgia G Clark 2, NE/IA/OH

 1910 Township 133, Morton, ND, p. 14A. Enmet E Clark 35, IA/PA/IL, farmer; Leta O Clark 32; Georgie G Clark 12, NE; Ceil M Clark 9, NE; Roscom C Clark 7, NE. M 13 yrs, 4 ch, 3 living.

 1915 ND State Census, Morton, Valley View, ND. Emmet J. Clark, 40 ; Leta O. 38 ; Georgie G. 17 ; Cecil E. 14; Roscoe G. 12; Edith I. 4.

 1920 Valley View, Grant, ND, p. 2B. Emmet Clark 45, IA/PA/IN, farmer - general farm; Leta O 42, OH; Cecel E 18, NE; Rosco G 17, NE; Edith I 9, ND.

 1930 Valley View, Grant, ND, p. 2A. Emmet Clark 55, farmer - general farm; O Leta 53; Florance Clark 26, dau-in-law, IA, m. age 19; Edith Clark 6, niece, ID; Ardith Clark 4 10/12, niece, ID; Gordon Clark 6/12, nephew, ND. [Children are actually grandchildren, children of his son Roscoe]

Military: WW I Draft Registration: James Emmet Clark, Leith, Grant Co, ND. age 43, b. 13 Dec 1874. Farmer, wife: Leta O Clark. Signed J. Emmet Clark. Medium height & build, blue eyes, light hair. Registered 12 Sep 1918.

Death: James Emmett Clark; b. 13 Dec 1874 Iowa; d. 30 Jan 1953, Marin Co; Mother's Maiden Name: Reed; Father's Surname: Clark. California Death Index, 1940-1997 [Ancestry.com]

Notes for Roxy Dale JONES #405

Info from Jones notes: "m. 2/6/1898 to Wm Jacob Evans at Wayne NE [b. 3/6/1877 PA] Resided (1930) Wayne NE"

Census:

 1900 Wilbur, Wayne, NE, p. 2a. William J. Evans, 23, Mar 1878, farmer; Roxy D. 10, 1 ch/1 liv.

1910 Precinct 5, Cedar, NE, p. 2a. William J Evans 33, farmer - general farm; Rosy D 30, m. 11 yrs, 5 ch/ 5 living; Orene 11; Fay O 9; Laura M 7; Dale E 4; Wilma J 2; William C Jones, 24, NE, hired man, farm labor - working out.

1920 Precinct 5, Cedar, NE, p. 16a. William J Evans 42, farmer; Roxy D 39; Orene G 20, NE, housekeeper; Fay O 18, housekeeper; Laura M 16; Dale E 13; Wilma J 11; Grace M 9; Dorotha G 7; Rex W 4 10/12. Children b. NE

1930 Wayne, Wayne Co, NE, p. 11a. William Evans 53, laborer, PA/PA/PA; Roxy 50, OH/OH/OH; Wilma 22; Grace 19; Rex 15; Fred Wohlman 25, son-in-law, NE/NE/NE; Dale Wohlman 23, dau; Eugene Wohlman 3 2/12, grandson; Blain Wohlman 1 ??/12, grandson; Kenneth Wohlman 5/12, grandson; Dorathea Evans 17, dau; William E Braisted 59, lodger, NY/NY/NY, minister - Baptist church. Children b. Nebraska; occupations of sons illegible.

No death information found.

Notes for William Jacob EVANS #405s

Family Tree of Elaine Edwards on Ancestry.com, gives his parents as Harrison & Elizabeth (Wentz) Edwards. No documentation.

Military: World War I Draft Registration Cards, 1917-1918 [Ancestry.com] William Jacob Evans, age 41, b. 6 Mar 1877; res: Wynot, Cedar Co, NE; occ: farming - self employed; contact: Roxy Dale Evans, same residence; tall, med. build, blue eyes, brown hair, no disabilities. Regis: 12 Sep 1918.

Notes for Edith Mary JONES #406

Jones notes: "m. 8/20/1916 to John Will at Leith ND [b. 1/21/1894 Menno SD; Resided ND 1930. He d. 7/23/1982; she d. 9/5/1961 Leith; bur Lewiston, MT]"

Death: Edith Will, Age: 79; Est. birth year: abt 1882; Death: 5 Sep 1961, Custer Co, MT. Res: Custer Co, MT. Married. Montana Death Index, 1860-2007 [Ancestry.com]

Notes for John WILL #406s

Census

1900 Township 97, Hutchinson, SD, p. 1B. Gottlieb Will 36, Russia; Fredericka 30, Russia; Emil 10; Gottlieb R 8; John 6, Feb 1894; Martha 5; Eugene E 10/12; Christine Will 70. 8 ch/5 living. Children all b. SD. [probably correct family - not proven but most facts fit]

1910 Menno Ward 1, Hutchinson, SD, p. 1A. same family; John 16, yardman. Parents immigrated 1873.

1920 Leith, Grant, ND, p. 8B. John Wille 26, SD, merchant - retail; Edith M 33, CO; Ineta M 1 7/12, ND; Manda F 3/12, ND.

1930 Bismarck, Burleigh, ND, p. 10A. John Will 38, SD/Rus/Rus, bank examiner - State Capitol; Edith 42, CO/OH/OH; Izeta 12, ND; Wanda 10, ND; Warren 9, ND.

Military: World War I Draft Registration Cards, 1917-1918 [Ancestry.com] John Will, Grant Co, ND; age 23, b. 21 Jan 1894, Memue?, SD. Merchant & asst. postmaster; married; short, stout, brown hair, brown eyes, disability: frequent attacks of rheumatism. Registered: Leith, ND, Jun 1917.

Death: John Will, Age: 88; Est. birth year: abt 1894; **death:** 23 Jul 1982, Cascade Co, MT; #516-03-1422; Widowed. Montana Death Index, 1860-2007 [Ancestry.com]

SS Death Index: John Will; #516-03-1422; Last Residence: Great Falls, Cascade, MT.

Notes for Marcellus Findly JONES #407

Jones notes. "d. 1975 Cal - does not say which of them"

Census:

1910 Strahan, Wayne, NE, p. 15A. Marcellus F Jones 28, farmer - gen farm, IA/OH/IN; Bertha Jones 24, NE/IA/WI; Clinton Jones 1; Marcellus Jones Jr 1/12; Roy Peterson 28; Deon Rathbun 17; Frances Stone 19. last 3 - farm labor.

1920 Strahan, Wayne, NE, p. 9A. Marcollos Jones 38, farmer; Bertha Jones 33; Clinton Jones 11; Marcollos Jones 9; Dale Jones 5; Floyd Jones 2; Loyd Jones 2

1930 Township 36, Bennett, SD, p. 1A. Marcellus Jones 47, farmer; Bertha Jones 44; Clinton Jones 21, farm labor; Marcellus Jones 19, farm labor; Dale Jones 16, farm labor; Floid Jones 13; Lloyd Jones 13; Hellen Jones 7. Ch all b. NE.

Military: WW I Draft Registration: Marcellous Findly Jones; Wayne, Wagner Co, NE; Birth: 7 Jul 1881, age 37; farmer, Contact: Bertha Mabel Jones. Medium build; medium height; blue eyes; brown hair. Registered: 12 Sep 1918.

Death: SS Death Index gives: Marcelles Jones; b. 7 Jul 1881; d. Jan 1964, CA; Issued: SD.

Death: Marcelle F Jones; #504075875; b. 7 Jul 1881, IA; d. 28 Jan 1964 Los Angeles; Mother's Maiden Name: Strahn. California Death Index [Ancestry.com]

Notes for Bertha Mabel CHERRY #407s

May be the Bertha Cherry in Iowa, Holt, NE, 1900 census, p. 3A. Birth date does not match, but she is only Bertha or Mabel Cherry in Nebraska. Dau of George & Marry Cherry.

No death information found.

Notes for Gayle E. JONES #408

Info from Jones notes.

Census: 1910 Wayne, Wayne, NE. George Sherbahn 28, PA, no occ; Gale Sherbahn 27. Living next to her parents - D. A. Jones.

1920 Wayne, Wayne, NE, p.7B. Doc A Jones 61, no occ; Lucy E Jones 60, IL; Dorathy Jones 18, NE; George Sherbahn 38, son-in-law, inspector - house, PA/PA/PA; Gail Sherbahn 36, dau, IA/OH/IL; Bernadine Sherbahn 9, dau, NE; Donald Sherbahn 7, son, NE.

1930 Wayne, Wayne, NE, p. 1B. D A Jones 72, farmer, widowed; Albert Jones 37, son, laborer ___ job; Edna Jones 37, dau-in law, saleslady - dry goods; Marion Jones 14, grandson; June Jones 12, granddau; Neva Jones 11, granddau; Bonnell Jones 8, granddau; George Sherbahn 43, son-in-law, advertising? - carnival; Gail Sherbahn 46; Bernadine Sherbahn 19, dau in law; Donald Sherbahn 17, grandson; Betty Meister 4 2/12, granddau; Cora Pratt 60, lodger.

Notes for George Garfield SHERBAHN #408s

Military: World War I Draft Registration Cards, 1917-1918 [Ancestry.com] George Garfield Sherbahn, age 36, b. 22 Sep 1881; res: Wayne, Wayne, NE; occ: laborer; relative: Mrs Gayle Sherbahn; med height & build; grey eyes, black hair; regis: 6 Sep 1918, Wayne Co, NE.

Notes for Jay Miller JONES #409

Info from Jones notes.

Census

1910 Strahan, Wayne, NE, p. 14A. Jay Jones 23, IA/OH/IL, farmer; Fern Jones 20 MO; Dorothy Jones 9/12, NE; Charles Mcmakin 33, farm labor; Charles Brietrom 21, farm labor

1920 Sioux City Precinct 2, Woodbury, IA, p. 14B. James M Jones 34, broker - real estate; Fern J Jones 30; Dorothy F Jones 10, NE; James M Jones 8, NE; Joe P Kirkendall 25, boarder, auto mechanic

Military: WW I Draft Registration [Ancestry.com] Jay Miller Jones, age 32, b. 19 Sep 188_; res: Sioux City, Woodberry Co, IA, Auto sales & repairman, D. A. Jones Auto; tall, med build, blue eyes, light hair, no defects. Register Sep 1918.

Notes for Fern BARLEY #409s

Census: 1910 Wayne, Wayne, NE, p. 2A. S M Barley 45, Apr 1855, PA, carpenter; Emma Barley 44, Jul 1855, IA; Joe Barley 21, Mar 1879, IA; Pearl Barley 18, Apr 1882 IA; Fern Barley 10, Oct 1890, MO. Not found on 1930 census - possibly remarried?

Notes for Roscoe Otis JONES #410

Info from Jones notes.

Census

1910 White Cloud, Mills, IA, p. 5. Rosco Jones 22 IA/OH/IL, farmer; Ellan 18, IA/IL/OH, married 1 year; Mildred 4m, NE; Fred Fisher 32, US, hired man; Sinnie Seaton 15, TN, hired girl.

1920 Strahan, Wayne, NE, p. 7A. Roscoe Jones 32, farmer; Ellem Jones 28; Mildred Jones 10; Jean Jones 7; Elizabeth Jones 5; Robert Jones 3; Elva Jones 6/12

1930 Wayne, Wayne, NE, p. 18B. Roscoe O Jones 42, IA, salesperson - service station; Ellen M Jones 38, m. age 18; Mildred G Jones 20, telephone operator; Jean E Jones 18; Elizabeth J Jones 16; Robert O Jones 13; Elva M Jones 10; Billy M Jones 9; Joan F Jones 1 11/12; Infant Jones 1/12. Ch b. NE.

Military: World War I Draft Registration Cards, 1917-1918 [Ancestry.com] Roscoe Otis Jones, age 29, b. 23 Dec 1888, Malvern, Iowa; res: Wayne, NE; dependents - wife & 4 children under 12; tall, med build, blue eyes, brown hair. Regis: Strahan, Wayne Co, NE; 5 Jun 1917.

Notes for Albert Doctor JONES #412

Info from Jones notes. "d. 1/24/1955 at Downey Cal"

Census:

1920 Strahan, Wayne, NE, p. 10A. Albert Jones 26, NE/OH/IL, farmer; Edna Jones 27, NE/IL/IN; Marion Jones 3; June Jones 2; Neva Jones 1; Payne Bert 33; Cora Pratt 48, m-in-law, IN/OH/OH. Ch b. NE.

1930 Wayne, Wayne, NE, p. 1B. D A Jones 72, farmer, widowed; Albert Jones 37, son, laborer ___ job; Edna Jones 37, dau-in law, saleslady - dry goods; Marion Jones 14, grandson; June Jones 12, granddau; Neva Jones 11, granddau; Bonnell Jones 8, granddau; George Sherbahn 43, son-in-law; Gail Sherbahn 46; Bernadine Sherbahn 19, dau in law; Donald Sherbahn 17, grandson; Betty Meister 4 2/12, granddau; Cora Pratt 60, lodger.

Military: World War I Draft Registration Cards, 1917-1918 [Ancestry.com] Albert Doctor Jones, age 24, b. 8 Jun 1892, Wayne Co, NE; res: Wayne, NE; farmer; dependents: wife & 2 children; medium height & build, blue eyes, brown hair. Regis: 4 Jun 1917, Strahan, Wayne Co, NE.

Death: Albert Doctor Jones, #507-01-4584; b. 8 Jul 1893, NE; d. 23 Jan 1955, Los Angeles; Mother's Maiden Name: Strahn; Father's Surname: Jones. California Death Index, 1940-1997 [Ancestry.com]

Notes for Edna Fae PRATT #412s

Census: 1900 Wayne, Wayne, NE, p. 4A. Ed Pratt 28, Jul 1871, IL, bartender; Cora Pratt 30, Jan 1870, IN; Edna Pratt 8, Jul 1892, NE; Arthur Pratt 6. M. 8 years.

Death: Edna Fae Jones [Edna Fae Pratt]; #507-01-4583; b. 8 Jul 1892, Nebraska; d. 3 Apr 1981, Los Angeles, CA; Mother's Maiden Name: Bloodhart; Father's surname: Pratt. California Death Index, 1940-1997 [Ancestry.com]

Notes for Dorothy F. JONES #413

Info from Jones notes.

Notes for John August MEISTER #413s
Not found on 1930 census; daugher Betty with grandparents.
Military: World War I Draft Registration Cards, 1917-1918 [Ancestry.com] John August Meister, b. 15 Oct 1892, West Point, NE; res: Dallas, Gregory, SD; occ: machinist - stationary engineer; single, tall, med build, blue eyes, light hair; regis: 5 Jun 1917, Dallas, Gregory Co, SD.
Death: John A Meister, b. 15 Oct 1893; d. 29 Dec 1971; Otter Tail Co, MN; Mother's Maiden Name: Kriger. Minnesota Death Index, 1908-2002 [Ancestry.com]
  SS Death Index gives a John Meister, same birth date, d. Dec 1971 in Ottertail, Otter Tail, MN. Card issued Nebraska.
Information: Ancestry Family tree "DM Bluechel Family Tree " gives death as 29 Dec 1971 in Ottertail, Otter Tail, Minnesota. Gives parents as Johannes August Meister 1859-1923 and Theresa Krienert 1864-1939. No documentation. John A. Meister is on 1900 census as a 6 year old, b. Oct 1893 with parents: John Meister 40; Theresa Meister 35

Notes for Selma GUYETTE #423
Information from Ancestry Web pages of Alan Case, whose wife is a descendant of William Guyette & Josephine Owens. 5/1/2010; states "4 living children".
Census:
  1920 East St Louis Ward 6, St. Clair, IL, p. 3A. Herschel Reeves 34, GA/GA/GA, salesman - stock; Selma Reeves 31, MO; Letha Reeves 5, IL; Herschel Reeves 2 6/12, IL.
  1930 East St Louis Ward 6, St. Clair, IL, p. 2A. Herschel Reeves 46; Selma Reeves 41; Letha Reeves 15; Herschel Reeves 12; Floyd L Reeves 6; Norman H Reeves 4 2/12
Death: Selma M. Reeves, 1944-10-03; East St Louis, St Clair, IL. Illinois Statewide Death Index 1916-1950

Notes for Hershel William REEVES #423s
Military: World War I Draft Registration Cards, 1917-1918 [Ancestry.com] Herschel William Reeves, age 34, b. 17 Jun 1884; res: East St Louis, St Clair, IL; occ: mule salesman - Harper Brothers; wife: Selma Reeves; tall, slender, blue eyes, brown hair. Regis: 12 Sep 1918, E. St Louis, IL.
No death information found.

Notes for Raymond Joseph GUYETTE #424
Information from great grandson via Ancestry Message Board and Case Family Tree [Ancestry.com]
Military: WW I Draft Registration [Ancestry.com] Ray Guyette, East St Louis, St Clair, IL; Age 25, b. 27 May 1892, IL. Clerk, Swift & Co, Natl Stock Yards; wife & 2 children; medium height, slender, dk brown eyes & hair.
Census: 1920 East St Louis Ward 6, St. Clair, IL, p. 11B. Raymond Guyett 27, yardmaster - stockyard, IL/France/IL; Sydona R Guyett 26; Raymond Guyett 8; Edward W Guyett 5
  1930 not found

Notes for Gussie E. HOLDERFIELD #426
Census
  1910 Ohio, Clermont, OH, p. 1A. John Gilfillan 30, dairyman; Gussie 29, wife; Ethelene 4, dau. next to Andrew A Light 54, farmer; Emma 51 (Gussie's parents).
  1920 Ohio, Clermont, OH, p. 2B. Andy Light 62, salesman - creamery, OH/US/Wales; Emma 61; John Gilfilen 40, son-in-law, widowed, foreman - novelty co, OH/MD/OH; Etheleen 13, grandchild.
Marriage: John G. Gilfillen, b. 1879, Moscow, Clermont Co, OH; parents: A.W. Gilfillen, Mary Hogan; spouse: Gussie E. Holderfield; marriage:14 Aug 1904, Clermont County, OH. Ohio County Marriages, 1790-1950 <familysearch.org>

Death: Gussie E. Gilfillen, d. 17 Dec 1918, New Richmond, Clermont, OH; b. 11 May 1880, Illinois; age: 38 years 7 months 6 days; married; Occ: House Work; Res: New Richmond, Clermont, OH; Burial: 20 Dec 1918, Green Mound Cem; father: Taylor Holdenfield, b. OH; mother: Mary Hicks, b. OH. d. of pneumonia; contributory cause: confinement. Ohio Deaths 1908-1953 <familysearch.org>. Evidently died just after birth of Mary Jane.

Notes for John Graham GILFILLEN #426s
Census:

1900 Moscow, Clermont, OH, p. 9B. Augustus Gilfillen 40; Marrie 51; Wm 25; John 21, Jun 1879 OH; James 18; Elsie 16; Tomas 12; Nellie 10.

1930 Ohio, Clermont, OH, p. 7A. John Gilfillan 50, foreman - coat hanger factory; Carris C Gilfillan 50; John Gilfillan 6; Mary F Gilfillan 4.

Military: World War I Draft Registration Cards, 1917-1918 [Ancestry.com] John Graham Gilfillen, age 39, b. 7 Jun 1879; machinist - __meminate Milling Machine Co, New Richmond, OH; nearest relative: Gussie Gilfillen; Med height & build, blue eyes, dark hair; deformed left foot & ankle; regis: Batavia, OH, Sep 12, 1918

Military: U.S. World War II Draft Registration Cards, 1942. John Gram Gilffillen, age 62, b. 11 Jun 1879, Moscow, Clermont, OH, wife: Carrie Gifillen; Residence: New Richmond, Clermont, OH

Information: Family tree of pesh527 on Ancestry gives death as 5 Oct 1946 in New Richmond, Clermont Co, OH. Not documented. "Married Carrie Judd 1920 - two children, both living."

Death: No death information found

Notes for Ethel HOLDERFIELD #427
Jones notes: "Resided at New Richmond, OH; no children"
Death: Ethel Beckman, birthplace: Salem, IL. Street address: 650 W. McMicken St. Married to August Beckman, housewife. Parents: Taylor Holderfield & Mary E. Hicks. <www.familysearch.org>
Census:

1920 Cincinnati Ward 11, Hamilton, OH, p. 1B. August J Beckman 37, OH/OH/OH, head - roofing & sheet metal works; Ethel 37; Gussie P 1, dau. two houses away from William Beckman, 70, OH/Baden/Baden, retired & Lena 67, OH/Alsace/Alsace.

1930 Cincinnati, Hamilton, OH, p. 5A. August J Beckman 47, tinner - roofing company; Ethel 48; Etheline 23, clerical work - roofing co; Mary Jane 11. Next to William (81) & Lena (78) Beckman. Both b. OH, parents b. Germany.

Notes for August John BECKMAN #427s
Death: August Beckman, b. 2 Oct 1883; d. Mar 1971; Cincinnati, Hamilton, OH; #284-16-1841; Card issued: Ohio. SS Death Index [rootsweb.com]
Military: WW I Draft Registration [Ancestry.com] August John Beckman, b. 2 Oct 1883, living in Cincinnati, OH, age 35, contact: Ethel Beckman: roofing contractor, working for William Beckman Co, Cincinnati, OH. Tall, medium build, gray hair, light complexion. Sept 1918.
Jones notes: "Resided at New Richmond, OH; no children"

Notes for Mary Edna H. MEENACH #428
Census
  1920 Maysville, Mason, KY. Robert F Cablish 37, grocer?; Edna Cablish 32; Evelyn Cablish 13; John Boulden 78, boarder. Indexed on Ancestry.com as Carlisle.
  1930 District 7, Mason, KY, p. 3A. Alexander H Calvert 23, farmer; Evelyn C Calvert 23; Alexander H Calvert, Jr 1 /12; Robt F Cablish 46 f-in-law, salesman - meat; Edna Cablish 42, m-in-law
Death: Edna Cablish; d. 3 Feb 1970, Jefferson Co, KY; Age: 84; Residence: Jefferson Co, KY. Kentucky Death Index, 1911-2000 [Ancestry.com]

Notes for Robert Fredrick CABLISH #428s
Military: World War I Draft Registration Cards, 1917-1918 [Ancestry.com] Robert Fredrick Cablish, age 36, b. 22 Feb 1882; res: Mason, KY; grocer, J. C. Cablish & Bro, Maysville, KY. Contact: Edna M. Cablish, wife. Short, slender, black eyes, dark hair. Registered 12 Sep 1918.
Death: R E Cablish, d. 5 Aug 1946, Mason, Residence: Mason. Age: 63, b. 22 Feb 1883, Maysville, KY; Spouse: Edna Meenach; Father: Jacob Cablish, b. Maysville, KY; Mother: Margaret Bodey, b. Maysville, KY. Kentucky Death Records, 1852-1953 [Ancestry.com]

Notes for Celia Mae HUTCHISON #430
Jones notes: "Resided (1972) 1026 Forest Av, Maysville, KY 41056"
Death: Celia M Cooper, age 84, Mason Co., 10-09-1972. KY Death Index [Ancestry.com]
Census: 1910 Maysville Ward 2, Mason, KY, p. 4B. C Marshall Cooper 27, wagon driver - express; Celia M 22, wife; Charles H Cooper, 60, father, widowed, janitor - school; Harris B Cooper 25, brother, brakeman - railroad. Married 2 years, 1 child / 1 living. All b. KY. (question - where is the child?)
  1920 not found
  1930 District 21, Mason, KY, p. 2B. Marshall Cooper 48, no occ; May Cooper 41

Notes for Charles Marshall COOPER #430s
Census: 1900 - Probably the Charles M. Cooper, age 18, b. Jan 1882, KY. Living in Maysville, Mason Co, KY with parents Charles H. 53, janitor - public school & Emma V, 43, siblings Natalie 19 & Harry 15.
Military: World War I Draft Registration Cards, 1917-1918 [Ancestry.com] Charles Marshall Cooper, age 36, b. 18 Jan 1882; res: Mason Co, KY; express manager - C. O. R. R.; contact: Celia May Cooper, Maysville, med. height, slender, brown hair & eyes. Registered: Sept 12, 1912.
Death: Charles Marshall Cooper, d. 31 Aug 1940, Mason Co, KY; Age: 58. b. 18 Jan 1882, Maysville, KY. wife Celia Mae, age 51, clerk. Father: Charles Henry Cooper, b. Fleming, KY?; mother - Emma Harris, b. Germantown, KY. Informant: Mrs. Anson McConnell, Key West, FL. Burial: Maysville, KY. Kentucky Death Records, 1852-1953 [Ancestry.com]

Notes for Edward Roy HUTCHISON #431
Jones notes: "Resides (1972) Rt 11, S. of Lewisburg, KY 41056"
Census: 1920 Not found
  1930 District 21, Mason, KY, p. Edward R Hutchinson 37, mechanic - garage; Lena 32; Mildred B 14; John M 11; Ruth V 7; Effie N 5; William E 3 2/12; Robert L 3 2/12 [indexed by Ancestry.com as Hutchins]
Military: World War I Draft Registration Cards, 1917-1918 [Ancestry.com] Edward Ray Hutchison, age 24, b. 13 Aug 1892, Maysville, KY; res: Maysville, Mason, KY; occ: chauffeur - Omar Dodson; dependents - wife & child aged 2; tall, med build, grey eyes, dk brown hair. Regis: Mason Co, KY, Jun 1917.

Death: Roy Hutchison, d. 25 Jan 1981; Mason Co, KY, age 88; [calculated birth year of 1893] Kentucky Death Index, 1911-2000 [Ancestry.com]
SS Death Index gives: Roy Hutchison, b. 13 Aug 1892; d, 1 Jan 1981; age 88; Maysville, Mason, KY; issued Kentucky; #404-07-9387

Notes for Lena BREEZE #431s
Death: Lena Hutchison, b. 24 Feb 1896; 25 Jun 1996; age 100; Maysville, Mason, KY; issued Kentucky; #401-54-6428. Social Security Death Index.

Notes for Leslie Brand HICKS #433
Jones notes: "Betty resides (1973) at 5461 Alexander Rd, Parma, OH"
Census: 1930 - Cuyahoga Co, OH. Leslie B. Hicks [indexed Hicko] 25, Ky/KY/KY, receiving clerk - dept store; Margaret 26, PA, Glenn H. 7, b. CA; Leslie W. 3 5/12, b. OH. Living with James P. & Emma Hicks & family - his parents? Next to James P. Glenn 54, PA, foreman - railroad, Emma M. 56. Her parents?
Death: Probably the Leslie Hicks who died in Ohio in November 1961, no location given in SS. Death Index. Birth date is off by 2 days (7 Jun 1905)
Obituary: *Leslie B. Hicks, Beloved husband of Mildred E. (nee Mitchell), father of Lesh Jr., Robert, David, Lynda, Becky Snodgrass and Glenn Kelly, and grandfather; son of William P. and the late Lillian, brother of William and Hazel Faloon, Saturday, Nov. 11, 1961. Friends may call Tuesday 2-5 And 7-10 P. M. at McGorray Bros. Lakewood Home, 14133 Detroit Ave. where services will be held Wednesday, Nov. 75, at 1 p. m. Rev. James Reeder officiating. Roosevelt Lodge Numher 650 will conduct Masonic services Tuesday evening, Nov. 14, at 8 p. m.* Nov 11 1961 **Plain Dealer**; Cleveland Necrology File.

Notes for Hazel Lee HICKS #434
Jones notes: "Resides (1972) at 8216 Russell Ln, Cleveland, OH"
Census: 1930 Cleveland, Cuyahoga, OH. Emma Hicks 56, widowed, gen housework - private house; William Hicks 16; Hazel Faloon 21, dau, married (at age 16), saleslady - dry goods. [Hazel's husband, John, is living with his parents and is listed as single]
Death: Hazel Lee Faloon [Hazel Lee Hicks], b. 9 Jan 1909, KY; d. 7 Mar 1993, Allen Memorial Hospital, Oberlin, Lorain Co, OH. Age: 84; Father's Surname: Hicks; Mother's Maiden Name: Dunbar; Widowed; Educ: 12 yrs; Occ: Miscellaneous printing machine operators. Ohio Deaths, 1908-1932, 1938-1944, and 1958-2007 [Ancestry.com]

Notes for John R. FALOON #434
Census:
- 1910 Cleveland Ward 4, Cuyahoga, OH, p. 10A. John R Faloon 31, ironer - laundry, Can/Scot/Scot; Francis Faloon 23, OH/OH/OH; William Faloon 7; John Faloon 5; Henry Faloon 3; Dorothy Faloon 4/12
- 1930 Cleveland, Cuyahoga, OH, p. 36a. John Faloon 24, single, is living in Cleveland, Cuyahoga, OH with parents John & Grace. He is a truck driver Why is she married but he isn't?

Obituary: *John R. Faloon of 7618 Lawn Ave., beloved husband of Hazel (nee Hicks), father of Janet Oberie and Richard, brother of Henry, Dorothy Dichold, Edun Tullar; grandfather of six. Died July 3. Friends may call at the Berg Funeral Service Home, 6318. Lorain Ave. From 2-5 And 7-10 P. M. Monday. All services private. Please omit flowers. Family suggests memorial contributions be sent to the Heart Association.* **Cleveland Press**; *Jul 5 1965. Cleveland Necrology File, Reel #107.*

Notes for William M. HICKS #435
Jones notes: "Resides (1972) at 238055 Amesburn Dr, N. Olmsted, OH"
Census: 1920 not found
  1930 Cleveland, Cuyahoga, OH. Emma Hicks 56, widowed, gen housework - private house; William Hicks 16; Hazel Faloon 21, dau, married (at age 16), saleslady - dry goods.
Death: William M Hicks, b. 16 Feb 1914 Hamilton, Butler Co, OH; d. 18 Feb 1998, Long-Term Care Facilities, North Olmsted, Cuyahoga Co, OH; Age : 84; Father's Surname: Hicks; Mother's Maiden Name: Hicks; Married; Educ: 9 yrs, Occ: Machine operators, motor vehicles. Ohio Deaths, 1908-1932, 1938-1944, and 1958-2007 [Ancestry.com]

Notes for Margaret Ethel HICKS #435s
Death: Ethel H. Hicks; #296-10-7770; Last Residence: San Pedro, Los Angeles, CA; b. 9 Jun 1909; d. 1 Jun 1999; card issued Ohio. Social Security Death Index [Ancestry.com]

Notes for Maria H. WILSON #438
Census
  1920 Seattle, King, WA, p. 3B. Robert J Wilson 59, OH/Ire/Ire, insurance agent; Lida 52, OH/OH/OH; Harold E Kerry 29, son in law, MI/Eng/Scot, salesman - paper; Marie Kerry 27, daughter, WA/OH/OH
  1930 Seattle, King, WA, p. 46A. Harold E Kerry 40, exporter - lumber; Maria 38; Harold E Jr, 1 3/12; Gladys Condit 25, servant - private family. Marriage age 28/26.
Death: Marie Wilson Kerry, d. 18 Jan 1947, Seattle, King Co, WA; Age: 54 years 11 months; Est. Birth Year: 1893, Married; Spouse's Name: Harold Wash [sic]; Father: Robert James Wilson; mother: Lida Hicks. Washington Death Certificates, 1907-1960 <familysearch.org>

Notes for Harold Edwin KERRY #438s
Birth: Michigan Births 1867-1902 [pilot.familysearch.org>. Gives date of birth, parents: Jane Kerry, b. Scotland; Aaron Kerry, b. England, blacksmith..
Census: 1900 Port Huron, Saint Clair, MI, p. 14B. Aaron Kerry 62, Jul 1837, Eng/Eng/Eng, blacksmith, imm. 1849, Na; Jane 48, May 1852, Scot/Scot/Scot, imm 1874; William 12, Apr 1888, MI; Harold 9, Feb 1891, MI. Married 20 yr, 6 ch/5 liv.
Passenger list: Harold Edwin Kerry, Arrival 4 Jun 1926, Age: 36; Birthplace: Marysville, Michigan, 8 Jan 1890; Ship Name: President Grant; Port of Arrival: Seattle, Washington; Port of Departure: Yokohama, Japan. Seattle Passenger and Crew Lists, 1882-1957 <ancestry.com>
Military: not found on WW I Draft registration
Death: Harold Kerry; #532-03-6199; Last Residence: 85351 Sun City, Maricopa, AZ, b. 8 Jan 1890; d. Apr 1984; issued: Washington. SS Death Index <rootsweb.com>:

Notes for Clarence Vern VERMILLION #439
Census
  1920 Kansas City Ward 7, Jackson, MO, p. 9B. Oscar E Herriott 48, bricklayer, NY/OH/NY; Luella Herriott 47, NE/US/VT; Lella Vermillion 23, dau, KS/NY/NE; Clarence Vermillion 24, son-in-law, MO/US/US, electrician - building
  1930 Kansas City, Wyandotte, KS, p. 44A. Oscar E Herriott 60, bricklayer; Alice L Herriott 59; Clarence Vermillion 34, son in law, MO, salesman - radio course; Zella Vermillion 34, dau, KS; John E Vermillion 4 3/12, KS; Shirley L Vermillion 6/12, KS; Estella Ebel 48, sister in law, widowed, tailoress - vest shop; Omar D Taylor 55, boarder, IA; Trena V Taylor 51, boarder, MN, foreman - contractor.

Military: World War I Draft Registration Cards, 1917-1918 [Ancestry.com] Clarence Vern Vermillion; age 22; b. 17 May 1895, Smithville, MO; res: Kansas City, Jackson, MO; occ: night wire chief, Home Telephone Co; married; military: seaman, electrician, 2 yrs; claims exemption "help keep up telephone service for the N___"; med height & build; dk brown hair & eyes. Regis: 5 Jun 1917, Kansas City, MO.
Death: Clarence Vermillion, #568-16-3152; Last Residence: Los Angeles, Los Angeles, CA, b. 17 May 1895; d. Apr 1986; issued: California. Social Security Death Index <rootswseb.com>
Death: Clarence Vermillion, b. May 17, 1895 Missouri; d. Apr 10, 1986, Los Angeles, CA; Age: 90; Mother's Maiden Name: Smith. California Death Index [Archives.com]

Notes for Clara Belle VERMILLION #440
Information on birth & death, children is from Verna Ruth (Vermillion) Coleman, granddaughter of Edgar Vermillion. "Clara Belle, b. 9 Mar 1901, Kansas; d. 21 Feb 1994, TX; married twice."
Census:
  1920 Kansas City Ward 16, Jackson, MO, p. 6A. Jess Brown 49; Pearl Brown 42; Audrey Brown 12; Eva Brown 9; Clara Virmiliam 19, boarder, MO/MO/MO, mail opener - mail order business. [Census taken 7 Jan 1920. It appears that Clara was enumerated in two places]
  1920 Marion, Grundy, MO, p. 5A. Chester Davis 20, MO/IL/IN, farm laborer - working out; Clara Davis 18. [Census taken 2 Jan 1920]
  1930 Trenton, Grundy, MO, p. 13A. Chester J Davis 31, B&B helper - RR construction; Clara E Davis 29; Harold R Davis 9; Allie M Davis 6. Children b. MO.
Death: Clara B. Davis, b. 9 Mar 1901; d. 21 Feb 1994; #513-01-8624; Last Residence: Houston, Harris, TX; issued: Kansas. Social Security Death Index [Ancestry.com]

Notes for John Ire Chester DAVIS #440
Military: World War I Draft Registration Cards, 1917-1918 [Ancestry.com] John Ire Chester Davis, age 19, b. 26 Mar 1899; farm laborer; Contact: Ella Davis, Loredo, Grundy Co, MO. Tall, slender, grey eyes, brown hair. Regis: Trenton, Grundy Co, MO 12 Sep 1918.

Notes for Maud Ella BRUBAKER #447
Jones notes: "She resides (1972) at 16004 Euclid, E. Cleveland OH, #213; went to Cleveland in 1920"
Death: Maud E Roden, b. 31 Jul 1899; d. 22 May 1988, age 88; Cleveland, Cuyahoga, OH; issued: Ohio; #290-20-8044. OH Deaths [ancestry.com]

Notes for James E. RODEN #447s
Census
  1900 Maysville, Mason, KY, p. 30A. Susan Roden 44, Apr 1856, wd, 4 children/ 4 living; Ernest Roden 23, Mar 1873, laundry man; Minnie Roden 19, Dec 1880, laundress; James Roden 10, Apr 1890.
  1910 Maysville Ward 3, Mason, KY, p. 9B. Susan Roden 54; James Roden 19
  1920 Maysville, Mason, KY, p. 10A. James E Roden 29, widowed, laundry man - own laundry; Bessie Roden 6, dau; Susan Roden 62, mother, widowed.
  1930 Mayfield Heights, Cuyahoga, OH, p. 8B. James E Roden 39, laundryman - supervisor Hospital; Maude Roden 30; Kenneth Roden 3 /12; Eleanor Roden 1 10/12; Herman Brunst 63, roomer, Ger/Ger/Ger, paper hanger.
Military: World War I Draft Registration Cards, 1917-1918 [Ancestry.com] James E Roden, b. 28 Apr 1890, Maysville, KY; res: Maysville, KY; occ: laundryman - Modern Laundry Co; dependents: child & mother; single; short, med. build, blue eyes, red hair. Reg: 5 Jun 1917, Mason, KY.
Death: James Roden, b. 28 Apr 1890; d. May 1966; age 76; Cleveland, Cuyahoga, OH; issued: Ohio; #270-10-0683. SS Death Index <rootsweb.com>

Notes for Bessie Salome BRUBAKER #448
Jones notes: "Resides (1972) at 1680 Wood Rd, Cleveland Hghts, OH 44121"
Census: 1930 Seven Mile, Butler, OH, p. 1A. Robert B Owens 34, TN/TN/TN, welder - automobile factory; Bessie 28; Alice 7, PA; Carrie Brubaker 58, mother in law.

Notes for Robert Brown OWENS #448s
Jones notes: "served in Co B, 330 Inf, WW I."
Military: World War I Draft Registration Cards, 1917-1918 [Ancestry.com] Robt Brown Owen, res: Birmingham, Jefferson Co, AL, b. 1 May 1895, Mt Pleasant, TN, single, pipe fitter, supporting father.
Military: U.S. World War II Draft Registration Cards, 1942 [Ancestry.com] Robert Brown Owen, b. 1 May 1895, MT Pleasant, TN; Res: E. Cleveland, Cuyahoga, OH; wife: Mrs. Bessie Owen; occ: Fisher Body, Cleveland.

Notes for Arthur B. BRUBAKER #449
Ancestry tree gives name as William Arthur Brubaker.
Twin of Bessie; SS Death Index gives same birth date for both, his name as William A..
Census: 1930 Maysville, Mason, KY, p. 6B. Arthur Brubaker 29, KY/KY/KY, clerk - milk c___t; Evelyn Brubaker 26, OK/OH/AR; Evelyn Ann Brubaker 4 2/12, KY
Death: Social Security Death Index: William Brubaker; b. 26 Jul 1901; d. Nov 1968; Last Res: Maysville, Mason, KY; #402-09-0491; issued: Kentucky

Notes for Evelyn DONALD #449s
Jones notes: "She resides (1972) at 7 W. 4th, Maysville, KY"
Death: SS Death Index: Evelyn D Brubaker; b. 7 Mar 1904; d. Nov 1993; Maysville, Mason, KY

Notes for Cecil N. BRUBAKER #450
Census: 1930 Maysville, Mason, KY, p. 9B. Cecil N Brubaker 25, office manager - pulley manuf.; Grace M Brubaker 26; Harriet J. Brubaker 6, dau. All Ky/KY/KY.
Marriage: Cecil N. Brubaker, m. 16 Dec 1922, Adams Co, OH; Age: 21; parents: James K. Brubaker; Carrie W. Hicks; Spouse: Grace M. Wallingford, Age: 19; Spouse's parents: George Wallingford; Anna Dawson. OH Marriages <familysearch.org>
Death: Cecil Brubaker; b. 16 Jul 1904; d. Dec 1966; #403-01-1208; issued Kentucky. Social Security Death Index:

Notes for Grace WALLINGFORD #450s
Jones notes: "She resides (1972) at Forest Av, Maysville, KY"
Death: May be the Grace W. Brubaker on SS death index who was b. 22 Aug 1903; d. 15 Feb 1999 at Sierra Vista, Cochise, AZ

Notes for Kyle Evans BRUBAKER #451
Jones notes: "Resided Hamilton, OH; operated Brubaker's Garage"
Census: 1930 Hamilton, Butler, OH, p. 15A. Kile Brubaker 22, labor - auto garage, OH/KY/KY; Ester Brubaker 22; Eiellene Brubaker 4 2/12; Shirley Brubaker 3 7/12. All b. OH. Both m. age 17.
Death: SS Death Index gives death as June 1957 but does not specify location

Notes for Esther CONOLD #451s
Census: 1910 Akron Ward 4, Summit, OH, p. 11A. Arthur W Conold 24; Marie L Conold 23; Ester L Conold 2; Mildred E Conold 8/12

Notes for Gladys Lee MERGARD #456

Marriage: 5 May 1921. Franklin County, OH; Winfield L Ohmert; age 38; Father: Geo. A. Ohmert; Mother: Elizabeth Fehr; to Gladys L. Mergard, age: 20; father: Morton H. Mergard; mother: Nancy O. Hicks. He has been previously married, no wife living; his occ: teacher; hers: stenographer

Census : 1930 Franklin, Franklin, OH, p. 3B. Winifred L Ohmert 48, IA/OH/IA, president - training school; Gladys L Ohmert 28, OH/KY/KY; Alice Ohmert 10; Aline Ohmert 10; Josephine Decarlo 18, servant, Ita/Ita/Ita

Passenger List - Feb 1936, ship Morazan from Vera Cruz, Mexico to New Orleans, LA. Gladys Ohmert, 32, b. Columbus, OH 14 Aug 1902; Winfield Ohmert, 53, b. Dubuque, IA; b. Feb 2, 1882. 48 E. Gay St, Columbus, OH.

Passenger List - 29 Oct 1937, ship Manhattan from Southampton, England and Cobh, Ireland to New York, Winifred L. Ohmert, b. Dubuque, IA, 22 Feb 1882; Gladys L. Ohmert, 36, b. Columbus OH; b. 14 Aug 1901. Res: 48 E. Gray, Columbus, OH.

Death: Gladys Lee Ohmert, d. Mar 1965, Broward Co, FL. Florida Death Index, 1877-1998 [Ancestry.com]

Notes for Winfield Leroy OHMERT #456s

Census:

1900 Table Mound, Dubuque, IA, p. 9A. George E Ohmert 49, OH/VA/VA, gardener; Elizabeth Ohmert 44, OH/Ger/Ger; Winfield S Ohmert 18, Feb 1882, IA/OH/OH; Millie M Ohmert 10; Harold G Ohmert 7; Laura I Ohmert 4

1910 Milwaukee Ward 22, Milwaukee, WI, p. 12A. Winfield L Ohmert 28, IA/IL/OH, teacher - public school; Lillian V Ohmert 21, IL/Swe/Swe, m. 3 years, no children; Sarah M Ollen 64, mother in law, Swe/Swe/Swe, widow, 8 ch / 5 liv.

College: Listed in Ohio State University Bulletin, 1909-10; College of Law, undergrad - special student, home address: Columbus, OH.

Marriage3: Winfield L Ohmert to Margaret Mackie; Mar 1966 ; Broward Co, FL

Living in Columbus, OH in 1920 - lodger, single, shoe designer - shoe company.

Military: Ohio Soldiers in WWI, 1917-1918 [Ancestry.com] Winfield L. Ohmert, b. 22 Feb 1882, Dubuque, IA; res: Gay St, Columbus, OH. Comments: 1 Lieutenant, Quartermaster Corps, 19 July 1918 from CL. 3 Detachment Labor Foreman, Cp Johnston, Fla to 3 Sept 1918; Student Co 7, Cp Johnston Fla to 6 Sept 1918; Office of Quartermaster General, Washington DC to 23 Oct 1918; Training Division Quartermaster Co; not found on draft records

Death: Winfield Leroy Ohmert; d. 28 Nov 1975, Dade Co, FL; Age: 93; b. 22 Feb 1882. Florida Death Index, 1877-1998 [Ancestry.com]

Death: Winfield Ohmert, b. 22 Feb 1882; d. Nov 1975; age 93. Last address of record: Fort Lauderdale, Broward, FL; card issued: Ohio; #291-09-7616. Social Security Death Index

Notes for Norma HICKS #450

Jones notes: "resides (1976) 1329 White Birch LN, Virginia Beach, VA 23456"

Census: 1930 Mifflin, Franklin, OH, p. 14A. Paul R Hott 30, musician - orchestra; Ruth B Hott 31; Clarence M Hicks 10, stepson; Norma C Hicks 8, step-dau; Marilyn J Hicks 6, step dau; Mary Kitzmiller 70, aunt. All OH/OH/OH

Possible Death: Norma Hill, b. 22 Oct 1921; d. Oct 1994; #287-14-2035, issued: Ohio ; Last Residence: Virginia Beach City, VA. Social Security Death Index.

Notes for Marilyn HICKS #463

Jones notes: "resides (1976) at 812 S. Waverly Rd, Columbus, OH 43027; notes mention letter from Mrs. Disbro giving names of sons"

Divorce: Marilyn J Disbro, Columbus, Franklin Co, OH; spouse: Richard D Disbro, Columbus, Franklin Co, OH. Marriage Duration (Years): 8; no minor children. Date of decree: 2 Dec 1970. Ohio Divorce Index, 1962-1963, 1967-1971, 1973-2007. [Ancestry.com]

Death: SS Death Index gives: Marilyn J Disbro, b. 27 Jan 1924; d. 08 Sep 2010; age: 86; Columbus, Franklin, OH; issued: Ohio; #300-16-0076

Notes for Rotheus Thomas ROGERS #469

Listed as daughter Rotheus on 1880 census; Rotheus, no relationship shown (possibly son crossed out) in 1900. Thomas in 1910 onward.

Census
- 1910 Galveston Ward 10, Galveston, TX, p. 8A. Thomas R Rogers 30, IN/SC/OH, forwarding - freight agent, m. 5 yrs; Syrene Rogers 29, wife, TX/MO/TN, 3 ch/3 living; Evalyan Rogers 4. OK; Loclins L Rogers 3, dau, TX; Paul G Rogers 1 6/12, TX; Lydia B Gibson 59, mother, OH/OH/IN, widow, 4 ch/3 living; Kenneth C Gibson 23, son, MO/IN/OH, check clerk - railroad; Mary M Gibson 20, dau, MO/IN/OH, stenographer - office.
- 1920 El Paso Precinct 7, El Paso, TX, p. 7B. Lydia A Gibson 60, OH/OH/OH, widow; Thomas R Rogers 40, son, widowed, IN/SC/OH, contractor - own office; Evelyn R Rogers 14, granddau, OK/IN/TX; Locleus L Rogers 13, granddau, TX/IN/TX; Paul G Rogers 11, grandson, TX/IN/TX; Mary M Rogers 9, granddau, TX/IN/TX; Claris L Rogers 7, granddau, TX/IN/TX. Rogers is crossed out - so surname of all may be Gibson
- *1930 Houston, Harris, TX, p. 28B. Thomas Rogers 55, OH; Viola Rogers 54; Lawrence J Rogers 20
*may not be right family...

Military: World War I Draft Registration Cards, 1917-1918 [Ancestry.com] Thomas Rotheus Rogers, age 38, b. 29 Oct 1879; billing clerk & forwarding agent, G. H. & S. A. Ry Co, El Paso; nearest relative: L. A. Gibson, El Paso. Med height & build; brown eyes, dark hair, no disability. Reg: El Paso, El Paso, TX 12 Jul 1918.

Death: Thomas Rotheus Rogers, d. 30 Oct 1960, Houston, Harris Co, TX; Age: 81 years; b. 29 Oct 1879, Spencer, IN; widowed; parents: Joseph Font Rogers & Lidia Tatmon. Informant: Evalyn McBride; burial: Forest Park Cem, Houston. Occ: special representative, Freight Line. Resident: 20 years. Texas Deaths, 1890-1976 <familysearch.org>

Death: Obituary, El Paso, Herald-Post, 8 Nov 1960. *Thomas R. Rogers - Funeral services and burial for Thomas R. Rogers, who died in Houston, Oct 30, were held there. He was 81. He is survived by a brother, Kenneth E. Gibson of El Paso and four daughters, a son, a sister, nine grandchildren and nine great-grandchildren. He was a special representative for Universal Carloading and Distributing Co, before retiring 16 years ago.*

Notes for **Syrene McADOO** #469s

Census: 1900 Titus Co, TX, p. 7A. Robert A Mcadoo 48, farmer; Laura Mcadoo 47; Lula Mcadoo 22; Sirene Mcadoo 19, Mar 1881, TX/TN/TN; Carry Mcadoo 16; Herman Mcadoo 14; Ethel Mcadoo 11; Earl Mcadoo 8

Death: Probably the Mrs. T. R. Rogers, age 33, who died in Galveston on 5 Mar 1914. Born 8 March 1881, father: William McAdoo; mother: not known. Buried Mt. Pleasant, Titus Co, TX on 9 Mar 1914. Cause of death: surgical shock, contributing ____ labor. Texas Death Index <familysearch.org>

Death of child: Infant Rogers, d. 08 Mar 1914, Galveston, Galveston, TX; Male, stillborn; Father: T. R. Rogers; b. El Paso, El Paso, TX; Mother: L. Mcadoo; Burial: Mount Pleasant, Titus, TX. Informant: R. E. Gibson. Texas Death Index <familysearch.org>

Notes for Frank L. TATMAN #470

Death: Jones notes: "Died Sept 18, 1924 in Tacoma, Pierce Co, WA from a fractured skull after falling from a shipping wharf. He was cremated"

Meade notes: "Frank L. Tatman (1st child of Frank and Flora and my great-grandfather) was in Pratt, Pratt Co, KS in 1910 census and moved to Bellingham, Whatcom Co, WA by the time his 2nd daughter was born. He moved to Tacoma, Pierce Co, WA by 1920 where he died in 1924. He married Ethel May Schaufler, daughter of Jacob Schaufler and Sarah Mack. Frank was also a tailor and owned his own dry cleaning / dye shop in Bellingham.

Frank and Ethel had 2 girls: 1. Leone Helen Tatman, b. Sept 30, 1909 in Pratt, Pratt Co, KS and d. Jan 9, 1994 in Chicago, Cook Co, IL. She was buried on Jan 16, 1994 in Homewood, Cook Co, IL. She was also married to Nicholas Roberts, but I don't believe they had any children. 2. Florence Marie Tatman, b. Oct 4, 1913 in Bellingham, Whatcom Co, WA and d. Jan 30, 1957 in Seattle, King Co, WA. She was buried on Feb 2, 1957 in Evergreen-Washelli Memorial Park, Seattle, King Co, WA."

Census

1910 Pratt Ward 2, Pratt, KS, p. 19A. Frank Tatman 25, cutter - tailor, IL/IL/IL; Ethel M Tatman 20, KS/Ger/IL; Leona H Tatman 8/12, KS/IL/KS. M. 2 years, 1 child.

1920 Tacoma Ward 2, Pierce, WA, p. 1B. Frank L Tatman 33, OK/OK/OK, longshoreman - ward? house; Ethel M Tatman 28; Leone H Tatman 10, KS/OK/KS; Florence M Tatman 6, WA

Notes for Ethel May SCHAUFLER #470s

May be the daughter of Hellen Stauffler Jackson, b. 1852, IL who was living in Coffeyville, Montgomery, KS in 1900. Ethel M. Stauffler, b. May 1891, KS/Ger/IL & her sister Anne, b. Apr 1886, were listed as step daughters of ____ Jackson.

Notes for Richard Bryon TATMAN #473

Meade notes: "He married a Ruby and also a Nell"

Census

1920 Coffeyville Ward 2, Montgomery, KS, p. 4A. Frank U Tatman 56, manager - bakery; Florence E Tatman 50; Richard B Tatman 20, OK, manager - Benery? Electric; William J Tatman 16, KS, apprentice - elec? bakery

1930 El Paso, El Paso, TX, p. 13A. R Richard Tatman 32, OK/OH/IL, broker - freight car? lots; B Nell Tatman 32, TX/US/US; U Franklin Tatman 66, father, married, OH/OH/IN, broker - freight car? lots.

Military: World War I Draft Registration Cards, 1917-1918 [Ancestry.com] Richard Bryan Tatman, age 19, b. 27 Jun 1899; res: Coffeyville, Montgomery, KS: occ: none; contact: Mrs Flora Tatman; med height (5'7"), slender, brown eyes & hair. Regis: Montgomery Co, KS, 7 Sep 1918.

Death: Richard B. Tatman; d. 06 Aug 1964, El Paso, El Paso, TX; Age: 65 years; b. 27 Jun 1899, Kansas; Married; Father: F. U. Tatman; mother: Flora Katherin Lewis; Occ: Freight Forwarding Firm; Res: El Paso, El Paso, TX; Cem: Rest Lawn Cem., El Paso, TX; Burial: 08 Aug 1964. Texas Deaths, 1890-1976 <familysearch.org>

Obituary: El Paso Herald-Post [El Paso, TX] 7 Aug 1964. *Tatman Rites Set Tomorrow, Funeral services for Richard B. Tatman, who died yesterday in a hospital, will be held under direction of the Masonic Lodge at 2 p.m. tomorrow in Martin Chapel. Burial will be in Restlawn. He was 65. Mr Tatman had lived in El Paso 41 years and retired from the freight business about two years ago. He lived at 5204 Pinehurst Road. He was associated with Masonic Lodge No 130, was a Knight Templar and had be active in El Maida Shrine since 1925. He served as potentate in 1946. He was a member of El Paso Aviation Assn, El Paso Chamber of Commerce and Downtown Rotary club. He was a Blue Lodge Mason, member of Sunset Lodge No 522 of Los Angeles, Calif., and a member of the El Paso Sheriff's Posse. Survivors include his widow, Mrs. Ruby Tatman; a son, Frank Tatman, of El Paso; two stepsons, Raymond Hays* *of Menlo Park, Calif, and Leslie Hays of Odessa, Tex,; a brother William J. Tatman of Rogers, Ark., a nephew and two nieces.*

Notes for Nell Beatrice MIXON #473s
Death: Nell Beatrice Tatman, d. 10 Dec 1956, El Paso, El Paso, TX; age: 60 years 1 month 25 days; b. 15 Oct 1896, Quanah, TX; Married; Father: William Henry Mixon, b. TN; Mother: Mary Alice McElreath, b. TX; Occupation: Housewife; Cem: Restlawn Memorial Park, El Paso, TX. Texas Deaths, 1890-1976 <familysearch.org>

Notes for Mrs. Ruby HAYS #473s2
Listed as widow of Richard Tatman in his 1964 obituary. She had sons, Raymond Hays of Menlo Park, CA and Leslie Hays of Odessa, TX, who were mentioned in Richard's obituary as stepsons. This is probably the Ruby Hays who was listed as the wife of Newell Raymond Hays in 1930. If so, the birth record of son, Newell Raymond Hays, Jr, gives her maiden name as Ruby Edith Campbell. She was apparently divorced from Newell Hays. Son Leslie's 2009 obituary states that, "From his mother, a pilot who won a cross-country derby, Leslie inherited curiosity and patience."

Notes for William Jennings TATMAN #474
Meade notes: "He married Marjorie Francis Wise in abt. 1924 and then married Ola Archer"
Census: 1930 Coffeyville, Montgomery, KS, p. 3B. William J Tatman 26, KS, still hooker - oil refinery, m. age 20; Margorie Tatman 26, KS/OH/KS; Gayl Tatman 4 1/12, KS; Richard Tatman 1 11/12, KS
Kansas State Census, 1925, Coffeyville, Montgomery Co, KS. Wm J Tatman 21; Marger F Tatman 22; Mary E Hall 58, mother?; George Hall 22, son; Murie Hall 17, dau in law; Raymer Taylor 26; Bulia Taylor 21. [relationships cannot be correct...]
Military: William J Tatman, b. 1903, KS; res: Montgomery Co, KS; Enlisted: 24 Sep 1942, Fort Levenworth, KS; Branch: Air Corps - Private; Education: 4 years of high school; Occ: Retail managers; Married; Height: 68"; Weight: 168. World War II Army Enlistment Records, 1938-1946 [Ancestry.com]
Marriage2: 02 Jul 1945, Sebastian, AK. William J Tatman, b, 1904, age 41; res: Coffeyville, Montgomery, KS; spouse: Mrs. Ola Archer Ballew, age 34, res: Coffeyville, Montgomery, KS; Arkansas County Marriages, 1837-1957 <familysearch.org>
Residence: Shown as living in Rogers, Ark. in obit of brother Frank in 1964.
Death: William Tatman, b. 22 Jul 1903; d. May 1966; age 62; death place not given, card issued: Kansas; #514-12-6419. Social Security Death Index

Notes for Nelly ALTMAN #475
Jones notes: "With grandfather Wm B. Brittingham in 1880, Tate Twp."
Census: 1900 Clermont Co, Franklin Twp, p. 42a. Dick Day, Aug 1873, 26, mar 8 yr, OH/OH/OH, farmer, rents farm; Nelli, wife, July 1873, 26, mar. 8 yr, 5 ch/4 living, OH/OH/OH; Roth, dau, Apr 1894, 6; Mary, dau, Oct 1895, 4; Cleyon, dau, Nov 1898, 2; Dorothy, dau, Feb 1900, 3/12. Ch. all b. OH.
  1910 Cincinnati, Hamilton, OH, p. 8B. Richard Day 36, laborer - stable; Nellie Day 36, 7 ch / 5 living; Ruth Day 16, sales lady - dry goods; Mary Day 14; Clessie Day 12; Dorothy Day 10; Samuel Day 7/12
  1920 Cincinnati Ward 24, Hamilton, OH, p. 9B. Richard Day 46, stable boss - ice company; Nellie Day 46; Ruth Day 26, nurse - Tramed? G.; Mary Day 23, nurse - graduate N; Joseph Day 21, driver - ice company; Dorothy Day 19, no occ. All OH/OH/OH
  1930 Cincinnati, Hamilton, OH, p. 12A. Richard Day 57, janitor- church; Nellie Day 57; Mary Day 34, chemist - lab.
Death: Nellie I Day, b. 21 Jul ___, Higginsport OH; d. 11 Feb 1946, Loveland, Clermont, OH; parents: Weslie Aultman, Cornellia Bettingham; spouse: Richard Day; informant: Mary Day
Ohio Deaths, 1908-1953 <familysearch.org>

Notes for Richard T. DAY #475s

Death: Richard T. Day, d. 23 Apr 1952, Loveland, Clermont, OH; b. 29 Aug 1873, Pt. Isabell, OH; Age: 78 years 7 months 24 days; Occ: retired horseman, widower, informant: Mary Day; father: Harrison Day; mother: Jenny Gray. Ohio Deaths, 1908-1953 <familysearch.org>

Notes for Millie Lou ALTMAN #479

Jones notes: "resides (1974) at Sardinia, OH"

Census

  1920 Scott, Boone, WV, p. 18A. C M Hall 34, dentist; Lou Hall 32

  1930 Madison, Boone, WV, p. 8B. Cicero M Hall 44, KY, dentist; M. Lou Hall 41, OH; Mildred R Hall 12, adopted dau, WV; Cicero S Hall 6, adopted son, WV

Death: Millie L Hall, b. 1889; res: Brown Co, OH; d. 27 Jun 1977, Brown County General Hospital, age 88, widowed. Ohio Deaths, 1908-1932, 1938-1944, and 1958-2007 [Ancestry.com]

Notes for Cicero Malcomb HALL #479s

Jones notes: "a dentist, practicing at Madison, WV for 25 years. D. 12/3/??."

Discrepancy in name of mother - Lou Elizabeth on death certificate; Salena on census records.

Census: 1900 Washington, Boone, WV, p. 3B. Manuel Hall 44, KY, farmer; Salena Hall 45, m 24 yrs, 7 ch/7 living; Alvin Hall 23, teacher; Allison Hall 21, teacher; Cairy L Hall 17; Cicero Hall 14; Alfonso E Hall 12, WV; John R Hall 10, WV; Joe E Hall 5, WV.

Military: World War I Draft Registration Cards, 1917-1918 [Ancestry.com] Cicero Malcolm Hall, age 33, b. 21 Jun 1885, res: Madison, Boone Co, WV; contact: Mrs. Lou Hall. Occ: dentist, self employed; med. height & build, blue eyes, dark hair. Reg: Racine, Boone Co, WV, 12 Sep 1918.

Death: Cicero Malcolm Hall; b. 22 Jun 1885, Pike Co., KY; d. 30 Dec 1936, Perry Township, Gallia Co, OH; burial: 2 Jan 1937, Bethel, OH; 51 years 6 months 8 days; occ: dentist; parents: Manuel Hall, Lou Elizabeth Osborne; spouse: Lou Altman Hall. Ohio Deaths, 1908-1953 <familysearch.org>

Notes for William Karl BRITTINGHAM #480

Discrepancy: birth year is given as 1892 in birth record, CA death record and 1900 census, 1890 in WW I Service records; 1889 in WW I Draft registration. Date is always 3 July.

Birth: William Brettingham, b. 3 Jul 1892, Washington Twp, Clermont, OH; Father: Jas. W. Brettingham; Mother: Mary Carr. Ohio Births and Christenings, 1821-1962 <familysearch.org>

Military: WW I Service - Ohio Military Men, 1917-18. William Karl Brittingham No Serial Number Race: W Residence: Cincinnati, O. Enlistment Division: United States Marine Corps; Enlistment Location: Cincinnati, O. Enlistment Date: 22 Jul 1918; Birth Place: Point Isabella, O.; Birth Date / Age: 3 July 1890; Assigns Comment: Parris Island Summary Court 22 July 1918; Co A 10 Separate Battalion 6 Nov 1918; Quantico Va 26 Nov 1918. Discharge 17 Apr 1919. Character excellent. File no 132220. Volume #: 22

Military: World War I Draft Registration Cards, 1917-1918 [Ancestry.com] William Karl Brittingham, b. 3 Jul 1889 Ohio; occ: foreman - Sanitary Manuf. Co; Kanoba, WV; supporting wife, child & sister; tall, slender, black hair & eyes. Disability: stiff fingers on right hand. Reg: Wayne, West Virginia 5 Jun 1917.

Census

  1920 Cincinnati Ward 8, Hamilton, OH, p. 3A. William Brittingham 32, sta fireman - plumbing co; Emrna Brittingham 26; Naomi Brittingham 4 9/12. All b. OH.

  1930 Cincinnati, Hamilton, OH, p. 2B. William Brittingham 42, govt worker - public health; Emma Brittingham 37, IN/IN/IN; Naomi Brittingham 14; Helen Brittingham 11; Robert Brittingham 8. children b. OH.

Death: Jones notes give death as 1930; California Death Index shows William K Brittingham; Birth: 7-3-1892 Ohio; Death: 4-6-1940, Los Angeles, CA, Age: 48; Mother's Maiden Name: Carr; Father's Name: Brittingham. California Death Index [archives.com]

Notes for Emma wife of William K. BRITTINGHAM #480
Possible Death: Emma E Brittingham [Emma E Craig]; b. 3 Apr 1893, Indiana; Residence: Cincinnati, Hamilton, OH; death: 16 Sep 1990, Cincinnati, OH; age 97; Father's surname: Craig; widowed, education: 8; homemaker. Ohio Deaths, 1908-1932, 1938-1944, and 1958-2007. Ancestry.com]
Question: This Emma is the daughter of Samuel & Mary F. Craig, b. Apr 1893. Living in Union, Ohio, Indiana in 1900. She may not be Emma who married William Brittingham. In the marriage information, the groom, William Brittingham, is listed as son of Isah Brittingham and Mary Jane Gray. If that is correct, this is the wrong Emma.

Notes for Bryan James BRITTINGHAM #483
Jones notes: "he resides (1974) at California"
Military: WW I - Bryan Brittingham # 417446; 750 W. Court St., Cincinnati, O. Enlistment: National Army, Cincinnati, OH, 10 May 1918; Birth: Hulington, OH, 15 Apr 1896; Assigns Comment: Headquarters Company, 54 Infantry to Discharge; Private, first class 4 July 1918; Corporal - 1 June 1919. Meuse-Argonne, Defensive Sector. American Expeditionary Forces 6 July 1918 to 10 June 1919. Honorable discharge: 18 June 1919. Ohio Military Men, 1917-18 [Ancestry.com]
Military: World War I Draft Registration Cards, 1917-1918 [Ancestry.com] Bryan Brittingham, age 21, b. 15 Apr 1896, Herlington?, OH; cabinet maker, Sanitary Manuf. Co, Kenoba, WV; single, tall, slender, brown eyes, lt brown hair; regis. Cincinnati, 1 Jun 1917.
Marriage: Groom: Bryan James Brittingham, b. 1896 Wellington, Ohio, age: 21; Bride: Gladys Henson, b. 1895 Cincinnati, O. Age: 22; Marriage Date: 25 Dec 1917, Hamilton Co, Ohio; Groom's parents: James Brittingham; Mary Carr; Bride's parents: John W. Parker, Jennie Higgins; Groom: Single; Bride: Divorced; Previous Husband's Name: Henson. Ohio Marriages, 1800-1958 <pilot.familysearch.org>
Census: 1930 Norwood, Hamilton, OH, p. 3B. Bryan Brittingham 32, salesman - window shades, OH/OH/KY; Eva Brittingham 28, KY/KY/KY; Mary L Brittingham 8/12, OH.

Notes for Gladys PARKER #483s
Census: 1900 Cincinnati Ward 22, Hamilton, OH, p. 2B. John Parker 45, garage packer; Jennie Parker 49; Gladys Parker 5. All OH/OH/OH.
Marriage1: 28 Jun 1911 to George Harrison Henson, Hamilton Co, OH. Bride age 18.
Death: Gladys E. Brittingham, b. 21 Feb 1895, Cincinnati, OH; d. 22 Jul 1918, Cincinnati, Hamilton, OH; Age: 23 years 5 months 1 day; married; Burial: 24 Jul 1918, Mt. Orab, OH; Father: John W. Parker b. OH; Mother: Jeinnie Higgins b. OH. Cause of Death: tuberculosis. Ohio Deaths, 1908-1953 <pilot.familysearch.org>

Notes for Melissa L. WALKER #484
Jones notes: "resides (1973) at Huntington, WV"
Census: 1930 Wrightsville, York, PA, p. 10A. Frank R Clement 29, NE/NE/NE, superintendent - bridge construction; Melissa M Clement 29, OH/OH/OH; Shirley M Clement 1, PA/PA/PA

Notes for Frank CLEMENT #484s
Not found on military draft records

Notes for Melva E. STEWART #488

Married Clarence Smith from Texas. Possibly died before 1930 as children are with grandparents.

Census: 1920 Manhattan Assembly District 11, New York, NY, p. 16A. Clarence Smith 34, IA, school teacher; Malva Smith 24. IA; Marilyne Smith 3/12, IA

  1930 Burlington, Des Moines, IA, p. 15A. John M Stewart 64, carpenter - house builder, IA/IN/IN; Carrie V Stewart 59, IN/IN/IN; Marilynne S Smith 10, gr dau, IA/TX/IA; Robert B Smith 7, gr son, NY/TX/IA

Notes for Ida May BENSON #489

Census

  1910 Buffalo, Garfield, OK, p.10B. Ora W Griggs 31, farmer, IA/NY/OH; May I Griggs 23, KS/OH/IL; William L Griggs 4/12, OK.

  1920 Buffalo, Garfield, OK, p. 11A. Orie Griggs 40, farmer; Ida May Griggs 33; Lloyd Griggs 10; Marie Griggs 4 5/12; Leta Griggs 0/12

  1930 Buffalo, Garfield, OK, p. 1A; Ida May Griggs 43, KS/IA/IA, Widow; Lois M Griggs 14, OK; Leta P Griggs 10, OK. No occ.

Notes for Orie William GRIGGS #489s

Census: 1880 Summit, Marion, IA, p. 498. Wm. Griggs 35, b. Jan; Phoeba E. Griggs 22, b. Mar; Ora W. Griggs 1, b. Apr; Clara A. Mercer 16, sister, b. July

Military: World War I Draft Registration Cards, 1917-1918 [Ancestry.com] Orie Wagerman Griggs, age 38, b. 7 Apr 1878, farmer, res: Hunter, Garfield Co, OK. Contact: Mrs. May Griggs. Med. height, med. build, blue eyes, light hair. Reg: Sep 1918, Garfield Co, OK.

Discrepancy: Draft registration gives middle name Wagerman; Jones notes give William

Notes for Paul Prosper PENNINGTON #490

Census

  1920 Noble, Garfield, OK, p. 9B. Paul P Pennington 32, KS/PA/?, farmer; Lettie Pennington 30, KS/IL/IA; Wayne Pennington 4 4/12, OK.

  1930 Colorado Springs, El Paso, CO, p. 3A. Paul P Pennington 42, carpenter - building contractor; Lettie P Pennington 40; Wayne B Pennington 14, messenger boy - telegraph Co; Wilma J Pennington 5

Military: Paul Prosper Pennington, age 30, b. 26 Aug 1887, Marion, KS; res: Hunter, Garfield, OK; occ: rural mail carrier - US Govt; dependents - wife and child; tall, med build, blue eyes, brown hair; regis: Noble, Garfield Co, OK. World War I Draft Registration Cards, 1917-1918 [Ancestry.com]

Notes for Roy Douglas BENSON #491

Census:

  1920 Hunter, Garfield, OK, p. 2B. Roy Benson 24, OK/MO/IA, manager - retail store; Alta Benson 22 OK/MO/IA; Douglas D Benson 1 3/12, OK

  1930 Hunter, Garfield, OK, p. 3A. Roy D Benson 34, salesman - grocery, m. age 20; Alta Benson 33; Douglas Benson 11; Fred Shepsherd 32, roomer, divorced, MO.

Military: WW I Draft Registration: Roy D. Benson, age 21, Enid, OK, b. Oct 27, 1895, Hunter, OK. Occ: Office work - Puritan Creamery Co. Enid, OK. Married. Medium height, slender build, blue eyes, brown hair. Registered Enid, OK 5 Jun [no year given]

Marriage: Jones notes give marriage as 26 May 1926; this date from Griggs book

Notes for Alta COGSWELL #491s

Census: 1900 Allison, Garfield, OK, p. 2B. Wm Cogsell 36, MO, farmer; Jennie Cogsell 28, IA; Alta Cogsell 1, OK. m. 6 yrs, 1 child.

Notes for Oran Ray MITCHELL #493

Census
- 1920 East San Diego, San Diego, CA, p. 3a. Oran R Mitchell 37, KS/IA/IA, no occ; Gracia 32, KS/ME/OH; Roy J 6, CA/KS/KS; Helen L 9/12.
- 1930 Enid, Garfield, OK, p. 6A. Roy Mitchell 45, mechanic - garage; Grace M Mitchell 37; Leroy J Mitchell 10

Military: World War I Draft Registration Cards, 1917-1918 [Ancestry.com] Oran Ray Mitchell, age 36, b. 6 Sep 1882; Res: San Diego, CA; occ: letter carrier - US Govt; relative: wife - Gracia Mitchell, San Diego, CA; tall, slender, blue eyes, dk brown hair; disability: heart & lungs weak. Regis: 11 Sep 1918, San Diego, CA.

Notes for William Jesse MITCHELL #495

Census
- 1910 Sumner, Reno, KS, p. 4. Jesse Mitchell 24, KS/IA/IA, farmer; Ida 18, KS/IN/IN. Married 2 years.
- 1920 Sumner, Reno, KS, p. 2B. W J Mitchell 33, KS/IA/IA, farmer; Ida M Mitchell 27, KS/PA/IN; Viola M Mitchell 7, dau
- 1930 Haven, Reno, KS, p. 4B. W J Mitchell 43, KS/IA/IA, farmer, m. age 21; Ida Mitchell 37; Viola Mitchell 18; Junior Mitchell 8; Wilma Mitchell 6; Oliver Mitchell 70, uncle, IA/PA/NY, no occ.

Military: World War I Draft Registration Cards, 1917-1918 [Ancestry.com]. William Jesse Mitchell, age 30, b. 11 Sep 1886, Haven, KS; res: Reno, KS; occ: farming; dependents - wife & child; tall, med build, blue eyes, light hair, bald. Regis: Haven, Reno Co, KS, 5 Jun 1917.

Notes for Ida May PRENE #495s

Census: 1900 Ninnescah, Reno, KS, p. 9B. Frank Prene 41, Apr 1859, farmer; Emma J Prene 31, Jul 1868, IN/Eng/IN; Ella E Prene 10; Ida M Prene 7, Jun 1892, KS/PA/IN; Mary N Prene 5; Fred Prene 3

Notes for George Henry MITCHELL #496

Census:
- 1910 Darling, Muskogee, OK, p. 14. George H Mitchell 22, farmer; Mary Neoma 15, wife, KS/PA/IN; Clara 46, mother, widow; Elmer 25, brother, farmer; Sarah Hopkins 70, grandmother, widow.
- 1920 Hutchinson Ward 6, Reno, KS. p. 7. George Mitchel 31, carter - salt plant; Neoma 25; Hazel 9; Glenn 6
- 1930 Spring, Butler, KS, p. 1. George H. Mitchell 42, farm operator; M Neoma 35, KA/PA/IN; Pearl H 19, OK/KS/KS; George L 7, KS/KS/KS; Clara E Wall 67, mother, IA/OH/Eng; Leon G M Chumina 17, hired man, CO/US/US.

Military: George Henry Mitchell, age 29, b. 30 Mar 1888, Haven, Kansas; res: Hutchison, Reno. KS; occ: Laborer - J. H. Shears & son; dependents: wife & 2 children; med height & build; blue eyes, lt brown hair; regis: 5 Jun 1917, Hutchison, KS. World War I Draft Registration Cards, 1917-1918 [Ancestry.com]

Notes for Mary Neoma PRENE #496s

Census: 1900 Ninnescah, Reno, KS, p. 9B. Frank Prene 41, Apr 1859, farmer; Emma J Prene 31, Jul 1868, IN/Eng/IN; Ella E Prene 10; Ida M Prene 7, Jun 1892, KS/PA/IN; Mary N Prene 5, Oct 1894; Fred Prene 3

Notes for Mollie E. LANHAM #502

Jones notes: "Mollie E. Johnston Mollie Lanham - Geo B. Patterson 5/14/1886; bur Vine St. Cemetery" (this was on page with Mildred Ruth Hall -- where does it fit & what does it mean?)

Census:
- 1900 Cincinnati, Hamilton Co, OH, p. 7B. William Kurtz, 32, b. Sep 1867, m. 10 yr, OH/Ger/Ger, stableman; Mary E., 28, Mar 1872, 2 ch/2 living; Marie L., 8, Sep 1891; Harry W., 5, Oct 1894. All b. OH.
- 1910 Cincinnati, Hamilton Co, OH, p. 1B. William Kurtz, 48, m. age 21, OH/Ger/Ger, night watchman - private police; Mollie, 38, 2 ch/2 living; Marie, 18; Harry, 15. All b. OH.
- 1920 Cincinnati, Hamilton Co, OH, p. 11A. William M. Kurtz 52, garage manager; Mollie E. 47.
- 1930 Cincinnati, Hamilton, OH, p. 9B. Mollie Kurtz 58, widow, no occ; Vivien Weigell 12, grand daughter; Delores Weigell 12, granddaughter

Death: Mollie Kurtz, b. 3 Mar 1872, Felicity, OH; d. 6 May 1945, Springfield Twp, Hamilton Co, OH; spouse: William Kurtz; parents: unknown; "widowed", "domestic", burial Vine Street Hill, death at Hamilton Co. Chronic Disease Hospital; informant: Dorothy Bent. OH Deaths, 1908-1953 <familysearch.org>.

Notes for William KURTZ #502s

Death: William Kurtz; b. 10 Sep 1866, Chilo, OH; death: 23 Jan 1928, Cincinnati, Hamilton, OH; burial: 25 Jan 1928; parents: Jacob Kurtz, Caroline Dice - both b. Germany. Occ: foreman, garage; spouse: Mollie E. Kurtz. Ohio Deaths, 1908-1953 <familysearch.org>

Notes for Lucy Florence UTTER #506

Jones notes: "she remarried -?- Arey; resides (1974) at 59 Union St, Felicity, OH 45120"

Birth: Lucy Florence Utter, b. 27 Jun 1903, Clermont, OH, parents: M. P. Utter, Anna B. Johnston. Ohio Births and Christenings, 1821-1962. <familysearch.org>

Census: 1930 Franklin, Clermont, OH, p. 3A. Harold M Edwards 27, farmer; Lucy F Edwards 26; Galen H Edwards 8; R Merrill Edwards 6; Harry M Edwards 3; Elfring E Edwards 15, brother.

Marriage: Lucy Edwards, Age: 76, Res: Clermont; Spouse: Louie Ayers, age: 78, Clermont; Marriage Date: 2 Oct 1979, Clermont Co, OH. Ohio Marriage Index, 1970, 1972-2007 [Ancestry.com]

Death: Lucy Florence Ayers [Lucy Florence Utter]; b. 27 Jun 1903; d. 18 Dec 1998, long term care facility, Clermont Co, OH. Age: 95, widow, father: Utter; mother: Johnston. Educ: 8th grade. Ohio Deaths, 1908-1932, 1938-1944, and 1958-2007 [Ancestry.com]

Notes for Harold M. EDWARDS #506s

Census: 1920 Washington, Clermont, OH, p. 6B. Arch A Edwards 46; Mary A 41; Hershal G 19; Harold M 17; Vern H 12; Beartric E 9; Elfring E 5;

Death: Harold Edwards, b. 15 May 1902; d. May 1975, Clermont, OH. U.S. Social Security Death Index <familysearch.org>

Death: Harold M Edwards, b. 1902, d. 6 May 1975, Brown Co Hospital; res: Clermont Co, OH; age 72; married. Ohio Deaths, 1908-1932, 1938-1944, and 1958-2007 [Ancestry.com]

Notes for Louis A AYERS #506s2

Death: Louis A. Ayers, b. 1901; d. 11 Jul 1988, Cincinnati, OH; res: Clermont Co, OH; farmer; married; age 87. Ohio Deaths, 1908-1932, 1938-1944, and 1958-2007 [Ancestry.com]

Notes for Mary Morgan UTTER #507

Jones notes: "resides (1974) at 420 Main St, Dayton, KY"

Census: 1930 Dayton, Campbell, KY, p. 6A. Jerry L Wing 26, truck driver; Mary Wing 25; Kathryne Wing 1 8/12; Jerry Wing 2/12.

Death: Mary M Wing, d. 3 Jul 1998, Dayton, Campbell Co, KY; Age: 93; Res: Campbell Co, KY. Kentucky Death Index, 1911-2000 [Ancestry.com]

Death: Mary M. Wing; b. 7 Feb 1905; d. 3 Jul 1998; #402-44-5868; Last Res: Dayton, Campbell, KY; issued: KY. Social Security Death Index [Ancestry.com]

Notes for Jeremiah L. WING #507s

Census: 1920 Dayton Ward 1, Campbell, KY, p. 4A. Jerry Wing 56, no occ; Caroline Wing 53; John Wing 28; Howard Wing 22; Jerry Wing 16, OH/OH/OH, collector, furnace co; Cartine Wing 12; Bertha Wing 7.

Death: Jeremiah Wing, b. 1903; d. 11 Nov 1960, Norwood, Hamilton Co, OH; married; res: Norwood, OH.

Notes for Robert Alexander UTTER #508

Birth: Robert Alexander Utter, b. 29 Mar 1907; Father: Morgan Utter; Mother: Amelia B. Johnson. Ohio Births and Christenings, 1821-1962 <familysearch.org>

Death: Robert Utter, d. April 1973; b. 29 March 1907; #270-03-0436, issued Ohio; Last Residence: Clermont, OH. Social Security Death Index <familysearch.org>

Death: Robert A Utter, b. 1907; Res: Clermont, OH; d. 21 Apr 1973, Brown County General Hospital, Brown County, OH; Age: 66; Married. Ohio Deaths, 1908-1932, 1938-1944, and 1958-2007 [Ancestry.com]

Notes for Margarite TURNER #508s

Jones notes: "she resides (1974) at Main St, Felicity, OH 45120"
No death information found.

Notes for Henry Johnston STEVENS #510

Census

1920 Franklin, Clermont, OH, p. 10A. Johnnie Stevens 25, KY/KY/OH, laborer - creamery; Lulu Stevens 24, OH/OH/OH; Elizabeth Stevens 3, OH; Charles Stevens 1/12, OH.

1930 Georgetown, Brown, OH, p. 11B. Johnston Stevens 35, agent - dry cleaning, KY/KY/OH; Lulu Stevens 34; Elizabeth E Stevens 13; Charles E Stevens 10; Wilma J Stevens 6; Lloyd J Stevens 1 7/12. Lulu & kids OH/OH/OH.

Military: World War I Draft Registration Cards, 1917-1918 [Ancestry.com] Henry Johnston Stevens, age 22, b. 8 Jan 1895, Falmouth, KY; res: Felicity, Clermont Co, OH; occ: railroad agent - Felicity & Bethel Railroad; married - wife & children; short, slender, blue eyes, light hair; regis: 5 Jun 1917, Felicity, OH.

Death: Henry J Stevens, b. 1895; Res: Clermont, OH; d. 31 May 1964, Christ Hospital, Cincinnati, Hamilton Co, OH; Age: 69; married. Ohio Deaths, 1908-1932, 1938-1944, and 1958-2007 [Ancestry.com]

Notes for Lulu O. REED #510s

Death: Lula O Stevens, b. 1896, res: Clermont, OH; d. 1 May 1971, Clermont Co, OH; Age: 75; Widowed. Ohio Deaths, 1908-1932, 1938-1944, and 1958-2007 [Ancestry.com]

Notes for Caroline Marie GLEASON #511

Jones notes: "resided at New Rochelle, NY"; gave death dates.

Census

1920 East Marion, Williamson, IL, p. 11B. William Charles 45, IN, rock quarry; Caroline Charles 34, OH; Mary Luise Charles 10, OH.

1930 New Rochelle, Westchester, NY, p. 2B. William S Charles unk, IN, construction - building; Caroline Charles 42, OH; Mary L Charles 20, OH.

Notes for William S. CHARLES #511s
Living in New Rochelle, NY, in 1930. William is a building contractor.

Notes for Marie W. WHITE #513
Jones notes: "resided at Batavia, OH"
Mentioned in 1941 Admin Docket "gr niece Marie Gregg of Batavia" but not in 1932 Will of Mary H. Kline; there is also a reference to "niece Marie (and James) Gregg of Batavia"
Marriage: George W. Gregg, b. 1882, Clermont, OH, Age: 25; Bride: Marie White b. 1886, Clermont, age 21; marriage 19 Mar 1907, Clermont Co, OH. Grooms parents: R. W. C. Gregg;: Clara Woodlief; Bride's parents: J. H. White, Maggie Atchley. Both single. Ohio Marriages, 1800-1958 <www.familysearch.org>
Census
  1910 Jackson, Clermont, OH, p. 2A. George W Gregg 28, farmer; Marie Gregg 24; married 3 years, no children
  1920 Batavia, Clermont, OH, p. 11B. George Gregg 37, farmer; Marie Gregg 34; Clark Gregg 9; James Gregg 7; Harry Morgan 22, laborer - farm
  1930 Batavia, Clermont, OH, p. 9B, George Gregg 48, proprietor - oil station; Marie Gregg 42; Clark Gregg 19; James Gregg 17
Death: Marie W Gregg, b. 1885; res: Clermont, OH; d. 26 Jun 1965, Cincinnati, Hamilton Co, OH, age 80, married. Ohio Deaths, 1908-1932, 1938-1944, and 1958-2002 [Ancestry.com]

Notes for George Woodlief GREGG #513s
Birth: George W. Gregg b. 16 Jan 1882, Batavia Tp., Clermont, OH, Father: R. W. C. Gregg; Mother: Clara W. Woodleef . Ohio Births and Christenings, 1821-1962 <pilot.familysearch.org>
Discrepancy on birth date - Jones notes gave 14 Dec 1881, which agrees with 1900 census and WW I draft registration; OH birth record gives: 16 Jan 1882
Census: 1900 Batavia, Clermont, OH. Missouri Gregg 64, Nov 1835, 1 ch/1 living; R W C Gregg 40, Oct 1859, son, printer; Clara W Gregg 39, Mar 1861, 1 ch/1 living; George W Gregg 18, Dec 1881, grandson.
Military: World War I Draft Registration Cards, 1917-1918 [Ancestry.com] George Woodlief Gregg, age 36, b. 14 Dec 1881, res: Batavia, Clermont, OH; farmer - self employed; contact: Marie Gregg, Batavia, OH. Tall, medium build, blue eyes, sandy hair. Reg: 12 Sep 1918, Batavia, OH.

Notes for Nicholas James WHITE #518
Jones notes: "she resides (1974) at 3817 Petosky, Apt 19, Mariemont, OH 45227"
Mentioned in 1941 Admin Docket "gr nephew Nich. White of Williamsburg"; not in 1932 Will of Mary H. Kline
Birth: Nicholas J. White, b. 10 Sep 1897, father: J... White; mother: Maggie Atchley. Ohio Births and Christenings, 1821-1962 <pilot.familysearch.org>
Marriage: Nicholas James White, married 6 Sep 1919, Delaware, OH; Age: 21; Est. Birth Year: 1898; Father: James H. White; Mother: Maggie Atchley; Spouse: Lucile Chatterton, Age: 24; Est. Birth Year: 1895; Father: Harry Chatterton; Mother: Sadie Moyer. Ohio County Marriages, 1790-1950 <familysearch.org>

Census
- 1920 Williamsburg, Clermont, OH, p. 8A. Nicholas White 21, bookkeeper- chair factory; Lucille White 24. Next to his parents.
- 1930 Williamsburg, Clermont OH. Nicholas J White 31, proprietor - chair factory; Lucile White 33; James White 8; Nicholas L White 4 9/12; Wanda Allen 20, servant. Next to his mother, Maggie & sister, Mina.

Military: World War I Draft Registration Cards, 1917-1918 [Ancestry.com] Nicholas James White, age 21, b. 10 Sep 1898; res: Williamsburg, Clermont, OH: occ: Manager, Williamsburg Chair Co, contact: J. A. White; med height & weight; brown eyes & hair; Regis: 12 Sep 1918, Batavia, OH.

Death: Nicholas J White, b. 1898; res: Clermont, OH; d. 12 Feb 1960, Hamilton Co, OH, age 62, married. Ohio Deaths, 1908-1932, 1938-1944, and 1958-2002 <ancestry.com>

Notes for Lucille C. CHATTERTON #518s

Census: 1910 Delaware Ward 2, Delaware, OH, p. 3A. John Moyer 74, own income; Mary J Moyer 67; Sadie C Chatterton 42, dau, widow; Bell M Colthar 39, dau, widow; Bertha B Chatterton 16; Lucile Chatterton 14, gr dau.

Possible Death: Sadie L White, b. 1894; Res: Clermont; d. 23 Mar 1968, Clermont, OH; Age: 74; Widowed. Ohio Deaths, 1908-1932, 1938-1944, and 1958-2007 [Ancestry.com]

Notes for Doyle Howard JOHNSTON #531

Jones notes: "resides (1974) at113 N. 13th, Cornelius, OR 97113"

Census: 1930 Washington, Bon Homme, SD, p. 3. Howard W Johnston 48, farmer - general farm; Cora 45; Doyle 20; Verle 18; Loren 15.

South Dakota State Census, 1935 - Doyle Johnston, 25; b. Iowa; Single; res: Capital, Hutchinson, SD; occ: farming; Father b. IL; Mother b. IL. Educ: high school; Methodist. Ancestry: Irish. [Ancestry.com]

Death: Doyle How Johnston, d. 7 Nov 1984, Washington Co, OR; Age: 75; b. 22 Jun 1909. Oregon Death Index, 1903-98 [Ancestry.com]

Notes for Helen L. SIMANTEL #531s

Census: 1920 Capital, Hutchinson, SD, p. 8B. George J Simantel 30; Bertha M Simantel 28; Hellen Simantel 7; Francis Simantel 2; Harrold Simantel 3/12

Death: Helen L Johnston, b. 20 Nov 1912;; d. 18 Jan 2007; age: 94; Gaston, Washington Co, OR; res: Cornelius, Washington, OR; issued: Oregon; #543-03-0430. SS Death Index [rootsweb.com]

Notes for Verle JOHNSTON #532

Jones notes: "resides (1974) at 403 Walnut, Bloomfield, IA 52537"

Census: 1930 Washington, Bon Homme, SD, p. 3. Howard W Johnston 48, farmer - general farm; Cora 45; Doyle 20; Verle 18; Loren 15.

South Dakota State Census, 1935: Verle Johnston, 23; Est. Birth Year: 1912; b. South Dakota; Single; res: Capital, Hutchinson, SD; Father b. Illinois; ;Mother b. Illinois. Educ: high school; Methodist. Ancestry: Irish [Ancestry.com]

Marriage: Verle Johnston, Age: 29; b. abt 1912; Marriage: 24 Jan 1941 Schuyler County, MO; Spouse: Gertrude Wiedenbach, Age: 25. Missouri Marriage Records, 1805-2002 [Ancestry.com]

Death: Verle Johnston, b. 08 May 1911; Mar 1985; age 73; Bloomfield, Davis Co, IA; issued Iowa; #485-42-7694. Social Security Death Index <rootsweb.com>

Notes for Gertrude WIEDENBACK #532s
Census: 1920 Kaylor, Hutchinson, SD, p. 5A. Emil Weidenbach 30, SD/Russ/Russ, farmer; Emma Weidenbach 27; Oliva Weidenbach 7; Ella Weidenbach 5; Gertrude Weidenbach 4; Loraine Weidenbach 3; Violet Weidenbach 4/12. All b. SD
Death: Gertrude Johnston, b. 06 Aug 1915; d. 10 Dec 2009; age 94; Bloomfield, Davis, IA; issued Iowa; #480-50-1786. Social Security Death Index <rootsweb.com>

Notes for Loren K. JOHNSTON #533
Jones notes: "resides (1974) at Scotland, SD"
South Dakota State Census, 1935 - Loren Johnston, 20; b. SD; Single; res: Capital, Hutchinson, SD; no occ; Father b. Illinois; Mother b. Illinois. Educ: high school; Methodist. Ancestry: Irish [Ancestry.com]
Marriage: Bon Homme Co, SD; 18 Jun 1937; Loren Johnston, Age: 22; to Ina Behl; Res: Bon Homme; Post Office: Scotland. South Dakota Marriages, 1905-1949. [Ancestry.com]
Death: Loren K Johnston, b. 11 Aug 1914; d. 27 Jan 1992, age 77; Scotland, Bon Homme Co, SD; #503-05-5819. SS Death Index [rootsweb.com]

Notes for Ina B. BEHL #533s
Census: 1920 Scotland, Bon Homme, SD, p. 5A. George Behl 27; Meredith Behl 25; Ina Behl 4
Death: Ina Blanche Johnston, b. 13 Jul 1915; d. 16 Sep 2006; age: 91; Scotland, Bon Homme, SD; issued: South Dakota; #503-46-4571. SS Death Index [rootsweb.com]

Notes for Willard Burnett HICKS #548
Information from daughter, "I am the daughter of Willard Burnett Hicks, who was the son of Charles Jefferson Hicks, who was the son of Albert Alden Hicks who was the son of Joshua Hicks. She provided death place and wife's name and data.

End notes - Generation 5

258. Ohio Deaths, 1908-1932, 1938-1944, and 1958-2002.
259. Ohio Deaths 1908-1953.
260. World War I Draft Registration Cards, 1917-1918.
261. Ohio Deaths 1908-1953.
262. Social Security Death Index.
263. Ibid.
264. World War I Draft Registration Cards, 1917-1918.
265. Social Security Death Index.
266. Ohio Marriages, 1800-1958.
267. Ibid.
268. Ohio Deaths, 1908-1932, 1938-1944, and 1958-2002.
269. Florida Death Index.
270. Social Security Death Index.
271. Ohio Military Men, 1917-18.
272. Ohio Deaths, 1908-1932, 1938-1944, and 1958-2002.
273. World War I Draft Registration Cards, 1917-1918.
274. Social Security Death Index.
275. Ohio Deaths 1908-1953.
276. Ibid.
277. Ibid.
278. Social Security Death Index.
279. Ohio Deaths 1908-1953.
280. World War I Draft Registration Cards, 1917-1918.
281. U.S. World War II Draft Registration Cards, 1942.
282. Social Security Death Index.
283. Ibid.
284. Ibid.
285. Ohio Deaths, 1908-1932, 1938-1944, and 1958-2002 [database on-line].
286. Ibid
287. Social Security Death Index
288. Ibid.
289. Ohio Deaths, 1908-1932, 1938-1944, and 1958-2002.
290. Ohio Deaths 1908-1953.
291. Alabama Deaths and Burials, 1881-1952.
292. Ibid.
293. Alabama Deaths, 1908-1974.
294. World War I Draft Registration Cards, 1917-1918.
295. Alabama Deaths, 1908-1974.
296. Ibid.
297. Ibid.
298. Alabama Marriages 1816-1957.
299. Bracken Co, KY Marriage Bonds.
300. Social Security Death Index.
301. World War I Draft Registration Cards, 1917-1918.
302. Social Security Death Index.
303. Ibid.
304. Ibid.
305. Ibid.
306. Ibid
307. Ibid.
308. Ibid.
309. Ibid
310. World War I Draft Registration Cards, 1917-1918.
311. Ohio Deaths 1908-1953.
312. World War I Draft Registration Cards, 1917-1918.
313. Social Security Death Index.
314. Ohio Deaths, 1908-1932, 1938-1944, and 1958-2002.
315. Ibid.
316. Ohio Marriages, 1800-1958.
317. Ohio Deaths 1908-1953.
318. Ohio Births and Christenings 1821-1962.
319. Ohio Deaths 1908-1953.
320. Social Security Death Index.
321. Ohio Deaths 1908-1953.
322. World War I Draft Registration Cards, 1917-1918.
323. Ohio Deaths 1908-1953.
324. World War I Draft Registration Cards, 1917-1918.
325. Ohio Deaths 1908-1953.
326. Ibid
327. Social Security Death Index.
328. Summit Co, OH - 1930 census.
329. Social Security Death Index.
330. Ohio Deaths, 1908-1932, 1938-1944, and 1958-2002 [database on-line].
331. Ibid.
332. Seipelt, Lvera - Records.
333. Hicks Family Bible.
334. Ohio Deaths, 1908-1932, 1938-1944, and 1958-2002 [database on-line].
335. Hicks Family Bible.
336. Ibid.
337. Social Security Death Index.
338. Seipelt, Lvera: Notes 1999.
339. Ibid.
340. Ohio Deaths 1908-1953.
341. Social Security Death Index.
342. Hicks Family Bible.
343. Social Security Death Index.
344. Ontario Death Index.
345. Levi Family Bible
346. Ibid.
347. World War I Draft Registration Cards, 1917-1918.
348. Social Security Death Index.
349. Ibid.
350. Levi, Lane - Interview & Email 1997.
351. World War I Draft Registration Cards, 1917-1918.
352. Levi, Lane - Interview & Email 1997.
353. Levi Family Bible.
354. Stalder, Mollie D. - Obituary.

355. Levi Family Bible.
356. Stalder, Mollie D. - Death Certificate.
357. Ibid.
358. Stalder/Levi Marriage license.
359. Stalder, William B. - Obituary.
360. World War I Draft Registration Cards, 1917-1918.
361. Stalder, William B. - Death Certificate.
362. Ibid.
363. Clermont Co, OH Birth records.
364. Zezula - Notes - abt 1990.
365. Clermont Co, OH Birth records.
366. Arizona Deaths, 1870-1951.
367. Clermont Co, OH Birth records.
368. Social Security Death Index.
369. World War I Draft Registration Cards, 1917-1918.
370. Social Security Death Index.
371. Ohio Deaths, 1908-1932, 1938-1944, and 1958-2002 [database on-line].
372. Social Security Death Index.
373. Ibid.
374. Missouri Marriage Records, 1805-2002.
375. Missouri Death Certificate [digital image].
376. Social Security Death Index.
377. World War I Draft Registration Cards, 1917-1918.
378. Ibid.
379. California Death Index.
380. Ibid.
381. Ibid.
382. U.S. World War II Draft Registration Cards, 1942.
383. World War I Draft Registration Cards, 1917-1918.
384. Social Security Death Index.
385. California Death Index.
386. Ibid.
387. Clermont County, Ohio 1980 Vol 1.
388. Ibid.
389. Information from daughter, Ann Lucas Geyer 10/15/05.
390. Ohio Deaths 1908-1953.
391. Ohio Deaths, 1908-1932, 1938-1944, and 1958-2002 [database on-line].
392. Indiana Marriage Collection, 1800-1941.
393. Ohio Deaths, 1908-1932, 1938-1944, and 1958-2002 [database on-line].
394. Clermont County, Ohio 1980 Vol 1.
395. World War I Draft Registration Cards, 1917-1918.
396. Clermont County, Ohio 1980 Vol 1.
397. World War I Draft Registration Cards, 1917-1918.
398. Ohio Deaths, 1908-1932, 1938-1944, and 1958-2002.
399. Social Security Death Index.
400. Clermont County, Ohio 1980 Vol 1.
401. Ibid
402. Ibid.
403. Ohio Deaths 1908-1953.
404. World War I Draft Registration Cards, 1917-1918.
405. Clermont County, Ohio 1980 Vol 1.
406. Social Security Death Index.
407. Clermont County, Ohio 1980 Vol 1.
408. Social Security Death Index.
409. Ohio Deaths, 1908-1932, 1938-1944, and 1958-2002.
410. Ohio Deaths 1908-1953.
411. Ohio Deaths, 1908-1932, 1938-1944, and 1958-2002.
412. Social Security Death Index.
413. Ohio Deaths, 1908-1932, 1938-1944, and 1958-2002.
414. World War I Draft Registration Cards, 1917-1918.
415. Ohio Deaths 1908-1953.
416. Ohio Deaths, 1908-1932, 1938-1944, and 1958-2002 [database on-line].
417. World War I Draft Registration Cards, 1917-1918.
418. Social Security Death Index.
419. Ibid.
420. Ibid.
421. Ibid.
422. Ibid.
423. World War I Draft Registration Cards, 1917-1918.
424. Social Security Death Index.
425. World War I Draft Registration Cards, 1917-1918.
426. Social Security Death Index.
427. Ibid.
428. World War I Draft Registration Cards, 1917-1918.
429. California Death Index.
430. World War I Draft Registration Cards, 1917-1918.
431. Social Security Death Index.
432. Illinois Statewide Death Index, 19161950.
433. World War I Draft Registration Cards, 1917-1918.
434. Ibid.
435. Social Security Death Index.
436. Social Security Death Index.
437. World War I Draft Registration Cards, 1917-1918.
438. Kentucky Death index, 1911-2000.
439. World War I Draft Registration Cards, 1917-1918.
440. Kentucky Death Records, 1852-1953.
441. Ibid.
442. Ibid.
443. Social Security Death Index.
444. Ibid.
445. World War I Draft Registration Cards, 1917-1918.
446. Social Security Death Index.
447. Ibid.
448. Social Security Death Index.
449. Ibid.
450. World War I Draft Registration Cards, 1917-1918.
451. Social Security Death Index.
452. World War I Draft Registration Cards, 1917-1918.

453. Social Security Death Index.
454. World War I Draft Registration Cards, 1917-1918.
455. Social Security Death Index.
456. Ibid.
457. Ibid.
458. Ibid.
459. Ibid.
460. Ibid.
461. Florida Death Index.
462. Ohio Military Men, 1917-18.
463. Social Security Death Index.
464. Florida Death Index.
465. El Paso Herald-Post, 8 Nov 1960.
466. Meade, Kevin.
467. Ibid.
468. Ibid.
469. World War I Draft Registration Cards, 1917-1918.
470. Meade, Kevin.
471. Ohio Deaths 1908-1953.
472. Clermont Co, OH - Census - 1900 [T623; #1247].
473. Ohio Deaths 1908-1953.
474. Ibid.
475. Ohio Deaths, 1908-1932, 1938-1944, and 1958-2002.
476. World War I Draft Registration Cards, 1917-1918.
477. Ohio Deaths 1908-1953.
478. Ohio Military Men, 1917-18.
479. California Death Index.
480. Ohio Military Men, 1917-18.
481. World War I Draft Registration Cards, 1917-1918.
482. Social Security Death Index.
483. Ohio Marriages, 1800-1958.
484. Social Security Death Index.
485. Griggs, *Levi W. & Sarah E. (Carter) Hopkins, their ancestors & descendants*.
486. Ibid.
487. World War I Draft Registration Cards, 1917-1918.
488. Griggs, *Levi W. & Sarah E. (Carter) Hopkins, their ancestors & descendants*.
489. Ibid.
490. World War I Draft Registration Cards, 1917-1918.
491. Griggs, *Levi W. & Sarah E. (Carter) Hopkins, their ancestors & descendants*.
492. Ibid.
493. Ibid.
494. Ibid.
495. Ibid.
496. World War I Draft Registration Cards, 1917-1918.
497. Ibid.
498. Ibid.
499. Social Security Death Index.
500. Ibid.
501. Ibid.
502. Ibid.
503. Social Security Death Index.
504. Ohio Marriages, 1800-1958.
505. World War I Draft Registration Cards, 1917-1918.
506. Ohio Births and Christenings 1821-1962.
507. Social Security Death Index.
508. Ohio Deaths 1908-1953.
509. World War I Draft Registration Cards, 1917-1918.
510. Social Security Death Index.
511. Ibid.
512. Ibid.

Generation Six
The 3rd great grandchildren of Joshua and Diana Hicks

Many members of the sixth generation are not even aware that they are descendants of the Clermont County Hicks family. They are scattered all over the United States and some are in other countries, as well.

For the purpose of this book, we have selected 1930 as the cutoff date for publishing personal information. Since the folks born before 1930 are listed on the easily-accessible 1930 census, this should satisfy the need for privacy. Where children of the 6th generation - or their offspring - were born after 1930 and may still be living, names are given but the symbols ## replace personal information. In many cases, we have more data on these folks and many of their descendants, so please contact the compiler for more information. If you have more information to add, please contact me as well.

Most of the known descendants still remained in the mid-west and west. Surprisingly few have been found on the east coast of the United States.

Occupations run the gamut – from hospital administrator, teachers, librarians, and physicists to farmers, bankers, grocers, mechanics and everything in between. Most have been outstanding citizens, but there have been a few criminals as well as several who died violent deaths. In other words, these folks are simply Americans.

Orville Guy Jones
(1908-1996)

Bill, Jeanette, Dick, Madge, Grace, Betty, Ruth
Kieser 25th anniversary - Feb 1961

Stalder Family

Eugene Martin Jennings, Jr
(1939-)

@@ see research notes at end of chapter   ## born after 1930 or known to be living

Betty Kieser cultivated gardens and memories of old Orlando

By MARTHA PHIFER
SENTINEL STAFF WRITER

Elizabeth "Betty" Kieser was fascinated by anything that grew.

An avid gardener, Kieser grew flowers and vegetables for more than 70 years and in the process had friendly competitions against her husband.

"She competed against my father to see who grew the best roses," said her daughter Betty Jo Stockton of Orlando. "She was planting in her garden just two weeks ago, well into her 90s."

Kieser died Friday of a heart attack. She was 95.

Born in Norwood, Ohio, Kieser and her family moved to Orlando in 1921. While in high school, she worked for a downtown dime store to help support her family during the Great Depression.

At 16, she met Robert J. Kieser at Delaney Street Baptist Church. They dated for four years and became the first couple to be married at that church.

Kieser stayed home taking care of their three children and their home and garden. She remained an active member of her church for 79 years, planting and taking care of its garden for more than 30 years.

"She worked as Sunday school teacher and even scrubbed the floor whenever necessary," Stockton said. "She did whatever was needed at the church. Last month, when the church celebrated its 80th anniversary, she was honored as its oldest living member."

Kieser had an unbelievable memory and could tell you anything that happened in Orlando since the time she moved here, her family said.

She often talked about her childhood, when she used to walk down Orange Avenue, then an 8-foot-wide brick road with very few buildings. She used to read a book on the way to Delaney Elementary and stop at the library on the way home to pick up a new one.

Her great-granddaughter Elisabeth Douberly of Orlando said Kieser was a great storyteller and never forgot the day the first airplane landed in Orlando. She got to miss school to go look inside the plane, Douberly said.

Kieser loved to travel and saw gardens all over the world. She went to Holland to see the tulips and to Holland, Mich., to see more tulips.

For the past 30 years, Kieser and her husband spent six months a year in North Carolina, and the other six months in Florida so that she could continue planting her garden.

"Her garden had just about everything, vegetables, some so big that she couldn't pull them. And 30 or 40 kinds of flowers," said Stockton. "Daisies and carnations were among her favorite."

"She was a doll," she said. "She was 4-foot-10 and would try anything. If there was a mountain, she wanted to see what was at the top. And if there was a valley, she wanted to check out the bottom."

Kieser also is survived by her brother Dick Stalder of Jacksonville; son Robert F. Kieser of Oklahoma; two grandchildren; and three great-grandchildren.

Carey Hand-Colonial Funeral Home, Orlando, is handling arrangements.

Martha Phifer can be reached at mphifer@orlandosentinel.com or 407-420-5259.

Betty (Stalder) Kieser (1913-2008)
mother of the compiler

Lindley & Mae Broadwell -
children: Leon, Lindley & Ruby

Lvera (Jennings) Seipelt
(1929-)

William Lloyd Griggs 1909-1975

@@ see research notes at end of chapter   ## born after 1930 or known to be living

Generation 6

555. Stanley Edward[6] PATTISON (Edward H.[5], Mary A. 'Mollie'[4] MANNING, Lucinda[3] TATMAN, Ruth[2] HICKS, Joshua[1]), born 17 Mar 1902 in Clermont Co, OH; died[513] 28 Oct 1951 in Cincinnati, Hamilton Co, OH; buried 31 Oct 1951 in Williamsburg Cemetery, Clermont, OH. He married (1) abt 1925 **Margaret ANSTAILT**, born 5 Feb 1906 in OH; died[514] 21 Apr 1932 in Cincinnati, Hamilton Co, OH; buried 24 Apr 1932 in Williamsburg Cemetery, Clermont, OH, daughter of Albert ANSTAILT and Lula HAUCK; (2) on 28 May 1936 in Clermont Co, OH **Florence ALLEN**, born 17 Mar 1908 in Brown Co, OH; died[515, 516] 16 Aug 1987 in Georgetown, Brown Co, OH.

Stanley Pattison was a school teacher in the public schools of Clermont County. His first wife, Margaret, died young, leaving small children. He remarried a few year later and had more children.@@

Children of Stanley Edward PATTISON and Margaret ANSTAILT were:

951   i   **Merrill John[7] PATTISON**, born 21 Apr 1926 in Batavia, Clermont Co, OH; died 7 Apr 1945 in Italy - WW II.

+ 952   ii   **Evelyn Grace[7] PATTISON**. born 2 Sep 1927 in Olive Brand OH; died 30 Jan 2004 in Mt Vernon, Knox Co, OH. She married on 3 Dec 1948 in Newport OH **Walter R. CASTRO**, born 14 Mar 1925 in Honolulu, HI; died Dec 1975 in Salt Lake City, Salt Lake Co, UT. Jones notes: "resides (1973) at PO Box 297, Oakley, CA 94561; he served 4 ½ years in WW II."

953   iii   **Glenn Edward[7] PATTISON**, born 28 Apr 1931; died 7 Jul 1942.
Jones notes: "drowned"
Death: Glenn Edward Pattison, d. 07 Jul 1942, Union, Clermont Co, OH; b. 28 Apr 1931, OH; Age: 11 years; Student; res: Batavia, Clermont Co., OH; Burial: 07 Jul 1942, Williamsburg, OH; father: Stanley Pattison b. OH; mother: Margaret Anst___t. Drowned in pond on farm. Ohio Deaths, 1908-1953 <familysearch.org>

954   iv   **Norma Jean[7] PATTISON**, ##. Jones notes: "she resides (1981) at 4062 Ellis Dr, Cincinnati OH 45244; married -?- Sweeney, divorced"

+ 955   v   **Keith[7] PATTISON**, ##. He married **Marilyn Jane WALKER**. Jones notes: "resides (1983) at RD 2, Box 28, Georgetown, OH 45121 (Old SR 68); served in OH National Guard"

956   vi   **Harold Ralph[7] PATTISON**, ##. Jones notes: "resides (1973) at 53 Betty Ln, Milford, OH 45150"

Children of Stanley Edward PATTISON and Florence ALLEN were:

957   i   **Stanley E.[7] PATTISON Jr.**, ##. Jones notes: "attending E. KY U 1973; resides (1973) Rt 1, Bethel, OH"

556. Thelma Myrtle[6] PATTISON (Edward H.[5], Mary A. 'Mollie'[4] MANNING, Lucinda[3] TATMAN, Ruth[2] HICKS, Joshua[1]), born 21 Jul 1903 in Clermont Co, OH; died Nov 1983 in Bethel, Clermont Co, OH. She married on 30 May 1922 in Clermont Co, OH **Ralph PARKER**, born 25 Apr 1902 in Clermont Co, OH; died Jun 1967 in Bethel, Clermont Co, OH.

Thelma Pattison married Ralph Parker, who managed a bakery in Bethel in 1930. @@

Children of Thelma Myrtle PATTISON and Ralph PARKER were:

+ 958   i   **Ralph K.[7] PARKER II**. born 13 Jan 1923 in Clermont Co, OH. He married (1) **Ruth LANE**, born Est. 1923; (2) **Ann HALL**, born Est. 1923.
Jones notes: "reside (1973) at 6830 LeConte, Cincinnati, OH (Mt. Washington)"

@@ see research notes at end of chapter   ## born after 1930 or known to be living

557. **Eunice Irene**[6] **PATTISON** (Edward H.[5], Mary A. 'Mollie'[4] MANNING, Lucinda[3] TATMAN, Ruth[2] HICKS, Joshua[1]), born 8 May 1916 in Clermont Co, OH. She married on 14 Oct 1951 in Clermont Co, OH **Ludwig FENKER**, born 13 Feb 1902 in Cincinnati, Hamilton Co, OH; died Apr 1964; buried in Bethel Tate Cemetery.

Children of Eunice Irene PATTISON and Ludwig FENKER were:
959 i **Edward Louis**[7] **FENKER**, born aft 1952; died 6 Feb 1954.

558. **John W.**[6] **PATTISON** (Edward H.[5], Mary A. 'Mollie'[4] MANNING, Lucinda[3] TATMAN, Ruth[2] HICKS, Joshua[1]), born 21 Apr 1918 in Clermont Co, OH; died 18 Feb 1971 in Ann Arbor, Washtenaw Co, MI; buried in Bethel Tate Cemetery He married (1) on 20 Jan 1940 in Cincinnati, Hamilton Co, OH **Audrey N. MCCLANAHAN**, born 15 Jan 1923 in Cincinnati, Hamilton Co, OH, daughter of Martin and Ida MCCLANAHAN; (2) **Audrey PETTIT**, born 6 Apr 1920.

Children of John W. PATTISON and Audrey PETTIT were:
960 i **James Edward**[7] **PATTISON**, ##. Jones notes: "reside (1973) in California"
961 ii **Caroline**[7] **PATTISON BICKEL**, ##. Jones notes: "resides (1973) at 4948 Beechwood Rd, Mt Carmel, OH; her mother remarried to Louis Bickel, who adopted her, so her name is Bickel"

559. **Robert John**[6] **PATTISON** (Ross John[5], Mary A. 'Mollie'[4] MANNING, Lucinda[3] TATMAN, Ruth[2] HICKS, Joshua[1]), born 5 May 1912 in Covington, Kenton Co, KY; died[5] 17 Jan 1985 in Covington, Kenton Co, KY. He married on 17 Apr 1937 in Covington, Kenton Co, KY **Emma Marie MOORE**, born 10 Feb 1916 in Dayton KY; died Feb 1984 in Covington, Kenton Co, KY. Jones notes: "resides (1973) at 1517 Eastern Av, Covington, KY 41014"

Children of Robert John PATTISON and Emma Marie MOORE were:
962 i **John Robert**[7] **PATTISON**, ##. Jones notes: "resides (1973) at 2232 Genevieve Ln, Covington, KY"
963 ii **Jo Ann**[7] **PATTISON**, ##. Jones notes: "reside (1973) at 14 Cobbler Ct, Erlanger, KY 41018"

560. **Grace**[6] **PATTISON** (Walter Cleavland[5], Mary A. 'Mollie'[4] MANNING, Lucinda[3] TATMAN, Ruth[2] HICKS, Joshua[1]), born 26 Mar 1906 in Cincinnati, Hamilton Co, OH; died 6 Jan 1929 in Cincinnati, Hamilton Co, OH; buried 9 Jan 1929 in Mt. Washington Cemetery. She married on 5 Dec 1923 in Cincinnati, Hamilton Co, OH **George Lester WYKOFF**, born 8 Aug 1905 in Clarksville, Clinton Co, OH; died 3 Apr 1996 in Cincinnati, Hamilton Co, OH, son of Edward D. WYKOFF and Anna ANSON.

Grace Pattison died at age 22, leaving two small children. Her husband, Lester Wykoff, was a machinist in a factory.@@

Children of Grace PATTISON and George Lester WYKOFF were:
964 i **Minnie M**[7] **WYKOFF**, born abt 1925 in OH.
965 ii **Thomas G**[7] **WYKOFF**, born abt 1926 in Cincinnati, Hamilton Co, OH.

561. **Edith May**[6] **PATTISON** (Walter Cleavland[5], Mary A. 'Mollie'[4] MANNING, Lucinda[3] TATMAN, Ruth[2] HICKS, Joshua[1]), born 30 Nov 1906 in OH; died 13 Jun 1994 in Maumee, Lucas Co, OH. She married abt 1920/23 probably in OH **William Carl HARRIS**, born 5 Sep 1886 in Coldwater, MI; died 26 Jul 1929 in Toledo, Lucas, OH; buried 28 Jul 1929 in Mt Pleasant Cemetery, son of William HARRIS and May BYERS.

@@ see research notes at end of chapter   ## born after 1930 or known to be living

Edith Pattison married young and was widowed by age 23, with 4 young children. Her husband, Carl Harris, died in fire/explosion in felt insulating company in Toledo, OH. Edith and her children lived with her father in 1930. @@

    Children of Edith May PATTISON and William Carl HARRIS were:
- 966 i **Rose M.**[7] **HARRIS**, born abt 1923 in OH.
- 967 ii **Carl W.**[7] **HARRIS**, born abt 1925 in OH.
- 968 iii **Charles E.**[7] **HARRIS**, born abt 1928 in OH.
- 969 iv **James F.**[7] **HARRIS**, born abt Oct 1929 in OH.

568. **Patricia**[6] **PATTISON** (Frank Lee[5], Mary A. 'Mollie'[4] MANNING, Lucinda[3] TATMAN, Ruth[2] HICKS, Joshua[1]), ##. She married **John Allen KARNOSH**, born 8 May 1934 in Cleveland, Cuyahoga Co, OH; died[518] 15 Apr 1991 in New Philadelphia, Tuscarawas Co, OH.

Jones notes: "resides (1974) at 1291 Crestview Dr, New Philadelphia, OH 44663". Her husband John's death record stated that he had 5+ years college and worked as a financial manager in miscellaneous fabricated metal products

    Children of Patricia PATTISON and John Allen KARNOSH were:
- 970 i **Melissa Lee**[7] **KARNOSH**, ##.
- 971 ii **Kenneth Allen**[7] **KARNOSH**, ##
- 972 iii **John Robert**[7] **KARNOSH**, ##.
- 973 iv **Richard Todd**[7] **KARNOSH**, ##.

571. **John C.**[6] **MANNING** (Ora Chasse[5], Charles William[4], Lucinda[3] TATMAN, Ruth[2] HICKS, Joshua[1]), born 6 Oct 1908 in Clermont Co, OH; died 8 Oct 1977 in New Richmond, Clermont Co, OH. He married (1) in 1929 in Hamilton Co, OH, divorced **Patricia VALKENSTOE**; (2) in 1938 in Clermont Co, OH **Mildred KABLER**, born abt 1908. @@

    Children of John C. MANNING and Mildred KABLER were:
- 974 i **Darlene May**[7] **MANNING**, ##. She married in Clermont Co, OH **Spencer SINGLER**. Jones notes: "resides (1973) at 3700 Rt 125, just east of rink"
- 975 ii **Virginia Ann**[7] **MANNING**, ##. She married in Clermont Co, OH **Arlie ROOT**. Jones notes: "resides (1983) at 2155 Donald Rd, Bethel, OH"

573. **Ruth N.**[6] **MANNING** (Ora Chasse[5], Charles William[4], Lucinda[3] TATMAN, Ruth[2] HICKS, Joshua[1]), born 11 Feb 1915 in Clermont Co, OH; died[519] 24 Jan 1999 in El Paso, El Paso Co, TX. She married on 21 Jul 1934 in Bethel, OH **Samuel A. HOLMES**, born 18 Sep 1898 in Mattoon, Coles Co, IL; died[520] 20 Mar 1970 in Bethel, Clermont Co, OH, son of Alph and Maud HOLMES.

Ruth Manning married Samuel Holmes, who was a shoemaker in Cincinnati in 1918. Ruth died in El Paso, TX. @@

    Children of Ruth N. MANNING and Samuel A. HOLMES were:
- 976 i **Winston A.**[7] **HOLMES**, ##. Jones notes: "career Army - Springfield recruiter 1973"

590. **Charles Edward**[6] **WOLF** (Pearl Diana[5] FITZPATRICK, Homer Jerome[4], Dianna[3] TATMAN, Ruth[2] HICKS, Joshua[1]), born 17 Mar 1919 in Amelia, Clermont Co, OH; died[521] 15 May 1999 in Amelia, Clermont Co, OH. He married on 26 Jan 1946 in Clermont Co, OH **Carrie MOORE**, born 11 May 1923 in Foster OH. Jones notes: "resides (1973) at 299 Chapel Rd, Amelia, OH"

Children of Charles Edward WOLF and Carrie MOORE were:

977   i   **Charles Edward**[7] **WOLF Jr**, ##.

978   ii   **Julie M.**[7] **WOLF**, ##. She married **Robert Thomas MOONEY**. Jones notes: "reside (1974) at 28 Day Circle"

979   iii   **Margaret**[7] **WOLF**, ##.

980   iv   **Katherine**[7] **WOLF**, ##.

591. Wayne Nichols[6] **FITZPATRICK** (John Charles[5], Homer Jerome[4], Dianna[3] TATMAN, Ruth[2] HICKS, Joshua[1]), born 14 Aug 1921 in Amelia, Clermont Co, OH; died[522] 4 Dec 1987 in Severna Park, Anne Arundel Co, MD. He married on 7 Jul 1947 in Hartford, CT **Hope BARTON**, born 25 Apr 1921 in Hartford, CT; died[523] 3 Apr 2001 in Cockeysville, Baltimore Co, MD, daughter of Malcolm and Cornelia BARTON.

Wayne Fitzpatrick served in the US Navy 1940-1969; retired as a Captain" @@

Children of Wayne Nichols FITZPATRICK and Hope BARTON were:

981   i   **David Wayne**[7] **FITZPATRICK**, ##. He married **Janice CRAIN**,

982   ii   **Diane**[7] **FITZPATRICK**, ##.

983   iii   **Lynne**[7] **FITZPATRICK**, ##.

984   iv   **Richard Douglas**[7] **FITZPATRICK**, ##.

985   v   **Steven Brewster**[7] **FITZPATRICK**, ##.

597. Frank Oliver[6] **HIGGINS** (Burton[5], Sarah Ellen[4] FITZPATRICK, Dianna[3] TATMAN, Ruth[2] HICKS, Joshua[1]), born 7 May 1900 in Alabama; died[524] 26 Feb 1965 in Deatsville, Elmore, AL. He married[525] on 2 Mar 1921 in Birmingham, Jefferson, AL **Marietta E. HOGAN**, born abt 1903 in Alabama.

Frank Higgins was a farmer in 1918 and later worked for the railroad in Cold Spring, AL. He was described in 1918 as "tall, med build, grey eyes, brown hair." @@

Children of Frank Oliver HIGGINS and Marietta E. HOGAN were:

\+ 986   i   **Frank**[7] **HIGGINS Jr**. born abt 1923 in Alabama. He married unknown.

987   ii   **Mary E.**[7] **HIGGINS**, born abt 1924 in Alabama.
Probable death: Evelyn Pennington, d. 16 Jun 1972, Montgomery, Montgomery, AL; Age: 48y; Est.. Birth Date: 1924; Spouse: Harry L; father: Frank O. Higgins; mother Mary E. Hogan. Alabama Deaths, 1908-1974 <familysearch.org>

620. Mary Laverne[6] **FITZPATRICK** (John Lee[5], John Lee[4], Sarah A.[3] TATMAN, Ruth[2] HICKS, Joshua[1]), born 8 Nov 1924 in Montgomery, AL. She married on 24 Jun 1944 in Valdosta, GA **Neighl GROGH**, born 26 Aug 1922 in Enid, Garfield Co, OK.

Children of Mary Laverne FITZPATRICK and Neighl GROGH were:

988   i   **Cathy Laverne**[7] **GROGH**, ##.

989   ii   **Luana**[7] **GROGH**, ##.

621. Sandra Louise[6] **FITZPATRICK** (John Lee[5], John Lee[4], Sarah A.[3] TATMAN, Ruth[2] HICKS, Joshua[1]), ##. She married **Robert Gordon KENDALL III**.

Jones notes: "reside (1973) 2308 Ashland Pl, Mobile, AL 36607"; Robert Kendall is probably the Robert Kendall who was a Circuit Court judge in Mobile County, AL. He died in 2006.

Children of Sandra Louise FITZPATRICK and Robert Gordon KENDALL III were:
990   i   **Elizabeth Lee[7] KENDALL**, ##.
991   ii   **Mary Margaret[7] KENDALL**, ##.
992   iii **Catherine Louise[7] KENDALL**, ##.

637. **Agnes Cleo[6] CRANE** (Alice B.[5] TAYLOR, Maud Blanche[4] TATMAN, John[3], Ruth[2] HICKS, Joshua[1]), born 17 Sep 1911 in Mt Washington, Cincinnati, Hamilton Co, OH. She married on 2 Mar 1935 in Bethel, OH **Robert Eberle SWING**, born 27 Jul 1908 in Bethel, OH; died Sep 1981 in Punta Gorda, Charlotte Co, FL.

Agnes Crane married Robert Swing, who served in the Bethel, OH post office for 42 years. @@

Children of Agnes Cleo CRANE and Robert Eberle SWING were:
+ 993   i   **Joyce Ann[7] SWING**, ##. She married (1) **Paul A. SCHNEIDER**; (2) **Dale J. ROBERTS**. Jones notes: "registered nurse; reside (1973) at 5903 Cottontail Ct, Cincinnati OH 45239"
+ 994   ii   **Joyce Renee[7] SWING**, ## . She married **Roger A. DECROW**, Jones notes: "registered nurse; reside (1973) at 1852 Allen Dr, Salem OH 44460"
+ 995   iii **Charles Robert[7] SWING**, ##. He married **Agnes A. KOEHNE**. Jones notes: "Marine Corp - Vietnam; resides (1973) at 511 Jackie Le, Cincinnati OH"

638. **Richard Taylor[6] BECK** (Alice B.[5] TAYLOR, Maud Blanche[4] TATMAN, John[3], Ruth[2] HICKS, Joshua[1]), born 7 Feb 1931 in Bethel, OH. He married on 29 May 1951 in Bethel, OH **Evelyn HOLDERFIELD**, born 15 Jun 1930 in Amelia, Clermont Co, OH. Jones notes: "resides (1973) at 2434 Dalton Rd, Akron OH 44313; served in US Navy 1948-1953"

Children of Richard Taylor BECK and Evelyn HOLDERFIELD were:
996   i   **Karen Sue[7] BECK**, ##.
997   ii   **Eric Richard[7] BECK**, ##.
998   iii **Jennifer Lynn[7] BECK**, ##.
999   iv   **Tracy Ann[7] BECK**, ##.

641. **Gwen[6] TAYLOR** (George Richard[5], Maud Blanche[4] TATMAN, John[3], Ruth[2] HICKS, Joshua[1]), ##. She married **J. Richard BENNETT**. Jones notes: "resides (1979) 56 Audubon Rd, Poland, OH 44514"

Children of Gwen TAYLOR and J. Richard BENNETT were:
1000 i   **Terrie Leah[7] BENNETT**, ##
1001 ii   **Richard James[7] BENNETT**, ##
1002 iii **Jill Stephens[7] BENNETT**, ##

644. **Ruth[6] HUTSON** (Carlos Stanley[5], Ledora Estelle[4] TATMAN, William Oliver[3], Ruth[2] HICKS, Joshua[1]), born Est. 1920. She married on 13 Mar 1945 in Mt Vernon, WA **Alvin FRY**, born Est. 1920.

Jones notes: "Reside (1984) at 1179 White Oak Rd, Clermont Co, OH"

Children of Ruth HUTSON and Alvin FRY were:
1003 i   **Amy[7] FRY**, ##. Jones notes: "graduate nurse"
1004 ii   **Harold[7] FRY**, ##. Jones notes: "resides (1973) at 696 McCormick Ln, Withamsville, OH; teacher"

@@ see research notes at end of chapter   ## born after 1930 or known to be living

645. Alice Mae[6] HUTSON (Carlos Stanley[5], Ledora Estelle[4] TATMAN, William Oliver[3], Ruth[2] HICKS, Joshua[1]), born 22 Aug 1926 in Cincinnati, Hamilton Co, OH. She married on 15 Jun 1946 in Clermont Co, OH **James Robert MCCARTY**, born 4 May 1925 in Cincinnati, Hamilton Co, OH. Jones notes: "Reside (1984) at 17 Laticia, Amelia, OH"

    Children of Alice Mae HUTSON and James Robert MCCARTY were:
1005 i **Debbie Ann[7] MCCARTY**, ##. She married **Thomas NICHODEMAS**. Jones notes: "resides (1973) at 273 Amelia-Olin Branch Rd, Clermont Co, OH"
1006 ii **Tammy[7] MCCARTY**, ##
1007 iii **Danny[7] MCCARTY**, ##.

646. Harriet[6] HUTSON (Carlos Stanley[5], Ledora Estelle[4] TATMAN, William Oliver[3], Ruth[2] HICKS, Joshua[1]), ##. She married **Gerald IDLET**. Jones notes: "Reside (1984) at 309 Sunset Dr, Bethel, OH"

    Children of Harriet HUTSON and Gerald IDLET were:
1008 i **Sandy[7] IDLET**, ##.
1009 ii **Jerry[7] IDLET**, ##.

647. Samuel Hodgson[6] GLOVER (Estella H.[5] HUTSON, Arizona T. "Arra"[4] TATMAN, William Oliver[3], Ruth[2] HICKS, Joshua[1]), born 26 Jul 1903 in Amelia, Clermont Co, OH; died 4 Jul 1965 in Hamilton Co, OH. He married on 4 May 1921 in Clermont Co, OH **Lulu FIGGINS**, born 23 May 1907 in Lindale OH; died Jun 1975 in Amelia, Clermont Co, OH, daughter of Edgar FIGGINS and Inez DONHAM.

Hodgson Glover was listed as a foreman in a pottery factory in 1930. He married Lulu Figgins and had one son, Darrell. @@

    Children of Samuel Hodgson GLOVER and Lulu FIGGINS were:
1010 i **Darrell[7] GLOVER**, born abt 1926 in OH; died 13 Nov 1983 in Cincinnati, Hamilton Co, OH. Jones notes: "resides (1973) at Lindale, OH."
    Death: Darrel H Glover, b. 1925 Ohio; Res: Clermont, OH; d. 13 Nov 1983, Veterans Adm. Med. Ctr, Cincinnati, Hamilton Co, OH; age: 58; married. Ohio Deaths, 1908-1932, 1938-1944, and 1958-2007 [Ancestry.com]

649. Julia Elsie[6] GLOVER (Estella H.[5] HUTSON, Arizona T. "Arra"[4] TATMAN, William Oliver[3], Ruth[2] HICKS, Joshua[1]), born 7 Sep 1906 in Clermont Co, OH; died[526] 1 May 2002 in Hamilton, Butler Co, OH. She married **Donald H. AULT**, born 11 Aug 1906 in London, Eng.

Julia Glover was a teacher in Amelia, OH. She married Donald Ault, who was born in England. @@

    Children of Julia Elsie GLOVER and Donald H. AULT were:
1011 i **Donald C.[7] AULT**, ##. Jones notes: "resides (1973) at 11350 Melissa Ct, Cincinnati, OH"
1012 ii **Julia[7] AULT**, ##. She married **Jens Allen HANSEN**. Jones notes: "resides (1973) at 185 Strathcoma, Cincinnati, OH 45230; Julie a speech & hearing therapist; BS from UC, MA from Stanford. Jens an attorney - BA from Yale; JD from Stanford Law School"

650. Dorothy H.[6] GLOVER (Estella H.[5] HUTSON, Arizona T. "Arra"[4] TATMAN, William Oliver[3], Ruth[2] HICKS, Joshua[1]), born 26 Apr 1908 in Amelia, Clermont Co, OH; died[527] 1 May 1971 in Cincinnati, Hamilton Co, OH. She married on 12 Aug 1937 in Clermont Co, OH **Leonard O. BILLINGSLEY**, born 19 Jun 1918 in Hinton, WV, son of Roy R BILLINGSLEY and Carrie WYANT.

Dorothy married Leonard Billingsley, who was driving a truck for a pottery company in 1930. @@

@@ see research notes at end of chapter   ## born after 1930 or known to be living

Children of Dorothy H. GLOVER and Leonard O. BILLINGSLEY were:
1013 i **Dorothy[7] BILLINGSLEY**, ##. Jones notes: "resides (1973) at 2141 Pace Dr, Clarksville, TN 37040; m. Colin Stewart"

651. **Charles Lee[6] GLOVER** (Estella H.[5] HUTSON, Arizona T. "Arra"[4] TATMAN, William Oliver[3], Ruth[2] HICKS, Joshua[1]), born 17 Oct 1910 in Clermont Co, OH; died 4 Dec 1960 in Amelia, Clermont Co, OH; buried in Amelia Meth. Cemetery He married (1) on 15 Mar 1942 in Clermont Co, OH **Inez Lucille BRILL**, born 12 Apr 1920 in Mt Piscah, OH, daughter of George and Elizabeth BRILL; (2) **Mrs. Givens WITHAM**, born 28 Jul 1916 in Hartford, WV.

Charles Glover was in the Army during World War II. He married Inez Brill and had 2 children. @@

Children of Charles Lee GLOVER and Inez Lucille BRILL were:
1014 i **Lena Lucille[7] GLOVER**, ##. She married **George G. SHRINE III**. Jones notes: "resides (1984) at 1697 OH, Amelia OH 45102"
1015 ii **Samuel Lee[7] GLOVER**, ##. He married **Wanda BATES**. Jones notes: "resides (1973) at 123 E. Main, Amelia, OH"

653. **Kenneth H.[6] MYRICK** (Gladys E.[5] HUTSON, Arizona T. "Arra"[4] TATMAN, William Oliver[3], Ruth[2] HICKS, Joshua[1]), born 16 Jan 1915 in Clermont Co, OH; died[528] 16 Apr 1997 in Amelia, Clermont Co, OH. He married on 31 Aug 1943 in La Flora Co, MS **Cecile Rose TURBYNE**, born 17 May 1917 in Waterville, ME; died 19 Jun 2006 in Clermont Co, OH, daughter of Alec TURBYNE and Maude RANCORT.

Kenneth Myrick enlisted as a private and served in the Army during World War II. He married Cecille Turbyne of Maine. @@

Children of Kenneth H. MYRICK and Cecile Rose TURBYNE were:
1016 i **Kenneth[7] MYRICK Jr**.
1017 ii **Michael[7] MYRICK**.

656. **Jessie Elizabeth (Betty)[6] MCNAIR** (Lloyd Edwin[5], Benjamin Edwin[4], Mary[3] TATMAN, Ruth[2] HICKS, Joshua[1]), born 1 Aug 1926 in Bethel, OH; died 7 Sep 2005 in Williamsburg, Clermont, OH. She married on 16 Jun 1949 in Clermont Co, OH **Leroy HERBST**, born 24 Feb 1926 in Coldspring, KY.

Betty McNair married Leroy Herbst and had 4 children. They lived in Williamsburg, OH. @@

Children of Jessie Elizabeth (Betty) MCNAIR and Leroy HERBST were:
1018 i **Roy Edwin[7] HERBST**, ##.
1019 ii **Theresa Lynn[7] HERBST**, ##.
1020 iii **Nancy Kay[7] HERBST**, ##.
1021 iv **Lee Anne[7] HERBST**, ##.

663. **Elizabeth Stewart[6] HITE** (Hattie Edna[5] HICKS, Orestes Daily "O.D."[4], Henry Melvin[3], Elijah[2], Joshua[1]), born 18 Aug 1914 in Clermont Co, OH; died 5 Jul 1986 in Felicity, Clermont Co, OH. She married (1) on 28 Apr 1934 in Clermont Co, OH **Floyd B. FUGETTE**, born 28 May 1912 in KY; died 24 Jul 1939 in Cincinnati, Hamilton, OH; buried 26 Jul 1939 in Felicity, Clermont Co, OH, son of Norman FUGETTE and Flora Mae TACKETT; (2) on 19 Feb 1943 in Covington, Kenton Co, KY **Eugene Locke POSTON**, born 18 Apr 1910 in Butler KY; died[529, 530] 17 Apr 1978 in Brown Co, OH.

Elizabeth Hite married Floyd Fugette, a metal worker, who died at age 26, as a result of appendicitis. She later married Eugene Poston. @@

@@ see research notes at end of chapter   ## born after 1930 or known to be living

Children of Elizabeth Stewart HITE and Floyd B. FUGETTE were:

+ 1022 i **Nancy Elizabeth**[7] **FUGETTE**, born 3 Mar 1936 in Clermont Co, OH; died 22 Aug 1995 in Felicity, Clermont Co, OH. She married on 19 Jun 1954 in Clermont Co, OH **Claude Thomas WILSON**, born 31 Oct 1932 in Clermont Co, OH; died 17 Apr 2008 in Felicity, Clermont, OH.
Jones notes: "reside (1972) at St Rt 133, 1 mi N of Felicity"

Children of Elizabeth Stewart HITE and Eugene Locke POSTON were:

+ 1023 i **Kenneth Eugene**[7] **POSTON**, ##. He married **Joan D. CAPPEL**.
Jones notes: "reside 1981 at 330 S. Perimeter Dr, Erlanger, KY"
+ 1024 ii **Patricia Lynne**[7] **POSTON**, ##. She married **Ernest Dale SCHWARTZ**
Jones notes: "reside (1972) at Rt 1, Felicity - Felicity-Higginsport Rd"

664. Melissa Rosaline[6] **HICKS**[531] (Hurdes Beeker[5], Elijah Franklin[4], Henry Melvin[3], Elijah[2], Joshua[1]), born 3 May 1920 in Chilo, Clermont Co, OH; died 20 Sep 2001 in Cincinnati, Hamilton Co, OH. She married on 25 Feb 1949 in Vanceburg KY **Russell S. BUSKIRK**, born 10 Jul 1909 in Vanceburg KY; died 4 Nov 1990 in Clermont Co, OH, son of Joseph B. and Cynthia BUSKIRK.

Rosaline Hicks married Russell Buskirk, who worked on the Ohio river boats. They had one son, Russell. @@

Children of Melissa Rosaline HICKS and Russell S. BUSKIRK were:

+ 1025 i **Russell E.**[7] **BUSKIRK**, ##. He married **Diana FRAZEE**, ##.
Jones notes: "resides (1972) at 1818 Sutton Cir, Cincinnati, OH"

666. Morris Hurdes[6] **HICKS**[532] (Hurdes Beeker[5], Elijah Franklin[4], Henry Melvin[3], Elijah[2], Joshua[1]), ##. He married (1), **Dorothy SHERMAN**; (2) **Veara Rose MOORE**, born 3 Mar 1933 in Batavia, Clermont Co, OH; died abt 1995.

Morris Hicks was a printer by profession and was living in Ocala, FL in 1999.@@

Children of Morris Hurdes HICKS and Dorothy SHERMAN were:

1026 i **Donna Lynn**[7] **HICKS**, ##.
Jones notes give name, dates, "lives with mother's family in El Monte, CA"
1027 ii **Janet**[7] **HICKS**, ##.
Jones notes: gives name, dates; "lives with mother's family in El Monte, CA"
1028 iii **Deborah**[7] **HICKS**, ##.
Jones notes give name, dates; "lives with their mother's family in El Monte, CA"

Children of Morris Hurdes HICKS and Veara Rose MOORE were:

1029 i **Rosalyn Lynn**[7] **HICKS**, ##. Jones notes give name, dates
1030 ii **Morris**[7] **HICKS Jr.**, ##. Jones notes give name, dates

667. Donald Rogers[6] **HICKS**[533] (Hurdes Beeker[5], Elijah Franklin[4], Henry Melvin[3], Elijah[2], Joshua[1]), born 15 Sep 1930 in Chilo, Clermont Co, OH. He married on 19 May 1955 in Maysville, Mason Co, KY **Helen STANTON**, died 4 Jan 1991.

Children of Donald Rogers HICKS and Helen STANTON were:

1031 i **Brenda Kay**[7] **HICKS**, ##. Jones notes give name, dates
1032 ii **Roger Wayne**[7] **HICKS**, ##. Jones notes give name, dates

@@ see research notes at end of chapter   ## born after 1930 or known to be living

1033 iii **Patricia Marie**[7] **HICKS**, ##. Jones notes give name, dates

668. Barbara Ann[6] **HICKS** (Hurdes Beeker[5], Elijah Franklin[4], Henry Melvin[3], Elijah[2], Joshua[1]), ##. She married **James Edward HALL**.

Jones notes give name, dates, spouse "resides (1972) at Felicity, OH"

Children of Barbara Ann HICKS and James Edward HALL were:
1034 i **James Edward "Rocky"**[7] **HALL Jr**, ##.

669. Eva Irlene[6] **DEVORE** (Irlene Evelyn[5] HICKS, Elijah Franklin[4], Henry Melvin[3], Elijah[2], Joshua[1]), born 16 Mar 1925 in Felicity, Clermont Co, OH. She married (1) on 18 Nov 1941 in Clermont Co, OH **Cecil Thomas GREGORY**, born 20 Jan 1918 in Maysville, Mason Co, KY, son of Thomas GREGORY and Grace PAUL; (2) **A. G. CLAYTON**, born Est. 1925.

Lvera (Jennings) Seipelt's notes (1999): living in Bradenton, FL; "this her second marriage; Bradenton, FL - retired". Cecil Gregory "resides (1972) at 5145 Sterling, Youngstown, OH"; "auto plant"

Children of Eva Irlene DEVORE and Cecil Thomas GREGORY were:
+ 1035 i **Melody Lynn**[7] **GREGORY**, ##. She married **Eugene WOODRUFF.**
    Jones notes: "reside (1972) at 5221 Belfast-Owensville Rd, Higginsport, OH"
+ 1036 ii **Richard Thomas**[7] **GREGORY**.##. He married **Barbara OWENS**,
    Jones notes: "reside (1972) at Youngstown, OH"
+ 1037 iii **Yvette**[7] **GREGORY**, ##. She married **Edward ZETTS**,
    Jones notes: "resides (1972) at 83 Duncan Ln, Youngstown, OH"

670. John Wilson "J. W."[6] **DEVORE** (Irlene Evelyn[5] HICKS, Elijah Franklin[4], Henry Melvin[3], Elijah[2], Joshua[1]), born 7 Jun 1931 in Felicity, Clermont Co, OH; died 12 Aug 1988 in Chelsea, Rogers, OK; buried in Claremore, OK. He married on 17 Sep 1951 in Clermont Co, OH, divorced **Jannette Anne LINDSEY**.

J. W. Devore raised miniature mules in Oklahoma. His funeral train was pulled by the miniature mules. @@

Children of John Wilson "J. W." DEVORE and Jannette Anne LINDSEY were:
1038 i **Pamela Sue**[7] **DEVORE**, ##. She married **Anthony OCCUZZA**.
    Jones notes: give names, dates, spouse "reside (1972) at Claremore, OK"
1039 ii **Dianna Jo**[7] **DEVORE**, ##. Jones notes give name, dates
1040 iii **John Wilson**[7] **DEVORE Jr.**, ##. Jones notes give name, dates
1041 iv **Allan Lewis**[7] **DEVORE**, ##. Jones notes give name, dates

673. Lvera Adrienne[6] **JENNINGS** (Georgia Elizabeth[5] HICKS, Elijah Franklin[4], Henry Melvin[3], Elijah[2], Joshua[1]), ##. She married **Victor Lloyd SEIPELT**, born 7 May 1920 in Ripley, OH; died 6 Dec 2008 in Georgetown, Brown Co, OH, son of Albert William SEIPELT and Parthena Mae FLAUGHER.

Lvera Jennings married Victor Seipelt, who was a "farmer 20 years; Farm Aide at OH Agricultural Research & Development Center, 30 years". Photo on page 305; Lvera supplied many of the photos for this book.@@

Children of Lvera Adrienne JENNINGS and Victor Lloyd SEIPELT were:
+ 1042 i **Victor Lloyd**[7] **SEIPELT Jr.**, ##. He married **Connie Nancy WILSON**,
+ 1043 ii **Leslie Galen**[7] **SEIPELT.**, ##. He married **Edna Marilyn FLORENCE**,
    "works for Browning Mfg since 1974 (1993)". Brown Co History

@@ see research notes at end of chapter   ## born after 1930 or known to be living

1044　iii **David Lyle⁷ SEIPELT**, born 14 Nov 1952; died 14 Nov 1952; buried in Maplewood Cemetery. Notes: "stillborn twins 11/14/1952". *Brown Co History*

1045　iv **Dale Lynn⁷ SEIPELT**, born 14 Nov 1952; died 14 Nov 1952; buried in Maplewood Cemetery. Notes: "stillborn twins 11/14/1952". *Brown Co History*

674. Irma Claire⁶ JENNINGS (Georgia Elizabeth⁵ HICKS, Elijah Franklin⁴, Henry Melvin³, Elijah², Joshua¹), born 27 Oct 1930 in east of Utopia, Brown Co, OH. She married on 14 Feb 1949, divorced **Lewis Ray PURDY**.

Irma Claire Jennings worked in the health care field for many years, at both nursing homes and the Georgetown Hospital. @@

Children of Irma Claire JENNINGS and Lewis Ray PURDY were:

1046　i　**Alan Lee⁷ PURDY**, ##.
1047　ii　**Danny Ray⁷ PURDY**, ##.
1048　iii　**Connie Sue⁷ PURDY**, ##.
1049　iv　**Dale Lynn⁷ PURDY**, ##.
1050　v　**John Russel⁷ PURDY**, ##.

675. Ivetta Faye⁶ JENNINGS (Georgia Elizabeth⁵ HICKS, Elijah Franklin⁴, Henry Melvin³, Elijah², Joshua¹), ##. She married, divorced **Robert William FRODGE**; married (2) Delbert Dawes, 24 May 2007.

Ivetta Jennings worked with an insurance company for 40 years. She remarried after she had retired. @@

Children of Ivetta Faye JENNINGS and Robert William FRODGE were:

1051　i　**Rhonda Yvetta⁷ FRODGE**, ##.
1052　ii　**Michael Robert⁷ FRODGE**, ##.
1053　iii　**Sheree Lee⁷ FRODGE**, ##.

676. Eugene Martin⁶ JENNINGS 2nd (Georgia Elizabeth⁵ HICKS, Elijah Franklin⁴, Henry Melvin³, Elijah², Joshua¹), ##. He married, divorced **Jacqueline Lou BERRY**.

Eugene Jennings worked in the Pepsi plant in Cincinnati for 25 years. He served in the Army. Photo on page 304. @@

Children of Eugene Martin JENNINGS 2nd and Jacqueline Lou BERRY were:

1054　i　**Clemons Michael⁷ JENNINGS**, ##.
1055　ii　**Eugene M.⁷ JENNINGS III**, ##.
1056　iii　**Kimberley Ann⁷ JENNINGS**, ##.

680. Harvey Clyde⁶ LEVI II (Clyde Harvey⁵, Lucy Ann⁴ HICKS, Henry Melvin³, Elijah², Joshua¹), born 18 Sep 1903 in Cincinnati, Hamilton Co, OH; died 12 Jan 1970 in Omaha, Douglas Co, NE. He married on 7 Oct 1935 in Glendale MS **Marvella Margaret TRUITT**, born 14 Sep 1917 in Muscatine, Muscatine Co, IA; died 2 Jan 1980 in Seattle, WA.

Clyde Levi was involved with the Silver States Carnivals for much of his life. He died in Omaha, NE. @@

Children of Harvey Clyde LEVI II and Marvella Margaret TRUITT were:

+　1057　i　**Harvey Clyde⁷ LEVI III**. born 25 Jan 1938 in Mercedes, TX; died 17 Mar 1995 in St Petersburg, FL. He married **Joanne Vivienne DUVAL**.
+　1058　ii　**Lane DeWitt⁷ LEVI**. ##. He married **Janet Ruth LEOPOLD**.
　　　　　　Jones notes: "a rocket scientist; 30 years in aerospace."
　1059　iii　**Paula Alora⁷ LEVI**, ##. "living in Montana (3/97) where she is a homemaker"

@@ see research notes at end of chapter　　## born after 1930 or known to be living

683. Elizabeth[6] STALDER (Mollie Dell[5] LEVI, Lucy Ann[4] HICKS, Henry Melvin[3], Elijah[2], Joshua[1]), born[534] 9 Mar 1913 in Norwood, Hamilton Co, OH; died 17 Oct 2008 in Orlando, Orange Co, FL; buried 20 Oct 2008 in Greenwood Cemetery, Orlando, FL. She married[535] on 2 Feb 1936 in Orlando, Orange Co, FL **Robert Julius KIESER**, born[536] 31 Jan 1909 in Columbus, Franklin Co, OH; died[537] 22 May 1995 in Orlando, Orange Co, FL; buried 25 May 1995 in Greenwood Cemetery, Orlando, FL, son of Charles Frederick KIESER and Jessie Marcella UMBAUGH.

Both Bob and Betty (Stalder) Kieser were avid gardeners, growing both flowers and vegetables. They were very active members of Delaney Street Baptist Church in Orlando for more than 50 years. Bob worked for the Naval Underwater Sound Lab for 35 years and, during World War II, helped dismantle a German submarine to discover how the sonar system worked and develop ways to combat it. Photo of Betty & Bob on dedication page; Betty & siblings on page 304; 4 generation photo on page 377; obituary on page 305. Parents of the compiler of this book. @@

Children of Elizabeth STALDER and Robert Julius KIESER were:

+ 1060 i **Robert Frederick[7] KIESER**, ##. He married, divorced **Nancy Elizabeth RUGG**, Master's degree in Science Education. Living in Choctaw, OK 1995. Retired Air Force officer.
+ 1061 ii **Elizabeth Joan[7] "Betty Jo" KIESER**, ##. She married **Robert Glenn STOCKTON**. Betty Jo has Master's degree in education; retired school librarian; compiler of this book; Glenn has Master's degree in math; operations researcher for Dept of the Army 30 yr. US Army 1961-1972, Vietnam veteran.
  1062 iii **Charles David[7] KIESER**, born 27 Oct 1946 in Orlando, Orange Co, FL; died 29 Jul 1967 in USS Forrestal, Vietnam; buried in Greenwood Cemetery, Orange Co, FL.
  Death: Killed in fire on USS Forrestal, off the coast of VietNam while serving in Navy.
  Burial: Greenwood Cemetery, Orlando, FL. Lot L.
  Obituary: *Charles David Kieser, 20, aviation and electricians mate 3rd class, 275 Prescott Dr, was killed July 29 in a fire on the carrier USS Forrestal. He was a native of Orlando and attended Orlando schools, Florida Military Academy, University of S. Florida and Orlando Junior College. He entered the Navy in 1966 and was attached to the FV-74 Flight Squadron. Survivors: Parents Mr & Mrs Robert J. Kieser, Orlando; brother Capt Robert F., Gunter AFB, AL; sister Mrs R. Glenn Stockton, Ft Belvoir, VA.* ***Orlando Sentinel****, 6 Aug 1967.*

684. Jeanette[6] STALDER (Mollie Dell[5] LEVI, Lucy Ann[4] HICKS, Henry Melvin[3], Elijah[2], Joshua[1]), born 22 Sep 1914 in Madeira, Hamilton Co, OH; died 5 Feb 1980 in Tallahassee, FL. She married on 18 Jan 1942 in Florida **Emmet Williams RHODES**, born 15 Oct 1917; died 17 Jul 1996 in Tallahassee, Leon, FL.

Jeanette Stalder trained as a beautician and worked in that field before she married Emmet Rhodes. They lived in Tallahassee, FL and had two daughters. @@

Children of Jeanette STALDER and Emmet Williams RHODES were:
  1063 i **Judith Ann[7] RHODES**, ##.
+ 1064 ii **Ellen Williams[7] RHODES**, ##. She married (1) abt 1962, divorced **Ronald CRAVEN**; (2) abt 1980 **John WEST**. "Living in Cordele, GA (1998)"

686. Grace Olive[6] STALDER (Mollie Dell[5] LEVI, Lucy Ann[4] HICKS, Henry Melvin[3], Elijah[2], Joshua[1]), born 11 Aug 1918 in Madeira, Hamilton Co, OH; died 14 Jun 2003 in Jacksonville, Duval Co, FL. She married on 22 Jun 1939 **Euthan Arthur WINDHAM**, born 23 Jul 1916 in Georgia; died[538] 22 Aug 1988 in Jacksonville, Duval Co, FL.

Grace Stalder married Euthan Windham, who worked for the Florida Times Union newspaper. Euthan served in the Army during World War II.

    Children of Grace Olive STALDER and Euthan Arthur WINDHAM were:
+   1065   i   **Marilyn Grace**[7] **WINDHAM**, ##. She married **Perry Hobart CARGAL**, Living in Jacksonville Beach, FL 1995.
+   1066   ii   **Douglas Arthur**[7] **WINDHAM**. He married **Ina Lynne JAUDON**, "Living in Lakeland, FL 1995.

687. Ruth Marilyn[6] **STALDER**[539] (Mollie Dell[5] LEVI, Lucy Ann[4] HICKS, Henry Melvin[3], Elijah[2], Joshua[1]), born 17 Nov 1919 in Madeira, Hamilton Co, OH; died 17 Feb 2000 in Jacksonville, Duval Co, FL. She married on 7 Feb 1941 in Jacksonville, Duval, Co, FL **Elkin Ewing "Jack" WATKINS**, born 11 May 1917 in Arlington, GA; died 17 Nov 1979 in Jacksonville, Duval Co, FL; buried in Arlington, GA.

Ruth Stalder married E. E. Watkins, called Jack. He worked as a pharmaceutical distributor.

    Children of Ruth Marilyn STALDER and Elkin Ewing "Jack" WATKINS were:
+   1067   i   **Thomas Taylor**[7] **WATKINS II**, ##. He married (1) divorced **Lucinda RITCHIE**; (2) **Louise HAGSED**. "3/1998 - District Service Manager, Mazda Motors of America"
     1068   ii   **William Benjamin**[7] **WATKINS**, ##.

688. Mary Madge[6] **STALDER** (Mollie Dell[5] LEVI, Lucy Ann[4] HICKS, Henry Melvin[3], Elijah[2], Joshua[1]), born 3 Feb 1921 in Madeira, Hamilton Co, OH; died 8 Apr 2006 in Jacksonville, Duval Co, FL. She married on 15 Jun 1946 in Folkston, GA **John Francis WASHELL**[540], born 10 Jul 1921 in Philadelphia, PA; died 18 Apr 1994 in Jacksonville, Duval, Co, FL; buried 22 Apr 1994 in Jacksonville, Duval, Co, FL; son of **Peter Joseph WASHELL** and **Mary KANDRAVI**.

Madge Stalder was only six weeks old when her family moved to Florida. She married John Washell, a carpenter, working on ships in the Jacksonville shipyards. @@

    Children of Mary Madge STALDER and John Francis WASHELL were:
+   1069   i   **John Phillip**[7] **WASHELL**, ##. He married **Mildred Carolyn EPPS**, "Living in Lakeland, FL; 1995 - a fireman."
+   1070   ii   **Mary Dell**[7] **WASHELL**, ##. She married **Walter Odis TEDDER**, "Living in Jacksonville, FL; 1995"
+   1071   iii   **Timothy J.**[7] **WASHELL**, ##. He married **Linda LANE** "Living in Lakeland, FL; 1995"

690. Elizabeth[6] **JOSLIN** (Archibald D. "Archie"[5], Mary Elizabeth[4] HICKS, Henry Melvin[3], Elijah[2], Joshua[1]), born 23 Jan 1918 in Norwood, Hamilton Co, OH; died 13 May 1975 in Cincinnati, Hamilton Co, OH. She married bef 1938 **Howard HAYDEN**, born[541] 10 Feb 1912; died[542] 9 Jun 1996 in Cincinnati, Hamilton Co, OH.

Elizabeth Joslin married Howard Hayden and lived in Clermont Co. They had four children. @@

    Children of Elizabeth JOSLIN and Howard HAYDEN were:
     1072   i   **Robert**[7] **HAYDEN**, ##. Jones notes give name, birth, "a surgeon, New York City - 124 E. 24th St (1972)
     1073   ii   **James**[7] **HAYDEN**, ##. Jones notes give name, birth, "resides (1972) 1725 N. Bronson, Hollywood, CA. not married."

    @@ see research notes at end of chapter   ## born after 1930 or known to be living

+ 1074 iii **John⁷ HAYDEN**. born 30 May 1939 in Clermont Co, OH; died 30 Jun 2000. He married (1), divorced **Saundra -?-**; (2) **Tina -?-**.
Jones notes "resides (1972) Painter at Covington, KY"
+ 1075 iv **Janie⁷ HAYDEN**, ##. She married (1) divorced **Tom GEIER**; (2) **Chris WILSON**.

692. **Marian⁶ WEST** (Adlara Leona 'Addie'⁵ JOSLIN, Mary Elizabeth⁴ HICKS, Henry Melvin³, Elijah², Joshua¹), born 14 Jun 1919 in Clermont Co, OH; died 14 Aug 1989 in Cincinnati, Hamilton Co, OH. She married on 1 Feb 1938 in Norwood, Hamilton Co, OH **Robert STARRETT**, born 3 Mar 1917 in Richmond, IN; died 20 Jul 1993 in Cincinnati, Hamilton Co, OH.

Marian West married Robert Starrett. They had five children.

Children of Marian WEST and Robert STARRETT were:
1076 i **Robert Howard⁷ STARRETT**, ##. He married **Nancy KURTZ**.
Jones notes: "resides (1980) at 4456 Glendale Dr, Clermont Co, OH 45203; no children"
1077 ii **Thomas Edwin⁷ STARRETT**, ##. He married in Wilmington **Janet SCHIELTZ**.
Jones notes: "resides (1974) at N. Binkley, Sherman, TX"
1078 iii **Virginia Joyce⁷ STARRETT**, ##. She married **Harry SCHMIDT**.
Jones notes: "resides (1974) at 11311 Ravenhurst, Cincinnati, OH.
1079 iv **Donna⁷ STARRETT**, ##. She married **Raymond REED**.
Jones notes: "resides (1974) at 801 Laverty Ln, Mt Washington, OH"
1080 v **Charles Clifford⁷ STARRETT**, ##. He married **Kathleen BROWN**.
Jones notes: "resides (1974) at 3325 Cardiff Av, Cincinnati"

693. **Margaret Anna⁶ MEEKER** (Lucy Mary Francis⁵ HICKS, Harvey Henry⁴, Henry Melvin³, Elijah², Joshua¹), born 20 Jan 1907 in Cincinnati, Hamilton Co, OH; died⁵⁴³ 1 Jun 1998 in Loveland, Clermont Co, OH. She married on 25 Jun 1923 in Newport KY **George Clement ORTH**, born 13 Nov 1905 in Cincinnati, Hamilton Co, OH; died⁵⁴⁴ Jan 1982 in Cincinnati, Hamilton Co, OH, son of George and Carrie ORTH.

Margaret Meeker married Clement Orth, who lived in Cincinnati, OH. The family had four children.@@

Children of Margaret Anna MEEKER and George Clement ORTH were:
+ 1081 i **James Clemens⁷ ORTH**, born 15 Dec 1924 in Cincinnati, Hamilton Co, OH. He married abt 1942 in Cincinnati, Hamilton Co, OH **Helen PIERNER?**, born 26 Jul 1927 in Covington, Kenton Co, KY.
Jones notes: "Resides (1972) 9447 McKinney Rd, Loveland; US Navy WW II"
+ 1082 ii **Frieda Mae⁷ ORTH**, born 22 Aug 1926 in Cincinnati, Hamilton Co, OH. She married on 15 Jun 1946 in Cincinnati, Hamilton Co, OH **Durwood Charles NICOLAY**, born 24 Apr 1922 in Norwood, Hamilton Co, OH; died 24 Sep 1990 in Montgomery, Hamilton Co, OH, son of **Chester** and **Hazel M. NICOLAY**.
Jones notes: "Resides (1972) Overbroook Av, Foster's Xing?; operates an antique shop"
+ 1083 iii **Donald Roy⁷ ORTH**, ##. He married **Angela CATALINA**.
Jones notes: "Resides (1972) at 1718 Pheasant Hills Dr, Loveland; USAF 1957-1958"
+ 1084 iv **Nancy Margaret⁷ ORTH**, ##. She married **John William HAMM Jr**.
Jones notes: "Resides (1972) at 336 Wiltsee Dr, Br. Hil?"

@@ see research notes at end of chapter   ## born after 1930 or known to be living

696. Rachel Matilda[6] **MEEKER** (Lucy Mary Francis[5] HICKS, Harvey Henry[4], Henry Melvin[3], Elijah[2], Joshua[1]), born 28 Apr 1911 in Cincinnati, Hamilton Co, OH; died 18 Feb 2002 in Louisville, Jefferson Co, KY. She married in Crown Point, IN **Philip NORMAN**, born 28 May 1906 in Cincinnati, Hamilton Co, OH; died 19 Jul 1979 in Cincinnati, Hamilton, OH.

Rachel Meeker married Phillip Norman. They had one son.

    Children of Rachel Matilda MEEKER and Philip NORMAN were:
    1085 i **Robert Phillp**[7] **NORMAN**, ##. "Press secretary to Sen. Ford of KY."

697. Robert[6] **MEEKER** (Lucy Mary Francis[5] HICKS, Harvey Henry[4], Henry Melvin[3], Elijah[2], Joshua[1]), born 28 Apr 1911 in Cincinnati, Hamilton Co, OH; died Apr 1984 in Cincinnati, Hamilton Co, OH. He married (1) on 24 Jun 1933 in Cincinnati, Hamilton Co, OH, divorced **Marcella B. HAGEN**, born 19 Dec 1909 in Cincinnati, Hamilton Co, OH; died 24 May 1989 in Cincinnati, Hamilton Co, OH, daughter of Henry and Anna HAGEN; (2) **Mary Ann VOYER**.

    Children of Robert MEEKER and Marcella B. HAGEN were:
    1086 i **Shirley**[7] **MEEKER**, ##. Notes from Lvera (Jennings) Seipelt (1998) "Lucy Meeker (Deceased 1964); Children: Robert Meeker (Deceased 1984): children: Shirley; William R."
    1087 ii **William R.**[7] **MEEKER**, ##. Notes from Lvera Seipelt (1998) list "Lucy Meeker (Deceased 1964); Children: Robert Meeker (Deceased 1984); children: Shirley; William R."

698. Helen[6] **HICKS** (Harvey John[5], Harvey Henry[4], Henry Melvin[3], Elijah[2], Joshua[1]), born 8 Oct 1918 in Cincinnati, Hamilton Co, OH. She married on 8 Aug 1937 in Covington, Kenton Co, KY **Wilson S. LUCKEY**, born 21 Feb 1915 in Madiera, Hamilton Co, OH; died 8 May 1985 in Amelia, Clermont Co, OH; buried 8 May 1985 in Pierce Township Cemetery, Locust Corner, OH, son of Wilson S. LUCKEY and Edna HAWLEY.

Helen Hicks married Wilson Luckey and lived in Clermont County. @@

    Children of Helen HICKS and Wilson S. LUCKEY were:
+ 1088 i **Barbara Jane**[7] **LUCKEY**, ##. She married **Ray MULLINS**,
    Jones notes: "resides (1972) at Maplewood Av, near Amelia, OH".
+ 1089 ii **Cynthia**[7] **LUCKEY**, ##. She married **Michael J. CLARK**.
    Jones notes: "resides (1972) at 890 Linda Sue Dr, Withamsville, OH?"
+ 1090 iii **Wilson Shannon**[7] **LUCKEY Jr.** ##. He married **Jacqueline HAZELIP**.
    Jones notes: "resides (1984) at 116 Arbor Ct, Cincinnati, OH 45013"
+ 1091 iv **Rebecca J.**[7] **LUCKEY**, ##. She married **Harlan G. CLIFTON**.
    Jones notes: "resides (1972) at 326 S.R. 132, Lindale, OH?"
    1092 v **Deborah L.**[7] **LUCKEY**, ##. She married **James B. SHELTON**.
    Jones notes: "resides (1972) New Concord, OH; leaving Aug 1972 to teach school a year in England; no children"
    1093 vi **Karen**[7] **LUCKEY**, ##.

699. Henrietta[6] **HICKS** (Harvey John[5], Harvey Henry[4], Henry Melvin[3], Elijah[2], Joshua[1]), born 13 Mar 1920 in Norwood, Hamilton Co, OH; died[545] 5 Aug 1993 in Cincinnati, Hamilton, OH. She married on 7 Dec 1940 in Cincinnati, Hamilton , OH **Albert WENGER**, born 17 Jul 1920 in Cincinnati, Hamilton, OH.

Henrietta Hicks married Albert Wenger of Cincinnati. Albert served in the Army Air Corps during World War II. They had one son, Peter. @@

@@ see research notes at end of chapter   ## born after 1930 or known to be living

Children of Henrietta HICKS and Albert WENGER were:

+ 1094 i **Peter[7] WENGER**, born 9 Aug 1947 in Cincinnati, Hamilton Co, OH; died 1982 in KY. He married bef 1976 in Cincinnati, Hamilton Co, OH **Sharon DENNLER?** Jones notes: "killed in a fall from a cliff in KY, 1982"

700. Harriet JoAnn[6] HICKS (Harvey John[5], Harvey Henry[4], Henry Melvin[3], Elijah[2], Joshua[1]), born 6 Oct 1928 in Norwood, Hamilton Co, OH; died 26 Oct 2009 in Miamisburg, OH. She married on 8 May 1948 in Cincinnati, Hamilton Co, OH **Richard Warren MCCRACKEN**, born 5 Apr 1926 in Cincinnati, Hamilton Co, OH.

Harriet Hicks married Richard McCracken. At the time of her death in 2009, she had five great grandchildren. @@

Children of Harriet JoAnn HICKS and Richard Warren MCCRACKEN were:

1095 i **Janice Lynne[7] MCCRACKEN**, ##. She married **Dennis Wayne HOLLAND**. Jones notes: "Resides (1984) at1214 Mina Dr, Olive Branch, OH"

1095a ii **James R. MCCRACKEN**, ##. He married **Debbie -?-**.

701. John Phillip[6] BEHAN (Minnie Clara[5] HICKS, Harvey Henry[4], Henry Melvin[3], Elijah[2], Joshua[1]), born 15 Nov 1917 in Norwood, Hamilton Co, OH; died 23 Nov 1981 in Peru, Miami Co, IN; buried in Mt. Hope Cemetery, Peru, Miami Co, IN. He married (1) on 27 Jun 1936 in Newport, Campbell KY **Dorothy Cloetill RAY**, born 3 Feb 1918 in Cincinnati, Hamilton Co, OH; died Nov 1974 in Kokomo, IN, daughter of **Monroe RAY** and **Mary MURPHY**; (2) **Maybelle STACKHOUSE**.

Phillip Behan was working as a landscaper in 1936. He ran a trailer park in Kokomo, IN for a number of years. @@.

Children of John Phillip BEHAN and Dorothy Cloetill RAY were:

+ 1096 i **Phyllis Marie[7] BEHAN**. She married **Willard CATTARON**,. Jones notes: "resides (1974) in Indiana"; Listed as Mrs. Keith Marks in her mother's 1974 obituary.
+ 1097 ii **Jacqualine Ray[7] BEHAN**, ##. She married **Phillip MCKIBBEN**, Jones notes: "resides (1974) in Indiana".
+ 1098 iii **Judith Lynn[7] BEHAN**, ##. She married **Larry THOMPSON**. Jones notes: "resides (1974) in Indiana"
  1099 iv **Nancy Lee[7] BEHAN**, ##. Jones notes: "resides (1974) in Indiana; m. Richard Lybrook; no children"

702. Dorothy Ann[6] BEHAN (Minnie Clara[5] HICKS, Harvey Henry[4], Henry Melvin[3], Elijah[2], Joshua[1]), born 10 Jan 1919 in Norwood, Hamilton Co, OH. She married on 9 Feb 1946 in Coronado, San Diego, CA **Adolph Edward ZEZULA**, born 29 Jan 1920 in Great Falls, Cascade Co, MT; died[546] Jan 1974 in California.

Dorothy Behan married Adolph Zezula, who was born in Great Falls, MT. He served in the US Navy. Their son, Norman, has done considerable research on the Hicks family and shared it willingly. @@

Children of Dorothy Ann BEHAN and Adolph Edward ZEZULA were:

1100 i **Norman Edward[7] ZEZULA**, ##. Jones notes: "He resides (1994) in Provo, UT; Graduated Univ. of Cal; Doctorate in Physics from Brigham Young"

+ 1101 ii **Duane Lindsay**[7] **ZEZULA**, ##. He married **Clarinda Rae JONES**,
Jones notes: "Resides (1974) at Sacramento, CA; Univ of CA - interested in politics & law"

+ 1102 iii **Deanne Lin**[7] **ZEZULA MD**, ##. She married **James Craig LEWIS**, MD.

703. **Laura Margaret**[6] **BEHAN** (Minnie Clara[5] HICKS, Harvey Henry[4], Henry Melvin[3], Elijah[2], Joshua[1]), born 10 Mar 1921 in Norwood, Hamilton Co, OH; died 27 Feb 2004; Cincinnati, Hamilton Co, OH. She married on 18 Dec 1943 in Hamilton Co, OH **John William ZINK Jr.**, born 5 Apr 1921 in Cincinnati, Hamilton Co, OH; died[547] 8 Aug 1998 in Cincinnati, Hamilton Co, OH.

Laura Behan married John William Zink. Laura died in Cincinnati at the age of 82. @@

Children of Laura Margaret BEHAN and John William ZINK Jr. were:
1103 i **Donald Allen**[7] **ZINK**, ##. He married **Mary Lee THIEMAN**.
Jones notes: "resides (1981) at 5908 Woodmont, Hyde Park, Cincinnati, OH; teacher"
1104 ii **Suzan Ellen**[7] **ZINK**, ##.
1105 iii **John Mark**[7] **ZINK**, ##.

704. **Donald James 'Bud'**[6] **BEHAN** (Minnie Clara[5] HICKS, Harvey Henry[4], Henry Melvin[3], Elijah[2], Joshua[1]), born 6 Jun 1923 in Norwood, Hamilton Co, OH. He married on 10 May 1952 in Ohio? **Dorothy LUEHRMANN**, born 2 Jun 1924.

Jones notes: "resides (1972) at 827 Larchview, Cincinnati 45236 (Dillonvale)"@@

Children of Donald James 'Bud' BEHAN and Dorothy LUEHRMANN were:
1106 i **John J.**[7] **BEHAN**, ##.
1107 ii **Lawrence R.**[7] **BEHAN**, ##.
1108 iii **Catherine A.**[7] **BEHAN**, ##.
1109 iv **Donald J.**[7] **BEHAN Jr.**, ##.
1110 v **Gary M.**[7] **BEHAN**, ##.

706. **Marjorie Claire "Margie"**[6] **BEHAN** (Minnie Clara[5] HICKS, Harvey Henry[4], Henry Melvin[3], Elijah[2], Joshua[1]), born 25 Feb 1928 in Norwood, Hamilton Co, OH; died 13 Aug 2009; in Orange Park, Clay Co, FL. She married on 31 May 1947 in Cincinnati, Hamilton Co, OH **Theodore Jackson ROGERS**, born 9 Dec 1928 in Cincinnati, Hamilton Co, OH.

Jones notes: "resides(1972) 2854 Brookwood Dr, Orange Park, FL; Theodore - a Navy chaplain" @@

Children of Marjorie Claire "Margie" BEHAN and Theodore Jackson ROGERS were:
1111 i **Richard Gary**[7] **ROGERS**, ##.
1112 ii **Gregory Kevin**[7] **ROGERS**, ##.
1113 iii **Rhonda Gayle**[7] **ROGERS**, ##.

708. **Dion**[6] **HICKS Jr.** (Dion Williams[5], Harvey Henry[4], Henry Melvin[3], Elijah[2], Joshua[1]), born 17 Jul 1929 in Millhauser, IN; died 6 Apr 2007 in Cincinnati, Hamilton Co, OH. He married on 10 Nov 1953 in Loveland OH **Jean WUNKER**.

Jones notes: "Served in Korean War; resides (1974) 203 W. 69th, Cincinnati, OH 45216" @@

Children of Dion HICKS Jr. and Jean WUNKER were:
1114 i **Byron Francis**[7] **HICKS**, ##.
1115 ii **Steven Dion**[7] **HICKS**, ##.

@@ see research notes at end of chapter   ## born after 1930 or known to be living

709. Daniel⁶ HICKS (Dion Williams⁵, Harvey Henry⁴, Henry Melvin³, Elijah², Joshua¹), born 6 Dec 1934 in Cincinnati, Hamilton Co, OH; died 1 Jun 1996. He married on 10 Nov 1953 in Loveland OH **Marjorie Geraldine MCATER**.

Jones notes: "served in Korean War; resides (1974) 2497 Ontario Dr, Mt Healthon, OH" @@

    Children of Daniel HICKS and Marjorie Geraldine MCATER were:
- 1116   i   **Daniel Richard⁷ HICKS**, ##.
- 1117   ii   **Shawn Dion⁷ HICKS**, ##.

711. Archie Milton⁶ ROSS (Mary Frances⁵ HOUSER, Minerva Elizabeth⁴ JONES, Mary³ HICKS, Elijah², Joshua¹), born 22 Sep 1885 in Missouri. He married abt 1919 in California **Maymie CONN**, born Sep 1879 in Iowa, daughter of Oliver C and Emma CONN.

Archie Ross was listed as a "pump man" on his draft registration in 1918. He was described as "tall, slender, blue eyes, brown hair; defect: loss of one eye." @@

    Children of Archie Milton ROSS and Maymie CONN were:
- 1118   i   **Milton⁷ ROSS**, born abt 1921 in Iowa.

713. Alma J.⁶ ROSS (Mary Frances⁵ HOUSER, Minerva Elizabeth⁴ JONES, Mary³ HICKS, Elijah², Joshua¹), born Nov 1893 in Downing, MO. She married 23 Dec 1916 in Burlington, IA **Clarence Harrison MARS**, born 14 Mar 1889 in Lisbon, ND; died April 1976 in Springfield, Greene Co, MO, son of **Rufus E. MARS** and **Mary Ellen LIEADY**.

Alma Ross married Clarence Mars, who was from North Dakota. Clarence was listed as a "mechanical dentist". @@

    Children of Alma J. ROSS and Clayton Harrison MARS were:
- 1119   i   **Clayton R.⁷ MARS**, born abt 1918 in Iowa.

714. William Clifford⁶ ROSS (Mary Frances⁵ HOUSER, Minerva Elizabeth⁴ JONES, Mary³ HICKS, Elijah², Joshua¹), born 10 Oct 1895 in Downing, MO. He married on 7 Mar 1928 in Moberly, Randolph Co, MO **Pauline WALDEN**, born abt 1901 in Missouri, daughter of Herbert and Julia WALDEN.

William Ross owned a service station in Sugar Creek, MO in 1930. On his WW I draft registration, he was described as "short, med build, blue eyes, brown hair." @@

    Children of William Clifford ROSS and Pauline WALDEN were:
- 1120   i   **Betty E.⁷ ROSS**, born abt 1929 in Missouri.

717. Ruby Alyce⁶ BROADWELL (Lindley Edward⁵, Minerva Elizabeth⁴ JONES, Mary³ HICKS, Elijah², Joshua¹), born 7 Jun 1906 in Kirksville, MO; died 1 Jan 1963 in San Antonio, Bexar, TX; buried in Ft Sam Houston Natl Cemetery, Bexar, TX. She married **Orville Paul CLARK**, born 23 Apr 1900 in Kansas; died 30 Nov 1972 in San Antonio, Bexar, TX.

Jones notes: "m. -?-- Ross [sic]; resided (1929) Ames IA". Ruby died in San Antonio, TX. @@

    Children of Ruby BROADWELL and Orville P. CLARK were:
- 1121   i   **Orville Paul⁷ CLARK**, born abt 1925 in Ames, Story Co, IA.

720. Chester Allen⁶ BROADWELL (Herbert Fay⁵, Minerva Elizabeth⁴ JONES, Mary³ HICKS, Elijah², Joshua¹), born 12 Oct 1892 in Downing, MO; died 8 Mar 1965 probably in Downing, Schuyler Co, MO;

@@ see research notes at end of chapter   ## born after 1930 or known to be living

buried in Coffey Cemetery. He married 25 Oct 1914 **Henrietta May BERGMAN**, married (2) 10 Jun 1951 La Belle, Lewis Co, MO **Ora NAYLOR**, born 16 Apr 1894 in MO; died 13 Jul 1966 probably in Downing, Schuyler Co, MO; buried in Coffey Cemetery.

Chester Broadwell was a mechanic in Prairie, MO in 1930. He married twice, first to Henrietta Bergman and later to Ora Naylor. @@

Children of Chester Allen BROADWELL and Henrietta May BERGMAN were:
- 1122 i **Bernie[7] BROADWELL**, born abt 1920 in MO.
- 1123 ii **Herbert P.[7] BROADWELL**, born abt 1924 in MO.
- 1124 iii **Ray C.[7] BROADWELL**, born abt 1927 in MO.
  Possible marriage: Raymond L. Broadwell, age 21, of Downing, MO who married Betty Louise Todlock, 18, of Lancaster, MO on 18 Dec 1945 in Schuyler Co, MO.

722. Harry[6] BROADWELL (Herbert Fay[5], Minerva Elizabeth[4] JONES, Mary[3] HICKS, Elijah[2], Joshua[1]), born 4 Nov 1895 in Downing, MO; died 2 Oct 1960 in Downing, Schuyler Co, MO; buried in Coffey Cemetery. He married abt 1923 **Myrtle ALDRIDGE**, born 23 May 1903 in MO; died Jun 1976 in Downing, Schuyler Co, MO.

Harry Broadwell was a farmer in Schuyler Co, MO. He served in World War I as a private. @@

Children of Harry BROADWELL and Myrtle ALDRIDGE were:
- 1125 i **Inez[7] BROADWELL**, born abt 1924 in MO.
- 1126 ii **Raymond[7] BROADWELL**, born abt 1925 in MO.
  See note for Ray C. Broadwell above for possible marriage.
- 1127 iii **Paul Eugene[7] BROADWELL**, born 16 Oct 1927 in Schuyler Co, MO; died[548] 2 Dec 1928 in Schuyler Co, MO; buried in Coffey Cemetery.
  Death: Paul Eugene Broadwell, b. 16 Oct 1927, near Queen City, Schuyler Co, MO; d. 2 Dec 1928, age 1 year, 1 month, 16 days. Cause of death: pneumonia, scarlet fever. Parents: Harry Broadwell; Myrtle Aldridge. Both b. MO. Burial: Coffee Cemetery. Missouri Death Records [Missouri digital Heritage]

723. Orma[6] BROADWELL (Herbert Fay[5], Minerva Elizabeth[4] JONES, Mary[3] HICKS, Elijah[2], Joshua[1]), born 14 Aug 1897 in Queen City, Schuyler, MO; died 25 Jan 1970 in Kirksville, Adair, M0. She married on 12 Apr 1918 in Schuyler County, MO **Ollie Willis MCELROY**[549], born 24 Jun 1895 in Independence, MO; died 4 Jul 1975 in Queen City, Schuyler, MO, son of Oscar MCELROY and Catherine L. EIFFERT.

Orma Broadwell married Ollie McElroy, who farmed in several areas of Missouri. He was described in 1917 as "med height, slender, light eyes & hair". @@

Children of Orma BROADWELL and Ollie Willis MCELROY were:
- 1128 i **Hazel E.[7] MCELROY**, born abt 1919 in MO.
- 1129 ii **Helen[7] MCELROY**, born abt 1920 in MO.
- 1130 iii **Marvin M.[7] MCELROY**, born abt 1922 in MO.
- 1131 iv **Lester L.[7] MCELROY**, born abt 1924 in MO.
- 1132 v **Wilma L.[7] MCELROY**, born abt 1926 in MO.

726. William Harold[6] BROADWELL (Percival[5], Minerva Elizabeth[4] JONES, Mary[3] HICKS, Elijah[2], Joshua[1]), born 18 Oct 1901 in Arizona; died 13 Nov 1989 in Fresno, CA. He married abt 1928 **Barbara LAIRD**, born 7 Oct 1901 in Vermont; died[550] 27 Feb 1994 in Fresno, CA.

@@ see research notes at end of chapter   ## born after 1930 or known to be living

William Broadwell was a house painter in Clovis, CA in 1930. @@

    Children of William Harold BROADWELL and Barbara LAIRD were:
1133   i   **Allen**[7] **BROADWELL**, ##.

731 Beulah Imogene[6] **BROADWELL**, born 19 Oct 1901 in Arkansas; died 6 Nov 1984 in Modesto, Stanislaus Co, CA; married 10 Aug 1920 **George MCKENZIE,** born 10 Feb 1900 in Arizona; died 30 Sep 1962 in Stanislaus Co, CA.

Beulah Broadwell married George McKenzie in Arizona, then moved to Turlock, CA before 1930. @@

    Children of Beulah Imogene Broadwell and George McKenzie were:
731a   I   **George E MCKENZIE,** born about 1922 in California.
731b   ii   **Layton A MCKENZIE** born about 1924 in California.
731c   iii   **Charlotte B MCKENZIE** born about 1928 in California.

732 Eunice[6] **Dale BROADWELL**, born 15 Dec 1905 in Arkansas; died 15 Dec 1995, Stanislaus Co, CA. Married (1) Robert B. **SAULS**, born abt 1895, Oklahoma, died 1965 Napa, CA; married (2) after 1965, Garrit **KOOY,** born 22 Nov 1895 in Harlem, Holland; died 10 Jan 1991, Modesto, Stanislaus Co, CA.

Eunice Broadwell married first Robert Sauls, who died in 1965. She married next Garrit Kooy, who had immigrated from Holland in 1911. @@

    Children of Eunice Dale Broadwell and Robert B. Sauls were:
732a   I   **Robert D. SAULS,** abt 1922 in California
732b   ii   **A. Fay SAULS,** abt 1924 in California
732c   iii   **Jack N. SAULS,** abt 1929 in California

733. Romba[6] **BROADWELL** (Nathaniel Dale[5], Minerva Elizabeth[4] JONES, Mary[3] HICKS, Elijah[2], Joshua[1]), born 1 Aug 1907 in Arkansas; died Dec 1972 in San Jose, Santa Clara, CA. She married bef 1927 **Harry JONES**, born abt 1909 in Kansas.

Romba Broadwell married Harry Jones, who was a state agricultural inspector. They were living in California by 1930. @@

    Children of Romba BROADWELL and Harry JONES were:
1134   i   **Harriet**[7] **JONES**, born abt 1927 in CA.
1135   ii   **Kent H.**[7] **JONES**, born abt 1930 in CA.

735 Karylton V.[6] **BROADWELL**, born abt 10 Jan 1910 in Arizona; died 29 Dec 1994 in Ceres, Stanislaus, CA; married bef 1942 **Althea E. PARRISH**, born 23 Jul 1918 in San Jose, CA; died 7 Feb 2004 in Turlock, Stanislaus Co, CA.

Karylton Broadwell was an author, editor and reporter when he enlisted for World War II in 1942. He was divorced from Althea in 1983 after nearly 40 years of marriage. @@

    Children of Karylton Victor BROADWELL and Althea Ethlyn PARRISH were:
735a   I   **Sherri BROADWELL**
735   ii   **Gail BROADWELL**

737. Effie Blanche[6] **WOOD** (Beatrice Gertrude[5] JONES, James Marcellus[4], Elizabeth[3] HICKS, Elijah[2], Joshua[1]), born 26 Apr 1897 in Clermont Co, OH; died[551, 552] 17 Apr 1992 in Richardson, Dallas Co, TX.

She married on 8 Jul 1920 **Walter Lloyd BAIRD**, born 12 Jun 1886 in Jellico, Campbell Co, TN, son of J. D. and Ella BAIRD.

Effie Wood married Lloyd Baird, who was a comptroller in wholesale hardware. @@

> Children of Effie Blanche WOOD and Walter Lloyd BAIRD were:
> 1136　i　**Glenna Gertrude[7] BAIRD**, born 25 Oct 1925 in Jellico, TN. She married on 30 Oct 1945, divorced **Julius Earl WILEY**, born 12 Nov 1923 in Ashland, AL; died[553] 4 Aug 1990. Jones notes: "Resides (1972) at 13839 Rolling Hills Ln, Dallas, TX"
> 1137　ii　**Ella Catherine[7] BAIRD**, ##. She married **John M. HUTCHINS Jr.**, born 27 Aug 1927 in Winston Salem, NC. Jones notes: "Resides (1972) at 13903 Rolling Hills Ln, Dallas, TX"

740. Wilbur Lewis[6] MCMAHON (Effie Maud[5] JONES, James Marcellus[4], Elizabeth[3] HICKS, Elijah[2], Joshua[1]), born 29 Jul 1896 in Lausche, OH; died 27 Jan 1990 in Cincinnati, Hamilton, OH. He married on 30 Jul 1921 in Hamilton Co, OH **Myrl M. EDWARDS**, born 25 May 1899 in OH; died 16 Sep 1986 in Madeira, Hamilton, OH; buried 18 Sep 1986 in Evendale, OH, daughter of Stanley D EDWARDS and Anna LIVINGSTON.

Wilbur McMahon was an newspaper editor in Cincinnati, OH. He died at the age of 93. @@

> Children of Wilbur Lewis MCMAHON and Myrl M. EDWARDS were:
> 1138　i　**Theodore Lewis[7] MCMAHON**, born 24 Jul 1922 in Indianapolis, Marion Co, IN. He married **Alma Mae BERGEN**, born 26 Nov 1922 in Cincinnati, Hamilton Co, OH, daughter of Harry A and Alma H. BERGEN.
> Jones notes: "Resides (1972) at 10681 Turfwood Ct, Sharonville, OH; Naval Air Corps, WW II". Not found on WW II enlistment records.
> 1139　ii　**James Edward[7] MCMAHON**, born 8 Nov 1926 in Cincinnati, Hamilton Co, OH. He married **Jean Elaine HEMMERLE**, born 9 Jun 1928 in Cincinnati, Hamilton Co, OH, daughter of George and Helen HEMMERLE.
> Jones notes: "Resides (1972) 7367 Hosbrook Rd, Cincinnati, OH; US Army WW II."
> 1140　iii　**Thomas Richard[7] MCMAHON**, ##. He married **Mary Ruth WEAVER**.
> Jones notes: "Resides (1972) at 7241 Thomas Dr, Madiera, OH; US Army Korean War"
> 1141　iv　**Kathleen Janet[7] MCMAHON**, ##. She married **James Edward MOUNTJOY**, born 13 Aug 1925 in Warsaw, Gallatin Co, KY, son of Edward and Helen MOUNTJOY. Jones notes: "Resides (1972) at 795 Mannington Av, Cincinnati, OH; He served in US Navy 1943-46"
> 1142　v　**Patrick Wilbur[7] MCMAHON**, ##. He married **Judith GERDES**.
> Jones notes: "Resides (1972) at 9617 Trafford Ct, Lexington Park, Mt Healthy, OH; US Army reserve 1957-62"

742. Lola Gayle[6] MCMAHAN (Effie Maud[5] JONES, James Marcellus[4], Elizabeth[3] HICKS, Elijah[2], Joshua[1]), born 1 Dec 1900 in Monterey, Clermont Co, OH; died[554] 7 Sep 1988 in Seaman, Adams Co, OH. She married on 21 Dec 1920 **Dewey Frank GARRISON**[555], born 6 Dec 1898 in Paulding, Paulding Co, OH; died 30 Oct 1948 in Winchester Twp, Adams, OH; buried 2 Nov 1948 in West Union, OH, son of Benjamin GARRISON and Mary COPPOCK.

Lola Gayle McMahan married Dewey F. Garrison, a farmer. He died at the age of 49 of a coronary thrombosis. @@

Children of Lola Gayle MCMAHAN and Dewey Frank GARRISON were:

1143 i **Mary Luis⁷ GARRISON**, born abt 1923 in IL.
This child was with family on 1930 census, but was not on the Jones notes. Possibly died young; no death information found.

1144 ii **Wayne Franklin⁷ GARRISON**, born 29 Jun 1924 in Warrensburg, Macon Co, IL. He married on 3 Feb 1945 **Hazel Faye STORER**, born 10 Jun 1921 in Peebles, Adams Co, OH; died[556] 26 Mar 2002 in Seaman, Adams Co, OH. Jones notes: "Resides (1967) at RR 1, Seaman, OH 45679". No death information found for him.

1145 iii **Jack L.⁷ GARRISON**, born 21 Mar 1921 in Warrensburg, Macon Co, IL. He married on 19 Sep 1953 **Mary Lee HILL**. Jones notes: "Resides (1967) at RR 1, Morrow, OH"

1146 iv **Jerry Carson⁷ GARRISON**, ##. He married **Dinah Lee WEBB**.
Jones notes: "Resides (1967) at RR 1, Yellow Springs, OH, c/o Camp Green"

743. Sarah Elizabeth⁶ MCMAHAN (Effie Maud⁵ JONES, James Marcellus⁴, Elizabeth³ HICKS, Elijah², Joshua¹), born 20 Dec 1908 in Monterey, Clermont Co, OH; died 27 Jul 1978 in Ocala, Marion Co, FL. She married on 25 Jun 1929 **Jack E. LUCAS**, born 20 Jul 1902 in Elyria, Lorrain Co, OH; died[557] Feb 1982 in FL, son of Jonas A and Ida LUCAS.

Sarah McMahan married Jack Lucas. Before she married, Sarah worked as a stenographer for a lumber shipping yard. @@

Children of Sarah Elizabeth MCMAHAN and Jack E. LUCAS were:

1147 i **Jack Elwood⁷ LUCAS Jr**, ##. He married **Doris Ann KEMPER**.
Jones notes: "Resides (1967) at 4935 Manlough Woods Dr NW, Canton, OH"

1148 ii **Ann Lorene⁷ LUCAS**, ##. She married **Rev G. R. GEYER**.
Jones notes: "Resides (1967) Freemont, OH"

1149 iii **Richard Russell⁷ LUCAS**, ##. He married **Darla Jean MITCHELL**.
Jones notes: "Resides (1967) at 973 Carnegie Av, Johnstown, PA 15905"

744. Hannah Elizabeth⁶ MYLER (Lola Agnes⁵ JONES, James Marcellus⁴, Elizabeth³ HICKS, Elijah², Joshua¹), born 18 Sep 1907 in Cincinnati, Hamilton Co, OH; died 6 Feb 2007 in Allen Co, OH. She married on 7 Aug 1927 in Clermont Co, OH **Thomas Gavin FOSTER**, born 18 Jan 1906 in Williamsburg, Clermont Co, OH; died 3 Mar 1968 in Clinton Co, OH, son of Theopholis and Jennie L FOSTER.

Hannah Myler Foster lived to be 99 years old, outliving her husband by almost 40 years. @@

Children of Hannah Elizabeth MYLER and Thomas Gavin FOSTER were:

+ 1150 i **Joann Elizabeth⁷ FOSTER**, born 8 Dec 1928 in Sabina, Clinton Co, OH. She married on 21 Sep 1951 in Sabina OH **Kenneth Conner GRAY**, born 25 Jun 1928 in Fayette Co, OH.
Jones notes: "Resides (1984) at 644 Kathryn Dr, Wilmington, OH 45177"; Kenneth a "Lt., US Air Force Reserve".

+ 1151 ii **Thomas Gavin⁷ FOSTER Jr**, ##. He married **Nancy J. BOWERS**,
Jones notes: "Resides (1984) at 440 Hana Av, Wilmington, OH 45177; US Air Force 1957-1963"

746. James Paul⁶ JONES (Orville Guy⁵, James Marcellus⁴, Elizabeth³ HICKS, Elijah², Joshua¹), born abt 1906 in Clermont Co, OH; died 18 Apr 1954; buried in Burlington Cemetery, Mt Healthy, OH. He married on 10 Oct 1931 in Hamilton Co, OH **Alma RUDD**, born 22 Mar 1908.

@@ see research notes at end of chapter   ## born after 1930 or known to be living

In 1930, Paul was working as a salesman for a lumber company. After his death in 1954, his widow remarried.

    Children of James Paul JONES and Alma RUDD were:
+   1152   i   **Robert Rudd**[7] **JONES**, ##. He married (1), divorced **Karen Sue WEIGEL**, (2) **Madella Jane BOUSE**. Jones notes: "Resides (1980) at 11704 NW 116th, Yukon, OK".

747. Orville William[6] **JONES**[558] (Orville Guy[5], James Marcellus[4], Elizabeth[3] HICKS, Elijah[2], Joshua[1]), born 22 Jun 1908 in Cincinnati, Hamilton Co, OH; died 18 Jul 1996 in Clermont Co, OH. He married on 28 May 1932 in Covington, Kenton Co, KY **Ruth D. NEVILLE**, born 18 Sep 1913 in Union City, Darke Co, OH; died Jan 1993 in Felicity, Clermont Co, OH; daughter of **Charles G. NEVILLE** and **LouEtta STEPHENS**.

Orville Jones was the compiler of the data which formed the nucleus for this book. At the time of his death, he had the 100+ page handwritten manuscript completed. He also had self-published a book on the Jones family. Photo on page 304 and on dedication page. @@

    Children of Orville William JONES and Ruth D. NEVILLE were:
    1153   i   **Charles Orville**[7] **JONES**, ##. Jones notes: "Resides (1972) at 2423 Ingleside Av, Cincinnati, OH; not married; draughtsman & river boat pilot"
+   1154   ii   **Walter Paul**[7] **JONES**, ##. He married **Diana RIEGLE**. Jones notes: "Resides (1972) at 2713 Erlene Dr, Apt 825, Cincinnati, OH". Living in family home on Neville Penn Rd, Felicity, OH (1999)

748. Hilda Louise[6] **JONES** (Orville Guy[5], James Marcellus[4], Elizabeth[3] HICKS, Elijah[2], Joshua[1]), born 16 Jun 1913 in Cincinnati, Hamilton Co, OH; died[559] Dec 1975 in Cincinnati, Hamilton Co, OH. She married on 21 Apr 1937 in Cincinnati, Hamilton Co, OH **Lewis METZ**, born 13 Oct 1914 in Hamilton Co, OH; died 24 Sep 2000 in Cincinnati, Hamilton Co, OH.

Jones notes: "Resides (1972) at 1241 Nagel Rd, Cincinnati, OH"

    Children of Hilda Louise JONES and Lewis METZ were:
    1155   i   **Joanne**[7] **METZ**, ##. She married **James WILLIAMS**. Jones notes: "Resides (1972) in Cincinnati, OH; she's a registered nurse, he a school teacher"

749. Alice Agnes[6] **JONES** (Carl Raymond[5], James Marcellus[4], Elizabeth[3] HICKS, Elijah[2], Joshua[1]), born 14 May 1916 in Cincinnati, Hamilton Co, OH; died[560] Jun 1992 in Los Angeles, Los Angeles Co, CA. She married on 5 May 1939 in Cincinnati, Hamilton Co, OH **James Thomas EUBANKS**, born 20 Nov 1900 in Cincinnati, Hamilton Co, OH; died Sep 1972, son of James L. and Laura EUBANKS.

Jones notes: "Resides (1972) at 5518 W. 96th St, Los Angeles CA 90045"

    Children of Alice Agnes JONES and James Thomas EUBANKS were:
    1156   i   **Raymond Lewis**[7] **EUBANKS**, ##. He married **Christine Theresa SIDEWELL**. Jones notes: "Resides (1972) at 4599 W. 136 St, Hawthorne, CA"

750. Calvin Marcellus[6] **BECKELHIMER** (Ethel Grace[5] JONES, James Marcellus[4], Elizabeth[3] HICKS, Elijah[2], Joshua[1]), born 12 Oct 1912 in Milford, Clermont Co, OH; died 30 Sep 1979; buried in Lebanon, Monroe Co, OH. He married on 2 Jul 1938 in Warren Co, OH **Sarah Blanche MONCE**, born 25 Dec 1913 in Lebanon, Monroe Co, OH, daughter of John and Electra S. MONCE.

Jones notes: "Resided (1972) at 512 Western Cir, Mason OH. @@

@@ see research notes at end of chapter   ## born after 1930 or known to be living

Children of Calvin Marcellus BECKELHIMER and Sarah Blanche MONCE were:

+ 1157 i **John Lee[7] BECKELHIMER**, ##. He married **Naomi JENKINS**
    Jones notes: "Resides (1967) at 7863 Hamilton Princeton Rd, Middletown, OH"
+ 1158 ii **Ruth Ann[7] BECKELHIMER**, ##. She married **Donald Clay BURNSIDE**,
    Jones notes: "Resides (1967) at 121 Lynnview Dr, Mason OH 45040"
+ 1159 iii **Jerry Monce[7] BECKELHIMER**, ##. He married **Barbara Sue RAINS**, born
    Jones notes: "Resides (1967) at 613 Lindeman Dr, Mason OH"

751. Harry Raymond[6] BECKELHIMER (Ethel Grace[5] JONES, James Marcellus[4], Elizabeth[3] HICKS, Elijah[2], Joshua[1]), born 14 Nov 1913 in Milford, Clermont Co, OH; died 6 Feb 1971 in Cincinnati, Hamilton Co, OH; buried in Mt Orab, OH. He married on 8 Apr 1940 in West Union OH **Mary L. JACKSON**, born 7 Mar 1921 in West Union, Adams Co, OH.

Jones notes: "US Army, WW II; She resides (1972) at 107 Oak St, Mt Orab, OH." @@

Children of Harry Raymond BECKELHIMER and Mary L. JACKSON were:

+ 1160 i **Robert Carl[7] BECKELHIMER**. He married **Mary JOHNSON**,
    Jones notes: "Resides (1969) at 703 DeWett St, Syracuse, NY"

752. Mary Elizabeth[6] BECKELHIMER (Ethel Grace[5] JONES, James Marcellus[4], Elizabeth[3] HICKS, Elijah[2], Joshua[1]), born 25 Jun 1921 in Utopia, Clermont Co, OH. She married on 4 Oct 1940 in Mt Orab, OH **Charles James JACOBS**, born 18 Mar 1920 in Sardinia, Brown Co, OH.

Jones notes: "Resides (1972) 9779 Rt 68, N. of Georgetown, OH; he served in US Army, WW II"

Children of Mary Elizabeth BECKELHIMER and Charles James JACOBS were:

+ 1161 i **Gary Clinton[7] JACOBS**, ##. He married **Linda Diana FULLER**,
    Jones notes: "Resides (1967) at 7060 Ashmore Dr, Dayton, OH; US Navy 1959-1863"
  1162 ii **Brian Harry[7] JACOBS**, born 2 Mar 1957 in Cincinnati, Hamilton Co, OH; died 2 Mar 1957 in Cincinnati, Hamilton Co, OH.
  1163 iii **Mary Beth[7] JACOBS**, ##. She married **Edward LOVETT**.

754. Jack Jones[6] BECKELHIMER (Ethel Grace[5] JONES, James Marcellus[4], Elizabeth[3] HICKS, Elijah[2], Joshua[1]), born 23 Jun 1925 in Utopia, Clermont Co, OH. He married on 9 Sep 1945 in Georgetown, Brown Co, OH, divorced **Fern Eileen BAUER**, born 16 Apr 1928 in Russellville, Brown Co, OH.

Jones notes: "Resides (1972) Rt 68, N. of Georgetown, OH" (same address as Mary Elizabeth Beckelhimer)

Children of Jack Jones BECKELHIMER and Fern Eileen BAUER were:

+ 1164 i **Velvet Jean[7] BECKELHIMER**, ##. She married, divorced **Harold Carl HONAKER Jr**. Jones notes: "Resides (1967) at Columbus, OH"
+ 1165 ii **Diana Lynne[7] BECKELHIMER**, ##. She married **Richard Lee COURTS**
    Jones notes: "Resides (1967) at 4241 Sunshine Rd, Georgetown, OH"
  1166 iii **Galen Wayne[7] BECKELHIMER**, ##.

755. James Marcellus[6] JONES (Lawrence Marcellus[5], James Marcellus[4], Elizabeth[3] HICKS, Elijah[2], Joshua[1]), born 4 Jan 1915 in Lexington, Fayette Co, KY; died abt 1970. He married on 10 Jul 1937 in Covington, Kenton Co, KY **Gertrude MOORE**, born 9 Aug 1917 in Philadelphia, Philadelphia Co, PA; died 4 Nov 1959.

Jones notes: "Resided (1970) 901 Scott St, Covington, KY"

Children of James Marcellus JONES and Gertrude MOORE were:

1167　i　**Mary Margaret "Dollie"**[7] **JONES**, ##. She married **Richard ASHCRAFT**.
　　　　Jones notes: "Resides (1972) at 7710 Montgomery Rd, Kenwood, Cincinnati, OH; No children"

1168　ii　**James Lawrence**[7] **JONES**, ##. He married **Donna Mae BRADFORD**.
　　　　Jones notes: "He was killed in auto accident in Cincinnati, OH 12/25/1965"

756. Beryl Josephine[6] **JONES** (Lawrence Marcellus[5], James Marcellus[4], Elizabeth[3] HICKS, Elijah[2], Joshua[1]), born 16 Jan 1932 in Burlington, Boone, KY. She married on 3 Dec 1949 **Wilfred D. GRUELLE**, born 15 Sep 1928 in Berry, Harrison Co, KY, son of Ferd and Ollie GRUELLE.

Jones notes: "Resides (1972) Hillsboro, OH"

Children of Beryl Josephine JONES and Wilfred D. GRUELLE were:

1169　i　**Durwood Timothy**[7] **GRUELLE**, ##. He married **Belinda Flo WEEKLY**.
1170　ii　**Joel Kevin**[7] **GRUELLE**, ##.
1171　iii　**Jerome Kent**[7] **GRUELLE**, ##.

757. John Lee[6] **JONES** (Lawrence Marcellus[5], James Marcellus[4], Elizabeth[3] HICKS, Elijah[2], Joshua[1]), ##. He married **Shirley Ann RYAN**.

Jones notes: "Resides (1972) at 46 N. Main, Walton, KY; 3 years in US Marines"

Children of John Lee JONES and Shirley Ann RYAN were:

1172　i　**Callie Ann**[7] **JONES**, ##.
1173　ii　**Yevanna Sue**[7] **JONES**, ##.
1174　iii　**Mark Mathew**[7] **JONES**, ##.
1175　iv　**Tanya Grace**[7] **JONES**, ##.
1176　v　**Moninca Lee**[7] **JONES**, ##.
1177　vi　**Mary Elizabeth**[7] **JONES**, ##.
1178　vii　**Stacy Lynn**[7] **JONES**, ##.

759. Virginia Marylin[6] **HODGES** (Genevieve Shinkle[5] JONES, James Marcellus[4], Elizabeth[3] HICKS, Elijah[2], Joshua[1]), born 9 Sep 1923 in Cincinnati, Hamilton Co, OH; died 29 Jul 2007 in Cincinnati, Hamilton, OH. She married on 27 Oct 1946 in Cincinnati, Hamilton Co, OH **William H. CUNNINGHAM**, born 13 May 1914 in Dayton OH; died abt 1970.

Jones notes: "She resides (1972) at 1267 Grace Ave, Cincinnati, OH; He served in US Army, WW II, decorated"

Children of Virginia Marylin HODGES and William H. CUNNINGHAM were:

1179　i　**Michael Thomas**[7] **CUNNINGHAM**, ##.
1180　ii　**William Bruce**[7] **CUNNINGHAM**, ##.
1181　iii　**Cynthia Carol**[7] **CUNNINGHAM**, ##. She married **Kirby Lee GEIER**.
　　　　Jones notes: "Resides (1972) at 2341 Buchmont Av, Cincinnati, OH"
1182　iv　**Cheryl Colleen**[7] **CUNNINGHAM**, ##.

760. Ralph Charles[6] **JONES**[561, 562] (Albert Essex[5], William A.[4], Elizabeth[3] HICKS, Elijah[2], Joshua[1]), born 24 Jan 1896 in Cincinnati, Hamilton Co, OH; died 31 Aug 1955 in Mt Orab, Clermont Co, OH; buried in Mt Orab, Clermont Co, OH. He married on 22 Jul 1915 in Covington, Kenton Co, KY **Grace Elenor STEPHENSON**, born 2 Apr 1894 in Boone Co, KY.

Jones notes: "Resided at Rt 1, Mt Orab, OH". He was timekeeper for a gas company and a candy company. He was described in 1942 as "5' 10", 165 pounds, brown eyes & hair, light complexion; no disabilities"@@

Children of Ralph Charles JONES and Grace Elenor STEPHENSON were:

+ 1183 i **Ralph William**[7] **JONES**, born 31 Aug 1918 in Covington, Kenton Co, KY; died bef 1972. He married on 3 Jan 1943 in Pascagoula, MS **Lydia Ethel MOORE**, born 27 Feb 1925 in Mobile, Mobile Co, AL.
  Jones notes: "Served in Army Air Force, WW II - 1943-1946. Graduated from Officer's Candidate School and was a Captain at time of discharge. Deceased before 1972; she resides (1972) at 223 Craigmont LN, San Antonio, TX 73213".

764. **Leta Grace**[6] **WILLIAMS** (Hertha Katherine[5] JONES, William A.[4], Elizabeth[3] HICKS, Elijah[2], Joshua[1]), born 14 Dec 1898 in Cumberland Gap, Claiborn Co, TN; died[563] Jan 1981 in Cincinnati, Hamilton Co, OH. She married on 30 Jul 1919 in Cincinnati, Hamilton Co, OH **Tate STEELE**[564], born 12 Jul 1891 in Griffin, Wayne Co, KY; died bef 1972, son of **John W. and Elzie STEELE.**

Jones notes: "Resides (1972) at 6434 Monalisa Ct, Cincinnati OH (Mt Airy) 45239; He served in WWI in Europe - deceased by 1972." @@

Children of Leta Grace WILLIAMS and Tate STEELE were:

+ 1184 i **Shirley Jean**[7] **STEELE**, born 17 Aug 1922 in Cincinnati, Hamilton Co, OH. She married on 18 Jan 1941 in Dayton OH **William Thomas GILBERT**, born 20 Jun 1918 in Winchester, Clark Co, KY.
  Jones notes: "Wm. was a pilot with 15h Air Force in WW II"
  1185 ii **Charles W.**[7] **STEELE**, born 25 Feb 1925 in Cincinnati, Hamilton Co, OH; died bef 1972. Jones notes: "Served with US Marines; badly wounded in WW II & never fully recovered; never married"

765. **Ezra Glenn Dale "Jack"**[6] **WILLIAMS** (Hertha Katherine[5] JONES, William A.[4], Elizabeth[3] HICKS, Elijah[2], Joshua[1]), born 11 May 1903 in Cincinnati, Hamilton Co, OH; died Sep 1973 in Cincinnati, OH. He married (1) on 14 Jun 1930 in Ft Thomas KY **Virginia E. DUGAN**, born Est. 1903; (2) on 20 Dec 1955 in Cincinnati, Hamilton Co, OH **Esther PENDERY**.

Jones notes: "Resides (1972) at 1317 Morton Av, Cincinnati OH"

Children of Ezra Glenn Dale "Jack" WILLIAMS and Virginia E. DUGAN were:

+ 1186 i **Tyler Glenn**[7] **WILLIAMS**, ##. He married **Sandra CLYDE**
  Jones notes: "Stephen & Tyler are own brothers, adopted by Jack Williams; resides (1973) at 3609 DeBolt, Newtown, OH 45244"
+ 1187 ii **Stephen**[7] **WILLIAMS**, ##. He married unknown.
  1188 iii **Kevin Daniel**[7] **WILLIAMS**, ##. He married **Nancy ROBINSON**. Jones notes: "Resides (1972) at 1211 Inglenook Pl, Cincinnati, OH; both are teachers"

768. **William Charles**[6] **BROWN** (Jessie Agnes[5] JONES, William A.[4], Elizabeth[3] HICKS, Elijah[2], Joshua[1]), born 27 Dec 1921 in Rossmoyne, Hamilton Co, OH; died[565] 29 Jun 2001 in Canoga Park, Los Angeles Co, CA. He married on 13 May 1939 in Lawrenceburg, Dearborn Co, IN **Edith Marion STREET**, born 22 Jan 1920 in Tazewell, Tazewell Co, VA.

@@ see research notes at end of chapter   ## born after 1930 or known to be living

Jones notes: "Resides (1972) at 22149 Cohasset St, Canoga Park, CA 91304"

    Children of William Charles BROWN and Edith Marion STREET were:

+   1189 i   **William Charles**[7] **BROWN Jr.**, ##. He married **Patricia Ann HOGAN**.
Jones notes: "Resides (1972) at 3151 Jacinto Av, Santa Susanna, CA 93063"

769. Rosslyn Earl[6] **MELVIN** (Anna Grace[5] JONES, William A.[4], Elizabeth[3] HICKS, Elijah[2], Joshua[1]), born 13 Apr 1903; died 1 Jun 1941 in Cincinnati, Hamilton, OH; buried 4 Jun 1941 in Laurel Cemetery, Madisonville, OH. He married (1) abt 1923 in Newport KY **Mabel MURPHY**, born 13 Aug 1907 in Newport, Campbell Co, KY; (2) on 13 Aug 1934 in Cincinnati, Hamilton Co, OH **Naomi PARTRIDGE**, born 12 Feb 1904 in Rockport, IN; (3) **Ruby TOWNSEND**, died aft 1941.

Ross Melvin owned a meat market in Cincinnati, OH in 1930. He died at the age of 40 in a parachuting accident.@@

    Children of Rosslyn Earl MELVIN and Mabel MURPHY were:

    1190 i   **Infant**[7] **MELVIN**, born 19 May 1925 in Cincinnati, Hamilton, OH; died 20 May 1925 in Cincinnati, Hamilton, OH; buried 21 May 1925 in St Michaels, Madisonville, OH.
Death: Infant Melvin, d. 20 May 1925, Cincinnati, Hamilton, OH; b. 19 May 1925, Cincinnati, OH; Age: 1 day; Male; Street address: 6761 Britton, Cincinnati, Hamilton, OH; Burial: 21 May 1925, Madisonville, OH; Cemetery: St Michaels; Father: Ross E Melvin, b. Cincinnati, OH; Mother: Mabel Murphy, b. Cincinnati, OH. Ohio Deaths, 1908-1953 <familysearch.org>

    1191 ii   **William Ross**[7] **MELVIN**, born 15 Sep 1927.
Jones notes: "Resides (1972) at 1430 Lyons Rd, Amelia, OH 45102"

+   1192 iii   **Violet Mae**[7] **MELVIN**, born 20 Oct 1929. She married **Harold STOWELL**
Jones notes: "Resides (1972) at 543 Gay St, Williamsburg, OH 45176"

770. Carl Starner[6] **PUGH** (Stella Blanche[5] JONES, William A.[4], Elizabeth[3] HICKS, Elijah[2], Joshua[1]), born 4 Mar 1908 in Galion, Crawford Co, OH; died[566] Feb 1981 in West Chester, Butler Co, OH. He married on 8 Mar 1938 in Cincinnati, Hamilton Co, OH **Margaret JENKINS**, born 8 Mar 1915 in Cincinnati, Hamilton Co, OH.

Jones notes: "Resides (1972) at 1198 Hempstead Dr, Cincinnati, OH 45231; m1 Lottie Garten; m2 Helen ?-; m3 Margaret Jenkins - children by 3rd marriage" @@

    Children of Carl Starner PUGH and Margaret JENKINS were:

+   1193 i   **Carl S. "Sandy"**[7] **PUGH Jr**, ##. He married **Merideth Margaret GOEBEL**.
Jones notes: "Resides (1984) at 9404 Meadow Ridge Dr, Cincinnati, OH 45241; USAF as fighter pilot"

+   1194 ii   **Carole Lee**[7] **PUGH**, ##. She married **James BICKNELL**,
Jones notes: "Resides (1984) at 7331 Shewango Way, Westchester, OH 45069"

    1195 iii   **Donna Sue**[7] **PUGH**, ##. She married **-?- BLACKWELL**,
Jones notes: "Resides (1972) at 3324 Cornelia Dr, Louisville, Ky 40225"

771. Julia M.[6] **JONES** (Alfred William[5], Elijah Hicks[4], Elizabeth[3] HICKS, Elijah[2], Joshua[1]), born 20 Apr 1906 in Clermont Co, OH; died[567] 29 Jan 1993 in Batavia, Clermont Co, OH. She married on 20 Aug 1927 in California, OH **Archie LANTER**, born 1903 in California, Hamilton Co, OH; died 15 May 1957 in Cincinnati, Hamilton Co, OH; buried in Graceland Memorial Cemetery, Cincinnati, OH.

@@ see research notes at end of chapter   ## born after 1930 or known to be living

Julie and her brother Alfred were raised by their uncle, William H. Simmons. Jones notes: "Resides (1972) at 4734 Eastern Ave, Cincinnati, OH". @@

Children of Julia M. JONES and Archie LANTER were:

+ 1196 i **Virginia[7] LANTER,** born 15 May 1928 in Cincinnati, Hamilton Co, OH; died Sep 1995 in Cincinnati, Hamilton Co, OH. She married on 22 Mar 1949 in Covington, Kenton Co, KY **Eugene BROWNING**, born Est. 1928.
Jones notes: "Resides (1972) at 4734 Eastern Ave, Cincinnati, OH".
+ 1197 ii **Dorothy[7] LANTER,** ##. She married (1) **Walter MISTISHAN**; (2) **Minor MCCROSBY**. Jones notes: "Resides (1972) at 4734 Eastern Ave, Cincinnati, OH"
+ 1198 iii **Archie[7] LANTER Jr,** ##. He married **Carol PRICE**
Jones notes: "Resides (1972) at 794 Danny Ln, Mt Carmel, OH 45245"

774. Leona I.[6] JONES (Alfred William[5], Elijah Hicks[4], Elizabeth[3] HICKS, Elijah[2], Joshua[1]), born 29 Nov 1909 in Cincinnati, Hamilton Co, OH; died[568] 24 Mar 1995 in Cincinnati, Hamilton Co, OH. She married on 14 Apr 1930 in Newport KY **Louis ROBERTS**, born 5 Jul 1902 in Monticello, Wayne Co, KY; died[569] May 1982 in Cincinnati, Hamilton Co, OH.

In 1930, Leona Jones, 10, was living with Elijah & Hattie Reeves, listed as grandniece. Jones notes: "Resides (1976) at 1712 Keeler, Chicago, IL 60639"

Children of Leona I. JONES and Louis ROBERTS were:

+ 1199 i **Harriett Juanita[7] ROBERTS,** ##. She married **John Robert BABB**.
Jones notes: "reside (1981) at 1811 Dellwood Dr, Norfolk, VA 23518"
+ 1200 ii **Mable Marie[7] ROBERTS,** ##. She married **Carl Irwin BLUST**,
Jones notes: "reside (1972) at 5335 Galley Hill Rd, Milford, OH 45150"
  1201 iii **Louis[7] ROBERTS,** ##. He married **Patricia KLEVINS**.
Jones notes: "reside (1972) at 1618 Campbell St, Chicago, IL 60647"
+ 1202 iv **Robert R.[7] ROBERTS,** ##. He married **Linda Rae DALE**
Jones notes: "Resides (1976) at 1701 Meadow Lake Dr, Norfolk, VA 23518. 3 years in US Marine Corps".
+ 1203 v **Rosalie[7] ROBERTS,** ##. She married **Robert JOHNSON**.
Jones notes: "Resides (1976) at 6162 E. Miami River Rd, Cleves?, OH 45002"
+ 1204 vi **Arthur Jack[7] ROBERTS,** ##. He married **Joan Carol GUNDERLACK**,
Jones notes: "Resides (1976) at 4110 N. Kilborn St, Chicago, IL. US Navy, 1958."
+ 1205 vii **Mary[7] ROBERTS,** ##. She married **Clyde WARREN**,
Jones notes: "Resides (1972) at 838 N. Marshfield, Chicago, IL 60622"
+ 1206 viii **Larry[7] ROBERTS,** ##. He married **Renata HUBER**
Jones notes: "Resides (1972) at 1027 N. Richmond St, Chicago, IL 60622"
  1207 ix **Pamela[7] ROBERTS,** ##. Jones notes: "Not married (1972) "

776. Julia Marie[6] JONES (Howard Hicks[5], Elijah Hicks[4], Elizabeth[3] HICKS, Elijah[2], Joshua[1]), ##. She married **Donald K. CRANK**

Jones notes: "resides (1973) at Boat Run Rd, Clermont Co, OH"

Children of Julia Marie JONES and Donald K. CRANK were:
1208 i **Donald[7] CRANK,** ##.
1209 ii **Dona Kay[7] CRANK,** ##.

@@ see research notes at end of chapter   ## born after 1930 or known to be living

  1210 iii **Sarah**[7] **CRANK**, ##.

781. Jessie Marie[6] **JONES** (Clifford O.[5], Elijah Hicks[4], Elizabeth[3] HICKS, Elijah[2], Joshua[1]), born 6 Sep 1913 in Hamilton Co, OH. She married on 25 Nov 1933 in Cincinnati, Hamilton Co, OH **John C. IRELAND Jr.**, born 13 Aug 1910 in Cincinnati, Hamilton Co, OH, son of John and Mayme IRELAND.

Jones notes: "Resides (1972) at 2536 Fleetwood, Cincinnati, OH"

  Children of Jessie Marie JONES and John C. IRELAND Jr. were:
+ 1211 i **John**[7] **IRELAND**. He married **Janet RICHTER**.
    Jones notes: "Resides (1984) at 2223 Van Blaircumb Rd, Hamilton Co, OH"
+ 1212 ii **Joyce**[7] **IRELAND**. She married **George F. STILT**.
    Jones notes: "Resides (1984) at 3425 Mayfair, Cincinnati, OH"

784. Georgia Gladys[6] **CLARK** (Leontine Orrene[5] JONES, George Washington[4], Elizabeth[3] HICKS, Elijah[2], Joshua[1]), born 10 Feb 1898; died 1 Jul 1966. She married on 4 Sep 1923 **Delbert Dewite BOSSINGHAM**, born 22 Apr 1899 in Iowa, son of Charles D. BOSSINGHAM and Lilian M. BALDWIN.

Delbert served in the Navy during World War I. He was listed as a "surfer" in the Coast Guard in 1930. Georgia's brother, Roscoe, married Delbert's sister, Florence. @@

  Children of Georgia Gladys CLARK and Delbert Dewite BOSSINGHAM were:
+ 1213 i **Madelaine Elaine**[7] **BOSSINGHAM**, born 14 Feb 1925. She married 4 Sep 19??, divorced **Ozzie BERTSCH**, born Est. 1925. Jones notes: "m1 9/4/1923 to Ozzie Bertsch, divorced [discrepancy - this is before she was born]; m2 Henry Stevens, divorced". May be the Madelyn Elaine (Bossingham) Wolfinger, b. 14 Feb 1925, Idaho; d. 25 Feb 1983, El Dorado, CA. CA Death Index [Ancestry.com]
+ 1214 ii **Delbert Leone "Leo"**[7] **BOSSINGHAM**, born 28 Jul 1926 in Algonia, IA; died Mar 1976. He married on 11 Nov 1949 **Rosa Imogene LEE**.

785. Cecil Emmett[6] **CLARK** (Leontine Orrene[5] JONES, George Washington[4], Elizabeth[3] HICKS, Elijah[2], Joshua[1]), born 27 Apr 1901 in Nebraska; died[570] 21 Jun 1970 in Concord, Contra Costa Co, CA. He married on 31 Dec 1922 **Amy Luella COOPER**, born 7 Aug 1902 in Iowa; died 30 Jul 1974 in Santa Clara, Santa Clara Co, CA.

Cecil Clark was a farmer in North Dakota in 1930. His oldest child was born in Idaho. @@

  Children of Cecil Emmett CLARK and Amy Luella COOPER were:
+ 1215 i **Laura Amy**[7] **CLARK**, born 11 Dec 1923 in Idaho; died 4 Feb 1992 in Creswell, Lane Co, OR. She married (1), divorced **George HENNIES**, born Est. 1923; (2) on 26 Mar 1949 **Henry LENNIE**, born 5 May 1915; died Feb 1980 in Santa Clara, Santa Clara Co, CA.
+ 1216 ii **Donna Beryl**[7] **CLARK**, born 20 Oct 1926 in North Dakota; died Mar 1973. She married **Johnny "Tex" DURDEN**, born Est. 1926.
+ 1217 iii **Avis Maude**[7] **CLARK**, born 18 Jul 1928 in North Dakota; died 20 Sep 2001 in Rohnert Park, Sonoma Co, CA. She married (1), divorced **Floyd MAJORS**, born Est. 1928; (2) on 4 Dec 1949 **Edwin BOURNE**, born 13 Dec 1925.
+ 1218 iv **Cecil Wayne**[7] **CLARK**, born 12 Oct 1930; died 21 Dec 1989 in Stafford, Stafford Co, VA. He married **Ruth Mary FLAHERTY**.

@@ see research notes at end of chapter ## born after 1930 or known to be living

786. Roscoe Glenn⁶ CLARK (Leontine Orrene⁵ JONES, George Washington⁴, Elizabeth³ HICKS, Elijah², Joshua¹), born 15 Sep 1902; died⁵⁷¹ Nov 1983 in Lead, Lawrence Co, SD. He married on 3 Aug 1922 **Florence Annette BOSSINGHAM**, born 5 Feb 1904 in IA; died Oct 1982 in Carson, Grant Co, ND, daughter of Charles D. BOSSINGHAM and Lilian M. BALDWIN.

In 1930, Roscoe Clark was working as a servant, his wife and 3 children were living with his parents. @@

    Children of Roscoe Glenn CLARK and Florence Annette BOSSINGHAM were:

	1219	i	**Edith Irene⁷ CLARK**, born 20 Jul 1923; died 20 Sep 1950.
+	1220	ii	**Ardith Faye⁷ CLARK**, born 6 May 1925. She married on 10 May 1945 **Robert JOHNSON**, born 31 May 1925.
+	1221	iii	**Gordon Glenn⁷ CLARK**, born 25 Oct 1929. He married on 3 Sep 1959 **Adele OSBURN**.
+	1222	iv	**Roscoe Delbert⁷ CLARK**, ##. He married **Veronica -?-**.
+	1223	v	**Maxine Elsie⁷ CLARK**, ##. She married **Charles CULVER**, born 21 Jan 1927; died 22 Dec 1997 in Deadwood, Lawrence Co, SD.
+	1224	vi	**Carol Deane⁷ CLARK**, ##. She married **Charles JENKINS**.
	1225	vii	**Elroy Emmett⁷ CLARK**, born 22 Mar 1941; died 26 Mar 1944.
	1226	viii	**Ray Gail⁷ CLARK**, ##. Jones notes: "not married, 1974"

787. Edith Zeta Mabel⁶ CLARK (Leontine Orrene⁵ JONES, George Washington⁴, Elizabeth³ HICKS, Elijah², Joshua¹), born 13 Jul 1910 in Saunders ND; died⁵⁷² 30 Jan 1999 in Petaluma, Sonoma Co, CA. She married on 7 Feb 1927 in Carson, ND **Earl Lloyd FAUBEL**, born 26 Nov 1904 in Pratt, Steele Co, MN; died⁵⁷³ 7 Jan 1995 in Petaluma, Sonoma Co, CA.

Jones notes: "resides (1974) at 1 Kendrick Dr, San Anselmo, Cal 94960".

    Children of Edith Zeta Mabel CLARK and Earl Lloyd FAUBEL were:

	1227	i	**Earl Lloyd⁷ FAUBEL, Jr.**, born 29 Sep 1927 in Elgin, Grant Co, ND. He married on 5 Apr 1974 **Rita HAVERMAAL**, born⁵⁷⁴ 1 Oct 1933; died⁵⁷⁵ 28 Sep 1988 in Downey, Los Angeles Co, CA. Jones notes: "resides (1974) at 10440 Paramount Blvd, Downey, CA 90241"
+	1228	ii	**Peggy Lu⁷ FAUBEL**, born 1 Jul 1929 in Mott, Hettinger Co, ND; died 8 Jul 1995 in Petaluma, Sonoma Co, CA. She married on 7 Nov 1947 **Donald Leroy MCCROSKEY**, born 22 May 1927; died 22 Nov 1965. Jones notes: "resides (1974) at 733 Compton Rd, Redwood City, CA".
+	1229	iii	**Dorla Deane⁷ FAUBEL)**, ##. She married **Arthur James CAMARA**, born 5 Apr 1927. Jones notes: "resides (1974) at 33 Spindrift Passage, Corte Madera, CA".
+	1230	iv	**James Everett⁷ FAUBEL**, ##. She married **Delona Jean MCKNIGHT**, born 24 Jan 1927; died 1 Mar 1995 in Petaluma, Sonoma Co, CA. Jones notes: "resides (1974) at 123 Birchway, San Rafael, CA".
+	1231	v	**Beverly Ann⁷ FAUBEL**, born, ##. She married **Howard Kenneth WILLIAMS**, born 10 Jun 1932; died 7 Aug 1981 in Redwood City, San Mateo, CA. Jones notes: "resides (1974) at 1742 Kentfield Av, Apt 2, Redwood City, CA".

790. Laura Mona⁶ EVANS (Roxy Dale⁵ JONES, George Washington⁴, Elizabeth³ HICKS, Elijah², Joshua¹), born 13 Aug 1903 in Wayne, Wayne Co, NE; died bef 1974. She married aft 1930 **Charles HARTFORD**, born 29 Mar 1903; died bef 1974.

In 1930, Laura Evans was working as a servant in the home of an elderly couple, John and Elizabeth Carhart, in Wayne Co, NE.@@

Children of Laura Mona EVANS and Charles HARTFORD were:

+   1232   i   **Bonnie Rae**[7] **HARTFORD, ##.** She married **Fred PRICE**.
Jones notes: "resides (1974) at Rt 6, Box 219, Shelby, NC 28150".

791. **Dale Elizabeth**[6] **EVANS** (Roxy Dale[5] JONES, George Washington[4], Elizabeth[3] HICKS, Elijah[2], Joshua[1]), born 31 May 1906 in Wayne, Wayne Co, NE; died Jun 1987 in Hartington, Cedar Co, NE. She married (1) on 21 Jun 1926 in Vermillion, SD **Fred WOHLMAN**, born 28 Sep 1910; died[576] 15 Aug 1993 in Grand Island, Hall Co, NE; (2) **Nick MITTEIS**, born Est. 1906.

Dale Evans married first, Fred Wohlman and had 3 children; she was divorced and then married Nick Mitteis. They were living with her parents in Wayne, NE in 1930. @@

Children of Dale Elizabeth EVANS and Fred WOHLMAN were:

+   1233   i   **Eugene William**[7] **WOHLMAN**, born 18 Jan 1927; died 2 Nov 2009 in Hartington, Cedar Co, NE. He married on 11 Nov 1952 **Alice Kay WEBER**, born 26 Feb 1931; died 1974.
Jones notes: "resides (1974) at Hartington, NE 68739".

+   1234   ii   **Blaine Evans**[7] **WOHLMAN**, born 16 Jul 1928; died 20 Aug 1992 in Grand Island, Hall Co, NE. He married on 6 Dec 1953 **Mary E. CASTOR**, born 9 Jan 1933; died 17 Jul 1999 in Grand Island, Hall Co, NE.
Jones notes: "resides (1974) at Grand Island, NE".

+   1235   iii   **Kenneth Fae**[7] **WOHLMAN**, born 22 Nov 1929. He married on 13 Aug 1949 **Arlene E. HOESING**. Jones notes: "resides (1974) at Hartington, NE".

793. **Grace**[6] **EVANS** (Roxy Dale[5] JONES, George Washington[4], Elizabeth[3] HICKS, Elijah[2], Joshua[1]), born 12 Jun 1910 in Wynot, Cedar Co, NE; died 14 Feb 1992 in Lakewood, Los Angeles Co, CA. She married on 21 Apr 1930 in Wayne, NE **Blaine ELLIS**, born 28 Jun 1910 in Wayne, Wayne Co, NE, son of Fred W. and Roxie ELLIS.

Jones notes: "resides (1975) at 4266 Lakewood Blvd, Long Beach, CA 90808" @@

Children of Grace EVANS and Blaine ELLIS were:

+   1236   i   **Darlene**[7] **ELLIS**, ##. She married, divorced **Walter SWENSON**.
Jones notes: "resides (1974) at 1245 Appleton St #1, Long Beach, CA 90802; m1 Walter Swenson, divorce; m2 Boatman, divorced".

+   1237   ii   **Gerald B.**[7] **ELLIS**, born 27 Jun 1933; died 12 Dec 1997 in Long Beach, Los Angeles Co, CA. He married in 1959 in Las Vegas, NV **Iris Joan SOUTHCOTT**, born 4 May 1929. Jones notes: "resides (1974) at 3607 Hungerford St, Long Beach, CA 90805; US Army 1950-53".

+   1238   iii   **Nancy Jo**[7] **ELLIS**, ##. She married **Ernie Charles OLSON**, born 18 Jul 1923 in Merrasha, WI. Jones notes: "resides (1974) at 222410 Horst St, Hawaii Gardens, CA 90716".

794. **Dorthea Gladys**[6] **EVANS** (Roxy Dale[5] JONES, George Washington[4], Elizabeth[3] HICKS, Elijah[2], Joshua[1]), born 30 Oct 1912 in Wynot, NE; died[577] 3 Feb 1997 in Anaheim, Orange Co, CA. She married on 23 Aug 1935 in Long Beach, CA **Nicholas Joseph WINGERT**, born 12 May 1912 in Laurel, NE; died[578] 28 Jan 1990 in Anaheim, Orange Co, CA.

Jones notes: "resides (1974) at 555 Sherwood Dr, Anaheim, CA 92805"

@@ see research notes at end of chapter   ## born after 1930 or known to be living

Children of Dorthea Gladys EVANS and Nicholas Joseph WINGERT were:

+ 1239 i **James Nicholas**[7] **WINGERT**, ##. He married **Delores Marie BENTON**.
Jones notes: "resides (1974) at 1424 James Way, Anaheim, CA"
+ 1240 ii **Kathleen Gale**[7] **WINGERT**, ##. She married (1), divorced **Robert L. KELLY**; (2) **Ronald W. LOUNSBURG**.
 1241 iii **Stephen Paul**[7] **WINGERT**, ##. Jones notes: "not married - 1974"

795. **Rex Willard**[6] **EVANS** (Roxy Dale[5] JONES, George Washington[4], Elizabeth[3] HICKS, Elijah[2], Joshua[1]), born 18 Feb 1915; died 8 Jul 1950. He married on 17 Mar 1937 **Romaine ZIMMERMAN**, born 7 Jan 1916.

Children of Rex Willard EVANS and Romaine ZIMMERMAN were:

+ 1242 i **Karen Lynn**[7] **EVANS**. She married **Larry SCHLICK**.
Jones notes: "resides (1974) at 2681 Montair, Long Beach, CA"

796. **Izeta Mae**[6] **WILL** (Edith Mary[5] JONES, George Washington[4], Elizabeth[3] HICKS, Elijah[2], Joshua[1]), born 2 May 1918 in Leith, Grant Co, ND. She married on 10 Jun 1944 in Laurin, MT **Robert Thomas MCGOWAN**, born 22 Feb 1908 in Great Falls, Cascade Co, MT.

Jones notes: "resides (1974) at Highwood, MT" @@

Children of Izeta Mae WILL and Robert Thomas MCGOWAN were:

+ 1243 i **Robin Jean**[7] **MCGOWAN**, ##. She married **Larry Edward STOLTZ**.
Jones notes: "resides (1974) at Valier, MT"
+ 1244 ii **John Casey**[7] **MCGOWAN**, ##. He married **Bonnie Patricia BOWMAN**.
Jones notes: "resides (1975) at Highwood, MT"
 1245 iii **Thomas Edward**[7] **MCGOWAN**, ##. Jones notes: "married Pat -?-"

797. **Wanda Fae**[6] **WILL** (Edith Mary[5] JONES, George Washington[4], Elizabeth[3] HICKS, Elijah[2], Joshua[1]), born 11 Sep 1919 in Leith, Grant Co, ND. She married on 26 Aug 1949 in Highwood, MT **John Phillip KISSINGER**, born 12 Feb 1924 in Clyde Park, Park Co, MT; died[579] Jun 1980 in Modesto, Stanislaus, CA.

Jones notes: "resides (1974) at 1421 Fordham St, Modesto, CA 95350"

Children of Wanda Fae WILL and John Phillip KISSINGER were:
 1246 i **Barbara Ann**[7] **KISSINGER**, ##.
 1247 ii **Coral Edith**[7] **KISSINGER**, ##.

806. **Donald G.**[6] **SHERBAHN** (Gayle E.[5] JONES, Doctor Albert[4], Elizabeth[3] HICKS, Elijah[2], Joshua[1]), born 13 Aug 1912 in Wayne, Wayne Co, NE; died 26 Feb 2005, Wayne, Wayne Co, NE. He married on 16 Jan 1941 in Papillion, NE **Bernita HINNERACHS**, born 14 Apr 1918 in Wakefield, Dixon Co, NE, daughter of Herbert and Lena HINNERACHS.

Jones notes. "Donald served in Army, WW II; resides (1975) at 218 Lincoln St, Wayne, NE 68787"

Children of Donald G. SHERBAHN and Bernita HINNERACHS were:

+ 1248 i **Nancy Caroline**[7] **SHERBAHN**, ##. She married **David WARNEMUNDE**,
Jones notes: "resides (1975) at Winside, NE"
+ 1249 ii **Donna Gayle**[7] **SHERBAHN**, ##. She married **Dennis E. JOHNSON**.
Jones notes: "resides (1975) at Plainview, NE"

@@ see research notes at end of chapter   ## born after 1930 or known to be living

810. **Mildred Gayle**[6] **JONES** (Roscoe Otis[5], Doctor Albert[4], Elizabeth[3] HICKS, Elijah[2], Joshua[1]), born 13 Dec 1909 in Wayne, Wayne Co, NE; died 3 Sep 2004 in Wayne, Wayne Co, NE. She married **Morris Verdon JENKINS**, born 28 Dec 1907 in Carroll, Wayne Co, NE; died[580] 25 Apr 2003 in Wayne, Wayne, NE, son of Samuel and Emily JENKINS.

Jones notes. "reside (1976) at 118 W. 12th, Wayne, NE"

    Children of Mildred Gayle JONES and Morris Verdon JENKINS were:

+   1250 i **Mary Faith**[7] **JENKINS**, ##. She married **Edward VERZAL Jr.**

812. **Elizabeth Jane**[6] **JONES** (Roscoe Otis[5], Doctor Albert[4], Elizabeth[3] HICKS, Elijah[2], Joshua[1]), born 5 Apr 1914 in Wayne, Wayne Co, NE; died[581] 7 Aug 1995 in Geneva, Fillmore Co, NE. She married **Laurence DOUD**, born 25 Nov 1913 in Geneva, Fillmore Co, NE; died[582] 21 Apr 2002 in Geneva, Fillmore Co, NE, son of George T. and Josephine DOUD.

Jones notes: "resides (1976) Geneva?"; Laurence graduated from pharmacy school, University of Nebraska, in 1938. @@

    Children of Elizabeth Jane JONES and Laurence DOUD were:

+   1251 i **Judith Ann**[7] **DOUD**, ##. She married **John L. PICARD**.
     1252 ii **Thomas Patrick**[7] **DOUD**, ##. He married **Christine MORIE**.
     1253 iii **Jane**[7] **DOUD**, ##.
     1254 iv **Deborali**[7] **DOUD**, ##.

813. **Robert Otis**[6] **JONES** (Roscoe Otis[5], Doctor Albert[4], Elizabeth[3] HICKS, Elijah[2], Joshua[1]), born 20 Aug 1916 in Wayne, Wayne Co, NE; died[583] Oct 1983 in Vallejo, Solano Co, CA. He married **Arleen Mae AGNEW**, born 7 Mar 1920 in Newman Grove, Madison Co, NE, daughter of Marshall and Mae AGNEW.

Jones notes: "resides (1976) Vallejo?"; no other information located. @@

    Children of Robert Otis JONES and Arleen Mae AGNEW were:

+   1255 i **Betty Jo**[7] **JONES**, ##. She married **John Richard STARKIE**.
         Jones notes: "resides (1974) at Colorado Springs?"
+   1256 ii **William Allen**[7] **JONES**, ##. He married **Karen Ethel RUSSELL**.
         Jones notes: "resides (1974) at Vallejo, Cal?"

814. **Elva Mae**[6] **JONES** (Roscoe Otis[5], Doctor Albert[4], Elizabeth[3] HICKS, Elijah[2], Joshua[1]), born 29 May 1919 in Wayne, Wayne Co, NE. She married **Delbert Ernest ALDERSON**, born 11 Feb 1920 in Wayne, Wayne Co, NE; died 30 Sep 1963 in Wayne, Wayne Co, NE, son of Ernest D. and Henrietta ALDERSON.

Delbert worked with the State Department of Roads in 1954-5. The Lake Park, IA newspaper reported a visit by the Aldersons to the home of his mother, Mrs A J. Frost, in 1955. @@

    Children of Elva Mae JONES and Delbert Ernest ALDERSON were:

+   1257 i **Debra Jean**[7] **ALDERSON**, ##. She married **Kerry Michael NOONAN**.
+   1258 ii **Clifford Lee**[7] **ALDERSON**, ##. He married, divorced **Nancy Ann -?-**.
+   1259 iii **Patricia Ann**[7] **ALDERSON**, ##. She married **Lawrence Richard DURFEE**.
+   1260 iv **Richard Alan**[7] **ALDERSON**, ##. He married **Paula -?-**.
     1261 v **Robert Dale**[7] **ALDERSON**, ##.

@@ see research notes at end of chapter   ## born after 1930 or known to be living

815. **William Morgan**[6] **JONES** (Roscoe Otis[5], Doctor Albert[4], Elizabeth[3] HICKS, Elijah[2], Joshua[1]), born 1 Nov 1920 in Wayne, Wayne Co, NE; died 24 Apr 1974 in Minneapolis, Hennipin Co, MN. He married[584] on 10 Jul 1949 in Huron, Beadle Co, SD **Dorothy RICHARDS**, born 26 Jan 1919 in Huron, Beadle Co, SD, daughter of Glen A. RICHARDS and Eva B. RICHARDS.

Jones notes give his name as Billy Morgan Jones; official records say William M. Jones. He served as a Staff Sergeant in World War II and is buried at the Ft Snelling National Cemetery in Minneapolis, MN. @@

Children of Billy Morgan JONES and Dorothy RICHARDS were:
- 1262 i **Ross Richards**[7] **JONES**, ##.
- 1263 ii **Shari Sue**[7] **JONES**, ##.
- 1264 iii **Steven William**[7] **JONES**, ##.

816. **Joan Faye**[6] **JONES** (Roscoe Otis[5], Doctor Albert[4], Elizabeth[3] HICKS, Elijah[2], Joshua[1]), born 22 Apr 1928 in Wayne, Wayne Co, NE. She married **Charles Victor CARHART**, born 25 Feb 1929 in Randolph, NE, son of Ralph M. and Fannie B. CARHART.

Jones notes: "resides (1976) at 628 Westwood Rd, Wayne, NE"; Charles was a bow hunter, noted in the Omaha newspaper in 1964, for a successful hunt for mule deer. @@

Children of Joan Faye JONES and Charles Victor CARHART were:
- \+ 1265 i **Kimberly Ann**[7] **CARHART**, ##. She married **Charles Gene HARGEN**.
- 1266 ii **Leslie Jill**[7] **CARHART**, ##.
- 1267 iii **William Charles**[7] **CARHART**, ##.

817. **Shirley Lou**[6] **JONES** (Roscoe Otis[5], Doctor Albert[4], Elizabeth[3] HICKS, Elijah[2], Joshua[1]), ##. She married **Gene L. FREDRICKSON**.

Jones notes: "resides (1976) RR#2, Wayne, NE 68787; Listed 2002 as president of Fredrickson Oil Co, with son Roger"

Children of Shirley Lou JONES and Gene L. FREDRICKSON were:
- 1268 i **Pamela Lou**[7] **FREDRICKSON**, ##. She married **Mark Kent MYERS**.
- \+ 1269 ii **Roger William**[7] **FREDRICKSON**, ##. He married **Denise Marie KAY**.
  Jones notes: "resides (1976) at RR 2, Wayne, NE"
- 1270 iii **Susan Kay**[7] **FREDRICKSON**, ##.
- 1271 iv **Ann Marie**[7] **FREDRICKSON**, ##.
- 1272 v **Thomas Gene**[7] **FREDRICKSON**, ##.

819. **June Gayle**[6] **JONES** (Albert Doctor[5], Doctor Albert[4], Elizabeth[3] HICKS, Elijah[2], Joshua[1]), born 3 Jun 1917 in Wayne, Wayne Co, NE; died 23 Dec 2004 in Paso Robles, San Luis Obispo Co, CA. She married on 4 Jan 1946 in Los Angeles, Los Angeles Co, CA **Arthur Lavorne WOOD**, born 17 Apr 1912 in Linwood, Butler Co, NE; died[585] 21 Oct 1991 in Los Angeles, CA. No other information found.

Children of June Gayle JONES and Arthur Lavorne WOOD were:
- \+ 1273 i **Sharon Pauline**[7] **WOOD**, ##. She married **Thomas Joseph WHITE Jr.**

820. **Neva Mae**[6] **JONES** (Albert Doctor[5], Doctor Albert[4], Elizabeth[3] HICKS, Elijah[2], Joshua[1]), born 24 Feb 1919 in Wayne, Wayne Co, NE; died[586] 13 Sep 1996 in Downey, Los Angeles Co, CA. She married on 25 Sep 1938 in Omaha, Douglas Co, NE **William Arnold AHERN**, born 15 Jul 1916 in Wayne, Wayne Co, NE; died[587] 9 Dec 1980 in Los Angeles, CA. No other information found.

Children of Neva Mae JONES and William Arnold AHERN were:
- \+ 1274 i **Patricia Ann**[7] **AHERN**, ##. She married **Kenneth Russell GRANVILLE**.

@@ see research notes at end of chapter   ## born after 1930 or known to be living

| + | 1275 | ii | **Connie June⁷ AHERN**, ##.. She married **Leslie Edward LACKERMAN**.. |
| + | 1276 | iii | **William Arnold⁷ AHERN Jr.**, ##. He married **Christy Lynn BENOIT**, |

821. Bonnell Elizabeth⁶ JONES (Albert Doctor⁵, Doctor Albert⁴, Elizabeth³ HICKS, Elijah², Joshua¹), born 12 Dec 1921 in Wayne, Wayne Co, NE; died⁵⁸⁸ 14 Nov 1994 in Paradise, Butte Co, CA. She married on 6 Apr 1941 in Omaha, Douglas Co, NE **Noah Chat MARSH**, born 16 Aug 1919 in Tekamah, Burt Co, NE; died⁵⁸⁹ 6 Dec 2000 in Saint Paul, Howard Co, NE.

Noah Marsh served in the Army during World War II. His civilian occupation was in the aviation industry.

Children of Bonnell Elizabeth JONES and Noah Chat MARSH were:
1277 i **Neil C.⁷ MARSH**, ##. He married **Trucy Ann LECKLIDER**
1278 ii **Robert Dale⁷ MARSH**, ##. He married **Rebecca Jean TERRY**.

830. Edward W.⁶ GUYETTE (Raymond Joseph⁵, Josephine⁴ OWENS, Nancy³ HICKS, Elijah², Joshua¹), born 6 Nov 1914 in E. St Louis, St Clair, IL; died 5 Jul 2002 in Columbus, Franklin Co, OH. He married on 18 Apr 1939 in St Louis, MO **Irene Dolly PLANK**, born 18 Jun 1918 in OK; died 14 Nov 1987 in Upper Arlington, Franklin Co, OH.

Most info from great grandson via Ancestry Message Board and Case Family Tree [Ancestry.com]. The Ohio Death Index indicates that he served in the Navy.

Children of Edward W. GUYETTE and Irene Dolly PLANK were:
1279 i **Daughter⁷ GUYETTE**.

837. Evelyn C.⁶ CABLISH (Mary Edna H.⁵ MEENACH, Nancy B.⁴ HICKS, Joshua³, Elijah², Joshua¹), born 1908; died 3 Feb 1954; buried in Maysville Cemetery, Maysville, KY. She married abt 1926, divorced **Alexander Hart CALVERT**, born 1906; died 26 Feb 1961; buried in Maysville Cemetery, Maysville KY, son of Pierce and Francis CALVERT.

Evelyn Cablish married Alexander Calvert, a farmer in Mason Co, KY. After their divorce, Alex married Allene Burline.

Children of Evelyn C. CABLISH and Alexander Hart CALVERT were:
+ 1280 i **Alexander Hart⁷ CALVERT, Jr**, born 4 Nov 1928 in Maysville, Mason Co, KY; died bef 1972. He married on 6 Mar 1948 in Jeffersonville, IN **Virginia NORTHNAGEL**, born 19 Sep 1929 in Indiana, PA, daughter of Charles and Virginia NORTHNAGEL.
Jones notes: "She resides (1972) at 218 Choctaw Rd, Louisville, KY 40207".

840. Mildred B.⁶ HUTCHISON (Edward Roy⁵, Nora Sureanth⁴ HICKS, James³, Elijah², Joshua¹), born 4 Jul 1915 in Maysville, Mason Co, KY; died 26 Sep 2005 in Maysville, Mason Co, KY. She married in 1938 in Maysville, Mason Co, KY **Albert JEFFERSON**, born 1 Mar 1916 in Mason Co, KY; died⁵⁹⁰ 30 Sep 1979 in Maysville, Mason Co, KY.

Jones notes: "Resides (1972) 460 W. 2nd, Riverview Ter, Maysville, KY 41056". Albert served in the Army during World War II.

Children of Mildred B. HUTCHISON and Albert JEFFERSON were:
+ 1281 i **John Charles⁷ JEFFERSON**, ##. He married **Donna Beth STROUP**.
Jones notes: "Resides (1972) at 8021 Wyatt Dr, White Settlement, Ft. Worth, TX "
+ 1282 ii **James Edward⁷ JEFFERSON**, ##. He married **Karen Lee ADELMAN**.

@@ see research notes at end of chapter   ## born after 1930 or known to be living

			Jones notes: "Resides (1972) at 1027 Springbrook Dr, Cincinnati OH 45224; he is a M.D., specializing in radiology"
+	1283	iii	**Susan Carol⁷ JEFFERSON**, ##. She married **Robert Scott CORRELL**, born 19 Sep 1945 in Los Angeles, Los Angeles Co, CA; died 22 Nov 1970. Jones notes: "Resides (1972) at 460 W. Second, Maysville, KY. Robert killed in highway accident 11/22/1970"
+	1284	iv	**Gerald Arthur⁷ JEFFERSON**, ##. He married **Mary Ester KILBOURN**, Jones notes: "Resides (1972) at 904 E. Second, Maysville, KY"

841. **John or Jack⁶ HUTCHISON** (Edward Roy⁵, Nora Sureanth⁴ HICKS, James³, Elijah², Joshua¹), born abt 1919 in KY. He married **Celia Mae TULLY**, born Est. 1920.

Jones notes: "Resides (1972) at Lewisburg, KY"

Children of John or Jack HUTCHISON and Celia Mae TULLY were:
1285 i   **Nancy Kay⁷ HUTCHISON**, ##.
1286 ii **Deborah⁷ HUTCHISON**, ##.

842. **Ruth Lenora⁶ HUTCHISON** (Edward Roy⁵, Nora Sureanth⁴ HICKS, James³, Elijah², Joshua¹), born 20 Nov 1923 in Mason Co, KY. She married on 16 Jun 1944 in Maysville, Mason Co, KY **Forest Allen BROWN**, born 6 Oct 1920 in Decatur, OH; died⁵⁹¹ 3 Jan 2001 in Homestead, Dade Co, FL.

Jones notes: "Resides (1972) at 545 NW 20th St, Homestead, FL 33030"

Children of Ruth Lenora HUTCHISON and Forest Allen BROWN were:
1287 i   **Patricia Kaye⁷ BROWN**, ##. She married **Rudolph R. FLORES**.
          Jones notes: "Resides (1972) at 112 Front St, Maysville, KY. Grad of U. of KY, a dental hygienist. Rudolph grad of Cal State, 3 yrs in Army."
1288 ii **Peggy Ann⁷ BROWN**, ##.
          Jones notes: "Resides (1972) at 9020 Hampshire Dr, Louisville, KY 40207"
1289 iii **William Robert⁷ BROWN**, ##. Jones notes: "(1972) attending college"
1290 iv **James Allen⁷ BROWN**, ##.

843. **Effie Nolean⁶ HUTCHISON** (Edward Roy⁵, Nora Sureanth⁴ HICKS, James³, Elijah², Joshua¹), born 3 Feb 1925 in Mason Co, KY. She married on 12 Nov 1946 in Maysville, Mason Co, KY **Albert Martin PARKER**, born 22 Jun 1925 in OH.

Jones notes: "She resides (1972) at Rt 3, Orangeburg, KY 41056"; "he resides (1972) at Lewisburg, KY (Rt 3, Maysville 41056)"

Children of Effie Nolean HUTCHISON and Albert Martin PARKER were:
1291 i   **Judy Kay⁷ PARKER**, ##. Jones notes: "lists child as Judy Kay Hutchinson"

845. **Robert L.⁶ HUTCHISON** (Edward Roy⁵, Nora Sureanth⁴ HICKS, James³, Elijah², Joshua¹), born abt Feb 1927 in Mason Co, KY. He married on 18 Jul 1953 in Maysville, Mason Co, KY **Gertrude ACKLEY**, born 1925 in Foxport, Lewis Co, KY, daughter of Alven M and Lina M. ACKLEY.

Jones notes: "Resides (1972) at Rt 3, Orangeburg, KY 41056"@@

Children of Robert L. HUTCHISON and Gertrude ACKLEY were:
1292 i   **Roy Alvin⁷ HUTCHISON**, ##.
1293 ii **Robin Ann⁷ HUTCHISON**, ##.

@@ see research notes at end of chapter   ## born after 1930 or known to be living

847. **Leslie William**[6] **HICKS** (Leslie Brand[5], William Pearce[4], James[3], Elijah[2], Joshua[1]), born 10 Oct 1926 in Oakland, CA; died 4 Feb 2007 in Cleveland, Cuyahoga, OH. He married on 6 Sep 1947 in Cleveland, Cuyahoga Co, OH **Bettie Ann CASTORA**, born 6 Jun 1921 in Cleveland, Cuyahoga Co, OH; died[592] Aug 1994 in Cleveland, Cuyahoga Co, OH, daughter of Stanley and Rose CASTORA.

Jones notes: "resides (1972) at 7406 Newport, Parma, OH. Maritime & Naval service, WW II." @@

    Children of Leslie William HICKS and Bettie Ann CASTORA were:
- 1294   i   **Ronald Leslie**[7] **HICKS**, ##. He married -?- **DOMBROWSKI**. Jones notes: "Resides (1972) at 6118 Ridge Rd, Parma OH 44129"
- \+ 1295   ii   **Bonnie Elaine**[7] **HICKS**, ##.. She married, divorced **Thomas John TOKAR**. Jones notes: "Resides (1972) at 7406 Newport Rd, Parma, OH"

848. **David Lee**[6] **HICKS** (Leslie Brand[5], William Pearce[4], James[3], Elijah[2], Joshua[1]), born 5 Oct 1938 in Cleveland, Cuyahoga Co, OH; died 18 May 1973; buried in West Park Cemetery, Cleveland. He married (1) on 18 Apr 1964 in Cleveland, Cuyahoga Co, OH **Betty KAUF**; (2) unknown.

Jones notes: "Murdered 5/18/1973; she resides (1973) at 7815 Eve Ave, Cleveland, OH 44102; served in US Army." @@

    Children of David Lee HICKS were:
- 1296   i   **Karen**[7] **HICKS** ##. Jones notes give surname "Winegar" - married name?
- 1296a   ii   **David HICKS**, ##. Not in Jones notes - mentioned in father's obit.

849. **Robert James**[6] **HICKS** (Leslie Brand[5], William Pearce[4], James[3], Elijah[2], Joshua[1]), ##. He married **Nancy MOORE**

Jones notes: "resides (1972) at AMS 5475744 Star Rte, Scotland, MD 20687; Career Navy man - 26 months Viet Nam duty"

    Children of Robert James HICKS and Nancy MOORE were:
- 1297   i   **Roberta Lynn**[7] **HICKS**, ##. Jones notes are not clear on this family, but I think this is the correct connection.
- 1298   ii   **Shirley Ann**[7] **HICKS**, ##.

850. **Becky Sue**[6] **HICKS** (Leslie Brand[5], William Pearce[4], James[3], Elijah[2], Joshua[1]), ##. She married **Palmer E. SNODGRASS**.

Jones notes: "resides (1973) at 556 Wesley Av, Elyria, OH 44035"

    Children of Becky Sue HICKS and Palmer E. SNODGRASS were:
- 1299   i   **Michael Dean**[7] **SNODGRASS**, ##.
- 1300   ii   **Steven Paul**[7] **SNODGRASS**, ##.

852. **Janet Lea**[6] **FALOON** (Hazel[5] HICKS, William Pearce[4], James[3], Elijah[2], Joshua[1]), ##. She married (1) **Marvin FENWICK**; (2) **Norman OBERLE**.

    Children of Janet Lea FALOON and Norman OBERLE were:
- 1301   i   **Carol**[7] **OBERLE**, ##. She married **Robert HADLEY**. Jones notes: " reside (1973) at Box 44, Sullivan, OH"

@@ see research notes at end of chapter   ## born after 1930 or known to be living

1302 ii **Sandra**[7] **OBERLE**, ##.
1303 iii **Denise**[7] **OBERLE**, ##.

853. **Richard Lee**[6] **FALOON** (Hazel[5] HICKS, William Pearce[4], James[3], Elijah[2], Joshua[1]), ##. He married **Frances CINA**.

Jones notes: "Resides (1973) at 15123 E. River Rd, Columbia St, OH 44028; both are teachers & part time farmers; US Navy - Korean War"

Children of Richard Lee FALOON and Frances CINA were:
1304 i **Susan**[7] **FALOON**, ##.
1305 ii **Frances**[7] **FALOON**, ##.
1306 iii **John**[7] **FALOON**, ##.
1307 iv **Karen**[7] **FALOON**, ##.

854. **Janie Marie**[6] **HICKS** (William M.[5], William Pearce[4], James[3], Elijah[2], Joshua[1]), ##. She married **Stephen CHOJNA**.

Jones notes: "Reside (1986) at 220 High St, Cuyahoga Falls, OH."

Children of Janie Marie HICKS and Stephen CHOJNA were:
1308 i **Stephen William**[7] **CHOJNA**, ##.
1309 ii **Craig Stephen**[7] **CHOJNA**, ##.
1310 iii **Susan Laura**[7] **CHOJNA**, ##.

855. **Jeanette Merle**[6] **HICKS** (William M.[5], William Pearce[4], James[3], Elijah[2], Joshua[1]), ##. She married **Edwin Hugh BARBOUR**.

Children of Jeanette Merle HICKS and Edwin Hugh BARBOUR were:
1311 i **Deborah Ann**[7] **BARBOUR**, ##.

863. **Kenneth Windsor**[6] **RODEN** (Maud Ella[5] BRUBAKER, Caroline Wise[4] HICKS, William Stephen[3], Elijah[2], Joshua[1]), born 2 Apr 1926 in Cleveland, Cuyahoga Co, OH. He married on 22 Jun 1946 in Cleveland, Cuyahoga Co, OH **Pauline MORTON**, born 28 Nov 1926 in Cleveland, Cuyahoga Co, OH.

Jones notes: "Resides (1972) at 10702 Chilicothe Rd, Chesterland, OH 44026; Marine Corp tail gunner WW II - corporal"

Children of Kenneth Windsor RODEN and Pauline MORTON were:
1312 i **Lee Ann**[7] **RODEN**, ##. She married **Larry Clayborn GLASSCOCK**.
       Jones notes: "Resides (1972) at 6365 Seminole Trail, Mentor, OH 44060"
1313 ii **Kyle Jean**[7] **RODEN**, ##.

864. **Eleanor Bernice**[6] **RODEN** (Maud Ella[5] BRUBAKER, Caroline Wise[4] HICKS, William Stephen[3], Elijah[2], Joshua[1]), born 5 Jun 1928 in Cleveland, Cuyahoga Co, OH; died[593] Jan 1986 in Chesterland, Geauga Co, OH. She married on 26 Jul 1947 in Cleveland, Cuyahoga Co, OH **Edward Howard GUY**, born 13 Sep 1919; died[594] 15 Feb 1996 in Cleveland, OH.

Jones notes: "Resides (1972) at 12850 Manchester Rd, Chesterland, OH 44026; Edward an Army Sgt, WW II, European Theater; operates interior decorating business"

@@ see research notes at end of chapter   ## born after 1930 or known to be living

Children of Eleanor Bernice RODEN and Edward Howard GUY were:

+   1314   i   **Gregory Howard**[7] **GUY**, ##. He married **Gayle Lynn WRIGHT**.
Jones notes: "reside (1972) at 481 E. Kenwood Dr, Euclid, OH 44123; US Marine Reserves"

+   1315   ii   **Cynthia Sue**[7] **GUY**, ##. She married OH **Reginald Price GOWER**.
Jones notes: "reside (1972) at 25 Trenton Sq, Euclid, OH 44123. Cynthia a registered nurse; Reginald a Chemical Engineer"

         1316   iii   **Lora Lynn**[7] **GUY**, ##.

866. Evelyn Ann[6] **BRUBAKER** (Arthur B.[5], Caroline Wise[4] HICKS, William Stephen[3], Elijah[2], Joshua[1]), born 1925 in Maysville, Mason Co, KY. She married on 14 Sep 1946 in Maysville, Mason Co, KY **George William DWYER**, born[595] 21 Jul 1923 in Mason Co, KY; died 5 Jun 1972 in Fayette Co, KY.

Jones notes: "Resides (1972) 7 W. 4th, Maysville, KY"

Children of Evelyn Ann BRUBAKER and George William DWYER were:

         1317   i   **Donald**[7] **DWYER**, ##.

870. Shirley[6] **BRUBAKER** (Kyle Evans[5], Caroline Wise[4] HICKS, William Stephen[3], Elijah[2], Joshua[1]), born 22 Dec 1926 in Massilon, Stark Co, OH; died[596] Nov 1983 in Fairfield, Butler Co, OH. She married on 24 Mar 1950 in Hamilton, OH **Eugene Bruce PEMBERTON**, born 4 Aug 1921 in Branchland, Lincoln Co, WV; died[597] 5 Jun 1997 in Fairfield, Butler Co, OH, son of George and Myrtle PEMBERTON.

Jones notes: "Resides (1972) at 1532 Marlene Dr, Fairfield, OH 45014; he served 4 years in USAF" @@

Children of Shirley BRUBAKER and Eugene Bruce PEMBERTON were:

         1318   i   **Marilyn Elizabeth**[7] **PEMBERTON**, ##.
         1319   ii   **Douglas Eugene**[7] **PEMBERTON**, ##.

874. Clarence M.[6] **HICKS III** (Clarence M.[5], Clarence Malcolm[4], Orestes Marion Polk[3], Elijah[2], Joshua[1]), born, ##. He married unknown.

Jones notes: "resides (1976) at Columbus, OH; 2 marriages, both Columbus - names not listed; notes seem to indicate that Angie is from 1st marriage, April & Clarence IV from 2nd"

Children of Clarence M. HICKS III were:

         1320   i   **Angie**[7] **HICKS**, ##.
         1321   ii   **April**[7] **HICKS**, ##.
         1322   iii   **Clarence M.**[7] **HICKS IV**, ##.

875. Thomas Kelly[6] **HILL II** (Norma[5] HICKS, Clarence Malcolm[4], Orestes Marion Polk[3], Elijah[2], Joshua[1]), ##. He married unknown.

Jones notes: "resides (1976) at Columbus, OH"

Children of Thomas Kelly HILL II were:

         1323   i   **Mathew**[7] **HILL**, ##.
         1324   ii   **Thomas Kelly**[7] **HILL III**, ##.

876. Walter H.[6] **WILKES Jr.** (Marilyn[5] HICKS, Clarence Malcolm[4], Orestes Marion Polk[3], Elijah[2], Joshua[1]), born 17 Oct 1943 in Columbus, Franklin Co, OH. He married unknown.

@@ see research notes at end of chapter   ## born after 1930 or known to be living

Jones notes: "resides (1976) at Columbus, OH; 2 marriages, both in Columbus; notes seem to indicate that Bradley was from 1st marriage, Wendy & Scott from 2nd "

Children of Walter H. WILKES Jr. were:
1325 i **Bradley Paul⁷ WILKES**.
1326 ii **Wendy⁷ WILKES**.
1327 iii **Scott⁷ WILKES**.

878. **Evalyn Rotheus⁶ ROGERS** (Rotheus Thomas⁵, Lydia Ann⁴ TATMAN, James³, Lydia² HICKS, Joshua¹), born 7 Sep 1905 in McAlester, Pittsburg Co, OK, and died 7 Sep 1993 in Fort Collins, Larimer Co, CO. She married bef 1925 in Texas **John Bradford WINN**, born 19 Nov 1903 in Texas; died 12 Apr 1991 in Llano Co, TX.

Evalyn Rogers married John Winn, who was an agent for a steamship line in 1930. Evalyn's mother had died young; her grandmother, Lydia Gibson, may have raised most of her grandchildren.@@

Children of Evalyn R. ROGERS and John B. WINN were:
1328 i **Kenneth R⁷ WINN**, 14 Nov 1924 in Texas.
1329 ii **John H⁷ WINN**, born abt 1930 in Texas.

879. **Locleus Laura⁶ ROGERS** (Rotheus Thomas⁵, Lydia Ann⁴ TATMAN, James³, Lydia² HICKS, Joshua¹), born 4 Nov 1906 in San Antonio, TX; died 30 Sep 1979 in Galveston Co, TX. She married abt 1928 **Oscar Thomas EKELUND**, born 20 Mar 1908 in Texas; died Aug 1980 in Galveston, Galveston, TX.

Locleus Rogers married Oscar Ekelund, who was a dry goods salesman in 1930. @@

Children of Locleus L ROGERS and Oscar EKELUND were:
1330 i **Dora Mae⁷ EKELUND**, born 19 Nov 1928 in Galveston, TX. She married **Thomas Robert BOYSEN**.
1330a ii **Oscar Thomas EKELUND, Jr**, ##. Not in Jones notes. He married **Joyce KLYNG**

882. **Claris⁶ ROGERS** (Rotheus Thomas⁵, Lydia Ann⁴ TATMAN, James³, Lydia² HICKS, Joshua¹), born abt 1913 in Texas. She married **Joseph Bailey AHLSCHIER**, born abt 1907 in Texas.

Jones notes had name as Ahlschies; official records give Ahlschier. In 1930, he and wife Claris were living with Claris's grandmother and Joseph was listed as a clerk, car loading ___. @@

Children of Claris ROGERS and Joseph B AHLSCHIES were:
1331 i **Joseph B⁷ AHLSCHIER**, born abt 1928 in Texas. Served in Army Corps of Engineer during World War II. Possibly the Joseph Ahlschier who is listed in Who's Who in the East; B.S., M.H.A. Medical College of VA; Hospital Administration; living in Cary, NC in 1995.
1331a ii **Thomas Courtney AHLSCHIER**, born 24 Mar 1934; died 29 Oct 1992 in Harris Co, TX. He married **Bonnie Edwina BANKHEAD**, born 14 Apr 1925; died 22 Oct 2005 in Hurst, TX.

884. **Florence Marie⁶ TATMAN**⁵⁹⁸ (Frank L.⁵, Franklin Ulyses⁴, James³, Lydia² HICKS, Joshua¹), born 4 Oct 1913 in Bellingham, Whatcom Co, WA; died 30 Jan 1957 in Seattle, King Co, WA; buried 2 Feb 1957 in Evergreen-Washelli Mem Park, Seattle, WA. She married in 1936 in Camas, Cowlitz Co, WA **Alvin William MEADE Jr**, born 22 Jun 1911 in WY; died 14 Jun 1944 in Naples, Italy, son of **Alvin William MEAD, Sr** and **Mary Elizabeth TIMMERMAN**.

@@ see research notes at end of chapter   ## born after 1930 or known to be living

Florence Tatman married Alvin Meade, Jr, who died in Italy during World War I. @@

    Children of Florence Marie TATMAN and Alvin William MEADE Jr were:
+   1332 i   **Curtis William^7 MEADE**. He married **Judith Mae QUINCER**

892. Dorothy Mildred^6 DAY (Nelly^5 ALTMAN, Cornelia Blanche^4 BRITTINGHAM, Lucinda^3 TATMAN, Lydia^2 HICKS, Joshua^1), born 4 Feb 1900 in Clermont Co, OH; died 17 Mar 1927 in Cincinnati, Hamilton Co, OH; buried 21 Mar 1927 in Spring Grove Cemetery, Cincinnati, OH. She married 18 Jun 1923 in Hamilton Co, OH **Thomas Raymond WATTS,** born about 1874 in Indiana

Jones notes gave spouse as Raymond Joseph Watts; official records give Thomas Raymond Watts. Thomas was listed as a bank president in 1930. @@

    Children of Dorothy DAY and Raymond Joseph WATTS were:
   1333 i   **Raymond D.^{7} WATTS**, born about 1904 in Iowa.
   1334 ii   **Anna Lou^7 WATTS**.

895. Ruth^6 DAY (Nelly^5 ALTMAN, Cornelia Blanche^4 BRITTINGHAM, Lucinda^3 TATMAN, Lydia^2 HICKS, Joshua^1), born 13 Apr 1895 in Clermont Co, OH. She married 17 Feb 1920 in Cincinnati, Hamilton Co, OH **Chester Franklin DITMAR**.

Jones notes: "resided in Oregon". No further information found.

    Children of Ruth DAY and Chester DITTMAN were:
   1335 i   **Florence^7 DITTMAN**, born est. 1930. Notes: not found on 1920 or 1930 census.

896. Cicero^6 HALL (Millie Lou^5 ALTMAN, Cornelia Blanche^4 BRITTINGHAM, Lucinda^3 TATMAN, Lydia^2 HICKS, Joshua^1), born 13 Jul 1923 in Huntington, WV. He married unknown.

Jones notes: "resides (1974) at Sardinia, OH, m. 1965 -?-."

    Children of Cicero HALL were:
   1336 i   **Samuel^7 HALL**, ##.
   1337 ii   **Denise^7 HALL**, ##.

897. Mildred Ruth^6 HALL (Millie Lou^5 ALTMAN, Cornelia Blanche^4 BRITTINGHAM, Lucinda^3 TATMAN, Lydia^2 HICKS, Joshua^1), born^{599} 13 May 1918 in Huntington, WV; died^{600} Mar 1986 in Lakewood, Los Angeles Co, CA. She married (1) on 31 Dec 1941 in New Richmond, Clermont Co, OH **Roy ERTLE**, born Est. 1917; died 1942/45 in Germany; (2) aft 1945 **Robert SILER**, born^{601} 8 Feb 1921; died^{602} 4 May 1996 in Lakewood, Los Angeles Co, CA.

Jones notes: "resides (1974) at 5213 Coke Av, Lakewood, CA 90712; Roy killed in Germany, WW II"

    Children of Mildred Ruth HALL and Roy ERTLE were:
   1338 i   **Roy^7 ERTLE**, ##.
   1339 ii   **Caroline Lou^7 ERTLE**, ##.

902. Shirley^6 CLEMENT (Melissa L.^{5} WALKER, Lydia May^4 BRITTINGHAM, Lucinda^3 TATMAN, Lydia^2 HICKS, Joshua^1), born Est. 1924 in Swickly, PA. She married on 15 Dec 1950 in Cincinnati, Hamilton Co, OH **E. Harvey SEAMAN II**, born in Cincinnati, Hamilton Co, OH.

@@ see research notes at end of chapter   ## born after 1930 or known to be living

Jones notes: "resides (1973) at 4930 New Harmony Rd, Evansville, IN 47712". May be the Shirley Seaman who was born 8 Aug 1928 and died 12 Jan 2002; Evansville, Vanderburgh, IN - based on last known address. SS card was issued in WV (her mother resided in WV)

    Children of Shirley CLEMENT and E. Harvey SEAMAN II were:
- 1340   i   **Ann⁷ SEAMAN**, ##.
- 1341   ii   **E, Harvey⁷ SEAMAN III**, ##.
- 1342   iii   **Robert Clement⁷ SEAMAN**, ##.
- 1343   iv   **Sue⁷ SEAMAN**, ##.
- 1344   v   **Paul Walker⁷ SEAMAN**, ##.

905. William Lloyd⁶ GRIGGS (Ida May⁵ BENSON, Sarah Lavina⁴ HOPKINS, Levi Whitcomb³, Elizabeth 'Betsy'² HICKS, Joshua¹), born 30 Dec 1909 in Hunter, Garfield Co, OK; died 16 Mar 1975 in Oklahoma City, Oklahoma Co, OK; buried in White Cemetery, Hunter, Garfield Co, OK. He married on 19 Oct 1928 in Enid, Garfield Co, OK **Annabell ANDERSON**, born 1 Oct 1909 in Hunter, Garfield Co, OK; died 3 Jul 1978 in Bethany, Oklahoma Co, OK; buried in White Cemetery, Hunter, Garfield Co, OK.⁶⁰³

Lloyd Griggs was a farmer in Oklahoma. He was seriously injured while training a race horse in the late 1940s and suffered from poor health for the remainder of his life. Photo on page 304. @@

    Children of William Lloyd GRIGGS and Annabell ANDERSON were:
- 1345   i   **Orville Mack⁷ GRIGGS**, born 7 Aug 1929 in Enid, Garfield Co, OK; died 18 Jun 1930 in Hunter, Garfield Co, OK; buried in Hunter, Garfield Co, OK. "Choked on a button from his father's overalls"
- + 1346   ii   **Richard Neil⁷ GRIGGS**, born 16 May 1931 in Hunter, Garfield Co, OK; died 23 Dec 1991 in Bloomington, MN. He married **Neva Jane NANCE**.
  Served in US Army 1954-1956. Worked for Honeywell, as installation manager for commercial buildings; Jones notes: "Neva living in Bloomington, MN (1994)"
- + 1347   iii   **Milton Dwight⁷ GRIGGS**, ##. He married **Jeannie SCHAFFER**.
  Dwight has a degree in Law from University of Oklahoma. Living in Arvada, CO (1994).
- + 1348   iv   **Glorene⁷ GRIGGS**, ##. She married **Lowell Leroy REDFERN**.
  Glorene a teacher in El Dorado, KS (1994); Lowell works for Coastal Corp and owns a bicycle shop.
- + 1349   v   **Ora Kendall⁷ GRIGGS**, ##. He married **Sylvia Jane LEAK**.
  Kendall is a mathematics professor at Hutchison Community in Hutchison, KS. He compiled a book, "**Descendants of Levi W. & Sarah E. (Carter) Hopkins**", published about 1994.
- 1350   vi   **Drucilla⁷ GRIGGS**, ##. She married **James Alfred GRAVES**.
  Drucilla has a degree in nursing from the University of OK and works as a nurse for the Oklahoma City schools (1994).
- 1351   vii   **Lois Meryle⁷ GRIGGS**, ##. She married **Archie Dean JONES**.
  Lois holds a Masters degree in Business from E. Texas State and teaches at Wylie, TX (1994).

906. Lois Marie⁶ GRIGGS (Ida May⁵ BENSON, Sarah Lavina⁴ HOPKINS, Levi Whitcomb³, Elizabeth 'Betsy'² HICKS, Joshua¹), born 18 Jul 1915 in Hunter, Garfield Co, OK; died 17 Jul 1990 in Homeland, Riverside Co, CA; buried in Oakdale Mem Park, Glendora, CA. She married 14 Jun 1940 in Las Vegas, NV **Telephus "Tex" GUINN**, born 10 Jan 1916 in Lubbock, Lubbock Co, TX; died 1 Sep 1990 in

Homeland, Riverside Co, CA; buried in Oakdale Mem Park, Glendora, CA, son of James A. GUINN and Naomi NORTHCUTT.

Lois Griggs married Tex Guinn in Las Vegas, NV. Tex was a foreman for Edison Electric Co. @@

>Children of Lois Marie GRIGGS and Telephus "Tex" GUINN were:
>1352 i **Gloria Marie^7 GUINN**, born 18 Feb 1942 in Maywood, CA; died 14 Nov 1982. She married **Steve FARRAND**, born 7 Aug 1942; died 18 Mar 1980.

919. **Marie L.^{6} KURTZ** (Mollie E.^{5} LANHAM, Lucinda Margaret^4 JOHNSTON, William J.^{3}, Margaret^2 HICKS, Joshua^1), born Sep 1891 in OH; died^{604} 23 Mar 1922 in Dade Co, FL; buried in Vine St. Hill Cemetery, Cincinnati, OH. She married in Cincinnati, Hamilton Co, OH **Robert Elliott WEIGHILL**^{605}, born 15 Apr 1883 in Cincinnati, Hamilton, OH; died 16 Feb 1943 in Cincinnati, Hamilton, OH; buried 18 Feb 1943 in Vine St. Hill Cemetery, Cincinnati OH, son of John Thomas WEIGHILL and Mary ELLIOTT.

Marie Kurtz married Robert Weighill and had two children. She died at age 29, leaving twin daughters. In 1930, the girls were living with their grandmother, Mollie Kurtz, in Cincinnati. @@

>Children of Marie L. KURTZ and Robert Elliott WEIGHILL were:
>1353 i **Delores^7 WEIGHILL**, born abt Jun 1917 in OH. She married -?-**SCHUMAKER**. Jones notes: "resides (1974) at 89 Frank Ln, Marietta GA"
>+ 1354 ii **Vivian Elliott^7 WEIGHILL**, born abt Jun 1917 in OH. She married on 20 Sep 1937 in Newport, KY **John CHACON**, born Est. 1916 in Bogota, Columbia, South America. Jones notes: "resides (1974) at Carrera 14-86 A 62, Bogota, Columbia, S. A.".

920. **Harry W.^{6} KURTZ** (Mollie E.^{5} LANHAM, Lucinda Margaret^4 JOHNSTON, William J.^{3}, Margaret^2 HICKS, Joshua^1), born 12 Oct 1893; died^{606} 23 Nov 1969 in Cincinnati, Hamilton Co, OH; buried in Vine St. Hill Cemetery, Cincinnati, OH. He married on 10 Jan 1934 in Lexington, KY **Anna W. EGLOFF**, born 11 Nov 1900 in Cincinnati, Hamilton Co, OH; died Mar 1995 in Las Vegas, Clark Co, NV.

Harry Kurtz was a chauffeur for a taxi company in 1930. Jones notes: "she resides (1974) at 1948 Raindance Way, Las Vegas, NE 89109"

>Children of Harry W. KURTZ and Anna W. EGLOFF were:
>+ 1355 i **Norman^7 KURTZ**. He married -?- **SCHNEIDER**. Jones notes: "resides (1974) at California"

930. **Edward M.^{6} UTTER** (Robert Alexander^5, Annie Belle^4 JOHNSTON, William J.^{3}, Margaret^2 HICKS, Joshua^1), ##. He married, divorced **Gloria (Kirby) BRYANT**.

Jones notes: "resides (1974) at Louisville, KY"

>Children of Edward M. UTTER and Gloria (Kirby) BRYANT were:
>1356 i **Edward Robert^7 UTTER**, ##.

932. **Charles E.^{6} STEVENS** (Henry Johnston^5, Mary Elizabeth^4 JOHNSTON, William J.^{3}, Margaret^2 HICKS, Joshua^1), born 5 Dec 1919 in Felicity, Clermont Co, OH; died^{607} 1 Jun 1997 in Sarasota, Sarasota Co, FL. He married on 26 May 1946 in Clermont Co, OH **Marilyn R. STAATS**, born 26 Mar 1927 in Pt. Pleasant, Clermont Co, OH, daughter of William C. and Louella M. STAATS.

Jones notes: "resides (1974) at 1105 Rosetree Ln,, Cincinnati, OH 45230"; "Marilyn is a sister to Martha Staats, who married Robert Merrill Edwards (#922)". Robert and Charles are 2nd cousins. @@

@@ see research notes at end of chapter   ## born after 1930 or known to be living

Children of Charles E. STEVENS and Marilyn R. STAATS were:
1357 i **Diana L.^{7} STEVENS**, ##.
1358 ii **Sharon S.^{7} STEVENS**, ##.
1359 iii **Patricia L.^{7} STEVENS**, ##. She married **Gregory COOKE**.
1360 iv **Carla J.^{7} STEVENS**, ##.

934. **Wilma J.^{6} STEVENS** (Henry Johnston^5, Mary Elizabeth^4 JOHNSTON, William J.^{3}, Margaret^2 HICKS, Joshua^1), born 29 Apr 1924 in Ohio. She married on 15 Feb 1947 **Ralph A. HOUGHTON**, born abt 1919 in Ohio, son of Charles L. and Mabel L. HOUGHTON.

Jones notes: "resides (1974) at 2966 Banning Rd, Cincinnati, OH 45230"

Children of Wilma J. STEVENS and Ralph A. HOUGHTON were:
1361 i **Jerry^7 HOUGHTON**, ##. He married **Janis WOODRUFF**.
1362 ii **Monica^7 HOUGHTON**, ##.
1363 iii **Denise^7 HOUGHTON**, ##.

935. **Lloyd J.^{6} STEVENS** (Henry Johnston^5, Mary Elizabeth^4 JOHNSTON, William J.^{3}, Margaret^2 HICKS, Joshua^1), born 9 Sep 1928 in Felicity, Clermont Co, OH. He married -?-.

Jones notes: "resides (1974) at 1642 Collinsdale, Cincinnati, OH 45230"

Children of Lloyd J. STEVENS were:
1364 i **Pamela^7 STEVENS**, ##.
1365 ii **Paul Johnston^7 STEVENS**, ##.
1366 iii **Laura Jacqueline^7 STEVENS**, ##.
1367 iv **Linda Jean^7 STEVENS**, ##.
1368 v **Kelly Jo^7 STEVENS**, ##.

936. **Delia^6 STEVENS** (Henry Johnston^5, Mary Elizabeth^4 JOHNSTON, William J.^{3}, Margaret^2 HICKS, Joshua^1), ##. She married **William MCCLANAHAN**.

Jones notes: "resides (1974) at 1389 Wolfangle Rd, Cincinnati, OH". May be the William R McClanahan b. 14 Jun 1928, d. 29 Dec 1985; Cincinnati, Hamilton, OH on SS Death Index.

Children of Delia STEVENS and William MCCLANAHAN were:
1369 i **Debbie^7 MCCLANAHAN**, ##. She married **Wayne HENDRICKS**
Jones notes: "resides (1974) at 256 Fosters-Maineville Rd, Warren Co, OH"
1370 ii **Darrel^7 MCCLANAHAN**, ##. He married **Christina REEVES**.
Jones notes: "resides (1974) at 6138 Benneville" town?
1371 iii **Teresa^7 MCCLANAHAN**, ##. She married **Timothy EVANS**.
1372 iv **Steven^7 MCCLANAHAN**, ##.
1373 v **Dwayne^7 MCCLANAHAN**, ##.

938. **Clarke W.^{6} GREGG** (Marie W.^{5} WHITE, James Hicks^4, Ann Maria^3 HICKS, James^2, Joshua^1), born 25 Jan 1911 in Batavia OH; died 17 Nov 1985 in Portsmouth, Scioto Co, OH. He married on 8 Jul 1937 in Clermont Co, OH **Dorothy M. HAMPEL**, born 5 Aug 1918 in St Bernard, OH; died 15 Sep 1982 in Portsmouth, Scioto Co, OH.

Jones notes: "resides (1970) at 1649 5th St, S. Portsmouth, OH"; Clarke's occupation is listed as "advertising" in his death record.

@@ see research notes at end of chapter   ## born after 1930 or known to be living

Children of Clarke W. GREGG and Dorothy M. HAMPEL were:
+ 1374 i **Darlene Fay**[7] **GREGG**, ##. She married (1) **James P. POPE**; (2) **Fred BLAIR**.
Jones notes: "resides (1974) at Portsmouth, OH"
+ 1375 ii **Jacqueline**[7] **GREGG**, ##. She married **Lenny COLE**
Jones notes: "resides (1974) at Portsmouth, OH"

939. **James Woodlief**[6] **GREGG** (Marie W.[5] WHITE, James Hicks[4], Ann Maria[3] HICKS, James[2], Joshua[1]), born 14 Jun 1912 in Afton, Franklin Co, OH; died 30 Jan 2005 in Batavia, Clermont, OH. He married (1) on 14 Oct 1937 in Clermont Co, OH, divorced **Dorothy L. CARSTENS**, born 7 Jun 1917 in Fairmount, Cuyahoga Co, OH; (2) on 6 Apr 1961 in Clermont Co, OH **Marilyn (Barnes) HERRLE**, born 18 Mar 1928 in Corbin, Whitley Co, KY.

Jones notes: "resides (1974) at 199 Spring St, Batavia, OH"

Children of James Woodlief GREGG and Dorothy L. CARSTENS were:
1376 i **Susanne**[7] **GREGG**, ##.
Jones notes: "resides (1974) at Thornville, OH; m1 -?-; m2 Warren Fluker"
1377 ii **Georgeanne**[7] **GREGG**, ##. She married **O. C. LEE**.
Jones notes: "resides (1974) at 212 Falcon Ln, Las Vegas, NE 89107"
1378 iii **Jill**[7] **GREGG**, ##. Jones notes: "resides (1974) at PO Box 26344, Tempe, AZ 85282; not married"

Children of James Woodlief GREGG and Marilyn (Barnes) HERRLE were:
1379 i **Mathew James**[7] **GREGG**, ##.

941. **James Chatterton**[6] **WHITE** (Nicholas James[5], James Hicks[4], Ann Maria[3] HICKS, James[2], Joshua[1]), born 10 Jan 1921 in Williamsburg, Clermont Co, OH; died 28 Jan 2006 in Grand Rapids, Kent, MI. He married on 26 Dec 1942 in Quantico, VA **Mildred MCCONNELL**, born 20 Oct 1921 in Delaware, OH; died[608] 6 Feb 1981 in Grand Rapids, Kent Co, MI.

Jones notes: "resides (1974) at 3004 Woodcliff Cir, SE; E. Grand Rapids, MI 49506; Capt, Marine Corp, WW II; both attended OH Weslyan"

Children of James Chatterton WHITE and Mildred MCCONNELL were:
1380 i **Nancy Chatterton**[7] **WHITE**, ##. She married **Donald R. MUELLER**.
Jones notes: "resides (1974) at 1937 Wilhelmina Rise, Hololu, HI 96816; no children"
1381 ii **Stephen McConnell**[7] **WHITE**, ##.
1382 iii **Constance Louise**[7] **WHITE**, ##. She married **James W. PUTNAM**.
Jones notes: "resides (1974) at 4716 Beau Bien Ln, E., Lisle, IL 60532; no children"
1383 iv **James Chatterton**[7] **WHITE Jr**, ##.
1384 v **Thomas McConnell**[7] **WHITE**, ##.

942. **Nicholas Lawrence**[6] **WHITE** (Nicholas James[5], James Hicks[4], Ann Maria[3] HICKS, James[2], Joshua[1]), born 5 Jul 1925 in Williamsburg, Clermont Co, OH. He married on 26 Jul 1947 in Williamsburg, Clermont Co, OH **Marjorie WILSON**, born 7 Feb 1929 in Athol, KY.

Jones notes: "resides (1974) at Inverness Woods, RR3, Bloomington, IN 47401; attorney - teaching at University of Indiana"

@@ see research notes at end of chapter   ## born after 1930 or known to be living

Children of Nicholas Lawrence WHITE and Marjorie WILSON were:

+ 1385 i **Nicholas James⁷ WHITE II**, ##. He married **Elizabeth Ann FRANNFELDER**. Jones notes: "resides (1974) at 518 Wachtel Av, Petoskey, MI 49770; served in US Marine corps; architect; attended OH Weslyan"; "she is a teacher; attended OH Weslyan"
 1386 ii **Cynthia Jane⁷ WHITE**, ##. She married **Steven GUDEMAN**,
 Jones notes: "resides (1974) at 266 Senator Pl, Cincinnati, OH 45220"
 1387 iii **Marcia Sue⁷ WHITE**, ##.
 1388 iv **Lawrence Wilson⁷ WHITE**, ##.

943. Gary Doyle⁶ JOHNSTON (Doyle Howard⁵, Cora⁴ NEWKIRK, William David³, Nancy² HICKS, Joshua¹), ##. He married **Janet E. OLSEN**.

Jones notes: "resides (1974) at 1625 Juniper St, Forest Grove, OR 97116"

Children of Gary Doyle JOHNSTON and Janet E. OLSEN were:
1389 i **Steven Douglas⁷ JOHNSTON**, ##.
1390 ii **David Allen⁷ JOHNSTON**, ##.

945. Barbara⁶ JOHNSTON (Verle⁵, Cora⁴ NEWKIRK, William David³, Nancy² HICKS, Joshua¹), ##. She married **Denny COLE**.

Jones notes: "resides (1974) at Rt 9, Bloomfield, IA"

Children of Barbara JOHNSTON and Denny COLE were:
1391 i **Terry Wynn⁷ COLE** [twin], ##.
1392 ii **Sherry Lynn⁷ COLE** [twin], ##.

946. Judith Kae⁶ JOHNSTON (Verle⁵, Cora⁴ NEWKIRK, William David³, Nancy² HICKS, Joshua¹), ##. She married **Thomas Harold HAWK**.

Jones notes: "resides (1974) at RR 6, Bloomfield (Mark), IA"

Children of Judith Kae JOHNSTON and Thomas Harold HAWK were:
1393 i **Thomas Jeremy⁷ HAWK**, ##.

Research Notes for Generation 6

Notes for Stanley Edward PATTISON #555
Census: 1930 Batavia, Clermont Co, OH, p. 11A. Stanley Pattison, 28, teacher - county schools; Marguerite 23; Merrill 3 11/12; Evalyn 2 6/12. Enumeration Apr 10, 1930.
Death: Stanley E. Pattison, RR5, Batavia, OH; b. 17 Mar 1902, Lindale, OH; d. 28 Oct 1951, Bethesda Hospital, Cincinnati. Teacher- public school. Father: E. E. Pattison; mother: Irene McKibben. Informant: Florence A. Pattison. Burial: Williamsburg Cemetery, 31 Oct 1951. <familysearch.org>

Notes for Margaret ANSTAILT #555s
Death: Marguerite A. Pattison, Mt Carmel, OH; b. 5 Feb 1906, OH; d. 21 Apr 1932, Bethesda Hosp, Cincinnati. Spouse: Stanley Pattison. Father: Albert Anstaott; mother: Lula Havck - both b. OH. Buried Williamsburg Cemetery, 24 Apr1932. <familysearch.org>

Notes for Florence ALLEN #555s2
Jones notes: "Florence resides (1973) at Davis Pk (SR 132); Rt 1, Bethel, OH"
Death: Florence A Pattison; b. 1908, Brown, OH; d. 16 Aug 1987, Brown County, OH; widow; occupation: homemaker, age 70. Ohio Deaths, 1908-1932, 1938-1944, and 1958-2002 [Ancestry.com]

Notes for Thelma Myrtle PATTISON #556
Jones notes: "resided (1972) at S Main St, Bethel, OH"
Census: 1930 Bethel, Clermont, OH, p. 10A. Ralph Parker 27, manager - bakery; Thelma Parker 26, school teacher; Ralph Parker 7. All OH/OH/OH.
Death: Thelma M Parker, b. 1903, Ohio; res: Clermont Co, OH; d. 24 Nov 1983, Clermont Co. Mercy Hospital; age 80; widow; Ohio Deaths, 1908-1932, 1938-1944, and 1958-2007 [Ancestry.com]

Notes for Ralph PARKER #556s
Census: 1910 Tate, Clermont, OH, p. 11B. George Parker 29, shoemaker - factory, IA/MO/OH; Delia Parker 33, KY/KY/KY; Ralph Parker 8, OH/IA/KY; Paul Parker 6.
Death: Ralph A Parker, b. 1902; res: Clermont Co, OH; d. 19 Jun 1967, Christ Hospital, Cincinnati, Hamilton Co, OH; age 65; married. Ohio Deaths, 1908-1932, 1938-1944, and 1958-2007 [Ancestry.com]

Notes for Eunice Irene PATTISON #557
Jones notes: "she resides (1973) at 3653 Shaw Av, Cincinnati OH"
Census
  1920 OH, Clermont, Tate, p. 1A. Edward Pattison, 42, Supt public schools; Gennie I, 36; Stanley E 17; Thelma M 16; Eunice T 3 8/12; John W 1 9/12.
  1930 OH, Clermont Co, Bethel, p. 11A. 423 Main St. Edward Pattison, 52; Irene 46; Eunice 18; John 11. Occ: Supt. public schools.
Death: Eunice I Fenker, b. 1917, Ohio; res: Norwood, Hamilton Co, OH; d. 10 Jan 1981, Deaconess Hospital, Cincinnati, OH; age: 64; married. Ohio Deaths, 1908-1932, 1938-1944, and 1958-2007 [Ancestry.com]

Notes for Ludwig FENKER #557s
Death: Ludwig J Fenker, b. 1902; res: Cincinnati, Hamilton Co, OH; d. 15 Apr 1964, Good Samaritan Hospital, Cincinnati, OH. Age 62; married. Ohio Deaths, 1908-1932, 1938-1944, and 1958-2007 [Ancestry.com]

Notes for John W. PATTISON #558
Death: John W Pattison, b. 18 Apr 1918; d. 18 Feb 1971, Ann Arbor, Washtenaw Co, MI. Michigan Deaths, 1971-1996 [Ancestry.com] This date matches date given in Jones notes

Notes for Audrey N. MCCLANAHAN #558s
Jones notes: "she resides (1972) at Bethel, OH"
Census: 1930 Cincinnati, Hamilton, OH, p. 14A. Martin Mcclanahan 35, commercial travel - automobile; Ida Mcclanahan 32; Burdella Mcclanahan 11; Thomas Mcclanahan 10; Audrey Mcclanahan 7. All b. OH.

Notes for Audrey PETTIT #558s2
Jones notes: "Cooper in ( )" after this entry - her remarriage?; married to Louis Bickel, who adopted dau Caroline.

Notes for Grace PATTISON #560
Marriage: Groom: Lester Wykoff, born Clarksville, OH; Bride: Grace Pattison, born 1906, Cincinnati, OH; Bride's Age: 17; Marriage: 5 Dec 1923, Hamilton Co, OH; Groom's parents: Edward C. Wykoff; Anna Anson; Bride's parents: Walter Pattison; Minnie Bauer; Both bride and groom: single: Ohio Marriages, 1800-1958 <familysearch.org>
Death: Grace Wykoff, b. 26 Mar 1906, Cincinnati, OH; d. 6 Jan 1929, Cincinnati, Hamilton, OH; Age: 22; Burial: 09 Jan 1929 Mt. Washington Cem; Spouse: Lester Wykoff; Father: Walter Pattison b. OH; Mother: Minnie Baur b. Ohio. Cause of death: myocarditis. Ohio Deaths, 1908-1953 <familysearch.org>

Notes for George Lester WYKOFF #560s
Census: 1930 Cincinnati, Hamilton, OH, p. Edward Wykoff 50, conductor - street railway; Anna Wykoff 49; Lester G Wykoff 24, widowed, machinist - factory; Charles N Wykoff 20, clerk - clothier; Sarah E Wykoff 17; Minnie M Wykoff 5, gr dau; Thomas G Wykoff 4 1/12, gr son; Clayton Wykoff 46, brother, tender- car shop
Birth: George Lester Wykoff, b. 8 Aug 1905 Clarksville, Clinton, OH; Father: Edward D. Wykoff; Mother: Anna Anson. Ohio Births and Christenings, 1821-1962 <familysearch.org>
Death: SS Death Index - Lester R G Wykoff, b. 8 Aug 1905; d. 3 Apr 1996; Cincinnati, Hamilton, OH; #269-03-9509; Issued: Ohio

Notes for Edith May PATTISON #561
Probably dau from 1st marriage as there is a large gap between children & Mada states on 1930 census that she was 24 when she married & is now 37. Thus Mada would not have been married to Walter when Edith was born.
Census: 1930 Bedford, Monroe Co, MI. On census with father, Walter C. Pattison, as Edith M. Harris, dau, widow, w/ dau Rose M. 6, sons Carl W. 5, Charles E. 2, James F. 4/12.
Information: From great granddaughter-in-law Lydia Harris [via Ancestry.com Message Board] "Edith was married to William Carl Harris, b. 5 Sept. 1886 in Coldwater, Michigan; died 26 July 1929 in fire/explosion in felt insulating company in Toledo, OH. Edith and William had 4 children. Rose M./ Carl W./ Charles Edward/ James F. My father-in-law is Carl W. He is the only one still living. After William's death, Edith lived with her father and stepmother in Michigan. She later married "Johnson" - not sure of first name; maybe my father-in-law will remember - I'll ask. Then in Edith's later years, she lived with a man named Owen Lewis but I don't think they ever married. Edith was born 30 Nov 1906 in Cincinnati, Ohio, and died 13 Jun 1994 in Maumee, Ohio. I have a picture of her in latter years in my tree. Maybe when Walter and Minnie split-up, Walter took Edith and Minnie took Grace. I just found a record in the Ohio Death Index for a Minnie M Pattison b.1882, d 25 Jun 1976 in Youngstown OH; not sure if this is Walter's Minnie or not."

Notes for William Carl HARRIS #561s
Wife Edith is listed as widowed on 1930 census.
Died in fire/explosion in felt insulating co in Toledo, OH.
Death: William Carl Harris, b. 5 Sep 1886, Scranton OH; d. 26 Jul 1929, Toledo, Lucas, OH; Age: 42; Married; Burial: 28 Jul 1929, Mt Pleasant; Spouse: May Harris; Father: Wm Harris, b. NE; Mother: May Bayer, b. OH. Ohio Deaths, 1908-1953 <familysearch.org>
Military: not found on WW I Draft registration.

Notes for John C. MANNING #571
Jones notes: "resided (1973) at Laurel, OH"
Not found on 1930 census.
Death: John C Manning, b. 1908; Res: Clermont Co, OH; d. 8 Oct 1977, Veterans Adm. Med. Ctr, Cincinnati, OH. age 69; divorced. Ohio Deaths, 1908-1932, 1938-1944, and 1958-2007 [Ancestry.com]

Notes for Ruth N. MANNING #573
Jones notes: "she resides (1973) at 111 Cherry St, Bethel OH"
Census: 1930 Williamsburg, Clermont, OH, p. 7B. Ora Munzing 50, farmer; Lida B Munzing 50; Glenn H Munzing 19, laborer - lumber factory; Ruth M Munzing 15. [should be Manning]

Notes for Samuel A. HOLMES #573s
Census: 1900 Mattoon, Coles, IL, p. 50B. Alph Holmes 49; Maud Holmes 25; Samuel Holmes 1, Sep 1898, IL.
Military: World War I Draft Registration Cards, 1917-1918 [Ancestry.com] Samuel Arthur Holmes, age 20, b. 18 Sep 1898; res: Bethel, Clermont, OH; occ: shoe maker - Cincinnati Shoe Co, Bethel, OH; relative: L Alfred Holmes; med. height, slender, brown eyes & hair. Regis: 12 Sep 1918, Batavia, OH.

Notes for Wayne Nichols FITZPATRICK #591
Living with grandfather Homer Fitzpatrick in 1930.
Jones notes: "resides (1973) at 645 Tewkesbury Le, Severna Park, MD 21146; US Navy 1940-1969, retired as a Captain"

Notes for Hope BARTON #591s
Census: 1930 Hartford, Hartford, CT. Malcolm Barton 43, elec engineer - elec light co; Cornelia Barton 40; Priscilla Barton 13; Hope Barton 8; Malcolm B Barton 3 1/12. All b. CT.

Notes for Frank Oliver HIGGINS #597
Military: World War I Draft Registration Cards, 1917-1918 [Ancestry.com] Frank Oliver Higgins, age 18, b. 7 May 1900; res: Deatsville, Elmore, AL; farmer - Bert Higgins; contact: Eula Higgins, mother. Tall, med build, grey eyes, brown hair. regis: 12 Sep 1918, Elmore, AL.
Census: 1930 Cold Spring, Elmore, AL, p. 26B. Frank O Higgins 29, station - railroad, AL/OH/AL; Mary E Higgins 27; Frank Higgins 7; Mary E Higgins 6. others AL/AL/AL
Marriage: F. O. Higgins, b. 1900, Age 21; Bride: Maeretta Hogan, b. 1903, age 18; marriage: 2 Mar 1921, Birmingham, Jefferson, AL. Alabama Marriages, 1816-1957 <familysearch.org>
Death: Frank O. Higgins, d. 26 Feb 1965, Deatsville, Elmore, AL, age 64, est. birth year: 1901; spouse: Mary E. Higgins; father: Burt Higgins; mother: Eulla P. Rawlinson
Probable death of daughter: Evelyn Pennington, d. 16 Jun 1972, Montgomery, Montgomery, AL; Age 48y; Est.. Birth Date 1924; Spouse: Harry L.; father: Frank O. Higgins; mother Mary E. Hogan. Alabama Deaths, 1908-1974 <familysearch.org>

Notes for Marietta E. HOGAN #597s
Census 1910 Precinct 9, Elmore, AL, p. 19A. Daniel Hogan 38, operator & f___ - railroad; Pearl Norris Hogan 30; Emmet O Hogan 9; Maretta Hogan 7; Linton D Hogan 5; Jeromie V Hogan 1
No death information found.

Notes for Agnes Cleo CRANE #637
Jones notes: "resides (1973) at 235 N. East St, Bethel, OH; he served in the Bethel P. O for 42 years"
Death: No death information found.

Notes for Robert Eberle SWING #637s
Death: SS Death Index gives: Robert Swing b. 27 Jul 1908; d. Sep 1981 Punta Gorda, Charlotte, FL #271-20-6206; issued: Ohio

Notes for Samuel Hodgson GLOVER #647
Birth: H...dgson Glover b. 26 Jul 1903; father: Samuel Glover; mother: Stella Hudson. Ohio Births and Christenings, 1821-1962 <pilot.familysearch.org>
Discrepancy: Jones notes gives birth as 26 Jul 1902; birth/christening record gives year as 1903
Census: 1930 Amelia, Clermont, OH p. 2B. Hodson Glover 26, foreman - pottery; Lula Glover 22; Darrel Glover 4
Death: Hodgson Glover, b. 1904; Residence: Clermont, OH; Death: 4 Jul 1965, Long-Term Care Facilities, Hamilton Co, OH. Age: 61, Married. Ohio Deaths, 1908-1932, 1938-1944, and 1958-2007 [Ancestry.com]

Notes for Lulu FIGGINS #647s
Census: 1910 Ohio, Clermont, OH, p. Jacob Donham 69, widowed, farmer; Edgar Figgins 25, son-in-law, farmer; Inez Figgins 24, dau; Lulu Figgins 3, gr dau. All b. OH.
Death: Social Security Death Index: Lula Glover, b. 23 May 1907; d. Jun 1975: Amelia, Clermont, OH

Notes for Julia Elsie GLOVER #649
Jones notes: "Teacher; she resides (1974) at 24 Church St, Amelia, OH"

Notes for Donald H. AULT #649s
Census: Jersey City Ward 10, Hudson, NJ, p. 26A. Charles H Ault 36, IL; Amy E Ault 33, Eng; Donald H Ault 13, Eng; Irine Ault 11, Eng; Margaruite Ault 4 4/12 NY; Reginald Ault 2 10/12 NY. Imm 1911; naturalized 1905 [sic].

Notes for Leonard O. BILLINGSLEY #650s
Census: 1930 Batavia, Clermont, OH, p. 3A. Roy R Billingsley 47, WV/TX/WV, farmer; Carrie M Billingsley 46; Leonard Billingsley 21, truck driver - pottery; Victor Billingsley 18; Mary Wyant 87

Notes for Charles Lee GLOVER #651
Jones notes: "US Army, WW II"

Notes for Inez Lucille BRILL #651s
Census: 1930 Ohio, Clermont, OH, p. 6A. George A Brill 44, farmer; Elizabeth Brill 49; Howard G Brill 17, laborer; Florine A Brill 15; Helen N Brill 12; Edwin L Brill 11; Walter K Brill 8; Inez L Brill 6
No death information found

Notes for Kenneth H. MYRICK #653
Jones notes: "resides (1983) at 27 Sperling Dr, Amelia, OH"

Notes for Cecile Rose TURBYNE #653s
Census: 1930 Waterville, Kennebec, ME, p. 25A. Alec Turbyne 48, Sco/Sco/Sco, repairman - paper mill; Maude Turbyne 47; John Turbyne 16; Frank Turbyne 15; Cecille Turbyne 12; Alexander Turbyne 10; Nathile Turbyne 4 6/12. Others b. Maine
Death: Cecile Rose Myrick, b. 17 May 1917; res: Clermont Co, OH; d. 19 Jun 2006; Age: 89; Father's Surname: Turbyne; Mother's Maiden Name: Rancort; Widowed; Education: 12. Ohio Deaths, 1908-1932, 1938-1944, and 1958-2007 [Ancestry.com]
Marriage: 31 Aug 1943, La Flora Co, MS

Notes for Jessie Elizabeth (Betty) MCNAIR #656
Jones notes: "resides (1973) at 350 Broadway, Williamsburg, OH"
Death: SS Death Index gives: Jessie Herbst, b. 1 Aug 1926; d. 7 Sep 2005 Williamsburg, Clermont, OH; #299-18-7186; issued: Ohio

Notes for Elizabeth Stewart HITE #663
Jones notes: give name, date, spouses, "resides (1972) at Rt 1, Felicity, Felicity-Higginsport Rd"
Married Floyd B. Fugette, son of Norman & Mae Tackett Fugette
Death: Elizabe S Poston, b. 1915, OH; d. 5 Jul 1986, Long-Term Care Facilities, Brown Co, OH; widowed; homemaker. Ohio Deaths, 1908-1932, 1938-1944, and 1958-2007 [Ancestry.com]

Notes for Floyd B. FUGETTE #663s
Death: Floyd Fugett, d. 24 Jul 1939, Cincinnati, Hamilton, OH; b. 28 May 1913 KY. Age: 26 years 1 month 27 days; Occ: Metal Worker; Bur: 26 Jul 1939, Felicity, OH; Spouse: Elizabeth Fugett; Father: Norman Fugett, b. KY; Mother: Flora Mae Tackett, b. KY. Ohio Deaths 1908-1953 <familysearch.org>
Discrepancy: Jones notes gave birthplace as CA; death certificate gives KY. KY seems more likely given that parents were both born & died there.

Notes for Melissa Rosaline HICKS #664
Jones notes: "resides (1972) at Rt 2, Box 302 New Richmond OH"
Hicks Bible: "Born to Mr. Hurdes Beeker Hicks and Mrs Bessie Hicks (nee Rogers) Melissa Rosaline Hicks, May 3, 1920"
Death: Rosalene M Buskirk [Rosalene M Hicks], b. 3 May 1920, Clermont Co, OH; Residence: Clermont Co, OH; d. 20 Sep 2001, Deaconess Hospital, Cincinnati, Hamilton, OH. Age: 81; father's surname: Hicks; mother's surname: Rogers; widow; education: 12 years. Ohio Deaths, 1908-1932, 1938-1944, and 1958-2007 [Ancestry.com]

Notes for Russell S. BUSKIRK #664s
Census: 1920 Bracken Co, KY, p. 6A. Joseph B Buskirk 45, farmer, KY/OH/OH; Cyntha A Buskirk 37; Willis J Buskirk 20; Emmet H Buskirk 16; Farris N Buskirk 13; Russell W Buskirk 10; Erma G Buskirk 7; Bruce B Buskirk 5. Other KY/KY/KY. Older boys farmhands.
Death: Russell U Buskirk, b. 10 Jul 1909 Kentucky; Residence: Clermont, OH; Death: 4 Nov 1990, Clermont County Mercy Hospital; Age: 81

Notes for Morris Hurdes HICKS #666
Jones notes give names of wives, dates of marriages. "resides (1972) at Rt2, Bethel OH, Sugar Tree Rd"; living in Ocala, FL 3/99
Hicks Bible: "Born to Mr. Hurdes Beeker Hicks and Mrs Bessie Hicks (nee Rogers) - Maurice Hurdes Hicks Sept 11, 1924"

Notes for Donald Rogers HICKS #667
Alive; living in Felicity, OH 1999
Jones notes give name of wife, marriage date, birthday as 9/12/1935; "Reside (1972) Clilo, OH"
Hicks Bible last known in possession of Addie Joslin West [copy sent to me by Lvera Jennings Seipelt, Georgetown OH]. "Born to Mr. Hurdes Beeker Hicks and Mrs Bessie Hicks (nee Rogers) - Donald Rogers Hicks, Mon. Sept 15, 1930"

Notes for John Wilson "J. W." DEVORE #670
Jones notes: gives nickname as Jay; resides (1972) at Rt1, Box 142B, Claremore, OK"
Lvera (Jennings) Seipelt's notes (1999): "divorced, M2 Dorothy Jean -?-, Claremore, OK"
Death: John W. Devore, b. 7 Jun 1931; d. 12 Aug 1988, Chelsea, Rogers, OK 74016 ;#281-28-1698; Issued Ohio. Social Security Death Index

Notes for Lvera Adrienne JENNINGS #673
Jones notes: give name, dates, spouse; "reside (1981) at 5766 Seip Rd, Georgetown 45167"
Lvera Seipelt's notes: "4 sons, resides (1975-1999) 5766 Seip Rd, Georgetown, OH"

Notes for Victor Lloyd SEIPELT #673s
Lvera Seipelt's notes: "farmer 20 years; Farm Aide at OH Agricultural Research & Development Center, 30 years"
Death: SSDI gives Victor Lloyd Seipelt, b. 7 May 1920; d. 6 Dec 2008; age 88; Georgetown, Brown, OH
Obituary: *Victor Lloyd Seipelt, Sr., age 87 of Georgetown, OH, died Saturday, Dec 6, 2008 at the Ohio Valley Manor Nursing and Rehabilitation Center near Ripley, OH. He worked at the Ohio Agricultural and Development Center near Ripley, OH, for 30 years and retired from there in 1987. He was also a farmer and a member of the Ripley Church of Christ. Mr. Seipelt was born on May 7, 1920 in Ripley, OH, the son of the late William Albert and Parthena (Flaugher) Seipelt. He was also preceded in death by twin sons, at birth, David Lyle and Dale Lynn Seipelt; 3 sisters - Clara Edith Frost, Ruby Seipelt, and Hazel Charles; and 2 brothers - Frances and Glenn Seipelt. Mr Seipelt is survived by his loving wife of sixty years, Lvera (Jennings) Seipelt; two sons - Victor L. Seipelt, Jr. and wife, Connie, of Ripley, OH and Leslie G. Seipelt and wife, Marilyn, of Georgetown, OH; 4 grandchildren and 6 great grandchildren. Interment in Shinkles Ridge Cemetery.* **Brown County Press**, December 11, 2008.

Notes for Irma Claire JENNINGS #674
Living 1999
Jones notes: give birth date as 1931, Brown Co. "reside (1972) Big Run Rd, Georgetown, OH"
Lvera Seipelt's notes: "1 dau, 4 sons; resides (1999) 80 Dell Acres Dr, Georgetown, OH 45121; divorced 1971"; gives baptism dates.

Notes for Ivetta Faye JENNINGS #675
Jones notes: give name, dates, spouse ", "div"; reside (1972) at 1027 Elm, Ripley, OH"
Living 1999
Lvera Seipelt's notes: "2 dau, 1 son; resides (1999) 1027 Elm St, Ripley. OH; divorced 1970"; gives baptism dates.
Lvera Seipelt's notes: Robert W. Frodge "shoe factory & life squad"
Marriage2: Dawes celebrate marriage. Bro. Delbert and Ivetta (Frodge) Dawes are pleased to announce they were joined together in marriage on Thursday, May 24, 2007...Bro. Dawes remains well-known in this area as he was a former minister of the Ripley Church of Christ from 1960 through 1966. He is now a retired minister in Springboro, Ohio where he remains active with revivals, counseling, weddings, funerals, etc. The new Mrs. Dawes is an insurance agent at John Wood Insurance Agency in Ripley, Ohio. **Brown County News**, May 2007.

Notes for Eugene Martin JENNINGS 2nd #675
Both living 1999
Jones notes: give name, dates, spouse; "reside (1981) Garden Acres Dr, Georgetown, OH"
Lvera Seipelt's notes: "2 sons, 1 dau; resides (1999) 188 Green Acres Dr, Georgetown, OH; divorced 1983; with Pepsi plant in Cincinnati 25 years"

Notes for Harvey Clyde LEVI II #680
Birth, Marriage: from Bible of Mollie Dell Levi, in possession of Betty Kieser, 2007
Children: Harvey Clyde; Irma Crystal. Names, no other information in Bible of Mollie Dell Levi.
Birth, death info from son, Lane Levi. "My father Harvey Clyde Jr was born in OH and also was involved with the Carnivals (Silver States Shows). My father left the carnival & we moved around TX, WV, NE & IA. He married my mother, Marvella, who ran away from home to join the carnival"
Buried Westlawn & Hillcrest Memorial Park, Omaha NE (photo of stones in my files).

Notes for Marvella Margaret TRUITT #680s
Birth, death info from son Lane Levi. Buried Sacramento, CA.

Notes for Elizabeth STALDER #683
Living in Orlando, FL 1992.
Birth: Birth Certificate; Norwood, Hamilton Co, OH, 9 Mar 1913.
Census: 1930 Orlando, Orange, FL, p. 4B. William B Stalder 51, age at marriage 35, IN/PA/IN, carpenter - house; Nellie D Stalder 46, age at marriage 24, OH/OH/OH; Curtis C Stalder 18, bookkeeper - motor transport; Elizabeth Stalder 17; Jennette Stalder 15; William Stalder 13; Grace Stalder 11; Ruth Stalder 10; Madge Stalder 5; Richard Stalder 2 10/12; Medora Cooper 81, mother, IN/IN/NY.
  1935 FL State Census, Orange Co, FL. W. B. Stalder, 56, husband, high school education, carpenter; Mrs. W. B. Stalder 50, wife, OH, high school education; D.J. Cooper 86, mother, high school education, retired; Mrs. Frank M. Levy 85, step mother in law; Bettie Stalder 22, dau, bookkeeper; Jeanette Stalder 21, salesclerk; Billie Stalder 19, paperman; Grace Stalder 17, nursemaid; Ruth Stalder 16, student; Madge Stalder 14, student; Dickie Stalder 8, b. FL, student.
  1945 FL State Census - Orlando, Orange Co, FL Robert J. Kieser 36, high school; Elizabeth Kieser 32, high school; Robert F Kieser 6, 1st grade; Elizabeth Joan Kieser 4. Rt 5, box 50C. Next to George & Lila Chapman and family.
Marriage: Delaney Street Baptist Church, Orlando FL; 2 Feb 1936. Certificate in file.
Obituary: *Elizabeth "Betty" Kieser, 95, of Orlando passed away Friday, Oct 17th in Orlando. Elizabeth Sunshine Stalder was born in Norwood, OH on Mar 9, 1913 to William Benjamin and Mollie Dell (Levi) Stalder. The family moved to Orlando in 1921. She married Robert J. "Bob" Kieser in 1936 and was the mother of three: Robert Frederick, Elizabeth Joan and Charles David. She was an active member of Delaney St Baptist Church for more than 79 years, serving in many capacities, including growing and arranging the flowers for the church for many years. An avid gardener, Betty raised a large garden for more than 70 years, growing vegetables and flowers that were envied by and shared with friends and neighbors. She was preceded in death by husband Bob and son David, as well as siblings: Curtis of Orlando; Jeanette Rhodes of Tallahassee, Bill of New Smyrna Beach, Grace Windham, Ruth Watkins, and Madge Washell, all of Jacksonville. Survivors include brother Dick Stalder and his wife Taeko of Jacksonville; son Robert F. of Choctaw, OK; daughter and son-in-law, Betty Jo and Glenn Stockton of Orlando; grandchildren Mary E. "Betsy" (Stockton) Douberley of Orlando and Robert G. "Greg" Stockton of Pittsburgh, PA; great grandchildren, Elisabeth, James and David Douberley of Orlando, as well as many nieces and nephews. Interment at Greenwood Cemetery. In lieu of flowers, family and friends are asked to plant a flower or tree in her memory.* [***Orlando Sentinel***, Oct 19, 2008]

Notes for Robert Julius KIESER #683s

Lived in Orlando, FL. Retired Civil Service, Naval Underwater Research Lab, Orlando.

Birth: Columbus OH, 31 Jan 1909. [Certificate 150586. State of OH, Registration District 186; Registered #269. Unnamed on original certificate, named in registration in Vital Statistics Division, OH Dept of Health.] Copy in file.

Occupation: Began working as child, delivering newspapers, to add income to family after death of father. After high school, worked for Cahoon Machinery - installing wells and irrigation for citrus groves. Hired by Columbia Labs for temporary position about 1940, designing equipment. During war years, this was taken over by the Navy, working on sonar and underwater sound equipment. This became the UN Navy Underwater Sound Lab on Lake Gem Mary in S. Orlando. He continued to work there until his retirement in 1971.

Education: Finished high school and took many college level courses in night school, but did not complete a degree. (When he retired, the lab hired two doctorate physicists to replace him).

Death: Heart attack at home, 22 May 1995. Died in emergency room, Orlando Regional Hospital. Death Certificate: #95-2566, State of Florida. Age 86, Physicist, US Govt; wife: Elizabeth Stalder. Born: 31 Jan 1909; father Charles Frederick Kieser, Mother: Jessie Umbaugh. Carey Hand Funeral Home.

Burial: Greenwood Cemetery, Orlando, FL. 25 May 1995. In family plot with parents, son David.

Church: Was first member of Delaney Street Baptist Church after its charter. Served in almost every role of church - chairman of deacons, Sunday School Supt., teacher, etc. Met Betty Stalder there at BYU meeting when she was 15. Married there and remained active until death.

Obituary: *Robert J. Kieser, 86, 275 Prescott Dr, Edgewood, died Monday, May 22. Mr. Kieser was retired from the Naval Research Lab, Orlando. Born in Columbus, OH, he moved to Central FL in 1911. He was a member of Delaney St Baptist Church. Survivors: wife, Elizabeth; son, Robert, Choctaw, OK; Dau, Elizabeth K. Stockton, Orlando; sister, Florence Dunlap, Orlando; 5 grandchildren; 4 great grandchildren. Carey Hand Funl. Home, Orlando.*

Notes for Jeanette STALDER #684

Married Emmet William Rhodes, 18 Jan 1942.

Census: 1945 FL State Census - Tallahassee, Leon Co, FL. Emmett Rhodes 28, tenant at practor?; Jeanette S. Rhodes 30, housewife; Judith Ann Rhodes 3. Both adults - high school. Address: 536 E. Georgia

Notes for Ruth Marilyn STALDER #687

Obituary: WATKINS - *Ruth Stalder Watkins, 80, passed away February 17, 2000 at her residence. She was born in Cincinnati, Ohio and lived all her life in Jacksonville, Florida. Mrs. Watkins retired in 1973 from the Social Security Administration and the Internal Revenue Service of the Federal Government after many years of service. Her husband Elkin E. Watkins preceded her in death in 1979. Survivors include two sons, Thomas T. Watkins (Louise), Young Harris, GA and William B. Watkins, Stanardsville, VA; four grandchildren, Jennifer Ruth Watkins, Travis Michael Watkins, Matthews Rosendale, and Shawna Rosendale Watkins; two brothers, William Stalder (Frances) and Richard Stalder all of FL; three sisters, Betty Kieser, Madge Washell, and Grace Windham. A funeral service will be held 2:30 PM Saturday, February 19, 2000 in the chapel of Arlington Park Funeral Home. . Interment will follow in Arlington Park Cemetery. In lieu of flowers, memorials may be made in her name to Habitat for Humanity.*

Notes for Mary Madge STALDER #688

Obituary: *Madge S. Washell, 85, passed away on Saturday, March 8, 2006 at her residence surrounded by her dear family. A gracious wife, mother, and grandmother, Madge was a member and past secretary of Terry Parker Baptist Church and was a retired Administrative Assistant at Florida Community College.. She was also an avid reader of anything that she could lay her hands on. Madge was preceded* *in death by her husband, John F. Washell. She is survived by her children - John (Carolyn) Washell, Mary (Walter) Tedder, Tim (Linda) Washell; 6 loving grandchildren; 3 great grandchildren; a sister Betty Kieser and brother Richard Stalder. The family will welcome friends at Arlington Park Funeral Home on Tuesday, April 11, 2006 from 6-8 p.m. The Homegoing Celebration will take place in the chapel of the funeral home on Wednesday, April 12, 2006 at 11 a.m. with Dr. Joe Courson and Reverend Virgil Jerrell officiating. Interment will follow in Arlington Park Cemetery where Madge will be laid to rest along side her husband. In lieu of flowers, memorial contributions can be made in Madge's name to Community Hospice of NE Florida.* **FL Times Union**, *Mar 10, 2006.*

Notes for Elizabeth JOSLIN #690
Obituary: *Elizabeth (nee Joslin) Hayden, dearly beloved wife of Howard Hayden & dau. of Archie & Josephine Joslin, joined her friends in Christ on 13 May 1975. Also survived by dau. Mrs. Jane Geir and sons Jim, John & Robert. Services at New Richmond First Bapt. Church. Lew F. White Funeral Home. Res. Cincinnati.* **Cincinnati Enquirer** 5/15/1975.

Notes for Howard HAYDEN #690s
Jones notes: gives birth date, spouse; "resides (1972) at 6251 Coachlight Way, Indian Hill, OH"

Notes for Margaret Anna MEEKER #693
Birth: Hamilton Co, OH delayed birth record: "Margaret Anna Meeker, b. 20 Jan 1907, F, at 5141 Section Ave., Cincinnati., Hamilton Co., OH also usual res. of mother; Parents: James Clarence Meeker (W, 21, b. Brown Co, OH, a carpenter), Lucie Mary Francis Hicks (W, 22, b. Clermont Co, OH, housewife); attested to on 10 Feb 1961 by Lucie Meeker, age 76 and Minnie Behan, age 69.
Notes from Lvera (Jennings) Seipelt 1998 list "Lucy Meeker (Deceased 1964); Children: Margaret Orth"
Jones notes: "resides (1972) 2224 Langdon Farm Rd, Cincinnati, OH"

Notes for George Clement ORTH #693s
Census: 1910 Cincinnati Ward 12, Hamilton, OH, p. 5B. George A Orth 38; Carrie D Orth 37; Frieda M Orth 12; Aurelia C Orth 10; Clemens G Orth 4

Notes for Rachel Matilda MEEKER #696
Notes from Lvera (Jennings) Seipelt 1998 list "Lucy Meeker (Deceased 1964); Children: Rachel Norman"
Marriage: Personal knowledge of Rachel Meeker.
Jones notes: "1 son; resides (1972) 2509 Kellerman Ave, Cincinnati, OH (Golf Manor)"
Death: SS Death Index: Rachel M. Norman; #079-09-9101; Last Residence: Louisville, Jefferson, KY; b. 28 Apr 1911; d. 18 Feb 2002; issued: New York.

Notes for Phillip NORMAN #696s
Death: Philip Norman, b. 1906 OH; Residence: Golf Manor, Hamilton Co, OH; death: 19 Jul 1979, Cincinnati, Hamilton, OH; Age: 73; Married. Ohio Deaths, 1908-1932, 1938-1944, and 1958-2007 [Ancestry.com]
SS Death index: Philip Norman, SSN: 076-01-6558; Last Residence: Cincinnati, Hamilton, OH; b. 28 May 1906; d. Jul 1979; issued: New York

Notes for Robert MEEKER #697
Birth: Lucy Hicks Meeker (his mother) supplied this birth date as part of the genealogy data she presented to members of the extended family
Notes from Lvera (Jennings) Seipelt 1998 list "Lucy Meeker (Deceased 1964); Children: Robert Meeker (Deceased 1984); children: Shirley; William R."
Jones notes: "1st marriage - 2 children; 2nd marriage - no children; resides (1972) 10916 Reading Rd, Cincinnati, OH."

Notes for Marcella B. HAGEN #697s
Census: 1910 Cincinnati Ward 13, Hamilton, OH, p. 13B. Henry Hagan 33; Anna Hagan 36; Micheal Hagan 11; Hilda Hagan 2; Marcella Hagan 4/12
Social Sec. Death Index gives birth as 11 Dec 1909

Notes for Mary Ann VOYER #697s2
May be the Mary Meeker on SS Death Index who was b. 8 Sep 1900 & d. Nov 1985 in Cincinnati, Hamilton, OH.

Notes for Helen HICKS #698
Notes from Lvera (Jennings) Seipelt 1998 list "Harvey John Hicks (deceased); children: Helen Luckey, Henrietta Wenger, Jo Ann McCracken."
Jones notes: "resides (1984) 14 Lori Lane, Amelia, OH 45102"

Notes for Wilson S. LUCKEY #698s
Jones notes give birth year as 1914. Social Security Death Index gives date of birth as 21 Feb 1915
Death: Wilson Shannon Luckey; d. 5 May 1985, Mariemont, Hamilton, Ohio; Age: 70; Burial: 8 May 1985, Pierce Township Cemetery, Locust Corner, OH; b. 21 Feb 1915, OH; Occ: Scrapper Hand Mach; married; parents: Wilson Shannon Luckey; Edna Hawley. Ohio Deaths and Burials, 1854-1997 <familysearch.org>

Notes for Henrietta HICKS #699
Jones notes: "resides (1972) 1962 Wanniger Ln, ?"; m. -?- Wenger
Notes from Lvera (Jennings) Seipelt 1998 list "Harvey John Hicks (deceased); children: Helen Luckey, Henrietta Wenger, Jo Ann McCracken."

Notes for Harriet JoAnn HICKS #700
Married: Richard McCracken
Notes from Lvera (Jennings) Seipelt 1998 list "Harvey John Hicks (deceased); children: Helen Luckey, Henrietta Wenger, Jo Ann McCracken."
Jones notes: "resides (1972) 1432 Clougle PK, Batavia, Children: Janice Lynne & Others - Richard?"
Obituary: *Harriett J. (Hicks)* **Mccracken***, 84 of Lebanon and formerly of Clermont County, Oh., passed peacefully on Monday, October 26, 2009 in Miamisburg. Born October 6, 1925 in Cincinnati, the daughter of Harvey J. and Beulah (Greene) Hicks, she was a loving wife, mother and grandmother. A resident of Lebanon since 1993, she had previously been active in Clermont County as a former member of the Amelia United Methodist Church, a teacher at the Mt. Moriah Methodist Church Montessori School and active as a Girl Scout and Boy Scout Leader. Preceded in death by her parents and two sisters, she is survived by her loving and devoted husband Richard McCracken of Lebanon, son James R. McCracken (Debbie) of Dayton and daughter Janice L. (Dennis) Holland of Ky., three grandchildren, Shelli Holland, Tricia Wilkerson and Jennifer Brantley and five great-grand children Kaitlynne, Allison, Michael, Matthew and Ashlyn. Visitation and funeral service was held Wednesday, October 28, 2009, all at the Stine & Kilburn Funeral Home, Lebanon with Pastor Alan Carroll officiating. Burial was in the Miami Valley Memorial Gardens, Centerville. The family requests memorials to your charity of choice.* **Hamilton Journal-News**, 29 Oct 2009.

Notes for John Phillip BEHAN #701
Jones notes: "resides (1972) at Maplelawn Village, Kokomo, IN"
Birth: Ohio birth record "John Phillip Behan, male, b. 15 Nov 1917 at 5107 Hunter St., Norwood, Hamilton, OH (parents res.); parents: John Joseph Behan (white; b. Co. Roscommon, Ireland; age 23, machinist); Minnie Hicks (white; b. Utopia, Clermont Co, OH; age 24)"

Marriage: (1) Dorothy Cloetill Ray. Campbell Co, KY marriage record; "John P. Behan (19, b. Norwood, Hamilton, OH; res. Madeira?, OH; landscaper; parents: John and Minnie Behan) to Dorothy Ray (18, b. Cincinnati, Hamilton, OH; parents: Monroe? Ray and ___ Murphy); both single; married at Newport, Campbell, KY, by G B Trainer, Methodist minister" (2) Maybelle Stackhouse - indicated as wife on his Indiana death certificate.
Death: Indiana death certificate - J. Phillip Behan, male; d. 23 Nov 1981 at Peru, Miami, IN; b. 15 Nov 1917 in OH; res. R R #3, Kokomo, Miami, IN; trailer park manager; parents: John J. Behan, Minnie Hicks; Maybelle Stackhouse (wife) was informant; bur. Mt. Hope Cemetery, Peru, IN."

Notes for Dorothy Cloetill RAY #701s
Birth: Personal knowledge of Laura (Behan) Zink (10 Jun 1991 letter to Norman Zezula)
Death: Phillip Behan died in 1981; his Indiana death certificate listed a second wife. Also, personal knowledge of Laura (Behan) Zink (10 Jun 1991 letter to Norman Zezula)
Obituary: *Kokomo Tribune*, 4 Nov 1974. *Mrs. Phillip Behan. Mrs. Dorothy C. Behan, 56, 415 Chatau Way, died at 2 p.m. Sunday in St Francis Hospital, following an extended illness. Born Feb 4 1918 in Cincinnati, OH, she was the daughter of Monroe and Mary (Murphy) Ray. She was married to Phillip Behan, who survives. She and her husband had operated a trailer park in Kokomo. Surviving with the husband are four daughters, Mrs. Richard Lybrook of Kokomo, Mrs Larry Thompson of Bunder Hill, Mrs Phillip McKibben of Kirklin and Mrs Keith Marks of Peru; four brothers and four sisters; 19 grandchildren and one great grand child. Burial in Washington Park East Cemetery.*

Notes for Dorothy Ann BEHAN #702
Birth: Ohio birth certificate - Dorothy Ann Behan, female, b. 10 Jan 1919 at 5107 Hunter, Norwood, Ham., OH (parents residence); parents: John Joseph Behan (white, 24, b. Ireland, a glazier); Minnie Hicks (white, 25, b. OH)
Marriage: Personal knowledge of Dorothy (Behan) Zezula
Jones notes: "reside (1972) at 2272 Canonita Dr, La Habra, CA 90631; he served in US Navy"

Notes for Laura Margaret BEHAN #703
Birth: Ohio birth certificate - "Laura Margaret Behan, female, b. 10 Mar 1921 at 4816 Oak St., Norwood, Hamilton Co, OH (at parents res.); parents: John Joseph Behan (white, 26, glazier); Minnie Clara Hicks (white, 27)"
Marriage: Hamilton Co, OH marriage certificate: "John W. Zink Jr.(22 on 4/5/1943; b. Cincinnati, Hamilton Co, OH) to Laura Behan (22 on 3/10/1943; b. Norwood, Hamilton Co, OH) on 18 Dec 1943 by Wilbur A. Vorhis, minister"
Jones notes: "Resides (1972) at 10948 Fernhill Dr, Cincinnati, OH 45241 (Sharonville)"
Death: Laura M. Zink, b. 10 Mar 1921; d. 27 Feb 2004; age 82; Cincinnati, Hamilton, OH; card issued Ohio; #283-16-8568. Social Security Death Index <rootsweb.com>

Notes for Donald James 'Bud' BEHAN #704
Jones notes: "resides (1972) at 827 Larchview, Cincinnati 45236 (Dillonvale)
Birth: Ohio birth certificate "Donald James Behan, male, b. 6 Jun 1923 at 1964 Ross St., Norwood, Ham., OH (at parents res.); parents: John Behan (white, 29 b. Ireland, glazier), Minnie Hicks (white, 25, b. OH)"
Marriage: Personal knowledge of Dorothy (Luehrmann) Behan--letter to Norman Zezula (10 Jun 1991)

Notes for Marjorie Claire "Margie" BEHAN #706
Birth: OH birth certificate "Marjorie Claire Behan, female, b. 25 Feb 1928 in Norwood, Ham., OH (no street given); parents: John Joseph Behan (white, 34, b. Ireland, glazier); Minnie C. Hicks (white, 34, b. OH). Both are residents of 5312 Section Ave in Norwood."

Marriage: Personal knowledge of Marjorie (Behan) Rogers (letter 12 Jun 1991 to Norman Zezula) Jones notes: "resides(1972) 2854 Brookwood Dr, Orange Park, FL 32073"
Death: Marjorie C Rogers, b. 25 Feb 1928; d. 13 Aug 2009; age 81; Orange Park, Clay, FL; card issued Ohio.

Notes for Dion HICKS #708
Death: Dion F Hicks, b. 17 Jul 1929; d. 6 Apr 2007; age 77; Cincinnati, Hamilton, OH; card issued Ohio; #268-26-1480. Social Security Death Index <rootsweb.com>

Notes for Daniel HICKS #709
Death: Daniel R Hicks, b. 6 Dec 1934; d. 1 Jun 1996; age 61; place not specified; card issued Ohio; #280-28-9163. Social Security Death Index <rootsweb.com>.
Ohio Death Index give place of death as Hamilton, Butler Co, OH; married, 2 years college; Army service; occ: science technician.

Notes for Archie Milton ROSS #711
Military: World War I Draft Registration Cards, 1917-1918 [Ancestry.com] Archie Milton Ross, age 32, b. 22 Sep 1885; occ: pump man - Douglas Co, Cedar Rapids, IA; relative: mother, Mary Frances Ross, Keokuk, IA; tall, slender, blue eyes, brown hair; defect: loss of one eye.
Census
   1920 Oakland, Alameda, CA, p. 15B. Archie M Ross 34. MO/OH/OH, house painter; Marnie B Ross 32, IA/OH/IL
   1930 Keokuk, Lee, IA, p. 22A. Archie Ross 45, MO/OH/OH, no occ, m. age 34; Mame Ross 47, IA/OH/MO; Milton Ross 9, IA/MO/IA; Francis Ross 67, mother, OH/OH/OH, widowed.
   1915 Iowa State Census: Keokuk, Lee, IA, unp. Archie M. Ross, 30, MO, single, occ: odd jobs; in IA 8 years.
   1925 Cedar Rapids, Linn Co, IA, p. Archie M. Ross, 39, Mayme Ross 37; Milton Ross 4. Archie's parents: Geo A. Ross & Frances Houser, both b. OH. Maymie's parents: Oliver L. Conn? b. OH & Emma Davis, b. MO. Archie & Maymie married in California.

Notes for Maymie CONN #711s
Census: 1910 Keokuk Ward 5, Lee, IA, p. 1B. Oliver S Conn 60, contractor - house, OH/PA/MD; Emma N Conn 51, MO/Eng/OH; Maymie B Conn 28, stenographer - lumber office, IA/OH/MO; Myrtle B Conn 20; Oliver G Conn 16; Davis S Conn 11; Dennis Ryan 60, boarder, Ireland.

Notes for Alma J. ROSS #713
Marriage: Clarence Harrison Mars, b. 1889 Lisbon, ND; Age: 27; Bride: Alma Imogene Ross, b. 1893 Downing, MO, age: 23; Marriage: 23 Dec 1916, Burlington, IA; Groom's parents: Rufus E. Mars / Mary Ellen Lieady; Bride's parents: George Allen Ross / Mary Francis Hansen. Iowa Marriages, 1809-1992 <familysearch.org>
Census
   1920 Keokuk Ward 2, Lee, IA, p. 8A. Geo A Ross 58, miller - cereal plant; Mary F Ross 56; Clarence H Mars 31, son in law, ND, plate maker - dental lab; Alma J Mars 26; Clayton R Mars 2 9/12, IA; Wm C Ross 24, machinist - rug factory; Walter H Ross 18, laborer - govt ?lock?
   1930 Keokuk, Lee, IA, p. 8A. Clarence Mars 41, ND/PA/PA, operator - dental laboratory; Alma Mars 36, MO/OH/OH; Clanton Mars 12, IA. M. 13 years.

Notes for Clarence Harrison MARS #713s
Military: World War I Draft Registration Cards, 1917-1918 [Ancestry.com] Clarence Harrison Mars, age 28, b. 14 Mar 1889, Sisbon, ND. occ: mechanical dentist - Tri state Dental Sales, Keokuk; married; crippled right hand; med height, slender, hazel eyes, brown hair. Regis: Lee Co, IA 3 Jun 1917

Notes for William Clifford ROSS #714
Military: World War I Draft Registration Cards, 1917-1918 [Ancestry.com] William Cliford Ross, age 21, b. 10 Oct 1895, Down, MO; res: Keokuk, IA, single, emp: labor, J. B. Humbinger? Co. Short, med build, blue eyes, brown hair. Regis: Lee Co, IA, 5 Jun 1917
Census: 1930 South Sugar Creek, Randolph, MO, p. 10B. William C Ross 37, MO/OH/OH, proprietor - service station; Pauline Ross 29, MO/MO/MO; Betty E Ross 1, MO.
Marriage: W. C. Ross, m. 7 Mar 1928, Moberly, Randolph Co, MO to Pauline Walden. Both over 21 and of Moberly, MO.

Notes for Pauline WALDEN #714s
Census: 1920 Moberly Ward 3, Randolph, MO, p. 16A. Herbert Walden 47, machinist foreman - railroad shop; Julia Walden 40; Pauline Walden 19, MO/IL/MO; George Walden 16; Otto Moeller 60; Carl Moeller 27

Notes for Ruby BROADWELL #717
Jones notes: "m. -?-- Ross; resided (1929) Ames IA"
Census: 1930 Kansas City, Jackson, MO, p. 3A. Orville P Clark 29, KS/MO/KS, engineer - power & light co; Ruby A Clark 24, MO/OH/MO; Orville P Clark 5, IA.
Death: Ruby A Clark, b. 7 Jun 1906, Kirksville, MO; d. 1 Jan 1963, San Antonio, Bexar, TX, Age: 56; Married; Father: Lindley Broadwell; Mother: Mae Zimmerman; Occ: Housewife; Res: Hill Country Village, Bexar, TX; Cemetery: Ft Sam Houston National, Ft Sam Houston, Bexar, TX; 4 Jan 1963. Texas Deaths, 1890-1976 <pilot.familysearch.org>

Notes for Orville P. CLARK #171s
Death: Orville P Clark; single; death: 30 Nov 1972. Bexar, TX. Texas Death Index, 1964-1998 <pilot.familysearch.org>
Death: Orville Clark, b. 23 Apr 1900; d. Nov 1972; age 72; San Antonio, Bexar, TX; card issued Minnesota; #469-20-1065. Social Security Death Index <rootsweb.com>

Notes for Chester Allen BROADWELL #720
Military: WW I Draft Registration: gives name as Chester Allen Broadwell, age 24, date & place of birth, married, tall, slender, blue eyes, lt brown hair. Registered 5 Jun 1917.
Census:
  1920 Prairie, Schuyler, MO, p. 2A. Chester Broadwell 27, day labor; Henritta Broadwell 26, MO/Ger/Ger
  1930 Prairie, Schuyler, MO. Chester Broadway, 37, mechanic - garage; Henreitta 36, MO/Ger/MO; Bernie, 10, dau, MO; Herbert P 6; Ray C 2 5/12. Children b. MO. M. 15 yrs.
Marriage: 25 Oct 1914, Queen City, Schuyler Co, MO. Chester Allen Broadwell to Hemietla May Bergman; both of Queen City. Missouri Marriage Records, 1805-2002 [Ancestry.com]
Marriage2: 10 Jun 1951; La Belle, Lewis Co, MO; Chester A Broadwell of Greentop to Ora Naylor of Kirksville. Missouri Marriage Records, 1805-2002 [Ancestry.com]
Death: Chester Broadwell, b. 13 Oct 1892; d. Mar 1965, #496-12-6194; Last Residence: Kirksville, Adair Co, MO. Social Security Death Index

Burial: Coffey Cemetery - Located South of Downing, MO on Rt. A, Schuyler Co. [freepages.genealogy.rootsweb.com]

   Chester Broadwell   13 Oct 1892 - 08 Mar 1965;   h/o Ora M Broadwell
   Ora M. Broadwell   16 Apr 1894 - 13 Jul 1966;   w/o Chester Broadwell
   Sarah M Broadwell   1867-1936   Mother

Notes for Harry BROADWELL #722

Military: WW I Draft Registration gives name as Harry Broadwell, age 21, date & place of birth, single, medium height, medium build, black eyes, black hair. Registered 5 Jun 1917.
Census: 1930 Prairie, Schuyler Co, MO, p. 7A. Harry Broadwell 37, farmer, MO/OH/KY; Myrtle Broadwell 25, MO/MO/MO; Inez Broadwell 6; Raymond Broadwell 5; married 7 years
Burial: Coffey Cemetery - Downing MO
Harry Broadwell   4 Nov 1895 - 2 Oct 1960; h/o Myrtle Broadwell; MO PVT US ARMY WWI
Paul Eugene Broadwell   6 Oct 1927 - 1 Dec 1928; s/o Harry & Myrtle Broadwell

Notes for Myrtle ALDRIDGE #722s

Maiden name from death certificate of son, Paul Eugene, Dec 1928.
Death: Myrtle Broadwell, b. 23 May 1903; d. Jun 1976; age 73; Downing, Schuyler, MO; issued Missouri; #487-48-6577 Social Security Death Index [Ancestry.com]

Notes for Orma BROADWELL #723

Marriage: Orma M Broadwell, 20; b. abt 1898; Marriage: 12 Apr 1918, Schuyler Co, MO; Spouse: Ollie M McElroy, 22. Missouri Marriage Records, 1805-2002 [Ancestry.com]
Census:
   1920 Mount Pleasant, Scotland, MO, p. 1B. Ollie McElroy 24, farmer, MO/MO/MO; Orma McElroy 22, MO/OH/KY; Hazel McElroy 10/12, MO.
   1930 Wyaconda, Clark, MO, p. 3B. Ollie W McElroy 34, farmer; Orma N McElroy 32; Hazel E McElroy 11; Helen I McElroy 10; Marvin N McElroy 8; Lester L McElroy 6; Wilma L McElroy 3 5/12

Notes for Ollie Willis MCELROY #723s

Information on Ollie's birth, death & parents from Ancestry.com site of Julie McElroy "August Julius Johann Mewes". She adds more children: Ralph 1934-2002; Bob 1936-2002, perhaps others who are still living. Undocumented.
Census: 1910 Independence, Schuyler, MO, p. 5B. Oscar S McElroy 37, farmer; Louesa McElroy 31; Ollie W McElroy 14; Cecil B McElroy 10; Mendon E McElroy 7; Haney L McElroy 2
Military: World War I Draft Registration Cards, 1917-1918 [Ancestry.com] Ollie Willis McElroy, age 21, b. 24 Jun 1895, Independence, MO; Res: Downing, Schuyler Co, MO; farmer for Oscar McElroy; claims exemption - "yes, bad"; med height, slender, light eyes & hair. Regis: 5 Jun 1917, Independence, Schuyler Co, MO.

Notes for William Harold BROADWELL #726

Census: 1930 Clovis, Fresno, CA, p. 14A. William H Brodwell 28, AR/OH/IL, painter - buildings; Barbara Brodwell 29, VT/VT/VT; Allen Bradwell, 0/12, CA [census taken 12 Apr 1930]
Death: William Harold Broadwell, b. 18 Oct 1901, Arkansas; d. 13 Nov 1989, Fresno, CA. age 88, Mother's Maiden Name: Wilson. California Death Index [archives.com]

Notes for Barbara LAIRD #726s

Death: Barbara Lucille Broadwell, b. 7 Oct 1901, Vermont; d. 17 Feb 1994, Fresno, CA; Age: 93; Mother's Maiden Name: Conner; Father's Last Name: Laird. California Death Index [archives.com]

Notes for Beulah Imogene BROADWELL #731

Marriage: George Mckenzie to Imogene Broadwell; marriage date: 10 Aug 1920, Phoenix, Maricopa, AZ. Arizona Marriages, 1888-1908 <familysearch.org>

Census: 1930 Turlock, Stanislaus, CA, p. 223. George W Mckenzie 30, AZ/MO/MO, farm labor - general farm; Beulah I Mckenzie 29, AK/OH/AK; George E Mckenzie 8; Layton A Mckenzie 4 10/12; Charlotte B Mckenzie 2. Children b. CA. Married age 20 / 18. Living next to Imogene's parents.

Death: Beulah Imogene McKenzie [Beulah Imogene Broadwell] ; #572017340; b. 19 Oct 1901, Arkansas; d. 6 Nov 1984, Stanislaus Co, CA. Mother's Maiden Name: Clark; Father's Surname: Broadwell. California Death Index, 1940-1997 [Ancestry.com]

Notes for George MCKENZIE #731s

Death: George W Mckenzie; b. 10 Feb 1900, Arizona; d. 30 Sep 1962, Stanislaus, CA; Age: 62; Mother's Maiden Name: Willis. California Death Index [Archives.com]

Notes for Eunice Dale BROADWELL #732

Census: 1930 Oakdale, Stanislaus Co, CA. Robert B Sauls 35, OK/US/US, salesman - washing machines; Eunice D Sauls 24, AK, age at 1st marriage - 14; Robert D Sauls 8; A Fay Sauls 6; Jack N Sauls 6/12. Children b. CA.

Death: Eunice Dale Kooy [Eunice Dale Broadwell]; #553561494, b. 15 Dec 1905, Arkansas; d. 15 Dec 1995, Stanislaus CA; Mother's Maiden Name: Clark; Father's Surname: Broadwell. California Death Index [Ancestry.com]

Notes for Robert B. SAULS #732s

Military: U.S. World War II Draft Registration Cards, 1942; Robert Boyer Sauls; b. 5 Apr 1895; Winnewood, OK; Res: Contra Costa, CA; Contact: Esther A. Sauls, Pittsburgh, CA.

Death: Robert B Sauls; Pfc: US Army World War I; b. 6 Apr 1895; d. 17 Jun 1965; Service Start Date: 26 Jun 1918; Interment Date: 22 Jun 1965; Cemetery: Golden Gate National Cemetery, Section I Site 4415-F. U.S. Veterans Gravesites, ca.1775-2006; [Ancestry.com]

Notes for Garrit KOOY #732s2

Military: World War I Draft Registration. Gerret Kooy, Kings Co, CA, b. 22 Nov 1895, Harlem, Holland; has 1st papers, farmer, single, tall, med. Build, grey eyes, brown hair. June 1917, Kings Co, CA.

Military: World War II (1942) Draft Registration. Garrit Kooy, age 46, b. 22 Nov 1895, Harlem, Holland. Contact Person: Lionel Broadwell, Modesto, CA

Death: Gerrit Kooy, #549055480; b. 22 Nov 1895, Other Country; d. 10 Jan 1991, Alameda, CA; Mother's Maiden Name: Gortzak. California Death Index, 1940-1997. [Ancestry.com]

Immigration: New York Passenger Lists, 1820-1957. Gerrit Kooy; Arrival Date: 22 Mar 1911; b. abt 1896, Haarlemmermeer, Holland, Netherlands; Age: 15; Dutch; Port of Departure: Rotterdam; Arrival: New York, New York; Ship: Potsdam

Notes for Romba BROADWELL #733

Census: 1930 Sacramento, Sacramento Co, CA, p. 9A. Harry A Jones 21, KS, inspector - state agriculture; Romba L Jones 32, AR; Harriet L Jones 2 4/12, CA; Kent H Jones 4/12, CA; Cecil L Broadwell 21, CA, bro-in-law, clerk - grocery.

Death: Romba Jones, b. 1 Aug 1907; d. Dec 1972; age 65; San Jose, Santa Clara, CA; issued California; #572-14-9843

Notes for Harry JONES #733s
Death: May be Harry V Jones, b. 15 Jul 1912, Kansas; d. 27 Nov1970, Santa Clara, CA; Age: 58. California Death Index [archives.com]   Note: There are several Harry Jones in the CA Death Index of about the right age, but this is the only one born in Kansas.

Notes for Karylton Victor BROADWELL #735
Military: Karylton V Broadwell, b. 1920; res: Stanislaus, CA; enlisted 10 Mar 1942, Merced Army Air Field, CA; Branch: Air Corps, private. Educ: 1 year college; civil occ: author, editor and reporter, married, 71" tall; 180 lbs. U.S. World War II Army Enlistment Records, 1938-1946 [Ancestry.com]
Divorce: Karylton V Broadwell vs Althea E; Stanislaus, CA. 21 Sep 1983. California Divorce Index, 1966-1984 [Ancestry.com]
Death: Karylton V. Broadwell, #567-07-2214; b. 10 Jan 1920; d. 29 Dec 1994, Ceres, Stanislaus, CA. Social Security Death Index

Notes for Althea Ethlyn PARRISH #735s
Obituary: *Althea Broadwell: A funeral service was held Friday at the Colonial Chapel of Franklin & Downs for Althea Ethlyn Parrish Broadwell, 85, of Ceres. She died Saturday, Feb. 7, 2004 at Emanuel Medical Center in Turlock. Burial was private.*
Born July 23, 1918, Mrs. Broadwell was a native of San Jose and lived in Ceres for 84 years. She was a caseworker for the Stanislaus County Department of Employment Development for 20 years. She was a member of Trinity Presbyterian Church in Modesto, the Thursday Bridge Club (since 1949) and PEO Chapter B.H. She enjoyed painting, reading and gardening.
She leaves behind two children, Sheri Massner of Ceres and Gail Ceciliani of Modesto; and three grandchildren and four great-grandchildren. She was preceded in death by her husband and one grandchild. Remembrances may be sent to the Arthritis Foundation, 3040 Explorer Drive, Suite 1, Sacramento, CA 95827. **Ceres Courier News**, Thursday, February 19, 2004

Notes for Effie Blanche WOOD #737
Jones notes: "Resides (1972) at 501 Notingham Dr, Richardson, TX"
Jones notes give name, marriage date
Census: 1930 Jellico, Campbell, TN, p. 15A. Lloyd Baird 33, comptroller - wholesale hardware, TN/TN/TN; Effie Baird 33; Glenna Baird 4 5/12; Merrie Wood 22, sister in law, stenographer - dry goods store.

Notes for Walter Lloyd BAIRD #737s
Not found in WW I Draft Registration 1917-18
Jones notes give first name, birth date, spouse, marriage date
Census: 1920 Jellico, Campbell, TN, p. 13A. J D Baird 57, president - Union Bank; Ella Baird 49; Jessie Lee Baird 20; Loyed Baird 23, salesman - hardware; Robert Baird 16; Eleanor Baird 10
No death information found

Notes for Wilbur Lewis MCMAHON #740
Jones notes: "Resides (1972) at 7225 Hosbrook Rd, Cincinnati, OH"
Census:
- 1920 May be the Wilmer McMahon, 22, living in Cincinnati, Ward 18; a lodger, stenographer - paper factory.
- 1930 Mount Healthy, Hamilton, OH, p. 5B. Wilber Mcmahan 33, editor - newspaper; Myrl Mcmahan 30; Theodore Mcmahan 7, IN/OH/OH; James Mcmahan 3, OH.

Marriage: Groom: Wilbur L. Mcmahan, b.1896 OH; Age: 25; Bride: Myrl M. Edwards, b. 1899 OH; Age: 22; Marriage: 30 Jul 1921, Hamilton Co, OH; Groom's parents: Lewis Mcmahan; Maude Jones; Bride's parents: Stanley Edwards; Anna Livingston. OH Marriages, 1800-1958 <pilot.familysearch.org>
No WW I Draft Registration found.
Death: Wilber L McMahan, b. 29 Jul 1896, OH; Res: Hamilton Co, OH; d. 27 Jan 1990, Deaconess Hospital, Cincinnati, OH; Age: 93; Widowed; 2 years college; Occ: Newspaper publishing and printing. Ohio Deaths, 1908-1932, 1938-1944, and 1958-2007 [Ancestry.com]

Notes for Myrl M. EDWARDS #740s
Census: 1900 Laura, Miami, OH, p. 2B. Stanley D Edwards 23, OH, barber; Anna Edwards 24; Myrl Edwards 1, May 1899; Rachel C Livingston 56, m-in-law; Jessie Livingston 14, s-in-law.
Death: Myrl Edwards Mcmahan, b. 25 May 1899, Madeira, Laura, OH; d. 16 Sep 1986, Hamilton, OH; Burial: 18 Sep 1986 Evendale, OH; Age: 87; Occ: Homemaker; Married; Spouse: Wilber L. Mcmahan; parents: Stanley D. Edwards; Anna Livingston. Ohio Deaths and Burials, 1854-1997 <familysearch.org>

Notes for Lola Gayle MCMAHAN#742
Jones notes: "Resides (1972) at 7225 Hosbrook Rd, Cincinnati, OH"
Census: 1930 Illini, Macon, IL, p. 4B. Frank Garrison 31, farmer; Lola G Garrison 29; Mary Luis Garrison 7; Wayne F Garrison 5

Notes for Dewey Frank GARRISON #742s
Military: World War I Draft Registration Cards, 1917-1918 [Ancestry.com]. Dewey Franklin Garrison, age 19, b. 6 Dec 1898; farmer for Mort Garrison; Res: W. Union, Adams, OH; contact: Mary Ann Garrison, tall, slender, brown eyes & hair. Registered: Sep 12 ___.
Death: Dewey Franklin Garrison, d. 30 Oct 1948, Winchester Twp, Adams, OH; b. 06 Dec 1898; age: 49 years 10 months 24 days; Married; farmer; Spouse: Gale Garrison; Father: Bengeman Garrison; Mother: Mary Ann Coppich. Ohio Deaths 1908-1953 <familysearch.org>

Notes for Sarah Elizabeth MCMAHAN #743
Jones notes: "Resides (1972) Summer: So. Dennis, MA 02660; Winter: 1922 Silver Springs Blvd, Ocala FL 32670"
Information: "I found your website while searching for ancestors of my father, Jack E Lucas of Elyria, OH. My mother was Sarah Elizabeth McMahan Lucas, the fourth and last child of Effie Maud Jones and Lewis Ozi McMahan. She was born in Monterey OH (her mother died in childbirth) in December 1909 and died in Ocala, FL July 27. 1978"
Census: 1930 Dayton, Montgomery, OH, p. 19B. Sarah E. McMahan, lodger, YWCA, 21, single, stenographer - lumber shipping yard.
Death: Sarah M Lucas; d. 27 Jul 1978, Marion Co, FL, age 68; b. 20 Dec 1909. Florida Death Index, 1877-1998 [Ancestry.com]

Notes for Jack E. LUCAS #743s
Census: 1910 Elyria Ward 4, Lorain, OH, p. 11B. Jonas A Lucas 37, Can, plumber - water; Ida Lucas 36; Russell A Lucas 11; Jack E Lucas 7, OH/Can/OH; Maxine J Lucas 2

Notes for Hannah Elizabeth MYLER #744
Jones notes: "Resides (1972) at 199 E. Elm St, Sabina, OH 45169"
Census: 1930 Sabins, Clinton, OH. Thomas G Foster 24, proprietor - dept store; Elisabeth H. 22; Joann E. 1 4/12. [Indexed on Ancestry.com as Fortes] Living near Elizabeth's mother, Lola (Jones) Myler Daily.

Death: Elizabeth H Foster [Elizabeth H. Myler]; b. 18 Sep 1907, OH; Res: Allen Co, OH; d. 6 Feb 2007; Age: 99; Father's Surname: Myler; Widowed; Homemaker, Own Home. Ohio Deaths, 1908-1932, 1938-1944, and 1958-2007 [Ancestry.com]

Notes for Thomas Gavin FOSTER #744s

Census: 1910 Williamsburg, Clermont, OH, p. 1B. Theophano G Foster 55, retail merchant - dry goods; Jannie L Foster 49; Edith G Foster 22; Isabel A Foster 19; Addaling L Foster 17; John W Foster 15; Dortha M Foster 12; Thomas G Foster 4

Death: Thomas G Foster, b. 1906; Residence: Clinton Co, OH; d. 3 Mar 1968, Home, Clinton Co, OH; Age: 62; Married. Ohio Deaths, 1908-1932, 1938-1944, and 1958-2007 [Ancestry.com]

Notes for Orville William JONES #747

Jones notes: "Resides (1972) 460 Neville-Penn Rd, Felicity, OH 45120; 83rd Naval CB's, WW II" Compiler of the manuscript upon which this book is based. Also compiled a book on the Jones family.

Census: 1930 Cincinnati Ward 2, Hamilton, OH, p.232A. Guy O Jones 48, conductor - street railroad; Lora Jones 40; Paul Jones 23, salesman - lumber co; Orville Jones 21, city s___; Hilda Jones 16.

No death information found

Notes for Ruth D. NEVILLE #747s

Census: 1930 Sidney, Shelby, OH, p. 10B. Charles G Neville 45, comm salesman - cigar factory; Etta Neville 44; Frank W Neville 20; Ruth D Neville 16; Richard H Neville 12; Kate Stephens 77, mother in law, widow.

Death: Ruth D Jones [Ruth D Neville], b. 18 Sep 1913, Darke Co, OH; d. 4 Jan 1993, Hospice of Cincinnati, Cincinnati, Hamilton, OH. Age: 79; #288-46-6752; Father's Surname: Neville; Mother's Maiden Name: Stephens; Married; Education: 12; Housewife/Homemaker. Ohio Deaths, 1908-1932, 1938-1944, and 1958-2007 [Ancestry.com]

Notes for Calvin Marcellus BECKELHIMER #750

Jones notes: "Resided (1972) at 512 Western Cir, Mason OH

Death: SS Death Index gives death as Sept 1977; res: Mason (Warren) OH.

Ohio Death Index gives death as "out of state".

Notes for Sarah Blanche MONCE #750s

John Tippet says "daughter of John Monce and Electra Hartman". Tippet Home Page <www.johntippet.com>

Census: 1920 Union, Butler, OH, p. 12A. John Monce 52, farmer; Electa S Monce 43; Isaac T Monce 13; William H Monce 11; Russel H Monce 7; Sarah B Monce 5; Ethel I Monce 2 3/12. All b. OH/OH/OH.

No definitive death information found. May be the S B Beckelhimer, b. 1915, Warren, OH; d. 7 Aug 1986, Cincinnati, Hamilton, OH on SS death Index.

Notes for Harry Raymond BECKELHIMER #751

Jones notes:"US Army, WW II"

Death: Harry R Beckelhimer, b. 1914; Res: Brown Co, OH; death: 6 Feb 1971, University Hospital, Cincinnati, OH. Ohio Deaths, 1908-1932, 1938-1944, and 1958-2002. [Ancestry.com]

Notes for Ralph Charles JONES #760

Jones notes: "Resided at Rt 1, Mt Orab, OH"

Census: 1920 Covington Ward 6, Kenton, KY, p. 10A. Ralph Jones 24, OH/OH/OH, time keeper - Gas Co; Grace Jones 25; KY/KY/KY Ralph W Jones 1 4/12, KY; Anna Walthall 34, roomer, Ky/KY/KY, clerk - publishing house?

    1930 not found

Military: World War I Draft Registration Cards, 1917-1918 [Ancestry.com] Ralph C Jones, age 21, b. 24 Jan 1896, Cincinnati, OH; res: Covington, Kenton, KY; occ: timekeeper - National Candy Co; married; tall, slender, brown eyes & hair; regis: Covington, Kenton Co, KY. 5 Jun 1917.
Military: World War II Draft Registration Cards 1942 [beta.familysearch.org] Ralph C. Jones, age 46, b. 24 Jan 1896, Cincinnati, OH; res: Mt Orab, Brown Co, OH; contact: Grace E. Jones, same residence; 5' 10", 165 pounds, brown eyes & hair, light complexion; no disabilities. Regis: 27 Apr 1942, Brown Co, OH.

Notes for Leta Grace WILLIAMS #764
Jones notes: "Resides (1972) at 6434 Monalisa Ct, Cincinnati OH (Mt Airy) 45239."
Census
   1920 Norwood Ward 3, Hamilton, OH, p. 2A. Tate Steele 28, KY/KY/KY, machinist - machine co; Leta G Steele 21, TN/VA/OH, asst office manager - ice co.
   1930 Cincinnati, Hamilton, OH, 3B. Tate Steele 38, machinist - lumber co; Lela G Steele 31; Shirley J Steele 8; Charles W Steele 5

Notes for Tate STEELE #764s
Jones notes: "He served in WWI in Europe - deceased by 1972."
Census: 1900 Parmleysville, Wayne, KY, p. 13B. John W Steele 38, Jan 1862, merchant; Elzie Steele 38, Aug 1861, m. 18 years, 6 ch/ 5 living; Camely Steele 15; George F Steele 11; Tate Steele 8, Jul 1891; Obie Steele 5; Gertie Steele 3. All KY/KY/KY
Military: World War I Draft Registration Cards, 1917-1918 [Ancestry.com] Tate Steele, age 26, b. 12 Jul 1891, Griffin, KY; res: Bent, Pulaski, KY; farmer; single; med height & build; brown eyes & hair; regis: 5 Jun 1917, Bent, Pulaski, KY.
Military: Ohio Soldiers in WWI, 1917-1918 [Ancestry.com] Tate Steele; Age: 26 5/12 ; b. abt 1891, Griffin, KY; Res: Norwood, OH; Enlistment Date: 13 Dec 1917, Fort Thomas, KY; Regular Army; 10 Co, Coast Defenses, San Francisco, Calif to 26 Jan 1918; Battery F 62, Artillery, Coast Artillery Corps to Discharge; Private American Expeditionary Forces, 14 July 1918 to 19 Feb 1919. Honorable discharge 10 March 1919.
Military: Ohio Military Men, 1917-18 [Ancestry.com] Tate Steele; Serial Number: 823987; Res: Norwood, O.; Enlistment Division: Regular Army, Enlistment: Fort Thomas, Ky. 13 Dec 1917; Birth Place: Griffin, KY; Assigns Comment: 10 Co Coast Defenses San Francisco Calif to 26 Jan 1918; Battery F 62 Artillery Coast Artillery Corps to Discharge; Private, American Expeditionary Forces 14 July 1918 to 19 Feb 1919. Honorable discharge 10 March 1919.
Death: No death information found.

Notes for Rosslyn Earl MELVIN #769
Census: 1930 Cincinnati, Hamilton, OH, p. 31A. Ross E Melvin 27, butcher - grocery; Mabel V Melvin 23, OH/OH/KY; William E Melvin 2; Violet M Melvin 6/12. Others OH/OH/OH. Married ages 20 / 17.
Death: Ross Melvin, d. 1 Jun 1941, Cincinnati, Hamilton, OH; b. 13 Apr 1901, Cincinnati, OH; Age: 40 years 1 month; Married; Burial: 4 Jun 1941, Laurel Cem; Spouse: Ruby Townsend Melvin; Father: Samuel Melvin, b. OH; Mother: Grace Jones, b. OH. Cause of death: internal injuries, parachute jump. Ohio Deaths, 1908-1953 <pilot.familysearch.org>

Notes for Carl Starner PUGH #770
Jones notes: "Resides (1972) at 1198 Hempstead Dr, Cincinnati, OH 45231; m1 Lottie Garten; m2 Helen ?-; m3 Margaret Jenkins - children by 3rd marriage"

Birth: Carl Starner Pugh, 4 Mar 1908, Galion, Crawford, OH; Father: Joseph Warren Pugh, b. Bellfountain, OH, age 29; Mother: Stella Blanche Jones, b. Utopia, Ohio. Ohio Births and Christenings, 1821-1962 <pilot.familysearch.org>

Notes for Julia M. JONES #771

Jones notes: "Resides (1972) at 4734 Eastern Ave, Cincinnati, OH".

Census:

- 1920 Pierce, Clermont, OH, p. 2A. Alfred Jones 12 and Julia Jones 13 were with William H. 74 & Sallie Simmons 67, listed as niece and nephew. Brother Roy Jones, 11, was 5 houses away as a boarder with George W. and Zouella Snider. Leona Jones, 10, was with Elijah and Hattie Reeves, listed as grandniece.
- 1930 Cincinnati, Hamilton, OH, p. 5B. Archie Lanter 26, carpenter helper - city; Julia M Lanter 23; Virginia L Lanter 1 10/12. All OH/OH/OH.

Notes for Georgia Gladys CLARK #784

Census: 1930 Georgia and children not found; Delbert was in Marin Co, CA - Fort Barry Coast Guard.

Notes for Delbert Dewite BOSSINGHAM #784s

Not found on WW I Draft Registration 1917-18 or WW II 1942 registration.

Census

- 1920 Leith, Grant, ND, p. 10A. Charlie D Bossingham 46, laborer; Lillian M 40; Delbert D 17; Florrence L 15; Merril M 12; Thelma J 10; Lester 7; Herman M Bossingham 43
- 1930 Marin Co, CA, p. 4A. Fort Barry Coast Guard Station. Delbert Dewite Bossingham, 29, b. IA, surfer - Coast Guard; m. at age 23.

Military: Delbert DeWitt Bossingham; Birth: 22 Apr 1900 Algonia, IA; Occ: laborer; Comment: enlisted in the Navy at Omaha, NE, on July 19, 1918; served at Naval Training Station, San Francisco, Calif., to Nov. 11, 1918. Grades: Apprentice Seaman, 44 days; Seaman 2nd Class, 71 days. Discharged at Puget Sound, WA, on June 9, 1919, as a Seaman. North Dakota Military Men, 1917-1918 [Ancestry.com]

Information: An Ancestry One World Tree <Lwells22> gives Delbert's parents as Charles D. Bossingham & Lillian Mae Baldwin of Wayne, Wayne Co, NE; his birth in Algona, Kossuth, IA; his second marriage to Living Carlson on 11 Feb 1968, in Winnamucca, NV.

Info: Delbert's sister Florence married Roscoe Clark, sister of Delbert's wife, Georgia.

Notes for Cecil Emmett CLARK #785

Census: 1930 Valley View, Grant, ND, p. 1A. E Cecil Clark 28, farm laborer, married age 21; L Amy 27, IA; A Lara 6, ID; B Bonna 3 5/12, ND; M Avie 1 8/12, ND.

Death: Cecil E Clark, #546268496; b. 27 Apr 1901 Nebraska; d. 21 Jun 1970, Contra Costa, CA. California Death Index, 1940-1997 [Archives.com]

Notes for Amy Luella CLARK #786s

Death: Amy L Clark; b. Aug 7, 1902 Iowa; d. Jul 30, 1974 Alameda, CA; Age: 71. California Death Index, 1940-1997 [Archives.com]

Notes for Roscoe Glenn CLARK #786

Jones notes: "Resides (1974) Box 312, Carson, ND 58529"

Census:

- 1930 Howard, Grant Co, ND, p. 1A. Roscoe G. Clark, 27, married at age 20, working as servant for Nick Schmartz?; his wife, Florence, and children are living with his parents

-370-

1930 Valley View, Grant, ND, p. 2A. Emmet Clark 55, farmer - general farm; O Leta 53; Florance Clark 26, dau-in-law, IA, m. age 19; Edith Clark 6, niece, ID; Ardith Clark 4 10/12, niece, ID; Gordon Clark 6/12, nephew, ND. [Children are actually grandchildren, children of his son Roscoe]

Notes for Florence Annette BOSSINGHAM #786s
Jones notes: "sister to Delbert (husband of Georgia Gladys Clark)"; gives death as 20 Sep 1950, ND.
Census: 1920 Leith, Grant, ND, p. 10A. Charlie D Bossingham 46, laborer, IA; Lillian M 40, MN; Delbert D 17; Florrence L 15; Merril M 12; Thelma J 10, ND; Lester 7, ND; Herman M Bossingham 43. Others b. IA.
Death: SS Death Index gives death as Oct 1982, Carson, ND - corresponds with last known residence.

Notes for Edith Zeta Mabel CLARK #787
Jones notes: "resides (1974) at 1 Kendrick Dr, San Anselmo, Cal 94960"
Census: 1930 Leith, Grant, ND, p. 1B. Lloyd Faubel 25 MN/Ger/MN, laborer - odd jobs; M Edith Faubel 19; L Earl Faubel 2 6/12; L Peggie Faubel 1. Others b. ND.

Notes for Earl Lloyd FAUBEL #787s
Death: Earl Lloyd Faubel; b. Nov 26, 1904 Minnesota; d. Jan 7, 1995, Sonoma, CA; Age: 90. Mother's name: Christensen. California Death Index [Archives.com]

Notes for Dale Elizabeth EVANS #791
Jones notes: "resides (1974) at Hartington, NE 68739"
Census: 1930 Wayne, Wayne, NE, p. 11A. William Evans 53, laborer, PA/PA/PA; Roxy 50, OH/OH/OH; Wilma 22; Grace 19; Rex 15; Fred Wohlman 25, son-in-law, NE/NE/NE; Dale Wohlman 23, dau; Eugene Wohlman 3 2/12, grandson; Blain Wohlman 1 -/12, grandson; Kenneth Wohlman 5/12, grandson; Dorathea Evans 17, dau; William E Braisted 59, lodger, NY/NY/NY, minister - Baptist church. Children b. Nebraska. occupations of sons illegible.
Information: Family tree of PW Phillips on Ancestry.com gives divorce from Fred Wohlman in 1946; death: Jun 1887 in Hartington, NE. No documentation.
Death: Dale Mitteis, b. 31 May 1906; d. Jun 1987, Hartington, Cedar, NE; #508-24-3156; issued Nebraska. SS Death Index <rootsweb.com>

Notes for Nick MITTEIS #791
Jones notes gave name as Mittern; SS death index for wife Dale gives Mitteis.

Notes for Grace EVANS #793
SS Death Index gives death as 14 Feb 1992; Lakewood, Los Angeles, CA

Notes for Blaine ELLIS #793s
Census: 1920 Strahan, Wayne, NE, p. 10B. Fred W Ellis 32; Roxie Ellis 29; Max Ellis 11; Blaine Ellis 9; Joe Ellis 6; Mary Ellis 1 4/12; Anna Frederickson 22
No death information found

Notes for Izeta Mae WILL #796
Jones notes: "resides (1974) at Highwood, MT"
Marriage: 10 Jun 1944, Laurin, Madison, MT; Robert T. Mcgowan, 37, of Highwood, MT; b. Great Falls, MT; parents: Frank M. Mcgowan, Thresa M. Casey to Izeta M. Will, 26, of Sheridan, MT, b. Leith, MT; parents: John Will, Edith M. Jones. Montana County Marriages, 1865-1950 <familysearch.org>
No death record found - Montana Death Index or SSDI.

Notes for Robert Thomas MCGOWAN #796s
Death: May be Robert McGowan, Age: 91; Est. birth year: abt 1908; d. 6 Feb 1999, Chouteau; Res: Chouteau Co, MT. Montana Death Index [Ancestry.com}

Notes for Donald G. SHERBAHN #806
Jones notes. "Donald served in Army, WW II; resides (1975) at 218 Lincoln St, Wayne, NE 68787"
Census: 1930 Wayne, Wayne, NE, p. 1B. D A Jones 72, farmer, widowed; Albert Jones 37, son, laborer ___ job; Edna Jones 37, dau-in law, saleslady - dry goods; Marion Jones 14, grandson; June Jones 12, granddau; Neva Jones 11, granddau; Bonnell Jones 8, granddau; George Sherbahn 43, son-in-law, __?__ - carnival; Gail Sherbahn 46; Bernadine Sherbahn 19, dau in law; Donald Sherbahn 17, grandson; Betty Meister 4 2/12, granddau; Cora Pratt 60, lodger.
Death: Donald G Sherbahn; b. 13 Aug 1912; d. 26 Feb 2005; Last Residence: Wayne, Wayne, NE; issued: Nebraska; #506-05-2171

Notes for Bernita HINNERACHS #806s
Census: 1920 Logan, Dixon, NE, p. 2B. Herbert Hinnericks 33, NE/Ger/IL, farmer; Lena Hinnericks 30, NE/Ger/WI; Gilbert Hinnericks 3 0/12; Bernetta Hinnericks 1 8/12, dau: Henry Hinnericks 70; Caroline Hinnericks 64; Lydia Hinnericks 26

Notes for Mildred Gayle JONES #806
Orville Jones notes. "reside (1976) at 118 W. 12th, Wayne, NE"
Death: Social Security Death Index: Mildred G. Jenkins b. 13 Dec 1909; d. 3 Sep 2004 Wayne, Wayne, NE; #507-56-6322; issued Nebraska

Notes for Morris Verdon JENKINS #806s
Census: 1910 Chapin, Wayne, NE. p. 11B. Samuel Jenkins 28, farmer, IA; Emily Jenkins 25, NE; Esther Jenkins 4; Morris Jenkins 2

Notes for Elizabeth Jane JONES #812
Jones notes: "resides (1976) Geneva? [NE]"

Notes for Laurence DOUD #812s
Census: 1920 Geneva Ward 2, Fillmore, NE, p. 2B. Geo T Doud 55. gardener - private estate; Josephine K Doud 39, Canada; Mary B Doud 11, NE; Lawrence J Doud 6, NE
SS Death index give name as: Lawrence J. Doud

Notes for Robert Otis JONES #813
Jones notes: "resides (1976) Vallejo?"

Notes for Arleen Mae AGNEW #813s
Census: 1930 Shell Creek, Madison, NE, p. 1B. Marshall Agnew 36. barber - own shop, MO; Mae Agnew 32, NE; Allien Agnew 10; Marshall Agnew 8; Eleanor Whinson 22, roomer.

Notes for Delbert Ernest ALDERSON #814s
Census: 1930 Precinct 20, Cedar, NE, p. 1B. Ernest D Alderson 37, farmer; Henrietta Alderson 34; Geneva H Alderson 13; Dale S Alderson 12; Delbert E Alderson 10; Argean A Alderson 5; Myra J Alderson 7/12. All b. NE.

Notes for Billy Morgan JONES #815
Listed as William M. Jones in Minnesota Death Index.

Marriage: Dorothy Richards, b. Iroquois, SD 26 Jan 1919 to William M. Jones, b. 1 Nov 1920, Wayne, NE, married 10 Jul 1949. Both 1st marriage. South Dakota Marriages, 1905-1949 [Ancestry.com]

Burial: William M Jones; Service: SSgt, US Army World War II; b. 1 Nov 1920; d. 24 Apr 1974; Service Start Date: 14 Sep 1942; Interment Date: 29 Apr 1974; Cemetery: Ft. Snelling National Cemetery; 7601 34th Avenue, South Minneapolis, MN 55450; Section N Site 4188. US Veterans Gravesites, [Ancestry.com]

Notes for Dorothy RICHARDS #815s

May be the Dorothy May Jones who died in Hennepin Co, MN 28 Jun 2001; gives birth date as 26 Jul 1919.

Census: *1930 Iroquois, Beadle, SD, p. 1B. Glen A Richards 38; Eva B Richards 37; Dorothy R Richards 9; Mae H Richards 6 [*may not be right family - right county, about the right age]

Notes for Joan Faye JONES #816

Jones notes: "resides (1976) at 628 Westwood Rd, Wayne, NE"

Notes for Charles Victor CARHART #816S

Census: 1930 Randolph, Cedar, NE, p. 9A. Ralph M Carhart 29, IA, manager - retail lumber; Fannie B Carhart 27, NE; Charles V Carhart 1 1/12, NE

Notes for Evelyn C. CABLISH #837

Census: 1930 District 7, Mason, KY, p. 3A. Alexander H Calvert 23, farmer; Evelyn C Calvert 23; Alexander H Calvert, Jr 1/12; Robt F Cablish 46 f-in-law, salesman - meat; Edna Cablish 42, m-in-law

Notes for Alexander Hart CALVERT #837s

Census: 1910 Dist 7, Mason, KY, p. 11B. Pierce Calvert 45, farmer; Francis Calvert 30; Katherine Calvert 7; Louise Calvert 3 [twin]; Alexander Calvert 3 [twin]; Josephine Walker 53, cook. All b. KY.

Jones notes: "Divorced; he remarried to Allene K. Burline"

Notes for Robert L. HUTCHISON #845

Jones notes: "Resides (1972) at Rt 3, Orangeburg, KY 41056"

Notes for Gertrude ACKLEY #845s

Census: 1930 Lewis Co, KY shows parents as Alven M Ackley 43 & Lina M Ackley 39. Both b. KY.

Death: Possible Death: Gertrude A Hutchison, d. 5 Aug 1999, Mason Co, KY; Age: 76. Kentucky Death Index, 1911-2000 [Ancestry.com]

SS Death Index gives: Gertrude Hutchison, b. 21 Apr 1923; d. 15 Aug 1999; age 76; Maysville, Mason, KY; card issued Kentucky; #402-38-8932

Notes for Leslie William HICKS #847

Jones notes: "reside (1972) at 7406 Newport, Parma, OH. Maritime & Naval service, WW II."

Death: Leslie William Hicks, b. 10 Oct 1926; d. 04 Feb 2007, Cleveland, Cuyahoga, OH 300-12-5563, issued Ohio. Social Security Death Index

Obit: *Leslie W Hicks, husband of late Bettie*; Obit in **Plain Dealer**, 05 Feb, 2007, pg. 4 sec. B; Cleveland Obit Index.

Notes for Bettie Ann CASTORA #847s

Census: 1930 Cleveland, Cuyahoga, OH, p. 12A. Stanley Castora 36, inspector - county roads; Rose Castora 31; Alice Castora 10; Betty Castora 8. All b. OH.

Notes for David Lee HICKS #848

Jones notes: "she resides (1973) at 7815 Eve Ave, Cleveland OH 44102; he served in US Army. Murdered 5/18/1973"

Obit: *David L. Hicks, beloved husband of Betty Lou (nee Kauff), father of David and Karen, son of Mrs. Margaret Kelso and the late Leslie B. Hicks, brother of Robert and Leslie Hicks, Glenn Kelly, Mrs. Becky Sue Snodgrass and Mrs. Linda Finley. Friends may call at The Nunn Funeral Home, 4434 Lorain Ave, Monday 2 to 4 And 7 to 9, where services will be held Tuesday, May 22, at 1:30 P.M.* Cleveland Necrology File, ***Cleveland Press***; May 21 1973.

Notes for Eugene Bruce PEMBERTON #870s

Census: 1930 Hamilton, Butler, OH, p. 6B. George M Pemberton 39, district superintendent - gas elec co.; Myrtle Pemberton 37; George M Pemberton 15; Max Pemberton 11, WV; Eugene Pemberton 8, WV; Henry Pemberton 6. Other b. OH.

Notes for Evalyn R. ROGERS #878

Census:
- 1920 El Paso Precinct 7, El Paso, TX, p. 7B. Lydia A Gibson 60, OH/OH/OH, widow; Thomas R Rogers 40, son, widowed, IN/SC/OH, contractor - own office; Evelyn R Rogers 14, granddau, OK/IN/TX; Locleus L Rogers 13, granddau, TX/IN/TX; Paul G Rogers 11, grandson, TX/IN/TX; Mary M Rogers 9, granddau, TX/IN/TX; Claris L Rogers 7, granddau, TX/IN/TX. Rogers is crossed out - so surname of all may be Gibson
- 1930 Houston, Harris, TX, p. 23A. Lydia Gibson 71, OH, widow; John B Winn 27, TX/TN/TX, grandson in law; Evalyn Winn 24, OK/IN/TX, granddau; Kenneth R Winn 5, TX, gr grandson; John H Winn 2/12, TX, gr grandson; Joseph B Ahlschies 23, grandson in law, TX/TX/TX; Claris Ahlschies 18, granddau, TX/IN/TX; Joseph B Ahlschies 1 4/12, gr grandson; Mary M Rogers 19, granddau, TX/IN/TX. Children b. TX

Notes for Locleus Laura ROGERS #879

Census: 1930 Galveston, Galveston, TX, p 12A. Oscar Ekelund, 22, TX/TX/TX, salesman - dry goods; Locleus Ekelund 24, TX/MO/TX, m. age 22; Dora M Ekelund 1 5/12

Notes for Claris ROGERS #882

Census: 1930 Houston, Harris, TX, p. 23A. Lydia Gibson 71, OH, widow; John B Winn 27, TX/TN/TX, grandson in law; Evalyn Winn 24, OK/IN/TX, granddau; Kenneth R Winn 5, TX, gr grandson; John H Winn 2/12, TX, gr grandson; Joseph B Ahlschies 23, grandson in law, TX/TX/TX; Claris Ahlschies 18, granddau, TX/IN/TX; Joseph B Ahlschies 1 4/12, gr grandson; Mary M Rogers 19, granddau, TX/IN/TX. Children b. TX

Death: Claris L Ahlschier, b. 15 Jan 1912; d. 3 Jun 1989; age 77; Austin, Travis, TX; issued Texas; #460-16-9465. Social Security Death Index <rootsweb.com>

Death: Joseph Ahlschier, b. 27 May 1906; d. Jun 1982; age 76; Houston, Harris, TX; issued Texas; #467-01-8110

Notes for Florence Marie TATMAN #884.

Meade notes: "Florence Marie Tatman (my grandmother) married Alvin William Meade, Jr. in the spring of 1936 in Camas, Cowlitz Co, WA. My father thinks they probably met in college while they were both in San Francisco. Alvin was son of Alvin William Mead(e) Sr. and Mary Elizabeth Timmerman, and he was born June 22, 1911 in WY and died in WWII on June 14, 1944 in Naples, Italy from pneumonia (caused by a gunshot wound). Florence and Alvin had 2 children, but their first child was a stillborn baby girl before my father was born."

Notes for Dorothy DAY #892

Marriage: Thomas Raymond Watts, b. Indiana; Bride: Dorothy Mildred Day, b. 1900, Felicity, Ohio; Age: 23; Marriage: 18 Jun 1923, Hamilton, OH; Groom's parents: Thos M. Watts / Blanche Harris; Bride's parents: Richard T. Day / Nellie Altman. Ohio Marriages, 1800-1958 <familysearch.org> Discrepancy: death certificate gives birth as 1899; 1900 census gave 1900.

Census: 1930 Junction, Greene, IA; Thomas R Watts, 56; OH/OH/OH, bank president; Dorothy Watts, IA/OH/IN, 55

Death: Dorothy Watts, d. 17 Mar 1927, Cincinnati, Hamilton, OH; b. 4 Feb 1899, OH; Age: 27 years 1 month; Address: 397 Elberon Ave; Burial: 21 Mar 1927, Spring Grove; Spouse: Thomas Raymond Watts; Father: Richard Day; Mother: Nellie Altman; cause of death: appendicitis. Ohio Deaths, 1908-1953 <pilot.familysearch.org>

Notes for Ruth DAY #895

Jones notes: "resided in Oregon"

Marriage: Ruth I. Day, b. 13 Apr 1895, Felicity, OH; marriage: Cincinnati, Hamilton, OH; parents: Richard T. Day, Nellie Altman; spouse: Chester Franklin Ditmar. Ohio County Marriages, 1790-1950 <familysearch.org>

Not found on 1920 or 1930 census.

Notes for William Lloyd GRIGGS #905

Census: 1930 Buffalo, Garfield, OK, p. 1B. Lloyd W Grigg 20, farmer; Annabelle Grigg 20; Orville Grigg 8/12

Notes for Annabell ANDERSON #905s

May be daughter of Ora & Anna Anderson living in Buffalo, Garfield, OK in 1910 with daughter Anna, b. 1909.

Notes for Lois Marie GRIGGS #906

Death: Lois Marie Guinn [Lois Marie Griggs]; #556133023; Female; b. 18 Jul 1915, Oklahoma; d. 17 Jul 1990, Riverside; Mother's Maiden Name: Benson; Father's Surname: Griggs. California Death Index, 1940-1997 [Ancestry.com]

Notes for Telephus "Tex" GUINN #906s

Census: 1930 Covina, Los Angeles, CA, p. 8B. James A Guinn 57, GA/GA/TN, retired; Naoma Guinn 51; Jasper J Guinn 32, electrician - Edison Co; Telephus Guinn 14; James E Guinn 11; W G Guinn 8. All but father born TX.

Death: Telephus Guinn, #552248422; Male; b. 10 Jan 1916, Texas; d. 1 Sep 1990, Riverside; Mother's Maiden Name: Northcutt. California Death Index, 1940-1997 [Ancestry.com]

Notes for Marie L. KURTZ #919

Census: 1920 Miami, Dade, FL, p. 7B. Robert E Weighell 37, no occ; Marie Weighell 27; Delores Weighell 2 6/12; Vivian Weighell 2 6/12. All OH/OH/OH

1930 Cincinnati, Hamilton, OH, p. 9B. Mollie Kurtz 58, widow, no occ; Vivien Weigell 12, granddaughter; Delores Weigell 12, granddaughter. (Marie & Robert not found on 1930 census)

Information: Family tree "Descendants Of James French Sussexon" on Ancestry.com gives death as 23 Mar 1922. Source is given as Cemetery Burial Records.

Death: FL Death index lists Mrs. Marie L. Weigle, d. Dade Co, FL 1922.

Notes for Robert Elliott WEIGHILL #919s
Military: World War I Draft Registration Cards, 1917-1918 [Ancestry.com]. Robert Elliott Weighill, age 35, b. 15 Apr 1883; res: Cincinnati, Hamilton, OH; occ: salesman: Jewel & Crocker Co; contact: Mrs. Robert Weighill; med height, slender, blue eyes, dk brown hair; Regis: 12 Sep 1918, Cincinnati.
Death: Robert Weighell, b. 15 Apr 1883, Cincinnati, OH; d. 16 Feb 1943, Cincinnati, Hamilton, OH; Age: 59 years 10 months 1 day; Widowed; Address: 3414 Telford Ave; Burial: 18 Feb 1943, Spring Grove; Spouse: Marie; Father: John Thomas Weighell, b. Cincinnati, OH; Mother: Mary Elliott, b. Cincinnati, OH. Ohio Deaths, 1908-1953 <pilot.familysearch.org>.

Notes for Harry W. KURTZ #920
Discrepancy: 1900 Census (Cincinnati, OH) gives his date of birth as Oct 1894.
Census: 1930 Cincinnati, Hamilton, OH, p. 6A. Harry Kurtz 35, OH/OH/OH, chauffeur - taxi co; Doretta Kurtz 34. m. age 23 / 22
Military: World War I Draft Registration Cards, 1917-1918 [Ancestry.com]. Harry William Kurtz, age 22, b. 12 Oct 1894, Felicity, Ohio; res: Cincinnati, Hamilton Co, OH; occ: chauffeur - Ballerman & V___; single, crippled in both legs; med height, stout, brown eyes & hair; regis: 5 Jun ___, Cincinnati, OH

Notes for Anna W. EGLOFF #920s
Jones notes: "she resides (1974) at 1948 Raindance Way, Las Vegas, NE 89109"
SS Death Index gives "Mar 1995, Las Vegas (Clark) NV"

Notes for Marilyn R. STAATS #932s
Jones notes: "resides (1974) at 1105 Rosetree Ln,, Cincinnati, OH 45230"; "Marilyn is a sister to Martha Staats" (#922s)
Census: 1930 Ohio, Clermont, OH, p. 9B. William C Staats 36, WV/WV/WV, body builder - automobile factory; Luella M Staats 28, OH/OH/OH; William S Staats 5; Martha M Staats 4; Marilyn Staats 3

Notes for Wilma J. STEVENS #934
Jones notes: "resides (1974) at 2966 Banning Rd, Cincinnati, OH 45230"

Notes for Ralph A. HOUGHTON #934s
Census: 1930 Felicity, Clermont, OH, p. 4A. Chas L Houghton 43, mail carrier - RFD; Mabel L Houghton 41; C Herman Houghton 21; Ralph A Houghton 11. All b. OH.

Notes for Clarke W. GREGG #938
Jones notes: "resides (1970) at 1649 5th St, S. Portsmouth, OH"
Death: Clarke W. Gregg, b. 1911; d. 17 Nov 1985, Portsmouth, Scioto Co, OH. age 74, widowed, occ: advertising. Ohio Deaths, 1908-1932, 1938-1944, and 1958-2002 [Ancestry.com]

Notes for Dorothy M. HAMPEL #938s
Death: Dorothy M Gregg, b. 1918, Ohio; res: Scioto, Ohio; d. 15 Sep 1982, Portsmouth, Scioto, OH, age 64, married. Ohio Deaths, 1908-1932, 1938-1944, and 1958-2002 [Ancestry.com]

Notes for James Woodlief GREGG #939
Jones notes: "resides (1974) at 199 Spring St, Batavia, OH"
Death: James W Gregg, b. 14 May 1912; d. 30 Jan 2005; Batavia, Clermont, OH; #300-05-1202; issued Ohio. Social Security Death Index <rootsweb.com>
Discrepancy: SSDI gives birth as 14 May 1912; Jones notes gave 14 Jun 1912.

Notes for Dorothy L. CARSTENS #939s
Death: Dorothy Gregg, b. 16 Sep 1917, d. May 1979, Florida ; #288-01-0967; issued: Ohio. Social Security Death Index <rootsweb.com>
Death: Dorothy P Gregg, d. 6 May 1979, Collier Co, FL, age 61; b. 16 Sep 1917. Florida Death Index, 1877-1998

Notes for James Chatterton WHITE #941
Jones notes: "resides (1974) at 3004 Woodcliff Cir, SE, E. Grand Rapids, MI 49506; Capt, Marine Corp, WW II; both attended OH Weslyan"
Death: SS Death Index gives: White, James C., b. 10 Jan 1921; d. 28 Jan 2006; age 85; Grand Rapids, Kent, MI; issued Ohio; #286-18-6412

And the line goes on...

Four Elizabeths
Elisabeth Ann Douberley "Lis"; Elizabeth Joan (Kieser) Stockton "Betty Jo";
Mary Elizabeth (Stockton) Douberley "Betsy";
front: Elizabeth (Stalder) Kieser "Betty" - March 2005

End Notes - Generation 6

513. Ohio Deaths 1908-1953.
514. Ibid.
515. Social Security Death Index.
516. Ohio Deaths, 1908-1932, 1938-1944, and 1958-2002 [database on-line].
517. Ibid.
518. Social Security Death Index.
519. Social Security Death Index.
520. Ibid.
521. Ibid.
522. Ibid.
523. Ibid.
524. Alabama Deaths, 1908-1974.
525. Alabama Marriages 1816-1957.
526. Ibid.
527. Ohio Deaths, 1908-1932, 1938-1944, and 1958-2002 [database on-line].
528. Social Security Death Index.
529. Social Security Death Index.
530. Ohio Deaths, 1908-1932, 1938-1944, and 1958-2002 [database on-line].
531. Hicks Family Bible.
532. Ibid.
533. Ibid.
534. Stalder, Elizabeth - Birth Certificate.
535. Kieser/Stalder - Marriage Certificate.
536. Kieser, Robert J. - Birth Certificate.
537. Kieser, Robert J. - Death Certificate.
538. Social Security Death Index.
539. Interview with Ruth (Stalder) Watkins.
540. Information from Madge (Stalder) Washell 4/1/1998.
541. Social Security Death Index.
542. Ibid.
543. Ibid.
544. Ibid.
545. Social Security Death Index.
546. Ibid.
547. Ibid.
548. Missouri Death Certificate [digital image].
549. World War I Draft Registration Cards, 1917-1918.
550. Ibid.
551. Social Security Death Index.
552. Texas Death Index 1964-1998.
553. Social Security Death Index.
554. Ibid.
555. World War I Draft Registration Cards, 1917-1918.
556. Social Security Death Index.
557. Social Security Death Index.
558. Clermont County, Ohio 1980 Vol 1.
559. Ibid.
560. Ibid.
561. World War I Draft Registration Cards, 1917-1918.
562. U.S. World War II Draft Registration Cards, 1942.
563. Social Security Death Index.
564. World War I Draft Registration Cards, 1917-1918.
565. Social Security Death Index.
566. Ibid.
567. Ibid.
568. Ibid.
569. Ibid.
570. Ibid.
571. Ibid.
572. Ibid.
573. Ibid.
574. Ibid.
575. Ibid.
576. Ibid.
577. Ibid.
578. Ibid.
579. Ibid.
580. Ibid.
581. Social Security Death Index.
582. Ibid.
583. Ibid.
584. South Dakota Marriages, 1905-1949.
585. Social Security Death Index.
586. Ibid.
587. Ibid.
588. Ibid.
589. Ibid.
590. Ibid.
591. Ibid.
592. Ibid.
593. Ibid.
594. Ibid.
595. Ibid.
596. Ibid.
597. Ibid.
598. Meade, Kevin.
599. Social Security Death Index.
600. Ibid.
601. Ibid.
602. Ibid.
603. Information on this family is from the book "Levi W. & Sarah E. (Carter) Hopkins, their ancestors & descendants
604. Florida Death Index.
605. World War I Draft Registration Cards, 1917-1918.
606. Social Security Death Index.
607. Ibid.
608. Ibid.

Index

Note: In a few cases, final formatting may have caused a line to slip to the page before or after.
If you do not find a name on the page listed in the index, please check the pages before and after.

ABERCROMBIE
   Beulah Gladys 276
   Beulah Gladys (1890-1973) . . 217
ACKLEY
   Alven M (1887-) 340, 373
   Gertrude (1925-) 340, 373
   Lina M. wife of Alven . 340, 373
ADAMS
   ___ 14, 80
   Diana (1768-1850) . 10, 14-16, 32
   Mina White 31, 79
ADELMAN
   Karen Lee (1945-) 339
ADRIAN
   Anne (1858-1918) 120, 175
   Sophia wife of William (1814-)
      120
   William (1813-) 120
AGNEW
   Arleen Mae (1920-) 337, 372
   Mae 372
   Marshall (1894-) 337, 372
AHERN
   Christy Lynn (BENOIT)
      (1949-) 339
   Connie June 339
   Patricia Ann 338
   Neva Mae (JONES)
      (1919-1996) 338
   William Arnold (1916-1980)
      . . . . 338, 339
AHLSCHIER / AHLSCHIES
   Claris (ROGERS) (1913-) . . . 344
   Claris L 168, 374
   Joseph 168, 374
   Joseph B (1907-) 344
   Joseph B (1928-) 344
   Joseph Bailey 344
   Thomas Courtney 344
ALDERSON
   Argean A 372
   Clifford Lee 337
   Dale S 372
   Debra Jean 337
   Delbert Ernest (1920-1963)
      . . . . 337, 372
   Elva Mae (JONES) (1919-) . . 337
   Ernest D. (1893-) 337, 372
   Geneva H 372
   Henrietta wife of Ernest D.
      (1896-) 337, 372
   Myra J 372

   Nancy Ann (UNKNOWN) . . 337
   Patricia Ann 337
   Richard Alan 337
   Robert Dale (1961-) 337
ALDRIDGE
   Myrtle (1903-1976) 323, 364
ALLEN
   Catherine 111, 164
   Florence (1908-1987) . . . 306, 351
   Mary Elizabeth 250
   Wanda 299
ALTMAN / AULTMAN
   Anna May (1881-1958) 115
   Aurelia M 170
   Bailey W. (1878-) 115, 170
   Barbara (1832-1854) 41
   C A 170
   Corna J 170
   Cornelia Blanche
      (BRITTINGHAM) (1854-1926)
      . . . . 115, 170
   Guy 172
   John 115, 172
   John S. (1841-1919) 116, 172
   John Wesley (1853-1900) 115, 170
   Lloyd Robison (1890-1915)
      . . . . 117, 172
   Louisa 170
   Maud 172
   Millie Lou (1888-1977)
      . . . . 116, 231, 292
   Missouri Mary (UTTER)
      (1864-1900) 116
   Nelly / Nellie
      . . . . 75, 115, 170, 230, 291, 375
   Nelly (1873-1946) 230
   Pearl M 172
   Pearl More (1884-) 117
   Percilla 172
   Ray 172
   Sam 170
   Samuel J. (1884-1947) 115
   Weslie 291
ANDERSON
   Anna 375
   Annabell (1909-1978) . . 346, 375
   Caroline (1839-) 95
   Elita 137
   Margaret 132
   Mary 92, 132
   Mary (KING) 41
   Melissa 61

   Melita or Melissa (1850-1918)
      . . . . 41, 61, 92
   Ora 375
   William 41, 61, 92, 132
ANSON
   Anna 307, 352
ANSTAILT / ANSTAOTT
   Albert 306, 351
   Lula (HAUCK) 306
   Margaret (1906-1932) . . . 306, 351
ARCHER
   Ola 230, 291
AREY
   -?- 296
ARNECKE
   August 156
ASHCRAFT
   Mary Margaret "Dollie"
      (JONES) (1938-) 329
   Richard (1937-) 329
ATCHLEY
   Daniel (1839-) 122, 178
   Maggie 298
   Margaret Pearl (1866-1958)
      . . . . 122, 178
   Mary wife of Daniel (1847-) . . 122
   Mary 178
   Minnie 178
AUBELL
   Frank 162
AUGUST
   John 6
AULT
   Amy E 354
   Charles H 354
   Donald C. (1940-) 311
   Donald H. (1906-) 311, 354
   Irine 354
   Julia (1942-) 311
   Julia Elsie (GLOVER)
      (1906-2002) 311
   Margaruite 354
   Reginald 354
AUSTIN
   Betty (1921-) 224
   Charles R 261
   Guy 261
   Mitilda (1856-1927) . . . 205, 261
   Pearl R. (1877-1953) . . . 205, 261
   Pearl Roser 261
   Lillie 260
   William (1849-) 205, 261

AYERS
- Louie / Louis 234, 296
- Lucy Florence 296

AYMES 4

BABB
- John Robert (1928-) 332

BACON
- Odessa (1906-1983) 109

BAIRD
- Effie Blanche (WOOD)
  (1897-1992) 324, 366
- Ella Catherine (1933-) 325
- Eleanor 366
- Ella 366
- Ella wife of J. D. (1871-) 325
- Glenna Gertrude (1925-) 325, 366
- J. D. (1863-) 325, 366
- Jessie Lee 366
- Loyed 366
- Robert 366
- Walter Lloyd (1886-) ... 325, 366

BALDWIN
- Lilian M. (1880-) ... 333, 334, 370

BALLEW
- Ola A. 230, 291

BALLON / BALLOU
- Elizabeth 71, 108

BALSIGER
- John 151

BANKHEAD
- Bonnie Edwina 344

BARBOUR
- Deborah Ann (1960-) 342
- Edwin Hugh 342
- Jeanette Merle (HICKS)
  (1941-) 342

BARLEY
- Emma (1855-) 219, 280
- Fern (1889-) 219, 280
- Joe 280
- S. M. (1855-) 219, 280

BARNES
- Charlie 67
- Emery 67
- Emma / Emily 68, 160
- Esther M. (1853-) 45, 67
- Jane 68
- John 68
- Lorinda 67
- Mary 68
- Minnie Martin 68
- Newton 67
- Serepttia 68

BARRETT
- Cora B 242

BARTLOW
- Nellie 47, 74

BARTON
- Cornelia 309, 353
- Hope (1921-2001) 309, 353
- Malcolm (1887-) 309, 353
- Priscilla 353

BATES
- Chas. L. 253
- Nora 253
- Wanda (1945-) 312

BAUER
- Ellen I 218
- Fern Eileen (1928-) 328
- James A 218
- Minnie 352

BAXTER
- Harriet Mary (1825-) 21, 31, 32, 50

BAYER
- May 353

BEALOCK
- Richard 4

BECK
- Alice 252
- Alice B. (TAYLOR) (1893-1944)
  199
- Angie C 252
- Charles H 252
- Clara E 252
- Eric Richard (1956-) 310
- Estel P 252
- Estel Rosco (1882-1940) 199, 252
- Evelyn (HOLDERFIELD)
  (1930-) 310
- Hannah Louise 252
- Horace 252
- Horace J. (1837-1917) 199
- Jennifer Lynn (1957-) 310
- Karen Sue (1954-) 310
- Phebe J 252
- Phoebe (WINTERROD)
  (1852-1915) 199
- Richard Taylor (1931-) .. 199, 310
- Tracy Ann (1961-) 310

BECKELHEIMER / BECKELHIMER
- Barbara Sue (RAINS)
  (1945-) 328
- Birtha 272
- Calvin 272, 273
- Calvin (1885-1946) 213
- Calvin Jr. 272
- Calvin Marcellus (1912-1979)
  .... 213, 327, 368
- Diana Lynne 328
- Elisabeth 272
- Elisabeth Ann (SUTTON)
  (1847-) 213
- Ethel 272, 273
- Ethel Grace (JONES)
  (1887-1963) 213
- Eva 272
- Fern Eileen (BAUER) (1928-) 328
- Galen Wayne (1952-) 328
- George 272, 273
- George W (1838-) 213
- George Washington 272
- Harriet (1914-) 213, 272, 273
- Harry R 272
- Harry Raymond (1913-1971)
  .... 213, 328, 368
- Jack J 272
- Jack Jones (1925-) 213, 328
- Jerry Monce 328
- John Lee 328
- Mary (JOHNSON) (1947-) .. 328
- Mary E 272
- Mary Elizabeth (1921-) . 213, 328
- Mary L (JACKSON) (1921-) . 328
- Naomi (JENKINS) (1940-) .. 328
- Robert Carl 328
- Ruth Ann 328
- S B 368
- Sarah Blanche (MONCE)
  (1913-) 327
- Velvet Jean 328
- Wilson 272

BECKEMEYER
- Benard J 266

BECKER
- Dora B 142
- Georgia E 142
- Melissa 142
- William 142

BECKETT
- Fannie L. (1888-1952) .. 194, 246
- Harry 246

BECKMAN
- A. J. Mrs. 158
- August 221-223, 282
- August John (1883-1971) 222, 282
- Emma Lucille 222
- Ethel 221-223, 282
- Ethel (HOLDERFIELD)
  (1882-1937) 222
- Ethelene (1907-) ... 221-223, 282
- Gussie M 223
- Gussie P. (1919-) ... 221, 223, 282
- John G 222
- Lena 223, 282
- Mary Jane (1918-) .. 221-223, 282
- William 223, 282

BECKNER
    Eva M. (1903-1993) 109
BECKTOLD
    Irene Caroline (1899-1988)
    . . . . 202, 256
BEEKER
    Dora H 141, 142, 147
    Elizabeth 88, 141, 147
    Elizabeth (BRADSHAW) (1837-
       1912) . . 100, 102, 141, 142, 147
    Emma Georgia Anna (1867-1928)
       . . . . 102, 147, 187
    Georgia . . . 87, 100, 102, 142, 143
    Melissa (1865-1949) 87, 100,
       . . . 102, 141-143, 148, 187, 259
    William 142, 147
    William (1831-) 100, 102
BEHAN
    Catherine A. (1958-) 321
    Deanne Lin 321
    Donald J. Jr. (1962-) 321
    Donald J. 266
    Donald James 'Bud' (1923-)
       . . . . 207, 321, 361
    Dorothy 266, 361
    Dorothy (LUEHRMANN)
       (1924-) 321
    Dorothy Ann (1919-)
       . . . . 207, 266, 320, 361
    Dorothy Cloetill (RAY)
       (1918-1981) 320, 361
    Duane Lindsay 321
    Gary M. (1966-) 321
    J. Phillip 361
    Jacqualine Ray 320
    John 207, 208, 266
    John J. (1955-) 266, 321, 361
    John Joseph . . 208, 266, 360, 361
    John Joseph (1891-1955) 207
    John Phillip (1917-1981)
       . . . . 207, 320, 360
    Judith Lynn 320
    Laura 361
    Laura Margaret (1921-)
       . . . . 27, 207, 266, 321, 361
    Lawrence 208
    Lawrence Harvey (1932-1933) 208
    Lawrence R. (1956-) 321
    Marjorie Claire "Margie"
       (1928-) 208, 266, 321, 361
    Maybelle (STACKHOUSE) . . 320
    Minnie 266, 359
    Minnie Clara (HICKS) (1893-
       1983) . . . 64, 145, 207, 264, 266
    Nancy Lee (1949-) 320

    Patrick 207, 266
    Phillip 361
    Phyllis Marie 320
    Richard 266
    Richard Melvin (1925-2002)
       . . . . 207, 208
BEHL
    George (1893-) 238, 300
    Ina B. (1915-) 238, 300
    Meredith (1895-) 238, 300
BEHYEMER / BEHYMER 25
    Hariet (1848-) 201
BELDEN
    George 31
    Georgia (HICKS) (1879-1954)
       . . . . 31, 53
    Guy Joseph (1878-1952) 53
    Moore H 53
BENFIELD
    Esky F 165
    Etta 72, 112, 165
BENNETT
    Billie 116
    Gwen (TAYLOR) (1935-) . . . 310
    J. Richard (1933-) 310
    Jill Stephens (1965-) 310
    Marie (BRITTINGHAM)
       (1895-1975) 116
    Otis (1895-) 116
    Richard James (1962-) 310
    Terrie Leah (1960-) 310
BENOIT
    Christy Lynn (1949-) 339
BENSON 375
    Alta (COGSWELL)
       (1898-1984) 233, 294
    Betty Ruth (MOORE) (1921-1990)
       233
    Douglas Dean (1918-1979) 233, 294
    George Hale (1835-) 118
    Hale T 173
    Ida 173, 232
    Ida May (1886-1947)
       . . . . 118, 232, 294
    Lettie Pearl (1889-1973)
       . . . . 118, 173, 232
    Lois Maurietta (1905-1978) 118, 173
    Neety Ann (ROBINSON) (1840-)
       118
    Roy 173, 233, 294
    Roy Douglas (1895-1960)
       . . . . 118, 233, 294
    Sarah Lavina (HOPKINS)
       (1861-1953) 118, 173

    Terry 209
    Thomas 173
    Thomas Hale (1869-1912) . . . 118
BENT
    Dorothy 296
BENTON
    Delores Marie (1938-) 336
BERGEN
    Alma H. (1896-) 325
    Alma Mae (1922-) 325
    Harry A (1894-) 325
BERGMAN
    Henrietta May 323, 363
BERRY
    Hargus (1899-) 193
    Jacqueline Lou (1942-) . .315, 357
    Jane 38
    John Rev. 265
    Milie wife of Hargus (1902-) . 193
    Norma Jean (MANNING)
       (1927-) 193
    Stanley H. (1922-1973) 193
BERT
    Payne 280
BERTLESMAN
    Lucy F 152
    Walker 152
    William H 152
BERTRAND
    Caroline (1830-) 53
BERTSCH
    Ozzie (1925-) 333
BICKEL
    Caroline (1953-) 307
    Louis 307, 352
BICKNELL
    James (1935-) 331
BIDDLE
    Fannie 270
    William 270
BIGGER
    Kenneth L 177
BILLINGSLEY
    Carrie (WYANT) (1884-) 311
    Dorothy (1938-) 312
    Dorothy H. (GLOVER)
       (1908-1971) 311
    Leonard O. (1918-) 311, 354
    Roy R (1883-) 311
BIRCHARD
    -?- 237
BLACK,
    Sarah Rebecca (1847-) . . .214, 274

BLACKWELL
- -?- (1946-) 331
- Donna Sue (PUGH) (1946-) . . 331

BLAIR
- Fred (1942-) 349

BLAND
- Clayton 246

BLANEY
- Dorothy Louise (BRITTINGHAM) (1893-1974) 116
- Edward A. (1869-) 116
- Geo S. 171

BLANEY
- Edward A. 171

BLOODHART
- Cora (1870-) 220

BLUST
- Carl Irwin (1932-) 332

BOARDMAN
- Medora 205

BODEY
- Margaret (1855-1920) . . 223, 283

BOGGESS
- Arch (1829-) 95, 135
- Caroline (ANDERSON) (1839-) 95
- Jane Louise (1870-1949) . 95, 135

BOICE
- Archie L 244
- Charles C 244
- Charles M. (1861-) 193
- Flossie L 244
- Hazel Marie (1900-1976) 193, 244, 245
- Mary E. (CORNELL) (1864-) 193, 244
- Myrtie M 244

BOLAN
- Samuel 30

BOLENDER
- Katherine (Shinkle) 11

BONER
- Nanney 199, 253

BOOK
- R. Mrs 170
- Rudolph 114
- Theodore R. 114

BOOTS
- Dolvia 216
- Joseph 216
- Monard 216
- Verlie 216

BORNHORST
- Catherine (SEVERING) (1855-1942). 108
- Henry (1851-1900) 108
- Rose (1889-1946) 108

BORSO / BOOSO
- -?- 82, 124
- Georgiana (1887-) 81, 82, 124, 179
- Luella (SMITH) (1873-1930) . 124

BOSSINGHAM
- Charles D. (1874-) 333, 334, 370, 371
- Delbert Dewite (1899-) 333, 370, 371
- Delbert Leone "Leo" 333
- Florence 370, 371
- Florence Annette (1904-1982) 334, 371
- Georgia Gladys (CLARK) (1898-1966) 333
- Herman M 370, 371
- Lester 370, 371
- Lilian M. (BALDWIN) (1880-) 333, 334, 371
- Madelaine Elaine 333
- Merril M 370, 371
- Rosa Imogene (LEE) (1926-) . 333
- Thelma J 370, 371

BOUGHNER
- Oliver 176

BOULDEN
- John 283

BOURNE
- Edwin (1925-) 333

BOUSE
- Madella Jane (1945-) 327

BOWER / BOWERS
- Harry 241
- Jennie 241
- Jerry (-1900) 189, 241
- Minnie M. (1882-1916) . 189, 241
- Nancy J. (1937-) 326
- Samatha (SHAW) (1860-) . . . 189

BOWLING
- Elijah 212
- Gladys R. (1906-1973) 212
- Louisa (MILLER) 212

BOWMAN
- Bonnie Patricia (1949-) 336
- Jean (1941-) 196
- Sadie Christine (FITZPATRICK) (1941-) 196

BOYSEN
- Thomas Robert 344

BRADEY
- Jennie 209

BRADFORD
- Donna Mae (1943-) 329
- W.G. Mrs 165

BRADSHAW
- Clement Jr 143
- Elizabeth (1837-1912) 100, 102, 141, 142, 147
- Lida 147

BRAGDON
- Anna Rebecca (1847-1922) . . . 99
- Rebecca 139

BRAGG
- Julia Rebica (1906-1971) 119

BRAISTED
- William E 278, 371

BRANDMAN
- Roxy 58

BRANNOCK
- J. L 143

BRANTLEY
- Jennifer 360

BRAWDWELL
- Lillie 267

BREEDING
- A 117
- Daisey 117
- Ella 117
- Herman 117
- Iola 117
- James 117
- L. E 117
- Lem 117
- Samuel E 117

BREEZE
- Lena (1896-1996) 224, 284

BRETZ
- H. J 61
- Harvey 61
- Harvey J. (1869-1958) 42, 61
- Ruie (TATMAN) (1871-1941) 42, 61

BREWER
- Sarah E 270

BRICKER
- Ella 192, 244

BRIEN
- -?- 253
- Laura 200

BRIETROM
- Charles 279

BRIGGS
- Pearson 80, 178
- Susan 61

BRILL
- Earl 73, 166
- Edwin L 354
- Elizabeth 312, 354
- Florine A 354
- George 312, 354
- Helen N 354

BRILL continued
   Howard G 354
   Inez Lucille (1920-) 312, 354
   Walter K 354

BRITTINGHAM
   Bryan 170, 293
   Bryan James (1896-1970)
      . . . . 116, 231, 293
   Cornelia 75, 115, 291
   Cornelia Blanche (1854-1926)
      . . . . 48, 115, 170
   Dorothy Louise (1893-1974)
      . . . . 116, 171
   Elizabeth 171
   Elizabeth Margaret (WARE)
      (1863-1941) 116
   Emma E 292, 293
   Emma (1894-) 231
   Eva (1902-) 231, 293
   Gladys (PARKER) (1895-1918)231
   Gladys E. 293
   Helen (1919-) 231, 292
   Isah 293
   James 75, 116, 170, 171, 292, 293
   James Winfield (1861-1943)
      . . . . 48, 116, 170
   Jane C 75
   Louise 170
   Lucinda (TATMAN) (1833-1912)
      . . . . 48, 75
   Lydia May (1857-1938)
      . . . . 48, 116, 171
   Marie 170, 171
   Marie (1895-1975) 116
   Mary "Mollie" (CARR) (1867-) 116
   Mary L. (1929-) 231, 293
   May 75, 116
   Mollie 75, 170
   Naomi (1916-) 231, 292
   Robert (1922-) 231
   William 75, 170, 171, 231, 291-293
   William Brown (1922-1900) . . . 48
   William Karl (1892-1940)
      . . . . 116, 231, 292
   Willie 170
   Winfield 75

BRITTON
   William 131

BROADWELL 365
   Allen (1930-) 324, 364
   Althea Ethlyn Parrish 366
   Andrew 148
   Andrew (-1919) 209
   Andrew J 148, 153, 269
   Andrew Jackson (1836-1930)
      . . . . 103, 105, 148, 149
   Arsnenia 148
   Baby 268
   Barbara 364
   Barbara (CONNER) (1901-1994)
      323
   Barbara Lucille 364
   Bernie (1920-) 323, 363
   Beulah Imogene . . . 211, 324, 365
   Broadwell 148, 365
   Catherine 148, 268
   Cecil L 211, 365
   Cecil Lionel (1909-1990) 211
   Chester . . 148, 149, 268, 363, 364
   Chester A. (1911-1983) 210
   Chester Allen (1892-1965) . . . 322
   Chester Allen 209, 363
   Clyde Lawrence (1900-1923)210, 268
   Dale / Dell 148, 269
   Elsie (CARLSON) (1913-1993) 209
   Elva 148, 269
   Elva Helen (CLARK) (1882-1953)
      . . . . 210, 269
   Eugene 267
   Eugenia (1908-) . . . 148, 210, 268
   Eunice 148, 211, 269
   Eunice (1906-) 211, 324
   Eunice Dale 365
   Fay H 268
   Ferdinand 153
   Glenn 148, 149, 268
   Glenn (1918-) 210
   Grace 210
   H F 268
   H Fay 268
   Harold 148, 268
   Harry 210, 268, 323, 364
   Harry (1895-1960) 323
   Henrietta (-1966) 323, 363
   Herbert 148, 268, 363
   Herbert Fay (1869-) 103, 209, 268
   Herbert P. (1924-) 323
   Hilbert F. 148
   Imogene (1902-)
      . . . . . . 148, 211, 269, 324, 365
   Inez (1924-) 323, 364
   Jackson J 148
   Joan 153
   Joanna (1823-) 105
   Karylton V. (1917-)
      . . . . . . 148, 211, 269, 324, 366
   Kathleen (1906-) 210, 268
   Kathleen A 149
   L. M 142, 147
   Lawrence (1874-1948)
      . . . . 103, 148, 149, 269
   Leander E. 148
   Leon 267, 305
   Leon (1911-) 209, 267
   Lindley 148, 153, 305, 363
   Lindley (1786-1880) 103
   Lindley E. (1904-1982) 209
   Lindley Edward (1867-1959) 209
   Lindley Edward 103, 267
   Lindley Jr 267
   Lionel 148, 269, 365
   M J 148
   Mabel (1894-1987) 209, 268
   Mae (ZIMMERMAN)
      (1878-1945) 209, 267, 305
   Millie S 268
   Minerva 148, 149, 268
   Minerva Elizabeth (JONES)
      (1844-1935) 103, 148
   Minnie 148
   Myrtle (ALDRIDGE)
      (1903-1976) 323, 364
   N. D 148
   Nathan 148, 268, 269
   Nathaniel Dale (1881-1966)
      . . . . 103, 210, 269
   Nellie / Nettie 148, 149, 268, 269
   Nettie E (WILSON) (1880-1963) 210
   Ora M 364
   Orma (1897-1970)
      . . . . 210, 268, 323, 364
   Paul Eugene (1927-1928) 323, 364
   Perce / Percy . 148, 149, 268, 269
   Percival (1877-1944)
      . . . . 103, 210, 268
   Perley L (1903-) 210, 268
   Preston 148
   Purcell 148
   Rawley 148
   Ray C. (1927-) 323, 363
   Raymond 323, 364
   Raymond (1925-) 323
   Raymond D. (1872-) 103
   Robert 148
   Romba (1907-1972)
      . . . . . . 148, 211, 269, 324, 365
   Ruby (1906-1963)
      . . . . 209, 305, 322, 363
   Ruby Alyce 322
   Sarah M 268, 364
   Sarah Millie (PINDELL)
      (1867-1936) 209
   Susan 153
   Susan wife of Lindley (1796-) . 103
   William H 364
   William Harold (1901-1989)
      . . . . 210, 323, 364

BROCKER
   Ella 243

BROSHEARS
   Judith 143
BROWN
   Andrew 215, 274
   Audrey 286
   Billy 274
   Charles E. (1874-1935) . 215, 274
   Charles Edwin 274
   Dorothea / Dorothy 215, 274
   Dorothy Jean (1918-2003) . . . 215
   Edith Marion (STREET)
     (1920-) 330
   Eva 286
   Forest Allen (1920-2001) 340
   James Allen (1960-) 340
   Jess / Jesse 274, 286
   Jessie Agnes (JONES)
     (1878-1922) 215
   John 5
   Josie 274
   Kathleen (1954-) 318
   Lois Maurietta (BENSON)
     (1905-1978) 118
   Margie 274
   Marjorie Lenore (1919-2004) . 215
   Patricia Ann (HOGAN) (1941-) 331
   Patricia Kaye (1946-) 340
   Pearl 286
   Peggy Ann (1950-) 340
   Raymond (1890-) 118
   Ruth Lenora (HUTCHISON)
     (1923-) 340
   William Charles (1921-2001) . 330
   William Charles 215
   William Charles Jr. 331
   William Robert (1952-) 340
BROWNEN
   Martha 42, 97, 137
BROWNING
   Eugene (1928-) 332
BROXTERMANN
   Katherine G 82
BRUBAKER
   Arthur 163, 287
   Arthur B. (1901-1968) 111, 227, 287
   Bessie 163, 287
   Bessie Salome (1901-1990)
     . . . . 111, 227, 287
   C. N. 163
   Caroline 71, 165
   Caroline Wise (HICKS)
     (1871-1952). 111
   Carrie 163, 287
   Cecil 163, 227
   Cecil N. (1904-1966)
     . . . . 111, 163, 227, 287
   David T (1842-1917) 111
   Eileen (1926-) 228, 287
   Esther (CONOLD) (1908-) 227, 287
   Evans 163, 164, 227
   Evelyn 287
   Evelyn (DONALD) (1904-1993)
     227
   Evelyn Ann (1925-) 227, 287, 343
   Grace 227, 287
   Grace (WALLINGFORD)
     (1900-) 227
   Harriet J. (1924-) 227, 287
   Hazel (IHLE) Mrs (1908-) . . . 227
   J. K. 163
   James 163, 287
   James Kyle (1867-1922) . 111, 164
   Kile / Kyle 163, 287
   Kyle Evans (1908-1957)111, 227, 287
   Lillia M 163
   Maud / Maude 163, 226
   Maud Ella (1899-1988)
     . . . . 111, 226, 286
   Nancy B. (1923-) 227
   Salome Arzela (CLARKE)
     (1846-1925) 111
   Shirley 228, 287
   Shirley (1926-1983) 343
   W. A. 163
   William 287
   William Arthur 163, 227, 287
BRUCE
   Mary F 117, 173
   Robert H. Cpt 170
BRUEN
   Cynthia (1847-1910) . . . 121, 175
BRUMELL
   Alma J 241
BRUNELL
   Minnie 241
BRUNK
   -?- 54
BRUNS
   Henry T. 82, 124, 179
   Jno. B. 82, 179
   Luella (SMITH) (1873-1930) . 124
BRUNST
   Herman 286
BRYANT
   Gloria (Kirby) (1942-) 347
BUCEY
   Delores Naomi (1903-1988) 191, 242
   Fredrick 191, 242
   Lois 191, 242
   Naoma D 242
   Ruth M 242
BULLARD
   Walter 129
BUNN
   Phillip R 165
BUNTON
   Thomas 73, 166
   William 73, 166
BURKE
   Elizabeth (1762-1822) 18
   James 59
   Rebecca 59
   Walter 59
BURKHARDT
   Alena 130
BURLINE
   Allene 339, 373
BURNGROVER
   Gretchen L. (1900-) 202, 257
BURNS
   Campbell 67, 68
   Emily 68
   Emily Ann (1839-1917) 45
   Emma 67
   Fannie C 81, 179
   Jane (MELVIN) 45
   John Campbell 45
   Telitha 71
BURNSIDE
   Donald Clay (1938-) 328
BUROW
   Fredrick R 169
BURR
   George 72
BUSKIRK
   Bruce B 355
   Cyntha A 355
   Cynthia wife of Joseph B. 313
   Emmet H 355
   Erma G 355
   Farris N 355
   Joseph B 313, 355
   Melissa Rosaline (HICKS)
     (1920-2001) . . 63, 143, 258, 313
   Rosalene . . . . iii, 258, 355
   Russell S. (1909-1990) . . 313, 355
   Willis J 355
BYERS
   May 307
CABANNE
   Stella (1856-) 204
CABLISH
   Edna 159, 283, 373
   Evelyn 159, 283, 339
   Evelyn C. (1908-1954)
     . . . . 223, 339, 373
   Fred 159

CABLISH continued
    Jacob (1845-1922) 223, 283
    Margaret (BODEY) (1855-1920)
        223
    Mary Edna H. (MEENACH)
        (1886-1970). 223, 283
    Robert 223, 283
    Robert Fredrick (1883-1946)
        . . . . 223, 283, 373
CALVERT
    Alexander 283, 339, 373
    Alexander Hart (1906-1961)
        . . . . 339, 373
    Alexander H Jr 283, 373
    Evelyn C. (CABLISH)
        (1908-1954) 283, 339, 373
    Francis (1880-) 339, 373
    Katherine 373
    Louise 373
    Pierce 339, 373
    Virginia (NORTHNAGEL) (1929-)
        339
CAMARA
    Arthur James (1927-) 334
CAMPBELL
    Eliza 69
    Ruby Edith 291
CANN
    (---) (KEESTER) (1870-) 49
    Anna 76
    Annie L. (1871-1875) 49
    Christian 76
    Cina 76
    Clinton 76
    Ella 76
    Emma 76
    Faye 76
    George 76
    Grover 76
    Irwin 76
    John 49, 76
    John (1838-1903) 49
    Margaret M 76
    Margaret Missouri (ROBINSON)
        (1844-1883) 49
    Melissa Blanche (1869-) . . 49, 76
    Missouri Belle (1878-) 49, 76
    Ott 76
    Otto Willard (1870-) 49
    Robert 76
    Robert Clayton or Clinton
        (1867-1892). 49
CANTER
    Sarah 136
CAPPEL
    Joan Dd. (1944-) 313

CARGAL
    Perry Hobart (1942-) 317
CARHART
    Charles Victor (1929-) . . 338, 373
    Fannie B 373
    Joan Faye (JONES) (1928-) . . 338
    John 334
    Kimberly Ann 338
    Leslie Jill (1954-) 338
    Ralph M. (1901-) 338, 373
    William Charles (1958-) 338
CALEY
    Carrie 82
CARLSON
    Elsie (1913-1993) 209
CARNES
    Grace 137
CARPENTER
    Sarah E 77
CARR
    -?- 293
    Mary 171, 293
    Mary "Mollie" (1867-) . . 116, 171
CARSTENS
    Dorothy L. (1917-) 349
CARSTENS
    Dorothy L 377
CARTER
    Andrew E 158
    Esther 158
    Louis 61
    Mary 158
    Sada 61
    Sarah E. 29
    Sarah Elizabeth (1839-1919) 51, 78
CASE
    Alan 66, 157
    Edith (1899-) 193
    Linda Guyette 157
CASTOR
    Mary E. (1933-1999) 335
CASTORA
    Alice 373
    Bettie Ann (1921-1994) . 341, 373
    Rose (1899-) 341, 373
    Stanley 341, 373
CASTRO
    Walter R. (1925-1975) 306
CATALINA
    Angela (1933-) 318
CATTARON
    Willard (1937-) 320
CATTEN
    John 6
CECILIANI
    Gail 366

CHACON
    John (1916-) 347
CHALFANT
    R. 23, 25
    Robert 23 24
CHAPMAN
    Blanche 76
    Christopher (1869-1910) 49
    George 357
    Lila 357
    Matilda 151
    Mary (1801-) 43
    Melissa Blanche (CANN) (1869-) 49
CHARLES
    Caroline Marie (GLEASON)
        (1880-1960) 236, 297
    Hazel 356
    Mary Louise (1910-) 236, 297
    William 236, 297
    William S. (1872-1961) . 236, 298
CHATTERTON
    Bertha B 299
    Harry 237
    Lucile 299
    Lucille C. (1900-) 237, 299
    Nellie / Nettie 31, 82
    Sadie C 299
CHERRY
    Bertha Mabel (1885-1930) 218, 279
CHIARA
    Margaret Ann (MCNAIR) (1932-)
        202
    Walter Raymond (1929-) 202
CHICHESTER
    Bethriah S wife of E. (1877-) . 218
    Eliphalet L (1873-) 218
    Faye Opal (EVANS)
        (1901-1974) 218
    Glenn V. (1901-1968) 218
CHOJNA
    Craig Stephen (1965-) 342
    Janie Marie (HICKS) (1939-) . 342
    Stephen (1938-) 342
    Stephen William (1961-) 342
    Susan Laura (1966-) 342
CHRISTENSEN 371
CHUMINA
    Leon G M 174, 295
CINA
    Frances (1939-) 342
    Civil War 26, 32, 42, 45-47,
        . . . . 54, 59, 62, 66-68, 72, 74, 84
    59th OVI 26
    Missionary Ridge 46

CLARK / CLARKE .. 211, 269, 365
  Adele (OSBURN) (1940-) .. 334
  Amy Luella (COOPER)
    (1902-1974) 333, 370
  Ardith Faye 334
  Avis Maude 333
  Benjamin M 208
  Carol Deane 334
  Cecil 186
  Cecil Emmett (1901-1970)
    .... 217, 333, 370
  Cecil Wayne 333
  Christie wife of John (1873-) . 208
  Donna Beryl 333
  Edith Irene (1923-1950) 334
  Edith Zeta Mabel (1910-1999)
    .... 217, 334, 371
  Edna 208, 267
  Edna Pauline (ROSS) (1883-) 208
  Elroy Emmett (1941-1944) ... 334
  Elva Helen (1882-1953) 210, 269
  Emmet 186, 371
  Florance 371
  Florence Annette (BOSSINGHAM)
    (1904-1982) 334
  Georgia 186, 370
  Georgia Gladys (1898-1966)
    .... 217, 333, 370
  Glen W. (1893-) 208, 267
  Gordon 371
  Gordon Glenn 334
  H C 85
  H. C. Mrs. 34
  Harvey 85
  Harvey (1859-1930) 56
  James Emmet (1874-1953) 217, 277
  John (1862-) 208
  Laura Amy 333
  Leontine Orrene (JONES)
    (1877-1964) 217
  Leta 186
  Lola 66
  Lucinda Mrs 44, 66
  Mark H 208
  Mary 66, 85
  Mary Elizabeth (HICKS)
    (1860-1931) 56
  Maxine Elsie 334
  Michael J. (1941-) 319
  Millie 85
  Nellie 85
  O Leta 371
  Orville 363
  Orville Dale (1897-1897) 217
  Orville P. (1925-) 322
  Orville P. (1901-) 322
  Orville Paul 322
  Ray Gail (1942-) 334
  Roscoe 186, 370
  Roscoe Delbert 334
  Roscoe Glenn (1902-1983)
    .... 217, 334, 370
  Ruby 267, 363
  Ruby (BROADWELL)
    (1906-1963) 322
  Ruth Mary (FLAHERTY)
    (1931-) 333
  Salome Arzela (1846-1925) .. 111
  Veronica (-?-) (1932-) 334
CLARKSON
  Ina (1869-) 110
CLAYTON
  A. G. (1925-) 314
  Eva Irlene (DEVORE) (1925-) 314
CLEM
  Edna (1894-1938) 127, 182
  Ethel 182
  Nancy E. wife of Willes (1874-)
    .... 127, 182
  Willes A (1869-) 127, 182
CLEMENT
  Frank (1899-) 231, 293
  Melissa L. (WALKER)
    (1900-1980) 231
  Melissa M 293
  Shirley (1924-) 232, 345
  Shirley M 293
CLIFTON
  Harlan G. (1942-) 319
CLINGLER
  Mary 77
  Minerva E 77
  William H 77
CLYDE
  Sandra (1935-) 330
COATE
  Mary 254
COBB
  Lelah (1893-) 196, 248
COCHLER
  Albert 31
COCHRAN / COCHORAN ... 167
  Everett 114
  John M. 114, 167
COCKRELL
  Levina 47, 73
COFFEE
  Martha 195, 248
COFFIN
  Thomas 4

COFFMAN
  Jennie wife of Wm (1872-) .. 233
  Nancy Ann 92, 132
COGSWELL / COGSELL
  Alta (1898-1984) 233, 295
  Jennie (1872-) 233, 295
  William (1864-) 233, 295
COLBURN
  Eliza 46
  Elizabeth 71
  Oliver C. 71
COLE
  Barbara (JOHNSTON) (1941-) 350
  Denny (1940-) 350
  Katherine 114, 167
  Lenny (1943-) 349
  Sherry Lynn [twin] (1960-) ... 350
  Terry Wynn [twin] (1960-) ... 350
COLEMAN
  Larry Vernon 226
  Verna Ruth (VERMILLION)
    .... 163, 226
COLTHAR
  Bell M 299
COLYER
  John 61
CONDIT
  Gladys 285
CONGER
  Ephraim L 150
CONN
  Emma N 362
  Maymie (1879-) 322, 362
  Oliver (1850-) 322, 362
CONNER 364
  Barbara (1901-1994) ... 323, 364
CONOLD
  Arthur (1886-) 227, 287
  Esther (1908-) 227, 287
  Marie L 287
COOKE
  Gregory (1952-) 348
  Patricia L. (STEVENS) (1952-) 348
COOPER 352
  Amy Luella (1902-1974) 333
  -?- 352
  Celia Mae (HUTCHISON)
    (1887-1972) 223, 283
  Charles H. (1845-1912) . 223, 283
  Charles Henry 283
  Charles Marshall (1882-1940)
    .... 223, 283
  D.J. 261, 357
  Emma V. (HARRIS) (1857-)
    .... 223, 283

COOPER continued
  Frances Marshall (1909-1930) 223
  Harris B 283
  Harry 283
  Marshall 223, 283
  May 283
  Medora 261, 357
  Milton Hutchison (1901-1919) 223
  Natalie 283
COPPICH
  Mary Ann 367
COPPOCK
  Mary (1865-) 325
CORNELL
  Mary E. (1864-) 193
CORRELL
  Robert Scott (1945-1970) 340
COSMAN
  Abraham 132
COUCH
  Joseph W 125
COUREY
  Linda (1892-1964) 198, 250
COURSON
  Joe Dr 359
COURTS
  Richard Lee (1947-) 328
COWLING
  Harriet M 193
COX
  Edwin 125, 180
  Inez (1906-) 125, 180
  James 84, 125
  James Hansford (1882-) . 125, 180
  Lena Gwendolyn (1920-2010) 238
  Mary A 125
  Mary Ellen (NEWKIRK)
    (1879-1912) 125
  Mildred (1908-) 84, 125, 180
  Mollie 180
  Nellie 180
  R. W. 180
  Roy 125
  Roy W. (1904-) 125, 181
CRAIG
  — 25
  Bill 25
  John 82
  Mary F. 293
  Samuel 293
CRAIN
  Janice (1948-) 309
CRANE
  Agnes 135, 252, 253
  Agnes Cleo (1911-) 199, 310, 354

  Alice B. (TAYLOR) (1893-1944)
    .... 135, 199, 252
  Birtha R 252
  Cortland C 252
  Forest T. (1893-) 199, 252
  Forest Theis 252
  George 252
  Hazel F 58
  James M 58
  Lena (THIES) (-1900) 199
  Maranda 252
  Mary Dr. 39, 58
  Matson 58
  W. E 252
  Wilen Ellsworth 252
  Wiley E. (1868-) 199, 252
CRANK
  Dona Kay (1964-) 332
  Donald (1963-) 332
  Donald K. (1936-) 332
  Julia Marie (JONES) (1947-) . 332
  Sarah (1971-) 333
CRAVEN
  Ronald (1946-) 316
CROME
  Emma 150
CULVER
  Charles (1927-1997) 334
CUMINS
  Benjamin 66
CUNNINGHAM
  Cheryl Colleen (1956-) 329
  Cynthia Carol (1950-) 329
  Michael Thomas (1947-) 329
  Virginia Marylin (HODGES)
    (1923-2007) 329
  William Bruce (1949-) 329
  William H. (1914-1970) 329
DAILEY / DAILY
  Emma 271
  Lola 271
  Lola (Jones) Myler 367
  Lola Agnes (JONES)
    (1880-1946) 212
  Nathaniel T. (1856-1929) 212, 271
  W. T. 271
DALE
  Linda Rae (1942-) 332
DANS
  Mabala 116
DAUGHERTY
  Bernice (1902-) 196
DAUGHTERS
  Adelia F. (LANHAM) (1881-1970)
    120
  Bruce T. (1877-1950) 120

  Delia F. 120
  Elizabeth (WEDDING) 120
  Turpin 120
DAVIDSON
  Adna 273
  Richard 273
DAVIS 171
  Allie M. (1924-) 226, 286
  Ann (1780-) 2, 8
  Chester 286
  Clara 286
  Clara Belle (VERMILLION)
    (1901-1994). 226
  Cora Jane (HICKS) (1860-1890) 45
  Elizabeth (1780-) 2, 7
  Ella 286
  Emma 362
  George (1905-) 205
  Harold A. (1921-) 226
  Harold R 286
  Irma Crystal (LEVI)
    (1905-1957) 205
  John Ire Chester (1899-) ..226, 286
  Linda Carol (1949-) 235
  Mary 246
  Sam'l 6
  Sarah 271
  William H. (1860-) 45
DAWSON
  Anna 227, 287
  Carl (1882-1929) 101, 187
  Charles W. 101
  Emarilla 'Rella' (JOSLIN)
    (1885-1919) 101, 187
  Emma (PIGMAN) 101
DAY
  Caroline (1927-1997) ... 205, 263
  Charles B. Mrs 165
  Cleon Joseph (1897-1920) ... 230
  Clessie 291
  Cleyon 291
  Dick 291
  Dorothy 230, 291, 375
  Dorothy (1900-1927) 345
  Dorothy Mildred 345, 375
  Fred R 165
  Harrison 230, 292
  Harry A. (1902-1906) 231
  Jenny wife of Harrison 230
  Joseph 291
  Mary 291, 292
  Mary (1895-) 230
  Nellie 291
  Nelly (ALTMAN) (1873-1946)
    230

DAY continued
- Richard 230, 291, 375
- Richard T. (1873-1952)
  .... 230, 292, 375
- Roy E. (1892-1897) 230
- Ruth 291, 375
- Ruth (1894-) 230
- Ruth (1910-) 345
- Samuel G. (1909-1912) 231
- Sarah 143

DEADMAN
- Elizabeth 6

DEAL / DEEL / DELL
- Carrie 139
- Charles Collins (1916-1953)
  .... 192, 243
- Collins 192
- Docia (1907-) 192, 243
- Edna 243
- Edna Edith (1914-) 192
- Ella (BRICKER) 192
- Estell (1908-1909) 192, 243
- Iva 243, 244
- Iva Lou (MANNING)
  (1881-1969) 192
- Jewel Virginia (SMITH) (1917-1996) 192
- Marjorie (1912-) 192, 243
- Mildred (1909-1908) ... 192, 243
- Miles Robert (1878-1951)
  .... 192, 243, 244

DEATLEY 269

DECARLO
- Josephine 288

DECROW
- Roger A. (1943-) 310

DELAY
- Gomer 72, 166

DENNISON
- Geo. W. Mrs. 29

DENNLER?
- Sharon (1947-) 320

DEVORE
- Allan Lewis (1960-) 314
- Dianna Jo (1953-) 314
- Dorothy Jean 356
- Eva D 258
- Eva Irlene (1925-) . 203, 258, 314
- Gerald Lee (1943-2007) 204
- Herbert L 258
- Herbert Leroy (1906-1970)
  .... 203, 259
- Irlene 142, 258, 259
- Irlene Evelyn (HICKS)
  (1904-2002) 203

- Jannette Anne (LINDSEY)
  (1936-) 314
- Jay 356
- John W. 356
- John Wilson "J. W." (1931-1988)
  .... 203, 314, 356
- John Wilson Jr. (1957-) 314
- John Wilson 258
- Lewis Abner (1884-1945) ... 203
- Melissa Rosetta (1933-1933) 203, 258
- Pamela Sue (1952-) 314
- Stella Rosetta (SHAW) 203

DEWALD
- George W. (1917-1986) 222
- Mary Jane (GILFILLEN)
  (1918-1994), ... 222

DICE
- Caroline 296

DICHOLD
- Dorothy 284

DISBRO
- Marilyn (HICKS) (1924-) 228
- Marilyn J 289
- Richard D 289
- Unknown (1924-) 228

DITTMAN / DITMAR
- Chester (1910-) 345
- Chester Franklin 345, 375
- Florence (1930-) 345
- Ruth (DAY) (1910-) 345

DODSON
- -?- 54

DOMBROWSKI
- (---) (1951-) 341

DONALD
- Evelyn (1904-1993) 227, 287

DONHAM
- Inez (1886-) 311
- Jacob 354
- Sarah (1800-1851) .. 38, 39, 57, 60

DONNALY
- Louise 246

DONNER
- Henry 155

DOOLEY
- John 275

DOOR
- John 6

DORRIS
- Jessie Lee (1921-) 197, 249

DOUBERLEY
- Betsy 377
- David 357
- Elisabeth Ann "Lis" 357, 377
- James 357

- Mary Elizabeth "Betsy"
  (STOCKTON) 357, 377

DOUD
- Christine (MORIE) (1946-) .. 337
- Deborah (1953-) 337
- Elizabeth Jane (JONES)
  (1914-1995) 337
- George T. (1865-) 337, 372
- Jane (1950-) 337
- Josephine (1881-) 337
- Judith Ann 337
- Laurence (1913-2002) .. 337, 372
- Lawrence J 372
- Mary B 372
- Thomas Patrick (1945-) 337

DROWN
- Olive A. (1883-) 46, 70

DUCKETT
- Lida 246

DUGAN
- Elizabeth (1824-1910) .. 203, 257
- Leanna (1856-1935) 96
- Susan Ann (1898-) . 203, 257, 258
- Virginia E. (1903-) 330

DUNBAR
- -?- 284
- Lillian 160
- Lillian [Emma?] (1872-) 109

DUNLAP
- Florence 358

DUNN
- Aletha E 277
- Frank L 277

DURDEN
- Johnny "Tex" (1926-) 333

DURFEE
- Lawrence Richard (1947-) ... 337

DURHAM
- Benedict (1854-1920) ... 108, 157
- Charles 139
- Charles Elliott (1940-) 202
- Charlie E. (1860-1941) 98
- David Joe (1939-) 202
- Effie 139
- Effie (TATMAN) (1870-1931)
  .... 98, 139
- Eleanor (SWING) (1905-) 99
- Ethel D 157
- Gretchen L. (BURNGROVER)
  (1900-) 202, 257
- John (1826-) 98, 139
- Josephine (OWENS) (1863-1926)
  .... 108, 157
- Josie M 157
- Mary (JONES) 98

DURHAM continued
- Phillip 99, 139, 257
- Phillip T. (1902-) 202
- Raymond 157
- Rogers Lynde (1936-) 202
- Selena H. 157
- Warren Tatman (1898-1978) . . 99

DUVAL
- H. C. 63
- Joanne Vivienne (1939-) 315

DWYER
- Donald (1947-) 343
- Evelyn Ann (BRUBAKER) (1925-) 343
- George William (1923-1972) . 343

EASTHAM
- D. D. 111
- Emma V (KINCAID) 111
- Georgia Kathryn (HICKS) (1900-1924) 111
- Paul Hargis (1884-1930) 111

EASYBUCK
- Elizabeth (POHLMAN) (1876-1942) 223
- Frances M. 224
- Frances Marshall (COOPER) (1909-1930) 223
- Joe (1874-1947) 223
- Lovell (1907-1995) 223, 224

EBEL
- Estella 285

EDWARDS
- Anna 367
- Anna (LIVINGSTON) (1876-) 325
- Anna (STATZMAN) 234
- Arch (1874-) 234, 296
- Beartric E 296
- Edna Clare (JOSLIN) (1889-1931) 144, 187, 206, 264
- Elfring E 296
- Elizabeth 278
- Galen Harold (1921-) . . 234, 296
- Harold M. (1902-1975) . 234, 296
- Harrison 278
- Harry M 296
- Harry Morgan (1926-1999) . . 235
- Hershal G 296
- Lilian (RUDD) (1932-) 235
- Lois Lucille (1930-2003) 235
- Lucy (UTTER) (1903-) 234
- Lucy F 296
- Martha M. (STAATS) (1926-) 234
- Mary (1930-) 206
- Mary A 296
- Mary A. (1879-) 234
- Merrill 296
- Myrl M. (1899-1986) . . . 325, 367
- Robert Merrill (1924-) . . 234, 347
- Stanley D (1867-) 325, 367
- Vern H 296
- W B 144, 264
- Wanita (HUFF) (1921-) 234
- William (1864-) 206
- Wm. B 264

EGLOFF
- Anna W. (1900-1995) . . 347, 376

EIFFERT
- Catherine L. 323

EKELUND
- Dora Mae 344
- Dora N (1928-) 344
- Locleus L (ROGERS) (1906-) 344
- Oscar (1904-) 344
- Oscar Thomas 344
- Oscar Thomas Jr 344

ELLIOTT
- Mary 347, 376

ELLIS
- Blaine (1910-) 335, 371
- Darlene 335
- Fred W. 335
- Grace (EVANS) (1910-1992) . 335
- Gerald B 335
- Iris Joan (SOUTHCOTT) (1929-) 335
- Mary 371
- Max 371
- Nancy Jo 335
- Roxie wife of Fred 335, 371

ELLSBERRY
- Bertha M 274

EMERY
- Ira J. 129

EMMONS / EMMENS
- David 42
- John Eselman (1867-1938) . 42, 62
- Lurena Dee (TATMAN) (1874-1960) 42 62
- Martha (MCNUTT) 42

ENSOR
- Clarence 165
- Russell 165

EPPS
- Mildred Carolyn (1952-) 317

ERTLE
- Caroline Lou (1945-) 345
- Mildred Ruth (HALL) (1918-1986) 345
- Roy (1917-1942) 345
- Roy (1945-) 345

ERWIN
- Nancy 178

ESSEX / ESSECKS
- Albert 105, 153
- Frances 105, 152
- Frances (1852-1930) 105, 153
- Francis 274
- Frank 152
- Joanna (BROADWELL) (1823-) 105, 153

EUBANKS
- Alice Agnes (JONES) (1916-1992) 327
- Christine Theresa (SIDEWELL) (1946-) 327
- James L. (1872-) 327
- James Thomas (1900-1972) . . 327
- Laura wife of James (1872-) . . 327
- Raymond Lewis (1943-) 327

EVANS
- Dale Elizabeth (1906-1987) 218, 278, 335, 371
- Dorthea Gladys (1912-1997) 218, 278, 335, 371
- Faye Opal (1901-1974) . . 218, 278
- Gayle Orene (1899-) 218
- Grace 218, 278, 371
- Grace (1910-1992) 335
- Karen Lynn 336
- Laura Mona (1903-1974) 218, 278, 334
- Orene G 218, 278
- Rex 278, 371
- Rex Willard (1915-1950) 218, 336
- Romaine (ZIMMERMAN) (1916-) 336
- Roxy Dale (JONES) (1880-) 217, 278, 371
- Teresa (MCCLANAHAN) (1953-) 348
- Timothy (1953-) 348
- William C 277, 278
- William Jacob (1877-) 217, 277, 278
- Wilma 278
- Wilma Jesse (1908-1987) 218

EVERTS 15

FAGIN
- Alpha (1898-) 128, 188
- Berdie 239
- Burl P 239
- Charles R. (1875-1916) . . 188, 239
- Cora (MANNING) (1878-1900) 188
- David M. 239
- Elizabeth 188
- Hazel L 239

FAGIN continued
- James 239
- Stanley W 239

FALOON
- Dorothy 284
- Frances (1957-) 342
- Frances (CINA) (1939-) 342
- Francis 284
- Francis wife of John (FALOON) (1879-) 225
- Grace 284
- Hazel 160, 284, 285
- Hazel (HICKS) (1909-1993) . 225
- Henry 284
- Janet Lea (1938-) 225, 341
- John 225, 284
- John (1961-) 342
- John R. (1905-1965) 225
- John R. (1879-) 225
- Karen (1967-) 342
- Richard 284
- Richard Lee (1934-) 225, 342
- Susan (1956-) 342
- William 284

FANCHER
- Hulda (1821-1873) 100

FARNHAM
- Erma (1879-) 56, 85
- Herbert (1859-1908) 56, 85
- Mary 85
- Mary Elizabeth (HICKS) (1860-1931) 56

FARRAND
- Steve 347

FAUBEL
- Beverly Ann 334
- Delona Jean (MCKNIGHT) (1927-1995) 334
- Dorla Deane 334
- Earl 371
- Earl Lloyd (1904-1995) .. 334
- Earl Lloyd Jr. (1927-) 334
- Edith Zeta Mabel (CLARK) (1910-1999) 334
- James Everett 334
- Lloyd 371
- M Edith 371
- Peggie 334, 371
- Rita (HAVERMAAL) (1933-1988) 334

FEE
- David 25
- Georgia 140
- Mary "Polly" (1805-1876) 42
- Mary 62

FEHR
- Elizabeth 288

FELENZ
- Harriett 267

FENKER
- Edward Louis (1952-1954) ... 307
- Eunice Irene (PATTISON) (1916-) 307, 351
- Ludwig (1902-1964) ... 307, 351

FENTON
- Addie (1855-1897) 100, 142
- Ida 100

FENWICK
- Janet Lea (FALOON) (1938-) 341
- Marvin (1929-) 341

FERRIE
- Imo (1891-) 201, 255

FEZER
- Amber C 221

FIGGINS
- Edgar (1885-) 311, 354
- Inez (DONHAM) (1886-) 311, 354
- Lulu (1907-1975) 311, 354

FINLEY
- Linda Mrs 374
- James 188
- Joseph I 188

FIRESTONE
- Cynthia (1813-) 46, 69

FISHER
- Elmirah (1803-) 52, 79
- James 31

FITZPATRICK 57
- Able 57
- Addie wife of Walter (1866-) .. 92
- Airee? (SEWARD) 196
- Ben 59, 60, 93
- Benjamin 60
- Benjamin F. (1860-1936) 40
- Bernice (DAUGHERTY) (1902-) 196
- Callie (MANNING) (1870-1966) 40
- Charles 131, 246
- Charles C. (1868-) 40
- Clifford 60
- Daisy B 93, 133, 249, 250
- Daisy B. (1901-1964) 197
- David Wayne (1948-) 309
- Diana 39, 57, 59, 92, 132
- Diane (1953-) 309
- Dianna (TATMAN) (1825-1867) 38
- Ella 246
- Ella Marie (NICHOLS) (1895-1928) 194, 246
- Emerine 57
- Ethel (1891-) 93
- Ethel G 132
- Fannie L. (BECKETT) (1888-1952) 194, 246
- Gail A. (1903-) 93, 133
- Galen A 249
- George (1941-) 196
- George 38, 57, 132, 137
- George E. (1854-1940) 132
- Gertrude (1866-1937) 39, 59
- H. T 249
- Hal (1895-) 93
- Hanley (1902-1992) .. 92, 196, 249
- Hannah 57
- Homer 91, 131, 133, 246, 249, 353
- Homer Jerome (1849-1935) 38, 57, 91, 131
- Homer Tatman (1908-1971) 93, 197, 249
- Hope (BARTON) (1921-2001) 309
- Hugh 57
- Ida 58, 60, 62, , 131 132, 137, 138
- Ida Blanche (1863-1937) .. 38, 58
- J. L 249
- J. L, Jr 249
- J. C 246
- Janice (CRAIN) (1948-) 309
- Jerome Homer 57, 131, 245
- Jessie Lee (DORRIS) (1921-) 197
- John ..... 24, 38, 39, 42, 57-60, ... 93, 131, 133, 246, 249
- John (1820-1911) 39
- John Charles (1888-1973) 92, 194, 245, 246
- John Lee (1856-1929) 93
- John Lee 40, 87, 93, 133, 249
- John Lee Jr (1900-1957) 196, 249
- John S. (1863-) 38
- John Sherman (1863-1937) 40, 93, 133
- John Willard (1915-1979) 93
- Jonathan 57
- Laverne 249
- Len.. 250
- Leorna L 133, 249
- Linda (MILLER) (1947-) 197
- Linda Margaret (1943-) 197
- Lynne (1955-) 309
- M M 249
- Mabel (1896-) 93
- Mabel (WEST) (1897-) 194
- Mabel L 132
- Maggie 93, 133, 249

FITZPATRICK continued
  Margaret 57, 93
  Margaret M. (MANNING)
    (1870-1949) 93
  Mary 59, 60, 249
  Mary Emma (1858-1905) 40
  Mary Laverne (1924-) 309
  Mary Laverne 197
  Mary Laverne (TANKERSLEY)
    (1905-1964) 196
  Mary Olive (1858-1908) ... 38, 57
  Minnie L. (1865-1937) 40, 59
  Minnie S 60
  Missouri 24, 58-60
  Missouri "Sue" (1850-1928) ... 39
  Nora 133
  Nora B. (VAIL) (1873-) 93
  Olive 57
  Oliver 40, 59, 60, 93
  Oliver L (1867-1936) 40, 59
  Ollie 75
  Ora D. (1881-1882) 92
  Pearl Diana (1882-1972)
    .... 92, 131, 193, 245
  Randolph (1849-1870) . 39, 59, 60
  Reece (1862-1890) 40, 59, 93
  Richard Douglas (1957-) 309
  Ruth 58, 59, 60, 131
  Ruth E. (1854-1905) 39
  Ruth Gertrude 58
  Ruth L. (1865-1920) 39, 58
  Sadie 132
  Sadie (HANLEY) (1855-1931) . 92
  Sadie Christine (1941-) 196
  Samuel (1851-) 38
  Sandra Louise (1941-) .. 197, 309
  Sara Ellen 248
  Sarah 58-60, 62, 87, 248
  Sarah (DONHAM) (1800-1851)
    .... 38, 39
  Sarah A (TATMAN) (1828-1890) 39
  Sarah Ellen (1850-1921) 92
  Sarah Ellen ... 131, 246, 247, 249
  Sarah Jane 57
  Sarah R. (1852-) 39, 60
  Sherman 133, 250
  Solomon (1793-1868) .. 38, 39, 57
  Steven Brewster (1961-) 309
  Susan 131, 246
  Susan A. (TEVEBAUGH)
    (1854-1931) 91
  Terry Baxter (1947-) 197
  Walter 38, 39, 58, 62, 132
  Walter (1861-1910) 92
  Wayne N, ... 131, 246
  Wayne Nichols (1921-1987)
    .... 194, 309, 353
  William 57
  William B. (1855-1900) 40, 59, 60
  Zachariah 39, 57-59, 132
  Zachariah (1826-1867) 38
  Zachariah (1856-1867) 38
  Zelphia E. (1907-) .. 93, 133, 249
FLAHERTY
  Ruth Mary (1931-) 333
FLAUGHER
  Parthena Mae (1886-1974) 314, 356
FLORENCE
  Edna Marilyn (1951-) 314
FLORES
  Patricia Kaye (BROWN) (1946-)
    340
  Rudolph R. (1946-) 340
FLOYD
  Mary 77
FLUKER
  Warren 349
FOLEY
  Cynthia 176
  James 176
FORESTER
  Charlie 205
FOSTER
  Addaling L 368
  Carl (1896-1969) 210
  Dortha M 368
  Edith G 368
  Electra Collins (1823-1893)
    .... 50, 54, 77, 84
  Elizabeth H 367, 368
  Hannah Elizabeth (MYLER)
    (1907-2007) 326
  Jennie L. wife of T. (1860-)
    .... 326, 368
  Joann E 367
  Joann Elizabeth 326
  John W 368
  Kathleen (BROADWELL)
    (1906-) 210
  Nancy J. (BOWERS) (1937-) . 326
  Theopholis (1855-) 326
  Thomas G 367, 368
  Thomas Gavin (1906-1968)
    .... 326, 368
FRANNFELDER
  Elizabeth Ann (1949-) 350
FRAZIER
  -?- 124. 256
  Anna Belle (1912-) 96, 136
  Florence J. (TATMAN)
    (1871-1919) 96, 136
  Lulu (REMLEY) (1889-1982) . 96
  Mildred (1902-1949) 96, 136
  Raymond T. (1892-1915) . 96, 136
  Rebecca 131
  Walter C. (1866-1961) ... 96, 136
  Walter P 136
FREDRICKSON
  Ann Marie (1960-) 338
  Anna 371
  Denise Marie (KAY) (1957-) . 338
  Gene L. (1932-) 338
  Roger William 338
  Shirley Lou (JONES) (1930-) . 338
  Susan Kay (1957-) 338
  Thomas Gene (1963-) 338
FREMONT
  General 68
FRENCH
  Florence Madlyn (1917-2000) . 205
FRISLER
  Edward 166
  Gordon 166
  Lulu 166
  Stanley 166
FRODGE
  Eugene Martin 357
  Ivetta Faye (JENNINGS) (1932-)
    .... 259, 315
  Jacqueline 357
  Michael Robert (1954-) 315
  Rhonda Yvetta (1952-) 315
  Robert W. 356
  Robert William (1931-) 315
  Sheree Lee (1955-) 315
FROST
  A. J. Mrs 337
  Clara Edith 356
FRY
  Alvin (1920-) 310
  Amy (1953-) 310
  Chas. 63
  Harold (1947-) 310
  Ruth (HUTSON) (1920-) 310
FUGAT / FUGETTE
  Elizabeth Stewart (HITE)
    (1914-1986) 312
  Flora Mae (TACKETT) 312
  Floyd B. (1912-1939) ...312, 355
  Nancy Elizabeth 313
  Norman 312, 355
FULLER
  Elizabeth L. (1876-) 194
  John P. (1839-) 194, 246
  Linda Diana (1949-) 328
FURY
  Mary 124, 179

GALLIUM
   Thomas 6
GANNON
   Anna 207, 266
GARRISON
   Benjamin (1860-) 325, 367
   Dewey Frank (1898-1948) 325, 367
   Dinah Lee (WEBB) (1947-) . . 326
   Frank 367
   Gale 367
   Hazel Faye (STORER)
     (1921-2002) 326
   Jack L. (1921-) 326
   Jerry Carson (1944-) 326
   Lola Gayle (MCMAHAN)
     (1900-1988) 325, 367
   Mary (1877-) 96
   Mary (COPPOCK) (1865-) . . 325
   Mary Ann 367
   Mary Lee (HILL) (1934-) 326
   Mary Luis (1923-) 326, 367
   Mort 367
   Wayne Franklin (1924-) . 326, 367
GARTEN
   Lottie 331
GATES
   -?- 251
   Emma (1862-) 199
GAYLORD
   Cecil R (1899-) 233
   Stanton Ray (1923-) 233
   Wilma June (PENNINGTON)
     (1925-1979) 233
GEIER
   Cynthia Carol (CUNNINGHAM)
     (1950-) 329
   Jane Mrs 359
   Kirby Lee (1946-) 329
   Tom 318
GERDES
   Judith (1940-) 325
GEST
   Nathaniel 25
GEYER
   Ann Lorene (LUCAS)
     (1937-) 326
GIBBONS 269
GIBSON
   Gertrude wife of Kenneth
     (1886-1968) 114, 169
   John William 168
   K. E. 170
   Kenneth (1886-1968) 114, 168, 289
   L. A. 289
   Lydia 168, 229, 289, 374

   Lydia Ann (TATMAN)
     (1858-1938) 114, 168, 169
   Mary M 168, 289
   Mary May (1889-) 114, 168
   R. E 289
   William (1834-) 114, 168
GILBERT
   William Thomas (1918-) 330
GILES
   Eliza 21, 32, 33
GILFILLEN
   A.W. 281
   August (1850-) 221, 282
   Carris C 282
   Elsie 282
   Emma Lucille (1911-1912) . . 222
   Ethelene (1906-) 158, 221, 222, 281
   Gussie E. (HOLDERFIELD)
     (1880-1918) . 158, 221, 222, 282
   James 282
   John 158, 221, 281, 282
   John Graham (1879-) . . . 221, 282
   Marie (1848-) 221, 282
   Mary F 282
   Mary Jane (1918-1994) . . . 222
   Nellie 282
   Tomas 282
   Wm 282
GILLENA
   Marian 273
GILLESPIE
   Marsha 55
GLASSCOCK
   Larry Clayborn (1948-) 342
   Lee Ann (RODEN) (1948-) . . 342
GLEASON
   Caroline M 177, 236
   Caroline Marie (1880-1960)
     . . . . 122, 236, 297
   Ella 31, 52, 177
   Ella F. (WHITE) (1859-1938)
     . . . . 122, 177
   Guy (1882-) 122
   Guy O 177
   Jno. C. (1857-1920) 122
   John C. 177
GLENN
   Emma M. 284
   James P. (1876-) 224
   Margaret (1904-) 224
   Margaret (RUDGERS) (1874-)
     . . . . 224, 284
GLOVER
   Charles 254
   Charles Lee (1910-1960)
     . . . . 254, 312, 354

   Darrell (1926-1983) 311, 354
   Dorothy H. (1908-1971)
     . . . . 201, 254, 311
   Elsie Julia 254
   Estella H. (HUTSON)
     (1883-1957) 200, 201, 254
   Givens (WITHAM) (1916-) . . 312
   Hodgson 254, 354
   Inez Lucille (BRILL) (1920-) . 312
   Julia Elsie (1906-2002)
     . . . . 201, 254, 311, 354
   Lena Lucille (1943-) 312
   Lulu (FIGGINS) (1907-1975)
     . . . . 311, 354
   Mary Elizabeth (1904-1913)
     . . . . 200, 201, 254
   Samuel 200, 254, 354
   Samuel (1879-1930) 200
   Samuel H. (1842-1913)
     . . . . 200, 201, 254
   Samuel Hodgson (1903-1965)
     . . . . 200, 311
   Samuel Lee (1943-) 312
   Sarah Elizabeth (ROUSCH)
     (1846-1932) 200
   Stella 254
   Wanda (BATES) (1945-) . . . 312
GODING
   Bertha May 205
GOEBEL
   Merideth Margaret (1939-) . . . 331
GOEDJKA
   Mayme 47, 74
GOINGS
   Margaret (TATMAN) (1907-) 100
   Robert (1907-) 100
GORDON
   Gracia (1887-1988) 233
GOREBRUND
   Carl 177
GORTZAK 365
GOTOS
   Josephine (1881-) 96
   Louis F. (1897-1984) 96
   Mildred (FRAZIER) (1902-1949) 96
GOWER
   Reginald Price (1951-) 343
GRANVILLE
   Kenneth Russell (1937-) 338
GRAVES
   James Alfred 346
GRAY
   Flora (1899-1974) 98
   Jenny 292
   Kenneth Conner (1928-) 326
   Mary Jane 293

GREEN / GREENE
  Beulah 360
  George 207, 265
  Ida Beulah (1891-1979) . 207, 265
GREENBURG 6
GREGG
  Clara (WOODLIEF) (1861-) 236, 298
  Clarke W. (1911-1985)
    . . . . 236, 298, 348, 376
  Darlene Fay 349
  Dorothy 377
  Dorothy L. (CARSTENS)
    (1917-) 349
  Dorothy M. (HAMPEL)
    (1918-1982) 348
  George 236, 298
  George Whitlock (1916-1916) 237
  George Woodlief (1882-1970)
    . . . . 236, 298
  Georgeanne (1941-) 349
  Jacqueline 349
  James 31, 298, 376
  James Woodlief (1912-2005)
    . . . . 236, 349, 376
  Jill (1947-) 349
  Marie 31, 298
  Marie W. (WHITE) (1885-1965) 236
  Marilyn (Barnes) (HERRLE)
    (1928-) 349
  Mathew James (1963-) 349
  Missouri 298
  R. W. C. (1859-) 236, 298
  Susanne (1938-) 349
GREGORY
  Barbara (OWENS) (1948-) . . . 314
  Cecil Thomas (1918-) 314
  Eva Irlene (DEVORE) (1925-) 314
  Grace (PAUL) (1898-) 314
  Melody Lynn 314
  Richard Thomas 314
  Thomas (1898-) 314
  Yvette 314
GRIGGS
  Annabell (ANDERSON)
    (1909-1978) 346, 375
  Drucilla (1941-) 346
  Glorene 346
  Ida May (BENSON) (1886-1947)
    . . . . 232, 294
  Jeannie (SCHAFFER) (1937-) 346
  Kendall 29, 51
  Leta P (1920-) 232, 294
  Lloyd 294, 375
  Lois M 294
  Lois Marie (1915-1990) 232, 346, 375
  Lois Meryle (1943-) 346
  Marie 294
  May 294
  Milton Dwight 346
  Neva Jane (NANCE) (1933-) . 346
  Ora Kendall 346
  Ora W 294
  Orie 232, 294
  Orie Wagerman 294
  Orie William (1879-1928) 232, 294
  Orville 375
  Orville Mack (1929-1930) . . . 346
  Phoeba E 294
  Phoebe wife of William (1858-) 232
  Richard Neil 346
  Sylvia Jane (LEAK) (1942-) . . 346
  William (1845-) 232
  William 294
  William Lloyd (1909-1975)
    . . . . 305, 346, 375
GROGH
  Cathy Laverne (1953-) 309
  Luana (1955-) 309
  Mary Laverne (FITZPATRICK)
    (1924-) 309
  Neighl (1922-) 309
GRUELLE
  Belinda Flo (WEEKLY) (1953-) 329
  Beryl Josephine (JONES) (1932-) 329
  Durwood Timothy (1952-) . . . 329
  Ferd (1880-) 329
  Jerome Kent (1956-) 329
  Joel Kevin (1956-) 329
  Ollie (1887-) 329
  Wilfred D. (1928-) 329
GUDEMAN
  Cynthia Jane (WHITE) (1951-) . 350
  Steven (1951-) 350
GUINN
  Gloria Marie (1942-) 347
  James A. (1874-) 347, 375
  James E 375
  Jasper J 375
  Lois Marie (GRIGGS) (1915-1990)
    . . . . 346, 375
  Naomi (NORTHCUTT) (1880-)
    . . . . 347, 375
  Telephus "Tex" (1916-1990) 346, 375
  W G 375
GUNDERLACK
  Joan Carol (1947-) 332
GUY
  Cynthia Sue 343
  Edward Howard (1919-1996) . . 342
  Eleanor Bernice (RODEN)
    (1928-1986) 342
  Gayle Lynn (WRIGHT) 343
  Gregory Howard 343
  Lora Lynn (1956-) 343
GUYETTE
  Adaline (HOUKE) (1809-1884) 108
  Augustus (1808-1880) 108
  Daughter 339
  Edward W (1914-2001) 157, 221, 339
  Ethel D. (1896-) 108
  Irene Dolly (PLANK)
    (1918-1987) 339
  Josephine (OWENS) (1863-1926) 108
  Josie Owens Mrs 157
  Linda 157
  Raymond 157
  Raymond J. (1911-1967) 221
  Raymond Joseph (1892-1952)
    . . . . 108, 221, 281
  Rosa 108, 157
  Selma (1889-1944)
    . . . . 108, 157, 221, 281
  Sydonia R (LEPAGE) (1893-1989)
    221
  William 157
  William (1836-1896) . 108, 157, 281

HAASE
  Harriet Mildred (1908-1999) . . . 119
HACKMAN
  Mildred L 136
  Ray R 136
HADLEY
  Ashton West 205
  Carol (OBERLE) (1956-) 341
  Frances (1919-2008) 205, 262
  Robert (1956-) 341
HAGEN
  Anna wife of Henry 319, 360
  Henry 319, 360
  Hilda 360
  Marcella B. (1909-1989) . 319, 360
  Micheal 360
HAGSED
  Louise (1945-) 317
HALCOMB
  Lawrence 6
HALCOURT
  Philimon 6
HALFHILL
  Lewis 76
HALL
  Alfonso E 292
  Allison 292
  Almira 67
  Alvin 292
  Ann (1923-) 306
  Barbara Ann (HICKS) (1940-)
    . . . . 258, 314

HALL continued
- C M 292
- Cairy L 292
- Cicero 231, 292
- Cicero (1923-) 345
- Cicero Malcomb (1885-1936) 231, 292
- Denise (1952-) 345
- George O'Neal 56
- James Edward "Rocky" Jr (1960-) 314
- James Edward (1935-) 314
- Joe E 292
- John R 292
- Julia Olive (1915-) 220
- Lou 292
- Lou Altman 292
- Lou Elizabeth 292
- Lou Elizabeth or Selena (OSBORNE) (1855-1948) . . 231
- Manuel (1856-1948) 231, 292
- Margaret Faye (1905-1999) 56
- Mayme Ethel (1884-1959) . . . 126
- Mildred R 292
- Mildred Ruth (1918-1986) 231, 296, 345
- Millie Lou (ALTMAN) (1888-1977) 231, 292
- Monone May (WATTS) 56
- Salena 292
- Samuel (1950-) 345

HAMILTON
- Dorothy Louis (BRITTINGHAM) (1893-1974) 116
- Hamilton 243
- Jasper M.D. (1893-) 116

HAMM
- John William Jr (1936-) 318

HAMMERLE
- Helen wife of George (1903-) . 325

HAMPEL
- Dorothy M. (1918-1982) 348, 376

HAMTON
- Wm 6

HANCOCK
- Eliza 136
- Elizabeth (1848-1868)! 41
- Henry 31
- Martha 31

HANLEY
- Caroline (1853-1944) 90, 128, 239
- Margaret (LIMING) 90
- Redmond 90, 132
- Sadie (1855-1931) 92,, 132
- Sarah F. 132

HANNAH
- Anna O 94, 134
- Eva 136

HANSEN
- Jens Allen (1941-) 311
- Julia (AULT) (1942-) 311
- Mary Francis 362

HARGEN
- Charles Gene (1952-) 338

HARRIS
- Blanche 375
- Carl W. (1925-) . . . 241, 308, 352
- Charles E. (1928-) . 241, 308, 352
- Charles Edward 352
- Edith (1838-1873) 39
- Edith M. 241, 352
- Edith May (PATTISON) (1906-1994) 307
- Elizabeth (1874-1939) 125
- Emma V. (1857-) 223, 283
- James F. (1929-) . . . 241, 308, 352
- Lydia 352
- May (BYERS) 307, 353
- Nancy E 180
- Rose M. (1923-) . . . 241, 308, 352
- William 307, 353
- William Carl (1886-1929) 307, 352, 353

HARTFORD
- Bonnie Rae 335
- Charles (1903-1974) 334
- Laura Mona (EVANS) (1903-1974) 334

HARTMAN
- Electra 368

HARVES
- William 275

HASTINGS
- Peter 28

HATFIELD
- George Bennett (1875-) 96
- Mary Louise (TATMAN) (1883-) 96

HAUCK
- Lula 306

HAULY
- ___ 239

HAUN
- Lena 174

HAUNCH
- Nancy 69
- Timothy 69

HAVCK
- Lula 351

HAVERMAAL
- Rita (1933-1988) 334

HAWK
- Judith Kae (JOHNSTON) (1951-) 350
- Thomas Harold (1950-) 350
- Thomas Jeremy (1971-) 350

HAWKINS
- Virginia B 169

HAWLEY
- Edna 360
- Edna (1880-) 319

HAYDEN
- Bob 263
- Elizabeth 144, 263, 359
- Elizabeth (JOSLIN) (1918-1975) 317
- Howard (1912-1996) 144, 317, 359
- James (1944-) 317
- Janie 318
- Jim 263, 359
- John 263, 318, 359
- Robert (1938-) 317, 359
- Saundra wife of John 318
- Tina wife of John 318

HAYS
- Leslie 291
- Newell Raymond 291
- Raymond 291
- Ruby Mrs 229, 291

HAZELIP
- Jacqueline (1943-) 319

HELMICK
- Dexter 114, 167
- Erma C 167
- Escalene R (1911-) 114, 167
- Frank T 167
- Fred C. 167
- Fred Cole (1879-) 114, 167
- Irma Clare (JONES) (1879-) 114, 167
- Katherine (COLE) 114
- Thomas [twin] (1913-) 114
- Wardie [twin] (1913-) . . 114, 167

HELVERING
- Alma 149-151
- E. G Mrs. 211
- Edward G 269
- Edwin G. (1871-) 104, 149, 211, 269
- Elsa 151
- Elsie (KAHLKE) (1887-1980) 104
- Ervin G 269
- Guy 149-151
- Guy Tresillian (1878-1946) 104, 150
- Ida (WILLIAMS) (1871-) 211, 269
- Kenneth M. (1894-) 211, 269
- Lillian Gertrude (1873-1878) . 104
- Mary Alma (1888-) 104, 151
- Nancy J. 149
- R. L Mrs 151
- Robert 149-151
- Robert Louis (1883-1961) 104, 151
- S J 149, 151

HELVERING continued
   Samantha Jane (JONES)
     (1850-) 103, 149-151
   Tinnie (KOESTER) (1878-)
     . . . . 104, 150
   W J 149-151
   William 149, 151
   William Joseph (1846-) . 103, 150
HEMMERLE
   George (1902-) 325
   Helen (1903-) 325
   Jean Elaine (1928-) 325
HENDRICKS
   Debbie (MCCLANAHAN)
     (1949-) 348
HENDRIXSON
   Allice 254
   Blanche (1898-1973) . . . 200, 254
   Charles 254
   Chas. F. (1876-) 200, 254
   Clark 254
   Minnie (SOLWALL) (1877-)
     . . . . 200, 254
HENNIES
   George (1923-) 333
HENSON
   -?- 293
   George Harrison 293
   Gladys 293
HERBST
   Jessie Elizabeth (Betty) (MCNAIR)
     (1926-2005) 312, 355
   Lee Anne (1961-) 312
   Leroy (1926-) 312
   Nancy Kay (1956-) 312
   Roy Edwin (1951-) 312
   Theresa Lynn (1952-) 312
HERRIOT
   Alice L. wife of Oscar (1872-)
     . . . . 225, 285
   Leila (1887-) 225
   Luella 285
   Oscar E. (1870-) 225, 285
HERRLE
   Marilyn (Barnes) (1928-) 349
HICKS / HIX 15
   (-) (DOMBROWSKI) (1951-) 341
   — 178
   A. G? 164
   Adda H. (PORTER) (1888-1920)
     . . . . 111, 112, 165
   Addie (FENTON) (1855-1897) 100
   Albert 33, 85, 127, 182
   Albert Alden (1857-1907)
     . . . . 22, 55, 85, 300
   Alexander 31
   Alfred 32
   Alif Maude (1877-) 47, 70
   Alonzo 33
   Angie (1964-) 343
   Ann (DAVIS) (1780-) 2
   Ann Maria (1839-1882) 21, 31, 52
   Anna 31, 66, 80, 82
   Anna Bertrand (MORSE)
     (1861-1938) 53
   Anna L. (1859-) 45
   Anna Marie 30
   April (1974-) 343
   Arthur 70, 71, 112
   Arthur S. (1878-)
     . . . . 47, 70, 111, 164, 165
   Barbara Ann (1940-)
     . . . . 203, 258, 314
   Becky Sue (1943-) 224, 341
   Benjamin (1768-1804) . . . 2-8, 14
   Bennett 127, 182
   Bernard 127, 182
   Bernard Russell (1919-1994) . 127
   Beryl L. wife of Frank S. (1883-)
     . . . . 47, 73
   Bessie 257, 258, 355
   Bessie Marie (RODGERS)
     (1899-1966) 203
   Bessie Mrs 355, 356
   Betsy (UTTER) (1804-1840)
     . . . . 17, 18, 29
   Bettie / Betty 112, 165, 284
   Bettie Ann (CASTORA)
     (1921-1994) 341
   Betty (AUSTIN) (1921-) 224
   Betty (KAUF) (1937-) 341
   Betty Ann (1919-) 112
   Betty Ann 165
   Beulah 265, 360
   Blaine 27, 35, 73, 145, 146
   Blaine Melvin (1895-1985) 102, 146
   Blanche E. (1883-1888) 55
   Bonnie Elaine 341
   Brenda Kay (1956-) 313
   Brittania 72
   Bryon (1898-1899) 102
   Burnett 182
   Byron Francis (1954-) 321
   C. R. J. 26, 167
   Callie 26, 161
   Callie James (1876-1979)
     . . . . 45, 109, 160
   Caroline 26, 27, 30, 72-74, 165-167
   Caroline (WHETSTONE)
     (1822-1894) 20
   Caroline Rebecca J. (1851-1928)
     . . . . 26, 47, 74
   Caroline W. 70
   Caroline Wise (1871-1952)
     . . . . 47, 111, 163
   Carrie 67, 81, 179, 287
   Carrie (1872-) 52
   Cecil 85
   Charles 33, 84, 85, 127, 182
   Charles James (1852-1893) . 22, 54
   Charles Jefferson (1894-1976)
     . . . . 56, 127, 182, 300
   Charley 33, 85
   Charley Frank (1862-1864) . . . 45
   Clara (HOPKINS) (1847-1920) 52
   Clarence 72, 167, 228, 288
   Clarence M. II (1920-) 228
   Clarence M. IV (1975-) 343
   Clarence M. III (1942-) 343
   Clarence Malcolm 47, 167
   Clarence Malcolm (1882-1925) 113
   Cora Jane (1860-1890) 45, 67
   Corrie 67
   Curtis 85, 182, 259
   Curtis Ivan (1889-1967) 55
   Daniel 7, 8, 208, 362
   Daniel (1934-1996) 322
   Daniel Richard (1958-) 322
   daughter 14, 18
   daughter (1819-) 14
   daughter (1882-) 55
   Daughter (1823-) 18
   Daughter (1889-1889) 100
   Daughter (1890-) 56
   Daughter (1940-) 228
   David 284, 341, 374
   David Lee (1938-1973)
     . . . . 224, 341, 374
   Deborah (1955-) 313
   Diana 10, 14-16, 23, 29, 32, 33, 35
   Diana (ADAMS) (1768-1850)
     . . . . 14, 33, 38
   Dion 145, 208, 267, 362
   Dion Jr. (1929-) 321
   Dion Williams (1898-1960)
     . . . . 102, 208, 267
   Dona L. (1906-) 113, 167
   Donald Rogers (1930-)
     . . . . iii, 203, 258, 313, 356
   Donna Lynn (1947-) 313
   Dorothy (SHERMAN) . . 124, 313
   E. 64, 68
   E. F. 63, 142, 147
   E. F. Mrs 147
   E. Franklin 141, 142, 147
   E. P. 166
   E.M. P. 26

HICKS continued
- Edna 63, 182, 257
- Edna (CLEM) (1894-1938) .. 127
- Edward Franklin 142
- Eleanor (1929-) 125
- Elijah   6, 8, 14-15, 17, 19, 21, 23,
  . 24, 26, 30, 32, 35, 63, 67-71, 105
- Elijah (1799-1853) 18
- Elijah (1837-1888) 45
- Elijah Franklin (1855-1935) 43, 87,
  ... 100, 141, 147, 187, 258, 259
- Eliza (1774-) 2, 6, 8
- Elizabeth ... 19, 26, 37, 43, 63-65,
  .. 66, 70, 71, 103, 141, 142, 147,
  152, 153, 163, 181, 185, 257, 258
- Elizabeth 'Betsy' (1804-1880) 14, 20
- Elizabeth (DAVIS) (1780-) 2
- Elizabeth Ann (MEENACH)
  (1840-1921) 46
- Elizabeth B. (MCDONALD)
  (1895-1931) 124
- Elizabeth Jane 6
- Elizabeth Macdonald 180
- Elizabeth Meenach 164
- Ella (YANCY) (1878-1967)
  .... 84, 85, 111, 164
- Ella Y. Dr 164
- Elsie 35, 47, 72, 73, 166
- Elsie (1874-1903) 113
- Elsie Glendora (PRICE)
  (1904-1993) 102
- Emil (1919-) 127, 182
- Emily Ann (BURNS)
  (1839-1917)' 45, 67, 68
- Emma 67, 143, 284, 285
- Emma Georgia Anna (BEEKER)
  (1867-1928) 102, 187
- Erastus 25, 27, 69
- Erlene 103
- Esther M. (BARNES) (1853-)
  .... 45, 66, 67
- Ethel 182, 285
- Eva Lou (1906-) 124, 179
- Fannie M 160
- Floriene (1903-1910) 109
- Frances (1925-) 124
- Frances [King] (MILLER) (1875-)
  109
- Frank   ... 63, 72, 73, 88, 89, 100,
  ...... 102, 141, 143, 147, 166,
  .... 257, 258, 261
- Frank St. Clair (1872-) 47
- Franklin 63
- Frederick 6
- G A 55, 182
- Gary Lynn 238
- Georgana 179
- George 27, 72, 158
- George W. (1847-1882) 19
- George W. ... 19, 25-27, 66, 69, 71
- Georgeta 80
- Georgia 80, 88, 89, 147, 164
- Georgia (1879-1954) 53
- Georgia Anna (1847-) 53
- Georgia Anna 21, 30, 81
- Georgia B. 141, 147, 148
- Georgia Elizabeth .. 100, 187, 259
- Georgia Elizabeth (1908-2000) 204
- Georgia Kathryn (1900-1924) 111
- Georgian 81
- Georgie 82, 179, 261
- Glen 85, 182
- Glenn Alvin (1882-1954)
  .... 55, 126, 182
- Glenn H. 284
- Glenn Kelly 224, 284
- Gordon B. (1890-) 53, 83
- Gordon Benavil 83
- Gordon R. 31
- Grace (TUCKER) (1893-) 55
- H. F. 64, 141, 143
- H. H. 63, 146, 147, 264-267
- H. M. 63, 143
- Hannah Francis (OWENS)
  (1821-1907) .. 37, 42, 63, 87, 89
- Harriet 31, 83
- Harriet JoAnn (1928-)207, 320, 360
- Harriet Mary (BAXTER) (1825-)
  .... 21, 50
- Harry 84, 85
- Harry (1887-) 55
- Harvey 63, 89, 146, 265, 266
- Harvey Henry (1862-1950)
  .... 27, 43, 102, 145, 267
- Harvey J 145, 265, 360
- Harvey John (1889-1979)
  .... 102, 207, 265, 266, 360
- Hattie 141
- Hattie Edna (1877-1938)
  .... 100, 203, 257
- Hattie Sarah (STEWART)
  (1855-1905) 100 141
- Hazel 109, 160, 225
- Hazel (1909-1993) 225
- Hazel Lee 225, 284
- Helen 83, 179, 207, 265, 360
- Helen (1899-) 124
- Helen (1918-) 319
- Helen (STANTON) (-1991) .. 313
- Helen R. (1891-) 54, 83
- Henrietta (1920-1993)
  .... 207, 265, 319, 360
- Henry ... 6, 8, 14, 15, 17, 23, 30,
  .... 35, 66, 73, 144, 145
- Henry (1795-1843) 18
- Henry M. .. 25, 27, 63, 69, 141, 147
- Henry Melvin (1826-1905)
  ..... 19, 27, 37, 42, 63, 87, 89
- Hurdes   ... 89, 141, 142, 147, 257
- Hurdes Beeker (1898-1984)   100,
  .. 187, 203, 257, 258, 355, 356
- Ida 66
- Ida (1866-1870) 45
- Ida Beulah (GREEN) (1891-1979)
  207
- Ida Fenton 100
- Irlene 141, 142, 187, 258
- Irlene Evelyn (1904-2002)
  .... 100, 203, 258
- J. J 63
- James . 2-4, 6, 7, 15-17, 19, 25-27,
  .. 30, 33, 67-69, 71, 74, 82, 160
- James (1770-1830) 2
- James (1811-1850) 20
- James (1836-1924) 45
- James Alphonse (1847-1899) .. 22
- James P. 284
- James R. (1886-1886) . 31, 53, 82
- James Reuben (1850-1938)
  .... 21, 53, 82
- James Walter (1843-) .. 21, 31, 83
- Janet (1951-) 313
- Janie Marie (1939-) 225, 342
- Jas. R 179
- Jean (WUNKER) 321
- Jeanette Merle (1941-) . 225, 342
- Joan 265
- John 6, 25-27, 33, 35,
  . 69, 74, 100, 102, 147, 158, 261
- John (1824-1863) 19
- John J. 141, 142, 147, 148
- John James (1864-1935) . 43, 63,
  . 87, 102 141-143, 146-148, 187
- Johnnie 141, 257
- Josephine (HOPKINS) (1851-1941)
  .... 50, 54 77, 84
- Joshua .. 2, 4, 5-8, 13-15, 17, 19,
  ... 23, 25-27, 30, 32, 33, 35, 38,
  .. 66, 69, 71, 73, 102, 158, 300
- Joshua (1765-1848) 14
- Joshua (1815-1900) 221
- Joshua (1833-1906) 45
- Joshua Jr. 14, 33
- Jossie 84
- Julian 85, 182
- Julian Stephen (1899-1981) ... 56
- Karen 374

-396-

HICKS continued
  L R 83
  Laban 3-7, 15
  Laura 146
  Laura Francis (RUMMEL)
    (1896-1952) 102
  Lavina Britana (1867-1949)
    . . . . 47, 72, 112, 165
  Layfiett 33
  Lena Gwendolyn (COX)
    (1920-2010) 238
  Lesh Jr. 284
  Leslie 284, 374
  Leslie Brand (1905-1961)
    . . . . 109, 224, 284
  Leslie William (1926-2007)
    . . . . 224, 341, 373
  Leslle B. 374
  Levina Caroline (UTTER)
    (1845-1928) 47, 73
  Lewis 31, 83
  Lida 69, 162, 285
  Lida H. (1867-) 46, 110, 162
  Lillian 284
  Lillian [Emma?] (DUNBAR)
    (1872-) 109
  Lilly 160
  Louis 21, 31, 32, 77, 83, 84
  Louis (1849-1920) 50, 54
  Louis Raymond (1886-1959) . . 53
  Louisa 31
  Louise 77, 84
  Lovina C. 166
  Lucie 265
  Lucie Mary Francis 359
  Lucy 63, 74, 87, 143, 145,
    . . . . 207, 265, 267, 359
  Lucy Ann (1857-1888) 43, 100, 143
  Lucy Mary Francis (1885-1964)
    . . . . 64, 102, 206, 264
  Lydia (1802-1861) . . 14, 17-19, 28
  Lynda Lee (1932-) 224, 284
  Mabel (1910-) 127, 182
  Madeline 145, 267
  Madelyn (VASKE) (1905-1988)
    . . . . 208, 267
  Malissa 141
  Mame 182
  Manda 30
  Marcella 88, 103, 147, 148,
    . . . . 187, 258, 259
  Marcella Delores (1908-2000)   103
  Margaret
    . . . 14, 27, 29, 31, 145, 267, 284
  Margaret (1810-1890) 20
  Margaret (GLENN) (1904-) . . 224
  Margaret Ethel (1909-) . 225, 285
  Margaret Faye (HALL)
    (1905-1999) 56
  Margaret Sarah (WELLS) (1864-
    1931) 102, 146, 186
  Marian 72
  Marilyn (1924-) . . . 113, 228, 288
  Marilyn J 167, 288
  Maris M 82
  Marjorie 73
  Marjorie Geraldine (MCATER)
    (1939-) 322
  Marsha Rose 238
  Martha . . 7, 25, 27, 33, 35, 69, 70
  Martha Ann (1840-1900) 46
  Martha Ann 19, 26, 69
  Martha E. (1862-1924) 22
  Mary 14, 15, 19, 28, 30, 33,
    . . . . 64, 145, 152, 263, 264, 282
  Mary (1803-1878) 19
  Mary (1827-1900) 43
  Mary Cecil (1890-1930)
    . . . . 55, 84, 126, 181
  Mary E 63, 66, 182, 282
  Mary E. (1922-) 127
  Mary Elizabeth (1860-1931) . . . 56
  Mary Elizabeth (1860-1955) . . 101
  Mary Elizabeth 22, 43, 85,
    . . . . 144, 187, 263, 264
  Mary Emma (1858-1934)
    . . . . 45, 108, 158
  Mary J (1845-1932) 21, 31
  Mary L. wife of Clarence (1886-)
    . . . . 113, 167
  Maurice Hurdes . . . 257, 258, 355
  Mayble E 182
  Mayme 74, 182
  Mayme Ethel (HALL)
    (1884-1959) 126
  Mayme (1877-) 47
  Mayne Goedjka 74
  Melissa . . . 88, 141, 142, 147, 258
  Melissa (BEEKER) (1865-1949)
    . . . . 100, 187, 258, 259
  Melissa Rosaline (1920-2001)
    . . . . 203, 258, 313, 355
  Merle (1908-) 126, 182
  Mildred E. (MITCHELL) (-1961)
    . . . . 224, 284
  Minerva (MARSHALL)
    (1830-1870) 45, 66
  Minna 266
  Minnie 26, 64, 67, 68, 145,
    . . . 160, 207, 208, 266, 360 361
  Minnie Clara (1893-1983)
    . . . . 102, 207, 264, 266, 361
  Minnie M 67
  Minnie Martin (1867-1944) . . . 45
  Miriam (1916-) 127, 182
  Morris 258
  Morris Hurdes (1924-)
    . . . . 203, 258, 313, 355
  Morris Jr. (1963-) 313
  Myrtle 257
  Nancy 16, 19, 25-27, 32-33, 35, 65,
    66, 69, 71, 74, 84, 108, 125, 157, 167
  Nancy (1817-1846) 21
  Nancy (1831-1865) 44
  Nancy (MELVIN) (1806-1903)
    . . . . 18, 37
  Nancy (MOORE) (1943-) 341
  Nancy B. (1862-1939) 45, 108, 158
  Nancy O. 288
  Nancy Olivia (1870-1937)
    . . . . 47, 112, 166
  Nathaniel 6
  Nettie W. (WHITAKER)
    (1846-1927) 53, 83
  Nora 45, 67, 179
  Nora (HUDDLESTON) (1877-)124
  Nora Sureanth (1865-1930)
    . . . . 45, 109, 160
  Norma (1922-) 113, 228, 288
  Norma C 167, 288
  O. D. 63, 187, 257, 261
  O. M. P 26, 27, 73, 165
  Olevia 72
  Opal Louise (1922-) 203, 258
  Orestes D. 63, 72, 141, 257
  Orestes Daily "O.D." (1851-1934)
    . . . . 43, 100, 140
  Orestes Marion Polk (1845-1902)
    . . . . 19, 27, 47, 72
  Orestus 74, 257
  Patricia Marie (1960-) 314
  Paul (1892-) 55, 84
  Poke / Polk   35, 67, 71-73 165-167
  Polly (1776-) 3, 6, 9
  Raymond (1913-1922) 103, 147, 148
  Rema 181
  Richard A. (1925-) 127, 182
  Robb A 179
  Robert   31, 52, 179, 284, 359, 374
  Robert A. (1874-) 124
  Robert James (1939-) . . . 224, 341
  Roberta Lynn (1961-) 341
  Roger Wayne (1957-) 313
  Ronald Leslie (1948-) 341
  Rosalane 63, 143, 257, 355
  Rosalyn Lynn (1962-) 313
  Roscoe 85, 182
  Roscoe (1880-1953) 55

HICKS continued
- Ruth 14, 24, 32, 35, 61, 83, 167 182
- Ruth (1797-1874) 18
- Ruth (1907-) 126
- Ruth (MORRISON) (1898-1957)
  113
- Ruth Babe 167
- Ruth wife of Lewis (1891-1970) 53
- Sadie 85, 182
- Sadie Bell (ROBERTS)
  (1858-1937) 55
- Sally 7, 80
- Samuel 3-6, 8, 14, 15
- Samuel (1745-1806) 2
- Sarah   7, 15, 16, 21, 30, 33, 80, 84
- Sarah (1843-) 52
- Sarah Ann . . . .
- Sarah Ann (MORGAN)
  (1824-1909) 15, 22, 34
- Sarah Ellen (REED) (1861-) . . 54
- Sarah F. (HOPKINS) (1849-1888)
  . . . . 50, 54
- Sarah Francis (1853-1859) 43
- Sarah L 31, 77, 84
- Sarah Louise (1886-1972) 54
- Shawn Dion (1961-) 322
- Sherman (1865-1932) 22, 33, 34, 56
- Shirley 359
- Shirley Ann (1963-) 341
- Solomon 7
- Stanley Markham (1902-1954) 111
- Steven Dion (1956-) 321
- Susan Ann (DUGAN) (1898-) 203
- Thomas 6, 74
- Uncle Hy 63
- Unknown (1745-) 2, 14
- Veara Rose (MOORE)
  (1933-1995) 313
- Verna 55, 84, 126, 181
- Verna (1886-1970) 126
- Victora 35, 69, 162
- Victoria E. (WARBINGTON)
  (1844-1916) 45, 69, 162
- W. A. 83
- W. H. 164
- W. H. Dr 164
- W. Morse 82
- W. Morse Dr. 180
- W. S. 165
- Walter P 72, 73
- Walter Polk (1878-1942) . . 47, 73
- Wendell (1914-1996) . . . 127, 182
- Willard Burnett (1919-1974)
  . . . . 238, 300
- William 2-6, 8, 14, 15, 17, 22,
  . 23, 25-27, 30-33, 67, 69, 71, 72,
  . . . 160, 164, 166, 225, 284, 285
- William (1772-1810) 2
- William (1816-1850) 21, 50
- William (1845-1906) 22
- William A 31, 83
- William Alexander (1845-1929)
  . . . . 21, 53, 83
- William H. (1876-1925) 70, 111, 164
- William J (1843-) 21, 31, 52,
  . . . . 80-82, 179
- William M 109, 285
- William M. (1914-1998) 225
- William Merle Jr (1946-) 225
- William Morse Jr (1924-) 124
- William Morse 53, 179
- William Morse (1887-) 124
- William P 160, 284
- William Pearce (1872-1962)
  . . . . 45, 109, 160
- William R 33, 359
- William S 70, 71, 164
- William Stephen (1842-1920)
  . . . . 19, 46, 70, 108
- Willis Albert (1916-2008) 127, 182
- Wm M. Dr. 31

HIGGENS / HIGGINS
- __ne (1929-) 195, 248
- A Jack 247
- Adeline E 132
- Anie M 247
- Annie 247
- B. F. 247
- Bert/ Burt 194, 247, 353
- Burton (1877-1947)
  . . . . 92, 131, 195, 247
- C Pearce 248
- Claude C. (1876-1893) . . . 92, 131
- Claude E 249
- Edith 248
- Edith Elizabeth (QUINN) (1890-
  1958) 195, 248
- Edith L. (1916-) 195, 248
- Edward N (1919-) 195, 248
- Elizabeth 194, 195, 246, 247
- Elizabeth (1900-) 195
- Elizabeth (1908-) 195
- Elizabeth L. (FULLER) (1876-) 194
- Elizabeth Linda 246
- Eugene H (1920-) 196
- Eula Pugh (RAWLINSON)
  (1879-1952) 195, 247, 353
- F. O. 353
- Frances Cullen 246
- Frank 92, 247, 309, 353
- Frank (1876-1973) 195
- Frank Oliver (1900-1965)
  . . . . 195, 309, 353
- Frederick (1879-1882) 92
- Frederick Allen 131, 249
- Glenn 247
- Gussie 194
- Gussie Rainer 194
- Guy 92, 131, 186, 195,
  . . . . 246, 247, 249
- Guy (1874-1951) 194
- Guy Jr (1910-1913)   194, 195, 246
- Herman A (1928-) 196
- Inez 247
- Irene L 248
- J B 194
- James 248, 249
- James M. (1915-) . . 131, 196, 248
- James Monroe (1890-1971)
  . . . . 92, 196, 248, 249
- Jane 248
- Jane wife of James M. (1889-) 196
- Jennie 231 293
- Joe 247
- John 194, 246
- John Burton (1898-) 194, 246
- Lela Estelle 248
- Lelah (COBB) (1893-) . 196, 248
- Leroy 92, 131, 248
- Leroy (1886-1951) 196
- Leroy? (1926-) 195
- Lida Frances (1909-) . . . 195, 248
- Lucille 248
- Lyda F 248
- Marietta E. (HOGAN) (1903-) 309
- Martha 194, 248
- Martha F. (1918-) 196, 248
- Mary (1905-) 195
- Mary E 132, 353
- Mary E. (1924-) 309
- Mary Ellen (1900-) 195
- Maury 247
- Milton 248
- Milton S. (1917-) 196, 248
- Morris W (1922-) 196, 248
- Nancy Ann (COFFMAN) 92
- Pearce C. (1915-) 196
- Pearry 248
- Robert Franklin 247
- Rosalia 249
- Roy 248
- Roy F. (1913-) 196, 248
- Ruth 248
- Ruth E. (1918-) 196
- Samuel O 132, 246, 248
- Samuel Oliver (1849-1929)
  . . . . 92, 132, 249
- Sarah E 131, 246
- Sarah E. (1909-1911) 194
- Sarah Elizabeth 194

HIGGENS / HIGGINS continued
   Sarah Ellen 132
   Sarah Ellen (FITZPATRICK)
     (1850-1921) 87, 92
   Virginia (1914-) 195, 248
   William . . . 92, 131, 132, 247-249
   William (1904-) 195
   William K. (1922-) 196
   William S (1912-) 195, 248
   William Zachary (1884-1973)
     . . . . 92, 195, 248

HILGE
   Elizabeth E. (STEVENS)
     (1916-2010) 236
   Herman H. (1875-) 236
   Jack Willis (1918-1999) 236
   Mary wife of Herman (1877-) . 236

HILL 5
   Mary Lee (1934-) 326
   Mathew (1967-) 343
   Norma 288
   Norma (HICKS) (1922-) 228
   Thomas Kelly (1922-) 228
   Thomas Kelly II (1947-) 343
   Thomas Kelly III (1969-) 343
   Thomas Kelly 228

HINKLE
   Jo Ann (PATTISON) (1938-) . 307

HINNERACHS
   Bernita (1918-) 336, 372
   Caroline 372
   Henry 372
   Herbert (1887-) 336, 372
   Lena (1890-) 336, 372
   Lydia 372

HITCH
   Maude 194, 246

HITE
   Bodman 187
   Charles 143, 257
   Charles Bodman (1867-1925)
     . . . . 203, 257
   Chas. B 257
   Edna 141, 257
   Elizabeth 257
   Elizabeth (DUGAN) (1824-1910)
     203
   Elizabeth Stewart (1914-1986)
     . . . . 203, 312, 355
   Hattie Edna (HICKS) (1877-1938)
     . . . . 203, 257
   James 257
   James (1817-1900) 203
   Mary . . . . iii, 143, 261

HOCK
   Frank (1878-) 207
   Laverne Joseph (1902-1964) . . 207

Ruth Melvin (MEEKER)
   (1908-1977) 207, 265

HODGES
   Alice 273
   Alice wife of Frank T. (1872-) 214
   Donald (1922-1969) 218
   F. T 273
   Frank 273
   Frank T. (1854-) 57, 214
   Genevieve 273
   Genevieve Shinkle (JONES)
     (1896-1996) 214
   George 273
   George Thomas (1896-1968)
     . . . . 214, 273
   Jacob 57
   John 57
   Mary J 57
   Thomas 57, 273
   Virginia Marylin (1923-2007)
     . . . . 214, 273, 329
   Wilma Jesse (EVANS) (1908-1987)
     218

HOESING
   Arlene E. (1930-) 335

HOGAN
   Daniel 354
   Emmet O 354
   Jeromie V 354
   Linton D 354
   Marietta E. (1903-) . 309, 353, 354
   Mary 281, 309, 353
   Patricia Ann (1941-) 331
   Pearl Norris 354

HOLDERFIELD
   America (1829-) 108
   Emma 158
   Ethel 108, 158, 222, 282
   Ethel (1882-1937) 222
   Evelyn (1930-) 310
   Gussie E. (1880-1918)
     . . . . 108, 158, 221, 281
   Jussie 222
   Mary E 158
   Mary Emma (HICKS)
     (1858-1934) 108
   Taylor 158, 282
   Taylor B. 158
   Taylor B. (1858-1900) 108
   William (1821-) 108

HOLLAND
   Allen 139, 140
   Anna 139, 140
   Anna Rebecca (BRAGDON)
     (1847-1922) 99
   Archer 140
   Archie 139, 140

Archie G. (1873-1974) . . . 99, 139
Carrie (TATMAN) (1872-1956)
   . . . . 42, 62, 99, 139, 140
De 320
Dennis 360
Ethel 139
Eva 139
Harlem 324, 365
Janice L. 360
Janice Lynne (MCCRACKEN)
   (1954-) 320
Keith T 140
Keith Thomas (1907-1993) 99
Lilly 139
Rebecca A 140
Thomas 139, 140
Thomas (1833-1916) 99

HOLME
   Elizabeth (1892-1971) 119

HOLMES
   Alph (1851-) 308, 353
   L Alfred 353
   Maud (1874-) 308, 353
   Ruth N. (MANNING)
     (1915-1999) 308
   Samuel A. (1898-1970) . 308, 353
   Winston A. (1941-) 308

HOMAN
   Rebecca (1842-1919) 191
   William G 242

HONAKER
   Harold Carl Jr (1944-) 328

HOPKINS
   Anna B 84
   Annabell (1849-1931) . 50, 77, 84
   Beleo 79
   Benjamin 81
   Betsy 17
   Caroline 77
   Carrie (1857-1886) 50, 77
   Clara 29, 78, 80-82
   Clara (1847-1920) 52
   Clara Elizabeth (1863-1956)
     . . . . 118, 173
   De Leo (RHODES) (1877-1964)
     . . . . 51, 78, 119
   Diana (1826-1897) 20, 50, 78
   Dina 173
   Electra Collins (FOSTER)
     (1823-1893) 50, 54, 77
   Elizabeth 29, 174
   Elizabeth 'Betsy' (HICKS)
     (1804-1880) 20
   Elizabeth (HOLME) (1892-1971)
     119
   Elizabeth Ann (1837-1844) . . . 20

HOPKINS continued
George Wesley (1866-1884)
.... 29, 51, 78
Georgiana 80
Gertie M. 29, 78
Gertrud 78, 173, 174
Gertrude May (1879-1969)
.... 51, 119, 174
Gladys Mary Rosezella
(1924-1927) 120
Josephine (1851-1941)
.... 50, 54, 77, 84
Joshua 20, 77, 84
Joshua H. (1823-1890) 50, 54
Julia 174
Julia Rebica (BRAGG)
(1906-1971) 119
Katheryn (WILLIAMS) 119
Lavina 29, 78
Leslie 78, 119
Leslie Frederick (1914-) 119
Levi 17, 29, 78
Levi (1803-1883) 20
Levi Whitcomb (1840-1883)
.... 20, 51, 78
Mariah M 81
Mariah wife of Robert (1843-) . 52
Mary 20, 77, 81, 172
Mary (1825-1894) 50
Preston Dale (1927-) ... 120, 174
Robert 80, 81
Robert A (1842-) 52
Sallie 77
Sarah 29, 77, 78, 84, 173, 174, 295
Sarah Elizabeth (CARTER)
(1839-1919) 51
Sarah F. (1849-1888) 50, 54
Sarah Lavina (1861-1953)
.... 51, 118, 173
W R 174
W. L 79
Walter 173, 174
Walter Ralph (1882-1958)
.... 51, 119, 174
William 29, 78, 119, 173, 174
William Lincoln (1879-1952)
.... 51, 79, 119
HOTT
Paul R 113, 167, 288
Ruth B 167, 288
HOUGHTON
C Herman 376
Charles L. (1887-) 348, 376
Denise (1951-) 348
Janis (WOODRUFF) 348
Jerry (1949-) 348
Mabel L 376

Monica (1950-) 348
Ralph A. (1919-) 348, 376
Wilma J. (STEVENS) (1924-) 348
HOUKE
Adaline (1809-1884) 108
HOUSER
Chris 15
Clifford 63, 148
F. M. 148
Frances 148. 362
Francis M. (1841-1866) . 103, 149
George W 149
Isaac R 149
Mary 148, 149
Mary Frances (1863-1930)
.... 103, 208, 267
Minerva Elizabeth (JONES)
(1844-1935) 103
Nancy (1817-) 103, 149
Sarah E 149
Sylvester J 149
William Clifford (1862-) 103
Wm 149
HUBER
Renata (1946-) 332
HUDDLESTON
Mary (FURY) 124
Nora (1877-) 124, 179
Rollin 124, 179
HUFF
Wanita (1921-) 234
HURDIS
Wm. D. 262
HUTCHINS
-?- 283
Ella Catherine (BAIRD) (1933-)325
John M. Jr. (1927-) 325
HUTCHISON
Betty J. (WATSON) (1938-) . 224
Celia M 160
Celia Mae (1887-1972) 223
Celia Mae (TULLY) (1920-) . 340
Celia Mae 223, 283
Deborah (1942-) 340
Edward 68, 160, 283
Edward Roy (1892-1981)
.... 109, 224, 283
Edward White (1860-1949) 109, 160
Effie Nolean (1925-) 224, 283, 340
Gertrude (ACKLEY) (1925-)
.... 340, 373
Glenn (1935-) 224
John M 283
John or Jack (1919-) 340
Lena 283, 284
Lena (BREEZE) (1896-1996) . 224

Mary E. (WORTHINGTON)
(1827-) 109
May 223
Mildred B. (1915-2005) . 224, 339
Nancy Kay (1940-) 340
Nora 67, 68, 160
Nora Sureanth (HICKS)
(1865-1930) 109, 160
Robert L. (1927-)
.... 224, 283, 340, 373
Robin Ann (1956-) 340
Roy 160, 284
Roy Alvin (1954-) 340
Ruth Lenora (1923-) 224, 340
Ruth V 283
William 160, 224, 283
William (1823-) 109
William E. (1927-) 224
HUTSON / HUDSON / HUTTO
Alberta 136, 254
Alice 136, 254
Alice Mae (1926-) 200, 311
Arizona T. "Arra" (TATMAN)
(1865-1933) 97, 137
Blanche (HENDRIXSON)
(1898-1973) 136, 200, 254
Carlos Stanley (1895-1973)
.... 97, 136, 200, 254
Charles 136, 137 254
Charles Wilmer (1859-1947)
.... 97, 136, 254
Clara B 136
David 255
Dora 136, 254
Effie 255
Estella H. (1883-1957) 97, 200, 254
Flora 136
Gladys 97, 137, 255
Gladys E. (1889-1945) 201
Harriet (1930-) 200, 311
Ida 136, 137
Imo (FERRIE) (1891-) .. 201, 255
Jennie Mae (1912-2000) . 201, 255
John F. (1862-1954) . 97, 137, 255
Ledora Estelle (TATMAN)
(1862-1935). . 97, 136, 137, 254
Lena Bell (1886-) 97, 137
Ruth (1920-) . 136, 200, 254, 310
Sarah L 136
Stella 137 354
Susan (KINDRICK) (1838-) 97, 136
Walter 136
William 136, 137, 255
William (1838-) 97
William Oliver (1887-)
.... 97, 136, 201, 255

HUTTER
    Lavina C. 165

IDLET
    Gerald (1931-) 311
    Harriet (HUTSON) (1930-) . . 311
    Jerry (1955-) 311
    Sandy (1953-) 311
IHLE
    Hazel Mrs (1908-) 227
IRELAND
    Janet (RICHTER) 333
    Jessie Marie (JONES) (1913-) 333
    John (1889-) 333
    John C. Jr. (1910-) 333
    Joyce 333
    Mayme wife of John (1891-) . 333

JACKSON
    Elizabeth 239
    Ellen C. 247
    Ellen Christina 195
    Hellen Stauffler 290
    Mary L. (1921-) 328
JACOBS
    Alfonso C. 243
    Brian Harry (1957-1957) . . . 328
    Charles James (1920-) 328
    Gary Clinton 328
    Lida / Lilla 243
    Lilla B. (Walker) (1885-) 191, 243
    Linda Diana (FULLER) (1949-) 328
    Mary Beth (1959-) 328
    Mary Elizabeth (BECKELHIMER)
        (1921-) 328
JAMES
    James 67
    Lucy 3
JAUDON
    Ina Lynne (1948-) 317
JEFFERIES
    Henry 5
    William 8
JEFFERSON
    Albert (1916-1979) 339
    Donna Beth (STROUP) (1940-) 339
    Gerald Arthur 340
    James Edward 339
    John Charles 339
    Karen Lee (ADELMAN)
        (1945-) 339
    Mary Ester (KILBOURN)
        (1948-) 340
    Mildred B. (HUTCHISON)
        (1915-2005) 339
    Susan Carol 340

JEFFERY
    William 4
JENKINS
    Charles (1935-) 334
    Emily (1885-) 337, 372
    Margaret (1915-) 331, 369
    Mary Faith 337
    Mildred Gayle (JONES)
        (1909-2004) 337, 372
    Morris Verdon (1907-2003)
        . . . . 337, 372
    Naomi (1940-) 328
    Nellie M 82
    Samuel (1882-) 337
JENNINGS
    Clemons Michael (1967-) 315
    Elizabeth 142, 258
    Elizabeth (Hicks)
        . . . . 26, 43, 63, 66, 67, 147, 185
    Elvira 259
    Emerson Everett (1880-) 204
    Eugene 185, 259
    Eugene M. III (1972-) 315
    Eugene Martin 204, 259
    Eugene Martin 2nd (1939-)
        . . . . 259, 304, 315
    Eugene Martin (1904-1984) . . 204
    Georgia Elizabeth (HICKS)
        (1908-2000) 204, 259
    Irma Claire (1930-) 204, 315, 356
    Ivetta Faye (1932-) 204, 315, 356
    Jacqueline Lou (BERRY) (1942-)
        315
    Kimberley Ann (1977-) 315
    Lillie Mae (SCOTT) (1880-) . 204
    Lvera 26, 63, 66, 147, 204, 263, 264
    Lvera Adrienne (1929-) . 314, 356
JERNEGAN 265
    Mary (1839-) 102, 146
JERRELL
    Virgil Rev 359
JOHNSON / JOHNSTON 3
    Alex 15, 25, 175
    Alexander 16, 23, 30, 79, 120
    Alexander (1809-1879) 20
    Anna 30, 79, 175, 296
    Anne (ADRIAN) (1858-1918) 120
    Annie Belle (1865-1931)
        . . . . 51, 121, 176
    Aterburt Elliot "Burt" (1872-1903)
        52
    Barbara (1941-) 237, 350
    Birt 79
    Bonitta K. (1939-) 238
    Cora (NEWKIRK) (1884-1982)
        . . . . 32, 125, 181, 299
    David Allen (1972-) 350
    Dennis E. (1942-) 336

    Doyle 125, 181, 299
    Doyle Howard (1909-1984)
        . . . . 126, 237, 299
    Edith 352
    Elizabeth 30, 114
    Frank 30, 79
    Frank (1862-1889) 51
    Franklin 30
    Gary Doyle (1939-) 237, 350
    George (1857-) 125, 181
    Gertrude (WIEDENBACK)
        (1915-2009) 237, 300
    Gloria Jane (1945-) 237
    Gordon K. (1942-) 238
    Helen L. (SIMANTEL) (1912-)
        . . . . 237, 299
    Howard 125, 181, 299
    Howard Washington (1881-1985)
        . . . . 125, 181
    Ina B. (BEHL) (1915-) 238
    Janet E. (OLSEN) (1947-) . . . 350
    Jennie 30, 79
    Judith Kae (1951-) 237, 350
    Kate (1847-) 125, 181
    Lena 79, 120, 175
    Lena (1882-1920) 121
    Loren .. 125, 126, 181, 299, 300
    Loren K. (1914-1992) 238
    Lucinda Margaret (1853-1883)
        . . . . 51, 120, 175
    Lucy 30, 79, 120
    Margaret 16, 30, 79
    Margaret (HICKS) (1810-1890) 20
    Mary 30, 79, 120, 175, 176
    Mary (1947-) 328
    Mary (MANNING) (1833-1923)
        51
    Mary Elizabeth (1869-1960)
        . . . . 51, 121, 176
    Mary M. (1882-) 120
    Mollie E 296
    Nancy Jane 'Jennie' (1859-1926)
        . . . . 51, 79
    Ora 181
    Pearl 181
    Robert (1925-) 334
    Robert (1935-) 332
    Steven Douglas (1970-) 350
    Verle 125, 126, 181, 299
    Verle (1911-1985) 237
    W. J. 176
    William . 20, 30, 51, 79, 175, 176
    William (1872-) 52
    William Alexander (1856-1918)
        . . . . 51, 120, 175
    William J. (1828-1883) . 30, 51, 79

JONES 268
  A Grace 152
  Albert 37, 65, 152, 273
  Albert Doctor (1893-1955)
    .... 107, 220, 280
  Albert Essex (1874-1962)
    .... 105, 214, 273
  Alford / Alfred 153, 216, 276
  Alfred W. Jr. (1907-) 216
  Alfred William (1879-1968) .. 216
  Alfred William 106, 276
  Alice 272
  Alice Agnes (1916-1992) 213, 327
  Alma (RUDD) (1908-) 326
  Althea (WALKER) (1896-) .. 217
  Anna E. (RARDIN) Mrs.
    (1893-1981) 106
  Anna Grace (1881-1971) 215, 275
  Archie C. (1883-1905) .. 105, 152
  Archie Dean 346
  Arleen Mae (AGNEW) (1920-) 337
  Arthur W 276
  Asbury 74
  Audrey 105, 152, 186
  Audrey Lucille (1894-1963) .. 105
  Audrey Lynn (1947-) 214
  Beatrice Gertrude (1875-)
    .... 104, 151, 211, 270
  Bertha Mabel (CHERRY)
    (1885-1930) 218, 278, 279
  Beryl Josephine (1932-) . 214, 329
  Betty Jo 337
  Beulah Gladys (ABERCROMBIE)
    (1890-1973) 217
  Beulah Madge (1890-1891) .. 107
  Billy M 280
  Billy Morgan (1920-1974)
    .... 220, 338, 372
  Bonnell 279, 280, 372
  Bonnell Elizabeth (1921-1994)
    .... 220, 339
  Callie 19, 26, 74
  Callie Ann (1961-) 329
  Carl 65, 152, 272
  Carl Raymond (1882-1955)
    .... 104, 213, 272
  Caroline 74, 168
  Caroline Rebecca J. (HICKS)
    (1851-1928) 26, 47
  Charles Orville (1936-) 327
  Charles Victor 373
  Chesley 153, 154, 276
  Chesley L. (1896-1978) 106
  Chester 154, 276
  Clarinda Rae (1954-) 321
  Clifford 106, 153, 276, 277
  Clifford O. (1892-) 217

Clinton 278
Clinton (1854-1855) 44
Clinton (1908-1990) 218
D A 155, 279, 280, 372
Dale (1915-) 218
Diana (RIEGLE) (1947-) ... 327
Doc 155, 279
Doctor Albert (1858-1942)
  .... 44, 107, 155
Dollie 153, 154, 276
Dollie M. (1876-1946) 106
Donna Mae (BRADFORD)
  (1943-) 329
Dorathy .. 107, 155, 220, 279, 280
Dorothy (RICHARDS) (1919-)
  .... 338, 373
Dorothy F. (1909-) 219
Dorothy F. (1902-1927) 220
Dorothy May 373
E Hicks 154
Earl (1915-1915) 217, 277
Edith M 154
Edith Mary (1887-1961)
  .... 106, 218, 278
Edna 155, 279, 280, 372
Edna Fae (PRATT) (1892-1981) 220
Effie Maud (1877-1909)
  .... 104, 151, 212, 270
Elijah Hicks (1852-1913)
  .... 44, 106, 153, 276
Elizabeth 64, 65, 280
Elizabeth (Hicks) 37
Elizabeth Jane (1914-1995)
  .... 220, 337, 372
Ellen Mae (MORGAN)
  (1891-1968) 219, 280
Elva Mae (1919-) .. 220, 280, 337
Enna 168
Essulene 168
Ethel 65, 152, 272
Ethel Grace (1887-1963)
  .... 104, 213, 272
Fern (BARLEY) (1889-) 219, 279
Finley E 65
Finley James (1867-) 44
Floyd Claire (1917-1988) 219
Forrest Allen (1904-1956)
  .... 214, 273, 274
Frances 152
Frances (ESSEX) (1852-1930) 105
Francis 65
Francis McClellen 'Mack' (1863-) 44
Frank 19, 26, 64, 74, 168
Frank (1941-) 217
Gale E 155
Gary G 152
Gay O 271
Gayle E. (1883-) 107, 219
Genevieve 186

Genevieve Shinkle (1896-1996)
  .... 105, 214, 273
George 19, 26, 48, 154, 167
George B. (1871-) 113
George Washington (1856-1942)
  .... 44, 106, 154
Gertrude (MOORE) (1917-1959)
  .... 270, 328
Grace 276, 368, 369
Grace Bell (WARD) (1881-1913)
  .... 216, 276
Grace Elenor (STEPHENSON)
  (1894-) 330
Guy 271, 368
Guy Orville 271
Harold (1891-) 113, 167
Harriet (1927-) 211, 324, 365
Harry 211, 365, 366
Harry (1909-) 324
Hazel (KIRTLEY) (1908-) ... 216
Hazel (PLANCK) 216
Helen Alberta "Peach" (1927-) 214
Helen Frances (1921-) 219
Helen L 274
Henry 37, 43, 64, 65, 74, 152, 153
Henry (1825-1904) 43
Hertha Katherine (1877-)
  .... 105, 214, 215, 274
Hicks 153
Hilda 271, 368
Hilda Louise (1913-1975) 213, 327
Howard 153, 154, 276
Howard Hicks (1887-1967)
  .... 106, 217, 276
Howard Stanley (1945-) 217
Infant 280
Irene (KEITHLER) (1874-1912)
  .... 214, 273, 274
Irma Clare (1879-) .. 48, 114, 167
Isaac 4, 5, 74
Isaac (1820-) 47
J C M 155
James 43, 272, 273
James (1854-1860) 43
James Lawrence (1943-1965) . 329
James M .. 65, 151, 272, 273, 279
James M. (1912-) 219
James Marcellus
  ..... 43, 89, 104, 151, 186, 214
James Marcellus (1847-1925) . 104
James Marcellus (1915-1970) . 328
James Paul (1906-1954) 213, 326
Jay 279
Jay Miller (1885-1928) 107, 219, 279
Jean 280
Jean Eleanor (1912-1977) 220

JONES continued
- Jenevieve 152
- Jennie V 152
- Jessie / Jesse ... 152-154, 276, 277
- Jessie (1881-1966) 106
- Jessie Agnes (1878-1922)
  .... 105, 215, 274
- Jessie Alfred 153, 276
- Jessie Marie (1913-) 217, 333
- Joan F 280
- Joan Faye (1928-) .. 220, 338, 373
- John 65, 74
- John (1801-) 43
- John Knox (1848-1866) 43
- John Lee (1938-) 214, 329
- Julia 106, 153, 154, 216, 276
- Julia (WILLIAMS)
  (1854-1936) 106
- Julia M 216, 276, 370
- Julia M. (1906-1993) 331
- Julia Marie (1947-) 217, 332
- Julia Mrs 154
- Julia Olive (HALL) (1915-) .. 220
- June 155, 279, 280
- June Gayle (1917-) 220, 338
- Karen Ethel (RUSSELL) (1945-)
  337
- Karen Sue (WEIGEL) (1944-) ... 327
- Kent H. (1930-) ... 211, 324, 365
- Laura A. (SHINKLE) (1855-1926)
  .... 106, 154, 155
- Lavinia (ROBINSON) (1887-1976)
  .... 213, 272
- Lawrence 65, 152, 271-273
- Lawrence Marcellus (1890-1964)
  .... 105, 213, 273
- Leona I. (1909-1995) 216, 276, 332
- Leontine Orrene (1877-1964)
  .... 106, 154, 217, 277
- Lewis Edward (1865-1867) ... 44
- Lloyd (1917-1983) 219
- Lois Marie (1916-1972) 214
- Lola Agnes (1880-1946)
  .... 104, 151, 212, 270
- Lora (ROGERS) (1889-1979)
  .... 213, 271, 272, 368
- Loretta 276
- Louise 274
- Lucy 3, 152, 155, 279
- Lucy E. (STRAHAN)
  (1859-1925) 107
- Lucy Florence (1891-) 105
- Lutie wife of George B. (1873-)
  .... 113, 167
- Lydia Ethel (MOORE) (1925-) 330
- M J 155
- M. Isadore 65
- Mabel 274
- Mabel I. (THORNTON)
  (1890-1995) 214
- Mabel Irene 274
- Madella Jane (BOUSE) (1945-)
  327
- Marcellus 152, 270, 271, 278
- Marcellus (1910-) 218
- Marcellus Findly (1881-1964)
  .... 107, 218
- Marcellus Findly 278, 279
- Marcellus Jr 278
- Margaret (SHARP) 213
- Marion 155, 279, 280, 372
- Marion Francis (1916-1970) .. 220
- Mark Mathew (1965-) 329
- Mary 26, 64, 74, 98,
  ... 139, 151, 152, 186, 272, 273
- Mary (CHAPMAN) (1801-) .. 43
- Mary (HICKS) (1827-1900) ... 43
- Mary (UNKNOWN) 213
- Mary Elizabeth (1892-1980) .. 105
- Mary Elizabeth (SHINKLE)
  (1854-1905). 104
- Mary Elizabeth (1972-) 329
- Mary Elizabeth 152
- Mary Margaret "Dollie" (1938-) 329
- Mary Mrs. 63
- Mary Olive 57
- Matilda 151
- Maude 212, 367
- Mildred 280
- Mildred Gayle (1909-2004)
  .... 220, 337, 372
- Minerva 64, 65, 105
- Minerva Elizabeth (1844-1935)
  .... 43, 103, 148
- Minerva Isadora 'Dora' (1859-1944)
  .... 44, 107, 156
- Minnie Ward "Wardy" (1888-)
  .... 48, 168
- Moninca Lee (1970-) 329
- Nellie (BARTLOW) 47
- Neva 155, 279, 280, 372
- Neva Mae (1919-1996) .. 220, 338
- O M 154
- Orpha 65
- Orpha Grace (1870-1960) .. 44, 65
- Orville 15, 23-25, 29, 30, 64,
  ..... 67, 74, 115, 161, 271, 368
- Orville Guy (1882-1940)
  .... 104, 213, 271, 304
- Orville William (1908-1996)
  .... i, iii, 327, 368
- Paul 271
- Paul Ralph (1945-) 217
- Pauline Joyce (1945-) 217
- R O 155
- Ralph 37, 273, 368, 369
- Ralph Charles (1896-1955)
  .... 214, 329, 368
- Ralph William 330
- Robert 280
- Robert Otis (1916-1983)
  .... 220, 337, 372
- Robert Rudd 327
- Romba (BROADWELL)
  (1907-1972) 211, 324, 365
- Rosco 280
- Roscoe Otis (1888-1968)
  .... 107, 219, 280
- Ross Richards (1954-) 338
- Roxy 154, 217
- Roxy Dale (1880-) . 106, 217, 277
- Roy 216, 276
- Roy E. (1908-) 216
- Ruth D. (NEVILLE) (1913-1993)
  .... 327, 368
- Sadie C 154
- Samantha Jane (1850-)
  .... 43, 64, 103, 149
- Sarah (RAHILLY) (1888-) ... 106
- Sarah K 154
- Shari Sue (1957-) 338
- Shirley Ann (RYAN) (1944-) . 329
- Shirley Lou (1930-) 220, 338
- Stacy Lynn (1973-) 329
- Stanley Hicks (1912-1913) ... 216
- Stanley L 153, 154
- Stanley Lee (1883-1940) . 106, 154
- Stella B 152
- Stella Blanche (1884-1967)
  .... 105, 216, 275, 370
- Steven William (1960-) 338
- Susan 167
- T. F. 167
- Tanya Grace (1967-) 329
- Thomas 74, 167
- Thomas Franklin (1840-1916) 47, 74
- Uertha K. 152, 274
- Walter Paul .... i, iii, 327
- Ward / Wardie 74, 168
- William . 19, 26, 64, 74, 105, 274
- William (1821-1891) 43
- William A 37, 43, 152, 153
- William A. (1851-1938) 105
- William Allen 337
- William M. 372, 373
- William Morgan 338
- William P. (1870-1871) 48
- William S. 65
- Yevanna Sue (1963-) 329

JOSLIN
- Addie 144, 258, 264
- Adlara Leona 'Addie' (1891-1971)
  . . . . 89, 102, 187, 206, 264
- Archibald D. "Archie" (1884-1918)
  . . . . 101, 206, 263
- Archie 89, 144, 263, 359
- Edna 187, 144, 264
- Edna Clare (1889-1931)
  . . . . 101, 206, 264
- Elizabeth 158, 206, 359
- Elizabeth (1918-1975) 317
- Elizabeth (Hicks) 63, 141
- Ella (1887-1887) 101
- Emarilla 'Rella' (1885-1919)
  . . . . 101, 144
- Eva 89, 144
- Eva May (1882-1912) 101
- Frances Emma (1885-) 101
- John 101, 144, 263, 264
- John D. (1855-1891) . . . 101, 263
- Josephine (RATCLIFF)
  (1884-1986) 206, 263, 359
- Josephine Mrs 144
- Leona 144
- Lina C. 144
- Lora J. 264
- Lucy (1887-1888) 101
- Mary 144, 264
- Mary Elizabeth (HICKS) (1860-
  1955) 101, 187, 263, 264
- Mary Mrs 63, 147
- Rella 89, 144, 187

JUDD
- Carrie 221, 282
- Elizabeth 32

KABLER
- Mildred (1908-) 308

KAHLKE
- Elsie (1887-1980) 104
- Fred (1864-) 104
- Metha wife of Fred (1868-) . . 104

KANDRAVI
- Mary 317

KANKIN
- William 165

KARNOSH
- John Allen (1934-1991) 308
- John Robert (1968-) 308
- Kenneth Allen (1965-) 308
- Melissa Lee (1961-) 308
- Patricia (PATTISON) (1936-) 308
- Richard Todd (1969-) 308

KAUF / KAUFF
- Betty (1937-) 341
- Betty Lou 374

KAY
- Denise Marie (1957-) 338

KEESTER
- (---) (1870-) 49

KEETHLER / KEITHLER
- Daniel S 274
- Emery E. 274
- Ida J. 274
- Irene (1874-1912) . . 214, 273, 274
- Mcdonold 274
- Riley W (1845-) 214, 274
- Sarah Rebecca (BLACK) (1847-) 214
- Sarah R. 274
- William W. 274

KELLEY
- Anna May (ALTMAN)
  (1881-1958) 115
- Henry (1881-) 115

KELLY
- Glenn 224, 374
- Robert L. (1943-) 336

KELSO
- Margaret Mrs. 374

KEMPER
- Barbara 253
- Doris Ann (1932-) 326

KENDALL
- Catherine Louise (1969-) 310
- Elizabeth Lee (1961-) 310
- Mary Margaret (1964-) 310
- Robert Gordon III (1939-) . . . 309
- Sandra Louise (FITZPATRICK)
  (1941-) 309

KENNEDY
- Lachlan 140

KERR
- Jas 15

KERRY
- Aaron (1837-1916) 225, 285
- Harold 162, 285
- Harold E. Jr (1928-) 225, 285
- Harold Edwin (1890-1984) 225, 285
- Jane 285
- Jane (MCCRACKEN) (1852-)
  . . . . 225, 285
- Maria H. (WILSON) (1892-1947)
  . . . . 225, 285

KETCHUM
- Clinton O. (1896-) 209
- Mabel (BROADWELL) (1894-
  1987) 209

KIDDER
- Mary (DAY) (1895-) 230
- Unknown (1895-) 230

KIESER / KEISER
- Betty 204, 260-262, 358, 359, 377
- Betty (Stalder) . . . . i, 305
- Betty Jo 316, 357, 377
- Bob . . . . i, 357
- Charles David (1946-1967)
  . . . . 316, 357
- Charles Frederick 316, 358
- David 357
- Elizabeth 357, 358
- Elizabeth (STALDER) (1913-2008)
  . . . . i, iii, 261, 316, 377
- Elizabeth Joan "Betty Jo"
  . . . . 316, 357, 377
- Elizabeth "Betty" 357
- Jessie Marcella (UMBAUGH) 316
- Nancy Elizabeth (RUGG) . . . 316
- Robert 357, 358
- Robert S Mrs 262
- Robert Frederick 316, 357
- Robert J. "Bob" 357
- Robert Julius (1909-1995) 316, 358

KILBOURN
- Mary Ester (1948-) 340

KINCAID
- Emma V 111

KINDRICK
- Susan (1838-) 97

KING
- __ Hicks 178
- Bessie (1878-) . . 52, 80, 123, 178
- Clifford 160
- E. M 178
- E. N. 80, 178
- Edward 80, 178
- Edward N. (1844-1937) 52
- Frances (Miller) 160
- Glada (1911-) 123, 178
- Gladys wife of Harlan (1903-) 123
- Grace 80, 178, 179
- Grace M (MAUFORT) (1878-) 123
- Harlan E. (1907-) . . . 80, 123, 178
- Helen 160
- Mary 41, 61
- Sara / Sarah 80, 178
- Sarah (HICKS) (1843-) 52
- Wakefield 31, 80, 178
- Wakefield Edward (1878-)
  . . . . 52, 123, 178, 179

KINGHT
- Clara 167
- Winfred F 167

KINGMAN
- Howard 150

KIRK
- James N. Mrs 165

KIRKENDALL
- Joe P 279

KIRTLEY
- Hazel (1908-) 216

KISSINGER
- Barbara Ann (1955-) 336
- Coral Edith (1959-) 336
- John Phillip (1924-1980) 336
- Wanda Fae (WILL) (1919-) . . 336

KITZMILLER
  Mary 167, 288
KLAPPER
  Albert 188, 239
  Laura 188, 239
KLEVINS
  Patricia (1936-) 332
KLINE
  Benneville (1821-1898) . . . 21, 31
  Elmer J 82
  Mary 31, 52, 53, 80, 82, 83,
    . . . . 122, 178, 179, 298
  Mary J. (HICKS) (1845-1932) . 21
  William J. 82
KLINGLER / KLINGER
  Mary (HOPKINS) (1825-1894) 50
  Mary E. (1844-1914) 50, 117, 172
  Minerva E (1842-) 50
  William H. (1815-1885) 50
KLINK
  Mary (MANNING) (1919-1979)
    193
  unknown (1919-) 193
KLUGAN
  Cornelia 154
KLUIGER
  Wm. 172
KLYNG
  Joyce 344
KNODEL
  Anna 105
  Charles 105
  Marie 105
KOCHEL
  Judy 209
KOEHLER 179
  Albert (1893-) 82, 124, 179
  Albert S 81, 179
  George 82, 124, 179
  Lulu 82, 179
  Luella (SMITH) (1873-1930)
    . . . . 82, 124, 179
KOEHNE
  Agnes A. (1942-) 310
KOEPPEL
  Paul Edward 246
KOESTER
  Charles (1841-) 104
  Jennie L 150
  Sylvia (1850-1885). 104
  Tinnie (1878-) 104
  Tinnie Ludawine 150
KOOY
  Eunice Dale 365
  Garrit 324, 365

KOPP
  Emma J 61
KRIENERT
  Theresa 281
KRIGER
  -?- 281
KUCH
  Sarah 139
KUHN
  George 189, 241
  Mada Mary (1891-1963)   189, 241
  Mady 241
  Mary (RAMMINGER) 189
  Nada 190
KURTZ
  -?- (SCHNEIDER) (1942-) . . . 347
  Anna W. (EGLOFF) (1900-1995)
    347
  Doretta 376
  Harry 234, 296, 376
  Harry W. (1893-1969) 347
  Harry William 376
  Jacob 296
  Marie L. (1891-1922)
    . . . . 234, 296, 347, 375
  Mary E 296
  Mollie E. (LANHAM) (1872-1945)
    . . . . 234, 296, 375
  Nancy (1942-) 318
  Norman 347
  William (1866-1928) . . . 234, 296

LACKERMAN
  Leslie Edward (1939-) 339
LAIRD 364
  Barbara 323
LANE
  Amanda 172
  Jane 121, 177
  Linda (1945-) 317
  Ruth (1923-) 306
LANHAM
  Adelia F. (1881-1970) 120
  Delia 79, 120
  John (1855-) 120, 175
  Lucinda Margaret (JOHNSTON)
    (1853-1883) 120, 175
  Mollie E. (1872-1945)
    . . . . 120, 175, 234
  Virginia 175
  William 175
LANTER
  Archie (1903-1957) 331, 332
  Carol (PRICE) 332
  Dorothy 332
  Julia M. (JONES) (1906-1993) 331
  Virginia 332

LAUGH
  Sarah Ella (1848-) 215, 275
LAUNSBERY
  William 158
LEAK
  Sylvia Jane (1942-) 346
LECKLIDER
  Trucy Ann (1949-) 339
LEE
  Georgeanne (GREGG) (1941-) 349
  O. C. (1941-) 349
  Rosa Imogene (1926-) 333
LEEDS
  Mabel (1892-1979) 122
LEIGHTY
  Daniel 172
LENNIE
  Henry (1915-1980) 333
LEONARD
  Pervilla K (1872-) 217, 277
LEOPOLD
  Janet Ruth (1940-) 315
LEPAGE
  Sydonia R (1893-1989) 221
LEVI / LEVY
  Amanda 143
  Clad H, Jr 260
  Clyde 260
  Clyde Harvey (1881-1948) . . . 205
  Clyde Harvey 101, 260
  Emma / Erma   141, 143, 144, 187
  Francis Marion 'Frank' (1854-1933)
    . . . . 100, 141, 143, 259
  Frank . . . 143, 144, 187 260-262
  Frank M. Mrs. 357
  Grandpa 261
  H. Clyde 260
  Harvey 143, 259, 260
  Harvey C Jr 260
  Harvey Clyde . 205, 261, 315, 357
  Harvey Clyde II (1903-1970)
    . . . . 315, 357
  Hulda (FANCHER) (1821-1873)100
  Huldy 143
  Irma . . . . iii, 143, 259, 260
  Irma Clair (1878-1928) 101, 204, 259
  Irma Crystal (1905-1957)
    . . . . 205, 260, 357
  Janet Ruth (LEOPOLD) (1940-)315
  Joanne Vivienne (DUVAL)
    (1939-) 315
  John 143, 144
  Lane 260, 261, 315, 357
  Lucy Ann (HICKS) (1857-1888)
    . . . . 87, 100, 141, 143

LEVI / LEVY continued
  Marvella Margaret (TRUITT)
    (1917-1980) 315, 357
  Mary 143, 259
  Mary Emma Townsley 143
  Mollie 63, 143, 259, 260
  Mollie Dell (1884-1947) ... 101,
     .... 141-145, 185, 205, 260, 261
  Paula Alora (1947-) 315
  Pearl R. (AUSTIN) (1877-1953)
    .... 205, 260, 261
  Pearl Roser 260
  Willis (1822-1915) 100, 143
LEWIS
  Decatur (1834-) 115, 170
  Flora Catherine (1866-1951)
    .... 115, 169, 170, 290
  Mabel 170
  Marshal M 170
  Mary A. 170
  Mary A. (1844-) 115
  Owen 352
  Richard 158
LEYPOLE
  Tabitha 30, 79
LIEADY
  Mary Ellen 322, 362
LIGHT
  Andrew A. (1856-1942)
    .... 108, 158, 281
  Benjamin (1806-) 108, 158
  John 158
  Mary Emma (HICKS) (1858-1934)
    .... 108, 158
LIMING
  Margaret 90, 128
LINDSAY / LINDSEY
  Jannette Anne (1936-) 314
  Madison D Mrs 165
LINGENFELSER
  Callie 67, 74, 161
  Callie James (HICKS) (1876-1979)
    .... 26, 109
  Elsie (HICKS) (1874-1903) 113, 166
  Emma Margaret (1899-) . 109, 161
  Eugene William (1903-2004)
    .... 109, 161
  Eva M. (BECKNER) (1903-1993)
    109
  Frank 161
  Gene 161
  George (1837-) ... 109, 113, 161
  John 161
  Joseph J. (1874-1938)
    .... 113, 161, 166, 167

  Kathryn R. (RICHTER) 109
  Katy 161
  Lula 167
  Margaret (MILLER) (1838-1915)
    .... 109, 113
  Margaret (1896-) 113
  Margarete 161
  Minnie 161
  Neva (MERS) (1898-1931) .. 109
  Odessa (BACON) (1906-1983) 109
  Stanley Joseph (1899-1934)
    .... 113, 166
  William 161, 167
  William (1873-1964) 109
LINNING
  M 132
LINVILLE
  Edward 164
LIPPS
  Jennie Mae (HUTSON)
    (1912-2000) 201
  William (1911-1986) 201
LISKA
  Emil 261
  Leanna 261
LIVINGSTON
  Anna (1876-) 325, 367
  Jessie 367
  Rachel C 367
LLOYD
  Robert 138
  Stella (1872-1958) ... 98 138 256
LOUNSBURG
  Ronald W. (1941-) 336
LOVETT
  Edward (1959-) 328
  Mary Beth (JACOBS) (1959-) 328
LUCAS
  Ann Lorene (1937-) 326
  Darla Jean (MITCHELL) (1942-)
    326
  Doris Ann (KEMPER) (1932-) 326
  Ida wife of Jonas (1884-) 326, 367
  Jack E. (1902-1982) 326, 367
  Jack Elwood Jr (1930-) 326
  Jonas A (1883-) 326, 367
  Maxine J 367
  Richard Russell (1939-) 326
  Russell A 367
  Sarah Elizabeth (MCMAHAN)
    (1908-1978) 326
  Sarah Elizabeth McMahan ... 367
  Sarah M 367
LUCKEY
  Barbara Jane 319
  Cynthia 319
  Deborah L. (1949-) 319
  Edna (HAWLEY) (1880-) ... 319

  Helen (HICKS) (1918-)265, 319, 360
  Jacqueline (HAZELIP) (1943-) 319
  Karen (1955-) 319
  Rebecca J 319
  Wilson S. 360
  Wilson S. (1879-) 319
  Wilson S. (1915-1985) . 319, 360
  Wilson Shannon 360
  Wilson Shannon Jr 319
LUEHRMANN
  Dorothy (1924-) 321
LYBROOK
  Richard 320
  Richard Mrs. 361

MACAY
  Jno 6
MACDONALD
  John 180
MACK
  Sarah 290
MACKIE
  Margaret 288
Maier & Mathews 160
MAJORS
  Floyd (1928-) 333
MANES
  Maria 176
MANNING
  Angie D. 133
  C. M. 245
  Callie 93, 133
  Callie (1870-1966) 40
  Carolina / Caroline 128, 188, 239
  Caroline (HANLEY)
    (1853-1944) 90, 239
  Charles 57, 130, 243-245
  Charles William (1855-1947)
    .... 38, 91, 130
  Chilton 91, 130, 244, 245
  Chilton H. (1885-1962) 192
  Chilton Henry 193, 244
  Chilton Jr (1929-1929) 192
  Cora 90, 188, 239
  Cora (1878-1900) 188
  Dana / Dane 242
  Dane C. (1909-1988) 191
  Darlene May (1939-) 308
  Daughter (1916-) 193
  Dorthea Bernadina (MASON)
    (1924-) 193
  Edith 130, 244, 245
  Edith L. (RILEY) (1858-) 91
  Eliza 93
  Elizabeth 57, 244
  Elizabeth (1928-) 192

MANNING continued
  Ethel M 90, 128, 239
  Ethel M. (1894-1993) 189
  Forest (1932-1932) 193
  Francis 38, 57, 128, 188, 239
  Francis M. (1844-1920) 90
  Francis William 188
  Frank 57
  Geneva Grace 193
  George 38, 57, 133
  George W. (1851-) 38
  George W. (1841-) 40, 93
  Georgia 93, 133
  Glenn 191, 243, 353
  Glenn (1910-1967) 191
  Grace (1890-) 90, 128
  Hazel 244
  Hazel Marie (BOICE)
    (1900-1976) 193
  Howard Metzzar (1888-) 91
  Ida Laron (1933-1933) 193
  Iva Lou (1881-1969) . 91, 192, 243
  James Chilton (1930-) 192
  Jane (BERRY) 38
  John . . 38, 57, 129, 191, 242, 353
  John C. (1908-1977) 308
  John Wesley (1849-) . 38, 91, 129
  Laura 129, 130 188
  Laura A. (WILLS) (1889-) . . . 188
  Laura Francis (VICKROY)
    (1851-1923) 91, 130
  Lewell 245
  Lida / Lila 243. 353
  Lilla B. (Walker) (JACOBS)
    (1885-) 191
  Lizzie M 133
  Lowell 130, 244, 245
  Lowell Burns (1896-1925)
    . . . . 91, 193, 245
  Lucinda 128
  Lucinda (1880-) 90
  Lucinda (TATMAN)
    (1824-1867) 38
  Lulu 57
  Lulu May (1867-) 38
  Maggie 93, 249
  Margaret 93, 133, 242
  Margaret M. (1870-1949) 93
  Margaret R. (SPRAGUE)
    (1876-1963) 191
  Mary 30, 51, 57, 79, 129,
    . . . . . . 133, 175, 176, 241, 244
  Mary (1833-1923) 51
  Mary (1919-1979) 193
  Mary A. 'Mollie' (1848-1913)
    . . . . 38, 90, 128

Mary Ann (WISBY) (1905-1962)
  192
Mary (1847-) 40, 93
May L. 244
Mildred (1908-) 188
Mildred (KABLER) (1908-) . . 308
Mollie 57
Norma J 244
Norma Jean (1927-) 193
O. L. 130
Onmeita (1907-1970) . . . 191, 242
Ora 130, 242, 353
Ora Chasse (1879-1939)
  . . . . 91, 191, 243
Orie 243
Orlando 243
Orville 129, 242
Orville Lorain (1876-1959)
  . . . . 91, 191, 242
Patricia (VALKENSTOE) . . . 308
Raleigh 244
Raleigh Clark (1896-1957)
  . . . . 91, 193, 244
Robert C 193, 244
Robert Chilton (1922-1967) . . 193
Rolland 243
Ruth 191 243 353
Ruth N. (1915-1999) 308
Sarah Elizabeth (1853-) . . . 38, 57
Tell (1887-1889) 91
Velma (PATTERSON)
  (1889-1920) 191, 242, 243
Virginia Ann (1941-) 308
Walter 90, 128, 130, 239, 245
Walter (1883-1913) 188
Walter L (1892-1966) 91
Wanda Lee (1931-) 193
Waunita 242
William 57, 128, 130
William (1815-1870) 38
William (1891-1931) 90
William Francis (1907-1989) . . 188
MAPP
  Charlei E. (1872-) 119
  Cora M. (1885-) 119
  Irene 119
  Joseph Benjamin (1900-1949) 119
  Lora Irene (SHUMWAY)
    (1907-1997) 119
MARGARD
  Gladys 73, 166
  Olivia 73, 166
  Ware H 73
  Wayne H 73, 166
MARKS
  Keith Mrs. 361

MARKSBERRY
  Albert 175
  Amos 175
  Anna / Annie 175, 176
  Cynthia (BRUEN) (1847-1910)
    . . . . 121, 175
  Emmie 176
  Essee 176
  James 175
  Lena (JOHNSTON) (1882-1920)
    . . . . 121, 175, 176
  Martha 175, 176
  Ray / Roy 175
  Russel B 175
  Sidney (1874-1951) 121, 175, 176
  Viola 175, 176
  William (1845-1910) 121, 175, 176
  Willis 175
MARLOW
  Murtle 150
MARNACH
  H G 159
  Rose 159
  Tully 159
MARS
  Alma J. (ROSS) (1893-)
    . . . . 267, 322, 362
  Clarence Harrison (1889-)
    . . . . 267, 322, 362, 363
  Clayton R. (1918-) . 267, 322, 362
  Rufus E. 322, 362
MARSH
  Bonnell Elizabeth (JONES)
    (1921-1994) 339
  Neil C. (1947-) 339
  Noah Chat (1919-2000) 339
  Rebecca Jean (TERRY) (1953-) 339
  Robert Dale (1950-) 339
  Trucy Ann (LECKLIDER)
    (1949-) 339
MARSHALL
  Gailon 252
  Jonnie 252
  Mannie 252
  Minerva (1830-1870) 45, 66, 67, 158
MARTIN
  Duke 27
  Eliza 27, 69, 162
  Emile 27, 69, 162
  George 27, 69, 162
  Joseph E. 69, 162
  Samuel D. 69, 162
MASON
  Ada F. (1884-) 107, 157
  Carrie 44, 156, 157
  Claude F. (1899-) 108, 157

MASON continued
- Dorthea Bernadina (1924-) ... 193
- Edith (CASE) (1899-) 193
- Edmund J 157
- Fred (1888-) 193
- Fred A 157
- Freddie 45, 156, 157
- Freddie (1873-) 107
- Ida M. (1876-) .. 45, 107, 156, 157
- Josie (1877-) ... 45, 108, 156, 157
- Julia 44, 156, 157
- Mary 44, 157
- Mary (OWENS) (1852-) 107, 108
- Mary C. (1886-) 107
- Nancy (1869-) 107, 156
- Nannie 44, 156, 157
- Peter (1836-1900) 44, 107, 156, 157
- Rosa 44, 156, 157
- Vera F. (1894-) 107, 157

MASSNER
- Sheri 366

MATTELS
- S. 25

MAUFORT
- Grace M (1878-) 123, 178
- J... 178

McADAMS
- Millie 85

McADOO
- Carry 289
- Earl 289
- Ethel 289
- Herman 289
- Infant 289
- L. 289
- Laura 289
- Lula 289
- Robert 229, 289
- Sirene / Syrene 229, 289
- T. R. 289
- William 289

McATER
- Marjorie Geraldine (1939-) ... 322

McBRIDE
- Evalyn 289

McCABE
- Baxter 156
- Dora 65, 156
- George W 156
- Harriet E 156
- J. B. 156
- James 65, 156, 221
- James Baxter (1856-1910) 107, 156
- James Robert 44, 221
- Minerva Isadora 'Dora' (JONES) (1859-1944) 107

- Orpha 44
- Raymond (1887-) ... 107, 156, 220
- Robert (1915-) 65, 220, 221
- Wilber 156

McCAFFREY
- Lillian 267

MCCALLA
- Anna Grace (JONES) (1881-1971) 215
- Oscar W. (1881-) 215, 275

McCARTER
- Rachiel 98, 138

McCARTY
- Alice Mae (HUTSON) (1926-) 311
- Danny (1959-) 311
- Debbie Ann (1947-) 311
- James Robert (1925-) 311
- Tammy (1956-) 311

McCLANAHAN
- Audrey N. (1923-) 307, 352
- Burdella 352
- Christina (REEVES) 348
- Darrel (1950-) 348
- Debbie (1949-) 348
- Delia (STEVENS) (1930-) ... 348
- Dwayne (1960-) 348
- Ida 352
- Martin (1895-) 307, 352
- Steven (1955-) 348
- Teresa (1953-) 348
- Thomas 352
- William (1930-) 348, 352

McCLELLAN
- Nancy 191, 243

McCONNELL
- Anson Mrs. 283
- Mildred (1921-1981) 349

McCRACKEN
- Debbie 360
- Harriet JoAnn (HICKS) (1928-) 320, 360
- James R. 320, 360
- Jane (1852-) 225
- Janice Lynne (1954-) ... 320, 360
- Jo Ann 265, 360
- Richard 360
- Richard Warren (1926-) 320

McCROSBY
- Minor (1932-) 332

McCROSKEY
- Donald Leroy (1927-1965) ... 334

McDONALD
- Elizabeth B. (1895-1931) 124, 180

McELREATH
- Mary Alice 229, 291

McELROY
- Bob 364
- Catherine L. (EIFFERT) 323

- Cecil B 364
- Haney L 364
- Hazel E. (1919-) 323, 364
- Helen (1920-) 323
- Helen I 364
- Julie 364
- Lester L. (1924-) 323
- Marvin M. (1922-) 323, 364
- Mendon E 364
- Ollie 364
- Ollie Willis (1895-1975) 323, 364
- Orma (BROADWELL) (1897-1970) 323, 364
- Oscar 323, 364
- Wilma L. (1926-) 323, 364

McGONAGLE
- Mary C 76

MCGOWAN
- Bonnie Patricia (BOWMAN) (1949-) 336
- Izeta Mae (WILL) (1918-) ... 336
- John Casey 336
- Robin Jean 336
- Robert Thomas (1908-) . 336, 372
- Thomas Edward (1954-) 336

McGRAW
- Laura A. (1846-1868) 48

McGREGOR
- Ida Mrs. 269

McINTYRE
- Charles 58
- Hazel 58

McKENNEY
- John A. 129

McKENZIE
- Beulah Imogene 365
- Charlotte B 324, 365
- George 324, 365
- Layton A 324, 365

McKIBBEN
- Albert 189
- Irene 351
- Jennie Irene (1883-1950) 189, 240
- Phillip (1940-) 320
- Phillip Mrs. 361
- Thresia (ROSS) 189

McKNIGHT
- Delona Jean (1927-1995) 334

McKOULE
- Jane 110, 162

McMAHAN / MCMAHON
- Alma Mae (BERGEN) (1922-) 325
- Byron 212, 270
- Byron Jones Ozar (1898-1963) 212
- Effie Maud (JONES) (1877-1909) 212, 270
- Gayle 270

McMAHAN / MCMAHON cont...
  Gladys R. (BOWLING)
    (1906-1973) 212
  James 366
  James Edward (1926-) 325
  Jean Elaine (HEMMERLE) (1928-)
    325
  Judith (GERDES) (1940-) . . . 325
  Kathleen Janet (1934-) 325
  L O 270
  Lewis 212, 270
  Lewis O. (1867-1930) . . .212, 270
  Lewis Ozi 367
  Lola Gayle (1900-1988)
    . . . . 212, 325, 367
  Mary Ruth (WEAVER) (1934-) 325
  Maud Effie 270
  Myrl 366
  Myrl M. (EDWARDS)
    (1899-1986) 325, 367
  Nona 212, 270
  Sarah 270
  Sarah Elizabeth (1908-1978)
    . . . . 212, 326, 367
  Theodore Lewis (1922-) 325
  Thomas Richard (1932-) 325
  Wilber 270, 366, 367
  Wilbur Lewis (1896-1990)
    . . . . 212, 325, 366
  Wilmer 366
McMAKIN
  Charles 279
McNAIR 76
  Alexander H. (1873-) 49
  Alma R. (WOOD) (1873-1940)
    . . . . 98, 137, 138
  Archibald 58, 60, 62, 75
  Archibald (1898-) 41, 42, 49
  Archy 61
  Benjamin Edwin (1870-1942)
    . . . . 42, 98, 138
  Betty J 256
  Charles (1869-) 49
  Dollie 137
  Eddie 58, 62, 132
  Edward / Edwin 138, 256
  Emily 75
  Flora (GRAY) (1899-1974) . . . 98
  Flora T 138
  Grant 58, 62, 98, 132, 138
  Hugh 75
  Infant (1865-1865) 42
  Infant (1869-1870) 42
  Irene C 256
  Irene Caroline (BECKTOLD)
    (1899-1988) 202

  Jane 61, 75, 134, 135, 136
  Jane (1834-1897) 41
  Jessie Elizabeth (Betty) (1926-2005)
    . . . . 202, 312, 355
  John . . . 39, 62, 75, 132, 137, 138
  John (1832-1910) 42
  John Lawrence (1898-1992)
    . . . . 98, 138
  Lawrence 137, 138
  Lloyd 137, 138, 256
  Lloyd Edwin (1900-1951)
    . . . . 98, 202, 256
  Lois E 256
  Lois Evelyn (1929-) 202
  Margaret Ann (1932-) 202
  Mary 75
  Mary (TATMAN) (1833-1895) 42
  Mary(1805-) 41, 42, 49
  Mitchel 62
  Nancy Emily (ROBINSON)
    (1846-1877) 49, 75
  Polly 62, 132
  Robert (1841-) 49, 75, 76
  Stella (LLOYD) (1872-1958)
    . . . . 98, 138
  Ulysses Grant (1866-1942) 98, 137
McNUTT
  Martha 42
MEADE
  Alvin William Jr (1911-1944)
    . . . . 344, 374
  Curtis William 345
  Florence Marie (TATMAN) (1913-
    1957) 344
  Kevin 169
MEEKER
  Clarence 265
  Cynthia (MURRAY) 206
  Harvey John Hicks 265
  James Clarence (1886-1961)
    . . . . 206, 265, 359
  Lucie / Lucy . . 206, 207, 265, 359
  Lucy Hicks 67, 74, 161,
    . . . . . . 206, 207, 265, 267, 359
  Lucy Mary Francis (HICKS)
    (1885-1964) 186, 206
  Mabel (1899-) 96, 135
  Marcella B. (HAGEN) (1909-1989)
    319
  Margaret 207, 265
  Margaret Anna (1907-1998)
    . . . . 206, 318, 359
  Mary 135, 360
  Mary (GARRISON) (1877-) . . . 96
  Mary Ann (VOYER) 319
  Napoleon 206, 265
  Rachael M 265

  Rachel Matilda (1911-2002)
    . . . . 207, 319, 359
  Robert 265, 319, 359
  Robert (1911-1984) 319
  Roy 206, 265
  Roy Murray (1908-1988) 206
  Ruth 265
  Ruth Melvin (1908-1977) 207
  Shirley (1934-) 265, 319
  William D. (1874-) 96
  William R. (1935-) 265, 319
MEENACH / MEERIACH /
MENACK
  Betty Ann 72
  Edna 283
  Eliza (COLBURN) 46
  Elizabeth 70, 108, 164, 166
  Elizabeth (BALLON) 108
  Elizabeth Ann (1840-1921) . 46, 71
  Harry 159
  Harry Gordon (1887-1966)
    . . . . 108, 159
  J. H. (1820-) 46, 71, 108
  James H. 71
  James Harvey Jr 71
  James Harvey 71
  Mary E 158
  Mary Edna H. (1886-1970)
    . . . . 108, 223, 283
  Maxey 159
  Nackie 158
  Nancy B. (HICKS) (1862-1939)
    . . . . 108, 158
  Rose (BORNHORST)
    (1889-1946) 108, 159
  William . . . 70, 71, 108, 158, 159
  W H 158
  William Harvey (1850-1932) . 108
MEFFORD
  W. P. 141
MEISTER
  Betty 220, 279-281, 372
  Betty Frances (1926-) 220
  Dorothy F. (JONES) (1902-1927)
    220
  Johannes August 281
  John 220, 281
  John August (1893-1971) 220, 281
  Patricia Yvonne (1927-) 220
  Theresa 281
MELVIN / MELVILLE
  A Grace 275
  Ada E. 275
  Anna G 275
  Anna Grace (JONES) (1881-1971)
    . . . . 215, 275
  Grace 275

MELVIN / MELVILLE continued
  Infant (1925-1925) 331
  James 63 275
  James S. (1850-1917) 215
  Jane 45, 68
  John 18, 275
  Mabel (MURPHY) (1907-) . . 331
  Mabel V 369
  Nancy (1806-1903)
    . . . . 18, 24, 26, 37, 64, 67, 70, 71
  Naomi (PARTRIDGE) (1904-) 331
  Ross 331, 369
  Rosslyn 275
  Rosslyn Earl (1903-1941)
    . . . . 215, 331, 369
  Ruby (TOWNSEND) (-1941)
    . . . . 331, 369
  Sallie A 275
  Samuel 275
  Samuel Elmore
    (1874-1937) 215, 275
  Sarah Ella (LAUGH) (1848-) . 215
  Violet Mae 331, 369
  William E 369
  William Ross (1927-) 331
  Winnie 275
MERCER
  Clara A. 294
MERGAN
  Mary A. 176
MERGARD / MERGUARD
  Elizabeth (SMITT) 112
  Emma 166
  Gladys 228
  Gladys Lee (1900-1965)
    . . . . 112, 228, 288
  Henry 112, 166
  Hermann 166
  Maggie 166
  Martin 112, 166
  Martin H. (1871-1908) 112
  Mattie 166
  Morton 166, 288
  Nancy Olivia (HICKS) (1870-1937)
    . . . . 112, 166
  Olivia 72, 166
  Wayne H. (1907-1966) 112
MERS
  Neva (1898-1931) 109
METZ
  Hilda Louise (JONES) (1913-1975)
    327
  Joanne (1945-) 327
  Lewis (1914-) 327
MILES
  Miles 243
MILLER
  Barbara 159
  Frances E 264
  Frances [King] (1875-) 109
  John 31, 52, 80
  Katharine (1850-1914) . 194, 245
  Linda (1947-) 197
  Louisa 212
  Margaret (1838-1915) . . 109, 113
MISTISHAN
  Walter (1930-) 332
MITCHELL
  Benjiman 174
  Clara 78, 173, 174, 295
  Clara Elizabeth (HOPKINS)
    (1863-1956) 118
  Darla Jean (1942-) 326
  Elmer 78, 173, 174, 295
  Elmer C. (1884-) 118
  George H 78, 173, 174, 295
  George Henry (1888-)
    . . . . 118, 234, 295
  George L. (1923-) . . 174, 234, 295
  Glenn (1914-) 234, 295
  Grace M 295
  Gracia (GORDON) (1887-1988)
    . . . . 233, 295
  Hazel Pearl (1911-) 234, 295
  Helen L. (1919-) 233, 295
  Ida 295
  Ida May (PRENE) (1892-) . . . 233
  Isaac 24
  Jane 75, 174
  Jesse / Jessie 173, 174, 295
  John 174
  Junior (1922-) 233, 295
  Leroy J 295
  M Neoma 174, 295
  Mary Louise 259
  Mary Neoma (PRENE) (1894-)
    . . . . 173, 234, 295
  Mildred E. (-1961) 224, 284
  Neoma 295
  Oliver 173, 174, 295
  Oran Ray (1882-1978)
    . . . . 118, 233, 295
  Pearl H 295
  Polly 173, 174
  Polly wife of Roland (1825-) . 118
  R. N. 173
  Ray 78, 173, 174
  Roland (1822-) 118, 174
  Roy 295
  Roy J. (1914-) 233
  Susan 174
  Viola M (1913-) 233, 295
  W J 295
  William 173, 174
  William Jesse (1886-) 118, 233, 295
  William Joseph (1854-1887) 118, 174
  Wilma (1924-) 233, 295

MITTEIS
  Dale Elizabeth (EVANS)
    (1906-1987) 335, 371
  Nick (1906-) 335, 371
MITTERN 371
MIXON
  Mary Alice (MCELREATH) . 229
  Nell Beatrice (1896-1956) 229, 291
  William Henry 229, 291
MOELLER
  Carl 363
  Otto 363
MOHR
  Lydia (1864-) 97
MONCE
  Electra S. (1876-) 327, 368
  Ethel I 368
  Isaac T 368
  John (1867-) 327, 368
  Sarah Blanche (1913-) . . 327, 368
  William H 368
MOONEY
  Julie M. (WOLF) (1950-) 309
  Robert Thomas (1947-) 309
MOORE
  Betty Ruth (1921-1990) 233
  Carrie (1923-) 308
  Emma Marie (1916-1984) . . . 307
  Gertrude (1917-1959) 328
  Guy 246
  Lydia Ethel (1925-) 330
  Nancy (1943-) 341
  Veara Rose (1933-1995) 313
MORGAN
  Ellen Mae (1891-1968) 219
  Harry 298
  Mary 176
  Sarah Ann (1824-1909) . . . 22, 34
MORIE
  Christine (1946-) 337
MORRISON
  Ruth (1898-1957) 113
MORRISON
  Ruth 167
MORSE
  Anna Bertrand (1861-1938) 53, 82
  Annie 82, 179
  Caroline (BERTRAND?) (1830-)
    . . . . 53, 82
  Cynthia 82
  Increase (1807-1880) 53
  Jessie 82
  John H 82
MORTON
  Pauline (1926-) 342
MOSS
  Polly 8

MOTES
　Alma 151
　Arthur O. (1853-) 104, 151
　Effie 151
　Huldiah J 151
　James E 151
　Leatha(1861-) 104, 151
　Mary Alma (HELVERING)
　　(1888-) 104
　Nora E 151
　Ray / Roy 151
　Roy Williard (1886-) 104
MOUNTJOY
　Edward (1900-) 325
　Helen (1903-) 325
　James Edward (1925-) 325
　Kathleen Janet (MCMAHON)
　　(1934-) 325
MOYER
　John 299
　Mary J 299
　Sadie 237
MUELLER
　Donald R. (1943-) 349
　Nancy Chatterton (WHITE)
　　(1943-), ... 349
MULLINS
　Ray (1937-) 319
MUNHILL
　Elizabeth A 164
MUNZING [see MANNING] .. 353
MURPHY
　-?- 361
　Mabel (1907-) 331
　Mary 320, 361
MURRAY
　Cynthia 206, 265
MYERS
　Mark Kent (1954-) 338
　Peter 6
MYLER / MYLOR
　Elizabeth 270, 271, 368
　Emma 271
　Frank 271
　Hannah 271
　Hannah Elizabeth (1907-2007)
　　............. 212, 326, 367
　Hannah wife of Joseph (1843-) 212
　Joseph 212, 270, 271
　Joseph Jr (1911-1911) 213
　Joseph Patrick (1875-1959)212, 271
　Katie A 271
　Lola 270, 271
　Lola Agnes (JONES)
　　(1880-1946) 212

　Patrick (1840-) 212, 271
MYRICK
　Cecile Rose (TURBYNE)
　　(1917-2006) 312, 355
　Clifford 255
　Clifford Behymer (1889-1930)
　　................... 201, 255
　Enock (1848-) 201, 255
　Eula P 247
　Gladys 255
　Gladys E. (HUTSON)
　　(1889-1945) 201
　Hariet (BEHYMER) (1848-)201, 255
　Kenneth 201, 255, 354
　Kenneth H. (1915-1997) 312
　Kenneth Jr 312
　Merta 255
　Michael 312
　W. W. 195
　William W 247
　Natl. Military Home 172

NAGEL
　Dorothy Louise (BRITTINGHAM)
　　(1893-1974) 116
　Ernest Gustav (1894-) ... 116, 171
　Wm. 171
NANCE
　Neva Jane (1933-) 346
NAYLOR
　Ora 363
NEAL
　Eliza Jane 105
　Mary Elizabeth (JONES)
　　(1892-1980) 105
　Mary J 105
　Olin Kennedy (1895-1965) ... 105
NEISER
　Ann C. (1887-1982) 189, 241
NEVILLE 368
　Charles G. 327, 368
　Etta 368
　Frank W 368
　John 15
　Richard H 368
　Ruth D. (1913-1993) ... 327, 368
NEWCOMB
　Francis 180
NEWKIRK
　A. N. 32
　Albert. L 32
　Alice 252
　Alice B (TAYLOR)
　　(1893-1944) 199
　Charles 32, 253
　Cora 54, 84, 181
　Cora (1884-1982) 125

　Daniel E 32
　Edith 252
　Edward (1874-1959) . 54, 125, 180
　Eliza 32
　Eliza Giles 32
　Elizabeth 180, 252
　Elizabeth (HARRIS) (1874-1939)125
　Emma 84
　Francis M 32
　Frank 32
　Hannah 33
　Harriet 32, 33
　Harriet Eliza (1841-) . 21, 252, 253
　James 32, 199
　John 21, 32, 35
　John C. (1843-1863) 21, 32
　Mack E. 252
　Malcolm (1892-1972)199, 252, 253
　Margaret 32
　Mary E. 84
　Mary Ellen (1879-1912)
　　............. 54, 125, 180
　Maysel 252
　Mollie 84, 125
　Nancy 33, 84
　Nancy (1887-1972) 54
　Nancy (HICKS) (1817-1846)
　　................. 21, 32, 35
　Nanney (BONER) 199
　Nannie 252
　Nelson14, 16, 17, 29, 32,, 33, 84, 125
　Nelson (1819-1905) 21
　Nora 253
　Ray E 180
　Raymond E. (1901-1964) 125, 180
　Sarah E. 84
　Sarah Emaline (WATKINS)
　　(1853-1921) 54
　W D 84
　William D 32, 33, 84, 125
　William David (1844-1932)
　　............. 21, 54, 84
NEWMAN
　Mary 70, 163
　Mildred 163
NICHODEMAS
　Debbie Ann (MCCARTY)
　　(1947-) 311
　Thomas (1947-) 311
NICHOLS
　Ann M. (1863-1937) 96, 136
　Annie 136
　Carrie 136
　Clayton B. 194, 246
　Ella Marie (1895-1928) 194
　Lewis H 136
　Maude (HITCH) 194

NICHOLS continued
   Nettie 136
   Perry (1840-) 96, 136
NICKS
   Ella 164
   Geo K 164
   Stanley 164
   William A 164
   Wm J 164
NICOLAY
   Chester (1895-) 318
   Durwoood Charles (1922-1990) 318
   Hazel M.(1893-) 318
NOONAN
   Kerry Michael (1941-) 337
NORMAN
   Phillip (1906-1979) 319, 359
   Rachel 265, 359
   Rachel Matilda (MEEKER)
    (1911-2002) 319, 359
   Rachel Mrs 265
   Robert Phillp 319
   Son 319
NORRIS
   Carrie L.(1896-1977) 138, 202, 256
   Fannie 98, 138, 139, 256
   Fanny (TATMAN) (1863-1944) 98
   Hugh 98, 138, 139, 256
   Hugh Elijah (1899-1994) 98, 202, 256
   Hugh L 138, 256
   Robert H. (1927-) .. 138, 202, 256
   William 98, 138, 139, 256
   William E. (1862-1943) 98
NORTHCUTT 375
   Naomi (1880-) 347
NORTHNAGEL
   Charles (1904-) 339
   Virginia (1929-) 339
   Virginia (1910-) 339

OBERLE
   Carol (1956-) 341
   Denise (1963-) 342
   Janet Lea (FALOON)
    (1938-) 284, 341
   Norman (1938-) 341
   Sandra (1961-) 342
OCCUZZA
   Anthony 314
   Pamela Sue (DEVORE) (1952-)314
Ohio Volunteer Infantry 39
OHMERT
   Ailine 228
   Alice (1920-) 228, 288
   Elizabeth 288
   Elizabeth wife of George (1856-)
    228
   George. 288
   George (1851-) 228

   Gladys Lee (MERGARD)
    (1900-1965) 228, 288
   Harold G 288
   Laura I 288
   Lillian V 288
   Millie M 288
   Olive (1910-) 228
   W. L. Mrs. 166
   Winfield Leroy
    (1882-1975) 228, 288
OLEPHANT
   Eugene L 167
   Flora 167
OLICH
   Hilda Mae (1927-) 190
OLIVER
   Betsy 9
   Elijah 3, 9
   Polly (HICKS) (1776-) 3
OLLEN
   Sarah M 288
OLSEN / OLSON
   Ernie Charles (1923-) 335
   Janet E. (1947-) 350
ORR
   -?- 253
   Blache 253
   Charles (1872-) 200, 253
   Grace (1909-) 200, 253
   Laura (1875-) 200
ORTH
   Angela (CATALINA) (1933-) 318
   Aurelia C 359
   Carrie D 359
   Carrie wife of George 318
   Clemens G 359
   Donald Roy 318
   Frieda Mae 318, 359
   George 318, 359
   George Clement (1905-1982)
    .... 318, 359
   Helen (PIERNER?) (1927-) .. 318
   James Clarence 186
   James Clemens 318
   Margaret 265, 359
   Margaret Anna (MEEKER)
    (1907-1998) 186, 318
   Nancy Margaret 318
OSBORNE / OSBURN
   Adele (1940-) 334
   Lou Elizabeth or Selena
    (1855-1948) 231, 292
OSWALT
   Josephine 188
OWEN / OWENS
   Alice 163, 287
   Alice Lorraine (1922-) 227
   Barbara (1948-) 314
   Belle 66

   Bessie 111, 163, 287
   Bessie Salome (BRUBAKER)
    (1901-1990) 227
   Emma 45, 66, 156, 157
   Emma (1861-) 44
   Fanny 64
   Father 42, 44
   Frances 66, 89
   Francis "Fanny" 64, 65
   Gertrude 66
   Hannah ... 37, 63, 142,, 145, 147
   Hannah Francis (1821-1907)
    .... 42, 63, 65, 89
   Isabel (1854-) 44, 65, 66
   James 65, 89
   James H. (1848-) 44
   John W. (1850-) 44, 65
   Josephine . 44, 66, 108, 157, 281
   Josephine (1863-1926) 108
   Joshua (1856-) 44, 65, 66
   Josie 45, 108, 157
   Lucinda 66
   Mary 44, 65, 107, 108, 156
   Mary (1852-) 107
   Nancy 65
   Nancy (HICKS) (1831-1865) 35, 44
   Nancy J. (1858-) 44
   Robert B 163, 287
   Robert Brown (1895-1955)
    .... 227, 287
   Robert Brown Mrs 164
   Sidney 66
   William 43, 65, 66, 157
   William F. (1824-1873) 44

PAELTZ
   Charles (1862-) 199
   Charlie J 251
   Emma (GATES) (1862-) 199
   Gladys A. (1893-1992) . 199, 251
   Gladys Armilda 251
   Louise 251
   Minnie 251
   Neomi 251
PAGE
   Julia (1902-1982) 198, 251
PARKER
   Albert Martin (1925-) 340
   Ann (HALL) (1923-) 306
   Delia 351
   Effie Nolean (HUTCHISON)
    (1925-) 340
   George 351
   Gladys (1895-1918) 231
   Jennie (HIGGINS) 231
   John W. 231, 293
   Judy Kay (1951-) 340

PARKER continued
  Nancy (NEWKIRK) (1887-1972) 54
  Nannie 84
  Ralph (1902-1967) 306, 351
  Ruth (LANE) (1923-) 306
  Thelma Myrtle (PATTISON)
    (1903-1983) 306
  William (1881-1942) 54, 84
PARRISH
  Althea Ethlyn 366
PARTELLO
  John 72, 166
PARTRIDGE
  Naomi (1904-) 331
PATTEN
  Mahala 191, 243
PATTERSON 6
  Geo B. 296
  John 191, 243
  Nancy (MCCLELLAN) 191
  Velma (1889-1920) 191, 243
PATTISON
  Albert P. (1922-1993) ... 190, 240
  Ann 240
  Ann C. (NEISER) (1887-1982) 189
  Audrey (PETTIT) (1920-) ... 307
  Audrey N. (MCCLANAHAN)
    (1923-) 307
  Caroline 307
  Clarence E. (1874-1951) .. 90, 129
  Daisy 129
  Dale L 128, 129
  Dale Lester (1887-1959) .. 91, 129
  Delores Naomi (BUCEY)
    (1903-1988) 191, 242
  E. E. 351
  E. H 129, 240
  Edith May (1906-1994)
    .... 190, 241, 307, 352
  Edward 90, 128, 129, 240
  Edward H. (1877-1961) 189
  Edwin L. (1923-) 190, 241
  Elmore W 190
  Elmore Walter (1916-1955) 190, 241
  Emma Marie (MOORE)
    (1916-1984) 307
  Eunice 240, 351
  Eunice Irene (1916-) 189, 307, 351
  Evalyn 351
  Evelyn Grace 306
  Florence 351
  Florence (ALLEN) (1908-1987) 306
  Frank 128, 242
  Frank Lee (1891-1954) 91, 191, 242
  Gennie I, ... 240, 351
  George E. (1920-) 190, 241
  Glenn Edward (1931-1942) .. 306
  Grace 190, 241, 352

Grace (1906-1929) 307
Harold Ralph (1940-) 306
Herbert L. 241
Herbert Leroy (1918-1941) 190, 241
Hilda Mae (OLICH) (1927-) .. 190
Irene 240, 351
J. S 241
James 129
James Edward (1951-) 307
Jennie I 240
Jennie Irene (MCKIBBEN)
  (1883-1950) 189
Jo Ann (1938-) 307
John 128, 129, 240, 241
John Robert (1941-) 307
John S. (1846-1906) 90
John W 189, 240, 351, 352
John W. (1918-1971) 307
Keith 306
Lizzie M. 128
Lorette 129
Mada 241, 352
Mada Mary (KUHN)
  (1891-1963) 189, 241
Margaret (ANSTAILT)
  (1906-1932), ... 306
Marguerite A. 351
Marilyn Jane (WALKER) (1939-)
  306
Mary A 128
Mary A. 'Mollie' (MANNING)
  (1848-1913) 90
Merrill John (1926-1945) 306, 351
Minnie M. (BOWER)
  (1882-1916) 189, 241, 352
Myrtle Elizabeth (1879-1956)
  .... 90, 128, 129
Nellie 91
Norma Jean (1934-) 306
Patricia (1936-) 191, 308
Robert 240
Robert John (1912-1985) 189, 307
Ross 240
Ross John (1882-1948) 90, 189, 240
Stanley 240, 351
Stanley E. Jr. (1952-) 306
Stanley Edward (1902-1951) . 306
Stanley Edward 189, 351
Thelma Myrtle (1903-1983)
  .... 189, 240, 306, 351
Walter 128, 190, 241, 352
Walter (1927-1927) 190
Walter Cleavland (1885-1973)
  .... 90, 189, 241
PAUL
  Grace (1898-) 314

PAYNE
  Helen wife of Edward (1903-) 325
  Thedora 66
PEFAH
  May Lena 174
PELHAM'S
  Mr. 27
PEMBERTON
  Douglas Eugene 343
  Eugene 374
  Eugene Bruce (1921-1997) 343, 374
  George (1891-) 343
  George M 374
  Marilyn Elizabeth 343
  Max 374
  Myrtle 374
  Shirley (BRUBAKER)
    (1926-1983) 343
PEMDUSON
  Meledia 61
PENDERY
  Esther 330
PENNINGTON
  Dorothy Louise (WOODEN)
    (1920-1992) 232
  Evelyn 309, 353
  Harry L 309, 353
  J. A. (1851-) 232
  Lettie Pearl (BENSON)
    (1889-1973) 232, 294
  Octavia H (1862-) 232
  Paul Prosper (1887-1972) 232, 294
  Wayne Benson (1915-1982)
    .... 232, 294
  Wilma June (1925-1979) 233
PETERSON
  Maggie (1838-) 41
  Mary W. (1870-1936) 41
  Roy 278
  William (1817-) 41
PETTIT
  Audrey (1920-) 307, 352
PHILIPS / PHILLIPS
  Georgia 140
  Edith (1882-1972) 99, 140
  Emerilla 206, 263
  Thomas 99
  Warren 140
PICARD
  John L. (1940-) 337
PIERNER?
  Helen (1927-) 318
PIGMAN
  Emma 101
PINDELL / PENDELL
  Jennie (BRADEY) 209
  Miqual M. 209
  Sarah Millie (1867-1936) 209, 268

PLANCK / PLANK
- Hazel 216
- Irene Dolly (1918-1987) 339

PLATT
- Dewey M 157
- Mary 157

POHLMAN
- Elizabeth (1876-1942) 223

POPE
- James P. (1940-) 349

PORTER
- Adda H. (1888-1920) 72, 111, 165
- Mary M. (1853-) 112, 165
- Samuel (1853-1920) 112

POSTON
- Elizabeth Fugatt 257, 265
- Elizabeth Stewart (HITE) (1914-1986) 312, 355
- Eugene Locke (1910-1978) .. 312
- Joan D. (CAPPEL) (1944-) .. 313
- John (1883-) 235
- John Holton Jr (1926-) 235
- Kenneth Eugene 313
- Lois Lucille (EDWARDS) (1930-2003) 235
- Patricia Lynne 313
- Stella wife of John (1887-) ... 235

POTTER
- Jacob 79

PRATT
- Cora (BLOODHART) (1870-) 155, 220, 279, 280, 372
- Ed (1871-) 220
- Edna Fae (1892-1981) .. 220, 280

PRENE
- Ella E 295
- Emma J 295
- Frank (1859-) 233, 234, 295
- Fred 295
- Ida May (1892-) 233, 295
- Mary Neoma (1894-) ... 234, 295

PRICE
- Carol 332
- Elsie Glendora (1904-1993) 102, 146
- Estelle M. (1881-) 102
- Fred 335
- Rachel (1864-) 90
- Robert (1877-) 102

PUCH/ PUGH
- Carl S 275, 331
- Carl Starner (1908-1981) 216, 331, 369, 370
- Carole Lee 331
- Donna Sue (1946-) 331
- Estella 275

James B. 216, 275
Joseph W 275
Joseph Warren (1879-1952) 216, 275, 370
Margaret (JENKINS) (1915-) . 331
Mary B. (SUTTLES) 216
Merideth Margaret (GOEBEL) (1939-) 331
Starner D 275
Stella 275
Stella Blanche (JONES) (1884-1967) 216

PULLIN
- Huldah 239

PURDY
- Alan Lee (1950-) 315
- Connie Sue (1954-1970) 315
- Dale Lynn (1955-) 315
- Danny Ray (1952-) 315
- Irma Claire (JENNINGS) (1930-) 259, 315
- John Russel (1957-) 315
- Lewis Ray 315

PUTNAM / PUTMAN
- P 117
- James W. (1949-) 349

QUINN
- Edith Elizabeth (1890-1958) 195, 248
- John V. 195, 248
- Martha (COFFEE) 195

RADER
- Charles H. 252
- Estel J 252
- Julia R 252
- Louise 252
- Walter 252

RAHILLY
- John 154
- Sarah (1888-) 106, 154
- William 154

RAINS
- Barbara Sue (1945-) 328

RALEIGH
- Sarah 154

RAMMINGER
- Mary 189, 241

RANCORT
- -?- 355
- Maude (1883-) 312

RARDIN
- Anna E. Mrs (1893-1981) 106, 154

RATCLIFF
- Charles (1835-) 206
- Cynthia J. (1841-) 206
- Josephine (1884-1986) .. 206, 263

RATHBUN
- Deon 278

RAWLINSON
- Ellen Christina (JACKSON) . 195
- Eula Pugh (1879-1952) . 195, 247
- Eulla P. 353
- Frank 247
- Frank B. 195

RAY
- Belle 66
- Dorothy Cloetill (1918-1981) 320, 361
- Elisha 66
- Emma 66
- Ergsmus 66
- Ida 66
- Margaret 66
- Martha J 66
- Mary 361
- Monroe 320, 361
- Ralph Ray 66
- Roy W 66
- Soloman 66

REDFERN
- Lowell Leroy (1932-) 346

REDGEN
- Frank 271

REED
- Donna (STARRETT) (1948-) 264, 318
- Lulu O. (1895-1971) 235, 236, 297
- Raymond 318
- Sarah Ellen (1861-) 54

REEDER
- James Rev. 284

REEVES
- Christina 348
- Elijah 276
- Floyd L (1924-) 221, 281
- Herschel 281
- Hershel William (1884-) . 221, 281
- Hershell (1917-1987) 221
- Leatha (1915-) 221, 281
- Norman H. (1926-) 221, 281
- Selma (GUYETTE) (1889-1944) 221, 281

REINHARDT
- Clarence H 90, 129
- Clarence Homer (1889-1963) .. 90
- Frank (1857-) 90
- Myrtle 129, 240
- Myrtle Elizabeth (PATTISON) (1879-1956) 90
- Rachel (PRICE) (1864-) 90

REINSTATLER
    Jack 201
    Lila Eleanor (WITSCHGER)
        (1919-) 201
REMLEY
    John (1847-1919) 96
    Leanna (DUGAN) (1856-1935) 96
    Lulu (1889-1982) 96
RETTICH / RETTESH
    Frances (1870-) 102, 146
RHOADES / RHODES
    De Leo (1877-1964) 51
    Ellen 78, 119
    Ellen Williams 316
    Emmet Williams (1917-1996)
        . . . . 316, 358
    Jeanette (STALDER) (1914-1980)
        . . . . 316, 357
    Judith Ann (1942-) 316, 358
    Vernon 78, 119
RICE
    Charles 25
RICHARDS
    Dorothy 373
    Dorothy (1919-) 338
    Eva B. (1893-) 338, 373
    Glen A. (1892-) 338, 373
    Mae H 373
RICHTER
    Janet 333
    Kathryn R 109, 161
RICKLES
    Herbert Donald (1931-1973) . . 197
    Linda Margaret (FITZPATRICK)
        (1943-) 197
RIEGLE
    Diana 327
RIESINGER
    Chris (1858-) 97
    Edward (1884-1960) 97
    Lelah T. (TAYLOR)
        (1897-1978) 97
    Lydia (MOHR) (1864-) 97
RILEY
    Edith 243, 245
    Edith L. (1858-) 91, 130
    Elizabeth V. 243
    Walter 244
RITCHIE
    Lucinda (1947-) 317
ROBERTS
    Arthur Jack 332
    Dale J. (1930-) 310
    Harriett Juanita 332
    Joan Carol (GUNDERLACK)
        (1947-) 332
    Larry 332
    Leona I (JONES) (1909-1995) 332
    Linda Rae (DALE) (1942-) . . . 332
    Louis (1902-1982) 332
    Louis (1936-) 332
    Mable Marie 332
    Mary 332
    Nicholas 229, 290
    Pamela (1949-) 332
    Patricia (KLEVINS) (1936-) . . 332
    Renata (HUBER) (1946-) 332
    Robert R 332
    Rosalie 332
    Sadie Bell (1858-1937) 55, 85
ROBERTSON
    Bess V 178
    Bessie (KING) (1878-)
        . . . . 31, 80, 123, 178
    Bessie L. 178
    Ella 178
    Fred 178
    Robert K. (1913-) 123, 178
    Robertson
        W.F. 178
    William 80, 178
    William Fernando (1877-1925)
        . . . . 123, 178
ROBINSON
    Alfonso (1852-) 20
    Alfred 29
    Alonzo (1848-1913)
        . . . . 20, 28, 40, 48, 57, 75
    Alvin 29, 75
    Clairmore (1863-1863) 48
    Dean M., ... 75
    Emily 29
    Homer E 272
    Ida A 272
    J. W. 29
    John 28, 29
    John W. (1817-1882) 19
    Laura A. (MCGRAW)
        (1846-1868) 48
    Lavinia (1887-1976) . . . 213, 272
    Lillie L. (1866-) 48, 75
    Malissa 29, 75
    Margaret Missouri
        (1844-1883) 20 49 76
    Martha 272
    Martha J. (1865-) 213
    Mary 28, 29
    Mary (HICKS) (1803-1878) 15, 19
    Mary Eliza (1848-1867) 20
    Melissa Jane (1842-1870)
        . . . . 20, 28, 48, 75
    Missorn 29
    Nancy (1943-) 330
    Nancy E. 29, 75
    Nancy Emily (1846-1877)
        . . . . 20, 49, 75
    Neety Ann (1840-) 118
    S. Miles Dr 144
    W. W. 29
    William J 272
    Willis J 272
    Winfield (1861-) 213
RODEN
    Bessie 286
    Eleanor Bernice (1928-1986)
        . . . . 226, 342
    Ernest 286
    James 226, 286
    James (1855-1900) 226
    James E. (1890-1966) . . . 226, 286
    James E. Mrs 164
    Kenneth 286
    Kenneth Windsor (1926-) 226, 342
    Kyle Jean (1952-) 342
    Lee Ann (1948-) 342
    Maud Ella (BRUBAKER)
        (1899-1988) 226
    Maude 286
    Minnie 286
    Pauline (MORTON) (1926-) . 342
    Susan 286
    Susan mother of James (1856-) 226
RODGERS / ROGERS
    Bessie 356
    Bessie Marie (1899-1966)
        . . . . 203, 257, 258
    Claris (1913-) . 168, 289, 344, 374
    Evalyan 168, 289
    Evalyn R.
        (1906-) . . . 229, 289, 344, 374
    Evalyn Rotheus 344
    Frank Tatman 114
    Gregory Kevin (1954-) 321
    John 271
    Joseph 168
    Joseph (1879-) 114
    Joseph Font 289
    Lawrence J 289
    Locleus L (1906-)
        . . . . . . 168, 229, 289, 344, 374
    Lora (1889-1979) 213, 271
    Lydia A 168
    Lydia Ann (TATMAN)
        (1858-1938) 114
    Marjorie 64
    Marjorie Claire "Margie"
        (BEHAN) (1928-) 321
    Mary M (1911-) 168, 229, 289, 374
    Paul G. (1909-) . . . 168, 229, 289
    Rhonda Gayle (1960-) 321
    Richard Gary (1948-) 321

RODGERS / ROGERS continued
  Rotheus 168, 289
  Rotheus Thomas (1879-1960)
  . . . . 114, 229, 289
  Sarah 271
  Syrene (1881-1920) . 168, 229, 289
  T. R. 169, 170
  T. R. Mrs. 289
  Theodore Jackson (1928-) . . . 321
  Thomas . . 168, 169, 229, 289, 374
  Thomas Rotheus 289
  Viola 289
ROLLINSON / ROLLISON
  Ella Pugh 247
  Ellen C 247
  Frank B. 247
Roosevelt's Rough Riders 169
ROOT
  Arlie 308
  Virginia Ann (MANNING)
  (1941-) 308
ROSENDALE
  Matthews 358
ROSS
  Alma 267
  Alma Imogene 362
  Alma J. (1893-) 209, 322, 362
  Archie 267, 362
  Archie Milton (1885-) 208, 322, 362
  Betty E. (1929-) 322, 363
  Edna Pauline (1883-) . . . 208, 267
  Francis 267, 362
  Frankie M 267
  Frankie Mrs 148
  G A 267
  Geo Allen 267
  George A 267, 362
  George Allen (1861-1926) 208, 362
  Mame 267, 362
  Marnie B 362
  Mary Ann (1830-) . . . 48, 74, 169
  Mary F 267, 362
  Mary Frances (HOUSER)
  (1863-1930) 208, 362
  Maymie (CONN) (1879-) 322, 362
  Milton (1921-) 267, 322, 362
  Pauline (WALDEN) (1901-)
  . . . . 267, 322, 363
  Thresia 189, 240
  W. C. 363
  Walter H. (1901-) 209, 267
  Welthie (1888-) 209, 267
  William C 267, 362, 363
  William Clifford (1895-)
  . . . . 209, 322, 363
  Willis 267

ROUSCH / ROUSH
  Elizabeth 254
  Sarah E. 254
  Sarah Elizabeth (1846-1932) . 200
RUDD
  Alma (1908-) 326
  Edna P. (VERMILLION)
  (1906-1985) 110
  Henry (1865-) 110
  Ina (CLARKSON) (1869-) . . . 110
  Lilian (1932-) 235
  Roscoe (1901-1984) 110
RUDGERS
  Margaret (1874-) 224
RUGG
  Nancy Elizabeth 316
RUMHARDL
  Myrtle E Mrs 129
RUMMEL
  Arthur (1864-) 102
  Frances (RETTICH) (1870-) . 102
  Laura Francis (1896-1952) 102, 146
RUMMEL
  Arthur 146
  D. H. Pvt 146
  Laura Francis 146
RUOLE
  Sarah 139
RUSH
  Mary "Polly" (FEE) (1805-1876)
  42
  Sarah 139, 140
  Sarah Ann (1844-1914) . . . 42, 62
  Thomas 62
  Thornton (1794-1862) 42
RUSSELL
  Karen Ethel (1945-) 337
RYAN
  Dennis 362
  Shirley Ann (1944-) 329

SAGASER
  Miriam (1818-) 91, 131
SATTERFIELD
  Dorothy Jean (BROWN)
  (1918-2003) 215
  Dow Enzor "Jack" (1912-1973) 215
SAULS
  A Fay 324, 365
  Esther A 365
  Eunice D 365
  Jack N 365
  Robert 324, 365
  Robert Boyer 365
SCHAEFER / SCHAFFER
  Jeannie (1937-) 346
  Milton 217
  Pauline Joyce (JONES) (1945-) 217

SCHARD
  Ruth 267
SCHATZMAN
  Margaret 171
SCHAUFLER
  Ethel May 229, 290
  Jacob 290
SCHAUSEN
  Lois Evelyn (MCNAIR)
  (1929-) 202
  Walter James (1927-) 202
SCHIELTZ
  Janet 318
SCHLICK
  Larry 336
SCHMARTZ
  Nick 370
SCHMIDT / SCHMITT
  Elizabeth 166
  Harry 318
  Virginia Joyce (STARRETT)
  (1946-) 318
SCHNEIDER
  -?- (1942-) 347
  Paul A. 310
SCHOTT
  John 241
  Oliver 241
  Samatha 241
SCHROER
  Eileen (BRUBAKER) (1926-) 228
  Raymond 228
SCHULTHEISS
  Lucy 171
SCHUMAKER
  Delores (WEIGHILL) (1917-) 347
  Unknown 347
SCHWARTZ
  Ernest Dale (1946-) 313
SCOTT
  Arthur J 150
  Jennie L 150
  Lillie Mae (1880-) 204
SEAMAN
  Ann (1955-) 346
  E. Harvey II 345
  E. Harvey III (1956-) 346
  Paul Walker (1967-) 346
  Robert Clement (1957-) 346
  Shirley (CLEMENT) (1924-) . 345
  Sue (1959-) 346
SEIPELT
  Albert William (1876-) 314
  Clara Edith 356
  Connie Nancy (WILSON) (1948-)
  . . . . 314, 356
  Dale Lynn (1952-1952) . 315, 356

SEIPELT continued
   David Lyle (1952-1952) . 315, 356
   Edna Marilyn (FLORENCE)
      (1951-) 314
   Frances 356
   Hazel 356
   Leslie Galen 314, 356
   Lvera . . . . . iii, 257-259, 264, 359
   Lvera (JENNINGS) (1929-) 26, 43,
      63, 66, 67, 147, 263, 264, 314, 356
   Marilyn 356
   Parthena Mae (FLAUGHER)
      (1886-1974) 314, 356
   Ruby 356
   Victor 259
   Victor L. Jr 356
   Victor Lloyd (1920-2008) 314, 356
   William Albert 356
SEVERING
   Catherine (1855-1942) 108
SEWARD
   Airee? 196
SHANIARA
   Richard 164
SHARP
   Margaret 213, 273
SHAW
   C 241
   Samatha (1860-) 189
   Stella Rosetta 203
SHEE
   Taeko (1924-) 205
   Warde 263
SHELTON
   Deborah L. (LUCKEY) (1949-) 319
   James B. (1949-) 319
SHEPHERD / SHEPSHERD
   Fred 294
   Hary E 242
SHERBAHN
   Bernadine 155, 279, 280, 372
   Bernadine L. (1910-2005) 219
   Bernita (HINNERACHS)
      (1918-) 336
   Donald 155, 279, 280
   Donald G. (1912-) . 219, 336, 372
   Donna Gayle 336
   Gail 155, 279, 280, 372
   Gayle E. (JONES) (1883-) . . . 219
   George 155, 279, 280
   George Garfield (1881-) . 219, 279
   Geraldine (1914-1915) 219
   Nancy Caroline 336
SHERMAN
   Dorothy 313

SHINKLE
   Elizabeth 151, 271, 270
   Katherine 11
   Laura A. (1855-1926) . . 106, 155
   Leroy R 151
   Mary E 151
   Mary Elizabeth (1854-1905) . . 104
   Mary R. (1820-) 104
   P. 26
   Solomon (1813-) 104, 151
SHOHER
   Helen Mrs 160
SHRINE
   George G. III (1942-) 312
   Lena Lucille (GLOVER) (1943-)
      312
SHUMWAY
   Fred Julian 174
   Frederick Julian (1878-1936)
      . . . . 119, 174
   Gertrude 174
   Gertrude May (HOPKINS)
      (1879-1969) 119
   Harriet Mildred (HAASE)
      (1908-1999) 119
   Irene 174
   Ivan 174
   Ivan Vernon (1904-1978) 119
   Lora Irene (1907-1997) 119
SIDEWELL
   Christine Theresa (1946-) 327
SILCOTT
   Frank 240
SILER
   Mildred Ruth (HALL) (1918-1986)
      345
   Robert (1921-1996) 345
SIMANTEL
   Bertha wife of George 237
   Bertha M 299
   Francis 299
   George J. 237, 299
   Harrold 299
   Helen L. (1912-) 237, 299
SIMMONS
   Anna Rebecca (1884-1972)198, 250
   Mary E. (1858-) 198, 250
   Sallie 216, 276
   William D (1850-) 198, 250
   William H 216, 276
SINGLER
   Anthony (1921-1986) . . . 197, 249
   Catherine 133
   Charles (1927-1947) 197, 249
   Daisy B. (FITZPATRICK)
      (1901-1964) 197, 249
   Darlene May (MANNING)
      (1939-) 308

   Donald (1925-2002) 197, 249
   Edward / Edwin 133, 249, 197, 250
   Edwin Joseph (1897-1966)197, 250
   Edwin Mrs 133
   George (1920-1976) 133, 197, 249
   Gladys (1923-) 197, 249
   Katherine wife of Edward 197, 250
   Spencer 308
SMITH
   Albert 53, 81, 82
   Albert Butler 82, 179
   Amos 82
   Bessie 77, 84
   Caroline A 82
   Carrie 31, 81, 82
   Catharine A 82
   Clarence (1896-) 232, 294
   Effie E 81
   Elmer J. 81, 179
   George C 81
   Georgia Anna (HICKS) (1847-) 53
   Georgiana 81, 82, 179
   Hattie 241
   Hicks William 81
   James 110
   Jewel Virginia
      (1917-1996) 192, 243
   Josephine 77
   Lew S. 81
   Luella (1873-1930)
      . . . . 53, 81, 82, 124, 179
   Luella Carrie 81
   Malva 294
   Marilyn (1920-) 232. 294
   Martha E. 81
   Melva E. (STEWART) (1895-) 232
   Mr 84
   Nora Ellen (1876-1930) . 110, 163
   Robert B. (1923-) . . 173, 232, 294
   Smith 32, 77
SMITT
   Elizabeth 112
SMITTKAMP
   Allen 181
   Cecil 181
   Charles (1915-) 126, 181
   Chester (1887-1931) 126, 181
   Chester Allen (1918-2010) . . . 126
   Fredrick F 181
   James (1924-1995) 126, 181
   John O 181
   Joseph (1863-) 126, 181
   Mary Cecil (HICKS)
      (1890-1930) 126
   Sabin 181
   Sophia 181

SNAKE
- Alice M 240
- Floyd H 240
- Hiram L 240
- Pearl B 240

SNEDIK
- Charles 73, 166

SNIDER
- George W 216, 276
- Zouella 216, 276

SNODGRASS
- Becky Sue (HICKS) (1943-)
  . . . . 284, 341, 374
- Michael Dean (1961-) 341
- Palmer E. (1938-) 341
- Steven Paul (1968-) 341

SNYDER
- Jos E 152

SOLWALL
- Minnie (1877-) 200, 254

SONDERS
- Lenora 165
- William 165

SOUDERS
- C. Nora (TUDOR) (1891-1978)
  . . . . 112, 165
- William 112, 165

SOUTHCOTT
- Iris Joan (1929-) 335

SPAIGHT
- Richd. D. 14

Spanish-American War 104, 115, 169

SPARKS
- Benjamin 2, 8, 9
- Eliza (HICKS) (1774-) 2

SPECHT
- Wilburn 274

SPEER 5

SPRAGUE
- Margaret R. (1876-1963) 191, 242
- Ora Chasse 242
- Rebecca (HOMAN) (1842-1919)
  . . . . 191, 242
- Wright (1839-1922) . 129, 191, 242

SPRIGGS
- Nona 212

STAATS / STATTS
- Louella M. (1902-) . . 234, 347, 376
- Marilyn R. (1927-) 347, 376
- Martha M. (1926-) . . 234, 347, 376
- William C. (1894-) . . 234, 347, 376

STABLER
- Krysten 40, 59

STACKHOUSE
- Maybelle 320, 361

STALDER
- Ben 205
- Betty 204, 261, 305, 357
- Bill 261, 305, 357
- Caroline (DAY) (1927-1997)
  . . . . 205, 263
- Curtis Clyde (1911-1996)
  . . . 143, 187, 205, 261, 262, 357
- Dick 261, 305, 357
- Elizabeth (1913-2008)
  . . . . 205, 261, 316, 357, 377
- Elizabeth Sunshine 357
- Florence Madlyn (FRENCH) (1917-2000) 205
- Frances (HADLEY) (1919-2008)
  . . . . 205, 261, 262, 358
- Grace Olive (1918-2003)
  . . . . 205, 261, 305, 316, 357
- Jeanette (1914-1980)
  . . . 205, 261, 305, 316, 357, 358
- Madge 205, 261, 357
- Mary M. 261
- Mary Madge (1921-2006)
  . . . . 205, 261, 305, 317, 358
- Medora (BOARDMAN) 205
- Mollie Dell (LEVI) (1884-1947)
  142-145, 185, 205, 261, 262, 357
- Mrs. B. 144
- Nellie D 261, 357
- Richard Benjamin (1927-)
  . . . . 261, 263, 205, 357-359
- Ruth Marilyn (1919-2000)
  . . . 205, 261, 305, 317, 357, 358
- Taeko (SHEE) (1924-)
  . . . . 205, 263, 357
- W. B. 261, 357
- W. B. Mrs 261, 357
- William 261, 262, 357, 358
- William Benjamin (1878-1948)
  . . . . 185, 205, 262, 357
- William Francis (1916-2005)
  . . . . 205, 261, 262
- William Henry Harriston 205

STANTON
- Helen (-1991) 313
- Stark Nursery 145

STARKIE
- John Richard (1939-) 337

STARRETT / STERRETT
- Charles Clifford (1950-) 264, 318
- Donna (1948-) 264, 318
- Janet (SCHIELTZ) 318
- Kathleen (BROWN) (1954-) . 318
- Marian (WEST) (1919-)
  . . . . 144, 264, 318
- Nancy (KURTZ) (1942-) 318
- Robert (1917-) 144, 264, 318
- Robert Mrs 264
- Robert Howard (1942-) 318
- Thomas Edwin (1944-) . 264, 318
- Virginia Joyce (1946-) . 264, 318

STATZMAN
- Anna 234

STAUFFLER
- Anne 290
- Ethel M. 290
- Hellen 290

STEELE
- Camely 369
- Charles W. (1925-1972)
  . . . . 274, 330, 369
- Elzie wife of John 330, 369
- George F 369
- Gertie 369
- John W. (1862-) 330, 369
- Leta G 274, 369
- Leta Grace (WILLIAMS)
  (1898-1981) 330
- Obie 369
- Queen 114, 167
- Shirley Jean 274, 330, 369
- Tate (1891-1972) . . 274, 330, 369

STEPHENS 368
- Esther E. (1902-1965) . . 199, 253
- Kate 368
- LouEtta 327

STEPHENSON
- Grace Elenor (1894-) 330

STEVENS
- Carla J. (1960-) 348
- Charles 177, 236, 297
- Charles E. (1919-1997) 347
- Charles Richard (1889-1973) . 121
- Delia (1930-) 236, 348
- Diana L (1947-) 348
- Edward 138
- Elizabeth 175, 177, 297
- Elizabeth E. (1916-2010) 236
- Frances 177
- Francis M 177
- H. J. 236
- Harry H. 176
- Henry 177, 297, 333
- Henry Harrison (1852-1916)
  . . . . 121, 177
- Henry Johnston (1895-1964)
  . . . . 121, 235, 297
- Jane (LANE) 121
- Johnnie 297
- Johnston 297
- Kelly Jo (1968-) 348
- Laura Jacqueline (1961-) 348
- Linda Jean (1963-) 348
- Lizzie 176
- Lloyd J. (1928-) 236, 348
- Lulu 297
- Lulu O. (REED) (1895-1971)
  . . . . 235, 297

STEVENS continued
   Margie Garnet (1921-1929) . . 236
   Marilyn R. (STAATS) (1927-) 347
   Marion 177
   Mary E 177
   Mary Elizabeth (JOHNSTON)
      (1869-1960) 121
   Pamela (1954-) 348
   Patricia L. (1952-) 348
   Paul Johnston (1957-) 348
   Samuel 121
   Sharon S. (1950-) 348
   Wilma J. (1924-) 236, 297, 348, 376
STEWART
   A.W 173
   Arthur 78
   Arthur W. (1828-1887) 50, 78
   Carrie 173
   Carrie V. wife of John (1867-) 117
   Colin 312
   Diana 78
   Diana (HOPKINS) (1826-1897) 50
   Elsworth 165
   Hattie Sarah (1855-1905) 100, 141
   J. M 173
   James W. (1857-1863) . . . 51, 78
   John 51, 78, 173
   John M. (1866-) 117
   Mary E. (1854-1863) 51, 78
   Melva E. (1895-) 117, 173, 232, 294
STILLWELL
   Bertha 177
STILT
   George F. (1942-) 333
STIPP
   Daniel W 133
   John D 133
STOCKTON
   Betsy 377
   Betty Jo 261, 377
   Elizabeth K. 358
   Elizabeth Joan (Kieser) 377
   Glenn 357
   Mary E. "Betsy" 357
   Mary Elizabeth 377
   Robert Glenn (1939-) 316
   Robert G. "Greg" 357
STOLTZ
   Larry Edward 336
STONE
   Dale 279
   Floyd 279
   Frances 278
   Loyd 279
STORER
   Hazel Faye (1921-2002) 326

STOWELL
   Harold 331
STRAHAN / STRAHN
   -?- 279
   James (1830-) 107, 156
   Frances 156
   Francis 156
   John 156
   Lorella 156
   Lucy 156
   Lucy E. (1859-1925) . . . 107, 156
   Rosetta 156
STREET
   Edith Marion (1920-) 330
STREITMEIR
   J. E. 105
   Lucy Florence (JONES) (1891-) 105
STROUP
   Donna Beth (1940-) 339
STUART
   Eliza 141
   Hattie 257
   Wm R. 141
SUSSEXON 375
SUTTLES
   Mary B. 216
SUTTON
   Elisabeth Ann (1847-) . . 213, 272
   Elizabeth 273
SWEENEY 306
   Norma Jean (PATTISON)
      (1934-) 306
SWEM
   Nancy 31
SWENSON
   Walter 335
SWING
   Agnes A. (KOEHNE) (1942-) 310
   Agnes Cleo (CRANE) (1911-) 310
   Archie T. (1893-1894) 94
   Barbara 199
   Charles Robert 310
   Charles W 94, 134
   Clifford John (1857-1951)
      . . . . 134, 94, 251
   Edna B (1891-1968) 94, 134
   Eleanor (1905-) 99
   Gladys(1901-) 199, 251
   Glen O'Hara (1889-1962)
      . . . . 94, 198, 250
   Glenn O 134, 250
   John C 134
   John Charles (1899-) 94, 199, 251
   Joyce Ann 310
   Joyce Renee 310
   Julia (PAGE) (1902-1982) . . . 198
   Julia E 251

   Katherine 251
   Katherine Jane (1926-) 199
   Kenneth (1919-1975) 198
   Linda (COUREY) (1892-1964) 198
   Linda C 250
   Marguerite R (1924-) 198
   Mary A (TATMAN) (1858-1929)
      94
   Mary Louise (1924-) 198, 251
   Mary / Mollie 134
   Page 199
   Phil 134
   Phillip B. (1895-1985) 94, 198, 251
   Phillip C 253
   Robert Eberle (1908-1981)310, 354
SYMMS
   Walter D. 260
SYMON / SYMONS
   David Watson (1875-1948)
      . . . . 204, 259, 260
   Emma 260
   Irma Clair (LEVI) (1878-1928) 204
   John 259, 260
   Robert Kenneth (1921-1993)
      . . . . 204, 259
   Watson 259
TACKETT
   Flora Mae 312, 355
   Mae 355
TALANAN
   Mary R. 251
TANKERSLEY
   Mary Laverne (1905-1964)196, 249
TATMAN / TATEMAN
   _?_ 128
   Alexander 246
   Alice 76, 134, 140
   Alice M (TAYLOR) (1853-1908)
      94
   Amanda C. (1853-) 18, 24
   Ann M (NICHOLS) (1863-1937)96
   Anna / Annie 135, 250, 255
   Anna Rebecca (SIMMONS)
      (1884-1972) 198
   Annie L. (1860-1880) 41
   Archibald (1862-1896) 41, 58, 60
   Arizona T. "Arra" (1865-1933)
      . . . . 41, 97, 137, 255
   B Nell 169, 290
   Barbara (ALTMAN) (1832-1854)
      41
   Benjamin 18 24 35
   Benjamin F. (1837-1864) 18
   Bessie 134, 140
   Bessie (1881-1960) 94
   Caroline 'Callie' (1869-1942)
      . . . . 42, 61, 97, 137

TATMAN / TATEMAN continued
  Carrie 42, 59, 62, 139
  Carrie (1872-1956) 99
  Clarice 114
  D. H. 135
  Dede 62
  Diana / Dianna
    . . . . 18, 39, 57-60, 132
  Dianna (1825-1867) 38
  Dick 169
  Dortha 28
  Durwood 250
  Dwight 61, 135
  Dwight Harrison (1899-1975)
    . . . . 96, 135
  Edith 58, 59, 140
  Edith (HARRIS) (1838-1873) . 39
  Edith (PHILLIPS) (1882-1972) . . 99
  Effie 24, 42, 58, 59, 62, 139
  Effie (1870-1931) 98
  Elijah 18, 24, 28, 39,
    . . . . 58, 59, 62, 139, 140
  Elijah (1835-1902) 42
  Eliza . . . . 28, 74 ,75
  Eliza (1836-1914) 19
  Elizabeth (HANCOCK)
    (1848-1868) 41
  Eloise (1916-2010) 198
  Ethel M 290
  Ethel May (SCHAUFLER) . . 229
  F. U. 290
  Fanny 24, 42, 58, 59, 62, 138
  Fanny (1863-1944) 98
  Flora 169, 290
  Flora Catherine (LEWIS)
    (1866-1951) 115
  Florence 60, 61
  Florence (1896-1904) 115
  Florence E 169, 290
  Florence E. (WILSON) (1877-) . . 41
  Florence J 41, 136
  Florence J. (1871-1919) 96
  Florence M 290
  Florence Marie 229, 290, 374
  Florence Marie (1913-1957) . . 344
  Florence Mrs 170
  Florence W 61
  Frank . . 169, 229-230, 250, 290-291
  Frank L 115, 290
  Frank L. (1862-1924) 229
  Frank M. 28
  Frank U 169, 290
  Franklin Ulyses (1862-1934)
    . . . . 48, 115, 169, 170
  Gayl (1925-) 230, 291
  George W. 24, 59, 62
  George Washington (1827-1899)
    . . . . 18, 39, 59
  Grace (1872-1873) 39
  Harriet (1865-1868) 41
  Hattie (1863-1868) 42
  Helena "Lena" (1879-1922) 76, 94
  Infant (-1869) 39
  J C 135
  J Louise 135
  James 19, 28, 74, 169
  James (1830-1869) 48
  James (1890-) 115
  James G. (1855-) 48
  James Sylvester 48, 114
  Jane . . . 39, 58, 60, 131, 135, 138
  Jane (MCNAIR) (1834-1897) . 41
  Jane Louise (BOGGESS)
    (1870-1949) 95
  Jennie (1883-1957) 94, 134
  John 18, 24, 25, 39, 58,
    . . . . . 60, 61, 92, 131, 134-136
  John (1830-1913) 41
  John C 1833-1895) 42
  John Charles (1857-1906)
    . . . . 41, 96, 135
  John Franklin (1885-1959)
    . . . . 94, 198, 250
  John W . . . . 62 ,140
  John Warren (1875-1961)
    . . . . 42, 99, 140
  Joseph 28
  L 139
  Ledora Estelle (1862-1935)
    . . . . 41, 97, 136
  Lena 94, 134
  Leone Helen (1909-1994) 229, 290
  Lewis 41, 60, 61, 135
  Lewis G. (1867-1949) 95
  Lieu 170
  Louis 58, 60, 131
  Louise 61, 135
  Lucinda 18, 19, 28, 57, 75, 170, 171
  Lucinda (1824-1867) 38
  Lucinda (1833-1912) 48
  Lurena Dee (1874-1960) 42
  Lydia 17, 18, 28, 168, 289
  Lydia (HICKS) (1802-1861) . . . 19
  Lydia Ann (1858-1938)
    . . . . 28, 48, 74, 114, 168
  Mabel (MEEKER) (1899-) 96
  Margaret . . . . 140 / 291
  Margaret (1907-) 100
  Mariam 114
  Marjorie Francis (WISE) (1903-)
    230
  Mary 18, 24, 41, 48,
    . . . 58, 60, 62, 74, 131, 134, 137
  Mary (1797-1875) 18
  Mary A. (1858-1929) 94
  Mary Ann 74
  Mary Ann (ROSS) (1830-) 48
  Mary Louise (1883-) 96
  Mary W. (PETERSON)
    (1870-1936) 41
  Maud / Maude 60, 95, 252
  Maud Blanche (1865-1915) 41, 94
  Melinda 130
  Melita / Melissa (ANDERSON)
    (1850-1918) . . . 41, 60, 61, 132
  Mollie 94
  Nell Beatrice (MIXON)
    (1896-1956) 229, 291
  Olive 61
  Oliver . . . 24, 58, 60, 61, 136, 137
  Oliver (1874-1952) 41
  Ora 254
  Orie 61
  R Richard 169, 290
  R. B. Mrs. 169
  R. B. 169, 230
  Reuben (1800-1840) . . 17-19, 28
  Richard 169, 290, 291
  Richard (1928-) 230
  Richard Bryon (1899-1964)
    . . . . 115, 169, 229, 290
  Richard Frank (1942-) 229
  Robert 140
  Ruby (HAYS) Mrs. 229
  Ruby 290, 291
  Ruie (1871-1941) 42, 61
  Russell Paul (1905-1908) 99
  Ruth 24, 28, 58
  Ruth (HICKS) (1797-1874) 18, 35
  Sallie 62
  Sara Ann 62
  Sarah 18, 24, 58, 59, 62
  Sarah A. (1828-1890) 39
  Sarah Ann (RUSH) (1844-1914) 42
  Solon 62
  Solon Elijah (1882-1942) . . 42, 62
  U Franklin 169, 290
  Ulyses 74
  W. Durwood 250
  Warren 62, 99, 140
  Washington 39, 58
  William 58, 60, 76, 92, 99,
    . . . 131, 134, 169, 170, 250, 291
  William Durwood (1919-1977) 198
  William J 169, 290, 291
  William Jennings (1903-1966)
    . . . . 115, 169, 230, 291
  William Oliver (1831-1876) 18, 41
  William W. (1853-1923) 94

TAYLOR 76
   Alice 95, 134, 250, 252
   Alice B. (1893-1944) 199
   Alice M. (1853-1908) 94
   Archie 134, 135, 251-253
   Archie McNair (1895-1932) . . . 95
   Arnold (1819-) 94
   Arnold F 134
   Arnold Tresttin 94
   Callie / Calla 97, 137, 255
   Caroline 'Callie' (TATMAN)
     (1869-1942) 97
   Charles 135, 251-253
   Charles Harrison (1888-1970)
     . . . . 95, 199, 251
   Charles T. (1944-) 200
   Charly H 134
   Dede 61
   Elizabeth Margaret (Ware) . . . 171
   Elmer (1865-1929) 61, 97,
     . . . . 134, 137, 255
   Esther E. (STEPHENS)
     (1902-1965) 199, 253
   Ethel 98, 137, 255
   Ethel G. (1895-1969) 201
   Frank 42, 97, 134, 137
   Gene Richard (1930-) 200
   George 134, 135, 252, 253
   George Richard (1898-1967)
     . . . . 95, 199, 253
   Gladys A. (PAELTZ)
     (1893-1992) 199
   Goldie L . . . 95, 134, 135, 252, 253
   Goldie Louise (1886-1963) 95
   Grace (ORR) (1909-) . . . 200, 253
   Gwen (1935-) 200, 310
   Harry 61
   Harry N. (1861-) 42
   Howard . . . 95, 134, 135, 252, 253
   Howard Tatman (1890-1922) . . 95
   J. Dwight (1936-) 200
   John 95, 134, 253
   John H 95, 134, 135, 252, 253
   John H. (1856-1926) 94
   John K 134, 135, 252, 253
   John Kenneth (1902-) 95, 200, 253
   Lelah T. (1897-1978) 97, 137
   Lella M 255
   Martha 134
   Martha (BROWNEN) 42, 97
   Martha wife of Arnold 94
   Maud Blanche (TATMAN)
     (1865-1915) 94, 134, 135
   Omar D 285
   Patricia Ann (1929-) 200, 253
   Ruie (TATMAN) (1871-1941)
     . . . . 42, 61, 62
   Sally L. (1934-1934) 199
   Theodore 171
   Trena V 285
TEDDER
   Mary 359
   Walter 359
   Walter Odis (1951-) 317
TEKULVA / TEKULVE
   Anthony 240
   Benjiman 240
   Elizabeth 240
   Ethel M. (MANNING)
     (1894-1993) . . 90, 128, 189, 239
   Henry 240
   Herman (1848-) 189
   Mary 239, 240
   Mary F. (1923-) 189
   Mary wife of Herman (1859-) . 189
   Mildred E. (1919-) . 128, 189, 239
   William 128, 239, 240
   William A. (1917-1967) 189
   William B (1891-1974) 189
   William Bernard 240
TERREL
   William 4
TERRY
   Rebecca Jean (1953-) 339
TEVEBAUGH / TEVEBOUGH
   John (1800-) 91
   Miriam (SAGASER) (1818-) . . 91
   Marion 131
   Susan A. (1854-1931) 91, 131, 245
   Theodore Roosevelt's Rough Riders
     170
THIEMAN
   Mary Lee (1950-) 321
THIES / THEIS
   Lena (-1900) 199, 252
Thomas
   Mary Kate 165
   Mary Kate 112
Thomas
   J J 165
   John 25
   Nola 165
THOMPSON
   Larry 320
   Larry Mrs. 361
   Medora 261
THORNTON 274
   Anna 274
   Mabel I. (1890-1995) . . . 214, 274
   Mabel Irene 273
TIMMERMAN
   Mary Elizabeth 344, 374
TINDELL
   Van 70
TINGLE
   James C 273
   Minnie D 273
TIPPET
   John 213, 368
TODLOCK
   Betty Louise 323
TOKAR
   Thomas John (1949-) 341
TOMPKINS
   Ella 49
TOWNSEND
   Ruby (-1941) 331
TOWNSLEY
   Emma 143
   Mary Emma 100, 143
TRACY / TRACEY
   Frank S 44, 65, 221
   Grace O 65
   Orpha Grace (JONES)
     (1870-1960) 44, 65, 221
TRESTTIN
   Arnold 94
TRISLER
   Lulu 166
   Nellie 166, 167
TROSHER
   Amasa S 150
TROY
   J. 15
TRUITT
   Marvella Margaret (1917-1980)
     . . . . 315, 357
TUCKER
   Grace (1893-) 55
TUDOR
   Bittie 165
   Brittania 165
   C. Nora (1891-1978) 72, 112, 165
   Caroline (WHITE) 112 165
   Edward 72, 165
   Edward N. (1867-1917) 112
   Lavina Britana (HICKS)
     (1867-1949) . 72, 112, 165, 166
   Thomas 112, 165
TULLAR
   Edun 284
TULLY
   Celia Mae (1920-) 340

TURBYNE
- Alec (1882-) 312, 355
- Alexander 355
- Cecile Rose (1917-2006) 312, 355
- Frank 355
- John 355
- Maude (RANCORT) (1883-)
  . . . . 312, 355
- Nathile 355

TURNER
- Margarite (1912-) 235

TURNER
- Margarite 297

UMBAUGH
- Jessie Marcella 316, 358

UNKNOWN
- Mary 213
- Nancy Ann 337
- Veronica (1932-) 334

UPTEGROVE
- ___ 178

UTTER
- Amelia B. 297
- Anna 176
- Annie Belle (JOHNSTON)
  (1865-1931) 121
- Betsy (1804-1840) 18, 23, 24
- Caroline 72, 167
- Dowty Col. 18, 24
- Edward M. (1940-) 347
- Edward Robert (1969-) 347
- Elizabeth (BURKE) (1762-1822) 18
- Gloria (Kirby) (BRYANT)
  (1942-) 347
- James I 75
- James T. (1834-) 48
- John 47
- Joseph (1766-1839) 18, 29
- Lavina 73
- Levina (COCKRELL) 47
- Levina Caroline (1845-1928)
  . . . . 47, 73, 166
- Linda Carol (DAVIS) (1949-) 235
- Lucy 121, 176,, 234
- Lucy (1903-) 234
- Lucy Florence 234, 296
- M. P. 296
- Margarite (TURNER) (1912-)
  . . . . 235, 297
- Mary 176
- Mary Morgan (1905-1998) 121, 235
- Melissa Jane (ROBINSON)
  (1842-1870) 48, 75
- Missouri Mary (1864-1900)
  . . . . 49, 116, 172
- Morgan (1853-1937) 121, 176, 297
- Robert 176, 235, 297
- Robert Alexander (1907-1973)
  . . . . 121, 235, 297
- Robert Eugene (1938-) 235
- W. P. 32
- Washington 28, 176

VAIL
- John 133
- Nora B (1873-) 93, 133
- Sarah 133

VALKENSTOE
- Patricia 308

VANDERGRIFF
- Betty 130

VANZANT
- Emma 82

VASKE
- Frank 267
- Lena 267
- Madelyn (1905-1988) . . . 208, 267

VAUDAL
- Laura 207, 265

VERMILLION
- Charles 69, 70
- Charles H. (1877-) 46
- Child (1855-) 46
- Clara 70, 162, 163, 286
- Clara Belle (1901-1994)
  . . . . 110, 226, 286
- Clarence . . 70, 162, 225, 285, 286
- Clarence Vern (1895-1986)
  . . . . 110, 225, 285
- E N 163
- Edgar 69, 70, 162, 163, 286
- Edgar Newton (1863-1954)
  . . . . 46, 110, 162
- Edna 70
- Edna P. (1906-1985) . . . 110, 163
- F M 163
- Frank 162, 163, 226
- Frank Marvin (1911-1993) 110, 226
- Grant 70
- Ignatius 69
- J E 163
- John 70, 162
- John A. (1915-) 110, 163
- John B. (1831-1910) . . 46, 69, 70
- John C. (1870-) 46, 69, 70
- John E. (1935-) 226
- Joseph 70, 162
- Joseph E. (1913-1982) . . 110, 163
- Julie B 69
- Leila (HERRIOT) (1887-) . . . 225
- Lella 285
- Lilly 69
- Lilly Or Julie (1857-) 46
- Martha 69, 70, 162
- Martha Ann (HICKS)
  (1840-1900) 35, 46
- Mary 69
- Mary mother of John (1794-) . . 46
- Mildred 163
- N E 163
- Nancy 69
- Nancy Or Mary (1861-) 46
- Nora 70, 162
- Nora Ellen (SMITH) (1876-1930)
  110
- Olive A. (DROWN) (1883-) . . 46
- R M 163
- Ruth 70, 162
- Ruth M. (1902-1998) 110
- Ruth Mildred (WILLIAMS)
  (1915-2002) 226
- Shirley L. (1929-) 226, 285
- U. S. Grant (1866-) 46, 69
- Verna Ruth 163, 226, 286
- William (1859-) 46
- Willie (1909-) 70, 110, 162
- Zella 285

VERZAL
- Edward 337

VICKREY / VICKROY
- Ellen 130
- Laura Francis (1851-1923) 91, 130
- Malvina 129, 130
- Nellie (PATTISON) 91
- Thomas 129
- Vina E 130
- William 91

VINSON
- Carrie 117, 173
- John 117, 173

VORHIS
- Wilbur A. 361

VOYER
- Mary Ann 319, 360

WAGLEMAN
- Rosana 53, 83

WALDEN
- George 363
- Herbert (1873-) 322, 363
- Julia (1880-) 322, 363
- Pauline (1901-) 322, 363

WALKER
- Aletha 276, 277
- Althea (1896-) 217
- George M. (1861-1928)
  . . . . 116, 171, 172
- Iola 277
- John 116, 172
- Lewis 191, 243

WALKER continued
  Lilla/Lida B. 243
  Lydia May (BRITTINGHAM)
    (1857-1938) 116, 171
  Marilyn Jane (1939-) 306
  May 171, 172, 277
  Melissa . . . 116, 171, 172, 293, 306
  Melissa L. (1900-1980) 231
  Ora W. (1872-) 217, 277
  Orie N 277
  Pervilla K (LEONARD) (1872-)217
  Rewilla 277
WALL
  Clara E 174, 295
WALLINGFORD
  George 287
  Grace (1900-) 227
WALLINGFORD
  George 227
  Grace 287
WALSH
  Francis Marion 'Frank' (1912-)
    . . . . 204, 259, 260
  Frank 259
  George 259, 260
  George Walter (1855-1921)
    . . . . 204, 260
  George Walter Jr (1886-1913)
    . . . . 204, 259
  Henriette 259
  Irma Clair (LEVI) (1878-1928)
    . . . . 204, 259, 260
  Judy 259
  Stella (CABANNE) (1856-)
    . . . . 204, 259, 260
  Walter Cabanni (1910-)
    . . . . 204, 259, 260
WALTHALL
  Anna 368
WARBINGTON / WARBLETON
  C. B. 68
  Charles B 69
  Cinta 69, 162
  Cynthia (FIRESTONE) (1813-)
    . . . . 27, 46, 69
  Eliza J 69
  John J 69
  Joseph (1811-) 45, 69
  Mrs. 68
  Victoria E. (1844-1916)
    . . . . 27, 45, 68, 69
WARD
  Grace 276
  Grace Bell (1881-1913) . 216, 276
  John 276
WARE
  Elizabeth 171

Elizabeth Margaret (1863-1941)
  . . . . 116, 171
  John 116, 170, 171
  Mabala (DANS) 116, 171
WARNEMUNDE
  David (1939-) 336
WARREN
  Clyde (1941-) 332
  Gay (1905-) 123, 124, 178
  Glada (KING) (1911-)123, 124, 178
WASH
  Harold 285
WASHELL
  Carolyn 359
  John Francis (1921-1994) 317
  John 359
  John Mrs 262
  John Phillip 317
  Linda (LANE) (1945-) . 317, 359
  Madge 357, 358
  Mary 359
  Mary Dell 317
  Mary Madge (STALDER)
    (1921-2006) 317
  Mildred Carolyn (EPPS)
    (1952-) 317
  Peter Joseph 317
  Tim 317, 359
WATERFIELD
  William 26
WATKINS
  E. E Mrs 262
  Elkin E. 358
  Elkin Ewing "Jack" (1917-1979)
    317
  Jennifer Ruth 358
  Louise (HAGSED) (1945-)317, 358
  Lucinda (RITCHIE) (1947-) . . 317
  Ruth Marilyn (STALDER)
    (1919-2000) 317, 357, 358
  Sarah Emaline (1853-1921) . . . 54
  Shawna Rosendale 358
  Thomas Taylor 317, 358
  Travis Michael 358
  William B. 358
  William Benjamin 317
WATSON
  Betty J. (1938-) 224
WATTS
  Anna Lou 345
  Dorothy (DAY) (1900-1927)
    . . . . 345, 375
  Monone May 56
  Raymond D. 345
  Raymond Joseph 345
  Thos M. 375
  Thomas Raymond 345, 375

WAYBRIGHT
  unknown 193
  Wanda Lee (MANNING) (1931-)
    193
WEAVER
  Charles F 165
  Mary Ruth (1934-) 325
WEBB
  Dinah Lee (1947-) 326
WEBER
  Alice Kay (1931-1974) 335
WEDDING
  Elizabeth 120
WEEKLY
  Belinda Flo (1953-) 329
WEGNER
  Henrietta 266
WEHMEYER
  Geneva 160
  Robert 160
WEIDENBACH
  Ella 300
  Emil 300
  Emma 300
  Gertrude 300
  Loraine 300
  Oliva 300
  Violet 300
WEIGEL / WEIGHILL
  Delores (1917-) . . . 296, 347, 375
  John Thomas 347, 376
  Karen Sue (1944-) 327
  Marie L. (KURTZ) (1891-1922)
    . . . . 347, 375, 376
  Mary (ELLIOTT) 347
  Robert Elliott (1883-1943)
    . . . . 347, 375, 376
  Vivien 296, 347, 375
WEINY / WINEY
  Amanda 172
  Ella (1875-) 117, 172
  Jno. 117
  Joseph (1832-1910) 117, 172
  Mary E. (KLINGLER)
    (1844-1914) 117, 172
WEISINGER
  Harvey 76
WELCH
  Ella 276
  Elvina 188
WELLS
  John Levi (1835-) 102, 146
  Madelyn 267
  Maggie 264-267
  Margaret 146, 265-267

WELLS continued
    Margaret Sarah (1864-1931)
        . . . . 102, 146
    Mary (JERNEGAN) (1839-)
        . . . . 102, 186, 265
WENGER
    Albert (1920-) 319
    Henrietta (HICKS) (1920-1993)
        . . . . 265, 319, 360
    Peter 320
    Sharon (DENNLER?) (1947-) 320
WENTX
    Elizabeth 278
WEST
    Adlara Leona 'Addie' (JOSLIN)
        (1891- 1971) 144, 187,
        . . . . 206, 258, 264, 356
    Bernadine L. (SHERBAHN)
        (1910-2005) 219
    Harold E. (1907-1972) 219
    Howard Arlie (1893-1976)
        . . . . 187, 206, 264
    Joanna 32
    John 316
    Lora 144, 264
    Mabel Mrs. (1897-) 194
    Marian (1919-) . 144, 206, 264, 318
    Susannah 74
WETHERS
    Susan 66
WHEELER
    Anna 181
    Belle 76
    Elizabeth P. (1919-) 126
    George 49
    Missouri Belle (CANN) (1878-) 49
    Myron (1874-) 49, 76
    Verna (HICKS) (1886-1970) . 126
    William Lafayette (1884-) 126, 181
WHETSTONE
    Caroline (1822-1894) . . 20, 30, 82
WHINSON
    Eleanor 372
WHITAKER
    Joseph T. 53, 83
    Nettie W. (1846-1927) 53
    Rosana (WAGLEMAN) 53
WHITE
    Ann Maria (HICKS)
        (1839-1882) 30, 52, 79
    Annie 247
    Caroline 112, 165
    Charles A. (1888-1888) 122
    Cynthia Jane (1951-) 350
    Elizabeth Ann (FRANNFELDER)
        (1949-) 350

Ella 79, 122
Ella F. (1859-1938) 52, 122
Elmirah (FISHER) (1803-) . 52, 79
J. 298
J. A. 299
J. H. 298
James . . . 25, 27, 69, 79, 177, 299
James Chatterton (1921-2006) 349
James Chatterton Jr (1953-) . . 349
James Chatterton 237, 377
James Hicks (1861-1928)
    . . . . 52, 122, 177
Joseph 52, 79
Lawrence 31, 177
Lawrence Webster (1889-1949) 122
Lawrence Wilson (1959-) 350
Lucille C. (CHATTERTON)
    (1900-) 237, 299
Mabel (LEEDS) (1892-1979) . 122
Maggie 80, 177, 299
Marcia Sue (1955-) 350
Margaret Pearl (ATCHLEY)
    (1866-1958) 122
Marie 79, 122, 177, 236, 237, 298
Marie W. (1885-1965) 236
Marjorie (WILSON) (1929-) . 349
Mildred (MCCONNELL)
    (1921-1981) 349
Mina 31, 79, 80, 177, 299
Mina Bell (1871-) 52, 79, 80
Mina P. (1891-1965) 123
Nancy Chatterton (1943-) 349
Nicholas . . . 31, 80, 177, 298, 299
Nicholas James (1897-1960)
    . . . . . . 123, 237, 298, 299, 350
Nicholas Lawrence (1925-)237, 349
Niny 177
Russell L. (1892-1902) . 123, 177
Sadie L 299
Stephen McConnell (1945-) . . 349
Thomas Joseph Jr. (1944-) . . . 338
Thomas McConnell (1955-) . . 349
William 31, 79, 80
William H. (1837-1912) . . 52
WHITTAKER
    Nettie 83
WICKLERY
    Andrew 171
WIEDENBACH / WIEDENBACK
    Emma wife of Emil
        (WIEDENBACH) (1893-) . 237
    Gertrude (1915-2009) 237, 299, 300
WILEY
    Glenna Gertrude (BAIRD) (1925-)
        325
    Julius Earl (1923-1990) 325
WILKERSON
    Tricia 360

WILKES
    Bradley Paul 344
    Marilyn (HICKS) (1924-) 228
    Scott 344
    Walter 228
    Walter H. Jr. (1943-) 343
    Wendy 344
    William Paul (1947-) 228
WILL / WILLE / WILLS
    Christine 278
    Edith Mary (JONES) (1887-1961)
        . . . . 218, 278
    Emil 278
    Eugene E 278
    Fredericka 278
    Gottlieb (1863-) 218, 278
    Ineta M 278
    Izeta Mae
        (1918-) 218, 278, 336, 371
    John (1894-1982) 218, 278
    Laura A. (1889-) 188, 239
    Manda F 278
    Martha 278
    Wanda Fae (1919-) 218, 278, 336
    Warren Howard (1921-) . 218, 278
WILLIAMS
    Charles 153, 194, 274
    Charles E. (1874-) 214
    Deborah (1836-) 106, 153
    Della 194
    Emerson 153
    Esther (PENDERY) 330
    Ezra Glenn Dale "Jack"
        (1903-) 215, 330
    Glen D 274
    Glendale 274
    Hanson 153
    Helen 76
    Hertha Katherine (JONES)
        (1877-) 214, 274
    Hester 153
    Howard Kenneth (1932-1981) 334
    Ida (1871-) 211
    Jack G. 274
    James (1943-) 327
    Joanne (METZ) (1945-) 327
    Joseph 153
    Julia (1854-1936) 106, 153
    Katherine 119, 274
    Katie H 274
    Kevin Daniel (1943-) 330
    Leta 274
    Leta Grace (1898-1981)
        . . . . 215, 274, 330, 369
    Maral 269
    Nancy (ROBINSON) (1943-) . 330
    Oliver P. (1834-) . . 106, 153, 154

WILLIAMS continued
  Ruth Mildred (1915-2002) . . . 226
  Sandra (CLYDE) (1935-) 330
  Stephen 330
  Tyler Glenn 330
  Virginia E. (DUGAN) (1903-) 330
WILLIS 365
  Walter 131
WILSON 364
  Agnes E 167
  Chris 318
  Claude Thomas (1932-) 313
  Connie Nancy (1948-) 314
  Everett 73, 166
  Florence E. (1877-) 41, 61
  James H 69
  Jane (MCKOULE) 110, 263
  John 110, 162
  Lena 162
  Lida H. (HICKS) (1867-)
    . . . . 69, 110, 162
  Mandal 167
  Maria H. (1892-1947)
    . . . . 69, 110, 162, 225, 285
  Marjorie (1929-) 349
  Nettie E (1880-1963) 210, 268, 269
  Ora B 162
  Robert J. (1861-1931)
    . . . . 69, 110, 162, 285
  Robert James 285
  Virginia S 167
  Wilson 210
WINDHAM
  Douglas Arthur 317
  E. A. Mrs 261
  Euthan Arthur (1916-1988) . . 316
  Grace Olive (STALDER)
    (1918-2003) . 261, 316, 357, 358
  Ina Lynne (JAUDON) (1948-) 317
  Marilyn Grace 261, 317
WINEGAR
  Karen (1962-) 341
WING
  Bertha 297
  Caroline 297
  Cartine 297
  Catharine Anna (1928-) 235
  Jeremiah L. (1903-) 235, 297
  Jerry 296, 297
  Jerry Laurence (1930-) 235
  John Raymond 235
  Kathryne 296
  Mary 296, 297
  Mary Morgan (UTTER)
    (1905-1998) 235, 296
  Robert Ralph 235

WINGERT
  Delores Marie (BENTON)
    (1938-) 336
  Dorthea Gladys (EVANS)
    (1912-1997) 335
  James Nicholas 336
  Kathleen Gale 336
  Nicholas Joseph (1912-1990) . 335
  Stephen Paul (1948-) 336
WINN
  Evalyn R. (ROGERS) (1906-)
    . . . . 168, 344, 374
  John B. (1903-) . . . 168, 344, 374
  John Bradford 344
  John H (1930-) 168, 344, 374
  Kenneth R (1925-) . 168, 344, 374
WINTERROD
  -?- 252
  Phoebe (1852-1915) 199
WIRWEL
  W. J. 239
WISBY
  Charles L. (1879-) 192 244
  Eliza A 244
  Ida A 244
  Mary 193 244
  Mary Ann (1905-1962) . . . 192 244
  Willard R 244
WISE
  Marjorie Francis (1903-) . 230, 291
WITHAM
  Mrs. Givens (1916-) 312
WITSCHGER
  Alice L. (1923-) 201, 256
  Ethel G. (TAYLOR) (1895-1969)
    . . . . 201, 255
  Fred 97, 137, 255, 256
  Frederick T 256
  Frederick Thurman (1895-1996)
    . . . . 201, 256
  Lila Eleanor (1919-)
    . . . . 137, 201, 255, 256
WOHLMAN
  Alice Kay (WEBER) (1931-1974)335
  Arlene E. (HOESING) (1930-) 335
  Blaine Evans 278, 335, 371
  Dale Elizabeth (EVANS)
    (1906-1987) 278, 335, 371
  Eugene 278
  Eugene William 335
  Fred (1910-1993) 278, 335
  Kenneth 278, 371
  Kenneth Fae 335
  Mary E. (CASTOR) (1933-1999) 335
WOLF / WOLF E
  Adam 245
  Anderson Alford (1873-) 22
  Angel Mrs. 34
  Carrie (MOORE) (1923-) 308

  Charles Edward Jr (1948-) . . . 309
  Charles Edward (1919-1999) . 308
  Charles Edward 194, 245
  Edward 245
  Edward (1882-1976) 194
  Illie 245
  John Adam (1834-1918) 194
  Julie M. (1950-) 309
  Katharine (MILLER)
    (1850-1914) 194
  Katherine 245
  Katherine (1963-) 309
  Margaret (1954-) 309
  Martha E. (HICKS) (1862-1924) 22
  Pearl 245
  Pearl Diana (FITZPATRICK)
    (1882-1972) 193, 245
WOLFORD
  Lois Marie (JONES)
    (1916-1972) 214
  Wayne W. 214
WOOD
  Alma 98, 137, 138
  Alma R. (1873-1940) 98
  Alpha M (1908-) 212, 270
  Arthur Lavorne (1912-1991) . . 338
  Beatrice Gertrude (JONES)
    (1875-) 211
  Edwin 137
  Effie 270
  Effie Blanche (1897-1992)
    . . . . 211, 324, 366
  Ellia 270
  Gertrude B. 270
  Grant 137
  John 98, 137, 138
  John Lawrence 98
  June Gayle (JONES) (1917-) . 338
  Katherine 270
  Katie 270
  Merrell 270
  Merrie 366
  Murel 270
  Rachiel (MCCARTER) 98
  Ruth Merrel (1901-) 211
  Sharon Pauline 338
  W. G. 270
  Wilber Glenn 211, 270
  Wilbur G. (1872-1960) . . 211, 270
WOODEN
  Dorothy Louise (1920-1992) . . 232
WOODLEEF / WOODLIEF
  Clara (1861-) 236, 298
WOODRIDGE
  Edward 4
  William 4, 5

WOODRUFF
 Eugene (1938-) 314
 Janis 348
WORKMAN
 Rachael 215, 274
World War I 55, 83, 124, 146
WORTHINGTON
 C. B. 68
 Mary E. (1827-) 109, 160
WRIGHT
 Capt 6
 Gayle Lynn 343
WUNKER
 Jean 321
WYANT
 Carrie (1884-) 311
WYKOFF
 Anna (ANSON) 307, 352
 Charles N 352
 Clayton 352
 Edward 307, 352
 George Lester (1905-1996) 307, 352
 Grace (PATTISON)
  (1906-1929) 307, 352
 Lester 352
 Minnie M (1925-) 307, 352

 Sarah E 352
 Thomas G (1926-) 307, 352
YANCY / YANCEY
 Andrew Jackson 111, 164
 Catherine Allen 111, 164
 Ella (1878-1967) 111, 164
 George 165
 Louis 165
YATES
 Harrison 26
YOUNG
 Iva A 168
 Rose 168
 William 168
ZETTS
 Edward (1942-) 314
ZEZULA
 Adolph Edward (1920-1974) . 320
 Clarinda Rae (JONES) (1954-) 321
 Dorothy Ann (BEHAN) (1919-)
  . . . . 320, 361
 Norman . . . iii, 14, 23, 25, 27, 29,
  . . 63, 64, 68, 141, 145, 162, 264,
  . . . . 266, 267, 320, 361

ZIMMERMAN
 Alfred C. 268
 Catharine E. 268
 Grafton 268
 James B. 268
 John 268
 Mae (1878-1945) . . 209, 268, 363
 Martha E 268
 Nettie M. 268
 Romaine (1916-) 336
ZINK
 Donald Allen (1949-) 27, 321
 John Mark (1961-) 321
 John William Jr. (1921-1998)
  . . . . 321, 361
 Laura Margaret (BEHAN) (1921-)
  . . . . 27, 321, 361
 Mary Lee (THIEMAN) (1950-) 321
 Suzan Ellen (1957-) 321

Notes

Place Index

Note: towns in Clermont County were omitted from the index, due to the great number of them

Alabama 87, 93
   Alexander City 196
   Birmingham 131, 195, 196,
       . . . . 247, 248, 309
   Blount Co 131, 132, 248
   Blount Springs 248
   Blountsville 131
   Chilton Co . . . 194, 246, 247, 249
   Clanton 194, 246, 247
   Culman Co 248
   Cold Spring 309
   Cooper 247
   Cullman Co . . 131, 132, 196, 248
   Deatsville 195, 247 309
   Decatur 195
   Elmore Co 195, 247, 309
   Garden City 131, 132,
       . . . . 195, 196, 247
   Jefferson Co . . 195, 247, 248, 309
   Montgomery 93, 196, 197,
       . . . . 249, 309
   Montgomery Co 309
   Morgan 131
   Thorsby 247, 249
Arizona 148, 324
   Cochise Co 287
   Higley 209 268
   Maricopa Co 109, 144, 149,
       . . . 206, 209, 264, 268, 269, 365
   Phoenix 144, 206, 264, 365
   Rogers 291
   Sierra Vista 287
   Sun City 109, 225, 253 285
   Wickenburg 109, 161
Arkansas 114, 268, 324, 364
   Grannis 210, 269
California 51, 269, 293,
       . . . . 307, 322, 366
   Alameda 218, 365, 370
   Alameda Co 362
   Anaheim 335
   Antioch 119
   Arcata 219
   Butte Co 219, 339
   Canoga Park 330
   Ceres 148, 269, 324, 366
   Clovis 148, 268, 269, 364
   Concord 333
   Contra Costa 56, 365, 370
   Contra Costa Co . . 119, 120, 333
   Coronado 320
   Covina 232, 375
   Downey 220, 338

El Cajon 118
El Monte 313
Fresno 119, 268
Fresno 210
Fresno Co 119, 269, 364
Glen Ellen 272
Glendora 346
Gracia 295
Hawthorne 327
Hollywood 317
Homeland 346
Humboldt Co 219
Huntington Beach 202
Kings Co 365
La Habra 361
Lakewood 335, 345
Lomita 231
Long Beach 335, 336
Los Angeles Co . . 207, 219, 220,
   . 225, 231, 232, 285, 330,
   . . . . . 334, 335, 338, 345
Los Angeles 116, 149,
   . 169, 171, 207, 218, 225,
   . 265, 272, 279, 286, 290,
   . . 293, 327, 338, 371, 375
Marin Co 370
Menlo Park 291
Modesto 148, 324, 336, 366
Napa 324
Nebraska 370
Oakdale 365
Oakland 341, 362
Oakley 120, 306
Paradise 219, 339
Paso Robles 338
Petaluma 334
Pittsburgh 365
Pomona 219
Redding 246
Redwood City 334
Riverside 375
Riverside Co 346
Rohnert Park 333
Sacramento . . . 211, 357, 365, 366
Sacramento Co 211, 365
San Anselmo 371
San Diego 220, 295, 320
San Diego Co 118, 220
San Francisco 55, 56, 374
San Jose 324, 365
San Luis Obispo Co 338
San Mateo Co 334
San Pedro 225, 285
Santa Clara 333

Santa Clara Co . . . 324, 333, 365
Shasta Co 246
Shirley J 371
Solano Co 337
Sonoma Co 149, 210,
   . . . 211, 269, 272, 333, 334, 366
Stanislaus Co 269, 324, 365
Turlock 269, 324, 365
Vallejo 337, 372
Canada . . . 107, 180, 204, 259, 260
   Ontario 260
   York 204, 260
Colorado 257
   Colorado Springs . 232, 294, 337
   Denver 93, 133
   Denver Co 133
   El Paso Co 232, 294
   Fort Collins 344
   Larimer Co 344
   Littleton 233
   Wray 218
   Yuma Co 218
Connecticut
   Hartford 309, 353
   Putnam 200
Dakota 54, 84
DC
   Washington 48, 75, 164
England 52, 78, 80
   London 311
   Southampton 288
   Upwell 51
Florida
   Alachua Co 119
   Avon Park 124
   Boca Raton 160
   Bradenton 203, 204
   Charlotte Co 354
   Dade Co . 190, 228, 340, 347, 375
   Daytona Beach 222
   Duval Co 205, 207, 261
       . . . . 262, 316, 317
   Gainesville 119
   Homestead 340
   Jacksonville 205, 207,
       . . . . 261, 262, 316, 317
   Leon Co 316, 358
   Manatee Co 203, 204
   Marion Co 326, 367
   Miami 190, 375
   Miami Beach 222

Florida continued
  New Smyrna 262
  Ocala 313, 326, 355, 367
  Orange Co 53, 78, 79, 119,
  . . . . 205, 261, 316
  Orange Park 321
  Orla Vista 119
  Orlando 51, 78, 205,
  . . . . 261, 262, 316
  Panama City 257
  Punta Gorda 354
  Sarasota 347
  Sarasota Co 347
  St Petersburg 204
  Tallahassee 316, 358
  Tampa 234
  Volusia Co 222
Georgia 221
  Andersonville Prison 26
  Arlington 317
  Augusta 132
  Chicamauga 26
  Donaldson 262
  Folkston 317
  Griffin 197
  Marietta 347
  Richmond Co 132
  Savannah 188
Germany 161, 345
Hawaii
  Hololu 349
  Honolulu 197, 306
Iowa 17, 51, 322, 333, 370
  Adams Twp 29 78
  Agency 54
  Algonia 333
  Ames 209, 267, 268, 322
  Appanoose 32
  Bloomfield . . . 125, 181, 237, 299
  Bonaparte 208
  Cedar Rapids 362
  Center 32
  Cerro Gordo Co 210
  Cleveland 180
  Davis 77
  Davis Co . . 50, 54, 78, 84, 110,
  117, 118, 172, 180, 181, 237, 299
  Des Moines 125
  Drakesville . . . 32, 50, 54, 77, 78,
  . . . . 84, 110, 118, 125
  Dubuque 228
  Fayette Co 174
  Fox River 180
  Harlan 219
  Illyria 174
  Keokuk 208, 209, 362, 363

  Lake Park 337
  Lee Co 208, 209, 362
  Louisa Co 51
  Malvern 156, 280
  Marion 180
  Marion Co 232, 294
  Mason City 210
  Mills Co 155, 156, 218, 219
  Monroe 232
  Muscatine 315
  Muscatine Co 315
  Ottawa 78
  Ottumwa 32, 54, 117, 173
  Perry 180
  Polk Co 125, 172
  Shelby Co, ... 219
  Silver Creek 218, 219
  Sioux City 49, 76, 279
  Soap Creek 77
  Story Co 209, 267
  Summit 294
  Wapello 51
  Wapello Co 29, 51,
  . . . . 54, 78, 117, 173
  White Cloud 280
  Woodbury Co 76, 279
  Wyacondah 117
Illinois 17, 44, 107, 207, 269
  Arcola 66
  Belleville 221
  Bloomfield 125
  Bremen 157
  Carroll Co 125
  Centralia 158
  Chicago 31, 53, 115, 123,
  . . . 157, 158, 170, 229, 290, 332
  Clark Co 182
  Coles Co 44, 66, 221, 353
  Cook Co   115, 123, 157, 229, 290
  Dennison 182
  Douglas Co 66, 74
  East Marion 297
  East St Louis 281
  Edgar Co 14, 17, 33, 55, 56,
  . . . . 84, 85, 126, 181
  Effingham 65
  Elbridge 33, 54-56, 84, 85
  Evanston 151
  Homecrest 151
  Homewood 229, 290
  Illini 367
  Lake Co 55
  Libertyville 55
  Lincoln 115, 169, 170
  Lisle 349
  Logan Co 115, 170

  Macon Co 367
  Marion Co 158
  Mattoon 44, 66, 221, 353
  McLean Co 118
  Moultrie 32
  Moultrie Co 54, 125
  Mt Carroll 125
  Paris 55, 56, 85, 126
  Redmon 126
  Rushville 156
  Salem 158, 282
  Sanford 55
  Sangamon Co 107
  Schuyler Co 156
  St Clair Co 221, 281, 339
  St Louis 339
  Stratton 56, 85
  Sullivan 54
  Symmes 181
  Vermillion 54, 84
  Whitley 32
  Williamson Co 297
  Windsor 84
Indian Territory 115, 168 169
  Choctaw Nation 168
  South McAlester 168, 169
Indiana 52, 53, 74, 123, 124,
  . . . . 178, 229, 293, 320
  Anderson 169
  Attica 55
  Bloomington 349
  Cambridge City 31, 179
  Centerville 81
  Clay 66
  Connersville . . 109, 160, 161, 240
  Daviess Co 48 168
  Dearborn Co 330
  Dillsboro 205
  Dublin 31, 32, 53, 80
  Evansville 231
  Fayette Co 109, 240
  Fountain Co 55
  Franklin Co 212
  Jackson 80, 179
  Jay Co 202, 257
  Jeffersonville 339
  Kokomo 360, 361
  Laurel 212
  Lawrenceburg 330
  Madison Co 169
  Miami Co 320, 361
  Millhauser 208, 321
  Milton 161
  Morgan Co 66
  Mt Auburn 179

Indiana continued
  New Goshen 238
  New Harmony 122
  Owen Co 168
  Paris 34
  Peru 235, 320, 361
  Portland 202, 257
  Richmond 31, 53, 80-82,
    . . . . 179, 236, 318
  Rush Co 109, 253
  Rushville 109, 161, 253
  Spencer 168
  Terre Haute . . 33, 55, 56, 85, 126
  Vanderburgh Co 231
  Vermillion 34
  Vigo 126
  Vigo Co 56, 126
  Wabash Co 235
  Wayne Co 62, 80, 81, , 124 179, 236
  Wilmington 262
Ireland 266
  Cobh 288
  Roscommon 207, 360
  Strokestown 207, 208
Italy
  Naples 344
Japan
  Yokohama 285
Kansas 50, 70, 290, 322, 324
  Allen Co 156
  Axtell 151
  Beattie 149-151
  Bonner Springs 163
  Butler Co 295
  Carlisle 268
  Coffeyville 115, 169, 170,
    . . . . 230, 290, 291
  Grainfield Gove 180
  Guittard 149-150
  Haven 295
  Haven 29, 51, 78, 173,
    . . . . 174, 233, 295
  Haynesville 174
  Hutchinson 295
  Iola 156
  Kansas City 46, 70, 162, 226, 285
  Kechi 119
  Kiowa Co 174
  Lawrence 104
  Leavenworth 70
  Lulu 151
  Marion Co 232, 294
  Marshall Co 104, 149-151
  Marysville 104, 150
  Mcpherson Co 119
  Mitchell Co 151
  Montgomery Co 115, 169,
    . . . . 230, 290, 291
  Murray 151
  National Military Home 70
  Nickerson 233
  Ninnescah 295
  Pratt 229, 290
  Pratt Co 174, 229, 290
  Reno Co 29, 51, 78, 118,
    . . . 119, 173, 174, 232, 233, 295
  Salina 104, 150
  Saline Co 150
  Sedgwick Co 119, 174
  Sheridan Co 125, 180
  Smithville 225
  Spring 295
  Stevens Co 174
  Sumner Twp 78, 173
  Thomas Co. 46
  Turon 119
  Vorhees 174
  Wellsford 174
  Wendell 46
  Wichita 119, 174
  Wyandotte Co . . 46, 70, 162, 285
Kentucky 30
  Athol 349
  Augusta 147
  Bent 369
  Berry 329
  Boone Co 272, 273, 329, 330
  Bracken Co . . 18, 43, 45, 63, 64,
    . . . . 69, 71, 175, 235, 355
  Bridgville 74
  Brooksville 63, 199
  Brown Co 199
  Burlington 272, 273, 329
  Butler 199, 252
  Butler Co 116
  Camp Springs 189
  Campbell Co . 30, 31, 53, 82, 96,
    . . . . . . 131, 135, 160, 198, 205,
    . . . . 235, 260, 297, 320
  Chester 67
  Citusso 235
  Coldspring 312
  Columbus 47
  Corbin 349
  Covington . . . 90, 129, 189, 198,
    . . . . . . 250, 262, 273, 307, 319,
    . . . . . . 327, 328, 330, 368, 369
  Dayton 235, 296, 297
  Dieterich 46, 160
  Elizaville 109
  Falmouth 235, 236, 253
  Fayette Co 328, 343
  Flag Springs 189, 206
  Fleming Co 109
  Flemingsburg 226, 228
  Fort Thomas 369
  Foxport 340
  Franklin Co 47
  Ft Thomas 330
  Gallatin Co 325
  Germantown 235
  Griffin 330
  Hanover 116
  Harrison Co 329
  Jefferson Co 223, 283, 359
  Kenton Co . . 129, 189, 198, 215,
    . . . . 250, 273, 307, 319,
    . . . . 327, 328, 330, 368, 369
  Lewis Co 111, 340, 373
  Lewisburg 283, 340
  Lexington 205, 328, 347
  Louisville 339, 340, 359
  Mason Co . . 18, 27, 45-47, 67-69,
    . 71, 72, 109, 111, 159, 161-163,
    . . 196, 223-227, 235, 283, 284,
    . . . . 286, 287, 313, 314,
    . . . . 339, 340, 343, 373
  Mays Lick 160
  Maysville . . 19, 27, 45-47, 67, 68,
    . 70, 74, 109, 111, 159-164, 166,
    196, 223-227, 235, 283, 284, 286,
    . . . 287, 313, 314, 339, 340, 343
  Milford 175
  Newport . 30, 31, 50, 53, 82, 91,
    . . . 96, 131, 135, 160, 197, 205,
    . . . . . . 260, 318, 320, 347, 361
  Orangeburg 70, 72, 340, 373
  Parmleysville 369
  Pekin 199
  Pendleton Co 116, 170, 171,
    . . . . 199, 235, 252
  Pike Co 231
  Somerset 207
  Vanceburg 313
  Warsaw 325
  Washington 161
  Wayne Co 330, 369
  Whitley Co 349
Louisiana
  New Orleans 197, 288
Maine 259
  Kennebec Co 355
  Waterville 312, 355
Massachusetts
  Attleborough 253
  Boston 161
  Bristol Co 253

Massachusetts continued
  S. Attleboro 200
  So. Dennis 367
Maryland
  Baltimore Co 309
  Cockeysville 309
  Severna Park 353
Mexico
  Vera Cruz 288
Michigan 225
  Ann Arbor 104, 307
  Bedford 241, 352
  Berrien Co 123, 178
  Coldwater 307, 352
  Flint 167
  Genesee Co 167
  Grand Rapids 349
  Kent Co 349
  Leonidas .. 31, 80, 124, 178, 179
  Marysville 285
  Mendon 123, 178
  Monroe Co 190, 241, 352
  Ottawa Lake 190
  Petoskey 350
  Port Huron 285
  Saint Clair Co 285
  Saint Joseph 123, 178
  St Joseph Co .. 80, 123, 124, 178
  Taylor 234
Minnesota 204, 371
  Hennepin Co 218, 338
  Minneapolis 218, 338, 373
  Minnetonka 238
  Otter Tail Co 220
  Ottertail 220
  Pratt 334
  Steele Co 334
Mississippi
  Glendale 315
  La Flora Co 312
Missouri 38, 148, 169,
  .... 208, 272, 322
  Adair Co 209, 268, 363
  Boonville 230
  Buchanan 151
  Caldwell 27
  Carroll 70
  Clark Co 364
  Columbia 210
  Downing ... 148, 208, 209, 213,
  .... 268, 322, 323, 362, 364
  Greentop 209, 363
  Grundy Co 286
  Independence 209, 268, 364
  Jackson Co ....
  .. 110, 162, 285, 286, 363

  Kansas City ....
  .. 110, 162, 285, 286, 363
  Kirksville 322, 363
  La Belle 323, 363
  Lancaster 237
  Lawrence Co 70, 114
  Lewis Co 323, 363
  Logan 114
  Macon 164
  Marion 286
  Moberly 322, 363
  Mount Pleasant 364
  Mt Vernon 70
  Parkville 70
  Pettis 268
  Platt City 46, 70
  Platte Co 46
  Prairie 364
  Queen City 268
  Randolph Co 322, 363
  Rockford 27
  Schuyler Co . 209, 213, 267, 268,
  .... 299, 322, 364
  Scotland Co 364
  Smithville 286
  Springfield 114
  St Louis 40, 46, 69, 162,
  .... 207, 221, 265
  St Louis Co 162
  Stateline 74
  Wyaconda 364
Montana 315
  Butte 259, 260
  Cascade Co 40, 218, 278, 320, 336
  Chouteau Co 371
  Clyde Park 336
  Custer Co 218, 278
  Great Falls 40, 208, 218,
  .... 278, 320, 336
  Highwood 371
  Laurin 336
  Lewiston 218, 278
  Silver Bow Co 260
  Valier 336
Nebraska 44, 219, 333
  Allen Co 156
  Burt Co 339
  Butler Co 338
  Carroll 337
  Cedar Co 278, 335, 371-373
  Chapin 372
  Cuming Co 220
  Dixon Co 336, 372
  Douglas Co 205, 339
  Fillmore Co 337, 372
  Geneva 337, 372
  Grand Island 335

  Hall Co 335
  Hartington 220, 335, 371
  Howard Co 339
  Linwood 338
  Logan 372
  Madison Co 156, 337, 372
  Newman Grove 337
  Norfolk 156
  North Loop 231
  Omaha 205, 339, 357
  Papillion 336
  Plainview 336
  Saint Paul 339
  Shell Creek 372
  Strahan 155, 278-280, 371
  Tekamah 339
  Wagner Co 279
  Wakefield 336
  Wayne 65, 154, 155, 217,
  220, 277-281, 334-339, 371, 372
  West Point 220, 281
  Wilbur 154, 277
  Winside 65, 156, 336
  Wynot 278, 335
Netherlands
  Haarlemmermeer 365
Nevada
  Clark Co 347
  Las Vegas 335, 347
New Jersey
  Hudson Co 354
  Jersey City 354
  Newark 180
New Mexico
  Albuquerque 124
  Bernalillo Co 124
  Sierra 169
New York 119, 139, 288, 359
  Manhattan 294
  New Rochelle 31, 122, 177,
  .... 236, 298
  New York 294, 317
  Oneida Co 119
  Westchester Co ... 122, 236, 298
North Carolina
  Brunswick 263
  Canton 205
  Cary 344
  Chatham Co 112
  Cobbs Creek 4
  Deep Creek 4
  Fort Caswell 263
  Haywood 111, 112, 165
  Hunting Creek 4
  Iredell Co 3, 6
  Rowan Co 14
  Surry Co 3, 7, 8, 14, 18

North Dakota 52, 123
  Bismarck 278
  Burleigh Co 278
  Carson 334
  Elgin 334
  Gilbert 80, 155, 178
  Grant Co   278, 334, 336, 370, 371
  Hettinger Co 334
  Howard 370
  Leith 155, 278, 336, 370, 371
  Lisbon 322, 362
  Memue 278
  Michigan 52
  Mott 334
  Rolette Co 80, 178
  Saunders 334
  Sisbon 363
  Valley View 370, 371
Ohio
  Aberdeen 18, 26, 45, 109
  Adams Co 110, 162, 212,
  . . . . 270, 272, 326, 367
  Afton 98, 138, 199, 200,
  . . . 202, 253, 256, 287, 310, 349
  Alexander 224
  Allen Co 326
  Athens 46
  Auglaize Co 108, 160
  Beachwood 198, 251
  Bellaire 242
  Bellefontaine 275, 370
  Belmont Co 242
  Blue Ash 189, 239
  Brown Co 18, 38, 41, 45,
  . . . . . . 54, 67, 74, 98, 109, 121,
  . . 143, 145, 146, 153, 177, 196,
  . . . 203, 204, 213, 214, 217, 231,
  . . 234, 259, 274, 292, 296, 297,
  . . . 306, 314, 328, 351, 355, 356
  Butler Co . . . 111, 138, 140, 170,
  . . . . . . 171, 212, 225, 270, 285,
  . . . 287, 311, 331, 343, 362, 374
  California 331
  Camp Dennison 214, 273
  Canton 326
  Cherry Grove 98
  Chesterland 342
  Chilicothe 41
  Cincinnati . 31, 40, 42, 66, 70, 75,
  . . . 81-83, 95, 98, 121, 128, 139,
  . . 170, 176, 188-189, 191, 192,
  . . . 196, 201, 205-208, 212-214,
  . . 216, 222, 231, 235, 236, 239,
  . . 241, 243, 246, 255, 256, 261,
  . . . 262, 265-267, 271, 272, 274,

Cincinnati continued
  . . . . . . 275, 282, 292, 293, 296,
  . . . 306, 307, 311, 317-319, 326,
  . . 345, 347, 348, 352, 355, 359,
  . . . . 360, 366, 375, 376
Clark Co 201
Clarksville 352
Clermont Co . . . . 14 , 28
Cleveland 160, 163, 224-227,
  274, 284-286, 308, 341, 373, 374
Cleveland Heights 227, 242
Clinton Co 271, 352, 368
Columbiana Co 191, 242
Columbus . . . 47, 58, 72, 73, 113,
  . . . . 228, 250, 289, 343, 358
Crawford Co 331, 370
Cuyahoga Co 160, 190, 191, 198,
  . . . . . . 215, 224-227, 242, 251
  . . . 284-286, 308, 341, 349, 373
Cuyahoga Falls . . . 202, 256, 342
Darke Co 327
Dayton 40, 95, 140, 159,
  . . . . 213, 360
Dayton State Hospital 95
Decatur 340
Deer Park 214, 215, 274
Delaware 349
Delaware Co 299
East Cleveland 191
Elyria 326
Elyria 367
Euclid 343
Fairfax 191
Fairfield 343
Fairlawn 253
Fairmount 349
Fayette Co 326
Franklin 73, 288
Franklin Co . . . 72, 74, 112, 113,
  . . . . . 196, 288, 289, 316,
  . . . . 339, 343, 349
Franklin Township 14
Freemont 326
Galion 331, 370
Gallia Co 231, 292
Geauga Co 342
Georgetown 26, 43, 63, 66,
  . . . . 203, 204, 297, 306, 314,
  . . . . 328, 356
Golf Manor 359
Green 274
Greene Co 40
Hamilton 75, 171, 212, 225,
  . . . 228, 235, 285, 311, 362, 374

Hamilton Co 30, 42, 53, 66,
  81-83, 95, 96, 98, 105, 116, 121,
  128, 138, 139, 143, 154 160 170,
  . . . 171, 176, 188, 189, 191, 192,
  . . . 200-201, 205-208, 212-215,
  . . 222, 231, 235, 236, 2 39, 241,
  . . . 246, 254, 261, 262, 265-267,
  . . 271, 272, 274-276, 282, 293,
  . . . 297, 306, 307, 316-321, 326,
  345, 352, 355, 359, 360, 367, 375
Higginsport 146, 153
Highland City 274
Hillsboro 329
Hulington 293
Independence 251
Indian Hill 359
Ivanhoe 143
Jacksonville 270
Jefferson 272
Jefferson 172
Kettering 140
Knox Co 306
Lakewood 251
Laura 367
Lausche 212
Lawrence Co 111
Lawshee 212
Lebanon 327, 360
Lewis 259
Lorain 367
Lorrain Co 225, 284, 326
Lucas Co 189, 241, 353
Madeira . 261, 316, 319, 317, 325
Madisonville 31, 215, 262,
  . . . . 275, 331
Mariemont 298
Mariemont Co 96
Marion 275
Mason 368
Massilon 343
Maumee 352
Mayfield Heights 286
Medina Co 98, 139
Meigs 270
Miami Co 159, 367
Miamiville 215
Middletown 140
Mifflin 288
Millcreek 239, 276
Millville 171
Monroe Co 327
Montgomery . . 159, 188, 214, 274
Montgomery Co . . . 95, 136, 140,
  . . . . 160, 172, 213, 254

Ohio continued
- Morrow 31, 326
- Mt Carmel 307
- Mt Healthon 322
- Mt Healthy 325, 326, 366
- Mt Vernon 306
- Muskingum 29
- N. Olmsted 225, 285
- New Philadelphia 308
- Nicholasville 162
- Nicholsville 116, 171
- North Olmsted 285
- Norwood . . . . 96, 105, 116, 138, 143, 146, 160, 171, 207, . . 208, 212, 215, 216, 235, 236, 262, 265, 266, 274, 275, . . 297, 316-320, 351, 369
- Nuncey 96
- Oberlin 225, 284
- Olive Branch 306, 320
- Oxford 236
- Parma 224, 341, 373
- Peebles 326
- Perry 231, 292
- Pike 274
- Point Pleasant 10
- Portage Co 98, 139
- Portsmouth 348
- Ravenna 139
- Reading 208, 240
- Ripley 314
- Ross Co 41, 61
- Rossmoyne 330
- Rural 73
- Russellville 328
- Sabina 326, 367
- Sardinia 231, 292, 328
- Scioto Co 348
- Scott Twp 213
- Scranton 353
- Seaman 326
- Seneca Co 188
- Seven Mile 287
- Sharonville 325, 361
- Sheridan Coal Works 111
- Sherman 191
- Silverton 106, 189
- Smith's Landing 43, 63
- St Bernard . . . . 154, 189, ... 239, 277, 348
- St Marys 108, 160
- St. Clair 212, 270
- Stark Co 343
- Sterling 217
- Summit Co . . . . 138, 199, ... 202, 253, 287
- Sycamore Twp 215
- Sylvania 189
- Symmes 105, 273
- Talmadge 98, 139
- Tiffin 188
- Toledo 189, 241, 353
- Tuscarawas Co 308
- Union 272, 293
- Union City 327
- Uniontown 200
- Upper Arlington 339
- Utopia 145
- Van Buren 136, 140, 254
- Van Wert 90
- Wadsworth 200
- Warren Co . . . 272, 327, 348, 368
- Wellsville 191. 242
- West Chester 331
- West Union 227. 328
- Westerville 112
- Westfield 139
- Westfield 98, 139
- Wilmington 326
- Winchester 367
- Youngstown 352
- Zanesville 29

Oklahoma 51, 229, 324
- Allison 295
- Bethany 346
- Buffalo 294, 375
- Chelsea 314, 356
- Claremore 356
- Custer Co 119
- Darling 78, 118, 174, 295
- Enid 232, 294, 309, 346
- Garfield 294
- Garfield Co . 118, 173, 232, 294, ... 309, 346, 375
- Hunter 118, 232, 294, 346
- Kingfisher 114
- Kingfisher Co 114
- Liberty 78
- McAlester 169, 344
- Muskogee 78, 170
- Muskogee Co 118, 295
- Noble 173, 294
- Oklahoma City 346
- Oklahoma Co 346
- Pawnee 78, 119, 120, 174
- Pawnee Co 119, 120, 174
- Pittsburg Co 344
- Pottawatomie Co 174
- Rogers Co 314, 356
- Texas Co 119, 174
- Thomas 119
- Tyrone 119
- Winnewood 365
- Yukon 327

Oregon 375
- Bon Homme Co 237
- Cornelius 237, 299
- Creswell 333
- Forest Grove 350
- Gaston 299
- Gresham 111
- Hillsboro 237
- Hood River, ... 218
- Lane Co 333
- Multnomah Co 111, 218
- Portland 44, 65, 218
- Washington Co 299

Pennsylvania 76, 202, 219
- Allegheny Co 227
- Beaver Co. 72
- Clairton 227
- Dowlestown 262
- Indiana 339
- Jeanette 224
- Johnstown 326
- Philadelphia 317, 328
- Philadelphia Co 328
- Planton 71
- Pleasant 274
- Richland 114
- Swickly 345
- Wrightsville 293
- York Co 293

Scotland 75, 49, 98
- Glasgow 139

South Dakota
- Bennett Co 279
- Bon Homme Co . . . . . . 181, 238, ... 299, 300
- Capital 125, 181, 299, 300
- Dallas 281
- Gregory Co 281
- Hellen 279
- Huron 338
- Hutchinson Co . . . 125, 181, 218, ... 237, 238, 278, 299, 300
- Iroquois 372
- Kaylor 300
- Lawrence Co 334
- Lead 333
- Lloyd 279
- Menno 218, 278
- Olivet 181, 237, 238
- Orient 238
- Scotland 238, 300
- Vermillion 335
- Washington 181, 237, 299

South America 347
- Bogota 347
- Columbia 347

Tennessee 114, 291
   Campbell Co 325, 366
   Claiborn Co 274, 330
   Clarksville 312
   Cumberland Gap 330
   Jellico 366
   Mt Pleasant 227, 287
   Nashville 73
   Smith Co 215
   Stone River 32
Texas 294, 344
   Alvin 156
   Austin 374
   Bexar Co 322, 363
   Brazoria Co 156
   Cameron Co 260
   El Paso 114, 115, 168, 169,
       ...... 229, 289, 290, 308, 374
   El Paso Co 308
   Galveston 168, 289
   Harlingen 260
   Harris Co ... 110, 160, 163, 168,
       .... 226, 229, 289, 374
   Hempstead 226
   Hidalgo Co 233
   Houston 110, 160, 163, 169,
       ...... 170, 226, 229, 289, 374
   Hurst 344
   Llano Co 344
   Lubbock 346
   Lubbock Co 346
   McAllen 233
   Mt Pleasant 229, 289
   Odessa 291
   Pharr 233
   Quanah 229, 291
   San Antonio .. 125, 322, 344, 363
   Sherman 318
Titus Co 229, 289
Travis Co 374
Victoria 124
Waller Co 226
Weatherford 119
Utah
   Murray Ward 76
   Salt Lake City 76, 306
   Salt Lake Co 306
Virginia
   Blacksburg 10
   Elizabeth City 269
   Newport News 211, 269
   Norfolk 332
   Oakwood Cemetery 26
   Quantico 292, 349
   Richmond 26
   Stafford 333
   Stafford Co 333
   Tazewell 330
   Tazewell Co 330
   Virginia Beach City 288
   Virginia Beach 288
   Warwick Co 211
   Wythe Co 269
Vermont 364
Washington
   Bellingham 290, 344
   Camas 344, 374
   Chehalis Co 149
   Cowlitz Co 344, 374
   King Co 69, 110, 162, 204,
       ...... 225, 259, 285, 290, 344
   Montesano 149
   Pierce Co 229, 290
   Seattle 46, 110, 162, 204,
       ... 225, 259, 285, 290, 315, 344
   Tacoma 229, 290
Whatcom Co 344
Yakima 260
Yakima Co 260
West Virginia 10, 82
   Boone 170
   Boone Co 115, 292
   Branchland 343
   Cabell Co 129
   Clay 167
   Gauley Bridge 341
   Gauley River 10
   Hinton 311
   Huntington 91, 129, 293, 345
   Kanawa River 10
   Kanawa Trace 10
   Kanoba 292, 293
   Lincoln Co 343
   Madison 292
   New River 10
   Ohio River 10
   Parkersburg 10
   Peterstown 11
   Ritchie Co 167
   Scott 170, 292
   Wayne 292
Wisconsin 123, 178
   Green Bay 135
   Merrasha 335
Wyoming 344, 374
   Careyhurst 44, 65
   Converse 44, 65
   Fremont Co 49
   Thermopolis 49

www.ingramcontent.com/pod-product-compliance
Lightning Source LLC
Chambersburg PA
CBHW081819280526
45789CB00007B/2267